MASTER Microsoft® Office 2000 VISUALLY™

From
maranGraphics®
&
Wiley Publishing, Inc.

Master Microsoft® Office 2000 VISUALLY™

Published by
Wiley Publishing, Inc.
909 Third Avenue
New York, NY 10022

Published simultaneously in Canada

Library of Congress Control Number: 98-75596

ISBN: 0-7645-6050-6

Manufactured in the United States of America

10 9 8 7 6 5 4

1V/RU/QU/QT/MG

Trademark Acknowledgments

maranGraphics Inc. has attempted to include trademark information for products, services and companies referred to in this guide. Although maranGraphics Inc. has made reasonable efforts in gathering this information, it cannot guarantee its accuracy.

The maranGraphics logo is a trademark or registered trademark of maranGraphics, Inc.. Wiley, the Wiley Publishing logo, Visual, the Visual logo, Simplified, Master VISUALLY, Teach Yourself VISUALLY, Visual Blueprint, In an Instant, Read Less - Learn More and related trade dress are trademarks or registered trademarks of Wiley Publishing, Inc. in the United States and other countries and may not be used without written permission. All other trademarks are the property of their respective owners. maranGraphics, Inc. and Wiley Publishing, Inc. are not associated with any product or vendor mentioned in this book.

Important Numbers

For U.S. corporate orders, please call maranGraphics at 800-469-6616 or fax 905-890-9434.

For general information on our other products and services or to obtain technical support, please contact our Customer Care Department within the U.S. at 800-762-2974, outside the U.S. at 317-572-3993 or fax 317-572-4002.

Permissions

Microsoft
Screenshots reprinted with permission from Microsoft Corporation.

Wal-Mart
Copyright © 1998 Wal-Mart Stores, Inc.

The following companies have also given us permission to use their screen shots:
Dicovery Channel Online
Minolta

U.S. Corporate Sales
Contact maranGraphics at (800) 469-6616 or fax (905) 890-9434.

U.S. Trade Sales
Contact Wiley at (800) 762-2974 or fax (317) 572-4002.

Praise for Visual books...

This is absolutely the best computer-related book I have ever bought. Thank you so much for this fantastic text. Simply the best computer book series I have ever seen. I will look for, recommend, and purchase more of the same.

–David E. Prince (NeoNome.com)

I have always enjoyed your Visual books, as they provide a quick overview of functions. Visual books are helpful even for technically inclined individuals who don't have the time to read thick books in order to get the job done. As a frequent traveler, I am extremely grateful to you for providing a pdf version of each book on a companion CD-ROM. I can easily refer to your book while on the road without much additional weight.

–Kin C. Wong (Calgary, Alberta, Canada)

I just want to let you know that I really enjoy all your books. I'm a strong visual learner. You really know how to get people addicted to learning! I'm a very satisfied Visual customer. Keep up the excellent work!

–Helen Lee (Calgary, Alberta, Canada)

These Visual Blueprints are great books! I just purchased ASP 3.0 – it could not have introduced programming with ASP any easier!

–Joseph Moglia (St. Louis, MO)

This book is PERFECT for me - it's highly visual and gets right to the point. What I like most about it is that each page presents a new task that you can try verbatim or, alternatively, take the ideas and build your own examples. Also, this book isn't bogged down with trying to "tell all" – it gets right to the point. This is an EXCELLENT, EXCELLENT, EXCELLENT book and I look forward purchasing other books in the series.

–Tom Dierickx (Malta, IL)

I have quite a few of your Visual books and have been very pleased with all of them. I love the way the lessons are presented!

–Mary Jane Newman (Yorba Linda, CA)

I am an avid fan of your Visual books. If I need to learn anything, I just buy one of your books and learn the topic in no time. Wonders! I have even trained my friends to give me Visual books as gifts.

–Illona Bergstrom (Aventura, FL)

I just had to let you and your company know how great I think your books are. I just purchased my third Visual book (my first two are dog-eared now!) and, once again, your product has surpassed my expectations. The expertise, thought, and effort that go into each book are obvious, and I sincerely appreciate your efforts.

–Tracey Moore (Memphis, TN)

Compliments to the chef!! Your books are extraordinary! Or, simply put, extra-ordinary, meaning way above the rest! THANK YOU THANK YOU THANK YOU! I buy them for friends, family, and colleagues.

–Christine J. Manfrin (Castle Rock, CO)

I write to extend my thanks and appreciation for your books. They are clear, easy to follow, and straight to the point. Keep up the good work! I bought several of your books and they are just right! No regrets! I will always buy your books because they are the best.

–Seward Kollie (Dakar, Senegal)

Thank you for making it clear. Keep up the good work.

–Kirk Santoro (Burbank, CA)

maranGraphics is a family-run business
located near Toronto, Canada.

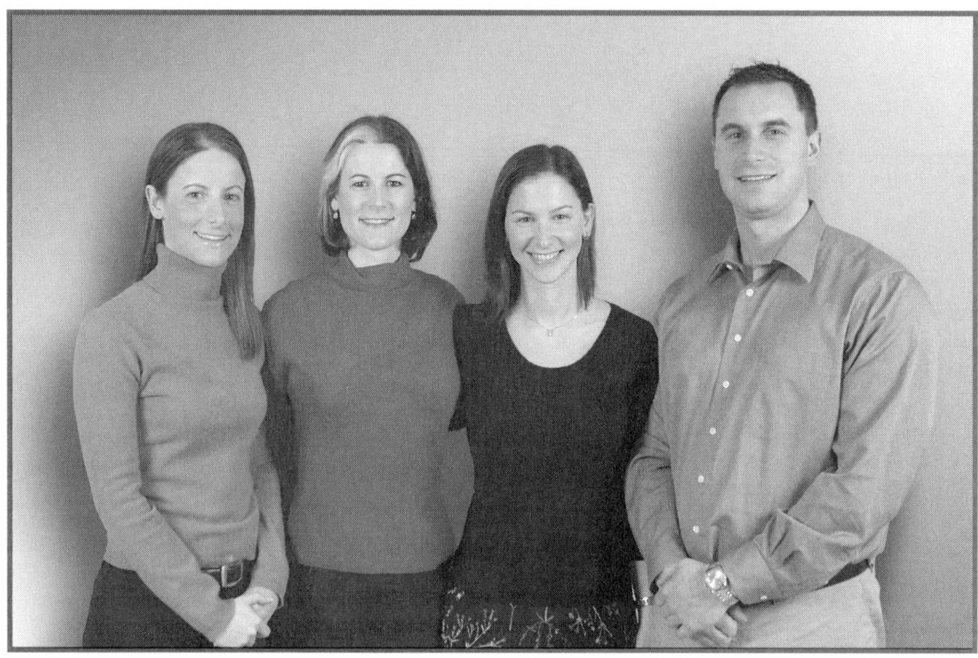

At maranGraphics, we believe in producing great computer books—one book at a time.

Each maranGraphics book uses the award-winning communication process that we have been developing over the last 25 years. Using this process, we organize screen shots, text and illustrations in a way that makes it easy for you to learn new concepts and tasks.

We spend hours deciding the best way to perform each task, so you don't have to! Our clear, easy-to-follow screen shots and instructions walk you through each task from beginning to end.

Our detailed illustrations go hand-in-hand with the text to help reinforce the information. Each illustration is a labor of love—some take up to a week to draw!

We want to thank you for purchasing what we feel are the best computer books money can buy. We hope you enjoy using this book as much as we enjoyed creating it!

Sincerely,

The Maran Family

Please visit us on the web at:

www.maran.com

CREDITS

Authors:
Ruth Maran and
Paul Whitehead

Directors of Copy Development:
Kelleigh Wing
Wanda Lawrie

Project Manager:
Judy Maran

Copy Developers:
Roxanne Van Damme
Cathy Benn

Editing & Screen Captures:
Raquel Scott
Janice Boyer
Michelle Kirchner
James Menzies
Frances Lea
Emmet Mellow

Layout Designers & Illustrators:
Jamie Bell
Treena Lees

Illustrators:
Russ Marini
Peter Grecco
Sean Johannesen
Steven Schaerer

Screen Artist:
Jimmy Tam

Indexer:
Raquel Scott

Post Production:
Robert Maran

Editorial Support:
Michael Roney

ACKNOWLEDGMENTS

Thanks to the dedicated staff of maranGraphics, including Jamie Bell, Cathy Benn, Janice Boyer, Francisco Ferreira, Peter Grecco, Jenn Hillman, Sean Johannesen, Michelle Kirchner, Wanda Lawrie, Frances Lea, Treena Lees, Jill Maran, Judy Maran, Maxine Maran, Robert Maran, Sherry Maran, Russ Marini, Emmet Mellow, James Menzies, Steven Schaerer, Raquel Scott, Jimmy Tam, Roxanne Van Damme, Paul Whitehead and Kelleigh Wing.

Finally, to Richard Maran who originated the easy-to-use graphic format of this guide. Thank you for your inspiration and guidance.

MICROSOFT® OFFICE 2000

I GETTING STARTED

1) Getting Started

II USING WORD

1) Getting Started
2) Edit Documents
3) Change View of Document
4) Format Text
5) Format Documents
6) Print Documents
7) Work With Tables
8) Work With Graphics
9) Mail Merge

III USING EXCEL

1) Getting Started
2) Edit Worksheets
3) Work With Formulas and Functions
4) Format Worksheets
5) Print Worksheets
6) Work With Multiple Worksheets
7) Work With Charts
8) Work With Graphics
9) Manage Data in a List
10) Using Macros

WHAT'S INSIDE

I. GETTING STARTED

II. USING WORD

1 Getting Started

TABLE OF CONTENTS

2 Edit Documents

3 Change View of Document

4 Format Text

5 Format Documents

6 Print Documents

7 Work With Tables

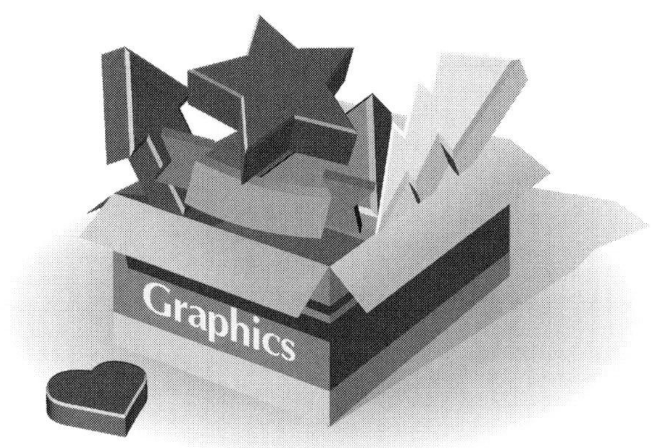

8 Work With Graphics

9 Mail Merge

TABLE OF CONTENTS

III. USING EXCEL

1 Getting Started

2 Edit Worksheets

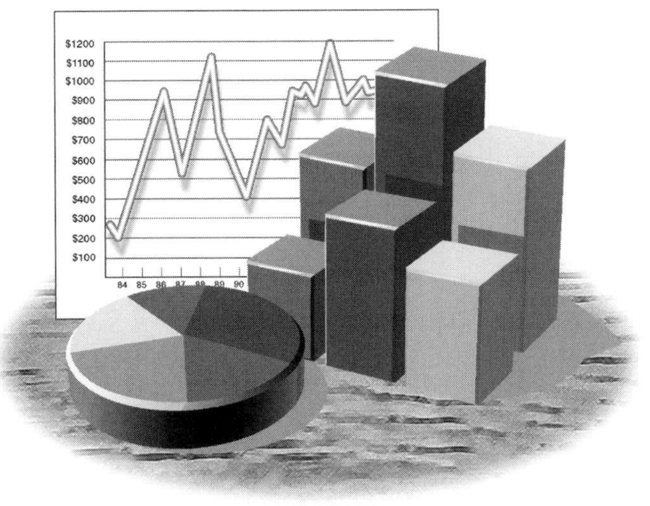

3 Work With Formulas and Functions

Jan
Feb
Product A
1254
1998
Product B
1245
1674
Product C
1356
1678
Product D
1675
1878
Product E
1785
1563
Product F
1674
1677
Product G
1876
1784
Product H
1467
1676

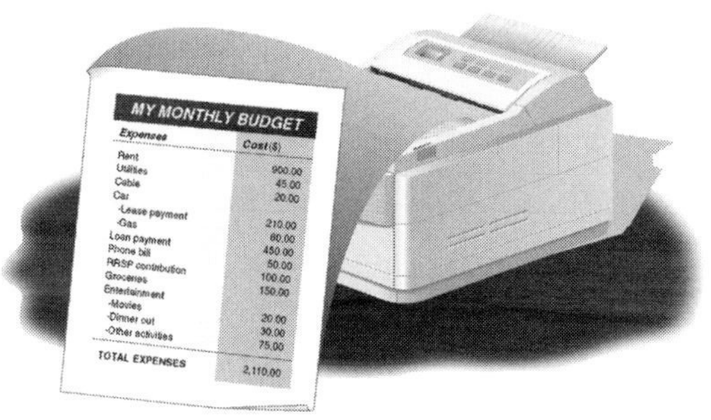

MY MONTHLY BUDGET
Expenses
Cost($)
TOTAL EXPENSES
2,110.00

TABLE OF CONTENTS

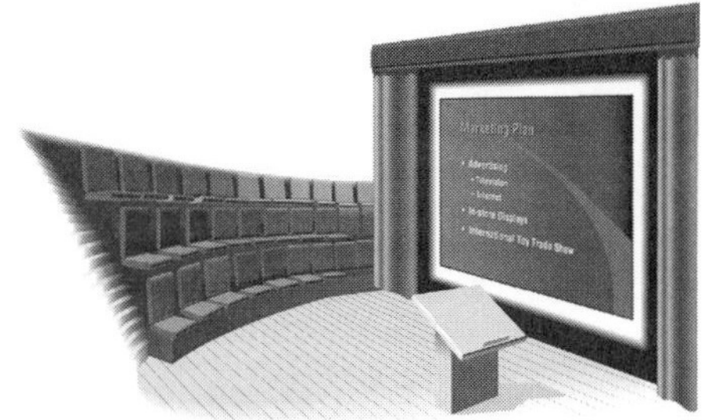

IV. USING POWERPOINT

3 Add Objects to Slides

4 Enhance a Presentation

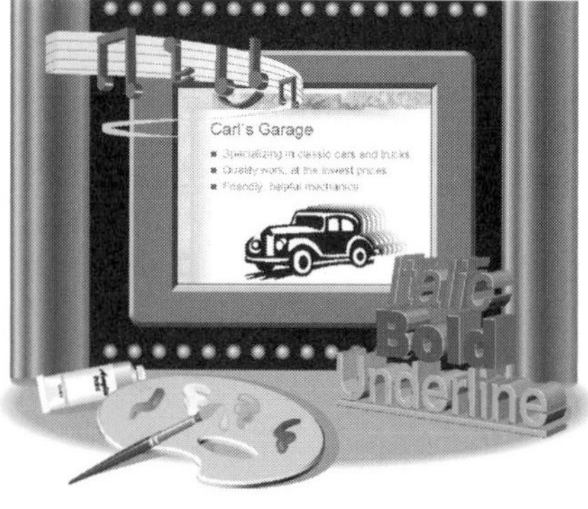

5 Fine-Tune a Presentation

TABLE OF CONTENTS

V. USING ACCESS

1 Getting Started

2 Create Tables

3 Design Tables

Title
Year Published
Pages
2 Escape from Reality
1990
400
3 Hugh's Haunted Castle
1994
315
1 Spaceships in Orbit
1996
360

Which wines were made before 1965?

TABLE OF CONTENTS

VI. USING OUTLOOK

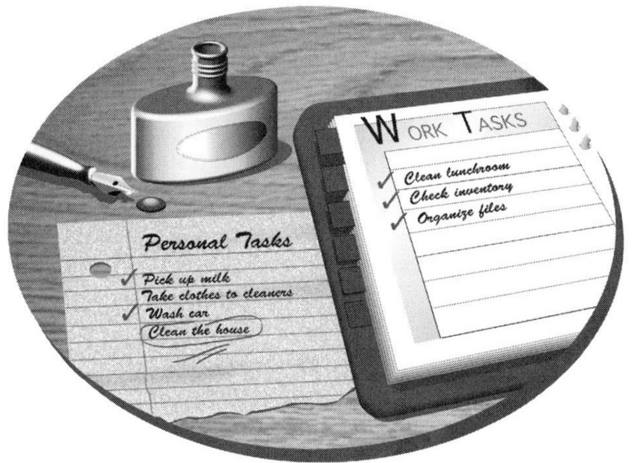

VII. USING PUBLISHER

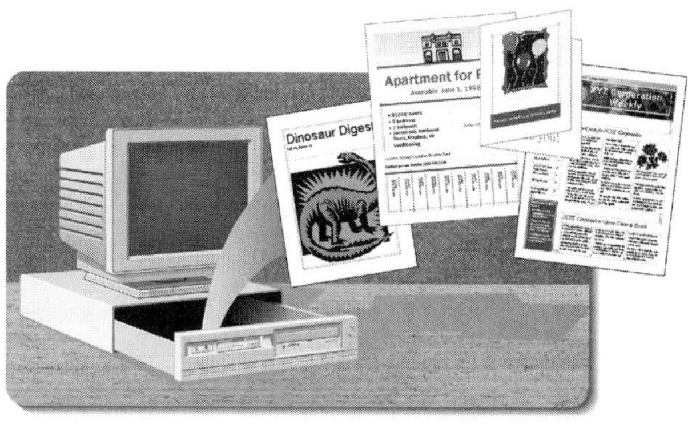

VIII. CREATE WEB PAGES

1 Manage a Web Site Using FrontPage

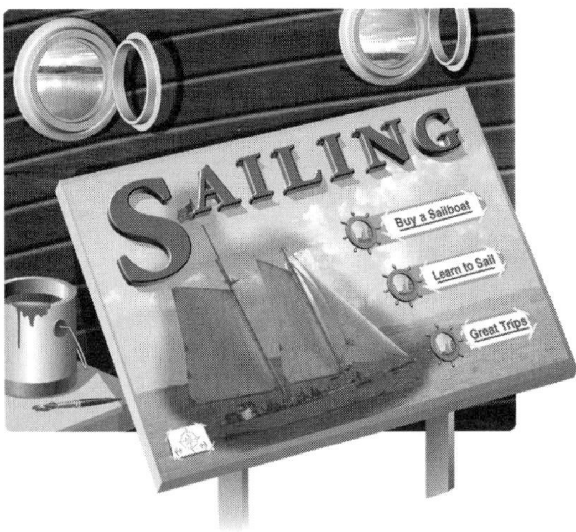

2 Enhance a Web Site Using FrontPage

3 Save Office Documents as Web Pages

TABLE OF CONTENTS

IX. EXCHANGE INFORMATION BETWEEN DOCUMENTS

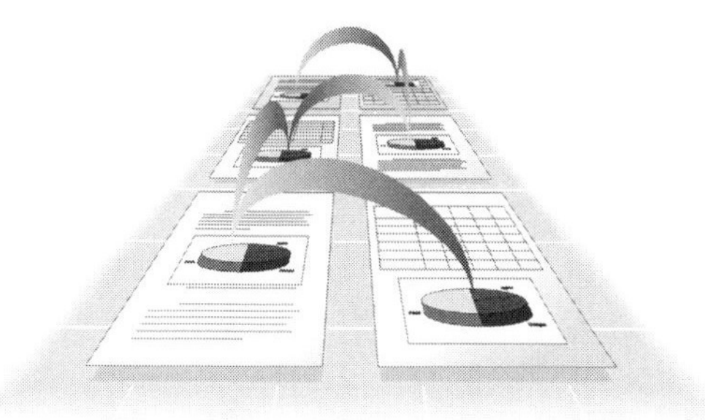

X. CUSTOMIZE OFFICE

APPENDIX

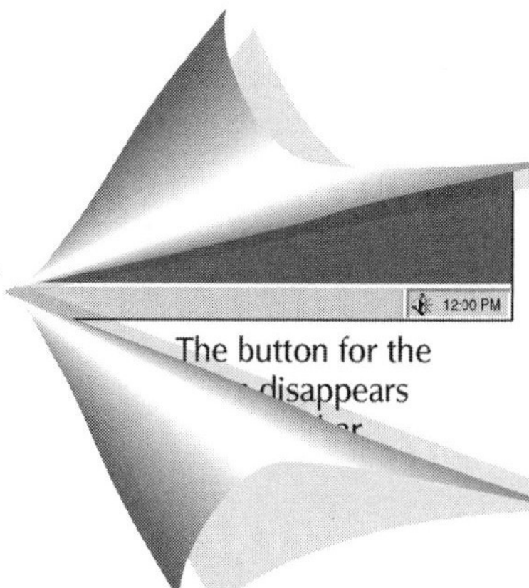

SECTION I

I) GETTING STARTED

GETTING STARTED

ABC CORPORATION

			Mar
Revenue	8745	11500	13670
Payroll	3850	4850	3552
Rent	1750	1750	1750
Su…			2030

Mountain Bike Tune-ups

This is my first year of mountain biking, and so far I've been doing my own tune-ups. But lately my bike hasn't performed well. For example, the chain slips when I switch gears. I'm wondering if I should pay a mechanic to do my tune-ups. Is it worth it?

George Arnoldson

Speaking of tune-ups, your friendly Mountai… Bike Stores are having one day semin… tune-ups. Look below for the location n…

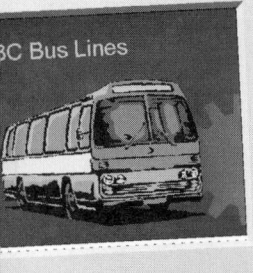

Mountain Mania Bike Store locations:

New York, NY
Boston, MA
Cincinnati, OH
Las Vegas, NV

Jacksonville, FL
Nashville, TN
Greenwich, CT
Salem, MA

Atlanta, GA
San Diego, CA
Los Ange…

Mounta…
Bik…

…C Bus Lines

INTRODUCTION TO MICROSOFT OFFICE 2000

Microsoft Office 2000 is a collection of programs sold together in one package, called a software suite. Purchasing a software suite is considerably less expensive than buying each program in the suite individually.

Microsoft Office 2000 is available at most computer stores. You will need a CD-ROM drive to install Office. If you purchase Office when buying a new computer, the retailer may install Office for you.

All Office 2000 programs share a common design and work in a similar way. Once you learn one program, you can easily learn the others.

Create Documents in Word

Word is a word processing program that lets you create documents such as letters, reports, manuals and newsletters.

Word can help you efficiently work with text in a document. You can edit text, rearrange paragraphs and check for spelling errors.

There are many formatting features available in Word that you can use to change the appearance of a document. You can use various fonts, center text and add page numbers to a document. You can also enhance a document by adding a graphic or creating a table to neatly display information.

Word's Mail Merge feature allows you to produce a personalized letter for each person on a mailing list.

Create Spreadsheets in Excel

Excel is a spreadsheet program you can use to organize, analyze and attractively present financial data, such as a budget or sales report.

Excel allows you to enter and edit data efficiently in a worksheet. You can use formulas and functions to calculate and analyze the data. A function is a ready-to-use formula that lets you perform a specialized calculation.

You can enhance the appearance of a worksheet by formatting numbers, changing the color of cells and adding graphics.

Excel can help you create colorful charts based on your worksheet data. Excel also provides tools you can use to manage and analyze a large amount of data in a list.

You can create and run macros in Excel. A macro saves you time by combining a series of commands into a single command. This is ideal for tasks you perform repeatedly.

Create Presentations in PowerPoint

PowerPoint is a program that helps you plan, organize and design professional presentations. You can use your computer screen, the Web, 35mm slides or overhead transparencies to deliver a presentation.

You can use the features in PowerPoint to edit and organize text in a presentation. PowerPoint also allows you to add objects to the slides in a presentation, including shapes, pictures, charts and tables. You can further enhance a presentation by changing the color scheme, animating slides or adding slide transitions.

PowerPoint includes presentation aids, such as speaker notes and timed rehearsals, that you can use to improve the delivery of a presentation. You can also print handouts to help the audience follow the presentation.

Create Databases in Access

Access is a database program that allows you to store and manage large collections of information. Many people use a database to store personal information such as addresses, music collections and recipes. Companies often use a database to store information such as client orders, expenses, inventory and payroll.

An Access database consists of tables, forms, queries and reports. A table is a collection of information about a specific topic, such as a mailing list. Forms provide a quick way to view, enter and change information in a database. Queries help you find specific information in a database. Reports allow you to create and print professionally designed copies of information in a database.

Manage Information in Outlook

Outlook is a program that helps you manage your e-mail messages, appointments, contacts, tasks and notes.

You can use the features included with Outlook to work with different types of information. The Inbox allows you to send and receive e-mail messages. The Calendar helps you keep track of your appointments. You can use the Contacts feature to store and manage information about the people you communicate with. The Tasks feature helps you create a list of duties you want to accomplish. You can use the Notes feature to create on-screen reminders, similar to paper sticky notes.

CONTINUED

INTRODUCTION TO MICROSOFT OFFICE 2000 CONTINUED

Create Publications in Publisher

Publisher is a desktop publishing program that helps you design professional publications, such as newsletters, brochures, catalogs, flyers, invitations and banners. Publisher includes many wizards to help you quickly get started creating your publication. The wizards can help you determine the layout, color scheme and content of a publication.

Publisher makes it easy to add text to a publication and provides a spell check feature to help make the publication more professional. Publisher also allows you to add objects to a publication, including clip art images, pictures, shapes and fancy text effects.

Create Web Pages in FrontPage

FrontPage is a program that helps you create, manage and maintain your own collection of Web pages, called a Web site.

You can use FrontPage to create Web pages that contain text, pictures, tables and hyperlinks. FrontPage also has many formatting features you can use. For example, you can change the color of text, add horizontal lines or use a theme to change the overall appearance of a page. When you finish creating the pages for your Web site, you can use FrontPage to publish the Web site.

In addition to FrontPage, other Office 2000 programs, such as Word, Excel and PowerPoint, also allow you to add hyperlinks to your documents and save your documents as Web pages.

Microsoft Office 2000 Editions

There are several editions of the Microsoft Office 2000 software suite available. The following table displays the programs included in each edition.

	MICROSOFT OFFICE 2000 EDITIONS				
Programs	**Standard**	**Small Business**	**Professional**	**Premium**	**Developer**
Word	✓	✓	✓	✓	✓
Excel	✓	✓	✓	✓	✓
PowerPoint	✓		✓	✓	✓
Access			✓	✓	✓
Outlook	✓	✓	✓	✓	✓
Publisher		✓	✓	✓	✓
FrontPage				✓	✓
PhotoDraw				✓	✓
Internet Explorer 5.0				✓	✓
Small Business Tools		✓	✓	✓	✓
Developer Tools					✓

USING THE MOUSE

A mouse is a handheld device that lets you select and move items on your screen. When you move the mouse on your desk, the mouse pointer on your screen moves in the same direction.

The mouse pointer assumes different shapes, such as ↖ or I, depending on its location on the screen and the task you are performing.

Click

Press and release the left mouse button. A click is used to select an item on the screen.

Double-click

Quickly press and release the left mouse button twice. A double-click is used to open a document or start a program.

Right-click

Press and release the right mouse button. A right-click is used to display a list of commands you can use to work with an item.

Drag and Drop

Position the mouse pointer over an item on the screen and then press and hold down the left mouse button. Still holding down the button, move the mouse to where you want to place the item and then release the button. Dragging and dropping makes it easy to move an item to a new location.

Cleaning the Mouse

You should occasionally remove the small cover on the bottom of the mouse and clean the ball inside the mouse. Make sure you also remove dust and dirt from the inside of the mouse to help ensure smooth motion.

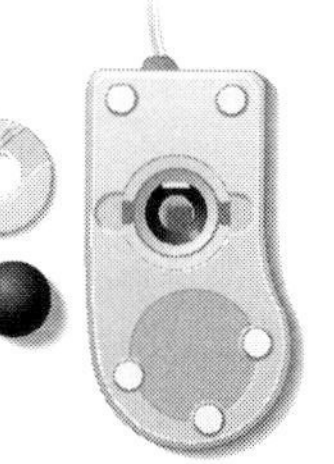

Wheeled Mouse

A wheeled mouse has a wheel between the left and right mouse buttons. Moving this wheel lets you quickly scroll through information on the screen. In some Office programs, you can zoom in or out with a wheeled mouse by holding down the Ctrl key as you move the wheel. The Microsoft IntelliMouse is a popular example of a wheeled mouse.

WINDOWS BASICS

Each program you start or item you open appears in a window on your screen. You can have many windows open on your screen at once.

If a window covers important items on your screen, you can move the window to a new location.

You can change the size of a window displayed on your screen. Increasing the size of a window allows you to view more of its contents. Reducing the size of a window lets you view items covered by the window.

Maximizing a window allows the window to fill your screen. You cannot move or size a maximized window. You can restore the window to its previous size at any time.

When you are not using a window, you can minimize the window to remove it from your screen. When you minimize a window, it reduces to a button on the taskbar. You can redisplay the window at any time.

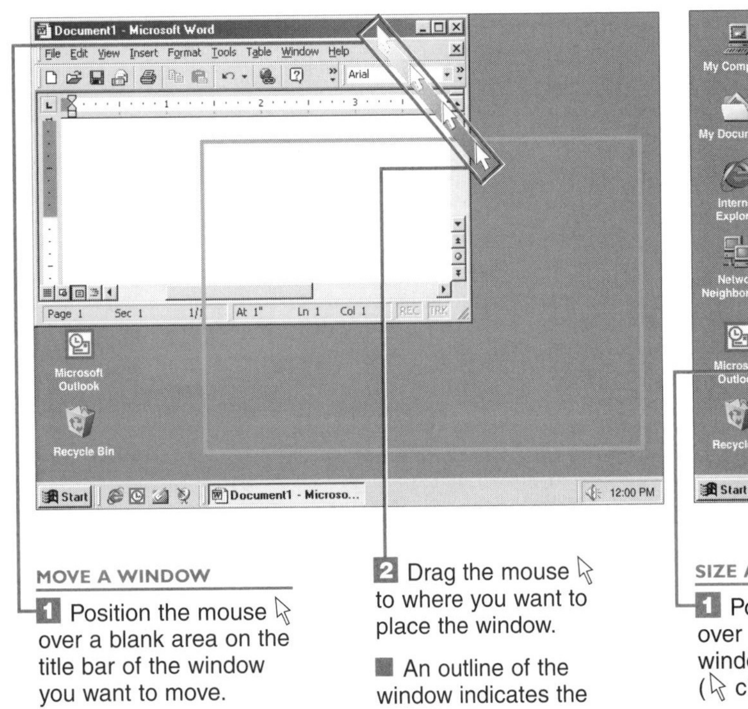

MOVE A WINDOW

1 Position the mouse over a blank area on the title bar of the window you want to move.

2 Drag the mouse to where you want to place the window.

■ An outline of the window indicates the new location.

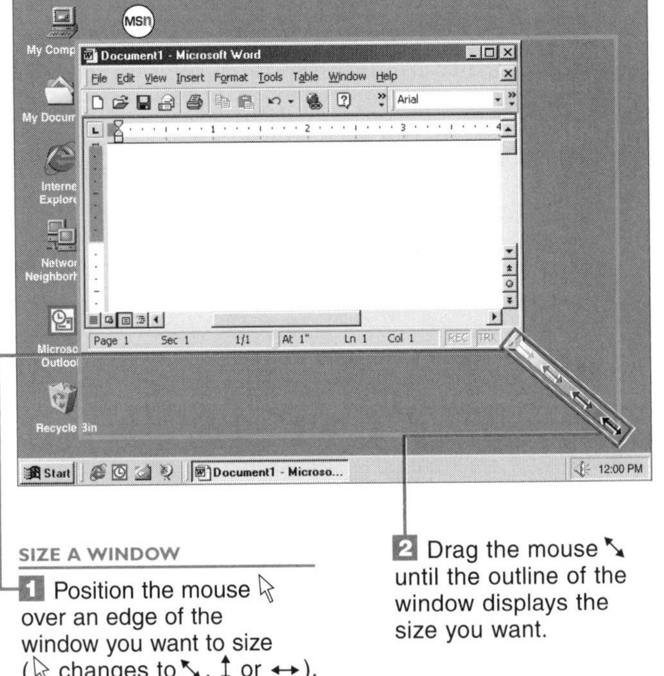

SIZE A WINDOW

1 Position the mouse over an edge of the window you want to size (changes to ↘, ↕ or ↔).

2 Drag the mouse ↘ until the outline of the window displays the size you want.

TIPS

Why do the Minimize (▁), Maximize (□), Restore (❐) or Close (☒) buttons appear more than once on my screen?

✔ These buttons appear for the program you are working in and for each open item within the program.

How can I view all the information in a window?

✔ When a window is not large enough to display all the information it contains, scroll bars appear in the window. To move through the information in the window, you can drag the scroll box (□) along a scroll bar or click an arrow button (▲ or ▼) at the end of a scroll bar.

How do I close a window?

✔ Click the Close button (☒) in the top right corner of the window you want to close.

How do I switch to another open window?

✔ To switch to another open window, click the button on the taskbar for the window you want to work with. The window appears in front of all other open windows.

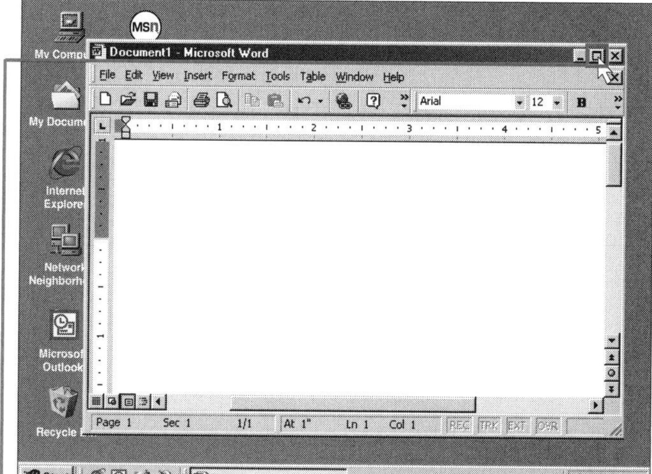

MAXIMIZE A WINDOW

1 Click □ in the window you want to maximize (□ changes to ❐).

■ The window fills your screen.

■ To return the window to its previous size, click ❐.

MINIMIZE A WINDOW

1 Click ▁ in the window you want to minimize.

■ The window reduces to a button on the taskbar. To redisplay the window, click the button.

SELECT COMMANDS USING MENUS

You can select commands from menus to perform tasks in Office. Each command performs a different task. Office programs share similar commands, which makes the programs easier to learn and use.

When you display a menu, a short version of the menu appears, displaying the most commonly used commands.

You can expand the menu to display all the commands on the menu. When you select a command from the expanded menu, the command is automatically added to the short version of the menu.

Some menu commands, such as Save or Undo, perform an action when they are selected. Other menu commands, such as Open or Print, display a dialog box.

A dialog box appears when a program needs more information to perform an action. Dialog boxes have areas where you can enter text or select options.

Most items on your screen, such as text or graphics, have a shortcut menu that appears when you right-click the item. The shortcut menu allows you to select frequently used commands for the item.

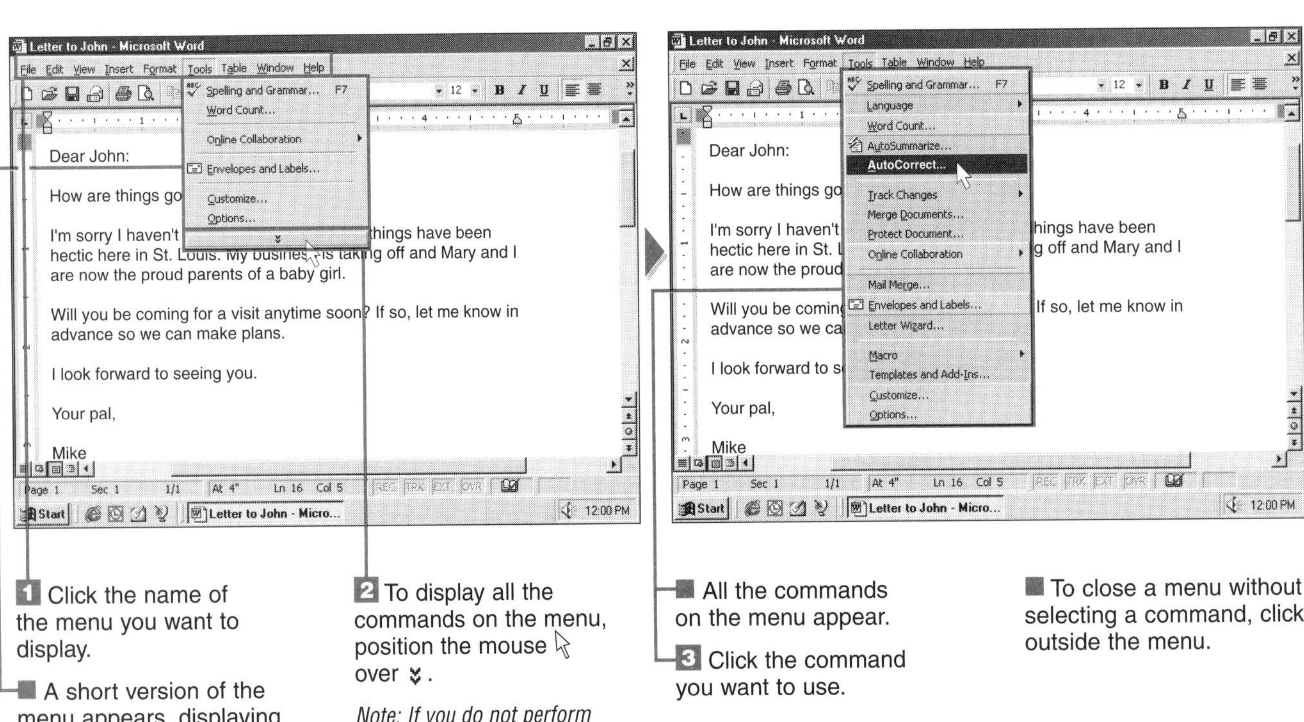

1 Click the name of the menu you want to display.

■ A short version of the menu appears, displaying the most commonly used commands.

2 To display all the commands on the menu, position the mouse ↖ over ⌄.

Note: If you do not perform step 2, all the commands on the menu will automatically appear after a few seconds.

■ All the commands on the menu appear.

3 Click the command you want to use.

■ To close a menu without selecting a command, click outside the menu.

TIPS

How can I redisplay the original short version of my menus?

✔ From the Tools menu, select Customize and then choose the Options tab. Select the Reset my usage data button, click Yes and then click Close.

Why do some menu commands have a dimmed appearance?

✔ Commands that have a dimmed appearance are currently not available. You must perform a specific task before you can select the commands. For example, you must select text to make the Cut and Copy commands in the Edit menu available in Word.

Are there shortcut keys for menu commands?

✔ Many menu commands offer keyboard shortcuts you can use to quickly select the commands. For example, Ctrl+S saves the current document in Word. If a keyboard shortcut is available, it appears beside the command in the menu.

Can I have Office always display all the commands on the menus?

✔ Yes. From the Tools menu, select Customize and then choose the Options tab. Click the Menus show recently used commands first option (☑ changes to ☐) and then click Close.

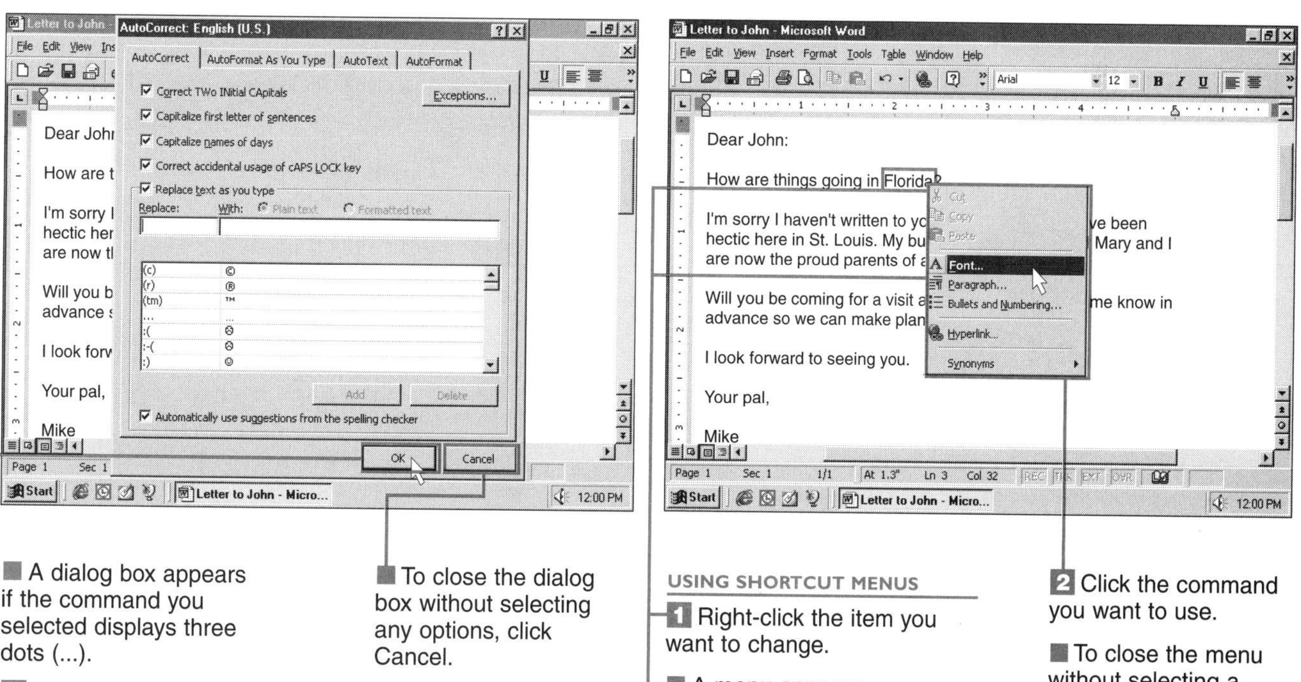

■ A dialog box appears if the command you selected displays three dots (...).

4 When you finish selecting options in the dialog box, click OK to confirm your changes.

■ To close the dialog box without selecting any options, click Cancel.

USING SHORTCUT MENUS

1 Right-click the item you want to change.

■ A menu appears, displaying the most frequently used commands for the item.

2 Click the command you want to use.

■ To close the menu without selecting a command, click outside the menu.

SELECT COMMANDS USING TOOLBARS

A toolbar contains buttons that you can use to select commands and access commonly used features.

When you first start an Office program, one or more toolbars automatically appear at the top of your screen. Office programs share similar toolbars, which makes the programs easier to learn and use.

You can display the name of a toolbar button in a yellow box. This can help you determine the task each button performs.

When multiple toolbars are displayed on the same row, the toolbars may not be able to display all of their buttons on the screen. You can display additional buttons for a toolbar at any time.

The toolbars in Office programs may change as you work. When you first start some Office programs, the most commonly used toolbar buttons appear. As you work with a program, the toolbars automatically adjust to remove buttons you rarely use and display the buttons you use most often.

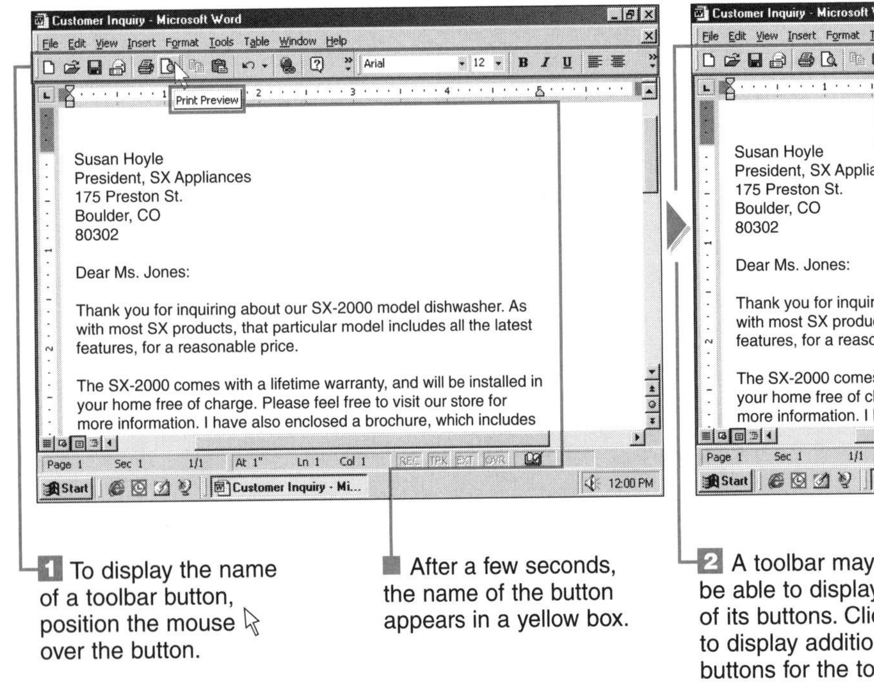

1 To display the name of a toolbar button, position the mouse over the button.

■ After a few seconds, the name of the button appears in a yellow box.

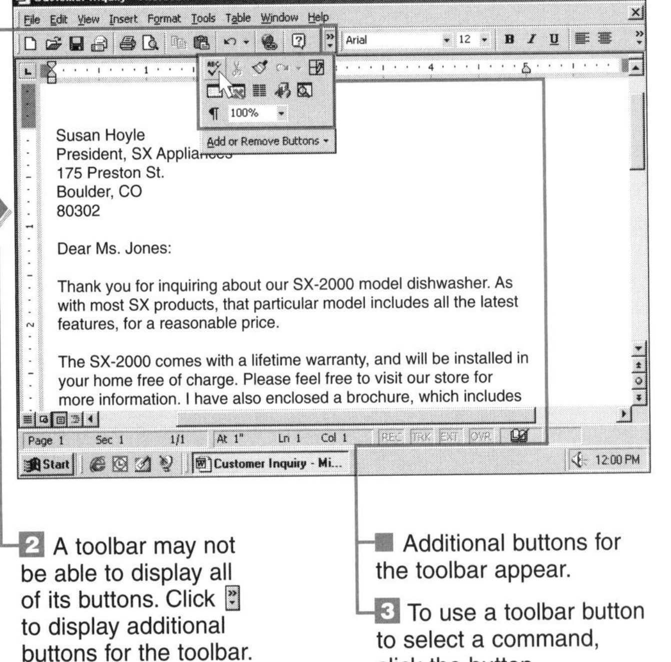

2 A toolbar may not be able to display all of its buttons. Click » to display additional buttons for the toolbar.

■ Additional buttons for the toolbar appear.

3 To use a toolbar button to select a command, click the button.

DISPLAY OR HIDE A TOOLBAR

Each Microsoft Office program offers several toolbars that you can display or hide at any time. Each toolbar contains buttons that help you quickly perform tasks.

When you first start an Office program, one or more toolbars automatically appear on your screen. Most programs display the Standard toolbar. The Standard toolbar contains buttons to help you select common commands, such as Save and Print. In some programs, the Formatting toolbar also automatically appears. The Formatting toolbar contains buttons to help you select formatting commands, such as Bold and Underline.

You can choose which toolbars to display based on the tasks you perform often. For example, if you frequently create and edit tables in Word, you may choose to display the Tables and Borders toolbar.

After you have displayed the toolbars you want, you can resize or move a toolbar to better suit your working area. To resize or move a toolbar, see page 14.

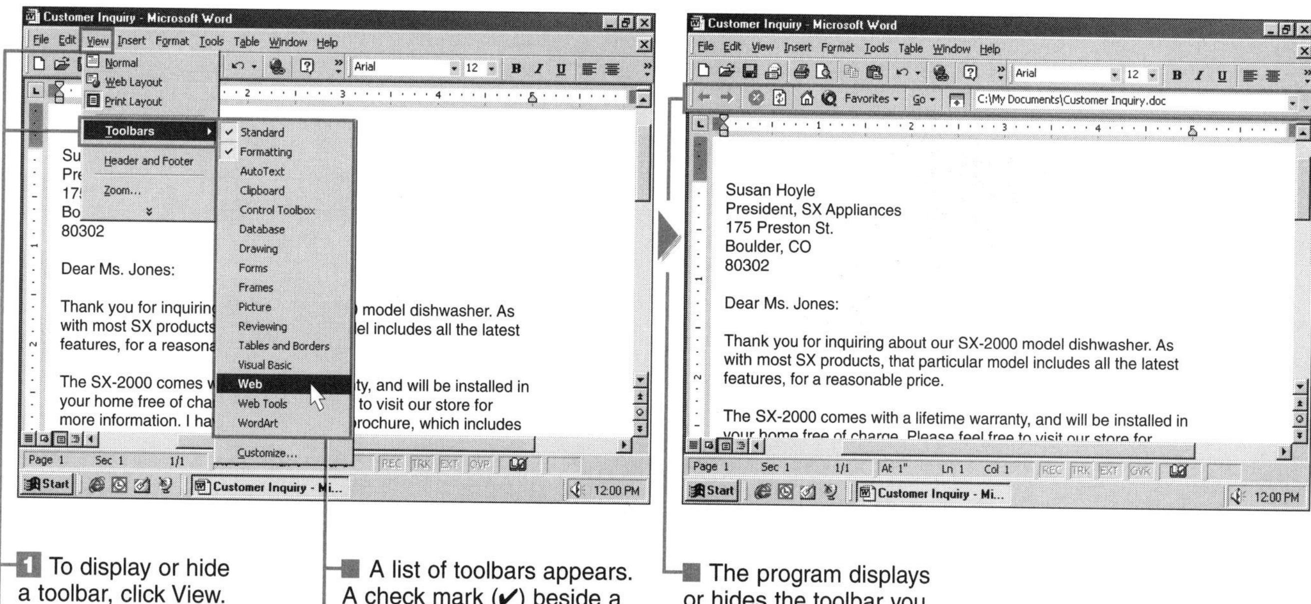

1 To display or hide a toolbar, click View.

2 Click Toolbars.

■ A list of toolbars appears. A check mark (✔) beside a toolbar name tells you the toolbar is currently displayed.

3 Click the name of the toolbar you want to display or hide.

■ The program displays or hides the toolbar you selected.

RESIZE OR MOVE A TOOLBAR

You can resize or move a toolbar to make the toolbar easier to work with.

When you first start an Office program, one or more toolbars automatically appear at the top of your screen. When multiple toolbars are displayed on the same row, the toolbars may not be able to display all of their buttons on the screen. You can increase the size of a toolbar to increase the number of buttons the toolbar can display.

Resizing a toolbar affects the location and size of other toolbars on the same row. When multiple toolbars are displayed on the same row, you cannot resize the toolbar at the left end of the row.

You can move a toolbar so the toolbar appears on its own row. This allows you to display most or all of the buttons on the toolbar. You cannot resize a toolbar that appears on its own row.

You can also move a toolbar to the top, bottom, right or left edge of your screen. You can choose the location that best suits your needs.

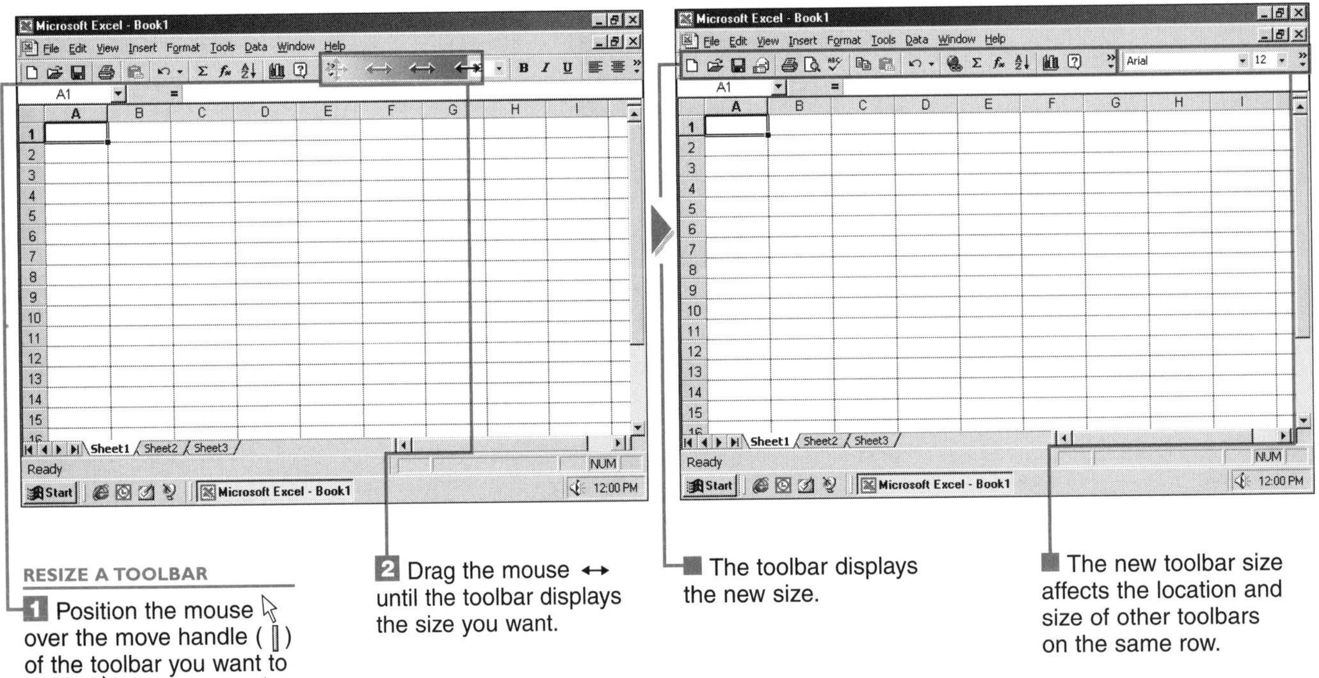

RESIZE A TOOLBAR

1 Position the mouse (↖) over the move handle (‖) of the toolbar you want to resize (↖ changes to ✥).

2 Drag the mouse ↔ until the toolbar displays the size you want.

■ The toolbar displays the new size.

■ The new toolbar size affects the location and size of other toolbars on the same row.

TIPS

Why does a toolbar I moved appear as if it is floating on my screen?

✔ When you drag a toolbar away from the edge of your screen, the toolbar appears as a floating toolbar. To return the floating toolbar to an edge of your screen, position the mouse pointer over the title bar of the toolbar and then drag the toolbar to the edge you want.

Can I increase the size of the buttons on toolbars?

✔ You can increase the size of buttons on toolbars to make the buttons easier to see. Click the Tools menu, select Customize and then click the Options tab. Select the Large Icons option (☐ changes to ☑) and then click Close.

How do I resize or move a floating toolbar?

✔ To resize a floating toolbar, position the mouse ⇖ over an edge of the toolbar (⇖ changes to ↔ or ↕) and then drag the edge until the toolbar is the size you want. To move a floating toolbar, position the mouse pointer over the title bar of the toolbar and then drag the toolbar to a new location.

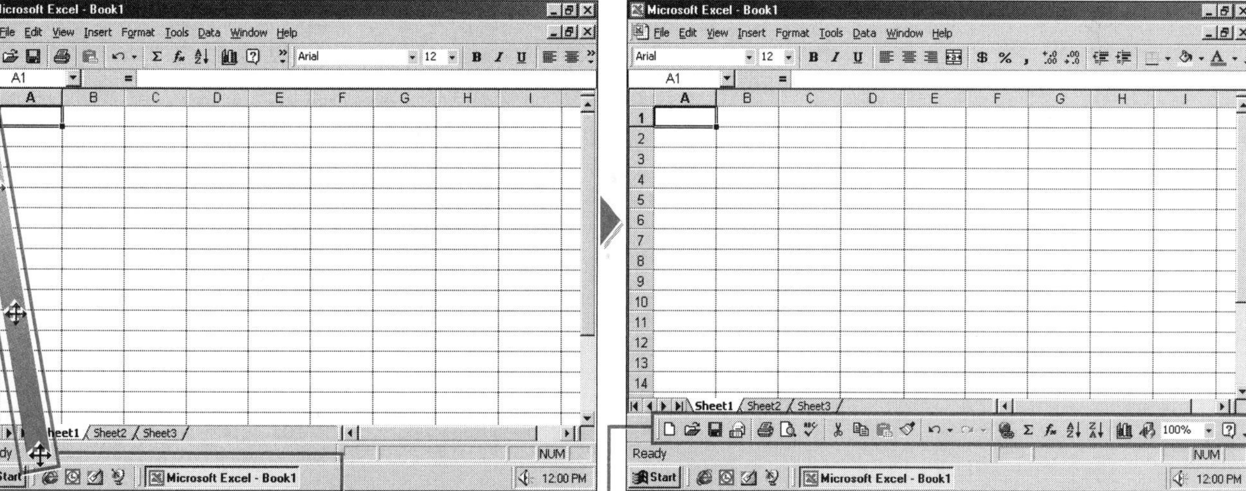

MOVE A TOOLBAR

1 Position the mouse ⇖ over the move handle (▯) of the toolbar you want to move (⇖ changes to ✥).

2 Drag the mouse ✥ to where you want the toolbar to appear.

■ The toolbar appears in the new location.

GETTING HELP USING THE OFFICE ASSISTANT

If you do not know how to perform a task, you can ask the Office Assistant for help. The Office Assistant provides help information specific to the program you are working in.

As you work, the Office Assistant automatically offers help information about how to perform tasks. For example, in Word, the Office Assistant offers help information when you begin writing a letter.

The Office Assistant also automatically displays a light bulb ( ) when it has a tip about how to use the current feature more effectively. You can click the light bulb to display the tip.

You can type a question to have the Office Assistant display a list of help topics related to the question. If you do not see a help topic of interest, you can try rephrasing your question.

When you select a help topic, help information appears in a window. You can select a word or phrase that appears in blue with no underline to display a definition of the word or phrase.

You can hide the Office Assistant to remove it from your screen at any time.

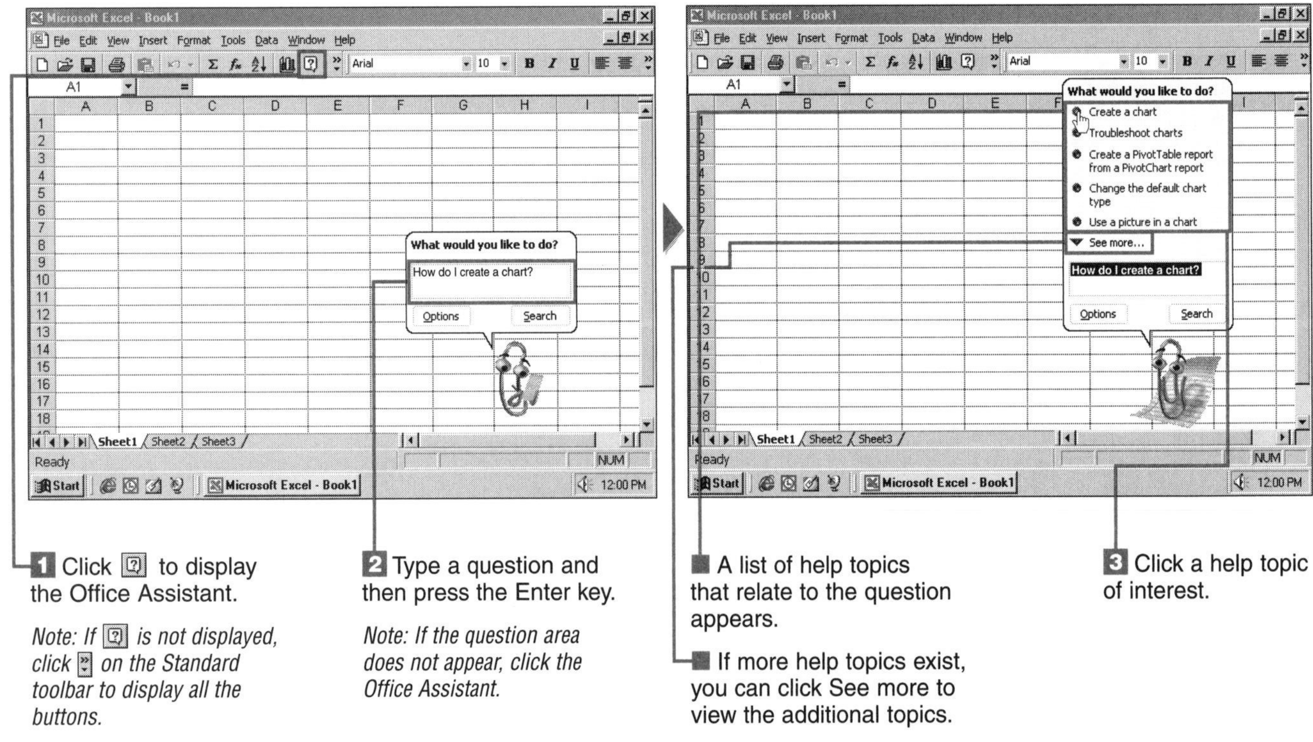

1 Click to display the Office Assistant.

Note: If is not displayed, click on the Standard toolbar to display all the buttons.

2 Type a question and then press the Enter key.

Note: If the question area does not appear, click the Office Assistant.

■ A list of help topics that relate to the question appears.

■ If more help topics exist, you can click See more to view the additional topics.

3 Click a help topic of interest.

TIPS

How can I view information related to the current help topic?

✔ You can click blue, underlined text in the Help window to display information related to the help topic you are currently viewing. To return to the previous help topic at any time, click the Back button ().

How do I move the Office Assistant?

✔ Position the mouse pointer over the Office Assistant and then drag the Office Assistant to a new location.

Can I print the help information?

✔ To print a copy of the help information in the Help window, click the Print button ().

Can I display help information for an item on my screen?

✔ Yes. Click the Help menu and then select What's This? (pointer changes to pointer with ?). Then click the item on your screen you want to display help information for.

How can I display help information for an item in a dialog box?

✔ Click [?] in the dialog box (pointer changes to pointer with ?) and then click the item you want to display help information for.

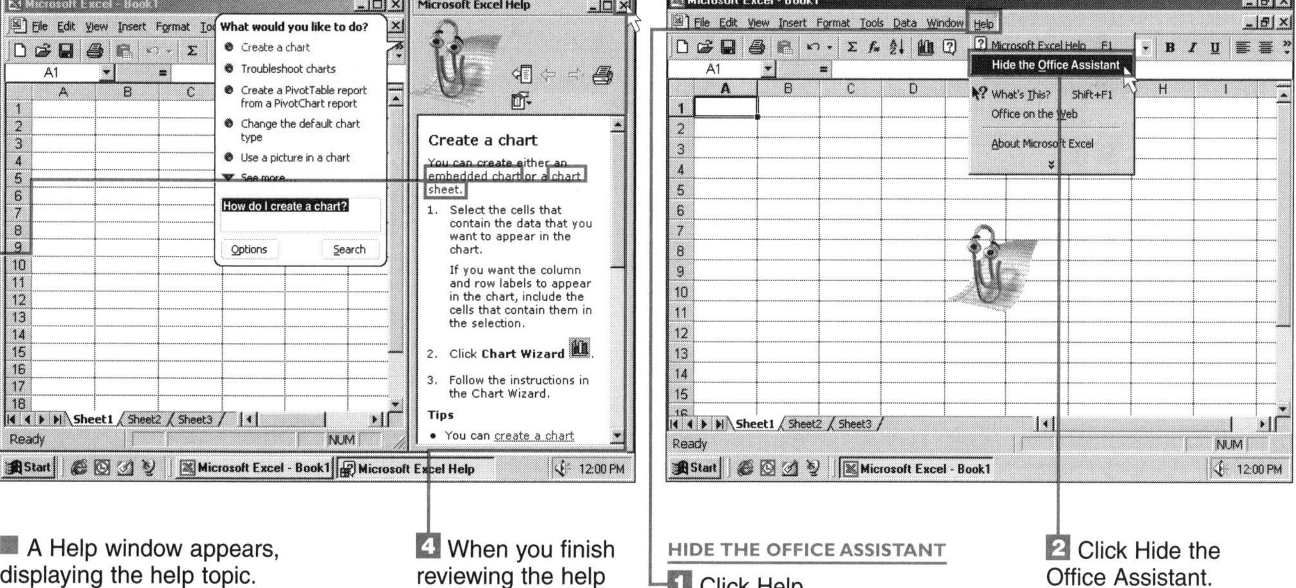

■ A Help window appears, displaying the help topic.

■ You can display a definition of a word or phrase that appears in blue with no underline. To display the definition, click the word or phrase. To remove the definition, click anywhere on the screen.

4 When you finish reviewing the help information, click ✕ to close the Help window.

HIDE THE OFFICE ASSISTANT

1 Click Help.

2 Click Hide the Office Assistant.

SECTION II

1) GETTING STARTED

2) EDIT DOCUMENTS

3) CHANGE VIEW OF DOCUMENT

USING WORD

4) FORMAT TEXT

5) FORMAT DOCUMENTS

6) PRINT DOCUMENTS

7) WORK WITH TABLES

8) WORK WITH GRAPHICS

9) MAIL MERGE

INTRODUCTION TO WORD

Word allows you to efficiently produce documents for business or personal use, such as newsletters, reports, letters and essays. Word offers many features that make it easy for you to create professional-looking documents.

For more information on Word, you can visit the following Web site: www.microsoft.com/word

Entering and Editing Text

Word offers many time-saving features to help you create documents. The templates and wizards included with Word save you time by setting up common types of documents, such as letters, memos and reports, for you. The AutoText feature stores text you frequently type, such as an address, so you do not have to repeatedly type the same text.

Word can help you efficiently work with text in a document. You can easily add or delete text, rearrange paragraphs and check for spelling and grammar mistakes. Word remembers the last changes you made to a document, so you can undo changes you regret.

When you finish entering and editing text, you can e-mail a document to another person.

Viewing Documents

You can change the view of a document to make the document easier to work with. Word offers four ways you can view a document. The Normal view simplifies a document so you can quickly enter, edit and format text. The Web Layout view displays a document as it will appear in a Web browser. The Print Layout view displays a document on the screen as it will appear on a printed page. The Outline view is useful for organizing the structure of a long document.

You can use the Zoom feature to magnify the view of a document so you can see an area of the document in more detail.

Formatting Text

Formatting allows you to enhance the appearance of text in a document. You can use various font sizes, styles and colors to help make important text stand out. You can also change the amount of space between lines of text or align text in different ways.

Formatting text can help you organize the information in a document. You can use tabs to line up columns of information or use bullets to separate items in a list. You can use one of Word's existing styles or create your own style to help you apply the same formatting to many areas of a document.

Formatting Documents

You can use Word's formatting features to enhance a document. For example, you can add page numbers to a document. You can also display text in newspaper-style columns.

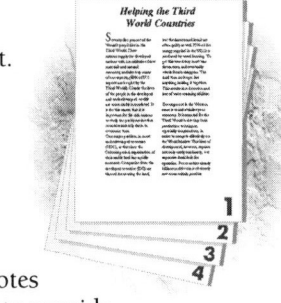

Features such as footnotes or endnotes allow you to provide additional information about text in a document. You can also add headers or footers to the top or bottom of a page to display information such as the date or the name of your company.

Word's formatting features can help you determine how you want a document to print on a page. You can change the margins for a document, center text on a page or specify whether you want to print a document in the portrait or landscape orientation.

Printing

After you finish editing and formatting a document, you can produce a paper copy of the document. You can preview the document before printing to see on the screen exactly what the printed document will look like. You can also use Word to create and print envelopes and mailing labels.

Tables

Tables help you organize and neatly display information in a document. Word lets you draw a table on the screen as you would draw a table with a pen and paper.

There are many ways you can enhance the appearance of a table, such as changing the cell borders, adding shading to cells and changing the position of text in cells. Word also offers ready-to-use designs you can use to enhance the appearance of a table.

Graphics

Word comes with many types of graphics you can use to enhance the appearance of a document. Graphics such as text effects, AutoShapes and professionally designed clip art can help make a document more interesting or help draw attention to important information.

After adding a graphic to a document, you can further enhance the document by wrapping text around the graphic.

Mail Merge

Word's Mail Merge feature allows you to quickly produce personalized letters and mailing labels for each person on a mailing list. This is useful if you want to send the same document, such as an announcement, change of address notification or advertisement, to many people.

START WORD

Word is a word processing program that lets you produce professional-looking documents quickly and efficiently. You can use Word to create documents such as letters, reports, manuals, newsletters and brochures.

When you start Word, a blank document appears on your screen. You can type text into this document. Typing text is only the beginning of word processing. Once you type the text for a document, you can change the content and appearance of the document. You can also produce a paper copy of the document.

The first time you start Word, the Office Assistant appears on your screen. The Office Assistant can provide you with information about performing many common tasks, including opening and saving documents. For more information on the Office Assistant, see page 16.

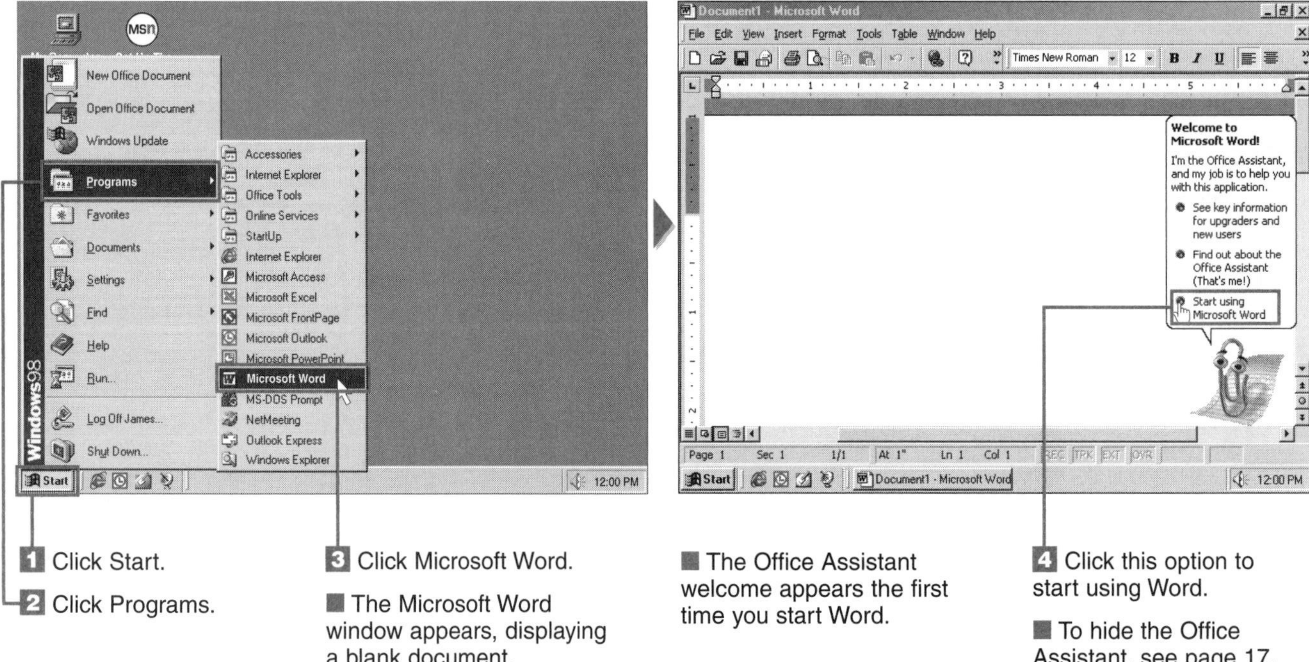

1 Click Start.

2 Click Programs.

3 Click Microsoft Word.

■ The Microsoft Word window appears, displaying a blank document.

■ The Office Assistant welcome appears the first time you start Word.

4 Click this option to start using Word.

■ To hide the Office Assistant, see page 17.

THE WORD SCREEN

The Word screen displays several items to help you perform tasks efficiently.

Standard Toolbar

Contains buttons to help you select common commands, such as Save and Print.

Menu Bar

Provides access to lists of commands available in Word.

Formatting Toolbar

Contains buttons to help you select formatting commands, such as Font Size and Underline.

Ruler

Allows you to change margin and tab settings for the document.

Insertion Point

The flashing line on the screen that indicates where the text you type will appear.

View Buttons

Allow you to quickly change the way the document is displayed.

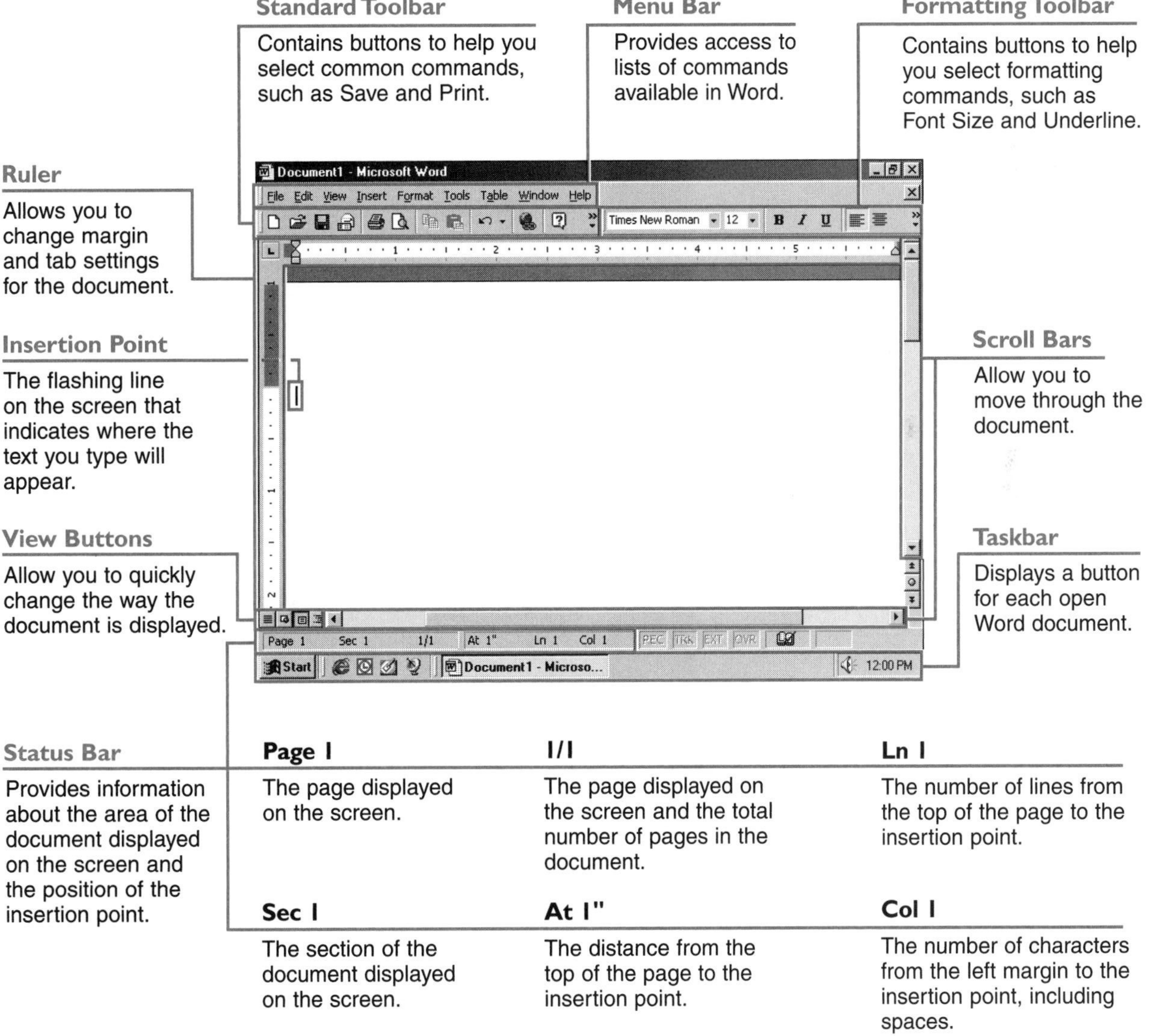

Scroll Bars

Allow you to move through the document.

Taskbar

Displays a button for each open Word document.

Status Bar

Provides information about the area of the document displayed on the screen and the position of the insertion point.

Page 1

The page displayed on the screen.

1/1

The page displayed on the screen and the total number of pages in the document.

Ln 1

The number of lines from the top of the page to the insertion point.

Sec 1

The section of the document displayed on the screen.

At 1"

The distance from the top of the page to the insertion point.

Col 1

The number of characters from the left margin to the insertion point, including spaces.

ENTER TEXT

Word allows you to type text into your document quickly and easily.

When the text you are typing reaches the end of a line, Word automatically wraps the text to the next line. You only need to press the Enter key when you want to start a new line or paragraph.

As you type, Word automatically checks your document for spelling and grammar errors and underlines any errors that are found. Word also corrects hundreds of common typing, spelling and grammar errors for you. For example, Word automatically replaces "insted" with "instead" as you type.

Word's AutoText feature helps you quickly enter common words and phrases in your document. For example, you can quickly enter greetings, such as "To Whom It May Concern:". You can also quickly enter the days of the week or months of the year. For more information on the AutoText feature, see page 62.

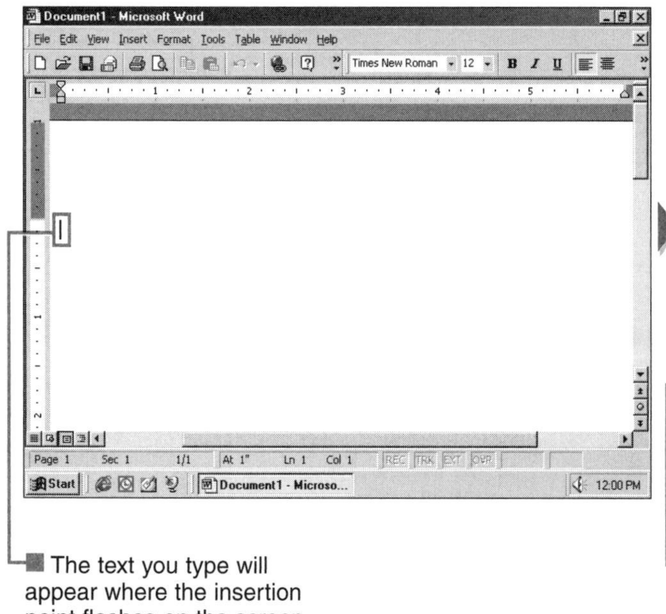

■ The text you type will appear where the insertion point flashes on the screen.

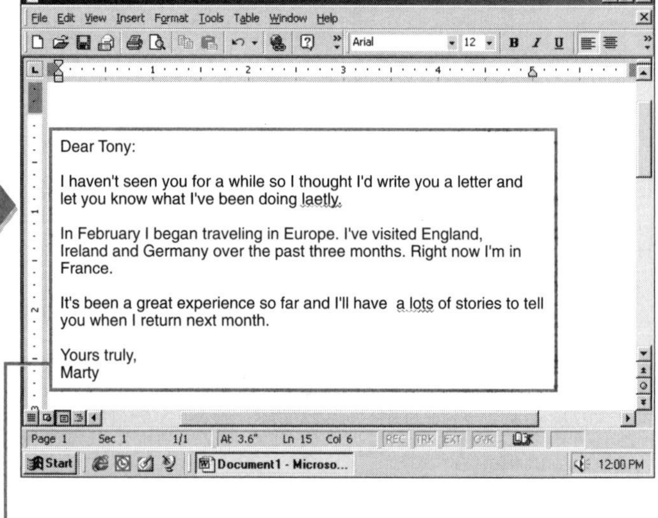

1 Type the text for the document.

■ Press the Enter key only when you want to start a new paragraph.

Note: In this example, the font of text was changed from Times New Roman to Arial to make the document easier to read.

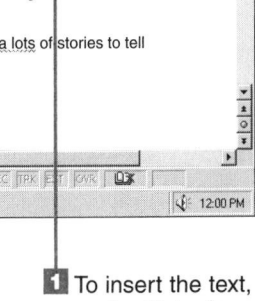

Can I enter text anywhere in my document?

✔ Word's Click and Type feature lets you quickly enter text in any part of your document. In the Print Layout or Web Layout view, double-click the location where you want to enter text. You can then type the text you want to add.

How can I quickly insert the current date and time in my document?

✔ Click where you want the date and time to appear in your document. Select the Insert menu and click Date and Time. Select the format you want to use for the date and time and then click OK.

Can I quickly enter symbols in my document?

✔ If you type one of the following sets of characters, Word will instantly replace the characters with a symbol. This lets you enter symbols in your document that are not available on your keyboard. For more information on inserting symbols, see page 64.

Characters	Symbol	Characters	Symbol
(c)	©	<--	←
(r)	®	-->	→
(tm)	TM	<==	⇐
:(	☹	==>	⇒
:)	☺	<=>	⇔
:|	😐		

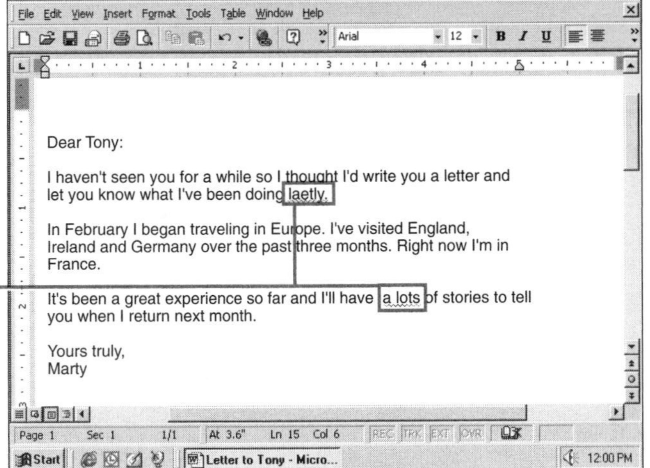

SPELLING ERRORS

■ Word underlines misspelled words in red and grammar mistakes in green. The red and green underlines will not appear when you print the document.

■ Word automatically corrects common spelling mistakes as you type, such as recieve (receive) and nwe (new).

ENTER TEXT AUTOMATICALLY

■ Word allows you to quickly enter common words and phrases.

■ When you type the first few characters of a common word or phrase, a box appears, displaying the text.

1 To insert the text, press the Enter key.

Note: To ignore the text, continue typing.

SELECT TEXT

Before performing many tasks in Word, you must select the text you want to work with. For example, you must select text you want to change to a different font.

Selected text appears highlighted on your screen. Word highlights selected text in a color that contrasts the background color of your document. This makes the selected text stand out from the rest of the text in your document.

You can select the part of your document you want to work with. You can select a single word, a sentence, a paragraph or any amount of text in your document.

After you finish working with selected text, you should deselect the text. If you begin typing when text on your screen is selected, Word will delete the selected text and replace it with the text you type.

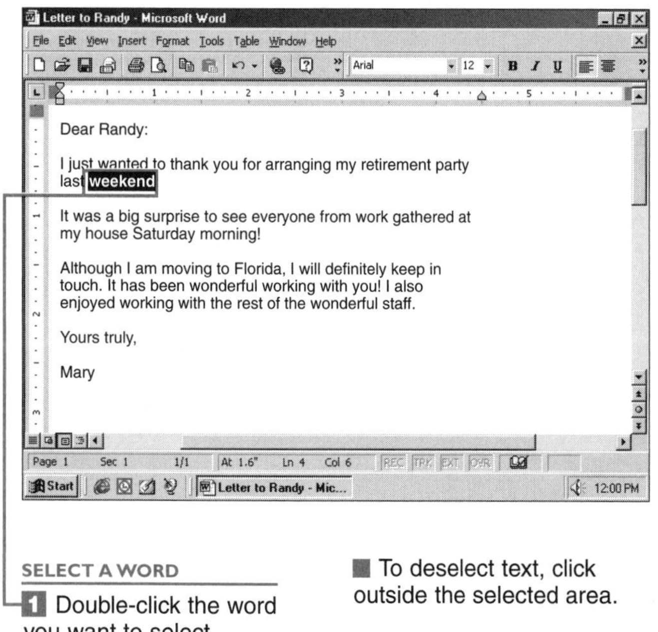

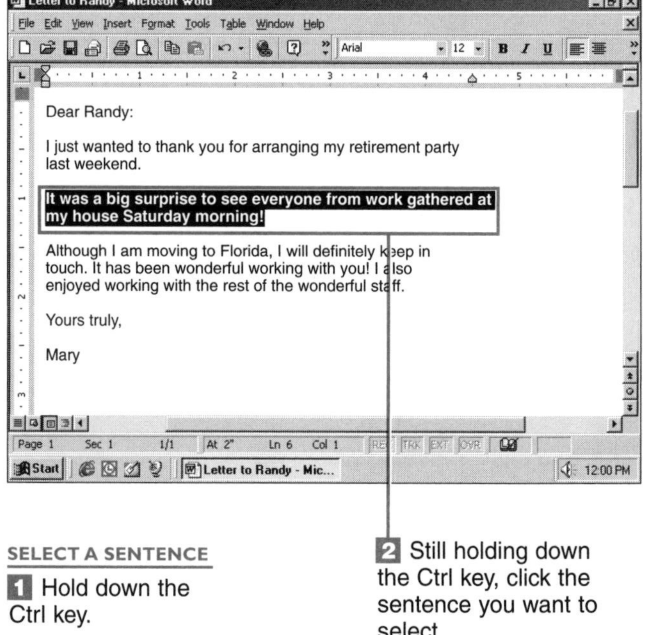

SELECT A WORD

1 Double-click the word you want to select.

■ To deselect text, click outside the selected area.

SELECT A SENTENCE

1 Hold down the Ctrl key.

2 Still holding down the Ctrl key, click the sentence you want to select.

TIPS

Can I select text using the keyboard?

✔ To select characters, hold down the Shift key as you press the ← or → key. To select words, hold down the Shift+Ctrl keys as you press the ← or → key.

How can I quickly select a large section of my document?

✔ Click to the left of the first word in the section you want to select and then scroll to the end of the section. Hold down the Shift key as you click to the right of the last character you want to select.

How do I select all the text in my document?

✔ If necessary, use the scroll bar to display the left edge of the document. Position the mouse pointer over the left edge of the document (↖ changes to ↗) and then triple-click to select all the text. You can also press the Ctrl+A keys to select all the text in your document.

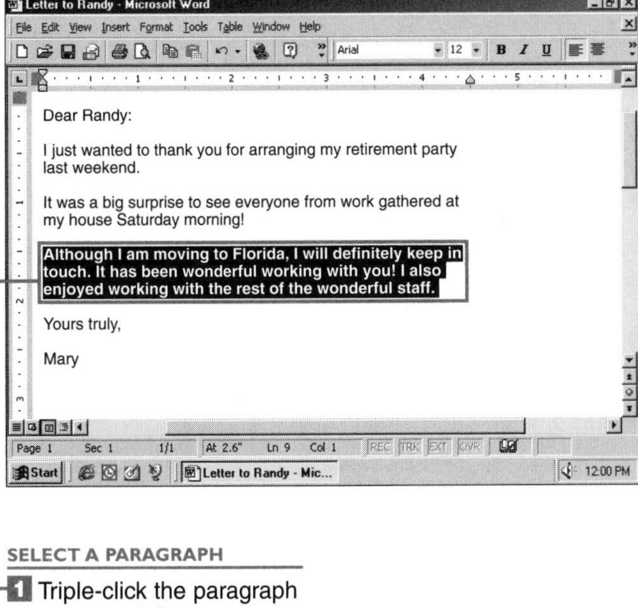

SELECT A PARAGRAPH

1 Triple-click the paragraph you want to select.

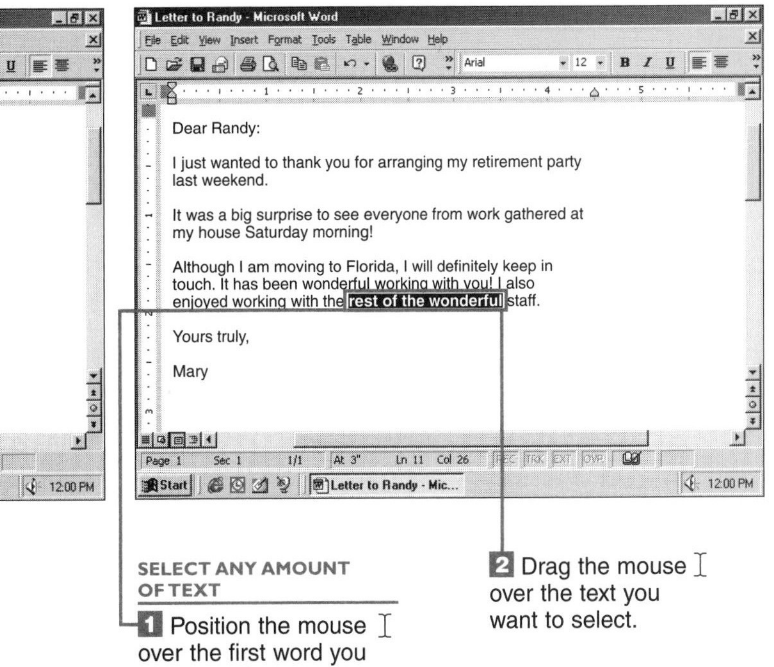

SELECT ANY AMOUNT OF TEXT

1 Position the mouse I over the first word you want to select.

2 Drag the mouse I over the text you want to select.

MOVE THROUGH A DOCUMENT

If your document contains a lot of text, your screen may not be able to display all the text at once. To view other areas of the document, you must move through the document.

The flashing line on your screen, called the insertion point, indicates where the text you type will appear. You can move the insertion point to another location in your document. If you begin typing text when the insertion point is not displayed on your screen, Word will automatically display the part of the document containing the insertion point.

Word allows you to move through your document one page at a time. This can help you quickly locate the page you want to work with.

You can also use the scroll bar to move through a document. Scrolling allows you to move to another location in the document but does not move the insertion point.

You can purchase a mouse with a wheel between the left and right mouse buttons. Moving this wheel lets you quickly scroll through your document.

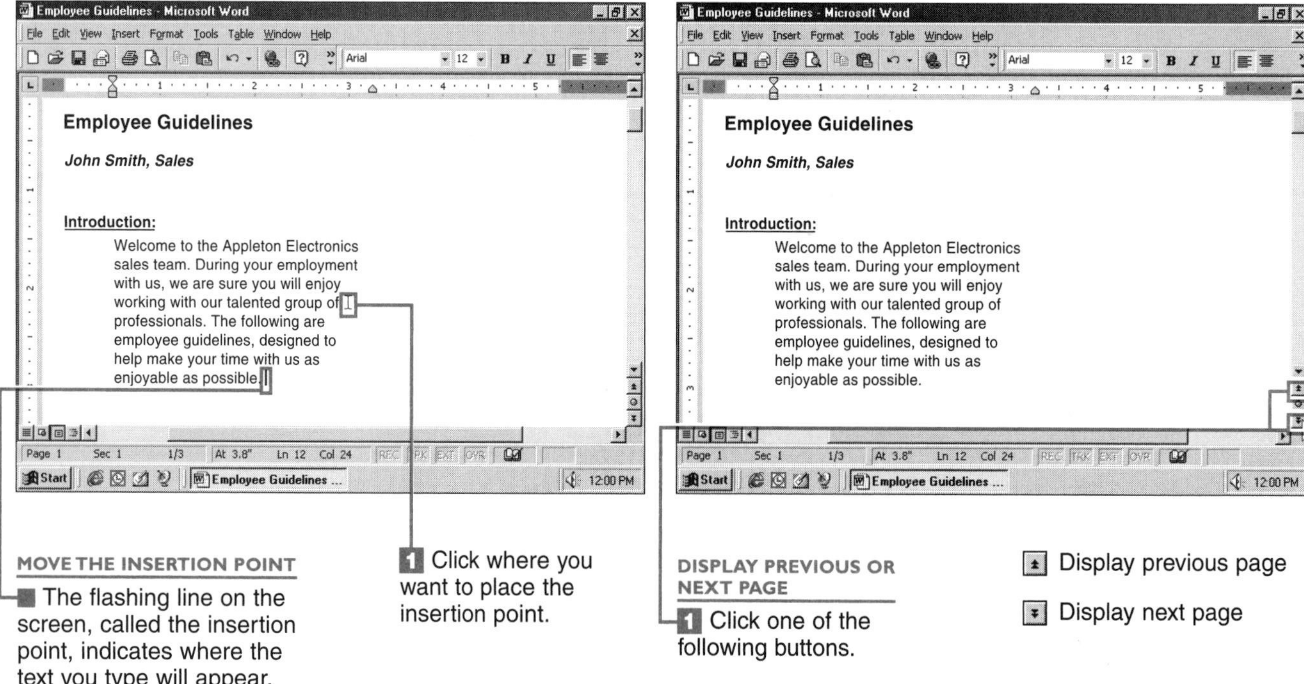

MOVE THE INSERTION POINT

■ The flashing line on the screen, called the insertion point, indicates where the text you type will appear.

1 Click where you want to place the insertion point.

DISPLAY PREVIOUS OR NEXT PAGE

1 Click one of the following buttons.

▲ Display previous page

▼ Display next page

TIPS

Why doesn't Word display the previous or next page when I click the ▲ or ▼ button?

✔ These buttons may be set to perform a different task. To use the buttons to display the previous or next page, click ○ located between the ▲ and ▼ buttons. Then select the Browse by Page option (□).

How can I use my keyboard to move through a document?

✔ You can press the ↑ or ↓ key to move through a document one line at a time. You can press the Page Up or Page Down key to move through a document one screen at a time.

Can I view two different parts of a document at the same time?

✔ Word lets you split your screen to view two parts of a document at the same time. Position the mouse pointer over the split box (▭) located above the scroll bar at the right of your screen (↖ changes to ÷). Then drag the split box to where you want to split the document. To remove the split, double-click the split bar.

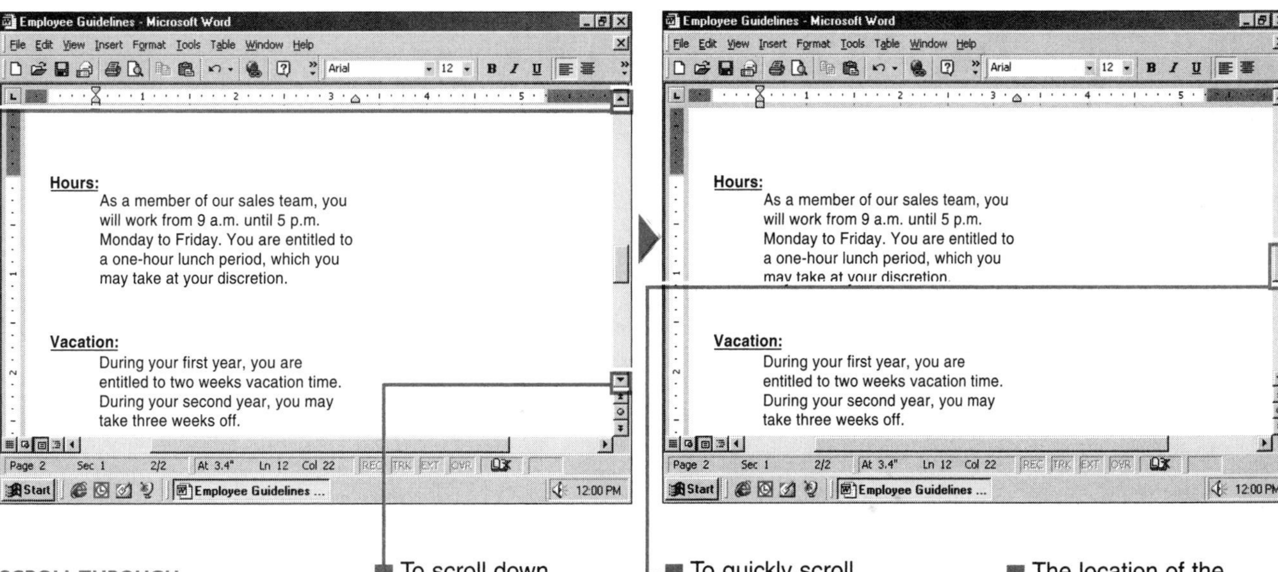

SCROLL THROUGH A DOCUMENT

■ To scroll up one line, click ▲.

■ To scroll down one line, click ▼.

■ To quickly scroll through the document, drag the scroll box (□) up or down the scroll bar.

■ The location of the scroll box indicates which part of the document you are viewing. To view the middle of the document, drag the scroll box halfway down the scroll bar.

SAVE A DOCUMENT

You can save your document to store it for future use. To avoid losing your work, you should regularly save changes you make to a document.

When you save a document, Word may suggest a name for the document based on the first line of the document. You can give the document another name.

You can specify where you want to save your document. The Places Bar in the Save As dialog box lets you quickly access commonly used folders. The History folder lets you access folders you recently used. The My Documents folder provides a convenient place to save your document. The Desktop folder lets you quickly save your document on the Windows desktop. The Favorites folder provides a place to save a document you will frequently access. You can use Web Folders to save your document on a computer called a Web server. Once the document is saved on a Web server, it will be available for other people to view.

When you finish using Word, you can exit the program. You should always exit all open programs and shut down Windows before turning off your computer.

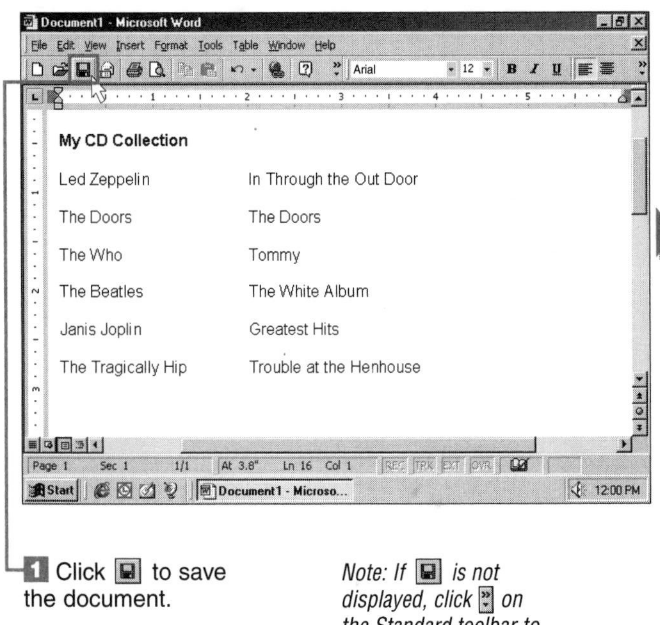

1 Click [save icon] to save the document.

Note: If [save icon] is not displayed, click [»] on the Standard toolbar to display all the buttons.

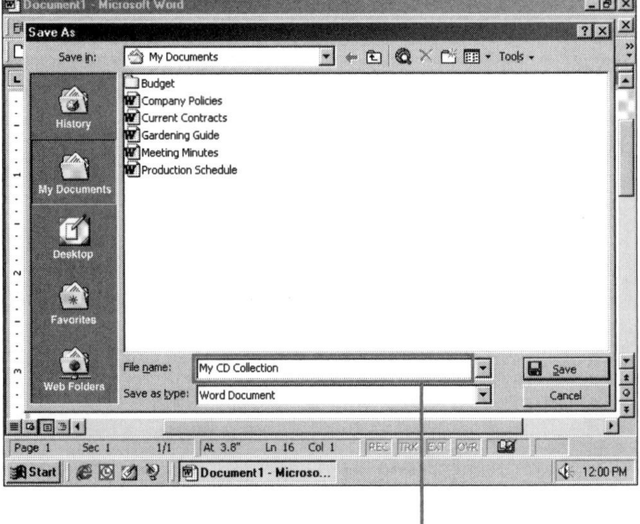

■ The Save As dialog box appears.

Note: If you previously saved the document, the Save As dialog box will not appear since you have already named the document.

2 Type a name for the document.

My colleagues do not use Word 2000. Can I save my document in a different format?

✔ Yes. In the Save As dialog box, click the Save as type area and then select a format. A dialog box appears if the file format converter is not installed. Click Yes to install the converter. A Microsoft Office 2000 dialog box will appear, asking you to insert the CD-ROM disc you used to install Office. Insert the CD-ROM disc and click OK.

In the Save As dialog box, what are the ⇦ and 📁 buttons used for?

✔ These buttons let you change where Word will store your document. The Back button (⇦) allows you to move back through the drives and folders you recently displayed. The Create New Folder button (📁) allows you to create a new folder to store the document.

I previously saved my document. How can I save a copy of the document with a different name?

✔ Click the File menu and then select Save As. Type the new name and then click Save.

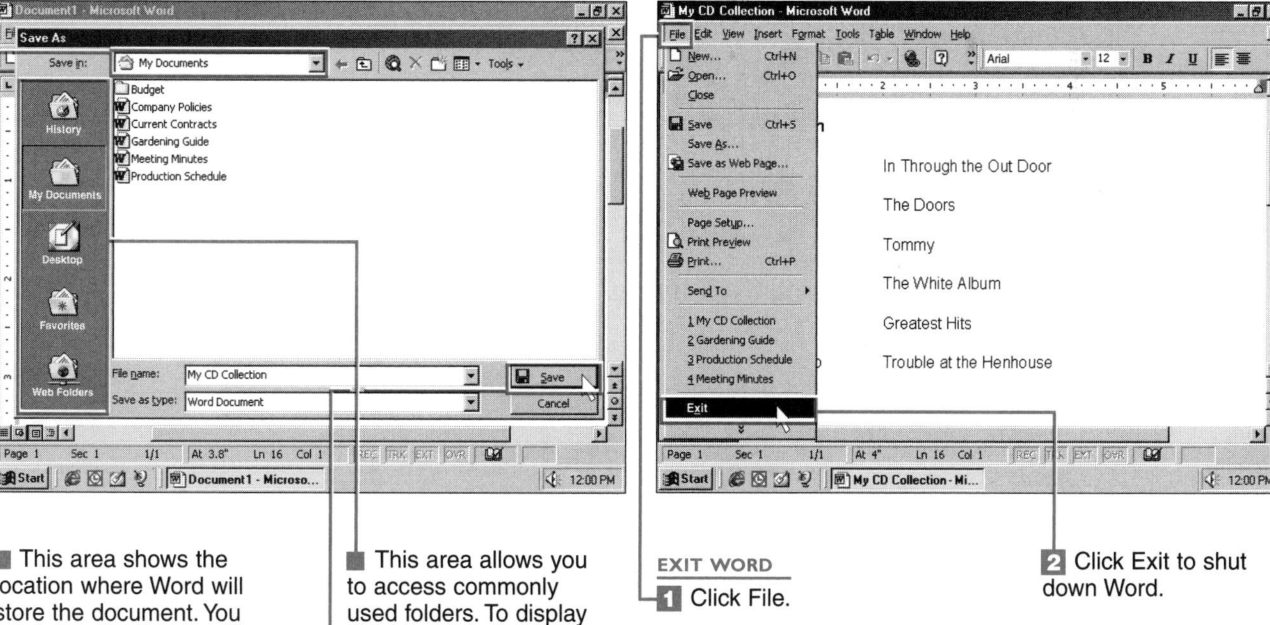

■ This area shows the location where Word will store the document. You can click this area to change the location.

■ This area allows you to access commonly used folders. To display the contents of a folder, click the folder.

3 Click Save.

EXIT WORD

1 Click File.

2 Click Exit to shut down Word.

OPEN A DOCUMENT

You can open a saved document and display it on your screen. This allows you to review and edit the document.

You can specify where the document you want to open is located on your computer. You can use the Places Bar to quickly display the contents of commonly used folders. For information on the Places Bar, see the top of page 32.

You can use Word to open and edit documents created in many different programs, such as WordPerfect and previous versions of Word. This is useful when you work with colleagues who use a word processor other than Word 2000. Word can also open documents saved as Web pages.

If you cannot see the document you want to open, make sure the correct type of document is selected. If you do not know which document type to use, select All Files.

After you open a document, Word displays the name of the document at the top of your screen.

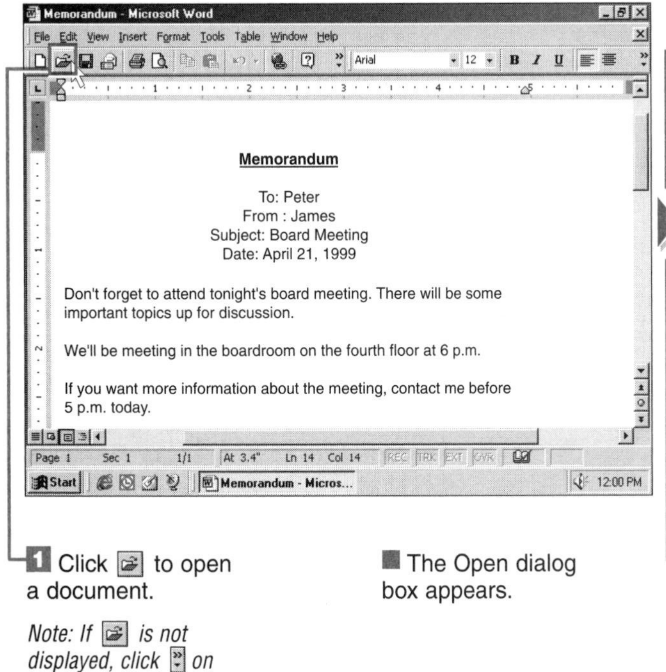

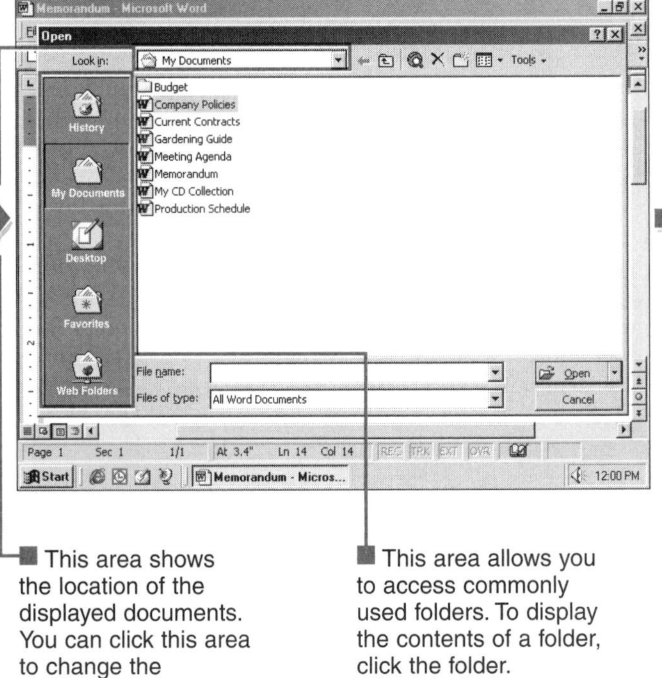

1 Click to open a document.

Note: If is not displayed, click on the Standard toolbar to display all the buttons.

■ The Open dialog box appears.

■ This area shows the location of the displayed documents. You can click this area to change the location.

■ This area allows you to access commonly used folders. To display the contents of a folder, click the folder.

TIPS

Can I open any type of document?

✔ Word allows you to open many types of documents, but a dialog box may appear if the necessary file format converter is not installed. Click Yes to install the converter. A Microsoft Office 2000 dialog box appears, asking you to insert the CD-ROM disc you used to install Office. Insert the CD-ROM disc and click OK.

Can I quickly open a document I recently worked with?

✔ Word remembers the names of the last four documents you worked with. To quickly open one of these documents, select the File menu and then click the name of the document you want to open.

How can I change the way documents are displayed in the Open dialog box?

✔ Click ▾ beside the Views button (▦▾) in the Open dialog box. To view the names of the documents, click List. To view information about the documents, such as size and type, click Details. To view information about the currently selected document, click Properties. To display a preview of the currently selected document, click Preview.

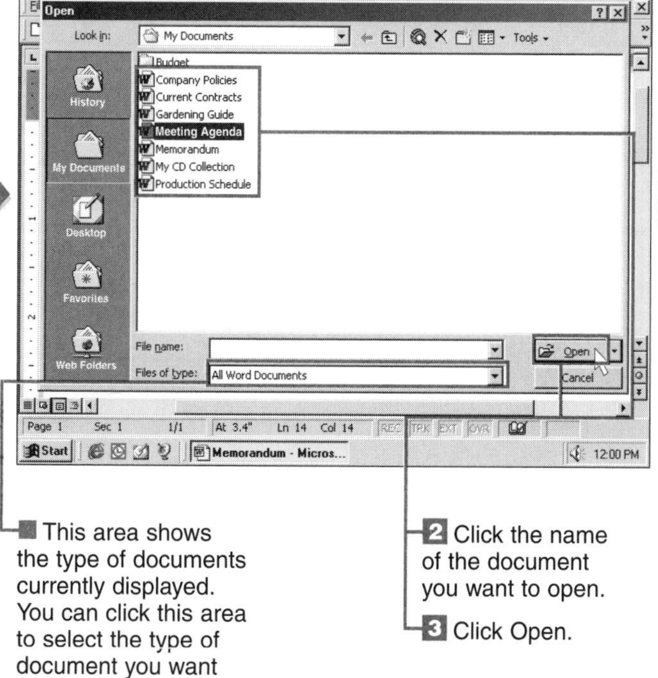

■ This area shows the type of documents currently displayed. You can click this area to select the type of document you want to open.

2 Click the name of the document you want to open.

3 Click Open.

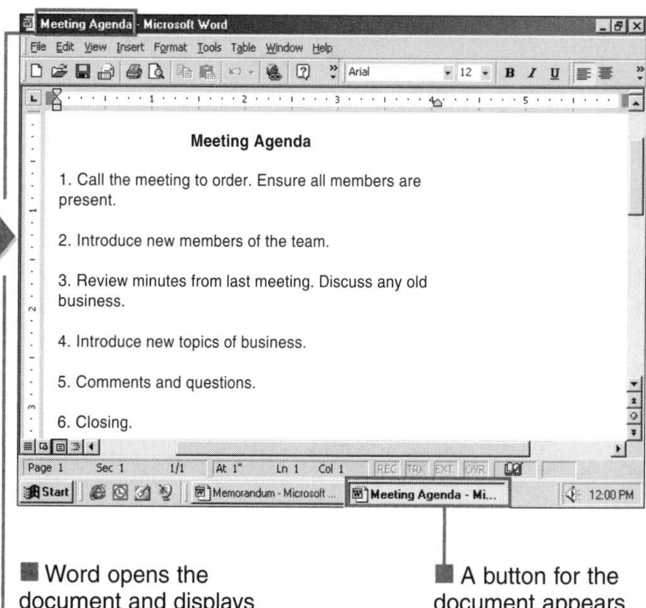

■ Word opens the document and displays it on the screen. You can now review and make changes to the document.

■ The name of the document appears at the top of the screen.

■ A button for the document appears on the taskbar.

FIND A DOCUMENT

If you cannot remember the name or location of a document you want to open, you can have Word search for the document using search criteria you specify.

To enter search criteria, you need to specify the property you want to use to find the document. For example, you can search for a document by the name of the document or the date the document was created.

After you select a property, you need to specify a condition for the search. The available conditions depend on the property you selected. For example, when you select the Last modified property, Word allows you to choose a condition such as yesterday, today or last week.

You may also need to specify a value to help Word determine what to search for. For example, you may need to specify text in the document's name or the total number of pages in the document. Some properties do not require you to specify a value for the search.

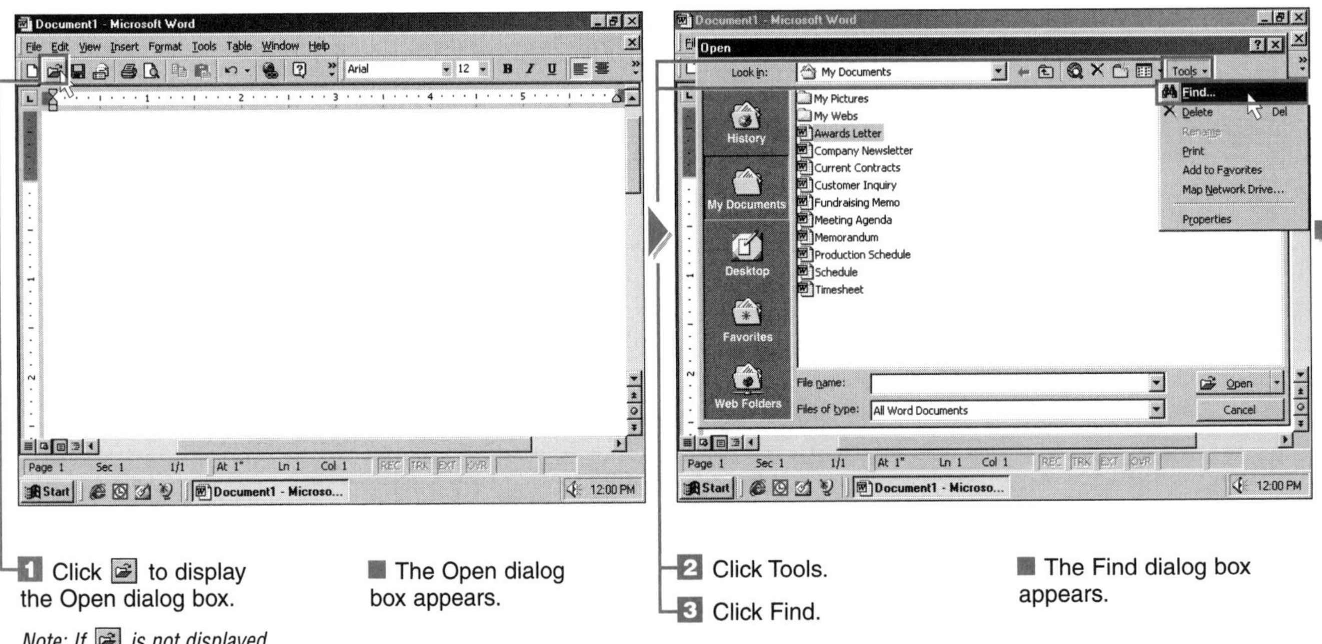

1 Click [Open icon] to display the Open dialog box.

Note: If [Open icon] is not displayed, click [More Buttons icon] on the Standard toolbar to display all the buttons.

■ The Open dialog box appears.

2 Click Tools.

3 Click Find.

■ The Find dialog box appears.

TIPS

Is there anything I should check before starting a search?

✔ You should make sure that the Files of type area in the Open dialog box displays the All Word Documents or All Files option. You can click the Files of type area to select the correct option.

How can I improve my search results?

✔ The results of a search depend on the properties of your documents. You should specify properties for your documents to ensure better search results later. When creating a document, click the File menu, select Properties and then enter the appropriate information for the document.

Can I have Word find the text I specified only when it is capitalized?

✔ You can have Word find a document containing text with exactly matching uppercase and lowercase letters. In the Find dialog box, click the Match exactly option (☐ changes to ☑).

How do I clear the search criteria I specified?

✔ To quickly clear the search criteria you specified and start a new search, click the New Search button in the Find dialog box.

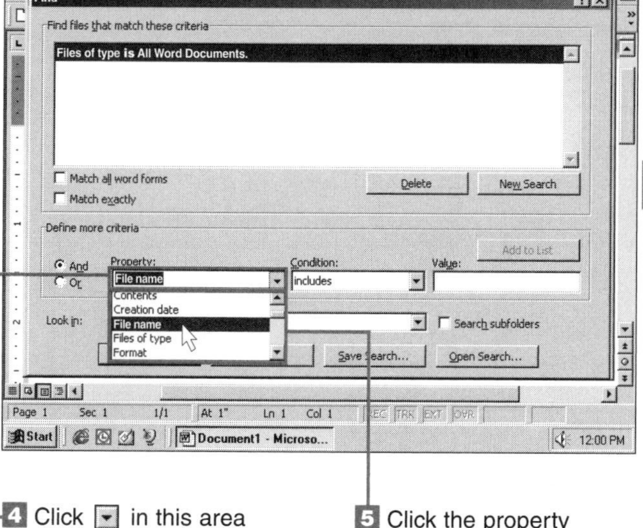

4 Click ▾ in this area to specify a property for the search.

5 Click the property you want to use.

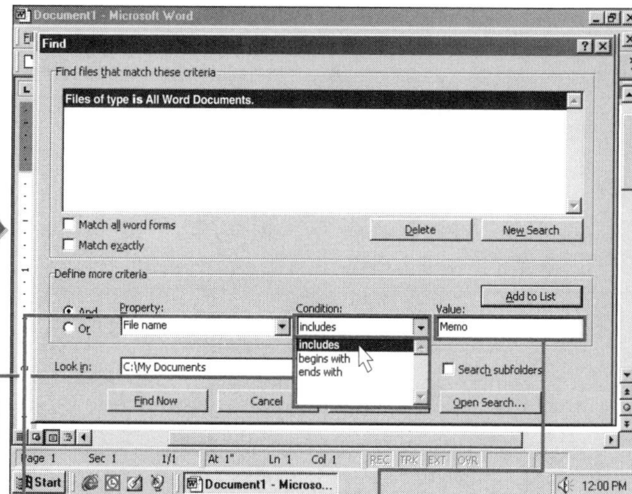

6 Click ▾ in this area to specify a condition for the search.

7 Click the condition you want to use.

Note: The available conditions depend on the property you selected in step 5.

8 Click this area and type the value you want to search for.

Note: If the value area is not available, you do not need to enter a value.

CONTINUED

FIND A DOCUMENT CONTINUED

You can specify the location where you want Word to search for a document. You can also have Word search the contents of all the subfolders in the location you specify.

When you finish specifying the criteria you want to use for the search, you must add the search criteria to a list of criteria in the Find dialog box. Word automatically adds the type of file displayed in the Open dialog box to the list of search criteria for you.

Word may take a few moments or several minutes to find a document. The search criteria you specified determines the length of time the search will take. Searching for a document on a network may also increase the length of a search.

When the search is complete, Word displays the names of all the documents it found. You can open a document Word found to review and make changes to the document.

If the search does not provide the results you were expecting, you may not have provided Word with enough information or you may have specified incorrect information.

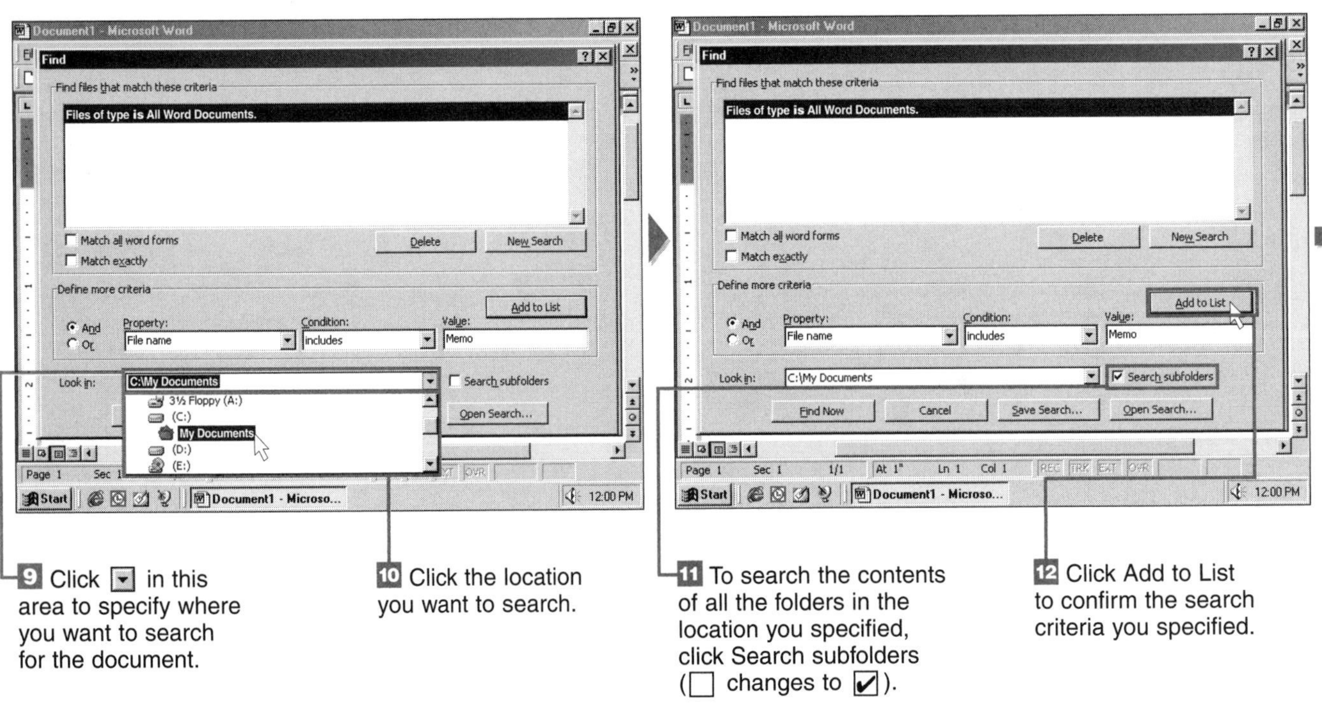

9 Click ▾ in this area to specify where you want to search for the document.

10 Click the location you want to search.

11 To search the contents of all the folders in the location you specified, click Search subfolders (☐ changes to ☑).

12 Click Add to List to confirm the search criteria you specified.

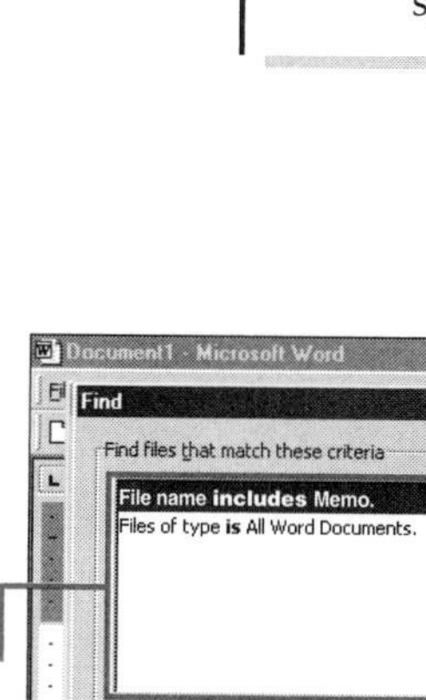

TIPS

Can I use more than one criteria in my search?

✔ Yes. Specify the first criteria you want to use and then click the "And" or "Or" option (○ changes to ⦿). Repeat steps 4 to 8 on page 37 to specify additional search criteria and then perform steps 12 and 13 below to complete the search. Select "And" to have Word search for documents that meet all of the search criteria you specified. Select "Or" to have Word search for documents that meet at least one of the search criteria you specified.

How do I remove criteria from the list of search criteria?

✔ Click the criteria you want to remove and then click the Delete button.

When I started the search, why did a dialog box appear, asking if I want to install FindFast?

✔ FindFast is a feature that can help speed up your searches. To install FindFast, click Yes and then insert the CD-ROM disc you used to install Office 2000 into your CD-ROM drive. Then click OK.

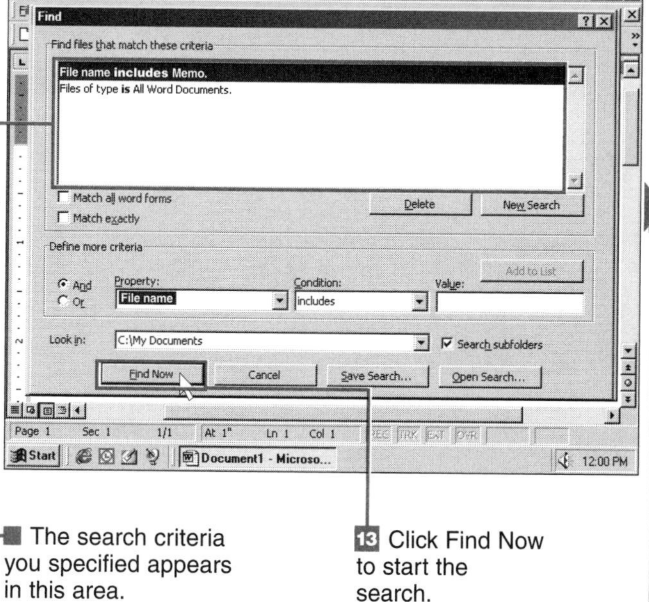

■ The search criteria you specified appears in this area.

13 Click Find Now to start the search.

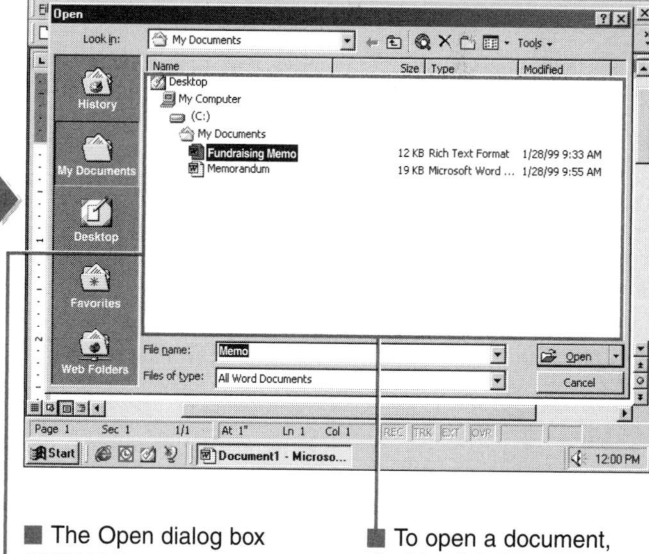

■ The Open dialog box reappears.

■ This area displays the names of the documents Word found.

■ To open a document, double-click the name of the document.

CREATE A NEW DOCUMENT

You can create a new document to start writing a letter, memo or report.

When you create a new document, Word displays a blank document on your screen. Each document is like a separate piece of paper. Creating a new document is like placing a new piece of paper on your screen.

If there is a document currently displayed on your screen, you do not have to close the document before creating a new document.

Word uses default settings, such as the Times New Roman font and the 12-point font size, for the new document. Word also gives each new document a temporary name, such as Document1, until you save the document. For information on saving a document, see page 32.

You can use Word's templates and wizards to create common types of documents. For information on templates and wizards, see page 44.

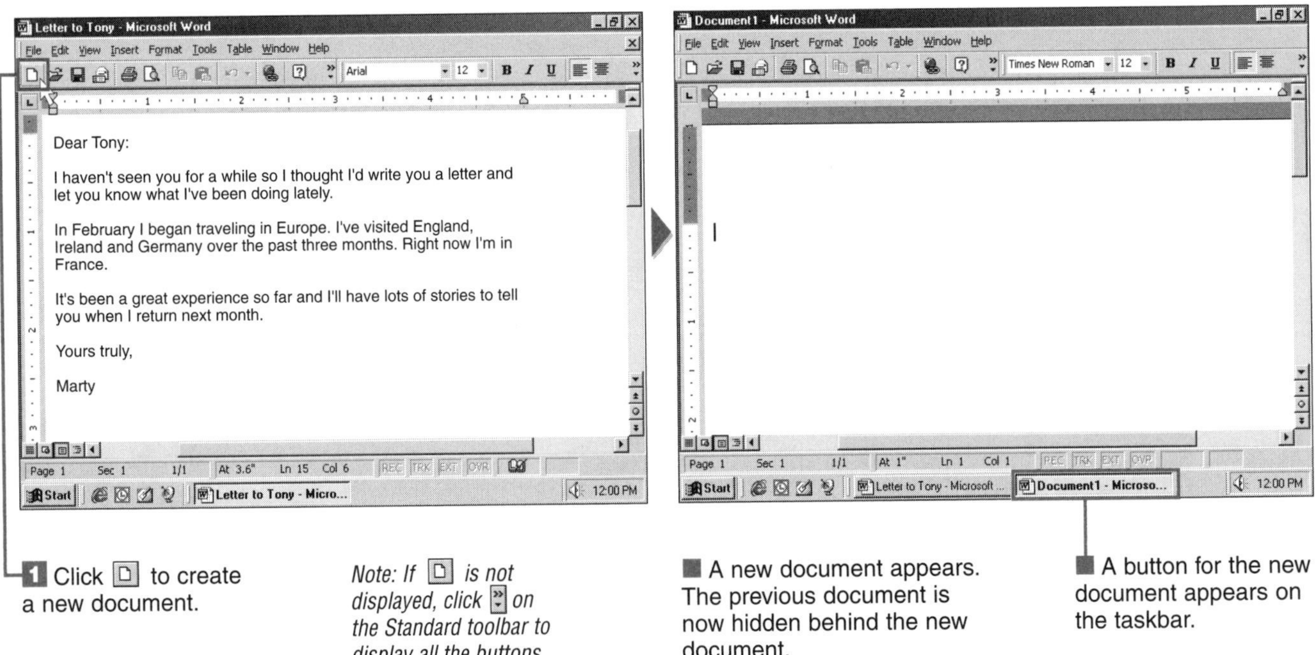

1 Click □ to create a new document.

Note: If □ is not displayed, click » on the Standard toolbar to display all the buttons.

■ A new document appears. The previous document is now hidden behind the new document.

■ A button for the new document appears on the taskbar.

SWITCH BETWEEN DOCUMENTS

Word lets you have many documents open at once. You can switch between all your open documents.

The ability to have multiple documents open and switch between them is very useful. For example, you can switch between open documents to consult a report while you write a letter.

You can display the names of all your open documents in a list and then select the name of the document you want to switch to.

You can also use the taskbar to switch between documents. The taskbar displays a button for each document you have open. To switch to the document you want to display on your screen, you can select the button for the document on the taskbar.

Word displays the name of the document you are currently working with at the top of your screen.

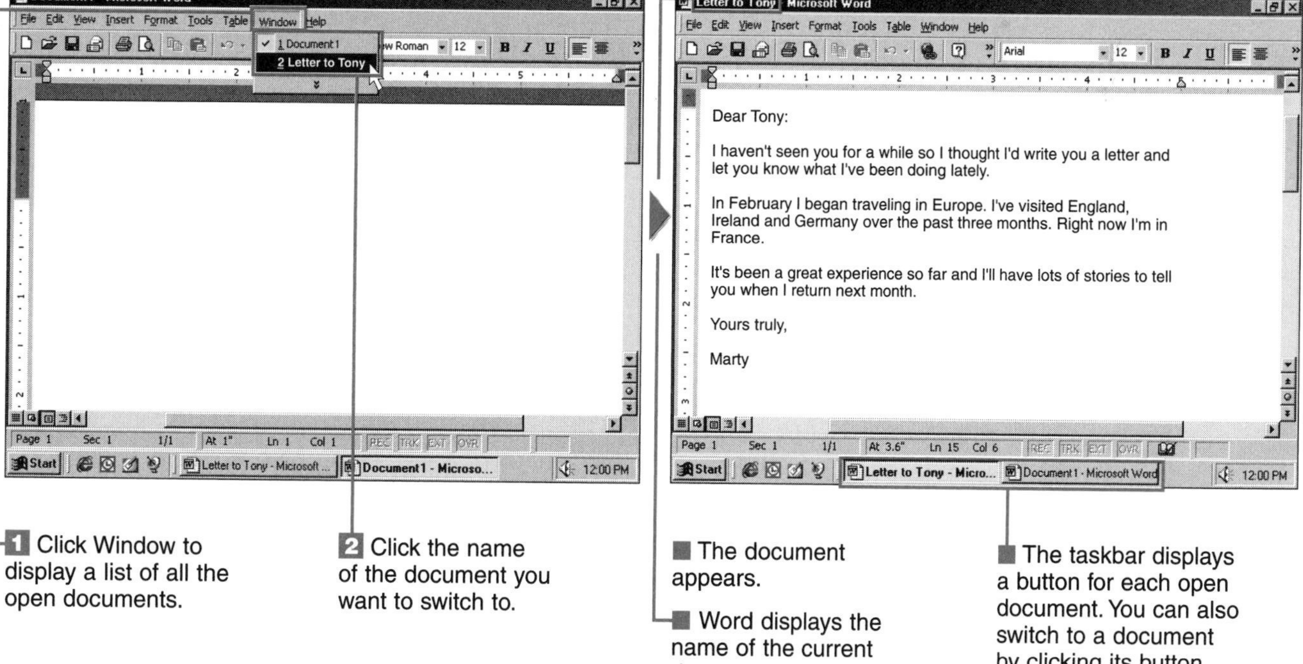

1 Click Window to display a list of all the open documents.

2 Click the name of the document you want to switch to.

■ The document appears.

■ Word displays the name of the current document at the top of the screen.

■ The taskbar displays a button for each open document. You can also switch to a document by clicking its button on the taskbar.

CLOSE A DOCUMENT

When you have finished working with a document, you can close the document to remove it from your screen.

You should save your document before you close the document. If you close a document without saving it, you will lose any changes you made to the document. For information on saving a document, see page 32.

If you try to close a document you have not saved, Word will remind you to save the document.

When you close a document, you do not exit the Word program. You can continue to work with other open documents. If you have more than one document open when you close your document, the second last document you worked with will appear on the screen. You can also create a new document or open an existing document after closing a document.

When you close a document, the button for the document disappears from the taskbar.

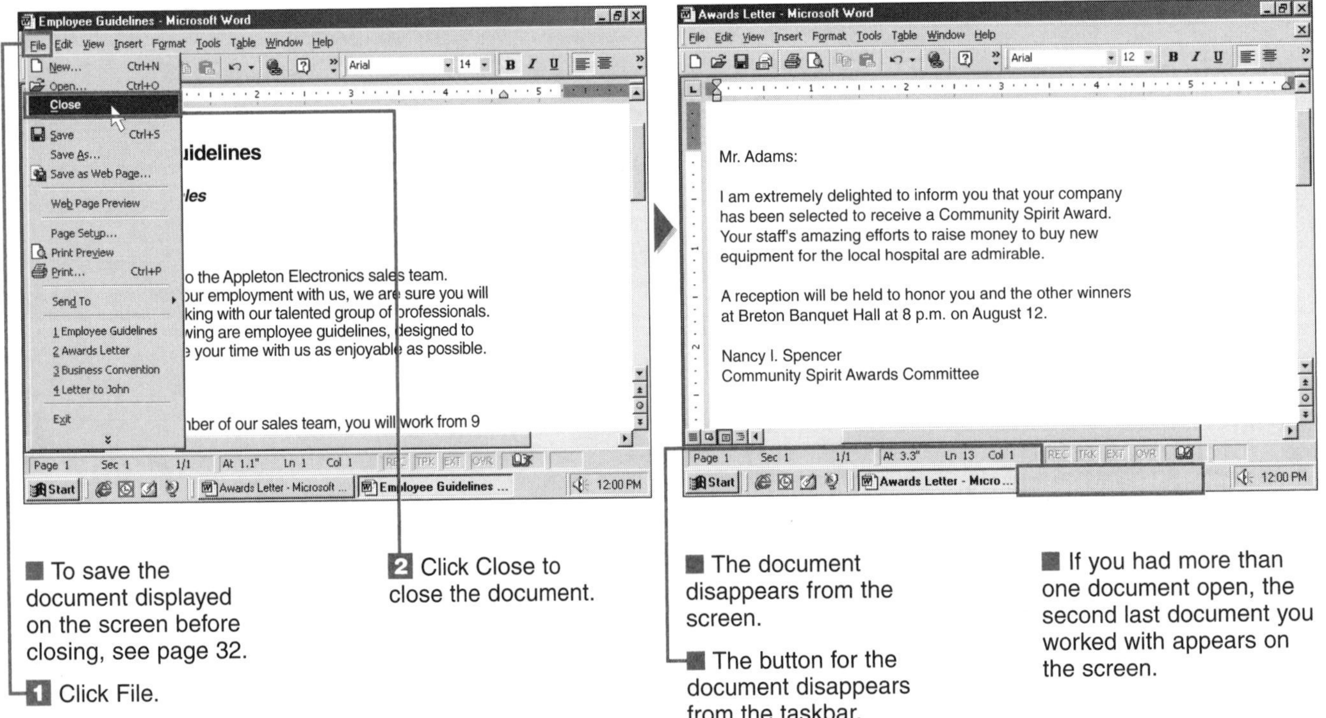

■ To save the document displayed on the screen before closing, see page 32.

1 Click File.

2 Click Close to close the document.

■ The document disappears from the screen.

■ The button for the document disappears from the taskbar.

■ If you had more than one document open, the second last document you worked with appears on the screen.

E-MAIL A DOCUMENT

You can e-mail the document displayed on your screen to other people on the Internet or your corporate intranet. The contents of the document will appear in the body of the e-mail message.

You can send a document to more than one person. You can enter the address of each person you want to receive the document in the To area. Entering an address in the Cc area allows you to send a copy of the document to a person who is not directly involved but would be interested in the document. Cc stands for carbon copy.

When you e-mail a document, Word may suggest a subject for the e-mail message based on the name of the document. You can enter a different subject. You should enter a subject that will help the recipient quickly identify the contents of the message.

Before you e-mail a Word document, you must set up Microsoft Outlook. For information on using Microsoft Outlook, see pages 508 to 521.

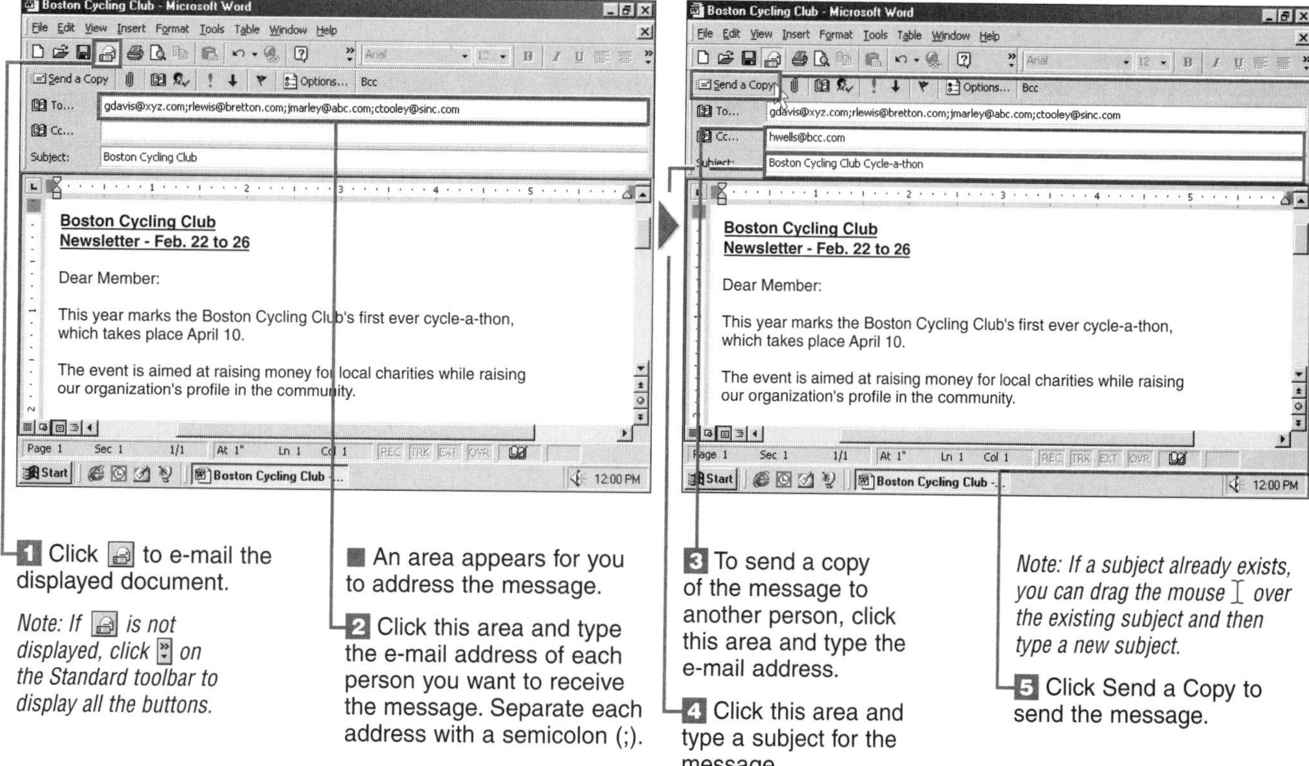

1 Click [icon] to e-mail the displayed document.

Note: If [icon] is not displayed, click [icon] on the Standard toolbar to display all the buttons.

■ An area appears for you to address the message.

2 Click this area and type the e-mail address of each person you want to receive the message. Separate each address with a semicolon (;).

3 To send a copy of the message to another person, click this area and type the e-mail address.

4 Click this area and type a subject for the message.

Note: If a subject already exists, you can drag the mouse I over the existing subject and then type a new subject.

5 Click Send a Copy to send the message.

USING TEMPLATES AND WIZARDS

You can use templates and wizards to save time when creating common types of documents, such as letters, faxes, memos and reports. Templates and wizards provide the layout and formatting so you can concentrate on the content of your document.

When you select a template, a document immediately appears on your screen with areas for you to fill in your personalized information. For example, the Contemporary Memo template provides areas for the name of the person you are sending the memo to, the date and the subject of the memo. You can replace the sample text in a template with the text you want to use.

Wizards guide you step by step through the process of creating a document. When you select a wizard, you will be asked a series of questions. The wizard uses your answers to create the document. For example, the Letter Wizard asks you for information such as the name and address of the person you are sending the letter to.

For additional templates and wizards, you can visit the following Web site: http://officeupdate.microsoft.com/downloadCatalog/dldWord.htm

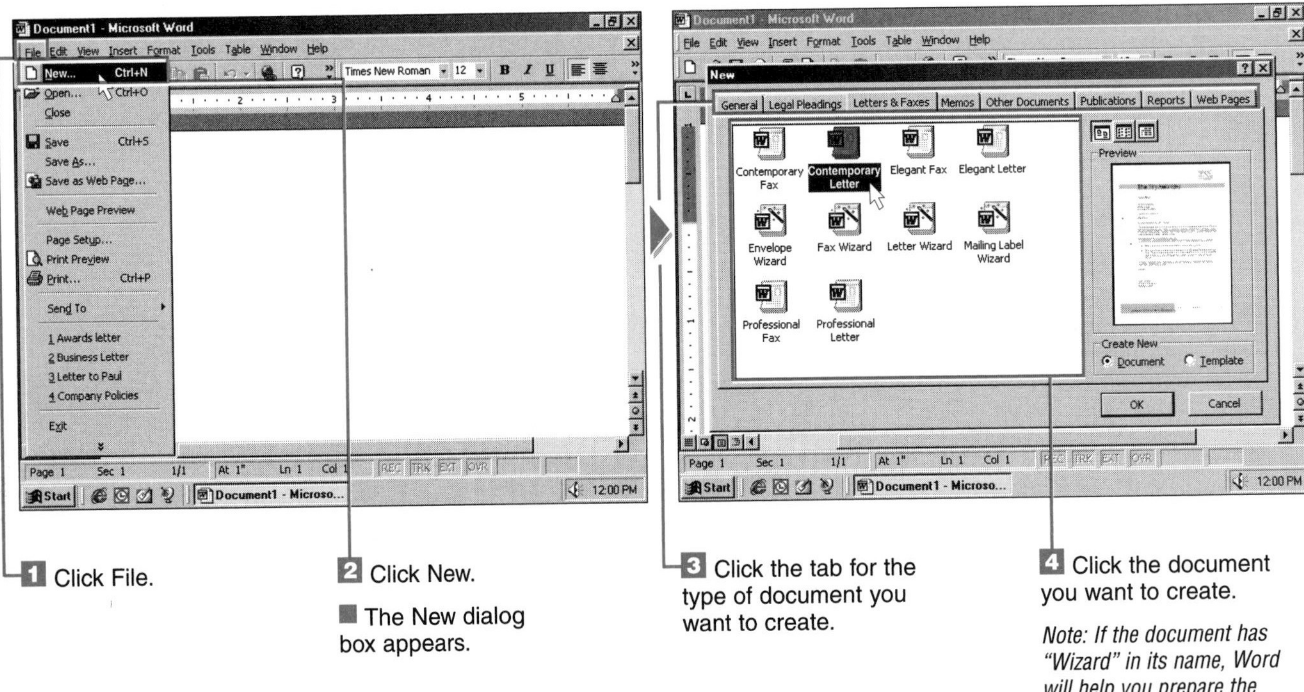

1 Click File.

2 Click New.

■ The New dialog box appears.

3 Click the tab for the type of document you want to create.

4 Click the document you want to create.

Note: If the document has "Wizard" in its name, Word will help you prepare the document step by step.

TIPS

Why does a Microsoft Office 2000 dialog box appear when I try to use a template or wizard?

✔ All of the templates and wizards may not have been installed on your computer. When you select a template or wizard that is not installed, Word asks you to insert the CD-ROM disc you used to install Office 2000 into your CD-ROM drive. Insert the CD-ROM disc and then click OK to install the template or wizard.

I create a lot of letters. How can I quickly display the Letter Wizard?

✔ To quickly display the Letter Wizard, select the Tools menu and then click Letter Wizard.

Can I create my own templates?

✔ Yes. Using a template you have created helps you create other documents that use the same formatting, page settings and text. Open the document you want to use as the basis for the template. Select the File menu and then click Save As. Type a name for the template and then click the Save as type area and select Document Template. Then click Save. The template will appear on the General tab in the New dialog box.

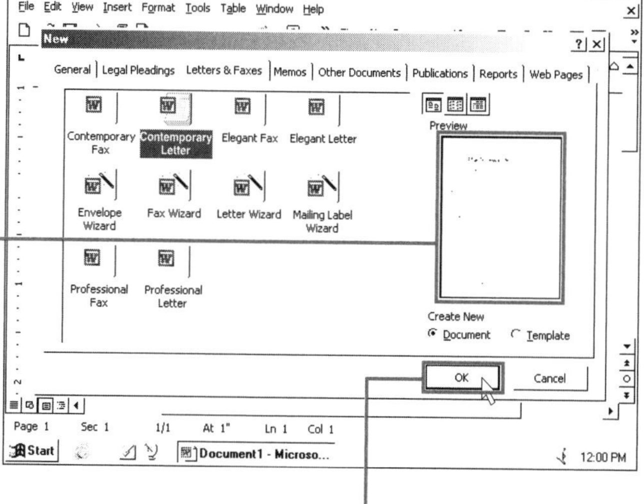

■ If a preview of the document you selected is available, the preview appears in this area.

5 Click OK to create the document.

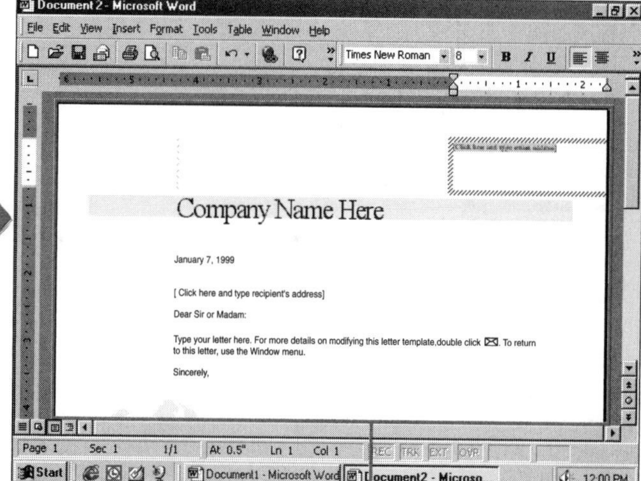

■ The document appears on your screen.

Note: If you selected a wizard in step 4, Word will ask you a series of questions before creating the document.

6 Type information where required to complete the document.

INSERT AND DELETE TEXT

You can insert and delete text in your document without having to retype the entire document. The ability to add and remove text in a document makes Word an efficient editing tool.

When you add new text to your document, the existing text moves to make room for the text you add.

You can also add a blank line to your document. Adding a blank line between paragraphs can help make your document easier to read.

You can remove text you no longer need from your document. You can select any amount of text you want to remove from your document, such as a few characters, a sentence or an entire paragraph. When you remove text from your document, the remaining text moves to fill any empty spaces.

You can also remove a blank line from your document. Removing a blank line is useful when you want to join two paragraphs.

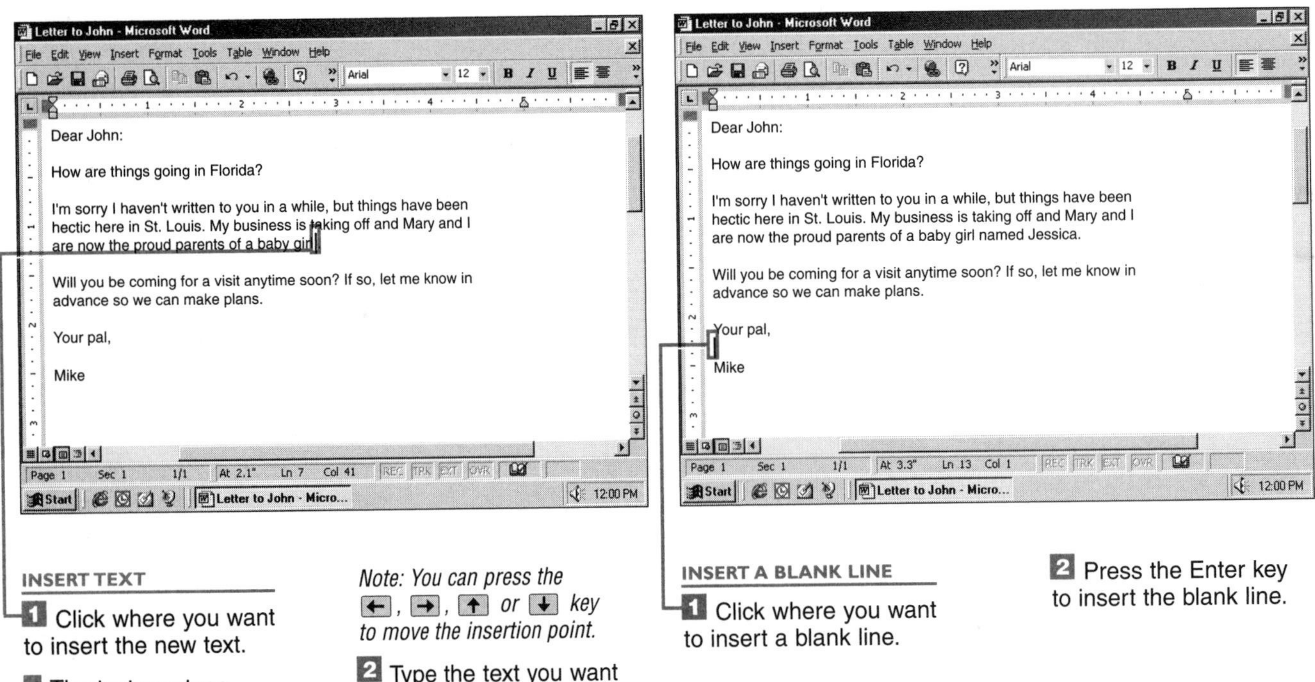

INSERT TEXT

1 Click where you want to insert the new text.

■ The text you type will appear where the insertion point flashes on the screen.

Note: You can press the ←, →, ↑ or ↓ key to move the insertion point.

2 Type the text you want to insert. To insert a blank space, press the Spacebar.

INSERT A BLANK LINE

1 Click where you want to insert a blank line.

2 Press the Enter key to insert the blank line.

TIPS

Can I recover text I accidentally deleted?

✔ Word remembers the last changes you made to your document. If you regret deleting text, you can click the Undo button (↶) on the Standard toolbar to recover the text. For more information on the Undo feature, see page 50.

Why does the existing text in my document disappear when I insert new text?

✔ The Overtype feature may be turned on. The Overtype feature allows Word to replace existing text with the text you insert. To turn off the Overtype feature, choose the Tools menu and then click Options. Select the Edit tab and then click the Overtype mode option (☑ changes to ☐).

Can I quickly change the text I inserted to uppercase letters?

✔ Word offers five case styles you can use to change the appearance of text in your document–Sentence case, lowercase, UPPERCASE, Title Case and tOGGLE cASE. Select the text you want to change. Choose the Format menu, click Change Case and then select the case you want to use (○ changes to ⊙).

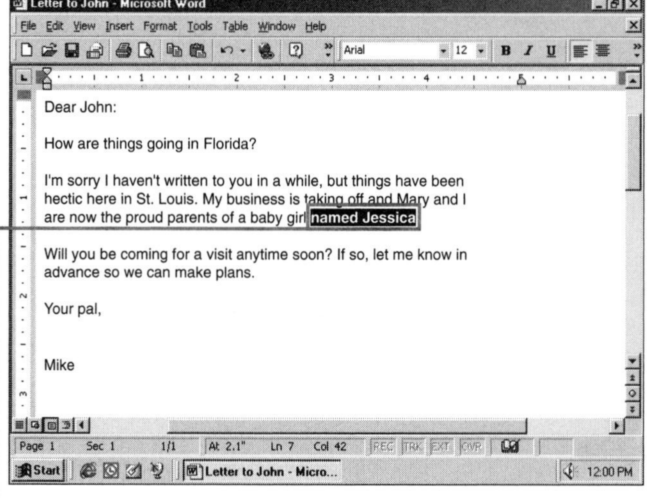

DELETE TEXT

1 Select the text you want to delete.

2 Press the Delete key to remove the text.

■ To delete one character at a time, click to the right of the first character you want to delete. Then press the Backspace key once for each character you want to delete.

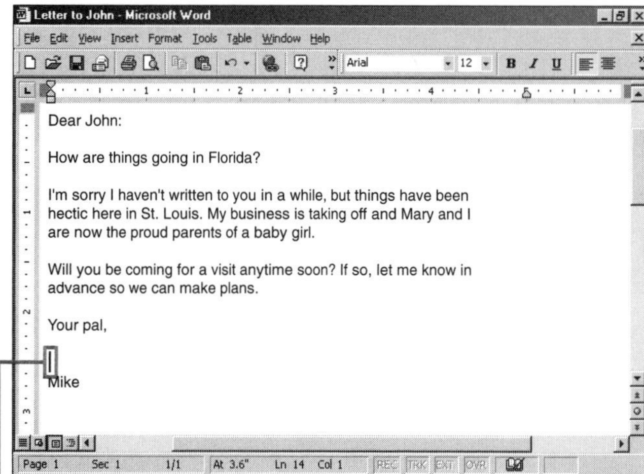

DELETE A BLANK LINE

1 Click the beginning of the blank line you want to delete.

2 Press the Backspace key to remove the blank line.

MOVE OR COPY TEXT

You can reorganize your document by moving text from one location to another. Moving text can help you find the most effective structure for your document. When you move text, the text disappears from its original location in your document.

You can also copy text to a different location in your document. This is useful when you want to use the same information, such as an address, in several locations in your document. When you copy text, the text appears in both the original and new location.

To move or copy text, you can drag text to a new location. When you drag text, Word displays a dotted insertion point to indicate the new location of the text you are moving or copying.

Word also allows you to use the Cut, Copy and Paste buttons on the Standard toolbar to move or copy text.

When you move or copy text to a new location in your document, Word shifts the existing text to make room for the text you move or copy.

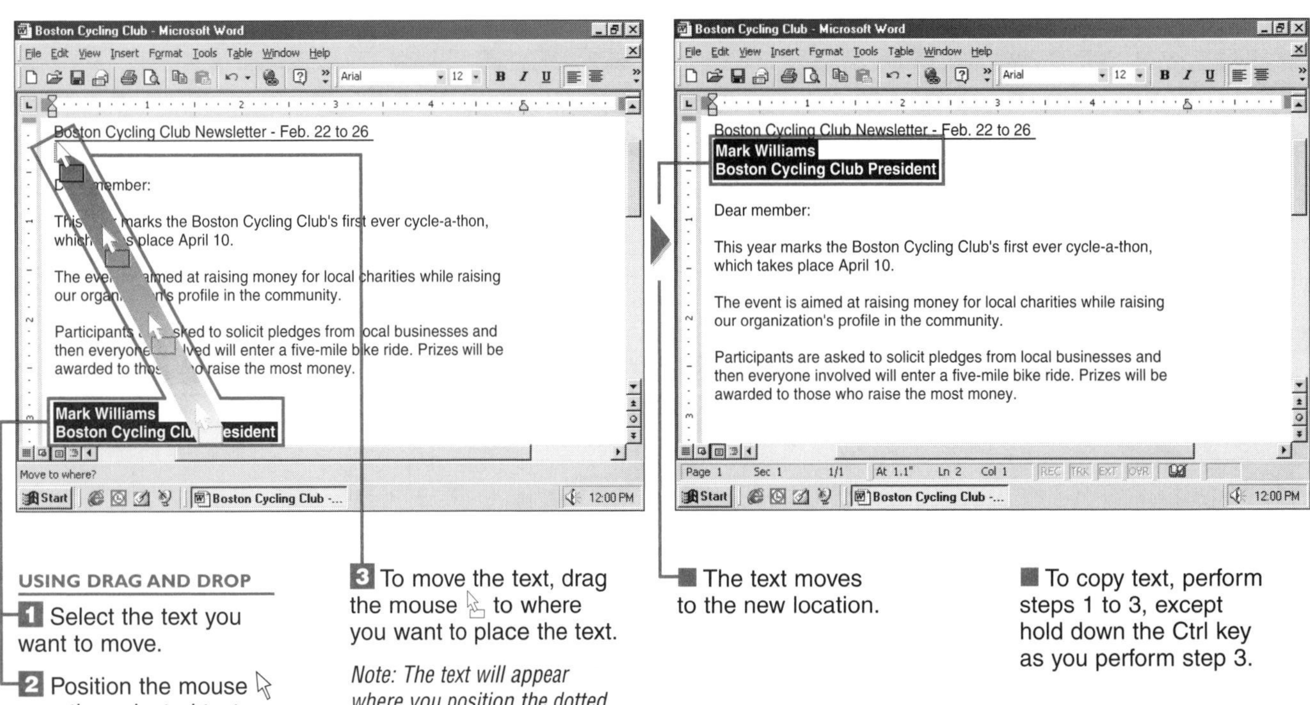

USING DRAG AND DROP

1. Select the text you want to move.
2. Position the mouse over the selected text.
3. To move the text, drag the mouse to where you want to place the text.

Note: The text will appear where you position the dotted insertion point on the screen.

■ The text moves to the new location.

■ To copy text, perform steps 1 to 3, except hold down the Ctrl key as you perform step 3.

TIPS

I dragged text to a new location, but I do not like the result. Can I cancel the change?

✔ You can immediately click the Undo button (↶) on the Standard toolbar to cancel the last change you made to your document.

While working with selected text, I often drag and drop the text by accident. Is there a way to turn off the drag and drop feature?

✔ Yes. Click the Tools menu and then select Options. Choose the Edit tab and click the Drag-and-drop text editing option (☑ changes to ☐). Then click OK.

Why does the Clipboard toolbar appear when I move or copy text using the toolbar buttons?

✔ The Clipboard toolbar may appear when you cut or copy two pieces of text in a row, copy the same text twice or place copied text in a new location and then immediately copy other text. To see the text an icon on the Clipboard toolbar represents, position the mouse pointer over the icon until the first few characters appear. To place the text in a new location, click the icon.

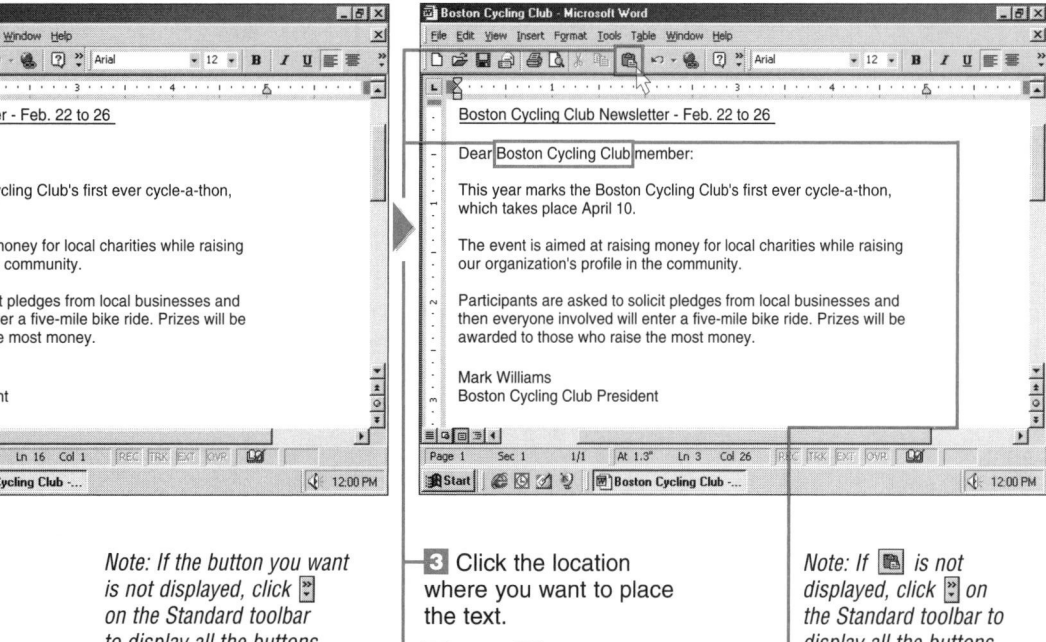

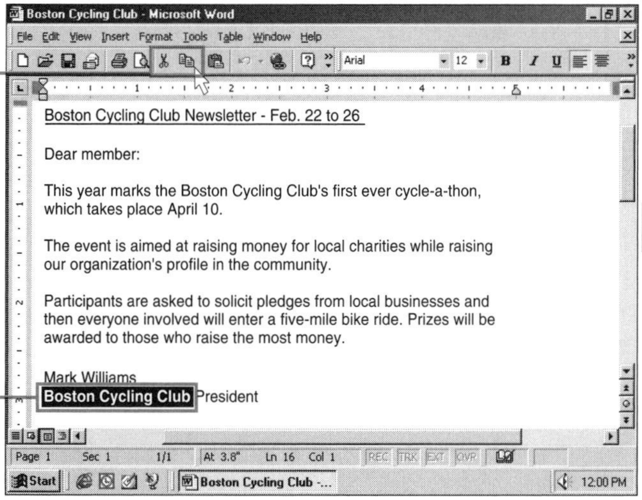

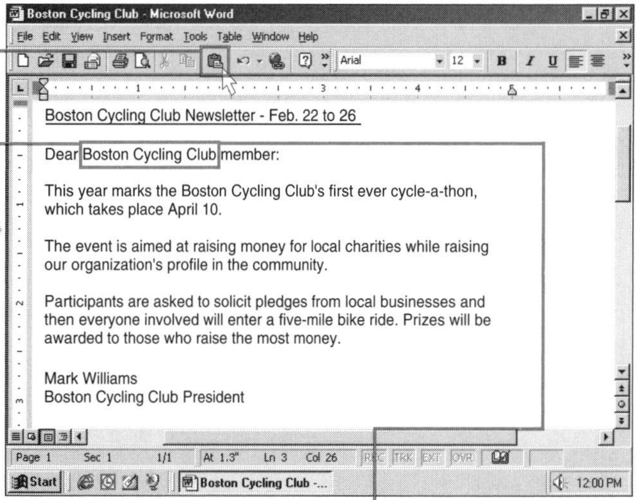

USING THE TOOLBAR BUTTONS

1 Select the text you want to move or copy.

2 Click one of the following buttons.

Move text

Copy text

Note: If the button you want is not displayed, click » on the Standard toolbar to display all the buttons.

3 Click the location where you want to place the text.

4 Click to place the text in the new location.

Note: If is not displayed, click » on the Standard toolbar to display all the buttons.

■ The text appears in the new location.

UNDO CHANGES

Word remembers the last changes you made to your document. If you regret these changes, you can cancel them by using the Undo feature.

The Undo feature can cancel your last editing and formatting changes. For example, you can cancel editing changes such as deleting a paragraph or typing a sentence. You can cancel formatting changes such as underlining a word or increasing the size of text.

You can also reverse the results of canceling an editing or formatting change.

You can use the Undo feature to cancel one change at a time or many changes at once.

Word stores a list of changes you made to your document. When you select the change you want to cancel from the list, Word cancels the change and all the changes you have made since that change.

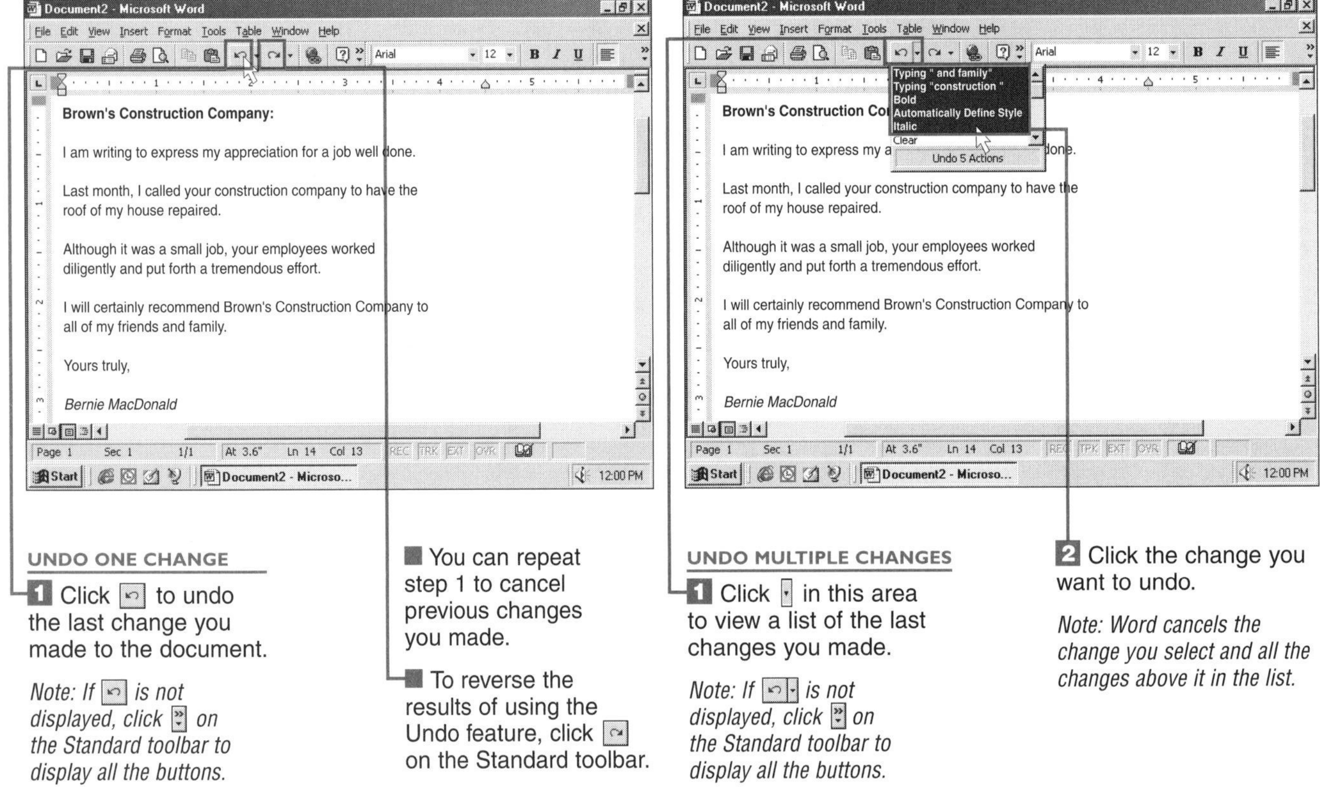

UNDO ONE CHANGE

1 Click ↶ to undo the last change you made to the document.

Note: If ↶ is not displayed, click » on the Standard toolbar to display all the buttons.

■ You can repeat step 1 to cancel previous changes you made.

■ To reverse the results of using the Undo feature, click ↷ on the Standard toolbar.

UNDO MULTIPLE CHANGES

1 Click ▾ in this area to view a list of the last changes you made.

Note: If ↶▾ is not displayed, click » on the Standard toolbar to display all the buttons.

2 Click the change you want to undo.

Note: Word cancels the change you select and all the changes above it in the list.

COUNT WORDS IN A DOCUMENT

You can quickly determine the number of words in your document. When you count the words in a document, Word also displays the number of pages, characters, paragraphs and lines in the document.

Counting words in a document is useful if your document must contain a specific number of words. For example, most newspapers and magazines specify that submissions must be a certain number of words before they will be accepted.

You can count the words in a specific section of text or your entire document. To count words in a specific section of text, select the text before you begin the word count. If you do not select any text, Word will count the words in the entire document.

When you count the words in an entire document, you can also include the words in any footnotes and endnotes in the document. To do this, select the Include footnotes and endnotes option (☐ changes to ☑).

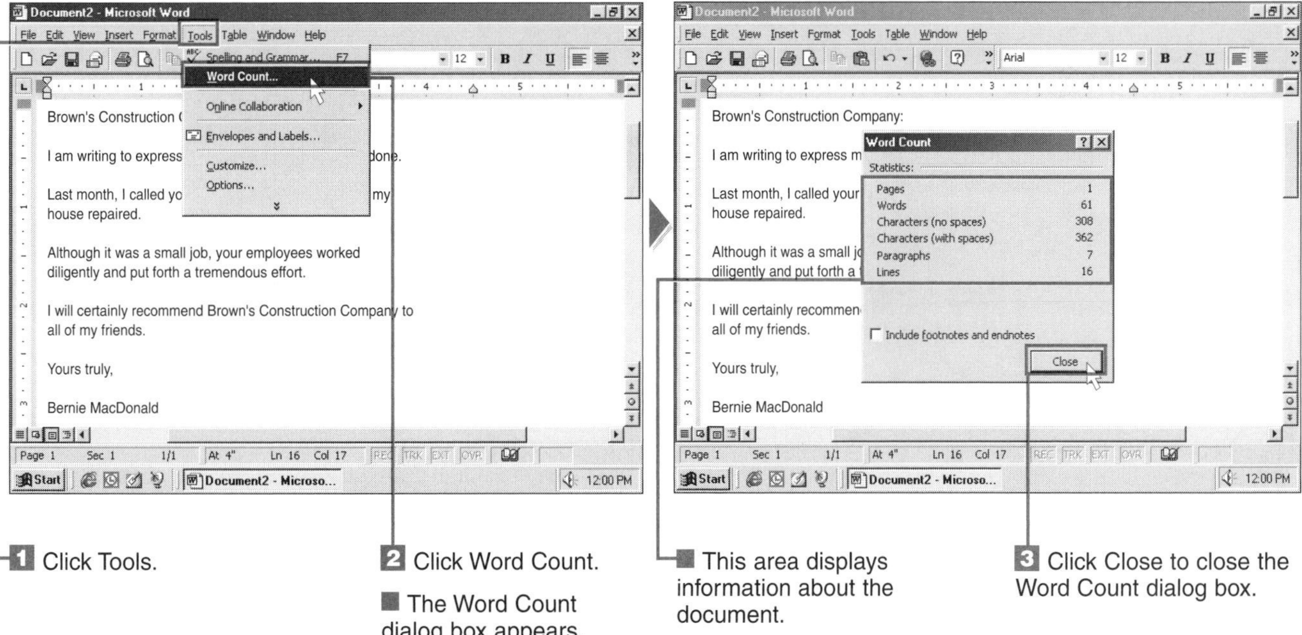

1 Click Tools.

2 Click Word Count.

■ The Word Count dialog box appears.

■ This area displays information about the document.

3 Click Close to close the Word Count dialog box.

FIND TEXT

You can use the Find feature to locate a word or phrase in your document.

You can search your entire document or only a specific section of text. To search a specific section of text, select the text before starting the search.

When you search for text in your document, Word will find the text even if it is part of a larger word. For example, if you search for "place", Word will also find "places", "placement" and "commonplace".

The word or phrase you want to find may appear in several locations in your document. After you start the search, Word finds and highlights the first instance of the word or phrase. You can continue the search to find the next instance of the word or phrase.

If your document is long, it may take a while for Word to search the entire document. You can cancel a search at any time.

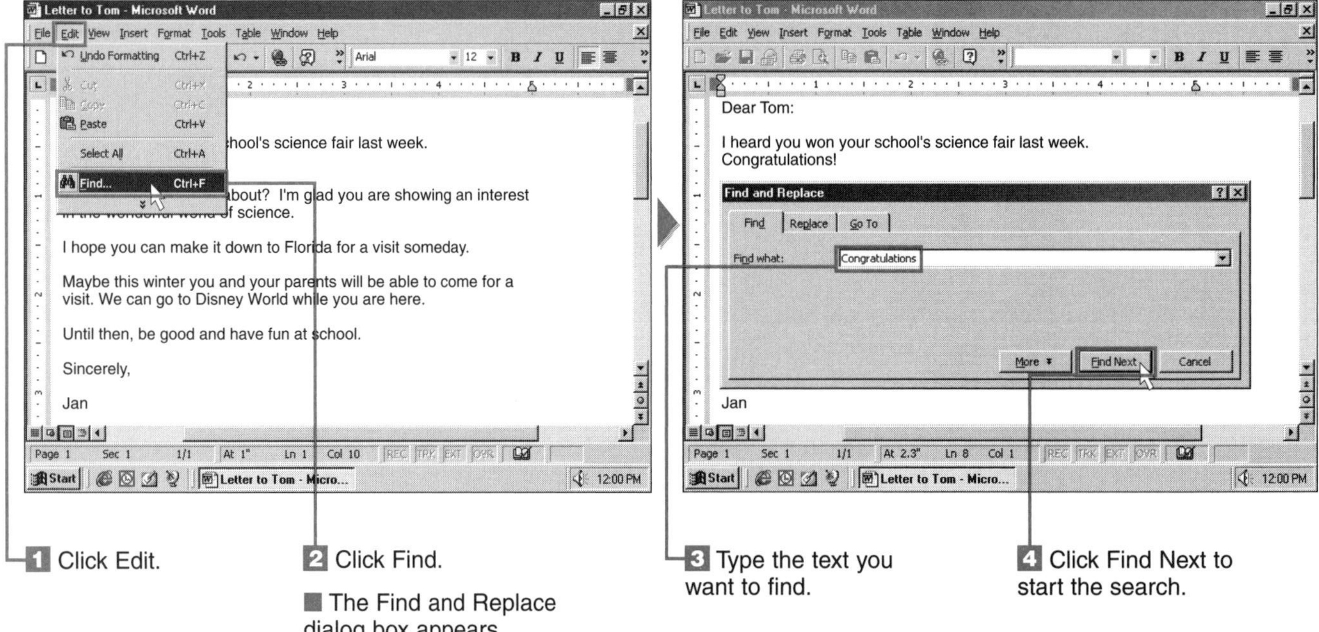

1 Click Edit.

2 Click Find.

■ The Find and Replace dialog box appears.

3 Type the text you want to find.

4 Click Find Next to start the search.

TIPS

How do I move the Find and Replace dialog box so I can view my document?

✔ Position the mouse pointer over the title bar of the Find and Replace dialog box and then drag the dialog box to a new location.

Does Word offer any options to help me refine my search?

✔ Word offers several options that can help narrow your search. In the Find and Replace dialog box, click the More button and then click each search option you want to use. Word will use each option that displays a check mark (✔).

The Match case option is useful for finding words with exactly matching uppercase and lowercase letters. For example, "Letter" will not find "letter" or "LETTER".

The Find whole words only option lets you search for words that are not part of a larger word. For example, "work" will not find "homework" or "coworker".

The Use wildcards option allows you to use wildcard characters to find words. The **?** wildcard represents a single character. For example, "h?t" will find "hit" and "hut". The * wildcard represents many characters. For example, "h*t" will find "heat" and "haunt".

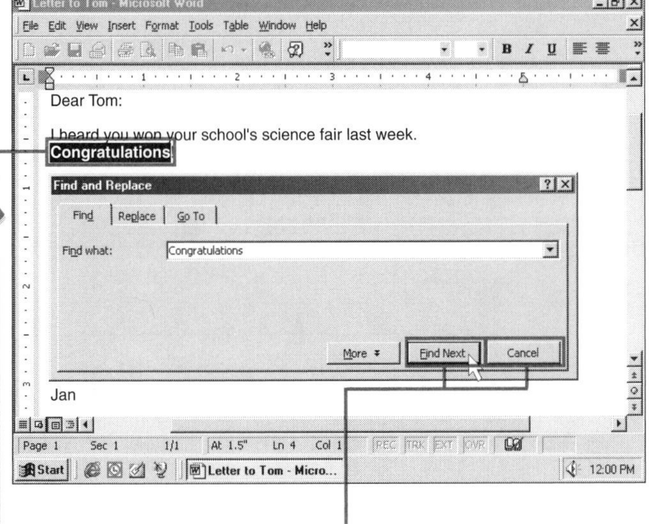

■ Word highlights the first matching word it finds.

5 Click Find Next to find the next matching word.

■ You can end the search at any time. To end the search, click Cancel.

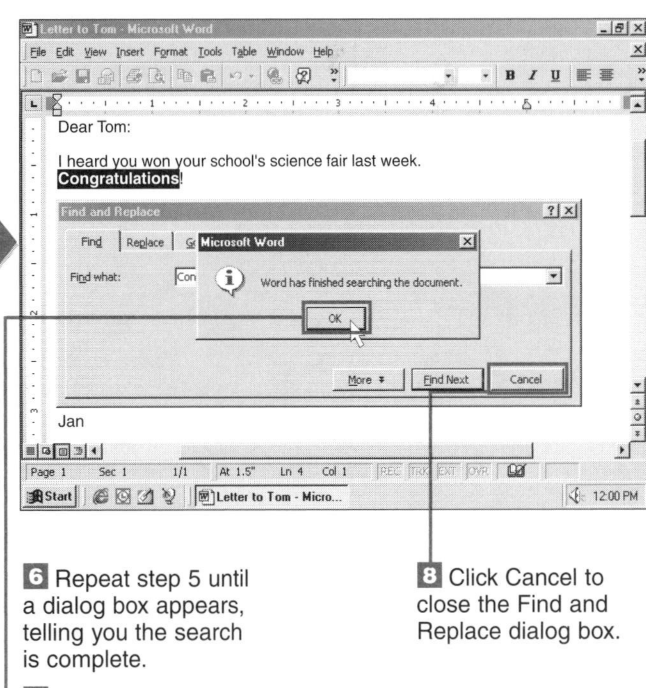

6 Repeat step 5 until a dialog box appears, telling you the search is complete.

7 Click OK to close the dialog box.

8 Click Cancel to close the Find and Replace dialog box.

REPLACE TEXT

The Replace feature can locate and replace every occurrence of a word or phrase in your document.

This is useful if you need to replace a name throughout a document. For example, if you have written a letter to ABC Inc. and you want to send the same letter to XYZ Corp., you can have Word replace ABC Inc. with XYZ Corp. throughout the document.

The Replace feature is also useful if you have repeatedly misspelled a name in your document. For example, you can quickly change all occurrences of McDonald to Macdonald.

Word locates and highlights each occurrence of the word or phrase in your document. You can replace a word or phrase Word locates or ignore a word or phrase you do not want to replace. You can also replace all the occurrences of the word or phrase in your document at once.

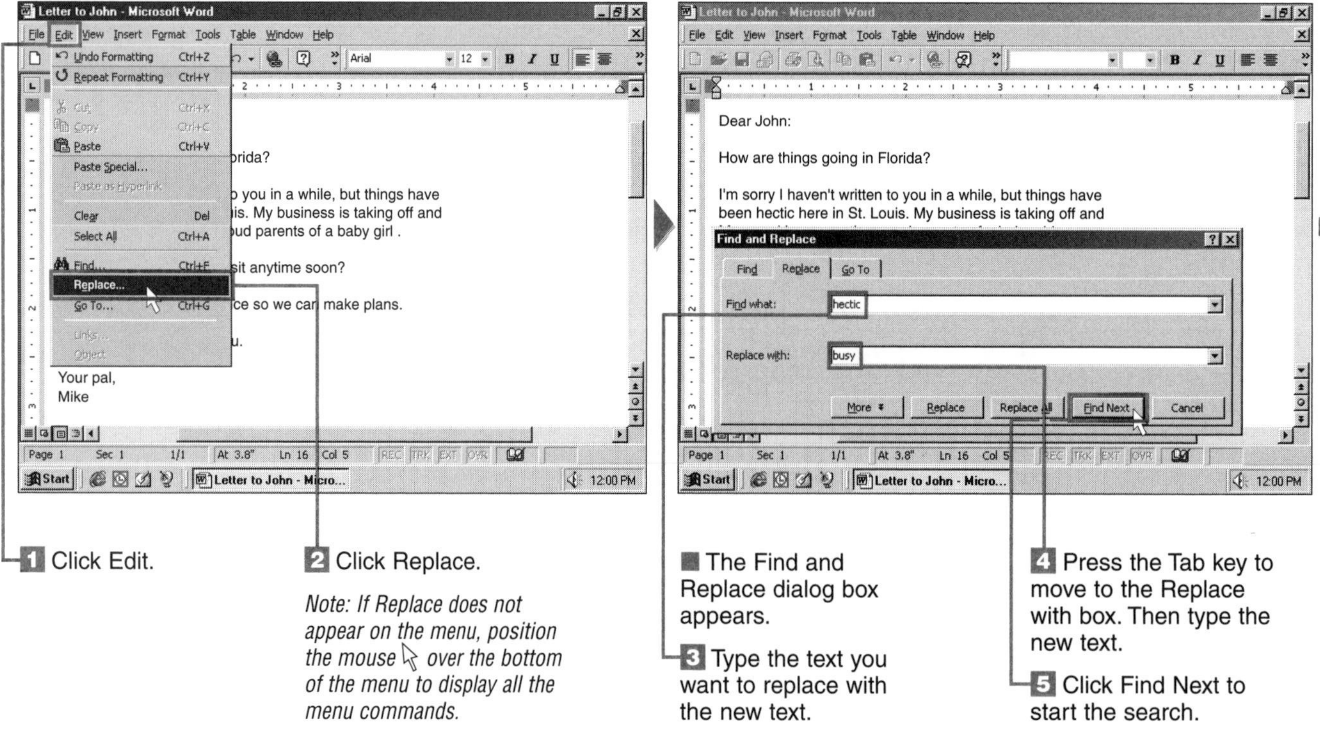

1 Click Edit.

2 Click Replace.

Note: If Replace does not appear on the menu, position the mouse over the bottom of the menu to display all the menu commands.

■ The Find and Replace dialog box appears.

3 Type the text you want to replace with the new text.

4 Press the Tab key to move to the Replace with box. Then type the new text.

5 Click Find Next to start the search.

TIPS

Can I use the Replace feature to change the formatting of text in my document?

✔ Yes. For example, you may want to remove all bold formatting from your document. In the Find and Replace dialog box, remove any text from the Find what and Replace with areas and then select the More button. Click the Find what area. Click the Format button and then choose Font. In the dialog box that appears, select the formatting you want to replace in your document and then click OK. Click the Replace with area and then repeat the steps above to specify the new formatting you want. To stop searching for formatting, click the Find what area and select the No Formatting button. Then click the Replace with area and select the No Formatting button.

Can I replace text in only part of my document?

✔ Yes. To use the Replace feature on only part of your document, you must first select the part of the document you want to search.

Is there another way to display the Find and Replace dialog box?

✔ You can press the Ctrl+H keys to display the Find and Replace dialog box at anytime.

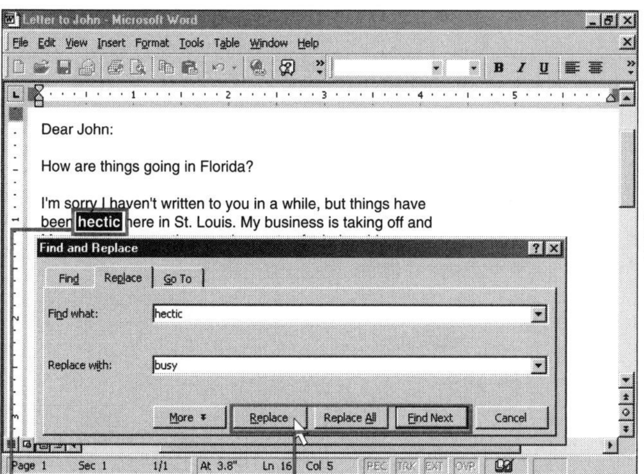

■ Word highlights the first matching word it finds.

6 Click one of these options.

Replace - Replaces the word

Replace All - Replaces the word and all other matching words in the document

Find Next - Ignores the word

■ In this example, Word replaces the text and searches for the next matching word.

Note: You can click Cancel to end the search at any time.

7 Repeat step 6 until a dialog box appears, telling you the search is complete.

8 Click OK to close the dialog box.

CHECK SPELLING AND GRAMMAR

Word checks your document for spelling and grammar errors as you type. You can correct the errors Word finds. Correcting spelling and grammar errors will make your document appear more professional.

Word's spell check feature compares every word in your document to words in its dictionary to find spelling errors. The grammar check feature finds errors such as capitalization problems, punctuation mistakes and misused words.

Word underlines spelling errors in red and grammar errors in green. The underlines only appear on the screen and will not appear when you print your document.

You can correct spelling and grammar errors one at a time as you create your document. You can also find and correct all spelling and grammar errors at once when you finish creating your document. Word offers suggestions for correcting the errors in your document.

Word automatically corrects common spelling errors, such as "adn" and "recieve", as you type. For information on the AutoCorrect feature, see page 60.

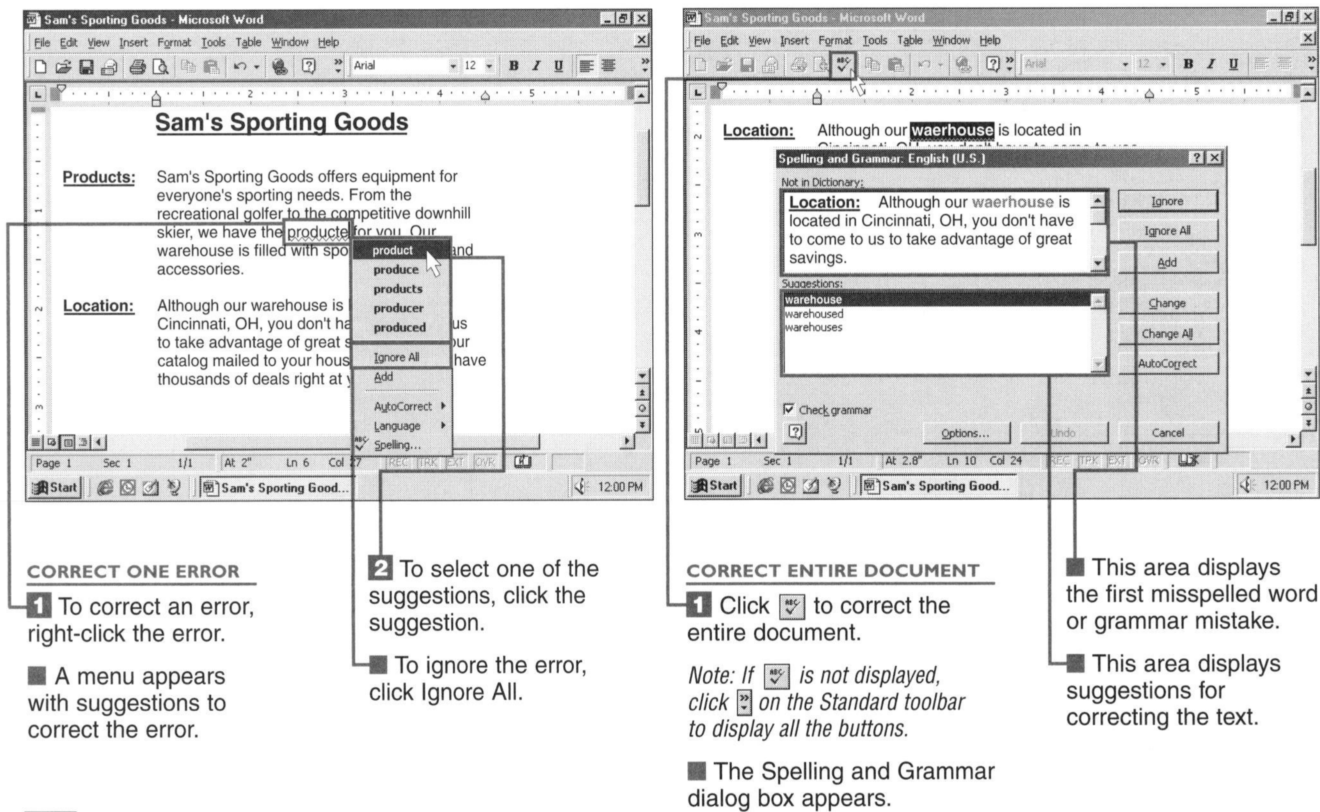

CORRECT ONE ERROR

1 To correct an error, right-click the error.

■ A menu appears with suggestions to correct the error.

2 To select one of the suggestions, click the suggestion.

■ To ignore the error, click Ignore All.

CORRECT ENTIRE DOCUMENT

1 Click the Spelling and Grammar button to correct the entire document.

Note: If the Spelling and Grammar button is not displayed, click the More Buttons button on the Standard toolbar to display all the buttons.

■ The Spelling and Grammar dialog box appears.

■ This area displays the first misspelled word or grammar mistake.

■ This area displays suggestions for correcting the text.

TIPS

Why did Word underline a correctly spelled word?

✔ Word considers any words that do not exist in its dictionary to be misspelled. You can add a word to the dictionary so Word will recognize the word during future spell checks. Right-click the word you want to add to the dictionary and then select Add.

Word found a grammar error that I do not know how to correct. What should I do?

✔ You can click the Help (?) button in the Spelling and Grammar dialog box to display a detailed explanation of the grammar error.

Can I prevent Word from underlining spelling and grammar errors?

✔ If you are distracted by the underlines Word uses to indicate spelling and grammar errors, you can hide the underlines in the document you are working with. Choose the Tools menu and then select Options. Select the Spelling & Grammar tab and then click the Hide spelling errors in this document option (☐ changes to ☑) and the Hide grammatical errors in this document option (☐ changes to ☑).

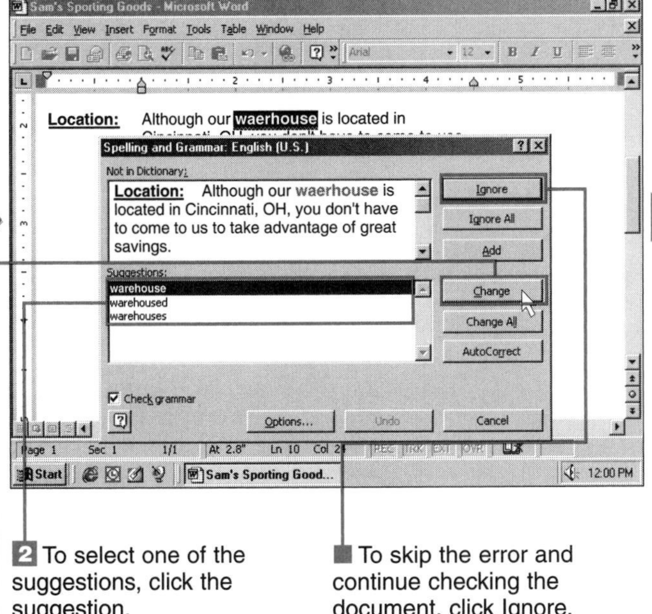

2 To select one of the suggestions, click the suggestion.

3 Click Change to correct the error.

■ To skip the error and continue checking the document, click Ignore.

Note: To skip all occurrences of the error, click Ignore All or Ignore Rule. The appearance of the button depends on whether Word found a spelling or grammar error.

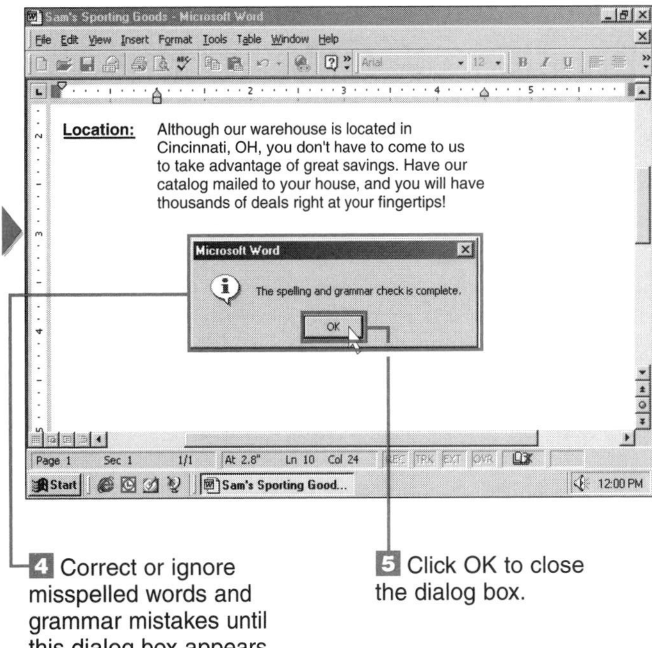

4 Correct or ignore misspelled words and grammar mistakes until this dialog box appears, telling you the spelling and grammar check is complete.

5 Click OK to close the dialog box.

USING THE THESAURUS

You can use a thesaurus to replace a word in your document with one that is more suitable. Using the thesaurus included with Word is faster and more convenient than searching through a printed thesaurus.

The thesaurus replaces a word in your document with a word that shares the same meaning. Words that share the same meaning are called synonyms.

Many people use the thesaurus to replace a word that they have used repeatedly in a document. Replacing repeatedly used words can help add variety to your writing and make your document appear more professional.

If the word you want to replace has more than one meaning, you can select the correct meaning. Word will display the synonyms for the meaning you select.

If the word you want to replace is not in the thesaurus, Word provides an alphabetical list of similar words you can choose from.

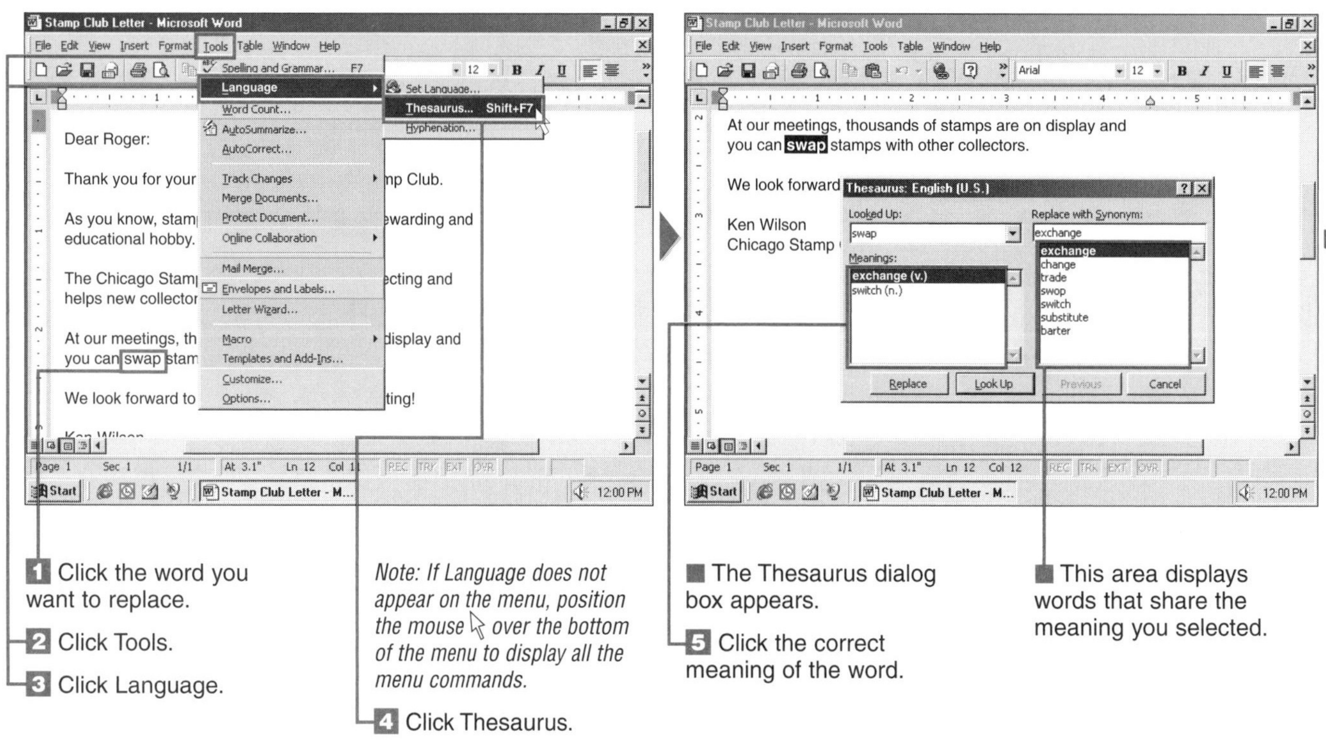

1 Click the word you want to replace.

2 Click Tools.

3 Click Language.

Note: If Language does not appear on the menu, position the mouse over the bottom of the menu to display all the menu commands.

4 Click Thesaurus.

■ The Thesaurus dialog box appears.

5 Click the correct meaning of the word.

■ This area displays words that share the meaning you selected.

TIPS

Can I find synonyms for a word displayed in the Thesaurus dialog box?

✔ Yes. Click the word you want to find synonyms for and then click the Look Up button. To return to the last word you looked up, click the Previous button.

Is there another way to quickly display common synonyms for a word?

✔ In your document, right-click the word you want to find synonyms for and then click Synonyms in the menu that appears. A list of common synonyms for the word appears. You can click a synonym to replace the word in your document.

Can I find the opposite meaning of a word?

✔ The Thesaurus dialog box may display words that have the opposite meaning of the word you want to replace. Words that have the opposite meaning are called antonyms. To find more antonyms, click a word in the Thesaurus dialog box that displays the word Antonym and then click the Look Up button.

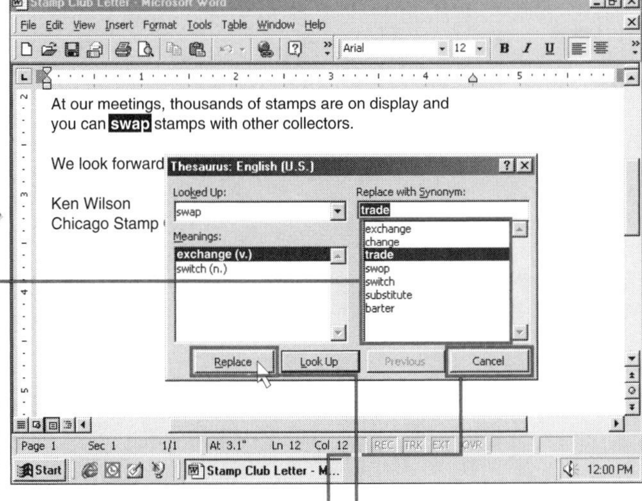

6 Click the word you want to replace the word in the document.

7 Click Replace to replace the word in the document.

■ If the Thesaurus does not offer a suitable replacement for the word, click Cancel to close the dialog box.

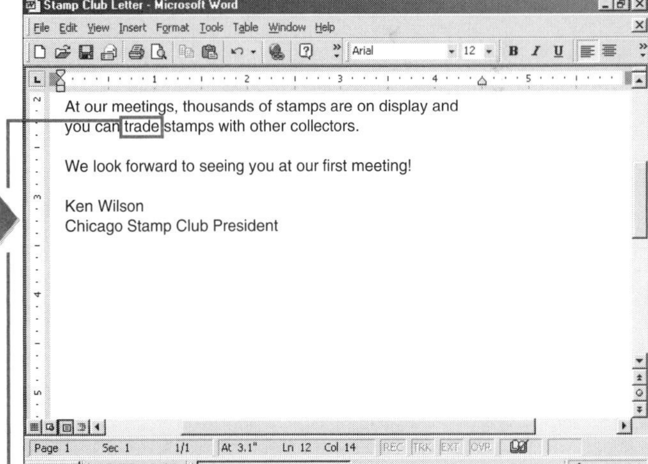

■ Your selection replaces the word in the document.

USING AUTOCORRECT

Word automatically corrects hundreds of typing, spelling and grammar errors as you type. The AutoCorrect feature uses its list of common errors and Word's dictionary to correct errors in your document. You can add your own words and phrases to the AutoCorrect feature.

The AutoCorrect feature replaces errors such as "aboutthe", "includ" and "may of been" with the correct word or phrase. The AutoCorrect feature also capitalizes the first letter of new sentences and the names of days.

The AutoCorrect feature inserts symbols into your document when you type certain characters. For example, when you type **(r)**, the ® symbol automatically appears in your document. This is useful when you want to quickly insert symbols into your document that do not appear on your keyboard.

You can create AutoCorrect entries for errors you often make or words and phrases you frequently use. For example, you can create an AutoCorrect entry for your name and title. This can save you time when typing business letters.

After you create an AutoCorrect entry, Word will automatically insert the entry into your document each time you type the corresponding text.

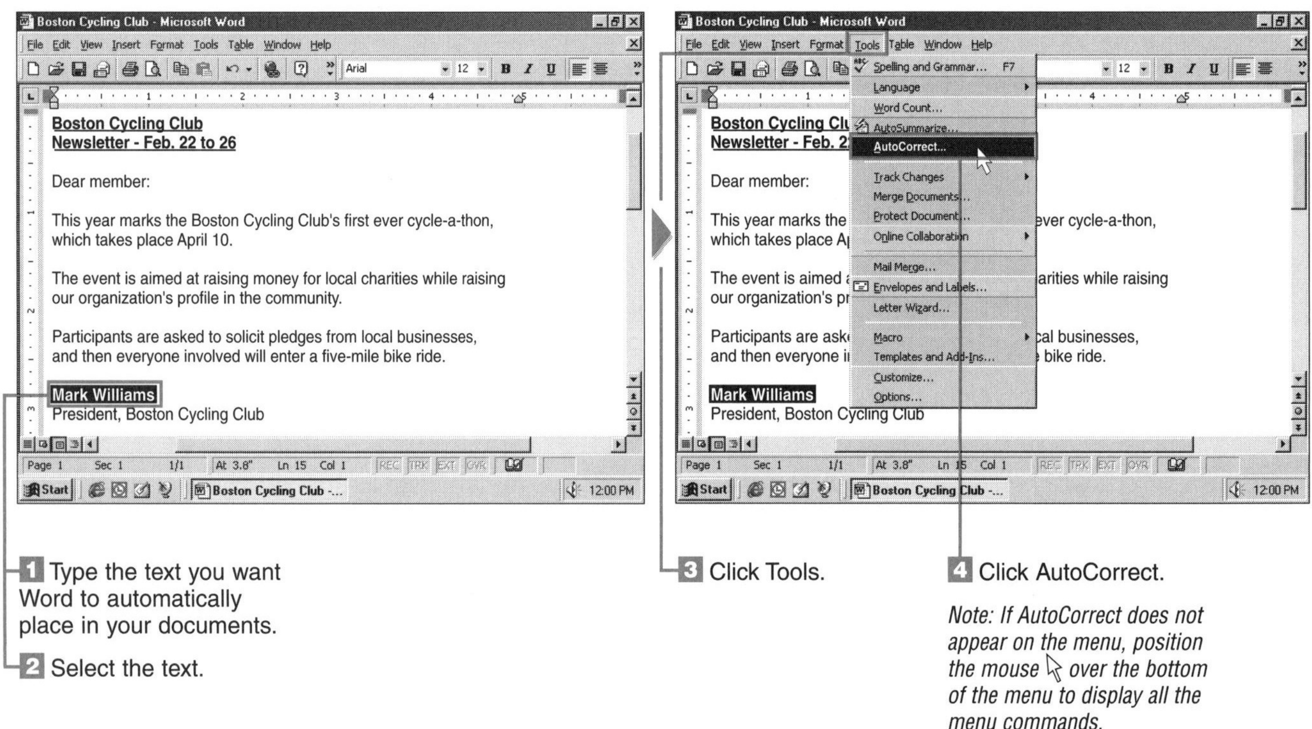

1 Type the text you want Word to automatically place in your documents.

2 Select the text.

3 Click Tools.

4 Click AutoCorrect.

Note: If AutoCorrect does not appear on the menu, position the mouse over the bottom of the menu to display all the menu commands.

TIPS

What other types of errors does the AutoCorrect feature correct?

✔ When you type two consecutive uppercase letters, the AutoCorrect feature converts the second letter to lowercase. Accidental usage of the Caps Lock key is also corrected. If you no longer want the AutoCorrect feature to automatically correct some types of errors, display the AutoCorrect dialog box and click each option you do not want to use (☑ changes to ☐).

Can I delete an AutoCorrect entry?

✔ Yes. In the AutoCorrect dialog box, select the entry you want to delete and then click the Delete button.

Why didn't the AutoCorrect feature replace a spelling error in my document?

✔ The AutoCorrect feature automatically replaces a spelling error when there is only one suggestion to correct the error. To have the AutoCorrect feature always correct a spelling error, right-click the misspelled word. Click AutoCorrect and then click the word you want to always replace the misspelled word.

Can I save text formatting, such as bold and italic, with my AutoCorrect entry?

✔ Yes. In the AutoCorrect dialog box, click the Formatted text option (○ changes to ⊙).

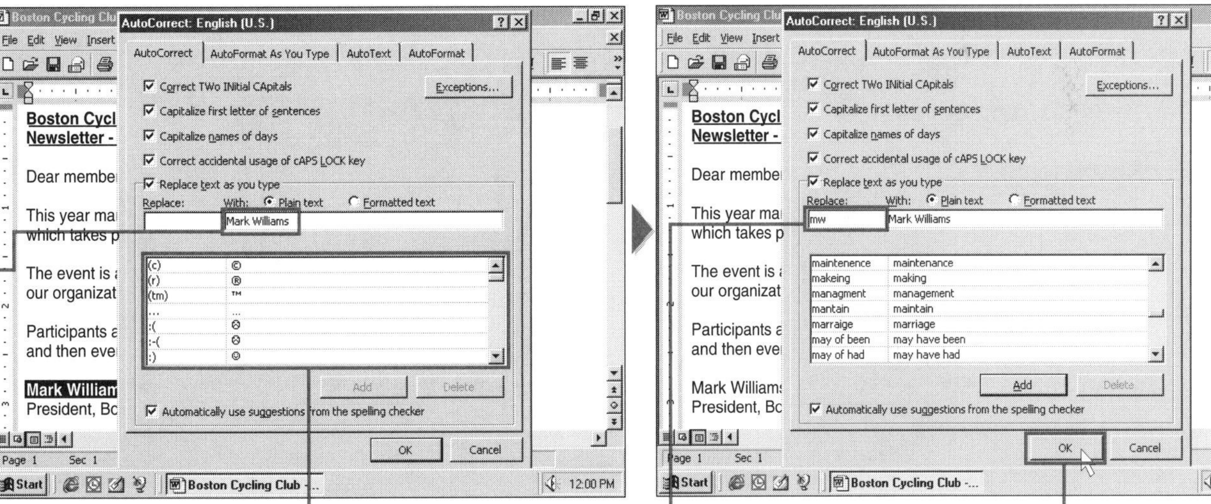

■ The AutoCorrect dialog box appears.

■ This area displays the text you selected in step 2.

■ This area displays a list of the AutoCorrect entries included with Word.

5 Type the text you want Word to replace automatically with the text you selected in step 2. The text should not contain spaces and should not be a real word.

6 Click OK to confirm your changes.

USING AUTOTEXT

You can use the AutoText feature to store text you use frequently. This lets you avoid typing the same text over and over again.

When you use AutoText, you only have to type a section of text once. You can create an AutoText entry for information such as a mailing address, legal disclaimer or closing remark. You can store text formatting, such as bold and underline, with your AutoText entry.

Word includes several categories of AutoText entries you can use in your document. For example, the Closing category stores entries such as "Best wishes," and "Thank you,". The Mailing Instructions category stores entries such as "CONFIDENTIAL" and "VIA FACSIMILE". The Salutation category stores entries such as "Dear Sir or Madam:" and "To Whom It May Concern:". Most AutoText entries you create are stored in the Normal category.

You can insert an AutoText entry you created or one included with Word into your document.

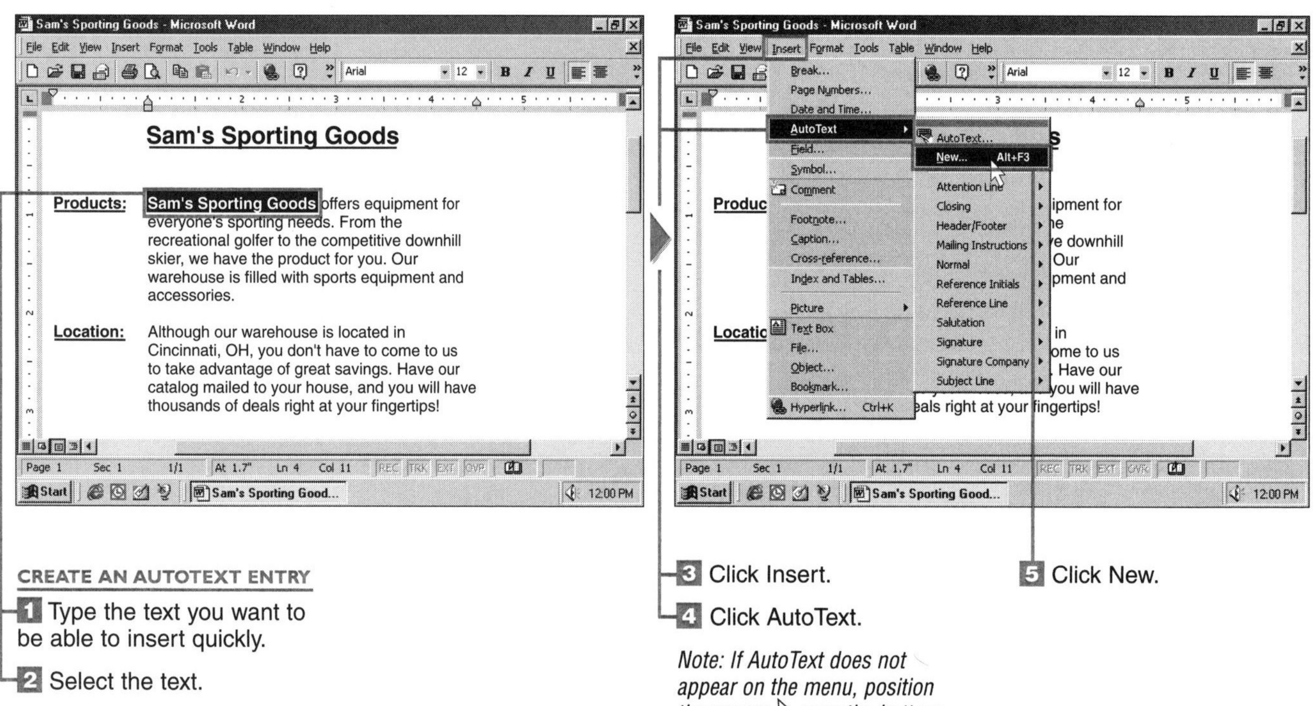

CREATE AN AUTOTEXT ENTRY

1 Type the text you want to be able to insert quickly.

2 Select the text.

3 Click Insert.

4 Click AutoText.

Note: If AutoText does not appear on the menu, position the mouse over the bottom of the menu to display all the menu commands.

5 Click New.

TIPS

How can I quickly insert an AutoText entry into my document?

✔ When you type the name of an AutoText entry in your document, a box may appear on your screen displaying the AutoText entry. To insert the AutoText entry, press the Enter key. To ignore the AutoText entry, continue typing.

Can I delete an AutoText entry?

✔ To delete an entry, select the Insert menu and then choose AutoText. In the menu that appears, click AutoText. Select the AutoText entry you want to delete and then click the Delete button.

I often use the AutoText feature. How can I access the feature more quickly?

✔ You can display the AutoText toolbar on your screen. The toolbar allows you to quickly access AutoText entries using a drop-down list. The AutoText toolbar also allows you to create new entries. To display the AutoText toolbar, select the View menu and then click Toolbars. Then select AutoText.

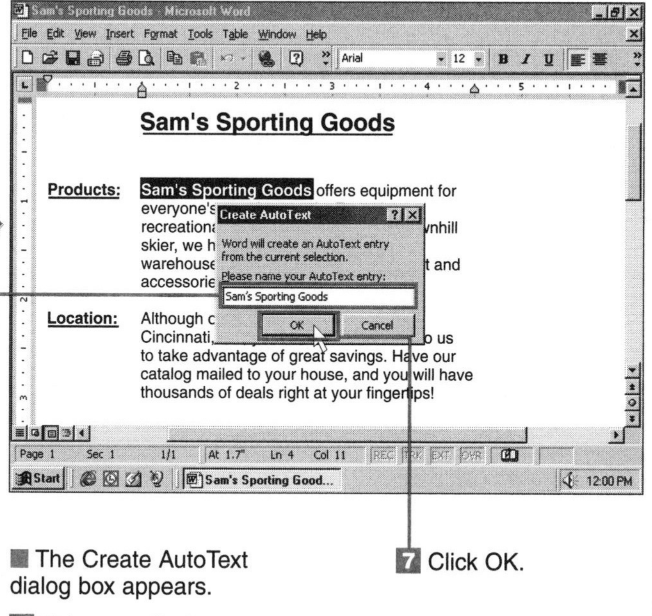

■ The Create AutoText dialog box appears.

6 This area displays a name for the AutoText entry. To use a different name, type the name.

7 Click OK.

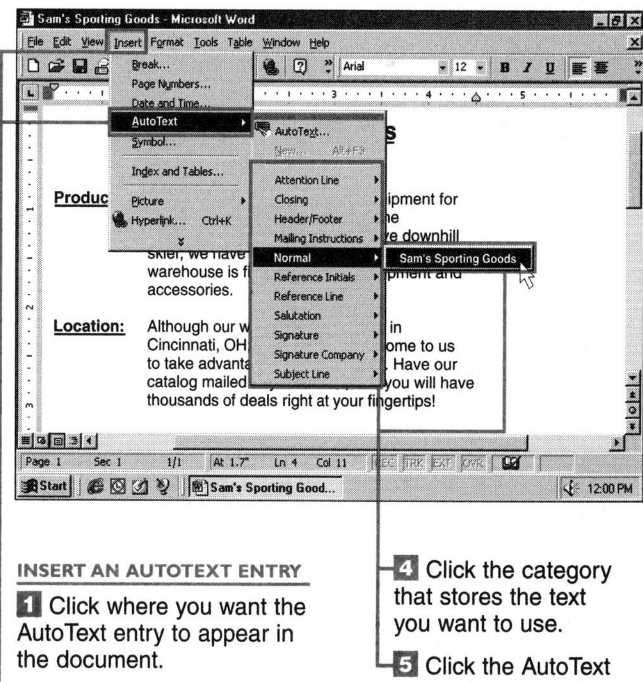

INSERT AN AUTOTEXT ENTRY

1 Click where you want the AutoText entry to appear in the document.

2 Click Insert.

3 Click AutoText.

4 Click the category that stores the text you want to use.

5 Click the AutoText entry you want to insert.

■ The text appears in the document.

INSERT SYMBOLS

You can insert symbols into your document that do not appear on a standard keyboard. Symbols you can insert into your document include uppercase and lowercase accented letters, arrows and one-character fractions such as ¼.

You can choose a symbol from one of the sets of symbols Word offers. Sets of symbols are called fonts. Two popular fonts that Word offers are Symbol and Wingdings. The Symbol font contains symbols for mathematical equations. The Wingdings font contains bullet and arrow symbols.

You can display an enlarged version of each symbol in a font. This allows you to view a symbol in more detail before you insert the symbol into your document.

You can insert as many symbols as you want while the Symbol dialog box is open.

Word's AutoCorrect feature can also help you quickly insert some symbols into your document. For example, when you type **(r)**, the AutoCorrect feature automatically inserts the ® symbol into your document. For more information on the AutoCorrect feature, see page 60.

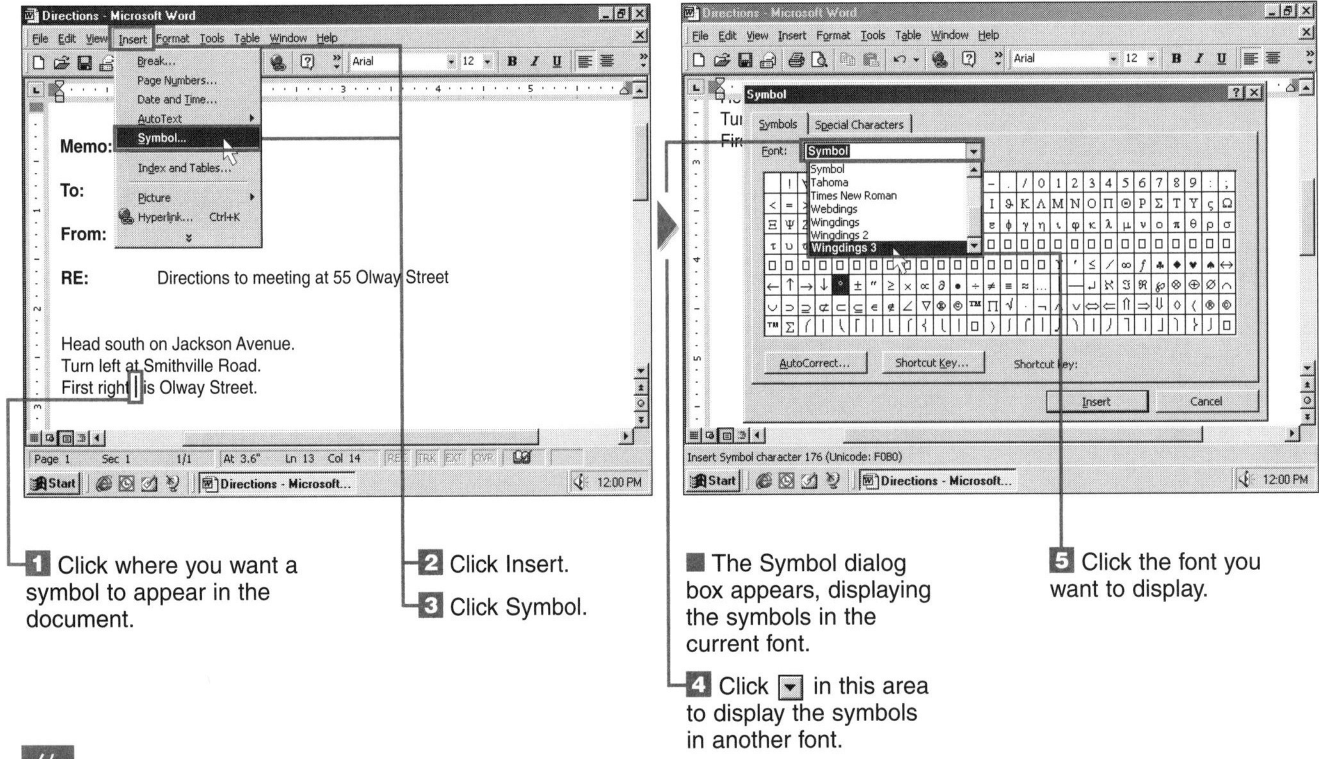

1 Click where you want a symbol to appear in the document.

2 Click Insert.

3 Click Symbol.

■ The Symbol dialog box appears, displaying the symbols in the current font.

4 Click ▼ in this area to display the symbols in another font.

5 Click the font you want to display.

TIPS

How can I quickly insert a symbol into my document?

✔ Some symbols have a shortcut key you can use to quickly insert the symbol as you type. Word displays the shortcut key for a symbol at the bottom of the Symbol dialog box. To insert a symbol with a shortcut key, click where you want the symbol to appear in your document and then press the shortcut key for the symbol.

How can I create my own shortcut key for a symbol?

✔ In the Symbol dialog box, select the symbol and then click the Shortcut Key button. Click the Press new shortcut key area and then press the keys you want to use, such as Alt+P. Click the Assign button and then click Close.

Why does the Symbol dialog box display a Subset area for some fonts?

✔ Fonts with many different symbols are often divided into subcategories, or subsets, to make the symbols easier to find and work with. You can click the Subset area to display the subsets for the current font. Click the subset of symbols you want to display in the dialog box.

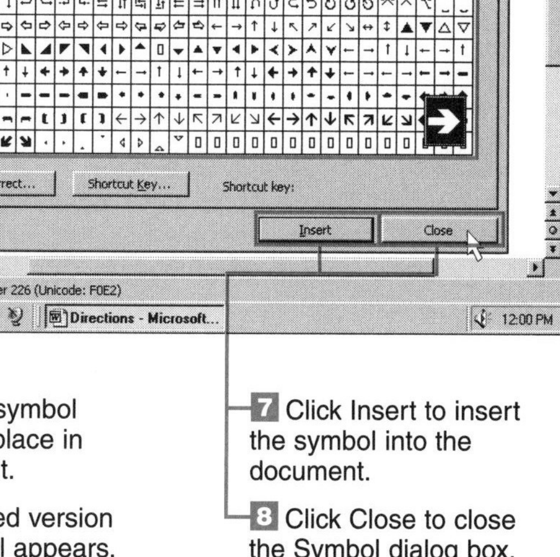

6 Click the symbol you want to place in the document.

■ An enlarged version of the symbol appears.

7 Click Insert to insert the symbol into the document.

8 Click Close to close the Symbol dialog box.

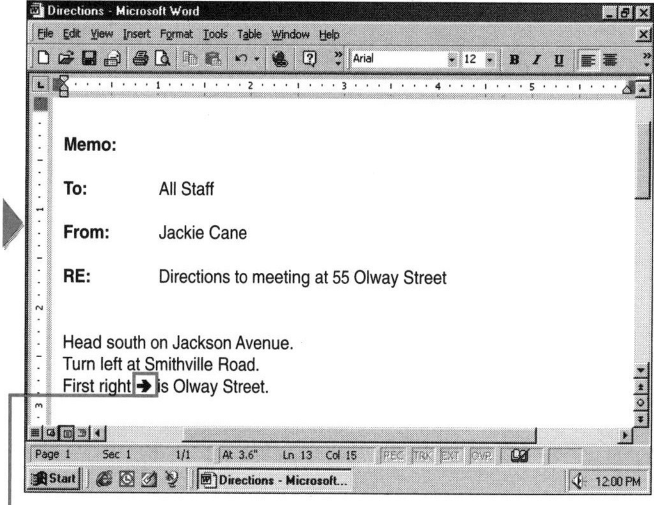

■ The symbol appears in the document.

CHANGE THE VIEW

Word offers several ways to display your document. You can choose the view that best suits your needs.

The Normal view simplifies your document so you can quickly enter, edit and format text. Word does not display top or bottom margins, headers, footers or page numbers in the Normal view.

The Web Layout view displays your document as it will appear in a Web browser. In this view, Word wraps lines of text to fit the width of the window and does not display page breaks.

The Print Layout view displays your document as it will appear on a printed page. The Print Layout view displays top and bottom margins, headers, footers and page numbers. When you first start Word, the document appears in the Print Layout view.

The Outline view allows you to focus on the structure of your document. This view lets you hide or display different levels of text in your document and is useful for working with long documents.

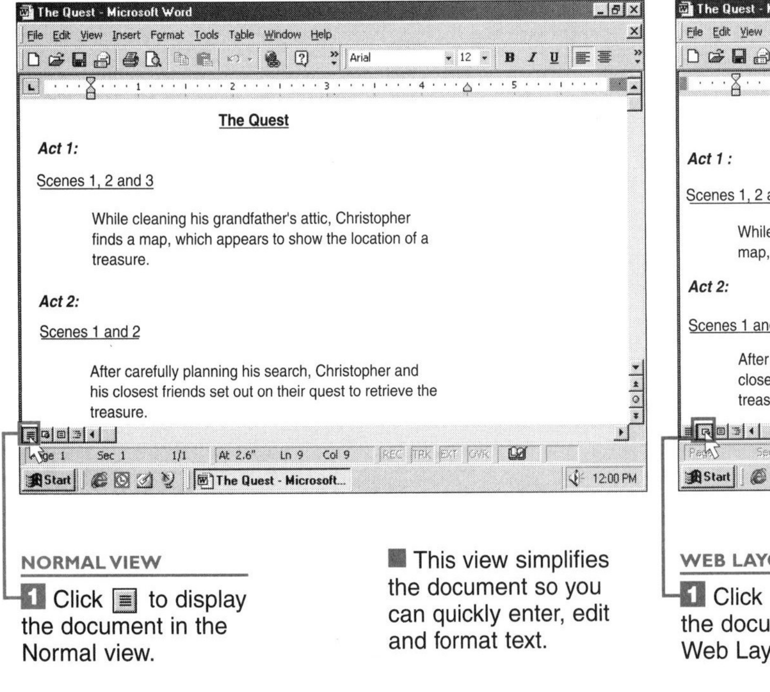

NORMAL VIEW

1 Click to display the document in the Normal view.

■ This view simplifies the document so you can quickly enter, edit and format text.

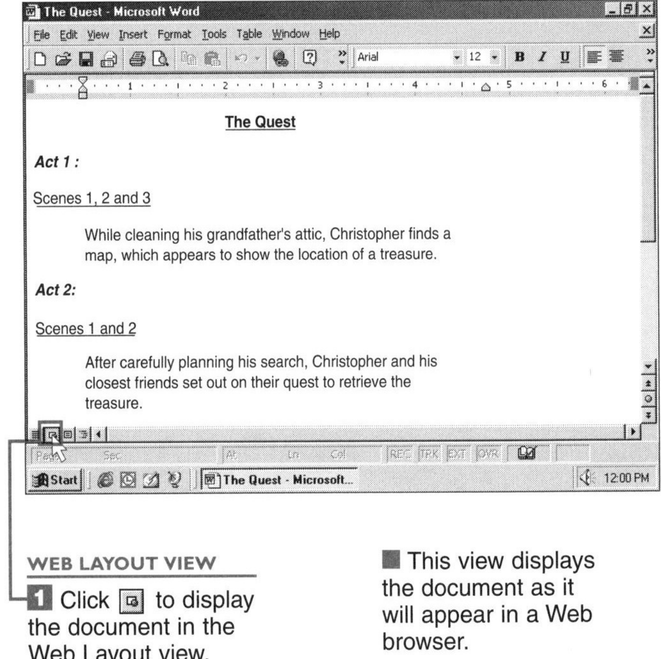

WEB LAYOUT VIEW

1 Click to display the document in the Web Layout view.

■ This view displays the document as it will appear in a Web browser.

TIPS

Why does it take so long to scroll through my document?

✔ If your document contains many elaborate graphics, such as clip art images, you may find it takes a long time to scroll through the document. You can hide graphics so you can scroll through your document faster. From the Tools menu, select Options and then choose the View tab. Click Picture placeholders (☐ changes to ☑) and then click OK. This does not hide simple graphics such as AutoShapes or text effects in your document.

How can I display more of my document on the screen?

✔ You can use the Full Screen view to hide items on your screen, such as the ruler, toolbars and scroll bars. This allows you to see more of your document at once. Select the View menu and then click Full Screen. To return to the previous view of your document, click Close Full Screen or press the Esc key.

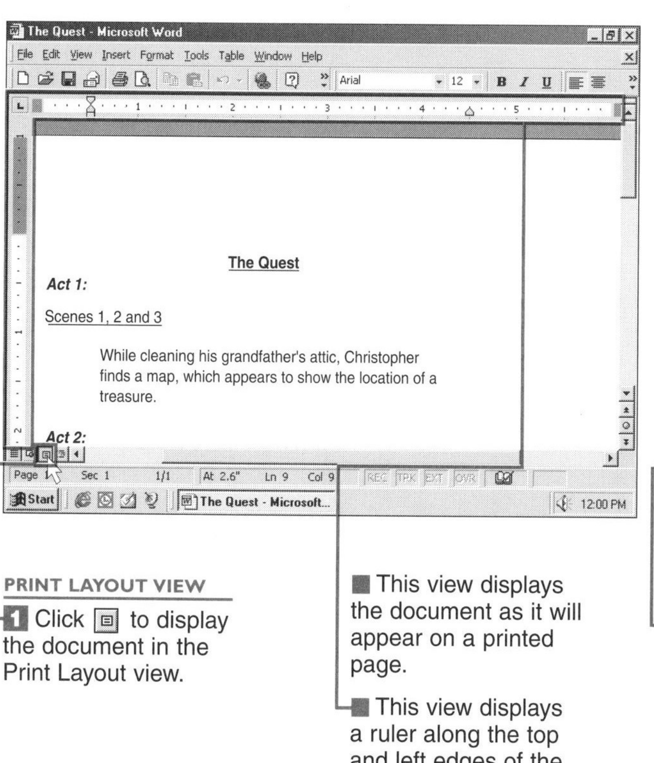

PRINT LAYOUT VIEW

1 Click ▤ to display the document in the Print Layout view.

■ This view displays the document as it will appear on a printed page.

■ This view displays a ruler along the top and left edges of the document.

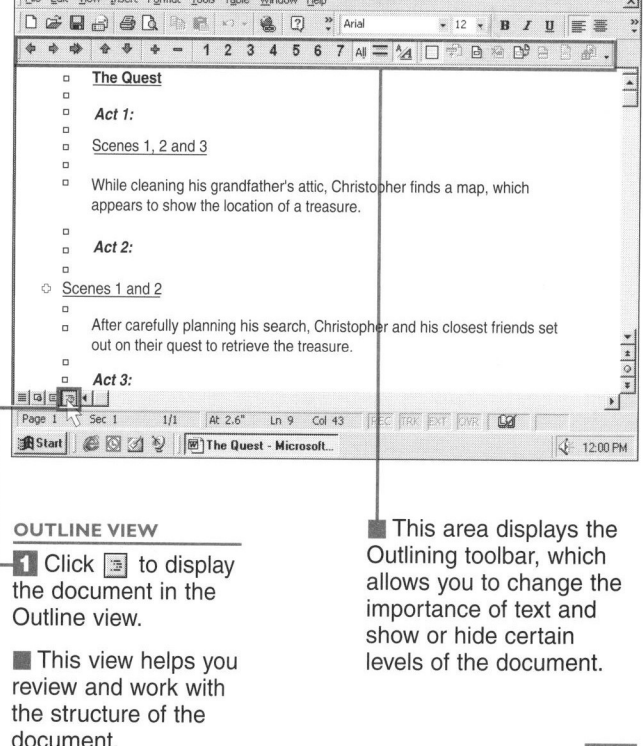

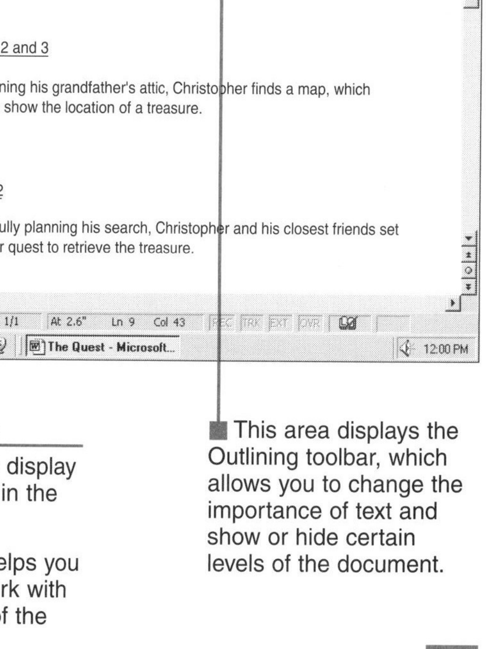

OUTLINE VIEW

1 Click ▤ to display the document in the Outline view.

■ This view helps you review and work with the structure of the document.

■ This area displays the Outlining toolbar, which allows you to change the importance of text and show or hide certain levels of the document.

DISPLAY OR HIDE THE RULER

Word offers a ruler you can use to set tabs and change margins for the text in your document. The ruler can also help you see where text and graphics in your document will appear on a printed page.

In the Print Layout view, Word displays the ruler along the top and left edges of your document. In the Normal and Web Layout views, Word only displays the ruler along the top edge of your document. The ruler is not available in the Outline view. For more information on the views, see page 66.

The default unit of measurement for the ruler is inches. To change the default unit of measurement, see the top of page 97.

If you no longer want to display the ruler, you can hide the ruler. Hiding the ruler provides a larger and less cluttered working area. You can once again display the ruler at any time.

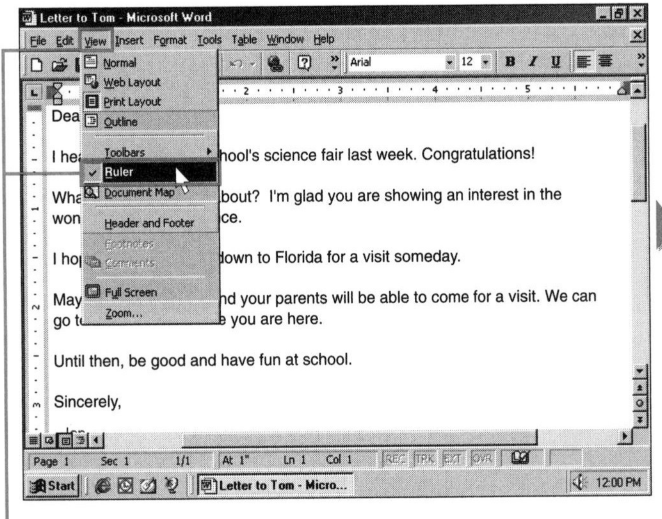

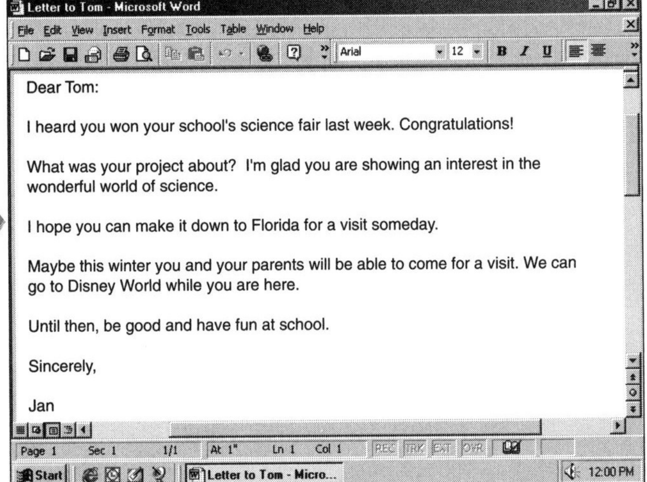

1 Click View.

2 Click Ruler. A check mark (✔) beside Ruler indicates the ruler is currently displayed.

Note: If Ruler does not appear on the menu, position the mouse over the bottom of the menu to display all the menu commands.

■ Word hides or displays the ruler.

ZOOM IN OR OUT

Word lets you enlarge or reduce the display of text on your screen. You can increase the zoom setting to view an area of your document in more detail or decrease the zoom setting to view more of your document at once.

Word offers specially designed zoom settings. The Page Width setting fits your document neatly across the width of your screen.

The Text Width setting ensures all text is visible across the width of your screen. The Whole Page and Two Pages settings display one or two full pages on your screen. The available zoom settings depend on which view your document is displayed in.

If the available zoom settings do not suit your needs, Word allows you to enter a specific zoom setting.

The zoom setting you use is saved as part of your document. The next time you open your document, it will appear in the zoom setting you selected.

Changing the zoom setting will not affect the size of your document when it is printed.

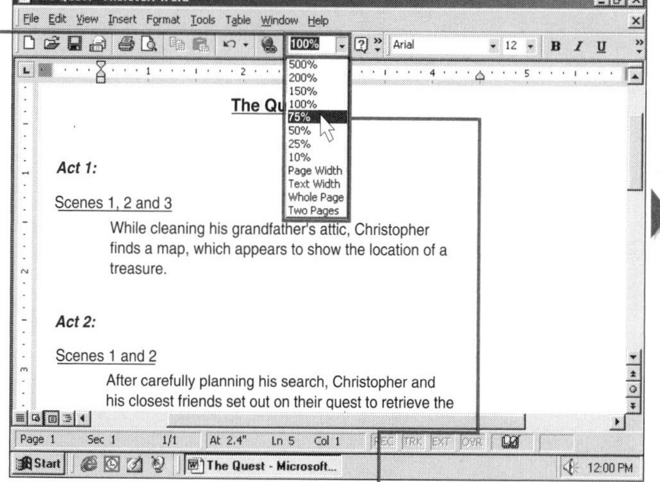

1 Click ▾ in this area to display a list of zoom settings.

Note: If the Zoom area is not displayed, click » on the Standard toolbar to display all the buttons.

2 Click the setting you want to use.

Note: Word initially displays the document in the 100% zoom setting.

■ The document appears in the new zoom setting. You can edit the document as usual.

■ You can also type a specific zoom setting. Click this area and type the zoom setting. Then press the Enter key.

DISPLAY OR HIDE FORMATTING MARKS

You can display formatting marks in your document. Formatting marks can help you edit your document and check for errors such as extra spaces between words.

Word displays several formatting marks. For example, the ¶ symbol indicates where you pressed the Enter key to start a new paragraph in the document.

A small arrow (→) indicates where you pressed the Tab key to indent text. The • symbol shows where you pressed the Spacebar to leave a blank space.

When you display formatting marks, Word also displays hidden text in your document. A dotted line (.....) under text indicates that the text is hidden. To hide text, see page 74.

Formatting marks only appear on your screen. Displaying formatting marks does not affect the way your document will appear on a printed page.

When you have finished reviewing your document with formatting marks, you can once again hide the formatting marks.

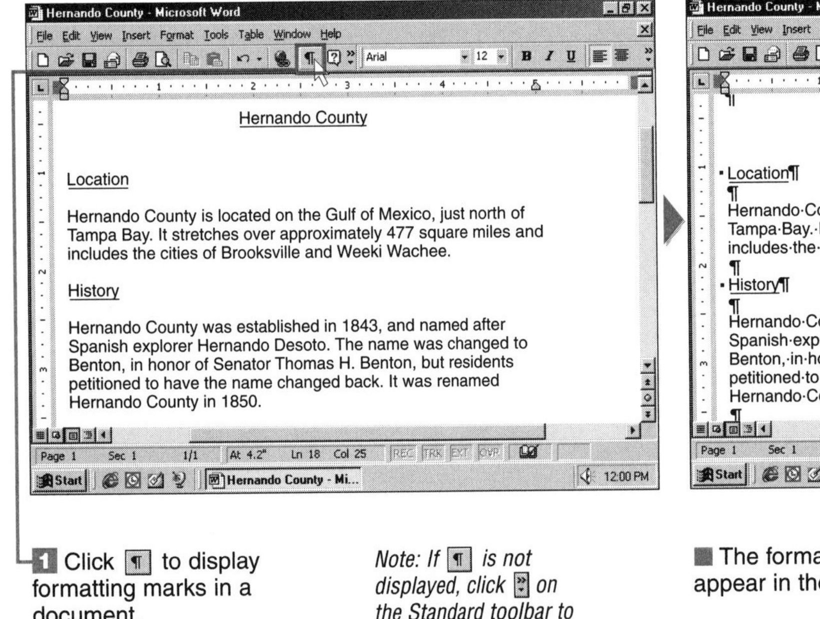

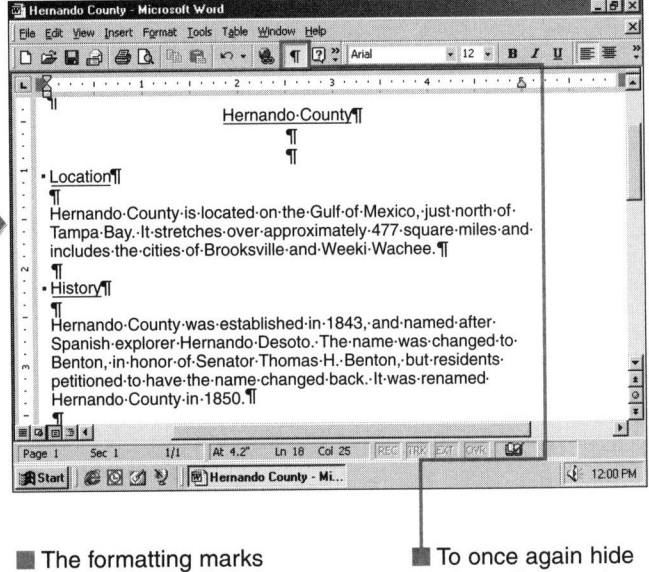

1 Click ¶ to display formatting marks in a document.

Note: If ¶ is not displayed, click » on the Standard toolbar to display all the buttons.

■ The formatting marks appear in the document.

■ To once again hide the formatting marks, click ¶.

USING THE DOCUMENT MAP

The Document Map creates an outline of your document and allows you to easily move through the document.

The Document Map lists all the headings and subheadings in your document. You can select a heading or subheading to quickly move to that part of your document. Word highlights the heading or subheading you select to indicate your location in the document.

When you display the Document Map, Word searches for headings in your document. If Word does not find any headings or subheadings in your document, the Document Map may be blank. For best results, you should apply styles to the headings and subheadings in your document. For information on applying styles, see page 92.

The Document Map may disappear from your screen when you change the view of the document. If you want to work with the Document Map in a different view, you must display the Document Map in the new view. For more information on the views, see page 66.

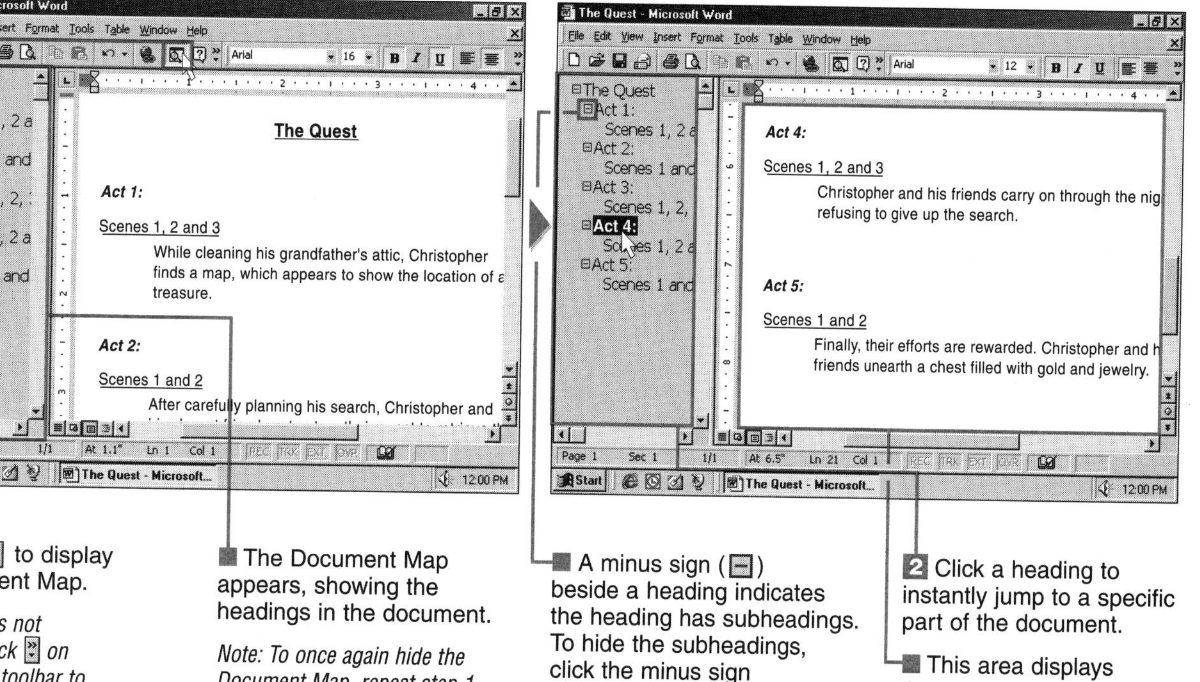

1 Click [icon] to display the Document Map.

Note: If [icon] is not displayed, click [»] on the Standard toolbar to display all the buttons.

■ The Document Map appears, showing the headings in the document.

Note: To once again hide the Document Map, repeat step 1.

■ A minus sign (⊟) beside a heading indicates the heading has subheadings. To hide the subheadings, click the minus sign (⊟ changes to ⊞).

Note: To once again display the subheadings, click the plus sign (⊞).

2 Click a heading to instantly jump to a specific part of the document.

■ This area displays the part of the document you selected.

CHANGE FONT AND SIZE OF TEXT

You can enhance the appearance of your document by changing the design, or font, of the text.

Word provides a list of fonts for you to choose from. Fonts you used most recently appear at the top of the list. This allows you to quickly select fonts you use often. The other fonts in the list appear in alphabetical order.

The fonts appear in the list as they will appear in your document. This lets you preview a font before you select it.

You can increase or decrease the size of text in your document. Larger text is easier to read, but smaller text allows you to fit more information on a page. Word measures the size of text in points. There are 72 points in an inch.

By default, Word uses the Times New Roman font and a text size of 12 points. You may want to change the font and size to draw attention to headings or emphasize important information in your document.

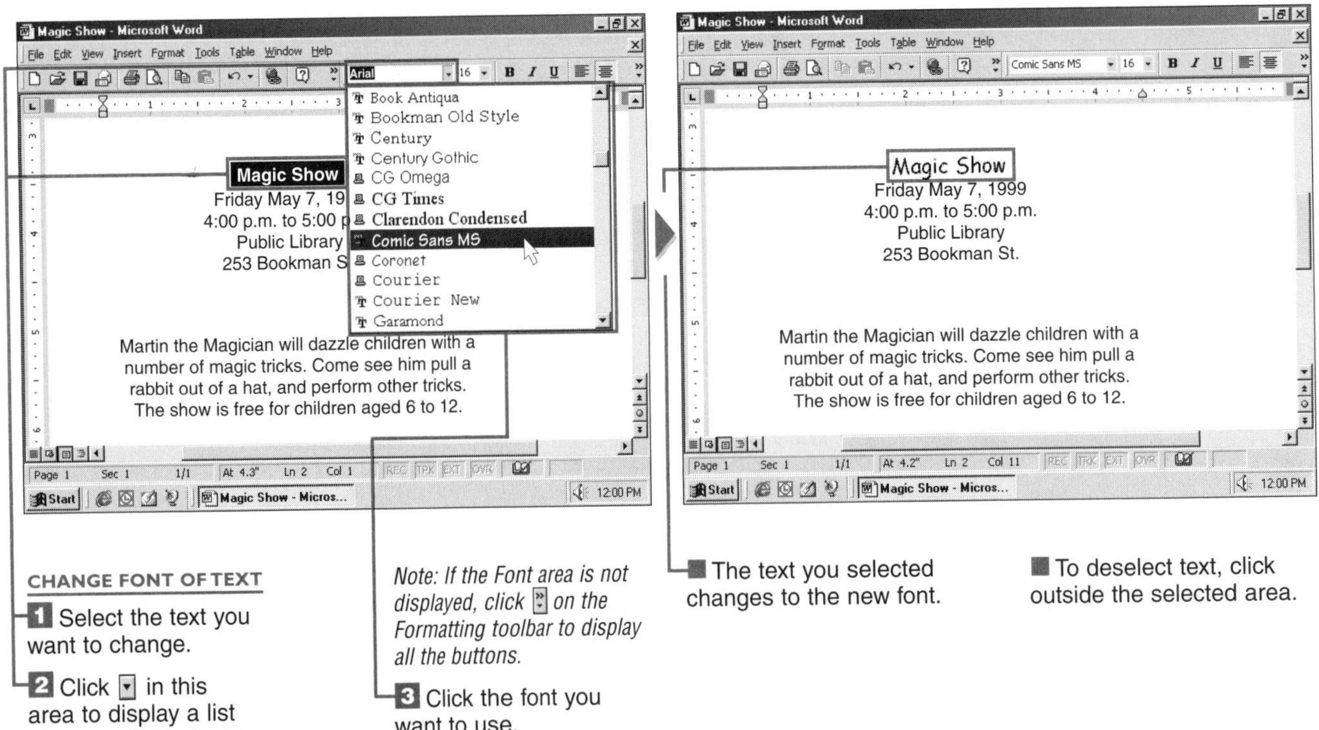

CHANGE FONT OF TEXT

1 Select the text you want to change.

2 Click ▾ in this area to display a list of the available fonts.

Note: If the Font area is not displayed, click » on the Formatting toolbar to display all the buttons.

3 Click the font you want to use.

■ The text you selected changes to the new font.

■ To deselect text, click outside the selected area.

TIPS

What does the symbol beside a font indicate?

✔ The 𝕋 symbol indicates the font is a TrueType font. This type of font prints exactly as it appears on your screen. The 🖶 symbol indicates the font is a printer font. This type of font may print differently than it appears on your screen. Documents you create using a printer font generally print faster.

How can I change the font and size of text while typing?

✔ Before you begin typing the text you want to display a different font and size, select the font and size you want to use. Any text you type after making the changes will display the new font and size.

Can I use other fonts with Word?

✔ You can add fonts to your computer that you can use in all your programs, including Word. You can obtain fonts from computer stores and on the Internet. Consult your Windows manual to add fonts to your computer.

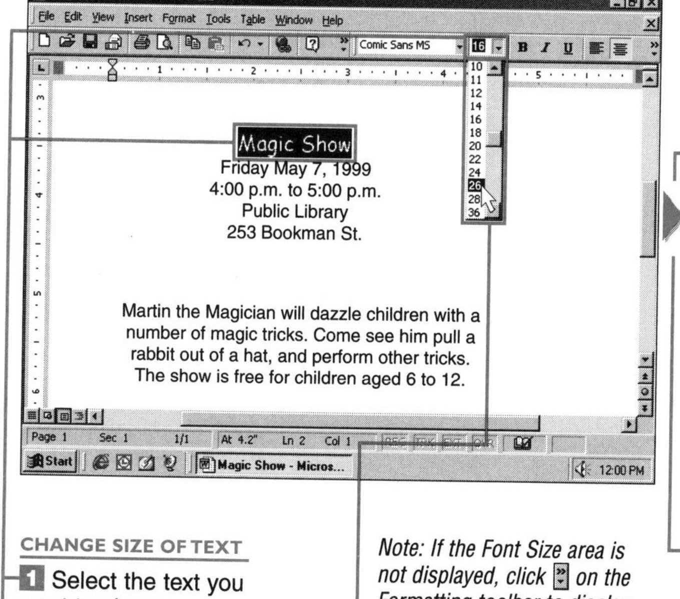

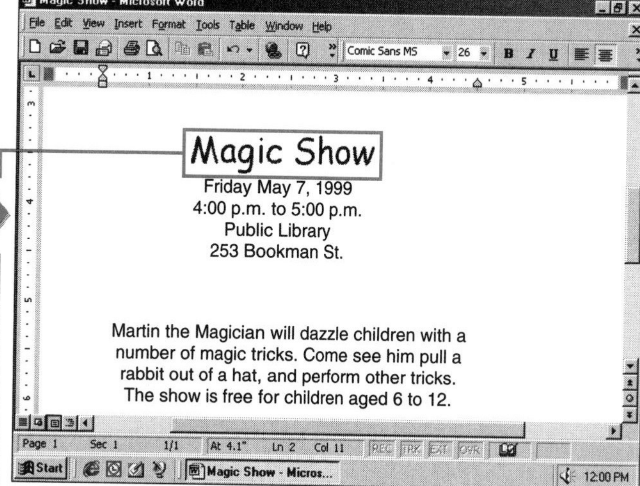

CHANGE SIZE OF TEXT

1 Select the text you want to change.

2 Click ▾ in this area to display a list of the available sizes.

Note: If the Font Size area is not displayed, click » on the Formatting toolbar to display all the buttons.

3 Click the size you want to use.

■ The text you selected changes to the new size.

■ To deselect text, click outside the selected area.

CHANGE APPEARANCE OF TEXT

You can make text in your document look more attractive by using various fonts, styles, sizes, colors and special effects.

You can change the font, size and color of text. This is useful when you want to make headings or important information stand out from the rest of the text in your document.

You can use a style, such as bold or italic, to draw attention to significant words and phrases in your document.

Special effects can enhance the appearance of your document. The Strikethrough options draw lines through text. The Superscript and Subscript options let you place text above or below the line of text. The Shadow, Emboss and Engrave options give text a three-dimensional look. The Outline option allows you to display an outline of each character. The Small caps and All caps options allow you to change text to different sizes of uppercase letters. You may not be able to select some special effects, depending on the other options you have selected.

You can see a preview of the text with all the formatting options you selected.

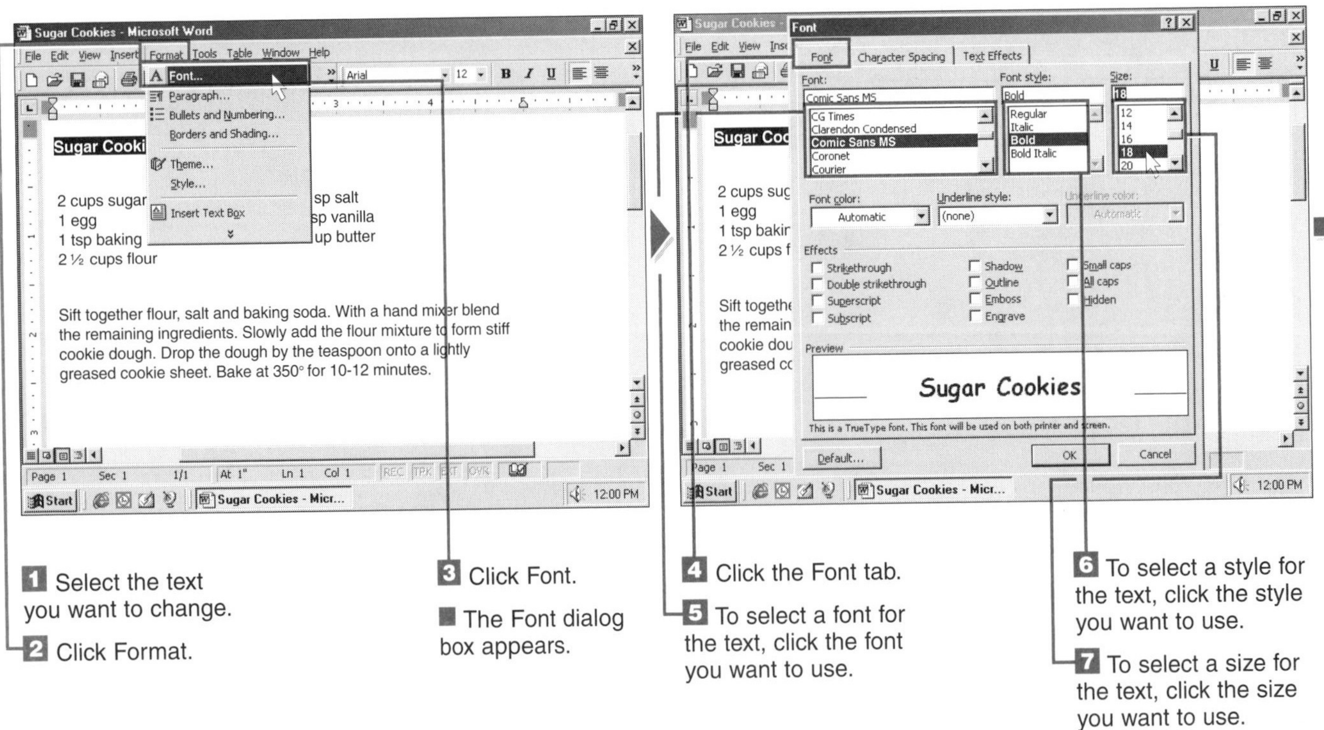

1 Select the text you want to change.

2 Click Format.

3 Click Font.

■ The Font dialog box appears.

4 Click the Font tab.

5 To select a font for the text, click the font you want to use.

6 To select a style for the text, click the style you want to use.

7 To select a size for the text, click the size you want to use.

TIPS

Can I use the Font dialog box to underline text?

✔ Yes. In the Font dialog box, click the box below Underline style and then select the underline style you want to use. You can also change the color of the underline. Click the box below Underline color and then select the color you want to use.

Can I quickly apply the formatting options I selected in the Font dialog box to other parts of my document?

✔ Yes. Select the text you want to format. Choose the Edit menu and then click Repeat Font Formatting.

Can I change the default font setting Word uses for all my new documents?

✔ You can change the default font setting to specify the font options you want Word to use for the text in new documents you create. In the Font dialog box, select the font options you want to use, such as font and size, and then click the Default button. In the dialog box that appears, click Yes. This will not affect documents you have already created.

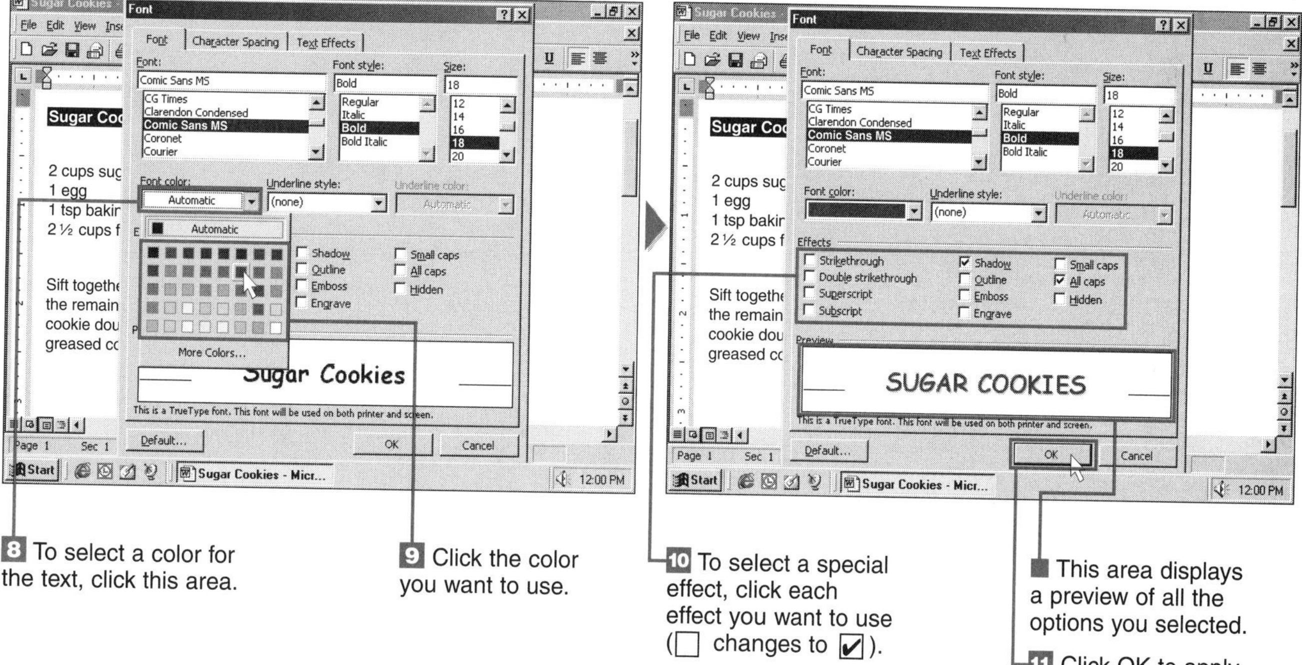

8 To select a color for the text, click this area.

9 Click the color you want to use.

10 To select a special effect, click each effect you want to use (☐ changes to ☑).

■ This area displays a preview of all the options you selected.

11 Click OK to apply the changes.

COLOR OR HIGHLIGHT TEXT

You can change the color of text in your document. Word provides many colors for you to choose from.

You can change the color of text to draw attention to headings or important information in your document. Changing the color of text also allows you to enhance the appearance of your document.

You can highlight text in your document to mark text you want to review or verify later. Word offers several colors you can use to highlight text.

When you highlight text, Word changes the background color of the text. This makes the highlighted text stand out from the rest of the text in your document.

When you print a document that contains colored or highlighted text using a black-and-white printer, the colored or highlighted text will appear in shades of gray. For best printing results, you should choose a light highlight color for text you intend to print on a black-and-white printer.

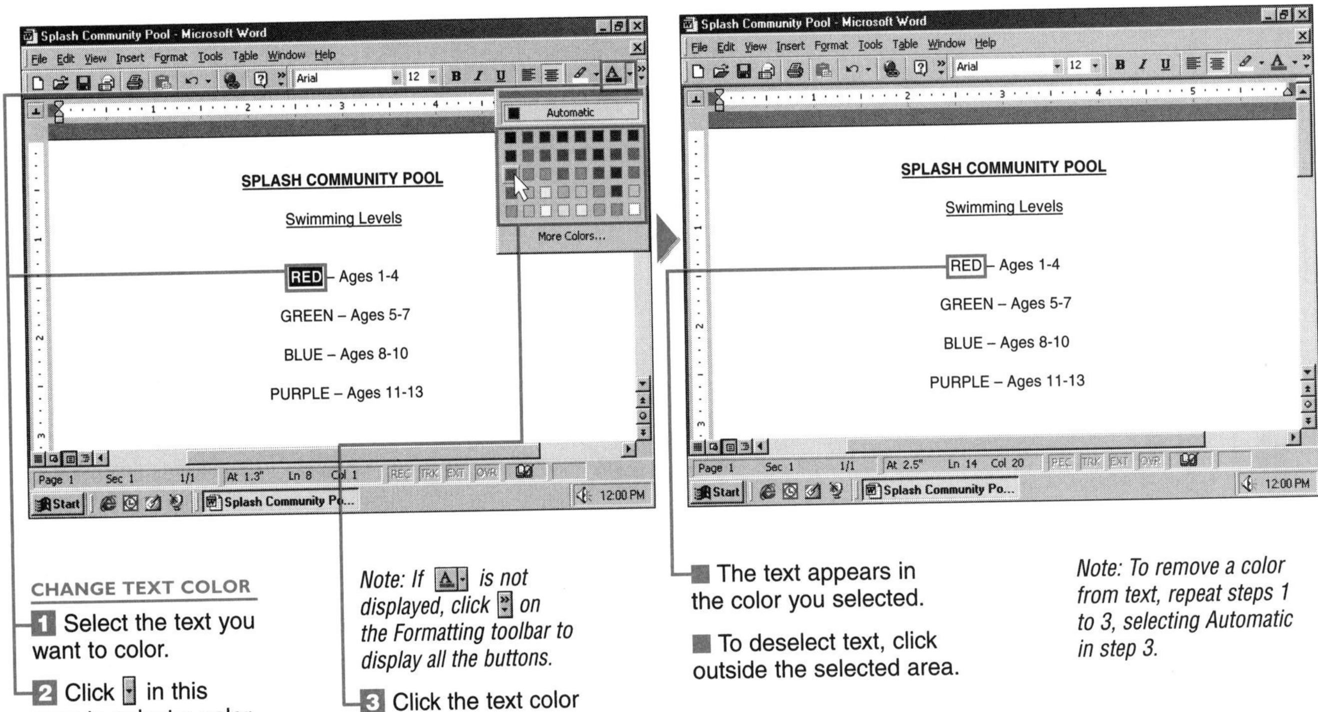

CHANGE TEXT COLOR

1 Select the text you want to color.

2 Click ▾ in this area to select a color.

Note: If A▾ is not displayed, click » on the Formatting toolbar to display all the buttons.

3 Click the text color you want to use.

■ The text appears in the color you selected.

■ To deselect text, click outside the selected area.

Note: To remove a color from text, repeat steps 1 to 3, selecting Automatic in step 3.

TIPS

How can I quickly change the color of text in my document?

✔ The Font Color button (A) on the Formatting toolbar displays the last font color you selected. To quickly add this color to text in your document, select the text you want to change and then click the Font Color button (A).

How can I quickly highlight text in my document?

✔ You can quickly highlight text using the color currently displayed on the Highlight button (✎) on the Formatting toolbar. Click the Highlight button (✎) and then select the text you want to highlight. When you finish highlighting text, click the Highlight button (✎) again.

Can I hide the highlighting in my document?

✔ Yes. Select the Tools menu and then click Options. Select the View tab, click the Highlight option (✔ changes to ☐) and then click OK.

Where can I find more text colors?

✔ Click ▾ on the Font Color button (A▾) and then click More Colors. A dialog box appears, displaying a color palette. Click the color you want to use and then click OK.

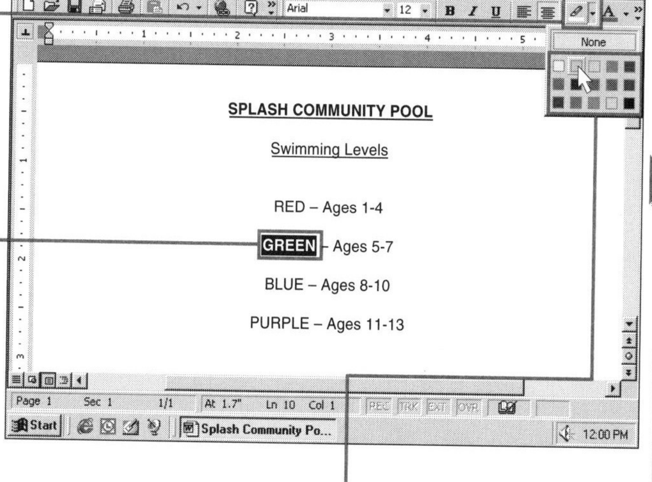

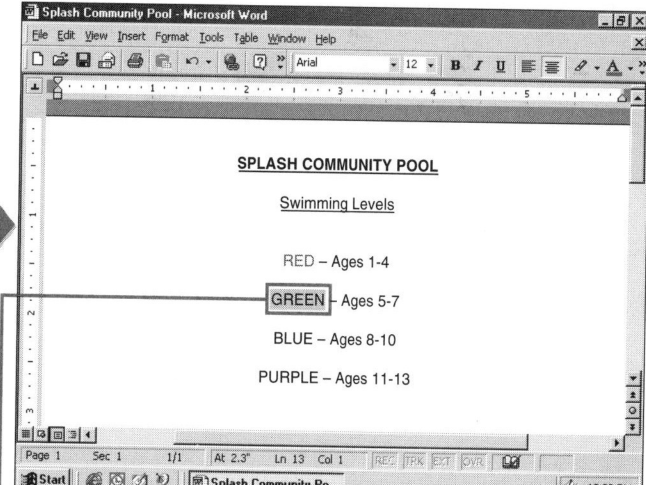

HIGHLIGHT TEXT

1 Select the text you want to highlight.

2 Click ▾ in this area to select a color.

Note: If ✎▾ is not displayed, click » on the Formatting toolbar to display all the buttons.

3 Click the highlight color you want to use.

■ The text appears highlighted in the color you selected.

Note: To remove a highlight, repeat steps 1 to 3, selecting None in step 3.

BOLD, ITALIC OR UNDERLINE

You can use the Bold, Italic and Underline features to change the style of text in your document. These features help you emphasize information and enhance the appearance of your document.

You can use one feature at a time or any combination of the three features to change the style of text.

The Bold feature makes text appear darker and thicker than other text. You can bold headings and titles to make them stand out from the rest of the text in your document.

The Italic feature tilts text to the right. You may want to italicize quotations and references in your document.

The Underline feature adds a line underneath text. This is useful for emphasizing important text, such as key words in your document.

You can also italicize or bold text as you type. To italicize text, type an underscore (_) before and after the text you want to appear italicized. For example, type **_maranGraphics_** to make the word appear in italics. To bold text, type an asterisk (*) before and after the text you want to appear bold.

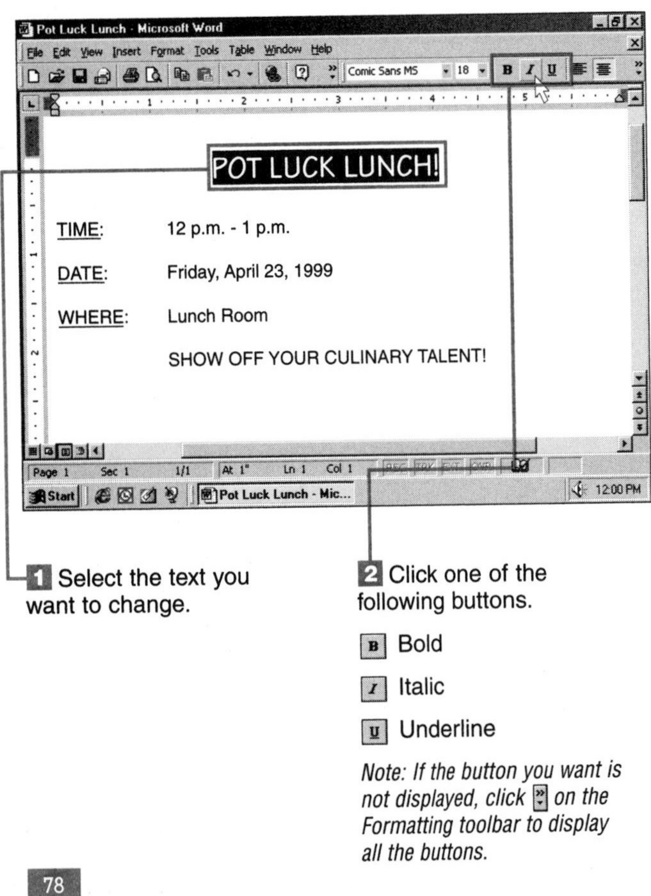

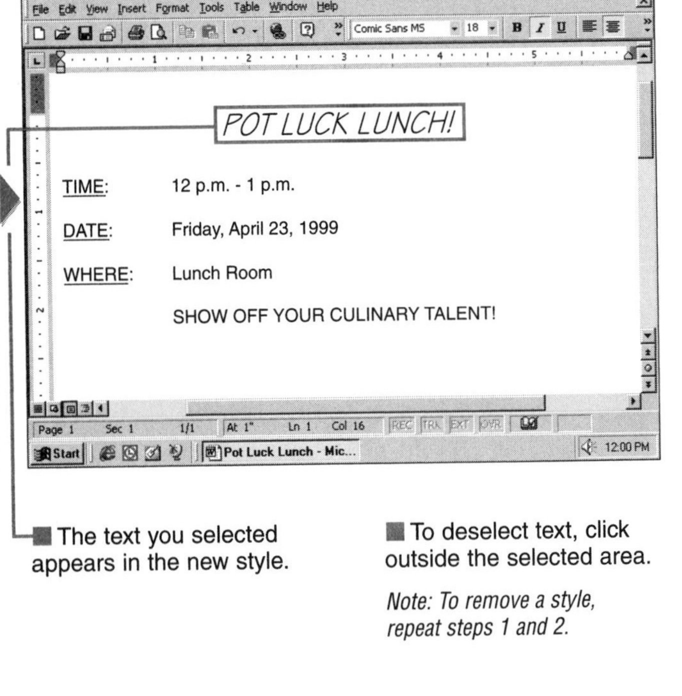

1 Select the text you want to change.

2 Click one of the following buttons.

B Bold

I Italic

U Underline

Note: If the button you want is not displayed, click » on the Formatting toolbar to display all the buttons.

■ The text you selected appears in the new style.

■ To deselect text, click outside the selected area.

Note: To remove a style, repeat steps 1 and 2.

COPY FORMATTING

You can make one area of text in your document look exactly like another.

You may want to copy the formatting of text to make all the headings or important words in your document look the same. This will give your document a consistent appearance.

If you copy the formatting of text that contains more than one type of the same formatting, such as multiple fonts, Word will only copy the first type of formatting. For example, if you select a paragraph that contains the Times New Roman font followed by the Arial font, Word will only copy the Times New Roman font.

You can copy formatting to several areas in your document at once. To do so, perform the steps below, except double-click the Format Painter button ( ) on the Standard toolbar in step 2. When you have finished selecting all the text you want to display the formatting, press the Esc key to stop copying the formatting.

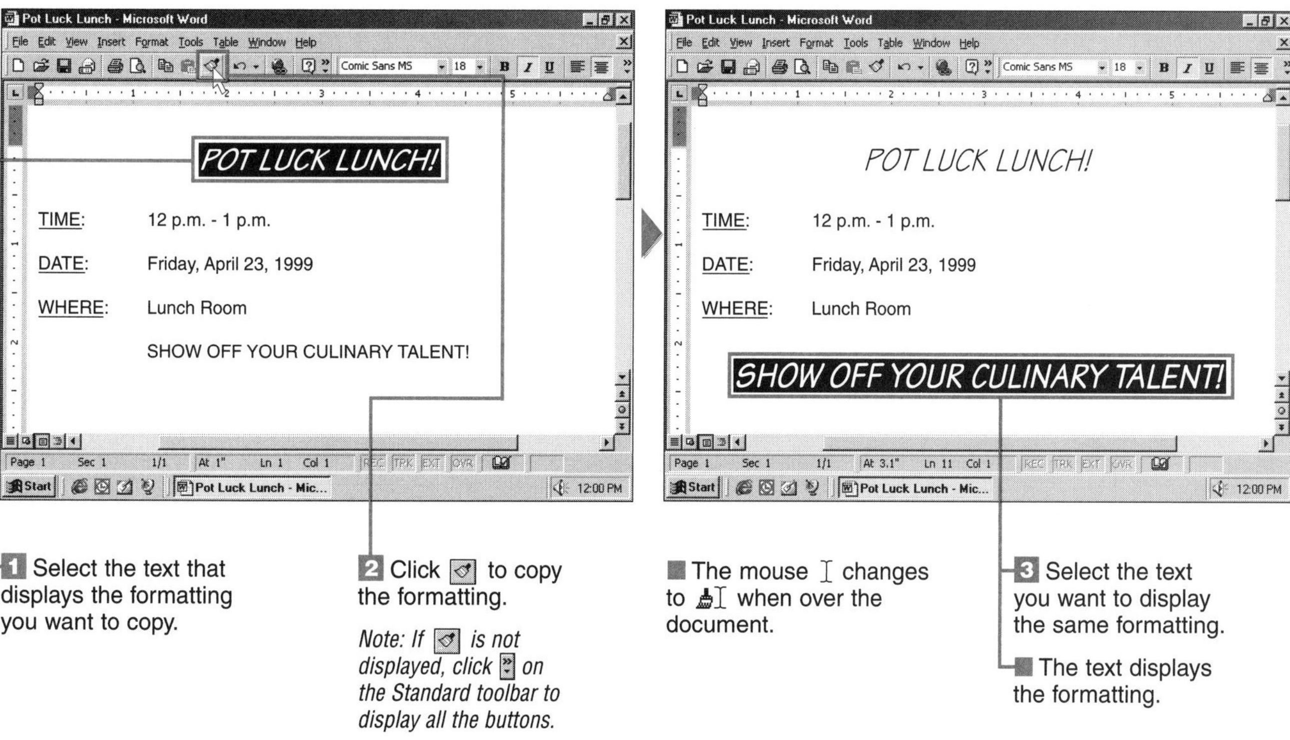

1 Select the text that displays the formatting you want to copy.

2 Click to copy the formatting.

Note: If is not displayed, click on the Standard toolbar to display all the buttons.

■ The mouse I changes to when over the document.

3 Select the text you want to display the same formatting.

■ The text displays the formatting.

CHANGE ALIGNMENT OF TEXT

You can use the alignment buttons on the Formatting toolbar to change the alignment of text in your document. By default, Word aligns text along the left margin.

Word allows you to center text between the left and right margins. This is useful for making headings and titles in your document stand out.

You can align text along the right margin. You may want to right align a return address that appears at the top of a letter you are creating.

You can justify text to align the text along both the left and right margins. When you justify text, Word spaces the text to make it fit neatly on a line. Justifying text is useful for text that appears in columns, such as newspaper columns.

You can also use Word's Click and Type feature to align text you enter in a document. The Click and Type feature lets you left align, center or right align new text. The Click and Type feature is only available in the Print Layout and Web Layout views. For more information on the views, see page 66.

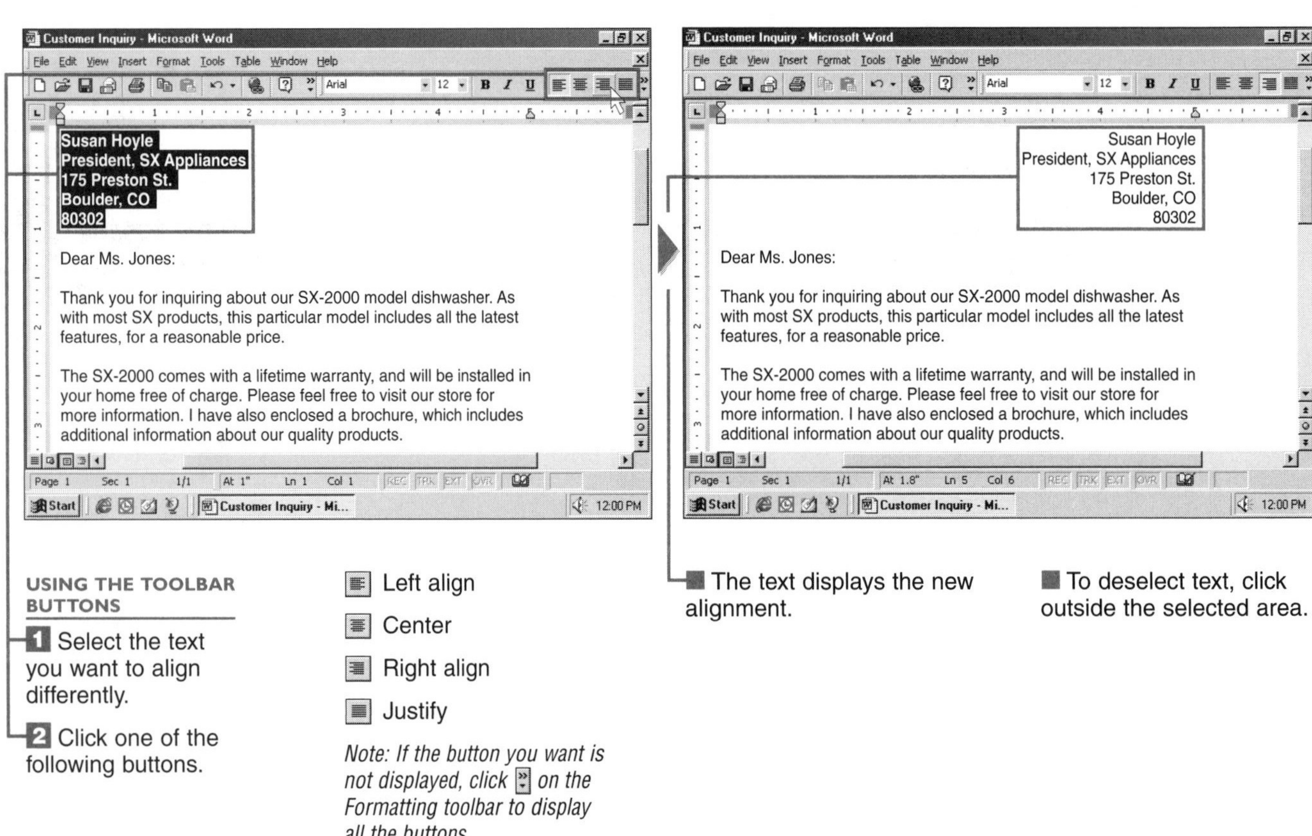

USING THE TOOLBAR BUTTONS

1 Select the text you want to align differently.

2 Click one of the following buttons.

- Left align
- Center
- Right align
- Justify

Note: If the button you want is not displayed, click » on the Formatting toolbar to display all the buttons.

■ The text displays the new alignment.

■ To deselect text, click outside the selected area.

TIPS

Why didn't Word justify the last line of my paragraph?

✔ By default, Word does not justify the last line of a paragraph to prevent the text from becoming too spread out. To have Word justify the last line of your paragraph, click at the end of the line and then press the Shift+Enter keys.

Can I use different alignments within a single line of text?

✔ You can use the Click and Type feature to vary the alignment within a line of text. For example, you can left align your name and right align the date on the same line.

Why didn't the Click and Type feature left align my text?

✔ You may not have positioned the mouse pointer properly. When the mouse pointer looks like I≡, Word will left align all the text you type. When the mouse pointer looks like I≡, Word will indent the first line of text.

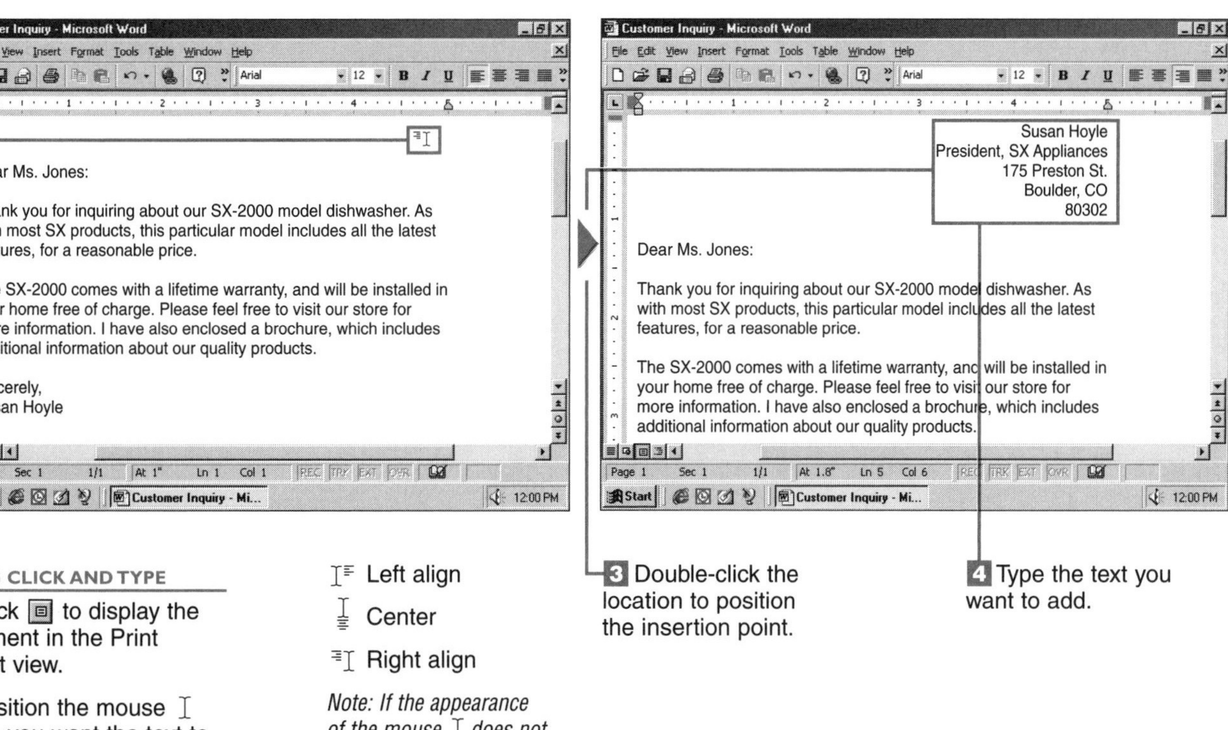

USING CLICK AND TYPE

1 Click ▤ to display the document in the Print Layout view.

2 Position the mouse I where you want the text to appear. The appearance of the mouse I indicates how Word will align the text.

I≡ Left align

I Center

≡I Right align

Note: If the appearance of the mouse I does not change, click where you want to add text.

3 Double-click the location to position the insertion point.

4 Type the text you want to add.

INDENT PARAGRAPHS

You can use the Indent feature to make paragraphs in your document stand out.

Word allows you to indent the left edge of a paragraph several ways. You can indent the first line of a paragraph. This saves you from having to press the Tab key at the beginning of new paragraphs.

Word also allows you to indent all but the first line of a paragraph. This is called a hanging indent. You may want to use hanging indents when creating a resume, glossary or bibliography.

You can indent all the lines in a paragraph. This is useful when you want to set quotations apart from the rest of the text in your document.

You can also indent the right edge of all the lines in a paragraph. This is useful when you want to emphasize a block of information in your document.

Word allows you to use the Decrease Indent button (⇤) or the Increase Indent button (⇥) on the Formatting toolbar to quickly move the left edge of all the lines in a paragraph to the left or right.

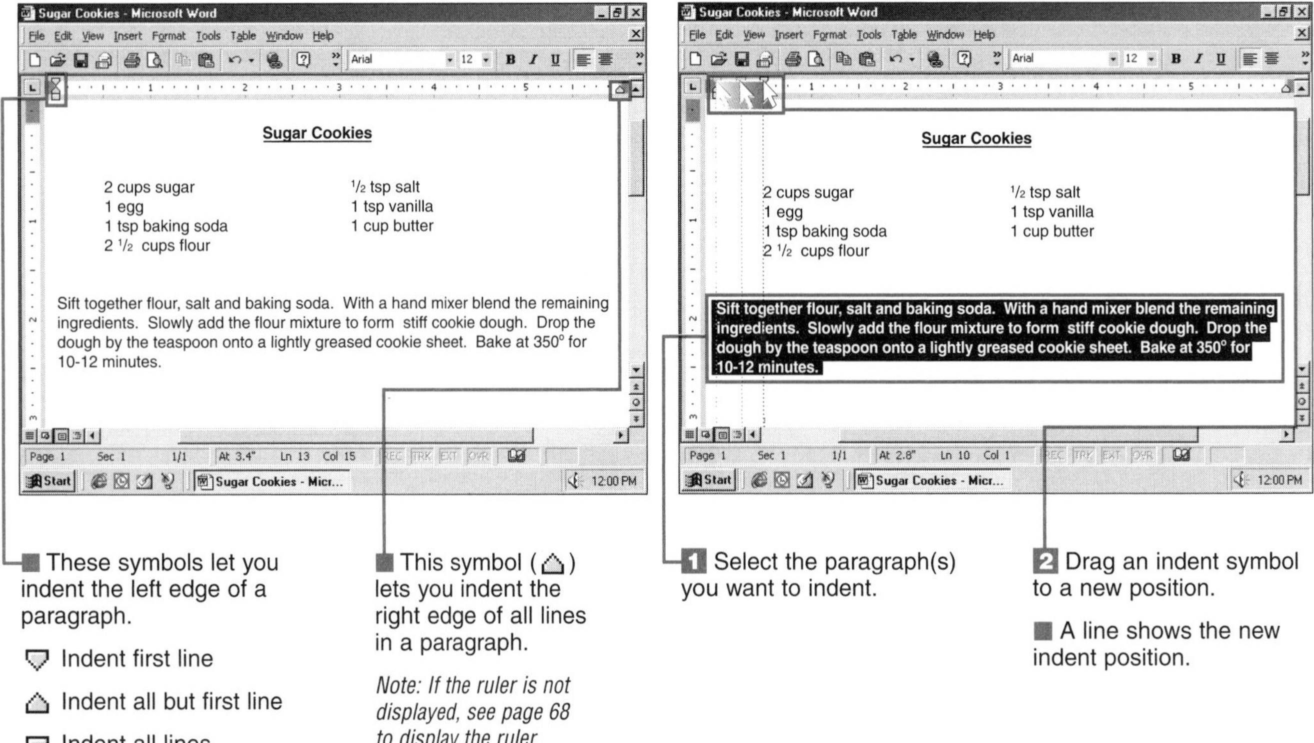

■ These symbols let you indent the left edge of a paragraph.

- ▽ Indent first line
- △ Indent all but first line
- □ Indent all lines

■ This symbol (△) lets you indent the right edge of all lines in a paragraph.

Note: If the ruler is not displayed, see page 68 to display the ruler.

1 Select the paragraph(s) you want to indent.

2 Drag an indent symbol to a new position.

■ A line shows the new indent position.

TIPS

Why are the indent symbols dimmed?

✔ Word dims the indent symbols when you select two or more paragraphs that contain different indent settings. Word can apply different indent settings to different paragraphs but can only display the indent symbols for one paragraph at a time. The dimmed symbols indicate the indent settings for the first selected paragraph.

Is there another way to create a first line or hanging indent?

✔ Yes. Select the paragraph(s) you want to change. Click ⌞ to the left of the ruler until the First Line Indent symbol (▽) or Hanging Indent symbol (□) appears. Then click the bottom half of the ruler where you want to create the indent.

Can I have Word automatically indent the first line of each paragraph I type?

✔ Yes. In the Print Layout view, click where you want to type the first paragraph and then position the mouse I until I changes to I≡. Double-click and then begin typing. Word will automatically indent the first line for each new paragraph you type.

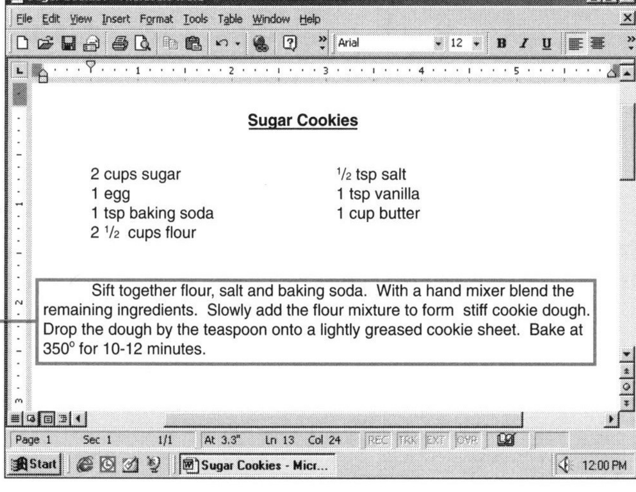

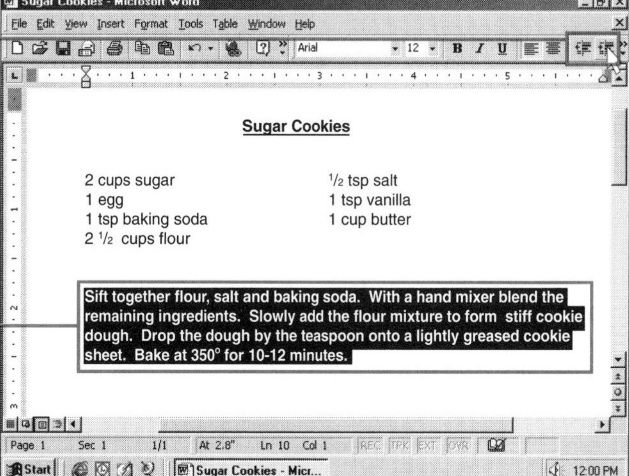

QUICKLY INDENT ALL LINES IN A PARAGRAPH

1 Select the paragraph(s) you want to indent.

2 Click one of the following buttons.

Move paragraph left.

Move paragraph right.

Note: If the button you want is not displayed, click » on the Formatting toolbar to display all the buttons.

■ Word indents the paragraph(s) you selected.

■ To deselect text, click outside the selected area.

CHANGE TAB SETTINGS

You can use tabs to line up columns of information in your document. Using tabs can help make your document easier to read.

Word automatically places a tab every 0.5 inches across a page.

Tabs allow you to accurately line up information at specific positions in your document. You should use tabs instead of spaces to line up information. If you use spaces, the information may not be lined up when you print your document.

Word offers several types of tabs for you to choose from. The tab you add depends on how you want to line up the information. When you choose the Left Tab, Word lines up the left side of your text with the tab. The Center Tab lines up the center of your text with the tab. When you choose the Right Tab, Word lines up the right side of your text with the tab. You can use the Decimal Tab to line up the decimal points in numbers.

When you no longer need a tab, you can remove it from your document.

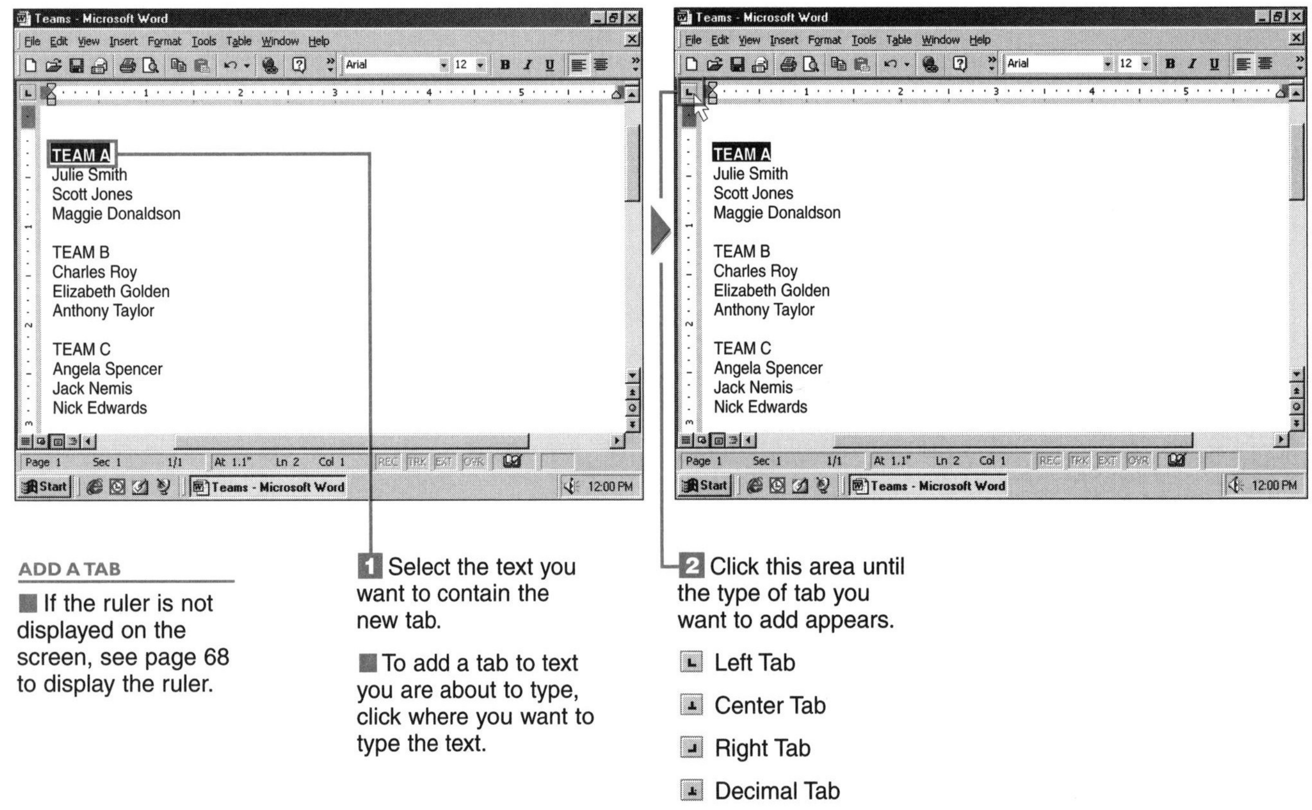

ADD A TAB

■ If the ruler is not displayed on the screen, see page 68 to display the ruler.

1 Select the text you want to contain the new tab.

■ To add a tab to text you are about to type, click where you want to type the text.

2 Click this area until the type of tab you want to add appears.

- Left Tab
- Center Tab
- Right Tab
- Decimal Tab

TIPS

What is the Bar Tab (▮) used for?

✔ The Bar Tab adds a vertical line to your document where you add the tab. You can use the Bar Tab to enhance the appearance of columns of information in your document. To add a Bar Tab, perform steps 1 to 3 on page 84, except select ▮ in step 2.

How can I move a tab?

✔ To move a tab, select the information containing the tab. Then drag the tab to a new location on the ruler.

How can I make the columns of information in my document easier to read?

✔ You can insert leader characters, such as a row of dots, before a tab to help lead the eye from one column of information to another. Leader characters make information such as a table of contents easier to read. Select the text containing the tab you want to add leader characters to. Select the Format menu and then click Tabs. Select the type of leader you want to use and then click OK.

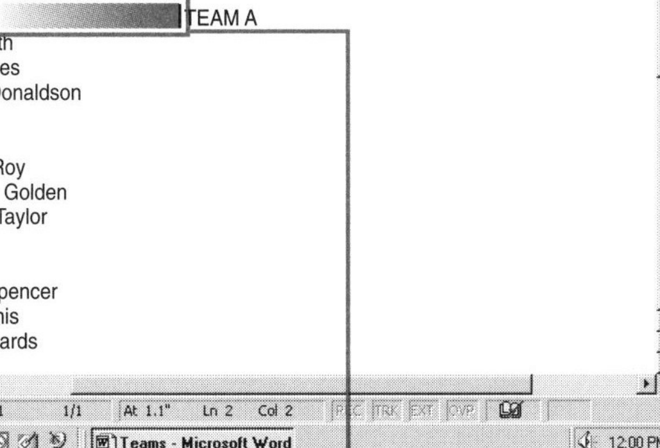

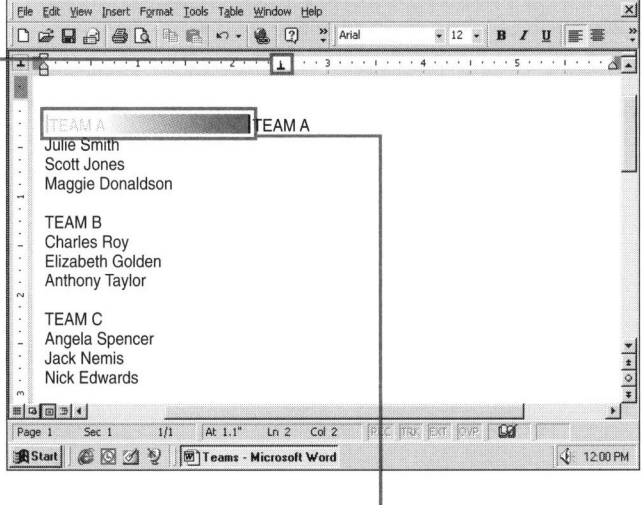

3 Click the bottom half of the ruler where you want to add the tab.

■ The new tab appears on the ruler.

4 Click the beginning of the line you want to move across and then press the Tab key. The insertion point and the text that follows move to the tab you set.

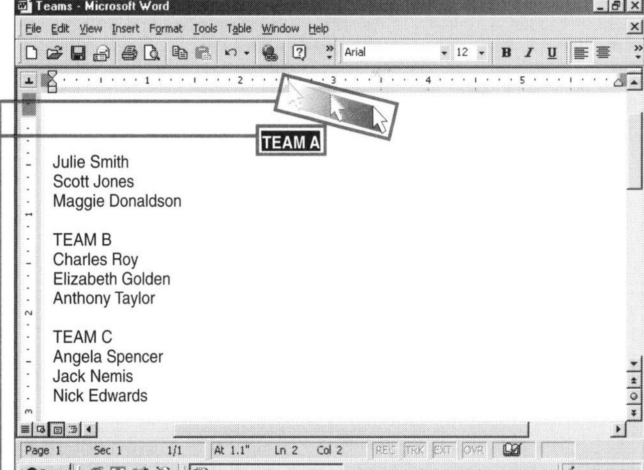

REMOVE A TAB

1 Select the text containing the tab you want to remove.

2 Drag the tab downward off the ruler.

■ The tab disappears from the ruler.

■ To move text back to the left margin, click to the left of the first character. Then press the Backspace key.

CHANGE LINE SPACING

You can change the amount of space between the lines of text in your document. Line spacing prevents the letters in a line of text from touching letters in the line above or the line below.

You can choose a line spacing option such as Single, 1.5 lines or Double. By default, each new document uses single line spacing.

Word uses the size of the text to determine the size of the line spacing and measures line spacing in points. For example, if you select single line spacing for text using a 10-point font size, the line spacing is approximately 10 points.

When you select 1.5 line spacing, Word increases the single line spacing by one-and-one-half times. For example, if you select 1.5 line spacing for text using a 10-point font size, the line spacing is approximately 15 points.

Double line spacing is twice that of single line spacing. For example, if you select double line spacing for a 10-point font size, the line spacing is approximately 20 points.

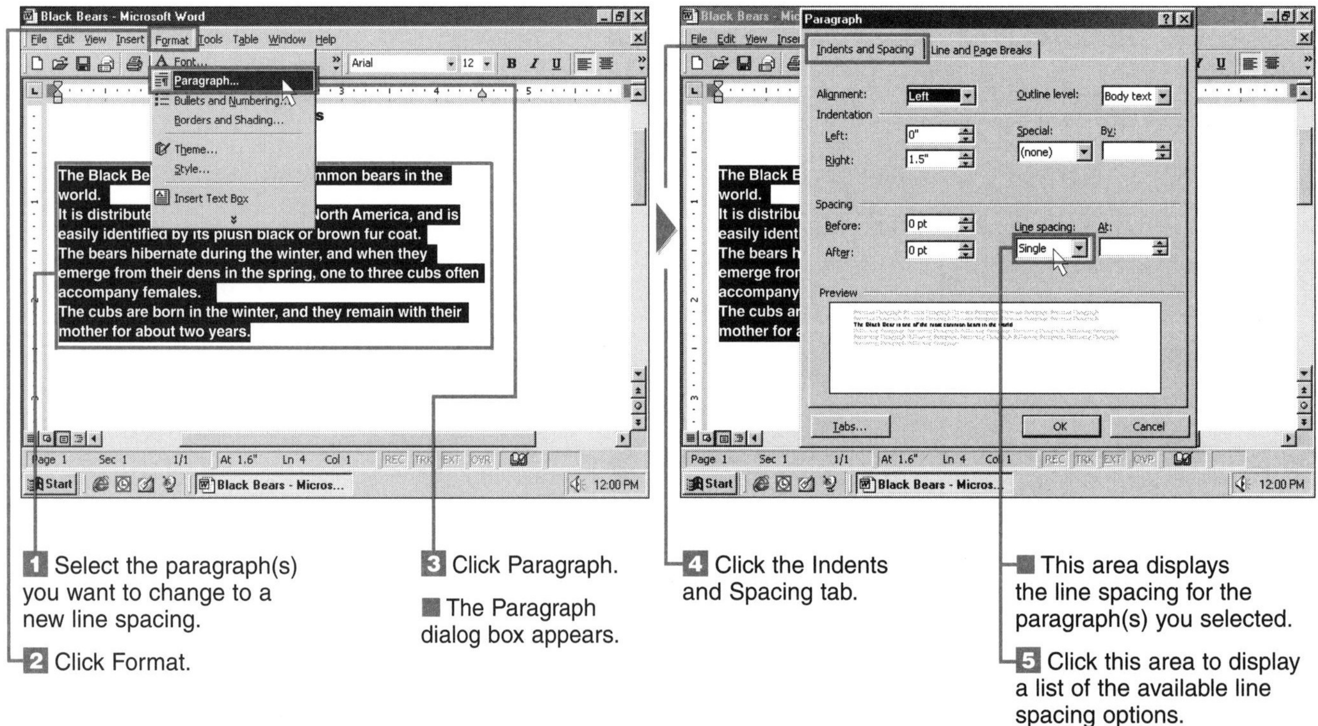

1 Select the paragraph(s) you want to change to a new line spacing.

2 Click Format.

3 Click Paragraph.

■ The Paragraph dialog box appears.

4 Click the Indents and Spacing tab.

■ This area displays the line spacing for the paragraph(s) you selected.

5 Click this area to display a list of the available line spacing options.

TIPS

What is the Multiple line spacing option in the Paragraph dialog box used for?

✔ You can use this option to specify a line spacing that is a multiple of single line spacing. For example, you can specify triple line spacing by selecting the Multiple option and entering 3 in the At area.

Can I use the keyboard to change line spacing?

✔ Select the text you want to change to a new line spacing. Press the Ctrl+1 keys to use single line spacing. Press the Ctrl+5 keys to use 1.5 line spacing. Press the Ctrl+2 keys to use double line spacing.

What are the At least and Exactly line spacing options in the Paragraph dialog box used for?

✔ You can select the At least option to specify the minimum point size you want to use for line spacing. In the At area, type the point size. You can select the Exactly option to ensure all lines are evenly spaced. In the At area, type the exact number of points you want to use for line spacing.

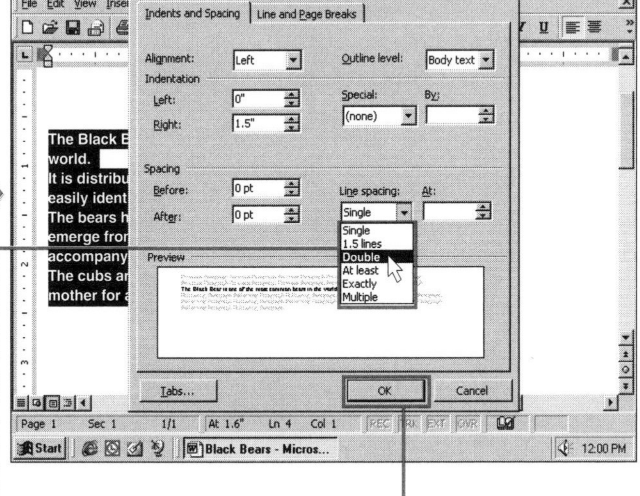

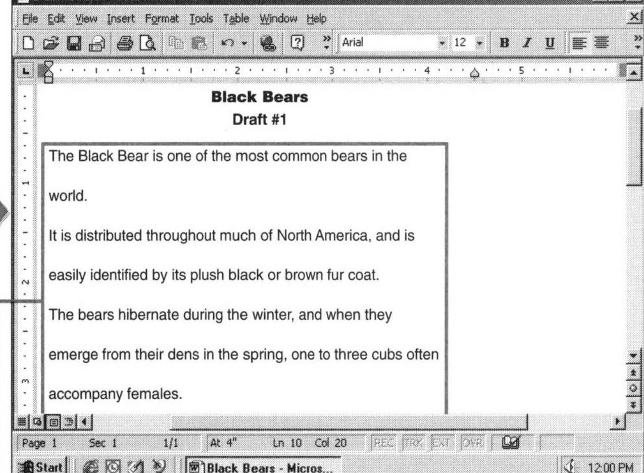

6 Click the line spacing option you want to use.

7 Click OK to confirm the change.

■ Word changes the line spacing of the paragraph(s) you selected.

■ To deselect text, click outside the selected area.

ADD BULLETS OR NUMBERS

You can begin each item in a list with a bullet or number. This can help make the list easier to read.

Bullets are useful for items in no particular order, such as items in a shopping list. Numbers are useful for items in a specific order, such as directions in a recipe.

You can choose a bullet style that suits your needs. For example, you may want to use round or square bullets in a formal business letter, while arrow or check mark bullets may be appropriate in an informal newsletter.

Word offers several number styles for you to choose from, including letters and Roman numerals.

Outline numbers allow you to use different types of number or bullet styles in one list. This is useful when your list contains sub-lists.

When you add a new item to a bulleted or numbered list, Word automatically adds a bullet or number to the new item.

Word also allows you to use the Bullets button (☰) or the Numbering button (☰) on the Formatting toolbar to quickly add bullets or numbers to selected text in your document.

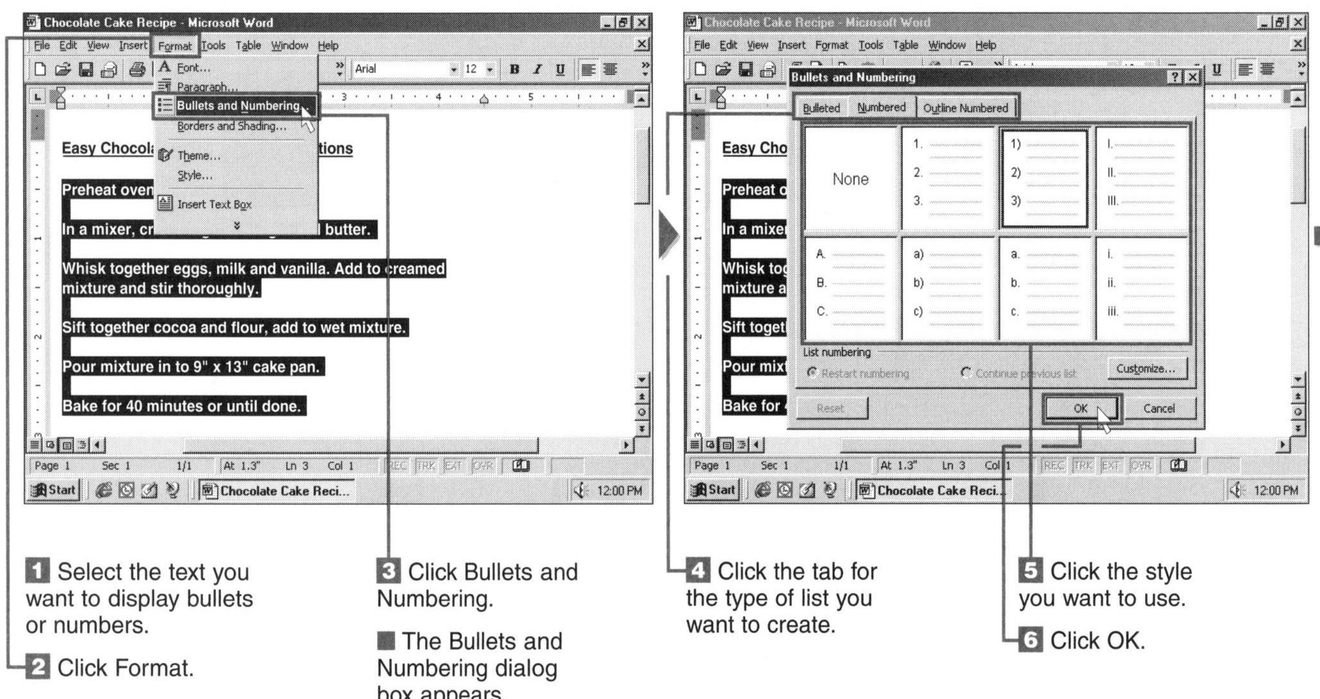

1 Select the text you want to display bullets or numbers.

2 Click Format.

3 Click Bullets and Numbering.

■ The Bullets and Numbering dialog box appears.

4 Click the tab for the type of list you want to create.

5 Click the style you want to use.

6 Click OK.

TIPS

How can I create a bulleted or numbered list as I type?

✔ To create a bulleted or numbered list as you type, type * or **1**. followed by a space. Then type the first item in the list. Press the Enter key and Word automatically starts the next item with a bullet or number. To end the bulleted or numbered list, press the Enter key twice.

Can I change the number Word uses to start my list?

✔ Yes. Perform steps 1 to 5 below and then click the Customize button. In the Start at area, enter the number you want to use to start the list and then click OK.

Can I add picture bullets to a list?

✔ Yes. Perform steps 1 to 4 below, selecting the Bulleted tab in step 4. Click the Picture button and then click the Pictures tab. Select the picture bullet you want to use and then click OK. You may need to insert the CD-ROM disc you used to install Office 2000 into your CD-ROM drive to access all the picture bullets.

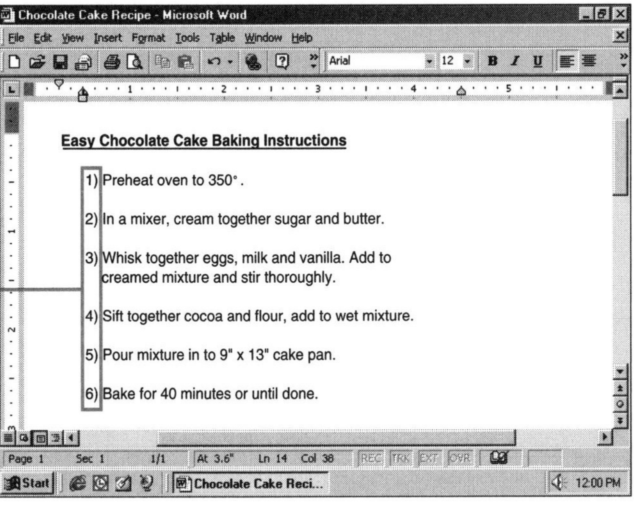

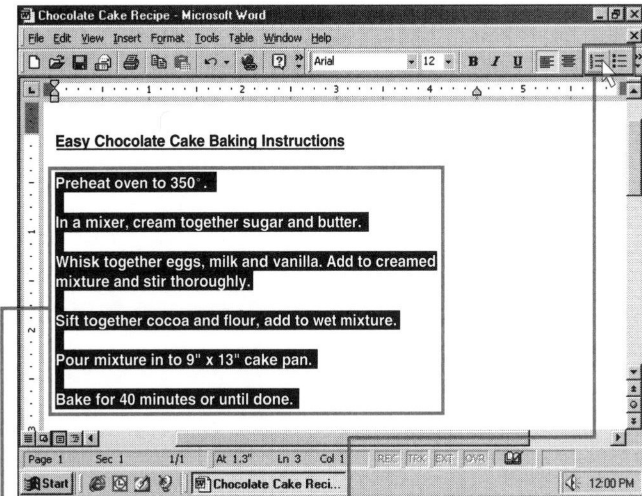

■ The bullets or numbers appear in the document.

■ To deselect text, click outside the selected area.

Note: To remove bullets or numbers from the document, perform steps 1 to 6, selecting None in step 5.

QUICKLY ADD BULLETS OR NUMBERS

1 Select the text you want to display bullets or numbers.

2 Click one of the following buttons.

Add numbers

Add bullets

Note: If the button you want is not displayed, click » on the Formatting toolbar to display all the buttons.

CREATE A STYLE

Styles allow you to save formatting you like and apply the formatting to text in one step. You can easily create your own styles.

Word allows you to create two types of styles—paragraph and character. A paragraph style includes formatting that changes the appearance of individual characters and entire paragraphs, such as text alignment, tab settings and line spacing.

A character style includes formatting that changes the appearance of individual characters, such as bold, underline and text color. A character style also includes the font and size of characters.

You can store your style so you can apply the style to text in new documents you create. If you do not store the style, you will only be able to apply the style to text in the current document. For information on applying a style, see page 92.

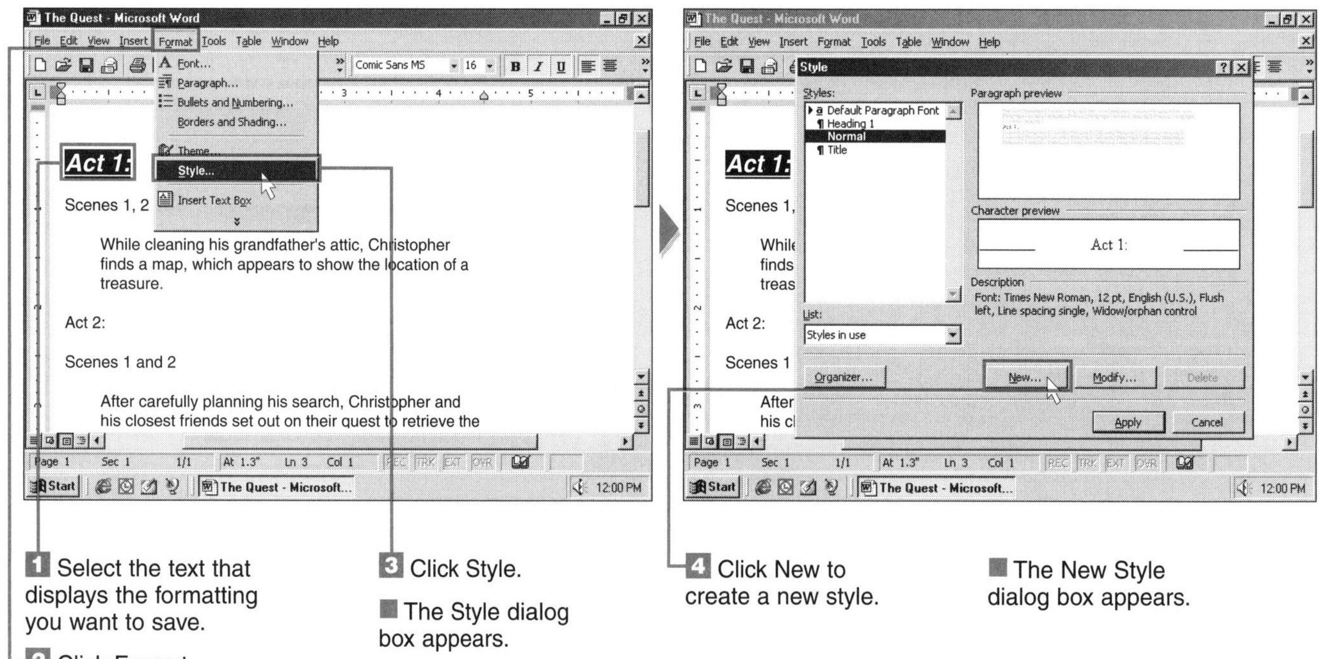

1 Select the text that displays the formatting you want to save.

2 Click Format.

3 Click Style.

■ The Style dialog box appears.

4 Click New to create a new style.

■ The New Style dialog box appears.

TIPS

How can I quickly create a paragraph style for the current document?

✔ Select the paragraph that displays the formatting you want to save. On the Formatting toolbar, click the Style area. Type a name for the new style and then press the Enter key.

Can I assign a keyboard shortcut to a style I created?

✔ Yes. In the Style dialog box, click the name of the style you want to assign a keyboard shortcut to. Click the Modify button and then select the Shortcut Key button. Click the Press new shortcut key area and then press the keys you want to use for the keyboard shortcut. Click the Assign button and then click Close.

Can I have Word automatically update my paragraph style?

✔ Yes. In the Style dialog box, click the name of the style you want Word to update automatically. Click the Modify button and then select the Automatically update option (☐ changes to ☑). When you change the formatting of a paragraph formatted with the style, Word automatically updates the style and all the paragraphs formatted with the style.

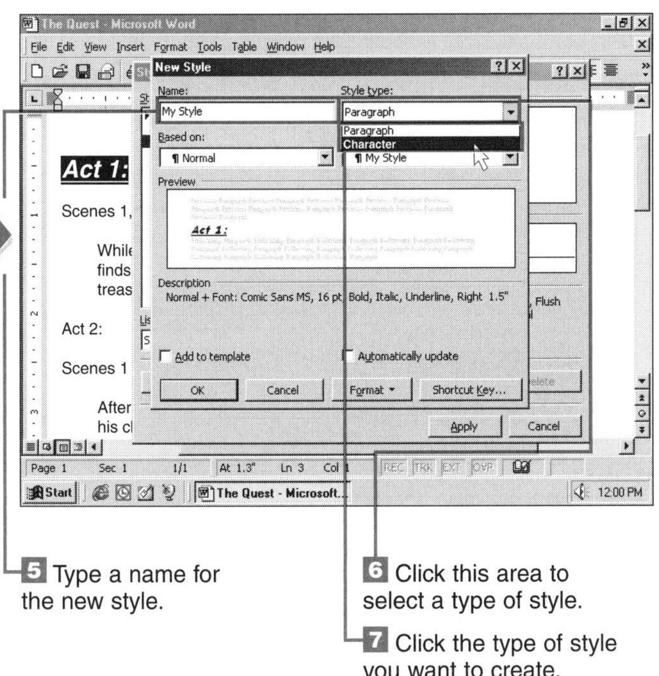

5 Type a name for the new style.

6 Click this area to select a type of style.

7 Click the type of style you want to create.

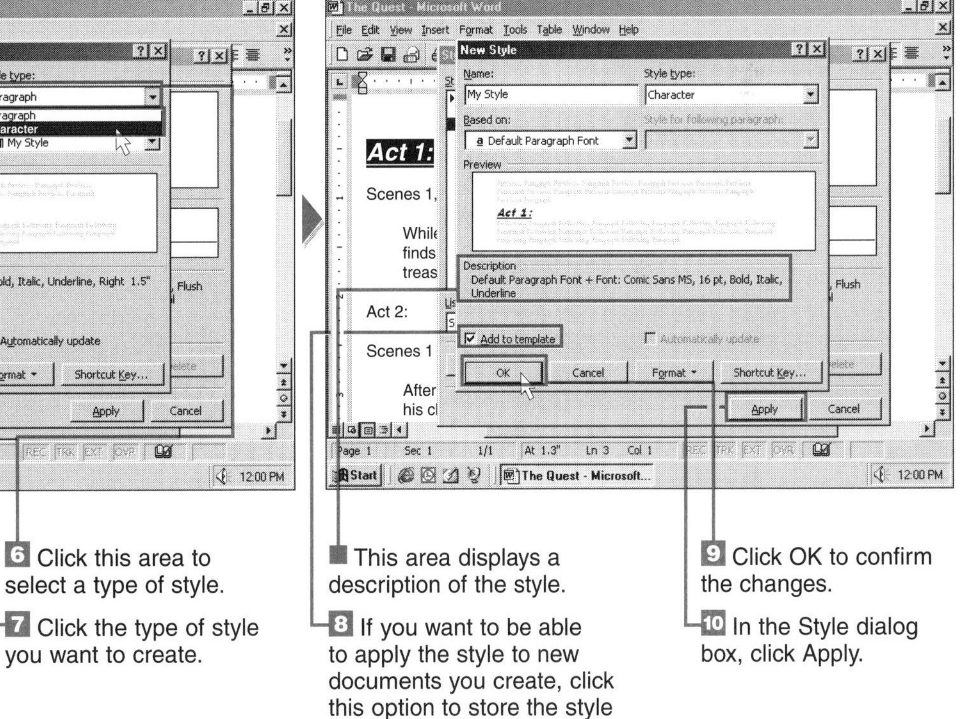

■ This area displays a description of the style.

8 If you want to be able to apply the style to new documents you create, click this option to store the style (☐ changes to ☑).

9 Click OK to confirm the changes.

10 In the Style dialog box, click Apply.

APPLY OR CHANGE A STYLE

You can apply a style to text in your document to quickly format the text.

Styles can save you time when you want to apply the same formatting to many different areas in a document. Styles also help you keep the appearance of text in a document consistent.

Word includes several styles you can apply to text in your document. You can also apply a style you created. To create a style, see page 90.

Word displays a list of the most common styles and styles you have most recently used. A symbol to the right of each style in the list indicates the type of style. The ¶ symbol indicates the style is a paragraph style. The a symbol indicates the style is a character style.

You can change a style you created. When you change a style, Word automatically changes all the text formatted using the style. This helps you quickly change the appearance of the document. You can experiment with several formats until the document appears the way you want.

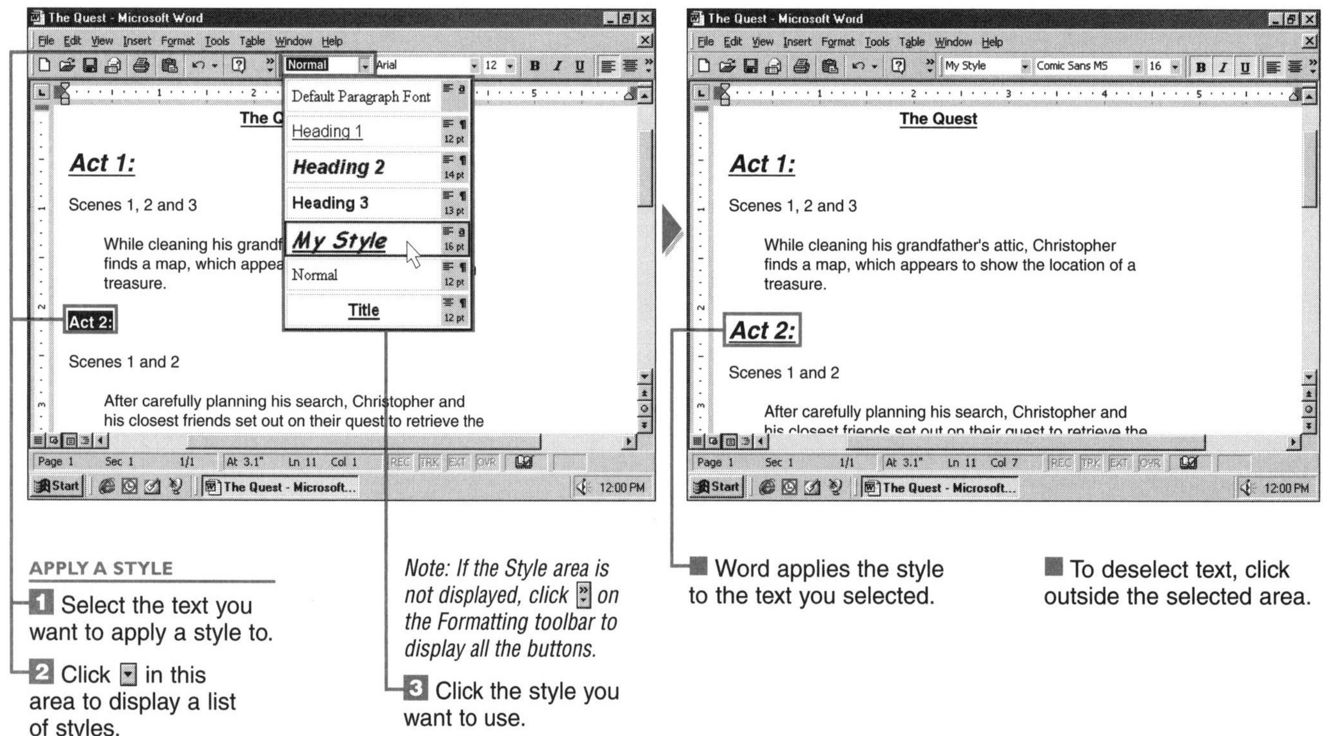

APPLY A STYLE

1. Select the text you want to apply a style to.
2. Click ▾ in this area to display a list of styles.

Note: If the Style area is not displayed, click » on the Formatting toolbar to display all the buttons.

3. Click the style you want to use.

■ Word applies the style to the text you selected.

■ To deselect text, click outside the selected area.

TIPS

How can I quickly display all the styles available in Word?

✔ To quickly display a complete list of the styles you can apply to your document, hold down the Shift key as you click ▾ in the Style area on the Formatting toolbar.

Can I view all the styles used in my document?

✔ Yes. Display your document in the Normal view. To change the view, see page 66. Select the Tools menu and then click Options. Select the View tab and in the Style area width area, type **0.5**. Then click OK. Word displays the styles used in your document at the left edge of your screen. To remove the styles from your screen, repeat the steps above, except type **0** in the Style area width area.

Why doesn't the style I applied look consistent throughout my document?

✔ The text in your document may have been formatted after the style was applied. To remove additional paragraph formatting, select the paragraph and then press the Ctrl+Q keys. To remove additional character formatting, select the text and then press the Ctrl+Spacebar keys.

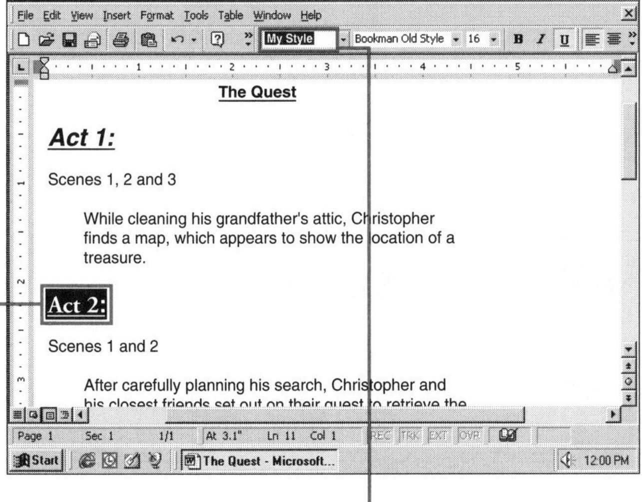

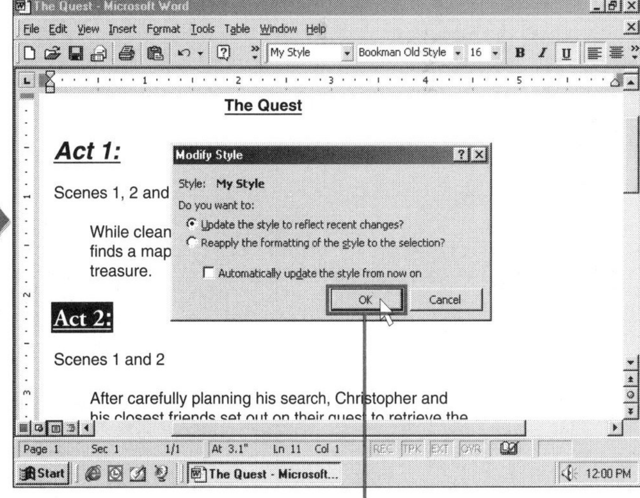

CHANGE A STYLE

1 Select an area of text that is formatted with the style you want to change.

2 Change the appearance of the text.

3 Click this area and then press the Enter key.

Note: If the Style area is not displayed, click » on the Formatting toolbar to display all the buttons.

■ The Modify Style dialog box appears.

4 Click OK to change the style.

■ All the text formatted using the style will display the changes.

INSERT A PAGE OR SECTION BREAK

If you want to start a new page at a specific place in your document, you can insert a page break. A page break shows where one page ends and another begins.

You can also divide your document into different sections. Dividing your document into sections allows you to apply formatting, such as page numbers or newspaper columns, to only part of your document.

There are four types of section breaks you can insert into your document. The Next page section break creates a new section on a new page. The Continuous section break creates a new section on the current page. The Even page and Odd page section breaks create a section break on the current page and start the next section on the next even or odd-numbered page.

When you display your document in the Normal view, a page break or section break line appears on the screen. You can delete this line to remove the page break or section break from your document.

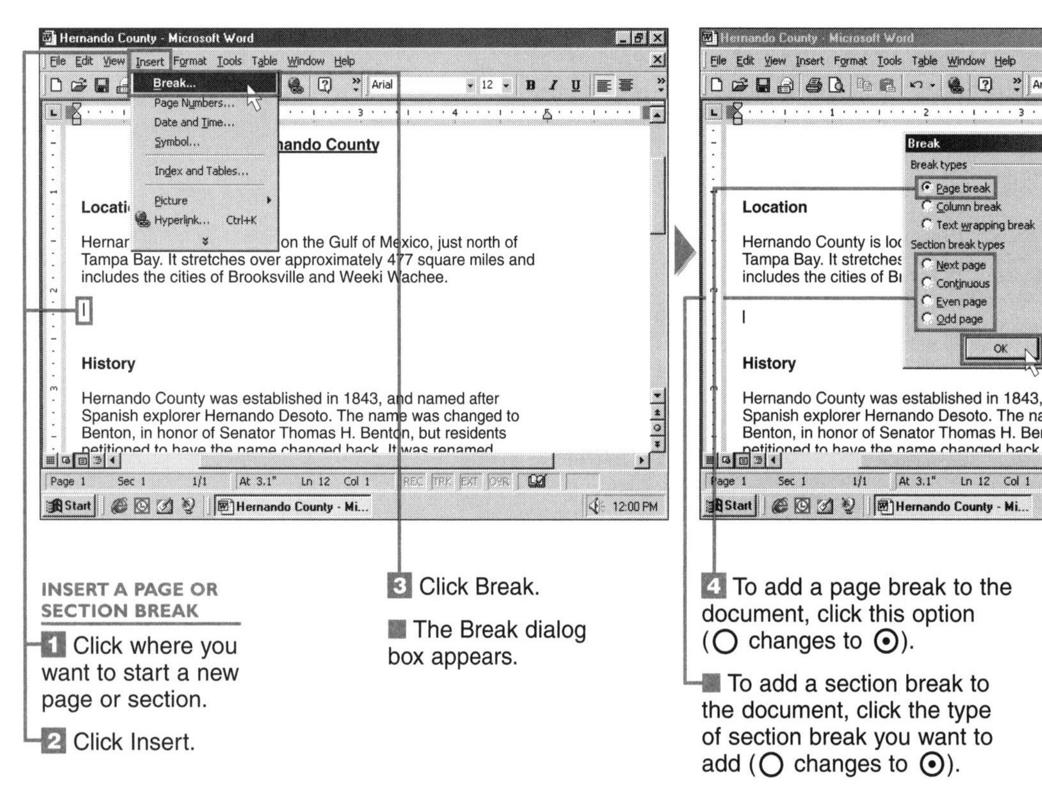

INSERT A PAGE OR SECTION BREAK

1 Click where you want to start a new page or section.

2 Click Insert.

3 Click Break.

■ The Break dialog box appears.

4 To add a page break to the document, click this option (○ changes to ⊙).

■ To add a section break to the document, click the type of section break you want to add (○ changes to ⊙).

5 Click OK to confirm your selection.

■ Word adds the page or section break to the document.

TIPS

Will Word ever insert page breaks automatically?

✔ Word automatically inserts a page break when you enter text past the bottom of a page. The length of the pages in your document is determined by the paper size and margin settings you are using.

Will the appearance of my document change when I remove a section break?

✔ When you remove a section break, the text above the break assumes the appearance of the text below the break. For example, if the text below the section break is displayed in columns, the text above the break will also appear in columns when you remove the break.

What are the Column break and Text wrapping break options in the Break dialog box used for?

✔ If you are displaying text in newspaper columns, the Column break option lets you move text to the next column. For information on newspaper columns, see page 106. The Text wrapping break option lets you move text to the next line in your document without starting a new paragraph.

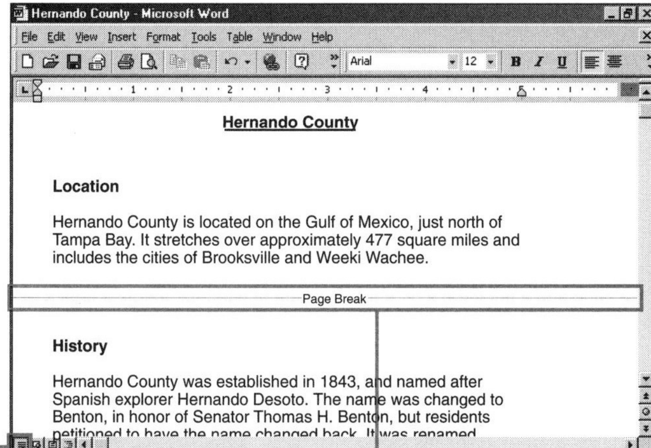

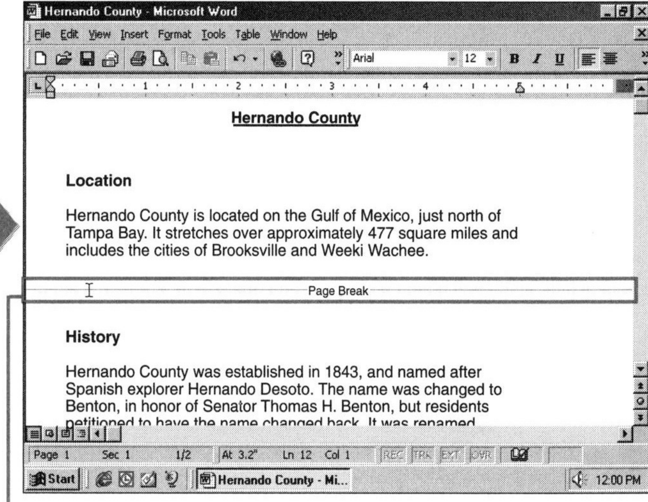

DELETE A PAGE OR SECTION BREAK

1 Click ▤ to display the document in the Normal view.

■ A line appears in the document, indicating the location of the page or section break.

Note: You may need to scroll through the document to view the line.

2 Click the page or section break line.

3 Press the Delete key to remove the page or section break.

CHANGE MARGINS

A margin is the amount of space between the text in your document and the edge of your paper.

There is a margin at the top, bottom, left and right edges of a page. Word automatically sets the top and bottom margins to 1 inch. Word sets the left and right margins to 1.25 inches. You can change the margins to suit your needs.

Increasing the size of margins increases the white space on your page. This can help make your document easier to read. Reducing the size of margins lets you fit more information on a page. Most printers cannot print right to the edge of a page and require that you use a margin of at least 0.25 inches on all sides. You can check the manual that came with your printer for more information.

When you change the margins, the changes affect the entire document. To change the margins for only specific pages in your document, you can divide your document into sections. To divide a document into sections, see page 94.

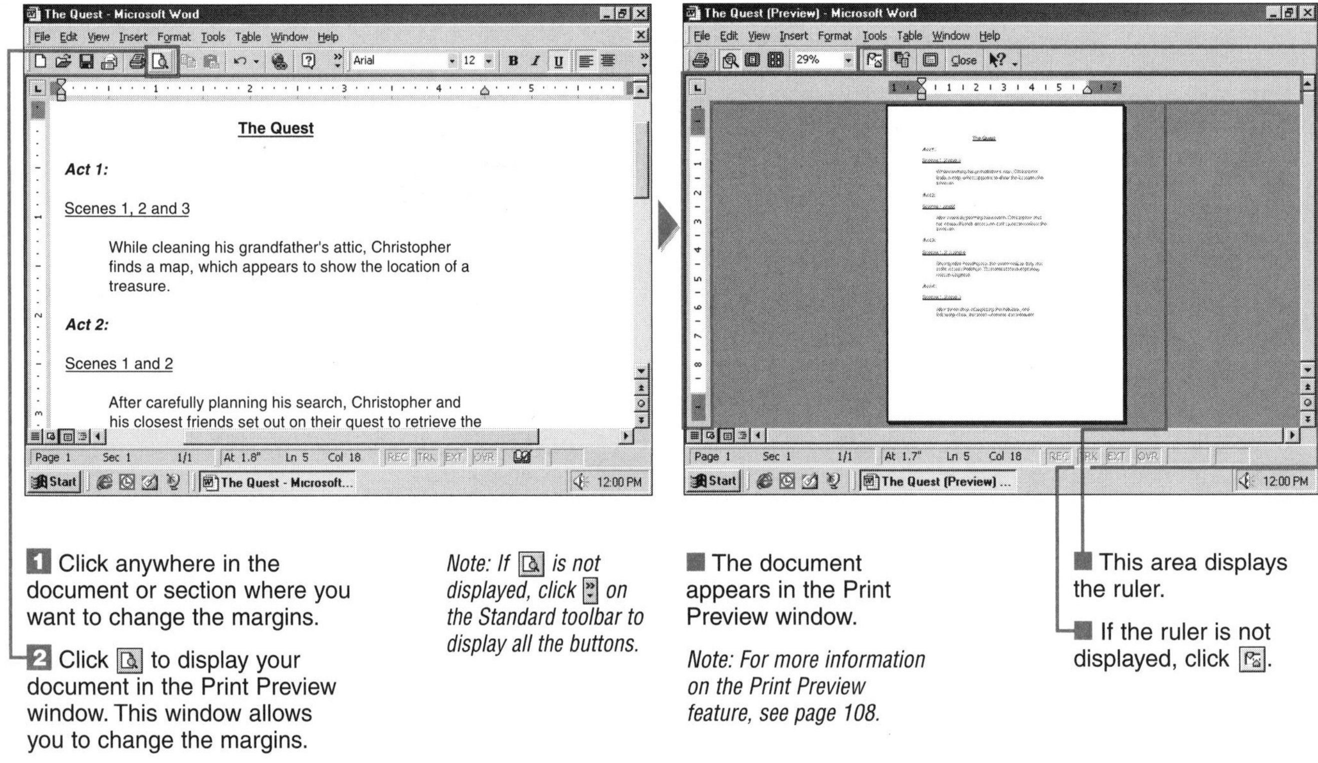

1 Click anywhere in the document or section where you want to change the margins.

2 Click [print preview icon] to display your document in the Print Preview window. This window allows you to change the margins.

Note: If [print preview icon] is not displayed, click [more buttons icon] on the Standard toolbar to display all the buttons.

■ The document appears in the Print Preview window.

Note: For more information on the Print Preview feature, see page 108.

■ This area displays the ruler.

■ If the ruler is not displayed, click [ruler icon].

TIPS

Can I change the left and right margins for only part of my document?

✔ If you do not want to divide your document into sections, you can change the indentation of paragraphs to change the left and right margins. For information on indenting, see page 82.

How can I specify exact measurements for my margins?

✔ Select the File menu and then click Page Setup. Click the Margins tab and then type the measurements in the Top, Bottom, Left and Right areas.

Can I change the units Word uses to measure a page?

✔ Yes. Select the Tools menu and then click Options. Click the General tab and in the Measurement units area, select inches, centimeters, millimeters, points or picas.

Is there another way to change the margins for my document?

✔ Yes. The Print Layout view displays a ruler you can use to change the margins. In the Print Layout view, position the mouse ↖ over the margin you want to change (↖ changes to ↕ or ↔). Then drag the margin to a new location.

Left Margin

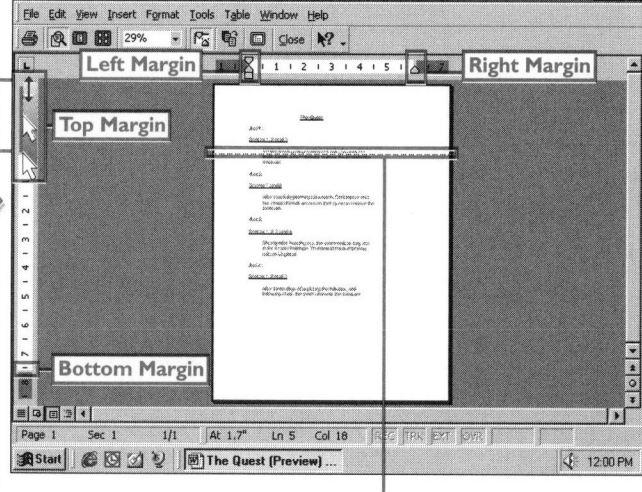

Right Margin

Top Margin

Bottom Margin

3 Position the mouse ↖ over a margin you want to change (↖ changes to ↕ or ↔).

4 Drag the margin to a new location.

Note: To view the exact measurement of a margin, hold down the Alt key as you drag the margin.

■ A line shows the new location.

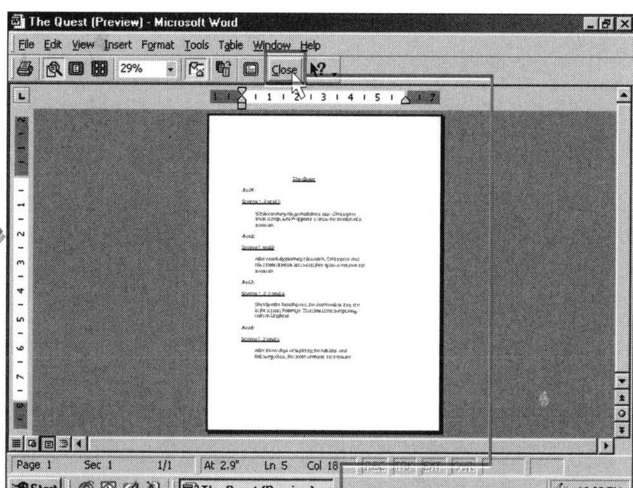

■ The margin moves to the new location.

5 Repeat steps 3 and 4 for each margin you want to change.

6 Click Close to close the Print Preview window.

ADD PAGE NUMBERS

You can have Word number the pages in your document. Numbering pages can help make a long document easier to organize when printed.

If you add, remove or rearrange text in your document, Word will automatically adjust the page numbers for you.

Word can display page numbers at the top or bottom of the pages in your document.

You can choose how you want the numbers aligned on your pages, including left, right or center. You may want to use the inside or outside alignment if your document will be bound. These alignment options display the numbers on the inside or outside edge of the pages in your document.

You can preview the position and alignment settings you choose for the page numbers.

You can also hide the page number on the first page of your document. This is useful if the first page is a title page.

Page numbers are only displayed on your screen in the Print Layout view. For information on the views, see page 66.

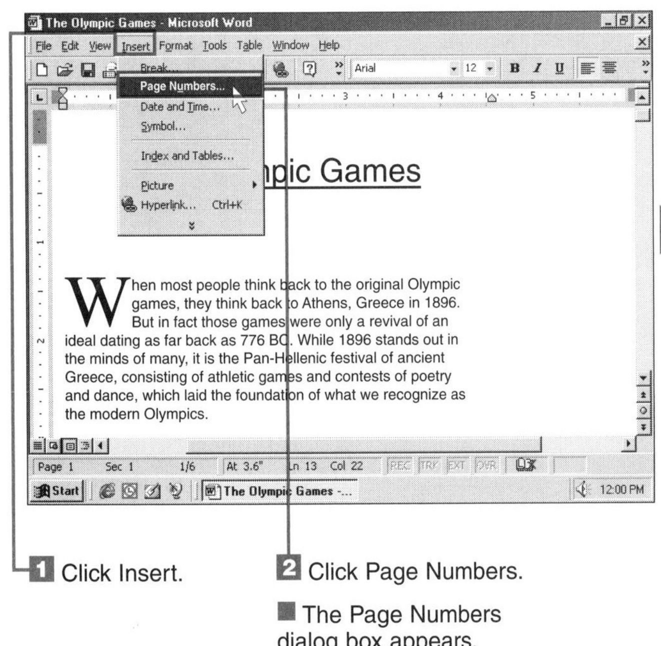

1 Click Insert.

2 Click Page Numbers.

■ The Page Numbers dialog box appears.

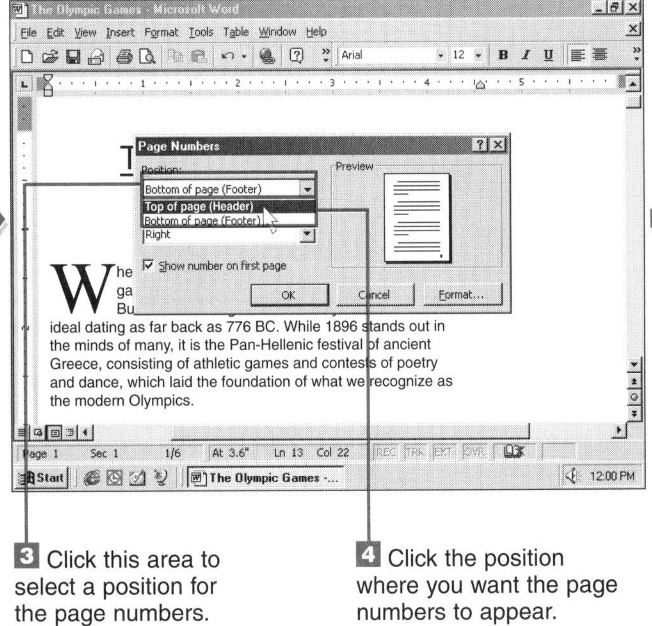

3 Click this area to select a position for the page numbers.

4 Click the position where you want the page numbers to appear.

TIPS

Can I specify a format for my page numbers, such as letters or Roman numerals?

✔ Yes. In the Page Numbers dialog box, click the Format button. Click the Number format area and select the format you want to use for the page numbers. Then click OK.

Can I have Word restart the page numbering for part of my document?

✔ Yes. To divide your document into sections, see page 94. Click in the section where you want to restart the page numbering. From the Insert menu, select Page Numbers and then click the Format button. Select the Start at option (◯ changes to ⊙) and then type the first page number you want the section to display.

How do I remove page numbers from my document?

✔ To remove page numbers, you must delete the page number from the document's header or footer. To display headers and footers, select the View menu and then click Header and Footer. Select the page number in the header or footer and then press the Delete key. For more information on headers and footers, see page 100.

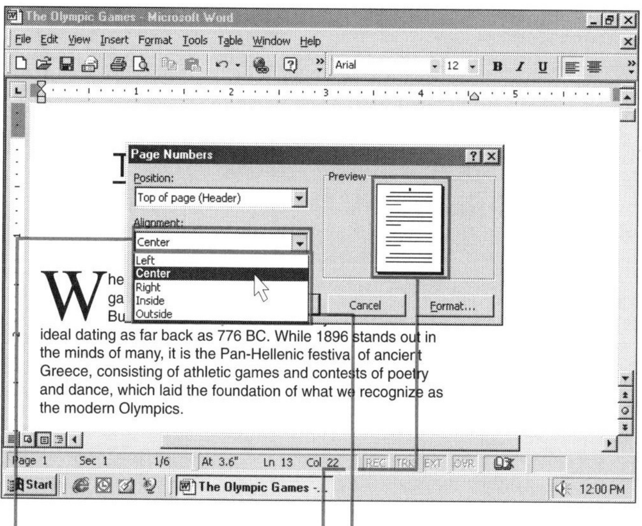

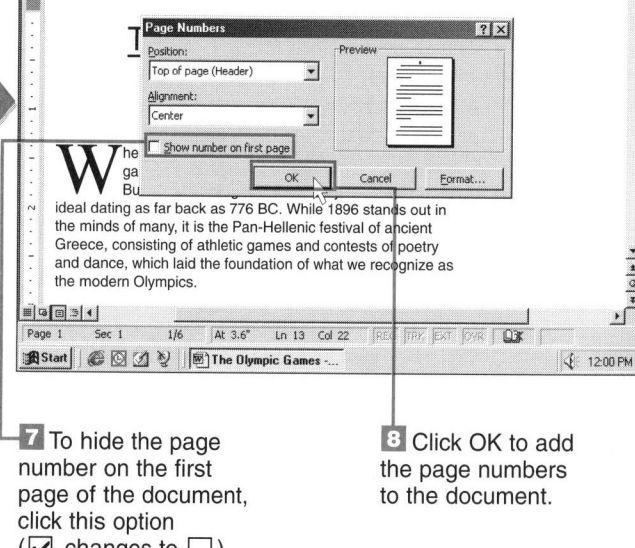

5 Click this area to select an alignment for the page numbers.

6 Click the alignment you want to use.

■ This area displays a preview of the position and alignment you selected for the page numbers.

7 To hide the page number on the first page of the document, click this option (☑ changes to ☐).

8 Click OK to add the page numbers to the document.

ADD A HEADER OR FOOTER

You can add a header and footer to every page in your document. A header appears at the top of each page. A footer appears at the bottom of each page.

A header or footer can contain information such as a company name, author's name or chapter title. You can edit and format the text in a header or footer as you would edit and format any text in your document.

You can quickly insert the page number and the total number of pages in your document into a header or footer. If you add, remove or rearrange text in your document, Word will automatically adjust the page numbers for you.

You can also quickly insert the date and time into a header or footer. Word will update the date and time every time you open or print your document.

Word only displays the headers and footers in a document in the Print Layout view. For more information on the views, see page 66.

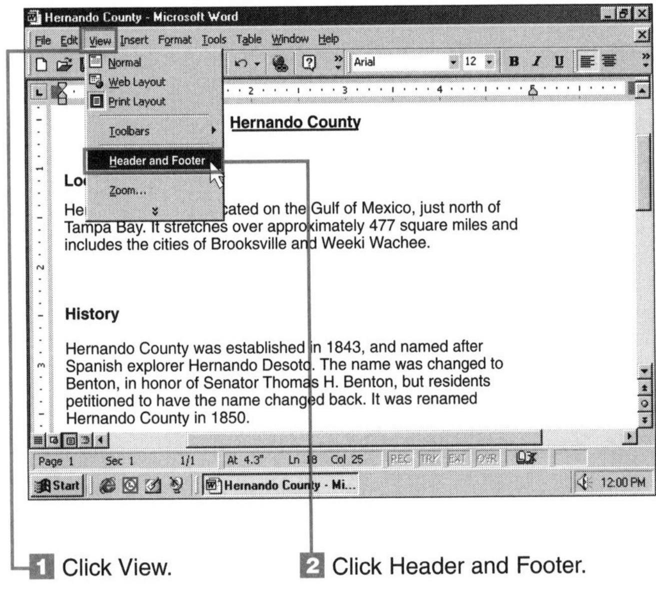

1 Click View.

2 Click Header and Footer.

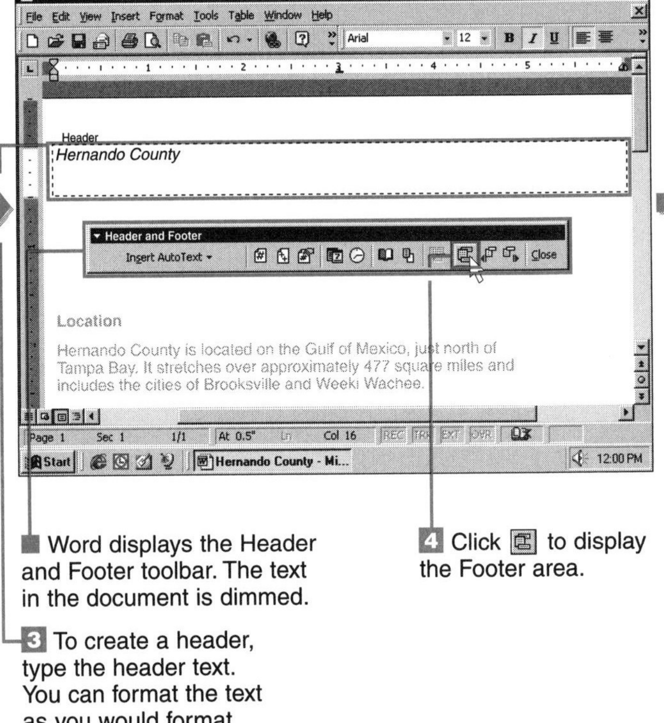

■ Word displays the Header and Footer toolbar. The text in the document is dimmed.

3 To create a header, type the header text. You can format the text as you would format any text in a document.

4 Click [icon] to display the Footer area.

TIPS

How can I prevent Word from adding a header or footer to the first page of my document?

✔ On the Header and Footer toolbar, click the Page Setup button (▣). Choose the Layout tab and then select the Different first page option (☐ changes to ☑). Then click OK. In your document, leave the First Page Header and First Page Footer areas blank.

How do I delete a header or footer?

✔ Select the View menu and then click Header and Footer to display the Header and Footer areas in your document. Select all the information in the Header or Footer area and then press the Delete key.

What other information can I quickly insert into a header or footer?

✔ You can quickly insert information such as the name of the person who created the document or the date and time the document was last printed. On the Header and Footer toolbar, click Insert AutoText and then select the information you want to insert.

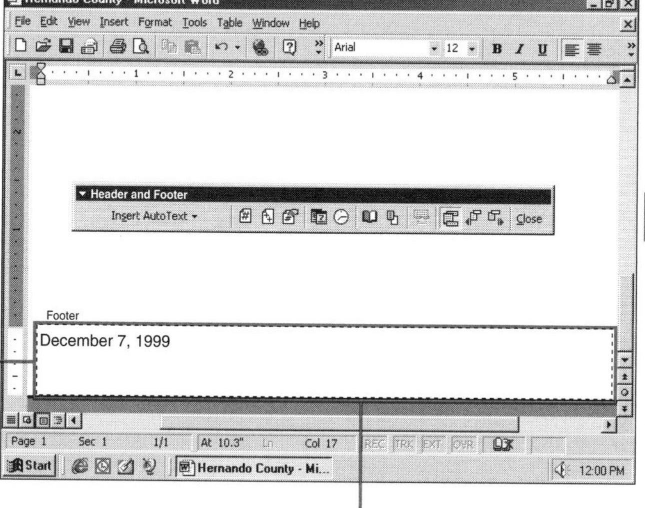

■ The Footer area appears.

Note: You can return to the Header area at any time by repeating step 4.

5 Type the footer text. You can format the text as you would format any text in a document.

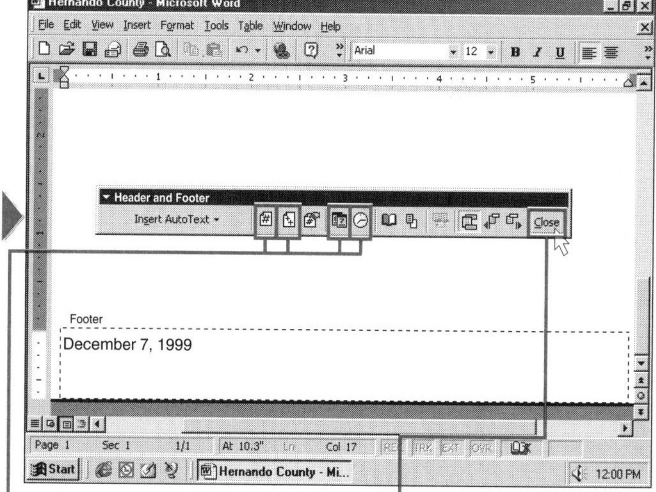

6 You can click one of the following buttons to quickly insert information.

- Page Number
- Total Number of Pages
- Date
- Time

7 Click Close when you have finished creating the header and footer.

Note: You can repeat steps 1 to 7 to edit the header or footer at any time.

ADD FOOTNOTES OR ENDNOTES

You can add a footnote or endnote to your document to provide additional information about specific text. Footnotes and endnotes can contain information such as an explanation, comment or reference for the text. Footnotes appear at the bottom of a page. Endnotes appear at the end of a document.

Word numbers the footnotes or endnotes you add, beginning with the number 1 or Roman numeral i. You can enter any amount of text for a footnote or endnote.

Word displays the footnote or endnote area of your document in the Print Layout view. To view the text for a footnote or endnote in any view, you can position the mouse pointer over the footnote or endnote number in your document. A box appears, displaying the footnote or endnote text.

If you add or remove footnotes or endnotes, Word automatically adjusts the numbers of the footnotes or endnotes in your document. Word also ensures that the text you type for a footnote always begins on the same page as the footnote number.

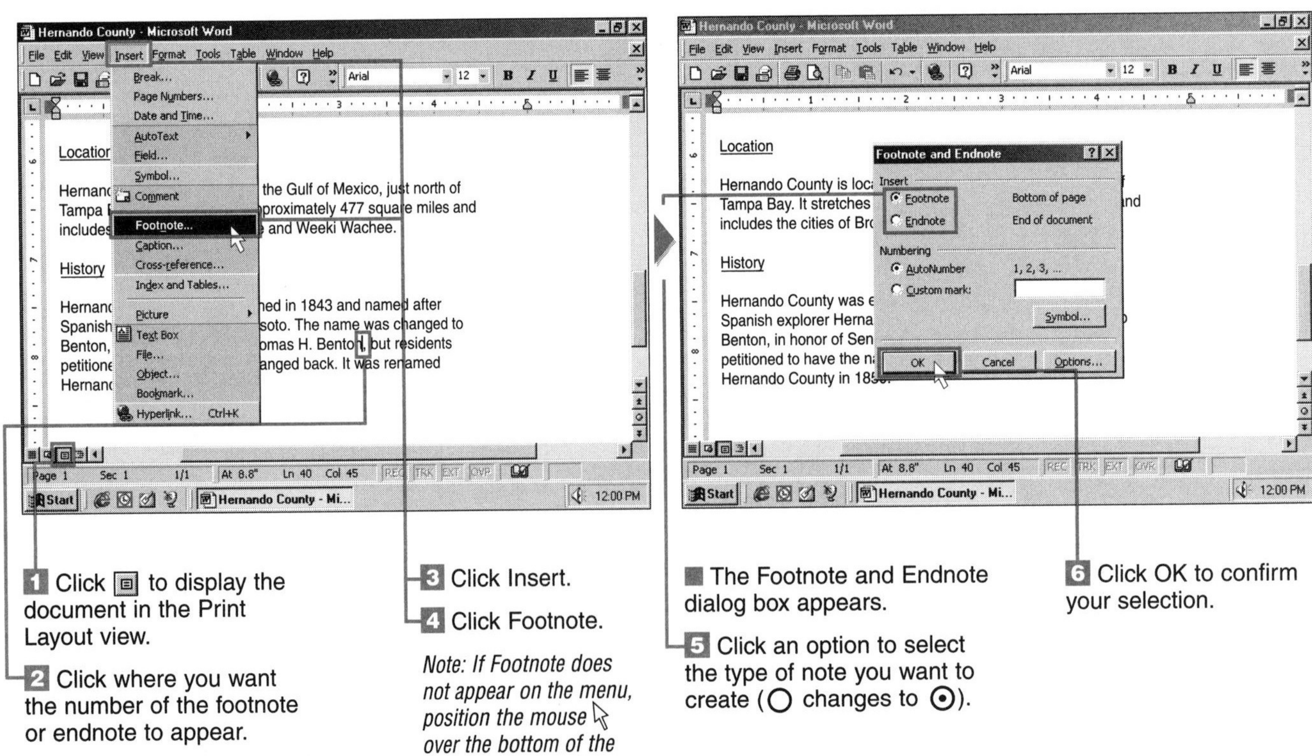

1 Click ▤ to display the document in the Print Layout view.

2 Click where you want the number of the footnote or endnote to appear.

3 Click Insert.

4 Click Footnote.

Note: If Footnote does not appear on the menu, position the mouse over the bottom of the menu to display all the menu commands.

■ The Footnote and Endnote dialog box appears.

5 Click an option to select the type of note you want to create (○ changes to ⦿).

6 Click OK to confirm your selection.

TIPS

How can I edit a footnote or endnote I added?

✔ You can edit a footnote or endnote as you would edit any text in your document. To quickly display the footnote or endnote area, double-click the footnote or endnote number in your document.

Can I have Word print endnotes on a separate page?

✔ To print endnotes on a separate page, insert a page break directly above the endnote area. To insert a page break, see page 94.

Can I convert all the footnotes in my document to endnotes?

✔ Yes. In the Footnote and Endnote dialog box, click the Options button. Click the Convert button and then select the Convert all footnotes to endnotes option (○ changes to ⦿). You can also convert all your endnotes to footnotes. Perform the steps above, except select the Convert all endnotes to footnotes option (○ changes to ⦿).

Can I delete a footnote or endnote?

✔ You can delete a footnote or endnote you no longer need. Select the footnote or endnote number in your document and then press the Delete key.

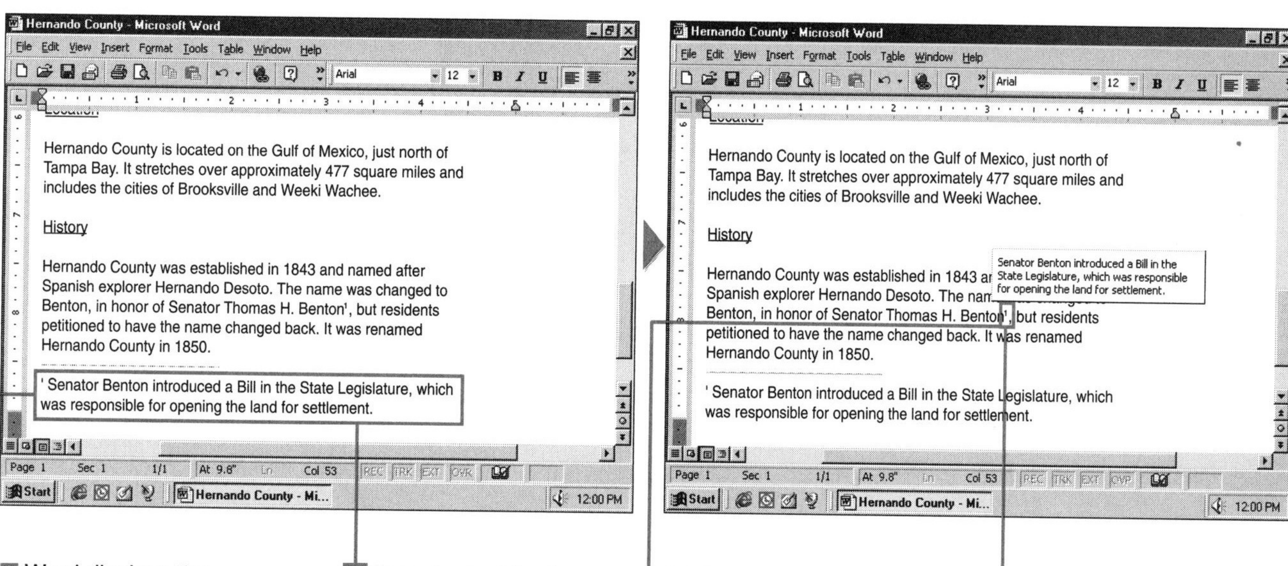

■ Word displays the footnote or endnote area.

7 Type the text for the footnote or endnote. You can format the text as you would format any text in a document.

■ The number of the footnote or endnote appears in the document.

■ To view the footnote or endnote text, position the mouse I over the footnote or endnote number in the document.

CENTER TEXT ON A PAGE

You can vertically center text on each page of your document. This is useful for creating title pages and short memos.

When you center text on a page, Word aligns the text between the top and bottom margins for the page. For information on margins, see page 96.

You cannot vertically center only part of the text on a page, but you can center the text on a single page in your document. To vertically center text on a single page, you must first divide your document into sections so the page you want to center is a separate section. To divide your document into sections, see page 94.

When your document is displayed in the Print Layout view, the text appears vertically centered on the page on your screen. If you are working in another view, vertically centering text does not affect the way the text appears on your screen. For more information on the views, see page 66.

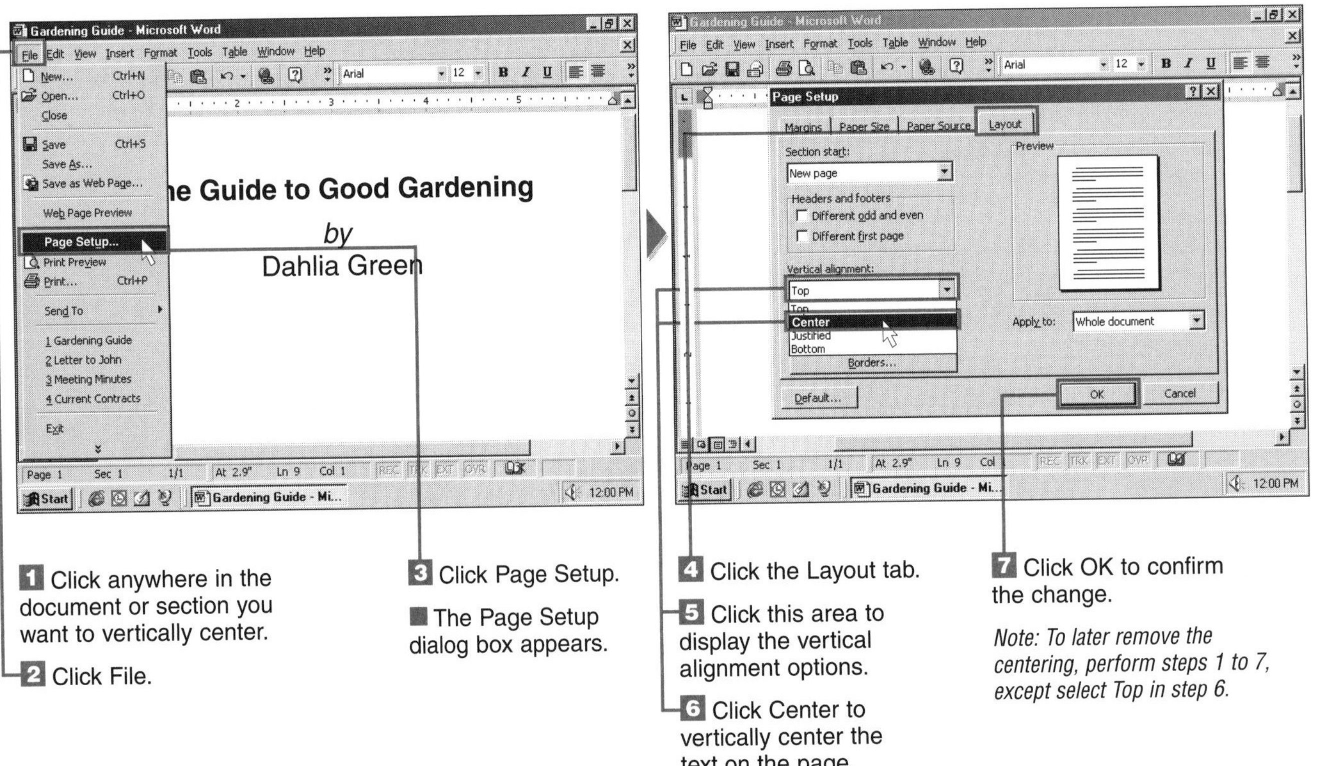

1 Click anywhere in the document or section you want to vertically center.

2 Click File.

3 Click Page Setup.

■ The Page Setup dialog box appears.

4 Click the Layout tab.

5 Click this area to display the vertical alignment options.

6 Click Center to vertically center the text on the page.

7 Click OK to confirm the change.

Note: To later remove the centering, perform steps 1 to 7, except select Top in step 6.

CHANGE PAGE ORIENTATION

You can change the orientation of pages in your document. Orientation refers to the way that information is printed on a page.

Portrait is the standard page orientation and is used to print most documents, such as letters, memos, reports and brochures. The portrait orientation prints information across the short side of a page.

Landscape orientation prints information across the long side of a page. Certificates and tables are often printed using the landscape orientation.

You can see a preview of the page orientation you selected.

You can change the page orientation for only specific pages in your document. For example, in a report, you can print a page displaying a table in the landscape orientation and print the rest of the pages in the report in the portrait orientation. To change the orientation for part of a document, you must first divide the document into sections. To divide a document into sections, see page 94.

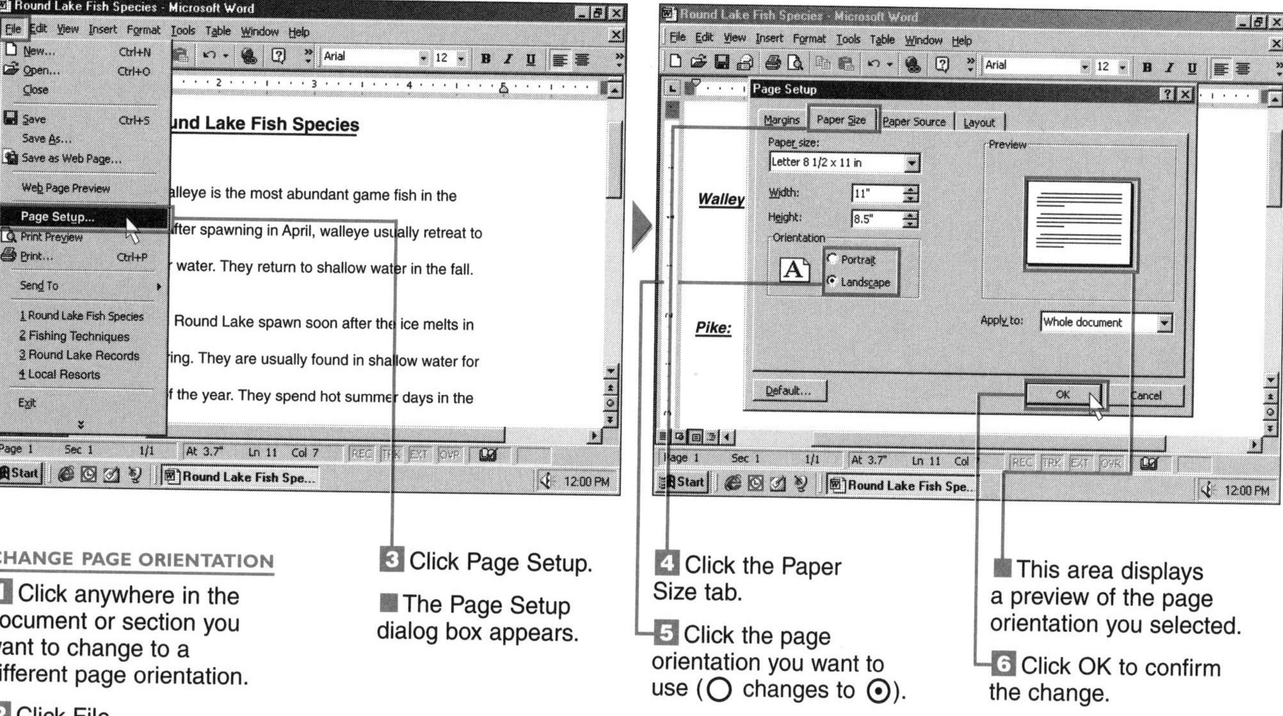

CHANGE PAGE ORIENTATION

1. Click anywhere in the document or section you want to change to a different page orientation.
2. Click File.
3. Click Page Setup.
   - The Page Setup dialog box appears.
4. Click the Paper Size tab.
5. Click the page orientation you want to use (○ changes to ⊙).
   - This area displays a preview of the page orientation you selected.
6. Click OK to confirm the change.

CREATE NEWSPAPER COLUMNS

You can display text in columns like those found in a newspaper. This is useful for creating documents such as newsletters and brochures. Displaying text in columns can make your document easier to read.

You can create one, two or three columns of equal size. You can also create two columns and have one column wider than the other. Using one wide column can add an interesting visual effect to your document. Regardless of the number of columns you create, Word fills one column with text before starting a new column.

You can also have Word display a vertical line between the columns.

In the Print Layout view, Word displays columns side-by-side. The Normal and Outline views display text in a single column. The Web Layout view does not display columns. For more information on the views, see page 66. The columns will all appear when you print your document, whether they are displayed on your screen or not.

To create columns for part of your document, you must first divide the document into sections. To divide a document into sections, see page 94.

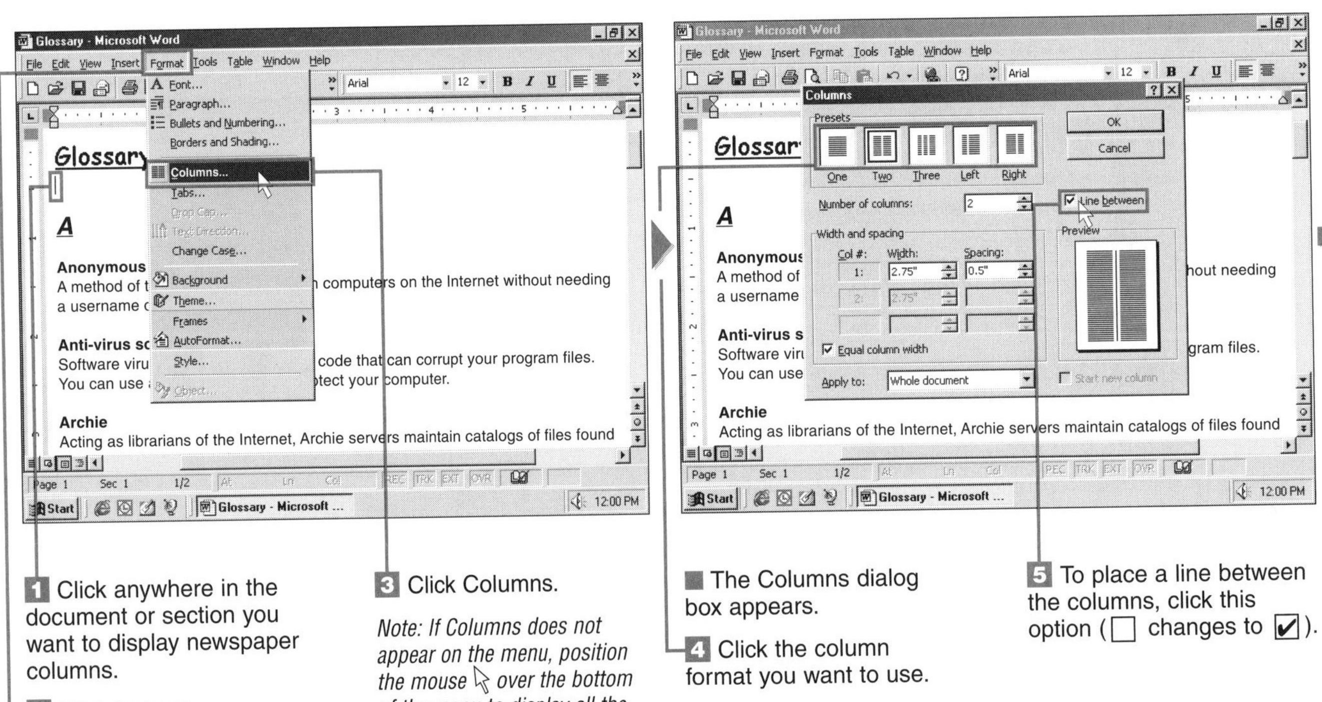

1 Click anywhere in the document or section you want to display newspaper columns.

2 Click Format.

3 Click Columns.

Note: If Columns does not appear on the menu, position the mouse over the bottom of the menu to display all the menu commands.

■ The Columns dialog box appears.

4 Click the column format you want to use.

5 To place a line between the columns, click this option (☐ changes to ☑).

TIPS

Can I create more than three columns?

✔ Yes. In the Columns dialog box, double-click the Number of columns area and then type the number of columns you want to create.

How do I move text from one column to the top of the next column?

✔ You can insert a column break to move text from one column to the top of the next column. Click to the left of the text you want to move. Select the Insert menu and then click Break. Click the Column break option (○ changes to ⦿) and then click OK.

How can I quickly create columns?

✔ To quickly create columns of equal size, click the Columns button (▥) on the Standard toolbar. Then drag the mouse pointer over the number of columns you want to create.

How do I change the width of the columns in my document?

✔ In the Print Layout view, the horizontal ruler displays the edges of the columns in your document. Position the mouse ↖ over the column edge you want to move (↖ changes to ↔). Then drag the column edge to a new position.

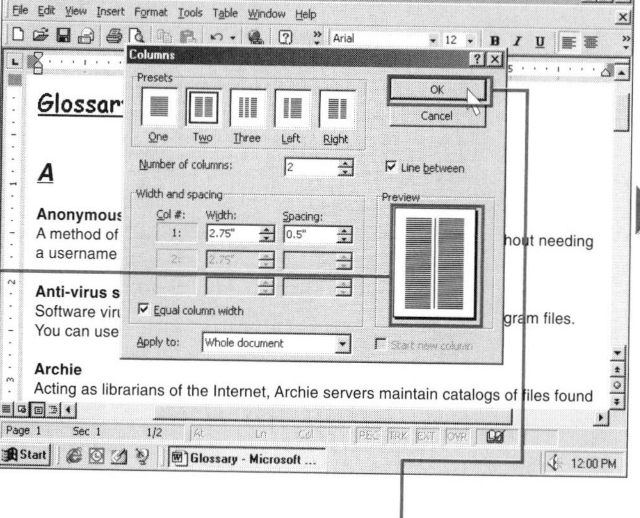

■ This area displays a preview of the options you selected.

6 Click OK to confirm your changes.

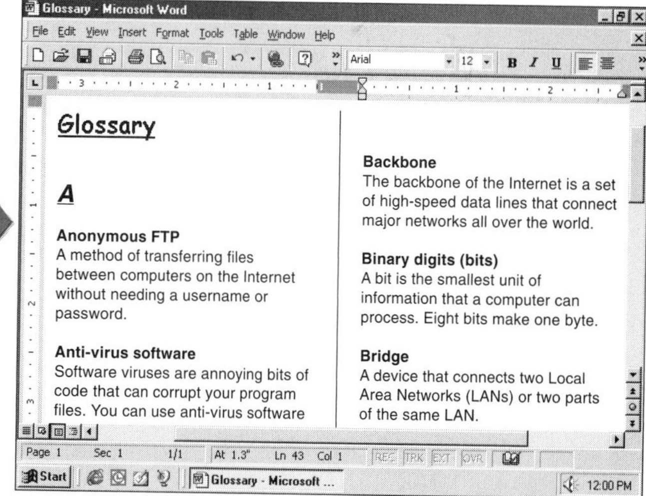

■ The text in the document appears in newspaper columns.

Note: To remove newspaper columns, repeat steps 1 to 6, selecting One in step 4.

PREVIEW A DOCUMENT

You can use the Print Preview feature to see how your document will look when printed.

The Print Preview feature allows you to view the layout of information on a page in your document. If your document contains more than one page, you can use the scroll bar to view the other pages.

You can magnify an area of a page in your document. This allows you to view the area in more detail.

You can have Word display several pages in the Print Preview window at once. Viewing several pages at once allows you to view the overall style of a long document. Depending on the setup of your computer, Word can display 12, 24 or more pages in the Print Preview window.

When you have finished using the Print Preview feature, you can close the Print Preview window to return to your document.

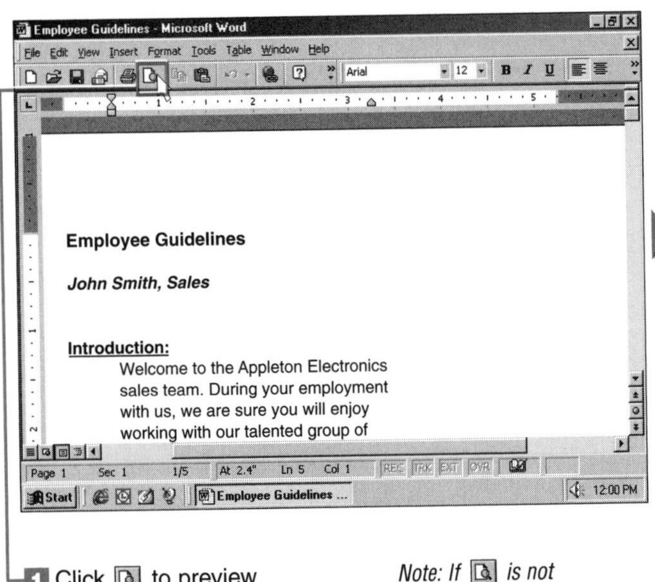

1 Click to preview the document.

Note: If is not displayed, click on the Standard toolbar to display all the buttons.

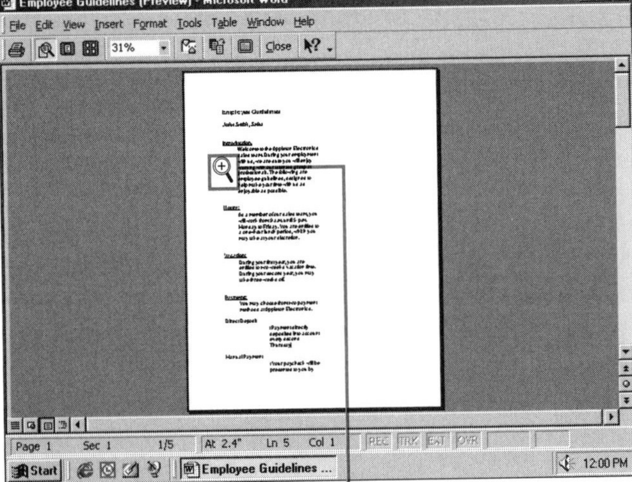

■ The Print Preview window appears, displaying a page from the document.

Note: You can use the scroll bar to view other pages.

MAGNIFY A PAGE

1 Position the mouse over the area of the page you want to magnify (changes to).

2 Click the area to magnify the area.

TIPS

Can I edit my document in the Print Preview window?

✔ Yes. If the mouse looks like I when over your document, you can edit the document. If the mouse looks like 🔍 or 🔍 when over your document, you can enlarge or reduce the size of the page displayed in the Print Preview window. To change the shape of the mouse, click .

Can I change the size of the paper my document will print on?

✔ Yes. Click the File menu, select Page Setup and then click the Paper Size tab. In the Paper size area, select the paper size you want to use and then click OK.

Can I shrink the text in my document to fit on fewer pages?

✔ If the last page in your document contains only a few lines of text, Word can shrink the text in your document to fit on one less page. In the Print Preview window, click the Shrink to Fit button () to shrink the text.

Can I print directly from the Print Preview window?

✔ To print your document directly from the Print Preview window, click the Print button ().

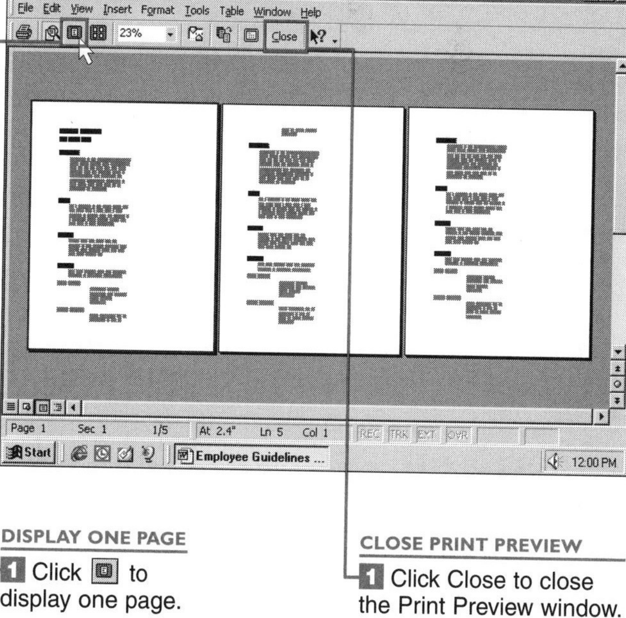

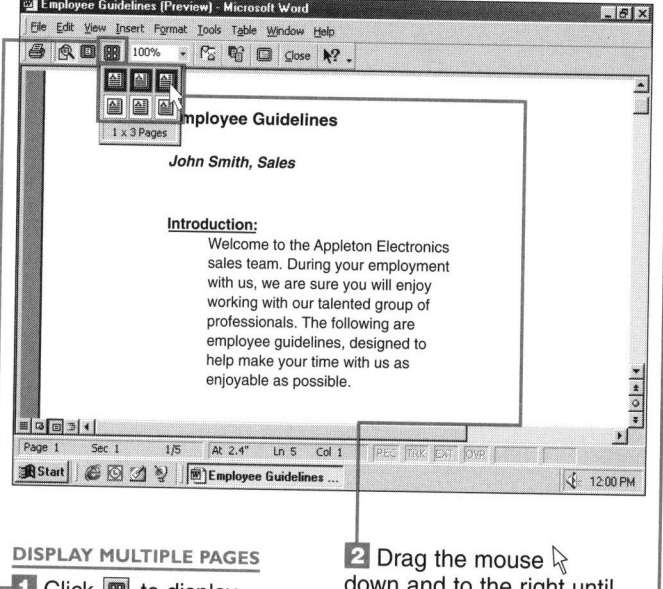

DISPLAY MULTIPLE PAGES

1 Click to display multiple pages of the document.

2 Drag the mouse down and to the right until you select the number of pages you want to display.

DISPLAY ONE PAGE

1 Click to display one page.

CLOSE PRINT PREVIEW

1 Click Close to close the Print Preview window.

PRINT A DOCUMENT

You can produce a paper copy of the document displayed on your screen. A paper copy is often referred to as a hard copy.

Before you print your document, make sure the printer is turned on and contains an adequate supply of paper.

If you use more than one printer, Word allows you to select which printer you want to use to print your document. This is useful if you want to use different printers to print different types of information. For example, you may want to use a black-and-white printer to print a draft of your document and a color printer to print the final version.

You can print multiple copies of your document. Printing multiple copies is useful if you are printing a brochure or handouts for a presentation.

Word allows you to specify the part of your document you want to print. You can print the entire document, the page containing the insertion point, a range of pages or selected text.

You can click the Print button (🖨) on the Standard toolbar to quickly print your entire document.

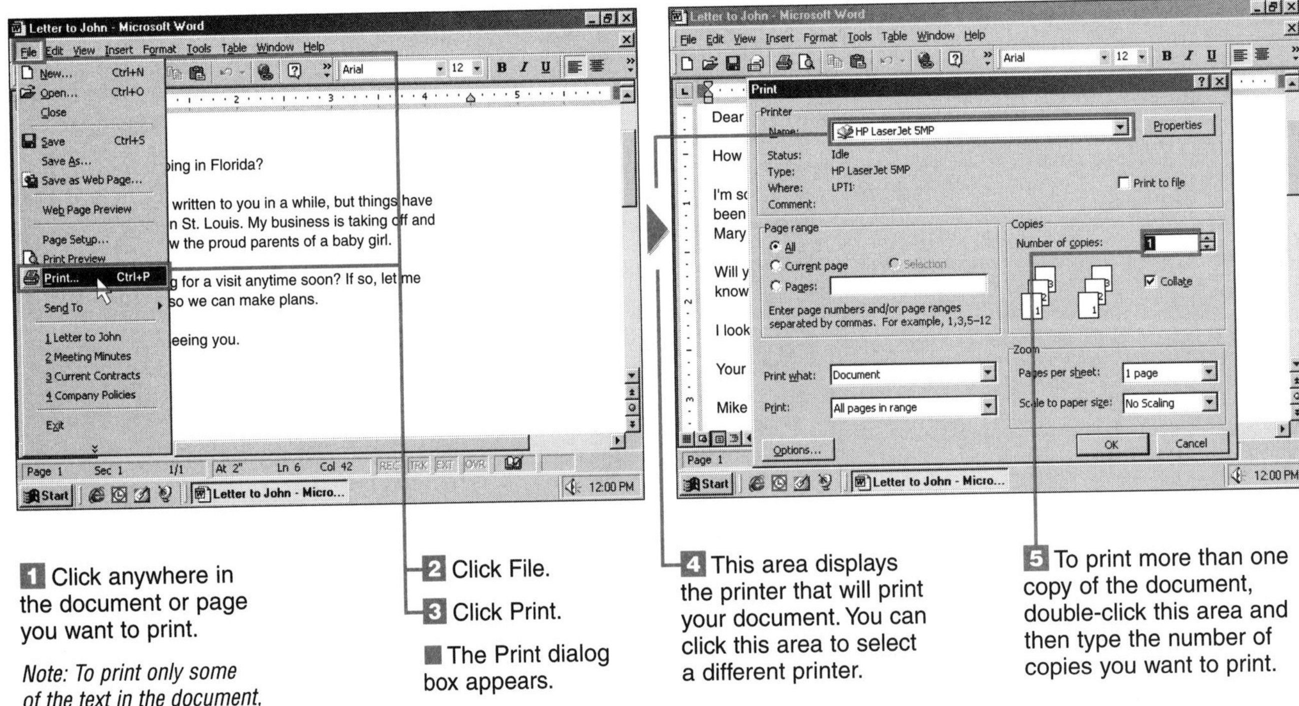

1 Click anywhere in the document or page you want to print.

Note: To print only some of the text in the document, select the text you want to print.

2 Click File.

3 Click Print.

■ The Print dialog box appears.

4 This area displays the printer that will print your document. You can click this area to select a different printer.

5 To print more than one copy of the document, double-click this area and then type the number of copies you want to print.

TIPS

How can I print my document on both sides of the paper?

✔ In the Print dialog box, click the Print area, select Odd pages and then click OK. When Word finishes printing the odd-numbered page(s), turn the paper over and put it back into the printer. Display the Print dialog box again and in the Print area, select Even pages.

Can I print multiple pages of my document on one sheet of paper?

✔ Yes. In Print dialog box, click the Pages per sheet area. Then select the number of pages you want to print on one sheet of paper.

Can I use letterhead as the first page of my document?

✔ Yes. When your printer stores specialty paper in one location and plain paper in another, you can change the location where Word will look for paper. From the File menu, select the Page Setup command and then click the Paper Source tab. Select a location for the first page and then select a location for the other page(s) in your document. Then click OK.

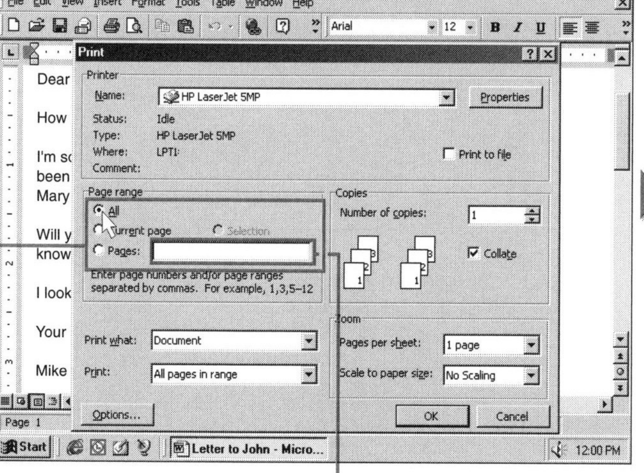

6 Click the print option you want to use (○ changes to ⊙).

■ If you selected Pages in step 6, type the pages you want to print in this area (example: 1,3,5 or 2-4).

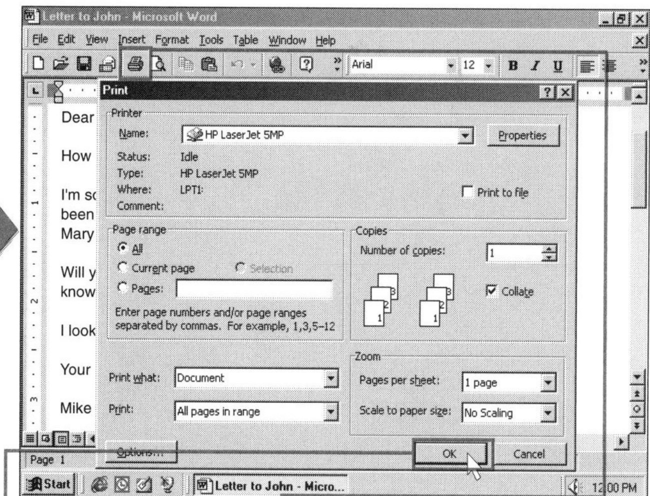

7 Click OK.

QUICKLY PRINT ENTIRE DOCUMENT

1 Click [print button] to quickly print an entire document.

Note: If [print button] is not displayed, click [»] on the Standard toolbar to display all the buttons.

PRINT AN ENVELOPE

You can use Word to print an address on an envelope. Printing an address directly on an envelope saves you from having to create a mailing label or use a typewriter to address the envelope.

Before you begin, make sure your printer is capable of printing envelopes. You can consult the manual that came with your printer to determine your printer's capabilities.

Word scans your document to find a delivery address for the envelope. You can use the address Word finds or enter another address.

You can enter a return address for the envelope. If you do not want Word to print the return address, you can omit the address. Omitting the return address is useful if your company uses custom envelopes that already display a return address.

If you enter a return address, Word allows you to save the return address. Word will then use the address as the return address every time you print an envelope. This saves you from having to type the same return address over and over again.

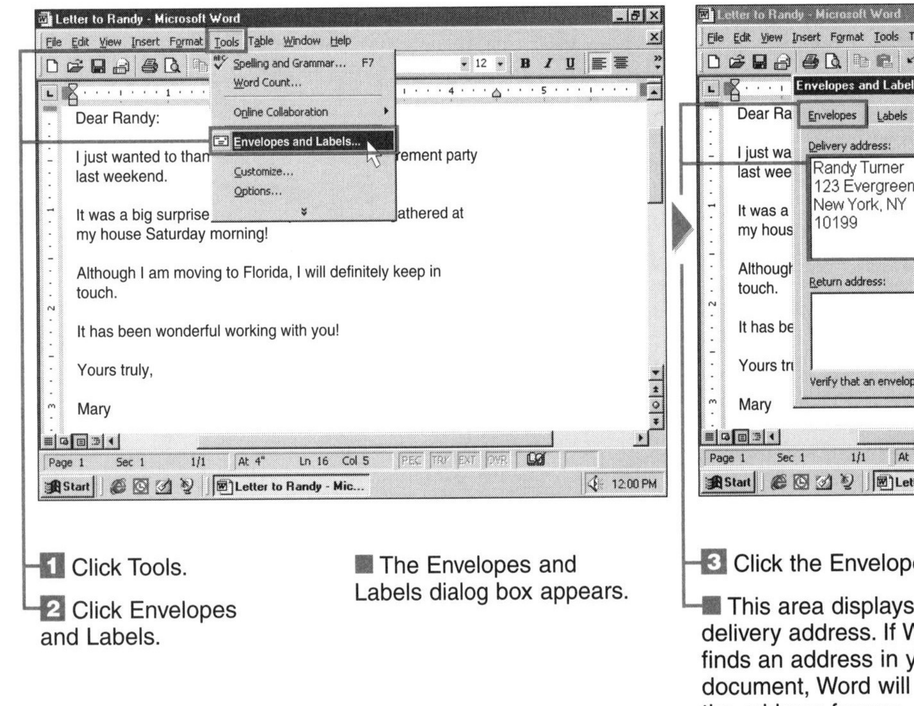

1 Click Tools.

2 Click Envelopes and Labels.

■ The Envelopes and Labels dialog box appears.

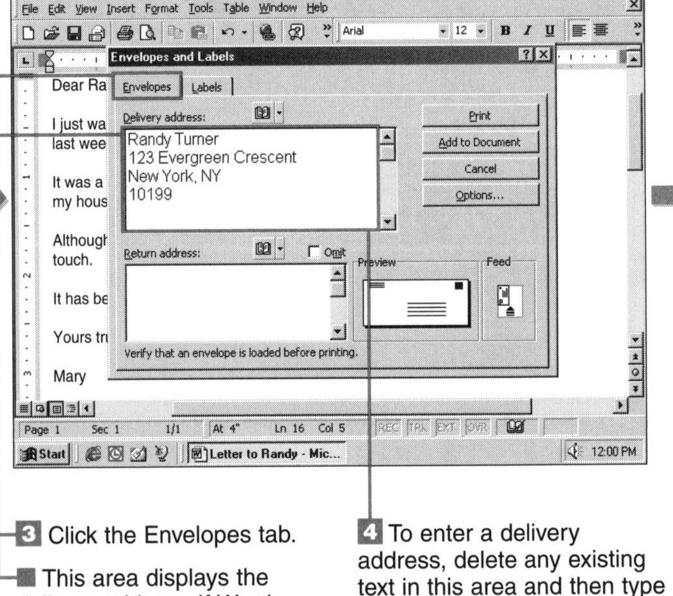

3 Click the Envelopes tab.

■ This area displays the delivery address. If Word finds an address in your document, Word will enter the address for you.

4 To enter a delivery address, delete any existing text in this area and then type the delivery address.

TIPS

How do I specify the size of the envelope I want to print?

✔ In the Envelopes and Labels dialog box, click the Options button. Click the Envelope size area and then select the envelope size you want to use. Then click OK.

How do I change the font used for my delivery or return address?

✔ In the Envelopes and Labels dialog box, click the Options button. Then click the Font button for the address you want to change. In the dialog box that appears, select the font options you want to use and then click OK.

Can I make an envelope part of my document?

✔ Yes. In the Envelopes and Labels dialog box, click the Add to Document button. The envelope appears before the first page of your document. You can then edit, format, save and print the envelope as part of your document.

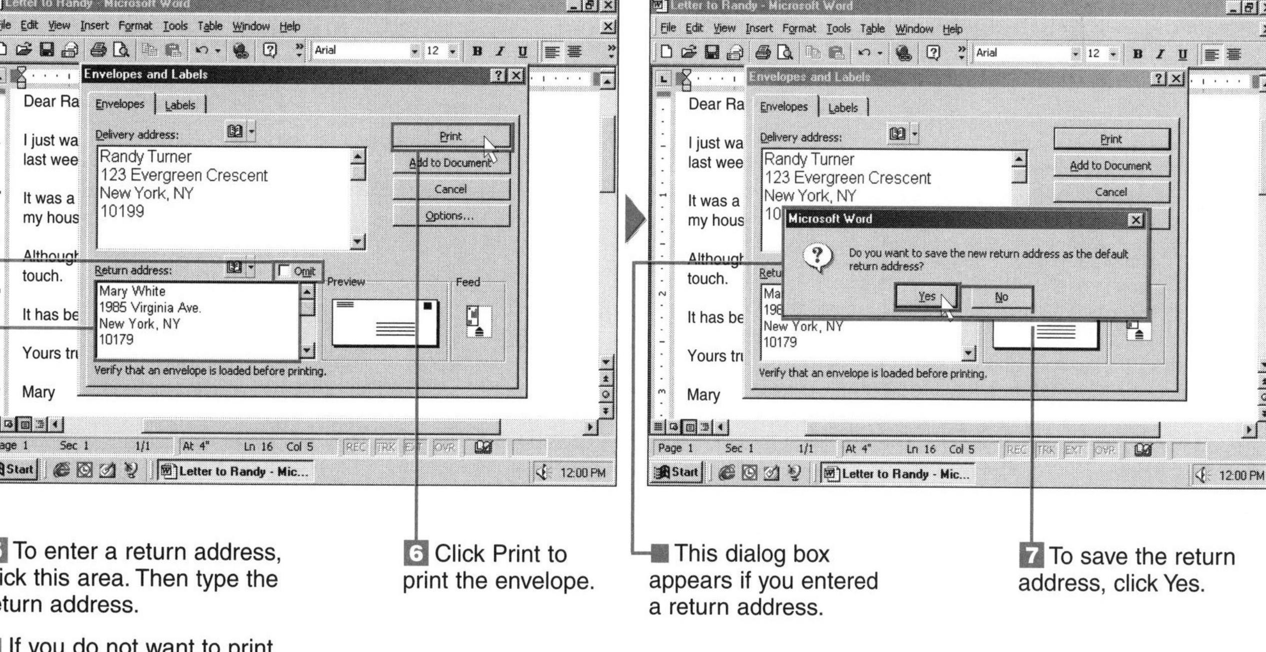

5 To enter a return address, click this area. Then type the return address.

■ If you do not want to print a return address, click Omit (☐ changes to ☑).

6 Click Print to print the envelope.

■ This dialog box appears if you entered a return address.

7 To save the return address, click Yes.

PRINT LABELS

You can use Word to print labels. Labels are useful for addressing envelopes, creating name tags, labeling file folders and much more.

Before you begin, make sure you consult the manual that came with your printer to determine if your printer can print labels. You should also consult the manual to find out which label products your printer can use.

Word can print on many popular label products and types of labels. You can check your label packaging to determine which label product and type of label you are using.

You can enter text for a label as you would enter text for any document. You can also format the text on a label. Word's formatting features can help you emphasize important information on labels or make text larger so it is easier to read.

If you want to quickly create a label for each person on your mailing list, you can use the Mail Merge feature included with Word. For information on using Mail Merge to print labels, see page 156.

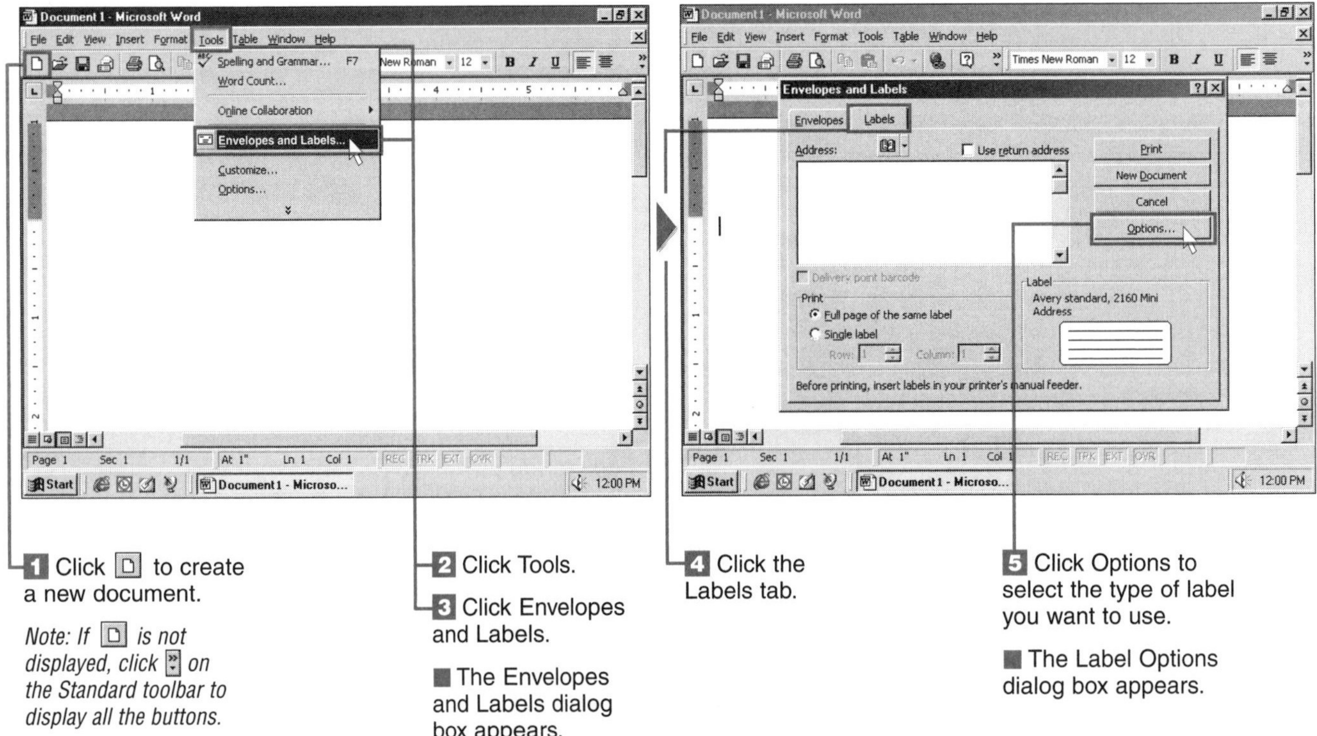

1 Click [New] to create a new document.

Note: If [New] is not displayed, click [»] on the Standard toolbar to display all the buttons.

2 Click Tools.

3 Click Envelopes and Labels.

■ The Envelopes and Labels dialog box appears.

4 Click the Labels tab.

5 Click Options to select the type of label you want to use.

■ The Label Options dialog box appears.

TIPS

Why can't I see the labels in my document?

✔ Word displays gray lines on your screen to separate the labels so you can view the labels more clearly. If the gray lines are not displayed, choose the Table menu and then select Show Gridlines.

Can I print the same information on every label?

✔ To print the same information on every label, perform steps 1 to 8 below. In the Envelopes and Labels dialog box, click the Address area and then type the text you want to appear on every label. Click New Document to view the labels.

Can I print a single label on a sheet of labels?

✔ Yes. Perform steps 1 to 8 below. In the Envelopes and Labels dialog box, click the Address area and then type the information you want to appear on the label. In the Print area, select Single label (○ changes to ⊙). In the Row area, enter the row number of the label you want to print on. In the Column area, enter the column number of the label. Then click the Print button.

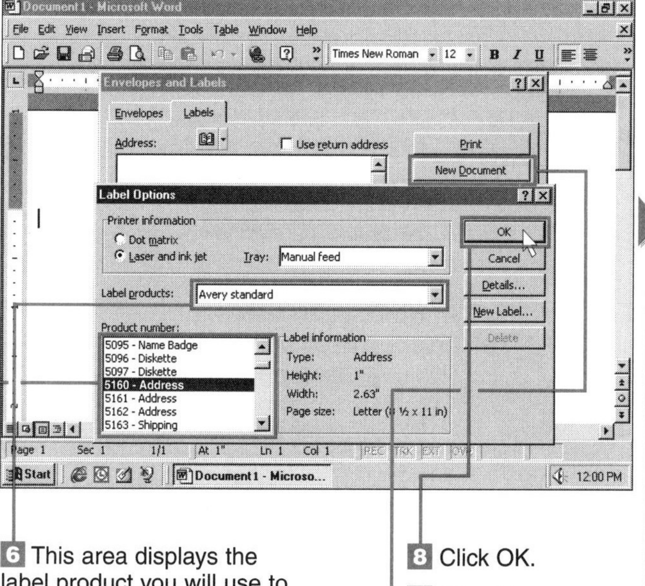

6 This area displays the label product you will use to print the labels. You can click this area to select a different label product.

■ This area displays the types of labels for the current label product.

7 Click the type of label you want to use.

8 Click OK.

9 Click New Document to add the labels to the new document.

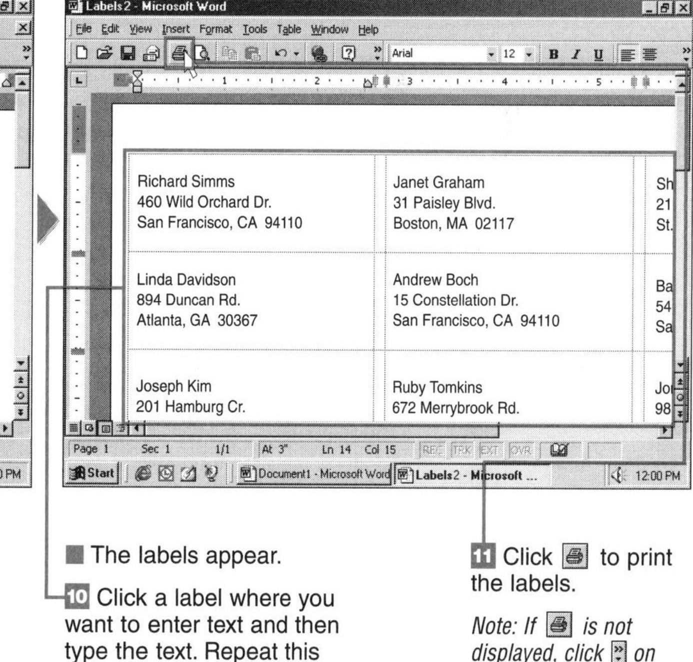

■ The labels appear.

10 Click a label where you want to enter text and then type the text. Repeat this step for each label you want to create.

11 Click 🖨 to print the labels.

Note: If 🖨 is not displayed, click » on the Standard toolbar to display all the buttons.

CREATE A TABLE

You can create a table to neatly display information, such as columns of numbers, in your document. Word lets you draw a table on the screen as you would draw a table with a pencil and paper.

A table is made up of rows, columns and cells. A row is a horizontal line of cells. A column is a vertical line of cells. A cell is the area where a row and column intersect.

You can enter any amount of text in a cell. When the text you enter reaches the end of a line, Word automatically wraps the text to the next line in the cell and increases the size of the cell to accommodate the text. Word also increases the width of a column to fit long words in a cell.

You can edit and format text in a table as you would edit and format any text in your document.

You can also use the steps below to create a table inside another table, called a nested table. Nested tables can help you better organize the information in a table.

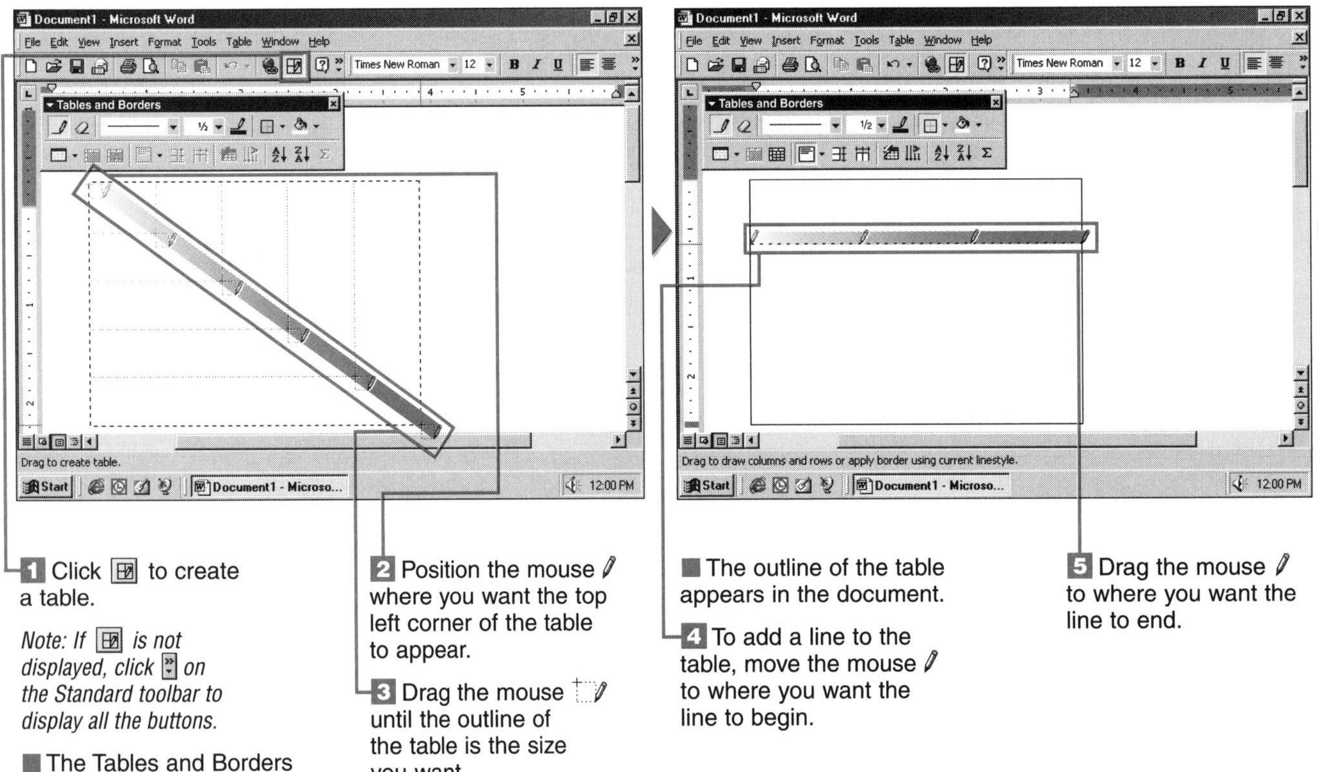

1 Click to create a table.

Note: If is not displayed, click on the Standard toolbar to display all the buttons.

■ The Tables and Borders toolbar appears.

2 Position the mouse where you want the top left corner of the table to appear.

3 Drag the mouse until the outline of the table is the size you want.

■ The outline of the table appears in the document.

4 To add a line to the table, move the mouse to where you want the line to begin.

5 Drag the mouse to where you want the line to end.

TIPS

Can I move the Tables and Borders toolbar out of the way?

✔ If the toolbar is displayed on top of information you want to view, you can move the toolbar out of the way. Position the mouse pointer over the title bar and then drag the toolbar to a new location.

How can I hide the Tables and Borders toolbar?

✔ To hide or display the Tables and Borders toolbar, click on the Standard toolbar.

Can I have text in my document wrap around a table I create?

✔ If you are creating a table near text in your document, you can have Word wrap the text around the table. Perform steps 1 to 7 on page 116, except hold down the Ctrl key as you perform step 3.

Is there another way to create a table?

✔ Yes. Click the Insert Table button ( ) on the Standard toolbar. Then drag the mouse pointer over the number of rows and columns you want the table to contain.

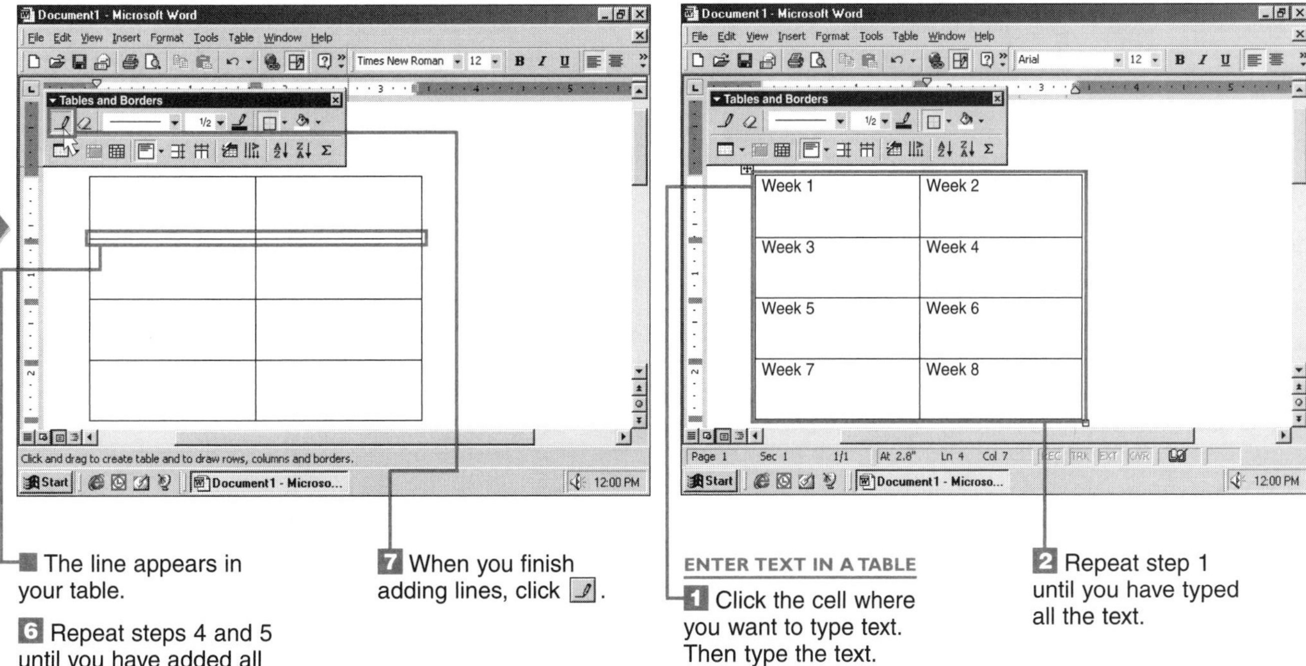

■ The line appears in your table.

6 Repeat steps 4 and 5 until you have added all the lines you want.

7 When you finish adding lines, click .

ENTER TEXT IN A TABLE

1 Click the cell where you want to type text. Then type the text.

2 Repeat step 1 until you have typed all the text.

CHANGE COLUMN WIDTH OR ROW HEIGHT

After you have created a table, you can change the width of columns and the height of rows.

Changing the width of a column or the height of a row can help improve the layout of your table. You cannot change the width or height of a single cell.

When you make changes to the column width or row height, all the cells in the column or row are affected.

When you change the width of a column or the height of a row, Word displays a dotted line on your screen to indicate the new width or height.

When you enter text in a table, Word may automatically increase the width of a column or the height of a row to accommodate the text you type. You may have to decrease the size of the text to decrease the height of the row. To change the size of text, see page 72.

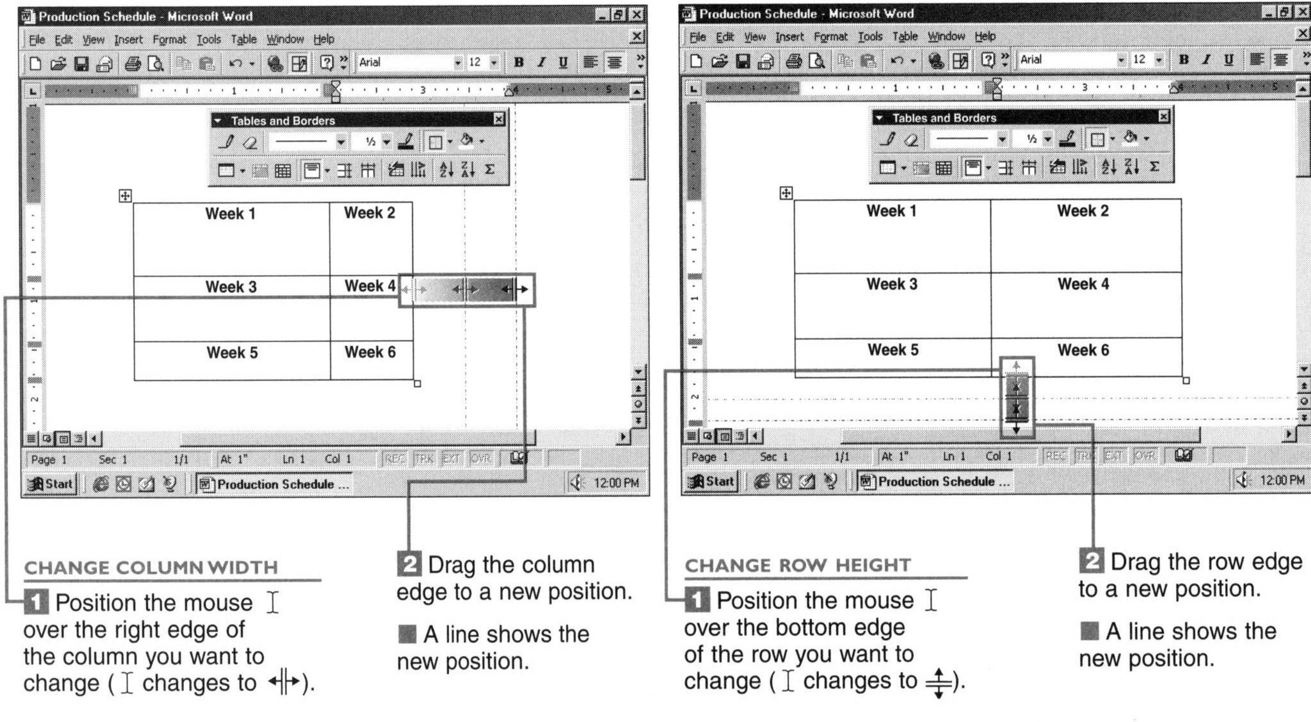

CHANGE COLUMN WIDTH

1 Position the mouse I over the right edge of the column you want to change (I changes to ◂||▸).

2 Drag the column edge to a new position.

■ A line shows the new position.

CHANGE ROW HEIGHT

1 Position the mouse I over the bottom edge of the row you want to change (I changes to ÷).

2 Drag the row edge to a new position.

■ A line shows the new position.

ERASE LINES

You can easily erase lines from your table. Word highlights the lines that you will erase.

You can erase the lines between two or more small cells to create one large cell. This is useful if you want to display a title in a cell at the top of your table.

If you erase a line between two cells that contain text, the text appears in the new, larger cell. If the text in the two cells was formatted differently, you can change the format of all the text in the new, larger cell. For information on formatting text, see pages 72 to 93.

You should not erase the lines that make up the outside of your table. If you erase these lines, the table will not have a solid border when you print the table.

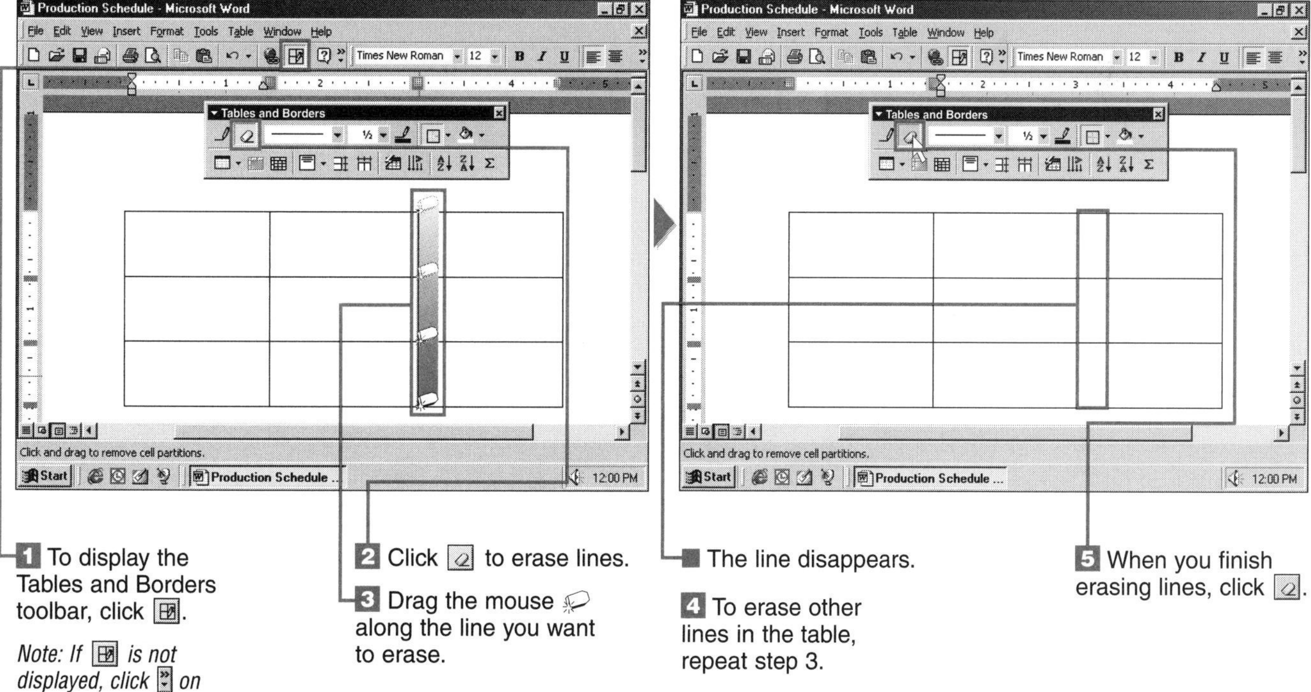

1 To display the Tables and Borders toolbar, click [button].

Note: If [button] is not displayed, click [button] on the Standard toolbar to display all the buttons.

2 Click [button] to erase lines.

3 Drag the mouse along the line you want to erase.

■ The line disappears.

4 To erase other lines in the table, repeat step 3.

5 When you finish erasing lines, click [button].

ADD OR DELETE A ROW OR COLUMN

If you want to insert additional information into your table, you can add a row or column.

Before you can add a row or column, you must select an existing row or column in your table. When you add a row, Word inserts the new row above the row you select. When you add a column, Word inserts the new column to the left of the column you select.

You can add several rows or columns to your table at once. The number of rows or columns you select determines the number of rows or columns Word will insert into your table.

You can delete a row or column you no longer need. When you delete a row or column from your table, all the information in the row or column is also deleted.

If you accidentally delete a row or column, you can use the Undo feature to restore the row or column. For more information on the Undo feature, see page 50.

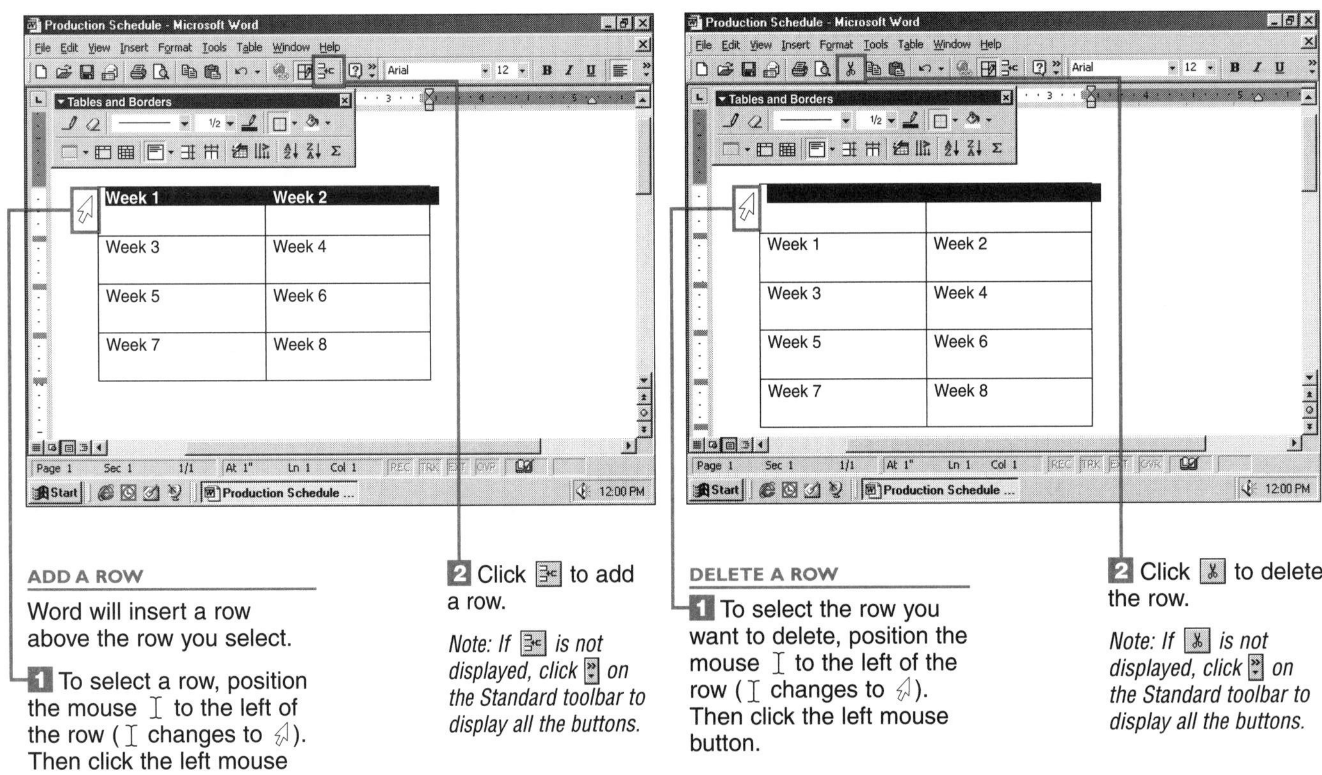

ADD A ROW

Word will insert a row above the row you select.

1 To select a row, position the mouse I to the left of the row (I changes to ↖). Then click the left mouse button.

2 Click to add a row.

Note: If is not displayed, click on the Standard toolbar to display all the buttons.

DELETE A ROW

1 To select the row you want to delete, position the mouse I to the left of the row (I changes to ↖). Then click the left mouse button.

2 Click to delete the row.

Note: If is not displayed, click on the Standard toolbar to display all the buttons.

TIPS

Can I add a row to the bottom of my table?

✔ Yes. Click the bottom right cell in your table and then press the Tab key. This allows you to quickly add rows to your table as you enter information.

Can I add a column to the right of the last column in my table?

✔ To add a column to the right of the last column in your table, click a cell in the last column. Select the Table menu, click Insert and then select Columns to the Right.

Is there another way to add a row or column to my table?

✔ You can add a row or column to your table by drawing a line for the new row or column. To display the Tables and Borders toolbar, click ▣ on the Standard toolbar. On the Tables and Borders toolbar, click the Draw Table button (▣). Position the mouse ✎ where you want the line to begin and then drag the mouse ✎ to where you want the line to end. For more information, see page 116.

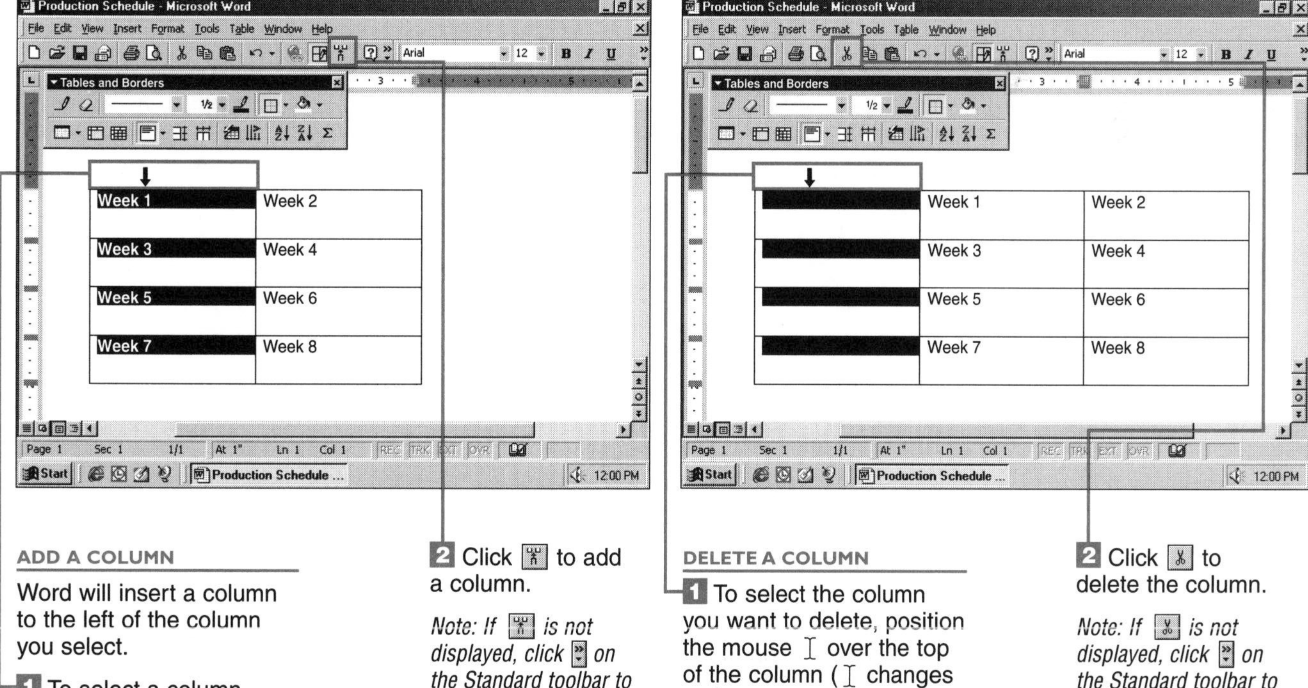

ADD A COLUMN

Word will insert a column to the left of the column you select.

1 To select a column, position the mouse I over the top of the column (I changes to ⬇). Then click the left mouse button.

2 Click ▣ to add a column.

Note: If ▣ is not displayed, click » on the Standard toolbar to display all the buttons.

DELETE A COLUMN

1 To select the column you want to delete, position the mouse I over the top of the column (I changes to ⬇). Then click the left mouse button.

2 Click ✂ to delete the column.

Note: If ✂ is not displayed, click » on the Standard toolbar to display all the buttons.

MOVE, RESIZE OR DELETE A TABLE

You can move a table from one location in your document to another. When you position the mouse pointer over a table, the table move handle (⊞) appears at the top left corner of the table. You can use this handle to move the table to a new location.

You can change the size of a table to suit your document. Changing the size of a table can also help to improve the layout of the table. Resizing a table does not change the size of the text or graphics in the table. When you position the mouse pointer over a table, the table resize handle (□) appears at the bottom right corner of the table. You can use this handle to resize the table.

You can delete a table you no longer need from your document. When you delete a table, you also remove the contents of the table from your document.

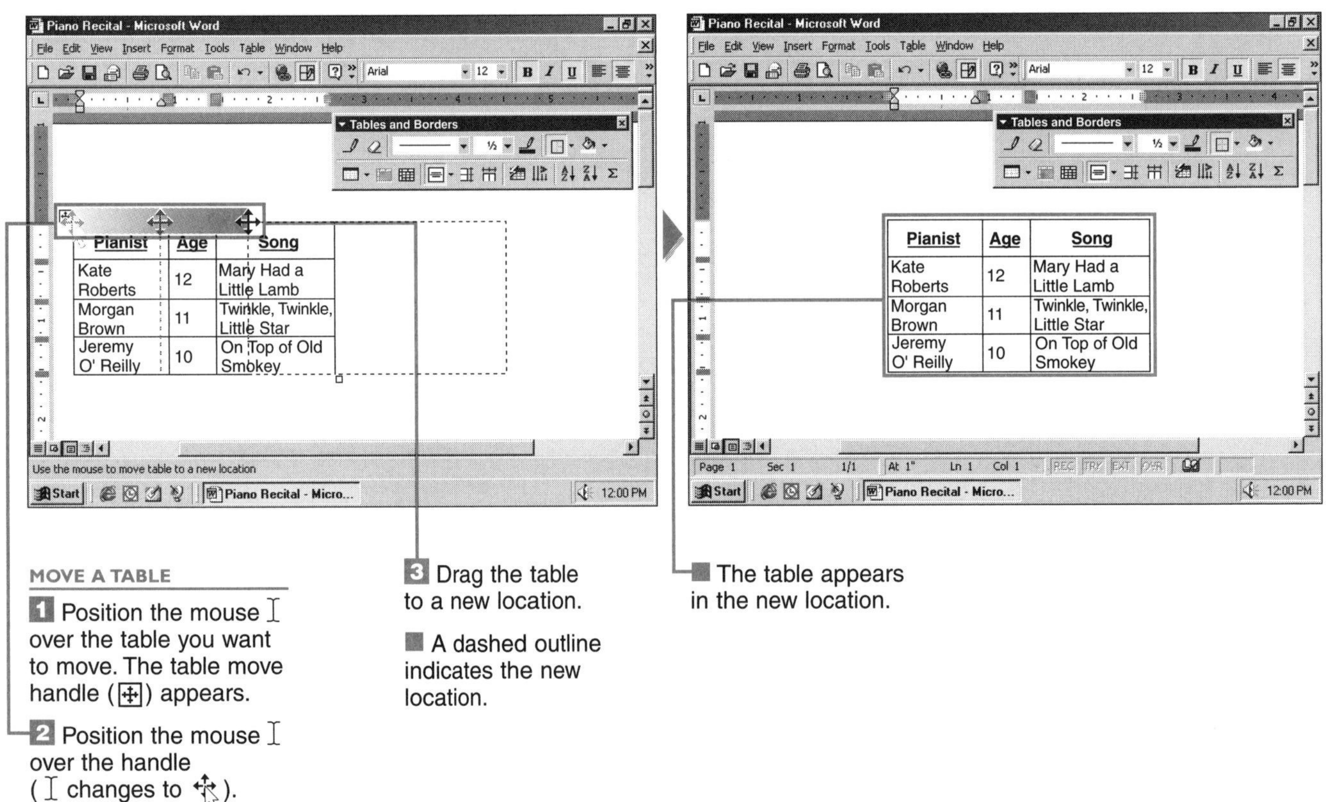

MOVE A TABLE

1 Position the mouse I over the table you want to move. The table move handle (⊞) appears.

2 Position the mouse I over the handle (I changes to ✥).

3 Drag the table to a new location.

■ A dashed outline indicates the new location.

■ The table appears in the new location.

TIPS

Why doesn't the table move handle (⊞) or table resize handle (□) appear when I position the mouse pointer over my table?

✔ Word can only display the handles in the Print Layout and Web Layout views. For more information on the views, see page 66.

Can I delete the contents of my table without removing the table from my document?

✔ Yes. To select the contents of the table, drag the mouse I over all the cells in the table. Then press the Delete key to delete the contents.

Can I change the alignment of my table?

✔ Yes. Word allows you to align a table to the left, center or right of a page. To select the table you want to align differently, position the mouse pointer over the table until the table move handle (⊞) appears. Then click the handle. To change the alignment of the table, click the Left align (≣), Center (≣) or Right align (≣) button on the Formatting toolbar.

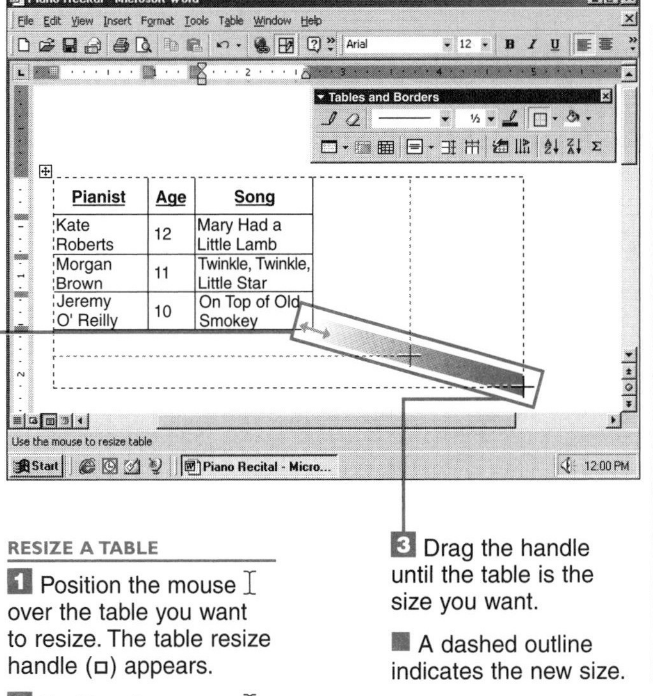

RESIZE A TABLE

1 Position the mouse I over the table you want to resize. The table resize handle (□) appears.

2 Position the mouse I over the handle (I changes to ↘).

3 Drag the handle until the table is the size you want.

■ A dashed outline indicates the new size.

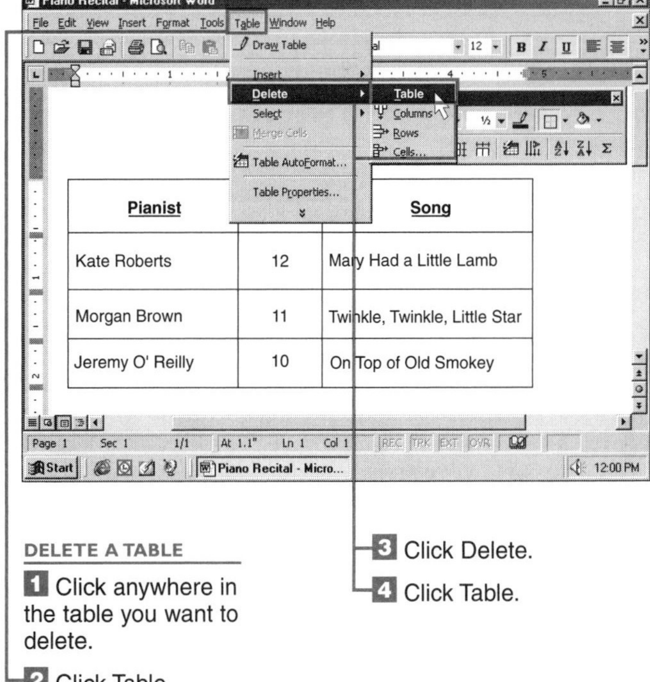

DELETE A TABLE

1 Click anywhere in the table you want to delete.

2 Click Table.

3 Click Delete.

4 Click Table.

CHANGE TABLE BORDERS

You can enhance the appearance of your table by changing the borders. By default, Word uses a solid, thin, black line for the border of your table.

You can change the border for a cell, a range of cells or your entire table. Changing the border for specific cells in your table can help you separate data or emphasize important information.

Word offers several line styles for you to choose from. You can also select a line thickness and color for the border. Word will use the line style, thickness and color you select for the border of all the new tables you create until you exit the program.

You can specify which border you want to change for the cells you selected. For example, you can change the outside border, the inside border, the right border or the left border. Changing only some of the borders for the cells you selected can give your table an interesting visual effect.

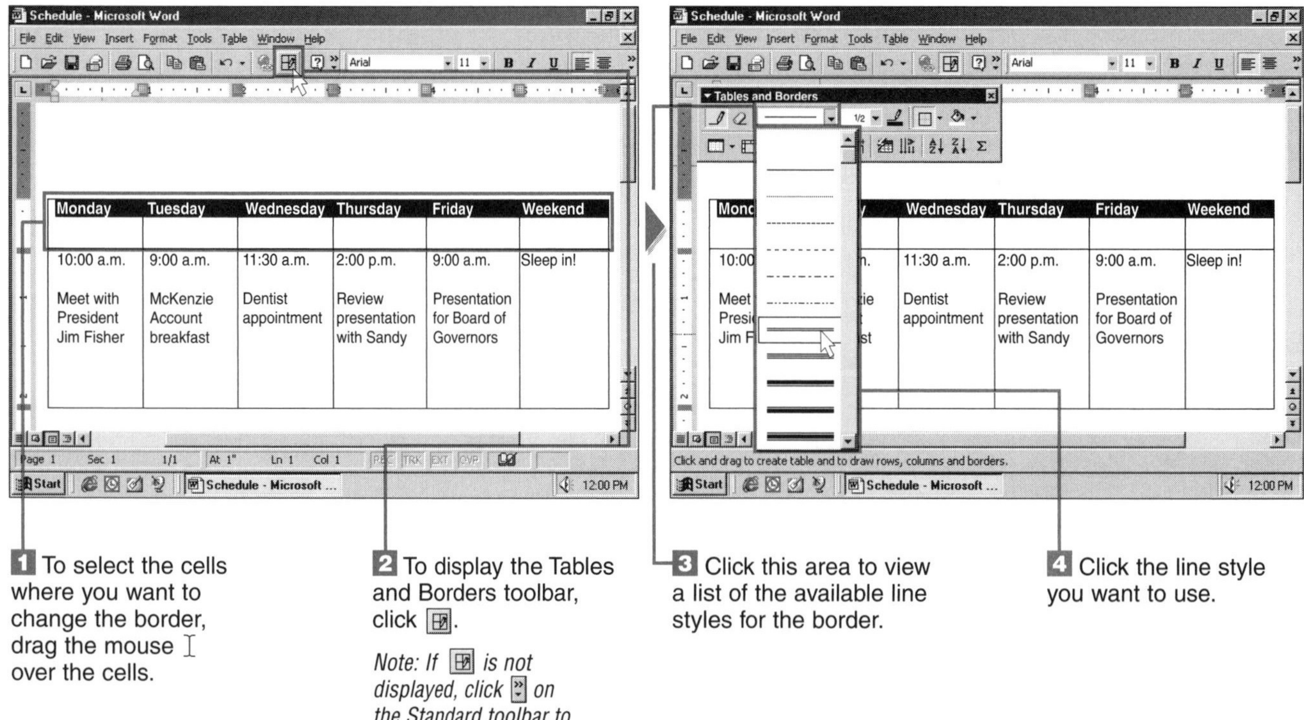

1 To select the cells where you want to change the border, drag the mouse over the cells.

2 To display the Tables and Borders toolbar, click .

Note: If is not displayed, click on the Standard toolbar to display all the buttons.

3 Click this area to view a list of the available line styles for the border.

4 Click the line style you want to use.

TIPS

How can I quickly enhance the appearance of my table?

✔ You can have Word automatically add formatting, such as borders and shading, to your table by using the Table AutoFormat feature. For more information on the Table AutoFormat feature, see page 128.

Can I remove a border from my table?

✔ You can remove a border that you do not want to appear when you print your table. This is useful if you used the table to organize the placement of information in your document. Select the cells you want to remove the border from. Then perform steps 8 and 9 below, except select the No Border button (▢) in step 9.

I removed a border from my table, but a faint border is still displayed on my screen. How do I remove the faint border?

✔ Word displays faint borders, called gridlines, for each table you create. To remove all the gridlines from a table, select the Table menu and then click Hide Gridlines. To once again display the gridlines, select the Table menu and then click Show Gridlines.

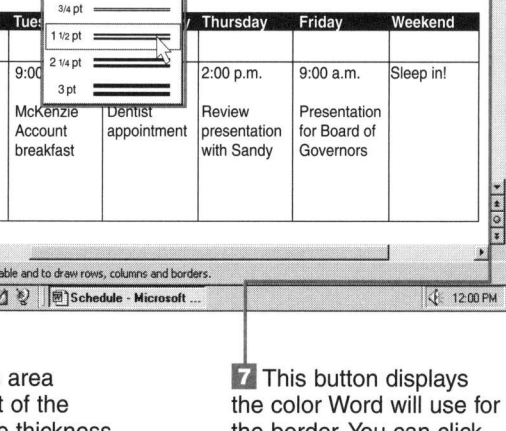

5 Click this area to view a list of the available line thickness options for the border.

6 Click the line thickness you want to use.

7 This button displays the color Word will use for the border. You can click the button to select a different color.

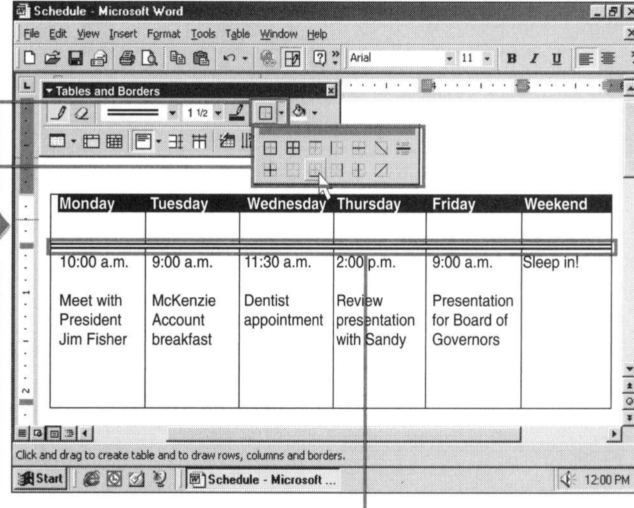

8 Click ▾ in this area to display the borders you can change.

9 Click the border you want to change for the cells you selected.

■ The border changes.

■ To deselect cells, click anywhere in the table.

ADD SHADING OR COLOR TO CELLS

You can draw attention to an area of your table by adding shading or color to cells. When you add shading or color, Word changes the background of the cells.

Word offers several shades of gray you can add to the cells in your table. The available shades of gray range from light gray to black.

Word also offers several colors you can use, including blue, yellow and violet. If you use a black-and-white printer, any color you add to cells will appear as a shade of gray when your table is printed.

Make sure the shading or color you want to add to cells will work well with the color of your text.

For example, black text on a violet background can be difficult to read.

If you no longer want cells in your table to display shading or color, you can easily remove the shading or color from the cells.

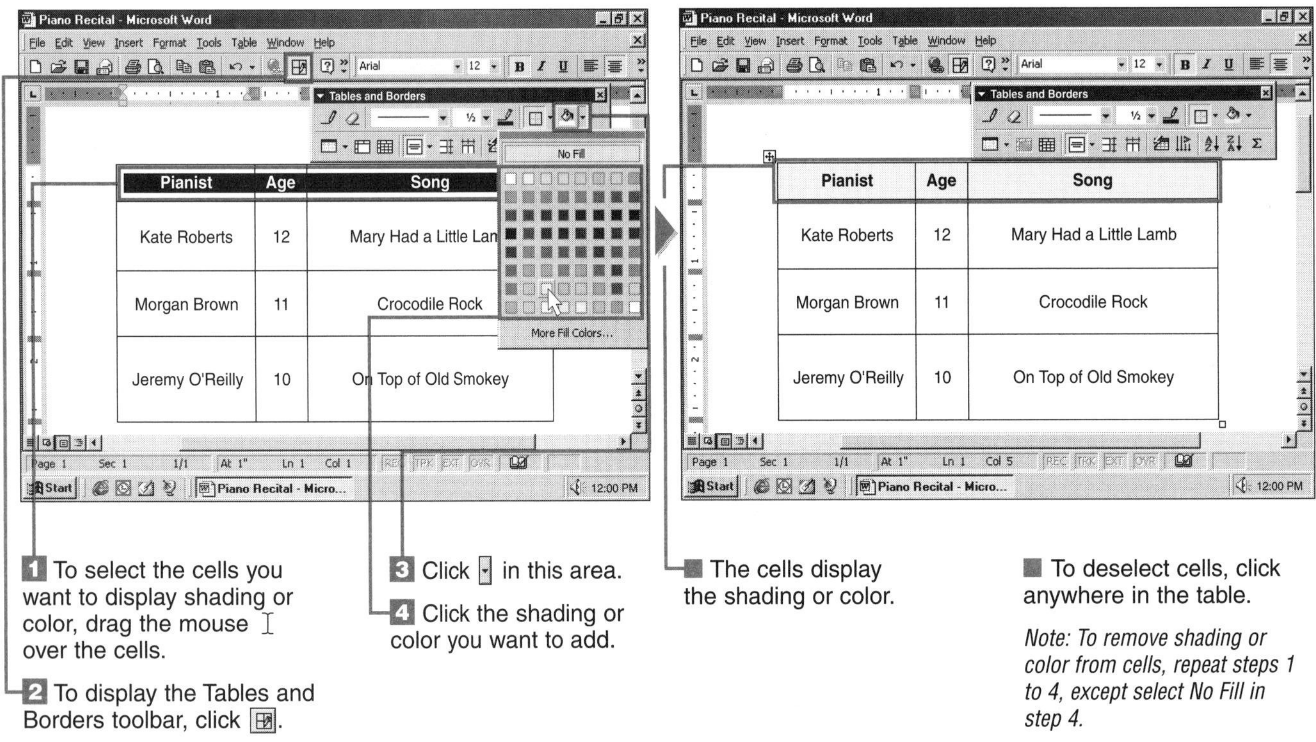

1 To select the cells you want to display shading or color, drag the mouse over the cells.

2 To display the Tables and Borders toolbar, click .

Note: If is not displayed, click on the Standard toolbar to display all the buttons.

3 Click in this area.

4 Click the shading or color you want to add.

■ The cells display the shading or color.

■ To deselect cells, click anywhere in the table.

Note: To remove shading or color from cells, repeat steps 1 to 4, except select No Fill in step 4.

CHANGE TEXT POSITION IN CELLS

You can enhance the appearance of your table by changing the position of text in cells.

Changing the position of text can also help you lay out the text in your table to suit your needs. By default, Word aligns text at the top left of a cell.

Word provides nine options that combine the left, right, center, top and bottom alignment positions. For example, you can center headings and titles horizontally and vertically in cells to make the text stand out.

Changing the position of text in cells can make long lists of information easier to read. For example, you can align chapter titles in a table of contents at the top left of cells and align the page numbers at the top right of the adjacent cells.

When you change the position of text that fills an entire cell, you may not see the change in position. You may need to increase the column width or row height to see the change. To change the column width or row height, see page 118.

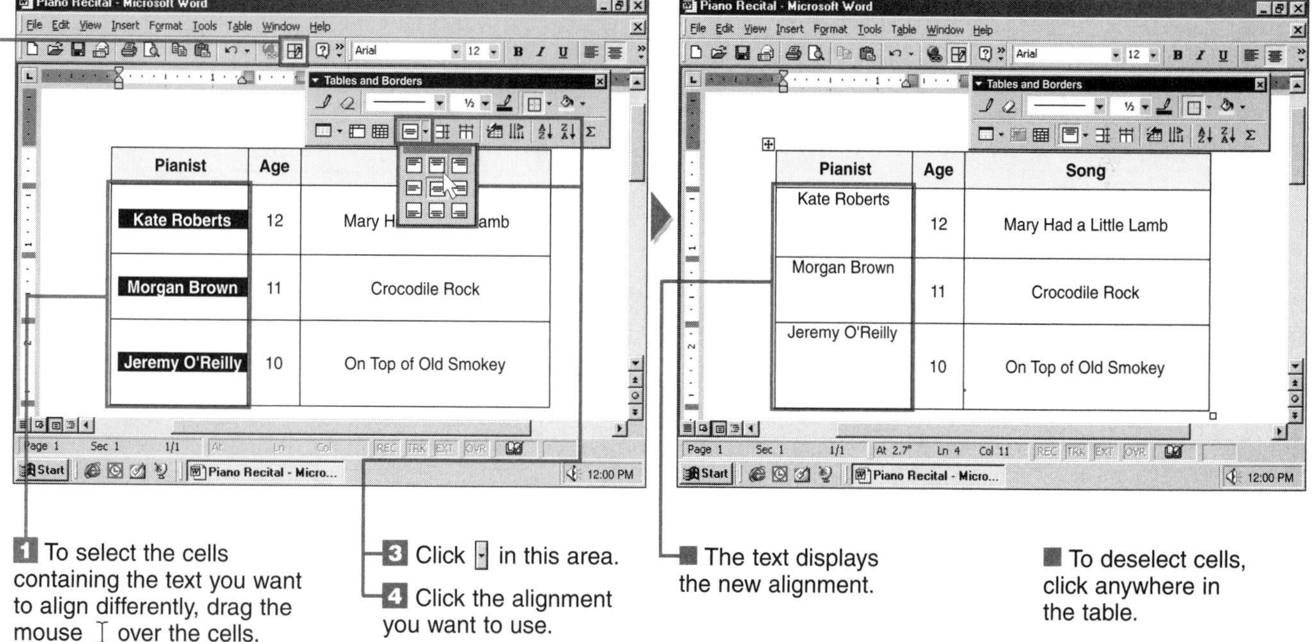

1 To select the cells containing the text you want to align differently, drag the mouse I over the cells.

2 To display the Tables and Borders toolbar, click ⊞.

Note: If ⊞ is not displayed, click » on the Standard toolbar to display all the buttons.

3 Click ▾ in this area.

4 Click the alignment you want to use.

■ The text displays the new alignment.

■ To deselect cells, click anywhere in the table.

FORMAT A TABLE

Word offers many ready-to-use designs that you can choose from to give your table a new appearance. These designs may also help make the information in your table easier to read.

Some of the types of table designs you can choose from include Simple, Classic, Colorful and 3-D effects. The Simple designs use only basic formatting. The Classic designs use simple borders and conservative colors. The Colorful designs use color combinations that make your table stand out. The 3-D effects designs give your table the appearance of depth.

A table design includes formatting options such as borders, fonts, shading and color. You can specify which formatting options you want Word to apply to your table.

You can have Word apply special formatting, such as italics, to the heading rows in your table. Word can also apply special formatting to the last row, first column and last column.

You can preview a table design. This allows you to determine if the design is suitable before you apply it to your table.

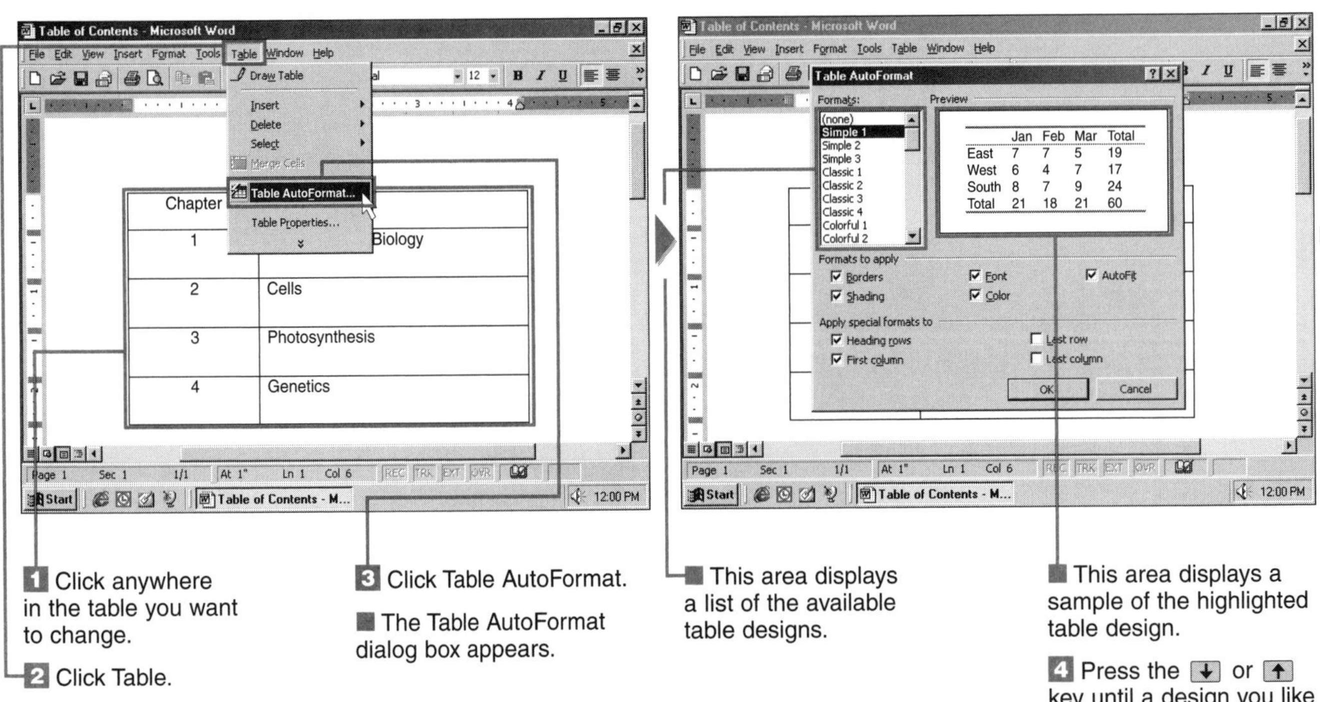

1 Click anywhere in the table you want to change.

2 Click Table.

3 Click Table AutoFormat.

■ The Table AutoFormat dialog box appears.

■ This area displays a list of the available table designs.

■ This area displays a sample of the highlighted table design.

4 Press the ↓ or ↑ key until a design you like appears.

TIPS

What is the AutoFit option used for?

✔ The AutoFit option changes the size of your table based on the amount of text in the table. This ensures that the text fits neatly in your table. If you later remove the table design using the steps below, your table will not return to its original size.

Can I apply a table design to only part of my table?

✔ No. You can only apply a table design to an entire table. To change only part of your table, you must select the cells you want to change and then format those cells. To change table borders, see page 124. To add shading or color to cells, see page 126.

Is there another way to display the Table AutoFormat dialog box?

✔ Yes. Click on the Standard toolbar to display the Tables and Borders toolbar. On the Tables and Borders toolbar, click the Table AutoFormat button ( ).

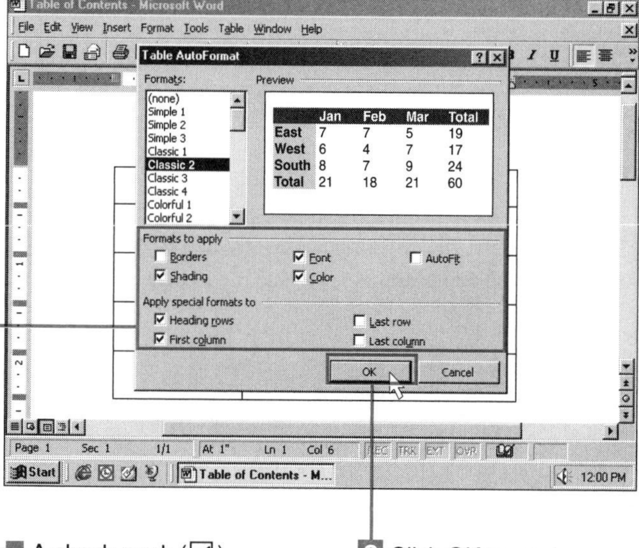

■ A check mark (☑) beside an option tells you that Word will apply the option to the table.

5 Click an option to add (☑) or remove (☐) a check mark.

6 Click OK to apply the design to the table.

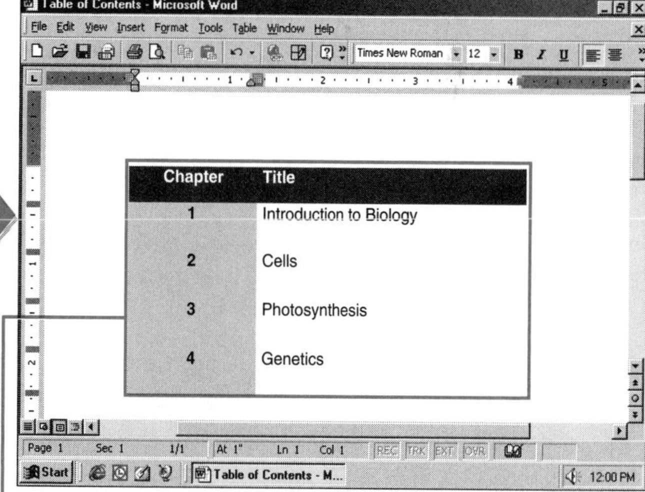

■ The table displays the design you selected.

REMOVE A TABLE DESIGN

■ Perform steps 1 to 4, except select Grid 1 in step 4. Then press the Enter key.

ADD AN AUTOSHAPE

Word provides many ready-made shapes, called AutoShapes, that you can add to your document. You can add AutoShapes to enhance the appearance of your document or draw attention to important information.

Word offers several categories of AutoShapes, including Lines, Basic Shapes and Stars and Banners. You can select a category to find the AutoShape you want to add to your document. You can add AutoShapes such as lines, rectangles, ovals and stars.

When you add an AutoShape to your document, Word lets you specify the location for the AutoShape and the size you want the AutoShape to display. You can later move and resize the AutoShape to better suit your needs. You can also delete an AutoShape you no longer need. For information on moving, resizing or deleting a graphic, see page 136.

Word can only display AutoShapes in the Print Layout and Web Layout views. For more information on the views, see page 66.

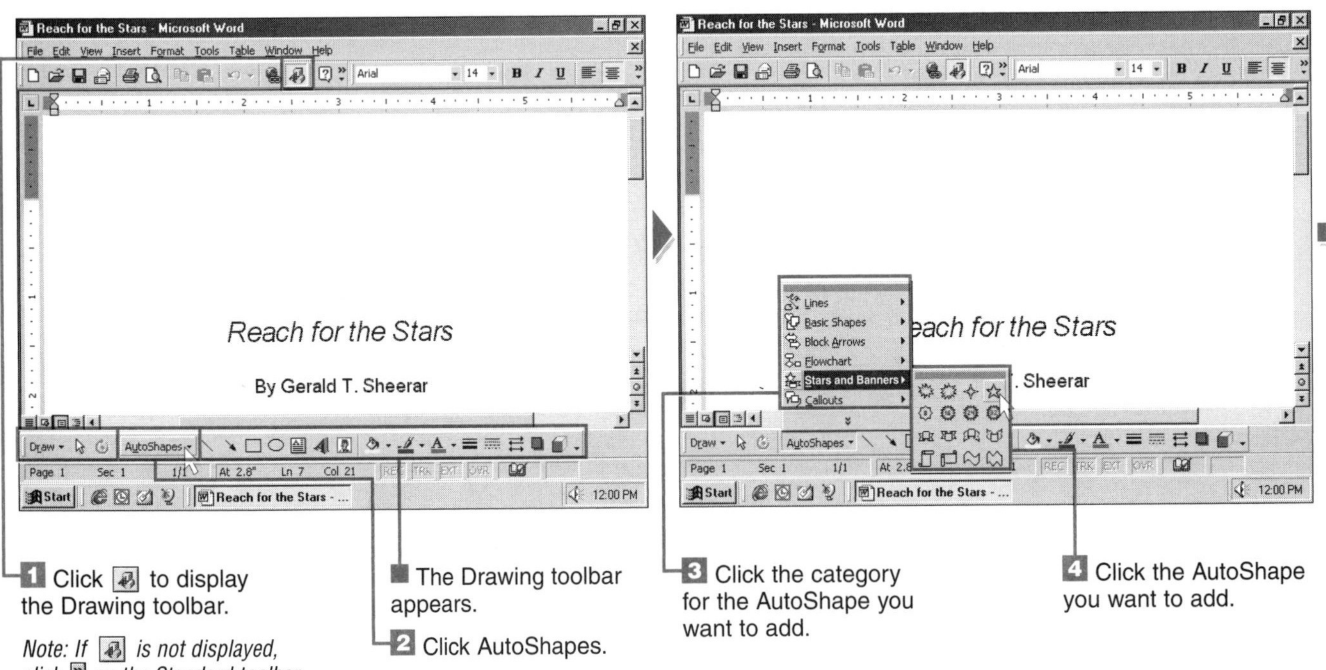

1 Click to display the Drawing toolbar.

Note: If is not displayed, click on the Standard toolbar to display all the buttons.

■ The Drawing toolbar appears.

2 Click AutoShapes.

3 Click the category for the AutoShape you want to add.

4 Click the AutoShape you want to add.

TIPS

How can I quickly draw a shape?

✔ You can use the buttons on the Drawing toolbar to quickly draw a simple shape. Click the Line button (◻) to draw a line. Click the Arrow button (◻) to draw an arrow. Click the Rectangle button (◻) to draw a rectangle. Click the Oval button (◻) to draw an oval.

How do I draw a square or circle?

✔ Click the Rectangle button (◻) on the Drawing toolbar to draw a square. Click the Oval button (◻) on the Drawing toolbar to draw a circle. Then hold down the Shift key as you draw the shape.

Can I add text to an AutoShape?

✔ Yes. Right-click the AutoShape you want to change. Click Add Text and then type the text you want the AutoShape to display. When you finish typing the text, click outside the AutoShape.

Can I draw my own shape?

✔ Yes. On the Drawing toolbar, click AutoShapes, select the Lines category and then click the Freeform option (◻). When you finish drawing your shape, double-click to stop drawing.

5 Position the mouse + where you want to begin drawing the AutoShape.

6 Drag the mouse + until the AutoShape is the size you want.

■ The AutoShape appears in the document. The handles (□) around the AutoShape let you change the size of the AutoShape.

7 To hide the handles, click outside the AutoShape.

Note: To hide the Drawing toolbar, repeat step 1.

ADD CLIP ART

Word includes professionally designed clip art images you can add to your document. You can add clip art images to make your document more interesting and entertaining.

The Microsoft Clip Gallery contains a wide variety of images divided into categories. Some of the categories are Animals, People at Work and Transportation. You can select a category to find the clip art image you want to add to your document.

Unlike other types of graphics, such as AutoShapes and text effects, Word can display most clip art images in the Normal and Outline views as well as the Print Layout and Web Layout views. For more information on the views, see page 66.

After you add a clip art image, you can move and resize the clip art image to suit your document. You can also delete a clip art image you no longer need. For information on moving, resizing or deleting a graphic, see page 136.

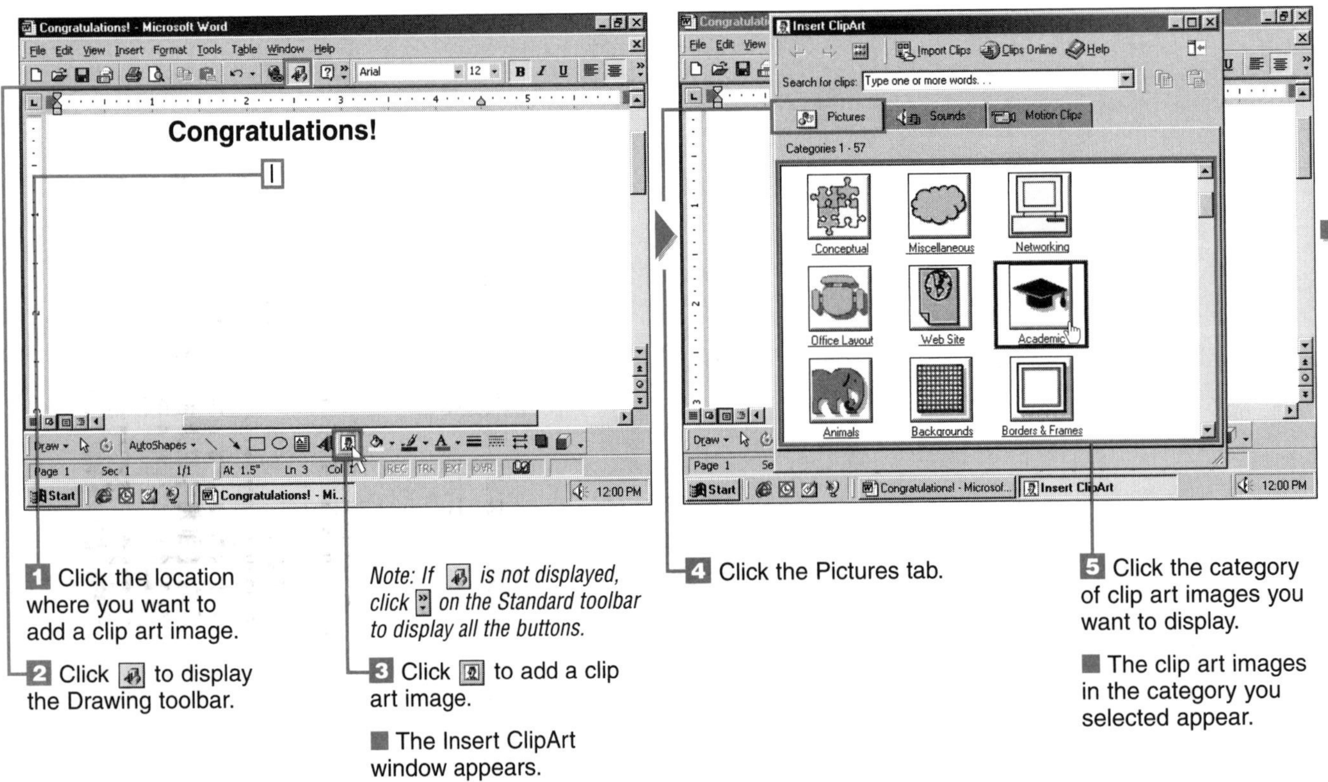

1 Click the location where you want to add a clip art image.

2 Click [Drawing] to display the Drawing toolbar.

Note: If [Drawing] is not displayed, click [»] on the Standard toolbar to display all the buttons.

3 Click [Insert Clip Art] to add a clip art image.

■ The Insert ClipArt window appears.

4 Click the Pictures tab.

5 Click the category of clip art images you want to display.

■ The clip art images in the category you selected appear.

TIPS

Is there another way to find clip art images in the Insert ClipArt window?

✔ You can search for clip art images of interest in the Insert ClipArt window. Click the Search for clips area, type a word or phrase describing the clip art image you want to find and then press the Enter key.

How do I use the Favorites category?

✔ You can add clip art images you frequently use to the Favorites category. This makes it easy to find the clip art images again later. In the Insert ClipArt window, click a clip art image you want to add to the Favorites category. A menu appears. Click and then click Add.

Where can I find more clip art images?

✔ If you are connected to the Internet, you can visit Microsoft's Clip Gallery Live Web site to find additional clip art images. In the Insert ClipArt window, click the Clips Online button and then follow the instructions on your screen.

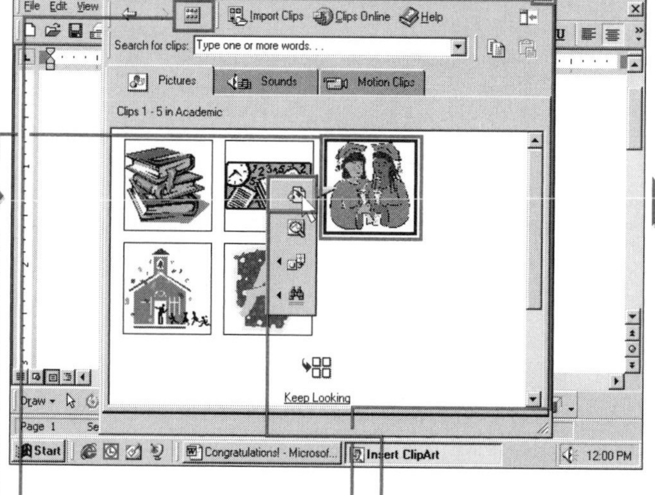

■ To once again view all the categories, click .

6 Click the clip art image you want to add to the document. A menu appears.

7 Click to add the clip art image to the document.

8 Click to close the Insert ClipArt window.

■ The clip art image appears in the document.

ADD A TEXT EFFECT

You can use the WordArt feature to add text effects to your document. You can work with a text effect as you would work with any graphic.

You can add text effects that shadow, stretch or make text appear three-dimensional. Text effects are useful for adding interesting headings to documents such as newsletters, flyers or brochures.

When typing the text for a text effect, you should be careful not to make any spelling errors. Word's spell check feature does not check the spelling of text effects.

Word can only display text effects in the Print Layout and Web Layout views. For more information on the views, see page 66.

After you add a text effect, you can move and resize the text effect to suit your document. You can also delete a text effect you no longer need. For information on moving, resizing or deleting a graphic, see page 136.

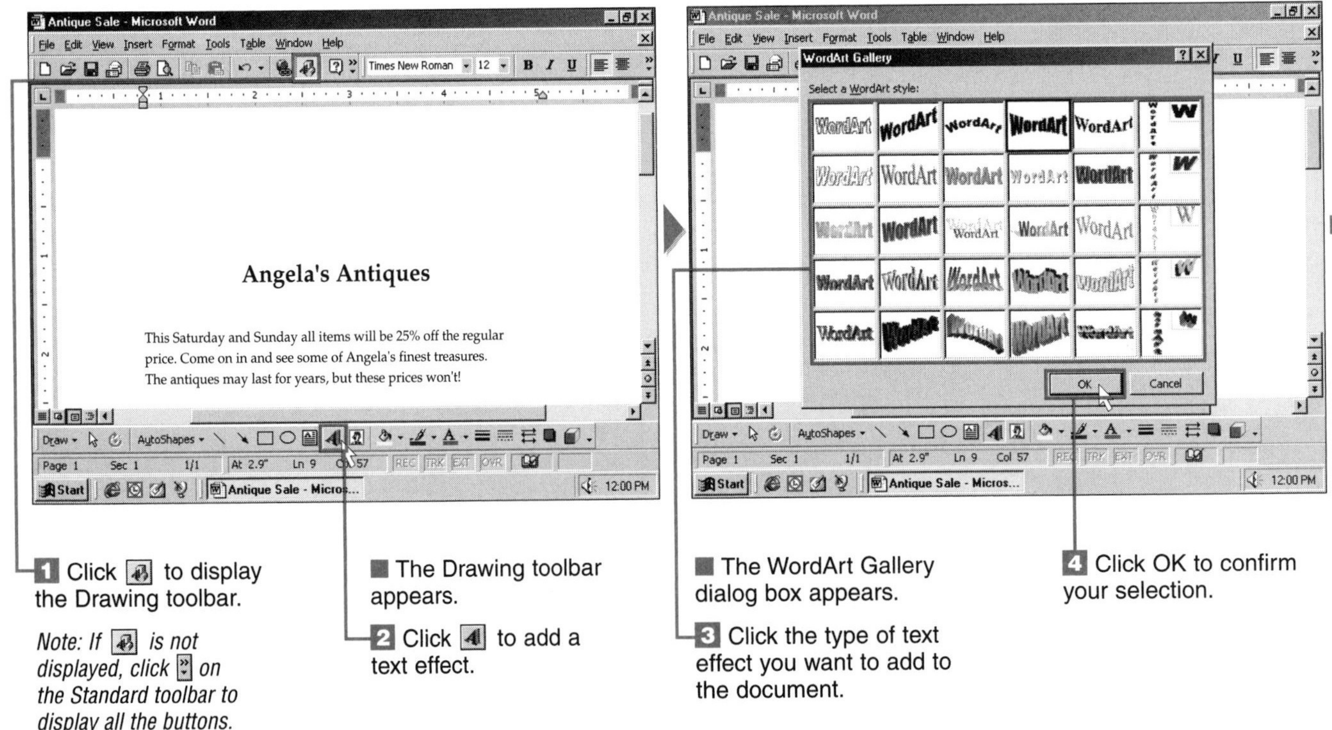

1 Click to display the Drawing toolbar.

Note: If is not displayed, click on the Standard toolbar to display all the buttons.

■ The Drawing toolbar appears.

2 Click to add a text effect.

■ The WordArt Gallery dialog box appears.

3 Click the type of text effect you want to add to the document.

4 Click OK to confirm your selection.

TIPS

Why does a toolbar appear on my screen when I add a text effect?

✔ When you add a text effect, Word automatically displays the WordArt toolbar. You can use the buttons on the toolbar to perform tasks such as changing the shape of a text effect ( ) or increasing and decreasing the space between characters ( ).

Can I add a text effect to existing text in my document?

✔ You can use existing text in your document to create a text effect. Select the text you want the text effect to display and perform steps 1 to 4 below. Then perform step 6 to display the text effect in your document.

Can I change a text effect?

✔ You can edit the text in a text effect or change the font and size of a text effect. You can also bold or italicize a text effect. To display the Edit WordArt Text dialog box so you can change a text effect, double-click the text effect.

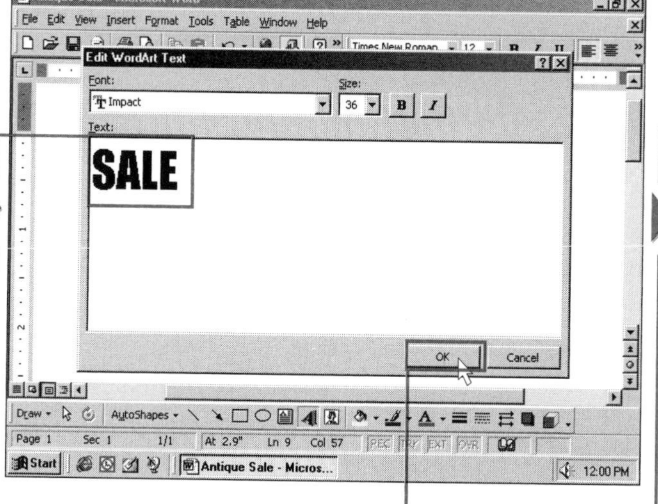

■ The Edit WordArt Text dialog box appears.

5 Type the text you want the text effect to display.

6 Click OK to add the text effect to the document.

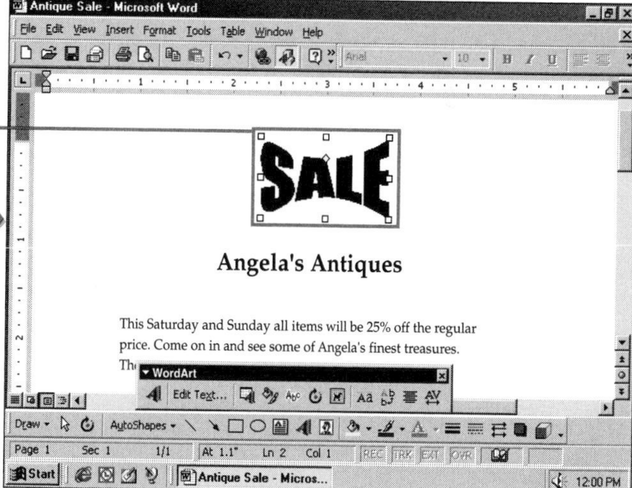

■ The text effect appears in the document. The handles (□) around the text effect let you change the size of the text effect.

7 To hide the handles, click outside the text effect.

Note: To hide the Drawing toolbar, repeat step 1.

MOVE, RESIZE OR DELETE A GRAPHIC

You can move or copy a graphic from one location in your document to another. When you move a graphic, the graphic disappears from its original location in your document. When you copy a graphic, the graphic appears in both the original and new locations.

You can change the size of a graphic to suit your document. The handles (□) that appear when you select a graphic allow you to change the size of the graphic. The handles at the top and bottom of a graphic allow you to change the height of the graphic. The handles at the sides of a graphic allow you to change the width of the graphic. The handles at the corners of a graphic allow you to change the height and width of the graphic at the same time.

You can delete a graphic you no longer need from your document.

Word can only display most graphics in the Print Layout and Web Layout views. For more information on the views, see page 66.

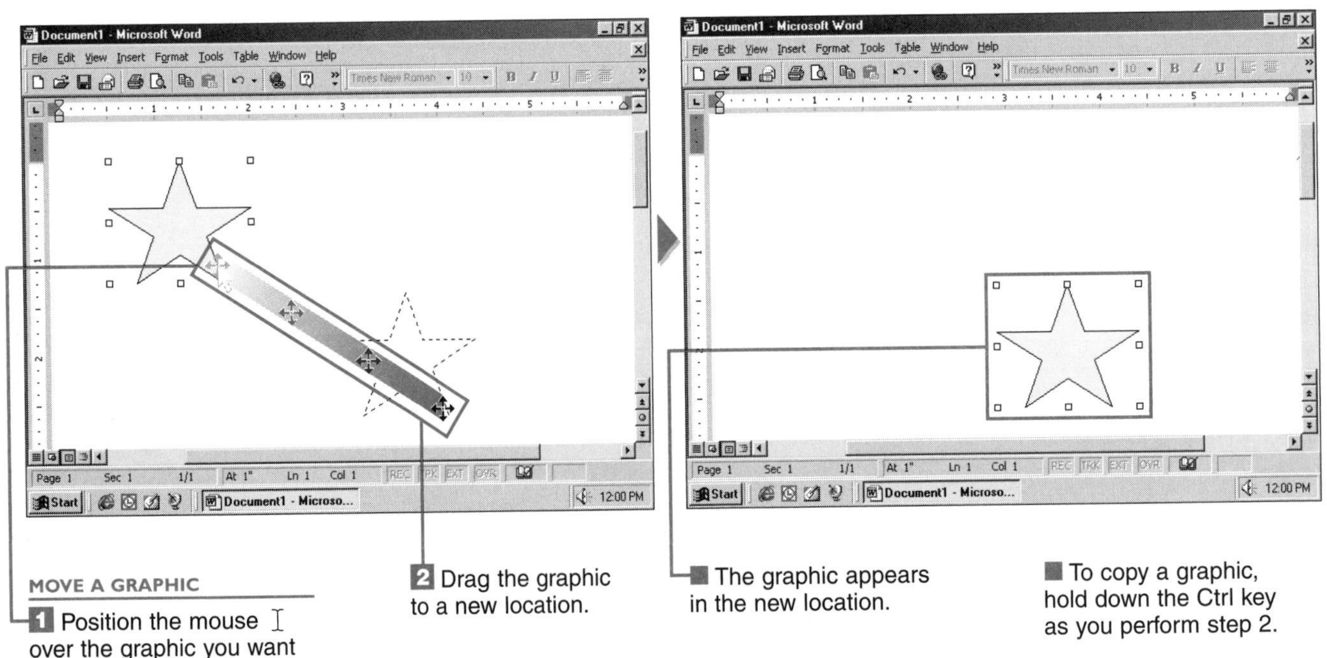

MOVE A GRAPHIC

1 Position the mouse I over the graphic you want to move (I changes to ✥).

2 Drag the graphic to a new location.

■ The graphic appears in the new location.

■ To copy a graphic, hold down the Ctrl key as you perform step 2.

TIPS

I am having trouble moving a clip art image. What is wrong?

✔ The clip art image may be an inline image. You can change an inline image to a floating image to make the image easier to work with. Click the image you want to change. Choose the Format menu and select Picture. Click the Layout tab and then choose an option other than In line with text in the Wrapping style area. For information on the Wrapping style options, see page 140.

How can I prevent a graphic from appearing distorted when I resize it?

✔ To maintain the height-to-width ratio of a graphic as you resize it, hold down the Shift key as you drag one of the corner handles.

Can I line up the graphics in my document?

✔ You can align graphics by their left, right, top or bottom edges. To display the Drawing toolbar, click [icon] on the Standard toolbar. Hold down the Shift key as you click each graphic you want to align. On the Drawing toolbar, select Draw. Click Align or Distribute and then select the alignment you want to use.

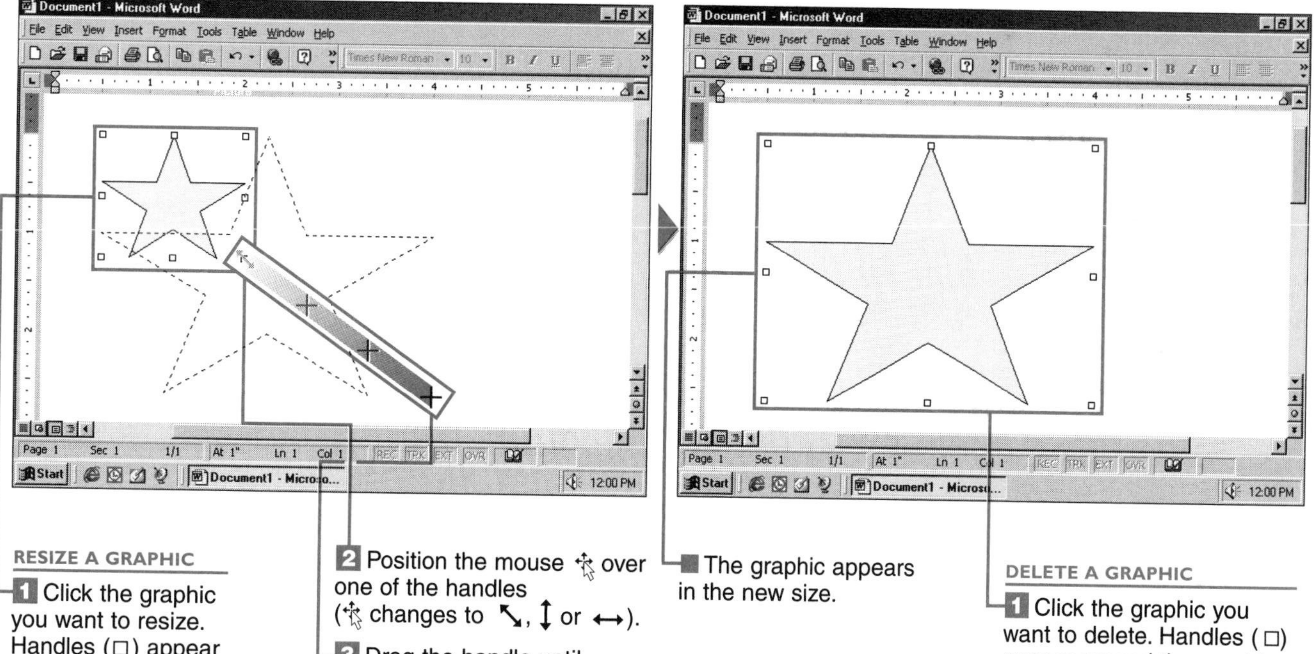

RESIZE A GRAPHIC

1 Click the graphic you want to resize. Handles (□) appear around the graphic.

2 Position the mouse ✥ over one of the handles (✥ changes to ↖, ↕ or ↔).

3 Drag the handle until the graphic is the size you want.

■ The graphic appears in the new size.

DELETE A GRAPHIC

1 Click the graphic you want to delete. Handles (□) appear around the graphic.

2 Press the Delete key.

ENHANCE A GRAPHIC

Word offers several ways you can enhance the appearance of certain graphics in your document. You will not be able to enhance some graphics, such as clip art images.

You can change the color that fills the inside of a graphic. You can also change the color of the line around a graphic.

You can select a new line style for a graphic. This allows you to use a thicker line or more than one line to outline a graphic.

To make a graphic appear as if it is raised off the page, you can add a shadow to the graphic. You can also make a graphic appear three-dimensional. This gives the graphic the appearance of depth. You cannot add a shadow and a 3-D effect to the same graphic.

You must display the Drawing toolbar before you can enhance a graphic. To display the Drawing toolbar, click the Drawing button (▣) on the Standard toolbar.

Word can only display most graphics in the Print Layout and Web Layout views. For information on the views, see page 66.

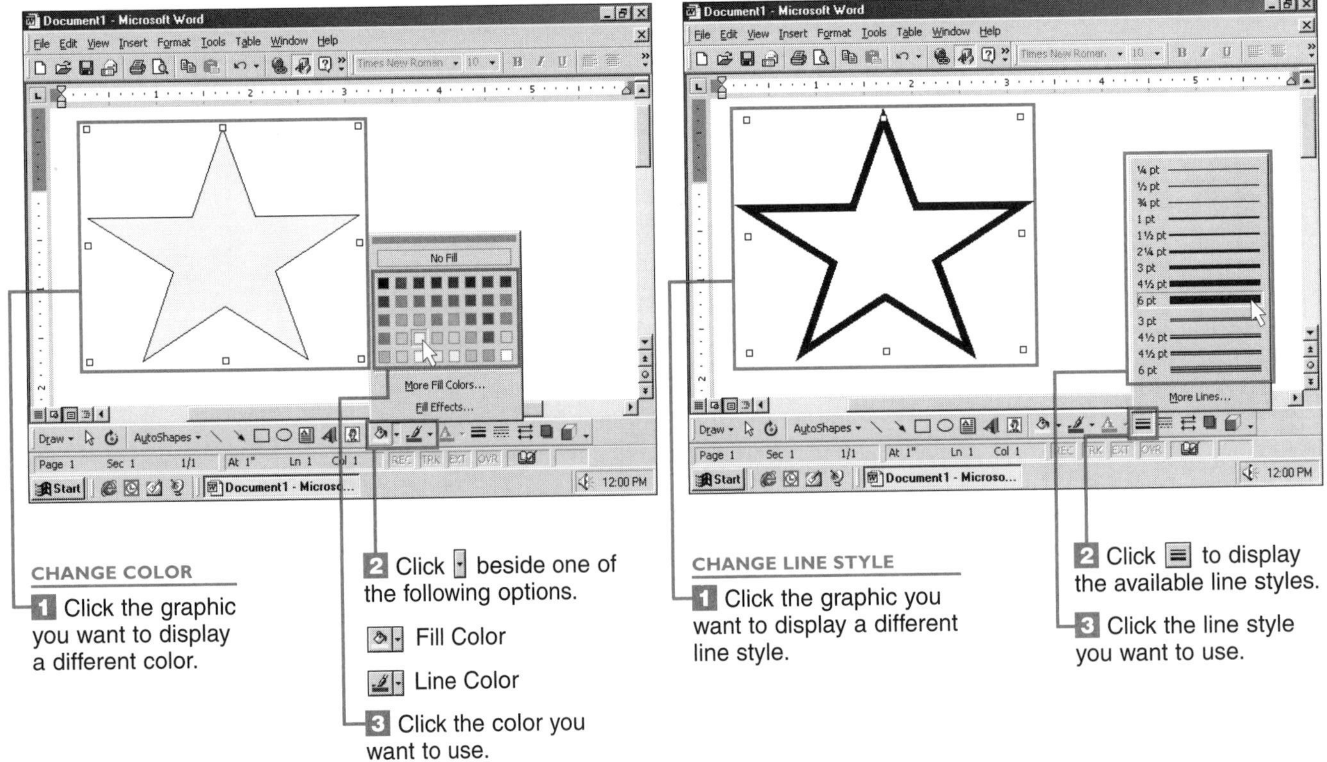

CHANGE COLOR

1 Click the graphic you want to display a different color.

2 Click ▾ beside one of the following options.

Fill Color

Line Color

3 Click the color you want to use.

CHANGE LINE STYLE

1 Click the graphic you want to display a different line style.

2 Click ▤ to display the available line styles.

3 Click the line style you want to use.

TIPS

Can I enhance more than one graphic at a time?

✔ Yes. You must first select all the graphics you want to enhance. To select multiple graphics, hold down the Shift key as you click each graphic you want to select. You can then enhance all the selected graphics at once.

Why does a yellow handle appear when I select certain graphics?

✔ Some graphics display a yellow handle (◇) that you can use to modify the shape of the graphic. For example, you can change the size of the arrowheads on some arrows. Position the mouse ▷ over the yellow handle and then drag the handle to a new location.

Can I rotate a graphic in my document?

✔ To rotate a graphic in your document, click the graphic and then select the Free Rotate button (⟳) on the Drawing toolbar. Green dots appear around the graphic. Position the mouse ⟳ over one of the green dots and then drag the dot to a new location.

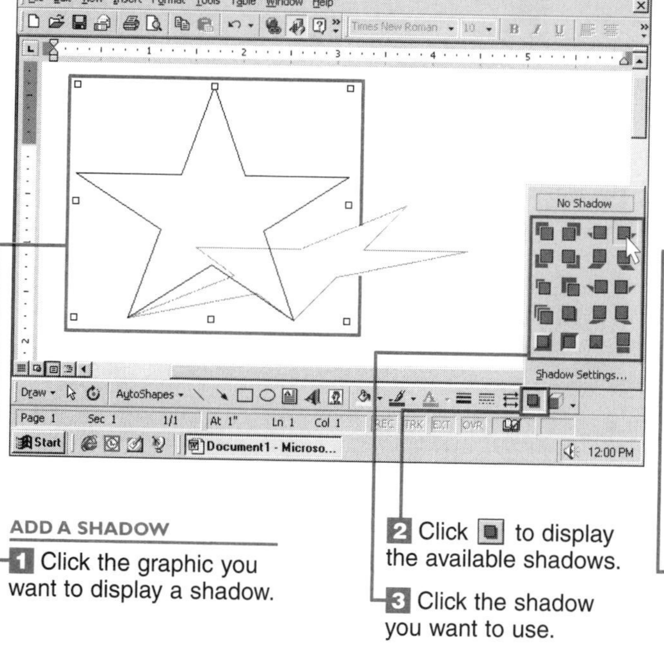

ADD A SHADOW

1 Click the graphic you want to display a shadow.

2 Click ■ to display the available shadows.

3 Click the shadow you want to use.

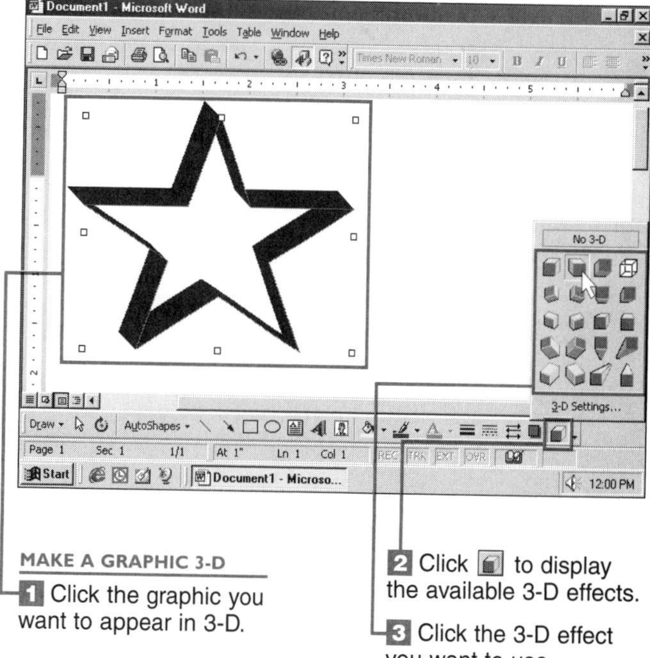

MAKE A GRAPHIC 3-D

1 Click the graphic you want to appear in 3-D.

2 Click ■ to display the available 3-D effects.

3 Click the 3-D effect you want to use.

WRAP TEXT AROUND A GRAPHIC

After you add a graphic to your document, you can wrap text around the graphic to enhance the appearance of the document.

Word offers several ways you can wrap text around a graphic. You can have Word wrap text to form a square around a graphic or fit tightly around the edges of a graphic. Word also lets you place a graphic behind or in front of text. You can also choose the In line with text option to have Word position the graphic within the text of the document.

You can choose how you want to align a graphic with the text in your document. This lets you specify which side(s) of the graphic you want the text to wrap around. Word can align the graphic to the left, center or right of the text. If you do not want Word to change the alignment of a graphic, you can choose the Other option.

Word can only display most graphics in the Print Layout and Web Layout views. For more information on the views, see page 66.

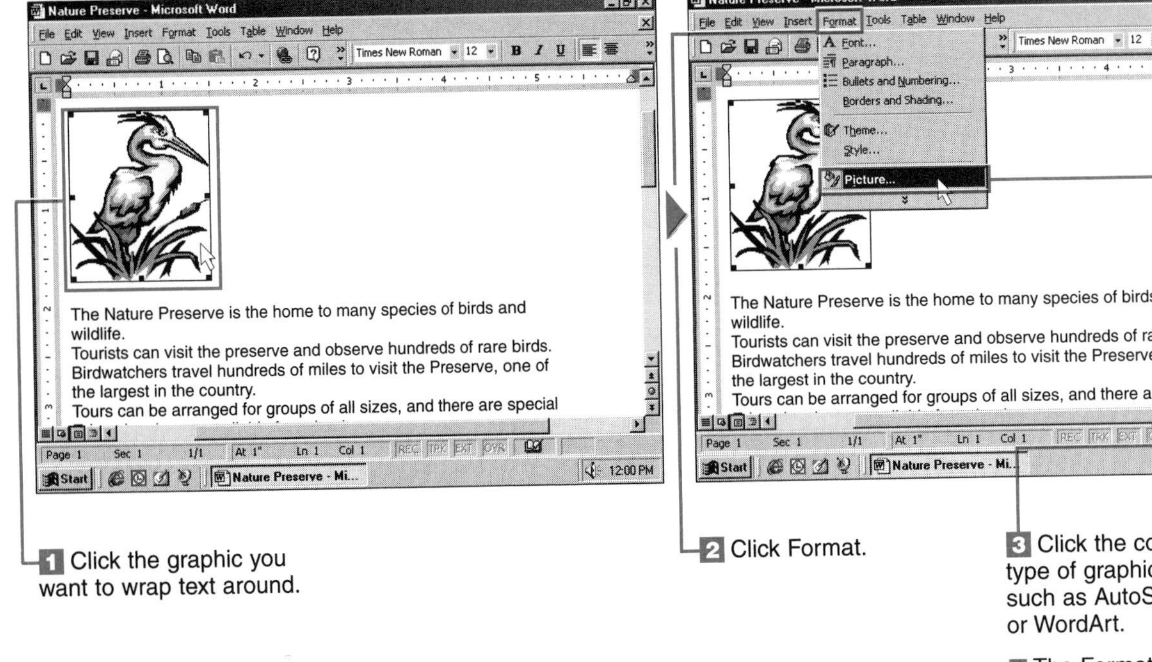

1 Click the graphic you want to wrap text around.

2 Click Format.

3 Click the command for the type of graphic you selected, such as AutoShape, Picture or WordArt.

■ The Format dialog box appears.

TIPS

Does Word offer any other wrapping styles?

✔ You can wrap text around a graphic using the Through or Top and bottom wrapping styles. To display the additional wrapping styles, click the Advanced button in the Format dialog box and then click the Text Wrapping tab.

I can't select the In line with text wrapping style. What is wrong?

✔ Word cannot position some graphics, such as AutoShapes, within the text of a document.

Can I change the amount of space between text and a graphic?

✔ For some wrapping styles, you can specify the amount of space you want to display between text and the edge of a graphic. Click the graphic you want to change. Display the Format dialog box and then click the Layout tab. Click the Advanced button and choose the Text Wrapping tab. In the Distance from text area, enter the amount of space you want to display in each of the appropriate boxes.

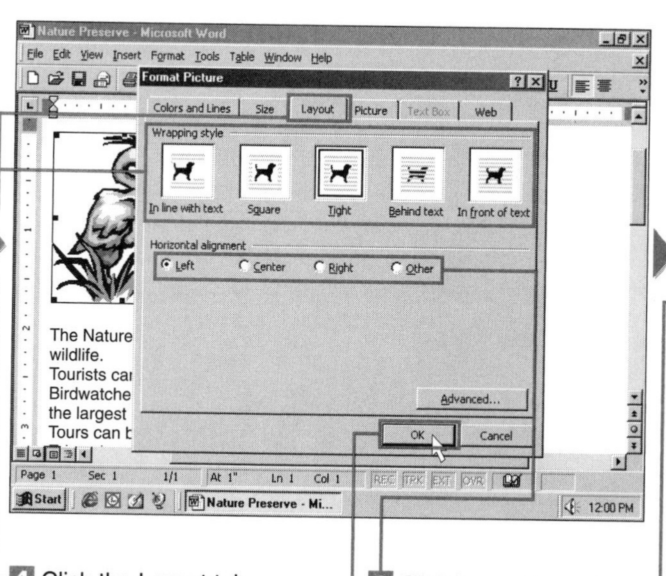

4 Click the Layout tab.

5 Click the way you want text to wrap around the graphic.

6 Click how you want to align the graphic with the text.

7 Click OK to confirm your changes.

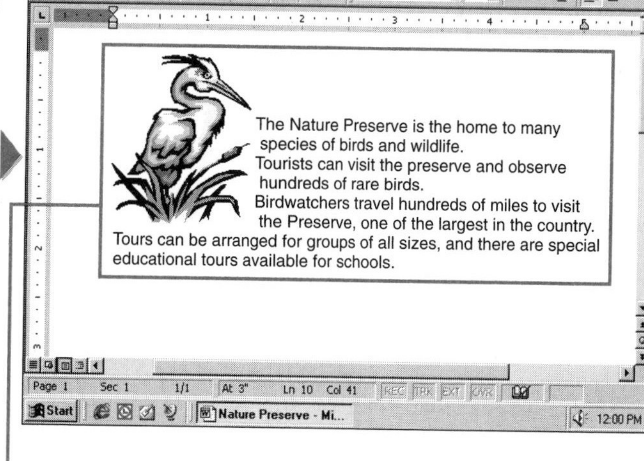

■ The text wraps around the graphic.

■ To deselect the graphic, click outside the selected area.

INTRODUCTION TO MAIL MERGE

You can use the Mail Merge feature to quickly produce a personalized letter for each person on your mailing list.

Performing a mail merge is very useful if you often send the same document, such as an announcement, notification or advertisement, to many people.

A mail merge saves you from having to type the information for a person, such as their name and address, on each letter.

You can also use the Mail Merge feature to print a mailing label for each person on your mailing list. You can use mailing labels on items such as envelopes and packages. Using the Mail Merge feature to create labels saves you from having to type each label individually.

Whether you use the Mail Merge feature to produce personalized letters or print mailing labels, the Mail Merge Helper will guide you through the steps of performing a mail merge.

STEP 1 Create a Main Document

The first step in performing a mail merge is to create a main document. A main document is a letter you want to send to each person on your mailing list. You can write the main document as if you are sending the document to one person.

You should carefully review the main document to make sure it is clearly written and does not contain any spelling or grammar errors. Remember that the main document will be read by every person on your mailing list.

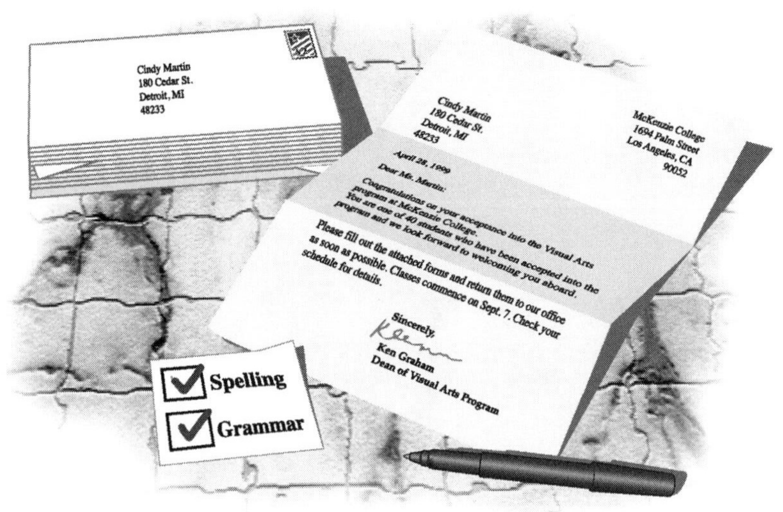

STEP 2 Create a Data Source

Once you have created a main document, you must create a data source. A data source contains the information that changes in each letter, such as the name and address of each person on your mailing list. Make sure you plan ahead and determine the information you want the data source to contain.

A data source is made up of fields and records. A field is a specific category of information. Each field has a name, such as LastName or City. A record is all the information for one person on your mailing list.

You only need to create a data source once. After you create a data source, you can use the data source in future mail merges. To use a data source you have previously created, you must open the data source after creating the main document.

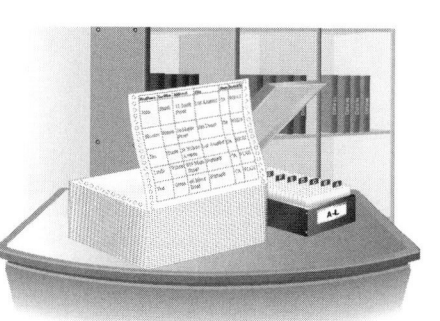

STEP 3 Complete the Main Document

Once you have created the main document and the data source, you can complete the main document. To complete the main document, you must insert special instructions into the main document. These instructions tell Word where to place the personalized information from the data source.

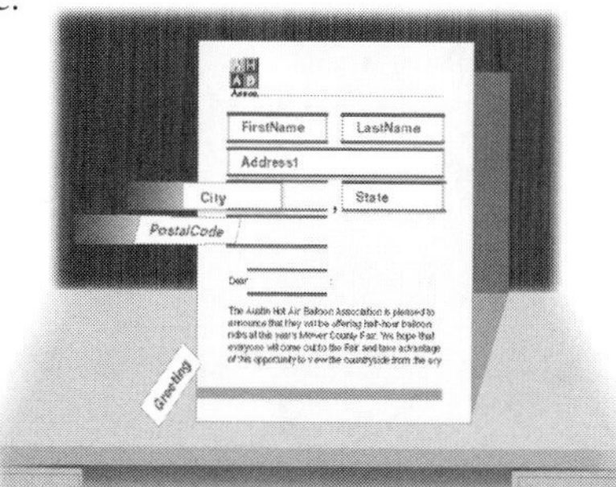

STEP 4 Merge the Main Document and Data Source

After you have completed the main document, you can combine, or merge, the main document and the data source to create a personalized letter for each person on your mailing list. Word replaces the special instructions in the main document with the personalized information from the data source.

CREATE A MAIN DOCUMENT

The main document contains the text that remains the same in each letter you will send to the people on your mailing list. A main document can be a new document or a document you previously created.

When you type the text for a main document, you can enter the personalized information for one person on your mailing list.

You can edit and format the text in a main document as you would edit and format the text in any Word document.

After you finish typing the text for a main document, make sure you carefully review the document. You should check for spelling and grammar errors and review the layout and formatting of the document. Remember that the main document will be read by every person on your mailing list.

Once you have created the main document, you must create a data source or open an existing data source to continue with the mail merge. A data source contains the personalized information that makes each letter unique.

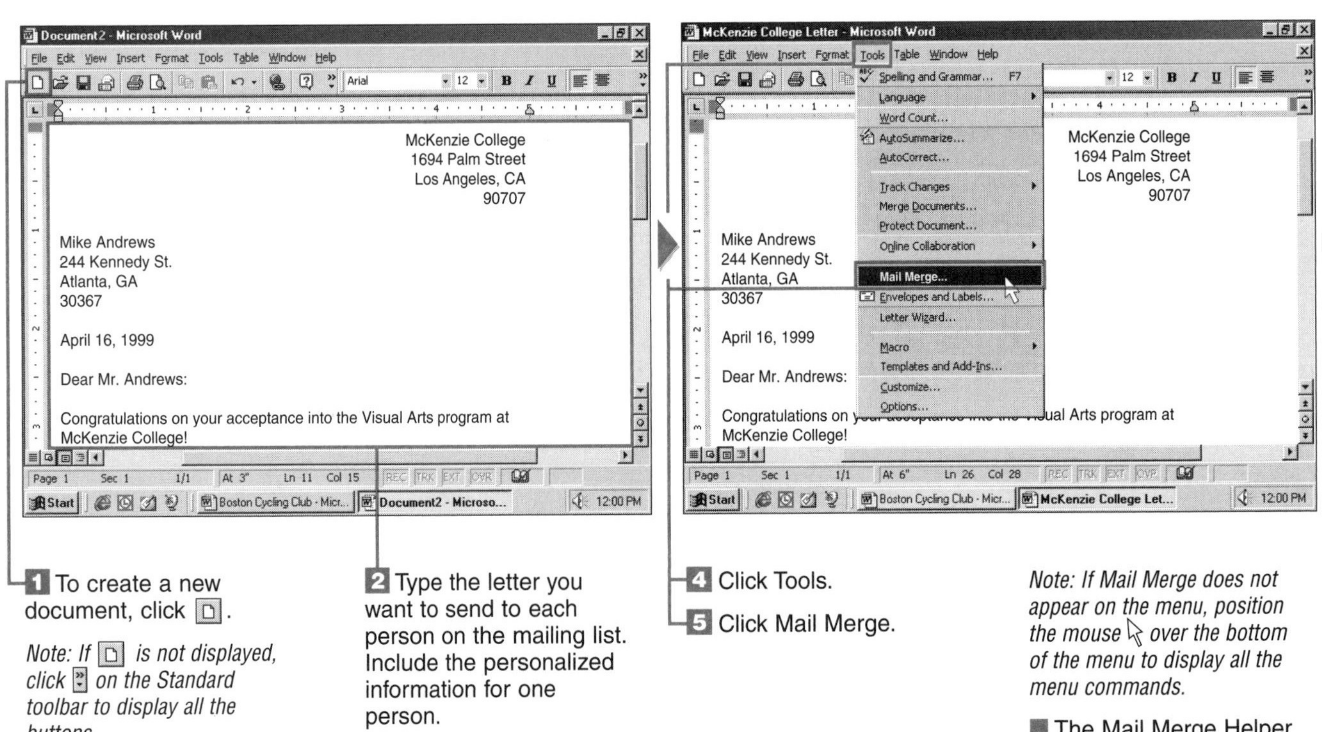

1 To create a new document, click [new document button].

Note: If [new document button] is not displayed, click [More Buttons] on the Standard toolbar to display all the buttons.

2 Type the letter you want to send to each person on the mailing list. Include the personalized information for one person.

3 Save the document. To save a document, see page 32.

4 Click Tools.

5 Click Mail Merge.

Note: If Mail Merge does not appear on the menu, position the mouse over the bottom of the menu to display all the menu commands.

■ The Mail Merge Helper dialog box appears.

TIPS

Can I have Word automatically insert the current date and time into a main document?

✔ Yes. Word will automatically update the information each time you open or print the document. Click where you want the date and time to appear. From the Insert menu, select Date and Time and then choose the format you want to use. Click the Update automatically option (☐ changes to ☑) and then click OK.

Can Word help me create a letter for the main document?

✔ You can use one of Word's templates or wizards to quickly create a letter for the main document. For information on using templates and wizards, see page 44.

I no longer want to use my document for a mail merge. Can I change the main document back to a normal Word document?

✔ Yes. Open the main document you want to change to a normal Word document. From the Tools menu, select Mail Merge. Click Create and then click Restore to Normal Word Document.

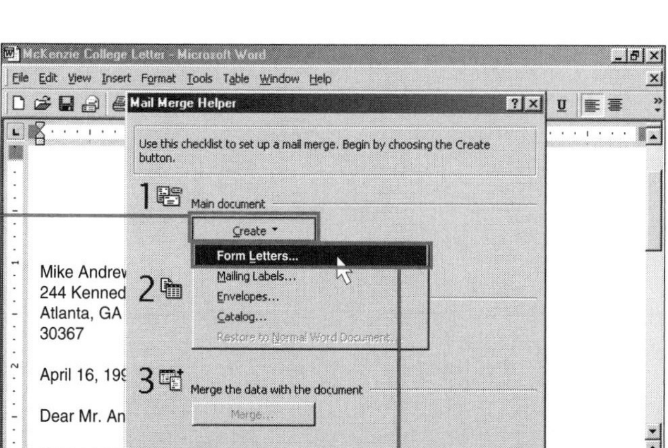

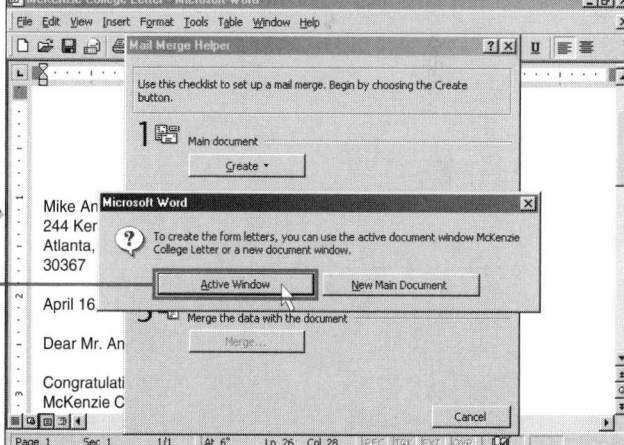

6 Click Create to select the type of main document you want to create.

7 Click Form Letters to create a letter you can send to each person on the mailing list.

■ A dialog box appears.

8 To make the document displayed on the screen the main document, click Active Window.

■ To continue, you must create a data source or open an existing data source. To create a data source, see page 146. To open an existing data source, see page 150.

CREATE A DATA SOURCE

The data source contains the personalized information that changes in each letter, such as the name and address of each person on your mailing list. You only need to create a data source once. To open an existing data source, see page 150.

A data source contains fields and records. A field is a specific category of information in a data source. For example, a field can contain the first names of all the people on your mailing list. A record is a collection of information about one person in a data source. For example, a record can contain the name, address, telephone number and account information for one person.

Make sure you take time to plan and properly set up the data source. Before you create a data source, you should determine the fields you will need.

Word provides a list of field names you can choose from. A field name is a name, such as LastName or City, that is given to a field. You can remove and add field names until you have all the field names you need.

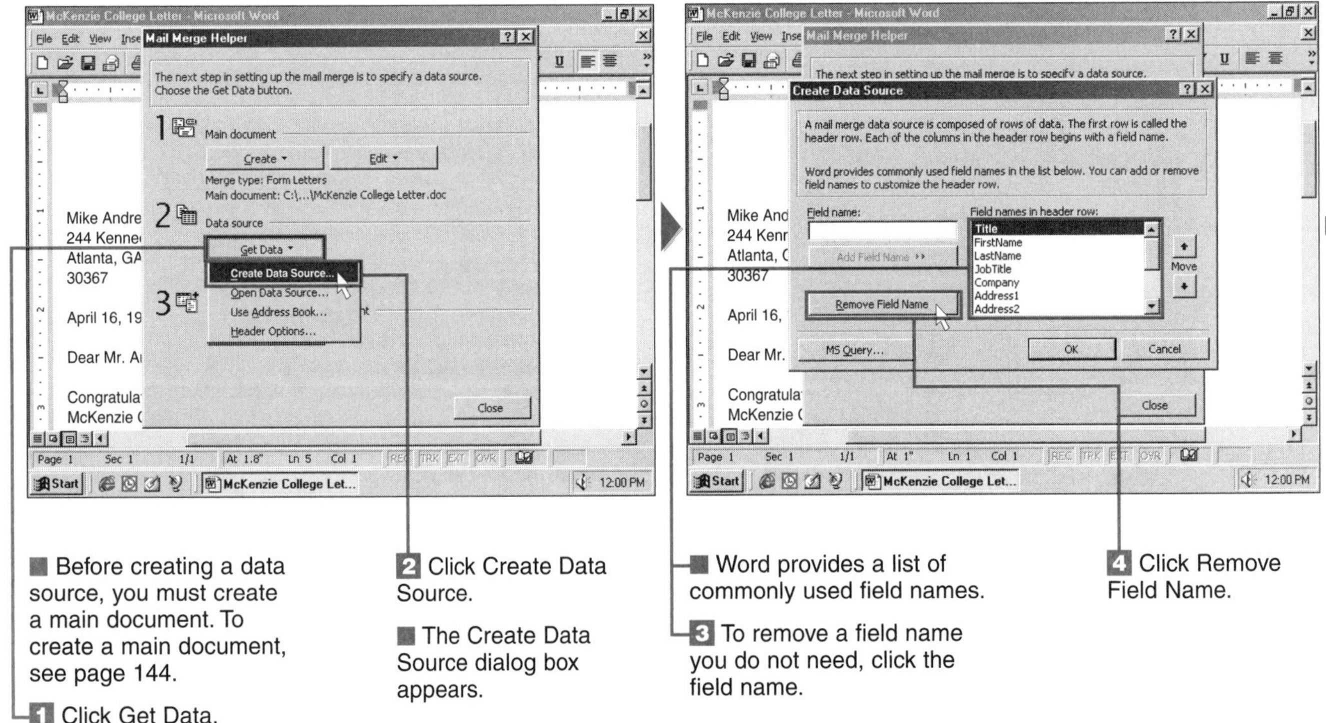

■ Before creating a data source, you must create a main document. To create a main document, see page 144.

1 Click Get Data.

2 Click Create Data Source.

■ The Create Data Source dialog box appears.

■ Word provides a list of commonly used field names.

3 To remove a field name you do not need, click the field name.

4 Click Remove Field Name.

TIPS

How many fields should I use?

✔ You should use as many fields as you need to store the personalized information for your letters. You should break down the information into its smallest parts and use a different field for each part. For example, you should have one field for first names and another for last names, rather than combining this information into one field.

Can I change the order of field names in the Create Data Source dialog box?

✔ To change the order of field names in the dialog box, select the field name you want to move and then click ⬆ or ⬇.

What field names should I use?

✔ You should use field names that accurately describe the contents of the field. Descriptive field names make it easier to work with a data source. For example, field names such as WorkPhone and HomePhone are more descriptive than Phone1 and Phone2. A field name must not contain any spaces and must begin with a letter.

5 To add a field name to the list, double-click this area.

6 Type the field name and then press the Enter key.

7 Remove and add field names until the list displays the field names you want to use.

8 Click OK to continue.

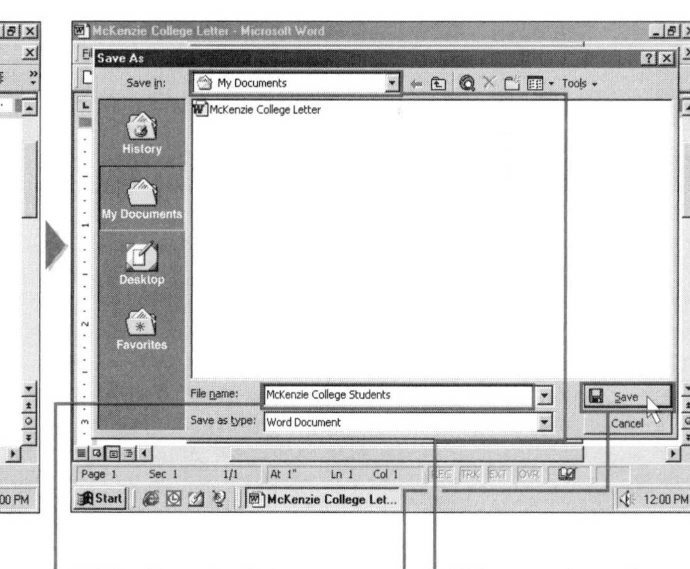

■ The Save As dialog box appears.

9 Type a name for the data source.

■ This area shows the location where Word will save the data source. You can click this area to change the location.

10 Click Save to save the data source.

CONTINUED

CREATE A DATA SOURCE CONTINUED

After you save a data source, you can enter information for each person on your mailing list in the data source. The Data Form dialog box allows you to easily enter information in the data source.

When you finish entering information in the data source, you can have Word display a table containing all the information. The first row of the table displays the field names you chose. Each of the following rows in the table contains the information for one person. Text that does not fit on one line in the table will appear on one line when you print the letters.

Once you have finished creating the data source, you must complete the main document to continue with the mail merge.

You can use the data source you created in future mail merges. Before using a data source again, you should make sure the information is up-to-date. You can open, edit and save a data source as you would any document.

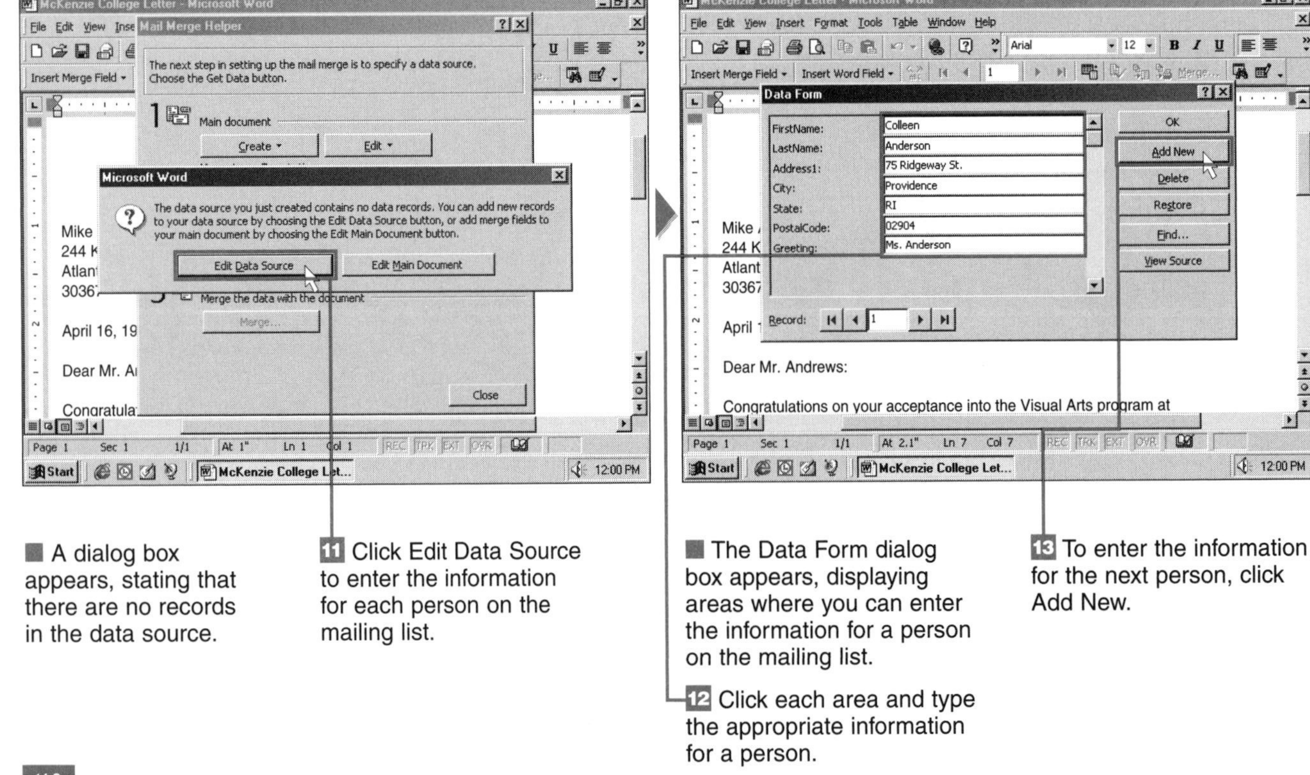

■ A dialog box appears, stating that there are no records in the data source.

11 Click Edit Data Source to enter the information for each person on the mailing list.

■ The Data Form dialog box appears, displaying areas where you can enter the information for a person on the mailing list.

12 Click each area and type the appropriate information for a person.

13 To enter the information for the next person, click Add New.

TIPS

How can I redisplay the Data Form dialog box?

✔ When viewing the data source information in a table, you can click the Data Form button (▣) to redisplay the Data Form dialog box. You can use the dialog box to add or change the information in your data source.

How do I browse through the information I have entered in the Data Form dialog box?

✔ The Record area displays the number of the record that is currently displayed. Click ⏮ to display the first record. Click ◀ to display the previous record. Click ▶ to display the next record. Click ⏭ to display the last record.

How do I delete a record in the Data Form dialog box?

✔ Display the record you want to remove and then click Delete.

Can I add or remove a field from my data source?

✔ When viewing the data source information in a table, you can click the Manage Fields button (▣) to manage your fields. You can then add, remove or rename a field.

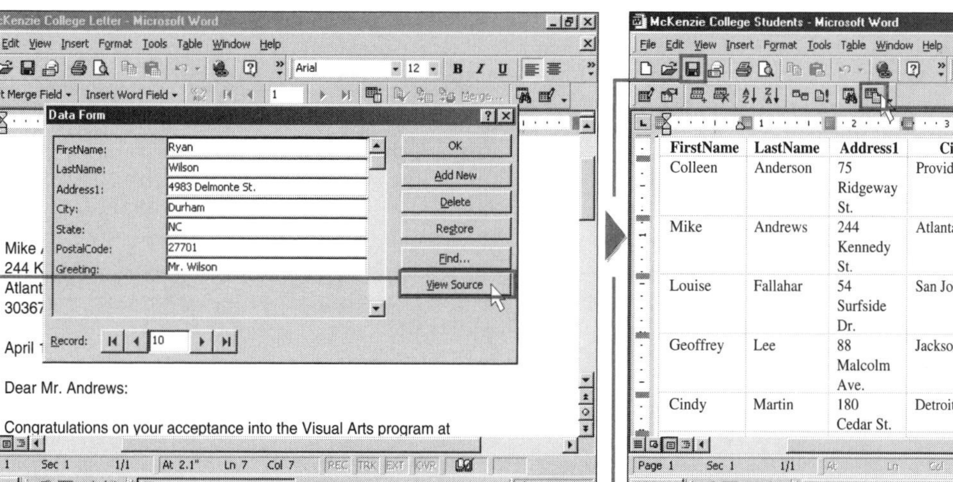

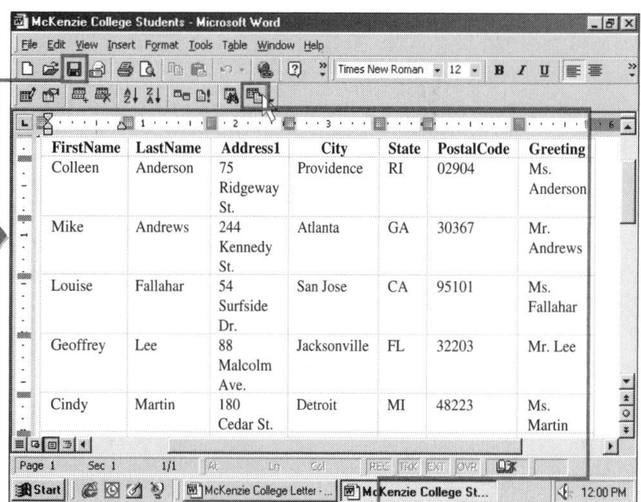

14 Repeat steps 12 and 13 for each person on the mailing list.

15 When you have entered the information for all the people on the mailing list, click View Source.

■ The information you entered appears in a table. The first row in the table contains the field names. Each of the following rows contains the information for one person.

16 Click 💾 to save the information.

Note: If 💾 is not displayed, click » on the Standard toolbar to display all the buttons.

17 Click ▣ to return to the main document.

■ To continue, you must complete the main document. To complete the main document, see page 152.

OPEN AN EXISTING DATA SOURCE

You can use a data source you previously created to perform a mail merge. A data source contains the information that changes in each letter, such as the name and address of each person on your mailing list. You must create a main document before you open an existing data source.

The ability to use one data source for multiple mailings saves you from having to create a new data source each time you perform a mail merge. For example, you can use the same data source for each newsletter, sales brochure and product list you send to your customers.

You should make sure the information in the data source is up-to-date. If a person on your mailing list has changed their address or phone number, you will need to update the information in the data source.

After you open the data source you want to use, you must complete the main document to continue the mail merge.

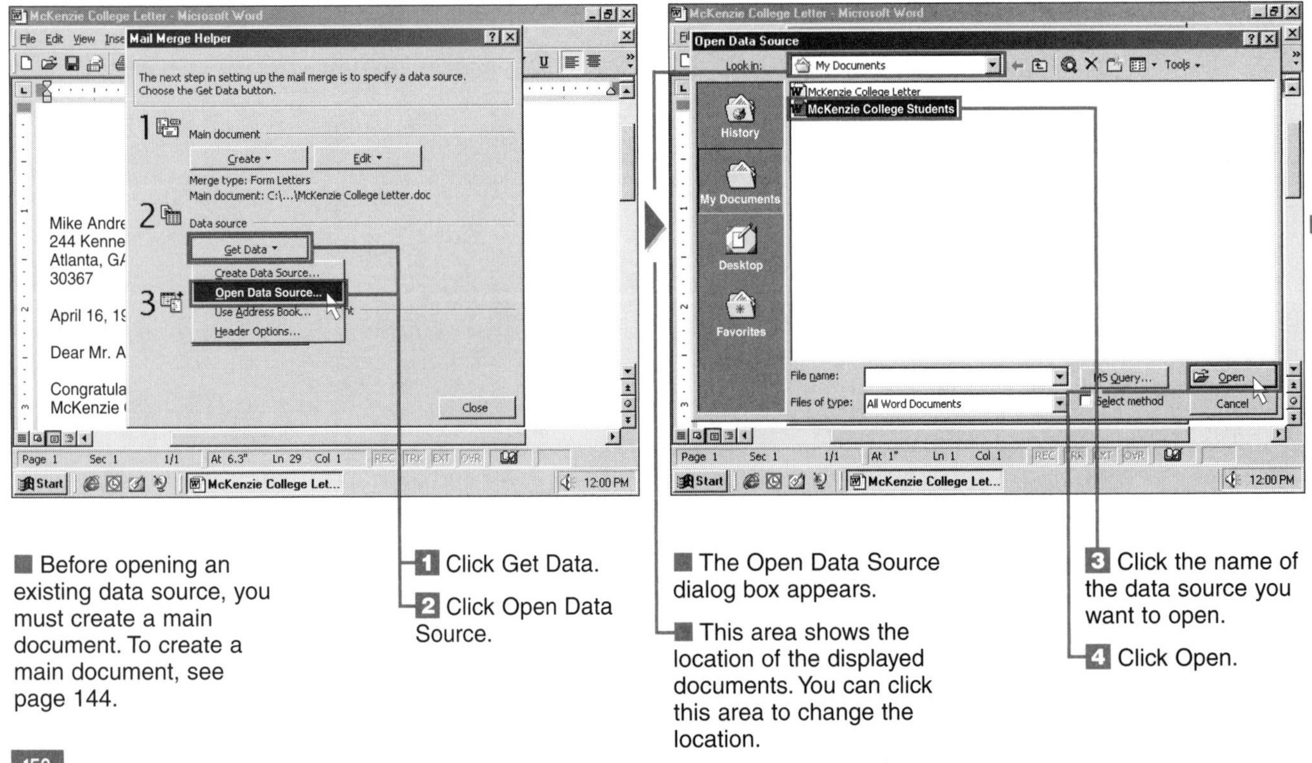

■ Before opening an existing data source, you must create a main document. To create a main document, see page 144.

1 Click Get Data.

2 Click Open Data Source.

■ The Open Data Source dialog box appears.

■ This area shows the location of the displayed documents. You can click this area to change the location.

3 Click the name of the data source you want to open.

4 Click Open.

TIPS

Can Word help me find a data source I previously created?

✔ If you cannot find the data source you want to use, you can have Word search for the data source. For information on finding a document, see page 36.

Can I use my Outlook Address Book as a data source?

✔ Yes. If you have added contacts to your Contacts list in Outlook, the contacts appear in your Outlook Address book. Click Get Data in the Mail Merge Helper dialog box and then click Use Address Book. Select Outlook Address Book and then click OK.

Can I use a file I created in another Office program as my data source?

✔ You can use an Excel worksheet or Access database as your data source. In the Open Data Source dialog box, click the Files of type area, select the type of file you want to use and then click Open. You can then select the Excel worksheet or the table in the Access database that contains the data you want to use.

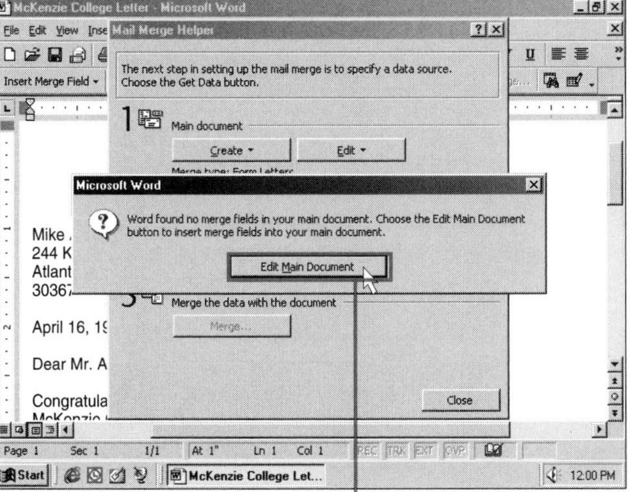

■ A dialog box appears.

5 Click Edit Main Document to return to the main document.

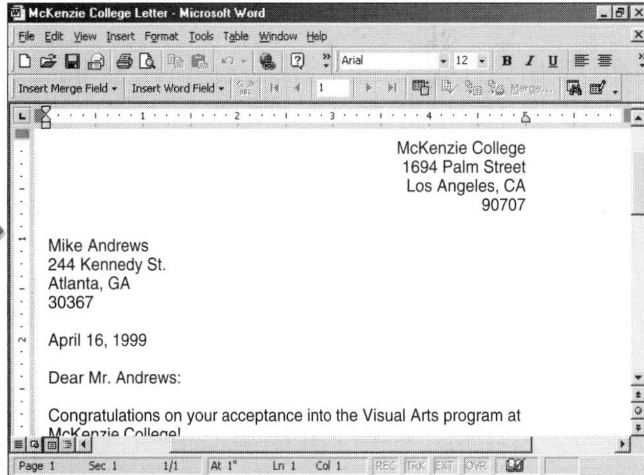

■ The main document appears on the screen.

■ To continue, you must complete the main document. To complete the main document, see page 152.

COMPLETE THE MAIN DOCUMENT

To complete the main document, you must insert special instructions into the document. These instructions tell Word where to place the personalized information from the data source that changes for each letter.

The instructions you insert into the main document are called merge fields. A merge field is a specific category of information in a data source, such as FirstName, City or State. The available merge fields are the same as the field names you specified when you created the data source.

You can insert as many merge fields as you need. The location of a merge field in the main document indicates where the corresponding information from the data source will appear when you print the letters. In the main document, a merge field begins with « and ends with ».

After you complete the main document, you can merge the main document and the data source to create your letters.

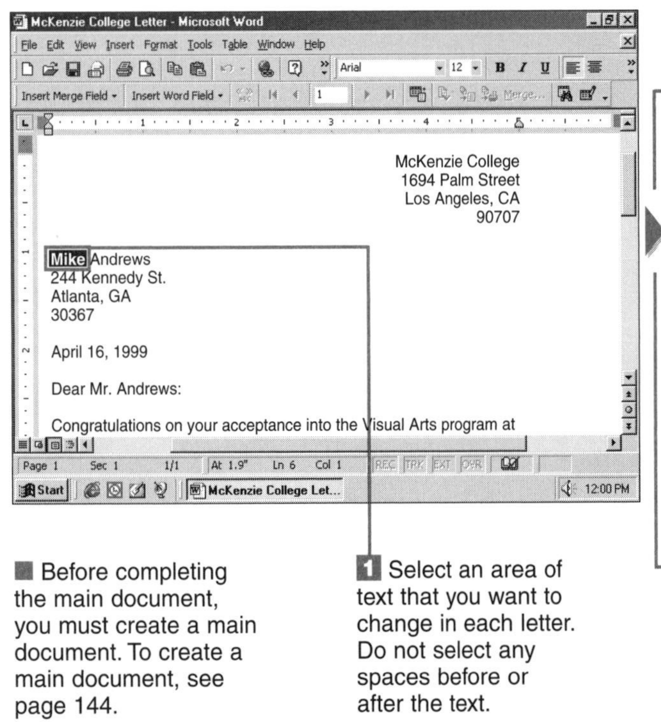

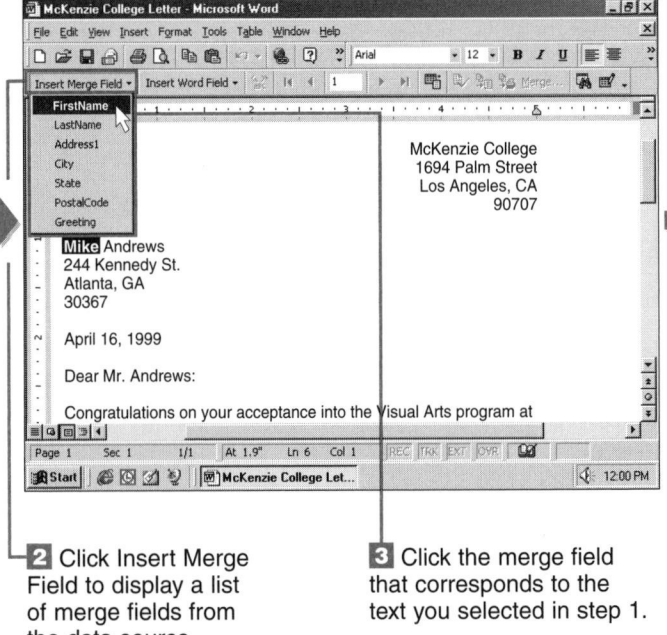

■ Before completing the main document, you must create a main document. To create a main document, see page 144.

1 Select an area of text that you want to change in each letter. Do not select any spaces before or after the text.

2 Click Insert Merge Field to display a list of merge fields from the data source.

Note: The merge fields that appear depend on the field names you specified when you created the data source.

3 Click the merge field that corresponds to the text you selected in step 1.

TIPS

How do I delete a merge field I accidentally inserted?

✔ You can delete a merge field as you would delete any text. Drag the mouse I over the merge field to select the field and then press the Delete key.

Can I format a merge field?

✔ You can format a merge field as you would format text in any document. When you merge the main document with the data source, the personalized information in each letter displays the formatting you applied to the merge field.

Can I test my main document and data source for errors before performing a mail merge?

✔ Yes. For example, if you have edited a field name in the data source after inserting merge fields into the main document, the merge field and field name may no longer match. Click the Check for Errors button (). Then select the Simulate the merge and report errors in a new document option (○ changes to ⦿) and click OK.

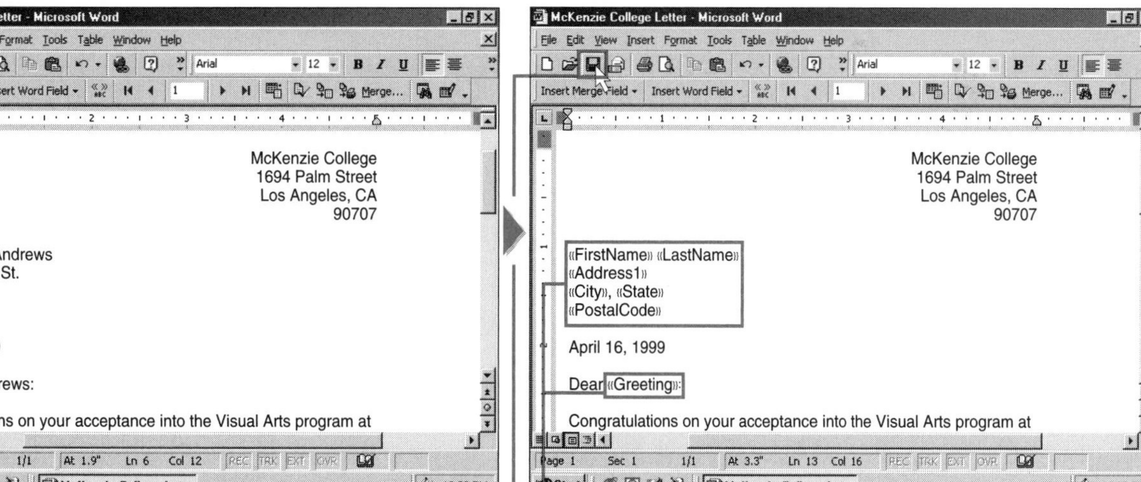

■ The merge field replaces the text you selected.

4 Repeat steps 1 to 3 for every area of text you want to change in each letter.

5 Click to save the document.

Note: If is not displayed, click » on the Standard toolbar to display all the buttons.

■ To continue, you must merge the main document and the data source. To merge the main document and the data source, see page 154.

MERGE THE MAIN DOCUMENT AND DATA SOURCE

After you complete the main document, you can preview how your letters will look when you merge the main document and the data source. Previewing lets you temporarily replace the merge fields in the main document with the information for a person on your mailing list.

You should preview the merged letters to make sure they look the way you want. This can help you find and correct any errors before you waste time and money printing the letters for every person on your mailing list.

After you preview the letters to ensure there are no errors, you can combine the main document and the data source to create a personalized letter for each person on your mailing list.

To conserve hard drive space, do not save the merged document. You can easily recreate the merged document at any time by merging the main document and the data source again.

You can print the personalized letters in the merged document as you would print any Word document.

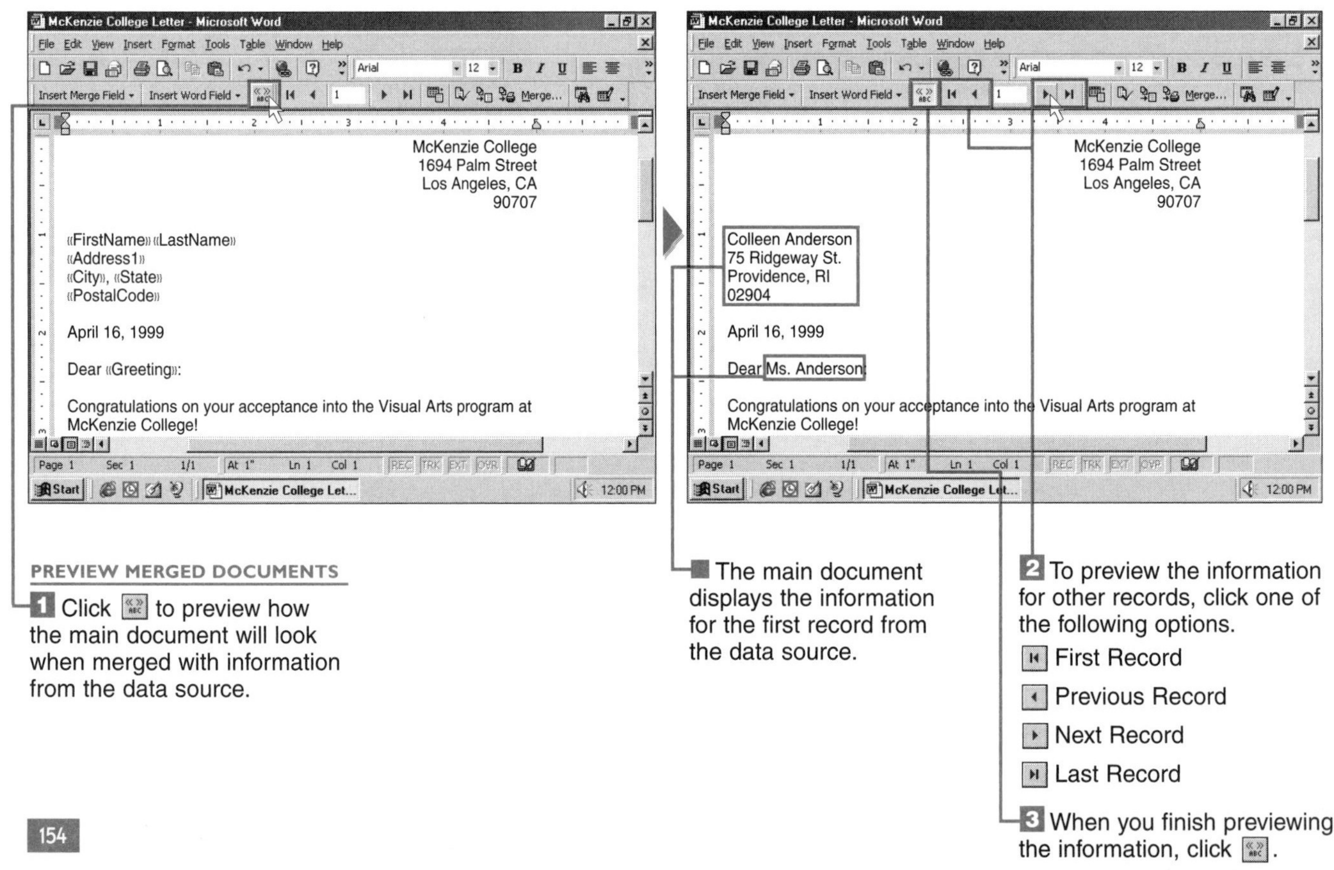

PREVIEW MERGED DOCUMENTS

1 Click [icon] to preview how the main document will look when merged with information from the data source.

■ The main document displays the information for the first record from the data source.

2 To preview the information for other records, click one of the following options.

[icon] First Record

[icon] Previous Record

[icon] Next Record

[icon] Last Record

3 When you finish previewing the information, click [icon].

TIPS

When previewing merged documents, how can I quickly display the information for a record of interest?

✔ Double-click the Go to Record area to the right of the Previous Record button (◂) and type the number of the record you want to display. Then press the Enter key.

Is it necessary to create a merged document on my computer before printing?

✔ No. Click the Merge to Printer button to merge the main document and the data source directly to the printer.

Can I e-mail the merged documents to the people on my mailing list?

✔ If your data source includes a field containing e-mail addresses, you can e-mail the merged documents to people on your mailing list. Click the Merge button. In the Merge dialog box, click the Merge to area and select Electronic mail. Then click Setup. Click the Data field with Mail/Fax address area and select the field containing e-mail addresses in your data source. Click the Mail message subject line area, type a subject for the messages and click OK. Then click Merge to e-mail the merged documents.

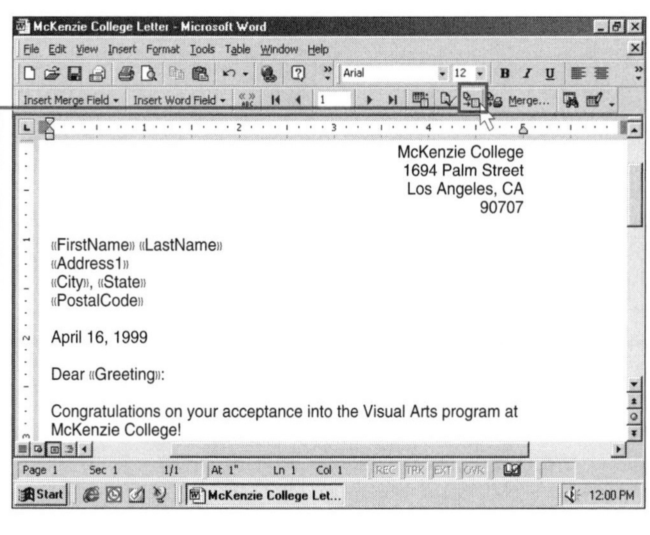

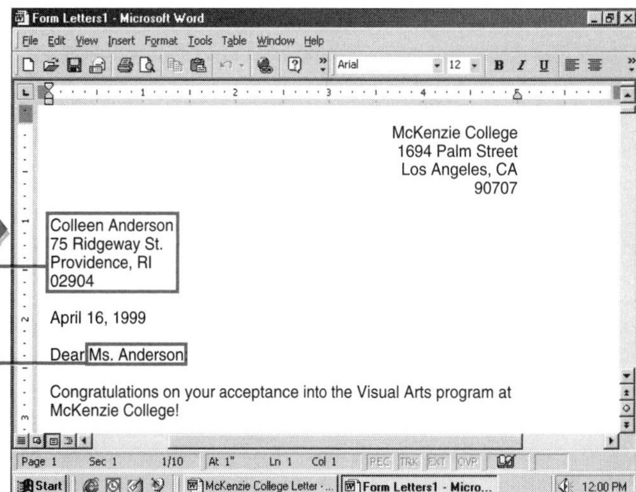

MERGE DOCUMENTS

1 Click the Merge to New Document button to merge the main document and the data source.

■ A new document appears, displaying a personalized letter for each person on the mailing list.

■ Word replaced the merge fields in the main document with the corresponding information from the data source.

■ You can edit the letters as you would edit any document. You may wish to add personalized comments to some letters.

USING MAIL MERGE TO PRINT LABELS

You can use the Mail Merge feature to print a label for every person on your mailing list. You can use labels for addressing envelopes and packages, labeling file folders and creating name tags.

You can use the information from an existing data source to print labels. A data source contains the personalized information that changes on each label, such as the name and address of each person on your mailing list. You should make sure the information in the data source you will use is up-to-date.

Before you begin, make sure you consult the manual that came with your printer to determine if the printer can print labels. You should also consult the manual to find out which label products the printer can use.

Word can print on many popular label products and label types. You can check your label packaging to determine which label product and type of label you are using.

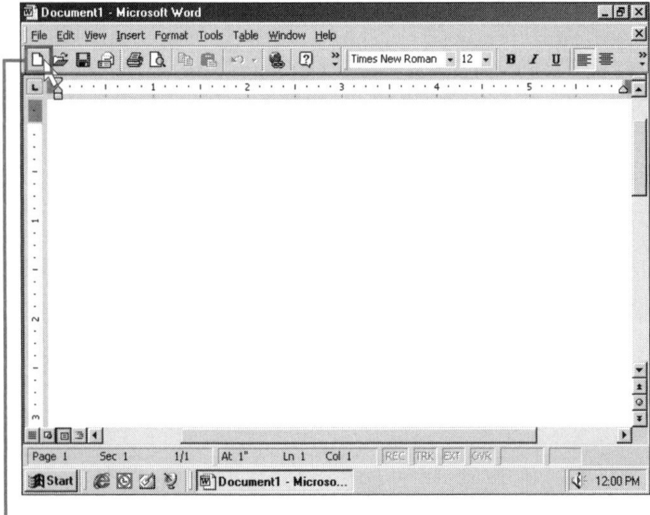

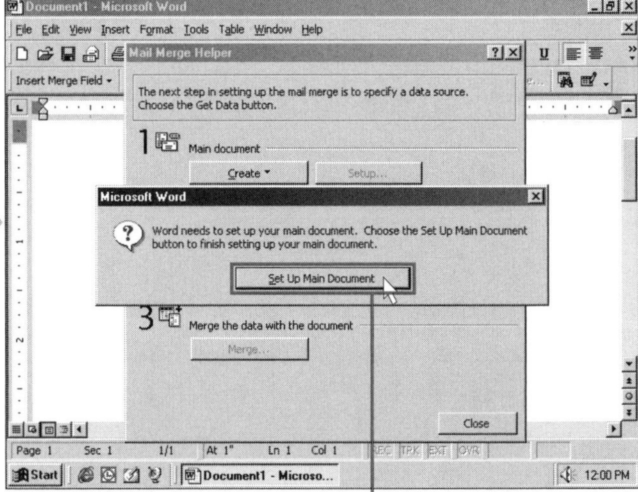

1 Click to create a new document.

Note: If is not displayed, click on the Standard toolbar to display all the buttons.

2 To tell Word that you want to create labels, perform steps 4 to 8 starting on page 144, except select Mailing Labels in step 7.

3 To open an existing data source, perform steps 1 to 4 on page 150.

4 Click Set Up Main Document to set up the labels.

■ The Label Options dialog box appears.

TIPS

Should I specify the kind of printer I am using?

✔ You should specify the kind of printer you are using so Word can display the appropriate label products and label types. In the Label Options dialog box, select the Dot matrix or Laser and ink jet option (○ changes to ⦿).

Can I create my own labels without using the Mail Merge feature?

✔ Yes. For information on printing labels without using the Mail Merge feature, see page 114.

Can I specify where I want Word to look for labels in my printer?

✔ If you are using a laser or ink jet printer, you can specify where you want Word to look for the labels. This is useful if you want to feed the labels into your printer manually or if your printer has more than one tray. In the Label Options dialog box, click the Tray area to specify where you want Word to look for the labels.

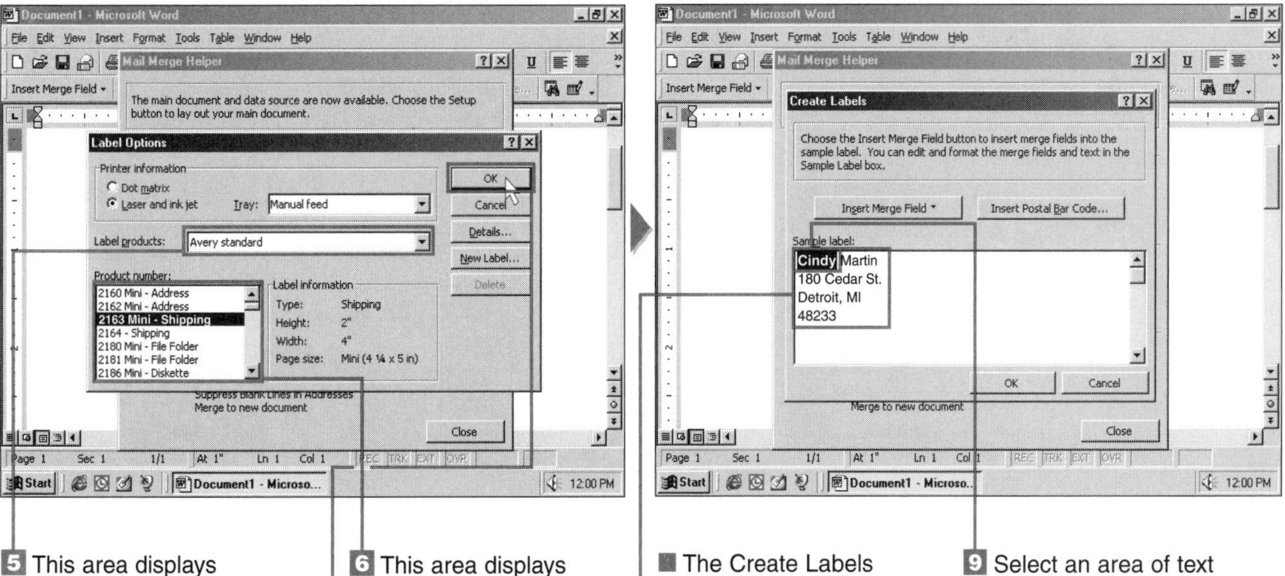

5 This area displays the label product you will use to print the labels. You can click this area to select a different label product.

6 This area displays the types of labels for the current label product. Click the type of label you want to use.

7 Click OK to continue.

■ The Create Labels dialog box appears.

8 Type a label for one person on the mailing list.

9 Select an area of text that you want to change in each label. Do not select any spaces before or after the text.

CONTINUED

USING MAIL MERGE TO PRINT LABELS CONTINUED

You must insert special instructions, called merge fields, into the labels to tell Word where to place the personalized information from the data source that changes in each label. A merge field is a specific category of information in a data source, such as FirstName, City or State. The available merge fields depend on the field names you specified when you created the data source.

The location of a merge field in a label indicates where the corresponding information from the data source will appear when you print the labels. You should make sure the information in the data source is not too long to fit on the labels when they are printed.

When you merge the labels and the data source, Word replaces the merge fields in the labels with the corresponding information from the data source. This creates a personalized label for each person on your mailing list. You can then print the merged labels.

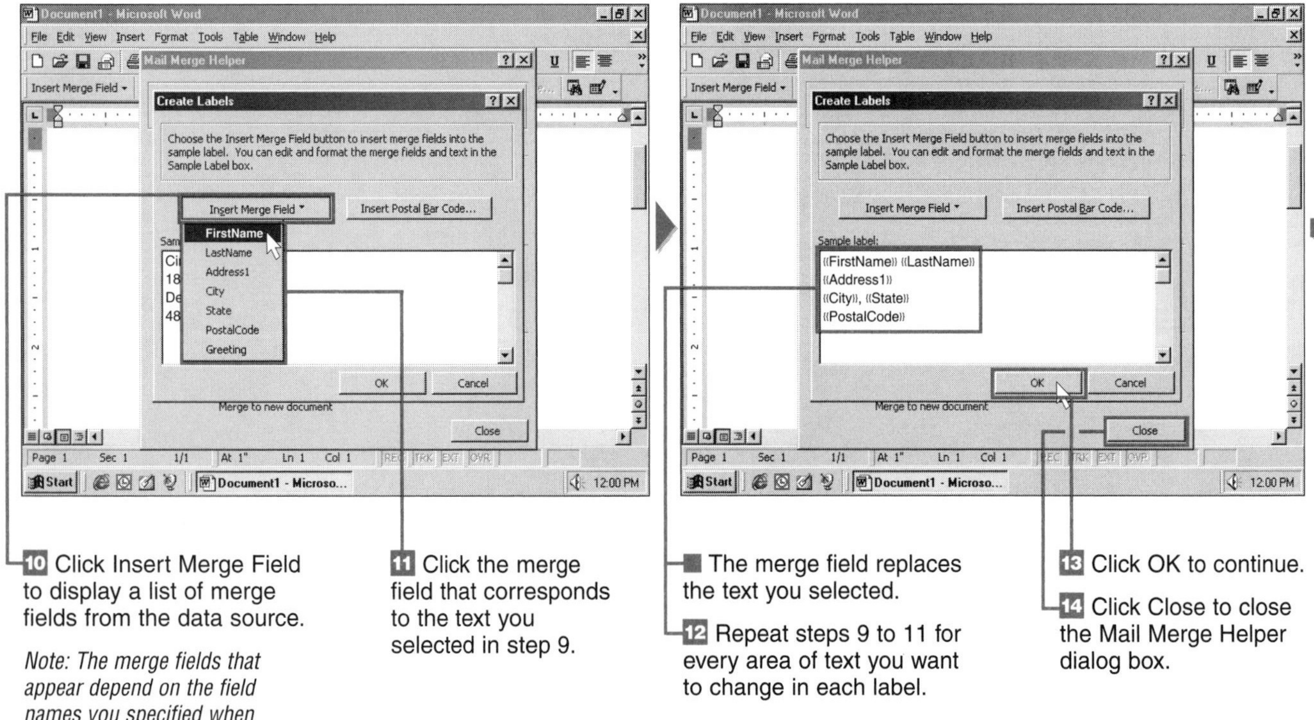

10 Click Insert Merge Field to display a list of merge fields from the data source.

Note: The merge fields that appear depend on the field names you specified when you created the data source.

11 Click the merge field that corresponds to the text you selected in step 9.

■ The merge field replaces the text you selected.

12 Repeat steps 9 to 11 for every area of text you want to change in each label.

13 Click OK to continue.

14 Click Close to close the Mail Merge Helper dialog box.

TIPS

Can I add bar codes to mailing labels?

✔ You can add bar codes that will help speed the delivery of your mail in the United States. In the Create Labels dialog box, click the Insert Postal Bar Code button. Click the Merge field with ZIP code area, select the field that contains zip codes and then click OK. The bar codes will appear after you merge the labels.

Can I preview the labels before I merge them with the data source?

✔ Yes. Click the View Merged Data button (   ) to preview the labels. To once again view the merge fields in the labels, click the button again.

Should I save the merged labels?

✔ To conserve space on your computer's hard drive, do not save the merged labels. You can easily recreate the merged labels at any time. To do so, open the label document you saved in step 15 below. Then click the Merge to New Document button (   ).

■ The labels appear, displaying the merge fields you selected.

15 Save the document. To save a document, see page 32.

16 Click   to merge the labels and the data source.

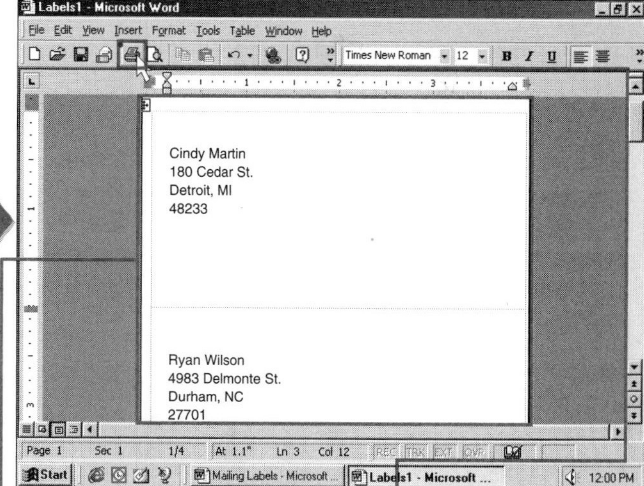

■ A new document appears, displaying a personalized label for each person on the mailing list.

■ You can edit the labels as you would edit any document.

17 Click   to print the labels.

Note: If   is not displayed, click   on the Standard toolbar to display all the buttons.

SECTION III

1) GETTING STARTED

2) EDIT WORKSHEETS

USING EXCEL

3) WORK WITH FORMULAS AND FUNCTIONS

4) FORMAT WORKSHEETS

5) PRINT WORKSHEETS

6) WORK WITH MULTIPLE WORKSHEETS

7) WORK WITH CHARTS

8) WORK WITH GRAPHICS

9) MANAGE DATA IN A LIST

10) USING MACROS

INTRODUCTION TO EXCEL

Excel is a spreadsheet program that helps you efficiently work with numerical data. You can use Excel to perform calculations, analyze data and present information. Excel can help you manage your business and personal finances.

An Excel file is called a workbook. A workbook contains several worksheets that you can use to store data. The worksheets in a workbook allow you to keep related data together.

For more information on Excel, you can visit the following Web site: www.microsoft.com/excel

Entering and Editing Data

Excel lets you efficiently enter and edit data in a worksheet. Excel can help you quickly enter data by completing a series of numbers or text for you. For example, Excel can complete a series of the days of the week for you.

After you enter data in a worksheet, you can add new data, delete data or move data to a new location. You can also check the text in a worksheet for spelling errors.

Excel remembers the last changes you made to a worksheet, so you can undo changes you regret.

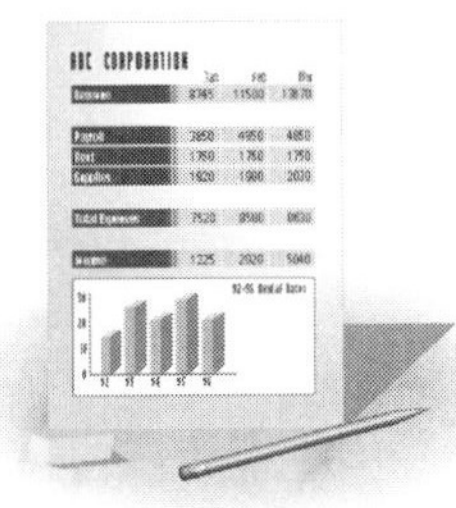

Formulas and Functions

Formulas and functions help you perform calculations and analyze data in a worksheet. Functions are ready-to-use formulas that let you perform specialized calculations on your data.

You can save time by copying a formula or function to other cells in a worksheet. Excel will automatically change the cell references in the new formulas or functions for you.

If you change a number used in a formula or function, Excel will automatically redo the calculation and display the new result.

Formatting Worksheets

Excel includes many formatting features that can help you change the appearance of a worksheet. You can change the width of columns and the height of rows to better fit the data in a worksheet. You can also add borders or color to cells.

Excel's formatting features can also help you enhance the data in a worksheet. The bold, italic and underline styles can emphasize important data. You can also make data in a worksheet easier to read by changing the font and size of the data or by changing the appearance of numbers to display formats such as currency or percent.

Printing

You can print a paper copy of an Excel worksheet. Excel lets you preview a worksheet on the screen to see how it will appear on a printed page.

You can add a header or footer to print additional information, such as your name or the date, at the top or bottom of each page. You can also specify how you want your data to appear on a page. You can adjust the margins for the worksheet or change the size of the printed data so it will fit on a specific number of pages.

Working With Worksheets

If you use more than one worksheet to store data in a workbook, you can switch between the worksheets to view and work with the data on different worksheets.

Excel makes it easy to change the order of worksheets or insert a new worksheet into a workbook. You can also rename a worksheet with a descriptive name to help you later identify the contents of the worksheet.

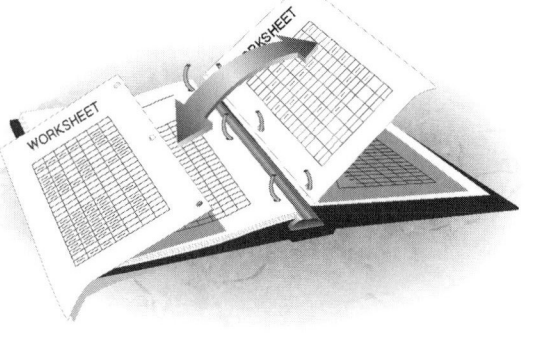

Charts

Excel helps you create colorful charts from your worksheet data. Charts can help better illustrate the data in a worksheet. You can choose from many chart types, such as Bar, Line, Area and Pie charts. If you change the data in the worksheet, Excel will automatically update the chart to display the changes. You can move and resize a chart on a worksheet to suit your needs.

Graphics

Excel includes many graphics, such as text boxes, text effects and AutoShapes, that you can use to enhance the appearance of worksheets and charts. AutoShapes include simple shapes, such as ovals and rectangles, and more complex shapes, such as stars and arrows.

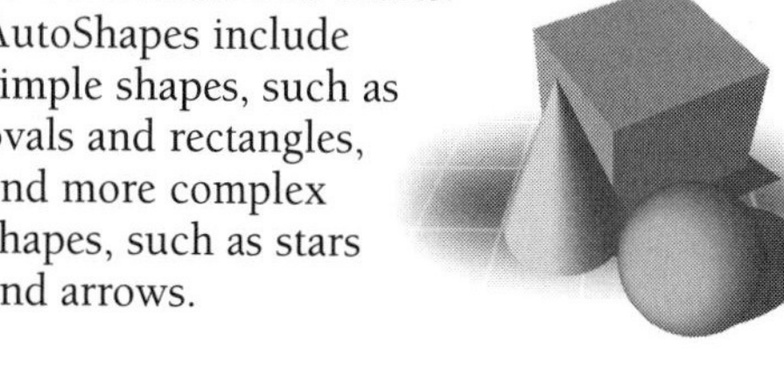

Managing Data in a List

Excel provides powerful tools that allow you to manage and analyze a large collection of data, such as a mailing or product list. After you organize data into a list, you can sort the data or filter the data to display only the data that meets certain criteria. You can also add subtotals to the list to help summarize the data.

START EXCEL

Excel is a spreadsheet program that helps you organize, analyze and attractively present data. You can use Excel to present data such as price lists, sales figures and budgets.

When you start Excel, a blank worksheet appears on your screen. The basic unit of a worksheet is called a cell. Cells store the data, such as text and numbers, you enter into a worksheet.

Once you enter the data for a worksheet, you can change the appearance of the worksheet, perform calculations on the data and produce a paper copy of the worksheet.

The first time you start Excel, the Office Assistant appears on your screen. The Office Assistant can provide you with information to help you perform tasks and understand the features Excel offers. For more information on the Office Assistant, see page 16.

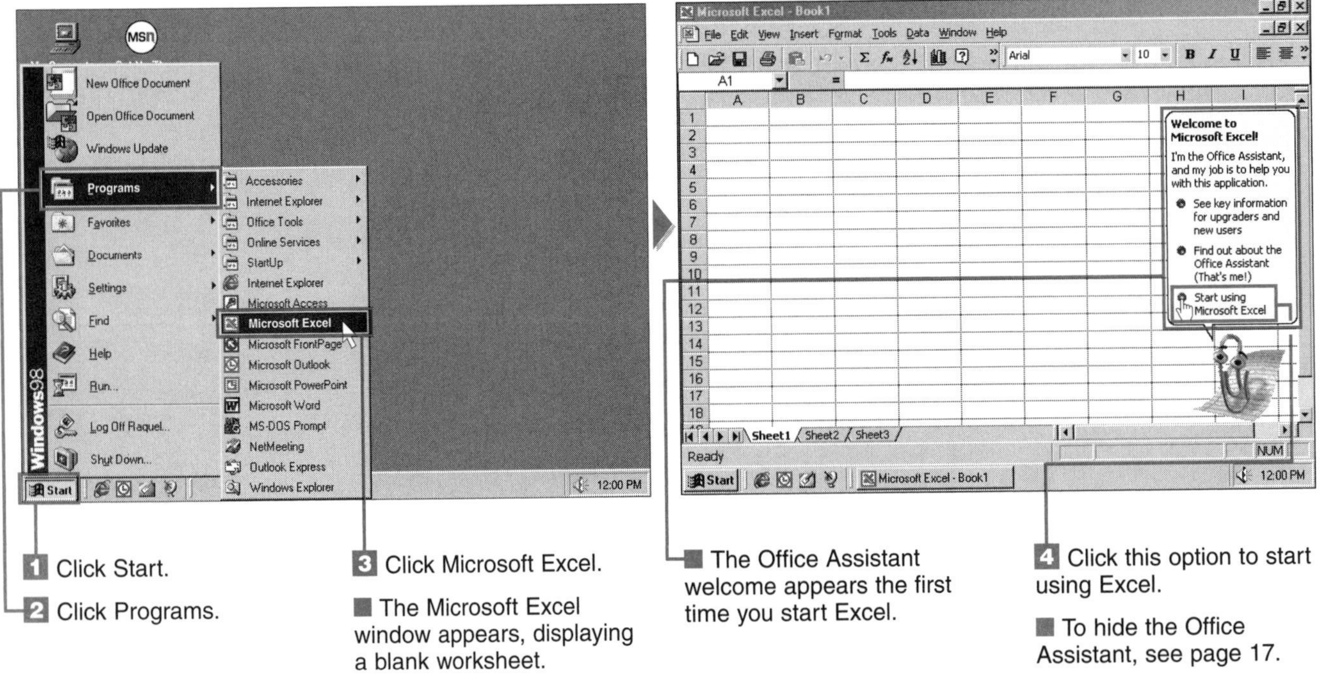

1 Click Start.

2 Click Programs.

3 Click Microsoft Excel.

■ The Microsoft Excel window appears, displaying a blank worksheet.

■ The Office Assistant welcome appears the first time you start Excel.

4 Click this option to start using Excel.

■ To hide the Office Assistant, see page 17.

THE EXCEL SCREEN

The Excel screen displays several items to help you perform tasks efficiently.

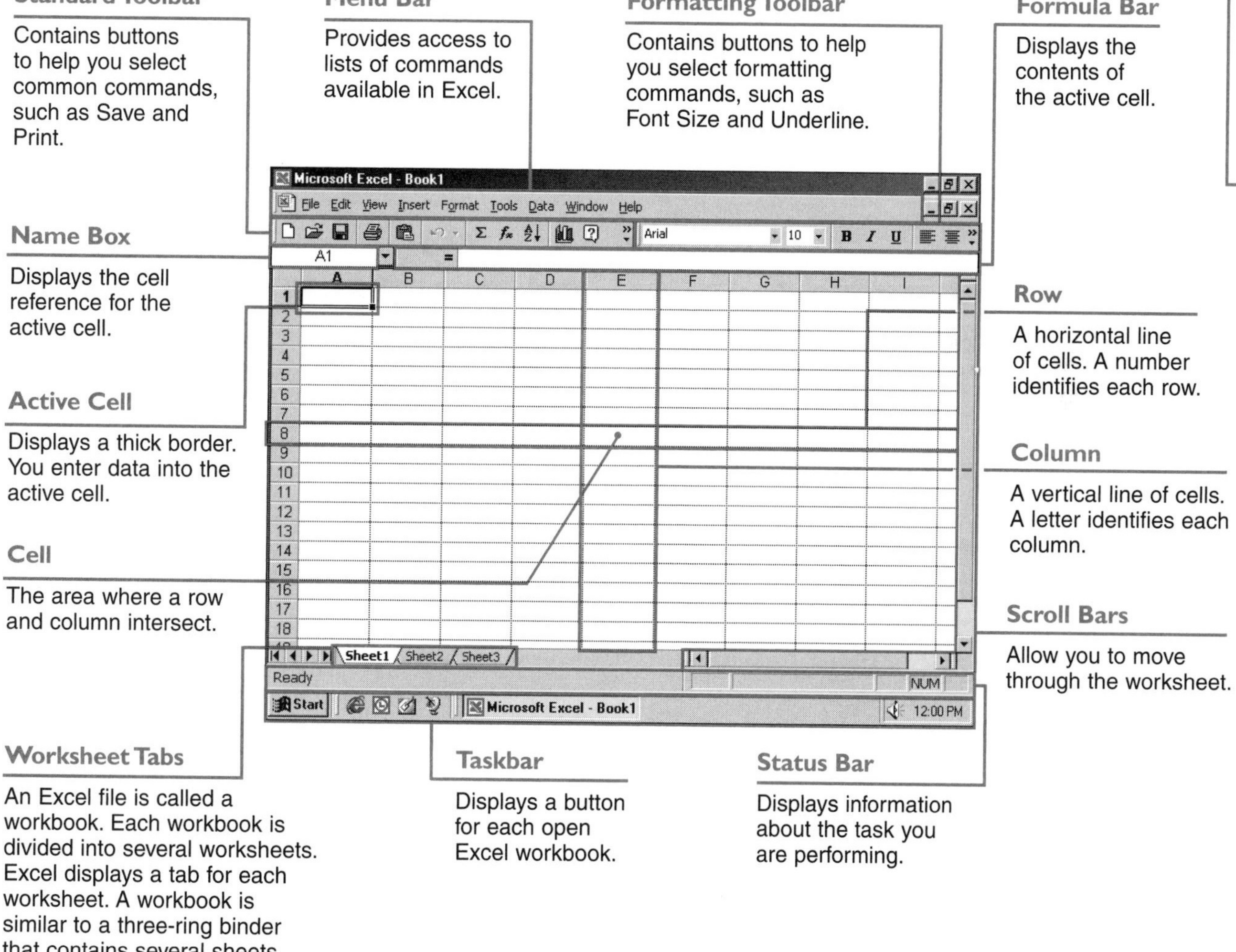

Standard Toolbar
Contains buttons to help you select common commands, such as Save and Print.

Menu Bar
Provides access to lists of commands available in Excel.

Formatting Toolbar
Contains buttons to help you select formatting commands, such as Font Size and Underline.

Formula Bar
Displays the contents of the active cell.

Name Box
Displays the cell reference for the active cell.

Active Cell
Displays a thick border. You enter data into the active cell.

Cell
The area where a row and column intersect.

Row
A horizontal line of cells. A number identifies each row.

Column
A vertical line of cells. A letter identifies each column.

Scroll Bars
Allow you to move through the worksheet.

Worksheet Tabs
An Excel file is called a workbook. Each workbook is divided into several worksheets. Excel displays a tab for each worksheet. A workbook is similar to a three-ring binder that contains several sheets of paper.

Taskbar
Displays a button for each open Excel workbook.

Status Bar
Displays information about the task you are performing.

ENTER DATA

You can enter data, such as text, numbers and dates, into your worksheet quickly and easily.

Excel automatically left aligns text and right aligns numbers and dates you enter in cells.

The data you type appears in the active cell and in the formula bar at the top of your worksheet.

Excel may not be able to display all of the text or numbers you type. The amount of data Excel can display in a cell depends on the width of the column and whether the cell to the right contains data. To change the width of a column, see page 216.

Excel compares the text you type to text in other cells in the column. If the first few letters you type match the text in another cell in the column, Excel may complete the text for you. This can save you time when you need to enter the same text into many cells in a column.

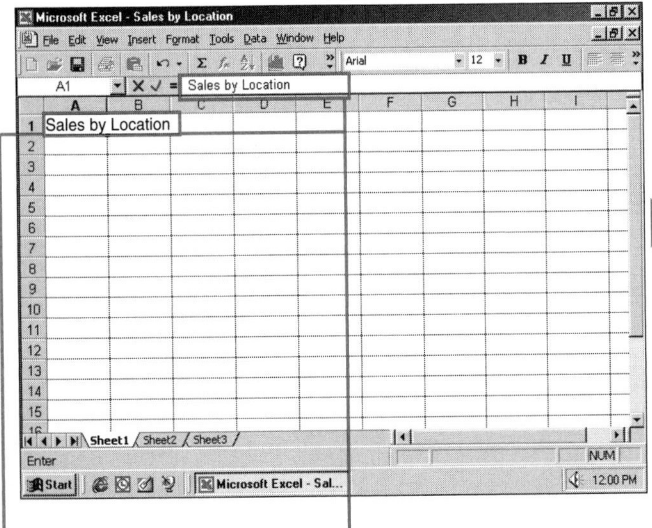

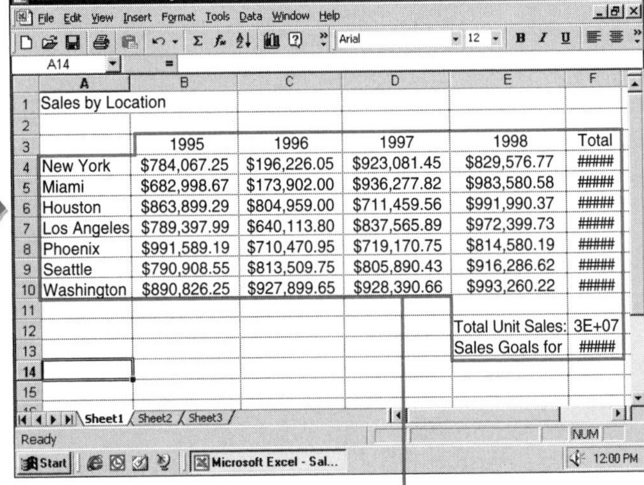

1 Click the cell where you want to enter data. Then type the data.

Note: In this example, the size of data was changed from 10 point to 12 point to make the worksheet easier to read.

■ If you make a typing mistake, press the Backspace key to remove the incorrect data. Then type the correct data.

■ The data you type appears in the active cell and the formula bar.

2 Press the Enter key to enter the data and move down one cell.

Note: To enter the data and move one cell in any direction, press the ↑, ←, ↓ or → key.

3 Repeat steps 1 and 2 until you finish entering all the data.

TIPS

Can I use the numeric keypad on my keyboard to enter numbers?

✔ Yes. Using the numeric keypad can help you quickly enter numbers. When NUM appears at the bottom of your screen, you can use the numeric keypad to enter numbers. To turn the display of NUM on or off, press the Num Lock key.

Can I enter numbers as text?

✔ When you enter a number that you want Excel to treat as text, such as a phone number or Zip code, type an apostrophe (') before the number. This will prevent Excel from trying to use the number in a calculation.

How can I quickly enter the date into a cell?

✔ Press the Ctrl+; (Semicolon) keys to enter the current date into the active cell.

How do I enter the same data into several cells at once?

✔ Select the cells where you want to enter the data. Type the data and then press the Ctrl+Enter keys.

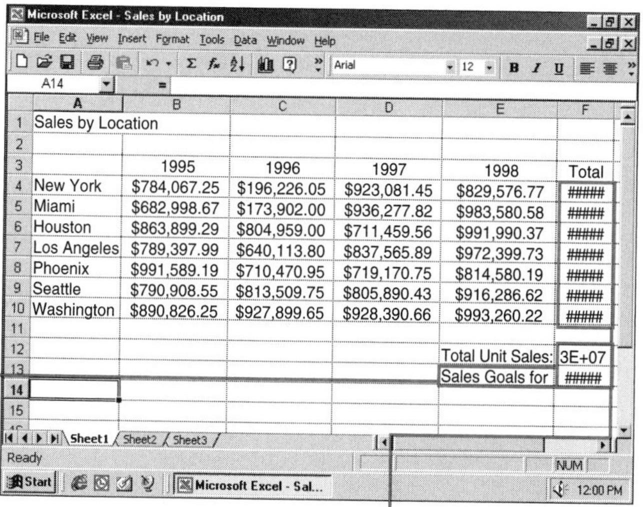

■ If text is too long to fit in a cell, the text will spill into the cell to the right. If the cell to the right contains data, Excel will display as much of the text as the column width will allow.

■ If a number is too long to fit in a cell, Excel will display the number in scientific form or as number signs (#).

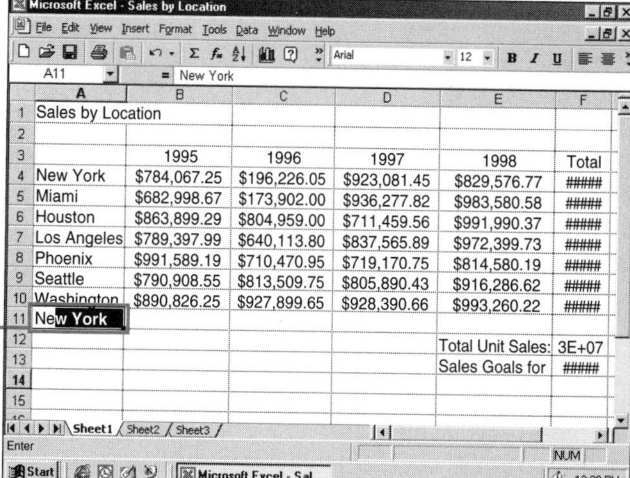

AUTOCOMPLETE

■ If the first few letters you type match another cell in the column, Excel may complete the text for you.

1 To enter the text Excel provides, press the Enter key.

Note: To enter different text, continue typing.

MOVE THROUGH A WORKSHEET

If your worksheet contains a lot of data, your computer screen may not be able to display all the data at once. You must move through your worksheet to view other areas.

You can use a scroll bar to scroll up and down or left and right. The location of the scroll box on the scroll bar indicates which area of the worksheet you are viewing.

When you drag a scroll box, Excel displays a yellow box containing the number of the row that will appear at the top of the screen or the letter of the column that will appear at the left of the screen.

Scrolling through your worksheet does not change the location of the active cell. If you begin entering data when the active cell is not displayed on your screen, Excel will automatically display the part of the worksheet containing the active cell. This allows you to see the data you enter.

You can use the mouse or keyboard to make any cell in your worksheet the active cell.

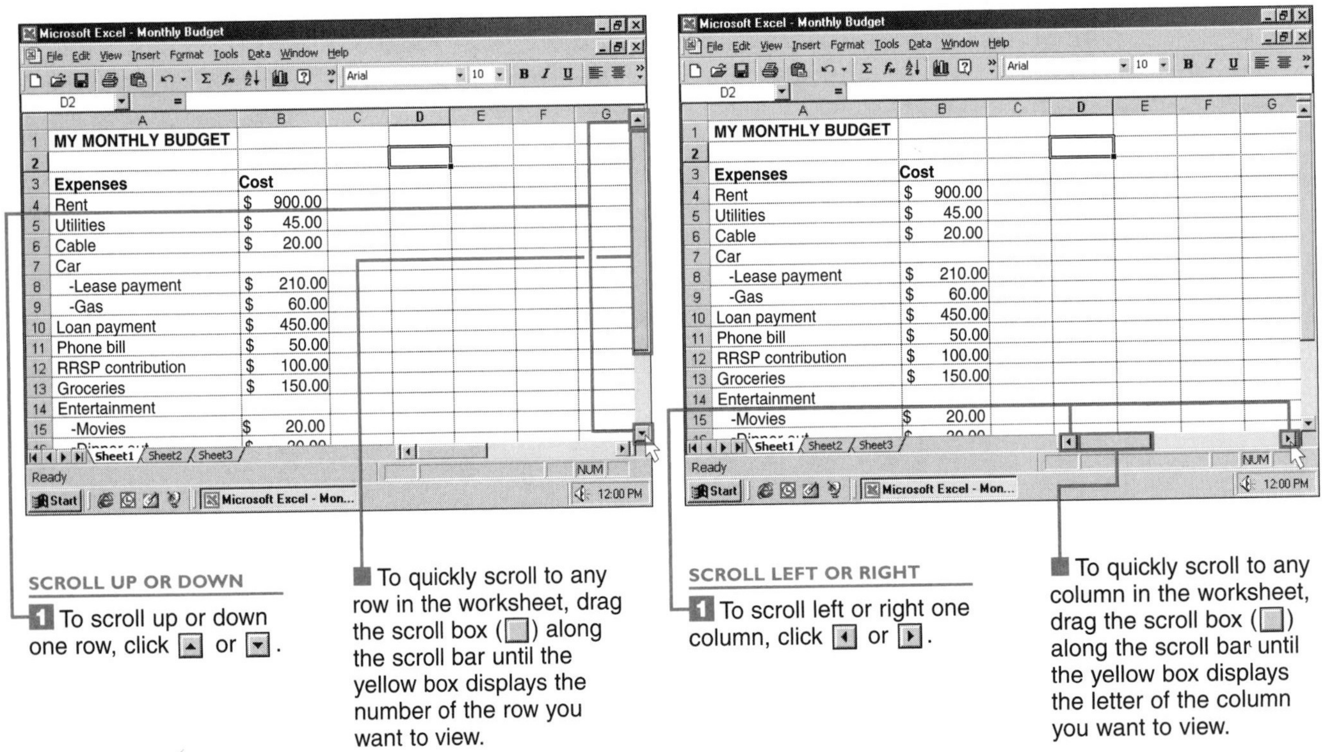

SCROLL UP OR DOWN

1 To scroll up or down one row, click ▲ or ▼.

■ To quickly scroll to any row in the worksheet, drag the scroll box (□) along the scroll bar until the yellow box displays the number of the row you want to view.

SCROLL LEFT OR RIGHT

1 To scroll left or right one column, click ◄ or ►.

■ To quickly scroll to any column in the worksheet, drag the scroll box (□) along the scroll bar until the yellow box displays the letter of the column you want to view.

TIPS

How do I use the keyboard to move through a worksheet?

✔ Press the Ctrl+Home keys to move to cell A1. Press the Ctrl+End keys to move to the last cell in the worksheet. Press the Alt+Page Up keys to move one full screen to the left. Press the Alt+Page Down keys to move one full screen to the right.

Is there another way to scroll through a worksheet?

✔ You can purchase a mouse that has a small wheel between the left and right mouse buttons. Moving this wheel lets you quickly scroll through a worksheet.

How can I quickly move to another cell?

✔ To quickly move to another cell, select the Edit menu and then click Go To. In the Reference area of the Go To dialog box, enter the column letter and row number of the cell you want to move to. Then press the Enter key.

How can I quickly display the active cell?

✔ To quickly display the active cell, press the Ctrl+Backspace keys.

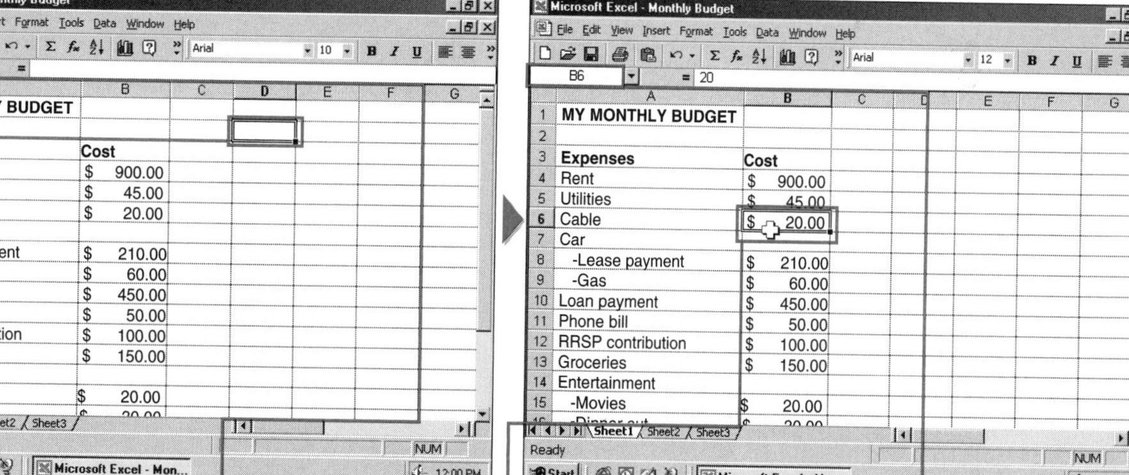

CHANGE THE ACTIVE CELL

■ The active cell displays a thick border.

■ The cell reference for the active cell appears in this area. A cell reference identifies the location of each cell in a worksheet and consists of a column letter followed by a row number.

1 To make another cell the active cell, click the cell.

Note: To use your keyboard to change the active cell, press the ↑, ←, ↓ or → key.

■ The cell reference for the new active cell appears in this area.

SELECT CELLS

Before performing many tasks in Excel, you must select the cells you want to work with. For example, you must select the cells containing data you want to change to a different font, size or color.

Selected cells appear highlighted on your screen. This makes cells you select stand out from the rest of the cells in your worksheet.

You can select a single cell you want to work with in your worksheet. The cell you select becomes the active cell and displays a thick border. You can also select a group of cells you want to work with. A group of cells is often called a range.

When you select more than one cell, the first cell you select becomes the active cell. Excel also lets you quickly select all the cells in a row or column.

After you finish working with selected cells, you can click any cell in the worksheet to deselect the cells.

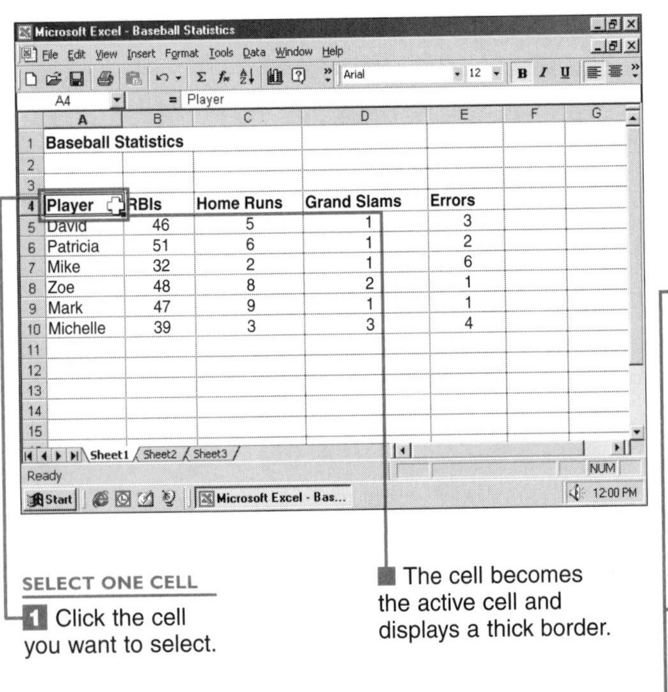

SELECT ONE CELL

1 Click the cell you want to select.

■ The cell becomes the active cell and displays a thick border.

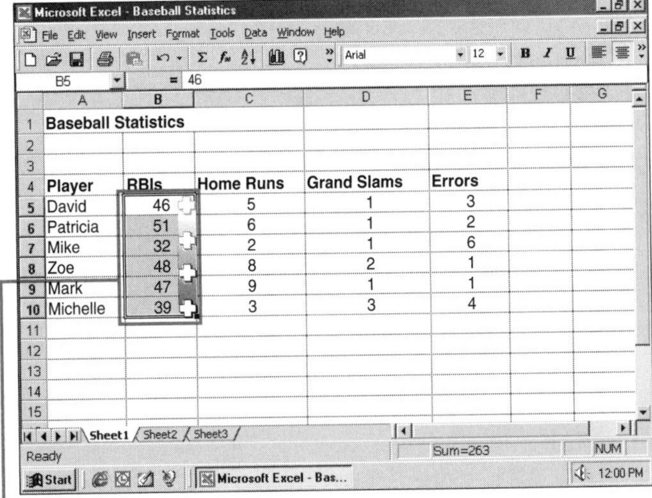

SELECT GROUPS OF CELLS

1 Position the mouse ✥ over the first cell you want to select.

2 Drag the mouse ✥ to highlight all the cells you want to select.

■ To select multiple groups of cells, hold down the Ctrl key as you repeat steps 1 and 2 for each group.

■ To deselect cells, click any cell.

TIPS

How do I select all the cells in my worksheet?

✔ To select all the cells in your worksheet, click the blank area (▭) to the left of the heading for column A. You can also press the Ctrl+A keys to select all the cells in your worksheet.

Can I quickly select a large group of cells?

✔ You can quickly select a large group of cells in your worksheet. Click the first cell in the group you want to select and then scroll to the end of the group. Hold down the Shift key as you click the last cell in the group. Excel highlights all the cells between the first and last cell you select.

How can I select rows or columns that are not beside each other?

✔ To select rows or columns that are not beside each other in your worksheet, hold down the Ctrl key as you click the numbers of the rows or letters of the columns you want to select.

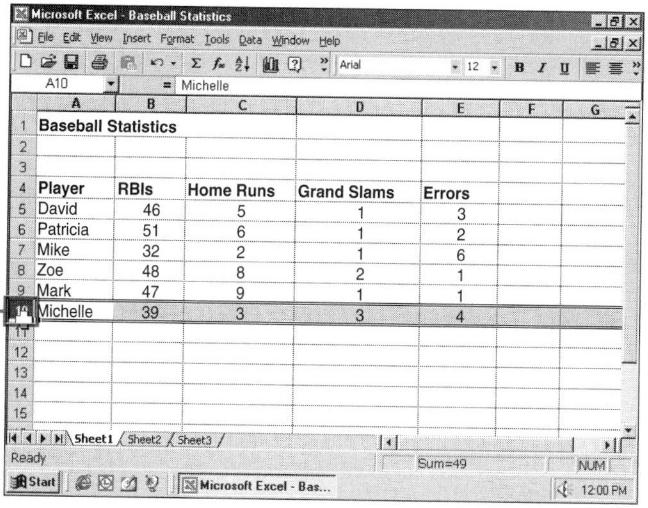

SELECT A ROW

1 Click the number of the row you want to select.

■ To select multiple rows, position the mouse ✥ over the number of the first row you want to select. Then drag the mouse ✥ to highlight all the rows you want to select.

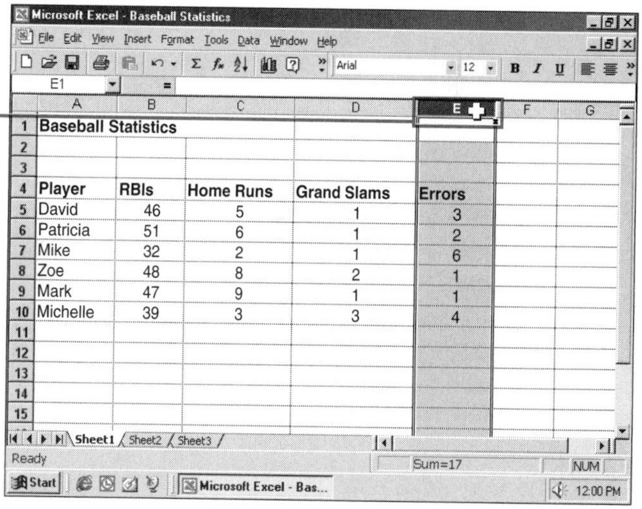

SELECT A COLUMN

1 Click the letter of the column you want to select.

■ To select multiple columns, position the mouse ✥ over the letter of the first column you want to select. Then drag the mouse ✥ to highlight all the columns you want to select.

COMPLETE A SERIES

Excel can save you time by completing a text or number series for you. A series is a sequence of data that changes, such as a range of consecutive numbers. You can complete a series in a row or column.

Excel completes a text series based on the text in the first cell. Excel can complete a text series such as the days of the week or the months of the year. This is useful for creating column labels. If Excel cannot determine the text series you want to complete, it will copy the text in the first cell to the cells you select.

Excel completes a number series based on the numbers in the first two cells. These numbers tell Excel how to change each number to complete the series. For example, you can create a series of even numbers by entering **2** in the first cell and **4** in the second cell.

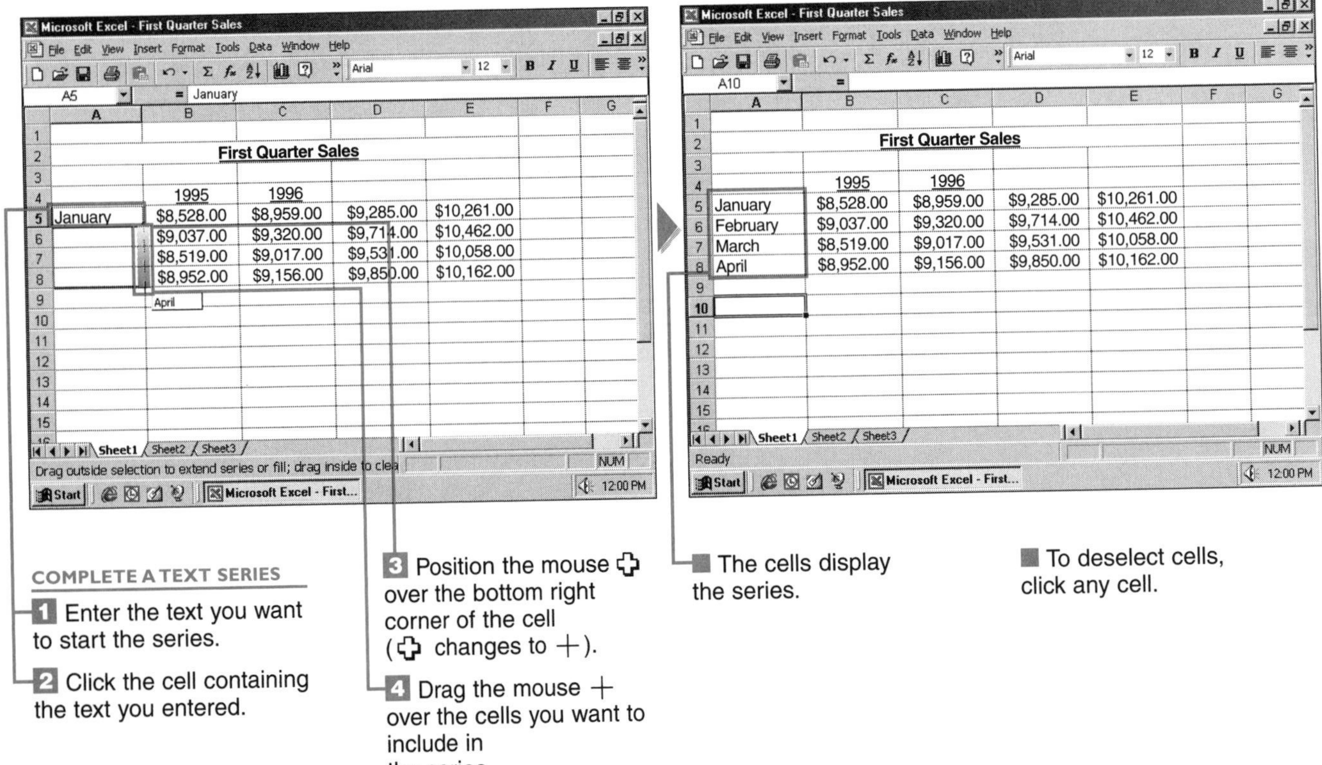

COMPLETE A TEXT SERIES

1 Enter the text you want to start the series.

2 Click the cell containing the text you entered.

3 Position the mouse ✥ over the bottom right corner of the cell (✥ changes to +).

4 Drag the mouse + over the cells you want to include in the series.

■ The cells display the series.

■ To deselect cells, click any cell.

TIPS

Can I complete a series in descending order?

✔ Yes. Select the cell(s) you want to start the series and then drag the mouse + up or to the left.

How can I complete a series for the days of the week without including Saturday and Sunday?

✔ Click the cell containing the day of the week you want to start the series. Hold down the right mouse button as you drag the mouse over the cells you want to include in the series. Then select Fill Weekdays from the menu that appears.

How can I copy the numbers in two cells without completing a series?

✔ Select the cells containing the numbers. Hold down the Ctrl key as you drag the mouse over the cells you want to copy the numbers to.

Can I create my own custom series?

✔ Yes. Select the cells containing the data you want to include in the series. Select the Tools menu and then click Options. Choose the Custom Lists tab and click the Import button. Then click OK.

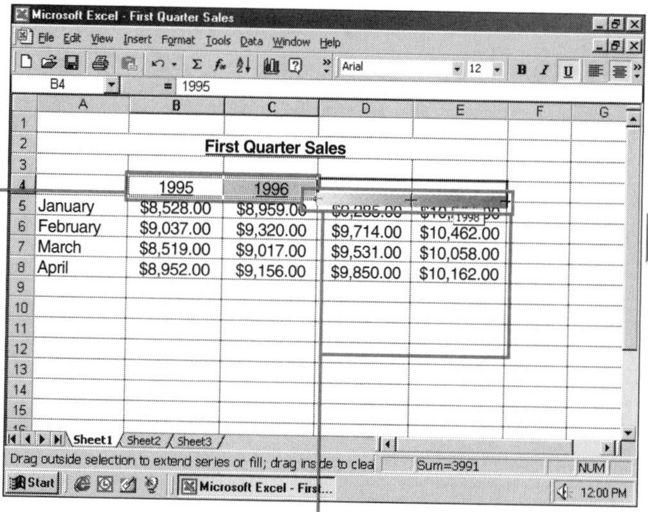

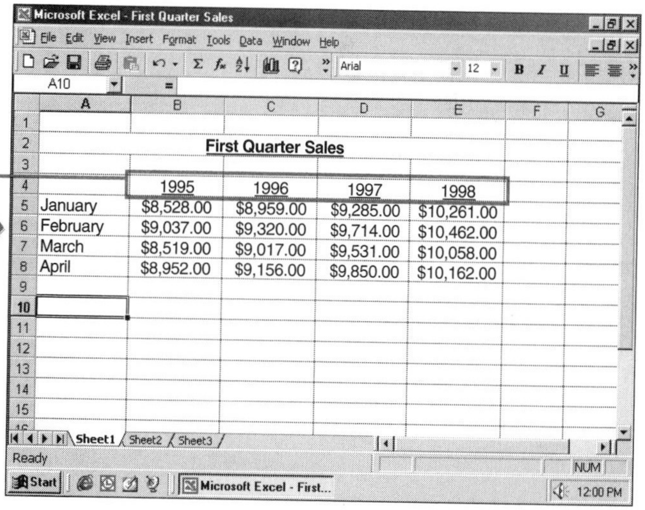

COMPLETE A NUMBER SERIES

1 Enter the first two numbers you want to start the series.

2 Select the cells containing the numbers you entered.

3 Position the mouse over the bottom right corner of the selected cells (changes to +).

4 Drag the mouse + over the cells you want to include in the series.

■ The cells display the series.

■ To deselect cells, click any cell.

SAVE A WORKBOOK

You can save your workbook to store it for future use. To avoid losing your work, you should regularly save changes you make to a workbook.

You can specify where you want to save your workbook. The Places Bar in the Save As dialog box lets you quickly access commonly used folders. The History folder lets you access folders you recently used. The My Documents folder provides a convenient place to save your workbook. The Desktop folder lets you quickly save your workbook on the Windows desktop. The Favorites folder provides a place to save a workbook you will frequently access. You can use Web Folders to save your workbook on a computer called a Web server. Once the workbook is saved on a Web server, it will be available for other people to view.

You can save a workbook in a different format. This lets you share your workbook with colleagues who do not use Excel 2000.

When you finish working with your workbook, you can close the workbook to remove it from your screen. You can continue working with other workbooks until you exit Excel.

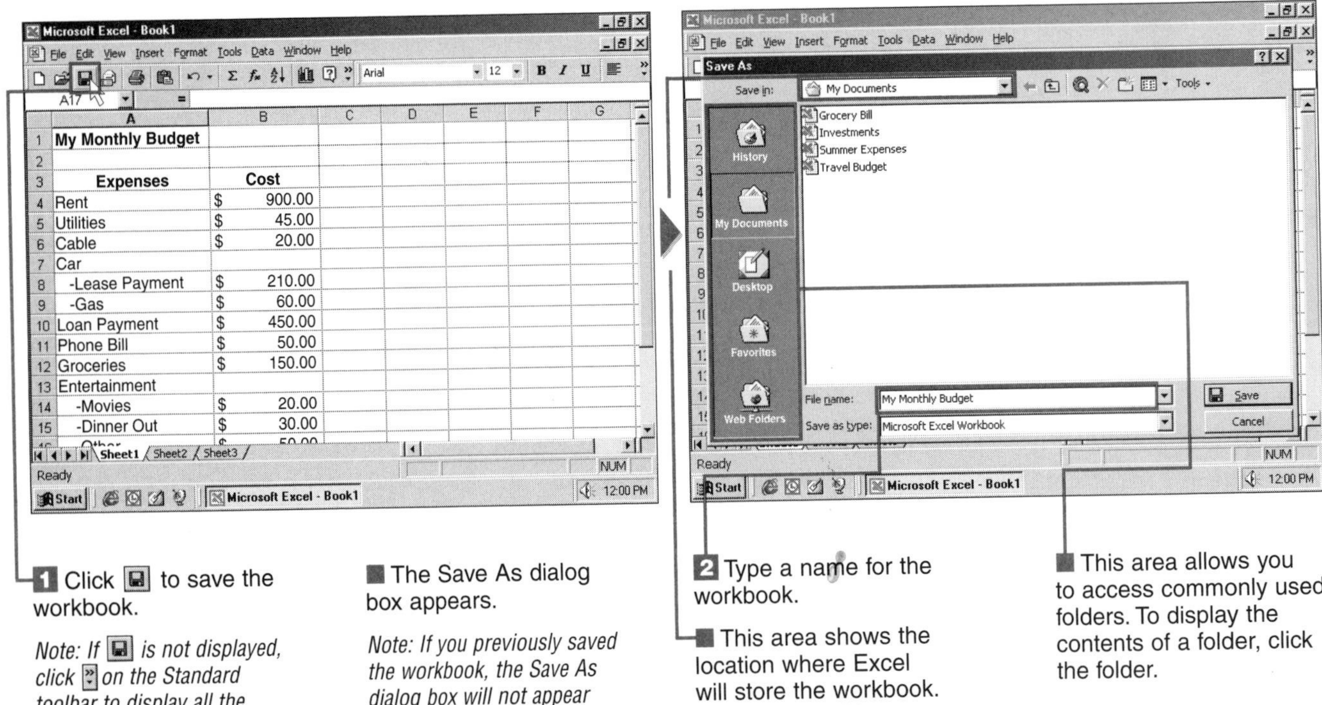

1 Click 💾 to save the workbook.

Note: If 💾 is not displayed, click » on the Standard toolbar to display all the buttons.

■ The Save As dialog box appears.

Note: If you previously saved the workbook, the Save As dialog box will not appear since you have already named the workbook.

2 Type a name for the workbook.

■ This area shows the location where Excel will store the workbook. You can click this area to change the location.

■ This area allows you to access commonly used folders. To display the contents of a folder, click the folder.

TIPS

I frequently use the same workbooks. How can I save them for quick access?

✔ You can save the workbooks you frequently use in a workspace file. Open all the workbooks you want to include in the workspace file. Click the File menu and then select Save Workspace. Type a name for the workspace file and then click Save. When you open the workspace file, all the workbooks you saved in the file open at once. You can open a workspace file as you would open any workbook. To open a workbook, see page 176.

I previously saved my workbook. How can I save a copy of the workbook with a different name?

✔ Click the File menu and then select Save As. Type the new name and then click Save.

Can I change the location where Excel automatically stores my workbooks?

✔ Yes. Select the Tools menu and then select Options. Click the General tab and in the Default file location area, type the drive and folder name you want to use. Then click OK.

■ This area displays the format Excel will use to save the workbook. You can click this area to change the format.

3 Click Save.

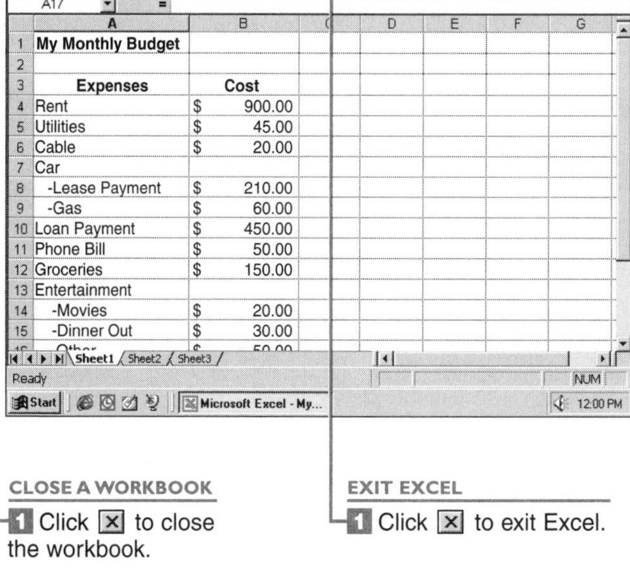

CLOSE A WORKBOOK

1 Click ☒ to close the workbook.

EXIT EXCEL

1 Click ☒ to exit Excel.

OPEN A WORKBOOK

You can open a saved workbook and display it on your screen. This lets you review and make changes to the workbook.

You can specify where the workbook you want to open is located. You can use the Places Bar in the Open dialog box to quickly display the contents of commonly used folders. For information on the Places Bar, see the top of page 174.

You can use Excel to open and edit many different types of workbooks. This is useful when you work with colleagues who do not use Excel 2000. Excel can open workbooks created in programs such as Lotus 1-2-3 and Quattro Pro. When you open a workbook created in another program, Excel converts the workbook into a format that it can use.

If you cannot see the workbook you want to open, make sure the correct type of workbook is selected. If you do not know which workbook type to use, select All Files.

After you open a workbook, Excel displays the name of the workbook at the top of your screen.

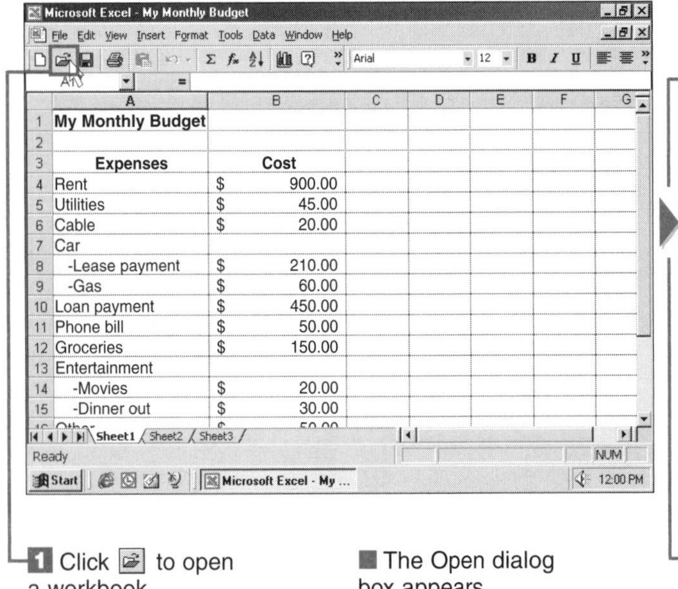

1 Click [icon] to open a workbook.

Note: If [icon] is not displayed, click [icon] on the Standard toolbar to display all the buttons.

■ The Open dialog box appears.

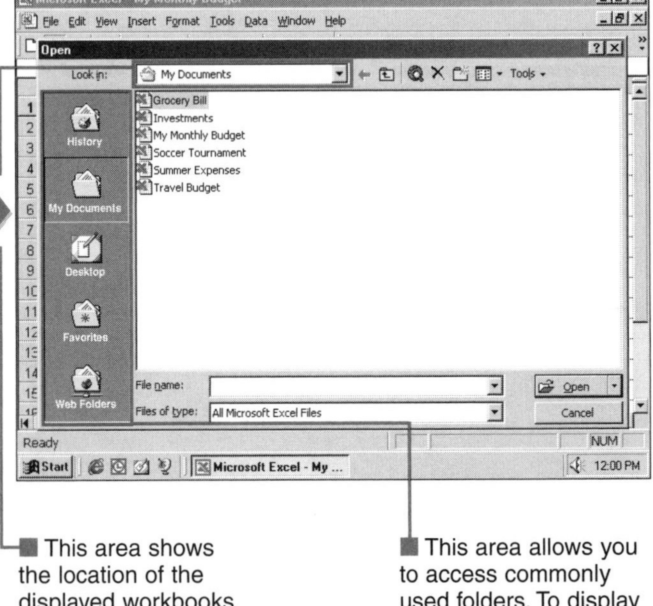

■ This area shows the location of the displayed workbooks. You can click this area to change the location.

■ This area allows you to access commonly used folders. To display the contents of a folder, click the folder.

TIPS

Can I quickly open a workbook I recently worked with?

✔ Excel remembers the names of the last four workbooks you worked with. To quickly open one of these workbooks, click the File menu and then select the name of the workbook you want to open.

How can I change the number of workbooks Excel remembers?

✔ Click the Tools menu and then select Options. On the General tab, double-click the Recently used file list area and type a number between 1 and 9. Then click OK.

Can I sort the icons displayed in the Open dialog box alphabetically by name?

✔ Yes. Sorting icons can help you find the workbook you want to open more easily. Click ▾ beside the Views button (▦▾) in the Open dialog box and then select Arrange Icons. Click the by Name option to sort the icons alphabetically by name. Excel also allows you to sort the icons by file type, by size or by the date the files were last modified.

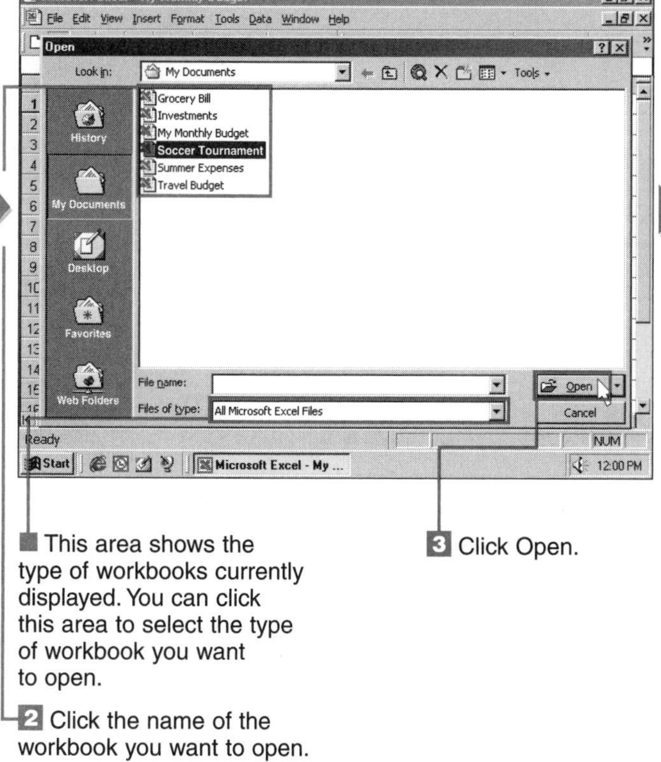

■ This area shows the type of workbooks currently displayed. You can click this area to select the type of workbook you want to open.

2 Click the name of the workbook you want to open.

3 Click Open.

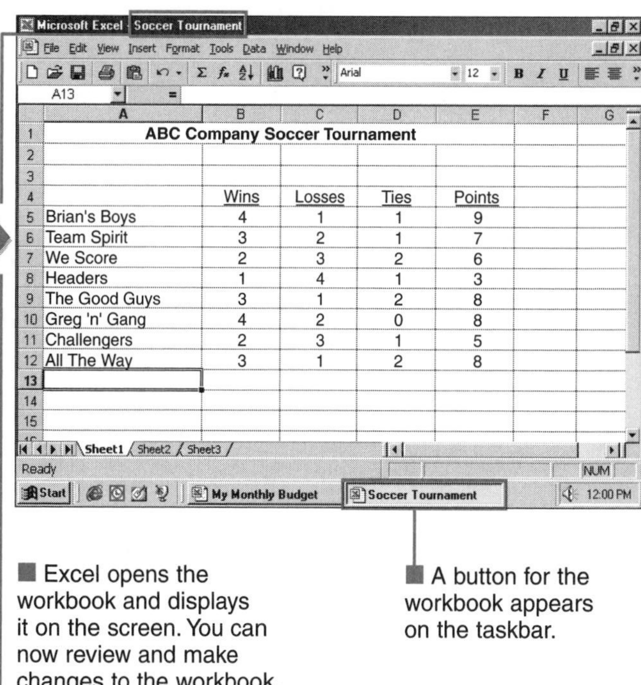

■ Excel opens the workbook and displays it on the screen. You can now review and make changes to the workbook.

■ The name of the workbook appears at the top of the screen.

■ A button for the workbook appears on the taskbar.

FIND A WORKBOOK

If you cannot remember the name or location of a workbook you want to open, you can have Excel search for the workbook using search criteria you specify.

To enter search criteria, you need to specify the property you want to use to find the workbook. For example, you can search for a workbook by the name of the workbook or the date the workbook was created.

After you select a property, you need to specify a condition for the search. The available conditions depend on the property you selected. For example, when you select the Last modified property, Excel allows you to choose a condition such as yesterday, today or last week.

You may also need to specify a value to help Excel determine what to search for. For example, you may need to specify text in the workbook's name or the name of the person who last saved the workbook. Some properties do not require you to specify a value for the search.

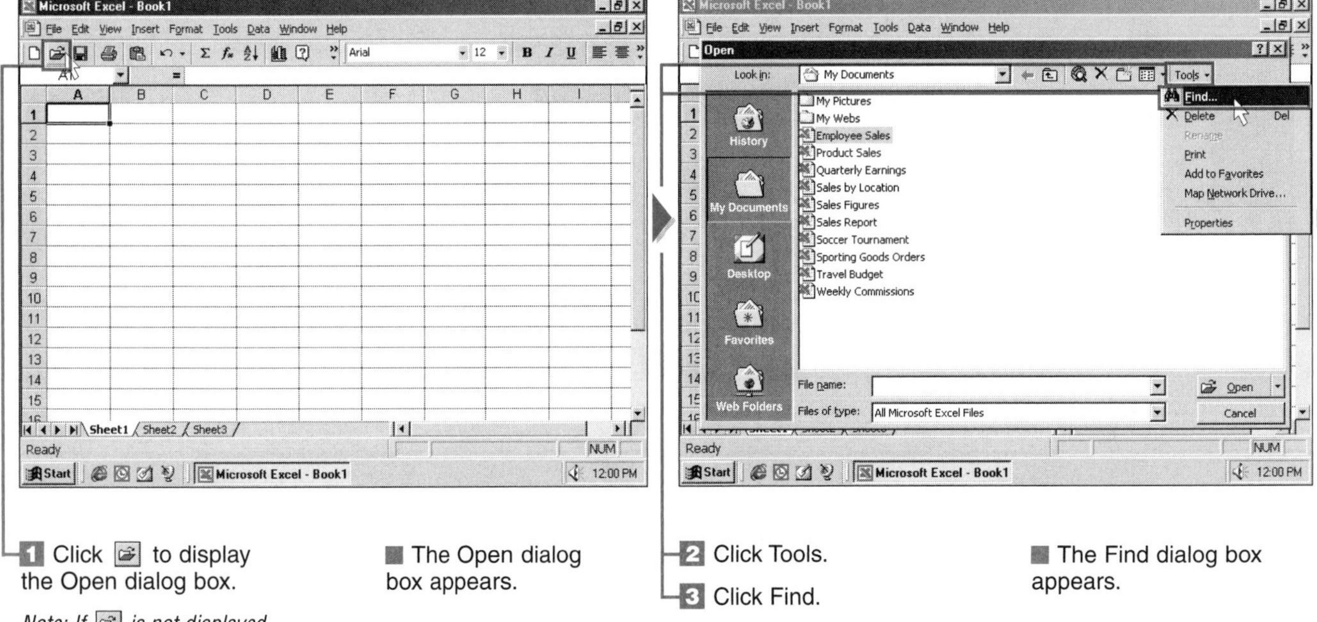

1 Click [open icon] to display the Open dialog box.

Note: If [open icon] is not displayed, click [more buttons icon] on the Standard toolbar to display all the buttons.

■ The Open dialog box appears.

2 Click Tools.

3 Click Find.

■ The Find dialog box appears.

TIPS

Is there anything I should check before starting a search?

✔ You should make sure that the Files of type area in the Open dialog box displays the All Microsoft Excel Files or All Files option. You can click the Files of type area to select the correct option.

How can I improve my search results?

✔ You can specify properties for your workbooks to improve your search results. When creating a workbook, click the File menu, select Properties and then enter the appropriate information for the workbook.

How can I refine my search?

✔ You can have Excel find all forms of a word. For example, if you search for the value "write", Excel will also search for "written" and "wrote". In the Find dialog box, perform steps 4 to 8 below to specify the value and then click the Match all word forms option (☐ changes to ☑).

How do I clear the search criteria I specified?

✔ To quickly clear the search criteria you specified and start a new search, click the New Search button in the Find dialog box.

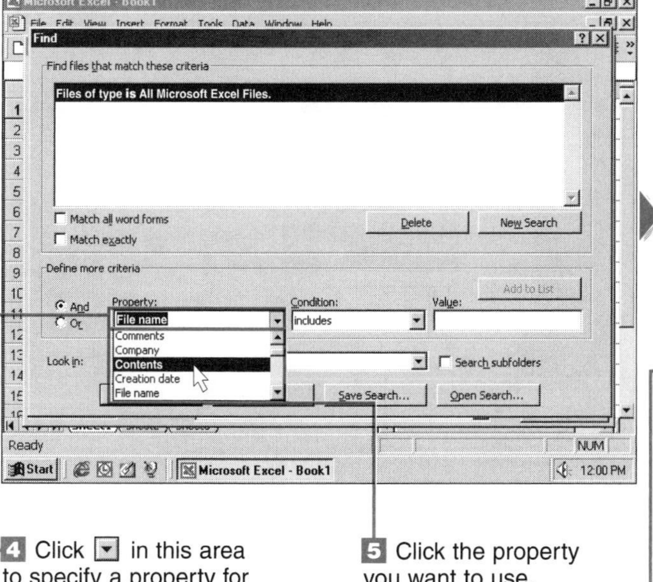

4 Click ▼ in this area to specify a property for the search.

5 Click the property you want to use.

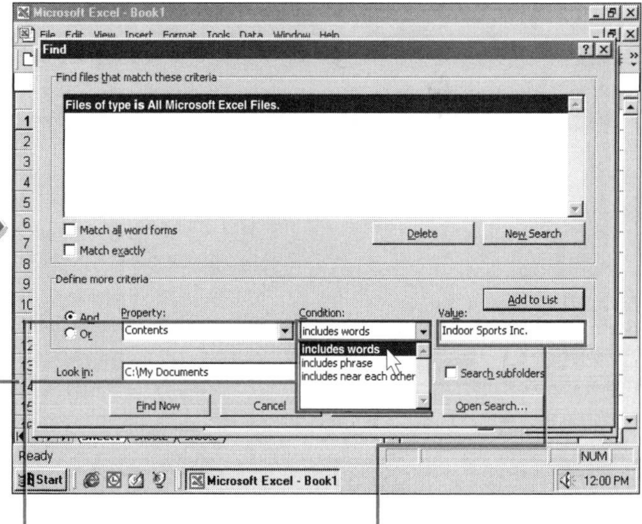

6 Click ▼ in this area to specify a condition for the search.

7 Click the condition you want to use.

Note: The available conditions depend on the property you selected in step 5.

8 Click this area and type the value you want to search for.

Note: If the value area is not available, you do not need to enter a value.

CONTINUED

FIND A WORKBOOK CONTINUED

You can specify the location where you want Excel to search for a workbook. You can also have Excel search the contents of all the subfolders in the location you specify.

When you finish specifying the criteria you want to use for the search, you must add the search criteria to a list of criteria in the Find dialog box. Excel automatically adds the type of file displayed in the Open dialog box to the list of search criteria for you.

Excel may take a few moments or several minutes to find a workbook. The search criteria you specified determines the length of time the search will take. Searching for a workbook on a network may also increase the length of a search.

When the search is complete, Excel displays the names of all the workbooks it found. You can open a workbook Excel found to review and make changes to the workbook.

If the search does not provide the results you were expecting, you may not have provided Excel with enough information or you may have specified incorrect information.

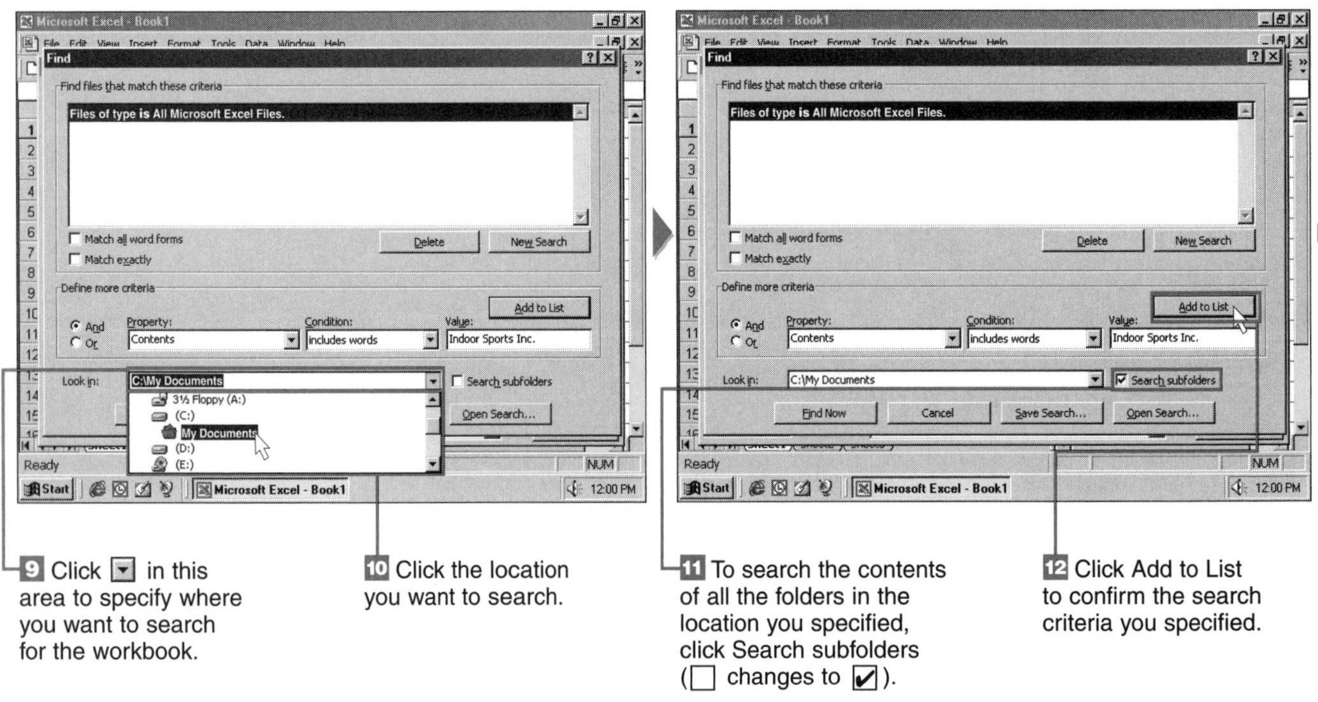

9 Click ▾ in this area to specify where you want to search for the workbook.

10 Click the location you want to search.

11 To search the contents of all the folders in the location you specified, click Search subfolders (☐ changes to ☑).

12 Click Add to List to confirm the search criteria you specified.

TIPS

How do I remove criteria from the list of search criteria?

✔ To remove the criteria you no longer want to include in a search, click the criteria you want to remove and then click the Delete button.

Can I save a search?

✔ Yes. After specifying the search criteria you want to use, click the Save Search button. Type a name for the search and press the Enter key. To open a saved search, click the Open Search button in the Find dialog box, select the name of the search and then click Open.

When I started the search, why did a dialog box appear, asking if I want to install FindFast?

✔ FindFast is a feature that can help speed up your searches. To install FindFast, click Yes and then insert the CD-ROM disc you used to install Office 2000 into your CD-ROM drive. Then click OK.

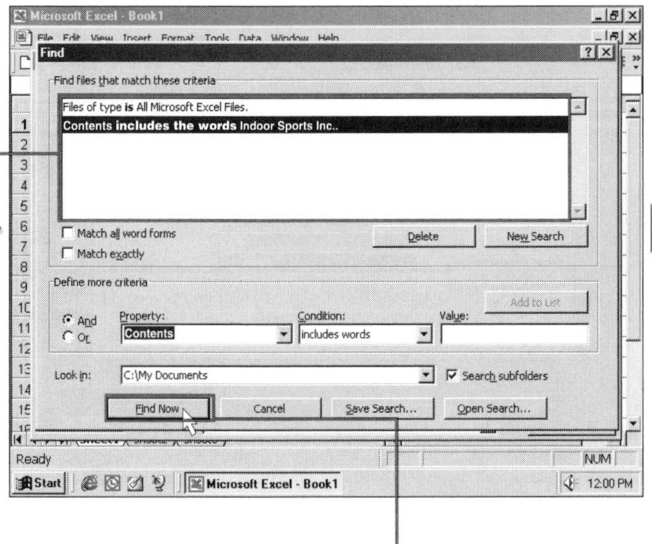

■ The search criteria you specified appears in this area.

13 Click Find Now to start the search.

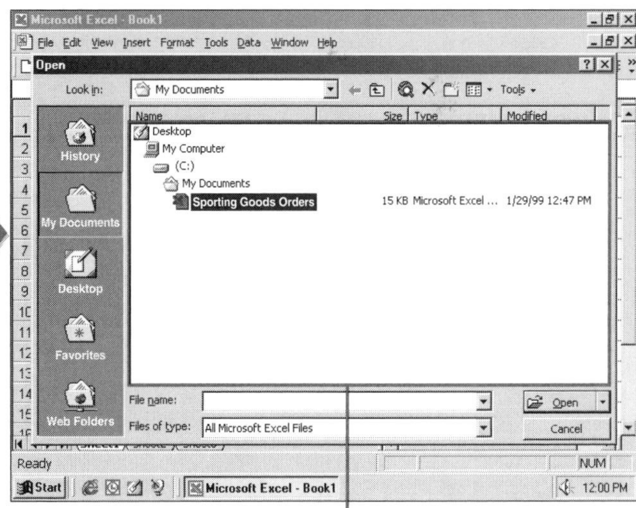

■ The Open dialog box reappears.

■ This area displays the names of the workbooks Excel found.

■ To open a workbook, double-click the name of the workbook.

CREATE A NEW WORKBOOK

You can easily create a new workbook to store data.

You do not have to close the workbook currently displayed on your screen before creating a new workbook. The new workbook will appear in front of the current workbook.

When you create a new workbook, Excel displays a blank worksheet on your screen. The blank worksheet displays the default font, data size and column width settings. You can change these and other settings to format the worksheet to suit your needs. To format a worksheet, see pages 216 to 235.

Excel gives the new workbook a temporary name, such as Book2. You can change the temporary name when you save the workbook. For information on saving a workbook, see page 174.

When you create a new workbook, the taskbar at the bottom of your screen displays a button for the new workbook.

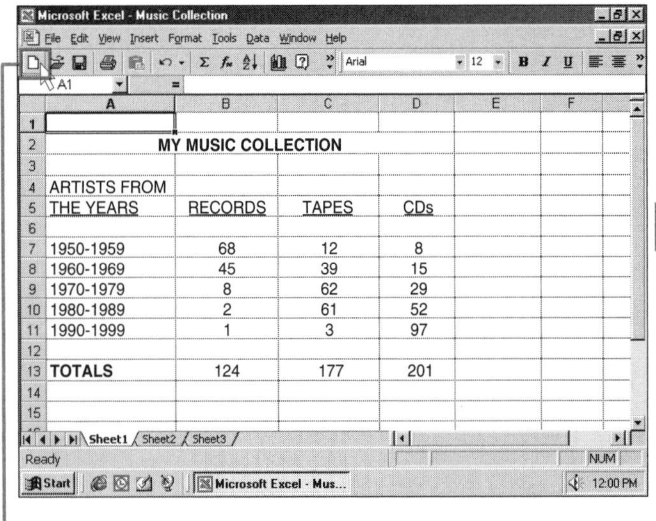

1 Click [new] to create a new workbook.

Note: If [new] is not displayed, click [»] on the Standard toolbar to display all the buttons.

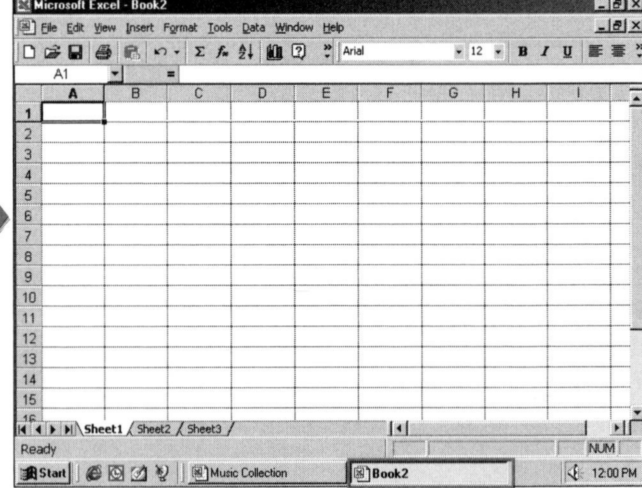

■ A new workbook appears. The previous workbook is now hidden behind the new workbook.

■ A button for the new workbook appears on the taskbar.

SWITCH BETWEEN WORKBOOKS

Excel lets you have many workbooks open at once. You can switch between all of your open workbooks.

The ability to have multiple workbooks open and switch between them is very useful. For example, if Excel is performing a calculation that will take a few moments, you can switch to another workbook and work on a different project while Excel performs the calculation.

You can display the names of all your open workbooks in a list and then select the workbook you want to switch to.

You can also use the taskbar to switch between workbooks. The taskbar displays a button for each workbook you have open. To switch to the workbook you want to display on your screen, you can select the button for the workbook on the taskbar.

Excel displays the name of the workbook you are currently working with at the top of your screen.

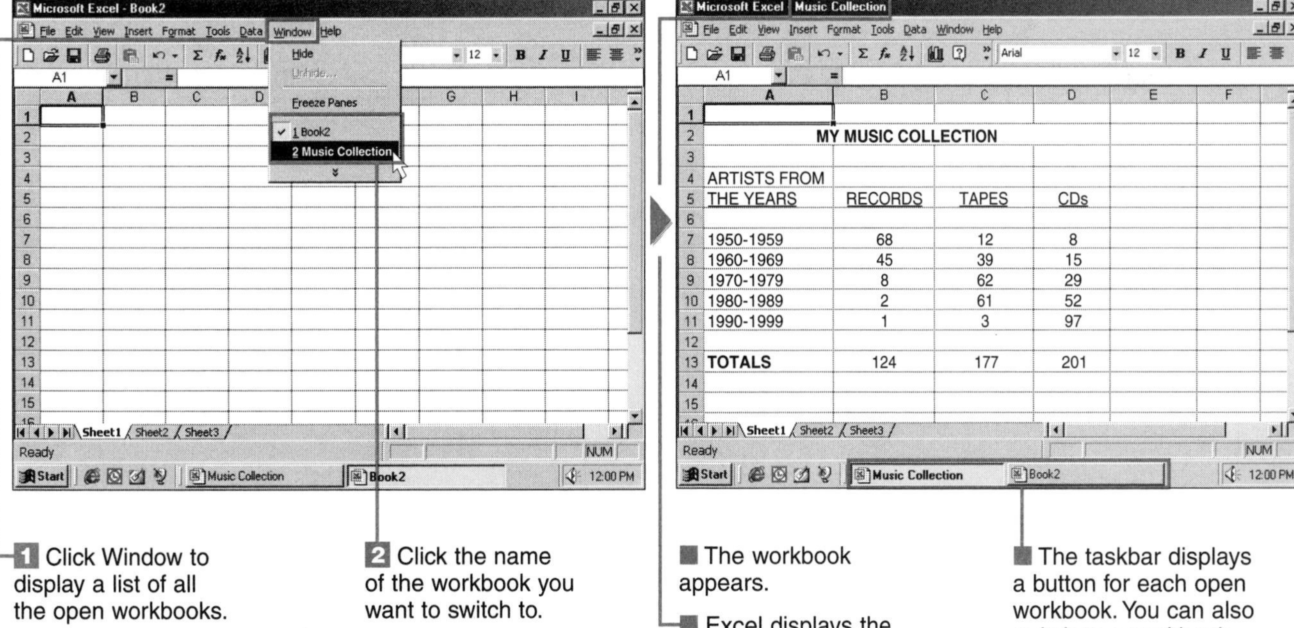

1 Click Window to display a list of all the open workbooks.

2 Click the name of the workbook you want to switch to.

■ The workbook appears.

■ Excel displays the name of the current workbook at the top of your screen.

■ The taskbar displays a button for each open workbook. You can also switch to a workbook by clicking its button on the taskbar.

E-MAIL A WORKBOOK

You can e-mail the worksheet currently displayed on your screen or the entire workbook you are working with. E-mailing a worksheet or workbook lets you quickly exchange data with other people on the Internet or your corporate intranet. You can send a worksheet or workbook to more than one person.

When you e-mail a single worksheet, the worksheet appears in the body of the e-mail message. When you e-mail an entire workbook, the workbook is sent as an attachment and appears as an icon in the message.

When you e-mail a worksheet or workbook, Excel may suggest a subject for the e-mail message based on the name of the workbook. You can enter a different subject. You should enter a subject that will help the recipient quickly identify the contents of the message.

Before you e-mail an Excel worksheet or workbook, you must set up Microsoft Outlook. For information on using Microsoft Outlook, see pages 508 to 521.

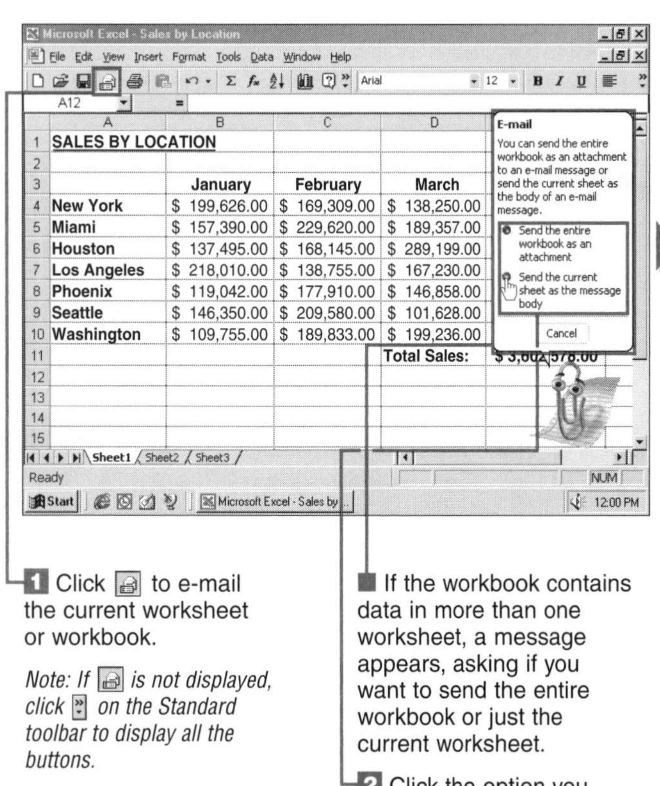

1 Click to e-mail the current worksheet or workbook.

Note: If is not displayed, click on the Standard toolbar to display all the buttons.

■ If the workbook contains data in more than one worksheet, a message appears, asking if you want to send the entire workbook or just the current worksheet.

2 Click the option you want to use.

■ If you chose to send the current worksheet in step 2, an area appears for you to address the message.

Note: If you chose to send the entire workbook in step 2, a window appears for the e-mail message.

TIPS

Excel did not offer me the option to e-mail my entire workbook. What is wrong?

✔ If you have previously sent the current worksheet in an e-mail message, Excel does not redisplay the message asking if you want to send the entire workbook. To e-mail the entire workbook, select the File menu, click Send To and then choose Mail Recipient (as Attachment).

How can I quickly enter an e-mail address for my worksheet or workbook?

✔ You can click the To button and then select a name from the address book to quickly enter an e-mail address. For more information on selecting names from the address book, see page 516.

Why can't the person I sent my worksheet or workbook to read the data?

✔ When you e-mail a worksheet, the worksheet data is converted to HTML format. The recipient must have an e-mail program that is capable of reading HTML to display the worksheet. When you e-mail a workbook, the workbook is sent as an attached file. The recipient must have a spreadsheet program that can open the file.

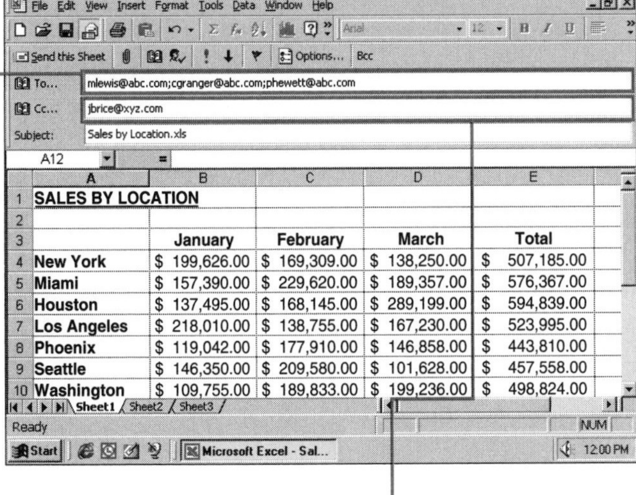

3 Type the e-mail address of each person you want to receive the message. Separate each address with a semicolon (;).

4 To send a copy of the message to another person, click this area and type the e-mail address.

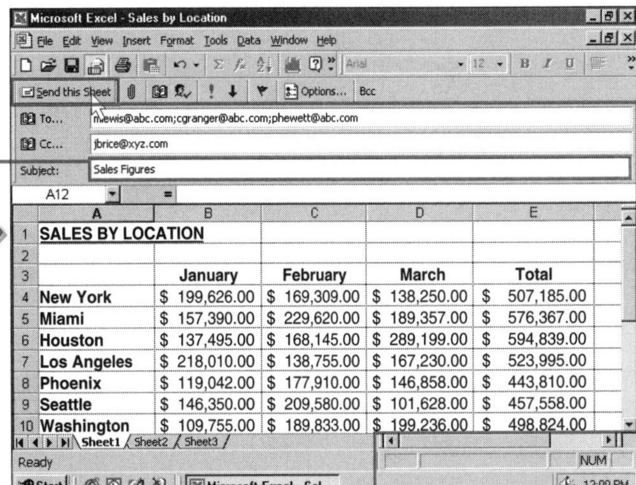

5 Click this area and type a subject for the message.

Note: If a subject already exists, you can drag the mouse I over the existing subject and then type a new subject.

6 To send the message, click Send this Sheet or Send.

Note: The button you use depends on the option you selected in step 2.

EDIT OR DELETE DATA

Excel allows you to edit the data in your worksheet. This lets you correct a mistake or update the data.

The flashing insertion point in the cell indicates where Excel will remove or add data. You can move the insertion point to another location in the cell.

When you remove data, Excel removes the characters to the left of the insertion point. When you add data, Excel inserts the characters you type at the location of the insertion point.

You can replace all the data in a cell at once. After you select the cell containing the data you want to replace, you can enter new data in the cell.

You can delete data you no longer need from the cells in your worksheet. You can delete the data in a single cell or group of cells.

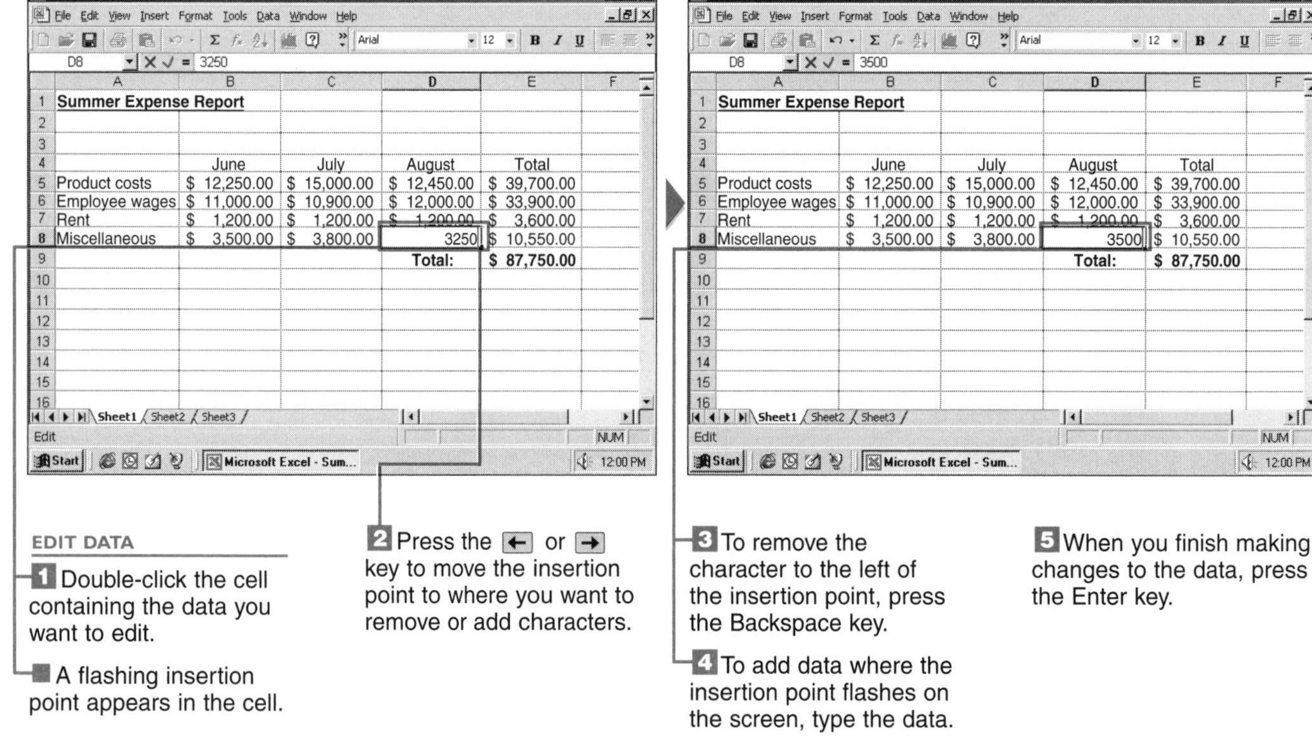

EDIT DATA

1 Double-click the cell containing the data you want to edit.

■ A flashing insertion point appears in the cell.

2 Press the ← or → key to move the insertion point to where you want to remove or add characters.

3 To remove the character to the left of the insertion point, press the Backspace key.

4 To add data where the insertion point flashes on the screen, type the data.

5 When you finish making changes to the data, press the Enter key.

TIPS

I want to edit data in a large worksheet. Can I display more of the worksheet on my screen?

✔ You can have Excel hide parts of the screen to display a larger working area. Select the View menu and then click Full Screen. You can repeat these steps to once again display the hidden parts of the screen.

Is there another way to edit data?

✔ Yes. Click the cell containing the data you want to edit. The data in the cell appears in the formula bar. Click in the formula bar and then perform steps 2 to 5 on page 186 to edit the data.

Does Excel remove the formatting from a cell when I delete the data in the cell?

✔ Excel does not remove the formatting and will apply the formatting to any new data you enter in the cell. To remove formatting from a cell, select the cell. Choose the Edit menu, select Clear and then click Formats.

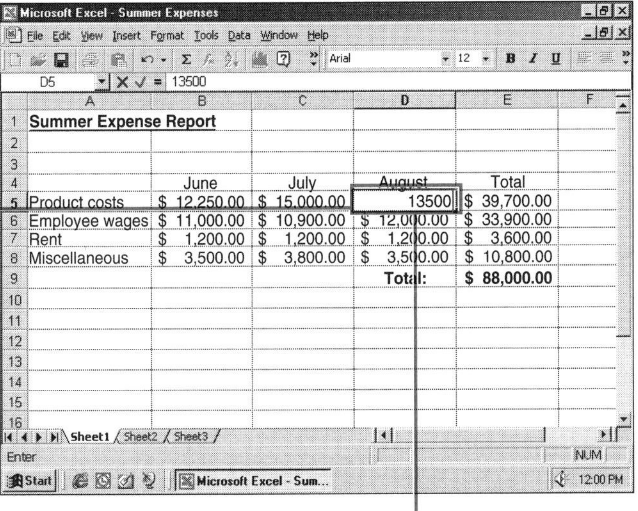

REPLACE DATA

1 Click the cell containing the data you want to replace with new data.

2 Type the new data and then press the Enter key.

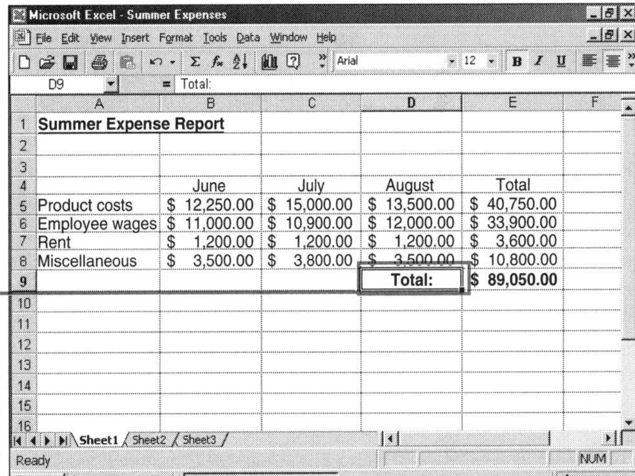

DELETE DATA

1 Select the cell(s) containing the data you want to delete.

2 Press the Delete key.

■ The data in the cell(s) you selected disappears.

MOVE OR COPY DATA

You can reorganize your worksheet by moving data from one location to another. Moving data can help you find the most effective structure for a worksheet. When you move data, the data disappears from its original location in your worksheet.

You can place a copy of data in a different location in your worksheet. This will save you time since you do not have to retype the data. When you copy data, the data appears in both the original and new location.

To move or copy data, you can drag data to a new location. When you drag data, Excel displays an outline to indicate the new location of the data you are moving or copying.

Excel also allows you to use the Cut, Copy and Paste buttons on the Standard toolbar to move or copy data.

If the cells you move or copy contain a formula, Excel may change the cell references in the formula so the formula still uses the correct cells. For more information on formulas, see page 208.

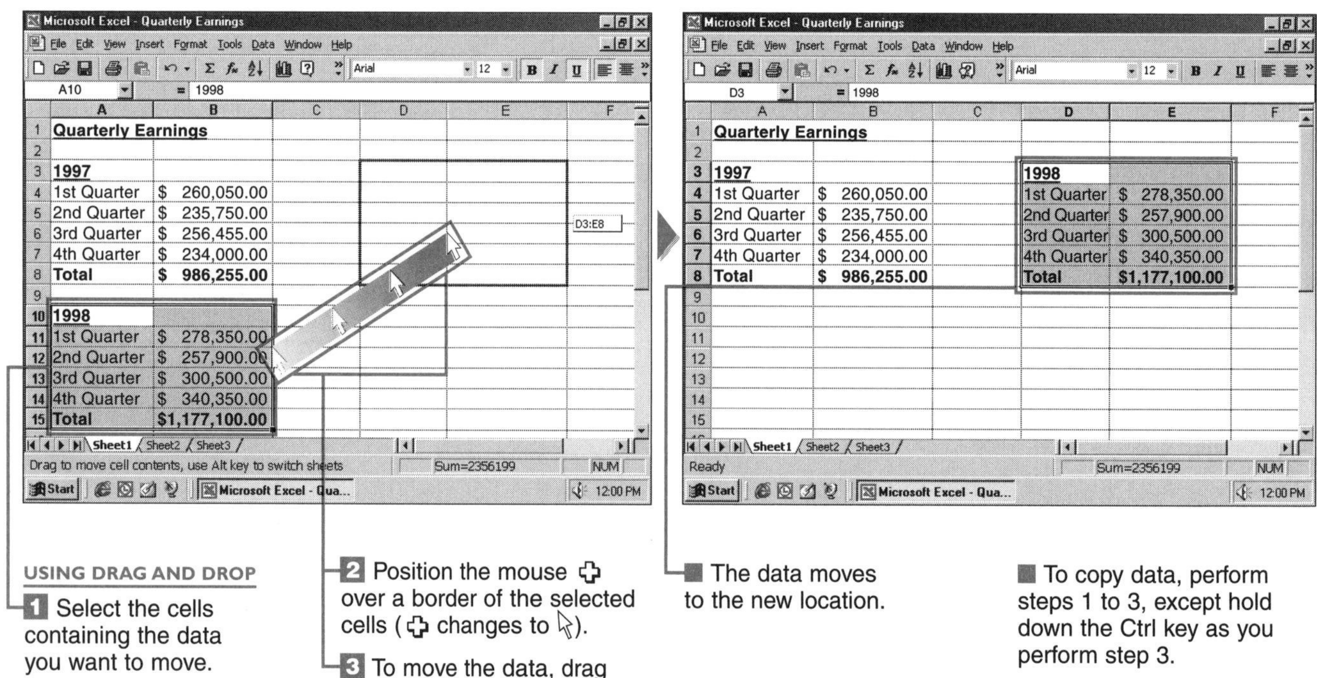

USING DRAG AND DROP

1 Select the cells containing the data you want to move.

2 Position the mouse ✥ over a border of the selected cells (✥ changes to ↖).

3 To move the data, drag the mouse ↖ to where you want to place the data.

■ The data moves to the new location.

■ To copy data, perform steps 1 to 3, except hold down the Ctrl key as you perform step 3.

TIPS

Why does Excel ask if I want to replace the contents of the destination cells?

✔ This message appears when you try to drag data to a location that already contains data. To replace the existing data with the data you are moving, click OK. To cancel the move, click Cancel.

How can I move or copy data to a different worksheet?

✔ Perform steps 1 and 2 on this page. Click the tab of the worksheet where you want to place the data and then perform steps 3 and 4.

Why does the Clipboard toolbar appear when I move or copy data using the toolbar buttons?

✔ The Clipboard toolbar may appear when you cut or copy two pieces of data in a row, copy the same data twice or place copied data in a new location and then immediately copy other data. To see what data an icon on the Clipboard toolbar represents, position the mouse pointer over the icon until a description of the data appears. To place data in a new location, click the icon for the data.

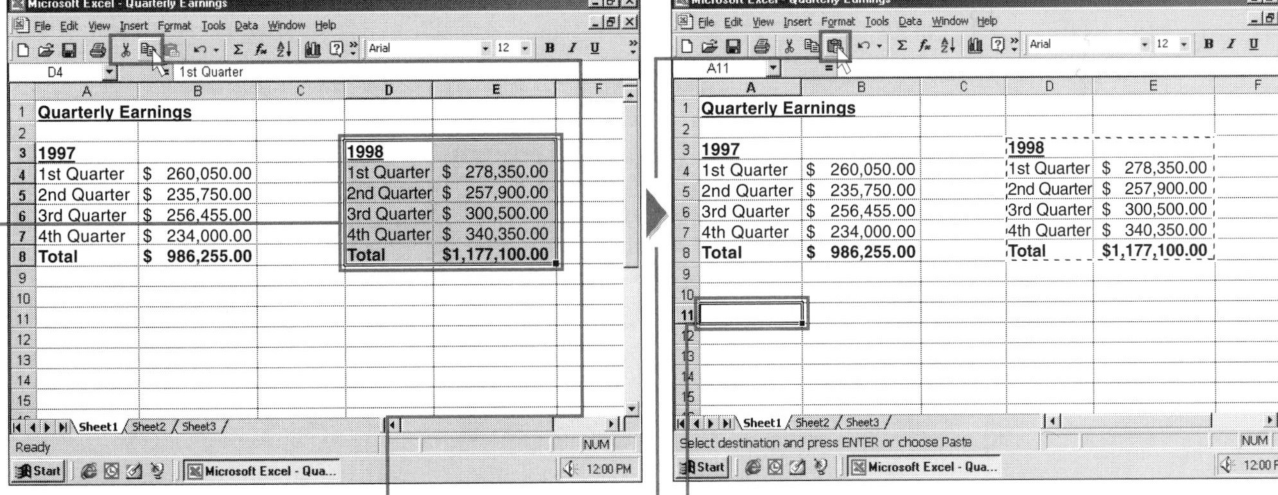

USING THE TOOLBAR BUTTONS

1 Select the cells containing the data you want to move or copy.

2 Click one of the following buttons.

Move data

Copy data

Note: If the button you want is not displayed, click on the Standard toolbar to display all the buttons.

3 Click the cell where you want to place the data. This cell will become the top left cell of the new location.

4 Click to place the data in the new location.

Note: If is not displayed, click on the Standard toolbar to display all the buttons.

■ The data appears in the new location.

CHECK SPELLING

You can quickly find and correct spelling errors in your worksheet.

Excel allows you to check the spelling of words in an entire worksheet or only specific cells. When you check the spelling of an entire worksheet, Excel automatically checks any charts in the worksheet for spelling errors. To check the spelling of only specific cells, you must select the cells before you begin.

Excel compares every word in your worksheet to words in its dictionary. If a word in your worksheet does not exist in Excel's dictionary, Excel considers the word misspelled.

Excel provides a list of suggestions for correcting a spelling error it finds.

You can choose the suggestion you want to replace the error in your worksheet. You can also ignore the error and continue checking your worksheet.

Excel automatically corrects common spelling errors as you type. For example, Excel automatically replaces "frmo" with "from" and "omre" with "more".

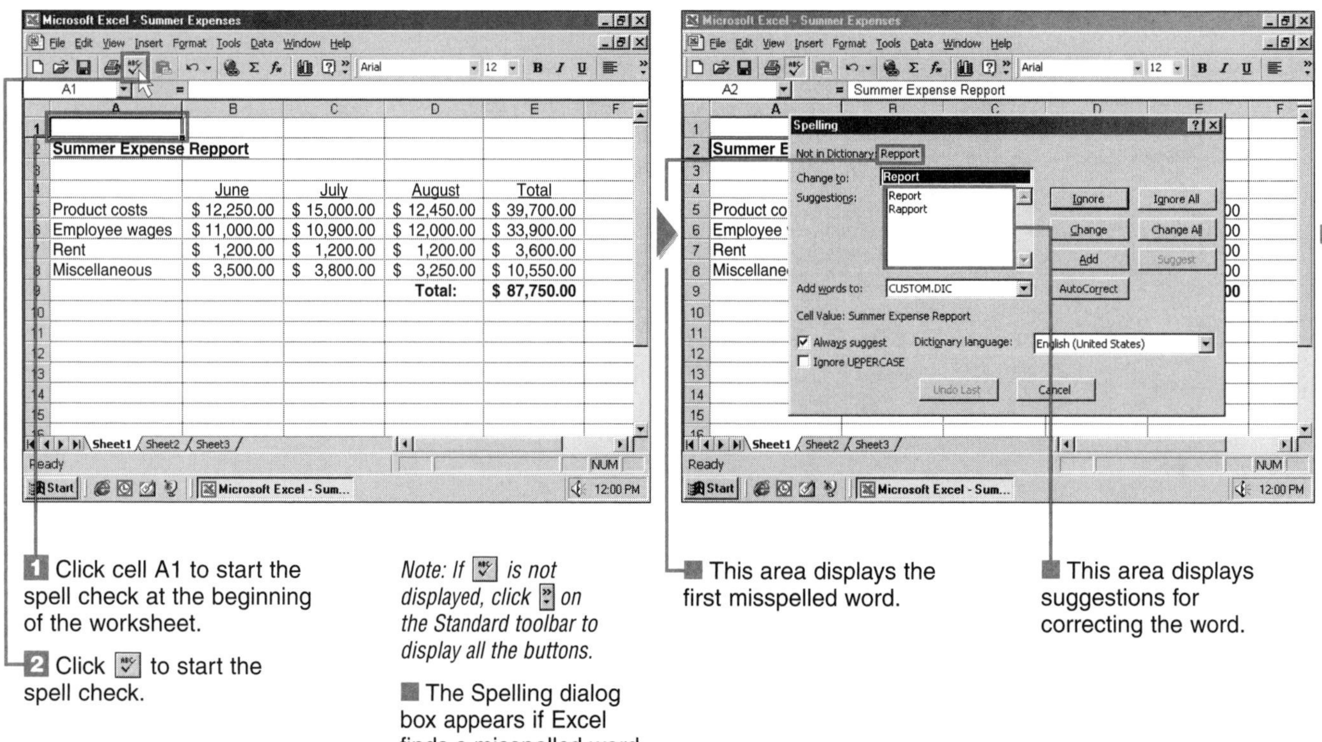

1 Click cell A1 to start the spell check at the beginning of the worksheet.

2 Click (spelling button) to start the spell check.

Note: If (spelling button) is not displayed, click (more buttons) on the Standard toolbar to display all the buttons.

■ The Spelling dialog box appears if Excel finds a misspelled word.

■ This area displays the first misspelled word.

■ This area displays suggestions for correcting the word.

TIPS

Can I add a word to Excel's dictionary?

✔ Many words, such as names or technical terms, are not in Excel's dictionary and will be considered misspelled. You can add a word to the dictionary so Excel will recognize the word during future spell checks. When Excel displays the word in the Spelling dialog box, click the Add button to add the word to the dictionary.

Can I have Excel automatically correct a spelling error I often make?

✔ Yes. When Excel displays the misspelled word in the Spelling dialog box, select the correct spelling of the word. Then click the AutoCorrect button. The next time you make the same error, Excel will automatically correct the error.

How can I check the spelling of several worksheets at once?

✔ Hold down the Ctrl key as you click the tab of each worksheet you want to check. Then perform steps 1 to 6 below. To later ungroup the worksheets, hold down the Ctrl key as you click each worksheet tab again.

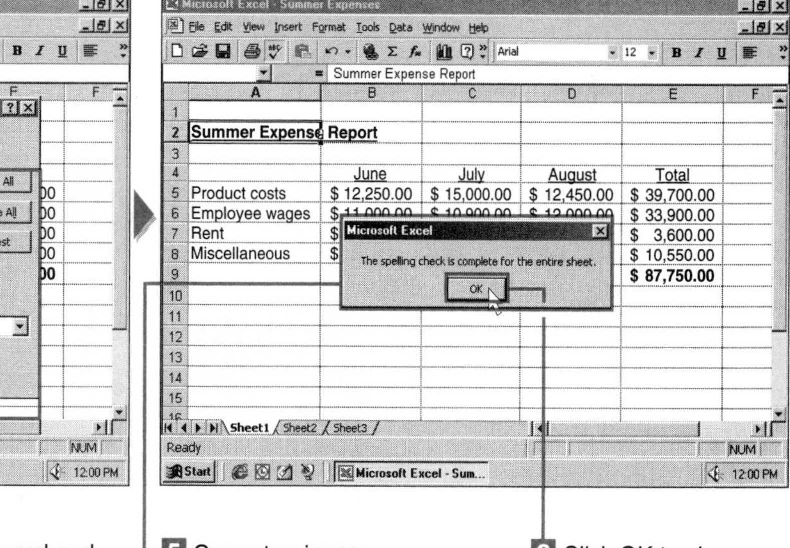

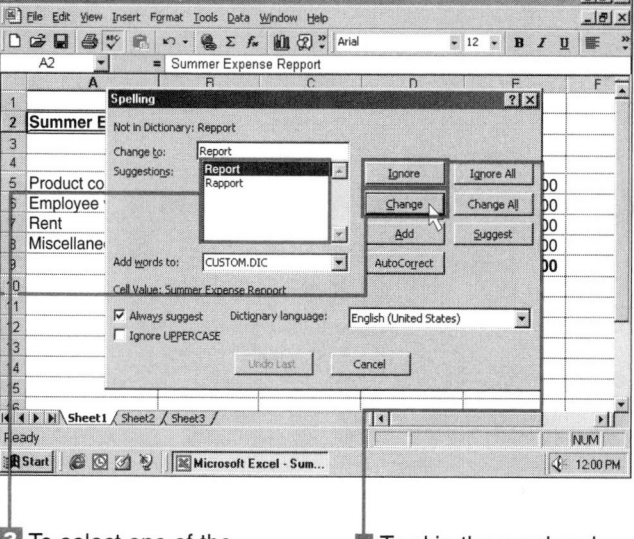

3 To select one of the suggestions, click the suggestion.

4 Click Change to correct the word in the worksheet.

■ To skip the word and continue checking the worksheet, click Ignore.

Note: To skip the word and all occurrences of the word in the worksheet, click Ignore All.

5 Correct or ignore misspelled words until this dialog box appears, telling you the spell check is complete.

6 Click OK to close the dialog box.

FIND DATA

You can use the Find feature to quickly locate a word or number in your worksheet.

You can have Excel search your entire worksheet or only specific cells. To have Excel search only specific cells, you must select the cells before starting the search.

Excel will find the data you specify even if it is part of a larger word or number.

For example, searching for the number 105 will locate cells that contain the numbers 105, 2105 and 1056.

The word or number you want to find may appear in several locations in your worksheet. After you start the search, Excel finds and highlights the cell containing the first instance of the word or number. You can continue the search to find the next instance of the word or number. You can also end the search at any time.

If Excel cannot find the word or number you are searching for, a dialog box will appear, directing you to check the data you specified.

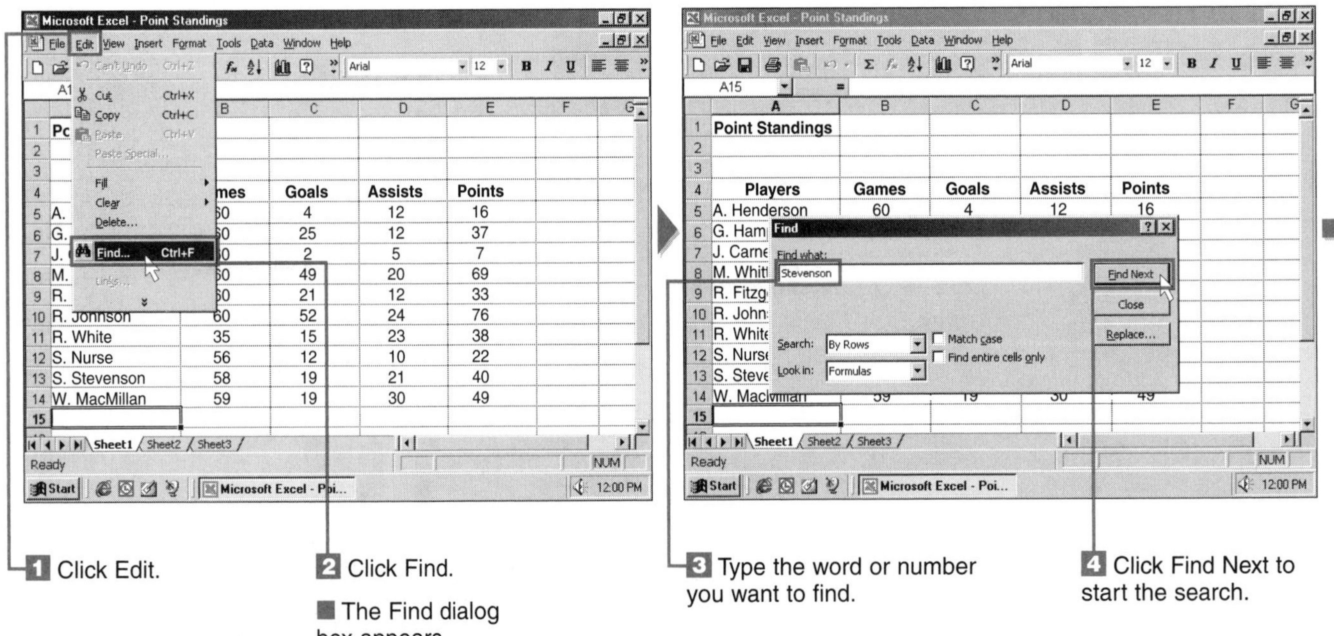

1 Click Edit.

2 Click Find.

■ The Find dialog box appears.

3 Type the word or number you want to find.

4 Click Find Next to start the search.

TIPS

Can I have Excel find a word only when it is capitalized?

✔ You can have Excel find words with exactly matching uppercase and lowercase letters. In the Find dialog box, click the Match case option (☐ changes to ☑).

Can I search for the exact contents of a cell?

✔ You can find only cells that contain an exact match for the data you specify. In the Find dialog box, click the Find entire cells only option (☐ changes to ☑).

Can I replace a word or number Excel finds in my worksheet with new data?

✔ Yes. Perform steps 1 to 3 below and then click the Replace button. In the Replace with area, type the new data. Click the Find Next button to start the search. To replace the word or number Excel finds in your worksheet with the new data, click the Replace button. To replace all occurrences of the word or number in your worksheet with the new data, click the Replace All button. To ignore the word or number and continue with the search, click Find Next.

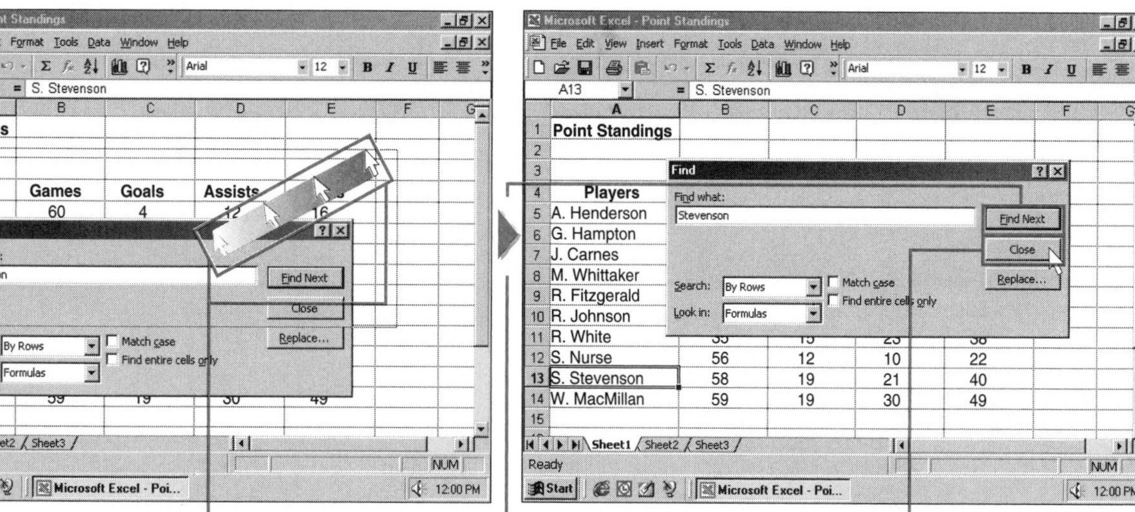

■ Excel highlights the first cell containing the word or number.

■ If the highlighted cell is hidden behind the Find dialog box, you can move the dialog box.

5 To move the Find dialog box, position the mouse over the title bar.

6 Drag the dialog box to a new location.

7 Click Find Next to find the next matching word or number.

8 To close the Find dialog box at any time, click Close.

INSERT A ROW OR COLUMN

When you want to insert additional data into your worksheet, you can add a row or column.

Before you can add a row or column, you must select an existing row or column in your worksheet.

When you insert a row, the row you selected and the rows that follow shift downward. When you insert a column, the column you selected and the columns that follow shift to the right. Excel automatically adjusts the row numbers and column letters in your worksheet for you.

The row you insert will be the same height as the row above it. The column you insert will be the same width as the column to its left.

When you insert a row or column, Excel automatically updates any formulas affected by the insertion. For information on formulas, see page 208.

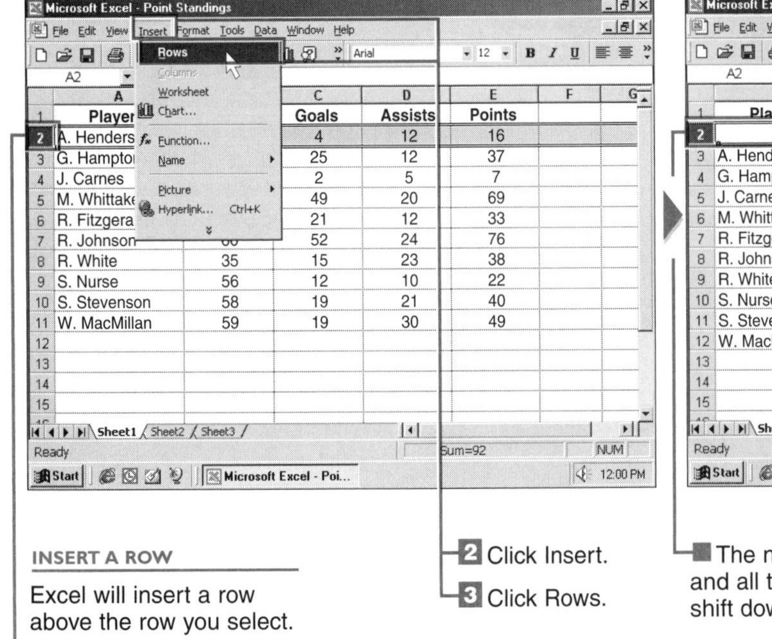

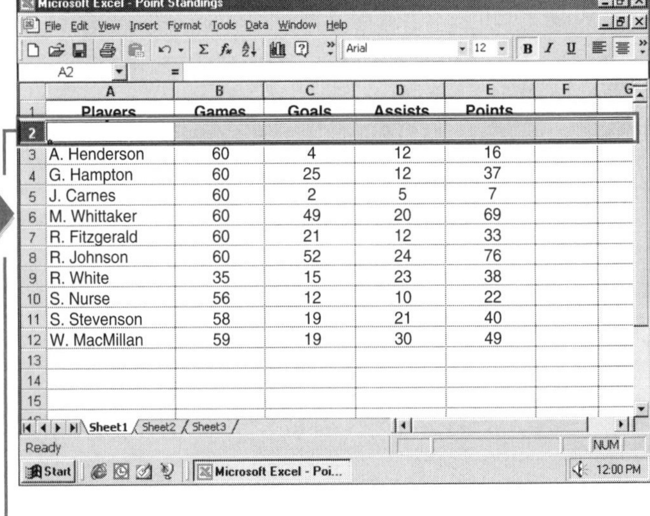

INSERT A ROW

Excel will insert a row above the row you select.

1 To select a row, click the row number.

2 Click Insert.

3 Click Rows.

■ The new row appears and all the rows that follow shift downward.

TIPS

How do I insert several rows or columns at once?

✔ Excel will insert as many rows or columns as you select. For example, to insert three columns, you must select three columns to the right of where you want the new columns to appear. Position the mouse ✥ over the letter of the first column you want to select. Then drag the mouse to highlight the three columns. Choose the Insert menu and then select Columns.

Can I insert a group of cells instead of an entire row or column?

✔ Yes. Select the cells where you want the new cells to appear. Select the Insert menu and click Cells. Then choose an option to specify whether you want to shift the existing cells down or to the right (○ changes to ⦿).

Can I increase the space between data in my worksheet without inserting a row or column?

✔ You can change the height of rows or width of columns to increase the space between data in your worksheet. For information on changing row height or column width, see page 216.

INSERT A COLUMN

Excel will insert a column to the left of the column you select.

1 To select a column, click the column letter.

2 Click Insert.

3 Click Columns.

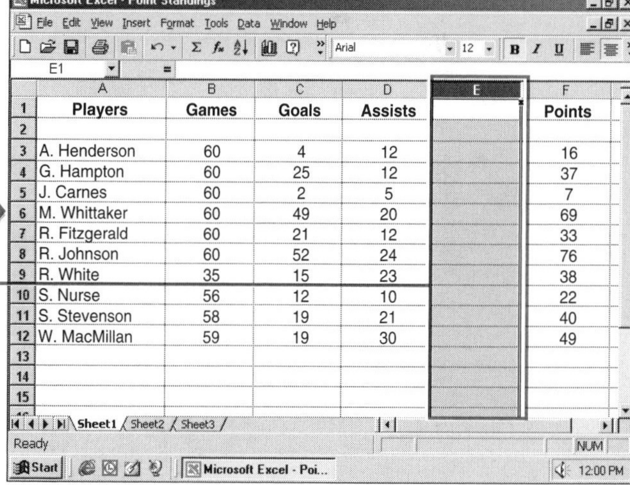

■ The new column appears and all the columns that follow shift to the right.

DELETE A ROW OR COLUMN

You can delete a row or column from your worksheet to remove data you no longer need. When you delete a row or column, all the data in the row or column is also deleted.

To delete a row or column, you must first select the row or column you want to delete.

The numbers along the left side of your worksheet identify each row. The letters along the top of your worksheet identify each column. When you delete a row, the remaining rows in your worksheet shift upward. When you delete a column, the remaining columns shift to the left. Excel automatically adjusts the row numbers and column letters in your worksheet for you.

If you regret deleting a row or column, you can use the Undo feature to immediately return the row or column to your worksheet. For more information on the Undo feature, see page 202.

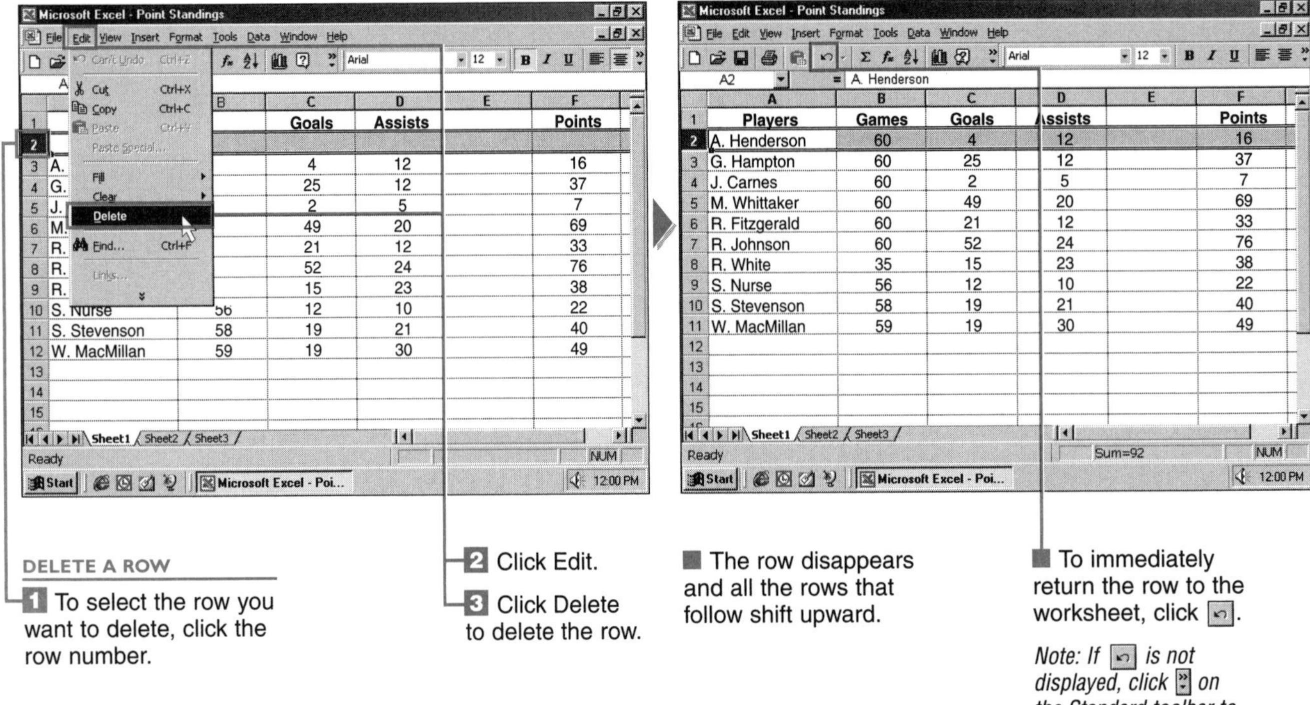

DELETE A ROW

1 To select the row you want to delete, click the row number.

2 Click Edit.

3 Click Delete to delete the row.

■ The row disappears and all the rows that follow shift upward.

■ To immediately return the row to the worksheet, click ↶.

Note: If ↶ is not displayed, click » on the Standard toolbar to display all the buttons.

TIPS

How do I delete several rows or columns at once?

✔ Click the row number or column letter of the first row or column you want to delete. Hold down the Ctrl key as you click the row numbers or column letters of the other rows or columns you want to delete. Select the Edit menu and then click Delete.

Can I delete a group of cells instead of an entire row or column?

✔ Yes. Select the cells you want to delete. Select the Edit menu and then click Delete. Then choose an option to specify whether you want to shift the remaining cells up or to the left (○ changes to ⊙).

Why did #REF! appear in a cell after I deleted a row or column?

✔ If #REF! appears in a cell in your worksheet, you may have deleted data needed to calculate a formula. Before you delete a row or column, make sure the row or column does not contain data that is used in a formula. For information on formulas, see page 208.

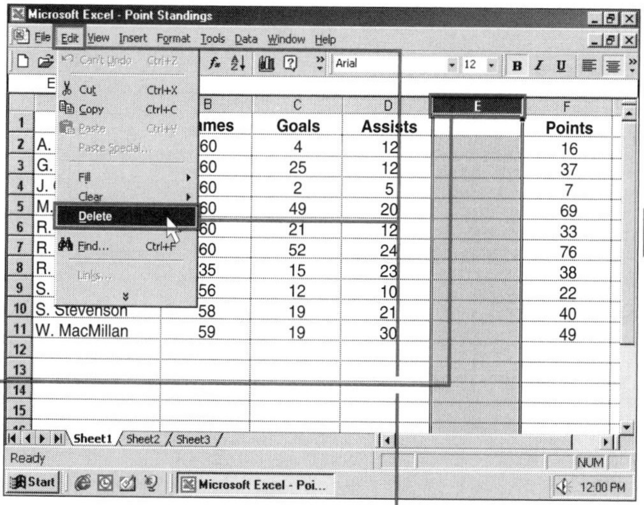

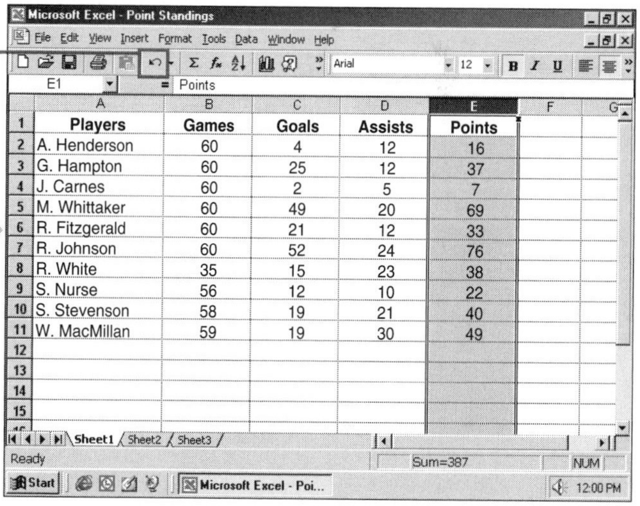

	Players	Games	Goals	Assists	Points
2	A. Henderson	60	4	12	16
3	G. Hampton	60	25	12	37
4	J. Carnes	60	2	5	7
5	M. Whittaker	60	49	20	69
6	R. Fitzgerald	60	21	12	33
7	R. Johnson	60	52	24	76
8	R. White	35	15	23	38
9	S. Nurse	56	12	10	22
10	S. Stevenson	58	19	21	40
11	W. MacMillan	59	19	30	49

DELETE A COLUMN

1 To select the column you want to delete, click the column letter.

2 Click Edit.

3 Click Delete to delete the column.

■ The column disappears and all the columns that follow shift to the left.

■ To immediately return the column to the worksheet, click ↶.

Note: If ↶ is not displayed, click » on the Standard toolbar to display all the buttons.

HIDE COLUMNS

If you do not want other people to view confidential data in your worksheet, you can hide the columns containing the data. You can also hide columns to reduce the amount of data displayed on your screen. This can help you work with specific data and can make your worksheet easier to read.

Hiding columns does not affect the data in a worksheet. Formulas and functions in the worksheet will continue to work when they are hidden. You can also use the data from cells in hidden columns when entering formulas and functions in your worksheet.

Hidden columns do not appear when you print your worksheet. This allows you to produce a printed copy of your worksheet without including confidential data.

Some macros may not work properly when you hide columns. For information on macros, see page 280.

You can redisplay hidden columns at any time to view the data in the columns.

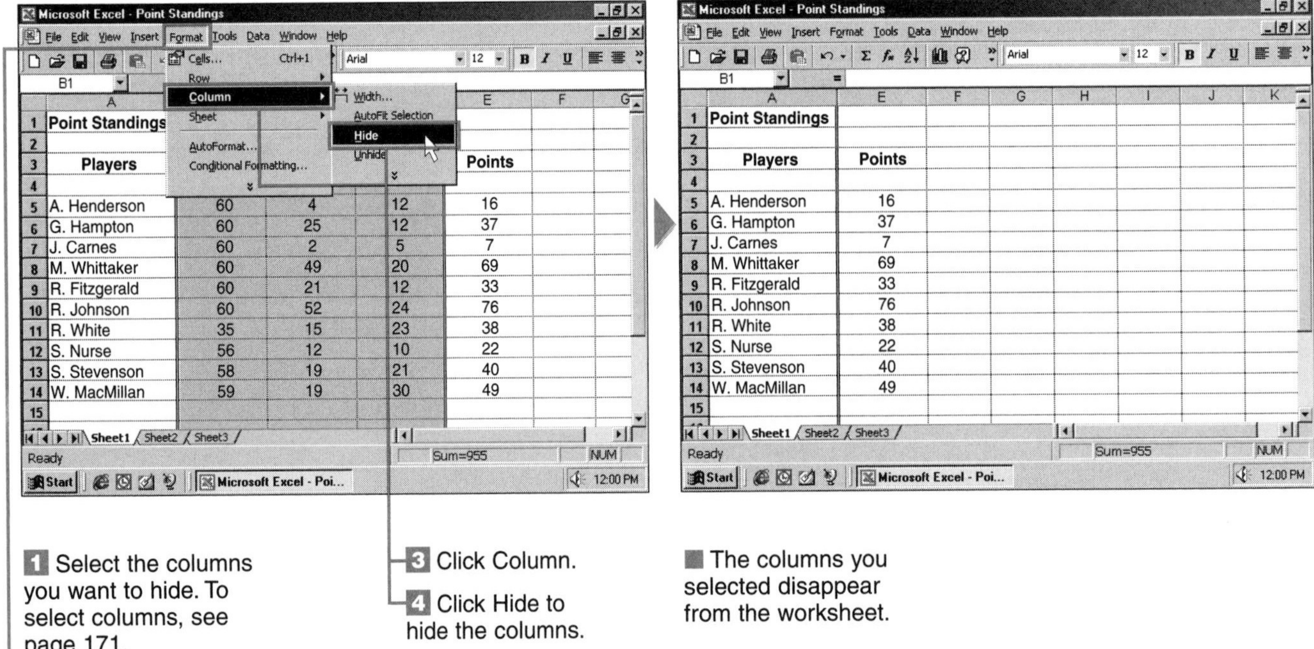

1 Select the columns you want to hide. To select columns, see page 171.

2 Click Format.

3 Click Column.

4 Click Hide to hide the columns.

■ The columns you selected disappear from the worksheet.

TIPS

Can I hide rows in a worksheet?

✔ Yes. Select the rows you want to hide. From the Format menu, select Row and then click Hide. To redisplay the rows, select the rows directly above and below the hidden rows. From the Format menu, select Row and then click Unhide.

If I hide column A, how do I redisplay the column?

✔ Choose the Edit menu and then select Go To. In the Reference area, type **A1** and then press the Enter key. From the Format menu, select Column and then click Unhide.

Can I hide an entire worksheet in my workbook?

✔ Yes. From the Format menu, select Sheet and then click Hide. To redisplay the worksheet, select the Format menu, click Sheet and then click Unhide. Click the name of the worksheet you want to redisplay and then click OK.

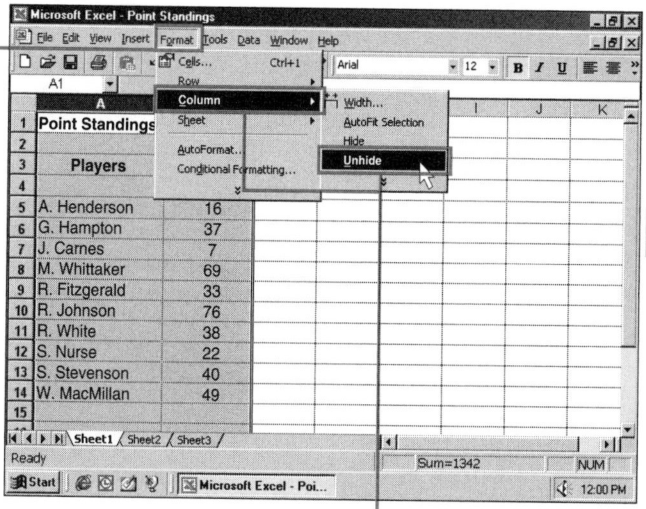

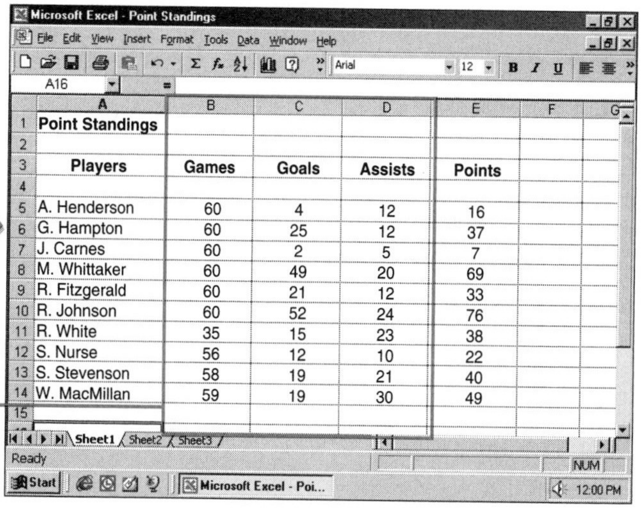

DISPLAY HIDDEN COLUMNS

1 Select the columns on each side of the hidden columns. To select columns, see page 171.

2 Click Format.

3 Click Column.

4 Click Unhide to display the hidden columns.

■ The columns reappear in the worksheet.

■ To deselect cells, click any cell.

NAME CELLS

You can give cells in your worksheet a meaningful name. Using named cells can save you time when selecting cells or entering formulas. You can name a single cell or a range of cells.

Cell names can be up to 255 characters in length. A cell name must begin with either a letter or an underscore character (_). The remaining characters can be any combination of letters, numbers, underscore characters or periods, but cannot include spaces. You cannot use a cell reference, such as D4, as a cell name.

After you name cells in your worksheet, you can use the name to quickly select the cells. When you select a cell name, Excel highlights the cell or range of cells in the worksheet.

Naming cells can help make formulas and functions easier to enter and understand. For example, if you name cell C4 "Income" and name cell D4 "Expenses", you can type the formula =Income-Expenses, instead of typing =C4-D4.

After you name cells in a worksheet, you can use the name in a formula in any worksheet in the workbook.

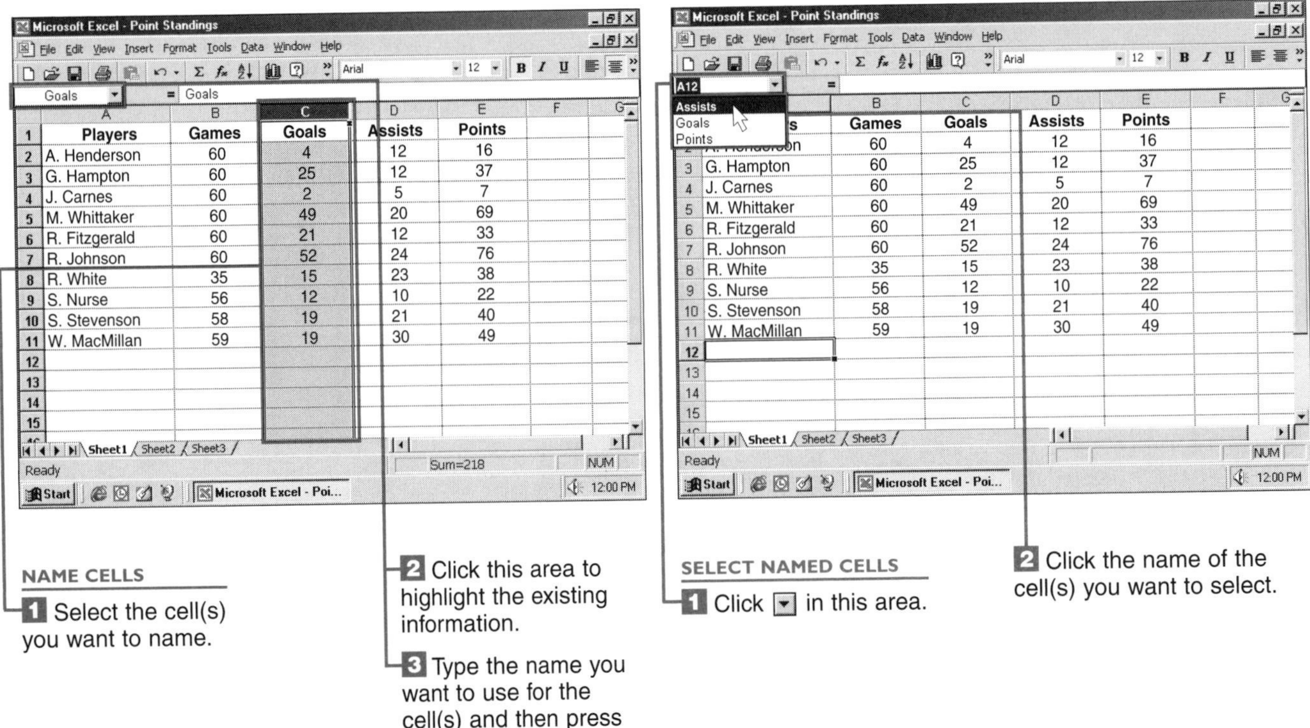

NAME CELLS

1. Select the cell(s) you want to name.
2. Click this area to highlight the existing information.
3. Type the name you want to use for the cell(s) and then press the Enter key.

SELECT NAMED CELLS

1. Click ▾ in this area.
2. Click the name of the cell(s) you want to select.

TIPS

Is there another way to insert a cell name in a formula?

✔ Select a cell and begin typing the formula. When you are ready to insert a cell name, choose the Insert menu, select Name and then click Paste. Select the name you want to insert in the formula and then click OK.

How do I delete a name I have assigned to cells?

✔ Choose the Insert menu, select Name and then click Define. Select the name you want to delete and click Delete. Then click OK.

Can I use column and row labels in my worksheet to name cells?

✔ Yes. Select the range of cells you want to name, including the column and row labels. Choose the Insert menu, select Name and then click Create. Excel will use each option that displays a check mark (✔) to name the cells. You can click an option to add or remove a check mark. Then click OK. You can now use the column and row labels to select named cells or to create formulas and functions.

Microsoft Excel - Point Standings

Assists = Assists

	A	B	C	D	E
1	Players	Games	Goals	Assists	Points
2	A. Henderson	60	4	12	16
3	G. Hampton	60	25	12	37
4	J. Carnes	60	2	5	7
5	M. Whittaker	60	49	20	69
6	R. Fitzgerald	60	21	12	33
7	R. Johnson	60	52	24	76
8	R. White	35	15	23	38
9	S. Nurse	56	12	10	22
10	S. Stevenson	58	19	21	40
11	W. MacMillan	59	19	30	49

Sum=169

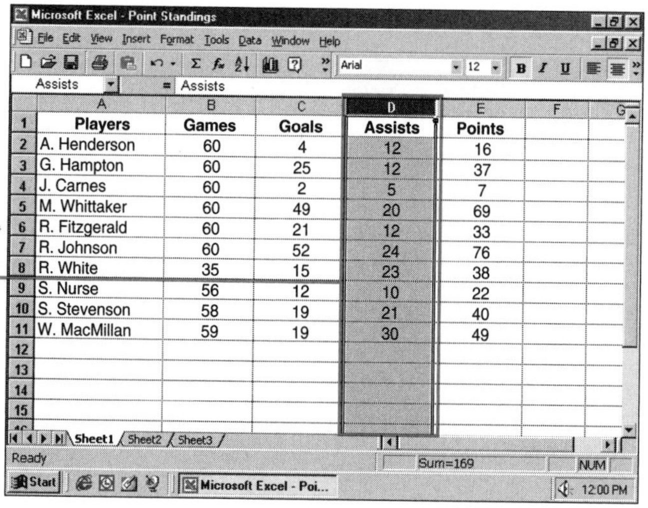

■ Excel highlights the cell(s) in the worksheet.

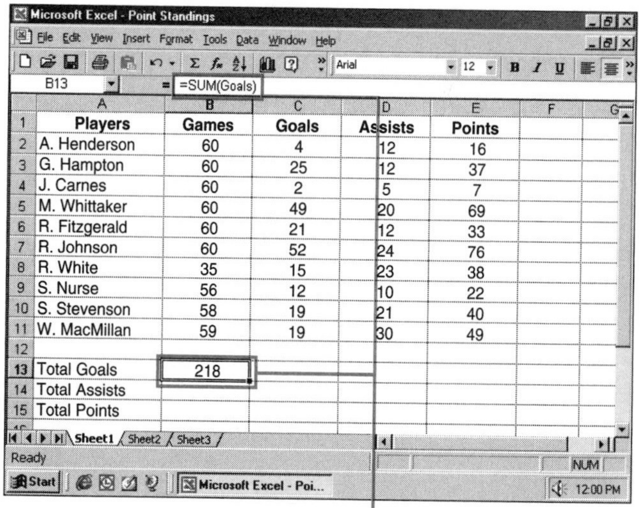

Microsoft Excel - Point Standings

B13 = =SUM(Goals)

	A	B	C	D	E
1	Players	Games	Goals	Assists	Points
2	A. Henderson	60	4	12	16
3	G. Hampton	60	25	12	37
4	J. Carnes	60	2	5	7
5	M. Whittaker	60	49	20	69
6	R. Fitzgerald	60	21	12	33
7	R. Johnson	60	52	24	76
8	R. White	35	15	23	38
9	S. Nurse	56	12	10	22
10	S. Stevenson	58	19	21	40
11	W. MacMillan	59	19	30	49
12					
13	Total Goals	218			
14	Total Assists				
15	Total Points				

USING NAMED CELLS IN FORMULAS AND FUNCTIONS

■ In this example, we named column C "Goals".

■ This cell contains the formula =SUM(Goals)

UNDO CHANGES

Excel remembers the last changes you made to your worksheet. If you regret these changes, you can cancel them by using the Undo feature.

The Undo feature can cancel your last editing and formatting changes, but certain actions, such as creating a chart, cannot be undone. You also cannot undo actions such as adding, moving and renaming worksheets. You will not be able to undo changes after you save your workbook or run a macro.

If you do not like the results of canceling an editing or formatting change, you can easily reverse the results.

You can use the Undo feature to cancel one change at a time or many changes at once.

Excel stores a list of the last 16 changes you made in all of your open worksheets and workbooks. When you select the change you want to cancel from the list, Excel cancels the change and all the changes you made since that change.

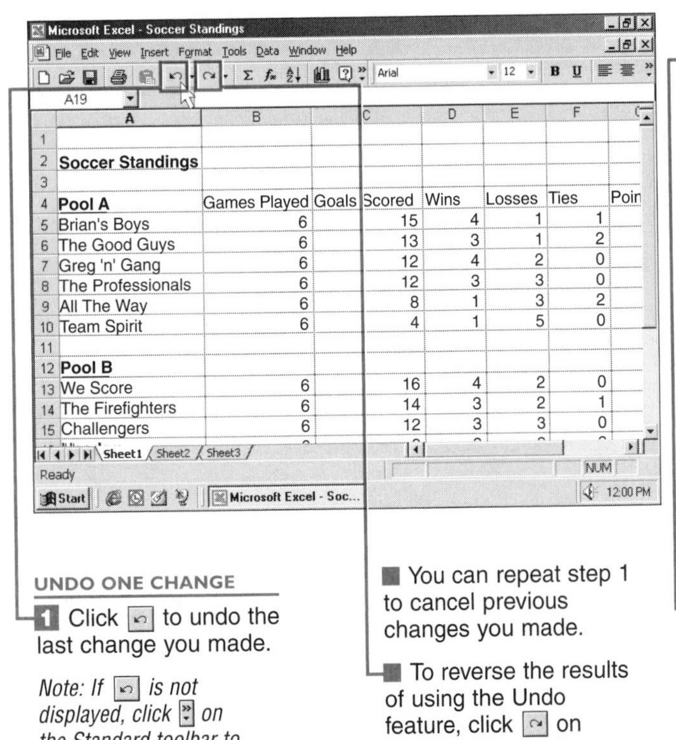

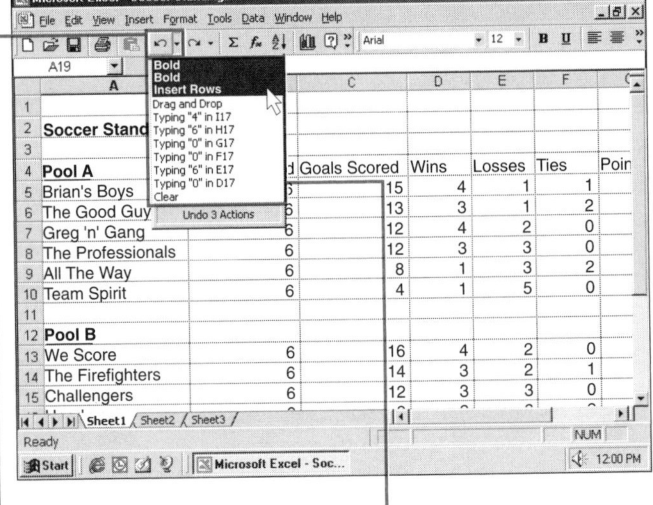

UNDO ONE CHANGE

1 Click [Undo] to undo the last change you made.

Note: If [Undo] is not displayed, click [»] on the Standard toolbar to display all the buttons.

■ You can repeat step 1 to cancel previous changes you made.

■ To reverse the results of using the Undo feature, click [Redo] on the Standard toolbar.

UNDO MULTIPLE CHANGES

1 Click [▾] in this area to view a list of the last changes you made.

Note: If [Undo ▾] is not displayed, click [»] on the Standard toolbar to display all the buttons.

2 Click the change you want to undo.

Note: Excel cancels the change you select and all the changes above it in the list.

ZOOM IN OR OUT

Excel lets you enlarge or reduce the display of data on your screen. Changing the zoom setting allows you to see data in more detail or display more data on your screen at once.

Zoom settings are measured in percentages. The higher the percentage, the more detail you will be able to view. By default, Excel displays your worksheets in the 100% zoom setting. You can choose any zoom setting you want. You can also choose the Selection setting to enlarge a group of cells you selected to fill your screen.

Changing the zoom setting will not affect the display of data in other worksheets in the workbook or in other workbooks. The zoom setting also does not change the way data appears on a printed page.

The zoom setting is saved as part of your worksheet. The next time you open your workbook, the worksheet will appear in the zoom setting you selected.

1 Click ▾ in this area to display a list of zoom settings.

Note: If the Zoom area is not displayed, click » on the Standard toolbar to display all the buttons.

2 Click the zoom setting you want to use.

Note: Excel initially displays the worksheet in the 100% zoom setting.

■ The worksheet appears in the new zoom setting. You can edit the worksheet as usual.

■ You can also type a specific zoom setting. Click this area and type the zoom setting. Then press the Enter key.

SPLIT A WORKSHEET

You can split your worksheet into separate sections. This lets you display different areas of a large worksheet at the same time. Each section contains a copy of your entire worksheet.

Excel allows you to split a worksheet vertically, horizontally or both.

A dividing line indicates where you split your worksheet. You can scroll through each section of a split worksheet.

A worksheet that is split vertically makes it easy to compare data in different columns in your worksheet. A worksheet that is split horizontally makes it easy to compare data in different rows. When you split your worksheet both vertically and horizontally, you can view data in four different areas of your worksheet at once.

The dividing lines that split your worksheet into sections will not appear when the worksheet is printed.

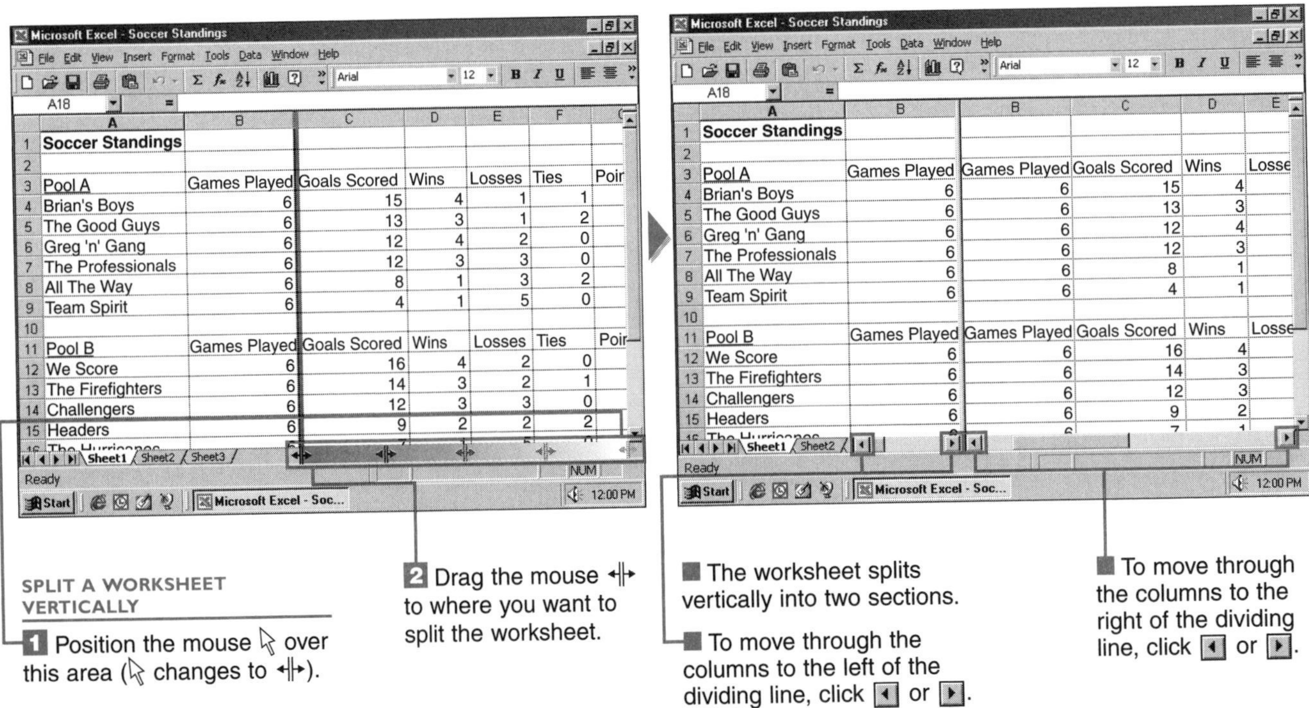

SPLIT A WORKSHEET VERTICALLY

1 Position the mouse ⇖ over this area (⇖ changes to ◂|▸).

2 Drag the mouse ◂|▸ to where you want to split the worksheet.

■ The worksheet splits vertically into two sections.

■ To move through the columns to the left of the dividing line, click ◂ or ▸.

■ To move through the columns to the right of the dividing line, click ◂ or ▸.

TIPS

How do I remove the split from my worksheet?

✔ To remove the split, click the Window menu and then select Remove Split.

How can I keep row or column labels displayed on my screen as I scroll through a large worksheet?

✔ You can freeze the row or column containing the labels you want to remain on your screen. Select the row below or the column to the right of the row or column you want to freeze. Click the Window menu and then select Freeze Panes. To later unfreeze the row or column, click the Window menu and then select Unfreeze Panes.

Can I compare the data on worksheets in different workbooks?

✔ Yes. Open the workbooks containing the worksheets you want to view. Click the Window menu and then select Arrange. To be able to clearly view and compare the data, click the Tiled option (○ changes to ⊙) and then click OK.

SPLIT A WORKSHEET HORIZONTALLY

1 Position the mouse over this area (changes to).

2 Drag the mouse to where you want to split the worksheet.

■ The worksheet splits horizontally into two sections.

■ To move through the rows above the dividing line, click ▲ or ▼.

■ To move through the rows below the dividing line, click ▲ or ▼.

INTRODUCTION TO FORMULAS AND FUNCTIONS

Formulas

Excel allows you to use formulas to calculate and analyze data in your worksheet. A formula always begins with an equal sign (=).

You can use arithmetic operators in formulas to perform mathematical calculations. Arithmetic operators include the addition (+), subtraction (-), multiplication (*), division (/), percent (%) and exponent (^) symbols.

You can use comparison operators in formulas to perform comparisons between two values. A formula containing comparison operators will return a value of TRUE or FALSE. Comparison operators include the greater than (>), less than (<), equal to (=), greater than or equal to (>=), less than or equal to (<=) and not equal to (<>) symbols.

In a formula, Excel performs calculations in a specific order. Excel calculates percentages first and then exponents, followed by multiplication and division. Excel then calculates addition and subtraction. Comparison operators are calculated last.

You can use parentheses ( ) to change the order in which Excel performs calculations. Excel will calculate the data inside the parentheses first. For example, in the formula =10*(1+2), the addition is performed before the multiplication.

Pizza Parlor

ORDERS

	A	B
1	Pizza	600
2	Spaghetti	200
3	Garlic Bread	400
4	TOTAL	1200

=B1+B2+B3

Functions

A function is a ready-to-use formula that you can use to perform a calculation on the data in your worksheet. Excel's functions allow you to perform calculations without having to type long, complex formulas.

A function always begins with an equal sign (=). The data Excel will use to calculate a function is enclosed in parentheses ( ).

Each cell or number used in a function is called an argument. When a comma (,) separates arguments in a function, Excel uses each argument to perform the calculation. For example, =SUM(A1,A2,A3) is the same as the formula =A1+A2+A3. When a colon (:) separates arguments in a function, Excel uses each of the specified arguments and all arguments between them to perform the calculation. For example, =SUM(A1:A3) is the same as the formula =A1+A2+A3.

Excel offers over 200 functions to help you analyze data. There are financial functions, math and trigonometry functions, date and time functions and statistical functions.

Examples of Formulas and Functions

	A
1	10
2	20
3	30
4	40
5	
6	

=A1+A2+A3*A4
=10+20+30*40 = 1230

=A1+(A2+A3)*A4
=10+(20+30)*40 = 2010

=A3/A1+A2+A4
=30/10+20+40 = 63

=A3/(A1+A2)+A4
=30/(10+20)+40 = 41

	A
1	10
2	20
3	30
4	40
5	
6	

=AVERAGE(A1:A4)
=(10+20+30+40)/4 = 25

=COUNT(A1:A4) = 4

=MAX(A1:A4) = 40

=SUM(A1:A4)
=10+20+30+40 = 100

Errors in Formulas

An error message appears when Excel cannot properly calculate a formula. Errors in formulas are often the result of typing mistakes. You can correct an error by editing the data in the cell containing the error.

indicates the column is too narrow to display the result of the calculation.

#DIV/0! indicates the formula divides a number by zero (0). Excel considers a blank cell to contain a value of zero.

#NAME? indicates the formula contains a function name or cell reference Excel does not recognize.

#REF! indicates the formula refers to a cell that is not valid. For example, a cell used in the formula may have been deleted.

#VALUE! indicates the formula contains a cell reference for a cell that Excel cannot use in a calculation. For example, the formula may refer to a cell containing text.

#N/A indicates the formula refers to a value that is not available.

#NULL! indicates the formula refers to an intersection of cells that do not intersect. This may occur when there is a space between two cell references instead of a comma (,) or colon (:).

A circular reference occurs when a formula refers to the cell containing the formula. Excel cannot calculate a formula that contains a circular reference and displays a warning message on your screen when it finds this type of error.

ENTER A FORMULA

You can enter a formula into any cell in your worksheet. A formula helps you calculate and analyze data in your worksheet. A formula always begins with an equal sign (=).

When entering formulas, you should use cell references instead of actual data whenever possible. For example, you should enter the formula =A1+A2 instead of =10+30. When you use cell references and you change a number used in the formula, Excel will automatically redo the calculations for you. For example, if you base your sales commissions on a value of 10% and then change the value to 12%, all the commissions in your worksheet will automatically change.

A cell displays the result of a formula, while the formula bar displays the formula itself.

You should always be careful to enter the correct cell references and mathematical symbols in a formula. Errors in formulas are often the result of typing mistakes. You can edit a formula to correct an error or change the formula. When you edit a formula, Excel outlines each cell used in the formula with a different color.

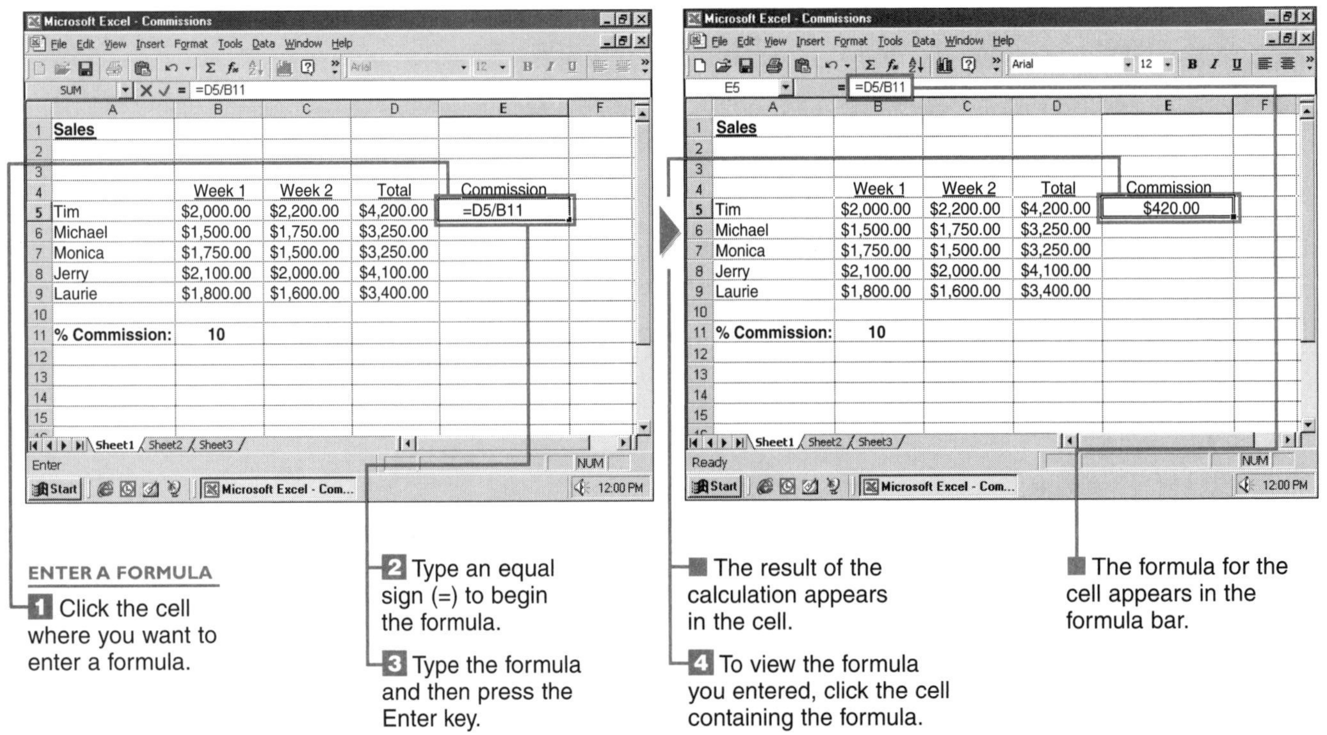

ENTER A FORMULA

1 Click the cell where you want to enter a formula.

2 Type an equal sign (=) to begin the formula.

3 Type the formula and then press the Enter key.

■ The result of the calculation appears in the cell.

4 To view the formula you entered, click the cell containing the formula.

■ The formula for the cell appears in the formula bar.

TIPS

How can I quickly enter cell references into a formula?

✔ Perform the steps on page 208, except click each cell you want to use instead of typing the cell references. This method can help minimize typing errors.

Can I reference a cell in another worksheet or another workbook?

✔ Yes. To reference a cell in another worksheet in the same workbook, type the worksheet name, followed by an exclamation mark and the cell reference. For example, type **Sheet1!A1**. To reference a cell in a worksheet in another workbook, type the workbook name in square brackets and then type the worksheet name, followed by an exclamation mark and the cell reference. For example, type **[Budget.xls]Sheet1!A1**.

Why do I get an error message when I try to reference a cell in another worksheet?

✔ If you have renamed a worksheet or workbook and included spaces, you must enclose the name of the worksheet in single quotation marks in the formula. For example, type **'My Sheet'!A1** or **'[My Budget.xls]Sheet1'!A1**.

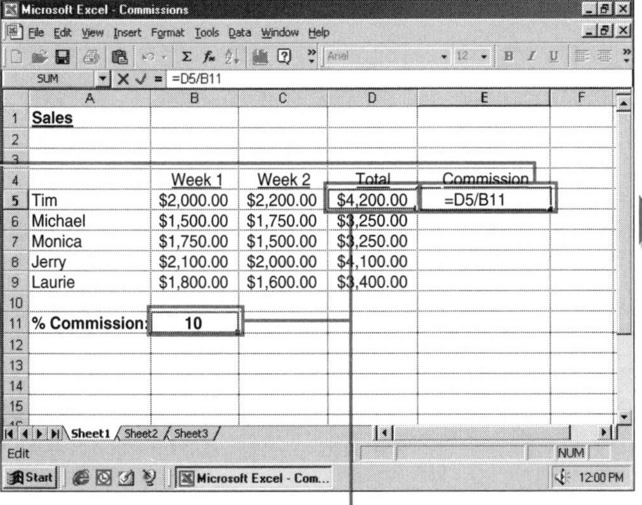

EDIT A FORMULA

1 Double-click the cell containing the formula you want to change.

■ The formula appears in the cell.

■ Excel uses different colors to outline each cell used in the formula.

2 Edit the formula.

Note: To edit data in a cell, perform steps 2 to 4 starting on page 186.

3 Press the Enter key when you have finished making changes to the formula.

ENTER A FUNCTION

A function is a ready-to-use formula that you can use to perform a calculation in your worksheet.

Excel offers over 200 functions for you to choose from. Excel groups the functions into categories according to their use. If you do not know which category contains the function you want to use, you can choose the All category to display a list of all the functions.

You can specify the cells containing the numbers you want to use in a function. Each cell or number in a function is called an argument. A function may require one or more arguments.

The arguments in a function are enclosed in parentheses and separated by commas (,) or a colon (:). When commas (,) separate arguments, Excel uses each argument to perform the calculation. For example, =SUM(A1,A2,A3) is the same as the formula =A1+A2+A3. When a colon (:) separates arguments, Excel uses the specified arguments and all arguments between them to perform the calculation. For example, =SUM(B1:B3) is the same as the formula =B1+B2+B3.

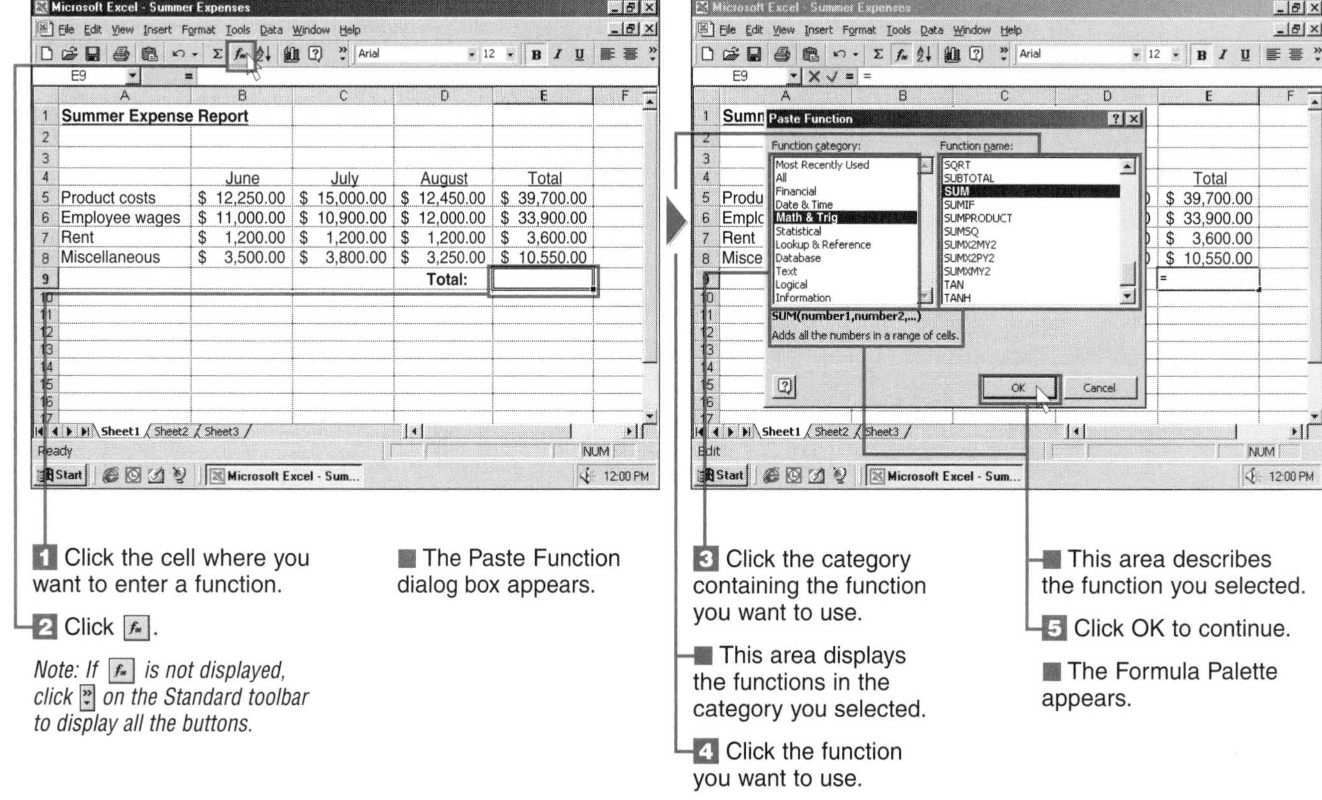

1 Click the cell where you want to enter a function.

2 Click [fx].

Note: If [fx] is not displayed, click [»] on the Standard toolbar to display all the buttons.

■ The Paste Function dialog box appears.

3 Click the category containing the function you want to use.

■ This area displays the functions in the category you selected.

4 Click the function you want to use.

■ This area describes the function you selected.

5 Click OK to continue.

■ The Formula Palette appears.

TIPS

How do I move the Formula Palette so it does not cover the cells I want to select?

✔ Position the mouse pointer over a blank area of the Formula Palette and then drag the palette to a new location on your screen.

How can I quickly enter the numbers I want to use for a function?

✔ When entering numbers for a function in the Formula Palette, you can select a group of cells rather than selecting each cell individually. For example, to sum the numbers in cells A1 to A5, you can drag the mouse pointer over the cells to quickly enter all the numbers.

Can I enter a function myself?

✔ If you know the name of the function you want to use, you can enter the function directly into a cell. You must start the function with an equal sign (=), enclose the arguments in parentheses ( ) and separate the arguments with commas (,) or a colon (:).

Can I edit a function?

✔ You can edit a function as you would edit any data in a cell. To edit data in a cell, see page 186.

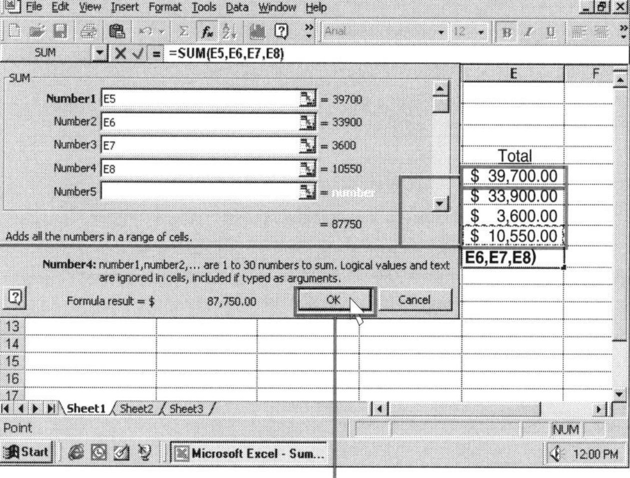

6 To enter the first number for the function, click the cell that contains the number and then press the Tab key. Repeat this step for each number you want to use in the function.

Note: If the number you want to use does not appear in the worksheet, type the number.

7 Click OK to enter the function in the worksheet.

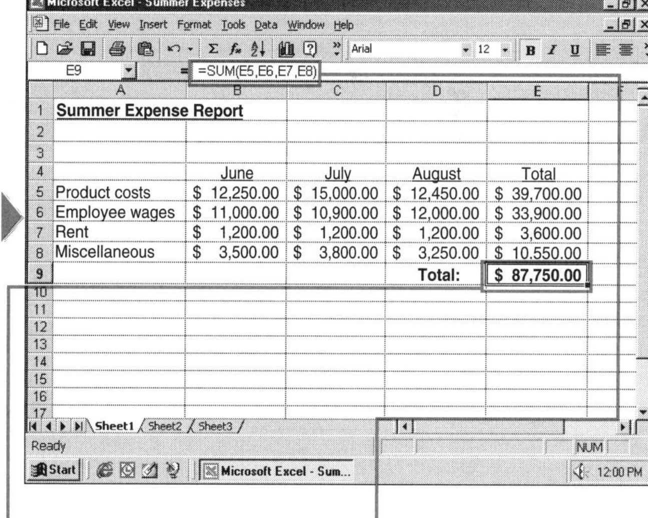

■ The result of the function appears in the cell.

■ The function for the active cell appears in the formula bar.

ADD NUMBERS

You can quickly calculate the sum of a list of numbers in your worksheet.

You can use the AutoSum feature to quickly add numbers in rows or columns. When you use the AutoSum feature, you can select a cell below or to the right of the cells containing the numbers you want to add. The AutoSum feature automatically inserts the SUM function in the cell you select.

Excel outlines the cells it will use in the AutoSum calculation with a dotted line. If Excel outlines the wrong cells, you can select the cells you want to use in the calculation.

You can use the AutoCalculate feature to display the sum of numbers without entering a formula in your worksheet. When you select two or more cells, AutoCalculate displays the sum of the selected cells in the bottom right corner of your screen.

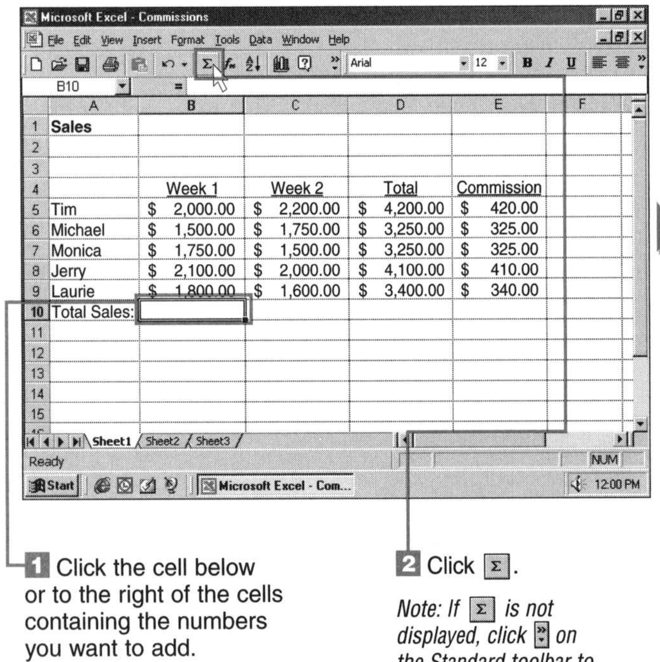

1 Click the cell below or to the right of the cells containing the numbers you want to add.

2 Click Σ.

Note: If Σ is not displayed, click » on the Standard toolbar to display all the buttons.

■ Excel outlines the cells it will use in the calculation with a dotted line.

■ If Excel does not outline the correct cells, select the cells containing the numbers you want to add.

TIPS

Can I have AutoCalculate perform other calculations?

✔ Yes. Select the cells you want to calculate and then right-click the area in the bottom right corner of your screen that displays AutoCalculate results. From the menu that appears, select the calculation you want to perform. Average calculates the average value of a list of numbers. Count calculates the number of items in a list, including text. Count Nums calculates the number of values in a list. Max finds the largest value in a list. Min finds the smallest value in a list.

Can Excel calculate a grand total?

✔ If your worksheet contains several subtotals, you can have Excel quickly calculate a grand total. Click the cell below or to the right of the cells containing the subtotals. Click the AutoSum button (Σ) on the Standard toolbar. Then press the Enter key to calculate the grand total.

Microsoft Excel - Commissions

File Edit View Insert Format Tools Data Window Help

C5 = 2200

	A	B	C	D	E	F
1	Sales					
2						
3						
4		Week 1	Week 2	Total	Commission	
5	Tim	$ 2,000.00	$ 2,200.00	$ 4,200.00	$ 420.00	
6	Michael	$ 1,500.00	$ 1,750.00	$ 3,250.00	$ 325.00	
7	Monica	$ 1,750.00	$ 1,500.00	$ 3,250.00	$ 325.00	
8	Jerry	$ 2,100.00	$ 2,000.00	$ 4,100.00	$ 410.00	
9	Laurie	$ 1,800.00	$ 1,600.00	$ 3,400.00	$ 340.00	
10	Total Sales:	$ 9,150.00				

Ready Sum= $ 9,050.00 NUM

USING AUTOCALCULATE

1 Select the cells you want to include in the calculation.

■ This area displays the sum of the cells you selected.

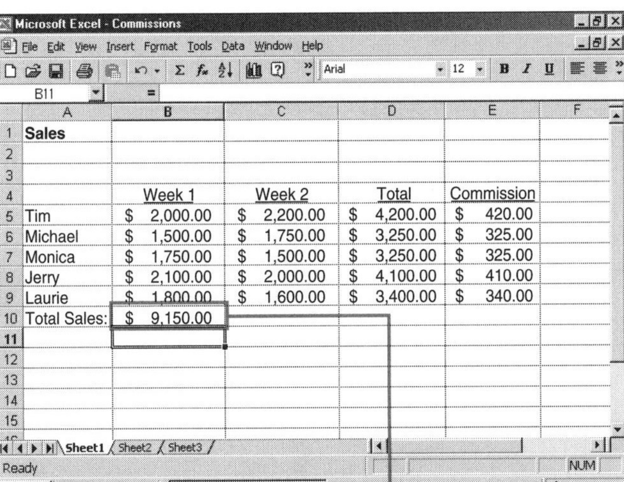

3 Press the Enter key to perform the calculation.

■ The result of the calculation appears.

COPY A FORMULA

If you want to use the same formula several times in your worksheet, you can save time by copying the formula.

There are two types of cell references you can use in a formula–relative and absolute.

A relative reference changes when you copy a formula. If you copy a formula to other cells in your worksheet, Excel automatically changes the cell references in the new formulas. For example, when you copy the formula =A1+A2 from cell A3 to cell B3, the formula changes to =B1+B2.

If you do not want Excel to change a cell reference when you copy a formula, you can use an absolute reference. This type of reference always refers to the same cell. You can make a cell reference absolute by typing a dollar sign ($) before both the column letter and row number. If you copy the formula to other cells in your worksheet, Excel does not change the absolute reference in the new formulas. For example, when you copy the formula =$A$7*B2 from cell B4 to cell C4, the formula changes to =$A$7*C2.

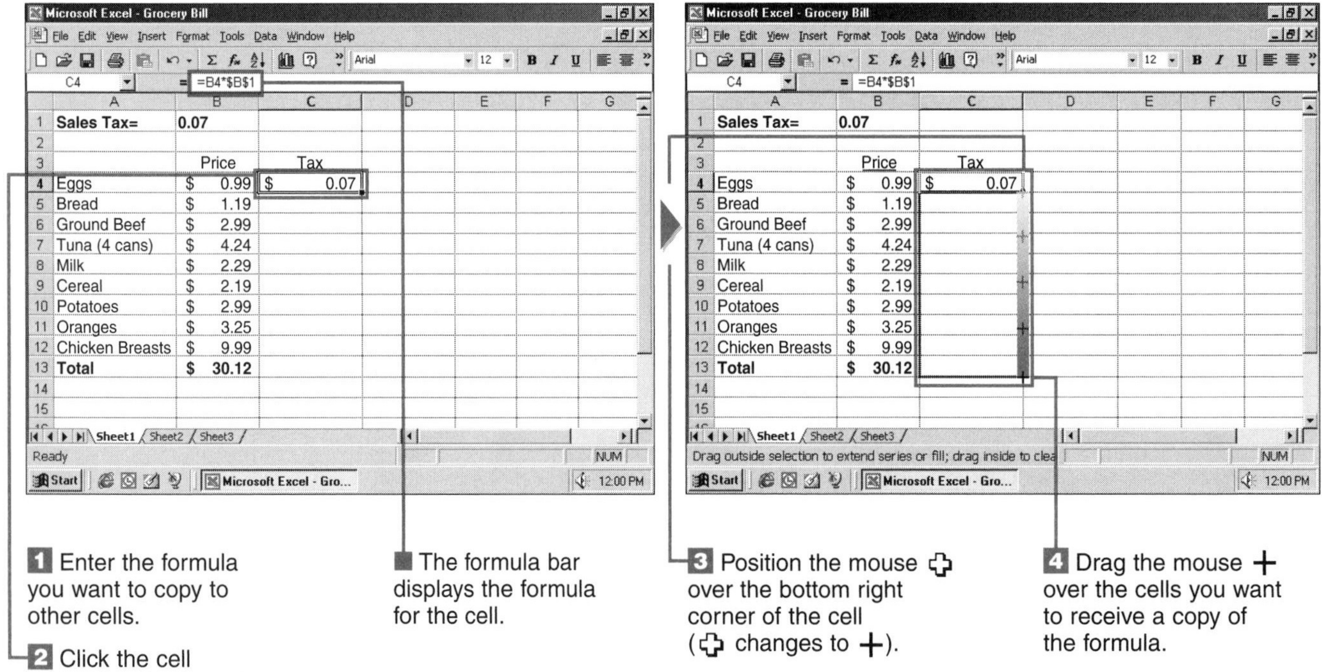

1 Enter the formula you want to copy to other cells.

2 Click the cell containing the formula.

■ The formula bar displays the formula for the cell.

3 Position the mouse ✥ over the bottom right corner of the cell (✥ changes to +).

4 Drag the mouse + over the cells you want to receive a copy of the formula.

TIPS

How do I copy a formula to a non-adjacent cell?

✔ Select the cell containing the formula you want to copy and then click the Copy button (📋) on the Standard toolbar. Select the cell you want to copy the formula to and then click the Paste button (📋) on the Standard toolbar.

Can I make only part of a cell reference absolute?

✔ Yes. Combining an absolute and a relative reference lets you prevent part of the cell reference from changing when you copy the formula. For example, you can use the reference $A1 to prevent only the column letter from changing. You can also use the reference A$1 to prevent only the row number from changing.

Is there an easier way to create an absolute reference?

✔ Yes. In a formula, select the cell reference you want to make absolute. Press the F4 key until dollar signs ($) appear in the appropriate places. You can repeat these steps for each cell reference you want to make absolute.

Microsoft Excel - Grocery Bill

C13 = =B13*$B$1

	A	B	C
1	**Sales Tax=**	**0.07**	
2			
3		Price	Tax
4	Eggs	$ 0.99	$ 0.07
5	Bread	$ 1.19	$ 0.08
6	Ground Beef	$ 2.99	$ 0.21
7	Tuna (4 cans)	$ 4.24	$ 0.30
8	Milk	$ 2.29	$ 0.16
9	Cereal	$ 2.19	$ 0.15
10	Potatoes	$ 2.99	$ 0.21
11	Oranges	$ 3.25	$ 0.23
12	Chicken Breasts	$ 9.99	$ 0.70
13	**Total**	**$ 30.12**	$ 2.11

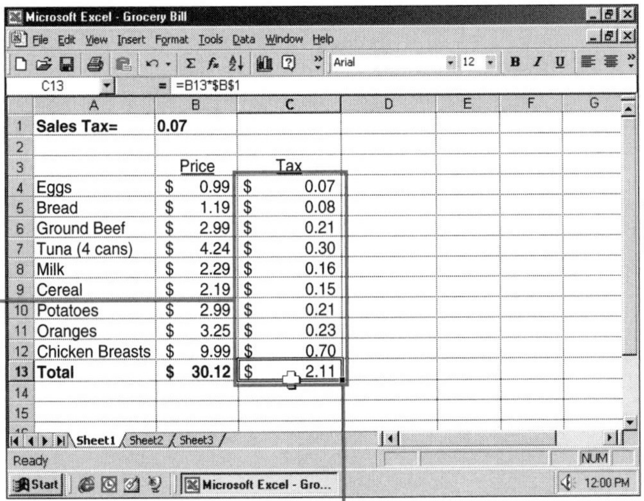

■ The results of the formulas appear.

5 To see one of the new formulas, click a cell that received a copy of the formula.

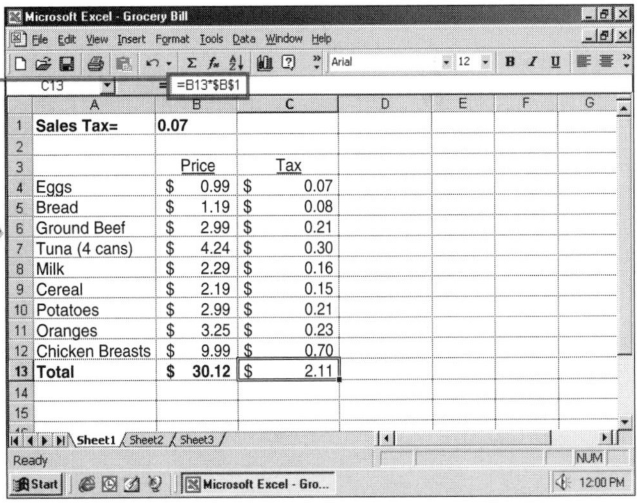

■ The formula bar displays the formula with the new cell references.

■ When you copy a formula containing an absolute reference, the absolute reference does not change.

CHANGE COLUMN WIDTH OR ROW HEIGHT

You can improve the appearance of your worksheet and display hidden data by changing the width of columns.

When text is too long to fit in a cell, the text spills into the cell to the right. If the cell to the right contains data, Excel will display as much of the text as the column width will allow. You can change the column width to display all the text in a cell. As you change the column width, Excel displays a small yellow box containing the average number of characters that will fit in the cell.

You can have Excel automatically adjust the column width to fit the longest item in the column.

You can change the height of rows to add space between the rows of data in your worksheet. As you change the row height, Excel displays a small yellow box containing the size of the row in points. There are 72 points in an inch.

You can have Excel automatically adjust the row height to fit the tallest item in the row.

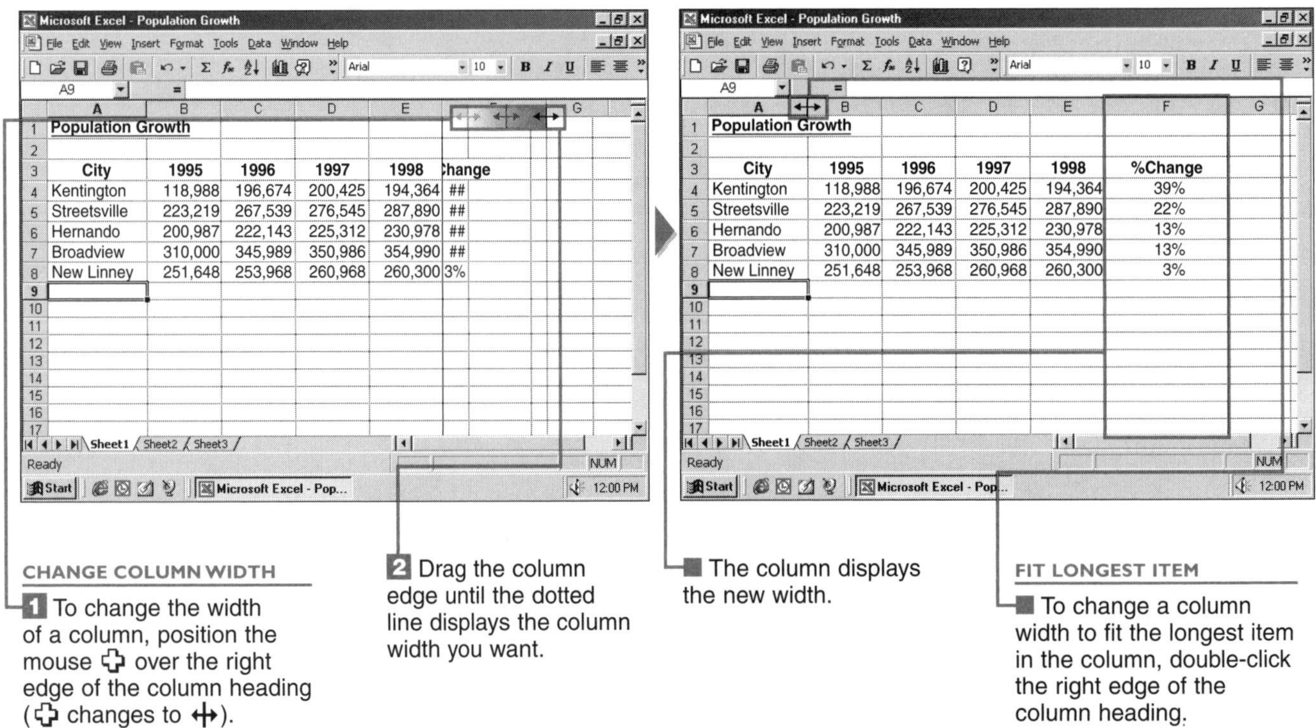

CHANGE COLUMN WIDTH

1 To change the width of a column, position the mouse ✣ over the right edge of the column heading (✣ changes to ↔).

2 Drag the column edge until the dotted line displays the column width you want.

■ The column displays the new width.

FIT LONGEST ITEM

■ To change a column width to fit the longest item in the column, double-click the right edge of the column heading.

TIPS

Can I change the width of several columns or the height of several rows at once?

✔ Yes. Drag the mouse pointer over the headings of the columns or the headings of the rows you want to change. Then drag the right edge of any column heading or the bottom edge of any row heading you selected.

Why does a cell in my worksheet display number signs (#)?

✔ Excel displays number signs (#) in a cell when the column is too narrow to display the whole number. To display the number, you must increase the width of the column.

How do I specify an exact column width?

✔ Click the heading of the column you want to change. From the Format menu, select Column and then click Width. Then type the width you want to use and click OK.

How do I specify an exact row height?

✔ Click the heading of the row you want to change. From the Format menu, select Row and then click Height. Then type the height you want to use and click OK.

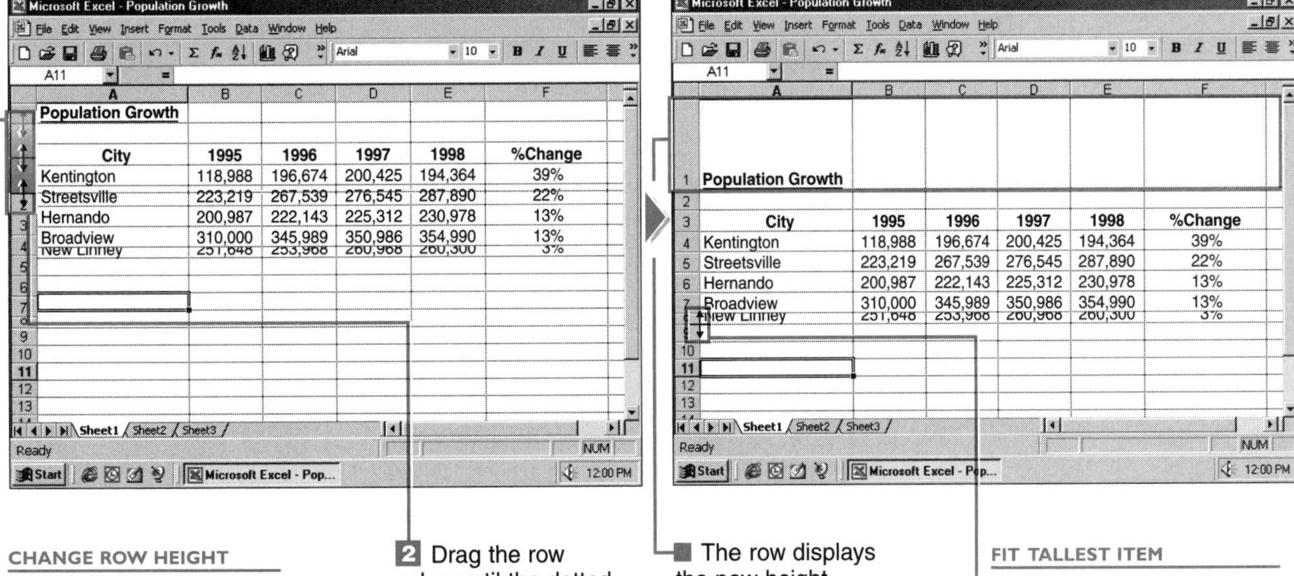

CHANGE ROW HEIGHT

1 To change the height of a row, position the mouse ✥ over the bottom edge of the row heading (✥ changes to ✛).

2 Drag the row edge until the dotted line displays the row height you want.

■ The row displays the new height.

FIT TALLEST ITEM

■ To change a row height to fit the tallest item in the row, double-click the bottom edge of the row heading.

CHANGE FONT AND SIZE OF DATA

You can enhance the appearance of your worksheet by changing the design, or font, of data.

By default, Excel uses the Arial font. You can use another font to draw attention to headings or emphasize important data in your worksheet.

Excel provides a list of fonts for you to choose from. The fonts appear in the list as they will appear in your worksheet. This lets you preview a font before you select it.

Most fonts in the list display a symbol. The TT symbol indicates the font is a TrueType font. This type of font prints exactly as it appears on your screen. The 🖶 symbol indicates the font is a printer font. This type of font may print differently than it appears on your screen.

You can increase or decrease the size of data in your worksheet. Larger data is easier to read, but smaller data allows you to fit more information on your screen and on a printed worksheet.

Excel measures the size of data in points. There are 72 points in an inch. By default, Excel uses a data size of 10 points.

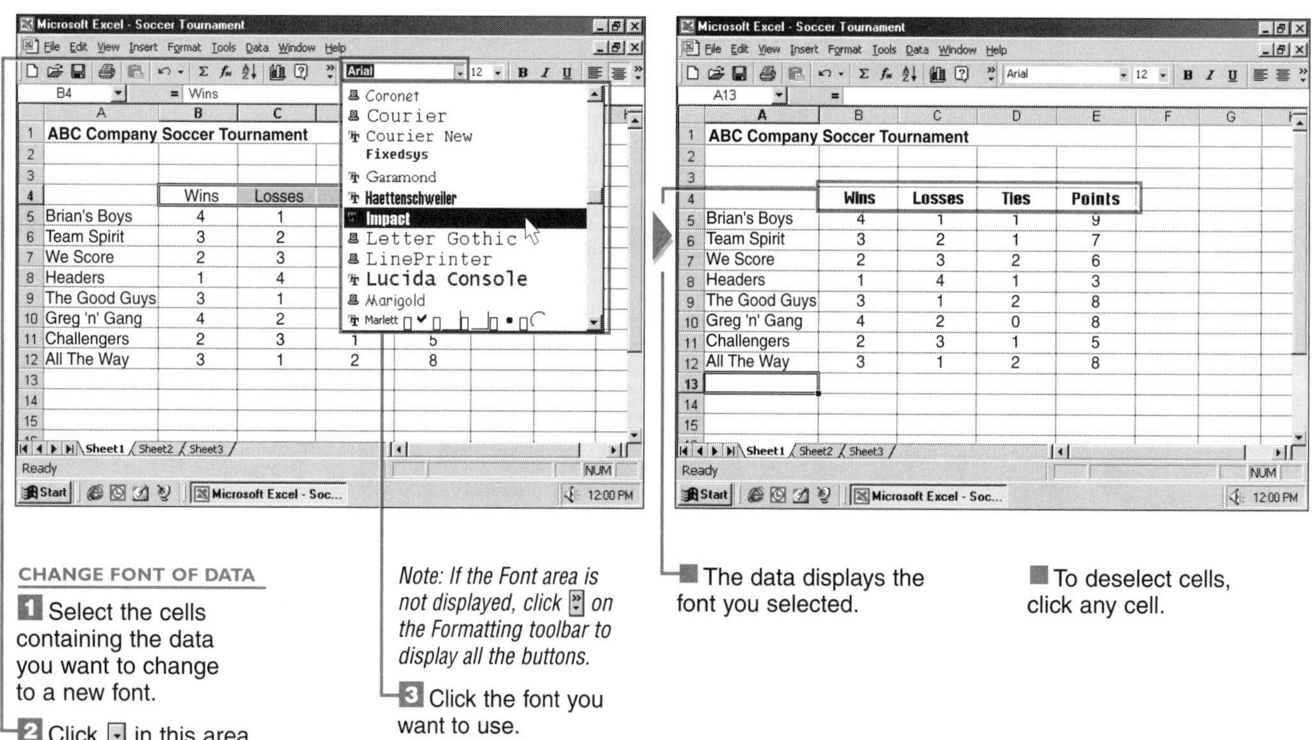

CHANGE FONT OF DATA

1 Select the cells containing the data you want to change to a new font.

2 Click ▾ in this area to display a list of the available fonts.

Note: If the Font area is not displayed, click » on the Formatting toolbar to display all the buttons.

3 Click the font you want to use.

■ The data displays the font you selected.

■ To deselect cells, click any cell.

TIPS

How do I change the font or size of only some of the data in a cell?

✔ Double-click the cell containing the data you want to change. Drag the mouse I over the data you want to change. To change the font of the data, perform steps 2 to 3 on page 218. To change the size of the data, perform steps 2 to 3 on this page.

Can I shrink data so it fits neatly in a cell?

✔ Yes. Select the cell containing the data you want to shrink. Choose the Format menu and then select Cells. Click the Alignment tab and then select the Shrink to fit option (☐ changes to ☑). Then click OK.

Can I decrease the size of data displayed on my screen without affecting the appearance of the data when I print the worksheet?

✔ You can use the Zoom feature to decrease the size of data displayed on your screen. Using the Zoom feature will not affect the appearance of the data when you print your worksheet. For more information, see page 203.

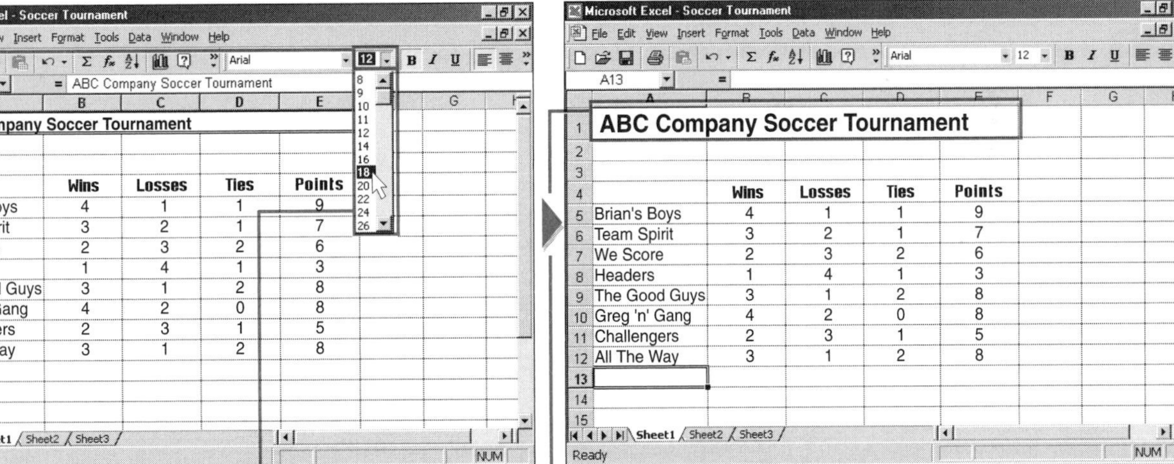

CHANGE SIZE OF DATA

1 Select the cells containing the data you want to change to a new size.

2 Click ▾ in this area to display a list of the available sizes.

Note: If the Font Size area is not displayed, click » on the Formatting toolbar to display all the buttons.

3 Click the size you want to use.

■ The data displays the size you selected.

■ To deselect cells, click any cell.

CHANGE APPEARANCE OF DATA

You can change the design, style and size of data in your worksheet at the same time. This allows you to quickly enhance the appearance of your worksheet.

Changing the design and style of data is useful when you want to make data, such as headings, stand out from the rest of the data in your worksheet. You can also increase or decrease the size of data in your worksheet.

Excel offers several underline styles you can use. An underline can help draw attention to important data, such as totals.

Excel includes three effects you can apply to data. The Strikethrough effect displays a line through the middle of the data. This is useful when you want to indicate revisions to data. The Superscript and Subscript effects decrease the size of the data and move it either slightly above or slightly below the line of regular-sized data. These effects are useful for displaying mathematical formulas.

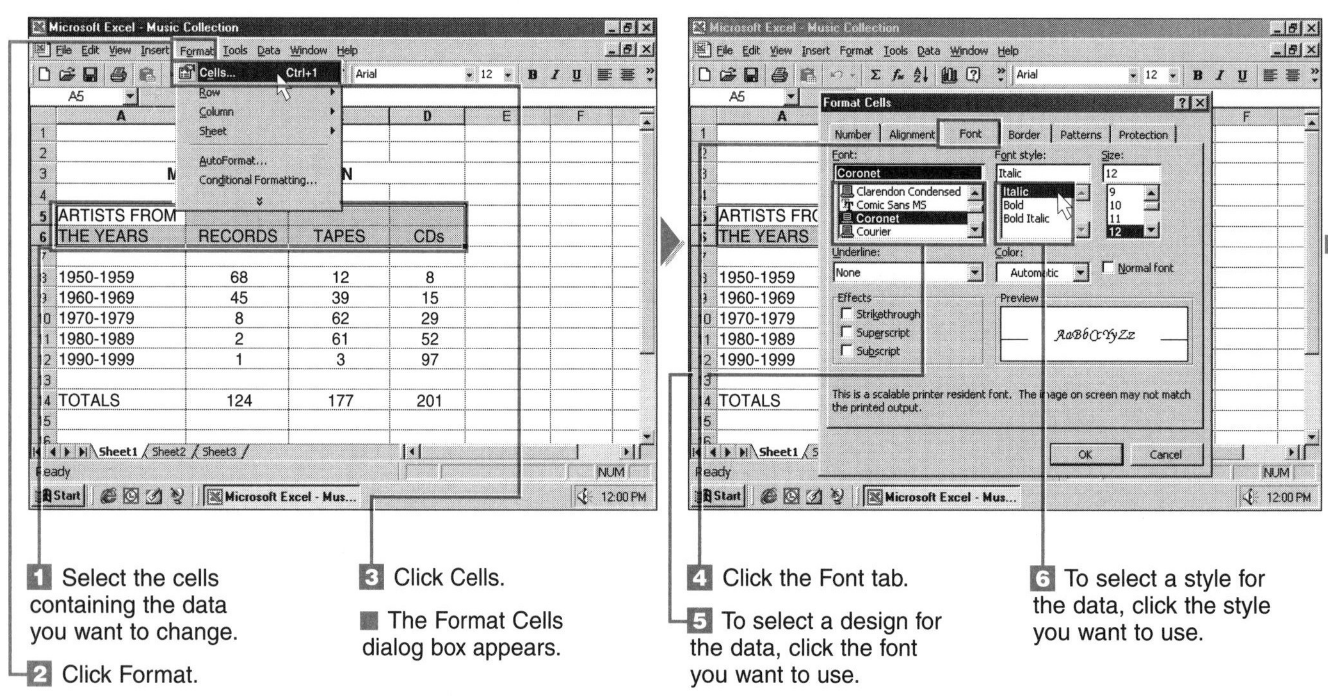

1 Select the cells containing the data you want to change.

2 Click Format.

3 Click Cells.

■ The Format Cells dialog box appears.

4 Click the Font tab.

5 To select a design for the data, click the font you want to use.

6 To select a style for the data, click the style you want to use.

TIPS

What determines which fonts are available in Excel?

✔ The available fonts depend on the fonts installed on your computer and printer. Excel includes several fonts, but additional fonts may be available from the other programs on your computer. Your printer may also have built-in fonts you can use.

How do I change the appearance of only some of the data in a cell?

✔ Double-click the cell containing the data you want to change. Drag the mouse pointer over the data you want to change and then perform steps 2 to 11 below.

How do I change the color of data in the cells I selected?

✔ In the Format Cells dialog box, click the Color area and then select the color you want to use.

Can I change the default font setting Excel uses for all my new workbooks?

✔ Yes. Select the Tools menu, click Options and then choose the General tab. In the Standard font area, select the font and size you want Excel to use for the default font setting. You must exit and restart Excel to apply the change.

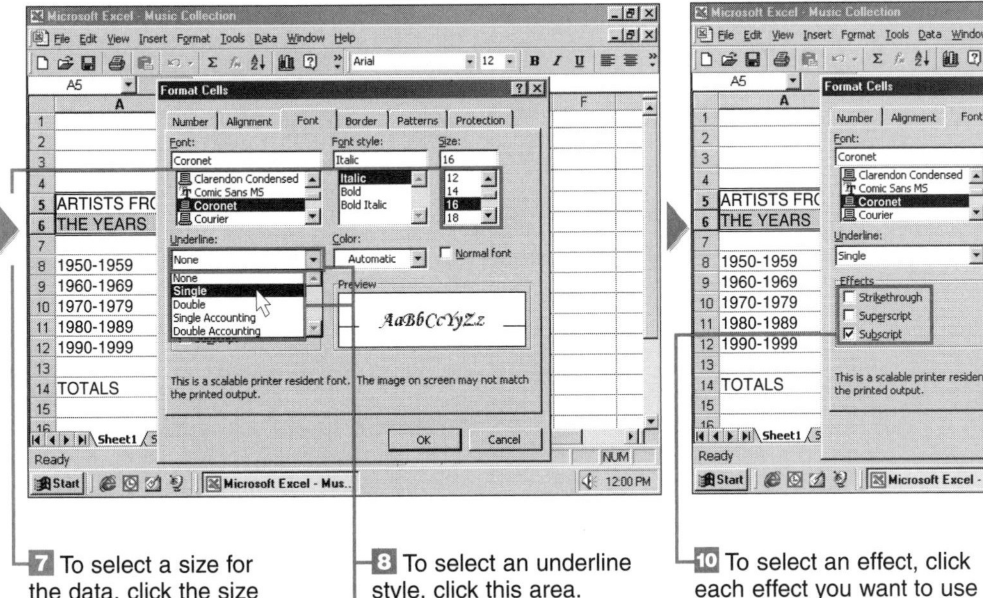

7 To select a size for the data, click the size you want to use.

8 To select an underline style, click this area.

9 Click the underline style you want to use.

10 To select an effect, click each effect you want to use (☐ changes to ☑).

■ This area displays a preview of all the options you selected.

11 Click OK to apply the changes.

BOLD, ITALIC OR UNDERLINE

You can use the Bold, Italic and Underline features to change the style of data in your worksheet. These features allow you to emphasize data and enhance the appearance of your worksheet.

The Bold feature makes the selected data appear darker and thicker than other data in your worksheet. You can use the Bold feature to emphasize row and column headings or other important information.

The Italic feature tilts the selected data to the right. You may want to italicize notes or explanations you add to your worksheet.

The Underline feature adds a line underneath the selected data.

Underlining data can be useful for emphasizing specific data in your worksheet, such as subtotals and totals.

You can use one feature at a time or any combination of the three features to emphasize the data in your worksheet.

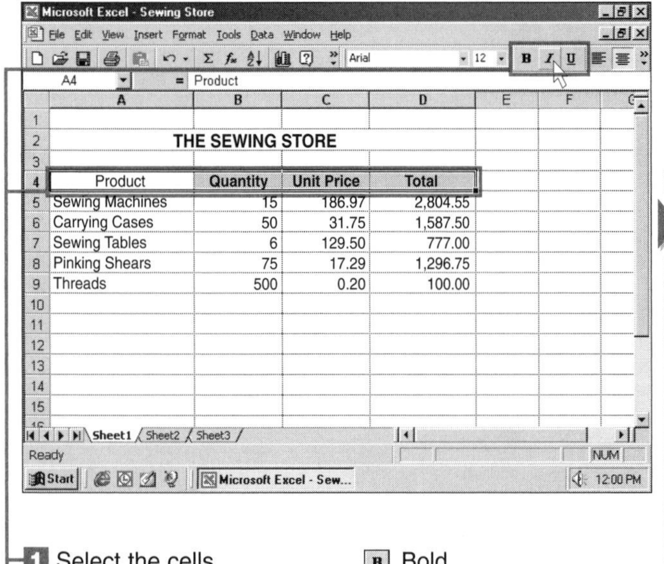

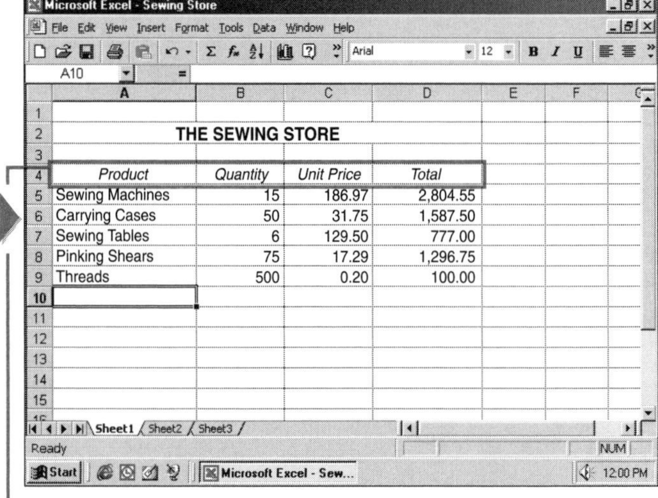

1 Select the cells containing the data you want to change.

2 Click one of the following buttons.

- B Bold
- I Italic
- U Underline

Note: If the button you want is not displayed, click » on the Formatting toolbar to display all the buttons.

■ The data displays the style you selected.

■ To deselect cells, click any cell.

Note: To remove a style, repeat steps 1 and 2.

FORMAT NUMBERS

You can quickly change the appearance of numbers in your worksheet without retyping the numbers. Changing the appearance of numbers can make it easier for other people to understand what the values in your worksheet represent. When you change the format of numbers, you do not change the value of the numbers.

The Currency format is useful for displaying a number as a monetary value. This format adds a dollar sign ($) and two decimal places to a number.

The Percent format changes a decimal number, such as 0.05, into a percentage that is easier to understand, such as 5%.

The Comma format makes a long number easier to read by adding commas and two decimal places to the number. For example, if you add the Comma format to the number 4273549, the number changes to 4,273,549.00.

You can increase or decrease the number of decimal places a number displays.

If you want more control over the format your numbers display, see page 224.

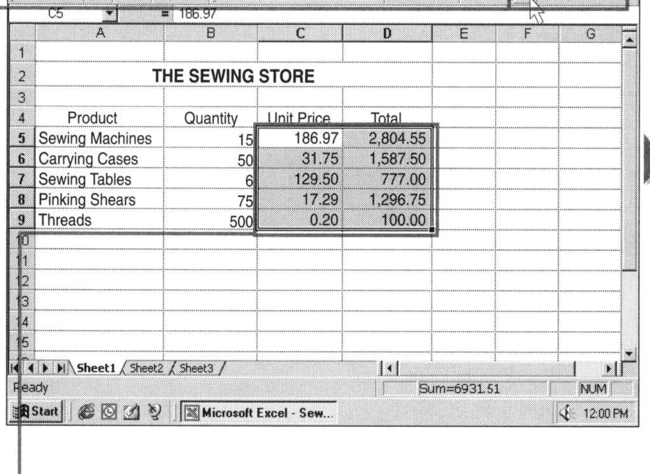

1 Select the cells containing the numbers you want to format.

2 Click one of the following buttons.

- Currency
- Percent
- Comma
- Add decimal place
- Remove decimal place

Note: If the button you want is not displayed, click » on the Formatting toolbar to display all the buttons.

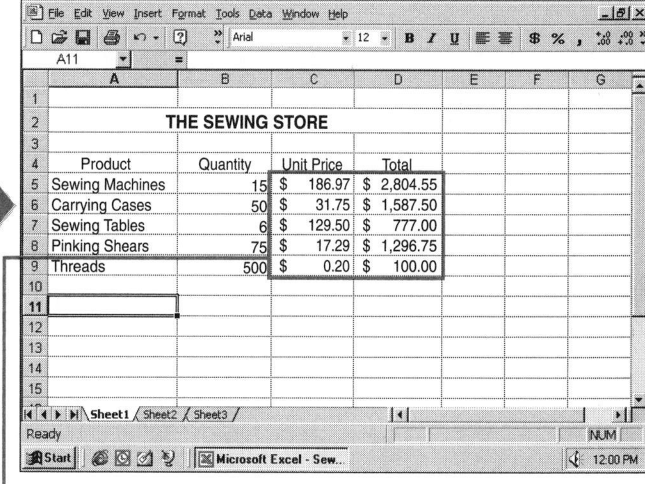

■ The numbers display the format you selected.

■ To deselect cells, click any cell.

FORMAT NUMBERS

You can display the numbers in your worksheet in many different ways. Changing the format of a number can help make the number easier to understand. For example, the number 11500 can also be displayed as $11,500.00. The number .075 can also be displayed as 7.5%.

When you change the format of a number, the value of the number does not change.

Excel offers several number format categories for you to choose from, including Currency, Date, Time, Percentage and Scientific. The category you choose determines the available options. For example, the Currency category allows you to select options such as the number of decimal places and how you want negative numbers to appear.

The Format Cells dialog box displays a sample of the formatting options you select. This allows you to see how numbers in your worksheet will appear in the new format.

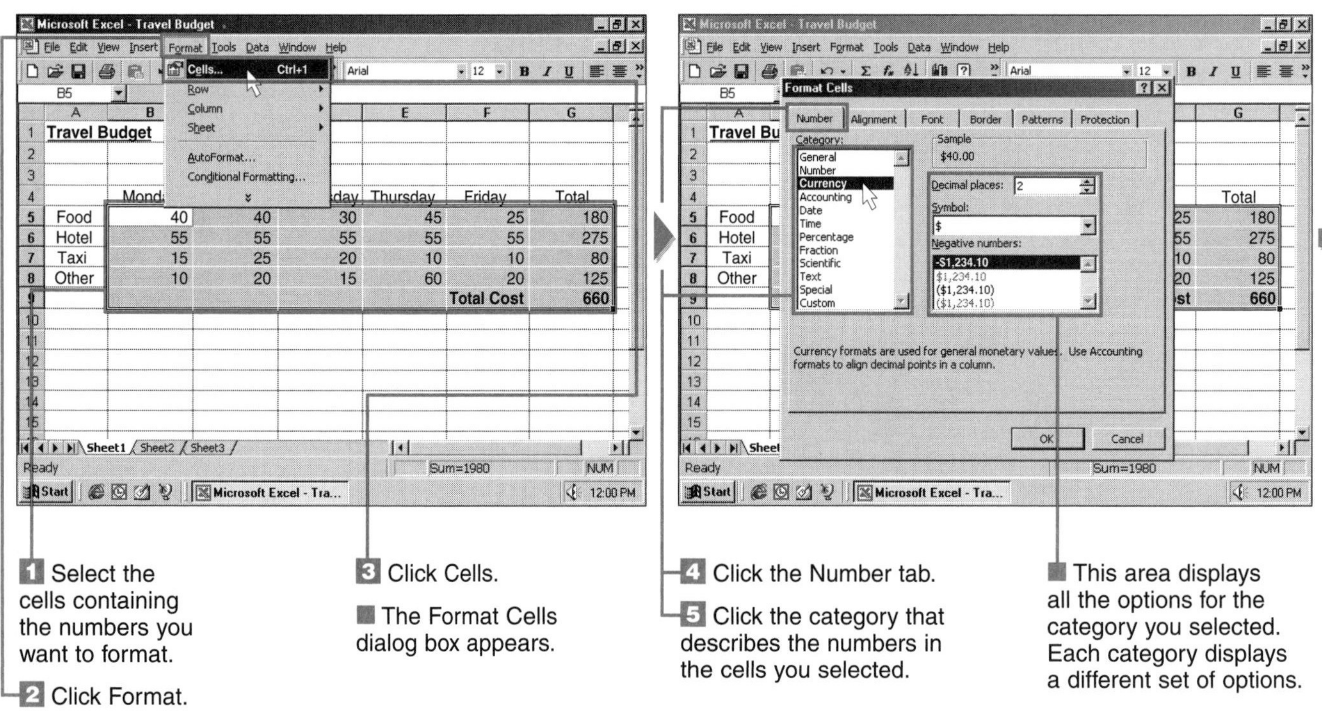

1 Select the cells containing the numbers you want to format.

2 Click Format.

3 Click Cells.

■ The Format Cells dialog box appears.

4 Click the Number tab.

5 Click the category that describes the numbers in the cells you selected.

■ This area displays all the options for the category you selected. Each category displays a different set of options.

TIPS

I formatted a column of numbers. Why do number signs (#) appear in each cell of the column?

✔ The column is not wide enough to display the numbers in the new format. To change the column width, see page 216.

How do I remove a number format I added to my data?

✔ Select the cells containing the data you want to remove a number format from. In the Format Cells dialog box, select the General category. Then click OK to remove the number format from the data.

Can I create a custom number format?

✔ Yes. You can base your custom number format on an existing number format. In the Format Cells dialog box, select the category for the type of number format you want to create and select any options you want to use. Then select the Custom category. The Type area displays a code for your custom number format. You can modify the code to further customize the number format.

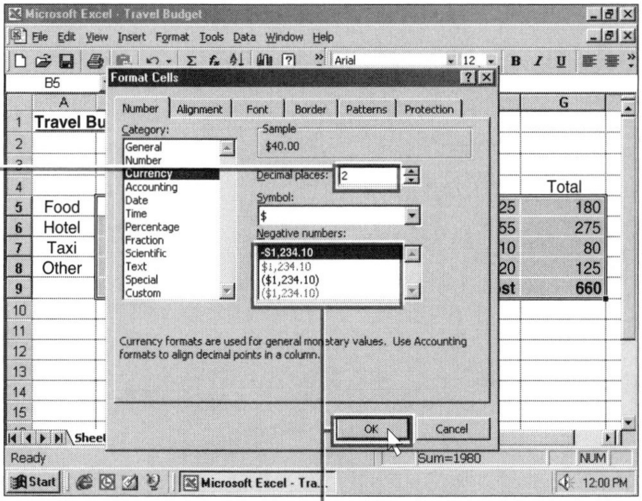

6 To select the number of decimal places you want the numbers to display, double-click this area. Then type the number of decimal places.

7 To select the way you want negative numbers to appear, click one of the available styles.

8 Click OK to apply the changes.

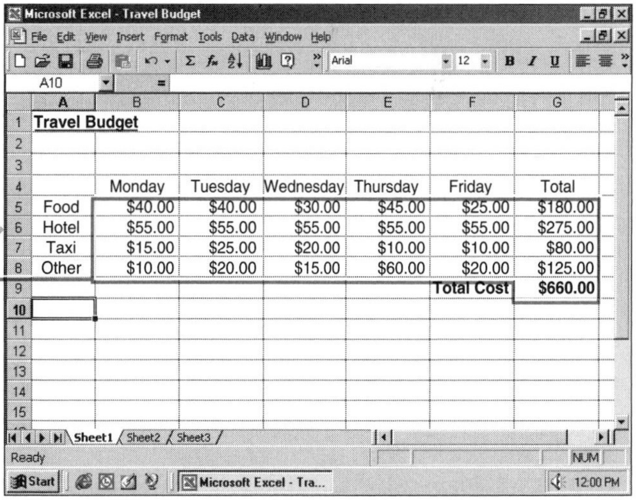

■ The numbers display the changes.

■ To deselect cells, click any cell.

CHANGE CELL OR DATA COLOR

You can add color to your worksheet to enhance the appearance of the worksheet. Excel offers a wide variety of colors for you to choose from.

You can change the background color of cells. Changing the background color of cells is useful when you want to distinguish between different areas in your worksheet. For example, in a worksheet that contains monthly sales figures, you can use a different background color for each month.

You can also change the color of data in a cell. This can help draw attention to titles or other important data in your worksheet.

When adding color to your worksheet, make sure you choose cell and data colors that work well together. For example, red data on a blue background is difficult to read.

If you are using a black-and-white printer, any colors you add will appear as shades of gray when your worksheet is printed.

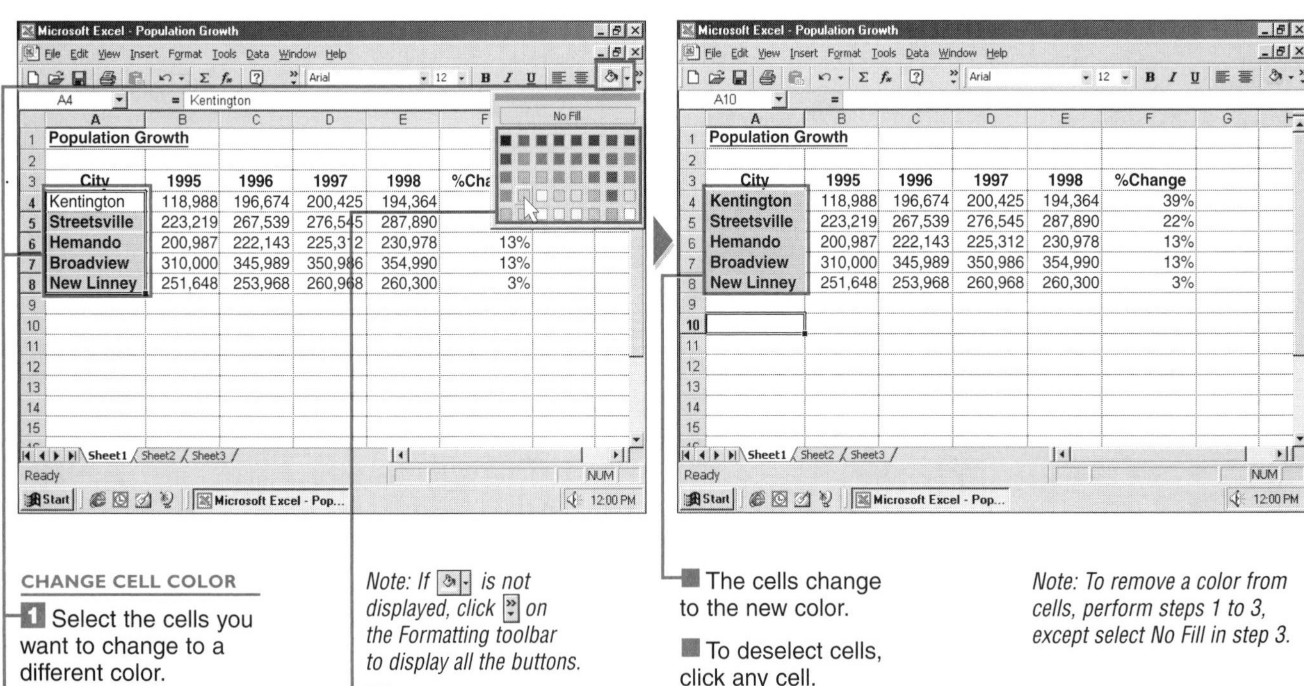

CHANGE CELL COLOR

1 Select the cells you want to change to a different color.

2 Click ▾ in this area to select a color.

Note: If [Fill Color] is not displayed, click » on the Formatting toolbar to display all the buttons.

3 Click the cell color you want to use.

■ The cells change to the new color.

■ To deselect cells, click any cell.

Note: To remove a color from cells, perform steps 1 to 3, except select No Fill in step 3.

TIPS

What other effects can I use to change the background of cells?

✔ You can add a pattern to the background of cells. Select the cells you want to display a pattern. Select the Format menu, click Cells and then choose the Patterns tab. Click the Pattern area and select the pattern you want to use. Then click OK.

How can I quickly change the color of data in my worksheet?

✔ The Font Color button (A) on the Formatting toolbar displays the last data color you selected. To quickly add this color to data in your worksheet, select the cells containing the data you want to change and then click the Font Color button (A).

Can I have negative numbers automatically appear in red?

✔ Select the cells that contain the data you want to appear in red when the data is a negative number. Select the Format menu, click Cells and then choose the Number tab. In the Category area, click Number or Currency. In the Negative numbers area, choose the option you want to use and then click OK.

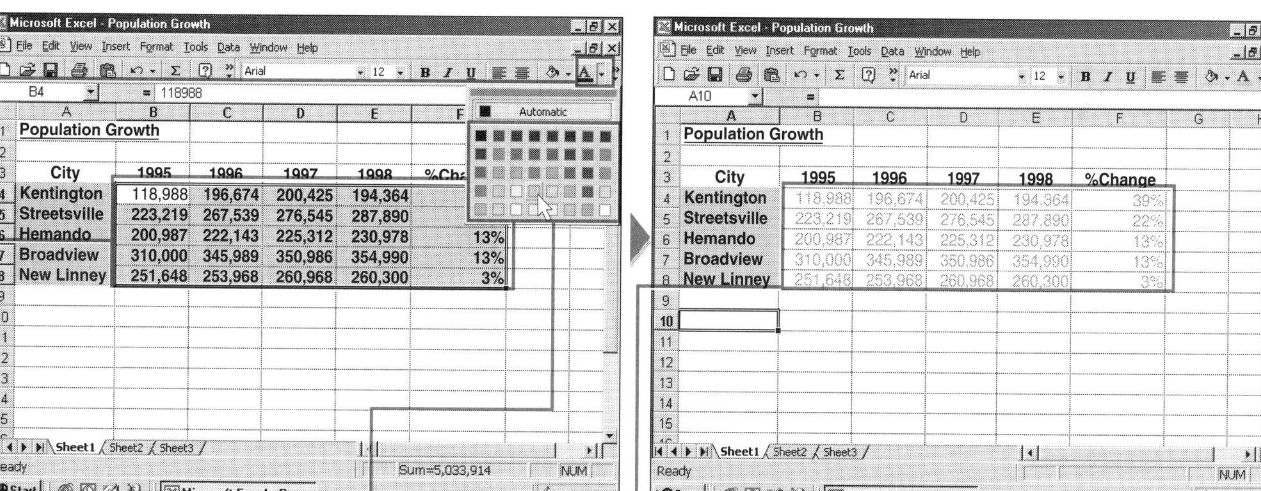

CHANGE DATA COLOR

1 Select the cells containing the data you want to change to a different color.

2 Click ▾ in this area to select a color.

Note: If A▾ is not displayed, click » on the Formatting toolbar to display all the buttons.

3 Click the data color you want to use.

■ The data changes to the new color.

■ To deselect cells, click any cell.

Note: To remove a color from data, perform steps 1 to 3, except select Automatic in step 3.

CHANGE ALIGNMENT OF DATA

You can change the way Excel aligns data within cells in your worksheet.

The left align option lines up data with the left edge of a cell. The right align option lines up data with the right edge of a cell. The center option aligns data between the left and right edges of a cell.

Excel automatically left aligns text and right aligns numbers and dates you enter in cells.

You can indent data to move data away from the left edge of a cell. When you indent data, you should make sure all the data is still visible in the cell. If the cell is not wide enough, Excel may hide part of the data. You can change the column width to display all the data in a cell. To change the column width, see page 216.

You can also center data across several columns in your worksheet. This is useful for centering titles over your data.

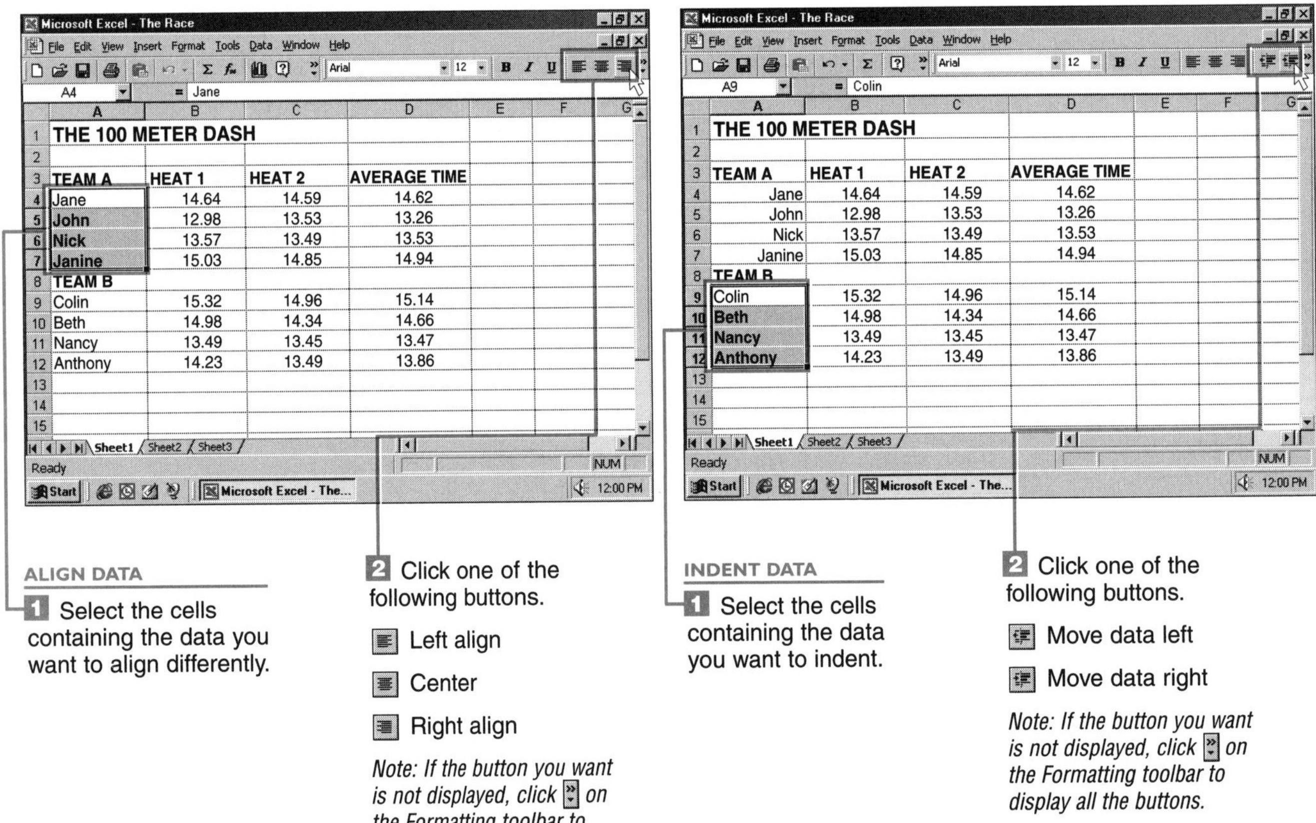

ALIGN DATA

1 Select the cells containing the data you want to align differently.

2 Click one of the following buttons.

- Left align
- Center
- Right align

Note: If the button you want is not displayed, click » on the Formatting toolbar to display all the buttons.

INDENT DATA

1 Select the cells containing the data you want to indent.

2 Click one of the following buttons.

- Move data left
- Move data right

Note: If the button you want is not displayed, click » on the Formatting toolbar to display all the buttons.

TIPS

How do I align data vertically in cells?

✔ Select the cells containing the data you want to align vertically. Select the Format menu, click Cells and then choose the Alignment tab. Click the Vertical area and select the alignment option you want to use. Then click OK.

How can I rotate data in cells?

✔ Select the cells containing the data you want to rotate. Select the Format menu, click Cells and then choose the Alignment tab. In the Orientation area, double-click the box beside Degrees and type the number of degrees you want to rotate the data. Then click OK.

Can I display long lines of text in a cell?

✔ You can display long lines of text in a cell by wrapping the text. Select the cell containing the text you want to wrap. Select the Format menu, click Cells and then choose the Alignment tab. Click the Wrap text option (☐ changes to ☑) and then click OK. This will change the height of the entire row.

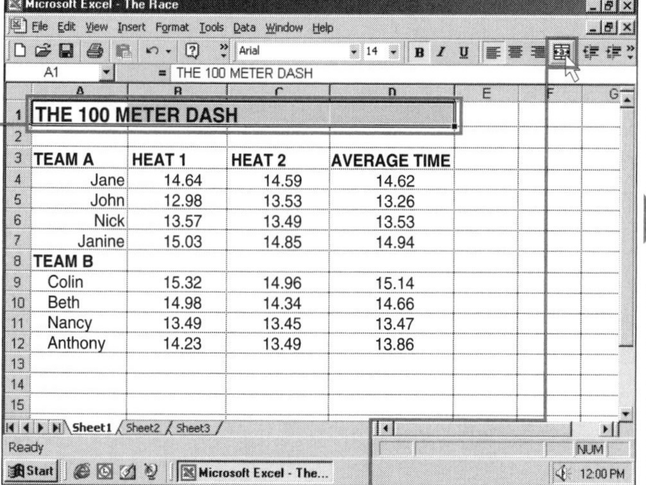

CENTER DATA ACROSS COLUMNS

1 Select the cells you want to center the data across.

Note: The first cell you select should contain the data you want to center.

2 Click ⊞ to center the data.

Note: If ⊞ is not displayed, click » on the Formatting toolbar to display all the buttons.

■ Excel centers the data across the cells you selected.

■ To deselect cells, click any cell.

ADD BORDERS

You can add borders to enhance the appearance of your worksheet. You can also use borders to divide your worksheet into sections.

Adding borders can help make important data in your worksheet stand out. For example, in a financial worksheet, you may want to add borders to the cells containing subtotals and totals.

Excel offers several line styles for you to choose from, including broken, bold and double lines.

The default color for borders is black. You can choose a color that better suits your worksheet.

You can specify which types of borders you want to add to the cells you have selected. For example, you can add a top, bottom, left or right border to cells. You can also add diagonal borders to cells. This is useful when you want to indicate that data in the cells is no longer valid.

You can preview the borders before you add them to your worksheet. This allows you to determine if the borders suit your needs.

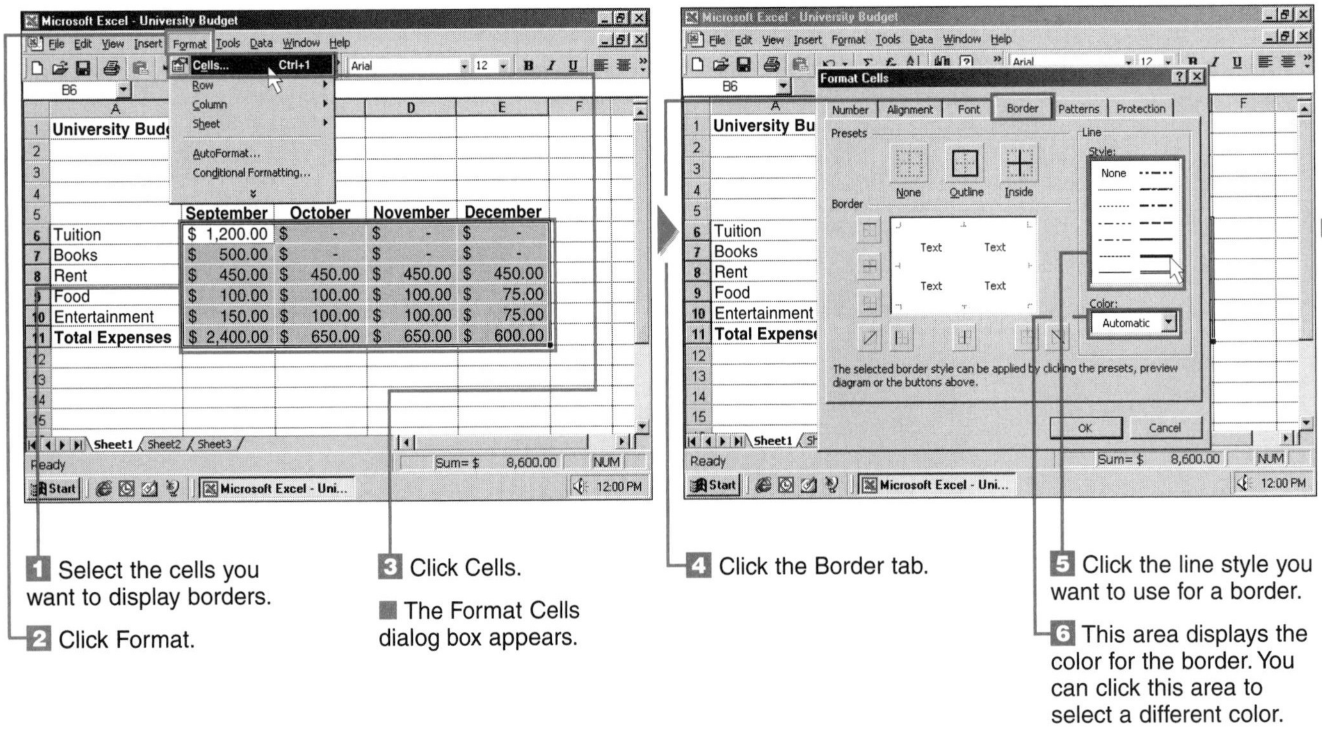

1 Select the cells you want to display borders.

2 Click Format.

3 Click Cells.

■ The Format Cells dialog box appears.

4 Click the Border tab.

5 Click the line style you want to use for a border.

6 This area displays the color for the border. You can click this area to select a different color.

TIPS

How can I quickly add borders to my worksheet?

✔ Select the cells you want to display borders. Click ▾ beside the Borders button (▦▾) on the Formatting toolbar. A selection of common border types appears. Select the type of border you want to use. You can also use Excel's AutoFormat feature to quickly add borders and color to your worksheet. For information on the AutoFormat feature, see page 234.

Can I print the gridlines displayed on my screen instead of adding borders?

✔ Yes. Click the File menu and then select Page Setup. Click the Sheet tab and select the Gridlines option (☐ changes to ☑). Then click OK.

Can I turn off the gridlines on my screen so I can more clearly see the borders I have added?

✔ Yes. Click the Tools menu and then select Options. Click the View tab and select the Gridlines option (☑ changes to ☐). Then click OK.

How do I remove borders I have added to my worksheet?

✔ Perform steps 1 to 4 below and then click the None button (▦).

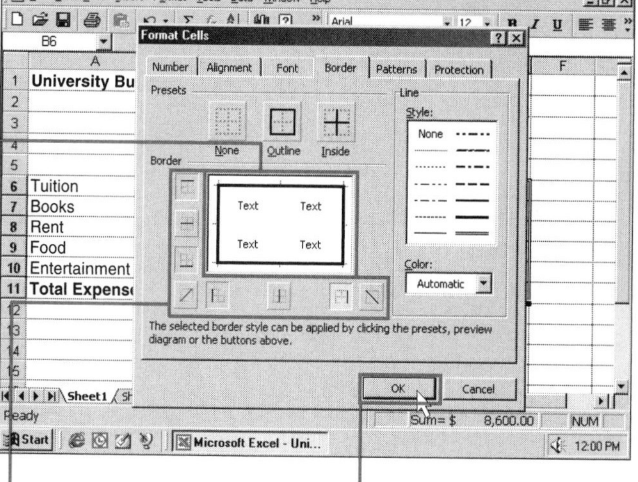

7 Click the button displaying the type of border you want to add.

■ This area displays how the border will appear in the worksheet.

8 Repeat steps 5 to 7 for each border you want to add.

9 Click OK to confirm the changes.

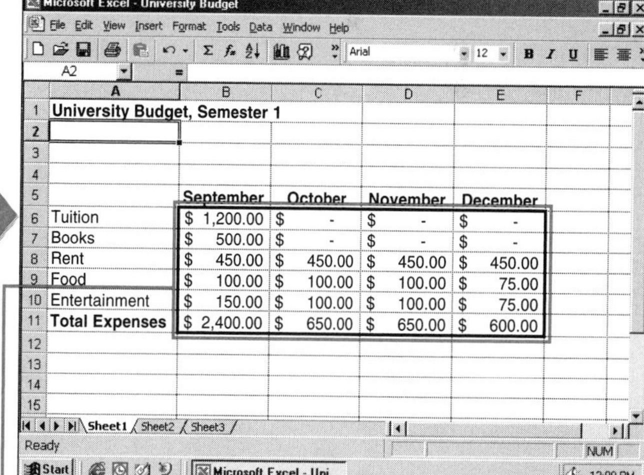

■ The cells display the border you selected.

■ To deselect cells, click any cell.

COPY FORMATTING

Once you have formatted one cell to suit your needs, you can use the Format Painter feature to copy the formatting to other cells in your worksheet.

You can copy formatting to make all the headings in your worksheet look the same. This will give your worksheet a consistent appearance.

You can copy number formatting, such as currency, date or percentage, and data formatting, such as font, size or alignment. Excel also allows you to copy cell formatting, such as cell color or borders. When you copy formatting, Excel does not copy the row height or column width of the cells.

You can copy formatting to several areas in your worksheet at once. To do so, perform the steps below, except double-click the Format Painter button (🖌) on the Standard toolbar in step 2. When you have finished selecting all the cells you want to display the formatting, press the Esc key to stop copying the formatting.

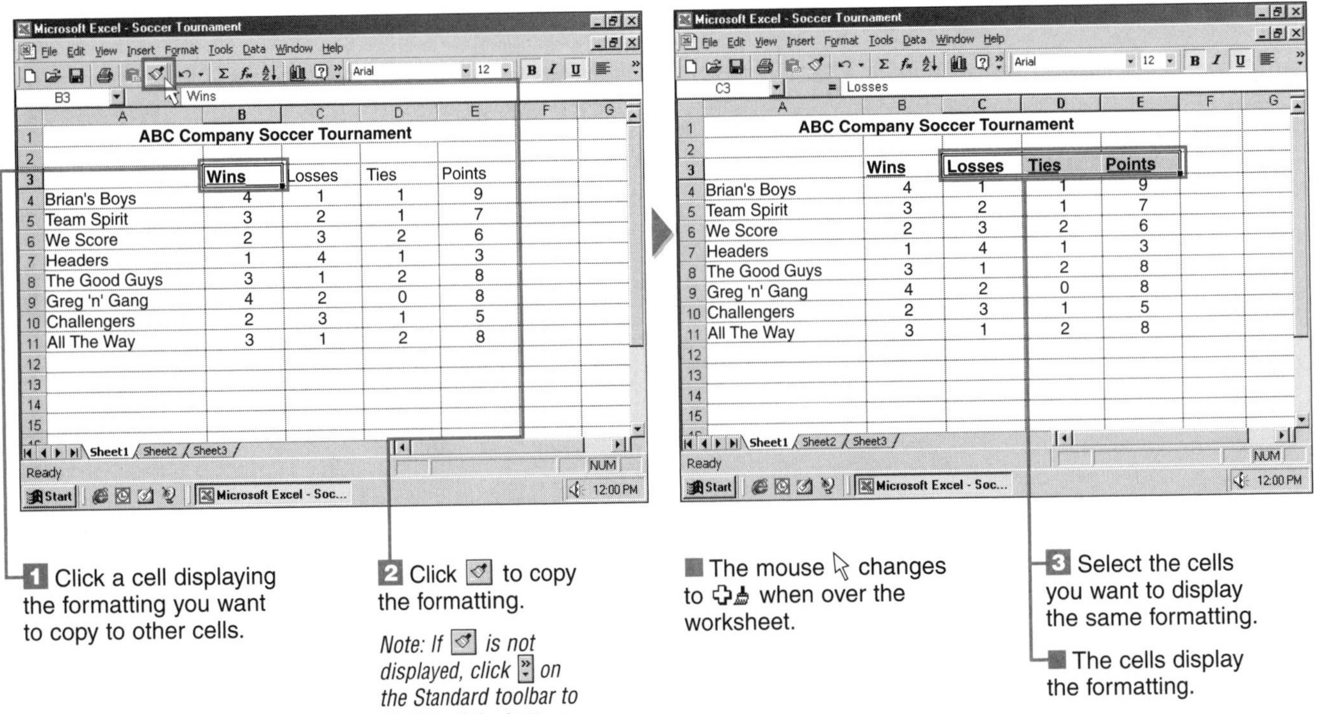

1 Click a cell displaying the formatting you want to copy to other cells.

2 Click 🖌 to copy the formatting.

Note: If 🖌 is not displayed, click » on the Standard toolbar to display all the buttons.

■ The mouse ↖ changes to ✥🖌 when over the worksheet.

3 Select the cells you want to display the same formatting.

■ The cells display the formatting.

CLEAR FORMATTING

You can remove all the formatting from cells in your worksheet. When you clear formatting from cells, the data in the cells appears as you originally entered it. If you clear the formatting from cells containing dates, the dates change to numbers.

You can clear many different types of formatting from cells, including currency, percentage, alignment, font and color. Clearing formatting will not reverse any changes you made to the row height or column width.

You may need to clear formatting after you use the Delete key to remove data from a cell. If you do not clear the formatting, Excel will apply the formatting to any new data you enter in the cell.

If two or more words or numbers in a cell display different formatting, Excel will clear the formatting from only the first word or number.

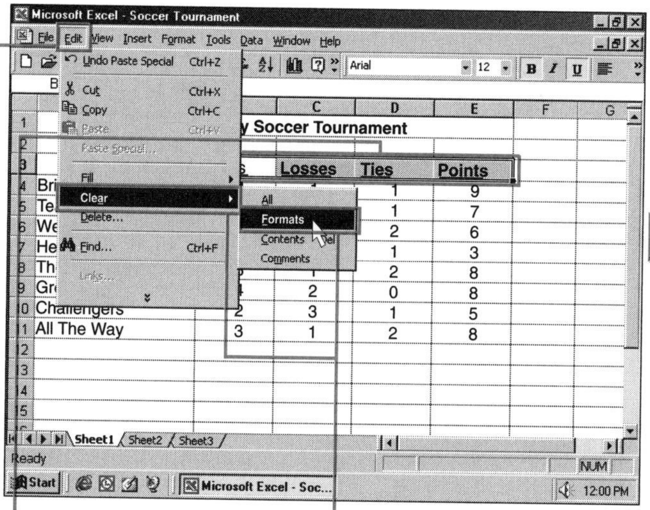

1 Select the cells containing the formatting you want to remove.

2 Click Edit.

3 Click Clear.

4 Click Formats to clear the formatting.

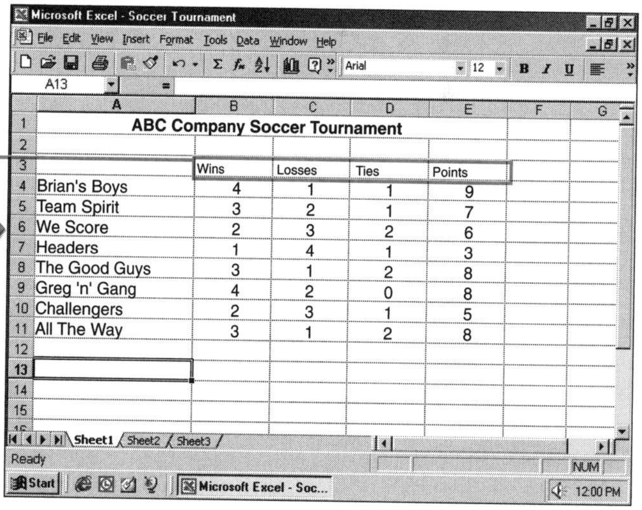

■ All the formatting disappears from the cells you selected.

■ To deselect cells, click any cell.

APPLY AN AUTOFORMAT

Excel offers many ready-to-use designs, called AutoFormats, you can choose from to give your worksheet a new appearance. An AutoFormat provides the formatting so you can concentrate on the content of your worksheet.

Some of the types of AutoFormats you can choose from include Accounting, Colorful and 3-D Effects. The Accounting AutoFormats format numbers as currency. The Colorful AutoFormats emphasize data by changing the color of the cells you selected. The 3-D Effects AutoFormats give the selected cells the appearance of depth.

Excel shows a preview of each available AutoFormat. This allows you to determine which AutoFormat suits the content, purpose and intended audience of your worksheet.

You can specify which formatting options you want Excel to apply to the selected cells. For example, you may not want to use the font or border options included in an AutoFormat.

When you apply an AutoFormat to your worksheet, Excel analyzes the cells you have selected to find the row or column labels and totals. Excel then applies the appropriate formatting options to the cells.

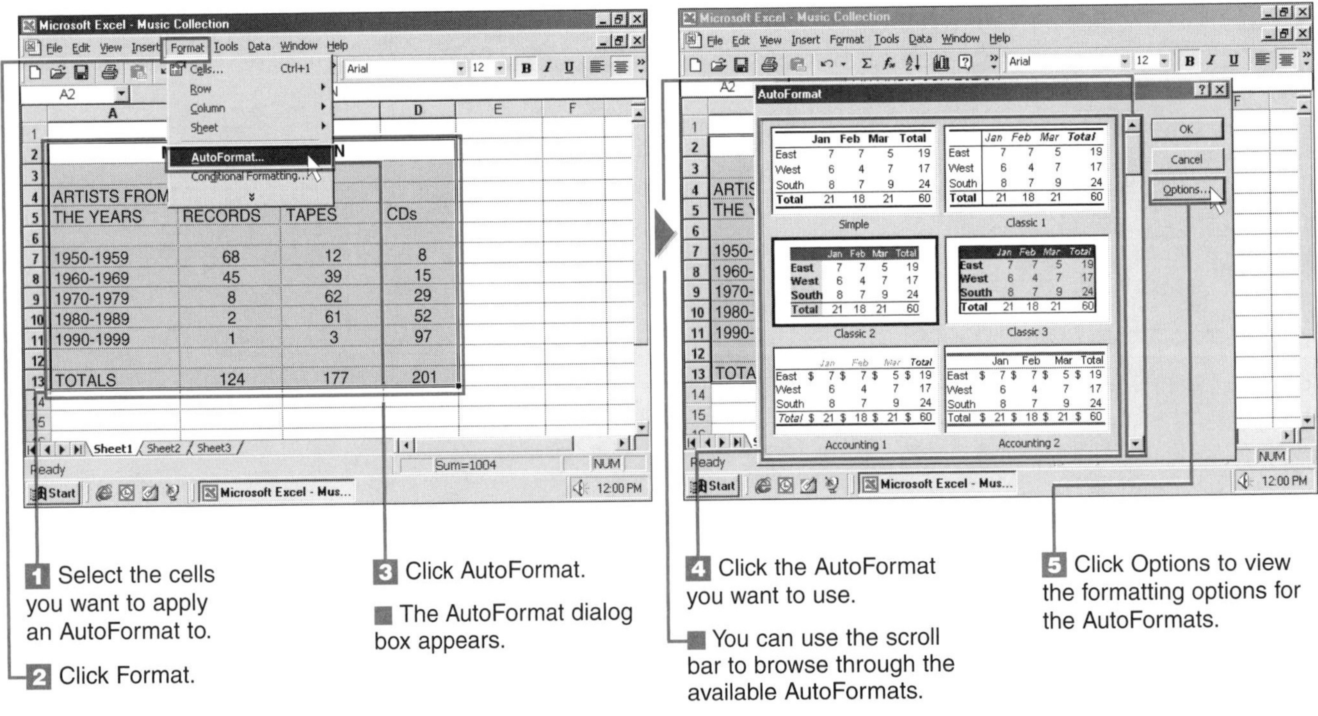

1 Select the cells you want to apply an AutoFormat to.

2 Click Format.

3 Click AutoFormat.

■ The AutoFormat dialog box appears.

4 Click the AutoFormat you want to use.

■ You can use the scroll bar to browse through the available AutoFormats.

5 Click Options to view the formatting options for the AutoFormats.

TIPS

Why do I get an error message when I select one cell?

✔ If you select only one cell, Excel may not be able to determine which cells in your worksheet you want to format and will ask you to select a range of cells. Excel will not apply an AutoFormat to a single cell.

What is the Width/Height option used for?

✔ The Width/Height option changes the column width and row height of the selected cells based on the amount of data in the cells. This ensures the data is neatly displayed in the worksheet. If you later remove an AutoFormat using the steps below, the columns and rows will not return to their original size.

When I enter data to the right or below the cells where I applied an AutoFormat, Excel automatically formats the new data. How can I stop this?

✔ To turn off the automatic formatting, select the Tools menu and then click Options. Select the Edit tab and click the Extend list formats and formulas option (☑ changes to ☐). Then click OK.

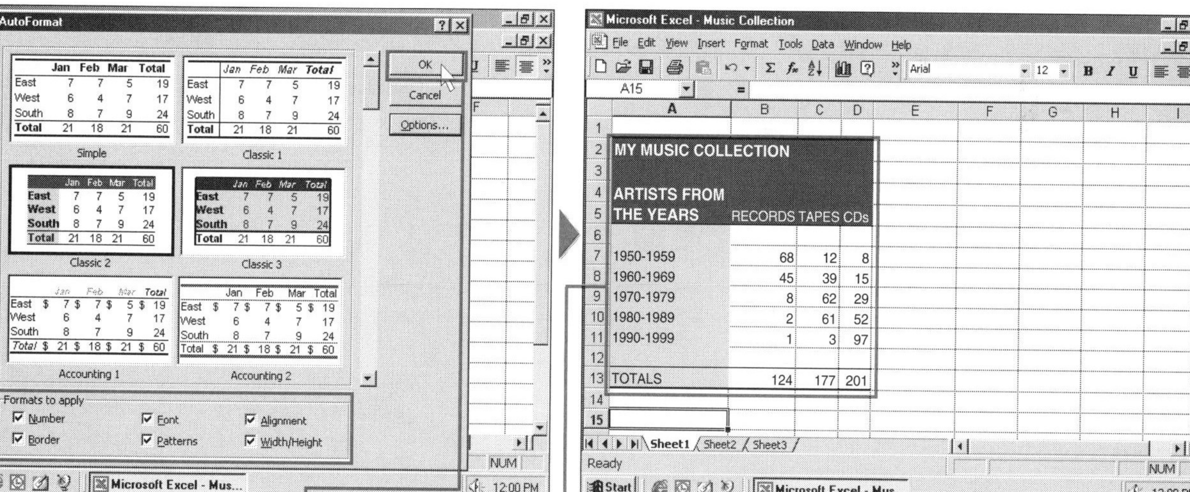

■ The formatting options appear in this area. A check mark (☑) beside an option indicates that Excel will apply the option to the cells.

6 Click an option to add (☑) or remove (☐) a check mark.

7 Click OK to apply the AutoFormat to the cells you selected.

■ The cells display the AutoFormat you selected.

■ To deselect cells, click any cell.

REMOVE AN AUTOFORMAT

■ Perform steps 1 to 4, except select None in step 4. Then press the Enter key.

PREVIEW A WORKSHEET

You can use the Print Preview feature to see how your worksheet will look when printed. Using the Print Preview feature can help you confirm that your worksheet will print the way you want. This can save you time and paper.

The Print Preview window indicates which page you are viewing and the total number of pages in your worksheet. If your worksheet contains more than one page, you can easily view the other pages.

You can magnify an area of a page in your worksheet. This allows you to view the area in more detail.

If you are using a black-and-white printer, the pages in the Print Preview window will be displayed in black and white. If you are using a color printer, the pages in the Print Preview window may be displayed in color.

When you finish using the Print Preview feature, you can close the Print Preview window to return to your worksheet.

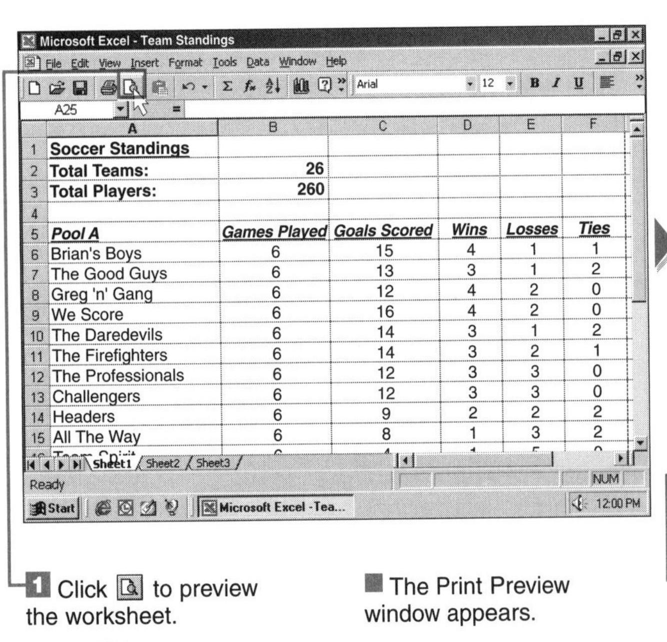

1 Click [preview button] to preview the worksheet.

Note: If [preview button] is not displayed, click [»] on the Standard toolbar to display all the buttons.

■ The Print Preview window appears.

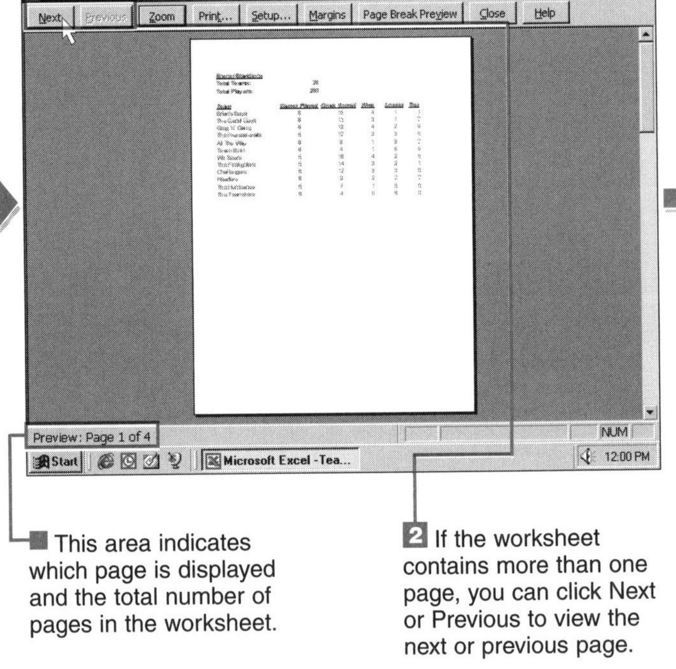

■ This area indicates which page is displayed and the total number of pages in the worksheet.

2 If the worksheet contains more than one page, you can click Next or Previous to view the next or previous page.

Note: You can also use the scroll bar to view other pages.

TIPS

Why aren't there any gridlines displayed in the Print Preview window?

✔ By default, Excel does not print gridlines. To print gridlines, click the Setup button in the Print Preview window. Select the Sheet tab and then click the Gridlines option (☐ changes to ☑). Then click OK.

Can I change the margins in the Print Preview window?

✔ You can click the Margins button to change the margins in the Print Preview window. For more information, see page 240.

How do I print my worksheet directly from the Print Preview window?

✔ Click the Print button. Excel returns to your worksheet and opens the Print dialog box. For information on printing, see page 238.

Why is the Print Preview window displaying only a chart from my worksheet?

✔ If you click a chart in your worksheet before you click the Print Preview button (🔍), the Print Preview window will display only the chart.

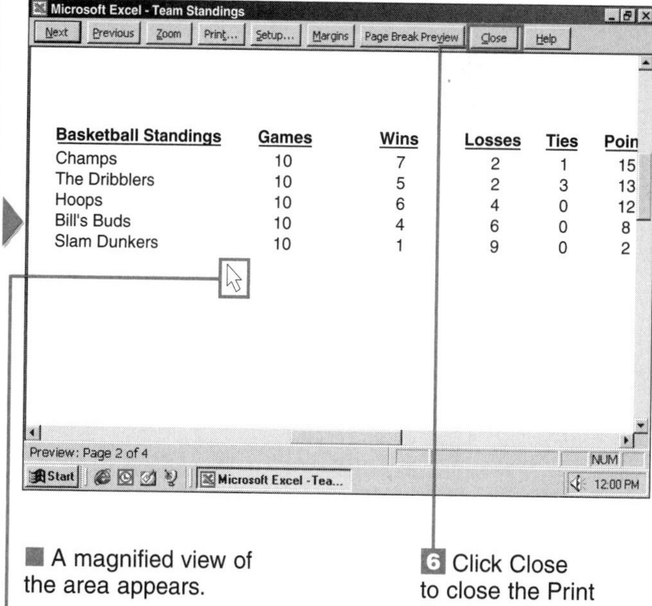

3 To magnify an area of the page, position the mouse ↖ over the area (↖ changes to 🔍).

4 Click the area to magnify the area.

■ A magnified view of the area appears.

5 To once again display the entire page, click anywhere on the page.

6 Click Close to close the Print Preview window.

PRINT A WORKSHEET

You can produce a paper copy of the worksheet displayed on your screen. This is useful when you want to present the worksheet to a colleague or refer to the worksheet when you do not have access to your computer.

If you have more than one printer installed on your computer, you can choose which printer you want to print your worksheet. Before printing, make sure the printer is turned on and contains an adequate supply of paper.

Excel allows you to specify the part of your workbook you want to print. You can print a selection of cells, an entire worksheet or all the worksheets in the workbook. To print a selection of cells, you must select the cells before you begin.

If the part of the workbook you want to print contains several pages, you can specify which pages you want to print.

You can click the Print button (🖨) on the Standard toolbar to quickly print the worksheet displayed on your screen.

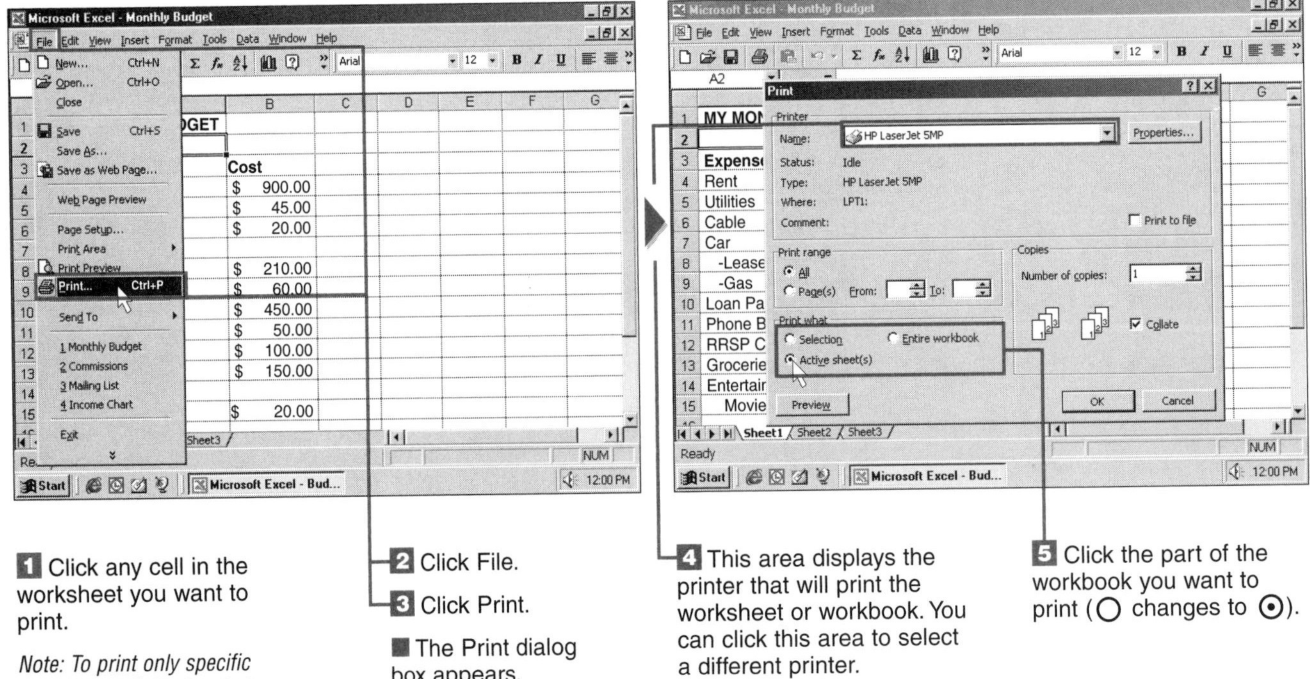

1 Click any cell in the worksheet you want to print.

Note: To print only specific cells in a worksheet, select the cells you want to print.

2 Click File.

3 Click Print.

■ The Print dialog box appears.

4 This area displays the printer that will print the worksheet or workbook. You can click this area to select a different printer.

5 Click the part of the workbook you want to print (○ changes to ⊙).

TIPS

Can I print multiple copies of a worksheet?

✔ You can print multiple copies of a worksheet, workbook or selection of cells. In the Print dialog box, double-click the Number of copies area and then type the number of copies you want to print.

Can I print more than one worksheet in my workbook?

✔ Yes. Hold down the Ctrl key as you click the tab for each worksheet you want to print. Then perform steps 2 to 7 below, except select Active sheet(s) in step 5.

I frequently print the same area of my worksheet. How can I quickly print this area?

✔ Select the area you frequently print. Choose the File menu, select Print Area and then click Set Print Area. When you click the Print button (🖨) on the Standard toolbar, Excel will print only the data in the print area you set. To later clear the print area, choose the File menu, select Print Area and then click Clear Print Area.

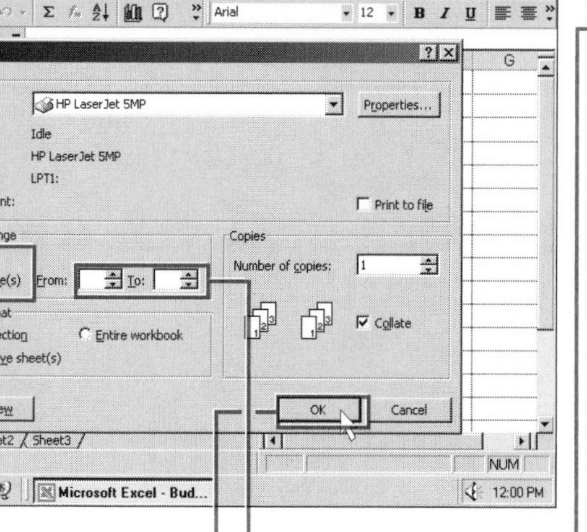

6 If the part of the workbook you selected to print contains more than one page, click an option to specify which pages you want to print (○ changes to ⊙).

■ If you selected Pages in step 6, type the first page you want to print. Press the Tab key and then type the last page you want to print.

7 Click OK.

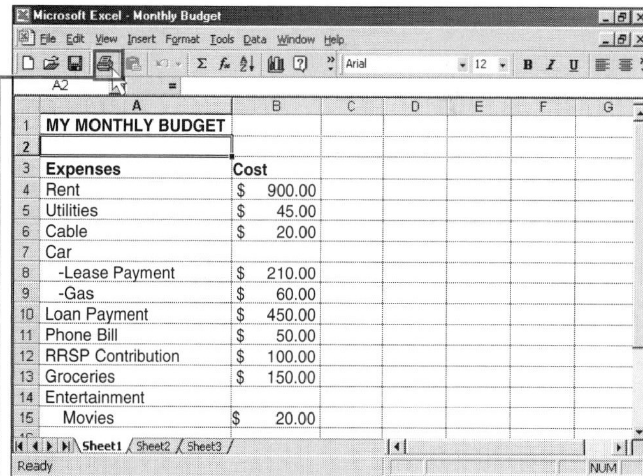

QUICKLY PRINT ENTIRE WORKSHEET

■ Click 🖨 to quickly print the worksheet displayed on the screen.

Note: If 🖨 is not displayed, click » on the Standard toolbar to display all the buttons.

CHANGE MARGINS

A margin is the amount of space between data and an edge of your paper.

There is a margin at the top, bottom, left and right edges of a page. Excel automatically sets the top and bottom margins to 1 inch and the left and right margins to 0.75 inches. You can change the margins to suit your needs.

Changing margins allows you to accommodate specialty paper. For example, if you are printing on company letterhead, you may need to increase the size of the top margin. If you are printing on paper that is three-hole punched, you may want to increase the size of the left margin.

You can also change the margins to fit more or less data on a page.

Most printers cannot print right to the edge of a page and require that you use a margin of at least 0.25 inches on all sides. You can check the manual that came with your printer for more information.

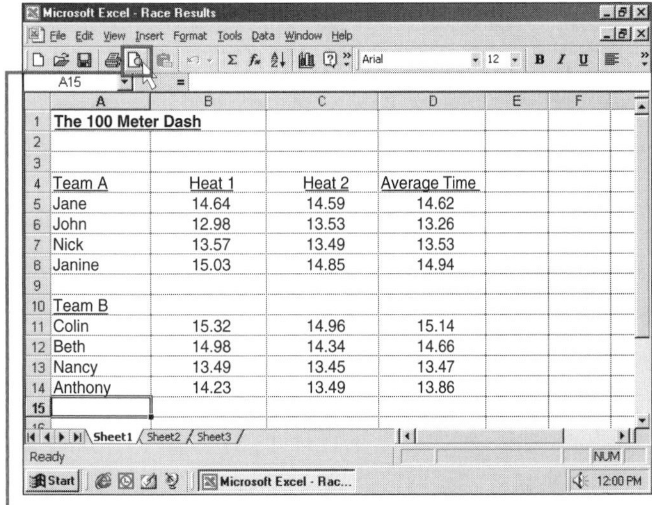

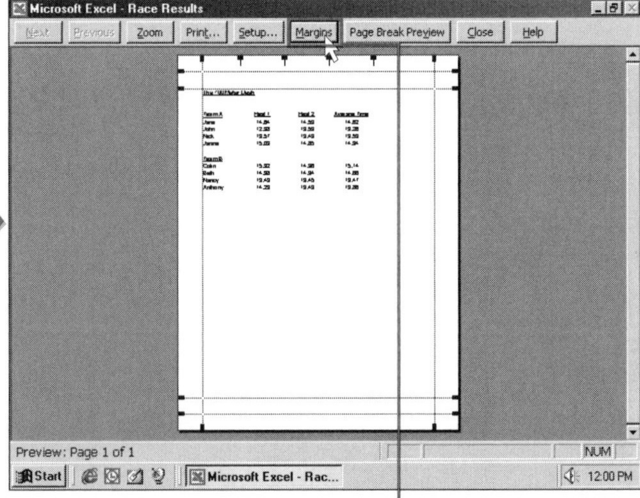

1 Click [icon] to display your worksheet in the Print Preview window. This window allows you to change the margins.

Note: If [icon] is not displayed, click [icon] on the Standard toolbar to display all the buttons.

■ The worksheet appears in the Print Preview window.

Note: For more information on the Print Preview feature, see page 236.

2 If the margins are not displayed, click Margins.

TIPS

How can I specify exact measurements for my margins?

✔ In the Print Preview window, click the Setup button. Select the Margins tab and type the measurements in the Top, Bottom, Left and Right areas. Then click OK.

What are the square markers (▼) along the top of a page used for?

✔ These markers allow you to change the width of columns in the Print Preview window. Position the mouse over the marker (▼) for the column you want to change (changes to ↔). Then drag the marker (▼) to a new location.

Can I center the data in my worksheet?

✔ You can center data horizontally and vertically between the margins on a page. In the Print Preview window, click the Setup button and then click the Margins tab. Click the option(s) for the way you want to center the data (☐ changes to ☑) and then click OK.

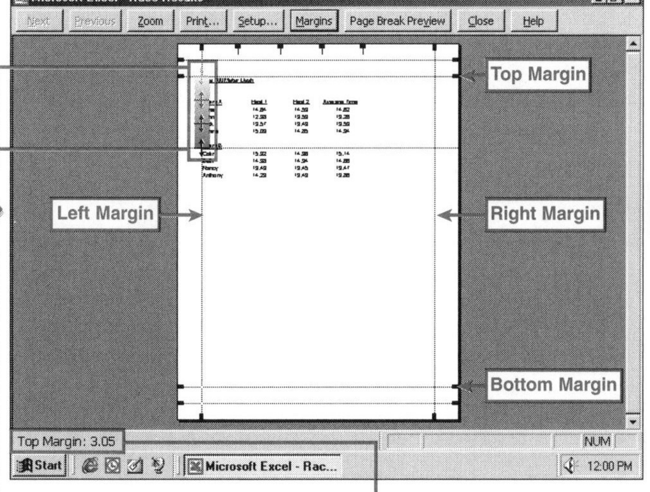

3 Position the mouse over a margin you want to change (changes to ↕ or ↔).

4 Drag the margin to a new location. A line shows the new location.

■ As you move the margin, this area displays the distance in inches between the margin and the edge of the page.

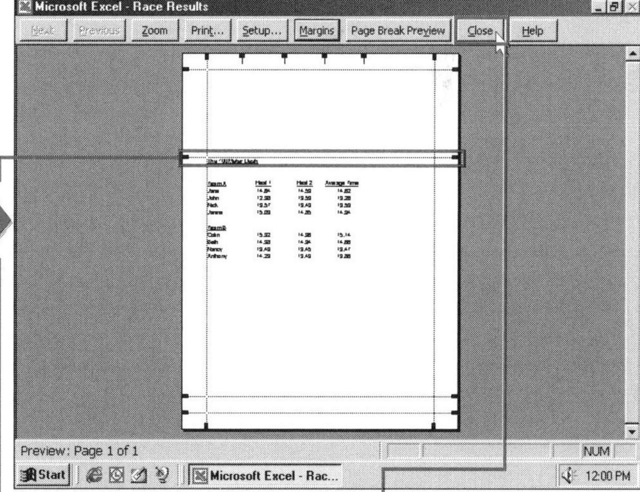

■ The margin moves to the new location.

5 Repeat steps 3 and 4 for each margin you want to change.

6 Click Close to close the Print Preview window.

CHANGE PAGE ORIENTATION

You can change the page orientation to change the way a worksheet prints on a page. Excel allows you to print worksheets using the portrait or landscape orientation.

By default, Excel prints worksheets across the short side of a page, in the portrait orientation. This orientation is useful for printing worksheets that have more rows than columns.

When you want to print a worksheet with more columns than rows, you can have Excel print the worksheet in the landscape orientation. This orientation rotates the worksheet so the data prints across the long side of a page.

Changing the page orientation affects the entire worksheet, but does not affect other worksheets in the workbook or other workbooks. Changing the page orientation also does not change the way the worksheet appears on your screen. You can use Print Preview to see how the worksheet will appear when printed. For more information on Print Preview, see page 236.

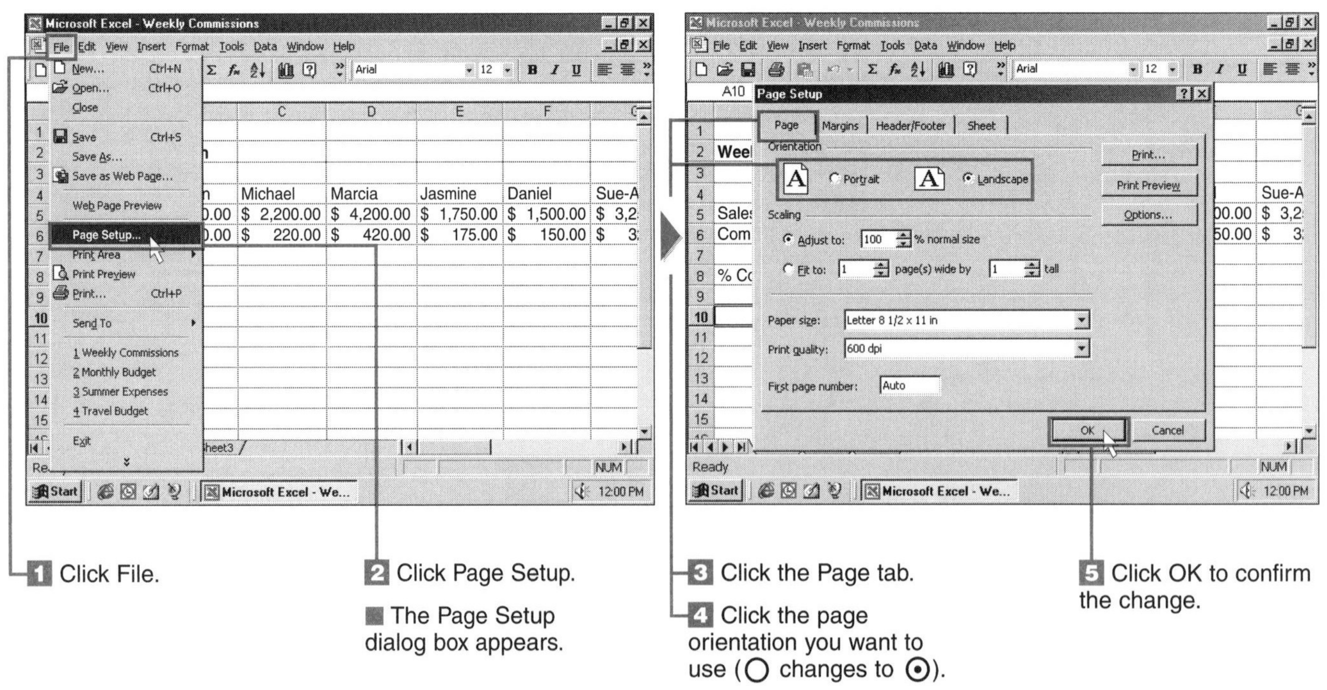

1 Click File.

2 Click Page Setup.

■ The Page Setup dialog box appears.

3 Click the Page tab.

4 Click the page orientation you want to use (○ changes to ⊙).

5 Click OK to confirm the change.

CHANGE PRINT OPTIONS

You can use the print options Excel offers to change the way your worksheet appears on a printed page. Changing the print options for your worksheet allows you to create a printout that suits your needs.

You can use the Gridlines option to have Excel print lines around each cell in a worksheet. This can help make the data in a large worksheet easier to read.

The Black and white option prints a colored worksheet in black and white. This is useful when you are using a color printer but want to print a black-and-white draft of a worksheet.

The Draft quality option helps reduce printing time by not printing gridlines and most graphics. This option is useful when you want to quickly print a rough draft of a worksheet.

When you select the Row and column headings option, Excel prints the row numbers and column headings in your worksheet.

Changing the print options only changes the way your worksheet appears on a printed page. The print options do not affect the way your worksheet appears on the screen.

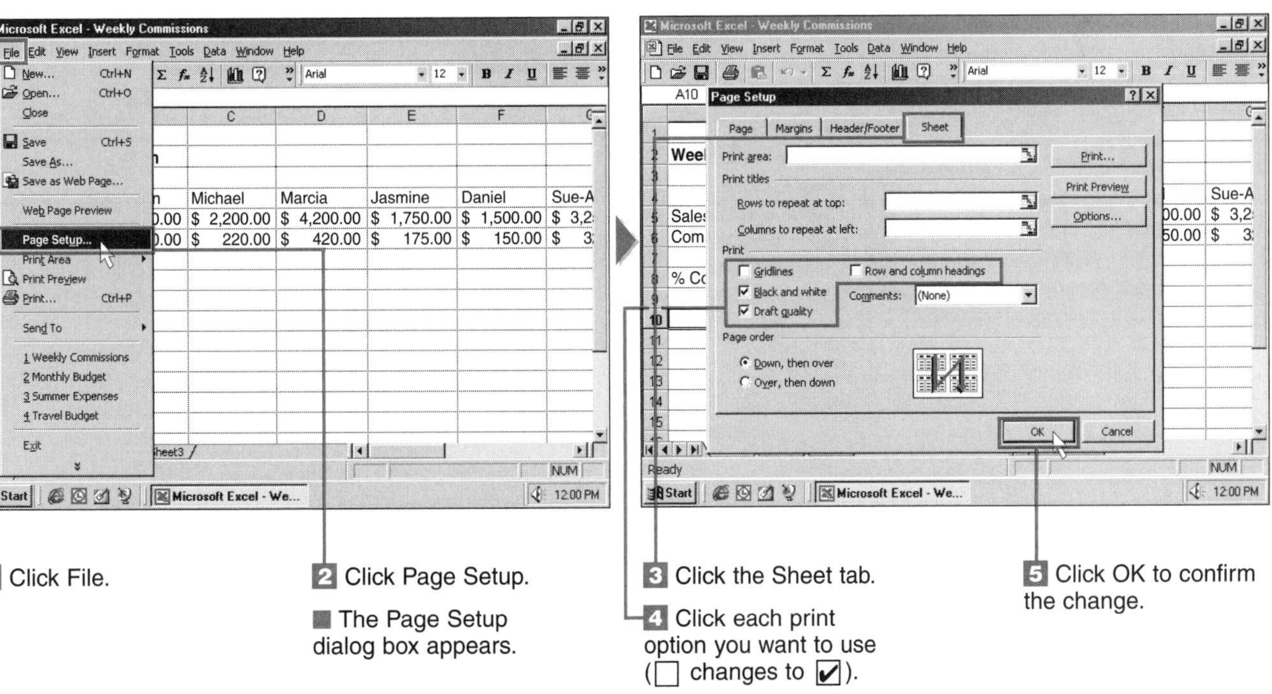

1 Click File.

2 Click Page Setup.

■ The Page Setup dialog box appears.

3 Click the Sheet tab.

4 Click each print option you want to use (☐ changes to ☑).

5 Click OK to confirm the change.

INSERT A PAGE BREAK

You can insert a page break when you want to start a new page at a specific place in your worksheet. A page break defines where one page ends and another begins.

When you fill a page with data, Excel automatically starts a new page by inserting a page break for you.

You may need to insert a page break to ensure that related data appears on the same page when you print your worksheet. You can insert a horizontal page break above a row to have Excel print the rows below the break on a new page. You can also insert a vertical page break to the left of a column to have Excel print the columns to the right of the break on a new page.

Before you print your worksheet, you can preview all the page breaks in the worksheet. Page breaks inserted by Excel appear as dotted blue lines. Page breaks you inserted appear as solid blue lines.

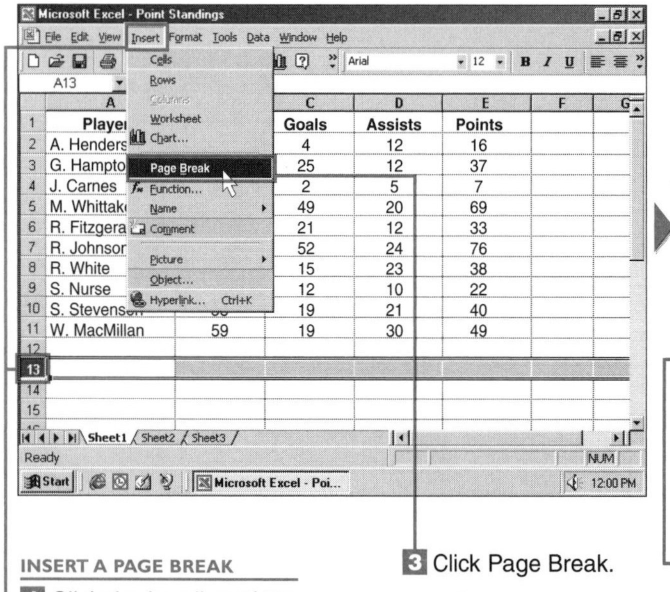

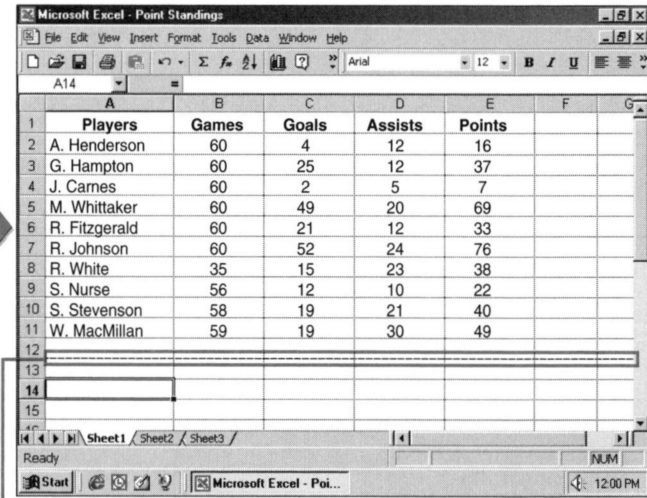

INSERT A PAGE BREAK

1 Click the heading of the row or column you want to appear at the beginning of the new page.

2 Click Insert.

3 Click Page Break.

Note: If Page Break does not appear on the menu, position the mouse over the bottom of the menu to display all the menu commands.

■ A dotted line appears on the screen. This line defines where one page ends and another begins.

■ To deselect a row or column, click any cell.

■ The page break line will not appear when you print the worksheet.

TIPS

How do I remove a page break?

✔ Select a cell that is directly below or directly to the right of the page break you want to remove. Select the Insert menu and then click Remove Page Break.

Can I remove all the page breaks I inserted in my worksheet at once?

✔ Yes. Click the blank area (▭) to the left of column A to select the entire worksheet. Select the Insert menu and then click Reset All Page Breaks.

How can I move a page break?

✔ Perform steps 1 to 3 on this page. Position the mouse ✥ over a blue page break line (✥ changes to ↔ or ↕) and then drag the line to a new location.

Can I insert horizontal and vertical page breaks at the same time?

✔ Yes. Click the cell that is directly below and to the right of where you want the horizontal and vertical page breaks to appear. Select the Insert menu and then click Page Break.

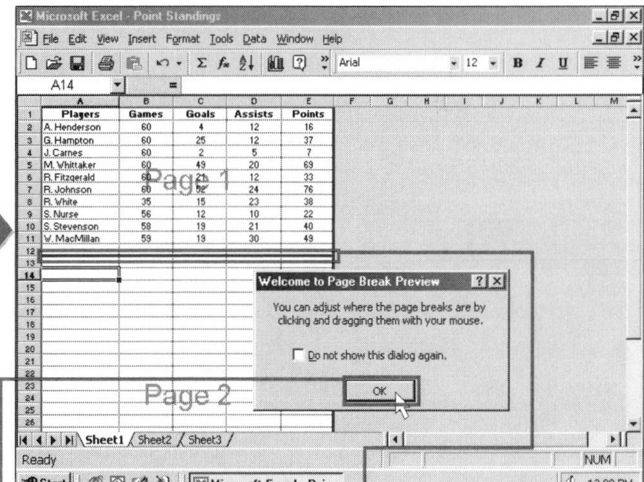

VIEW ALL PAGE BREAKS

1 Click View.

2 Click Page Break Preview to display all the page breaks in the worksheet.

■ A Welcome dialog box appears.

3 Click OK to close the dialog box.

■ Blue lines show the location of page breaks in the worksheet.

Note: To return to the normal view at any time, repeat steps 1 and 2, except select Normal in step 2.

CHANGE SIZE OF PRINTED DATA

You can have Excel reduce the size of printed data to print your worksheet on a specific number of pages. This is useful when the last page of your worksheet contains a small amount of data that you want to fit on the previous page.

To change the size of printed data, you must specify how many pages you want the data to print across and down. Excel will resize the data in your worksheet to print on the number of pages you specify. If you try to fit the data on too few pages, the data may become too small to read.

When you change the size of printed data, Excel ignores any page breaks you have inserted in your worksheet. For information on page breaks, see page 244.

Changing the size of printed data does not affect the way your worksheet appears on the screen. You can use the Print Preview feature to preview how your worksheet will appear when printed. For information on the Print Preview feature, see page 236.

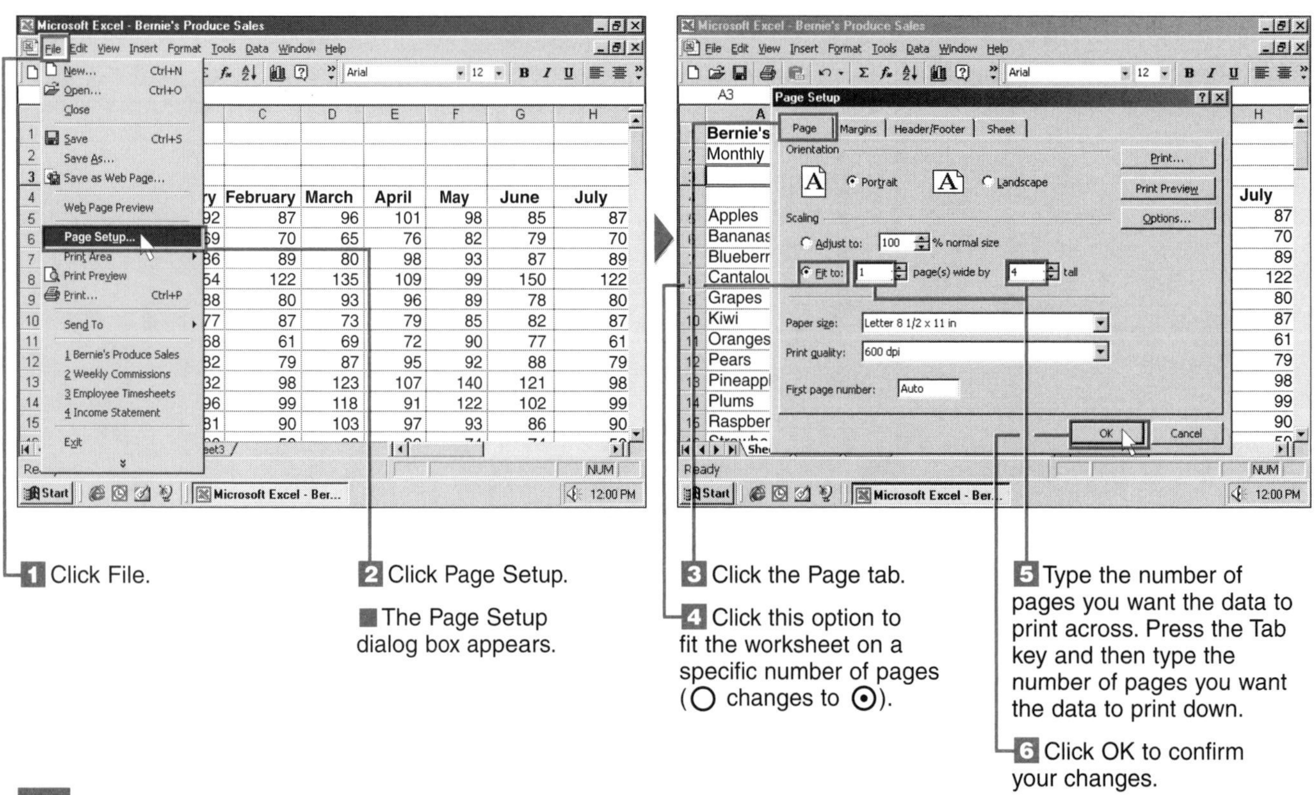

1 Click File.

2 Click Page Setup.

■ The Page Setup dialog box appears.

3 Click the Page tab.

4 Click this option to fit the worksheet on a specific number of pages (○ changes to ⊙).

5 Type the number of pages you want the data to print across. Press the Tab key and then type the number of pages you want the data to print down.

6 Click OK to confirm your changes.

REPEAT LABELS ON PRINTED PAGES

If your worksheet prints on more than one page, you can print the same row or column labels on every page.

Repeating row or column labels can help make the data in a long worksheet easier to understand. For example, repeating column labels in a worksheet containing product information can help you avoid confusing data in the "Quantity Sold" column with data in the "Quantity in Stock" column.

You only need to select one cell in each row or column of labels you want to print on every page. If the Page Setup dialog box covers the labels you want to repeat, you can move the dialog box to a new location.

Repeating labels on printed pages does not affect the way your worksheet appears on the screen. You can use the Print Preview feature to preview how the repeated labels will look when you print your worksheet. For information on the Print Preview feature, see page 236.

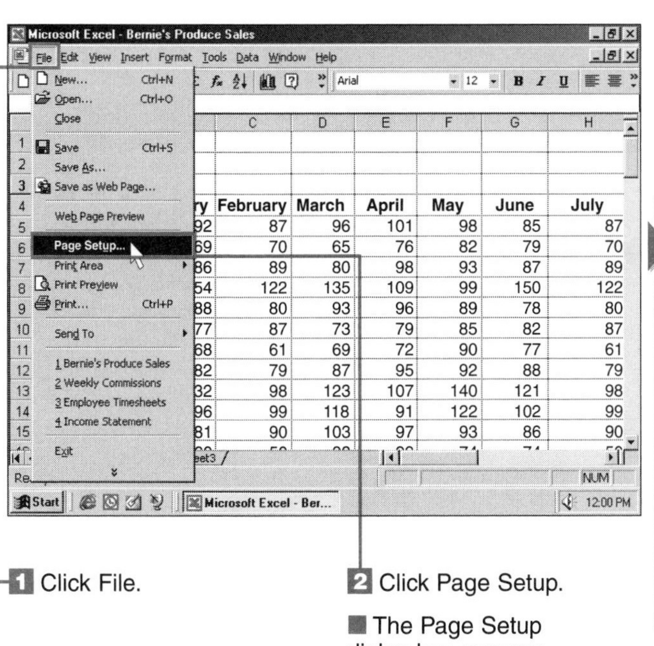

1 Click File.

2 Click Page Setup.

■ The Page Setup dialog box appears.

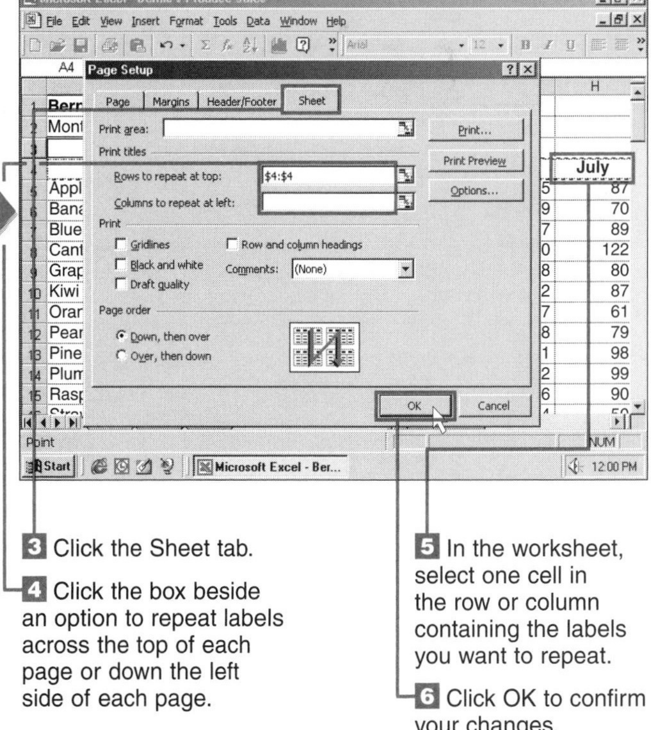

3 Click the Sheet tab.

4 Click the box beside an option to repeat labels across the top of each page or down the left side of each page.

5 In the worksheet, select one cell in the row or column containing the labels you want to repeat.

6 Click OK to confirm your changes.

ADD A HEADER OR FOOTER

You can add a header or footer to display additional information on each page of your worksheet. A header or footer can contain information such as your name, the page number and the current date.

By default, a header appears 0.5 inches from the top of a printed page and a footer appears 0.5 inches from the bottom of a printed page. A worksheet can contain only one header and one footer.

Excel provides many headers and footers for you to choose from. If your worksheet contains budget or financial information, you may want to choose a header that contains the word "Confidential". If you frequently update the data in your worksheet, you may want to choose a footer that includes the current date every time the worksheet is printed.

To see how a header or footer will appear before you print your worksheet, you can use the Print Preview feature. For information on the Print Preview feature, see page 236.

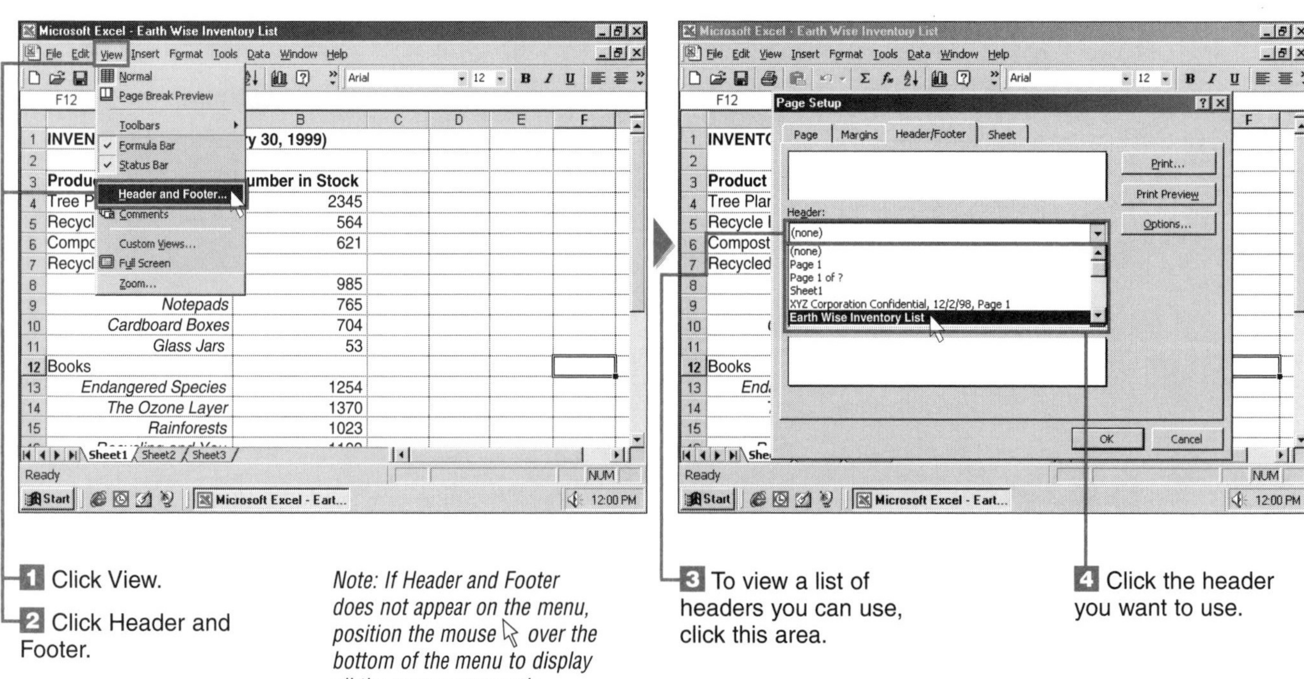

1 Click View.

2 Click Header and Footer.

Note: If Header and Footer does not appear on the menu, position the mouse over the bottom of the menu to display all the menu commands.

■ The Page Setup dialog box appears.

3 To view a list of headers you can use, click this area.

4 Click the header you want to use.

TIPS

How do I remove a header or footer?

✔ Select the View menu and then click Header and Footer. To remove a header, click the Header area and then select (none). To remove a footer, click the Footer area and then select (none).

Can I create a custom header or footer?

✔ Yes. Select the View menu and then click Header and Footer. Click the Custom Header or Custom Footer button. You can enter text in the left, center and right sections of the header or footer. The buttons can help you insert information, such as the page number (▣), total number of pages (▣), date (▣) and time (▣), into your header or footer.

My custom header runs into the data in my worksheet. What can I do?

✔ You can increase the top or bottom margin to allow more space for a header or footer. Select the File menu and click Page Setup. Then click the Margins tab. Double-click the Top or Bottom area and enter a larger number. Then click OK.

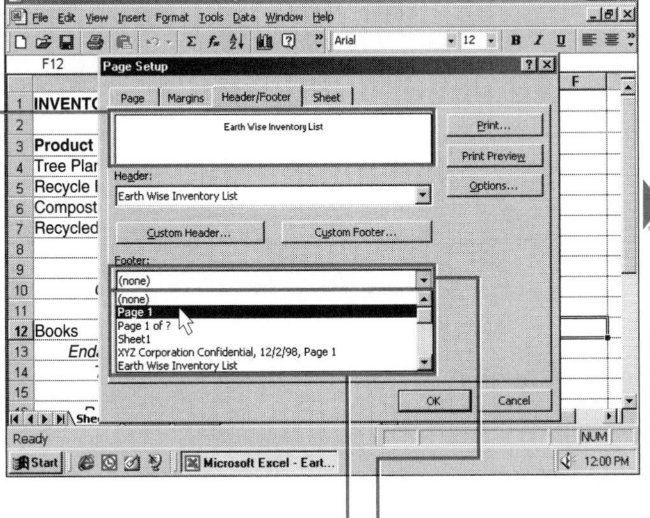

■ This area displays how the header will appear at the top of a page.

5 To view a list of footers you can use, click this area.

6 Click the footer you want to use.

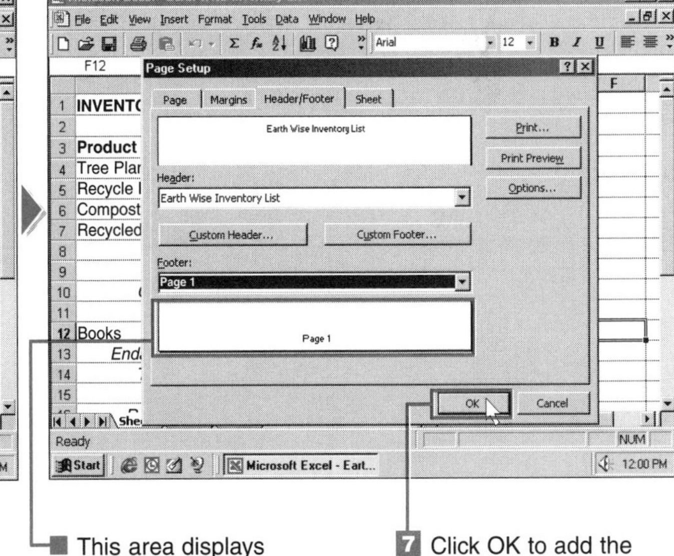

■ This area displays how the footer will appear at the bottom of a page.

7 Click OK to add the header or footer to the worksheet.

Note: You can repeat steps 1 to 7 to change the header or footer at any time.

INSERT A WORKSHEET

The worksheet displayed on your screen is one of several worksheets in your workbook. You can insert a new worksheet to add related information to your workbook.

By default, workbooks contain three worksheets, but you can insert as many new worksheets as you need. You can insert a new worksheet anywhere in your workbook.

Inserting a new worksheet can help you better organize the information in your workbook. For example, information for each division of a large company can be stored on a separate worksheet in one workbook. As the company grows, you may find that you need to add more worksheets.

When you no longer need a worksheet, you can delete the worksheet from your workbook. Once you delete a worksheet, it is permanently removed from your workbook and cannot be restored.

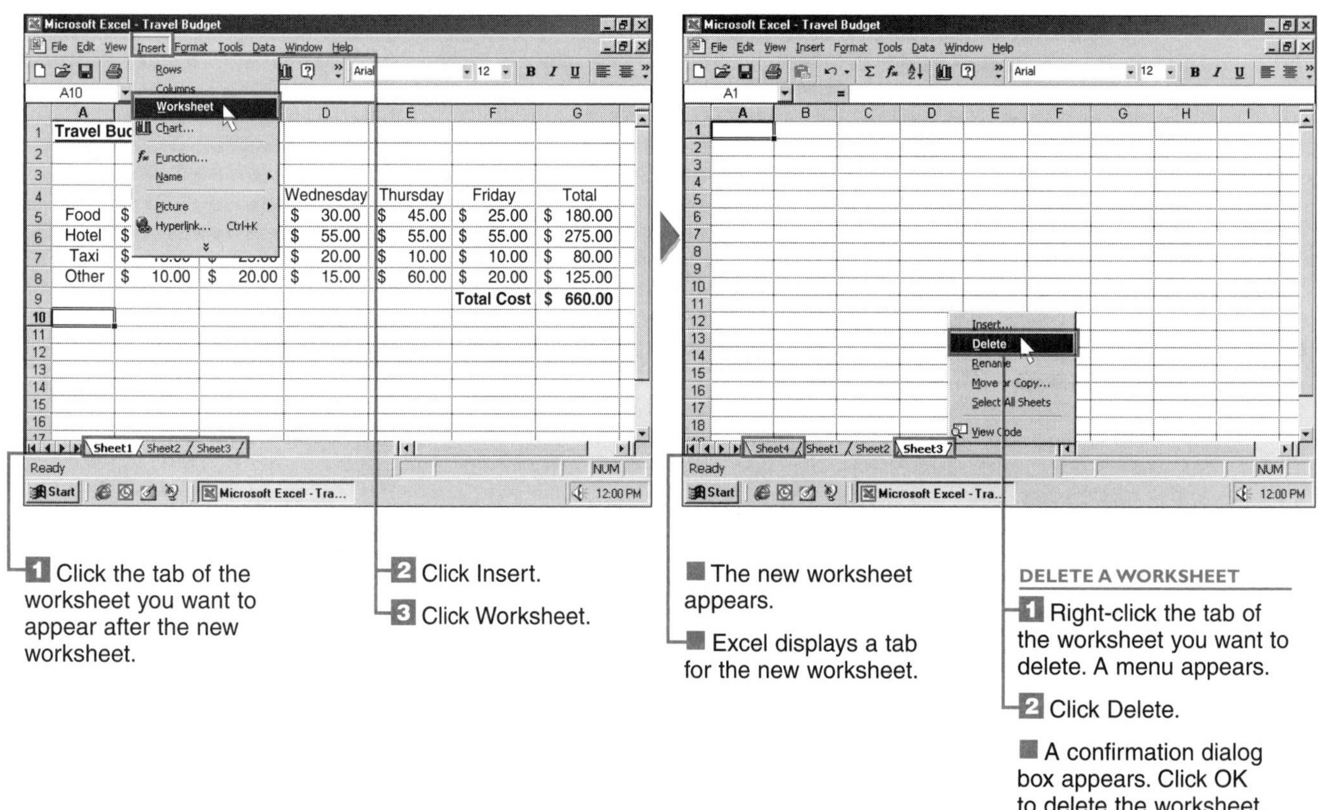

1 Click the tab of the worksheet you want to appear after the new worksheet.

2 Click Insert.

3 Click Worksheet.

■ The new worksheet appears.

■ Excel displays a tab for the new worksheet.

DELETE A WORKSHEET

1 Right-click the tab of the worksheet you want to delete. A menu appears.

2 Click Delete.

■ A confirmation dialog box appears. Click OK to delete the worksheet.

SWITCH BETWEEN WORKSHEETS

You can switch between the worksheets in your workbook to view and compare all the data.

For example, if each worksheet in a financial workbook contains the sales figures for one month, you can switch between the worksheets to compare the sales figures for each month.

Each worksheet in your workbook has a tab that displays the name of the worksheet. The worksheet currently displayed on your screen has a white tab. The other worksheets in the workbook have gray tabs. The contents of the other worksheets are hidden from view.

You can switch between worksheets in your workbook by selecting the tab of the worksheet you want to view. If you have many worksheets in your workbook, some of the worksheet tabs may be hidden from view. You can use the tab scrolling buttons to display hidden tabs.

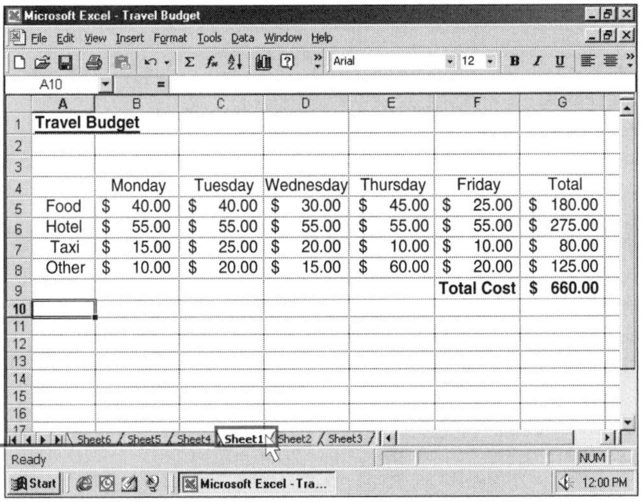

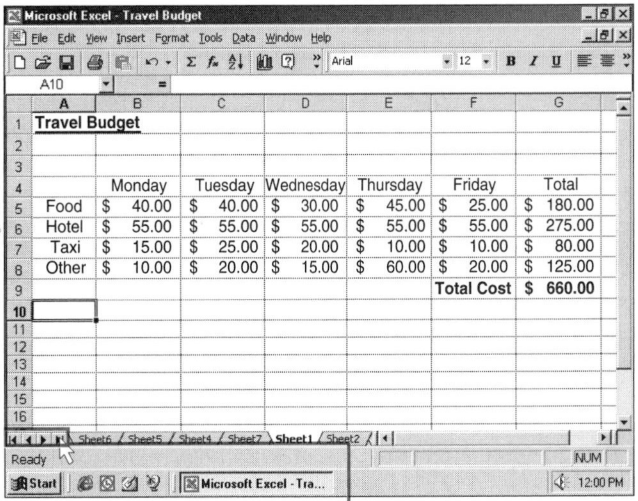

Microsoft Excel - Travel Budget

	A	B	C	D	E	F	G
1	Travel Budget						
2							
3							
4		Monday	Tuesday	Wednesday	Thursday	Friday	Total
5	Food	$ 40.00	$ 40.00	$ 30.00	$ 45.00	$ 25.00	$ 180.00
6	Hotel	$ 55.00	$ 55.00	$ 55.00	$ 55.00	$ 55.00	$ 275.00
7	Taxi	$ 15.00	$ 25.00	$ 20.00	$ 10.00	$ 10.00	$ 80.00
8	Other	$ 10.00	$ 20.00	$ 15.00	$ 60.00	$ 20.00	$ 125.00
9						Total Cost	$ 660.00

Sheet6 / Sheet5 / Sheet4 / Sheet1 / Sheet2 / Sheet3

1 To display the contents of a worksheet, click the tab of the worksheet.

■ The worksheet you selected has a white tab.

■ The contents of the worksheet appear. The contents of the other worksheets in the workbook are hidden.

■ If you have many worksheets in the workbook, you may not be able to see all the tabs.

2 Click a button to browse through the tabs.

- Display first tab
- Display tab to the left
- Display tab to the right
- Display last tab

RENAME A WORKSHEET

You can give each worksheet in your workbook a descriptive name.

Excel automatically provides a name, such as Sheet1, for each worksheet in a workbook. You can rename a worksheet to better describe the contents of the worksheet. This helps you and other users more easily identify and find worksheets of interest.

Excel allows you to use up to 31 characters, including spaces, to name a worksheet. You cannot use the \ / : ? * [or] characters in a worksheet name. Each worksheet in a workbook must have a unique name.

Generally, short worksheet names are better than long worksheet names. Short names allow you to display more worksheet tabs on your screen at once.

After you rename a worksheet, you cannot use the Undo feature to return the worksheet to its original name.

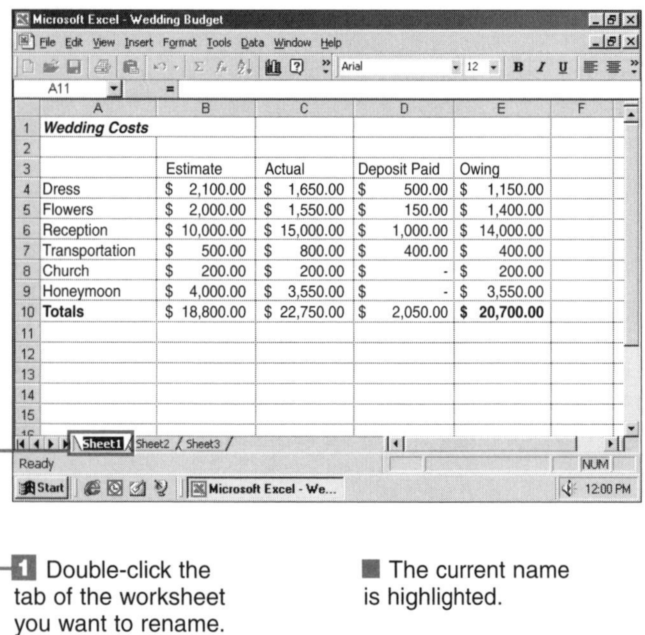

1 Double-click the tab of the worksheet you want to rename.

■ The current name is highlighted.

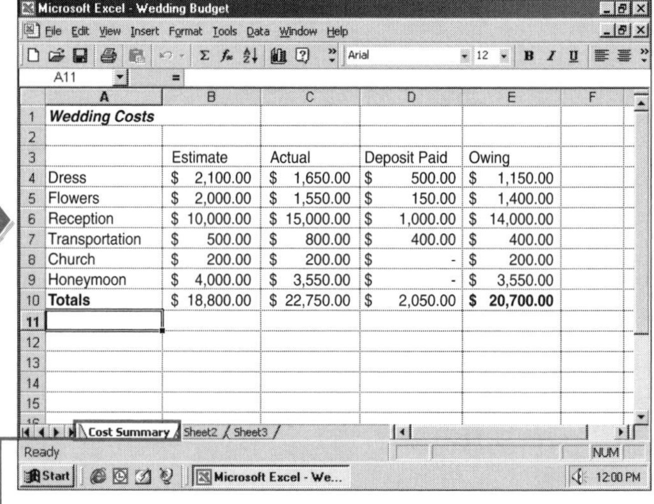

2 Type a new name and then press the Enter key.

Note: A worksheet name can contain up to 31 characters, including spaces.

MOVE A WORKSHEET

You can move a worksheet to a new location in your workbook. This allows you to reorganize the data in a workbook.

Moving worksheets allows you to place two worksheets you frequently switch between beside each other.

You should be careful when moving worksheets in a workbook. Calculations or charts based on the data in a worksheet could become inaccurate if the worksheet is moved. For example, in a formula that contains references to other worksheets, the result may change if you move any of the worksheets referenced in the formula.

Once you move a worksheet, you cannot use the Undo feature to return the worksheet to its original location in the workbook.

You can copy a worksheet. Copying a worksheet is useful if you plan to make major changes to a worksheet and you want to have a copy of the worksheet without the changes.

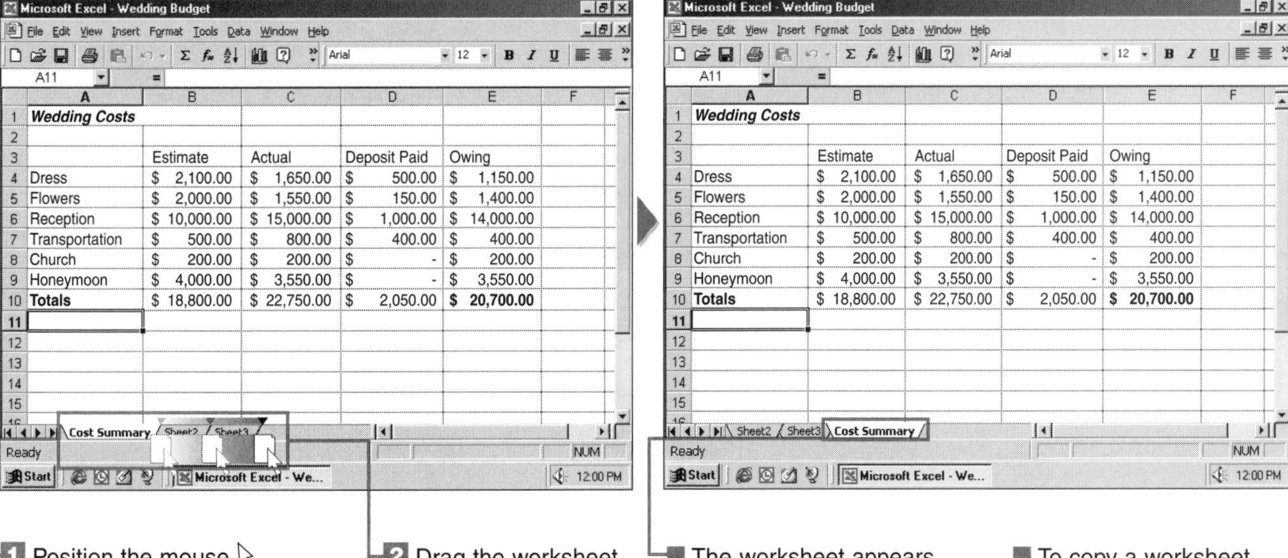

1 Position the mouse over the tab of the worksheet you want to move.

2 Drag the worksheet to a new location.

■ An arrow (▼) shows where the worksheet will appear.

■ The worksheet appears in the new location.

■ To copy a worksheet, perform steps 1 and 2, except hold down the Ctrl key as you perform step 2.

CREATE A CHART

You can create a chart to graphically display your worksheet data. A chart can help make data easier to understand.

The data you use to create a chart should be organized into rows and columns in your worksheet. You can use data in rows and columns that are not beside each other. When selecting the data, make sure you include the row and column labels you want to appear in the chart.

The Chart Wizard takes you step-by-step through the process of creating a chart. You can select the type of chart you want to create, such as a Column, Pie or Area chart. You can also specify whether you want to plot your worksheet data by rows or columns.

You can add titles to a chart. The Chart title identifies the subject of the chart. The X-axis title indicates the categories used in the chart. The Y-axis title indicates the unit of measure used in the chart. If you create a 3-D chart, you may be able to add a title to the Z-axis.

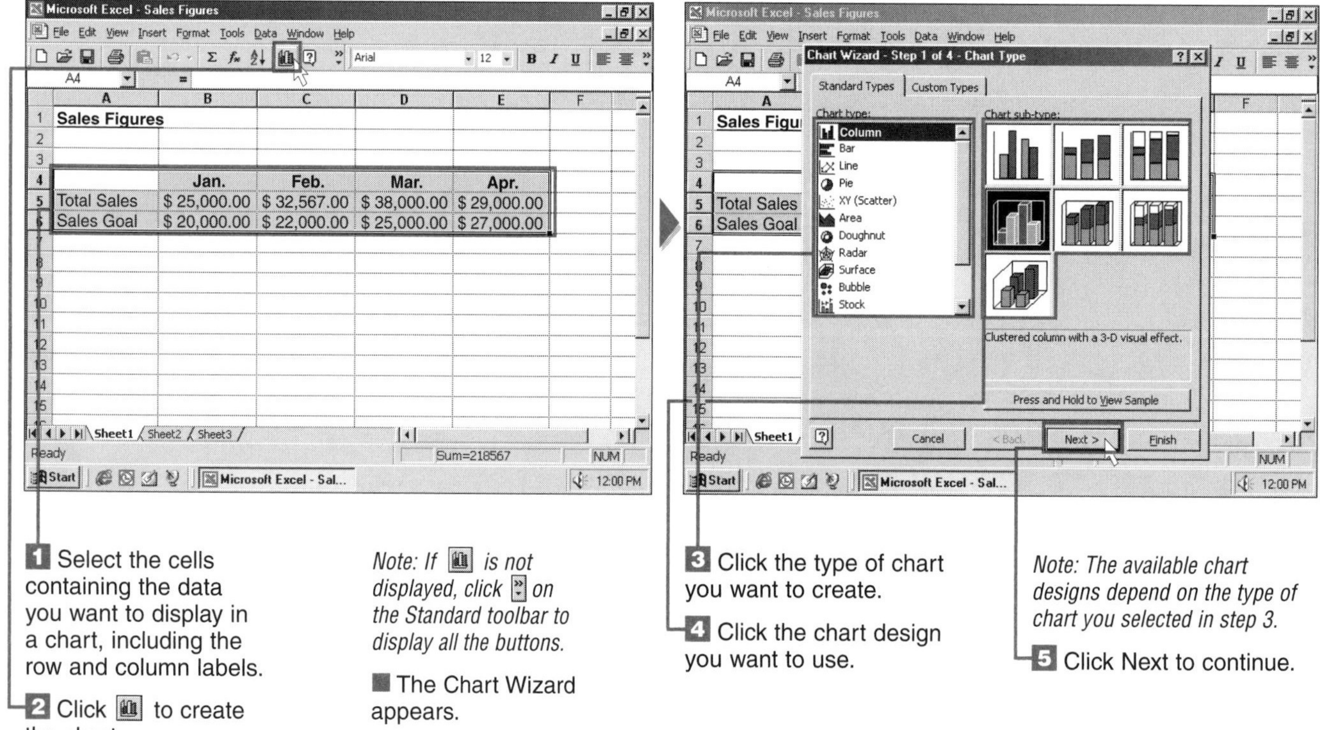

1 Select the cells containing the data you want to display in a chart, including the row and column labels.

2 Click [chart icon] to create the chart.

Note: If [chart icon] is not displayed, click [» icon] on the Standard toolbar to display all the buttons.

■ The Chart Wizard appears.

3 Click the type of chart you want to create.

4 Click the chart design you want to use.

Note: The available chart designs depend on the type of chart you selected in step 3.

5 Click Next to continue.

TIPS

How can I see what my chart will look like when I select a chart type in the Chart Wizard?

✔ After you select a chart type and design for your chart, you can use the Press and Hold to View Sample button to see what the chart will look like in your worksheet.

Can I change the chart type after I create a chart?

✔ You can change the chart type at any time after creating a chart. To change the chart type, see page 258.

Can I change the chart titles after I create a chart?

✔ Yes. In the completed chart, click the title you want to change. Type the new title and then press the Enter key.

Is there another way to quickly create a chart?

✔ You can quickly create a chart that displays Excel's default chart settings. Select the cells containing the data you want to display in the chart and then press the F11 key. The chart will appear on its own sheet in your workbook.

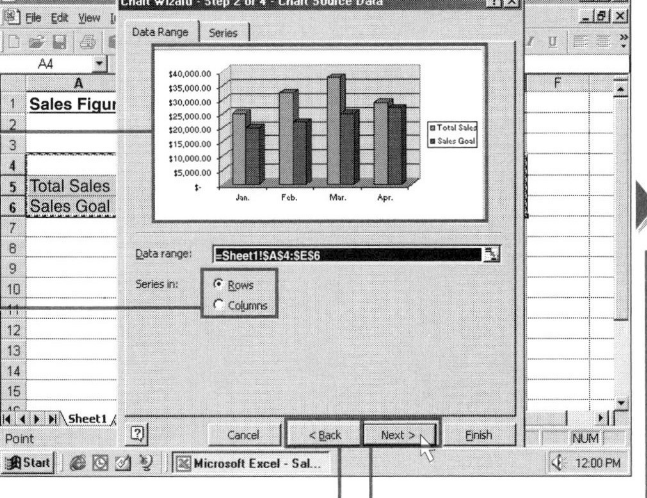

6 Click an option to select the way you want Excel to plot the data from the worksheet (○ changes to ⦿).

■ This area displays a sample of the chart.

7 Click Next to continue.

■ You can click Back at any time to return to a previous step and change your selections.

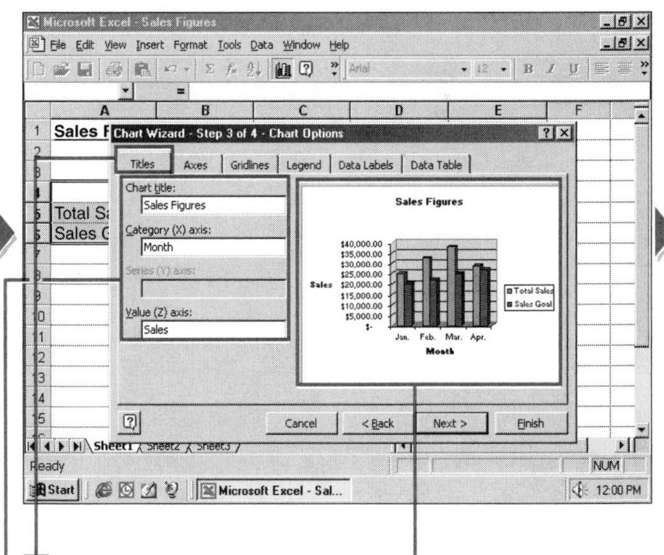

8 To add titles to the chart, click the Titles tab.

9 Click the box for a title you want to add and then type the title. Repeat this step for each title you want to add.

■ This area shows how the titles will appear in the chart.

CONTINUED

CREATE A CHART CONTINUED

You can choose how you want to display the legend for a chart you create. You can display the legend at the bottom, top, right, left or top-right corner of the chart.

The legend identifies the color, pattern or symbol used for each data series in a chart. A data series is a group of related data representing one row or column from your worksheet. When there is more than one data series in a chart, Excel uses different colors, patterns or symbols to help you identify each data series.

You can display a chart on the same worksheet as the data or on its own sheet, called a chart sheet.

After you create a chart, Excel displays the chart on your screen. Excel also displays the Chart toolbar. The Chart toolbar automatically appears on your screen each time you select the chart.

The handles (■) that appear around a chart allow you to resize the chart. For information on resizing a chart, see page 260.

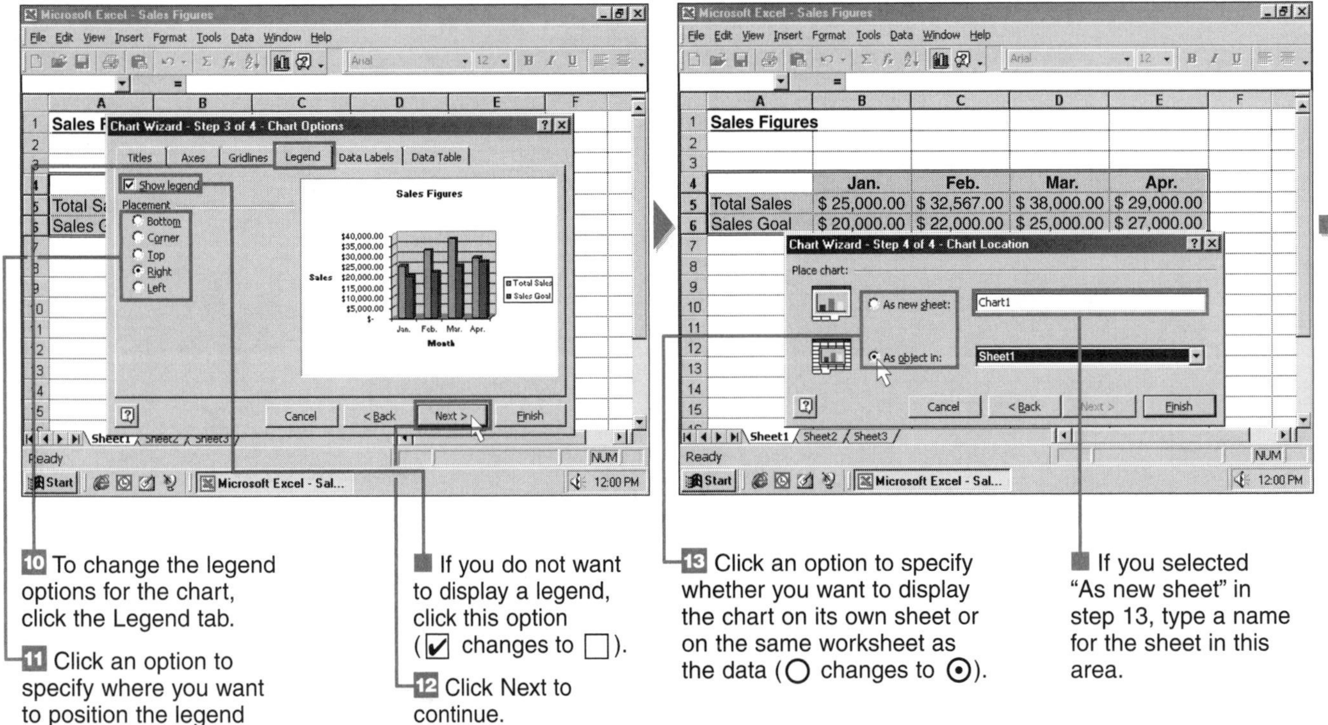

10 To change the legend options for the chart, click the Legend tab.

11 Click an option to specify where you want to position the legend (○ changes to ⦿).

■ If you do not want to display a legend, click this option (☑ changes to ☐).

12 Click Next to continue.

13 Click an option to specify whether you want to display the chart on its own sheet or on the same worksheet as the data (○ changes to ⦿).

■ If you selected "As new sheet" in step 13, type a name for the sheet in this area.

TIPS

What happens if I change data used in a chart?

✔ If you change data used in a chart, Excel will automatically update the chart.

Can I move the Chart toolbar?

✔ Yes. Position the mouse pointer over the title bar of the Chart toolbar and then drag the toolbar to a new location on your screen.

How can I hide the legend for my chart?

✔ Click a blank area of the chart. On the Chart toolbar, click the Legend button (▤) to hide or display the legend.

Can I add a data table to my chart?

✔ Yes. Click a blank area of the chart. On the Chart toolbar, click the Data Table button (▦) to add or remove a data table at any time.

How can I format a chart?

✔ You can format each area of a chart individually. Double-click the area of the chart you want to format. The Format dialog box appears and displays the available options for the area you selected.

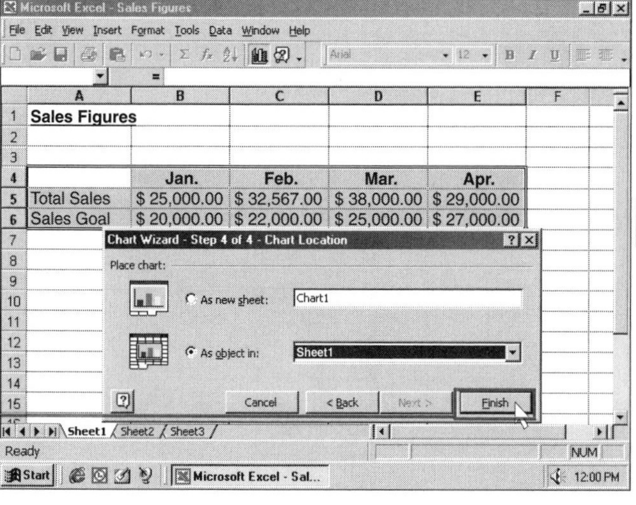

14 Click Finish to complete the chart.

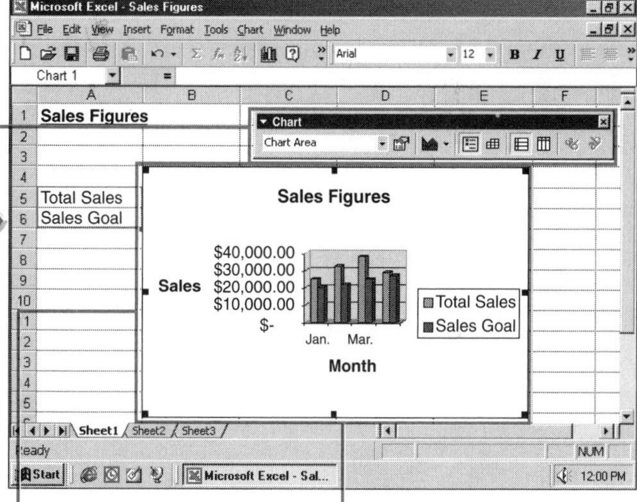

■ The chart appears.

■ The Chart toolbar also appears, displaying buttons that allow you to change the chart.

Note: If the Chart toolbar does not appear, see page 13 to display the toolbar.

■ The handles (■) around a chart let you change the size of the chart. To hide the handles, click outside the chart.

CHANGE CHART TYPE

You can change the chart type to present your data more effectively. Excel provides 14 standard chart types and approximately 70 designs for you to choose from. Column, Bar, Line, Area and Pie charts are popular chart types.

The chart type you should use depends on your data. Each chart type presents data in a specific way.

A column chart is useful for showing changes to data over time or comparing individual items. Each column represents an item in a data series.

A bar chart is useful for comparing individual items. Each bar represents an item in a data series.

A line chart is useful for showing changes to data at regular intervals. Each line represents a data series.

An area chart is useful for showing the amount of change in data over time. Each line represents a data series.

A pie chart is useful for showing the relationship of parts to a whole. Each piece of a pie represents an item in a data series. A pie chart can show only one data series at a time.

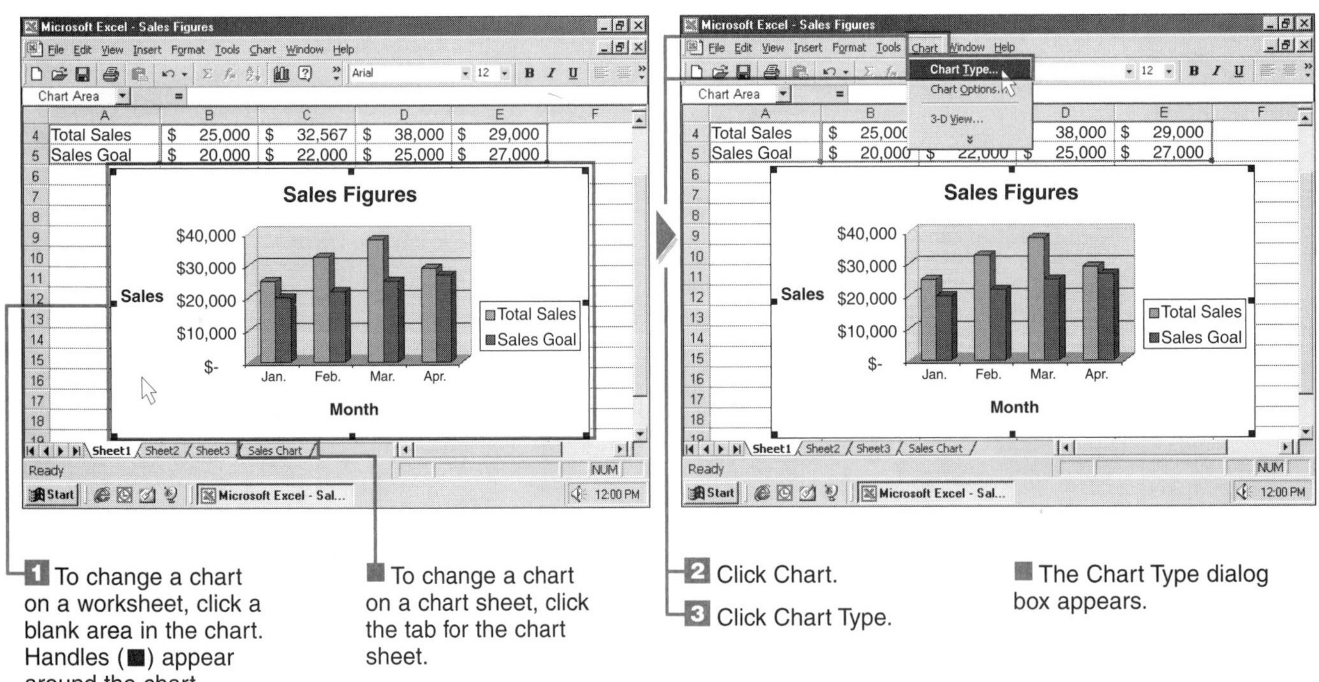

1 To change a chart on a worksheet, click a blank area in the chart. Handles (■) appear around the chart.

■ To change a chart on a chart sheet, click the tab for the chart sheet.

2 Click Chart.

3 Click Chart Type.

■ The Chart Type dialog box appears.

TIPS

What is the difference between the Pie and Doughnut chart types?

✔ While pie and doughnut charts are both useful for showing the relationship of parts to a whole, they differ in the amount of information they can display. A pie chart can display only one data series, but a doughnut chart can display multiple data series. Each ring of a doughnut chart represents a data series.

What chart types are available on the Custom Types tab in the Chart Type dialog box?

✔ The Custom Types tab contains custom chart types that are based on standard chart types but include additional formatting. For example, the Columns with Depth custom chart type can be used to create a two-dimensional chart with three-dimensional columns.

How can I quickly change the chart type?

✔ Click a blank area in the chart you want to change. On the Chart toolbar, click ▾ beside the Chart Type button (▾) and then select the chart type you want to use. If the Chart toolbar is not displayed, see page 13 to display the toolbar.

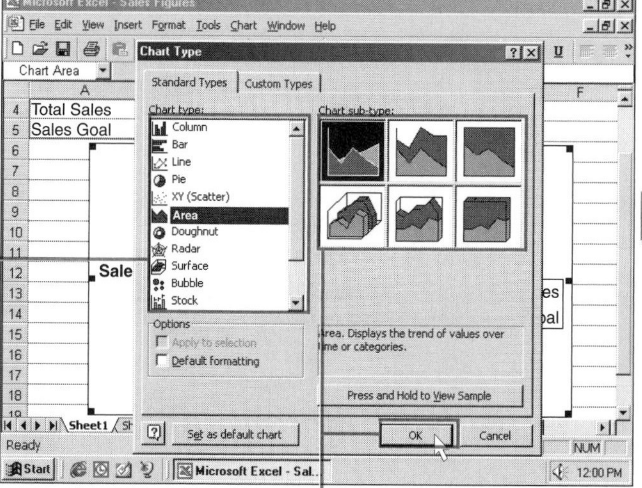

4 Click the chart type you want to use.

5 Click the chart design you want to use.

6 Click OK to confirm your changes.

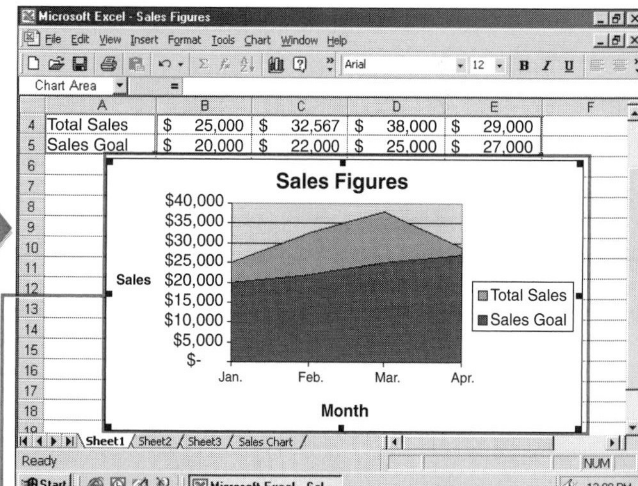

■ The chart displays the new chart type.

MOVE, RESIZE OR DELETE A CHART

After you create a chart, you can move, resize or delete the chart.

You can move a chart to another location in your worksheet. This is useful if the chart covers your data. You can also copy a chart in your worksheet.

You can change the size of a chart. Increasing the size of a chart is useful if the information in the chart is too small to read.

The handles around a chart let you change the size of the chart. The handles at the top and bottom of a chart allow you to change the height of the chart.

The handles at the sides of a chart allow you to change the width of the chart. The handles at the corners of a chart allow you to change the height and width of the chart at the same time.

You can also delete a chart you no longer need from your worksheet.

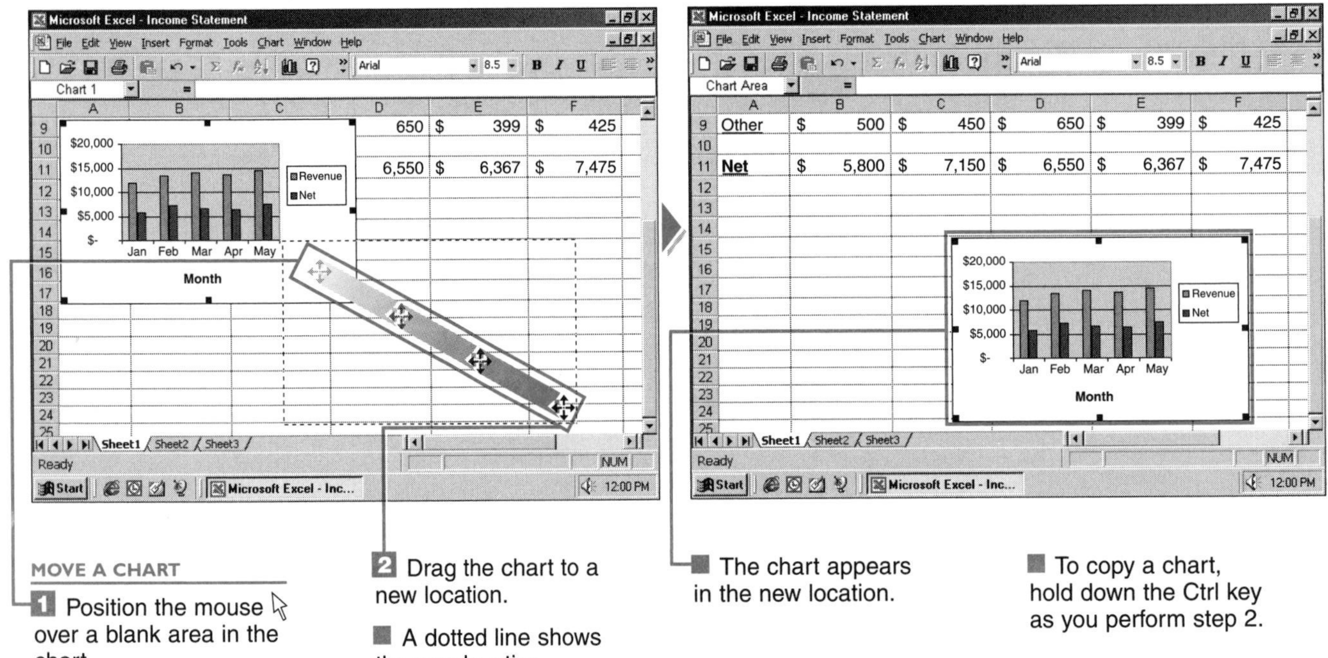

MOVE A CHART

1 Position the mouse over a blank area in the chart.

2 Drag the chart to a new location.

■ A dotted line shows the new location.

■ The chart appears in the new location.

■ To copy a chart, hold down the Ctrl key as you perform step 2.

TIPS

Can I resize a chart without changing the height-to-width ratio?

✔ Yes. Hold down the Shift key as you drag a corner handle of the chart.

Can I move the slices in a pie chart?

✔ You can move, or pull out, the slices in a pie chart. Click the pie chart and then click the slice you want to pull out. Handles (■) appear around the slice. Position the mouse pointer over the slice and then drag the slice away from the chart.

Can I move a chart to its own chart sheet?

✔ Yes. Click a blank area in the chart. Select the Chart menu and then click Location. Click the As new sheet option (○ changes to ⦿). Type a name for the chart sheet and then click OK.

How do I delete a chart that is on a chart sheet?

✔ You must delete the chart sheet. Right-click the tab for the chart sheet you want to delete. Click Delete on the menu that appears. Then click OK in the confirmation dialog box that appears.

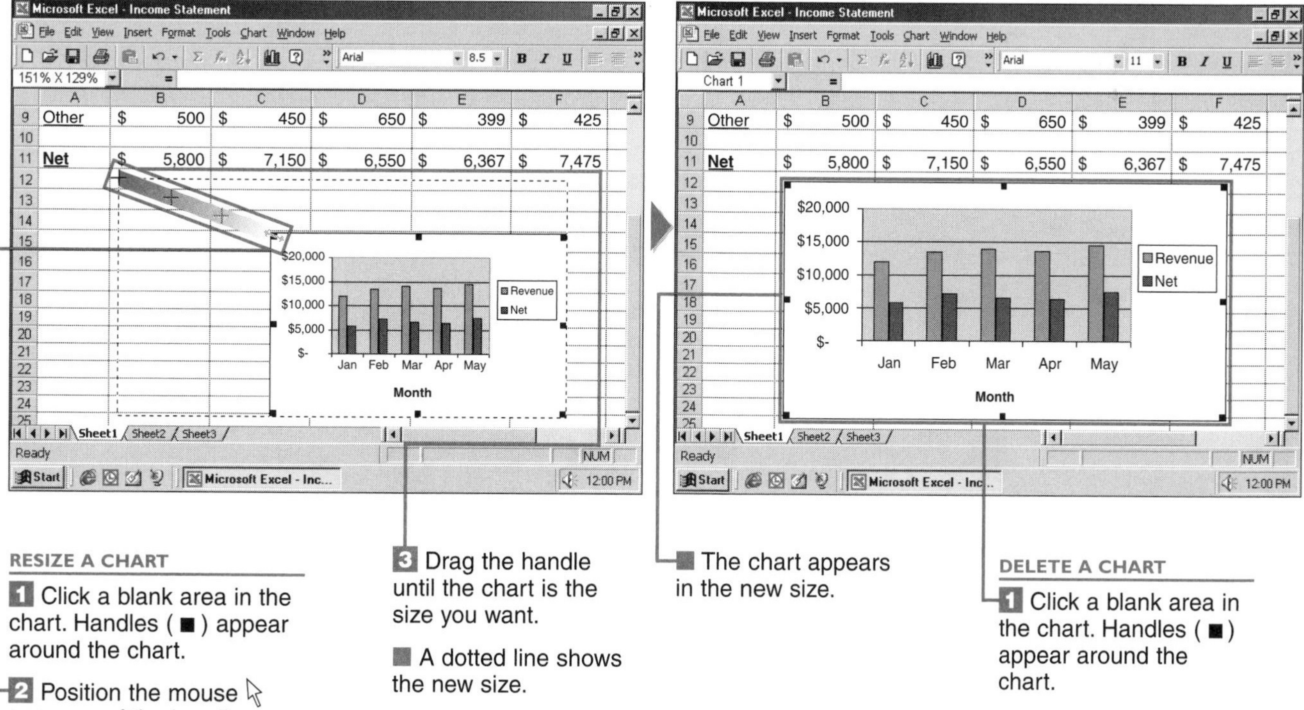

RESIZE A CHART

1 Click a blank area in the chart. Handles (■) appear around the chart.

2 Position the mouse over one of the handles changes to ↖, ↕ or ↔).

3 Drag the handle until the chart is the size you want.

■ A dotted line shows the new size.

■ The chart appears in the new size.

DELETE A CHART

1 Click a blank area in the chart. Handles (■) appear around the chart.

ADD DATA TO A CHART

After you create a chart, you can add a new data series to the chart. You do not need to create a new chart to include a new data series. A data series is a group of related data representing one row or column from your worksheet.

You cannot add another data series to a pie chart. A pie chart can display only one data series.

The ability to add a new data series to a chart is useful when the chart will need to be updated over time. For example, a chart containing monthly sales figures will need to be updated with a new data series each month.

Excel automatically updates the legend when you add a new data series to a chart.

You can delete a data series you no longer need in a chart.

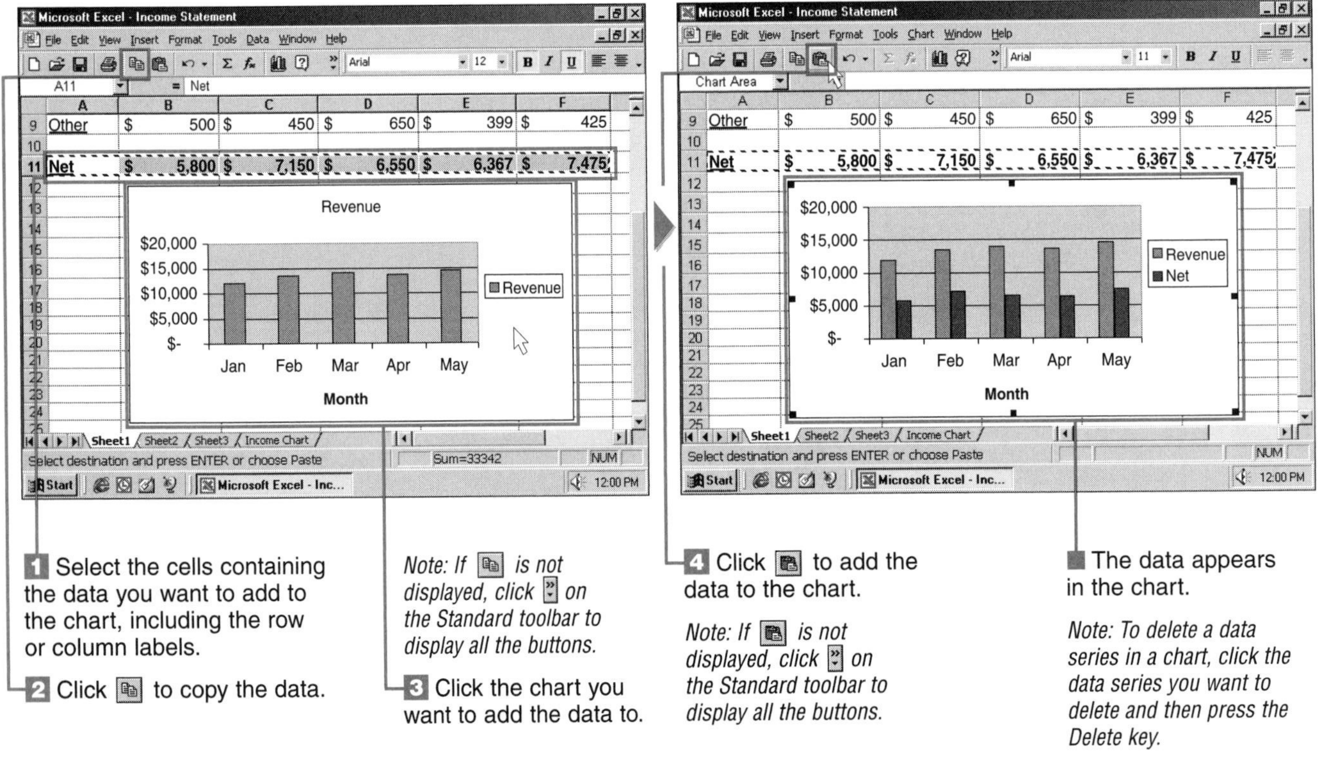

1 Select the cells containing the data you want to add to the chart, including the row or column labels.

2 Click to copy the data.

Note: If is not displayed, click on the Standard toolbar to display all the buttons.

3 Click the chart you want to add the data to.

4 Click to add the data to the chart.

Note: If is not displayed, click on the Standard toolbar to display all the buttons.

■ The data appears in the chart.

Note: To delete a data series in a chart, click the data series you want to delete and then press the Delete key.

PRINT A CHART

You can print a chart with the worksheet data or on its own page.

Printing a chart with the worksheet data is useful if you want the data and the chart to appear on the same page.

When you print a chart on its own page, the chart will expand to fill the page. The printed chart may look different from the chart on your screen. For example, you may find that the chart's legend is smaller.

If you are using a black-and-white printer to print the chart, the colors in the chart will appear as shades of gray.

You can preview a chart as you would preview a worksheet. This allows you to see what the chart will look like when printed. For information on previewing a worksheet, see page 236.

For more information on printing a worksheet, see page 238.

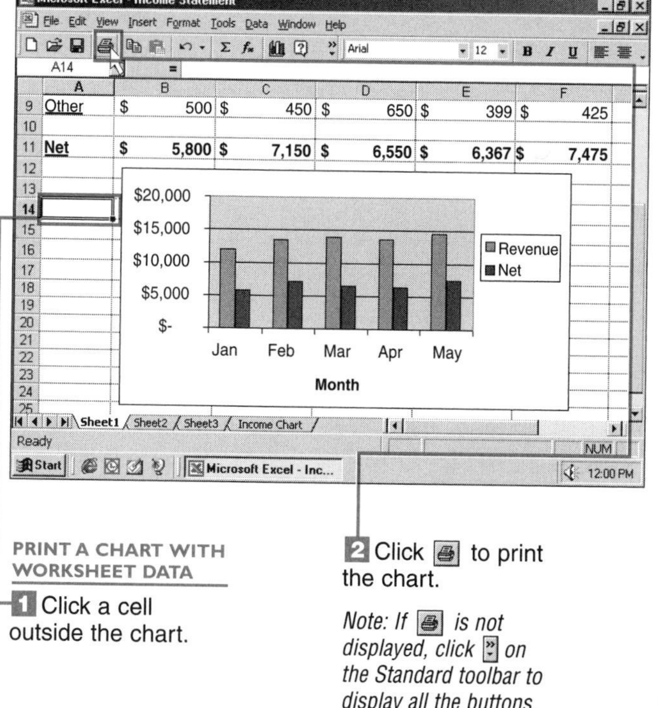

PRINT A CHART WITH WORKSHEET DATA

1 Click a cell outside the chart.

2 Click 🖨 to print the chart.

Note: If 🖨 is not displayed, click » on the Standard toolbar to display all the buttons.

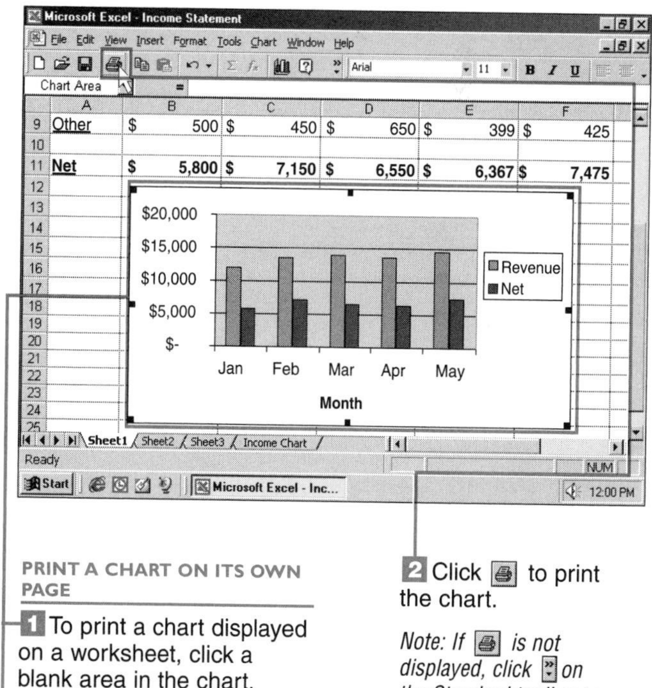

PRINT A CHART ON ITS OWN PAGE

1 To print a chart displayed on a worksheet, click a blank area in the chart.

■ To print a chart displayed on a chart sheet, click the tab for the chart sheet.

2 Click 🖨 to print the chart.

Note: If 🖨 is not displayed, click » on the Standard toolbar to display all the buttons.

ADD AN AUTOSHAPE

Excel provides many ready-made shapes, called AutoShapes, that you can add to your worksheet or chart.

Adding an AutoShape is a fast and easy way to enhance the appearance of your worksheet. You can also add AutoShapes to help illustrate information or draw attention to important data.

Excel offers several categories of AutoShapes for you to choose from. You can select a category to find the AutoShape you want to add. For example, the Lines category contains lines and arrows. The Basic Shapes category contains rectangles, ovals, crosses and hearts. The Stars and Banners category contains ribbons and stars with 8, 16 or 32 points.

When you add an AutoShape to your worksheet, Excel lets you specify the location for the AutoShape and the size you want the AutoShape to display. You can later move and resize the AutoShape to suit your worksheet. You can also delete an AutoShape you no longer need. For information on moving, resizing or deleting a graphic, see page 270.

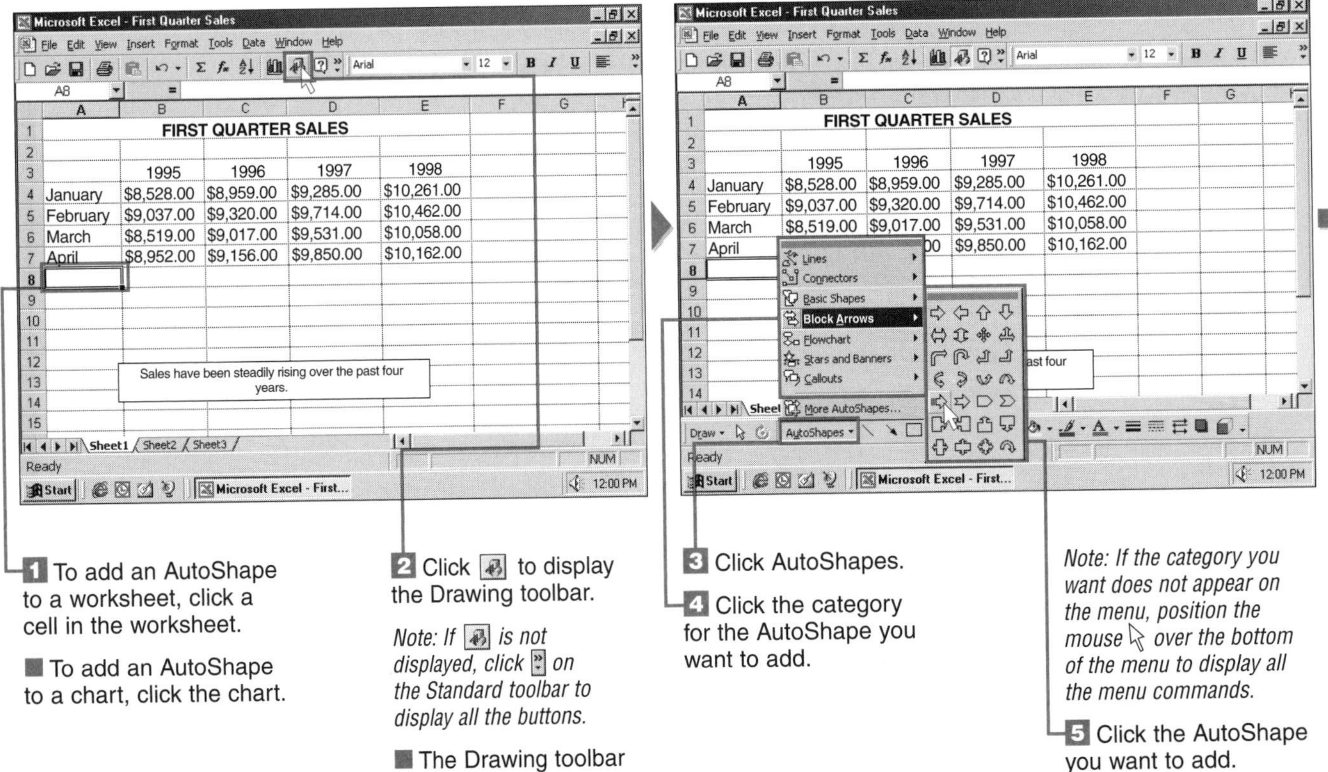

1 To add an AutoShape to a worksheet, click a cell in the worksheet.

■ To add an AutoShape to a chart, click the chart.

2 Click [drawing icon] to display the Drawing toolbar.

Note: If [drawing icon] is not displayed, click [»] on the Standard toolbar to display all the buttons.

■ The Drawing toolbar appears.

3 Click AutoShapes.

4 Click the category for the AutoShape you want to add.

Note: If the category you want does not appear on the menu, position the mouse over the bottom of the menu to display all the menu commands.

5 Click the AutoShape you want to add.

TIPS

Can I control how an AutoShape will appear?

✔ When drawing an AutoShape, you can hold down the Alt key to have an AutoShape fit perfectly within cell borders. You can hold down the Ctrl key to draw an AutoShape from the center outward. You can hold down the Shift key to maintain the height-to-width ratio of an AutoShape.

Can I add text to an AutoShape?

✔ Yes. Click the AutoShape and then type the text you want to add. You cannot add text to some AutoShapes.

How can I change the appearance of an AutoShape?

✔ You can use the buttons on the Drawing toolbar to change the appearance of an AutoShape. Click the AutoShape you want to change. To change the color of an AutoShape, click ▾ beside the Fill Color button (🖌▾) and then select a color. To add a shadow, click the Shadow button (■) and then select a shadow. To add a 3-D effect, click the 3-D button (■) and then select a 3-D effect.

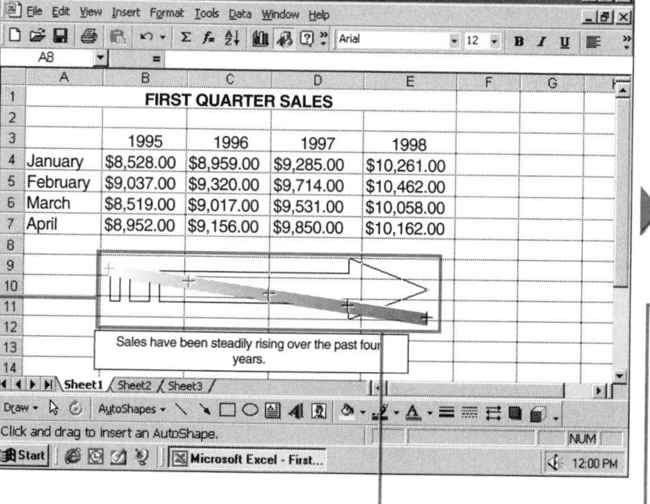

6 Position the mouse + where you want to begin drawing the AutoShape.

7 Drag the mouse + until the AutoShape is the size you want.

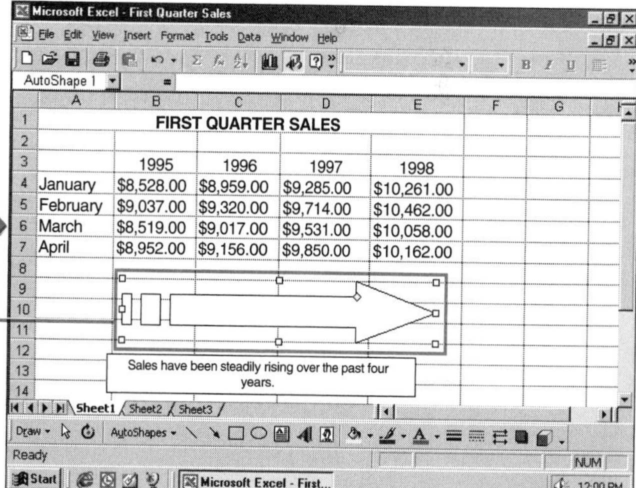

■ The AutoShape appears. The handles (□) around the AutoShape let you change the size of the AutoShape.

8 To hide the handles, click outside the AutoShape.

Note: To hide the Drawing toolbar, repeat step 2.

ADD A TEXT BOX

You can add a text box to your worksheet or chart to display additional information.

Text boxes are useful for displaying your comments. You can also use text boxes to label, identify or describe specific items in your worksheet or chart.

The text you type in a text box wraps to fit the width of the text box.

After you add a text box, you can move and resize the text box to suit your worksheet. You can also delete a text box you no longer need. For information on moving, resizing or deleting a graphic, see page 270.

In addition to text boxes, Excel offers AutoShapes that are specifically designed to display text, such as the AutoShapes in the Stars and Banners or Callout categories. These AutoShapes let you neatly display additional text in your worksheet. For more information on AutoShapes, see page 264.

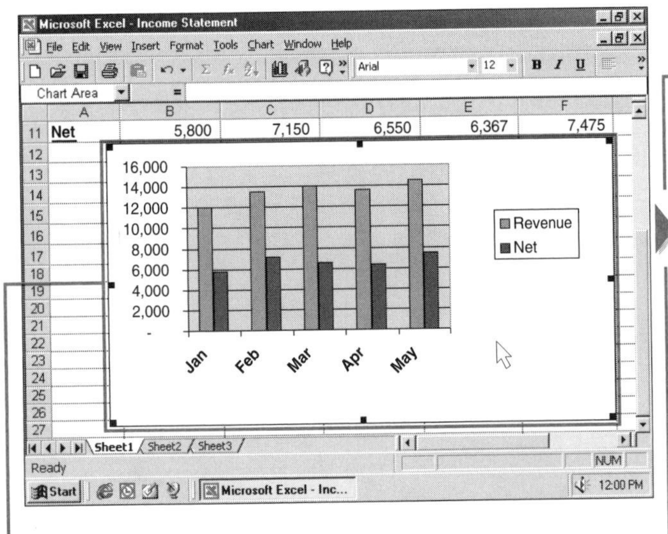

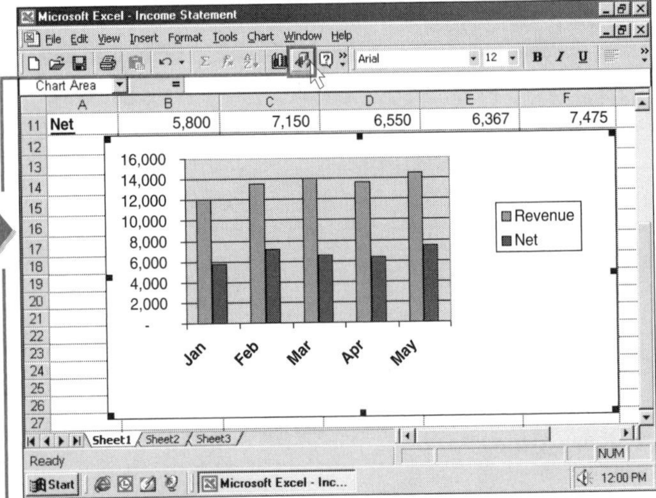

1 To add a text box to a chart, click the chart.

■ To add a text box to a worksheet, click a cell in the worksheet.

2 Click to display the Drawing toolbar.

Note: If is not displayed, click on the Standard toolbar to display all the buttons.

■ The Drawing toolbar appears.

TIPS

How do I format the text in a text box?

✔ Select all the text you want to format in the text box. You can then use the buttons on the Formatting toolbar, such as Bold (B), Italic (I) or Center (≡), to format the text.

How can I change the border of a text box?

✔ Select the text box and then use the buttons on the Drawing toolbar to change the border. To change the color of the border, click ▾ beside the Line Color button (✎▾) and then select the color you want to use. To give the text box a dashed border, click the Dash Style button (┅) and then select the dash style you want to use.

Can I prevent a text box from printing?

✔ Yes. This is useful if a text box contains a note you wrote to yourself. Right-click the border of the text box and then select Format Text Box. Select the Properties tab, click the Print object option (✔ changes to ☐) and then click OK.

3 Click ▤ to add a text box.

4 Position the mouse ↓ where you want to begin drawing the text box.

5 Drag the mouse + until the text box is the size you want.

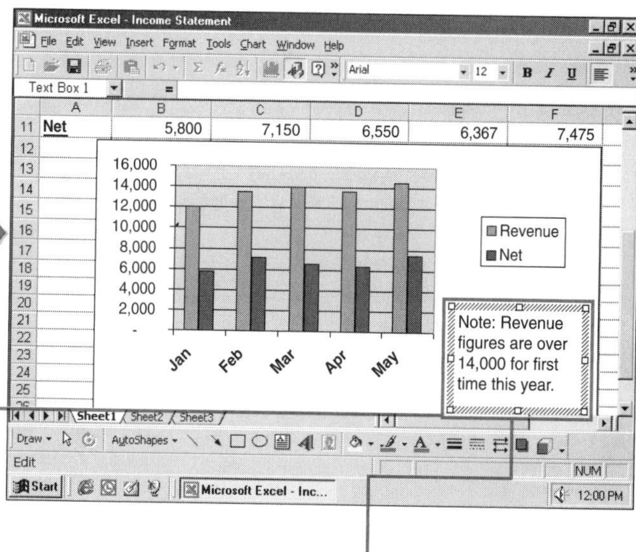

■ The text box appears.

6 Type the text you want to appear in the text box.

■ The handles (□) around the text box let you change the size of the text box.

7 To hide the handles, click outside the text box.

Note: To hide the Drawing toolbar, repeat step 2.

ADD A TEXT EFFECT

You can use the WordArt feature to add special text effects to your worksheet or chart. Adding a text effect is an easy way to create eye-catching titles, headings or notes.

The WordArt feature offers several text effects you can choose from. For example, you can add text effects that skew, shadow, stretch or rotate text. You can also make text appear three-dimensional.

When typing the text for a text effect, you should be careful not to make any spelling errors. Excel's spell check feature does not check the spelling of text effects.

After you add a text effect, you can work with the text effect as you would work with any other graphic. You can move and resize the text effect to suit your worksheet. You can also delete a text effect you no longer need. For information on moving, resizing or deleting a graphic, see page 270.

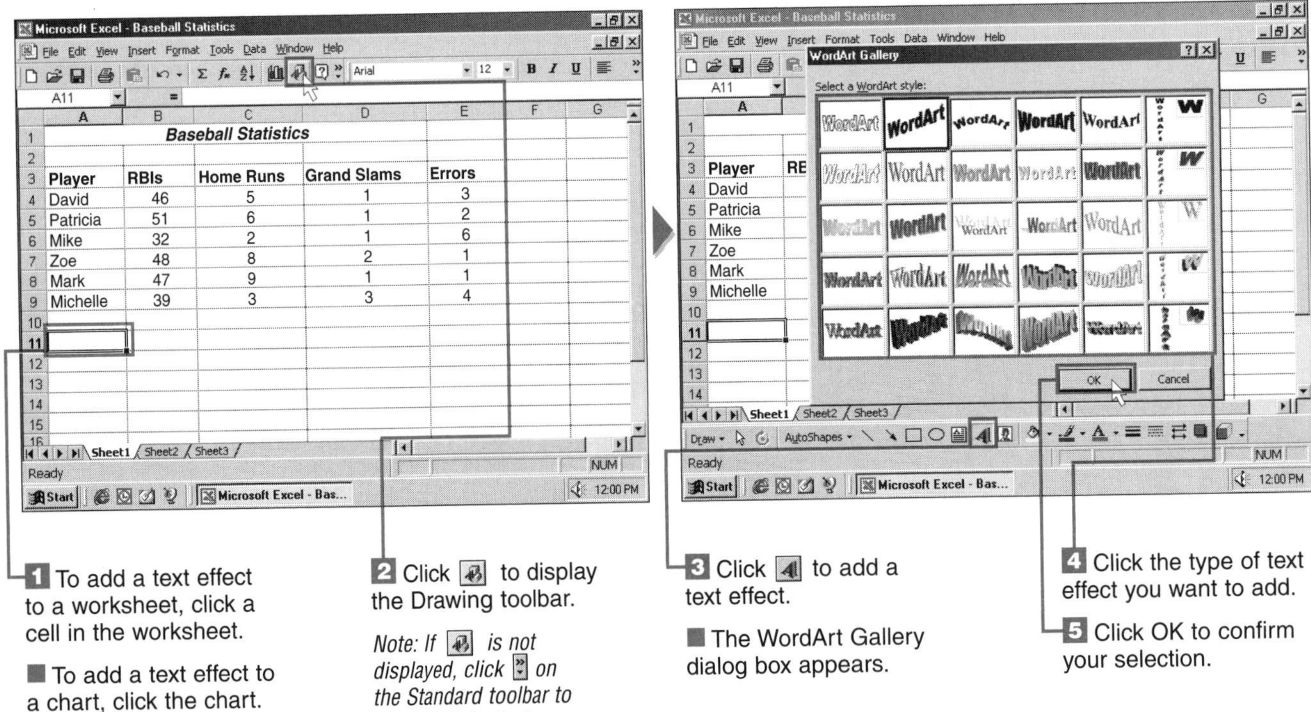

1 To add a text effect to a worksheet, click a cell in the worksheet.

■ To add a text effect to a chart, click the chart.

2 Click [icon] to display the Drawing toolbar.

Note: If [icon] is not displayed, click [icon] on the Standard toolbar to display all the buttons.

■ The Drawing toolbar appears.

3 Click [icon] to add a text effect.

■ The WordArt Gallery dialog box appears.

4 Click the type of text effect you want to add.

5 Click OK to confirm your selection.

TIPS

Why does a toolbar appear on my screen when I add a text effect?

✔ When you add a text effect, Excel automatically displays the WordArt toolbar. You can use the buttons on the toolbar to perform tasks such as changing the color of a text effect ( ) or rotating a text effect ( ).

The WordArt toolbar is not displayed on my screen. How do I display the toolbar?

✔ From the View menu, select Toolbars and then click WordArt.

How do I edit a text effect?

✔ Double-click the text effect you want to edit. The Edit WordArt Text dialog box appears. You can use this dialog box to edit the text effect or change the font and size of the text effect.

How can I change the appearance of a text effect?

✔ Click the text effect you want to change. On the WordArt toolbar, click the WordArt Gallery button ( ) and then select a different text effect.

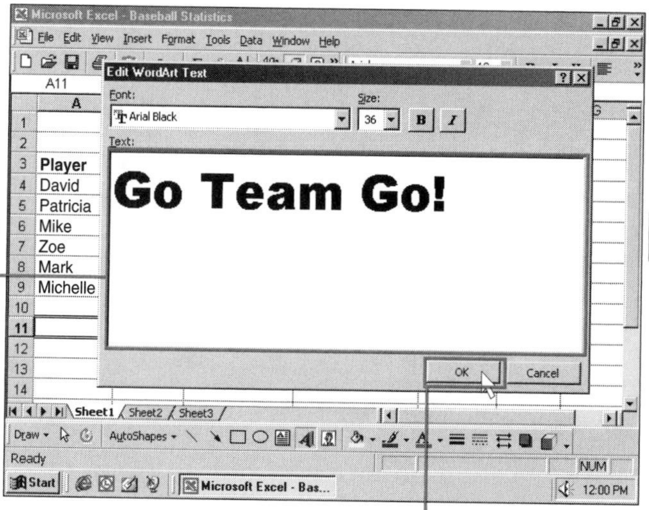

■ The Edit WordArt Text dialog box appears.

6 Type the text you want the text effect to display.

7 Click OK to add the text effect to the worksheet or chart.

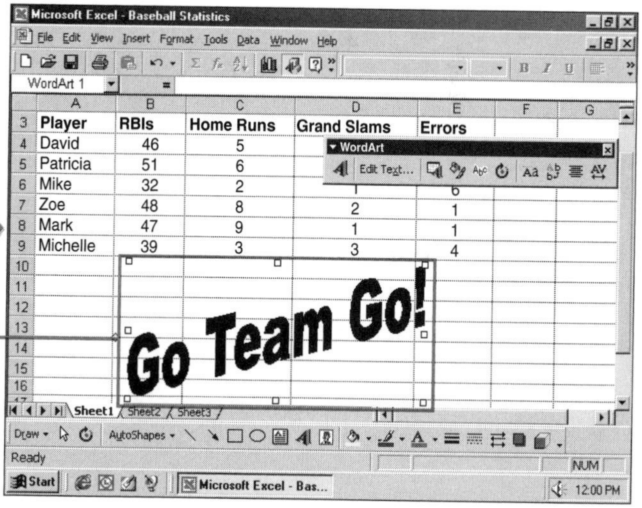

■ The text effect appears in the worksheet or chart. The handles (□) around the text effect let you change the size of the text effect.

■ To hide the handles, click outside the text effect.

Note: To hide the Drawing toolbar, repeat step 2.

MOVE, RESIZE OR DELETE A GRAPHIC

You can move, resize or delete a graphic you added to your worksheet or chart to suit your needs.

You can move a graphic to another location in your worksheet. If you added a graphic to a chart, you cannot move the graphic outside the chart area.

When you select a graphic, handles (□) appear around the graphic. The handles allow you to change the size of the graphic. The handles at the top and bottom of a graphic allow you to change the height of the graphic. The handles at the sides of a graphic allow you to change the width of the graphic. The handles at the corners of a graphic allow you to change the height and width of the graphic at the same time.

You can also delete a graphic you no longer need from your worksheet.

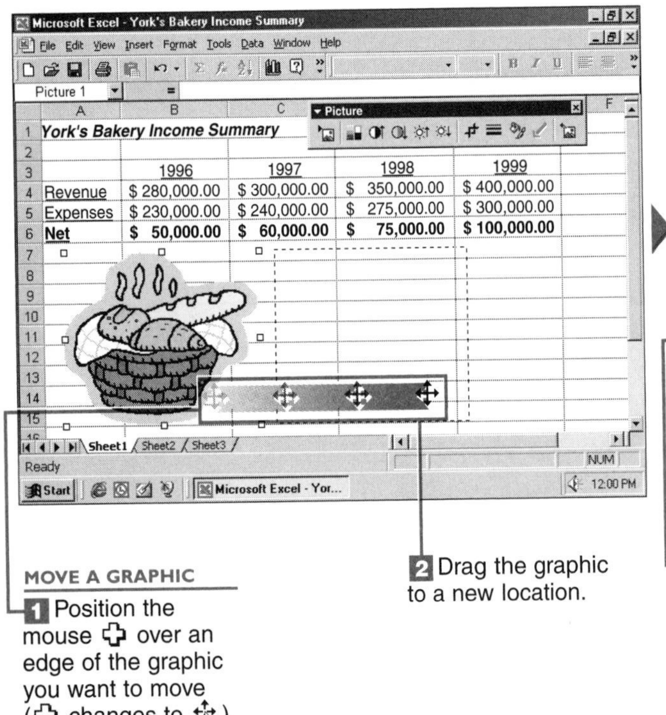

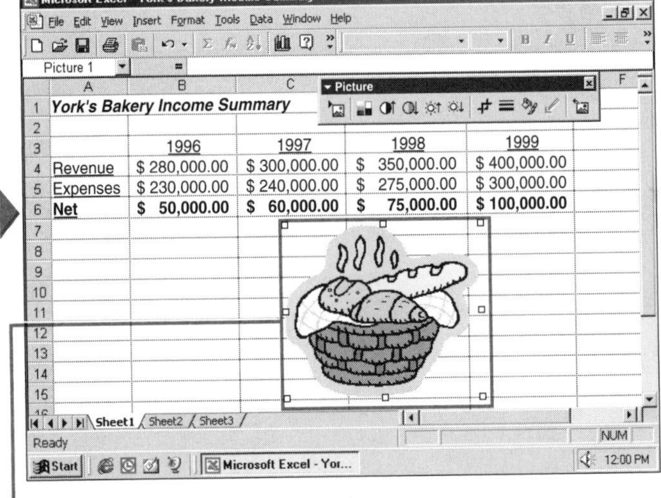

MOVE A GRAPHIC

1 Position the mouse ✛ over an edge of the graphic you want to move (✛ changes to ✥).

2 Drag the graphic to a new location.

■ The graphic appears in the new location.

Note: You cannot move a graphic you added to a chart outside the chart area.

■ To copy a graphic, hold down the Ctrl key as you perform step 2.

TIPS

How can I maintain the height-to-width ratio of a graphic I am resizing?

✔ To maintain the height-to-width ratio, hold down the Shift key as you drag one of the corner handles.

How do I rotate a graphic?

✔ Click the graphic you want to rotate. If the Drawing toolbar is not displayed, click (Drawing button) on the Standard toolbar. Then click the Free Rotate button (Free Rotate button) on the Drawing toolbar. Green dots appear around the graphic. Drag one of the green dots to rotate the graphic. You cannot rotate some graphics.

Can I change several graphics at the same time?

✔ Yes. Click the first graphic you want to change. Hold down the Shift key as you click the other graphics. You can now move, resize or delete all the graphics at the same time.

Can I cancel a change I made to a graphic?

✔ Excel remembers the last changes you made. Click the Undo button (Undo button) on the Standard toolbar to immediately cancel a change you made to a graphic.

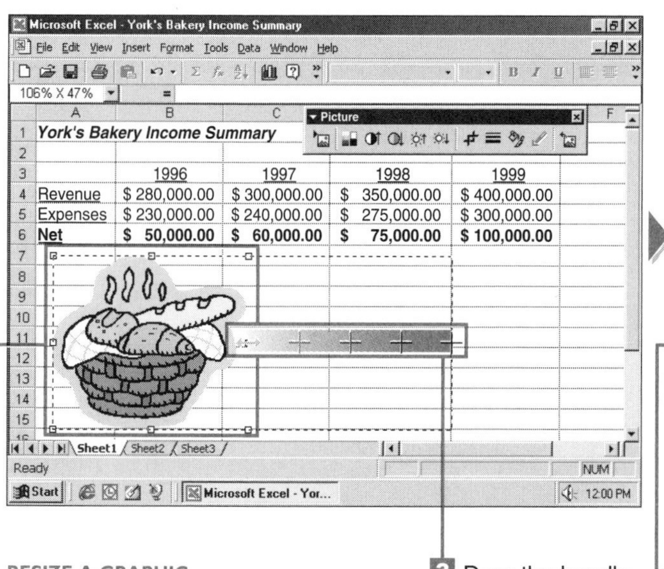

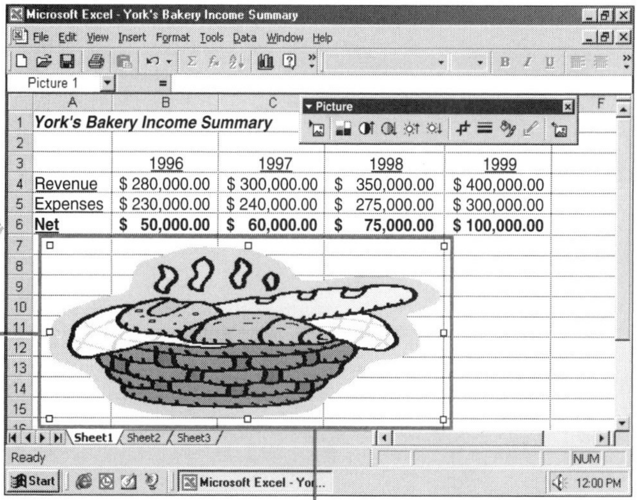

RESIZE A GRAPHIC

1. Click the graphic you want to resize. Handles (□) appear around the graphic.
2. Position the mouse (mouse pointer) over one of the handles (mouse pointer changes to ↔, ↕ or ↘).
3. Drag the handle until the graphic is the size you want.

■ The graphic appears in the new size.

DELETE A GRAPHIC

1. Position the mouse (mouse pointer) over an edge of the graphic you want to delete (mouse pointer changes to move pointer). Then click the graphic. Handles (□) appear around the graphic.
2. Press the Delete key.

CREATE A LIST

Excel provides powerful tools for organizing and analyzing a large collection of data in a list.

Common lists include mailing lists, phone directories, product lists, library book catalogs, music collections and wine lists.

The first row in a list contains column labels. Column labels describe the data in each column.

Each row in a list contains one record. A record is a group of related data, such as the name and address of one person on a mailing list.

You can create and store a list of data in a worksheet. You can enter data in a list by typing the data directly in the worksheet. You can also use a data form to enter data in a list. A data form allows you to focus on one record at a time.

You should create only one list in a worksheet. If you use the worksheet for other data or calculations, you should leave at least one blank column and row between the list and the other data to prevent unwanted data from appearing in the data form.

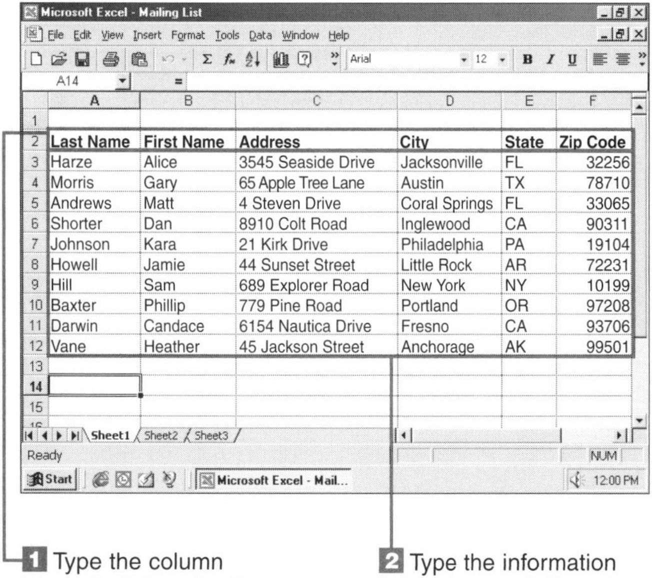

1 Type the column labels that describe the data you will enter into each column. You should format the column labels to ensure that Excel will recognize the text as column labels.

2 Type the information for each record. Do not leave any blank rows in the list.

3 Save the workbook. For information on saving, see page 174.

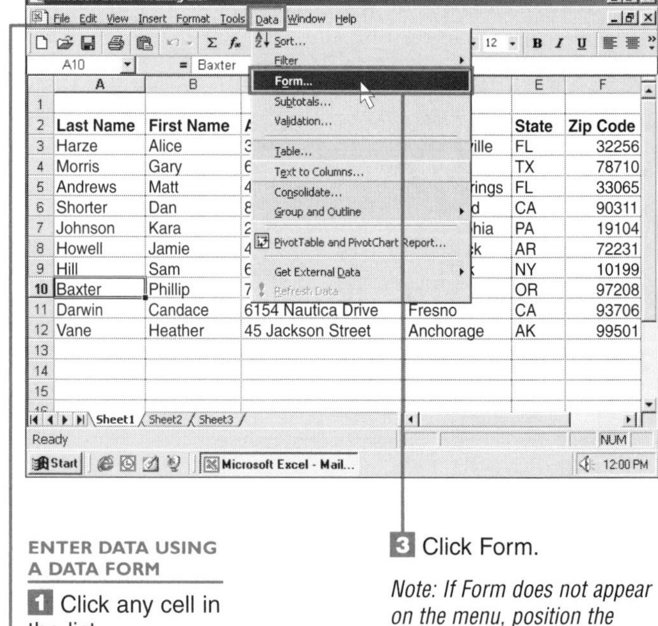

ENTER DATA USING A DATA FORM

1 Click any cell in the list.

2 Click Data.

3 Click Form.

Note: If Form does not appear on the menu, position the mouse over the bottom of the menu to display all the menu commands.

TIPS

Can I edit a record in a data form?

✔ Yes. Display the record you want to edit. Click the area containing the data you want to change and then edit the data as you would edit any data. If you regret changes you make to a record, you can click the Restore button to undo the changes. You must use the Restore button before you move to another record.

How do I delete a record using a data form?

✔ You can click the Delete button to delete the currently displayed record. The record is permanently deleted and cannot be restored.

How do I search for a specific record using a data form?

✔ Click the Criteria button. Click the area beside the label of the column you want to use to find the record. Then type the data you want to find. Click the Find Prev or Find Next button to display the previous or next matching record.

■ A data form dialog box appears.

4 Click New to add a new record.

5 Type the data that corresponds to the first column label and then press the Tab key. Repeat this step until you have entered all the information for the record.

6 Repeat steps 4 and 5 for each record you want to add.

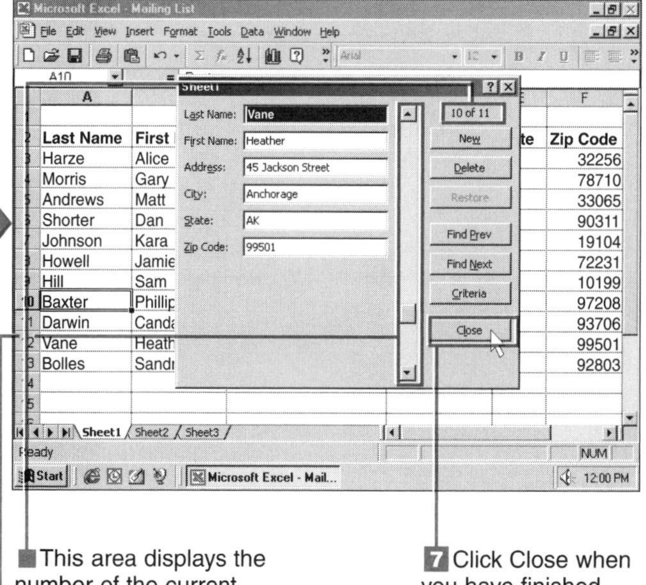

■ This area displays the number of the current record and the total number of records.

■ You can drag the scroll box (□) along the scroll bar to browse through the records.

7 Click Close when you have finished entering records.

SORT DATA IN A LIST

You can organize a list by changing the order of the records.

You can select the column you want to use to sort the data in a list. For example, you can sort a mailing list by the name, company name, state or zip code column. You can also sort data by more than one column. For example, if you are sorting by the last name column and a last name appears more than once, you can sort by a second column, such as the first name column. You can sort the data in a list by up to three columns.

You can sort the data in a list by letter, number or date. An ascending sort arranges data from lowest to highest. For example, 0 to 9, A to Z or Jan-99 to Dec-99. A descending sort arranges data from highest to lowest. For example, 9 to 0, Z to A or Dec-99 to Jan-99.

You should save your workbook before sorting data in case you do not like the results of the sort. To save a workbook, see page 174.

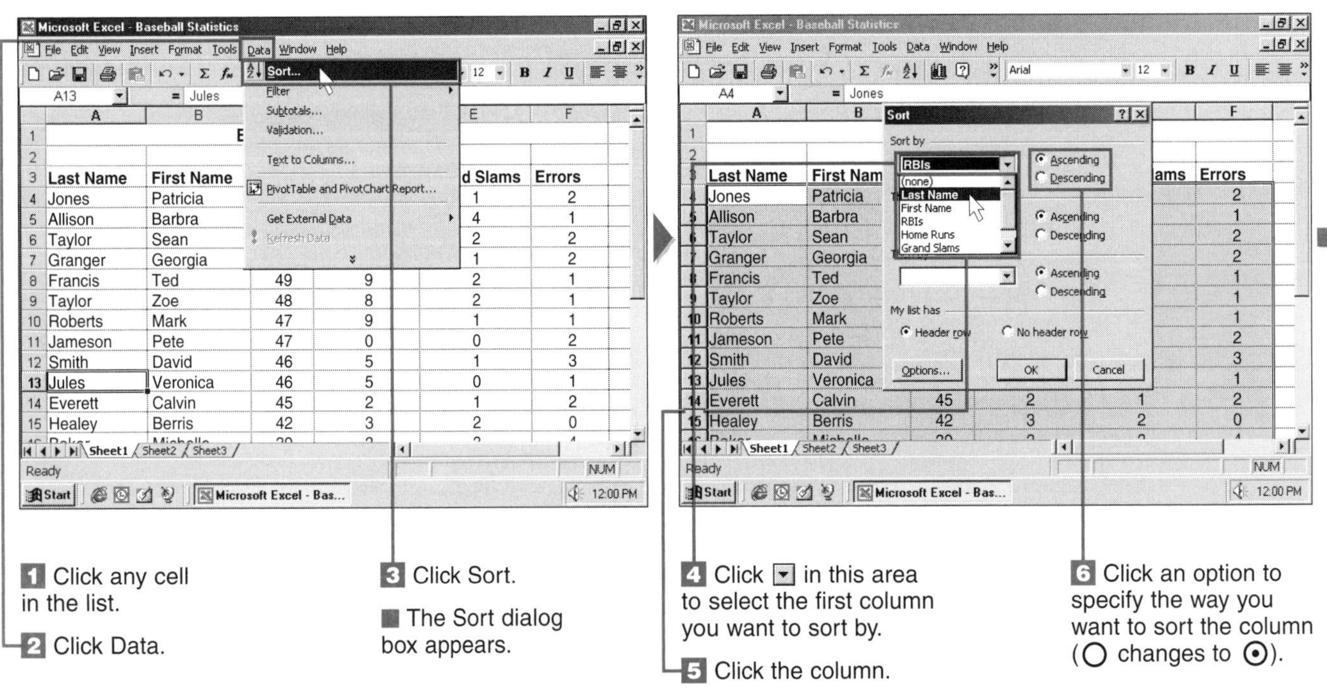

1 Click any cell in the list.

2 Click Data.

3 Click Sort.

■ The Sort dialog box appears.

4 Click ▼ in this area to select the first column you want to sort by.

5 Click the column.

6 Click an option to specify the way you want to sort the column (○ changes to ⊙).

TIPS

How can I quickly sort a list?

✔ Click any cell in the column you want to sort by. To sort from 0 to 9 or A to Z, click the Sort Ascending button (A↓Z) on the Standard toolbar. To sort from 9 to 0 or Z to A, click the Sort Descending button (Z↓A) on the Standard toolbar.

How do I sort a column of weekdays or months according to their calendar order?

✔ By default, Excel sorts weekdays and months alphabetically. To sort weekdays or months according to their calendar order, select the Options button in the Sort dialog box. Click the First key sort order area and then select the sort order you want to use.

Can I perform a case sensitive sort?

✔ Yes. A case sensitive sort sorts data by capitalization. For example, a case sensitive ascending sort would place "ann" before "Ann". Click the Options button in the Sort dialog box and then select the Case sensitive option (☐ changes to ☑).

How do I undo a sort?

✔ To immediately reverse the results of a sort, click the Undo button (↶) on the Standard toolbar.

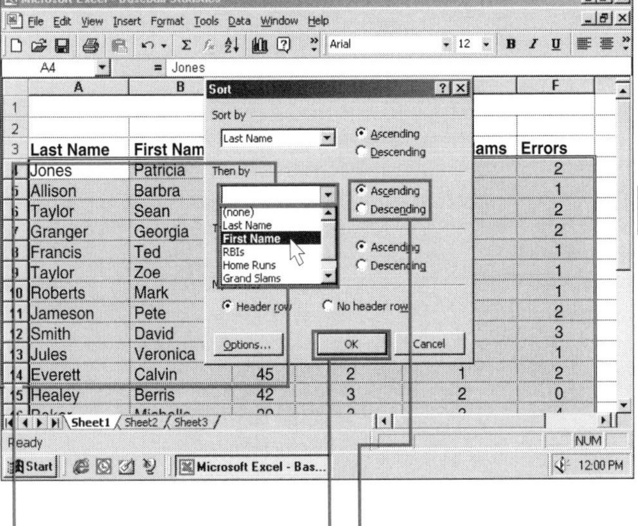

7 To select a second column you want to sort by, click ▼ in this area.

8 Click the column.

9 Click an option to specify the way you want to sort the column (○ changes to ◉).

10 Click OK to sort the list.

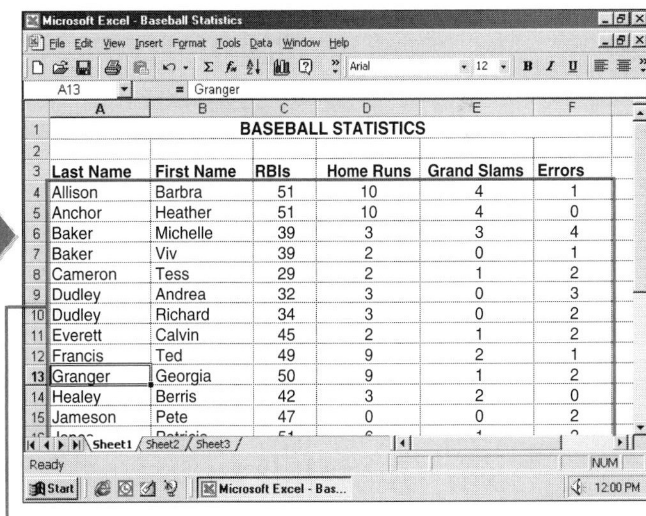

■ The list appears in the new order.

FILTER DATA IN A LIST

You can filter a list to display only the records containing the data you want to review.

The AutoFilter feature allows you to analyze data by placing related records together and hiding the records you do not want to review.

You can select the column containing the data you want to use to filter the list. You can also specify the data you want Excel to compare to each record in the list and how Excel should compare the data to each record. Telling Excel how to compare the data allows you to display records containing data within a specific range. For example, in a list containing customer names and purchase amounts, you can display only customers whose purchases were greater than $1,000.00.

After you filter a list, the row numbers of the records that match the condition you specified are displayed in a different color.

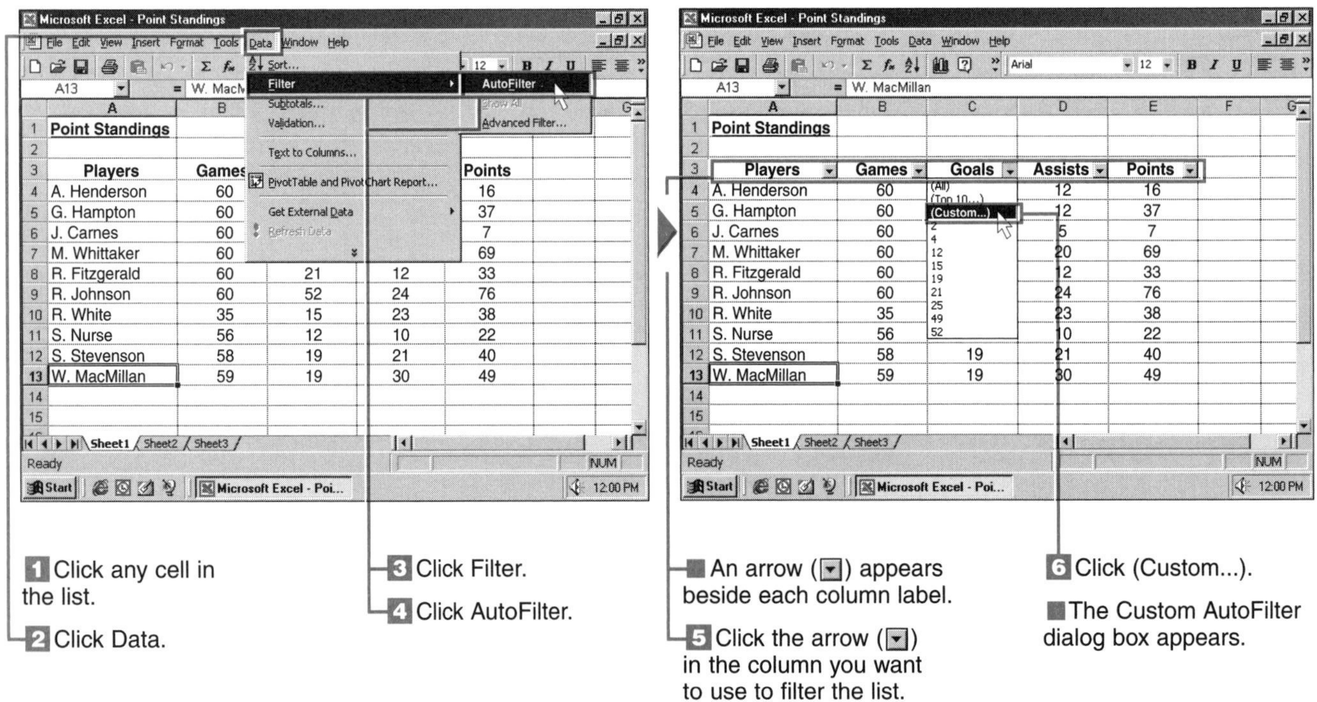

1 Click any cell in the list.

2 Click Data.

3 Click Filter.

4 Click AutoFilter.

■ An arrow (▼) appears beside each column label.

5 Click the arrow (▼) in the column you want to use to filter the list.

6 Click (Custom...).

■ The Custom AutoFilter dialog box appears.

TIPS

How can I quickly filter data in a list?

✔ Click the arrow (▾) in the column you want to use to filter the list and then select the data you want to use to filter the list. The list displays only the records containing the data you selected.

How do I display the top 10 records in a list?

✔ Click the arrow (▾) in the column you want to use to filter the list and then select (Top 10...). In the Top 10 AutoFilter dialog box, click the Items area. To display the top 10 records, select Items. To display the top 10% of the records, select Percent.

Can I use two conditions to filter data?

✔ Yes. Perform steps 1 to 9 below to specify the first condition. In the areas below the first condition, repeat steps 7 to 9 to specify the second condition. If you want both conditions to be met, click the And option (○ changes to ⦿). If you want either condition to be met, click the Or option (○ changes to ⦿).

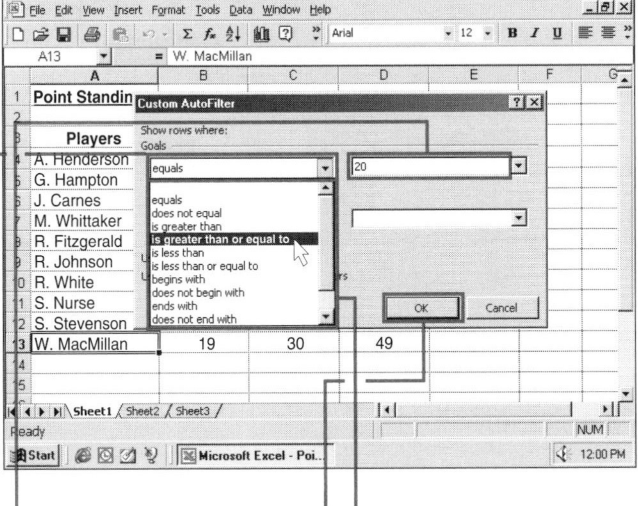

7 Type the data you want Excel to compare to each record in the list.

8 To select how you want Excel to compare the data, click this area.

9 Click the way you want Excel to compare the data.

10 Click OK.

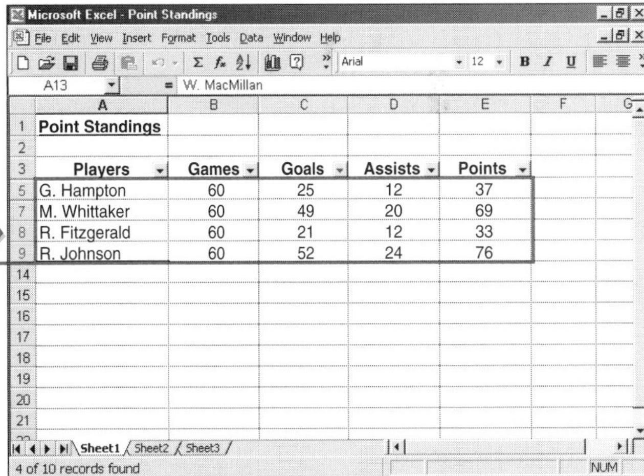

■ The list displays only the records matching the data you specified. The other records are temporarily hidden.

■ To turn off the AutoFilter feature and redisplay the entire list, perform steps 2 to 4.

ADD SUBTOTALS TO A LIST

You can quickly summarize data by adding subtotals to a list.

You can use subtotals to help you analyze the data in a list and quickly create summary reports for the data. For example, in a list containing employee names and sales figures, you can use subtotals to find the total sales made by each employee and the grand total of all the sales.

Before you add subtotals to a list, you should sort the column you want to use to group the records.

You can use the Subtotals feature to perform several types of calculations, such as calculating the sum of values, counting the number of values, calculating the average value or finding the maximum or minimum value.

After adding subtotals to a list, you can display just the grand total, the subtotals and the grand total or all the data. By default, Excel displays subtotals below each group of data in a column.

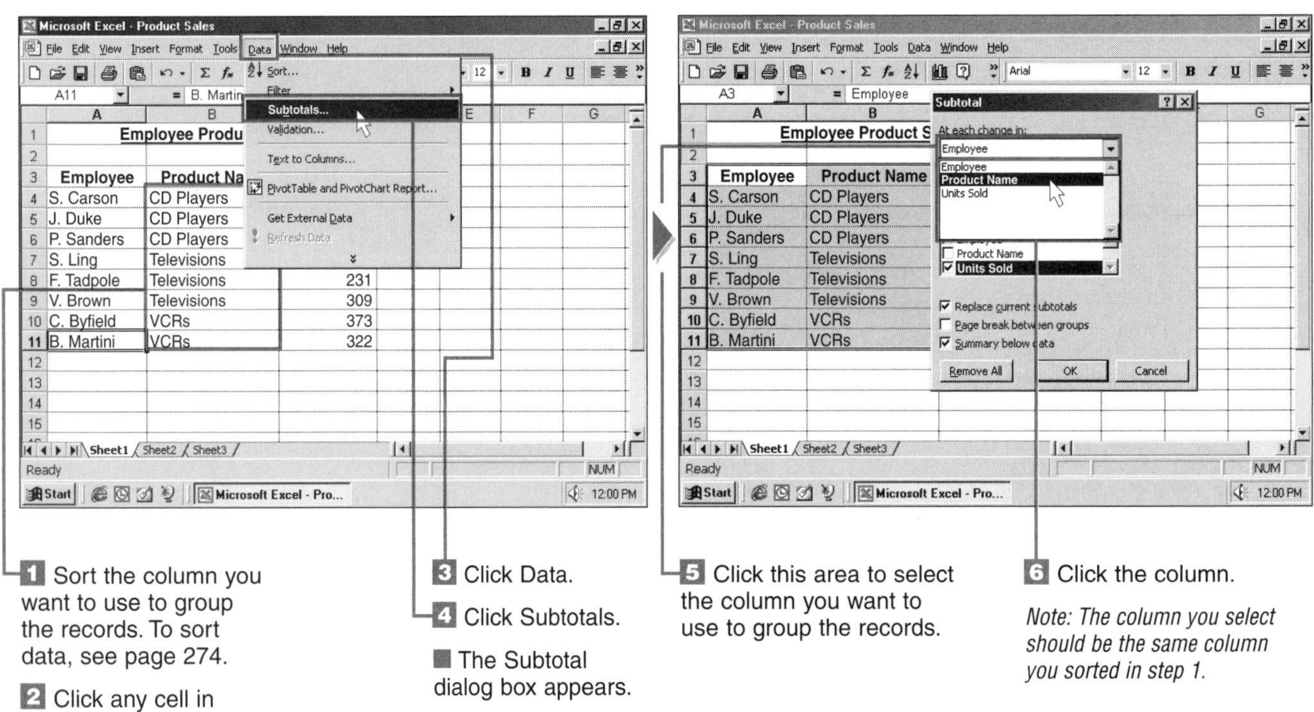

1 Sort the column you want to use to group the records. To sort data, see page 274.

2 Click any cell in the list.

3 Click Data.

4 Click Subtotals.

■ The Subtotal dialog box appears.

5 Click this area to select the column you want to use to group the records.

6 Click the column.

Note: The column you select should be the same column you sorted in step 1.

TIPS

Can I create a chart based on the subtotals in my list?

✔ Yes. Click 2 to display only the subtotals and grand total. Select the cells containing the subtotals and row labels you want to display in the chart. Then perform steps 2 to 14 starting on page 254 to create a chart. If you later hide or display data in the list, Excel will automatically hide or display the data in the chart.

How do I display subtotals above each group of data in a column?

✔ Perform steps 2 to 4 below and then select the Summary below data option (☑ changes to ☐).

Can I hide the data used in a subtotal?

✔ Yes. Minus signs (⊟) appear to the left of your subtotaled list. Click a minus sign (⊟) to hide the data used in a subtotal (⊟ changes to ⊞). Click the plus sign (⊞) to redisplay the data (⊞ changes to ⊟).

How do I remove subtotals from my list?

✔ Perform steps 2 to 4 below and then click the Remove All button.

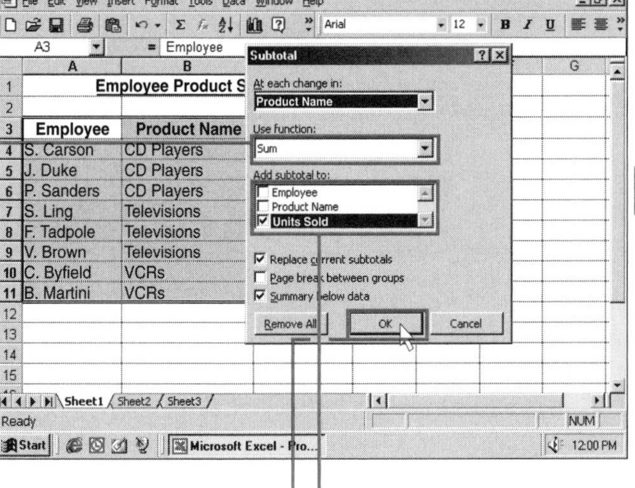

■ This area displays the calculation Excel will perform. You can click this area to select a different calculation.

■ This area displays a check mark (✔) beside each column Excel will subtotal. You can click the box beside a column to add (☑) or remove (☐) a check mark.

7 Click OK to add the subtotals to the list.

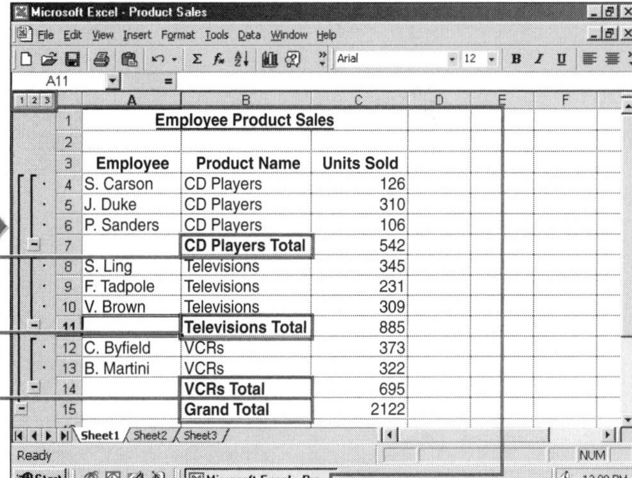

■ The list displays the subtotals and a grand total.

■ You can click one of these options to hide or display data.

1 Display only grand total

2 Display only subtotals and grand total

3 Display all data

RECORD A MACRO

A macro saves you time by combining a series of commands into a single command. For example, you can create a macro to enter column labels and apply formatting to the labels.

You can create a name and description for a macro. You can also assign a keyboard shortcut that you can use to run the macro. You can use Ctrl+any letter.

You can choose where you want to store a macro. If you store the macro in the current workbook, you will only be able to use the macro when this workbook is open. If you want to use the macro with all your workbooks, you can store the macro in the Personal Macro Workbook. You can also have Excel create a new workbook to store the macro, but you will only be able to use the macro when the new workbook is open.

By default, a macro will run in the cells where you recorded the macro. If you want the macro to be able to run in any cell in a worksheet, you can click ▣ on the Stop Recording toolbar before performing the actions you want the macro to include.

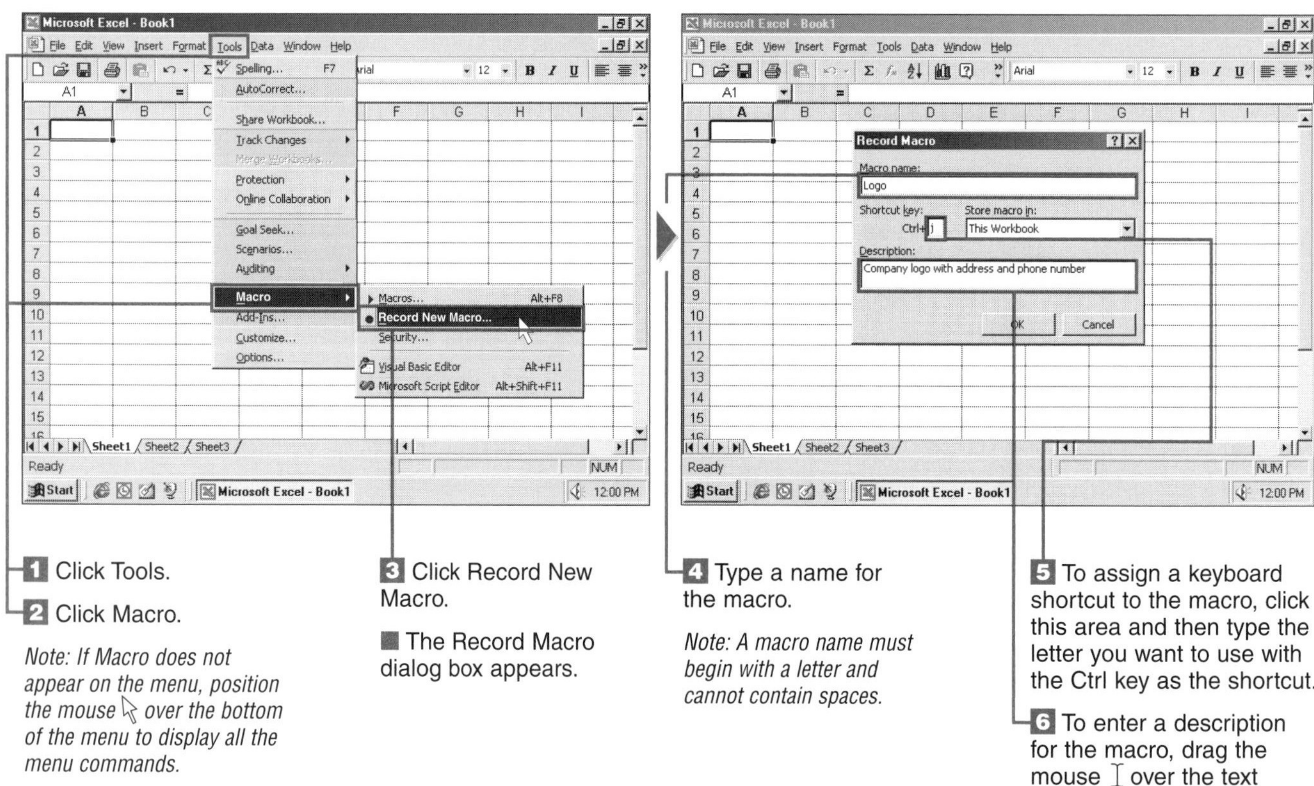

1 Click Tools.

2 Click Macro.

Note: If Macro does not appear on the menu, position the mouse over the bottom of the menu to display all the menu commands.

3 Click Record New Macro.

■ The Record Macro dialog box appears.

4 Type a name for the macro.

Note: A macro name must begin with a letter and cannot contain spaces.

5 To assign a keyboard shortcut to the macro, click this area and then type the letter you want to use with the Ctrl key as the shortcut.

6 To enter a description for the macro, drag the mouse over the text in this area and then type a description.

TIPS

What happens if I make a mistake while recording?

✔ Macros play back very quickly, so most mistakes you make will not be noticeable. For example, if you correct typing mistakes or open the wrong dialog box and then click Cancel while the macro is recording, these mistakes will not affect the way the macro runs. If the finished macro has a noticeable error, you must record a new macro.

What happens if I choose a keyboard shortcut that is already assigned to a command in Excel?

✔ While the workbook that stores the macro is open, the macro keyboard shortcut will override the Excel keyboard shortcut. Using the keyboard shortcut will run the macro.

How do I change the keyboard shortcut for a macro?

✔ Open the workbook where you stored the macro. Click the Tools menu, select Macro and then choose Macros. In the dialog box that appears, select the name of the macro you want to change and then click the Options button. Type a new keyboard shortcut and then click OK.

7 Click this area to specify the location where you want Excel to store the macro.

8 Click the location where you want to store the macro.

9 Click OK to continue.

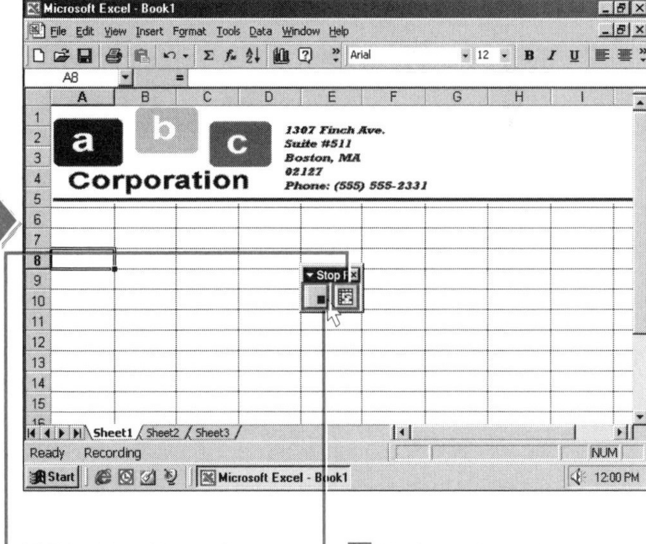

■ The Stop Recording toolbar appears.

10 If you want to be able to run the macro in any cell in a worksheet, click ▦.

11 Perform the actions you want the macro to include.

12 Click ■ when you have completed all the actions you want the macro to include.

RUN A MACRO

When you run a macro, Excel automatically performs the series of actions you recorded.

You can run a macro by viewing the names of all the available macros and choosing the macro you want to run. You can also run a macro using the keyboard shortcut you assigned to the macro.

Before running a macro, you should save changes to your workbook. After the macro runs, you will not be able to use the Undo feature to reverse the results of the macro or any changes you made before running the macro.

If you want the macro to affect specific cells in the worksheet, you can select the cells you want to change before you run the macro.

If you realize you selected the wrong macro or that you no longer need to use the macro, you can stop the macro by pressing the Esc key before the macro completes the actions you recorded.

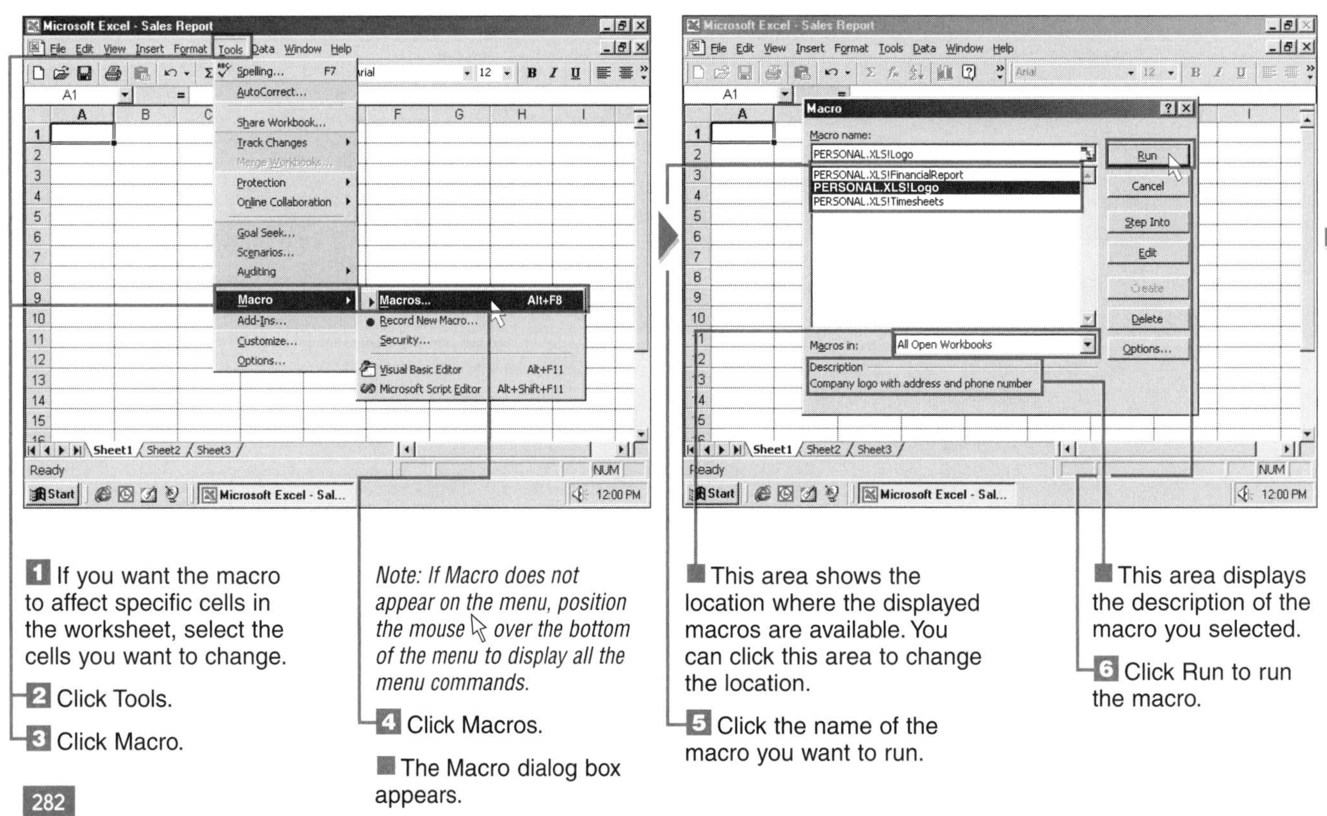

1 If you want the macro to affect specific cells in the worksheet, select the cells you want to change.

2 Click Tools.

3 Click Macro.

Note: If Macro does not appear on the menu, position the mouse over the bottom of the menu to display all the menu commands.

4 Click Macros.

■ The Macro dialog box appears.

■ This area shows the location where the displayed macros are available. You can click this area to change the location.

5 Click the name of the macro you want to run.

■ This area displays the description of the macro you selected.

6 Click Run to run the macro.

TIPS

Why does a warning dialog box appear when I open a workbook containing a macro?

✔ Macros can contain viruses, which can perform unwanted tasks on your computer. If the workbook is from a trusted source, click Enable Macros. If the workbook is not from a trusted source and you want to open the workbook without the macros, click Disable Macros.

How can I remove a macro I no longer need?

✔ Click the Tools menu, select Macro and then click Macros. Select the macro you want to delete and then click the Delete button. You cannot use this method to remove a macro you stored in the Personal Macro Workbook.

Can I use a toolbar button to run a macro?

✔ Yes. To add a button for the macro to a toolbar, perform steps 1 to 9 on page 632, except select Macros in step 5 and Custom Button in step 6. Click the button you added to the toolbar and then double-click the macro you want to assign to the button. You can now click the button at any time to run the macro.

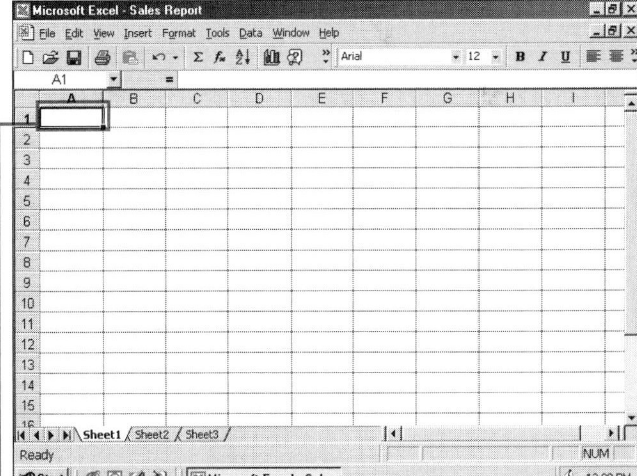

■ The macro performs the actions you recorded.

■ In this example, the macro entered a picture at the top of the worksheet.

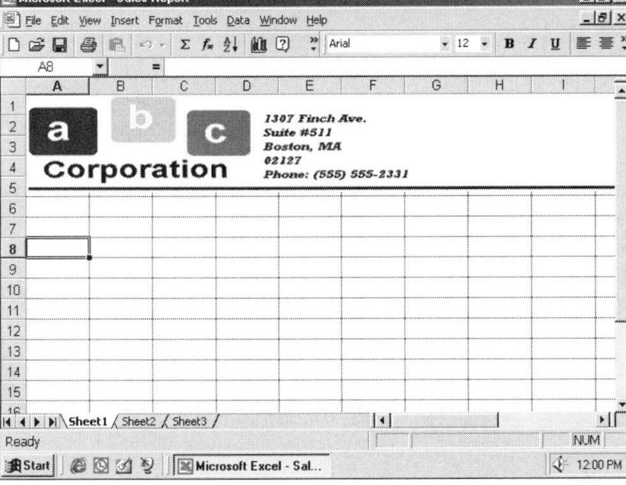

RUN A MACRO USING THE KEYBOARD

1 If you want the macro to affect specific cells in the worksheet, select the cells you want to change.

2 Press the keyboard shortcut you assigned to the macro.

■ The macro performs the actions you recorded.

SECTION IV

1) GETTING STARTED

2) EDIT SLIDES

3) ADD OBJECTS TO SLIDES

USING POWERPOINT

4) ENHANCE A PRESENTATION

5) FINE-TUNE A PRESENTATION

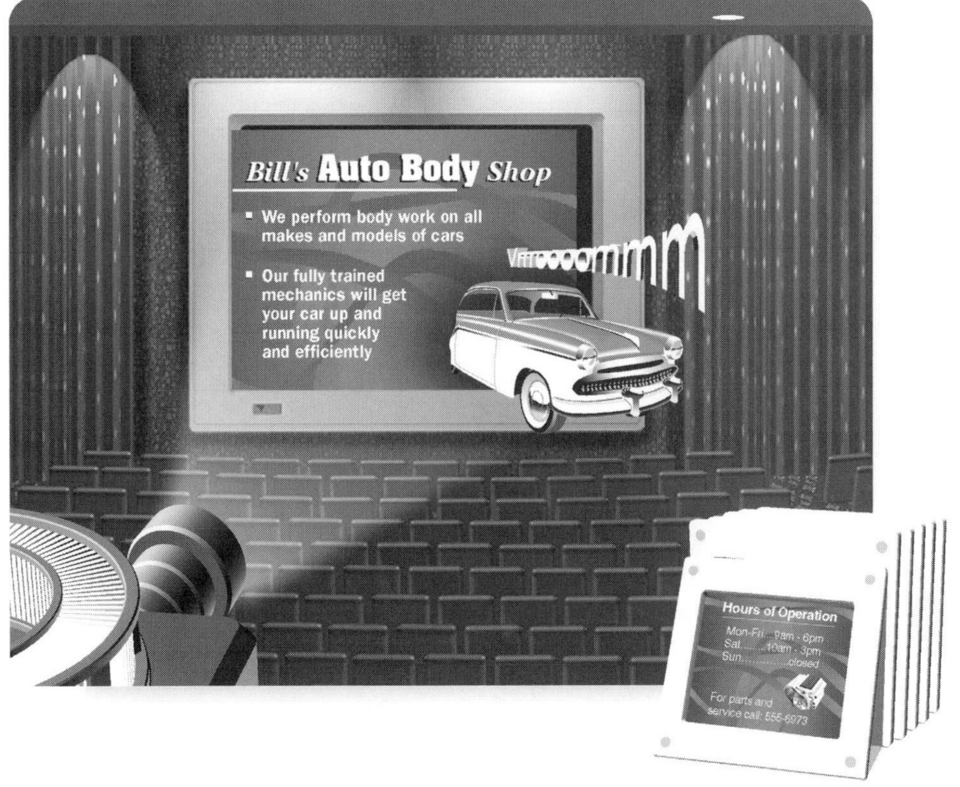

INTRODUCTION TO POWERPOINT

PowerPoint helps you plan, organize, design and deliver professional presentations. You can use a computer screen, the Web, 35mm slides or overhead transparencies to deliver a presentation. PowerPoint also allows you to create handouts for the audience and speaker notes to help you deliver the presentation.

For more information on PowerPoint, you can visit the following Web site: www.microsoft.com/powerpoint

Creating Presentations

PowerPoint offers several ways to create a presentation. The AutoContent Wizard takes you through the process of creating a presentation step by step. The design templates PowerPoint offers can also help you get started by allowing you to choose a pre-designed look for the presentation.

PowerPoint offers four ways you can view a presentation on the screen. The Normal view displays all the text in a presentation, the current slide and the speaker notes for the current slide. This view allows you to work with all the parts of a presentation in a single screen. The Outline view displays all the text in a presentation and is useful for developing the content and organization of the presentation. The Slide view displays one slide at a time, which allows you to easily change the formatting and layout of individual slides. The Slide Sorter view displays a miniature version of each slide, giving you an overview of the entire presentation.

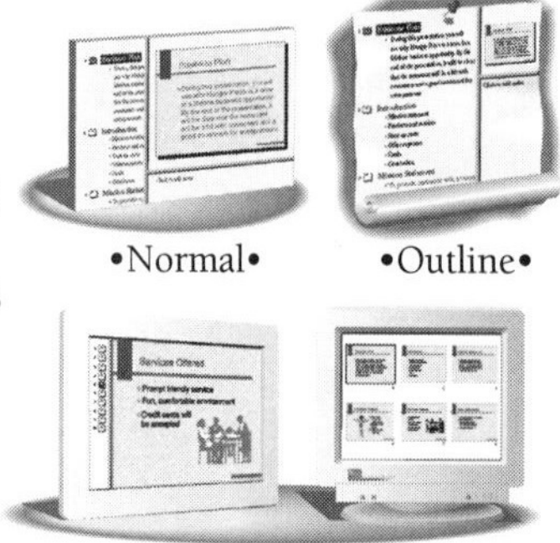

•Normal• •Outline•

•Slide• •Slide Sorter•

Editing Slides

When you create a presentation using the AutoContent Wizard, each slide displays sample text you can use as a guide for preparing the content of the presentation. You can replace the sample text with the information for your own presentation.

You can add new text to a slide or remove text you no longer need. PowerPoint also allows you to move text within a presentation so you can easily reorganize the ideas.

You can find and correct spelling errors in a presentation. PowerPoint can also automatically correct common spelling errors as you type.

PowerPoint remembers the last editing and formatting changes you made to the slides. If you regret a change, you can undo the change.

When editing slides, you may want to display just the titles for each slide and hide the remaining text. This can help you work more easily with the structure of the presentation.

Adding Objects to Slides

PowerPoint allows you to add objects to slides to enhance a presentation.

Professionally designed clip art images can help make a presentation more interesting and entertaining. Adding AutoShapes, such as arrows and stars, can help make a slide more appealing. You can also add pictures stored on your computer, such as your company logo or a picture of a product.

You can add a chart to a slide in a presentation. Charts are useful for displaying trends and comparing data on a slide. Charts are often easier to understand than a list of numbers. You can also add a table to a slide to neatly display information such as a table of contents or a price list.

Enhancing Presentations

There are many ways to make the information on a slide stand out. You can emphasize the text on a slide using bold, italic, underline or shadow formatting. You can also change the font, size and color of text. Changing the appearance of bullets can help you emphasize important points on a slide.

You can use one of PowerPoint's many ready-to-use designs to give the slides in a presentation a new appearance. You can also change the color scheme of a single slide or an entire presentation.

You can add movement and sound effects to objects on a slide. Animation can help emphasize important points and keep the audience's attention throughout an on-screen presentation.

Fine-Tuning Presentations

When you have finished organizing the ideas and formatting the slides in a presentation, you can fine-tune the presentation. If you are going to view the presentation as an on-screen slide show, you can add special effects, called transitions, to help you move from one slide to the next.

PowerPoint can help you create a summary slide that lists the title of each slide in the presentation. You can use the summary slide to quickly explain the content of the presentation to the audience.

You can also create speaker notes that contain all the ideas you want to discuss when delivering a presentation. The speaker notes can include statistics and supporting information you may need to answer questions from the audience.

START POWERPOINT

PowerPoint is a program that helps you plan, organize and design professional presentations.

Each time you start PowerPoint, the PowerPoint dialog box appears. This dialog box allows you to create a new presentation or open an existing presentation.

You can create a new presentation using the AutoContent Wizard, a design template or a blank presentation. The AutoContent Wizard helps you create your entire presentation, including sample text and formatting for each slide. A design template lets you create a presentation one slide at a time using formatting included in one of PowerPoint's ready-to-use designs. A blank presentation lets you create a presentation one slide at a time without any sample text or formatting provided by PowerPoint.

The first time you start PowerPoint, the Office Assistant appears on your screen. The Office Assistant can provide you with information to help you perform tasks and understand the features PowerPoint offers. For more information on the Office Assistant, see page 16.

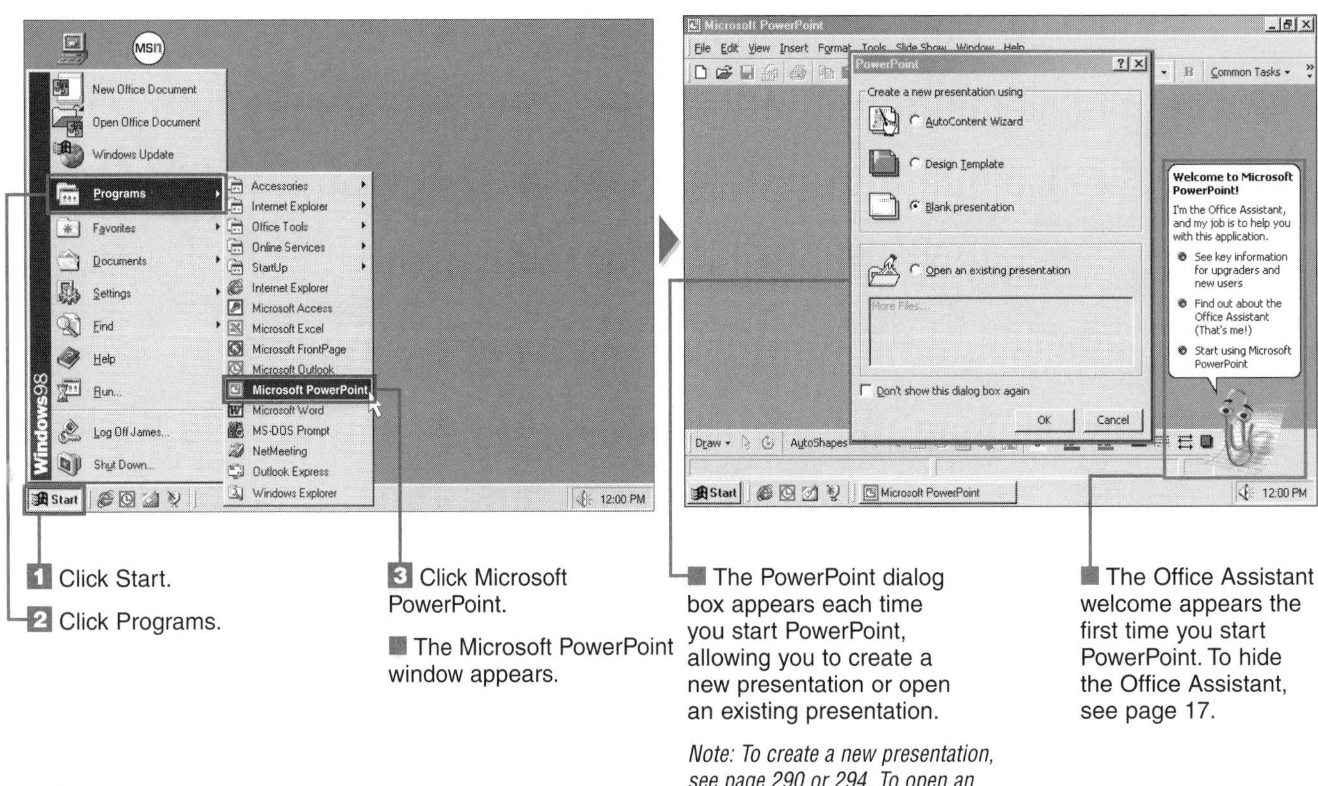

1 Click Start.

2 Click Programs.

3 Click Microsoft PowerPoint.

■ The Microsoft PowerPoint window appears.

■ The PowerPoint dialog box appears each time you start PowerPoint, allowing you to create a new presentation or open an existing presentation.

Note: To create a new presentation, see page 290 or 294. To open an existing presentation, see page 302.

■ The Office Assistant welcome appears the first time you start PowerPoint. To hide the Office Assistant, see page 17.

THE POWERPOINT SCREEN

The PowerPoint screen displays several items to help you perform tasks efficiently.

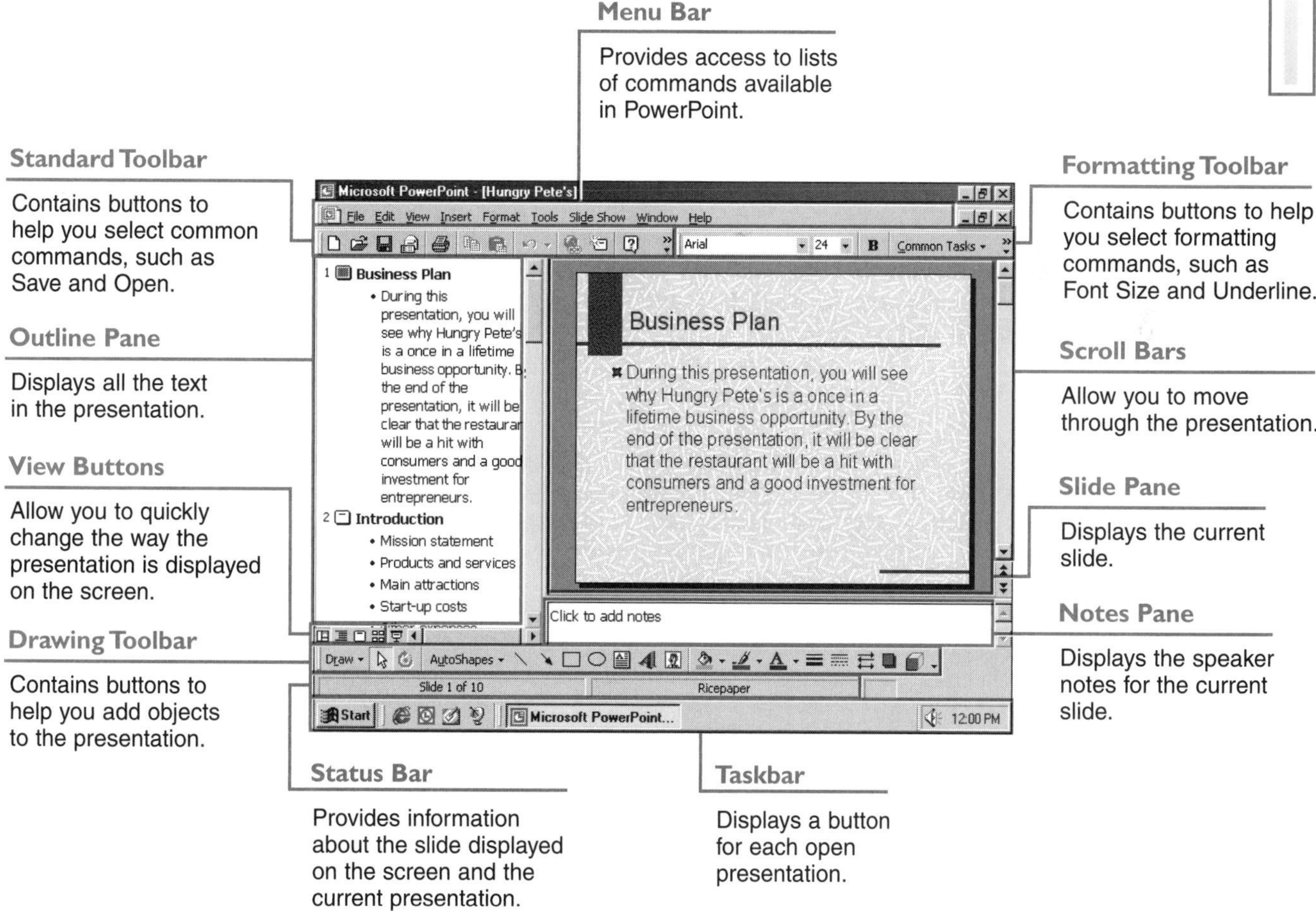

CREATE A PRESENTATION USING THE AUTOCONTENT WIZARD

You can use the AutoContent Wizard to quickly create a presentation. The wizard asks you a series of questions and then sets up a presentation based on your answers. The AutoContent Wizard provides a design and sample text for the slides in the presentation.

The wizard offers several categories of presentations for you to choose from, including General, Corporate, Projects, Sales/Marketing and Carnegie Coach. The Carnegie Coach category contains presentations provided by Dale Carnegie Training®, which include tips on how to improve your presentations. If you are not sure which category to choose, you can select the All category to list all the available presentations.

After you choose a category, you can select the presentation that best suits your needs.

The AutoContent Wizard asks how you want to output your presentation. You can choose to output your presentation as an on-screen presentation, Web presentation, black-and-white overheads, color overheads or 35mm slides.

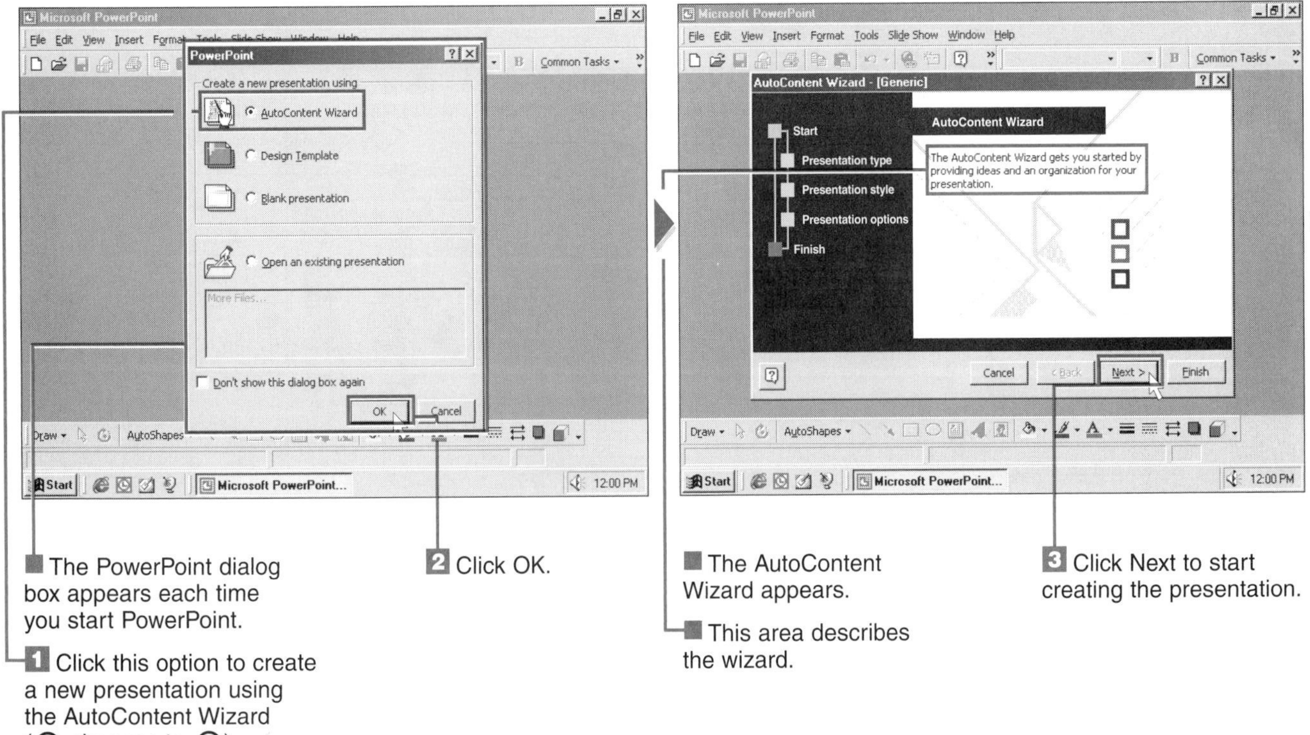

■ The PowerPoint dialog box appears each time you start PowerPoint.

1 Click this option to create a new presentation using the AutoContent Wizard (○ changes to ⊙).

2 Click OK.

■ The AutoContent Wizard appears.

■ This area describes the wizard.

3 Click Next to start creating the presentation.

TIPS

Why does a dialog box appear when I select a presentation in the AutoContent Wizard?

✔ All of the presentations may not have been installed on your computer when you installed Office 2000. Click Yes to install the presentation. A Microsoft Office dialog box appears, asking you to insert the CD-ROM disc you used to install Office 2000. Insert the CD-ROM disc and click OK.

How do I start the AutoContent Wizard while working in PowerPoint?

✔ Choose the File menu and then click New. Select the General tab and then double-click AutoContent Wizard.

Are there other ways to create a presentation using the PowerPoint dialog box?

✔ Yes. Select the Design Template option if you know what information you want to include but want to use one of PowerPoint's designs for your slides. PowerPoint will create a slide with a design but no sample text. For more information, see page 294.

Select the Blank presentation option if you know what information you want to use and want to create your own design. PowerPoint will create a blank slide with no design or sample text.

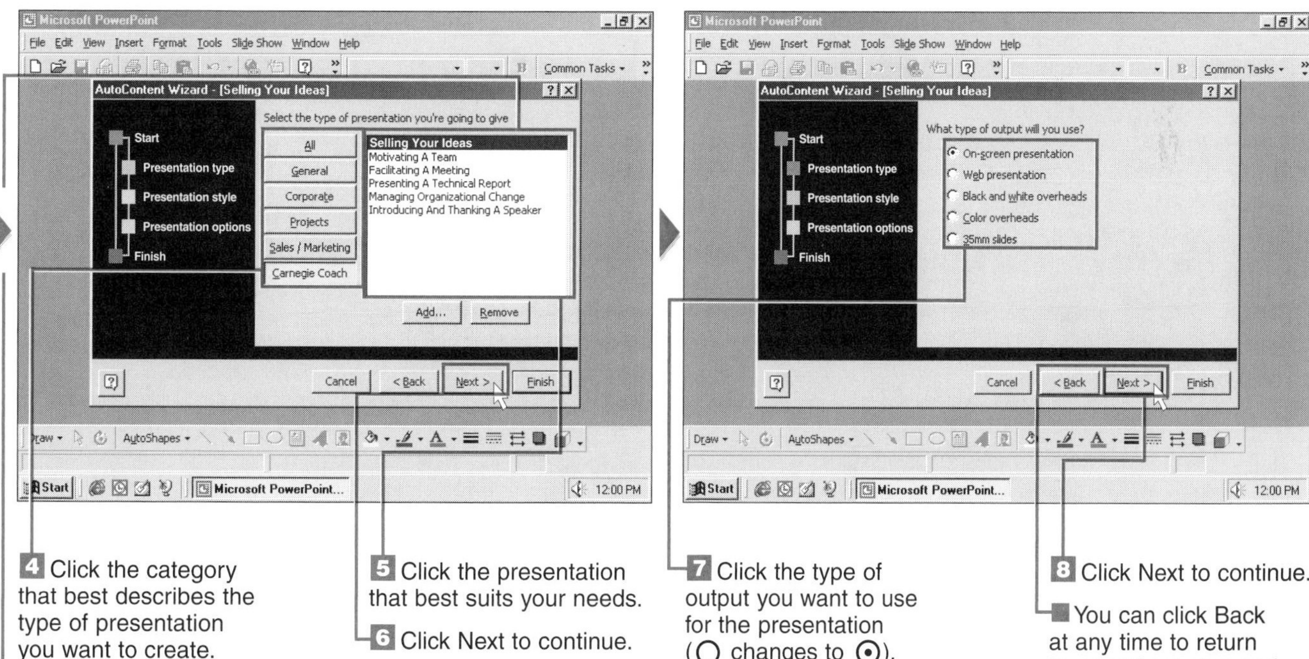

4 Click the category that best describes the type of presentation you want to create.

■ This area displays the presentations in the category you selected.

5 Click the presentation that best suits your needs.

6 Click Next to continue.

7 Click the type of output you want to use for the presentation (○ changes to ⊙).

8 Click Next to continue.

■ You can click Back at any time to return to a previous step and change your answers.

CONTINUED

CREATE A PRESENTATION USING THE AUTOCONTENT WIZARD CONTINUED

The AutoContent Wizard allows you to specify a title for your presentation. The title will appear on the first slide in the presentation.

You can choose to display footer text on each slide. Footer text is useful when you want the audience to keep certain information in mind during your presentation, such as your name or the name of your company.

You can also choose to include the date and slide number on each slide. If you include the date, PowerPoint will automatically update the date each time you open the presentation.

After you create your presentation, PowerPoint displays the presentation in the Normal view. The Normal view displays the sample text in the presentation and the current slide. The sample text and the appearance of the slides depend on the information you supplied the AutoContent Wizard. You can replace the sample text PowerPoint provides with your own information. To edit text, see page 308.

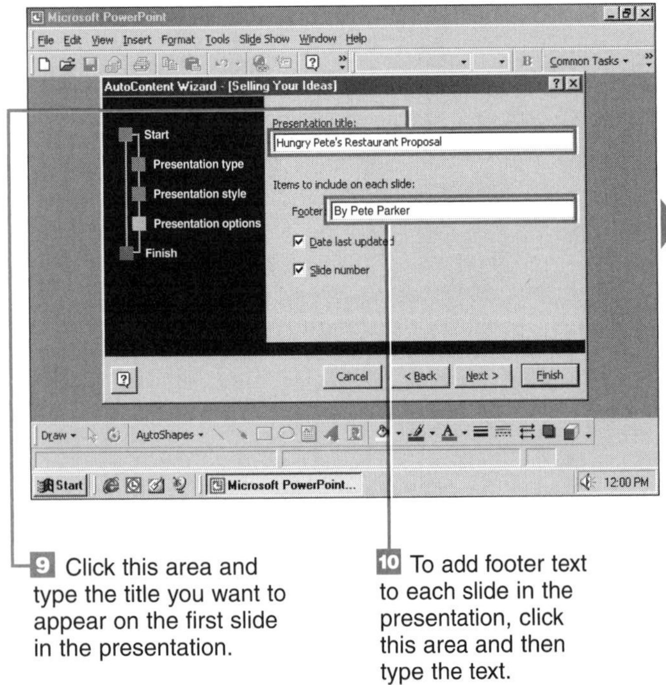

9 Click this area and type the title you want to appear on the first slide in the presentation.

10 To add footer text to each slide in the presentation, click this area and then type the text.

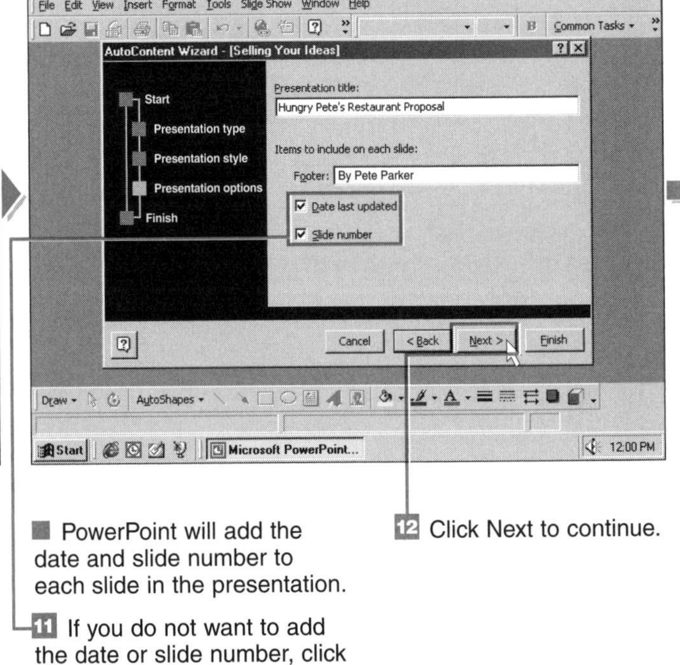

■ PowerPoint will add the date and slide number to each slide in the presentation.

11 If you do not want to add the date or slide number, click the option you do not want to add (☑ changes to ☐).

12 Click Next to continue.

TIPS

Do I have to answer all the questions in the AutoContent Wizard?

✔ No. You can click the Finish button at any time to create a presentation based on the answers you have provided so far. The AutoContent Wizard will use default settings for the questions you did not answer.

Can I later change the footer text on my slides?

✔ Yes. Click the View menu and then select Header and Footer. For more information, see page 352.

Why is there a yellow light bulb on a slide in my presentation?

✔ A yellow light bulb indicates the Office Assistant has a suggestion on how to improve an aspect of the slide, such as the text style or slide design. Click the light bulb to display the Office Assistant's suggestion. You can then select the option you want to use. To ignore the options and remove the light bulb from the slide, click OK. This feature is not available if the Office Assistant is turned off.

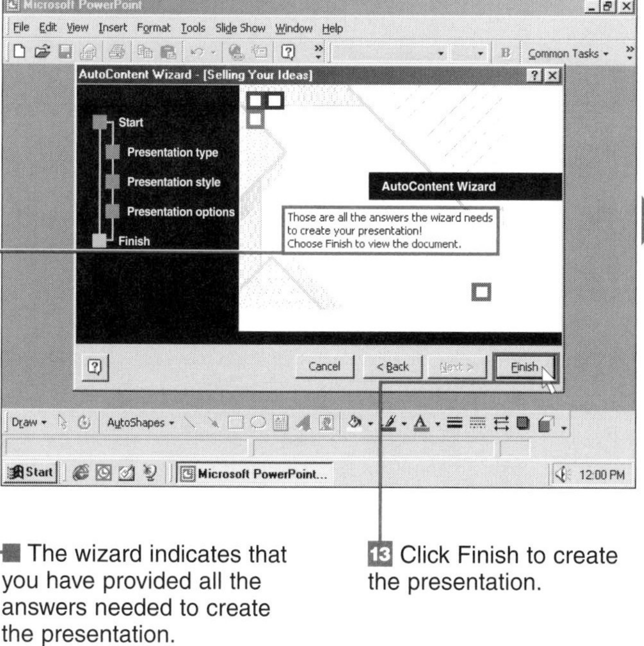

■ The wizard indicates that you have provided all the answers needed to create the presentation.

13 Click Finish to create the presentation.

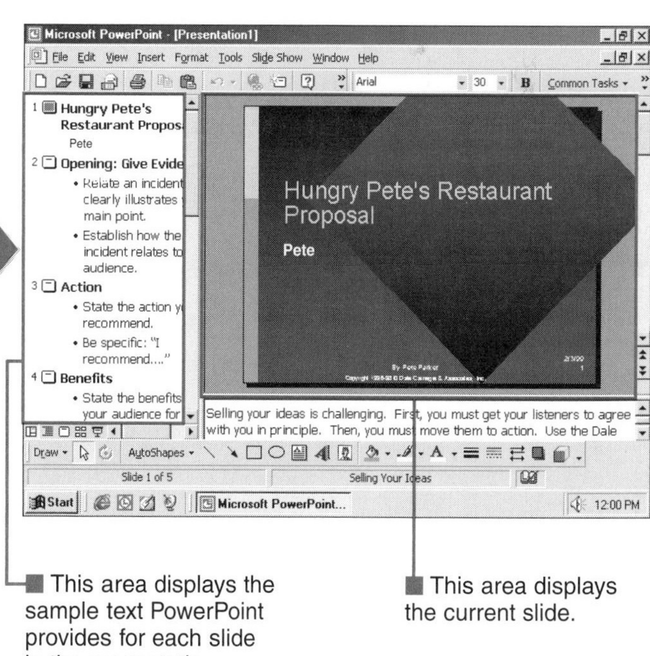

■ This area displays the sample text PowerPoint provides for each slide in the presentation.

■ This area displays the current slide.

CREATE A PRESENTATION USING A DESIGN TEMPLATE

You can use a design template to help create a professional-looking presentation. Design templates are useful when you know what information you want to include in your presentation, but you want to choose a design for the slides.

When you create a presentation using a design template, PowerPoint creates only the first slide. You can add additional slides to your presentation as you need them.

PowerPoint provides several design templates for you to choose from. Each design template conveys a specific mood and includes fonts, text colors and a background that work well together. You can preview a design template to determine if it is appropriate for your presentation. For additional design templates, you can visit the following Web site: http://officeupdate.microsoft.com/downloadCatalog/dldPowerPoint.htm

You can select a layout for the first slide in your presentation. A slide layout allows you to easily add text and objects to a slide.

PowerPoint displays the slide in the Normal view. PowerPoint will apply the same design template to each additional slide you add to your presentation.

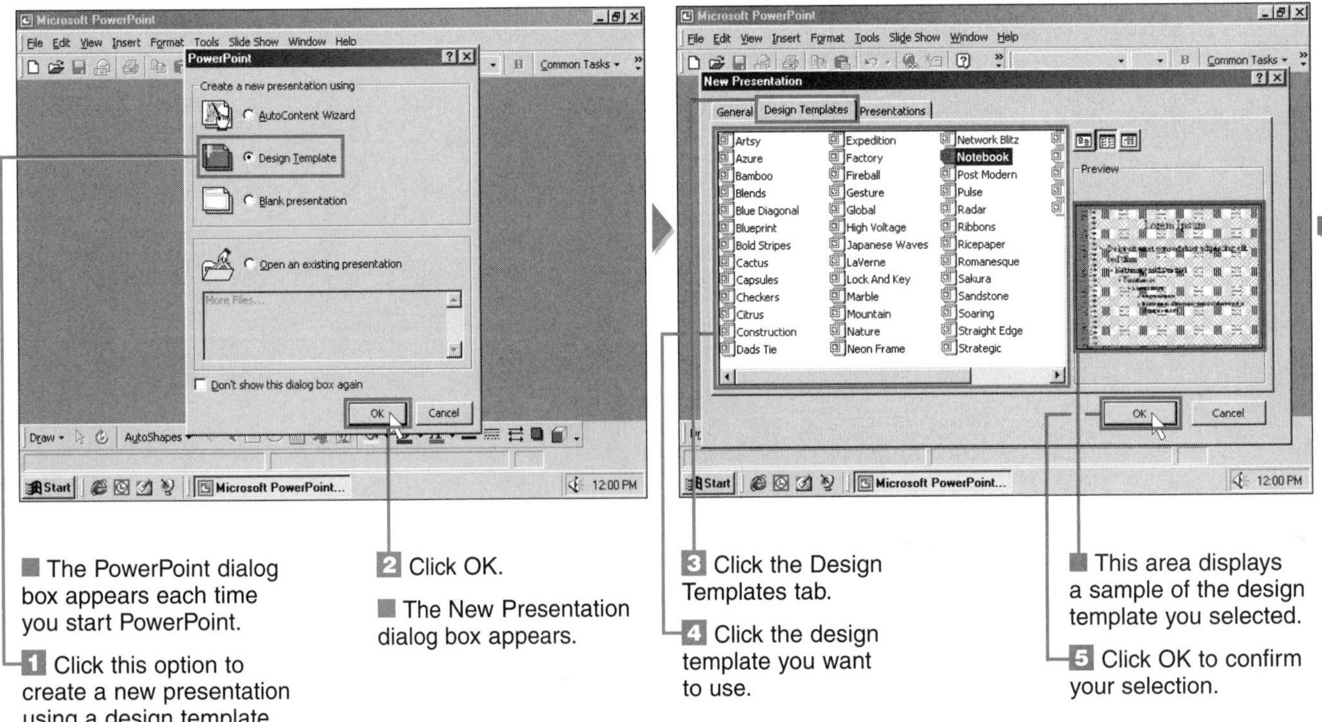

■ The PowerPoint dialog box appears each time you start PowerPoint.

1 Click this option to create a new presentation using a design template (○ changes to ⊙).

2 Click OK.

■ The New Presentation dialog box appears.

3 Click the Design Templates tab.

4 Click the design template you want to use.

■ This area displays a sample of the design template you selected.

5 Click OK to confirm your selection.

TIPS

Why does a Microsoft Office 2000 dialog box appear when I try to create a presentation using a design template?

✔ All of the design templates may not have been installed on your computer when you installed Office 2000. When you select a design template that is not installed, PowerPoint asks you to insert the CD-ROM disc you used to install Office 2000 into your CD-ROM drive. Insert the CD-ROM disc and click OK to install the design template.

Can I use two different design templates in a presentation?

✔ No. A PowerPoint presentation can contain only one design template.

Can I create a new presentation while working in PowerPoint?

✔ Yes. Click the File menu and then select New. Perform steps 3 to 7 below to create a new presentation using a design template.

Can I change a design template later?

✔ You can change the design template for a presentation at any time. Click Common Tasks on the Formatting toolbar and then select Apply Design Template. For more information, see page 346.

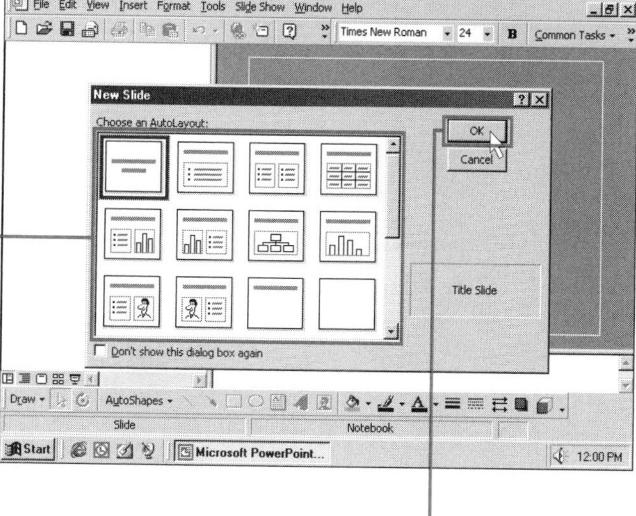

■ The New Slide dialog box appears.

6 Click the layout you want to use for the first slide in the presentation.

7 Click OK to create the first slide.

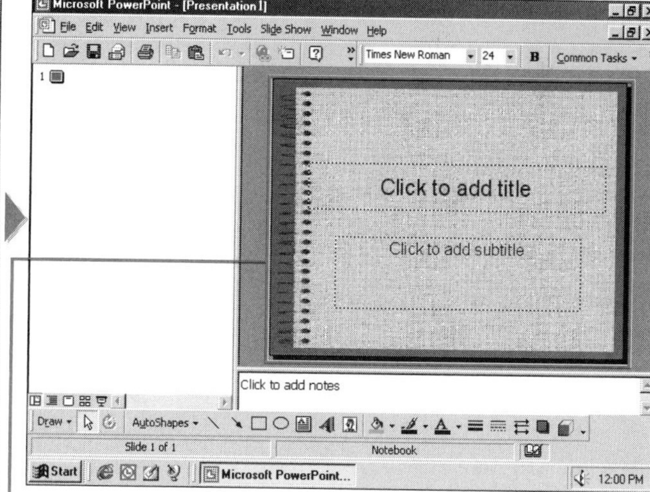

■ The slide appears, displaying the design template and the layout you selected.

■ To add additional slides to the presentation, see page 316.

CHANGE THE VIEW

PowerPoint offers several ways to display your presentation on the screen. You can choose the view that best suits your needs. Each view displays the same presentation. If you make changes to a slide in one view, the other views will also display the changes.

The Normal view displays all the text in your presentation, the current slide and the speaker notes for the current slide. This view allows you to work with all the parts of your presentation in a single screen.

The Outline view displays all the text in your presentation, a miniature version of the current slide and the speaker notes for the current slide. This view is useful for developing the content and organization of your presentation.

The Slide view displays one slide at a time. This view is useful for changing the formatting and layout of individual slides.

The Slide Sorter view displays a miniature version of each slide to provide an overview of your entire presentation. This view is useful for adding, deleting and reorganizing slides.

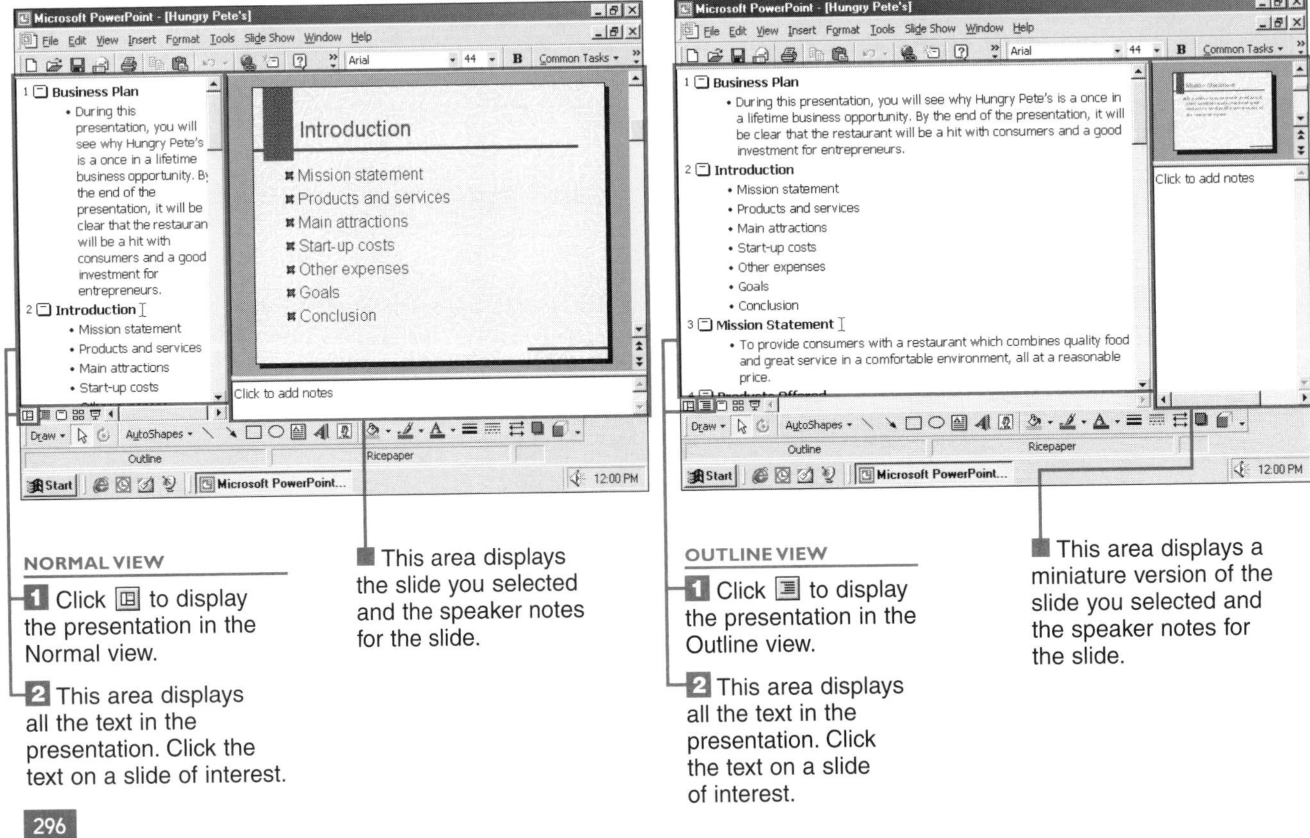

NORMAL VIEW

1 Click [icon] to display the presentation in the Normal view.

2 This area displays all the text in the presentation. Click the text on a slide of interest.

■ This area displays the slide you selected and the speaker notes for the slide.

OUTLINE VIEW

1 Click [icon] to display the presentation in the Outline view.

2 This area displays all the text in the presentation. Click the text on a slide of interest.

■ This area displays a miniature version of the slide you selected and the speaker notes for the slide.

TIPS

Does PowerPoint offer any other views?

✔ PowerPoint also offers the Notes Page view. The Notes Page view displays the current slide and the speaker notes for the current slide. To display your presentation in the Notes Page view, select the View menu and then click Notes Page.

What is the Slide Show button (▣) used for?

✔ The Slide Show button (▣) allows you to view a slide show of your presentation on your screen. For information on viewing a slide show, see page 366.

Can I change the size of an area of the screen in the Normal view?

✔ In the Normal view, the PowerPoint screen is divided into panes. You can change the size of the panes to display more of the pane you want to work in. Position the mouse ↖ over the vertical or horizontal bar that separates the panes (↖ changes to ↔ or ↕) and then drag the bar to a new location.

Can I magnify part of my presentation?

✔ Yes. Magnifying part of a presentation can make text on the screen easier to read and work with. Click the area you want to magnify. In the Zoom area on the Standard toolbar, click ▾ to display a list of zoom settings. Then click the zoom setting you want to use.

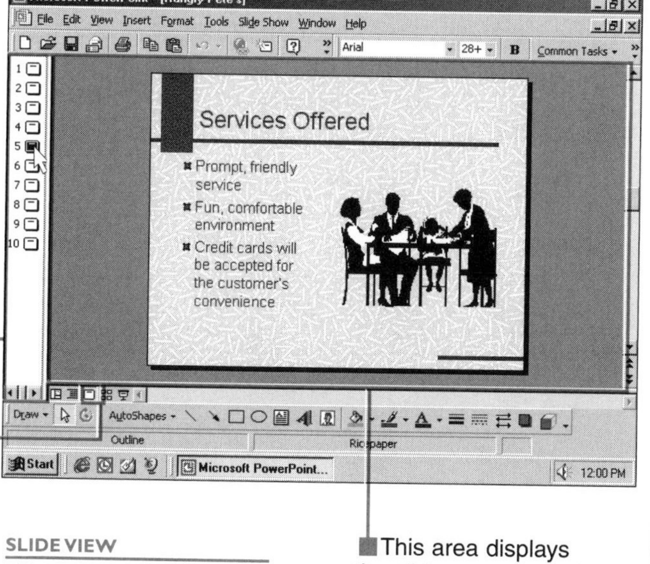

SLIDE VIEW

1 Click ▢ to display the presentation in the Slide view.

2 This area displays the numbers of all the slides in the presentation. Click the number of a slide of interest.

■ This area displays the slide you selected.

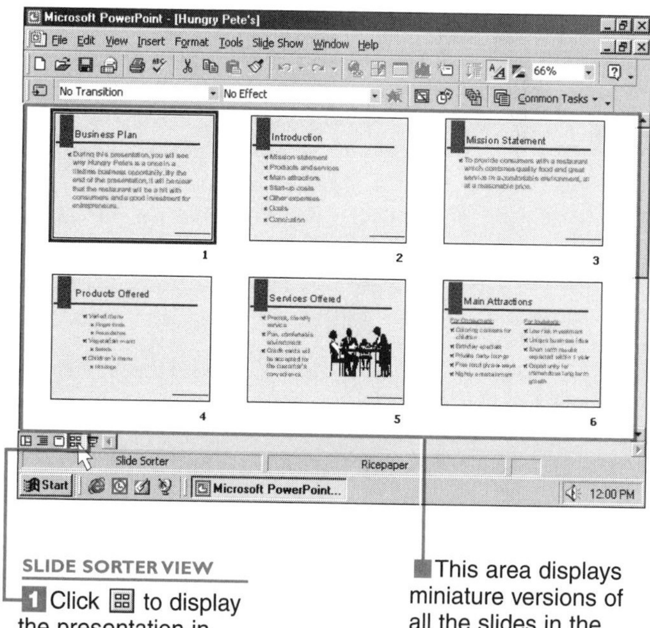

SLIDE SORTER VIEW

1 Click ▦ to display the presentation in the Slide Sorter view.

■ This area displays miniature versions of all the slides in the presentation.

BROWSE THROUGH A PRESENTATION

Your computer screen cannot display your entire presentation at once. You must browse through the presentation to view the text or slides not displayed on your screen.

In the Normal view, you can use the scroll bar in the Outline pane to browse through all the text in your presentation. You can scroll up or down one line of text at a time.

You can also use the scroll bar in the Slide pane to browse through all the slides in your presentation. You can scroll up or down one slide at a time. When you are working in the Slide pane, the Status bar displays the number of the current slide and the total number of slides in the presentation.

To quickly browse through your presentation, you can drag the scroll box along the scroll bar in the Outline or Slide pane. When you drag the scroll box in the Slide pane, PowerPoint displays a yellow box containing the number and the title of the slide that will appear on your screen.

You can also display the previous or next slide in your presentation.

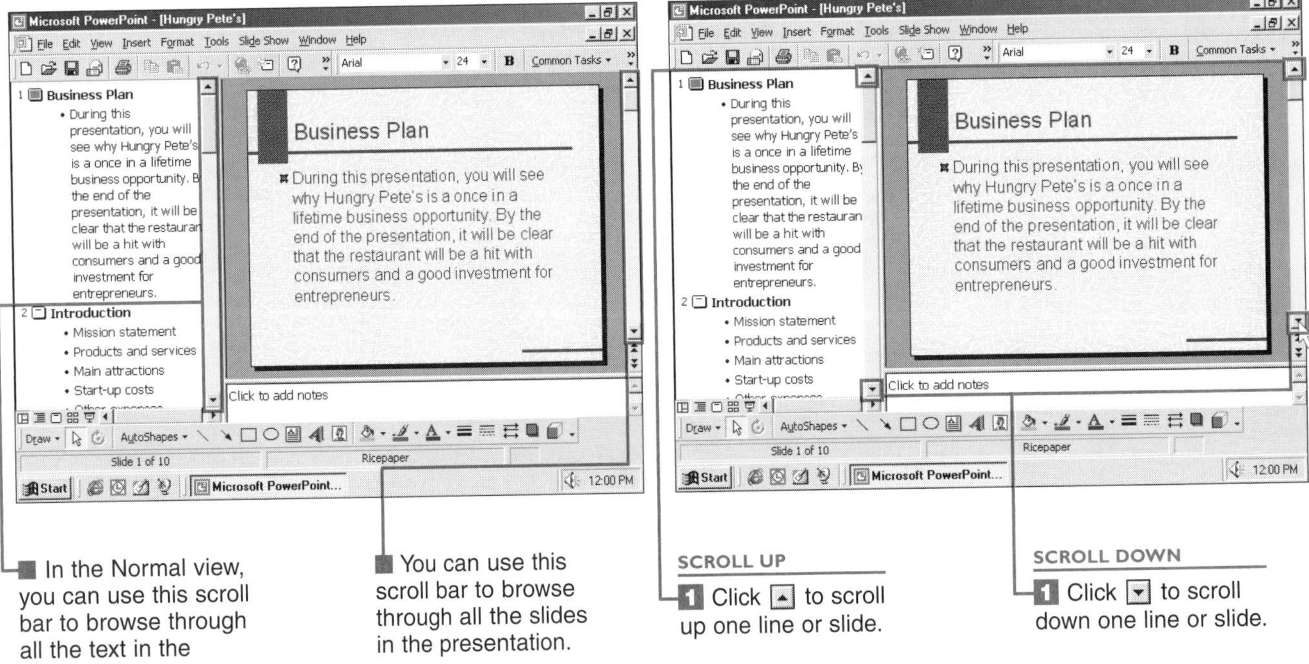

■ In the Normal view, you can use this scroll bar to browse through all the text in the presentation.

■ You can use this scroll bar to browse through all the slides in the presentation.

SCROLL UP

1 Click ▲ to scroll up one line or slide.

SCROLL DOWN

1 Click ▼ to scroll down one line or slide.

TIPS

How can I browse through the speaker notes in my presentation?

✔ In the Normal view, the Notes pane at the bottom of the window displays the speaker notes for the current slide. You can click ▲ or ▼ in the Notes pane to browse through the speaker notes.

How do I use a wheeled mouse to browse through my presentation?

✔ A wheeled mouse has a wheel between the left and right mouse buttons. Moving this wheel lets you quickly browse through your presentation. The Microsoft IntelliMouse is a popular example of a wheeled mouse.

How can I use my keyboard to browse through my presentation?

✔ When working in the Outline pane, you can press the ↑ or ↓ key to browse through your presentation one line at a time.

When working in the Slide pane, you can press the Page Up or Page Down key to browse through your presentation one slide at a time. You can also press the Home key to move to the first slide in your presentation or the End key to move to the last slide in your presentation.

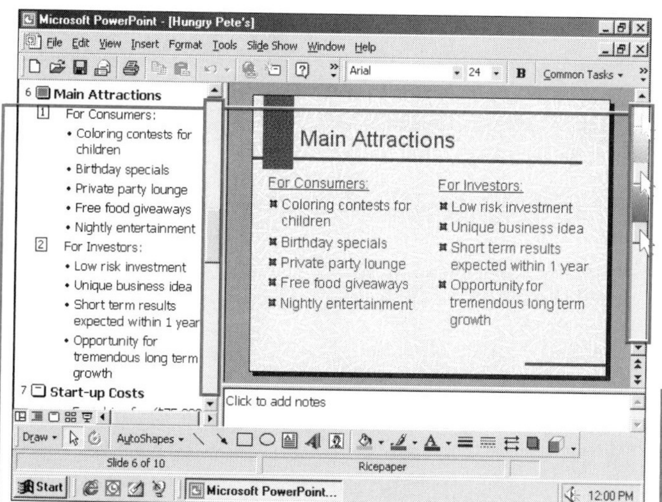

QUICKLY SCROLL

1 To quickly scroll through the presentation, drag the scroll box (□) along the scroll bar.

■ The location of the scroll box indicates which part of the presentation you are viewing. To view the middle of the presentation, drag the scroll box halfway down the scroll bar.

DISPLAY PREVIOUS OR NEXT SLIDE

1 Click one of the following buttons.

⇞ Display previous slide

⇟ Display next slide

SAVE A PRESENTATION

You should save your presentation to store it for future use. This allows you to later review and make changes to the presentation. To avoid losing your work, you should regularly save changes you make to your presentation.

You can specify where you want to save your presentation. The Places Bar in the Save As dialog box lets you quickly access commonly used folders. The History folder lets you access folders you recently used. The My Documents folder provides a convenient place to save your presentation. The Desktop folder lets you quickly save your presentation on the Windows desktop. The Favorites folder provides a place to save a presentation you will frequently access. You can use Web Folders to save your presentation on a computer called a Web server. Once the presentation is saved on a Web server, it will be available for other people to view.

When you finish working with a presentation, you can close the presentation to remove it from your screen. You can continue to work with other presentations until you exit PowerPoint.

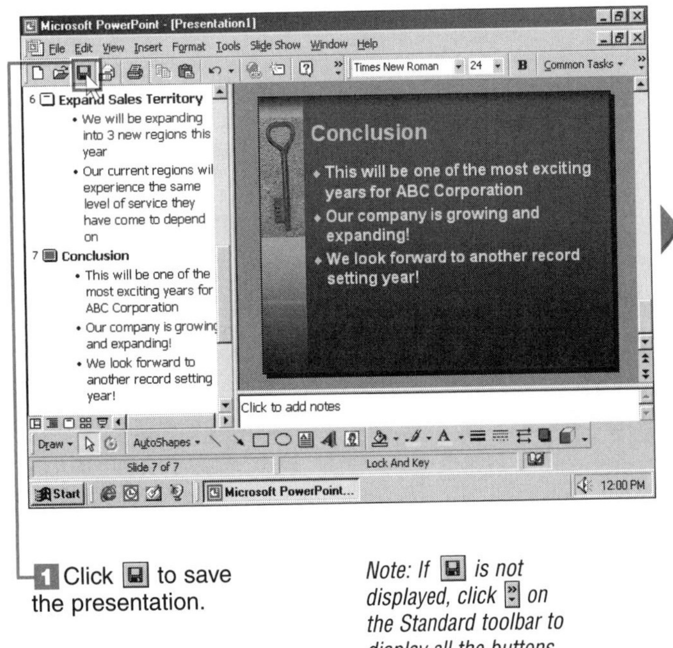

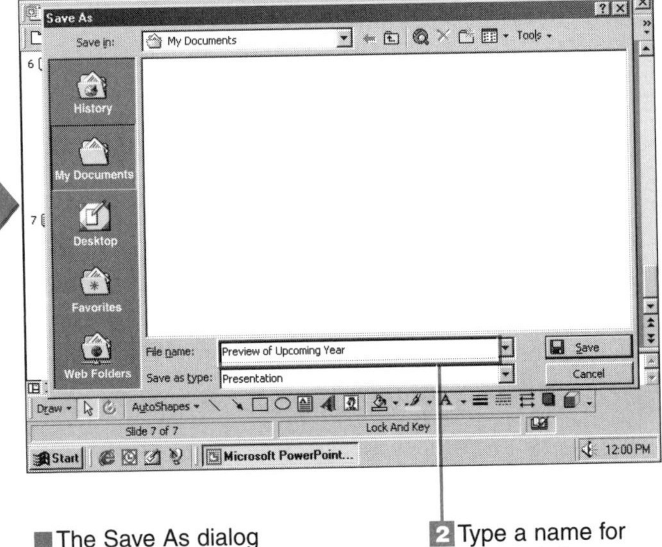

1 Click (save icon) to save the presentation.

Note: If (save icon) is not displayed, click (more buttons icon) on the Standard toolbar to display all the buttons.

■ The Save As dialog box appears.

Note: If you previously saved the presentation, the Save As dialog box will not appear since you have already named the presentation.

2 Type a name for the presentation.

TIPS

My colleagues do not use PowerPoint 2000. Can I save my presentation in a different format?

✔ Yes. In the Save As dialog box, click the Save as type area and then select a format. A dialog box appears if the file format converter is not installed. Click Yes to install the converter. A Microsoft Office 2000 dialog box will appear, asking you to insert the CD-ROM disc you used to install Office. Insert the CD-ROM disc and click OK.

I previously saved my presentation. How can I save a copy of my presentation with a different name?

✔ Click the File menu and then select Save As. Type the new name and then click Save.

How can I ensure the fonts I used in my presentation will appear properly when I view the presentation on another computer?

✔ You can embed the fonts in the presentation to ensure they appear properly on another computer. In the Save As dialog box, click Tools and then select Embed TrueType Fonts. Some fonts cannot be embedded due to license restrictions.

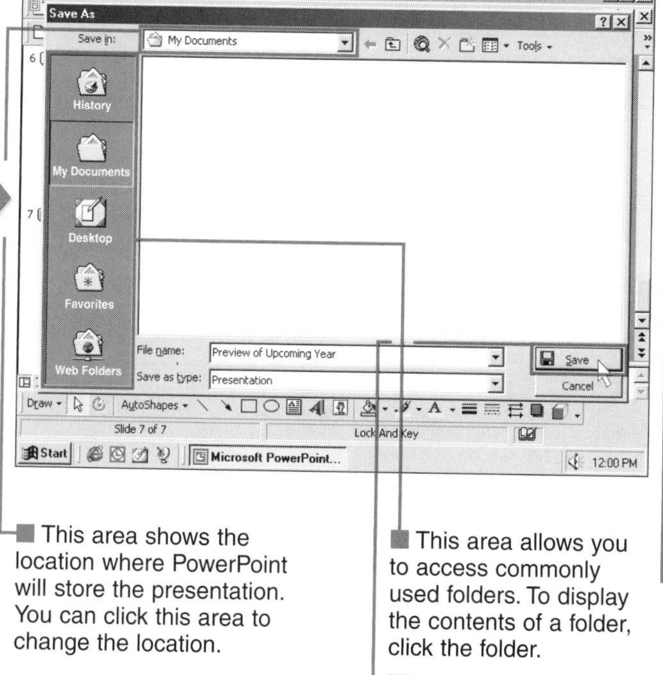

■ This area shows the location where PowerPoint will store the presentation. You can click this area to change the location.

■ This area allows you to access commonly used folders. To display the contents of a folder, click the folder.

3 Click Save.

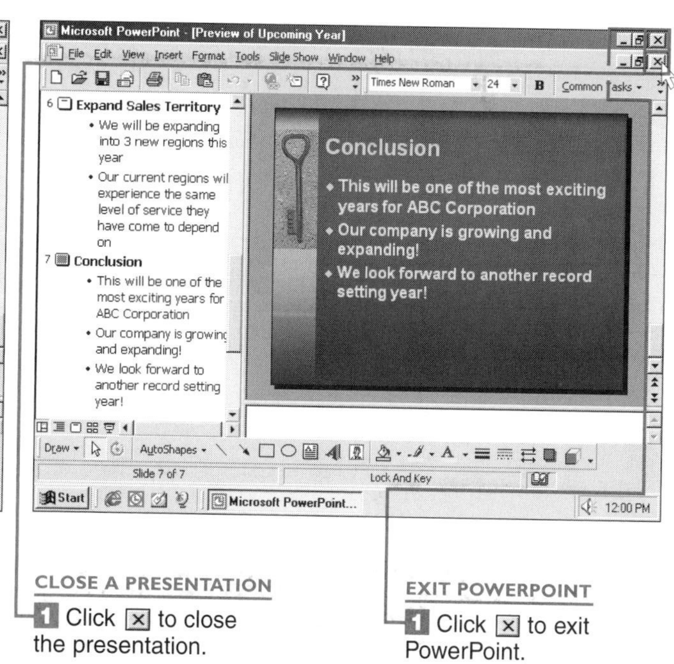

CLOSE A PRESENTATION

1 Click ☒ to close the presentation.

EXIT POWERPOINT

1 Click ☒ to exit PowerPoint.

OPEN A PRESENTATION

You can open a saved presentation and display it on your screen. This lets you review and make changes to the presentation.

Each time you start PowerPoint, the PowerPoint dialog box appears, displaying a list of presentations you recently worked with. You can quickly open one of these presentations. If the presentation you want to open is not in the list, you can use the Open dialog box to open the presentation.

The Open dialog box allows you to specify the drive or folder where the presentation you want to open is located. You can use the Places Bar to quickly display the contents of commonly used folders. For information on the Places Bar, see the top of page 300.

After you select a presentation you want to open, the Open dialog box displays a preview of the first slide in the presentation. Previewing the first slide allows you to verify that you selected the correct presentation.

After you open a presentation, PowerPoint displays the name of the presentation at the top of your screen.

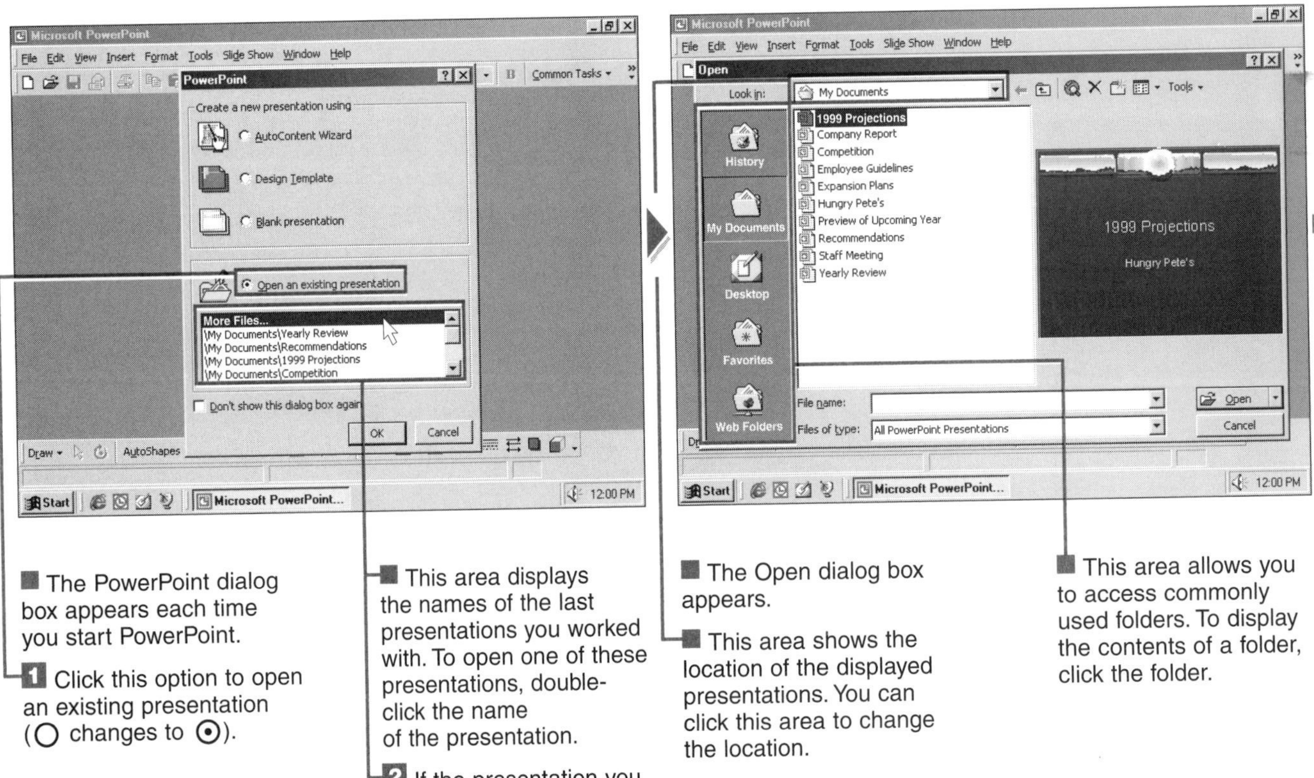

■ The PowerPoint dialog box appears each time you start PowerPoint.

1 Click this option to open an existing presentation (○ changes to ⦿).

■ This area displays the names of the last presentations you worked with. To open one of these presentations, double-click the name of the presentation.

2 If the presentation you want to open is not listed, double-click More Files.

■ The Open dialog box appears.

■ This area shows the location of the displayed presentations. You can click this area to change the location.

■ This area allows you to access commonly used folders. To display the contents of a folder, click the folder.

TIPS

Are there other ways to open a presentation?

✔ Yes. In the Open dialog box, click ▾ beside Open. If you only want to review the contents of the selected presentation without making changes, select Open Read-Only. If you want to create a copy of the selected presentation that you can work with, select Open as Copy.

Can I change the location where PowerPoint automatically looks for my presentations?

✔ Yes. Select the Tools menu and then click Options. Click the Save tab and in the Default file location area, type the drive and folder name you want to use. Then click OK.

How can I open a presentation while working in PowerPoint?

✔ Click the Open button (📂) on the Standard toolbar to display the Open dialog box. Click the name of the presentation you want to open and then click Open. If you want to open a presentation you recently worked with, click the File menu and then select the name of the presentation you want to open.

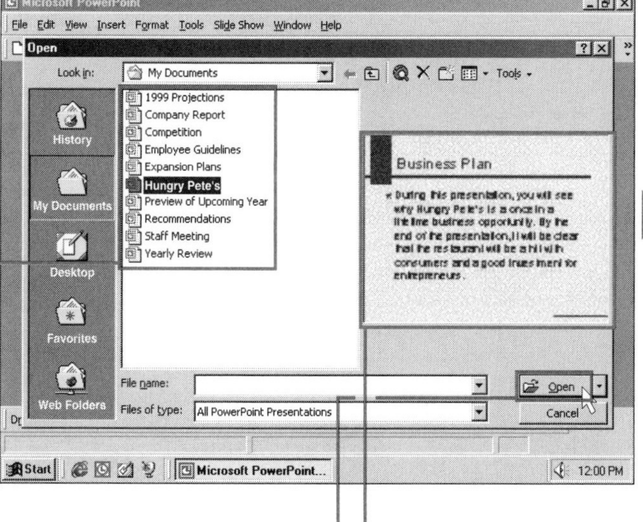

3 Click the name of the presentation you want to open.

■ This area displays the first slide in the presentation you selected.

4 Click Open to view the presentation.

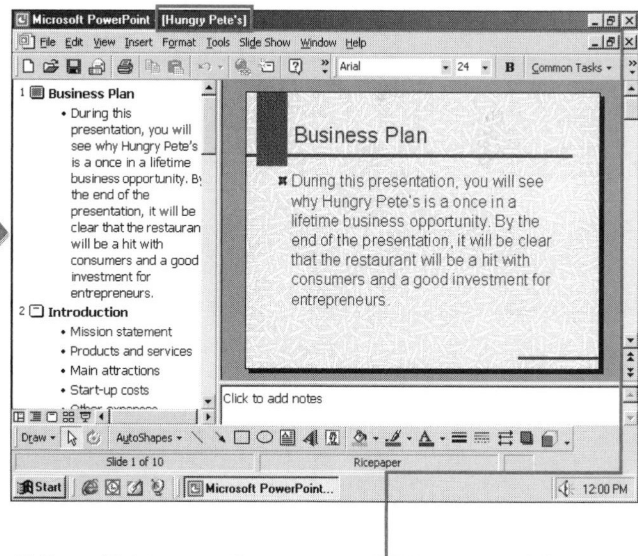

■ PowerPoint opens the presentation. You can now review and make changes to the presentation.

■ The name of the presentation appears at the top of the screen.

E-MAIL A PRESENTATION

You can send the presentation you are working with in an e-mail message. You can also e-mail the slide currently displayed on your screen. E-mail is a fast and convenient method of exchanging information with other people.

When you e-mail an entire presentation, the presentation is sent as an attachment and appears as an icon in the message. When you e-mail a single slide, the slide appears in the body of the e-mail message.

You can e-mail a presentation or slide to more than one person. You can also send a copy of the message to a person who is not directly involved but would be interested in the message.

When you e-mail a presentation or slide, PowerPoint may suggest a subject for the e-mail message based on the name of the presentation. You can enter a different subject. You should enter a subject that will help the recipient quickly identify the contents of the message.

Before you e-mail a presentation or slide, you must set up Microsoft Outlook. For information on using Microsoft Outlook, see pages 508 to 521.

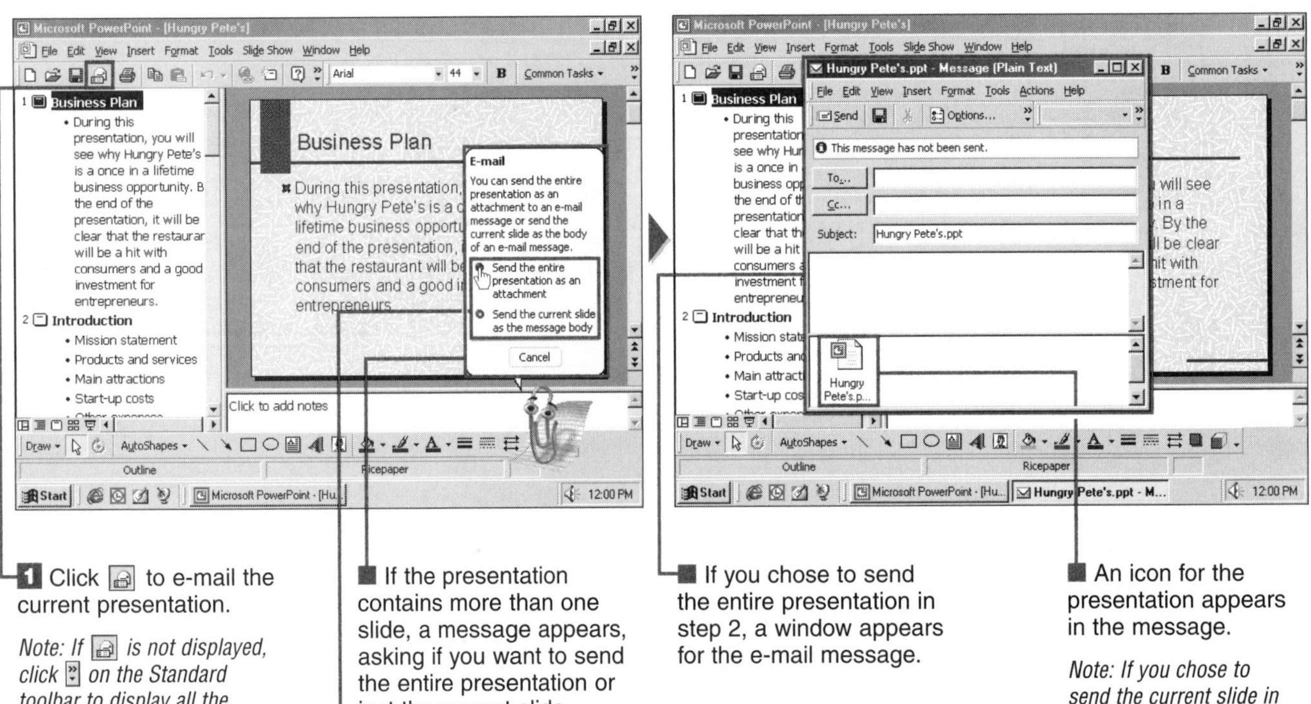

1 Click the e-mail button to e-mail the current presentation.

Note: If the button is not displayed, click » on the Standard toolbar to display all the buttons.

■ If the presentation contains more than one slide, a message appears, asking if you want to send the entire presentation or just the current slide.

2 Click the option you want to use.

■ If you chose to send the entire presentation in step 2, a window appears for the e-mail message.

■ An icon for the presentation appears in the message.

Note: If you chose to send the current slide in step 2, an area appears for you to address the message.

TIPS

PowerPoint did not offer me the option to e-mail my entire presentation. What is wrong?

✔ If you have previously e-mailed a slide from the presentation, PowerPoint does not redisplay the message asking if you want to send the entire presentation. To e-mail the entire presentation, select the File menu, click Send To and then choose Mail Recipient (as Attachment).

How can I quickly enter an e-mail address for my presentation or slide?

✔ You can click the To button and then select a name from the address book to quickly enter an e-mail address. For more information on selecting names from the address book, see page 516.

Why can't the person I sent my presentation or slide to view the information?

✔ When you e-mail a presentation, the presentation is sent as an attached file. The recipient must have PowerPoint 2000 to open the file. When you e-mail a slide, the slide is converted to HTML format. The recipient must have an e-mail program that is capable of reading HTML to display the slide.

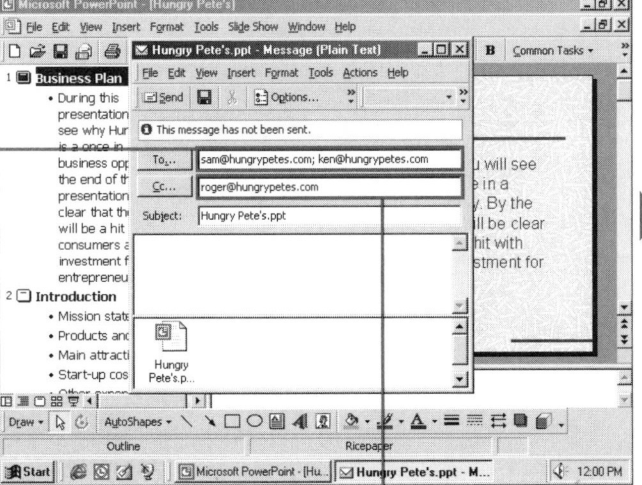

3 Type the e-mail address of each person you want to receive the message. Separate each address with a semicolon (;).

4 To send a copy of the message to another person, click this area and type the e-mail address.

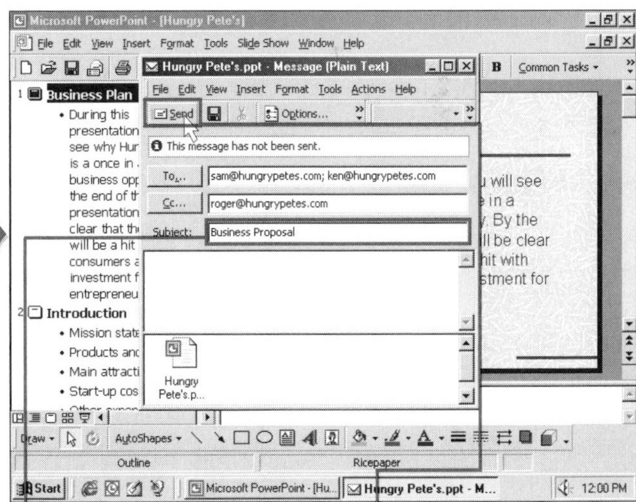

5 Click this area and type a subject for the message.

Note: If a subject already exists, you can drag the mouse I over the existing subject and then type a new subject.

6 To send the message, click Send or Send this Slide.

Note: The button you use depends on the option you selected in step 2.

SELECT TEXT

Before changing text in a presentation, you will often need to select the text you want to work with. For example, you must select the text you want to move, delete or change to a new font. You can select a single word, a point, any amount of text or an entire slide. Selected text appears highlighted on your screen.

The Normal view allows you to select and work with text efficiently on all the slides in your presentation or just the current slide. You can select text in the Outline pane to work with large portions of your presentation at once. You can also select text on the current slide displayed in the Slide pane.

After you finish working with selected text, you should deselect the text. If you begin typing when text on your screen is selected, PowerPoint will delete the selected text and replace it with the text you type.

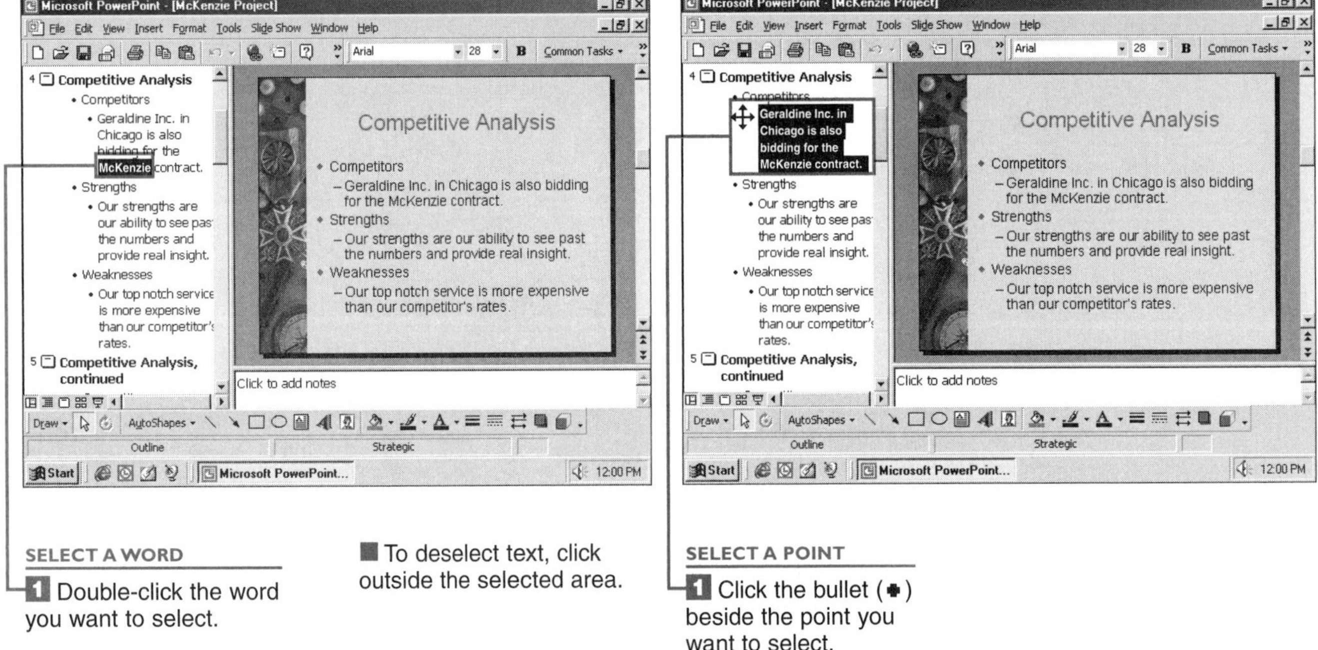

SELECT A WORD

1 Double-click the word you want to select.

■ To deselect text, click outside the selected area.

SELECT A POINT

1 Click the bullet (•) beside the point you want to select.

TIPS

Can I select text using the keyboard?

✔ To select characters, hold down the Shift key as you press the ← or → key. To select words, hold down the Shift+Ctrl keys as you press the ← or → key.

How do I select all the text in my presentation?

✔ Click the text in the Outline pane and then press the Ctrl+A keys. You can also select the Edit menu and then click Select All.

How do I select all the text on the current slide?

✔ Click a blank area on the slide in the Slide pane and then press the Ctrl+A keys. PowerPoint does not highlight the text, but displays a thick border around all the selected text.

Can I select text in other views?

✔ You can select text in the Outline or Slide view as you would select text in the Normal view. You cannot select text in the Slide Sorter view. For more information on the views, see page 296.

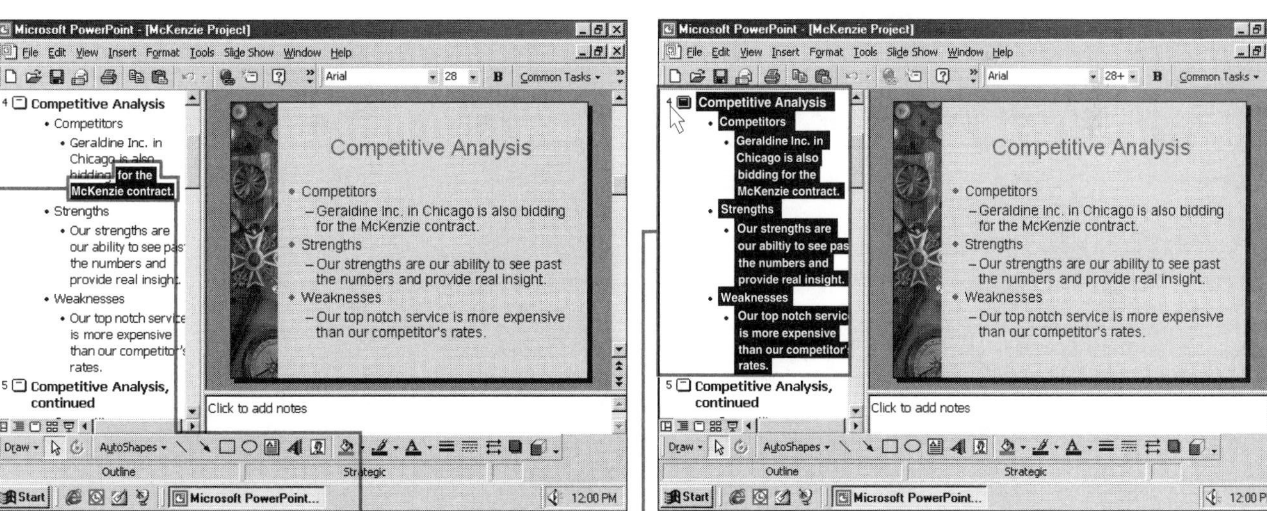

SELECT ANY AMOUNT OF TEXT

1 Position the mouse over the first word you want to select.

2 Drag the mouse over the text you want to select.

SELECT A SLIDE

1 Click the number of the slide you want to select.

EDIT TEXT

PowerPoint lets you edit the text in your presentation. This is useful when you need to correct a mistake or update the information on a slide.

The Normal view displays the text on all the slides in your presentation in the Outline pane. The Normal view also displays the current slide. You can edit the text in the Outline pane or directly on the current slide. Editing the text in one area will change the text in the other.

You can replace text in your presentation with new text. This allows you to replace the sample text supplied by the AutoContent Wizard with your own text.

You can also add new text to your presentation at any time. The text you type will appear where the insertion point flashes on your screen.

If you forgot to include an idea when you created your presentation, you can add a new point to a slide.

You can remove text you no longer need from your presentation. PowerPoint allows you to delete a character, word, point or entire slide.

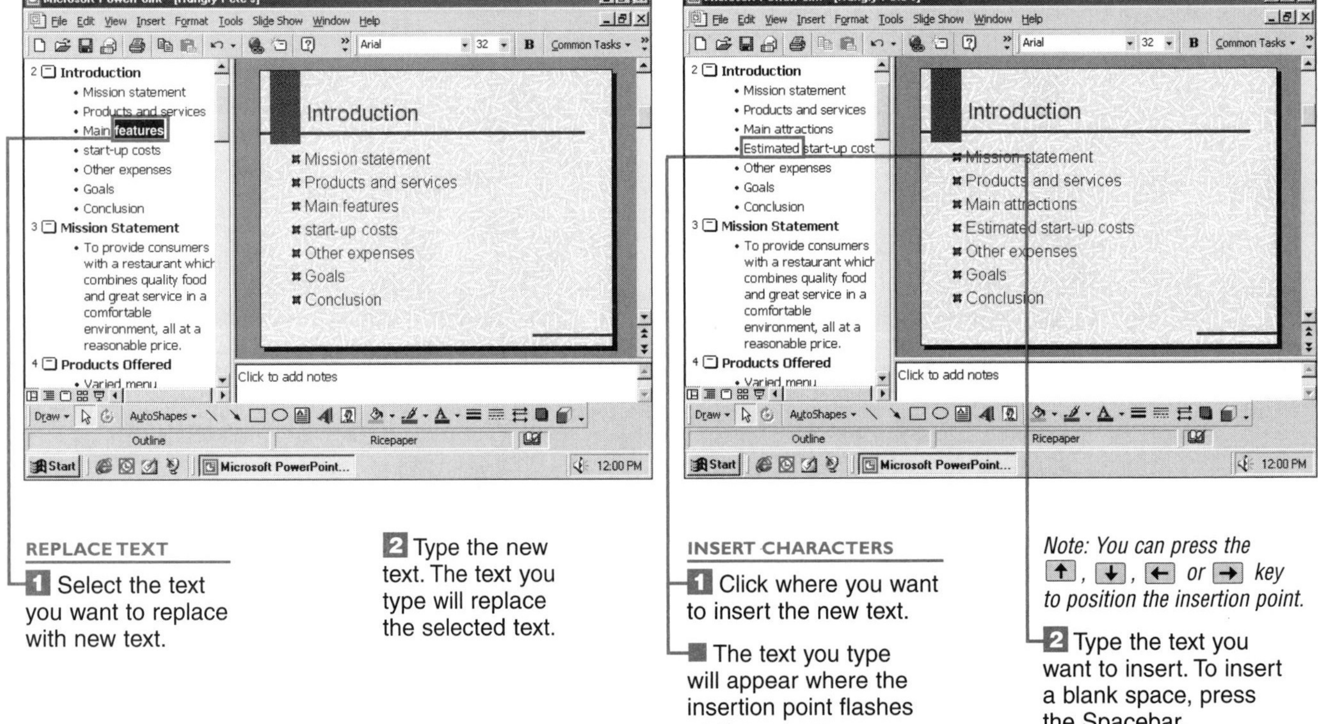

REPLACE TEXT

1 Select the text you want to replace with new text.

2 Type the new text. The text you type will replace the selected text.

INSERT CHARACTERS

1 Click where you want to insert the new text.

■ The text you type will appear where the insertion point flashes on the screen.

Note: You can press the ↑, ↓, ← or → key to position the insertion point.

2 Type the text you want to insert. To insert a blank space, press the Spacebar.

TIPS

Why do some words in my presentation display a red underline?

✔ If PowerPoint does not recognize a word in your presentation, it considers the word misspelled and underlines the word with a red line. To spell check your presentation and remove the red underlines, see page 310.

Can I edit text in other views?

✔ You can edit text in the Outline and Slide views the same way you edit text in the Normal view. You cannot edit text in the Slide Sorter view. For more information on the views, see page 296.

Can I add a new slide to my presentation?

✔ Yes. To add a new slide to your presentation, see page 316.

Can I quickly change the text I inserted to uppercase letters?

✔ PowerPoint offers five case styles you can use to change the appearance of text in your presentation–Sentence case, lowercase, UPPERCASE, Title Case and tOGGLE cASE. Select the text you want to change. Choose the Format menu, click Change Case and then select the case you want to use (○ changes to ⊙).

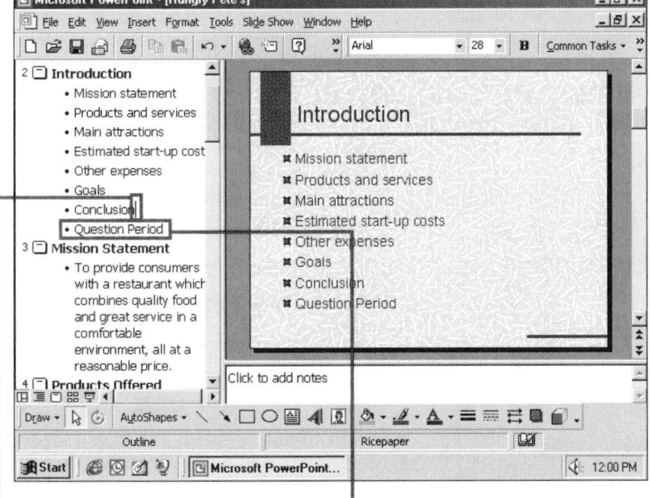

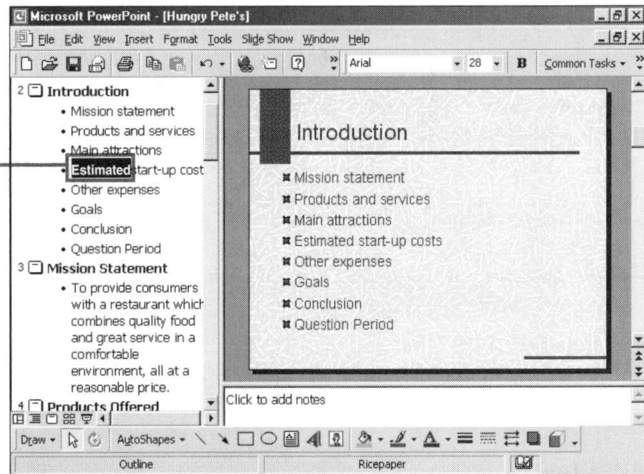

INSERT A NEW POINT

1 Click at the end of the point directly above where you want to insert a new point.

2 Press the Enter key to insert a blank line for the new point.

3 Type the text for the new point.

DELETE TEXT

1 Select the text you want to delete.

2 Press the Delete key to remove the text.

■ To delete one character at a time, click to the right of the first character you want to delete. Then press the Backspace key once for each character you want to delete.

CHECK SPELLING

You can correct spelling errors in your presentation. This can help make your presentation appear more professional.

PowerPoint's spell check feature compares every word in your presentation to words in its dictionary. If a word in your presentation does not exist in PowerPoint's dictionary, PowerPoint considers the word misspelled.

PowerPoint automatically checks your presentation for spelling errors as you type and underlines misspelled words in red. The underlines appear only on your screen and will not appear when you print your presentation or run the slide show.

When you finish entering text for your presentation, you can locate and correct all the spelling errors at once. When PowerPoint finds a misspelled word, it provides a list of suggestions to correct the word. You can replace the word with a suggestion or ignore the word and continue checking your presentation. If PowerPoint repeatedly finds a misspelled word you know is correct, such as a name, you can choose to ignore all occurrences of the word in your presentation.

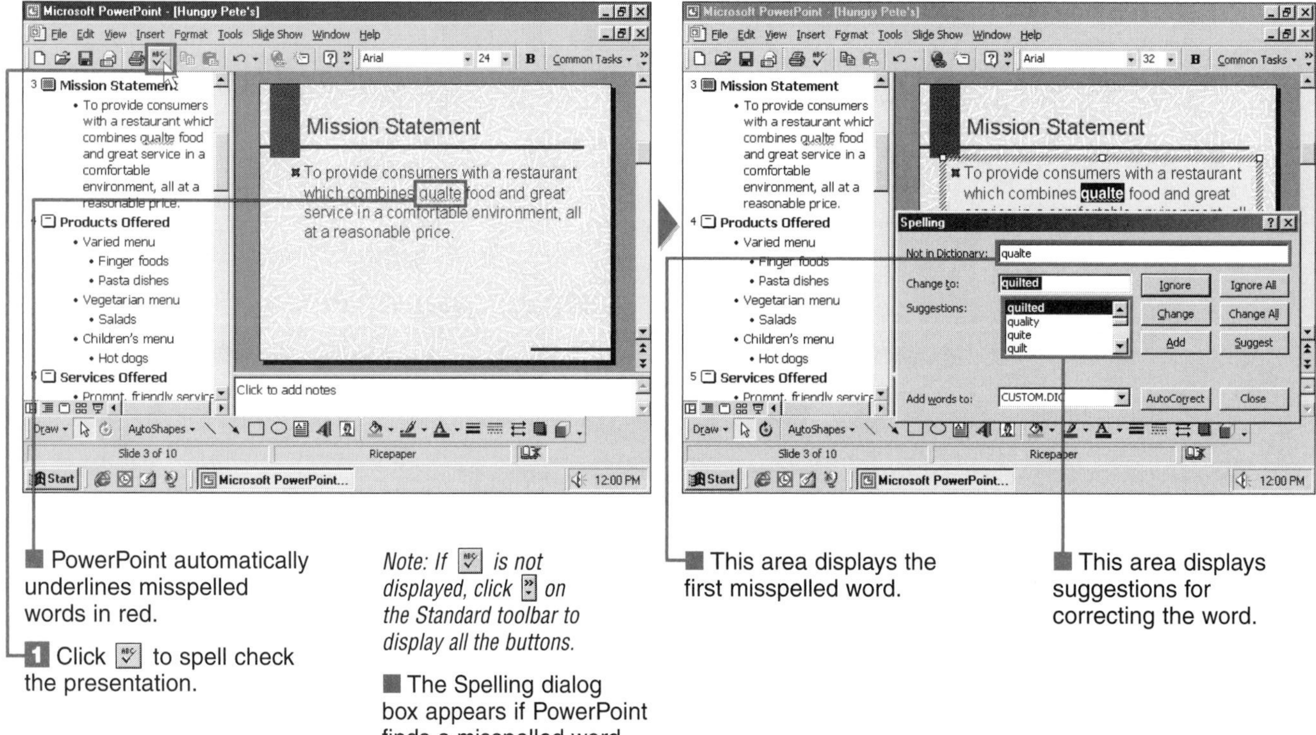

■ PowerPoint automatically underlines misspelled words in red.

1 Click [spelling icon] to spell check the presentation.

Note: If [spelling icon] is not displayed, click [»] on the Standard toolbar to display all the buttons.

■ The Spelling dialog box appears if PowerPoint finds a misspelled word.

■ This area displays the first misspelled word.

■ This area displays suggestions for correcting the word.

TIPS

Why does PowerPoint automatically correct some of my spelling errors?

✔ PowerPoint's AutoCorrect feature automatically corrects common spelling errors as you type. For example, PowerPoint automatically replaces "compair" with "compare" and "importent" with "important". To see a list of errors PowerPoint automatically corrects, select the Tools menu and then click AutoCorrect.

Can I correct a single error in my presentation?

✔ Yes. Right-click a word that displays a red underline. A list of suggestions to correct the error appears. Click the suggestion you want to use.

Can I have PowerPoint automatically correct a spelling error I often make?

✔ Yes. When PowerPoint displays the misspelled word in the Spelling dialog box, click the correct spelling. Then click the AutoCorrect button. The next time you make the same error, PowerPoint will automatically correct the error.

How can I correct spelling errors without using the Spelling dialog box?

✔ On the status bar, double-click [icon] to move to the first misspelled word in your presentation. A list of suggestions to correct the error appears. Click the suggestion you want to use. You can repeat these steps for each error you want to correct.

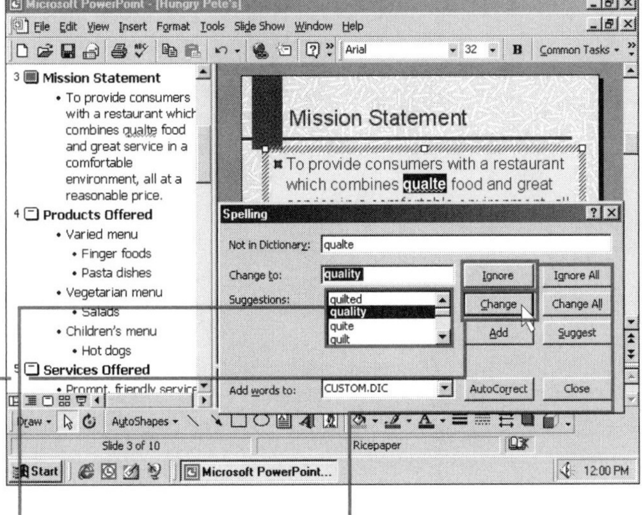

2 To select one of the suggestions, click the suggestion.

3 Click Change to correct the word in the presentation.

■ To skip the word and continue checking the presentation, click Ignore.

Note: To skip the word and all occurrences of the word in the presentation, click Ignore All.

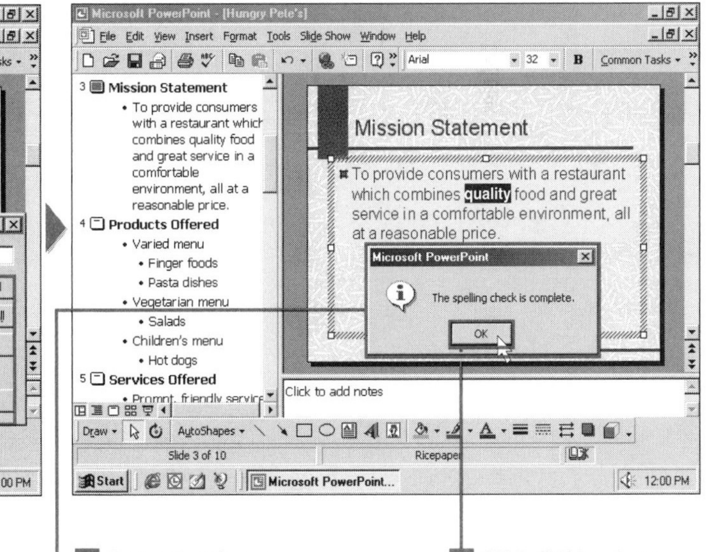

4 Correct or ignore misspelled words until this dialog box appears, telling you the spell check is complete.

5 Click OK to close the dialog box.

MOVE TEXT

You can move text in your presentation to reorganize your ideas. When you move text, the text disappears from its original location in your presentation.

You can move a word, phrase, point or entire slide to a new location in your presentation. Before you can move text, you must select the text you want to move. A solid line or dotted insertion point indicates where the text you are moving will appear.

When you move a slide, PowerPoint automatically renumbers the slides in the presentation for you.

The Outline pane in the Normal view displays the text on all the slides in your presentation. This allows you to easily move text to a new location in the presentation.

You can also move text on the slide currently displayed in the Slide pane.

You can copy text from one location in your presentation to another. This saves you time since you do not have to retype the text. When you copy text, the text appears in both the original and new locations.

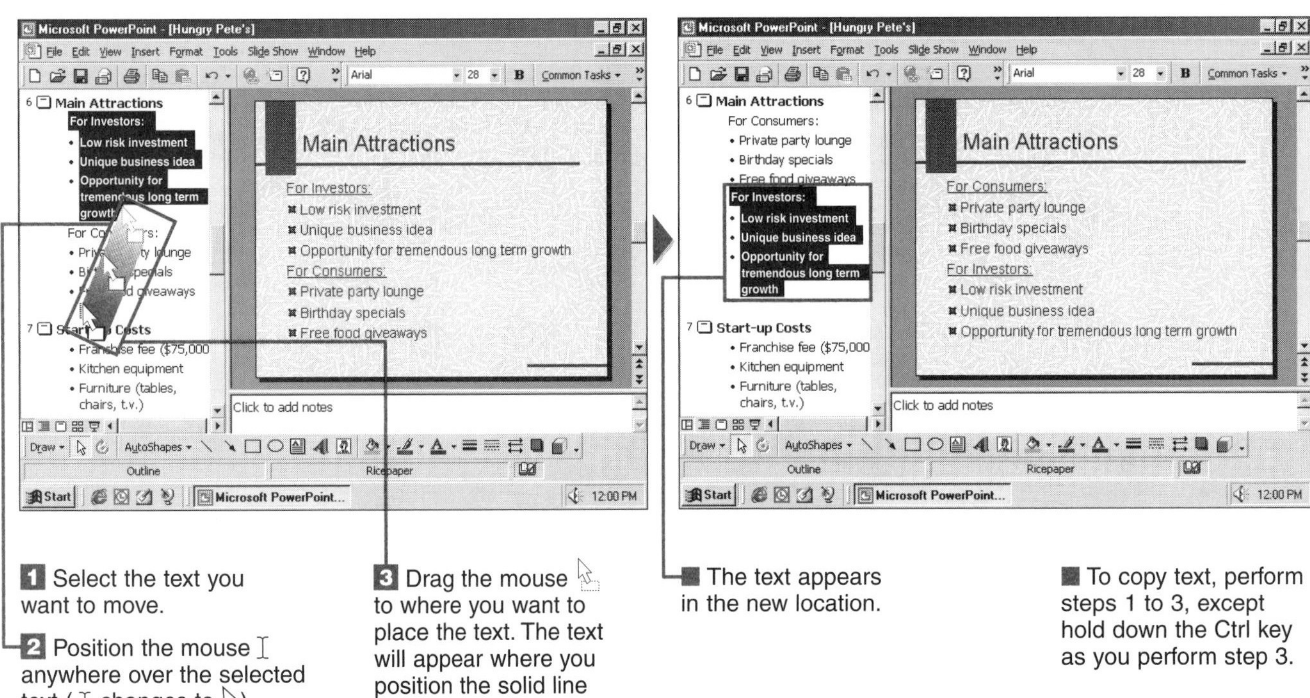

1 Select the text you want to move.

2 Position the mouse I anywhere over the selected text (I changes to ↖).

3 Drag the mouse ↖ to where you want to place the text. The text will appear where you position the solid line or dotted insertion point on the screen.

■ The text appears in the new location.

■ To copy text, perform steps 1 to 3, except hold down the Ctrl key as you perform step 3.

UNDO CHANGES

PowerPoint remembers the last changes you made to your presentation. If you regret these changes, you can cancel them by using the Undo feature.

The Undo feature can cancel your last editing and formatting changes. For example, you can cancel editing changes such as deleting text or adding a new point to a slide. You can cancel formatting changes such as bolding a slide title or increasing the size of text.

If you do not like the results of canceling an editing or formatting change, you can easily reverse the results.

You can use the Undo feature to cancel one change at a time or many changes at once.

PowerPoint stores a list of changes you made to your presentation. When you select the change you want to cancel from the list, PowerPoint cancels the change and all the changes you have made since that change.

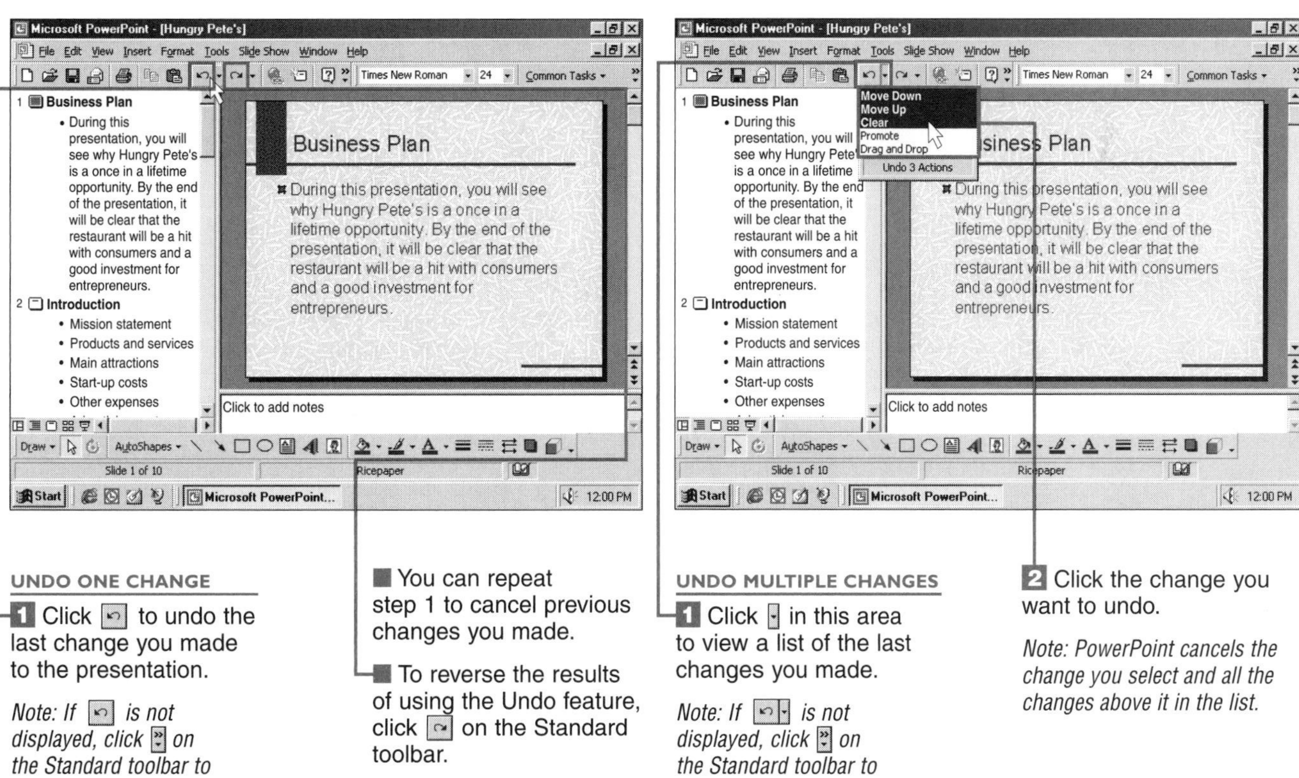

UNDO ONE CHANGE

1 Click [undo] to undo the last change you made to the presentation.

Note: If [undo] is not displayed, click [»] on the Standard toolbar to display all the buttons.

■ You can repeat step 1 to cancel previous changes you made.

■ To reverse the results of using the Undo feature, click [redo] on the Standard toolbar.

UNDO MULTIPLE CHANGES

1 Click [▾] in this area to view a list of the last changes you made.

Note: If [undo▾] is not displayed, click [»] on the Standard toolbar to display all the buttons.

2 Click the change you want to undo.

Note: PowerPoint cancels the change you select and all the changes above it in the list.

CHANGE IMPORTANCE OF TEXT

You can increase or decrease the importance of text in your presentation. Changing the importance of text can help you group related ideas together.

You can use six different levels of importance to display the text on a slide. The title of the slide displays the highest level of importance.

When you decrease the importance of text, the text becomes indented and displays a smaller font size. You can decrease the importance of text to make the text a sub-point of a main point.

When you increase the importance of text, the indent decreases and the text displays a larger font size. You can increase the importance of text you want to make a main point on a slide.

You can also increase the importance of text until PowerPoint makes the text a title on a new slide. You cannot use this method to create a new slide when working in the Slide pane in the Normal view.

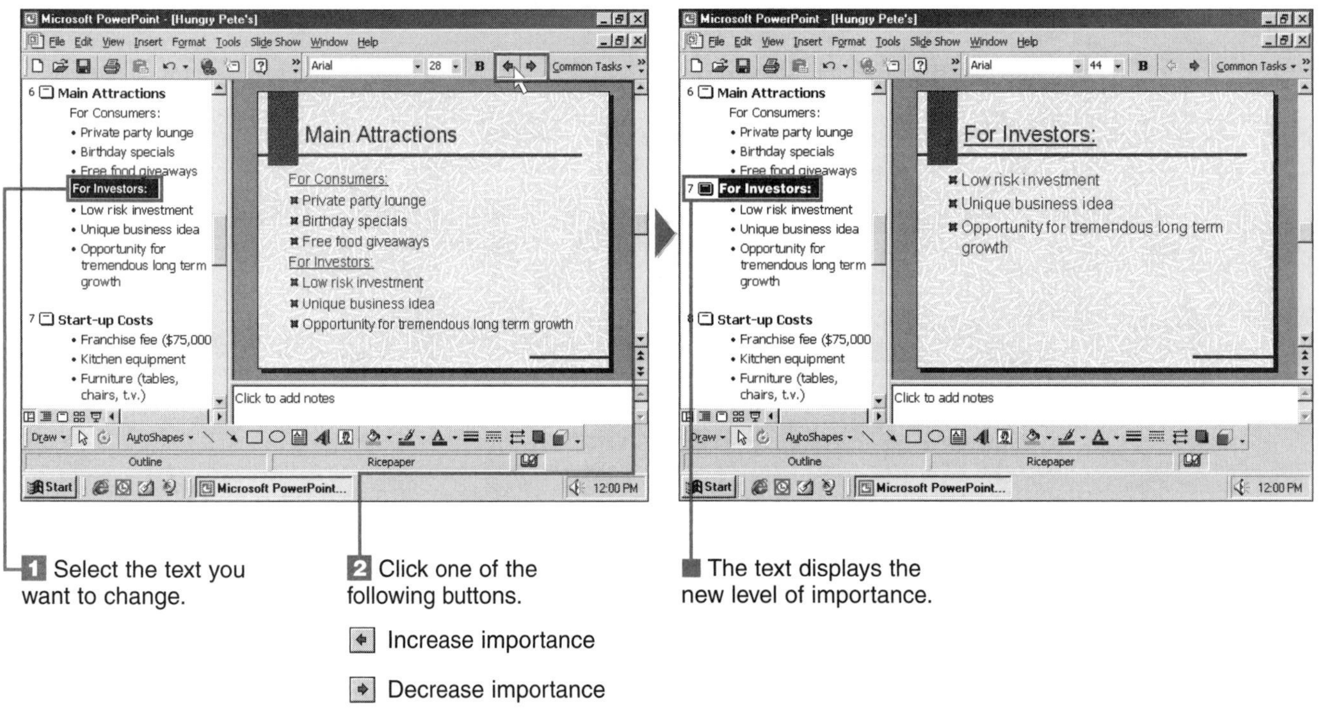

1 Select the text you want to change.

2 Click one of the following buttons.

- Increase importance
- Decrease importance

Note: If the button you want is not displayed, click » on the Formatting toolbar to display all the buttons.

■ The text displays the new level of importance.

HIDE SLIDE TEXT

You can display just the titles for each slide in your presentation and hide the remaining text. This lets you clearly view the overall structure of your presentation.

By default, the Normal view displays all the text on each slide of your presentation. If your presentation contains numerous slides, your screen will not be able to display all the slides at the same time. This can make organizing the slides in your presentation difficult. You can hide the text on slides to make your presentation more manageable.

When you hide the text on slides, only the slide titles remain visible on your screen. You can focus on the content of one slide by displaying just the text on that slide. When you want to once again view the text on all the slides, you can redisplay all the text.

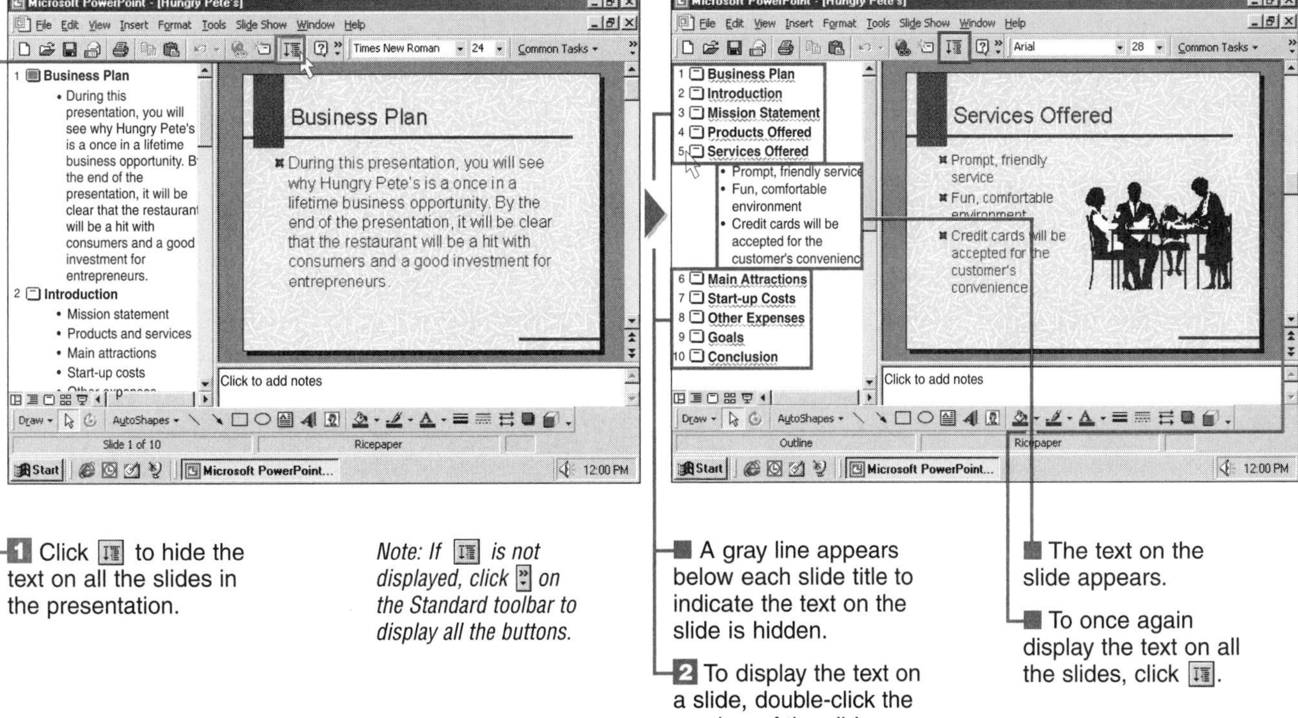

1 Click [icon] to hide the text on all the slides in the presentation.

Note: If [icon] is not displayed, click [icon] on the Standard toolbar to display all the buttons.

■ A gray line appears below each slide title to indicate the text on the slide is hidden.

2 To display the text on a slide, double-click the number of the slide.

■ The text on the slide appears.

■ To once again display the text on all the slides, click [icon].

ADD A NEW SLIDE

You can insert a new slide into your presentation to add a new topic you want to discuss.

In the Normal view, the new slide will appear after the slide displayed on your screen.

Each slide in your presentation should present information in a clear, concise and easy-to-understand format. Too much text on a slide can make the slide difficult to read and minimize the impact of important ideas. If a slide contains too much text, you can add a new slide to accommodate some of the text.

You can specify the layout you want the new slide to display. Using a slide layout saves you from having to arrange and position items on a slide. If you select a slide layout that does not suit your needs, you can change the layout later. To change the slide layout, see page 318.

After PowerPoint adds a new slide to your presentation, you can add the items you want to appear on the slide.

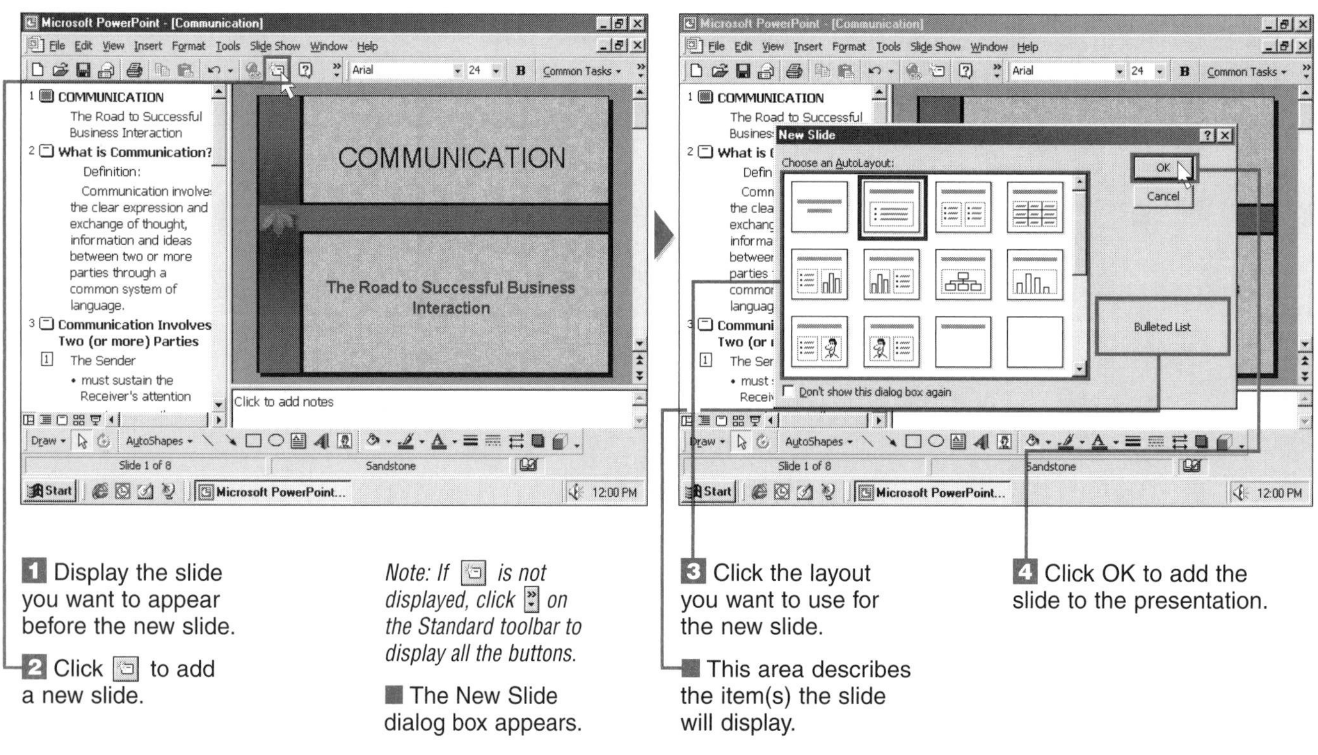

1 Display the slide you want to appear before the new slide.

2 Click to add a new slide.

Note: If is not displayed, click on the Standard toolbar to display all the buttons.

■ The New Slide dialog box appears.

3 Click the layout you want to use for the new slide.

■ This area describes the item(s) the slide will display.

4 Click OK to add the slide to the presentation.

Can I add a slide from another presentation?

✔ Yes. Click the text on the slide you want to appear before the new slide. Click the Insert menu and then select Slides from Files. Click the Browse button to locate the presentation containing the slide you want to add. Select the name of the presentation and then click Open. Click the Display button and then select the slide you want to add to your presentation. Click the Insert button to add the slide and then click the Close button. When you add a slide from another presentation, PowerPoint automatically changes the design of the slide to match the design of the current presentation.

Can I create a new slide based on an existing slide?

✔ You can duplicate a slide in your presentation to create a new slide based on the content and appearance of an existing slide. Click the text on the slide you want to duplicate. Then click the Insert menu and select Duplicate Slide.

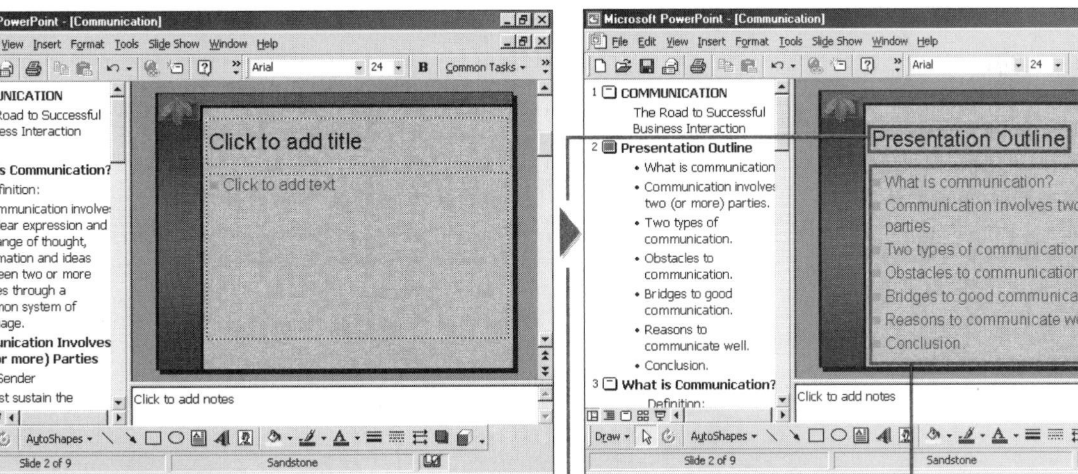

■ The new slide appears, displaying the layout you selected.

5 If the slide layout provides an area for a title, click the area and then type the title.

6 If the slide layout provides an area for a list of points, click the area and then type a point. Press the Enter key each time you want to start a new point.

CHANGE THE SLIDE LAYOUT

You can change the layout of a slide in your presentation to accommodate text and objects you want to add.

PowerPoint offers 24 slide layouts for you to choose from. Each slide layout displays a different arrangement of placeholders. Placeholders allow you to easily add objects you want to appear on a slide. There are slide layouts available that allow you to add objects such as a bulleted list, table, chart, clip art image or media clip. If you want to design your own slide layout, you can use the blank layout.

PowerPoint displays a description of the slide layout you select, indicating the type of placeholders the layout will add to the slide.

After you apply a layout to a slide, you can add the appropriate object to a placeholder on the slide. Any text a placeholder contains will disappear when you enter your text or add an object.

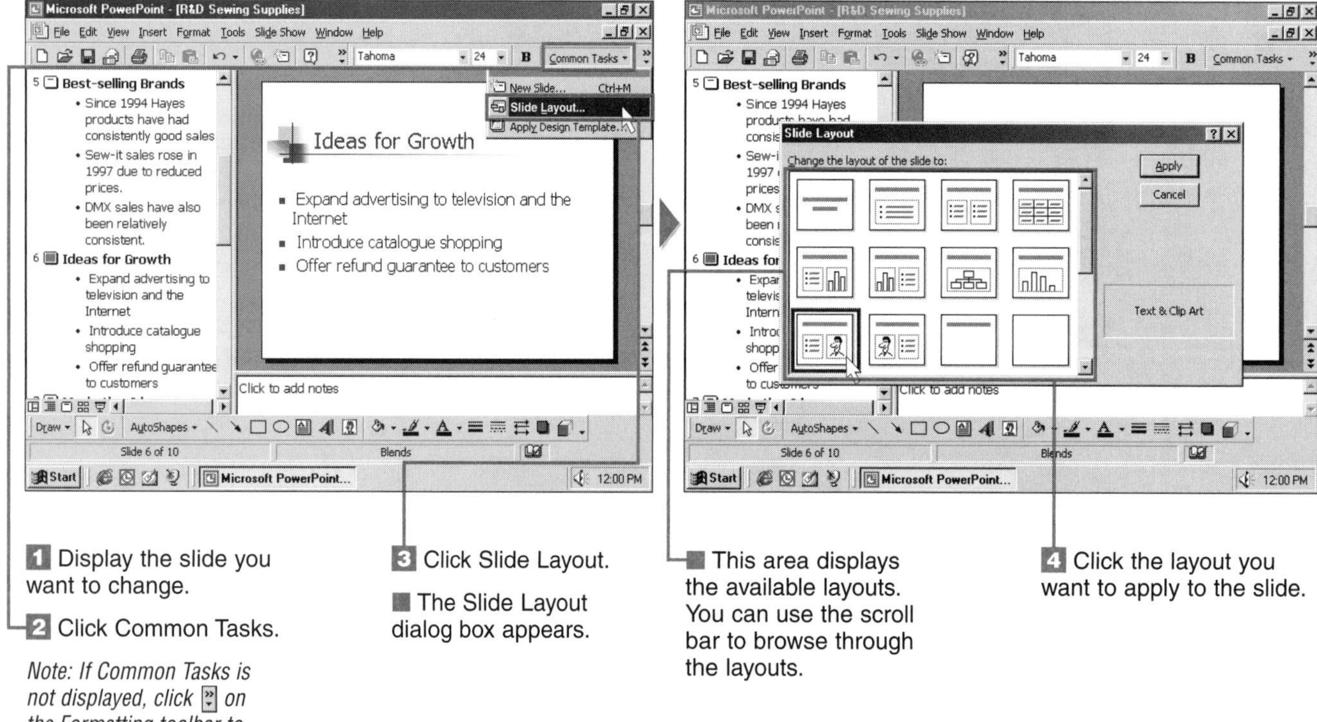

1 Display the slide you want to change.

2 Click Common Tasks.

Note: If Common Tasks is not displayed, click » on the Formatting toolbar to display all the buttons.

3 Click Slide Layout.

■ The Slide Layout dialog box appears.

■ This area displays the available layouts. You can use the scroll bar to browse through the layouts.

4 Click the layout you want to apply to the slide.

TIPS

Can I change the size of a placeholder on a slide?

✔ Yes. Click the placeholder you want to change. Handles (□) appear around the placeholder. You can drag a handle to resize the placeholder. For more information on resizing objects, see page 336.

Can I change the slide layout at any time?

✔ You should not change the slide layout after you have added an object to a slide. An object you have added will remain on the slide even after PowerPoint adds the placeholders for the new slide layout. This can cause the slide to become cluttered with overlapping objects and placeholders.

I rearranged the placeholders on a slide, but I do not like the result. How can I change back to the last slide layout I applied?

✔ Display the slide you want to change. Click Common Tasks on the Formatting toolbar and then select Slide Layout. Click the Reapply button to move the placeholders back to their default positions for the slide layout.

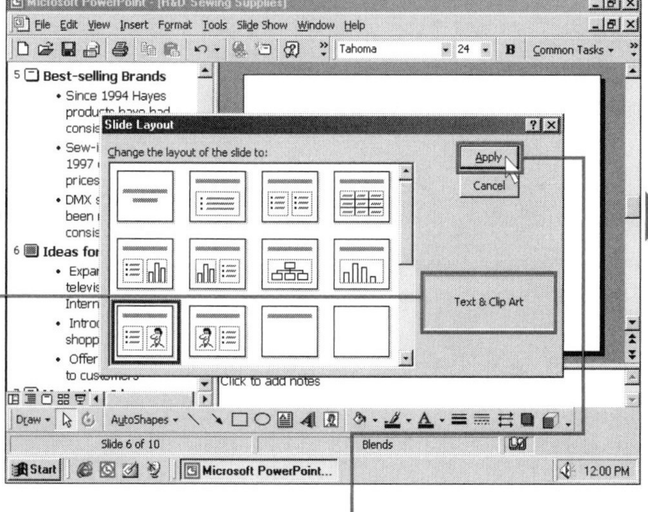

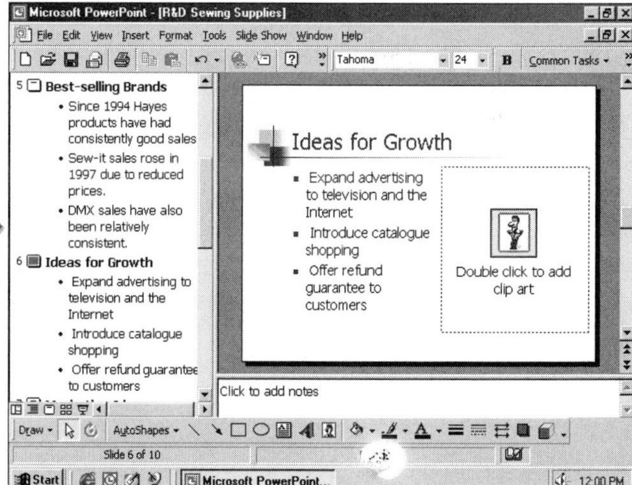

■ This area describes the object(s) the slide will display.

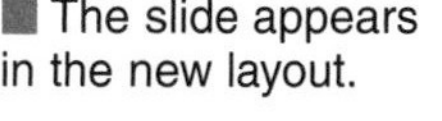

5 Click Apply to apply the layout to the slide.

■ The slide appears in the new layout.

ADD AN AUTOSHAPE

You can add simple shapes, called AutoShapes, to the slides in your presentation. Adding AutoShapes can help emphasize important information on your slides.

PowerPoint offers several categories of AutoShapes for you to choose from. You can select a category to find an AutoShape you want to add. For example, in the Basic Shapes category, you can find rectangles, ovals and triangles. In the Block Arrows category, you can find bent and curved arrows. The Stars and Banners category includes stars and ribbons. The Callouts category contains AutoShapes you can use to add captions. Captions are useful for displaying explanations or comments about items on your slides.

When you add an AutoShape to a slide, PowerPoint lets you specify the location for the AutoShape and the size you want the AutoShape to display. You can later move and resize an AutoShape to suit your slide. You can also delete an AutoShape you no longer need. For information on moving, resizing or deleting an object, see page 336.

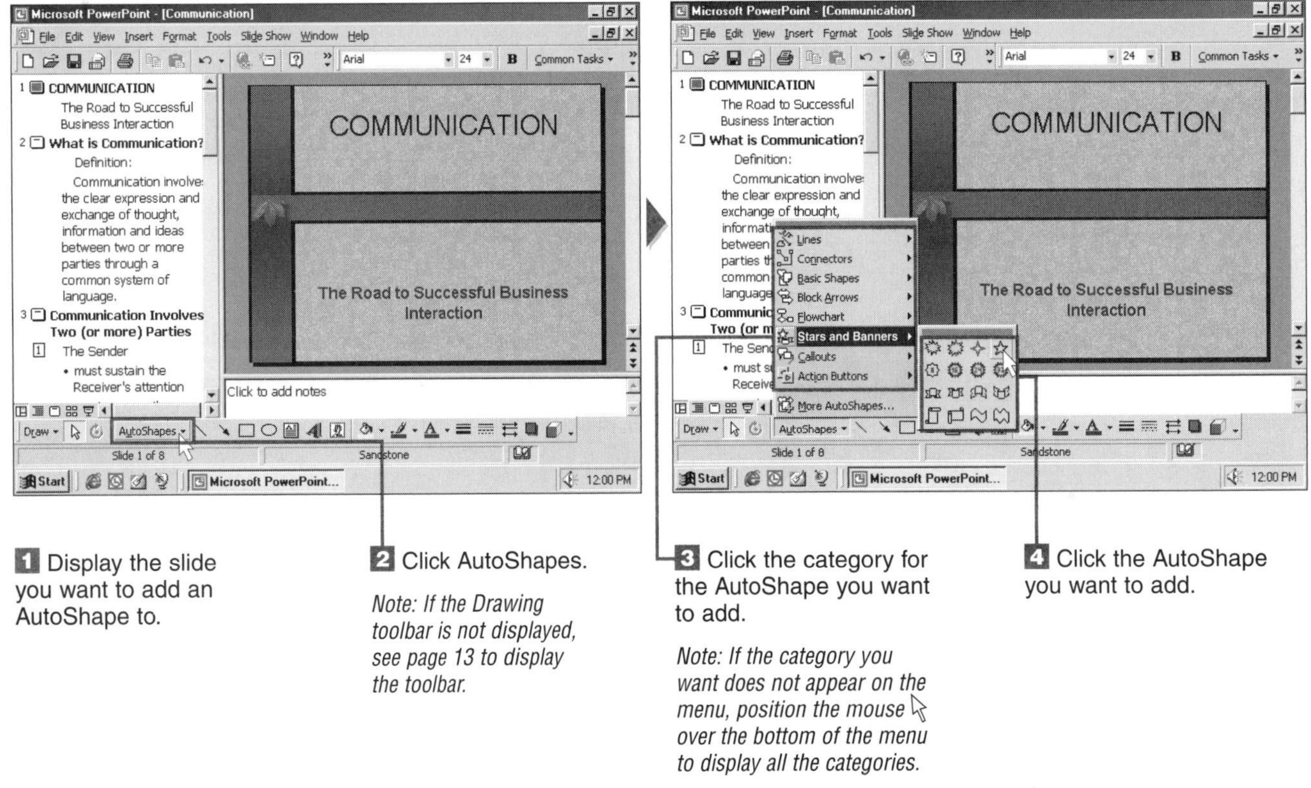

1 Display the slide you want to add an AutoShape to.

2 Click AutoShapes.

Note: If the Drawing toolbar is not displayed, see page 13 to display the toolbar.

3 Click the category for the AutoShape you want to add.

Note: If the category you want does not appear on the menu, position the mouse over the bottom of the menu to display all the categories.

4 Click the AutoShape you want to add.

TIPS

How can I change the appearance of an AutoShape?

✔ You can use the buttons on the Drawing toolbar. Click the AutoShape you want to change. To change the inside color, click ▾ beside the Fill Color button (▾) and then select a color. To change the outline color, click ▾ beside the Line Color button (▾) and then select a color. To add a shadow, click the Shadow button (■) and then select a shadow. To add a 3-D effect, click the 3-D button (■) and then select a 3-D effect.

Can I add a texture to an AutoShape?

✔ Yes. PowerPoint offers several textures, such as marble and canvas, which you can use to enhance an AutoShape. Click the AutoShape you want to change. Click ▾ beside the Fill Color button (▾) and then select Fill Effects. Click the Texture tab and select the texture you want to use. Then click OK.

Can I add text to an AutoShape?

✔ Yes. Click the AutoShape and then type the text you want to add. You cannot add text to some AutoShapes.

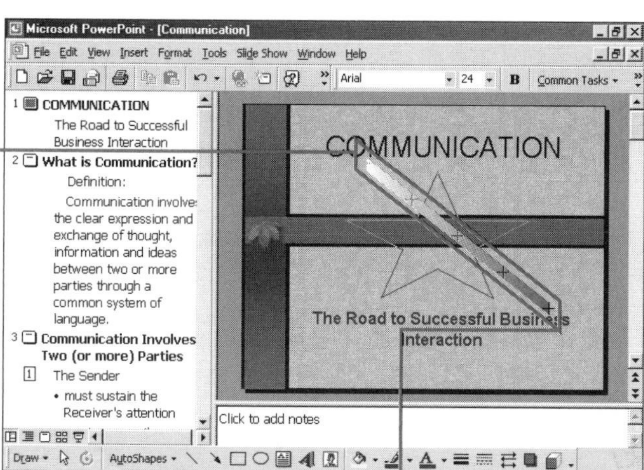

5 Position the mouse + where you want to begin drawing the AutoShape.

6 Drag the mouse + until the AutoShape is the size you want.

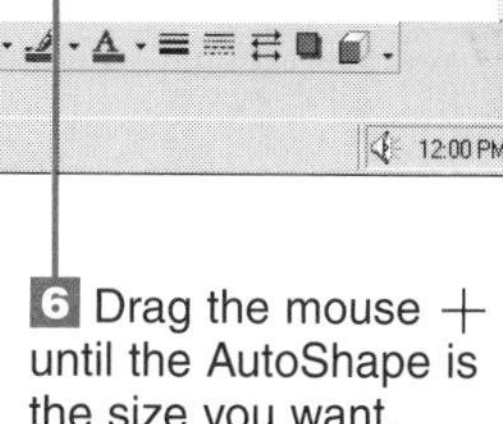

■ The AutoShape appears on the slide. The handles (□) around the AutoShape let you change the size of the AutoShape.

7 To hide the handles, click outside the AutoShape.

ADD A TEXT EFFECT

You can use the WordArt feature to add text effects to your slides. A text effect can help enhance the appearance of a title or draw attention to an important point in your presentation.

If changing the font, size and color of text does not allow you to achieve the look you want, you can add a text effect that skews, rotates, shadows or stretches the text. You can also make text appear three-dimensional.

When typing the text for a text effect, you should be careful not to make any spelling errors. PowerPoint's spell check feature does not check the spelling of text effects.

When you add a text effect, PowerPoint automatically displays the WordArt toolbar. You can use the buttons on the toolbar to change the appearance of the text effect.

You can also move and resize a text effect to suit your slide or delete a text effect you no longer need. For information on moving, resizing or deleting an object, see page 336.

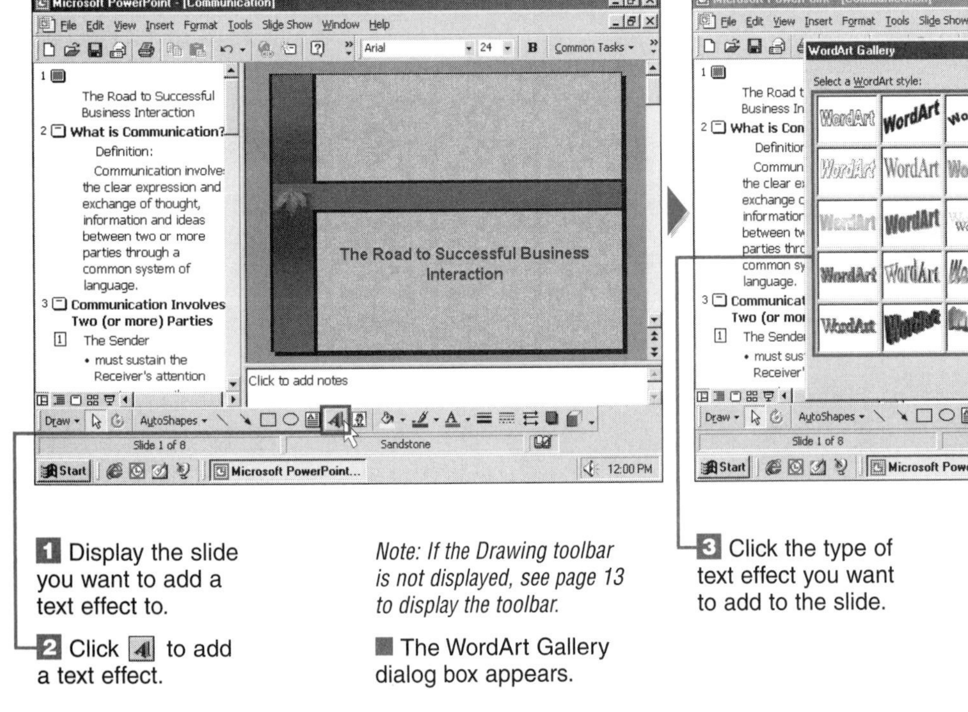

1 Display the slide you want to add a text effect to.

2 Click ![WordArt button] to add a text effect.

Note: If the Drawing toolbar is not displayed, see page 13 to display the toolbar.

■ The WordArt Gallery dialog box appears.

3 Click the type of text effect you want to add to the slide.

4 Click OK to confirm your selection.

■ The Edit WordArt Text dialog box appears.

TIPS

Can I add a text effect to existing text on a slide?

✔ Yes. Select the text you want the text effect to display and then perform steps 2 to 4 below. In the Edit WordArt Text dialog box, click OK. You can then delete the original text to remove it from the slide.

How do I edit a text effect?

✔ Double-click the text effect you want to edit. The Edit WordArt Text dialog box appears. You can use this dialog box to edit the text effect or change the font and size of the text effect. You can also bold and italicize the text effect.

How can I change the color of a text effect?

✔ Click the text effect you want to change and then use the buttons on the Drawing toolbar. To change the inside color, click ▾ beside the Fill Color button (▾) and then select the color you want to use. To change the outline color, click ▾ beside the Line Color button (▾) and then select the color you want to use.

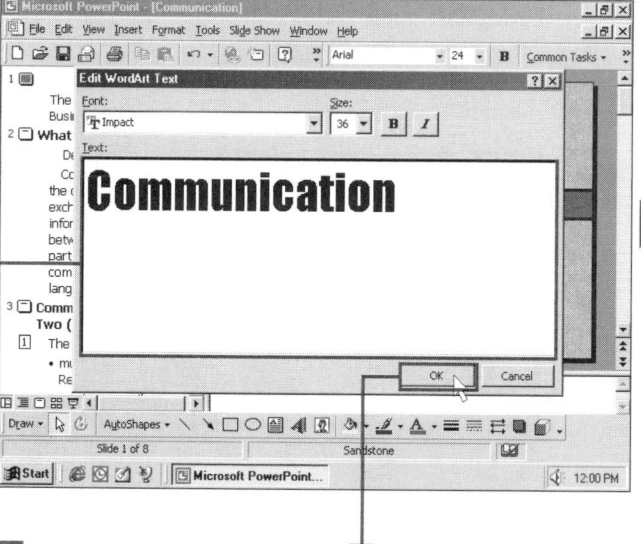

5 Type the text you want the text effect to display.

6 Click OK to add the text effect to the slide.

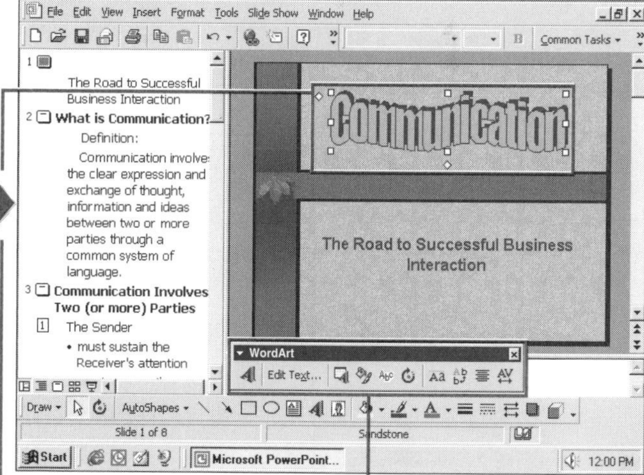

■ The text effect appears on the slide. The handles (□) around the text effect let you change the size of the text effect.

■ The WordArt toolbar also appears, providing tools to help you work with the text effect.

7 To hide the handles and the WordArt toolbar, click outside the text effect area.

ADD CLIP ART

You can add a clip art image to a slide to make your presentation more interesting and entertaining. A clip art image can illustrate a concept and help the audience understand the information in your presentation.

Before you add a clip art image to a slide, you should change the layout of the slide to create space for the clip art image.

The Microsoft Clip Gallery contains a wide variety of images divided into categories. Some of the categories are Animals, Entertainment, Home & Family, Nature, Sports & Leisure and Transportation.

The Picture toolbar automatically appears on your screen when you add a clip art image to a slide. You can use the buttons on the Picture toolbar to make changes to the clip art image.

You can move or resize a clip art image you add to a slide. You can also delete a clip art image you no longer need. For information on moving, resizing or deleting an object, see page 336.

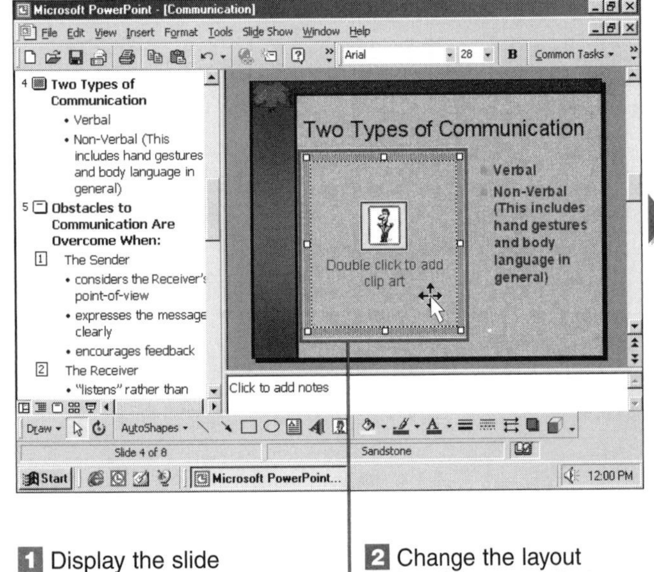

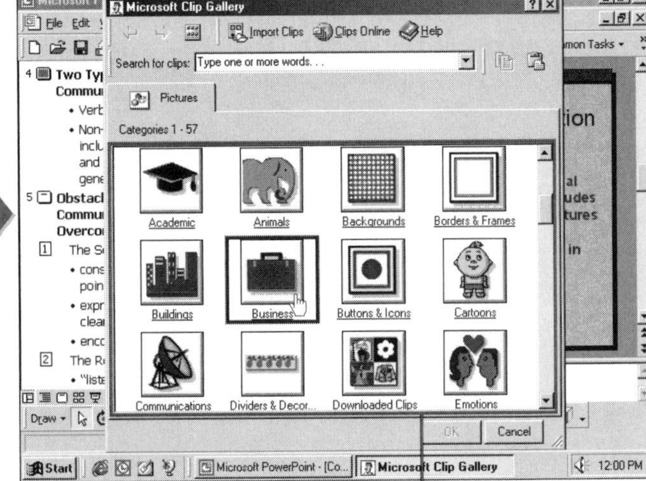

1 Display the slide you want to add a clip art image to.

2 Change the layout of the slide to one that includes a placeholder for a clip art image. To change the slide layout, see page 318.

3 Double-click the clip art area to add a clip art image to the slide.

■ The Microsoft Clip Gallery dialog box appears.

4 Click the category of clip art images you want to display.

TIPS

Can I have the same clip art image appear on each slide in my presentation?

✔ You can add a clip art image to the Slide Master to have the image appear on each slide in your presentation. For information on the Slide Master, see page 354.

How can I quickly find a clip art image of interest?

✔ You can search for clip art images in the Microsoft Clip Gallery dialog box. Click the Search for clips area, type a word or phrase describing the clip art image you want to find and then press the Enter key.

Can I add a clip art image without changing the layout of my slide?

✔ Yes. Click the Insert Clip Art button (▣) on the Drawing toolbar and perform steps 4 to 6 below. Then click ☒ in the Insert ClipArt window.

Where can I find more clip art images?

✔ If you are connected to the Internet, you can visit Microsoft's Clip Gallery Live Web site to find additional clip art images. In the Microsoft Clip Gallery dialog box, click the Clips Online button and then follow the instructions on your screen.

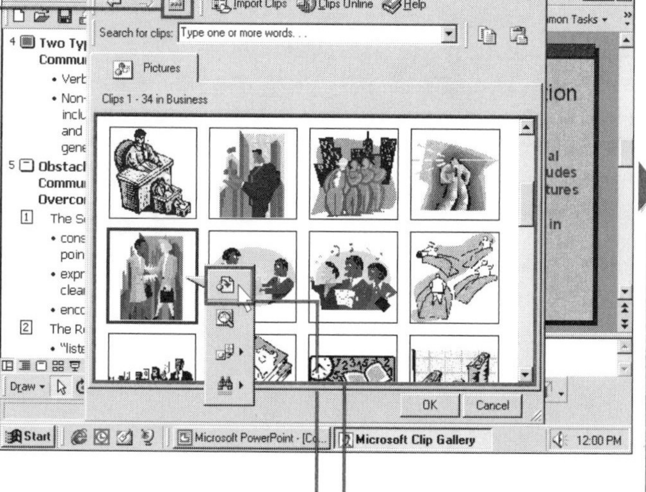

■ The clip art images in the category you selected appear.

■ To once again view all the categories, click ▦.

5 Click the clip art image you want to add to the slide. A menu appears.

6 Click ▣ to add the clip art image to the slide.

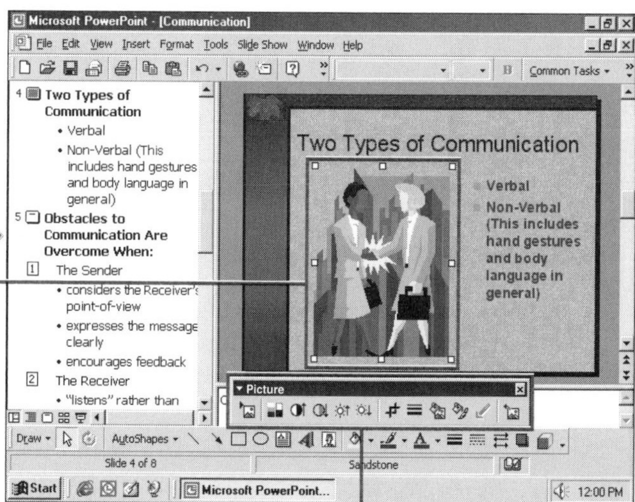

■ The clip art image appears on the slide. The handles (□) around the image let you change the size of the image.

■ The Picture toolbar also appears, providing tools to help you work with the clip art image.

7 To hide the handles and the Picture toolbar, click outside the clip art image.

ADD A PICTURE

You can add a picture stored on your computer to a slide in your presentation. Adding a picture is useful if you want to display your company logo or a picture of your products on a slide.

PowerPoint allows you to use several popular graphics file formats, including Enhanced Metafile (.emf), Graphics Interchange Format (.gif), JPEG (.jpg), Portable Network Graphics (.png), Windows Bitmap (.bmp) and Windows Metafile (.wmf).

You can specify where the picture you want to add is located on your computer. You can use the Places Bar to quickly locate the picture in a folder you frequently use. For information on the Places Bar, see the top of page 300.

The Picture toolbar automatically appears on your screen when you add a picture to a slide. You can use the buttons on the Picture toolbar to change the appearance of the picture.

You can move and resize a picture to suit your slide. You can also delete a picture you no longer need. For information on moving, resizing or deleting an object, see page 336.

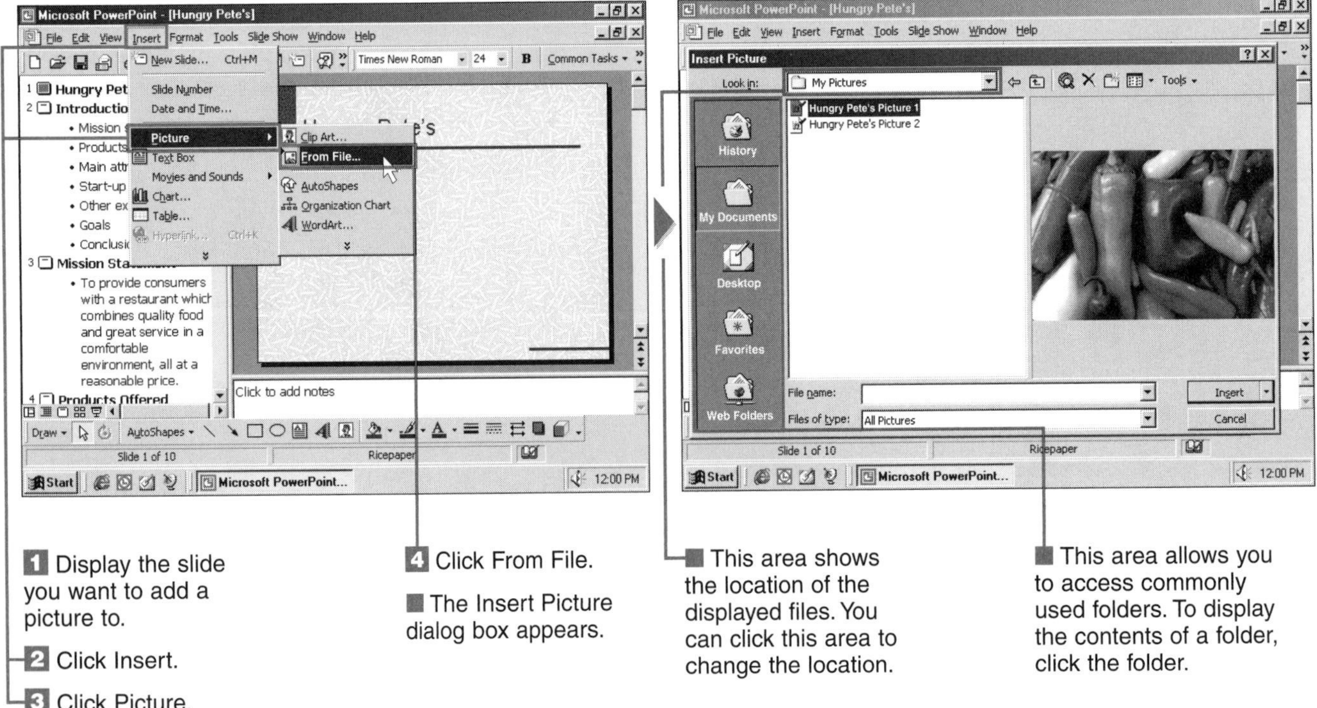

1 Display the slide you want to add a picture to.

2 Click Insert.

3 Click Picture.

4 Click From File.

■ The Insert Picture dialog box appears.

■ This area shows the location of the displayed files. You can click this area to change the location.

■ This area allows you to access commonly used folders. To display the contents of a folder, click the folder.

TIPS

The picture I added covers text on my slide. How can I move the picture behind the text?

✔ You can change the order of objects on the slide. Click the picture. On the Drawing toolbar, click the Draw button. Select Order and then choose Send to Back.

Can I have the same picture appear on each slide in my presentation?

✔ You can add a picture to the Slide Master to have the picture appear on each slide in your presentation. For information on the Slide Master, see page 354.

How can the buttons on the Picture toolbar help me change the appearance of a picture?

✔ You can use the More Contrast button (◐) or Less Contrast button (◑) to change the contrast of a picture. You can use the More Brightness button (☼) or Less Brightness button (☼) to change the brightness of a picture. The Crop button (#) allows you to trim the edges of a picture.

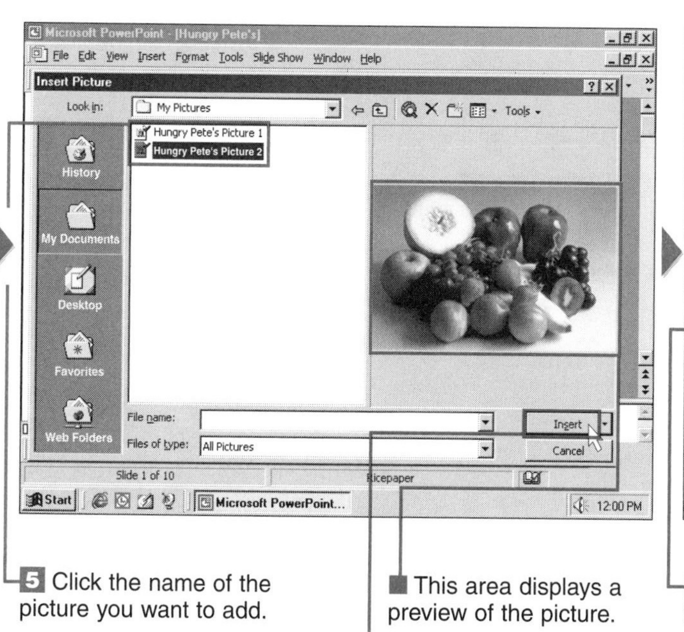

5 Click the name of the picture you want to add.

■ This area displays a preview of the picture.

6 Click Insert to add the picture to the slide.

■ The picture appears on the slide. The handles (□) around the picture let you change the size of the picture.

■ The Picture toolbar also appears, providing tools to help you work with the picture.

7 To hide the handles and the Picture toolbar, click outside the picture.

ADD A CHART

You can add a chart to a slide to show trends and compare data. Adding a chart is useful when a slide in your presentation contains numerical data. A chart is more appealing and often easier to understand than a list of numbers.

The Microsoft Graph program allows you to add a chart to a slide in your presentation. This program is automatically installed on your computer when you install Office.

When you add a chart to a slide, the menus and toolbars from Microsoft Graph appear on your screen. Microsoft Graph also displays a datasheet for the chart. A datasheet is similar to an Excel worksheet, with rows, columns and cells. You cannot use formulas in a Microsoft Graph datasheet. You can replace the sample data in a datasheet with the text and numbers you want your chart to display. As you enter data in the datasheet, the chart on the slide automatically changes to display the new data.

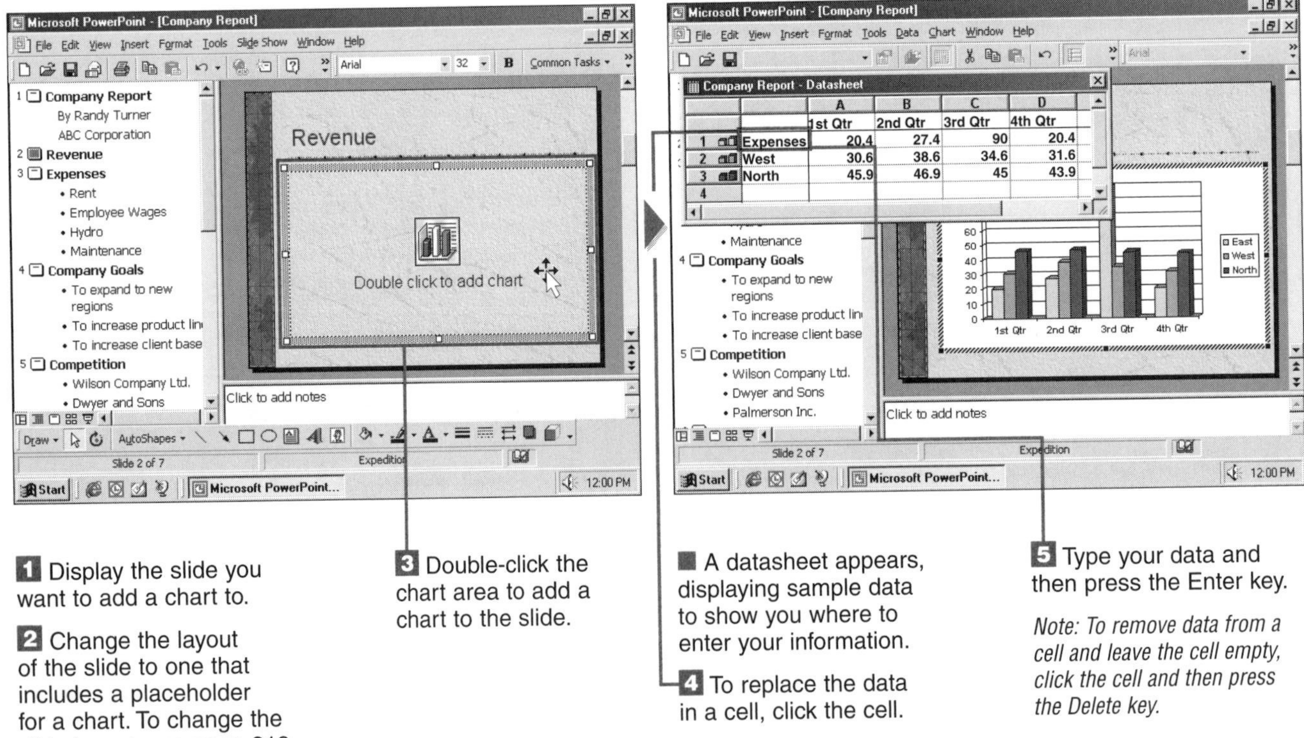

1 Display the slide you want to add a chart to.

2 Change the layout of the slide to one that includes a placeholder for a chart. To change the slide layout, see page 318.

3 Double-click the chart area to add a chart to the slide.

■ A datasheet appears, displaying sample data to show you where to enter your information.

4 To replace the data in a cell, click the cell.

5 Type your data and then press the Enter key.

Note: To remove data from a cell and leave the cell empty, click the cell and then press the Delete key.

TIPS

How can I add a chart without changing the slide layout?

✔ You can click the Insert Chart button (📊) on the Standard toolbar and then perform steps 4 to 7 below to add a chart to any slide.

Can I move, resize or delete a chart I added?

✔ You can move, resize or delete a chart as you would any object on a slide. For more information, see page 336.

Can I add a chart from Excel?

✔ Yes. In Excel, click a blank area of the chart and then select the Copy button (📋) on the Standard toolbar. In PowerPoint, display the slide you want to add the chart to and then click the Paste button (📋) on the Standard toolbar. When you use this method to add a chart, you cannot use Microsoft Graph to change the data displayed in the chart.

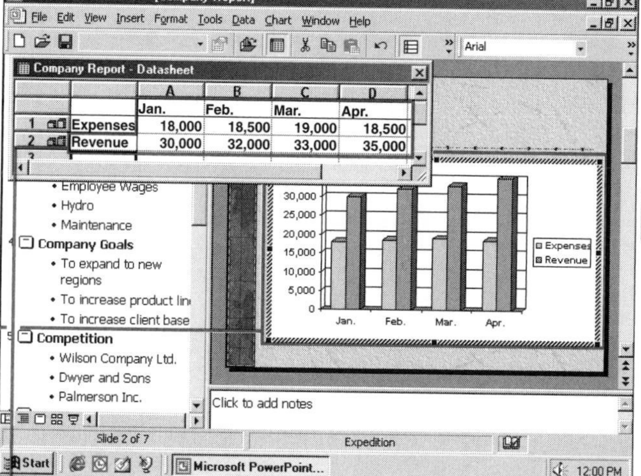

6 Repeat steps 4 and 5 until you finish entering all of your data.

■ As you enter data, PowerPoint updates the chart on the slide.

7 When you finish entering data for the chart, click a blank area on the screen to hide the datasheet.

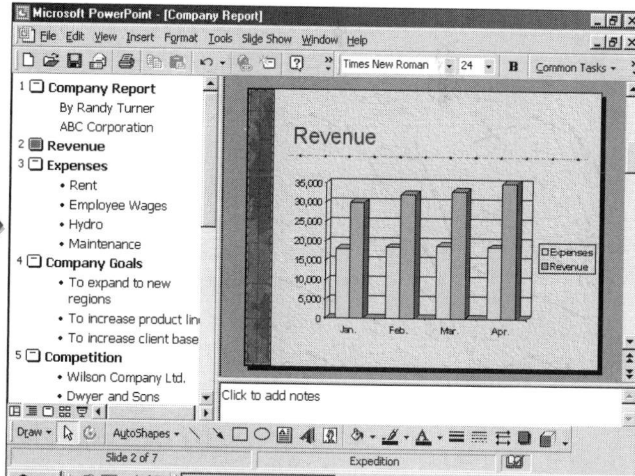

■ The datasheet disappears and you can clearly view the chart on the slide.

ADD A CHART CONTINUED

You can change a chart you added to a slide. To make changes to a chart, the chart must be active. An active chart is surrounded by a thick border and handles (■).

You can edit the data in the datasheet at any time to update the data plotted in the chart.

Microsoft Graph allows you to change the chart type to suit your data. There are several chart types available for you to choose from. The area, column and line charts are useful for showing changes to values over time. A pie chart is ideal for showing percentages.

You can plot data by row or column. Changing the way data is plotted determines what information appears on the X-axis.

You can change the format of numbers on an axis to help make the numbers easier to read. You can use the Currency ($1,000.00), Percent (50%) or Comma (1,000.00) number format. You can also increase or decrease the number of decimal places a number displays.

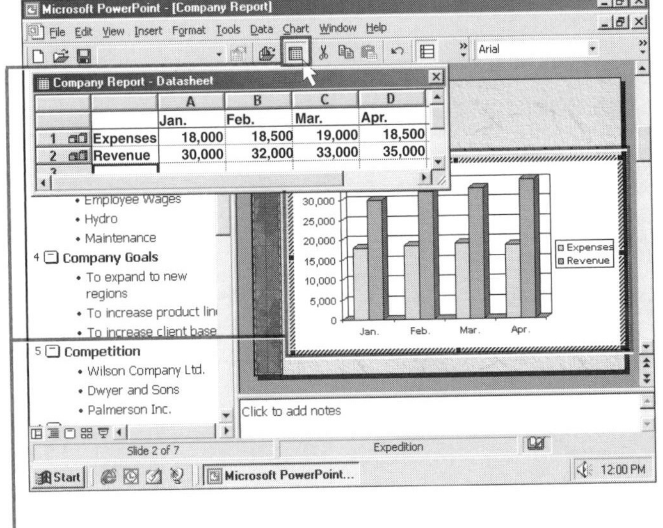

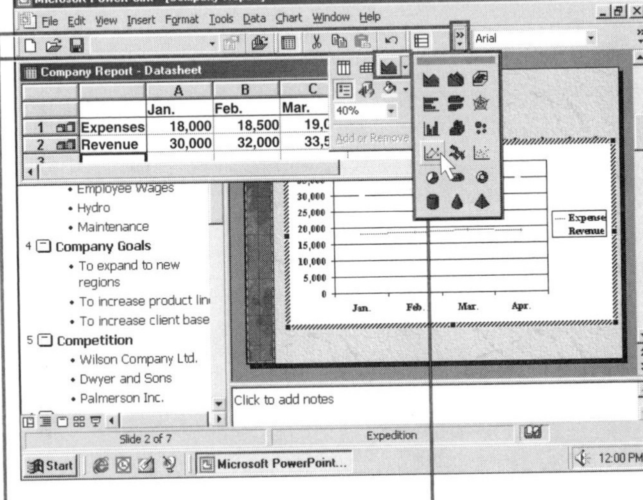

EDIT A CHART

1 Double-click the chart area to activate the chart.

2 To display the datasheet for the chart, click ▦.

Note: If ▦ is not displayed, click » on the Standard toolbar to display all the buttons.

■ You can now edit the data in the datasheet and change the appearance of the chart.

CHANGE CHART TYPE

1 Click » on the Standard toolbar to display all the buttons.

2 Click ▾ in this area to select the type of chart you want to use.

3 Click the type of chart you want to use.

TIPS

Why does a dialog box appear instead of the datasheet when I double-click a chart?

✔ The chart is already active. When you double-click an active chart, a Format dialog box appears.

Will the datasheet appear in my on-screen presentation?

✔ The datasheet will not appear in your on-screen presentation or when you print your presentation. To make the data in the datasheet part of your on-screen and printed presentation, click the Data Table button (▦) on the Standard toolbar.

Where can I find more chart types?

✔ To display more chart types, click the Chart menu and then choose Chart Type. Click the chart type and then select the design you want to use.

How do I add a title to a chart?

✔ From the Chart menu, select Chart Options and then choose the Titles tab. Click the Chart title area and type a title for the chart. You can also add a title for each axis in your chart.

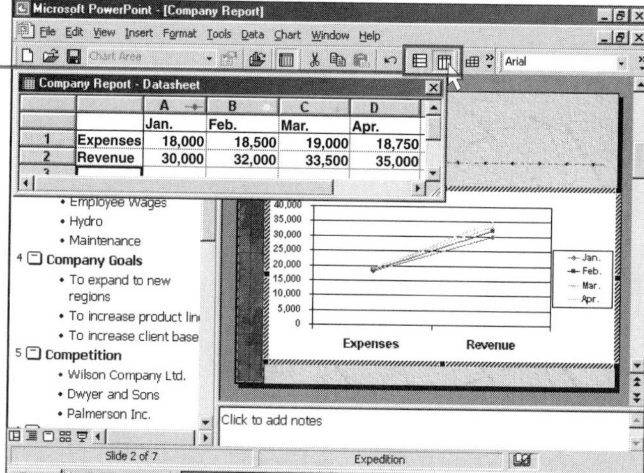

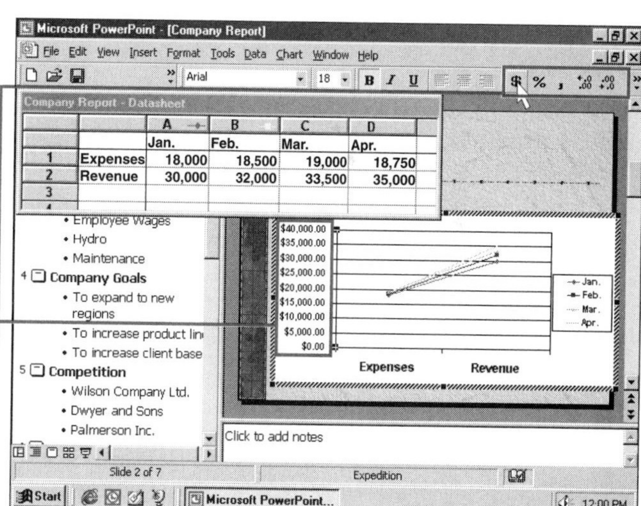

PLOT DATA BY ROW OR COLUMN

1 Click a button to change the way data is plotted in the chart.

- ▤ Plot data by row
- ▥ Plot data by column

Note: If the button you want is not displayed, click » on the Standard toolbar to display all the buttons.

CHANGE NUMBER FORMAT

1 Click the axis displaying the numbers you want to change.

2 Click the number format you want to use.

- $ Currency
- % Percent
- , Comma
- Add decimal place
- Remove decimal place

Note: If the button you want is not displayed, click » on the Formatting toolbar to display all the buttons.

ADD A TABLE

You can create a table to neatly display information on a slide. Tables can help you organize lists of information, such as a table of contents or a price list.

Before you add a table to a slide, you should change the layout of the slide to create space for the table.

A table is made up of rows, columns and cells. A row is a horizontal line of cells. A column is a vertical line of cells. A cell is the area where a row and column intersect.

You can enter any amount of text in a cell. When the text you enter reaches the end of the cell, PowerPoint may automatically wrap the text to the next line in the cell. If PowerPoint does not automatically wrap the text, you may have to press the Enter key at the end of each line. The height of the cell will increase to accommodate the text you type.

You can edit and format text in a table as you would edit and format any text in your presentation.

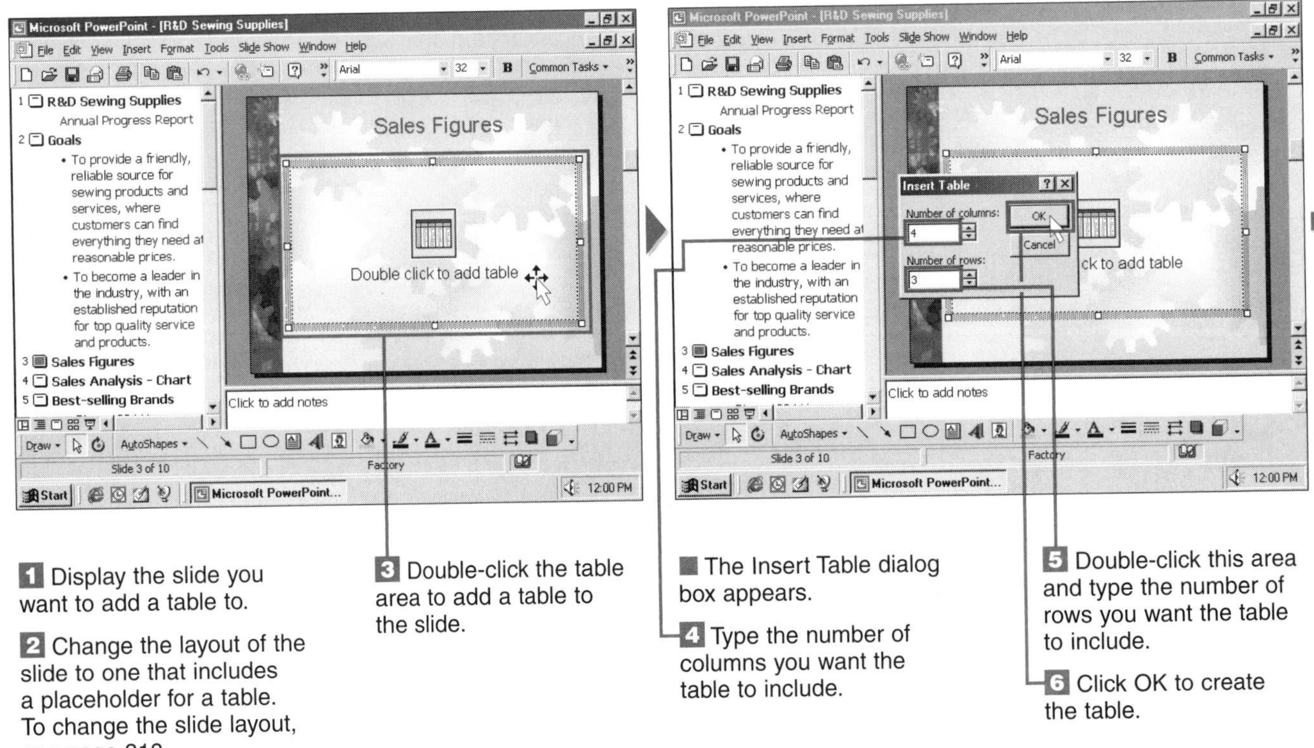

1 Display the slide you want to add a table to.

2 Change the layout of the slide to one that includes a placeholder for a table. To change the slide layout, see page 318.

3 Double-click the table area to add a table to the slide.

■ The Insert Table dialog box appears.

4 Type the number of columns you want the table to include.

5 Double-click this area and type the number of rows you want the table to include.

6 Click OK to create the table.

TIPS

Can I add a table without changing the layout of the slide?

✔ Yes. Click the Insert Table button (▤) on the Standard toolbar. Then drag the mouse pointer over the number of rows and columns you want the table to contain.

How do I delete the contents of cells in a table?

✔ To select the contents of the cells, drag the mouse I over the cells. Then press the Delete key to delete the contents of the cells you selected.

Can I rotate the text within a cell?

✔ You can rotate text within cells in your table by 90 degrees. This can help you emphasize column labels or give the table an interesting visual effect. Click the cell containing the text you want to rotate. Choose the Format menu and then select Table. Click the Text Box tab and select the Rotate text within cell by 90 degrees option (☐ changes to ☑). Then click OK.

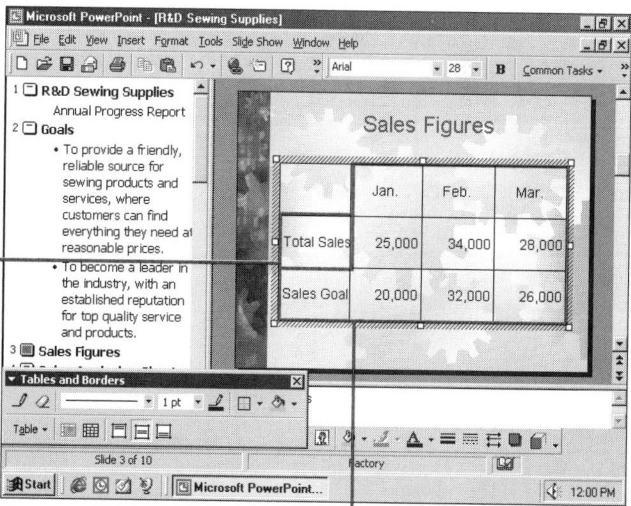

■ The table appears on the slide. The handles (□) around the table let you change the size of the table.

7 To hide the handles, click outside the table.

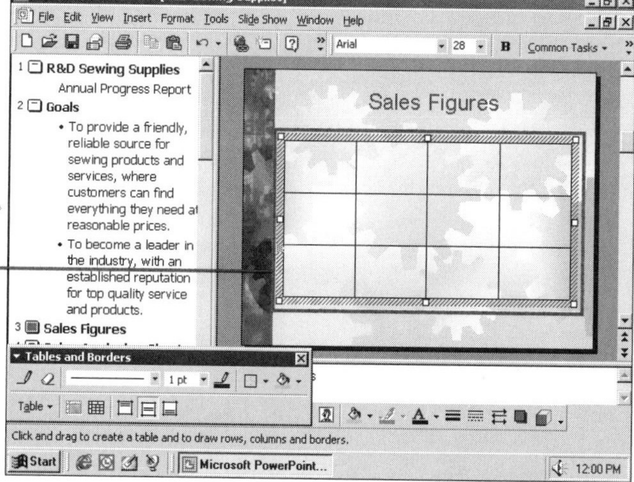

ENTER TEXT IN A TABLE

1 Click a cell where you want to type text in the table. Then type the text.

2 Repeat step 1 until you have typed all the text.

ADD A TABLE CONTINUED

After you add a table to a slide, you can change the width of columns and the height of rows. This can help improve the layout of your table.

When you change the width of a column or the height of a row, PowerPoint displays a dashed line on your screen to indicate the new width or height.

You cannot change the width or height of a single cell. When you make changes to the column width or row height, all the cells in the column or row are affected.

If you want to insert additional information into your table, you can add a row to the table.

After you add a row, the table may no longer fit on the slide. You may need to move or resize the table to make the table fit on the slide. For information on moving or resizing an object, see page 336.

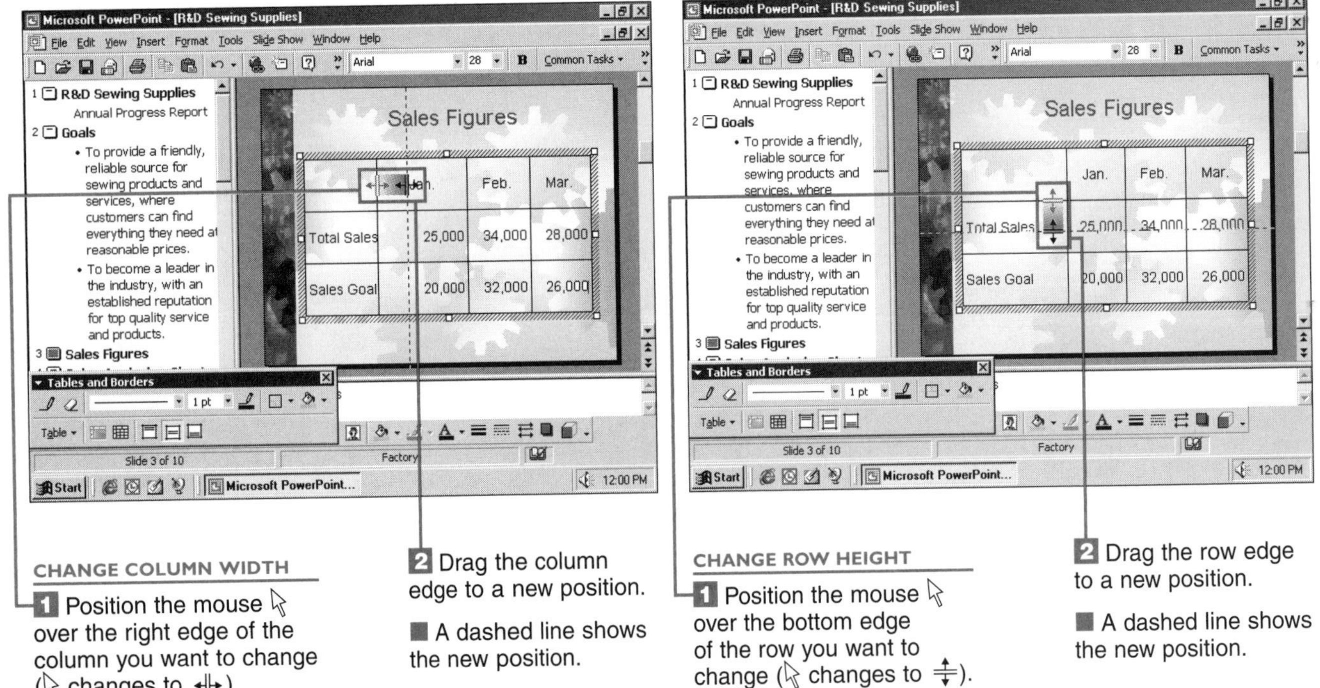

CHANGE COLUMN WIDTH

1 Position the mouse ↖ over the right edge of the column you want to change (↖ changes to ↔).

2 Drag the column edge to a new position.

■ A dashed line shows the new position.

CHANGE ROW HEIGHT

1 Position the mouse ↖ over the bottom edge of the row you want to change (↖ changes to ↕).

2 Drag the row edge to a new position.

■ A dashed line shows the new position.

TIPS

Can I add a column to my table?

✔ Yes. PowerPoint will insert a column to the left of the column you select. To select a column, drag the mouse over the cells in the column. Right-click anywhere in the selected column and then click Insert Columns.

Can I join multiple cells together?

✔ You may want to join, or merge, cells together to create space for a long line of text, such as a title across the top of a table. To select the cells you want to join, drag the mouse over the cells. Right-click anywhere in the selected cells and then select Merge Cells.

How do I delete a row or column?

✔ To select the row or column you no longer need, drag the mouse over all the cells in the row or column. Click the Cut button ( ) on the Standard toolbar to delete the row or column.

Can I delete an entire table from a slide?

✔ Yes. You can delete a table as you would delete any object on a slide. For more information, see page 336.

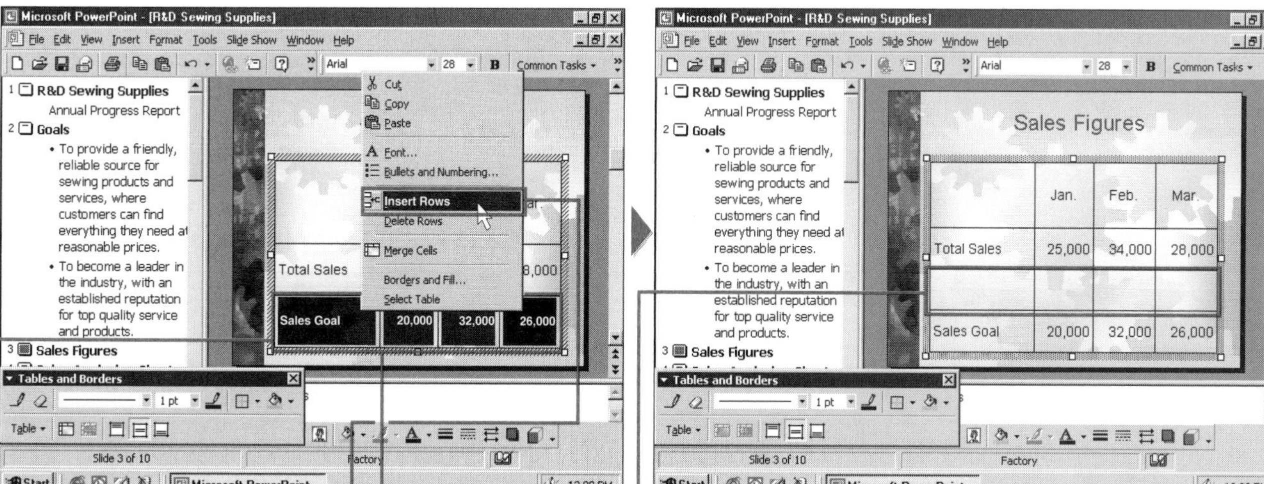

ADD A ROW

PowerPoint will insert a row above the row you select.

1 To select a row, drag the mouse over all the cells in the row.

2 Right-click anywhere in the row. A menu appears.

3 Click Insert Rows.

■ The new row appears and all the rows that follow shift downward.

■ You may need to move or resize the table to fit the table on the slide. To move or resize an object, see page 336.

■ To add a row to the bottom of a table, click the bottom right cell in the table and then press the Tab key.

MOVE, RESIZE OR DELETE AN OBJECT

You can move, resize or delete an object on a slide. An object can include an AutoShape, chart, clip art image, picture, table, text box or text effect.

PowerPoint allows you to move an object to another location on a slide. This is useful if an object covers other items on a slide. You can also copy an object from one location to another. This allows you to use the same object in more than one location on a slide.

When you select an object, handles (□) appear around the object. These handles allow you to resize the object. The handles at the top and bottom of an object allow you to change the height of the object. The handles at the sides of an object allow you to change the width of the object. The handles at the corners of an object allow you to change the height and width of the object at the same time.

You can also delete an object you no longer need from a slide.

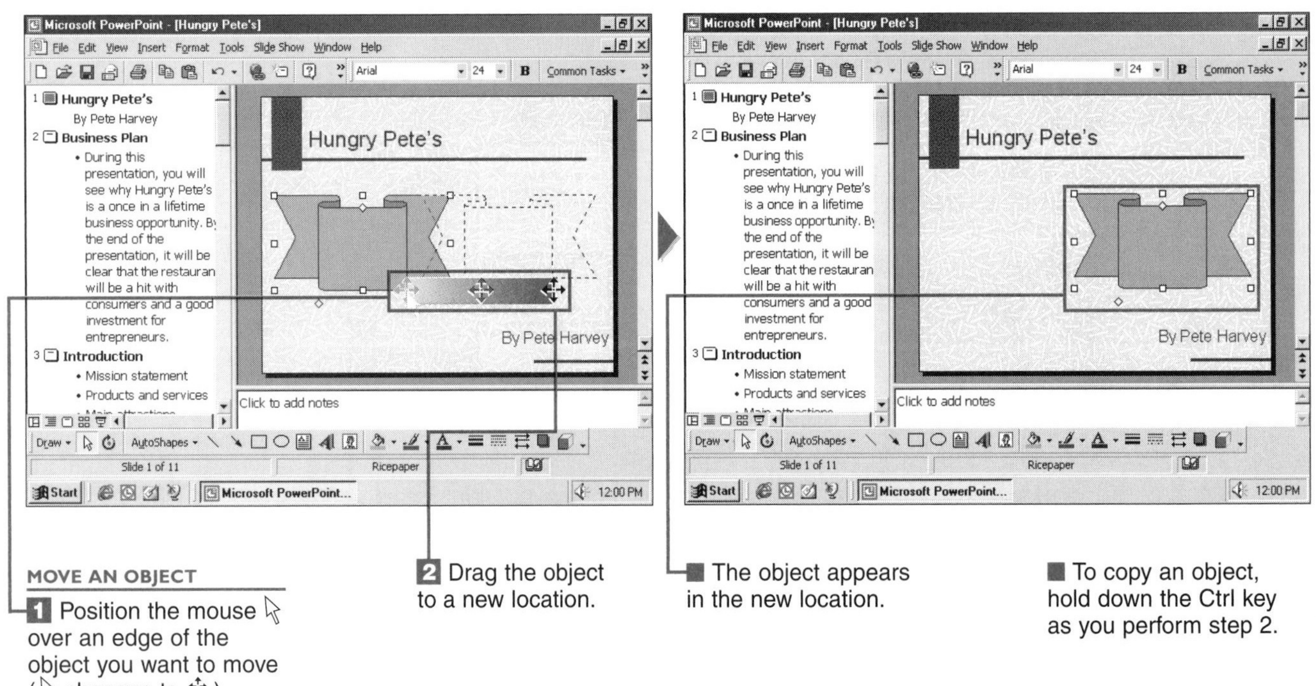

MOVE AN OBJECT

1 Position the mouse ↖ over an edge of the object you want to move (↖ changes to ✥).

2 Drag the object to a new location.

■ The object appears in the new location.

■ To copy an object, hold down the Ctrl key as you perform step 2.

Can I move or copy an object from one slide in my presentation to another?

✔ Yes. Select the object you want to move or copy. On the Standard toolbar, click the Cut button (✂) to move the object or the Copy button (📋) to copy the object. Display the slide you want to move or copy the object to and then click the Paste button (📋) on the Standard toolbar.

How can I move an object exactly where I want it to go?

✔ If you are having difficulty moving an object using the mouse, you can nudge the object using the keyboard. Select the object you want to move. Hold down the Ctrl key and press the ↑, ←, ↓ or → key to move the object.

How can I cancel a change I made to an object?

✔ PowerPoint remembers the last changes you made. You can click the Undo button (↶) on the Standard toolbar to immediately cancel a change you regret.

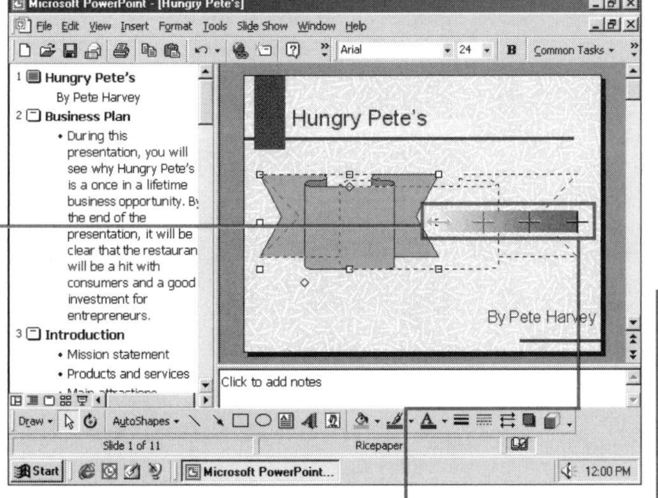

RESIZE AN OBJECT

1 Click the object you want to resize. Handles (□) appear around the object.

2 Position the mouse ↖ over one of the handles (↖ changes to ↔, ↕ or ↘).

3 Drag the handle until the object is the size you want.

■ The object appears in the new size.

DELETE AN OBJECT

1 Position the mouse ↖ over an edge of the object you want to delete (↖ changes to ✥). Then click the object. Handles (□) appear around the object.

2 Press the Delete key.

Note: You may need to press the Delete key again to remove the placeholder for the object from the slide.

CHANGE FONT AND SIZE OF TEXT

You can enhance the appearance of a slide by changing the design, or font, of text.

PowerPoint provides a list of fonts for you to choose from. Fonts you used most recently appear at the top of the list. This allows you to quickly select fonts you use often.

The fonts appear in the list as they will appear in your presentation. This lets you preview a font before you select it.

You should consider your audience when choosing a font. For example, you may want to use an informal font, such as Comic Sans MS, for a presentation you will be delivering to your co-workers. A conservative font, such as Times New Roman, may be more appropriate for a presentation you will be delivering to clients.

You should not use more than three different fonts in your presentation. Using too many fonts can make your presentation difficult to follow.

PowerPoint allows you to increase or decrease the size of text in your presentation. Larger text is easier to read, but smaller text allows you to fit more information on a slide.

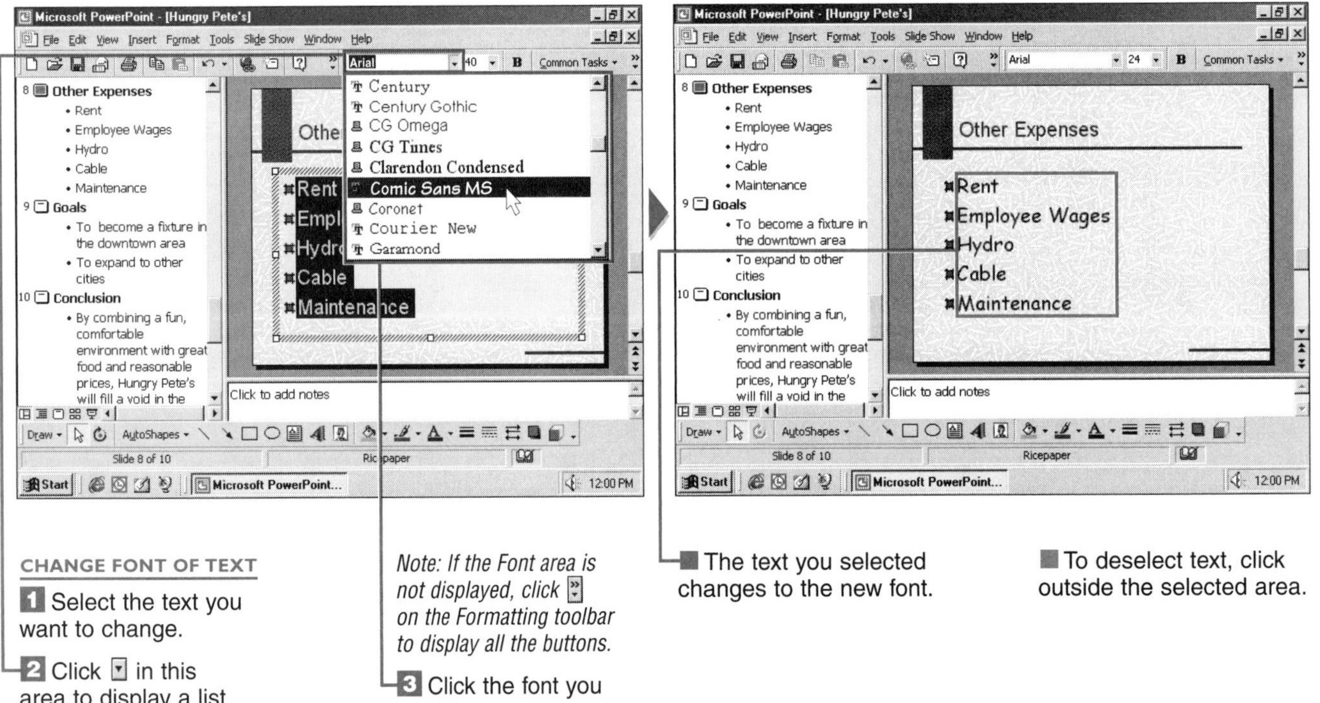

CHANGE FONT OF TEXT

1 Select the text you want to change.

2 Click ▾ in this area to display a list of the available fonts.

Note: If the Font area is not displayed, click » on the Formatting toolbar to display all the buttons.

3 Click the font you want to use.

■ The text you selected changes to the new font.

■ To deselect text, click outside the selected area.

TIPS

I plan to deliver my presentation on a computer screen. Which font should I use?

✔ You should use a font that is easy to read on a computer screen, such as Arial, Tahoma, Times New Roman or Verdana.

Can I replace a font throughout my presentation?

✔ You can replace a font on all the slides in your presentation with another font. From the Format menu, select Replace Fonts. Click the Replace area and then select the font you want to replace. In the With area, click ▾ and then choose the font you want to use. Click Replace and then click Close.

Is there another way to change the size of text?

✔ You can use the Increase Font Size button (A) or Decrease Font Size button (A) on the Formatting toolbar to change the size of text. Select the text you want to change. To increase the size of the text, click A until the text displays the size you want. To decrease the size of the text, click A until the text displays the size you want.

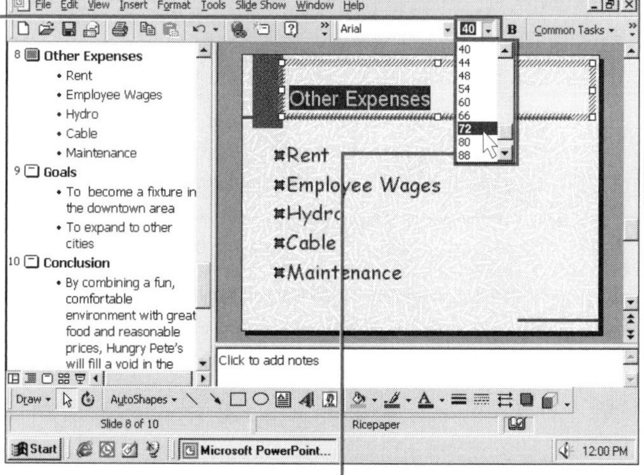

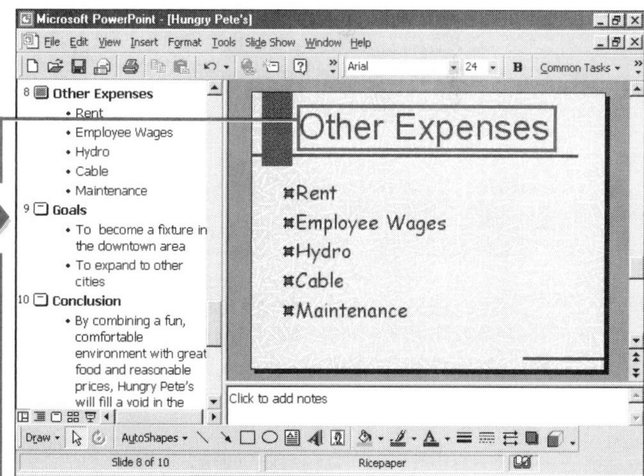

CHANGE SIZE OF TEXT

1 Select the text you want to change.

2 Click ▾ in this area to display a list of the available sizes.

Note: If the Font Size area is not displayed, click » on the Formatting toolbar to display all the buttons.

3 Click the size you want to use.

■ The text you selected changes to the new size.

■ To deselect text, click outside the selected area.

EMPHASIZE TEXT

You can use the Bold, Italic, Underline and Shadow features to change the style of text on slides in your presentation. Changing the style of text allows you to emphasize important information and enhance the appearance of slides.

You can use one feature at a time or any combination of the four features to change the style of text.

The Bold feature makes text appear darker and thicker than other text. You can bold headings and titles to make them stand out from the rest of the text on your slides.

The Italic feature tilts text to the right. You may want to italicize quotations on your slides.

The Underline feature adds a line underneath text. This is useful for emphasizing important words or phrases on your slides.

The Shadow feature adds a three-dimensional effect to text and is useful for creating eye-catching slide titles.

You should avoid overusing the Bold, Italic, Underline and Shadow features, as this can make the text on your slides difficult to read and diminish the effectiveness of the features.

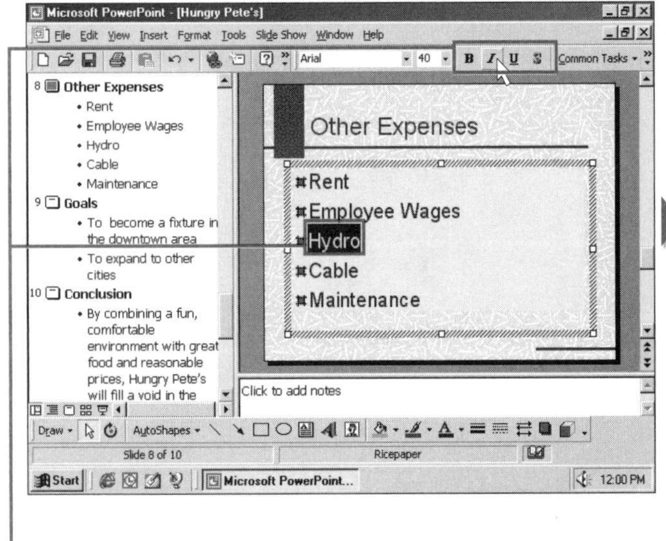

1 Select the text you want to emphasize.

2 Click one of the following buttons.

- **B** Bold
- *I* Italic
- U Underline
- S Shadow

Note: If the button you want is not displayed, click » on the Formatting toolbar to display all the buttons.

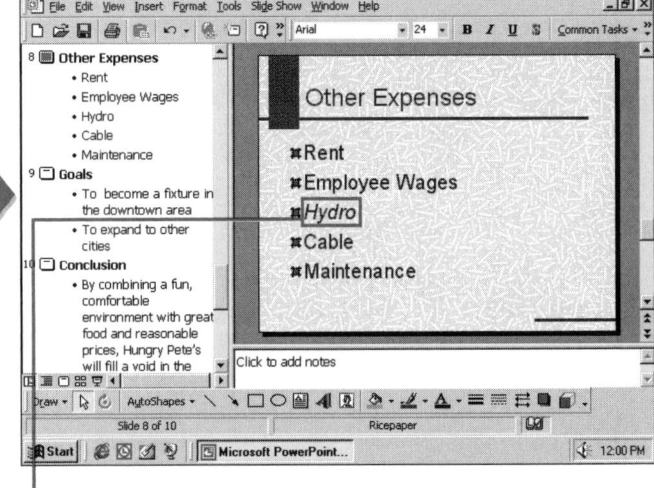

■ The text you selected appears in the new style.

■ To deselect text, click outside the selected area.

Note: To remove a style, repeat steps 1 and 2.

CHANGE ALIGNMENT OF TEXT

You can use the alignment buttons on the Formatting toolbar to change the alignment of text on a slide. Changing the alignment of text can make the text on your slides easier to read and help your audience distinguish between different types of information in the presentation.

PowerPoint uses text boxes to display text on a slide. When you change the alignment of text, you change the position of the text in the text box.

You can use the left align option to line up text along the left edge of a text box. You may want to left align the main points on a slide.

The center option lets you center text between the left and right edges of a text box.

This is useful for making headings and titles on a slide stand out.

You can use the right align option to line up text along the right edge of a text box. You may want to right align short lists of information on a slide.

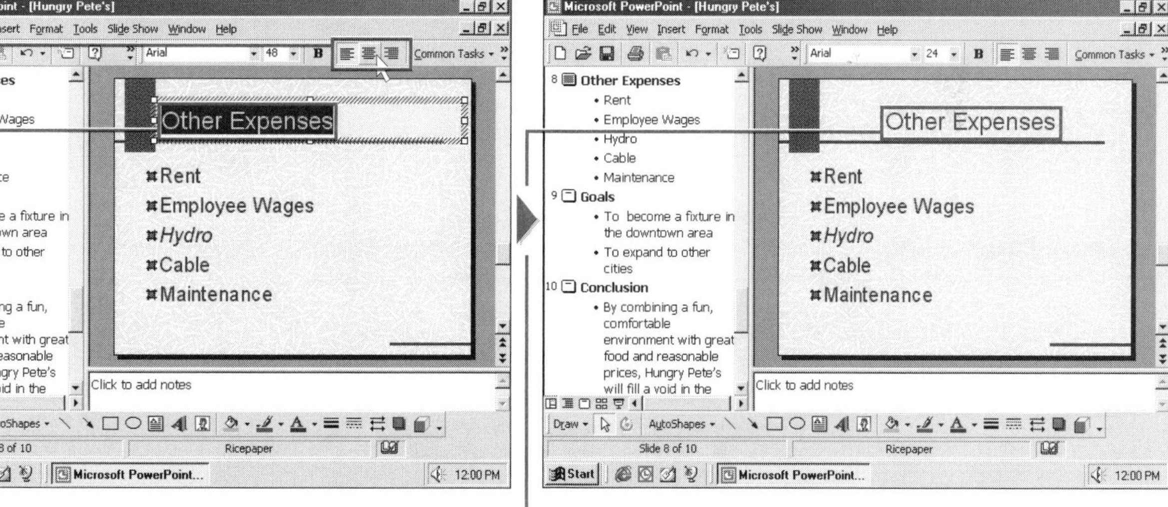

1 Select the text you want to align differently.

2 Click one of the following buttons.

Left align

Center

Right align

Note: If the button you want is not displayed, click » on the Formatting toolbar to display all the buttons.

■ The text displays the new alignment.

■ To deselect text, click outside the selected area.

CHANGE COLOR OF TEXT

You can change the color of text on a slide. This can help enhance the appearance of a slide or draw attention to important information.

You can choose the text color you want to use from a color palette. The top row of the color palette contains the eight colors used in the color scheme of the current slide. A color scheme is a set of coordinated colors for items such as the background, text, shadows and titles of a slide. For more information on color schemes, see page 348.

Make sure the text color you choose works well with the background color of the slide. For example, red text on a blue background can be difficult to read.

When you change the color of text in the Normal view, the text in the Slide pane displays the new color. The text in the Outline pane does not display the new color.

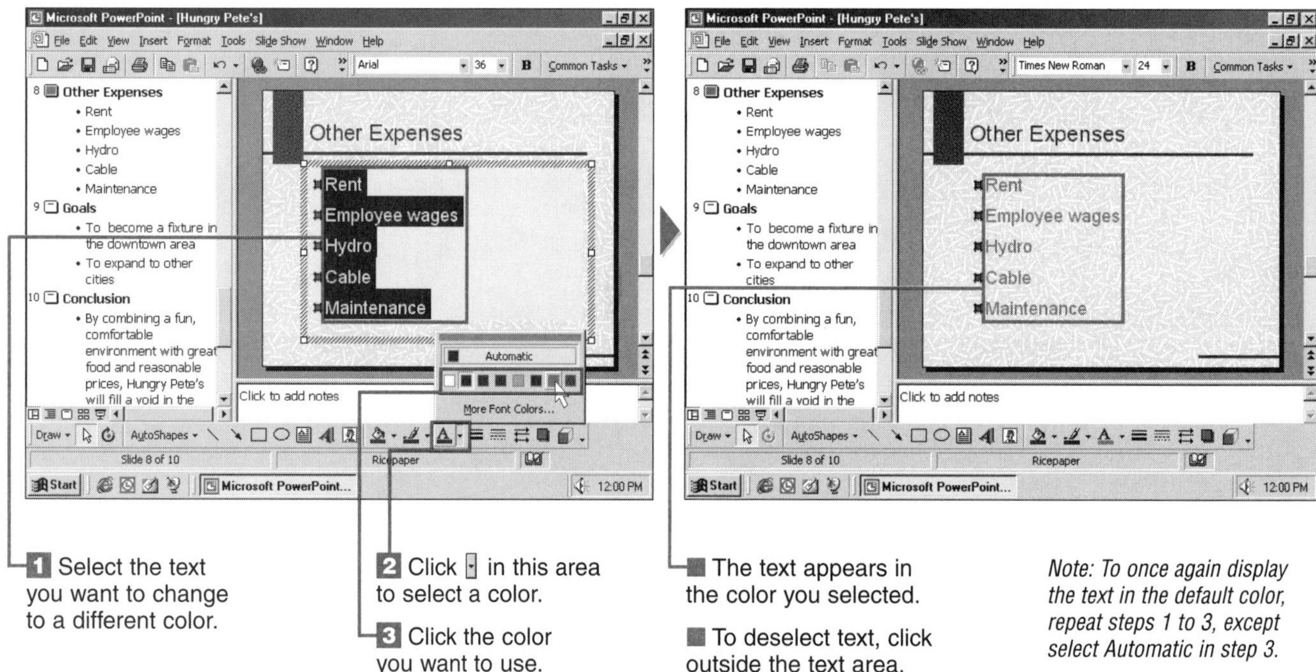

1 Select the text you want to change to a different color.

2 Click ▾ in this area to select a color.

3 Click the color you want to use.

■ The text appears in the color you selected.

■ To deselect text, click outside the text area.

Note: To once again display the text in the default color, repeat steps 1 to 3, except select Automatic in step 3.

COPY FORMATTING

You can make the text on one slide in your presentation appear exactly like the text on another slide.

You may want to copy the formatting of text to make all the titles or important information on your slides look the same. This can help give your presentation a consistent appearance.

If you copy the formatting of text that contains more than one type of the same formatting, PowerPoint will only copy the first type of formatting. For example, if you select a point that contains bold formatting followed by italics, PowerPoint will only copy the bold formatting.

You can copy formatting to text on several slides in your presentation at once. To do so, perform the steps below, except double-click the Format Painter button (🖌) on the Standard toolbar in step 2. When you have finished selecting all the text you want to display the formatting, press the Esc key to stop copying the formatting.

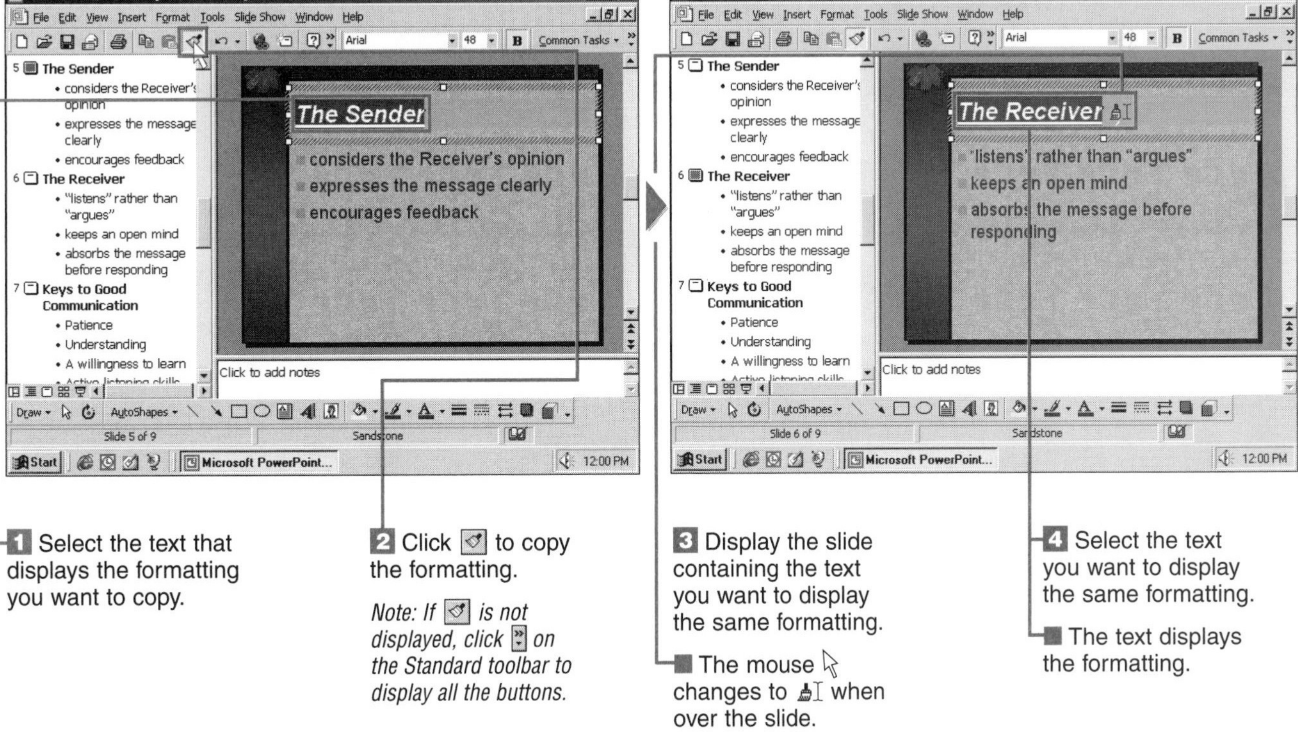

1 Select the text that displays the formatting you want to copy.

2 Click 🖌 to copy the formatting.

Note: If 🖌 is not displayed, click » on the Standard toolbar to display all the buttons.

3 Display the slide containing the text you want to display the same formatting.

■ The mouse ↖ changes to 🖌I when over the slide.

4 Select the text you want to display the same formatting.

■ The text displays the formatting.

CHANGE BULLET CHARACTER

You can change the appearance of the bullets on a slide. You can also change the bullets to numbers. Bullets are useful for items in no particular order, such as a list of expenses. Numbers are useful for items in a specific order, such as the steps required to complete a project.

You can change one, some or all of the bullets on a slide.

PowerPoint offers several bullet styles for you to choose from, including dots (•), squares (■) and check marks (✓). PowerPoint also provides several number styles you can use, including letters and Roman numerals.

You can change the color of the bullets or numbers you select. The available colors depend on the color scheme of the slide. If you want to make the bullets or numbers the same color as the default text color on the slide, you can choose the Automatic option.

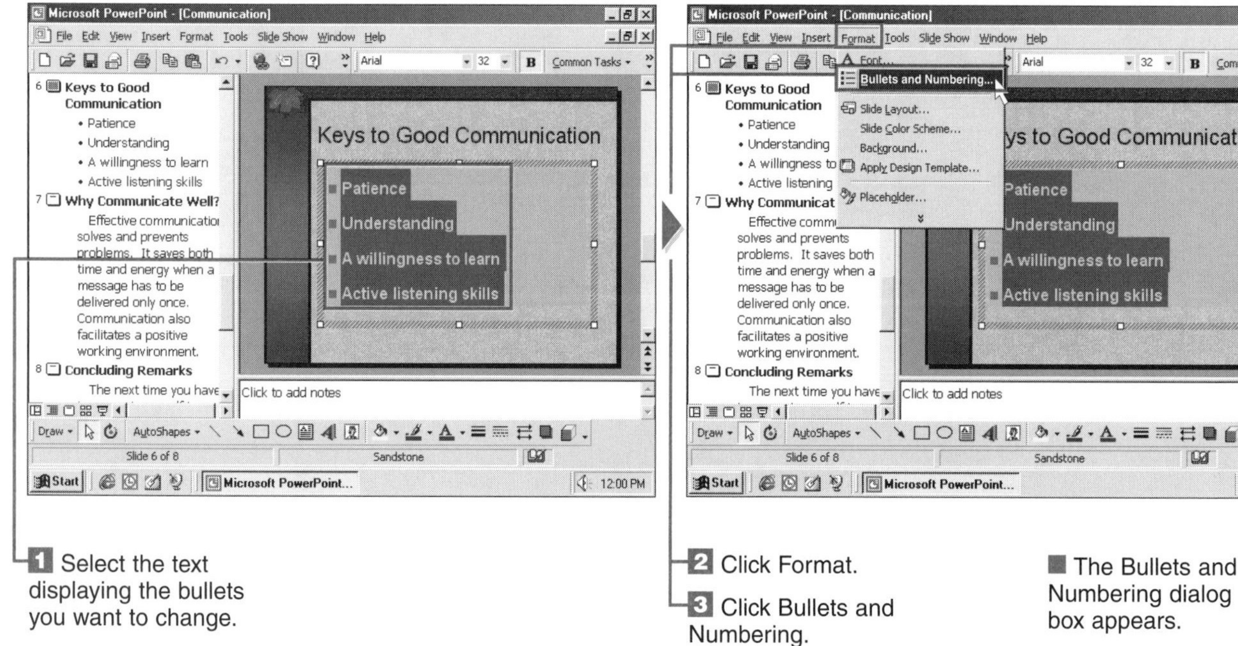

1 Select the text displaying the bullets you want to change.

2 Click Format.

3 Click Bullets and Numbering.

■ The Bullets and Numbering dialog box appears.

TIPS

How can I quickly add bullets or numbers to text?

✔ Select the text you want to display bullets or numbers. On the Formatting toolbar, click the Bullets button (☰) to add bullets or click the Numbering button (☰) to add numbers. Repeat this procedure to remove the bullets or numbers.

Are there more bullet styles I can choose from?

✔ Yes. In the Bullets and Numbering dialog box, select the Bulleted tab and then click the Character button. In the Bullets from area, click ▼ and then select the font containing the bullet style you want to use. Click the bullet style you want to use and then click OK.

How can I change the bullets on all my slides at once?

✔ Choose the View menu, select Master and then click Slide Master. Perform the steps below to change the bullets for one or more levels of text. The bullets on all your slides will change, except those you have previously changed. For information on the Slide Master, see page 354.

4 Click a tab to specify whether you want to select a bullet or number style.

5 Click the style you want to use.

■ This area displays the color for the bullets or numbers. You can click this area to select a different color.

6 Click OK to confirm your selection.

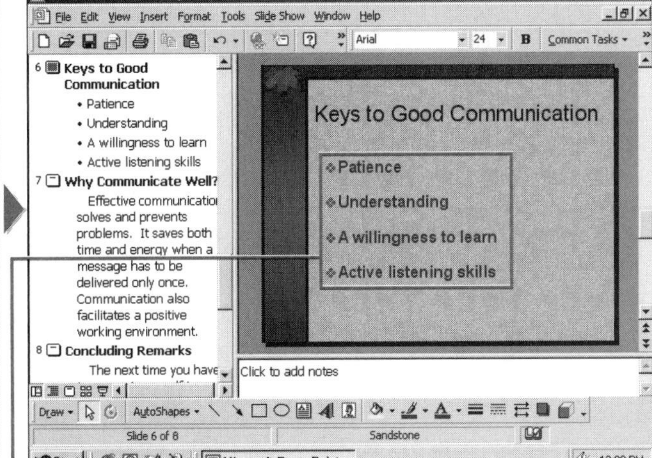

■ The text you selected displays the new bullets or numbers.

■ To deselect text, click outside the selected area.

Note: To remove bullets or numbers from text, perform steps 1 to 6, except select None in step 5.

CHANGE DESIGN TEMPLATE

PowerPoint offers many design templates that you can choose from to give the slides in your presentation a new appearance. Changing the design of your slides can help make your presentation more effective.

Some of the available design templates are Blueprint, Expedition and Marble. Each design template contains fonts, text colors and a background that work well together. You can choose the design template that best suits the content of your presentation and your intended audience. The design template you select changes only the appearance of the slides. The content of the slides will not change.

Changing the design template will not affect any formatting you have applied directly to a slide. For example, if you change the color of text on a slide and then change the design template, the text color you chose will not be affected by the new design.

After you change the design template, you should review your entire presentation to ensure that your slides appear the way you want.

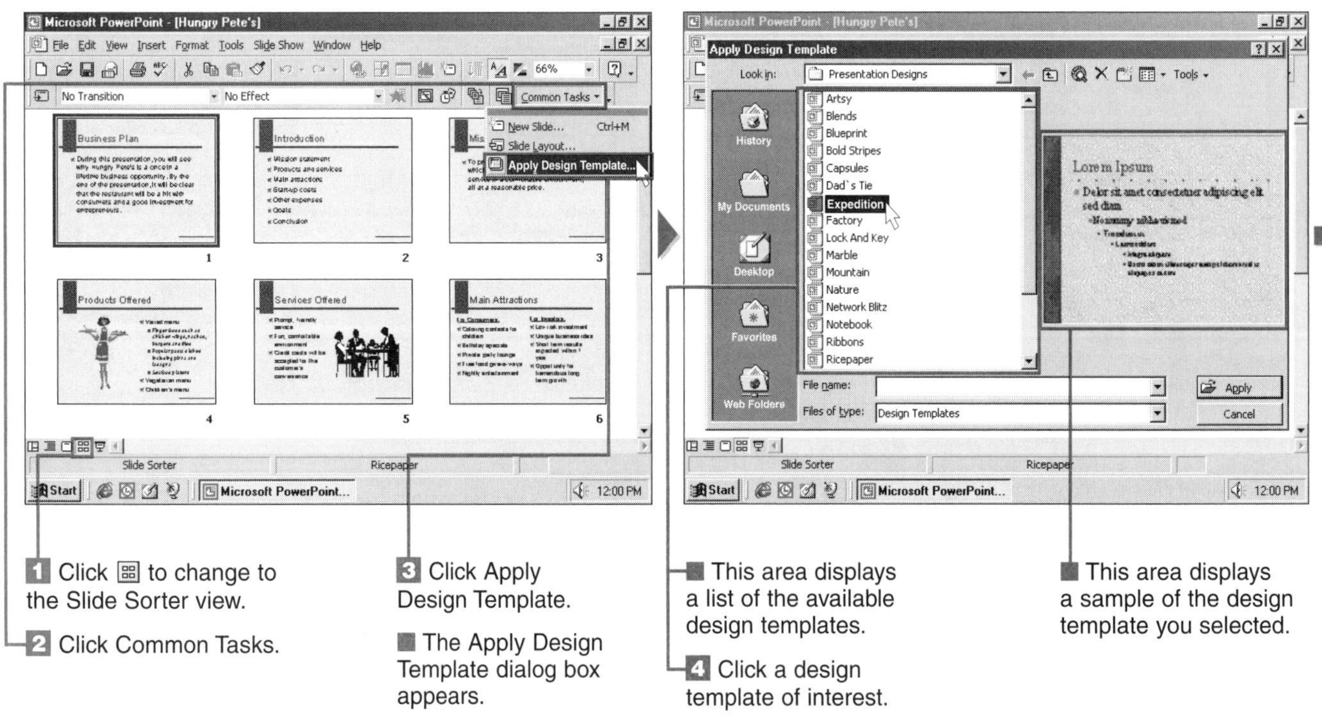

1 Click ⊞ to change to the Slide Sorter view.

2 Click Common Tasks.

3 Click Apply Design Template.

■ The Apply Design Template dialog box appears.

■ This area displays a list of the available design templates.

4 Click a design template of interest.

■ This area displays a sample of the design template you selected.

TIPS

How can I return to the previous design template?

✔ If you regret changing the design template for your presentation, you can click the Undo button (↶) to immediately return to the previous design template.

Can I change the color scheme for my presentation after changing the design template?

✔ Yes. PowerPoint provides several different color schemes for each design template. For more information on changing the color scheme, see page 348.

Can I change the background color of a slide after changing the design template?

✔ Yes. From the Format menu, select Background. In the Background fill area, click ▼ and select a new color. Then click the Apply button. To change the background color of all the slides in the presentation, click the Apply to All button.

Can I preview how the new design will look when I print my slides on a black-and-white printer?

✔ You can click the Grayscale Preview button (◩) to preview how your slides will look when printed on a black-and-white printer.

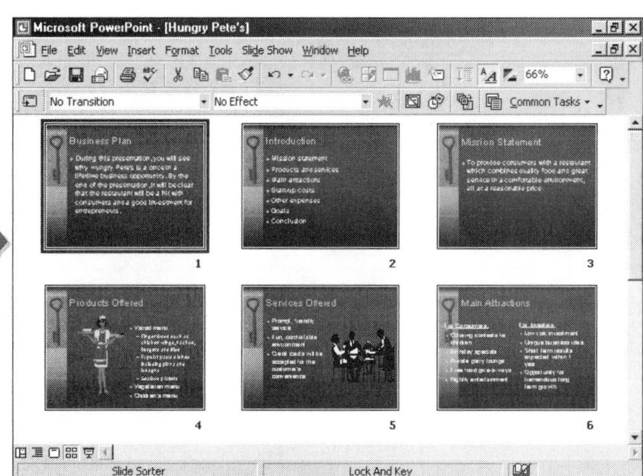

5 Repeat step 4 until the design template you want to use appears.

6 Click Apply to apply the design template to all the slides in the presentation.

■ The slides in the presentation display the new design.

CHANGE COLOR SCHEME

You can select a new color scheme for an individual slide or all the slides in your presentation. Changing the color scheme for an individual slide is useful when you want to make an important slide stand out from the rest of the slides in your presentation. Changing the color scheme for all the slides is useful when you want to keep the appearance of the presentation consistent.

The design template you are using for the presentation determines the available color schemes. For information on design templates, see page 346.

Each color scheme contains a set of eight coordinated colors, including background, text, shadow, title text and accent colors.

When selecting a color scheme, you should consider the type of presentation you will be giving. If you will be using overheads, you should choose a color scheme with a light background and dark text. If you will be using 35mm slides, you should choose a color scheme with a dark background and light text.

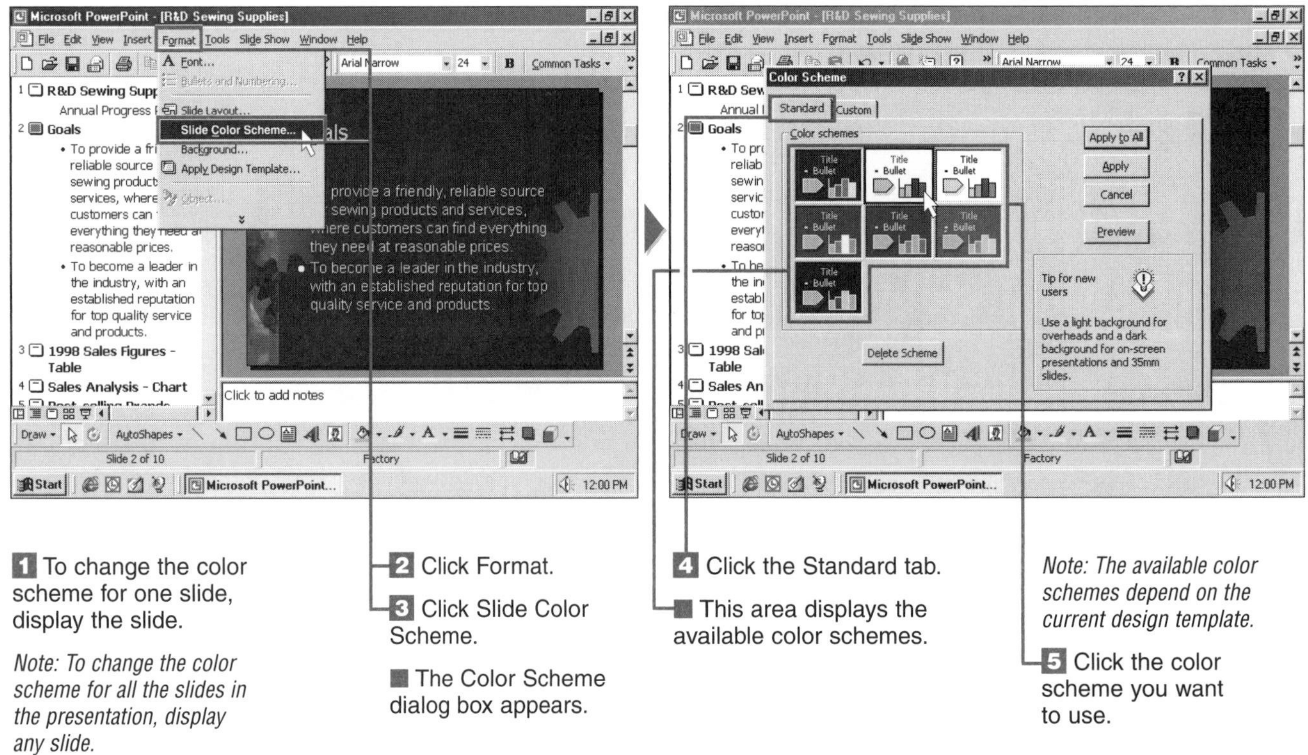

1 To change the color scheme for one slide, display the slide.

Note: To change the color scheme for all the slides in the presentation, display any slide.

2 Click Format.

3 Click Slide Color Scheme.

■ The Color Scheme dialog box appears.

4 Click the Standard tab.

■ This area displays the available color schemes.

Note: The available color schemes depend on the current design template.

5 Click the color scheme you want to use.

TIPS

How can I change a color in a color scheme?

✔ In the Color Scheme dialog box, click the Custom tab. Click the color you want to change and then click the Change Color button. Click the color you want to use and then click OK.

Can I change just the background color for a slide?

✔ Yes. Choose the Format menu and then select Background. Click ▼ in the Background fill area and then select the background color you want to use. Click Apply to apply the color to the current slide.

Can I copy a color scheme from one slide to another?

✔ To copy a color scheme from one slide to another, display your presentation in the Slide Sorter view. To change to the Slide Sorter view, see page 296. Select the slide that displays the color scheme you want to copy. Click the Format Painter button (🖌) and then click the slide you want to change.

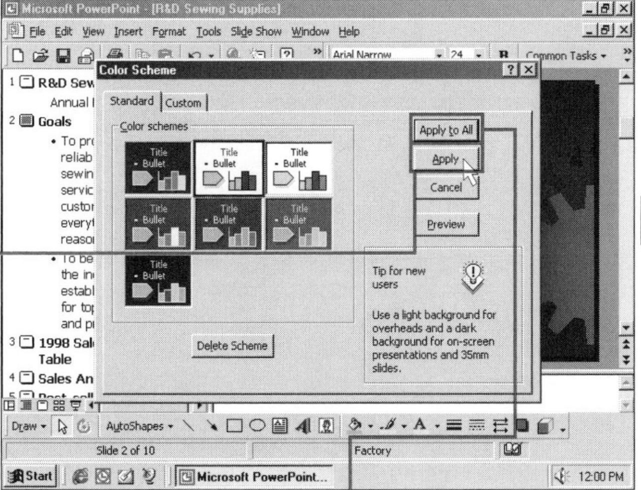

6 Click Apply to apply the color scheme to the current slide.

■ To apply the color scheme to all the slides in the presentation, click Apply to All.

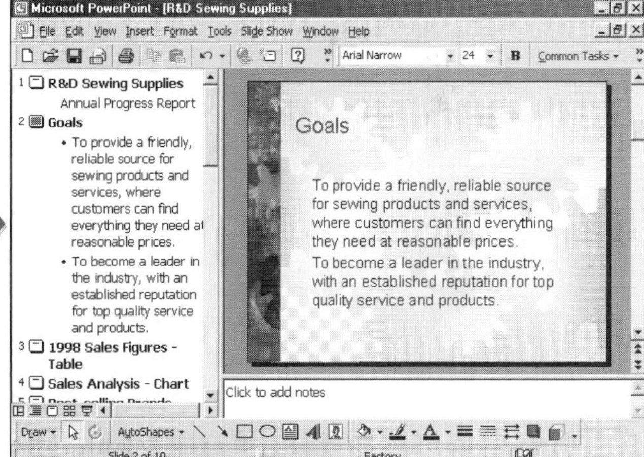

■ The slide displays the new color scheme.

ANIMATE SLIDES

You can add movement and sound to the objects on your slides. This can help you emphasize important points and keep your audience's attention throughout a presentation.

You can animate objects such as a title, list of points, AutoShape, text effect, table, picture or clip art image.

PowerPoint offers several animation effects for you to choose from. The Drive-In Effect and Flying Effect cause objects to fly onto a slide. The Laser Text Effect and Drop-In Text Effect add points to a slide one at a time. The available animation effects depend on the object you select.

You can preview an effect to see the animation and hear the sound. If you add more than one effect to a slide, PowerPoint will display the effects in the order you added them to the slide.

When you use the AutoContent Wizard to create a presentation, PowerPoint may automatically include animated objects in the presentation.

To display an animated object during a slide show, you must click the slide that contains the object. For information on viewing a slide show, see page 366.

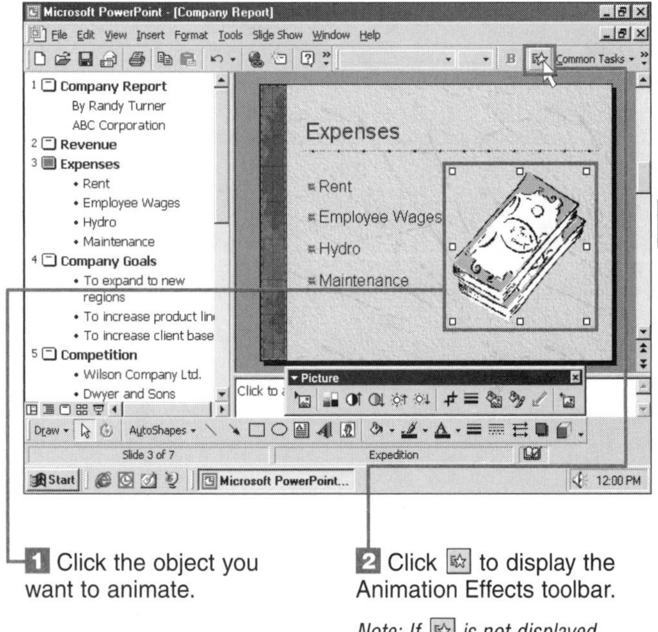

1 Click the object you want to animate.

2 Click to display the Animation Effects toolbar.

Note: If is not displayed, click on the Formatting toolbar to display all the buttons.

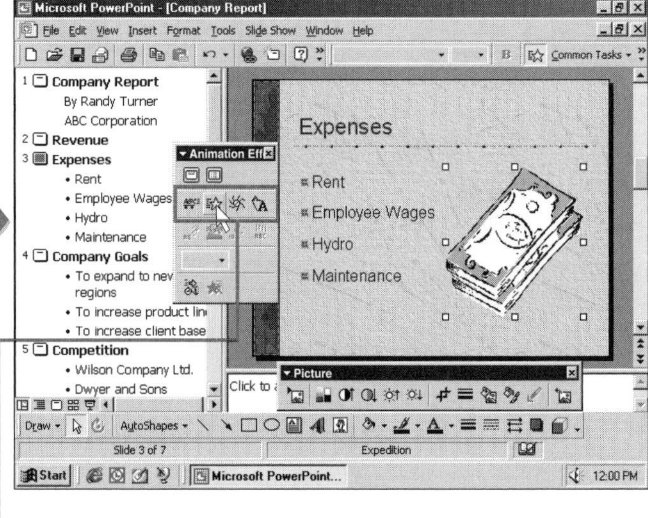

3 Click the animation effect you want to use.

Note: The available animation effects depend on the type of object you selected in step 1.

TIPS

How can I have an animated object appear automatically during a slide show instead of waiting for a mouse click?

✔ Click the animated object you want to change. From the Slide Show menu, select Custom Animation. Select the Order & Timing tab and then click the Automatically option (○ changes to ⦿). Click ▲ or ▼ to enter the number of seconds after the previous event you want the animation to occur.

How do I change the order of animations on a slide?

✔ From the Slide Show menu, select Custom Animation. Select the Order & Timing tab and in the Animation order area, click the object you want to move. Click ⬆ or ⬇ to move the object up or down in the animation order.

How do I turn off an animation?

✔ From the Slide Show menu, select Custom Animation. In the Check to animate slide objects area, a check mark (☑) appears beside each object PowerPoint will animate. Click the box beside the object you do not want to animate (☑ changes to ☐).

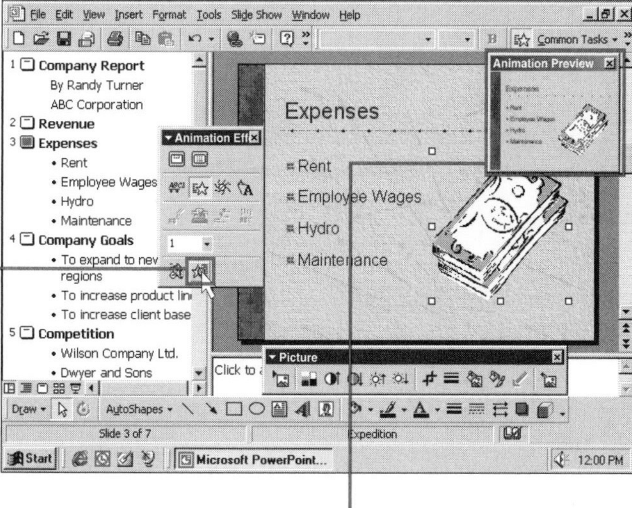

4 Click [icon] to preview the animation.

■ The Animation Preview window appears, displaying the animation. You can click the window to preview the animation again.

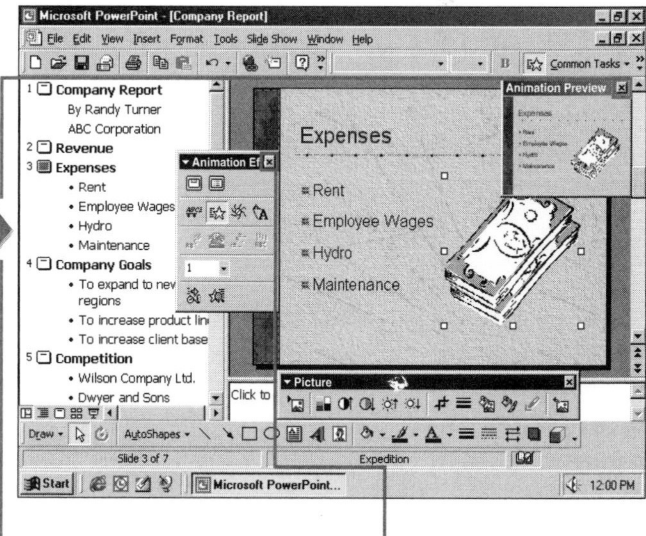

■ Click ☒ to close the Animation Preview window.

■ Click ☒ to close the Animation Effects toolbar.

CHANGE A HEADER OR FOOTER

You can display additional information at the top or bottom of every slide in your presentation. This is useful when you want the audience to keep certain information, such as the name of your company, in mind during your presentation.

You can display the date and time, a slide number and footer text on every slide in your presentation.

A footer appears at the bottom of each slide. When you use the AutoContent Wizard to create a presentation, PowerPoint may automatically add this information to your slides for you.

You can have the date and time update automatically each time you open your presentation. You can also display a fixed date and time, such as the date the presentation was created. If you choose to update the date and time automatically, PowerPoint allows you to choose from several formats, such as 4/22/99 3:59 PM.

You can also add the date and time, a page number, footer text and header text to the speaker notes and handouts for your presentation. A header appears at the top of each page.

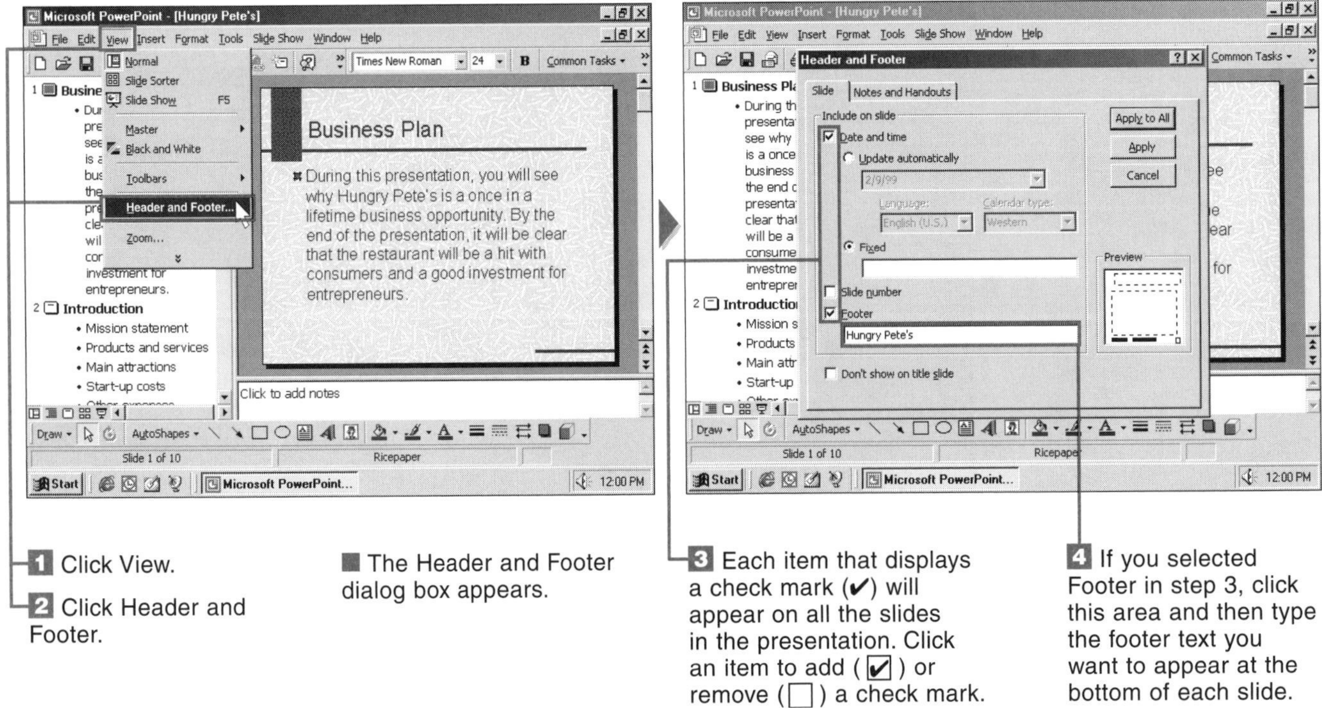

1 Click View.

2 Click Header and Footer.

■ The Header and Footer dialog box appears.

3 Each item that displays a check mark (✔) will appear on all the slides in the presentation. Click an item to add (☑) or remove (☐) a check mark.

4 If you selected Footer in step 3, click this area and then type the footer text you want to appear at the bottom of each slide.

TIPS

How can I prevent a footer from appearing on the first slide in my presentation?

✔ In the Header and Footer dialog box, select the Don't show on title slide option (☐ changes to ☑). This also removes the date and time and the slide number from the first slide.

Can I change the appearance and position of text in a header or footer?

✔ You can change the appearance and position of text in a header or footer on your slides, speaker notes and handouts. Click the View menu, select Master and then choose the appropriate Master. For more information on the Slide Master, see page 354.

Can I start numbering the slides in my presentation at a number other than 1?

✔ Yes. Click the File menu and then select Page Setup. Double-click the Number slides from area and then type the number you want to display on the first slide of the presentation. Then click OK.

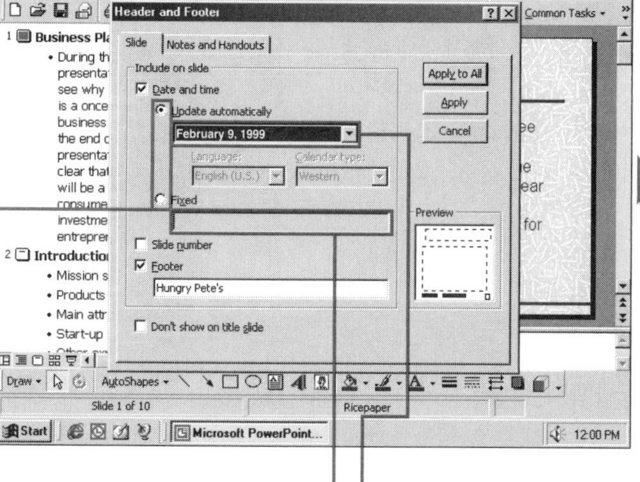

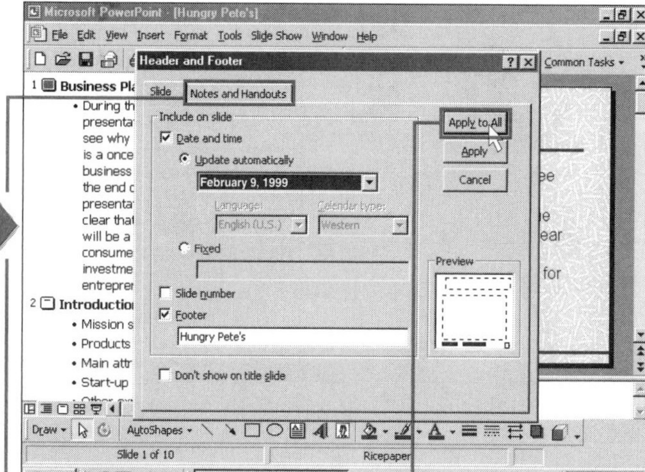

5 If you selected Date and time in step 3, click an option to have the date update automatically or display a fixed date (○ changes to ⦿).

6 If you selected Update automatically, click this area to change the format of the date.

■ If you selected Fixed, type the date in this area.

■ To specify the information you want to appear on the speaker notes and handout pages, click this tab. Then repeat steps 3 to 6 to specify the information.

7 Click Apply to All to apply the changes to the entire presentation.

Note: To apply the changes to only the current slide, click Apply.

USING THE SLIDE MASTER

You can use the Slide Master to change the appearance of all the slides in your presentation at once. This can help you apply a consistent style to your presentation.

The Slide Master contains a placeholder for the title, points, date, footer text and slide number on each slide in your presentation. You can format the sample text in a placeholder to format text on all your slides. For example, changing the font of the title sample text will change the font of all the titles in your presentation. Formatting text on the Slide Master does not affect text you previously formatted on individual slides.

You can add an object to the Slide Master, such as a clip art image, picture or chart, you want to appear on all your slides.

You can move, resize or delete items on the Slide Master as you would any object in your presentation. For more information, see page 336.

After changing the Slide Master, you should review your entire presentation to make sure text and objects do not look out of place.

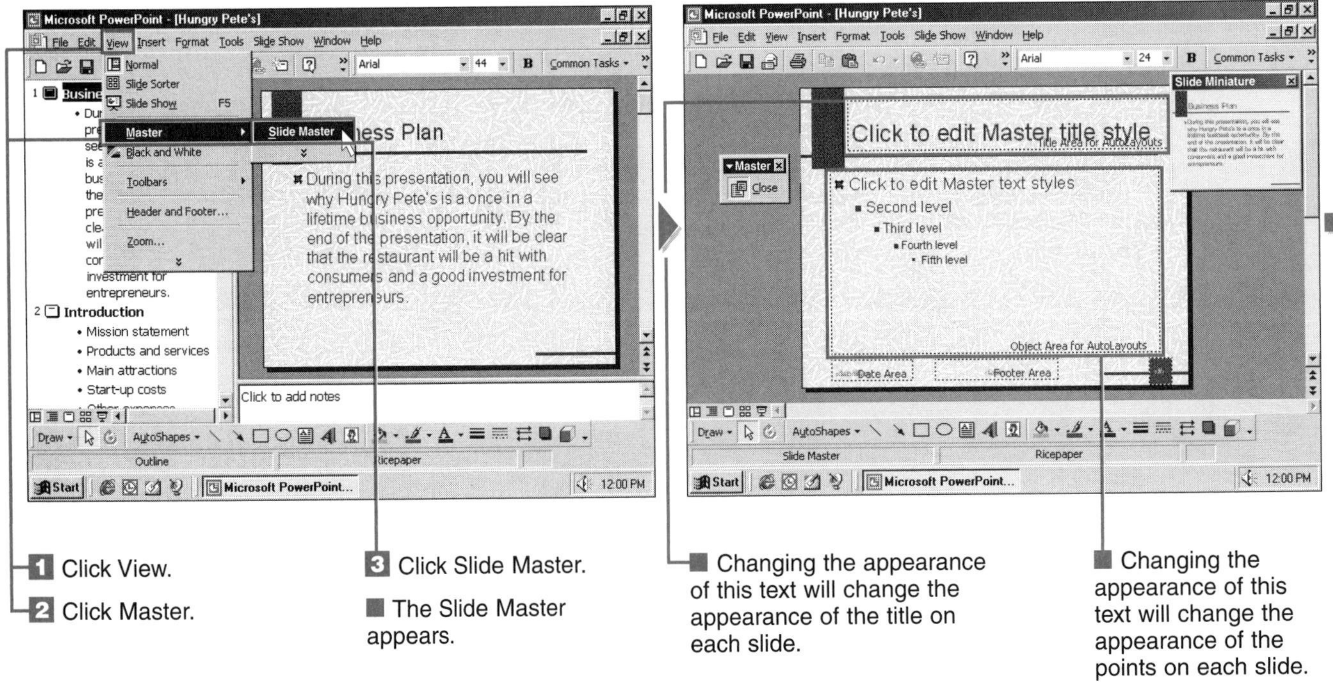

1 Click View.

2 Click Master.

3 Click Slide Master.

■ The Slide Master appears.

■ Changing the appearance of this text will change the appearance of the title on each slide.

■ Changing the appearance of this text will change the appearance of the points on each slide.

TIPS

How do I display the slide miniature?

✔ If a miniature version of a slide is not displayed on your screen, select the View menu and then click Slide Miniature.

Are there other masters available?

✔ Yes. The Title Master allows you to change the appearance of the title slide. The Handout Master allows you to change the appearance of handouts. The Notes Master allows you to change the appearance of speaker notes. To use one of these masters, choose the View menu and click Master. Then select the master you want to use.

Is there a faster way to display the Slide Master and Handout Master?

✔ To display the Slide Master, hold down the Shift key and then click the Slide View button (□). To display the Handout Master, hold down the Shift key and then click the Outline View button (☰).

Can I restore a placeholder I accidentally deleted from the Slide Master?

✔ Yes. Choose the Format menu and then select Master Layout. Click the placeholder you want to restore (☐ changes to ☑) and then click OK.

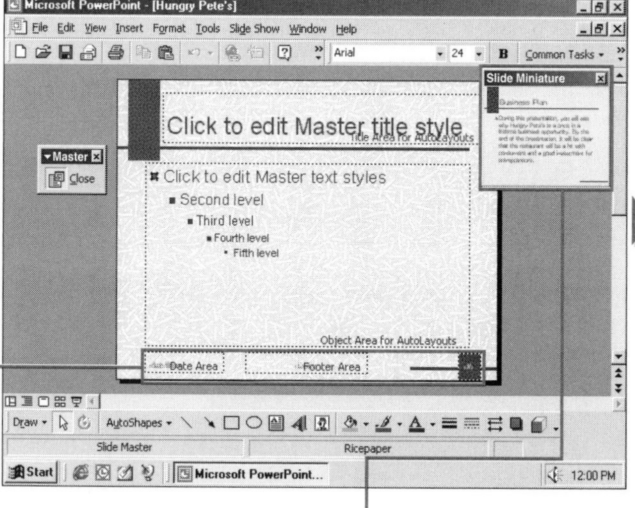

■ These areas display the date, footer text and slide number on each slide.

■ You can add objects to the Slide Master that you want to appear on each slide.

■ This area displays a miniature version of a slide in the presentation. This allows you to preview any changes you make.

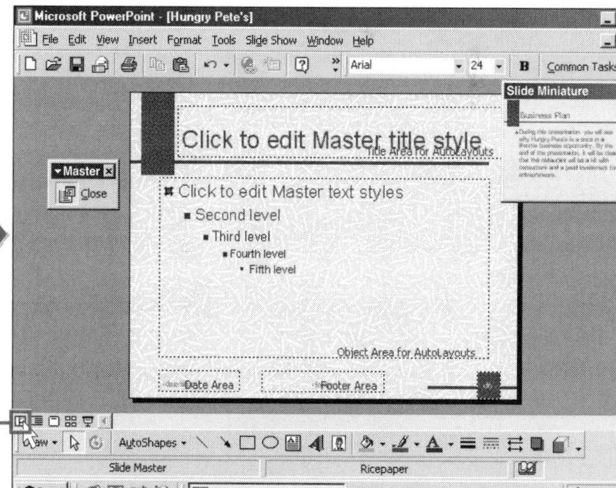

4 When you finish making changes to the Slide Master, click ⊞ to close the Slide Master and return to the Normal view.

REORDER SLIDES

You can change the order of the slides in your presentation. This is useful when you have finished creating your presentation and realize you want to present the slides in a different order.

The Slide Sorter view displays a miniature version of each slide so you can see a general overview of your presentation. This view allows you to easily reorder your slides. For more information on the views, see page 296.

A slide number appears below each slide in your presentation. When you move a slide, PowerPoint automatically renumbers the slides for you.

You can move one slide or several slides at once. To move several slides at once, you must first select the slides you want to move. PowerPoint displays a line to indicate the new location of the slides in the presentation.

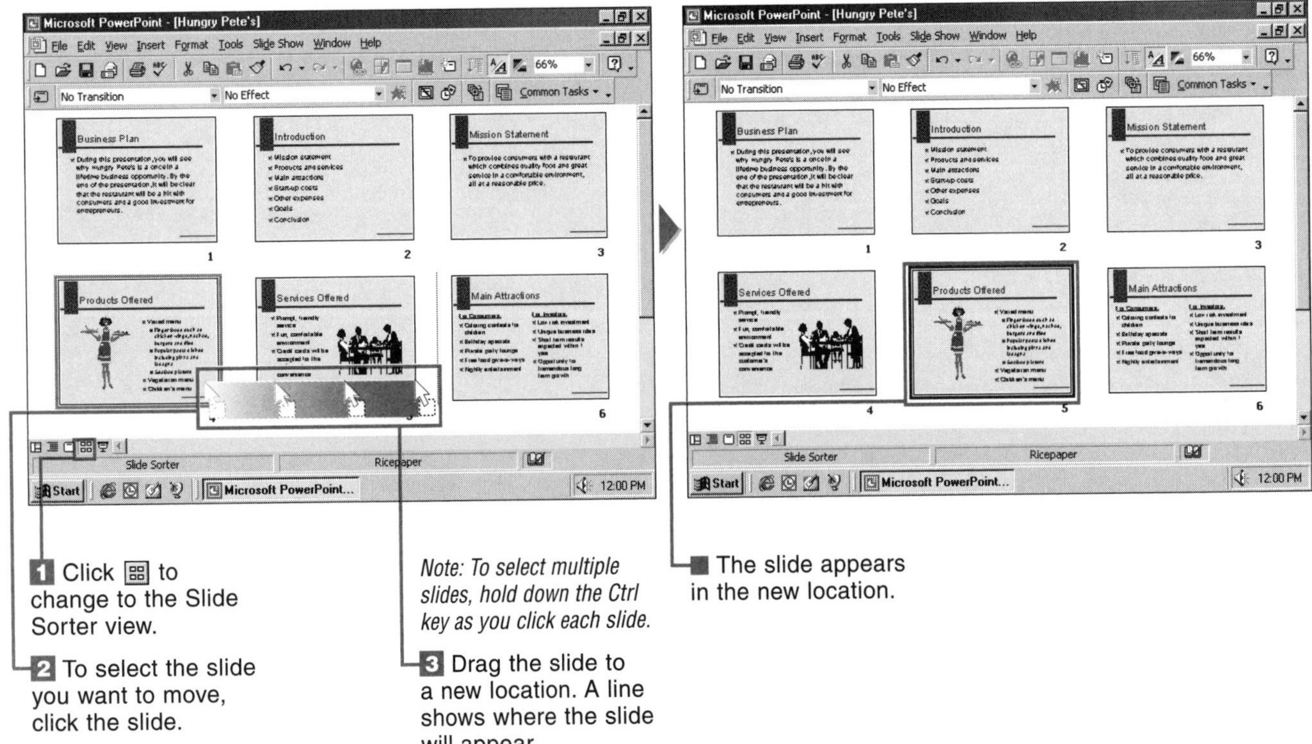

1 Click ▦ to change to the Slide Sorter view.

2 To select the slide you want to move, click the slide.

Note: To select multiple slides, hold down the Ctrl key as you click each slide.

3 Drag the slide to a new location. A line shows where the slide will appear.

■ The slide appears in the new location.

DELETE A SLIDE

You can remove a slide you no longer need in your presentation. This is useful when you are reviewing your presentation and realize a slide contains incorrect or outdated information.

The Slide Sorter view displays a miniature version of each slide in your presentation. This view allows you to easily see the slide you want to delete. For more information on the views, see page 296.

When you delete a slide, PowerPoint automatically renumbers the remaining slides in your presentation for you.

You can delete one slide or several slides at once. To delete several slides at once, you must first select the slides you want to delete.

PowerPoint remembers the last changes you made to your presentation. If you regret deleting a slide, you can use the Undo feature to immediately cancel the deletion.

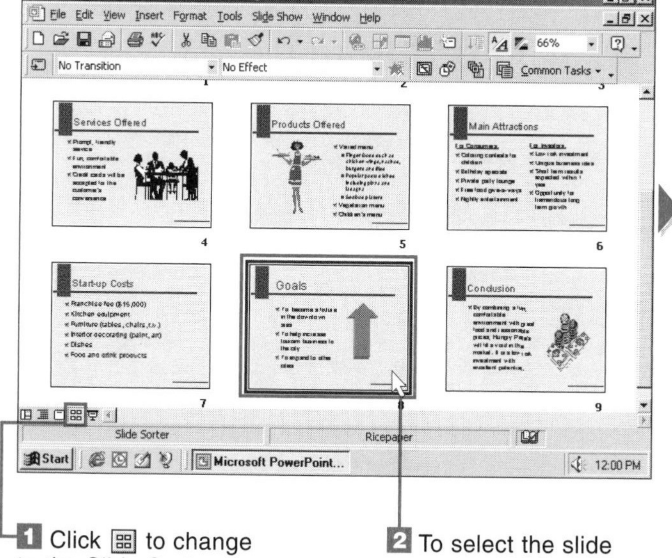

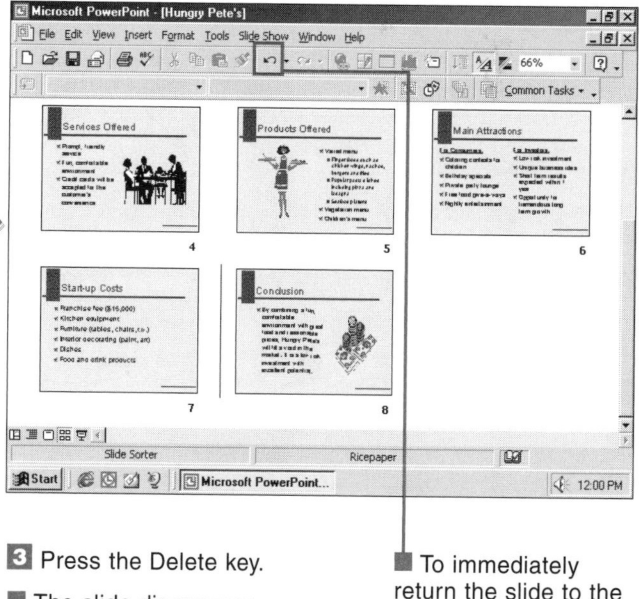

1 Click ▦ to change to the Slide Sorter view.

2 To select the slide you want to delete, click the slide.

Note: To select multiple slides, hold down the Ctrl key as you click each slide.

3 Press the Delete key.

■ The slide disappears.

■ To immediately return the slide to the presentation, click ↶.

CREATE A SUMMARY SLIDE

You can create a summary slide containing the titles of the slides in your presentation. A summary slide is useful for giving your audience an overview of your presentation before you begin the presentation.

Before creating a summary slide, you can select all the slides in your presentation to include all the slide titles on the summary slide. Depending on the length of your presentation, the summary slide may be more than one slide.

PowerPoint places the summary slide at the beginning of your presentation. If you want to use the summary slide to conclude your presentation, you can move the slide to the end of the presentation. For information on moving slides, see page 336.

After creating a summary slide, you can edit the summary slide as you would edit any slide in your presentation. For example, you can remove a slide title you do not want to appear on the summary slide. For information on editing text on a slide, see page 308.

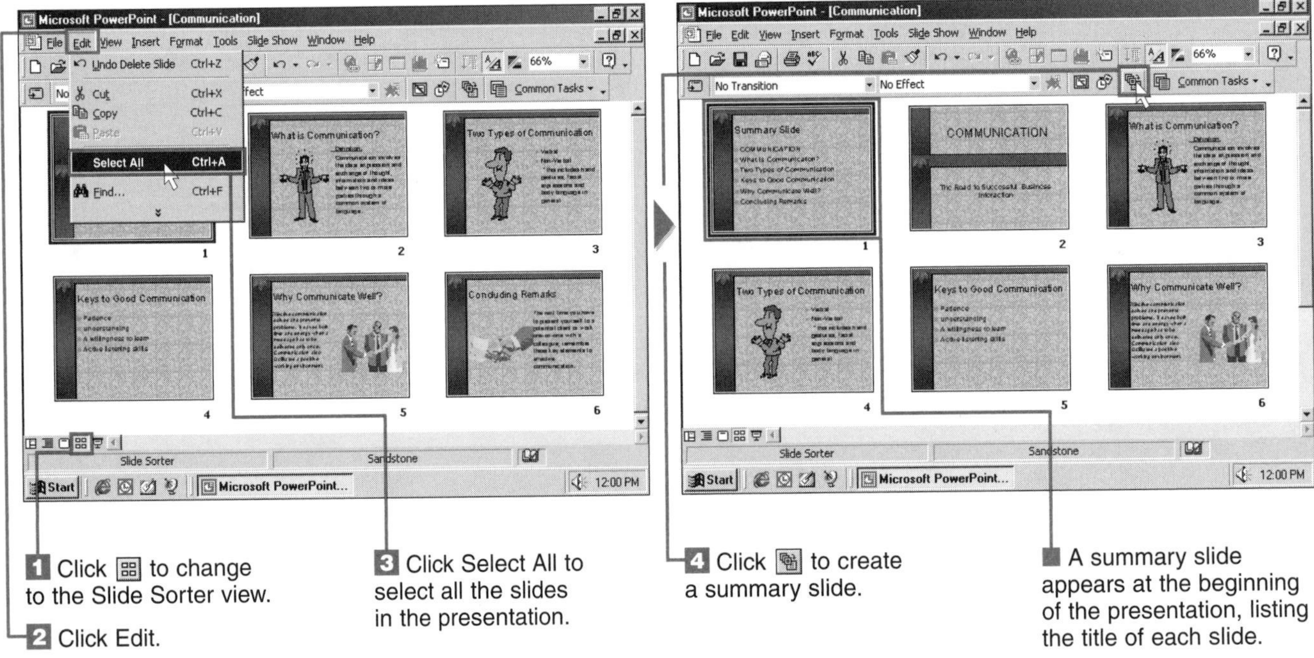

1 Click ⊞ to change to the Slide Sorter view.

2 Click Edit.

3 Click Select All to select all the slides in the presentation.

4 Click ▣ to create a summary slide.

■ A summary slide appears at the beginning of the presentation, listing the title of each slide.

HIDE A SLIDE

You can hide a slide in your presentation so the slide will not be displayed when you deliver the presentation.

Hiding a slide is useful when a slide in your presentation contains supporting information you do not want to include unless the audience requires clarification. For example, you may not want to show your audience a slide containing sensitive financial information unless they ask to see the information.

Hiding a slide can also help you prepare for questions from the audience. You can create slides that answer common questions and then display the slides only when necessary.

When you hide a slide in your presentation, the symbol appears through the number for the slide in the Slide Sorter view.

If you want to present the information on a hidden slide during a slide show, you can easily display the hidden slide. For information on viewing a slide show, see page 366.

1 Click to change to the Slide Sorter view.

2 Click the slide you want to hide.

3 Click to hide the slide.

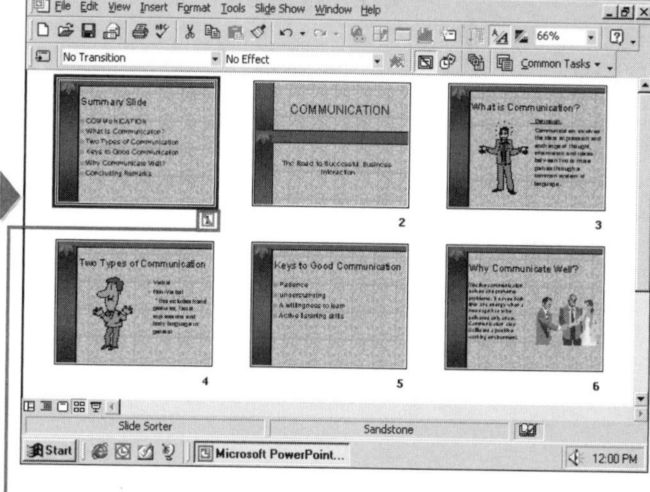

■ A symbol ( ) appears through the slide number.

■ To unhide the slide, repeat steps 1 to 3.

■ To display a hidden slide during a slide show, press the H key when viewing the slide before the hidden slide.

ADD SLIDE TRANSITIONS

You can use effects called transitions to help you move from one slide to the next. A transition determines how one slide is removed and the next slide is presented on the screen.

Using transitions can help you introduce each slide during an on-screen slide show, add interesting visual effects to your presentation and signal to the audience that new information is appearing. When you use the AutoContent Wizard to create a presentation, PowerPoint may automatically add slide transitions to the presentation for you.

PowerPoint offers many slide transitions for you to choose from, including Blinds Vertical, Checkerboard Across, Dissolve and Uncover Down. You can preview a slide transition to determine if it is appropriate for your presentation.

You can set the speed of a slide transition to slow, medium or fast.

You can add a transition to one slide or to your entire presentation. PowerPoint will display the transition when you rehearse or present your slide show.

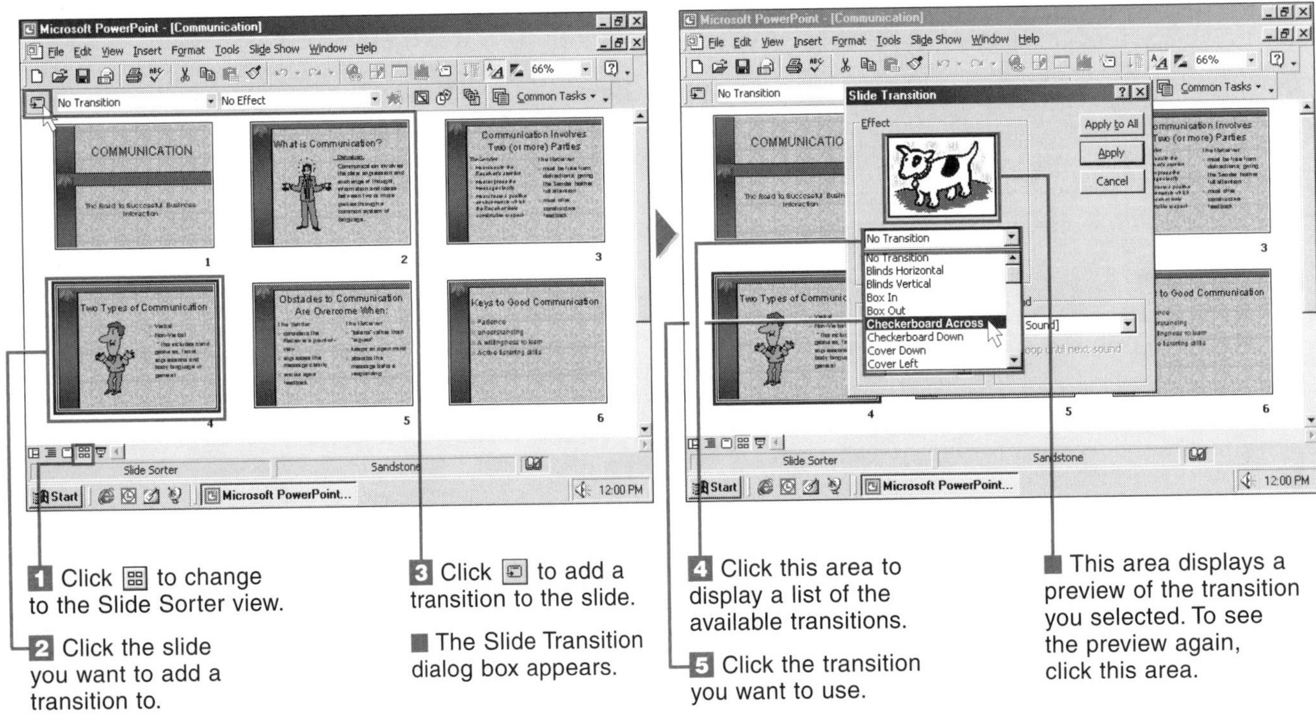

1 Click ▦ to change to the Slide Sorter view.

2 Click the slide you want to add a transition to.

3 Click ▣ to add a transition to the slide.

■ The Slide Transition dialog box appears.

4 Click this area to display a list of the available transitions.

5 Click the transition you want to use.

■ This area displays a preview of the transition you selected. To see the preview again, click this area.

TIPS

Is there another way to add a transition?

✔ Yes. Click the slide you want to add a transition to. On the Slide Sorter toolbar, click the Slide Transition Effects area to the right of the Slide Transition button. Then select the transition you want to use.

How do I remove a transition?

✔ Click the slide you want to remove a transition from. Perform steps 3 to 5 below, except select No Transition in step 5. Then click Apply.

How do I add a sound to a transition?

✔ In the Slide Transition dialog box, click the Sound area and then select the sound you want to use.

Can I have a transition sound keep playing?

✔ You can have a transition sound keep playing until a slide with a new sound is displayed. In the Slide Transition dialog box, click the Loop until next sound option (☐ changes to ☑).

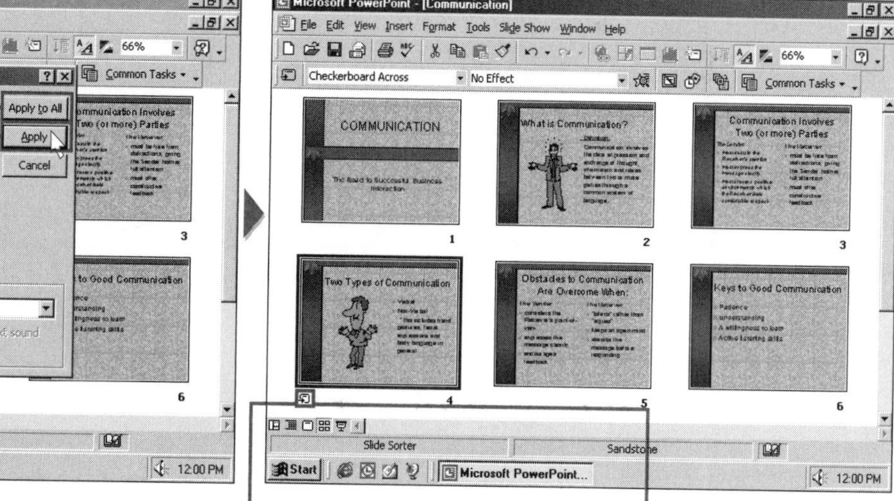

6 To change the speed of the transition, click the speed you want to use (○ changes to ⊙).

7 Click Apply to add the transition to the slide.

■ To add the transition to every slide in the presentation, click Apply to All.

■ The symbol appears below the slide.

■ To preview the transition for the slide, click below the slide.

REHEARSE A SLIDE SHOW

You can rehearse your slide show and have PowerPoint record the amount of time you spend on each slide. Timing your slide show can help you decide if you need to add or remove information.

While you rehearse your slide show, PowerPoint displays the time you spend on the current slide and the total time for the slide show. If you make a mistake while rehearsing and want to begin a slide again, you do not have to restart the entire rehearsal. You can restart the timer for the current slide as many times as necessary.

When you finish rehearsing your slide show, PowerPoint displays the total time for the slide show. You can choose to record the time you spent on each slide.

If you record the timings for each slide, the timings will appear below each slide in the Slide Sorter view. PowerPoint will use the timings to advance your slides automatically during a slide show.

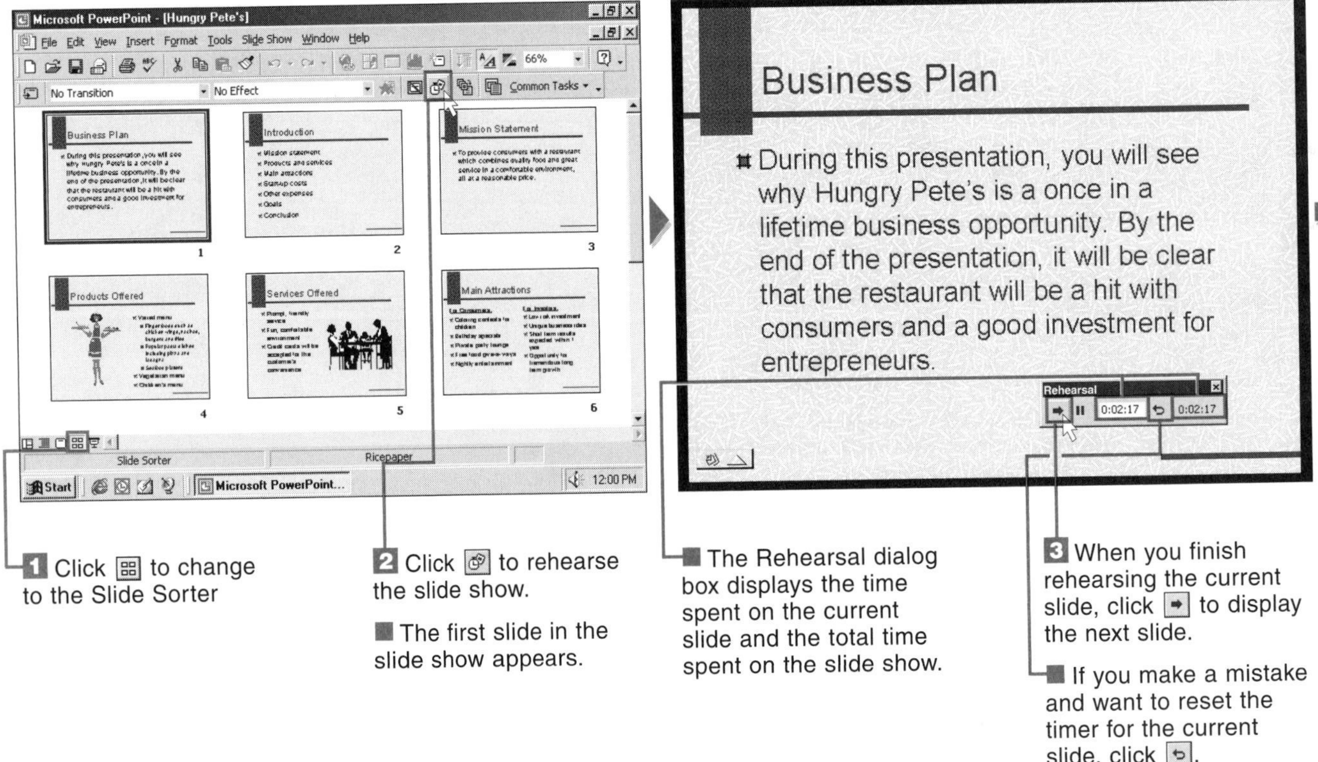

1 Click ⊞ to change to the Slide Sorter

2 Click to rehearse the slide show.

■ The first slide in the slide show appears.

■ The Rehearsal dialog box displays the time spent on the current slide and the total time spent on the slide show.

3 When you finish rehearsing the current slide, click ➡ to display the next slide.

■ If you make a mistake and want to reset the timer for the current slide, click ↺.

TIPS

Can I pause the timer during a rehearsal?

✔ Yes. In the Rehearsal dialog box, click the Pause button (⏸) to temporarily stop the timer. To restart the timer, click the Pause button (⏸) again.

Can I change the timing for a slide after rehearsing my slide show?

✔ If you are dissatisfied with the timing you recorded for a slide, you can change the timing for the slide. Click the slide and then click the Slide Transition button (). In the Automatically after area, drag the mouse pointer over the current timing and type the new timing. Then click Apply to save the new timing for the slide.

I do not want to use my timings to advance my slides automatically during a slide show. How can I advance my slides manually?

✔ From the Slide Show menu, select Set Up Show. In the Advance slides area, select the Manually option (○ changes to ⦿) and then click OK.

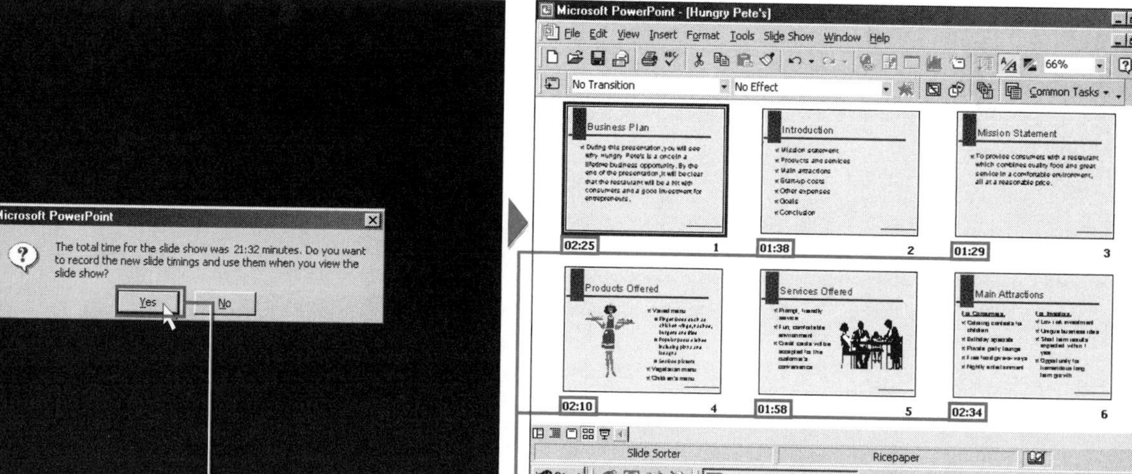

■ When you finish rehearsing the slide show, a dialog box appears, displaying the total time for the slide show.

4 To record the time you spent on each slide and use the timings when you later view the slide show, click Yes.

■ The time you spent on each slide appears below the slides.

TIPS

Can I increase the height of the notes pane in the Normal view?

✔ Yes. Position the mouse over the horizontal bar above the notes pane (changes to) and then drag the bar to a new location.

Can I enter speaker notes in other views?

✔ You can enter speaker notes in the Outline and Slide Sorter views. Like the Normal view, the Outline view provides a pane where you can enter speaker notes. To enter speaker notes in the Slide Sorter view, click a slide and then click the Speaker Notes button ( ). For more information on the views, see page 296.

I am having trouble formatting my speaker notes in the Normal view. What is wrong?

✔ To view the formatting for speaker notes in the Normal view, click the Show Formatting button ( ) on the Standard toolbar.

How can I display speaker notes on my screen during a slide show?

✔ Right-click the slide you want to display speaker notes for and then select Speaker Notes.

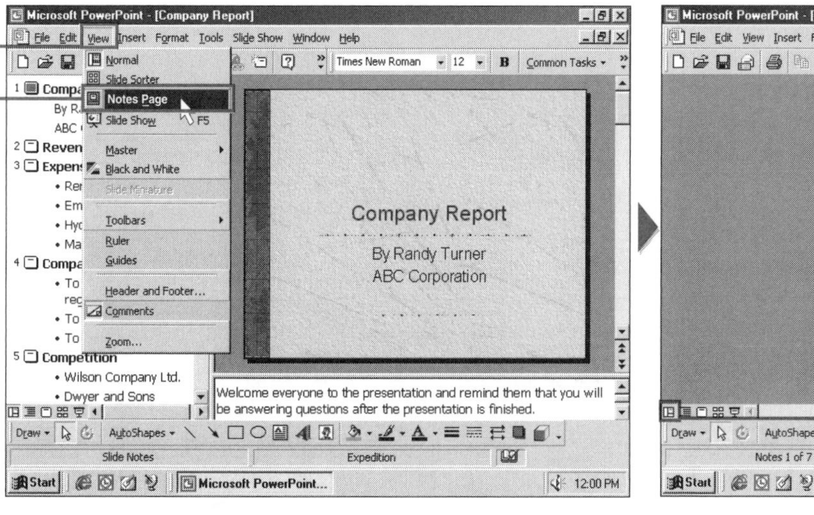

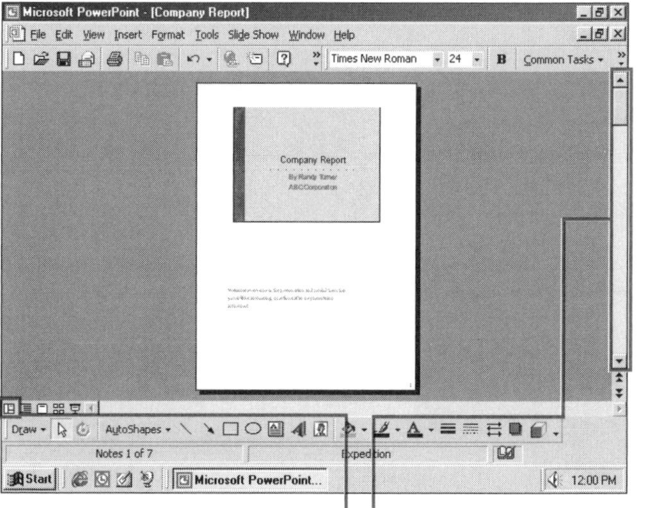

USING THE NOTES PAGE VIEW

1 Click View.

2 Click Notes Page to display the presentation in the Notes Page view.

Note: If Notes Page does not appear on the menu, position the mouse over the bottom of the menu to display all the menu commands.

■ The notes page for the current slide appears on the screen.

■ You can edit and format the speaker notes as you would any text in the presentation. To magnify the page so you can clearly view the text, see page 296.

■ You can use the scroll bar to view the notes pages for other slides in the presentation.

■ When you finish reviewing the notes pages, click to return to the Normal view.

SET UP A SLIDE SHOW

You can specify how you want to present a slide show on a computer.

There are three ways your slide show can be delivered. A slide show can be presented by a speaker, browsed by an individual or set up to run at a kiosk. Kiosks are often found at shopping malls and trade shows.

You can have your slide show run continuously until you press the Esc key. This is useful if your slide show will run at a kiosk.

If your presentation contains voice narration or animation, you can choose not to include these effects in your slide show.

You can set up your slide show to display all the slides in your presentation or only a specific range of slides.

During a slide show, the slides can be advanced manually or automatically. If you choose to advance slides manually, you must perform an action, such as clicking the mouse, to move to the next slide. If you choose to advance slides automatically, you must set timings for your slides. To set timings for your slides, see page 362.

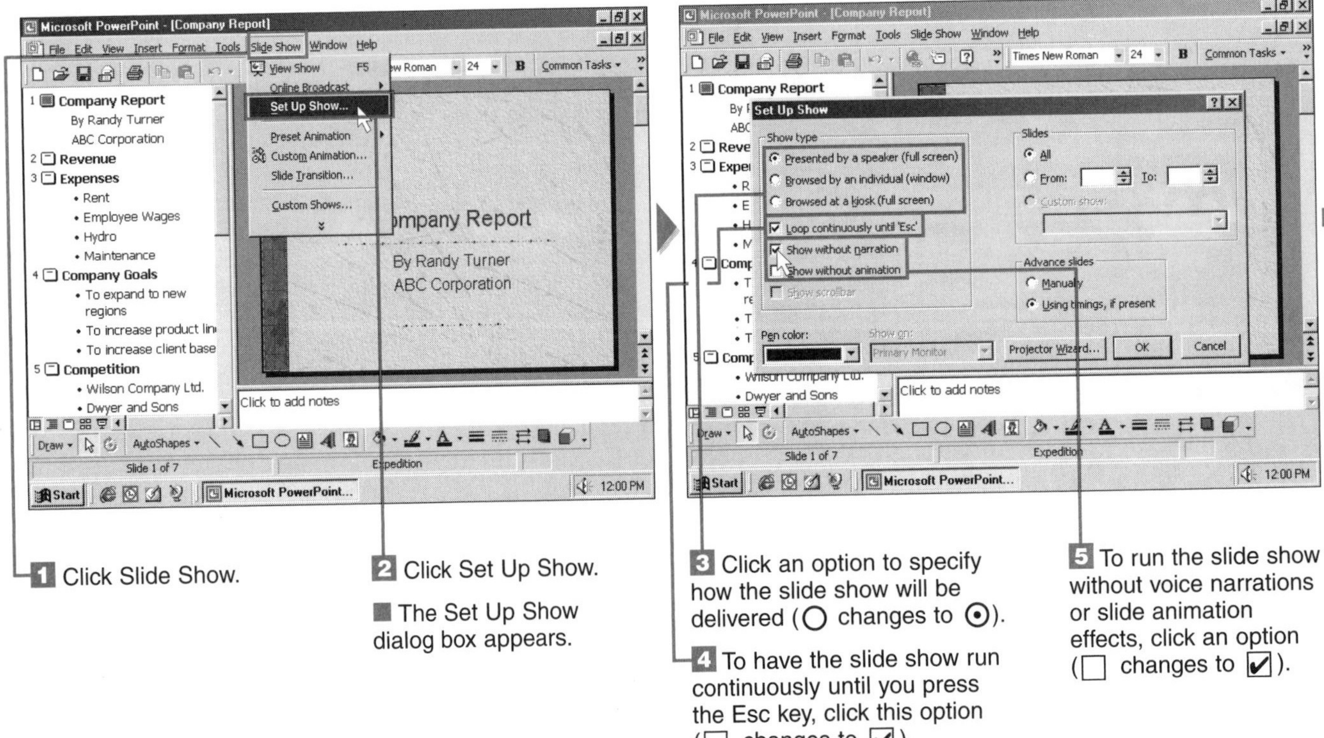

1 Click Slide Show.

2 Click Set Up Show.

■ The Set Up Show dialog box appears.

3 Click an option to specify how the slide show will be delivered (○ changes to ⊙).

4 To have the slide show run continuously until you press the Esc key, click this option (☐ changes to ☑).

5 To run the slide show without voice narrations or slide animation effects, click an option (☐ changes to ☑).

TIPS

What is the Show scrollbar option in the Set Up Show dialog box used for?

✔ If you select the Browsed by an individual option, you can choose to display a scroll bar during the slide show. This allows an individual to easily move through the slide show.

Can I use multiple monitors to present my slide show?

✔ If you are running Windows 98 and are using multiple monitors, the audience can view the slide show on one monitor while you view the outline, speaker notes and slides on another monitor. In the Set Up Show dialog box, click ▼ in the Show on area to select the monitor the audience will view.

How can I present my slide show to a large audience?

✔ You can connect a computer to a projector to display your slide show on a screen. In the Set Up Show dialog box, click Projector Wizard and then follow the instructions on your screen to set up your computer to work with the projector.

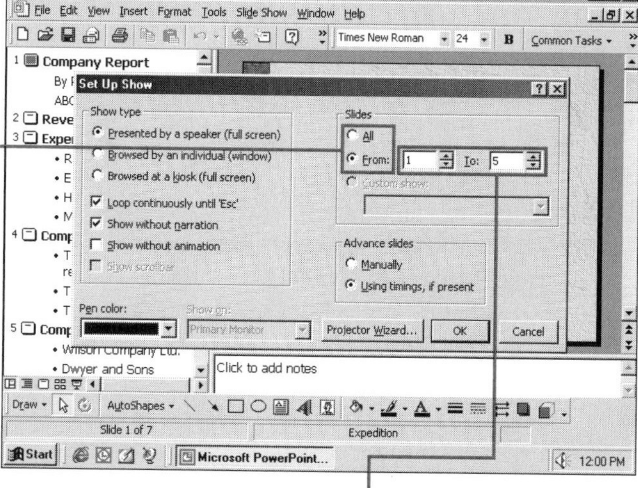

6 Click an option to specify which slides you want to present in the slide show (○ changes to ⦿).

7 If you selected the From option in step 6, double-click these areas and then type the starting and ending slide numbers.

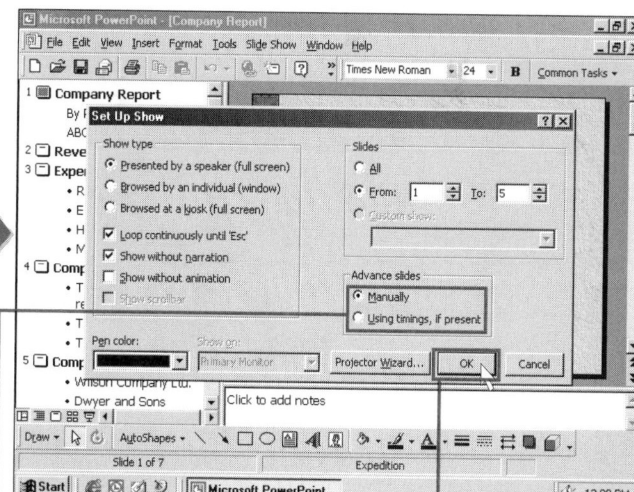

8 Click an option to specify whether you want to advance the slides manually or automatically using timings you have set (○ changes to ⦿).

9 Click OK to save your changes.

VIEW A SLIDE SHOW

You can view a slide show of your presentation on a computer screen. A slide show displays one slide at a time using the entire screen.

If your presentation was created for on-screen viewing, a slide show allows you to preview how your slides will look and rehearse the pace of your presentation.

Any objects or enhancements you added to your slides, including clip art, animations or transitions, will appear during the slide show.

You can display the next slide or return to the previous slide while viewing a slide show. You can also end the slide show at any time.

PowerPoint allows you to draw on the slides during a slide show. This is useful if you want to add a check mark beside an important point or circle a key word on a slide. If a slide becomes cluttered with drawings, you can erase all the drawings. The drawings you add during a slide show are temporary and will not appear on the slides when the slide show is over.

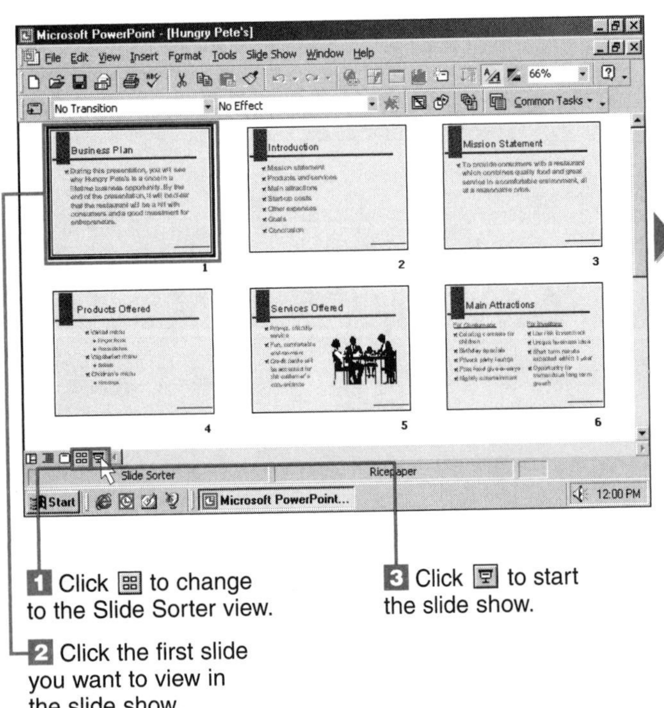

Business Plan

During this presentation, you will see why Hungry Pete's is a once in a lifetime business opportunity. By the end of the presentation, it will be clear that the restaurant will be a hit with consumers and a good investment for entrepreneurs.

1 Click ▦ to change to the Slide Sorter view.

2 Click the first slide you want to view in the slide show.

3 Click ▣ to start the slide show.

■ The first slide fills the screen.

Note: You can press the Esc key to end the slide show at any time.

4 To display the next slide, click the current slide or press the Spacebar.

■ To return to the previous slide, press the Backspace key.

TIPS

How can I use my keyboard to display a specific slide during a slide show?

✔ To display a specific slide, type the number of the slide and then press the Enter key.

Can I take meeting minutes during a slide show?

✔ You can take meeting minutes to record important ideas discussed during the slide show. Right-click a slide and then select Meeting Minder. Type the meeting minutes and then click OK. To view the meeting minutes after the slide show, select the Tools menu and click Meeting Minder.

Can I create speaker notes during a slide show?

✔ Yes. Right-click the slide you want to create speaker notes for and then select Speaker Notes. Type the speaker notes for the slide and click Close. For more information on speaker notes, see page 368.

How can I pause a slide show?

✔ Press the B key to turn the screen black and pause the slide show. This is useful if you want to discuss an idea in detail or answer questions from the audience. You can press the B key again to resume the slide show.

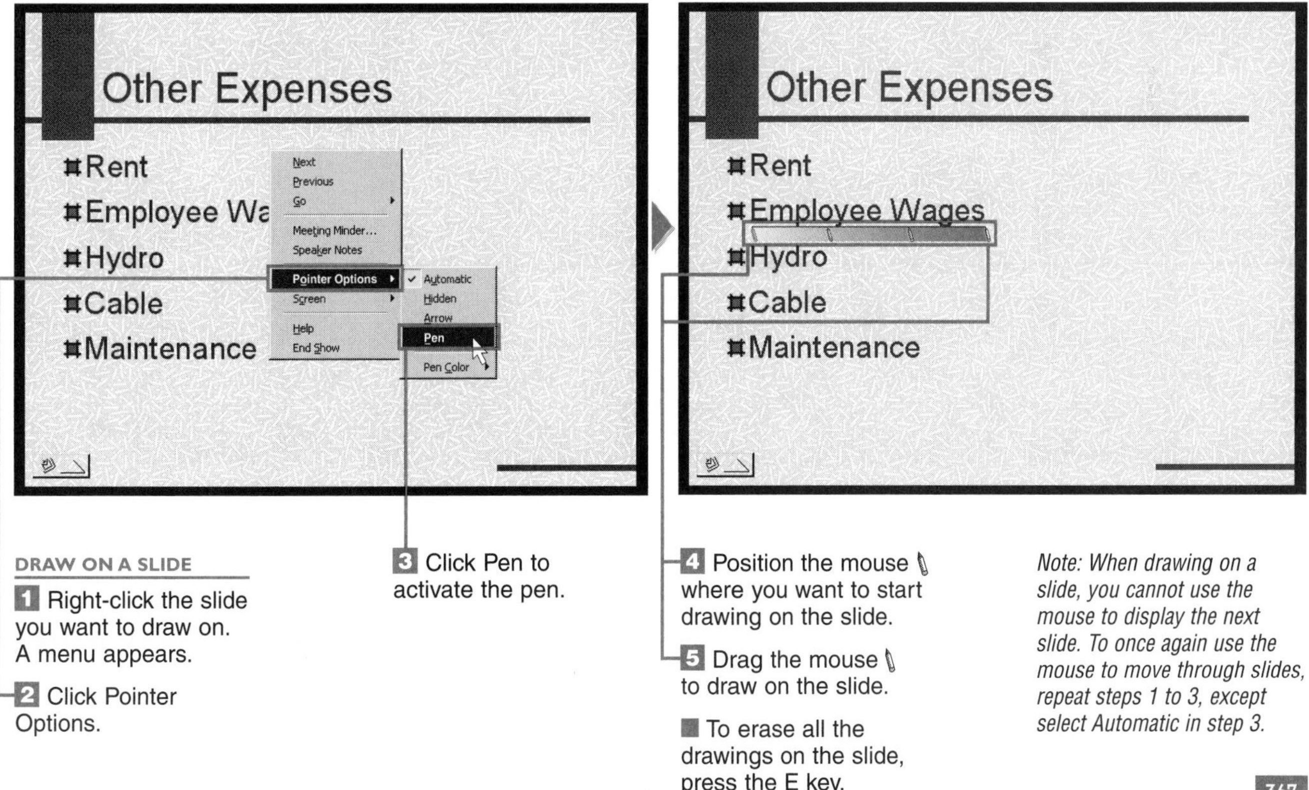

DRAW ON A SLIDE

1 Right-click the slide you want to draw on.

A menu appears.

2 Click Pointer Options.

3 Click Pen to activate the pen.

4 Position the mouse where you want to start drawing on the slide.

5 Drag the mouse to draw on the slide.

■ To erase all the drawings on the slide, press the E key.

Note: When drawing on a slide, you cannot use the mouse to display the next slide. To once again use the mouse to move through slides, repeat steps 1 to 3, except select Automatic in step 3.

CREATE SPEAKER NOTES

You can create speaker notes that contain copies of your slides with all the ideas you want to discuss. You can use these notes as a guide when delivering your presentation.

You can create speaker notes in the Normal and Notes Page views. The Normal view provides a notes pane where you can enter speaker notes while creating your slides. This lets you record your ideas while working on your presentation.

The Notes Page view is useful for editing and formatting your speaker notes. Each notes page includes a small version of a slide and a text area. You can magnify the text area to make it easier to see the text. You can edit and format text in the text area as you would any text in the presentation.

When you have finished creating your speaker notes, you can print the notes pages so you have a paper copy of your notes to refer to while delivering your presentation. For information on printing a presentation, see page 372.

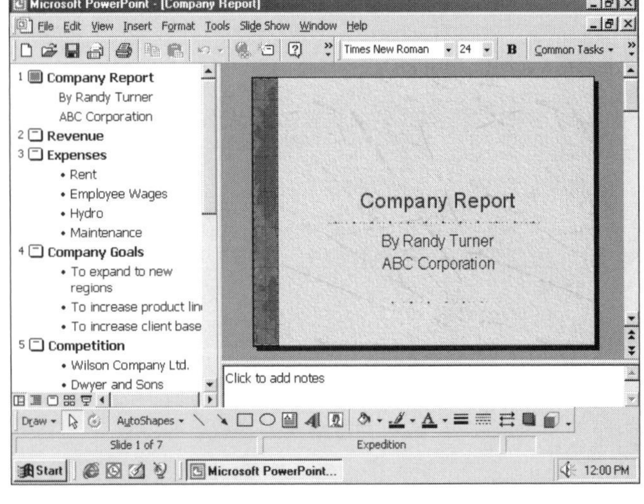

USING THE NORMAL VIEW

1 Display the slide you want to create speaker notes for.

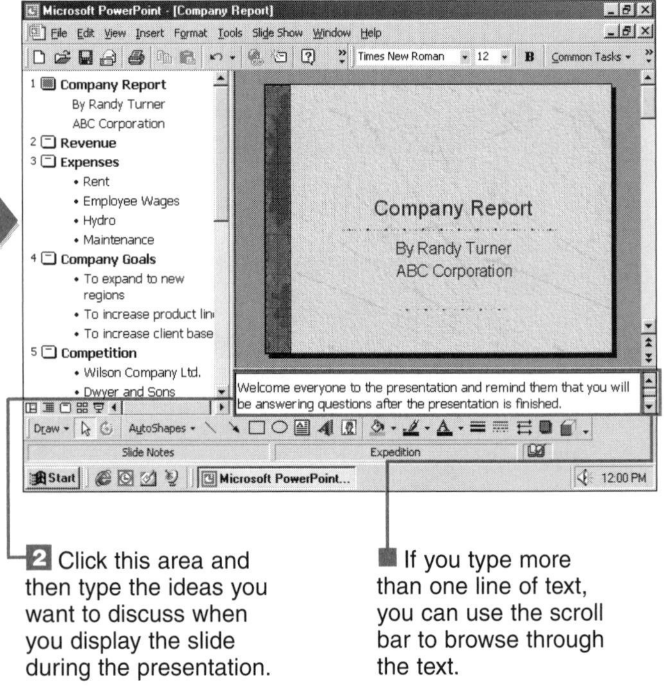

2 Click this area and then type the ideas you want to discuss when you display the slide during the presentation.

■ If you type more than one line of text, you can use the scroll bar to browse through the text.

SET UP A PRESENTATION FOR PRINTING

Before printing your presentation, you can change the setup of the presentation.

PowerPoint allows you to specify how you want to output your presentation, such as on paper, 35mm slides or overheads.

You can choose the orientation you want to use when printing your presentation. Orientation refers to the way information is printed on a page. The orientation you select for the slides will affect every slide in your presentation. Portrait orientation prints information across the short side of a page. Landscape orientation prints information across the long side of a page and is the standard orientation for slides.

You can also choose the orientation you want to use for speaker notes, handouts and the outline of your presentation. Portrait is the standard orientation for speaker notes, handouts and the outline.

After you set up your presentation for printing, PowerPoint will adjust the presentation to reflect the new settings.

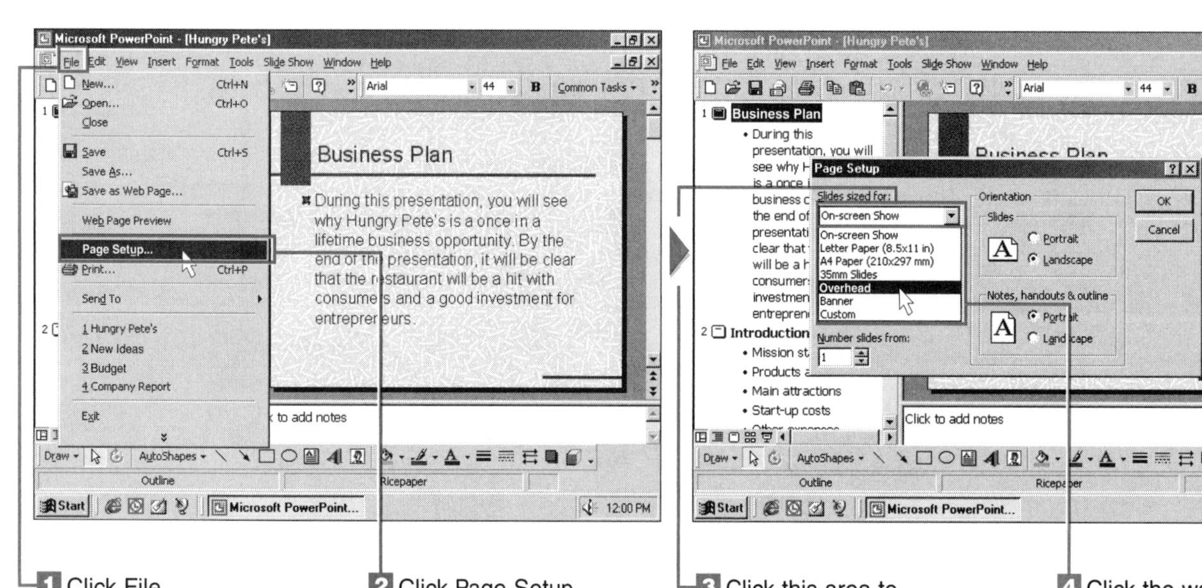

1 Click File.

2 Click Page Setup.

■ The Page Setup dialog box appears.

3 Click this area to display the ways you can output the slides.

4 Click the way you want to output the slides.

TIPS

Should I review my presentation after setting it up for printing?

✔ You should review your presentation after changing the output or orientation of slides to ensure that the information on your slides still appears the way you want.

The layout of information on my slides does not suit the new orientation. What can I do?

✔ You can move and resize text placeholders and objects on the Slide Master to better suit the new orientation of the slides. Choose the View menu, select Master and then click Slide Master. For information on using the Slide Master, see page 354.

Can I start numbering the slides in my presentation at a number other than 1?

✔ Yes. Changing the numbering of slides is useful if your presentation is part of a larger presentation. In the Page Setup dialog box, double-click the Number slides from area and then type the number you want to use for the first slide of the presentation.

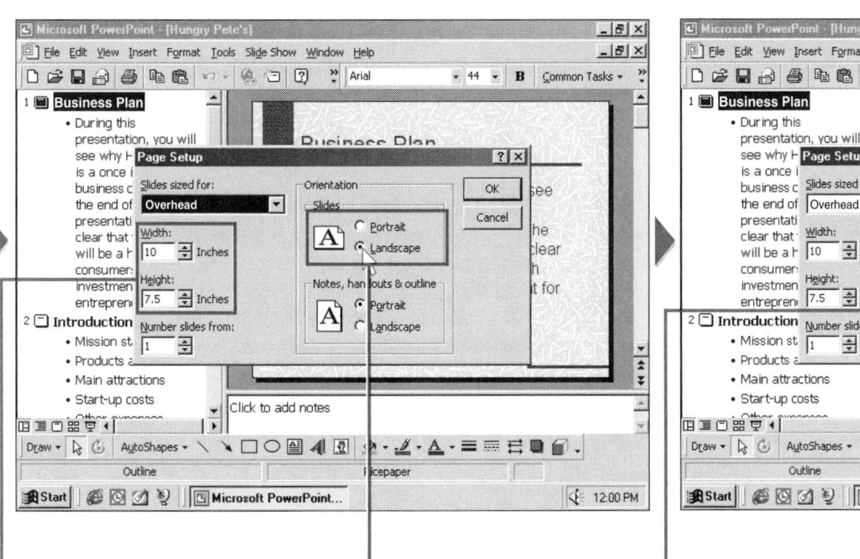

■ This area displays the width and height PowerPoint will use for the slides.

5 Click the orientation you want to use for the slides (○ changes to ⦿).

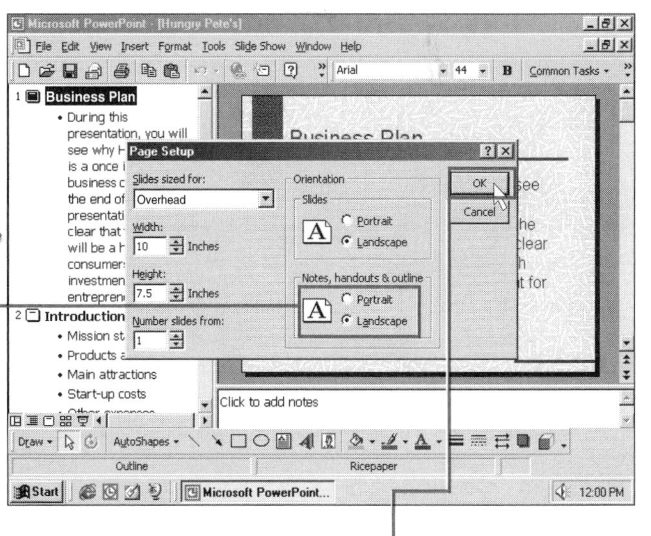

6 Click the orientation you want to use for speaker notes, handouts and the outline of the presentation (○ changes to ⦿).

7 Click OK to confirm your changes.

PRINT A PRESENTATION

You can produce a paper copy of your presentation.

PowerPoint lets you specify the part of the presentation you want to print, such as slides, handouts, notes pages or the text displayed in the Outline pane. When printing handouts, you can choose the number of slides you want to appear on each printed page.

You can print every slide in your presentation, the current slide or a series of slides.

PowerPoint offers several options you can use to change the appearance of your printed presentation. The Grayscale option improves the appearance of color slides printed on a black-and-white printer. The Pure black and white option eliminates shades of gray and prints in black and white. The Include animations option prints slides as they will appear when animated. For information on animating slides, see page 350. The Scale to fit paper option adjusts the size of slides to fill a printed page. The Frame slides option adds a border around your slides, handouts and notes pages. The Print hidden slides option prints slides you have hidden. For information on hiding slides, see page 359.

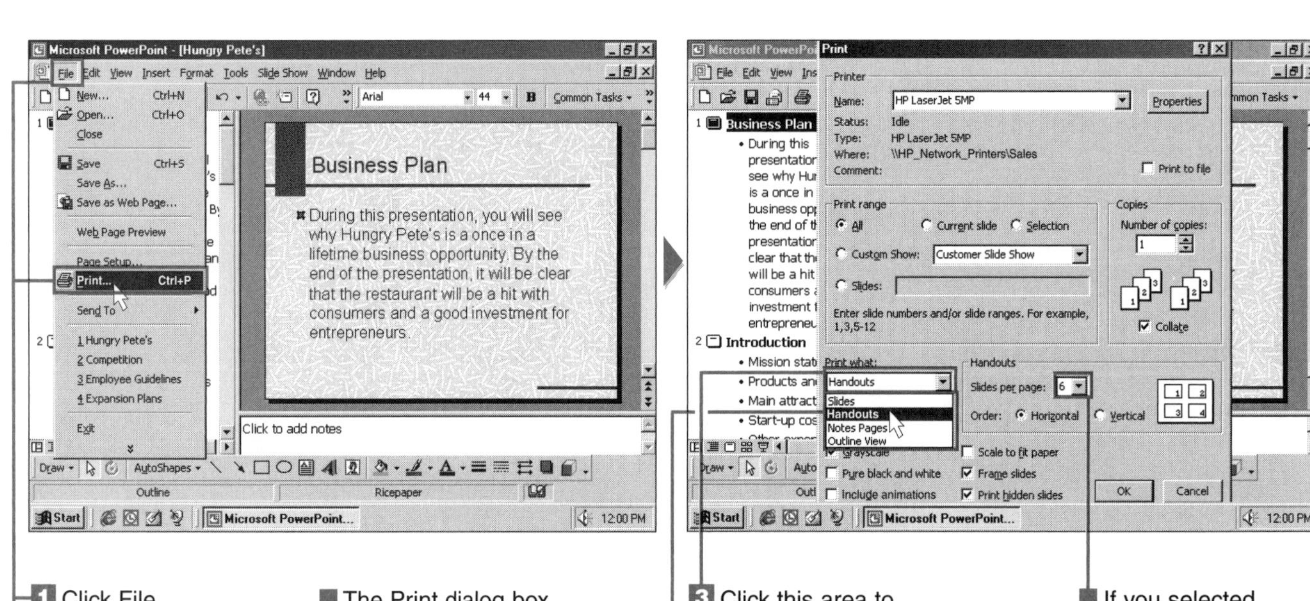

1 Click File.

2 Click Print.

■ The Print dialog box appears.

3 Click this area to select the part of the presentation you want to print.

4 Click the part of the presentation you want to print.

■ If you selected Handouts in step 4, this area displays the number of slides that will print on each page. You can click this area to change the number.

Why doesn't my entire outline print?

✔ Your outline prints as it appears in the Outline pane. If you have hidden text, click the Expand All button (▤) on the Standard toolbar to display all the text. For information on hiding slide text, see page 315.

Can I preview how my slides will look when printed on a black-and-white printer?

✔ Yes. Click the Grayscale Preview button (◩) on the Standard toolbar to preview your slides in shades of gray. To once again view your slides in color, click the button again.

How do I produce 35mm slides?

✔ You can send your presentation to a service bureau to create 35mm slides. If you do not have a service bureau, you can use the Genigraphics Wizard to send your presentation to Genigraphics. From the File menu, select Send To and then click Genigraphics. The first time you select this option, you may have to install the wizard. Insert the CD-ROM disc you used to install Office 2000 into your CD-ROM drive and click OK. Then follow the instructions on your screen.

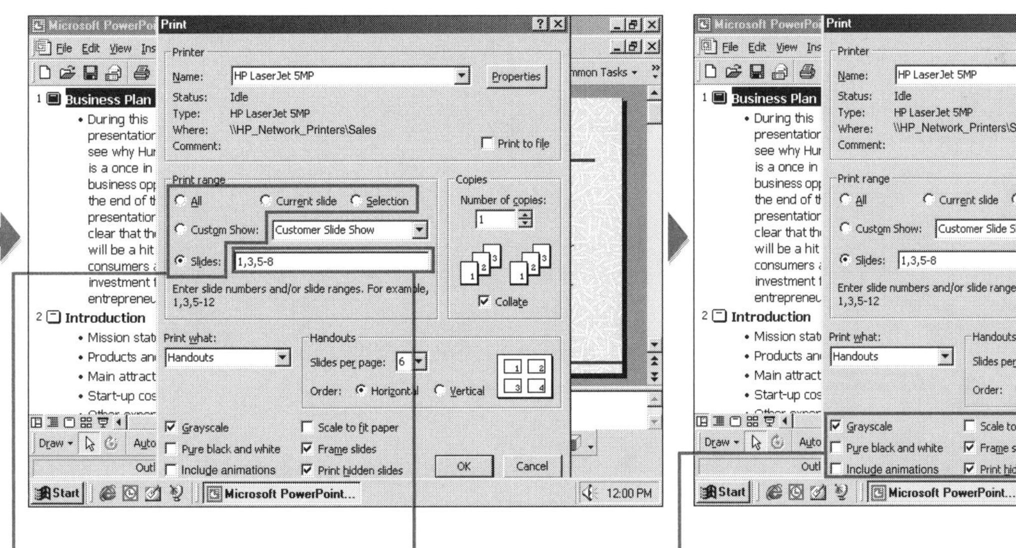

5 Click a print range option to specify which slides you want to print (○ changes to ⊙).

6 If you selected Slides in step 5, type the numbers of the slides you want to print in this area (example: 1,3,4 or 2-4).

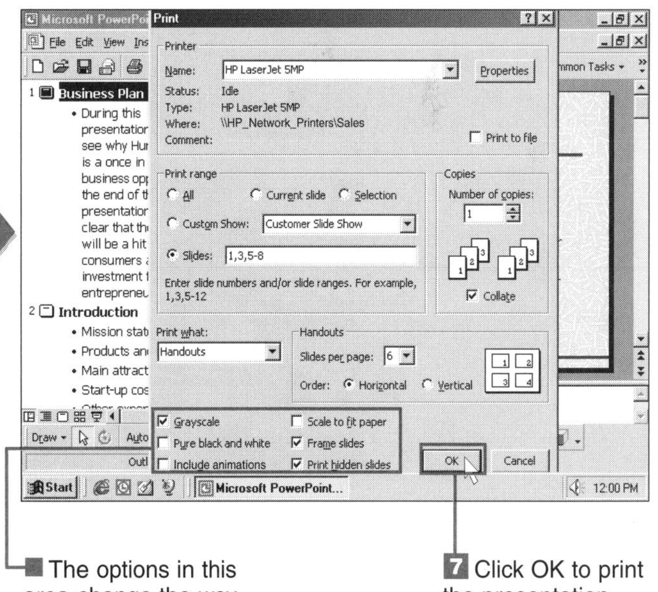

■ The options in this area change the way the presentation appears when printed. You can click an option to turn the option on (☑) or off (☐).

7 Click OK to print the presentation.

SECTION V

1) GETTING STARTED

2) CREATE TABLES

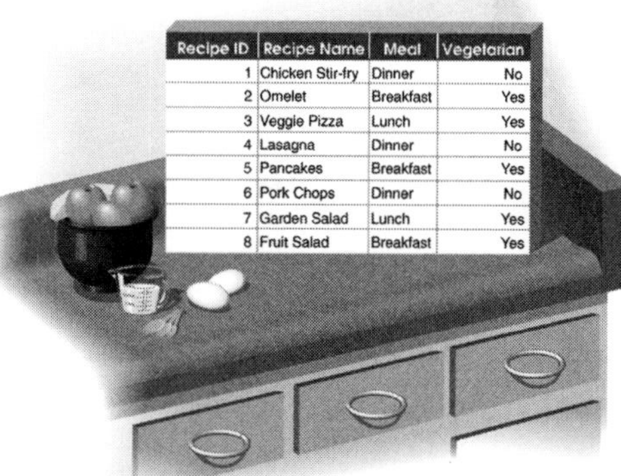

Recipe ID	Recipe Name	Meal	Vegetarian
1	Chicken Stir-fry	Dinner	No
2	Omelet	Breakfast	Yes
3	Veggie Pizza	Lunch	Yes
4	Lasagna	Dinner	No
5	Pancakes	Breakfast	Yes
6	Pork Chops	Dinner	No
7	Garden Salad	Lunch	Yes
8	Fruit Salad	Breakfast	Yes

USING ACCESS

3) DESIGN TABLES

4) CREATE FORMS

5) FIND DATA

6) CREATE QUERIES

7) CREATE REPORTS

8) PRINT

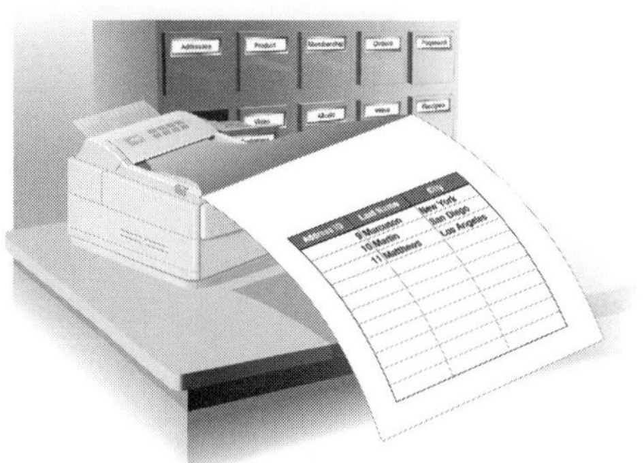

INTRODUCTION TO ACCESS

Microsoft Access is a database program that allows you to store and manage large collections of information. Access provides you with all the tools you need to create an efficient and effective database.

Databases are very useful for finding specific data in a large collection of information.

Databases also allow you to perform calculations on the information they contain.

For more information on Access, you can visit the following Web site: www.microsoft.com/access

Personal and Business Uses

Many people use a database to store personal information such as addresses, music and video collections, recipes or a wine list. Using a database to store and organize information is much more efficient than using sheets of paper or index cards.

Companies use a database to store information such as mailing lists, billing information, client orders, expenses, inventory and payroll. A database can help a company effectively manage information that is constantly being reviewed, updated and analyzed.

Types of Databases

Flat file databases store information in one large table. This type of database often contains duplicate information. A flat file database is easy to set up, but is not very flexible or efficient for storing large amounts of information.

Relational databases store information in separate tables. You can use relationships to bring together information from different tables. This type of database is powerful, flexible and effectively stores large amounts of information. A relational database is faster and easier to maintain than a flat file database. You can use Access to create a relational database.

Database Applications

A database stores and manages a collection of information related to a particular subject or purpose. You can efficiently add, update, view and organize the information stored in a database.

You can instantly locate information of interest in a database. For example, you can find all clients with the last name Smith. You can also perform more advanced searches, such as finding all clients who live in California and who purchased more than $100.00 worth of supplies last year.

You can perform calculations on the information in a database to help you make quick, accurate and informed decisions. You can neatly present the information in professionally designed reports.

PARTS OF A DATABASE

Databases consist of objects such as tables, forms, queries, reports, pages, macros and modules.

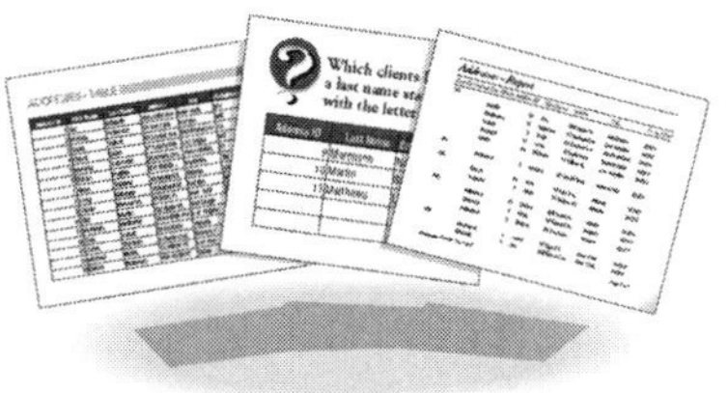

Tables

A table is a collection of related information about a specific topic. You can have one or more tables in a database. A table consists of fields and records. A field is a specific category of information in a table such as the first names of all your clients. A record is a collection of information about one person, place or thing such as the name and address of one client.

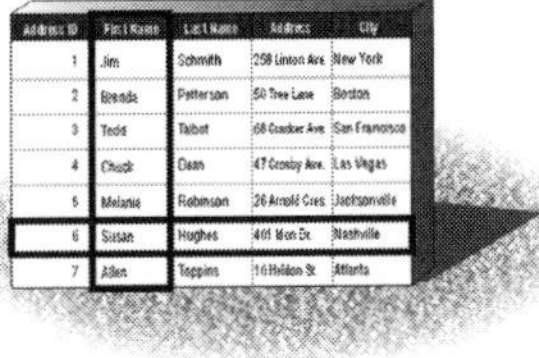

Address ID	First Name	Last Name	Address	City
1	Jim	Schmith	258 Linton Ave	New York
2	Brenda	Petterson	50 Tree Lane	Boston
3	Todd	Talbot	68 Cracker Ave	San Francisco
4	Chuck	Dean	47 Crosby Ave	Las Vegas
5	Melanie	Robinson	26 Arnold Cres	Jacksonville
6	Susan	Hughes	401 Main Dr.	Nashville
7	Allen	Toppins	16 Hildon St.	Atlanta

Forms

Forms provide a quick way to view, enter and modify information in a database by presenting information in an easy-to-use format. A form displays boxes that clearly show you where to enter or modify information. Forms usually display one record at a time.

Queries

Queries allow you to find information of interest in a database. When you create a query, you ask Access to find information that meets the criteria, or conditions, you specify. For example, you can create a query to find all items that cost less than $100.00.

Reports

Reports are professional-looking documents that summarize data from your database. You can perform calculations, such as averages or totals, in a report to summarize information. For example, you could create a report that displays the total sales for each product.

Pages

Pages allow you to access a database on the Internet or an intranet using a Web browser. When you add pages to a database, other users can view and enter information in the database even if they do not have Access installed on their computers.

Macros

A macro saves you time by combining a series of actions into a single action. Macros are ideal for tasks you perform frequently. For example, you can create a macro that calculates and prints daily sales figures. Instead of having to perform each action individually, you can have a macro automatically perform all the actions for you.

Modules

Modules are programs created in Visual Basic for Applications (VBA), which is a programming language. Modules allow you to efficiently control a database.

PLAN A DATABASE

You should take the time to properly design a database. A good database design ensures that you will be able to perform tasks efficiently and accurately. As you add information and objects to a database, the database becomes larger and more complex. A database that is designed properly will be easier to modify and work with as it grows. Good planning can also make it easier for other users to work with a database you create.

STEP 1 Determine the Purpose of the Database

Decide what you want the database to do and how you plan to use the information. If others will be using the database, you should consult with them and consider their needs. This can help you determine what information you need to include to make the database complete.

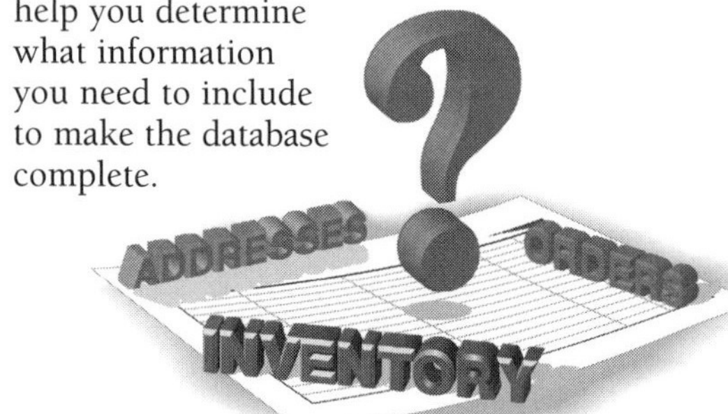

STEP 2 Determine the Tables You Need

Gather all the information you want to store in the database and then divide the information into separate tables. A table should contain related information about one subject only. The same information should not appear in more than one table in a database. You can work more efficiently and reduce errors if you only need to update information in one location.

STEP 3 Determine the Fields You Need

Each field should relate directly to the subject of the table. When adding fields, make sure you break down information into its smallest parts. For example, break down names into two fields called First Name and Last Name.

Try to keep the number of fields in a table to a minimum. For example, do not include a field containing data you can calculate from other fields. Tables with many fields increase the time it takes to process information in a database.

STEP 4 Determine the Relationships Between Tables

A relationship tells Access how to bring together related information stored in separate tables. You can use the primary key to form a relationship between tables. A primary key is one or more fields that uniquely identifies each record in a table. For example, the primary key for a table of employees could be the social security number for each employee.

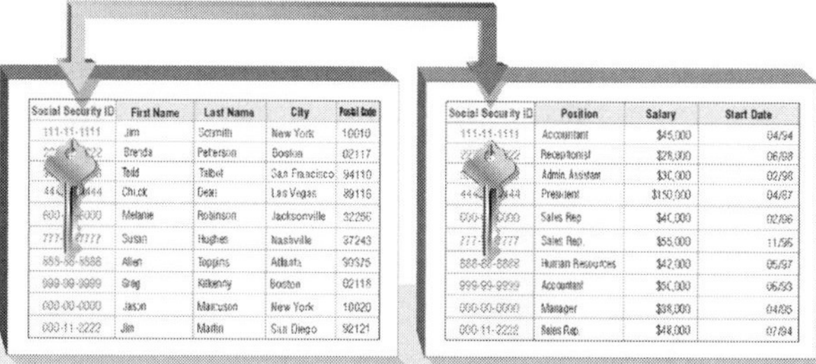

Social Security ID	First Name	Last Name	City	Postal Code
111-11-1111	Jim	Schmith	New York	10010
[illegible]	Brenda	Peterson	Boston	02117
[illegible]	Todd	Talbot	San Francisco	94110
[illegible]	Chuck	Dean	Las Vegas	89116
[illegible]	Melanie	Robinson	Jacksonville	32256
[illegible]	Susan	Hughes	Nashville	37243
888-88-8888	Allen	Toppins	Atlanta	30375
999-99-9999	Greg	Kilkenny	Boston	02118
000-00-0000	Jason	Marcuson	New York	10020
000-11-2222	Jim	Martin	San Diego	92121

Social Security ID	Position	Salary	Start Date
111-11-1111	Accountant	$45,000	04/94
[illegible]	Receptionist	$28,000	06/98
[illegible]	Admin. Assistant	$30,000	02/98
[illegible]	President	$150,000	04/87
[illegible]	Sales Rep	$40,000	02/96
[illegible]	Sales Rep.	$55,000	11/96
888-88-8888	Human Resources	$42,000	05/97
999-99-9999	Accountant	$50,000	06/93
000-00-0000	Manager	$38,000	04/95
000-11-2222	Sales Rep.	$48,000	07/94

START ACCESS

You can start Access to create a new database or work with a database you previously created.

Each time you start Access, the Microsoft Access dialog box appears. This dialog box allows you to create a blank database or use a Database Wizard to create a database. A Database Wizard will guide you step-by-step through the process of creating a new database.

You can also use the Microsoft Access dialog box to open an existing database. The dialog box displays a list of the databases you most recently used. This allows you to quickly open a database you use often.

The first time you start Access, the Office Assistant appears on your screen. The Office Assistant can provide you with information to help you perform tasks and understand the features Access offers. For more information on the Office Assistant, see page 16.

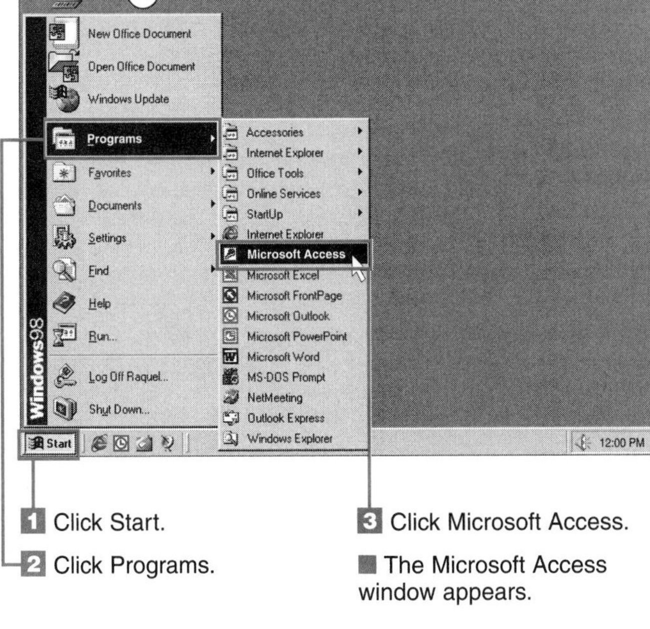

1 Click Start.

2 Click Programs.

3 Click Microsoft Access.

■ The Microsoft Access window appears.

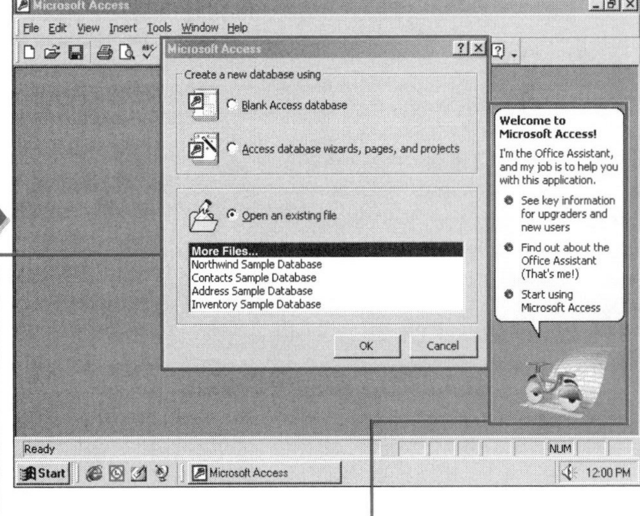

■ The Microsoft Access dialog box appears each time you start Access, allowing you to create a new database or open an existing database.

Note: To create a database, see page 380 or 382. To open an existing database, see page 390.

■ The Office Assistant welcome appears the first time you start Access. To hide the Office Assistant, see page 17.

CREATE A BLANK DATABASE

If you want to design your own database, you can create a blank database.

Each time you start Access, a dialog box appears, allowing you to create a blank database or use the Database Wizard to create a simple database. Creating a blank database is useful when you have experience using Access or when you want to create a complex database.

To store the database as a file on your computer, you must give the database a name. Access assigns a default name, such as db1, to each database you create. You should give the database a more descriptive name to help you recognize the database later.

Access automatically stores the database in the My Documents folder, but you can specify another folder. The Places Bar lets you quickly access many commonly used folders.

Access displays the blank database on your screen. The database does not contain any objects such as forms, reports or tables. You can create the objects you want to use in the database.

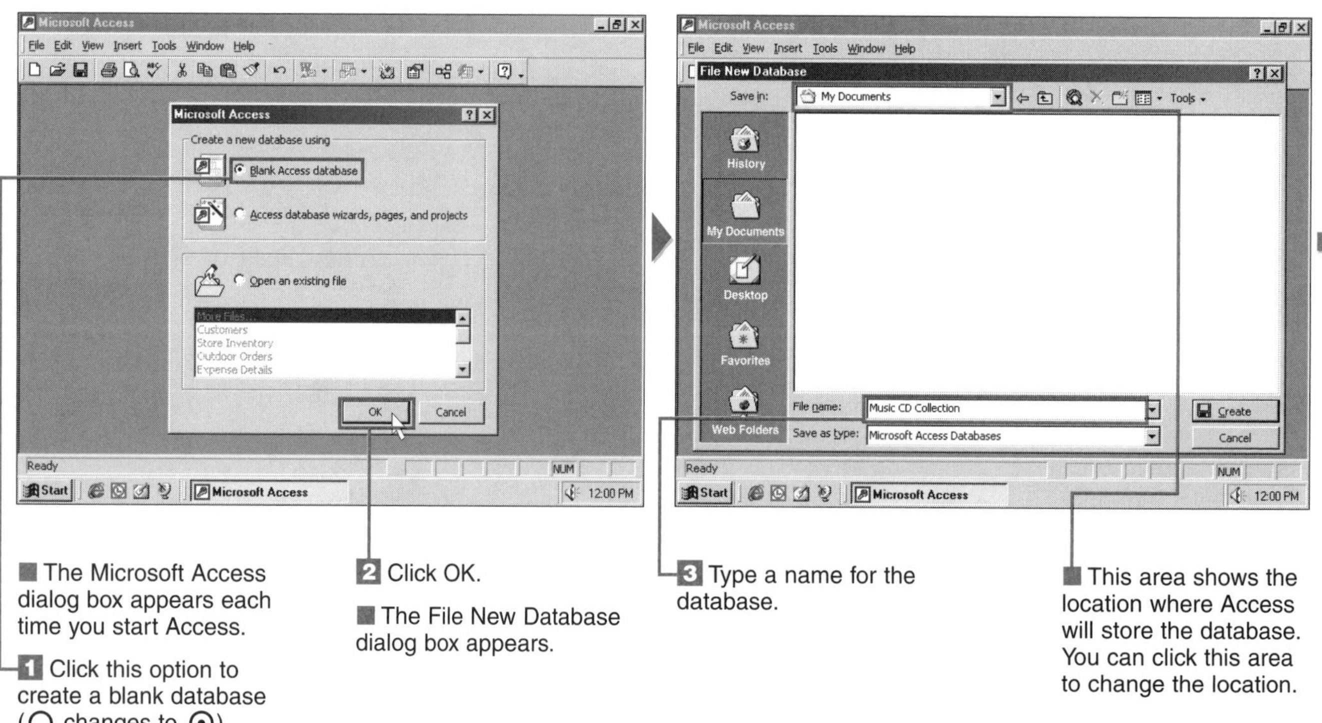

■ The Microsoft Access dialog box appears each time you start Access.

1 Click this option to create a blank database (○ changes to ⊙).

2 Click OK.

■ The File New Database dialog box appears.

3 Type a name for the database.

■ This area shows the location where Access will store the database. You can click this area to change the location.

TIPS

Can I create a blank database while working in Access?

✔ Yes. Click the New button (□) to display the New dialog box. Click the General tab and then double-click Database. Type a name for the database and then click Create. Access will close a database displayed on your screen when you create a new database.

How do I create a new folder to store my database?

✔ In the File New Database dialog box, click the Create New Folder button (□). Type a name for the folder and then press the Enter key.

What folders can I access using the Places Bar?

✔ The History folder lets you access folders you recently used. The My Documents folder provides a convenient place to store your database. The Desktop folder lets you store your database on the Windows desktop. The Favorites folder provides a place to store a database you will frequently access.

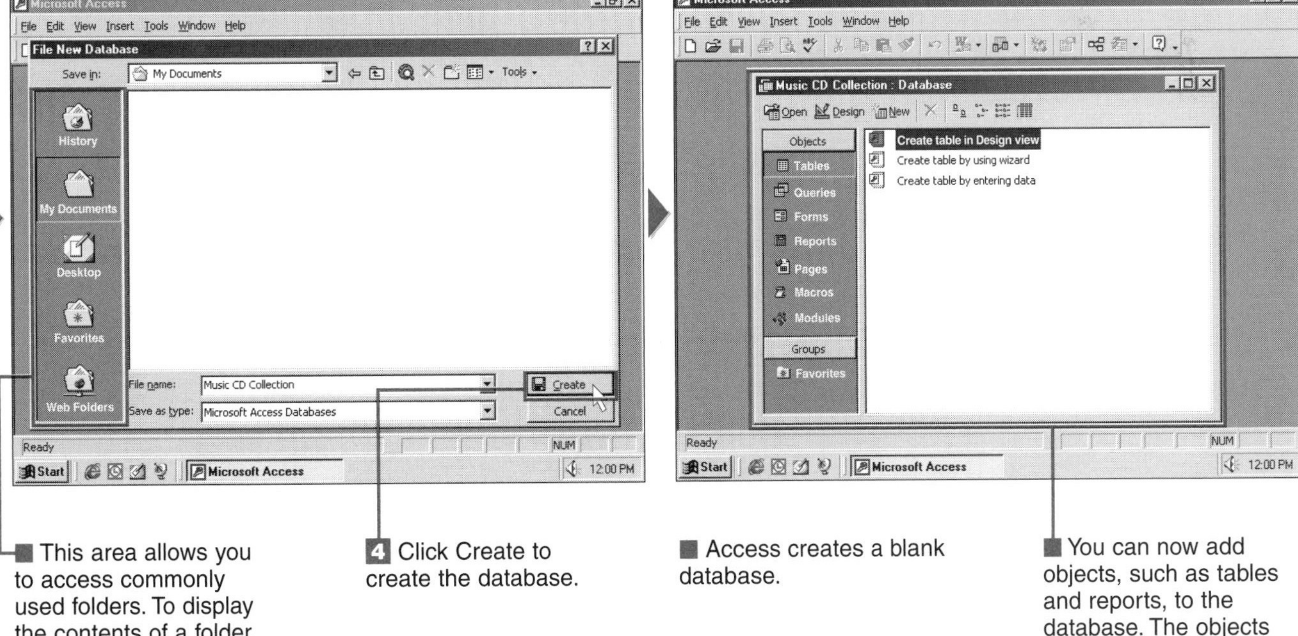

■ This area allows you to access commonly used folders. To display the contents of a folder, click the folder.

4 Click Create to create the database.

■ Access creates a blank database.

■ You can now add objects, such as tables and reports, to the database. The objects you add will appear in the Database window.

CREATE A DATABASE USING THE DATABASE WIZARD

The Database Wizard lets you create a database quickly and efficiently. The wizard saves you time by providing ready-to-use objects, such as tables, forms, queries and reports.

Access offers ten databases, such as the Contact Management, Expenses, Inventory Control and Order Entry databases. You can choose the database that best suits the type of information you want to store. For additional databases, you can visit the following Web site: http://officeupdate.microsoft.com/downloadCatalog/dldAccess.htm

To store the new database as a file on your computer, you must give the database a name. Using a descriptive name will help you recognize the database later.

Access automatically stores the database in the My Documents folder, but you can specify another folder. Access lets you quickly access several commonly used folders, such as Desktop and Favorites.

The Database Wizard will ask you a series of questions to determine how to set up the database to suit your needs. When you start the wizard, the wizard describes the type of information the database will store.

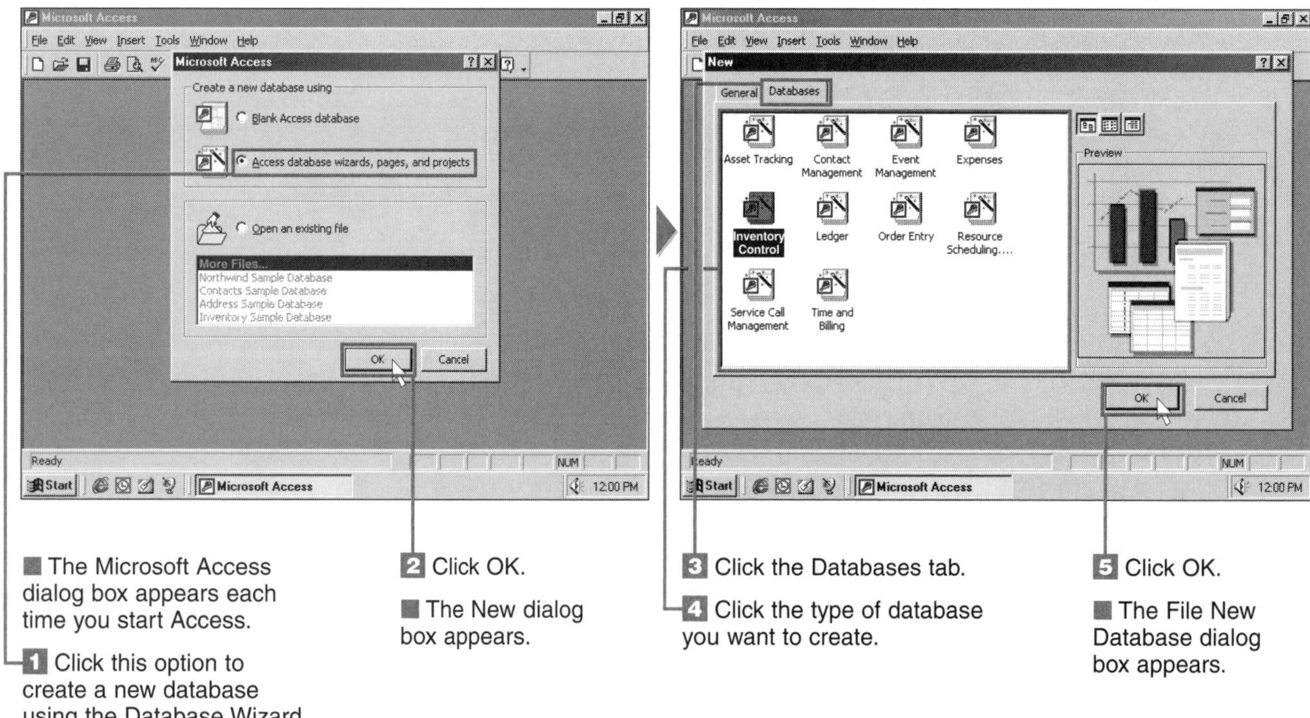

■ The Microsoft Access dialog box appears each time you start Access.

1 Click this option to create a new database using the Database Wizard (○ changes to ⊙).

2 Click OK.

■ The New dialog box appears.

3 Click the Databases tab.

4 Click the type of database you want to create.

5 Click OK.

■ The File New Database dialog box appears.

TIPS

The Microsoft Access dialog box offers the "Access database wizards, pages, and projects" option. What are pages and projects?

✔ Pages are Web pages you can create to access a database on an intranet or the Internet using a Web browser. Projects allow you to create an Access database that can work with more sophisticated programs, such as network database programs.

In the New dialog box, click the General tab. To create a page, click the Data Access Page icon. To create a project, click a Project icon. Then click OK.

How can I start the Database Wizard while working in Access?

✔ Click the New button (🗋) to display the New dialog box. Then perform steps 3 to 7 below. Access will close a database displayed on your screen when you create a new database.

Can I change the way databases appear in the New dialog box?

✔ Yes. Click ▣ to display the databases as large icons. Click ▦ to display the databases as small icons in a list. Click ▤ to display additional information about the databases.

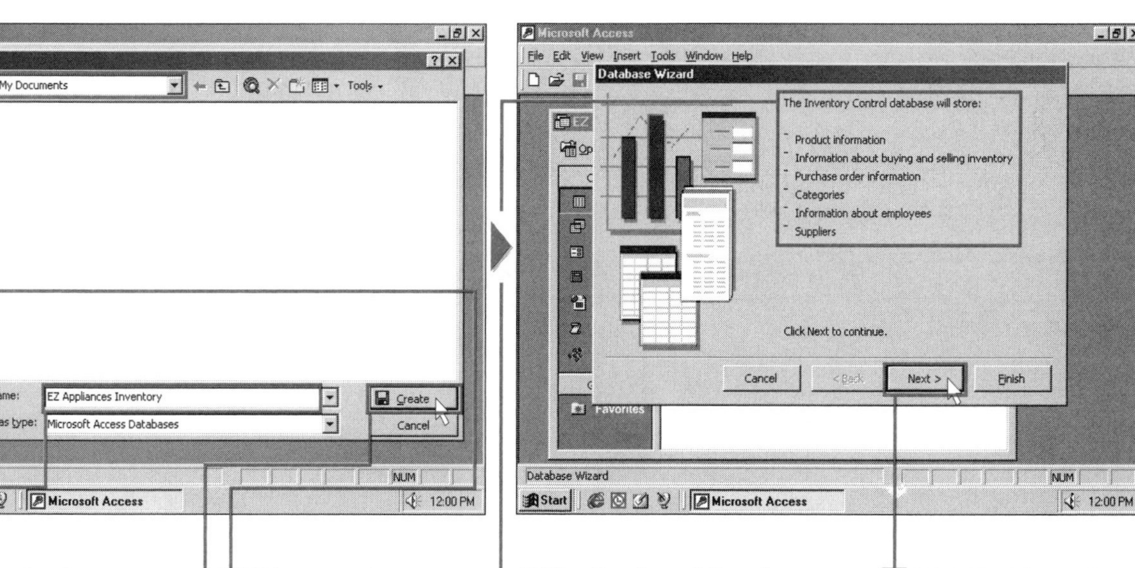

6 Type a name for the database.

■ This area shows the location where Access will store the database. You can click this area to change the location.

■ This area allows you to access commonly used folders. To display the contents of a folder, click the folder.

7 Click Create.

■ The Database Wizard appears.

■ This area describes the type of information the database will store.

8 Click Next to continue.

CONTINUED

CREATE A DATABASE USING THE DATABASE WIZARD CONTINUED

When using the Database Wizard to create a database, the wizard displays all the tables that Access will create. The wizard also displays the fields that will be included in each table. A field is a specific category of information in a table.

The wizard automatically includes required fields in each table. You can choose to include other optional fields. For example, in the Order Entry database, the Customer information table includes required fields such as Company Name, Billing Address and Phone Number. You can include optional fields in the table, such as Email Address and Notes.

The Database Wizard asks you to select the style you want to use for screen displays. A screen display style gives the database a consistent look. There are several screen display styles for you to choose from, including Blends, International and Stone.

The wizard also asks you to select a style for printed reports. Using a report style helps you create professional-looking reports. The wizard offers several report styles for you to choose from, including Bold, Corporate and Formal.

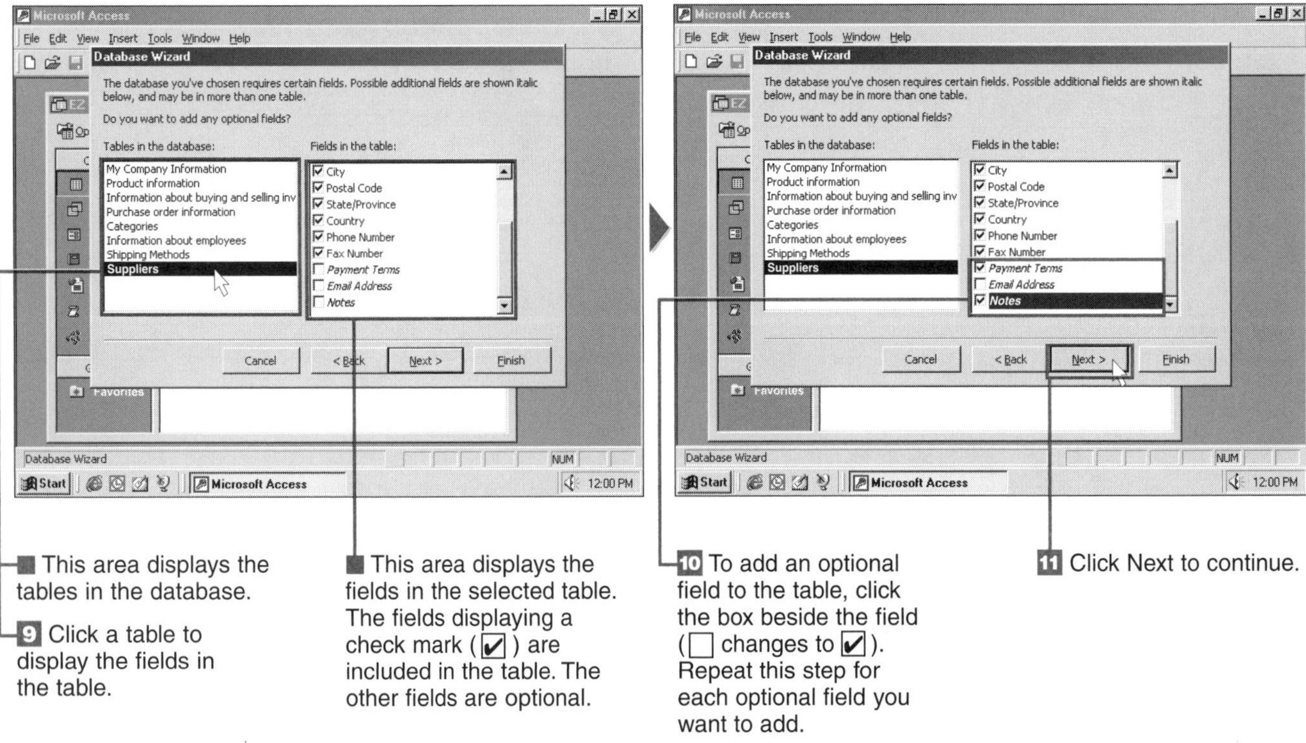

■ This area displays the tables in the database.

9 Click a table to display the fields in the table.

■ This area displays the fields in the selected table. The fields displaying a check mark (✔) are included in the table. The other fields are optional.

10 To add an optional field to the table, click the box beside the field (☐ changes to ✔). Repeat this step for each optional field you want to add.

11 Click Next to continue.

Do I have to answer all the questions in the Database Wizard?

✔ No. You can click the Finish button at any time to create a database based on the answers you have provided so far. If you are using the Database Wizard for the first time, the wizard will use default settings for the questions you did not answer. If you have used the Database Wizard before, the wizard will use the last answers you provided.

Can I change the style of my screen displays later on?

✔ You can easily change the style of your screen displays after you create a database. For more information, see page 463.

Can I remove a required field from the Database Wizard?

✔ You can only remove a required field after you finish creating the database. When you try to remove a required field from the Database Wizard, a dialog box appears, stating that the field is required and must be selected. To remove a field from a database you have created, see page 402.

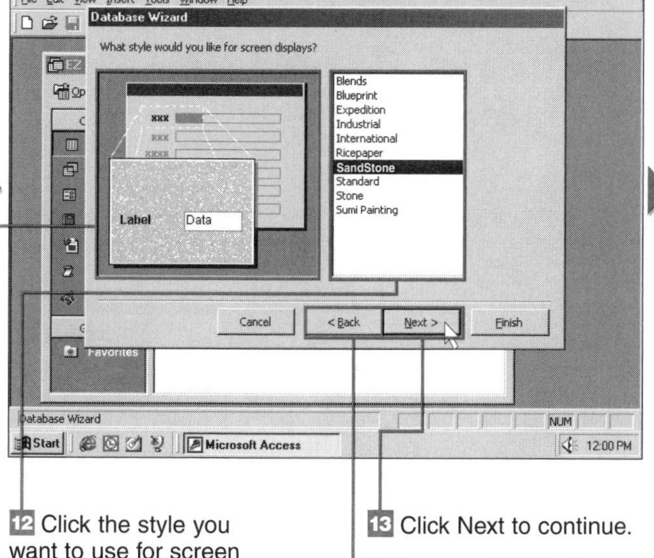

12 Click the style you want to use for screen displays.

■ This area displays a sample of the style you selected.

13 Click Next to continue.

■ You can click Back at any time to return to a previous step and change your answers.

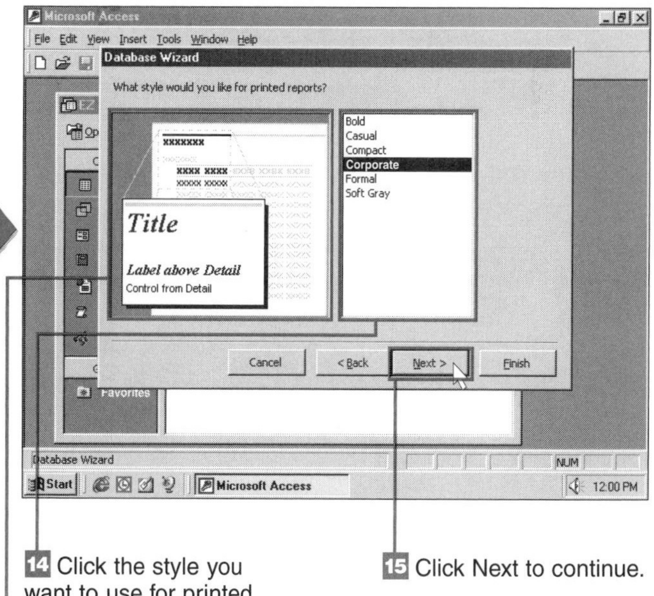

14 Click the style you want to use for printed reports.

■ This area displays a sample of the style you selected.

15 Click Next to continue.

CREATE A DATABASE USING THE DATABASE WIZARD CONTINUED

The Database Wizard asks you to specify a title for the database. Do not confuse the title of the database with the name of the database. The title of the database appears on the switchboard, which is similar to a main menu for the database. The name of the database is the name you used to store the database as a file on your computer.

After the wizard has finished creating the database, the wizard will start the database. You can specify whether or not you want to start using the database immediately after it is created.

The Database Wizard automatically creates objects for the database, such as tables, forms, queries and reports.

When the wizard is complete, the switchboard appears on your screen. You can use the switchboard to perform common tasks, such as adding records to the database and exiting the database.

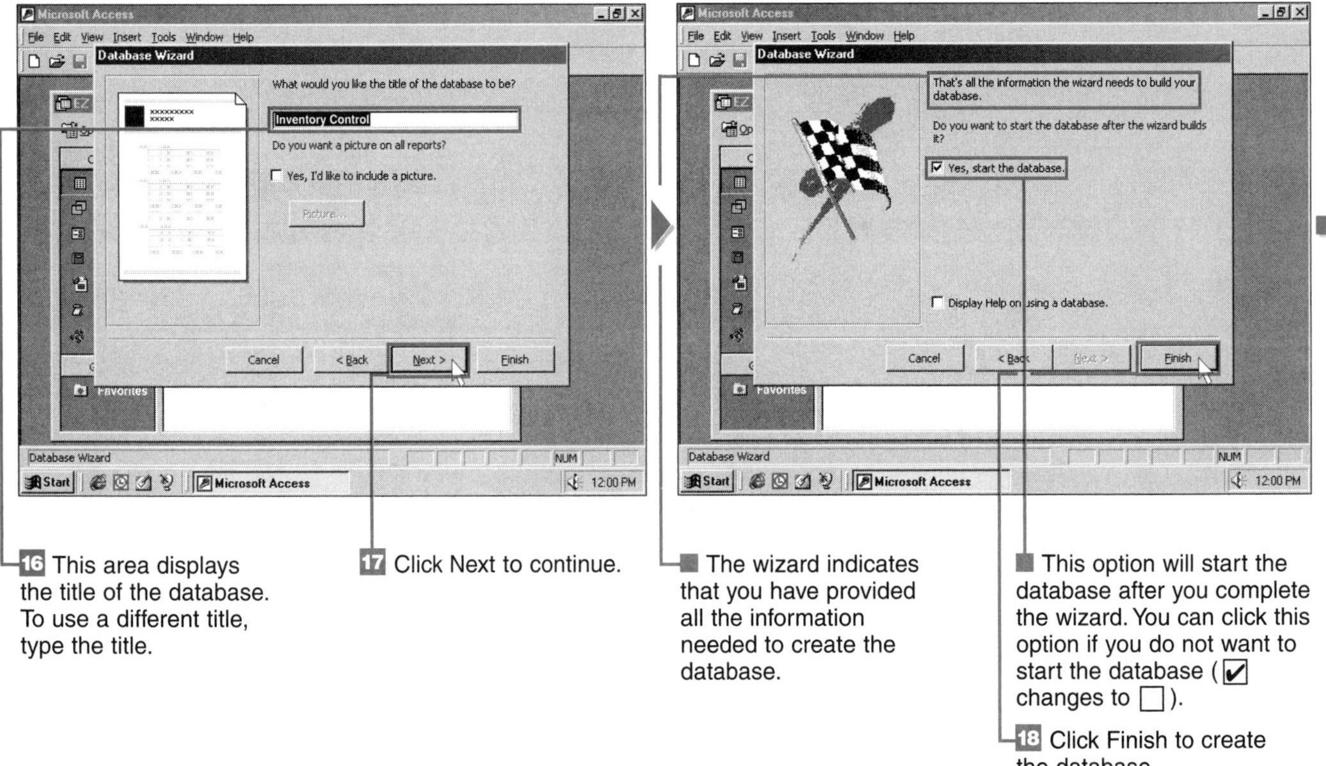

16 This area displays the title of the database. To use a different title, type the title.

17 Click Next to continue.

■ The wizard indicates that you have provided all the information needed to create the database.

■ This option will start the database after you complete the wizard. You can click this option if you do not want to start the database (☑ changes to ☐).

18 Click Finish to create the database.

TIPS

Can I get help with my new database?

✔ Access can display help information when it starts your newly created database. In the last dialog box of the Database Wizard, click the Display Help on using a database option (☐ changes to ☑).

Why does Access ask for information when the database starts?

✔ Access may ask you to enter information, such as your company name and address, to finish setting up the database.

Can I include a picture on all my reports?

✔ You can include a picture, such as a company logo, next to the title on your reports. After you specify a title for the database in the Database Wizard, select the Yes, I'd like to include a picture option (☐ changes to ☑). Then click the Picture button to find the picture on your computer. The picture you select will appear in the Database Wizard.

■ Access creates the objects for the database, including tables, forms, queries and reports.

■ The Main Switchboard window appears, which helps you perform common tasks.

19 To perform a task, click the task you want to perform.

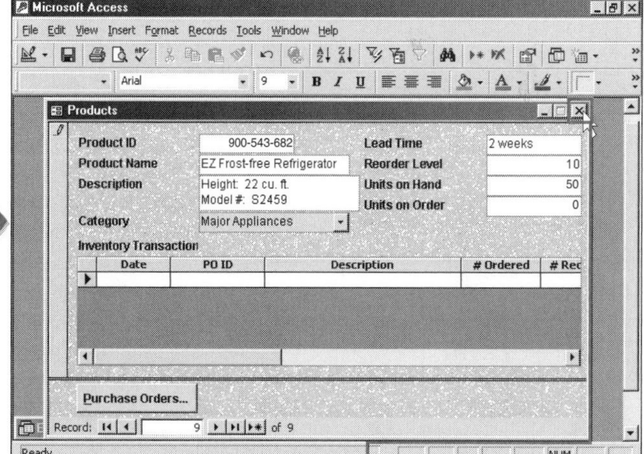

■ The object in the database that allows you to perform the task appears.

20 When you finish using the object and want to return to the switchboard, click ☒ to close the object.

USING THE DATABASE WINDOW

You can use the Database window to view and work with all the objects in a database, including tables, queries, forms, reports, pages, macros and modules. Each type of object in the Database window displays a different icon, such as a table (▦), query (▦), form (▦) and report (▦).

The Database window allows you to quickly open an object in the database to perform a task, such as adding a record to a table or changing a form.

You can change the name of an object displayed in the Database window to help you better identify the object.

You can delete an object you no longer need from your database. Before you can delete a table with a relationship to another table, you must first delete the relationship. For more information on relationships, see page 442.

When the Database window is hidden, you can press the F11 key to place the Database window in front of all the open windows in Access.

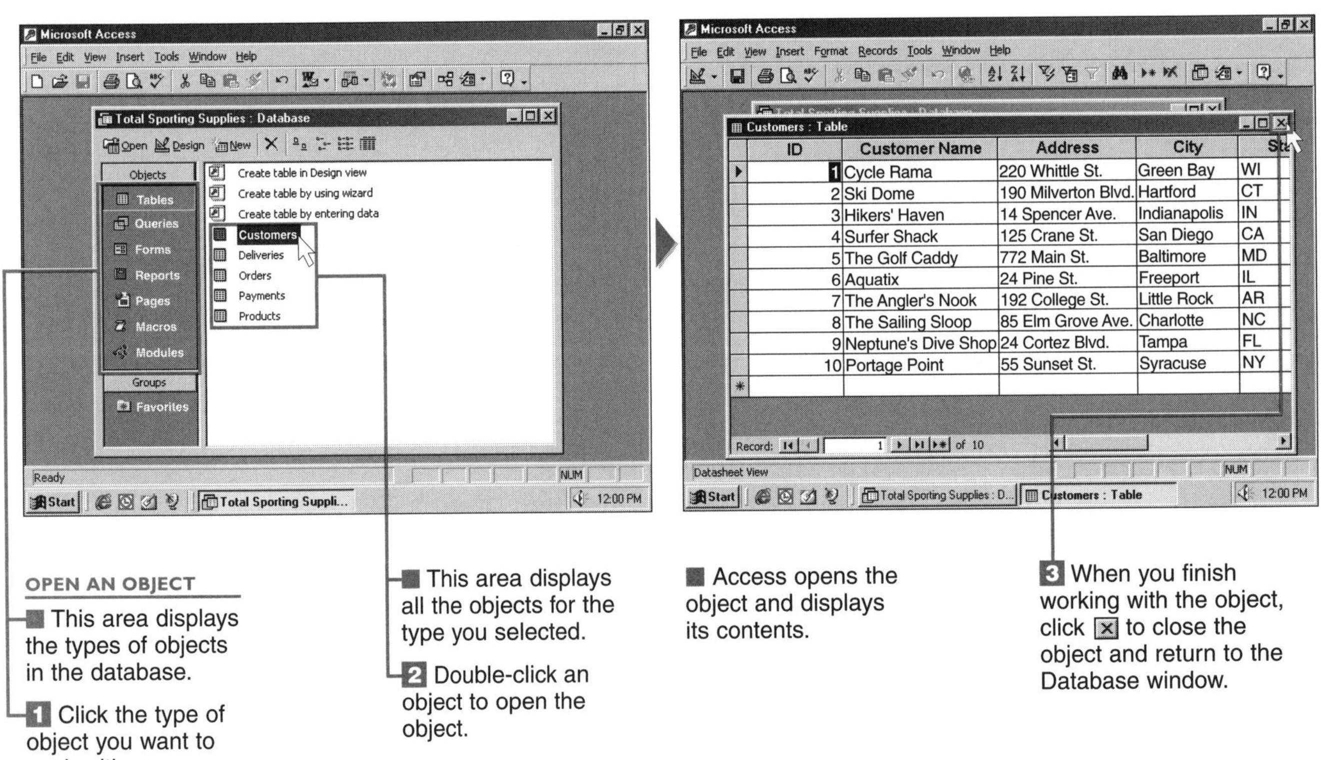

OPEN AN OBJECT

■ This area displays the types of objects in the database.

1 Click the type of object you want to work with.

■ This area displays all the objects for the type you selected.

2 Double-click an object to open the object.

■ Access opens the object and displays its contents.

3 When you finish working with the object, click ☒ to close the object and return to the Database window.

TIPS

Is there a more efficient way to work with the objects in the Database window?

✔ You can create groups to keep related objects in one place. For example, you can create a group named Sales to hold the tables and forms for your sales data. To create a group, click the Groups bar in the Database window. Right-click the area below the Groups bar and then select New Group. Type a name for the group and then click OK. To add an object to the group, drag the object from the right pane of the Database window to the name of the group below the Groups bar.

To display the objects in a group, click the group. You can work with an object in a group as you would work with any object in the Database window.

Can I change the way objects appear in the Database window?

✔ Yes. Click [icon] to display the objects as large icons. Click [icon] to display the objects as small icons. Click [icon] to display the objects as small icons in a list. Click [icon] to display additional information about the objects.

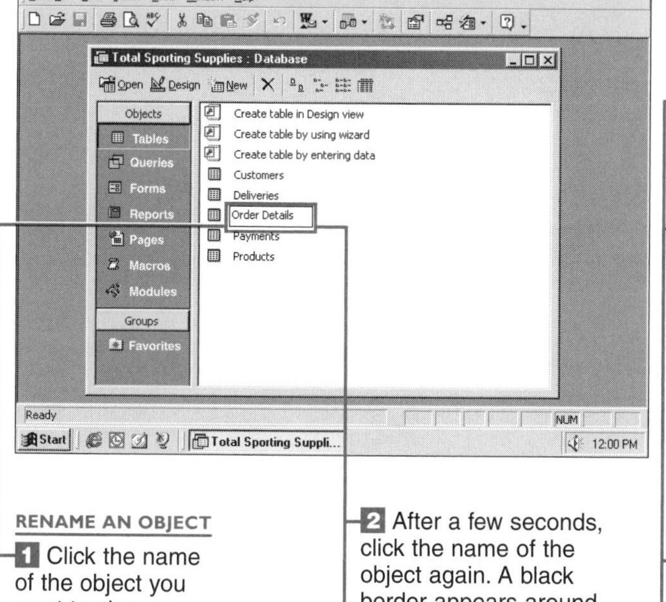

RENAME AN OBJECT

1 Click the name of the object you want to change.

2 After a few seconds, click the name of the object again. A black border appears around the name of the object.

3 Type a new name for the object and then press the Enter key.

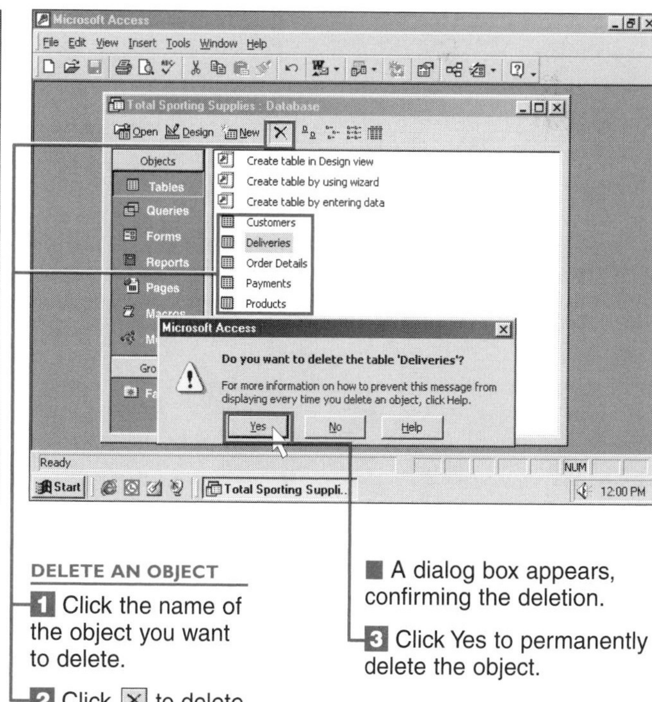

DELETE AN OBJECT

1 Click the name of the object you want to delete.

2 Click [X] to delete the object.

■ A dialog box appears, confirming the deletion.

3 Click Yes to permanently delete the object.

OPEN A DATABASE

You can open a database you previously created and display it on your screen. This lets you review and make changes to the database.

Each time you start Access, a dialog box appears, displaying a list of the databases you recently worked with. The names of sample databases, such as Contacts Sample Database, may also appear in the list. You can quickly open one of these databases. If the database you want to open is not in the list, you can use the Open dialog box to open the database.

The Open dialog box allows you to specify where the database you want to open is located. You can use the Places Bar to quickly display the contents of commonly used folders, such as the Desktop and Favorites folders.

In the Open dialog box, the icon appears beside the name of each database.

You can have only one database open at a time. Access will close a database displayed on your screen when you open another database.

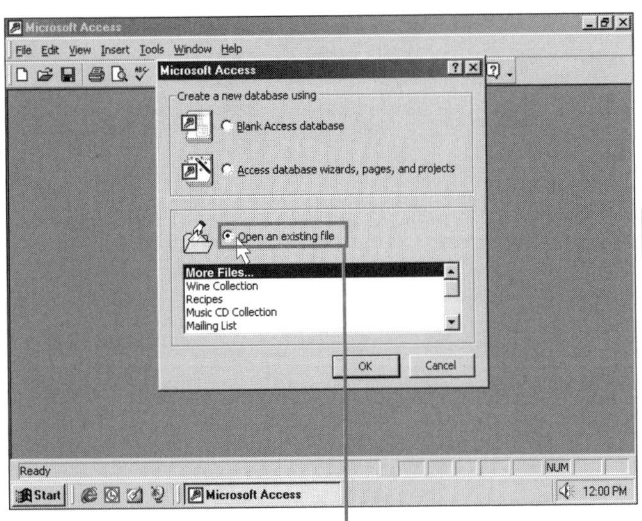

■ The Microsoft Access dialog box appears each time you start Access.

1 Click this option to open an existing database (○ changes to ⊙).

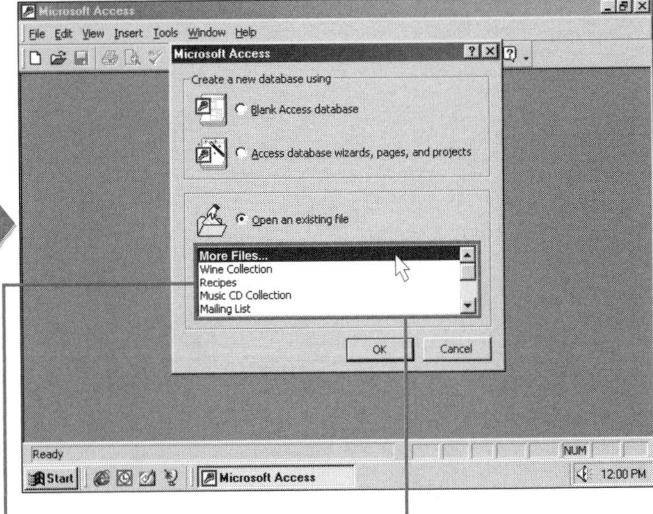

■ This area displays the names of the last databases you worked with. To open one of these databases, double-click the name of the database.

Note: The names of sample databases may also appear in the list.

2 If the database you want to open is not listed, double-click More Files.

■ The Open dialog box appears.

TIPS

How can I open a database while working in Access?

✔ Click the Open button (📂) on the Database toolbar to display the Open dialog box. Click the name of the database you want to open and then click Open. If you want to open a database you recently worked with, click the File menu and then select the name of the database you want to open.

Can I prevent other people on a network from opening a database?

✔ If the database is saved on a network, other people may be able to open the database while you are using it. To prevent others from opening the database, in the Open dialog box, click ▾ beside Open and then select Open Exclusive.

Why does a dialog box appear when I try to open a sample database?

✔ All of the sample databases may not have been installed on your computer when you installed Office 2000. Click Yes to install the sample database. A Microsoft Office 2000 dialog box appears, asking you to insert the CD-ROM disc you used to install Office. Insert the CD-ROM disc and click OK.

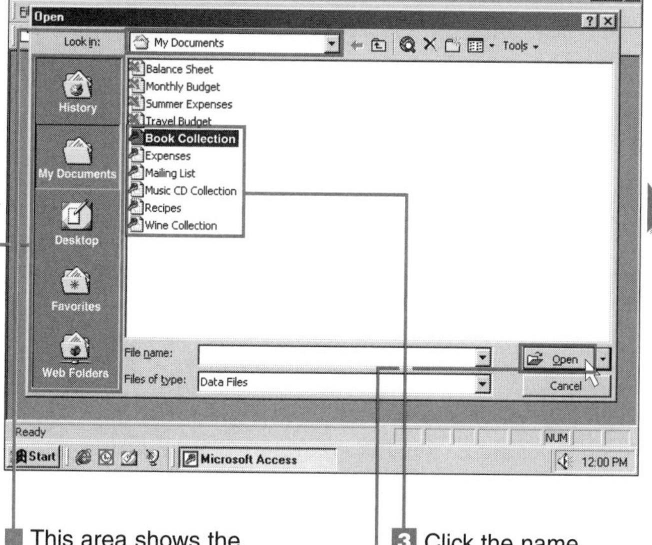

■ This area shows the location of the displayed files. You can click this area to change the location.

■ This area allows you to access commonly used folders. To display the contents of a folder, click the folder.

3 Click the name of the database you want to open.

4 Click Open.

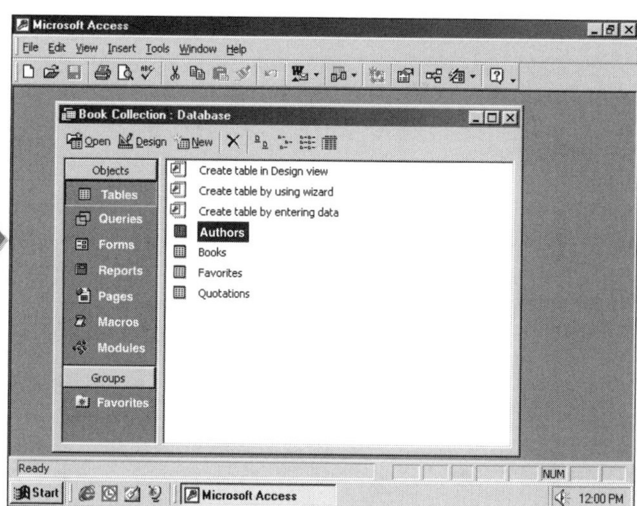

■ Access opens the database. You can now review and make changes to the database.

CREATE A TABLE IN THE DATASHEET VIEW

A table in a database stores a collection of information about a specific topic, such as a list of client addresses. You can create a table in the Datasheet view to store new information in rows and columns.

A table consists of records, fields and field names. A record is a collection of information about one person, place or thing in a table. For example, a record can contain the name, address and account number for one client.

A field is a specific category of information in a table. For example, a field can contain the first names of all your clients.

A field name identifies the information in a field. You can use up to 64 characters to name a field. You should avoid using long field names that will be difficult to remember and refer to later.

When you save a table, you give the table a name. You can use up to 64 characters to name a table. A descriptive name can help you recognize the table in a large database.

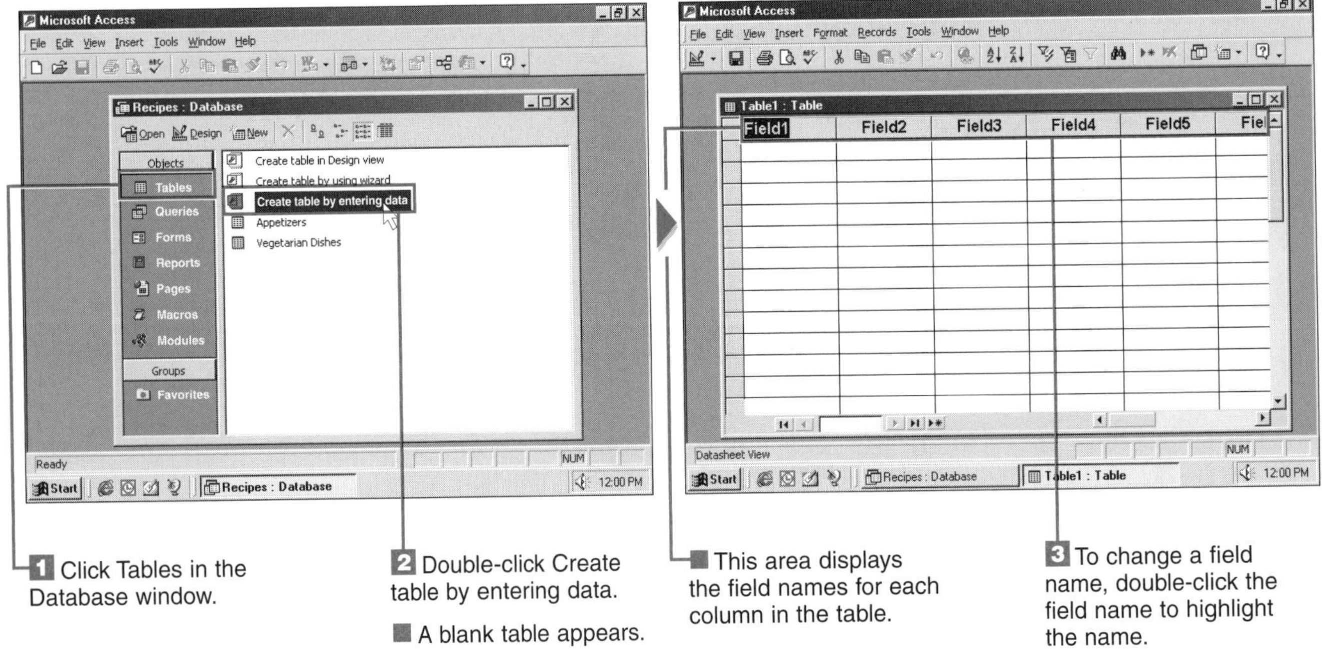

1 Click Tables in the Database window.

2 Double-click Create table by entering data.

■ A blank table appears.

■ This area displays the field names for each column in the table.

3 To change a field name, double-click the field name to highlight the name.

TIPS

Is there another way to create a table?

✔ You can create a table in the Design view. In the Database window, click Tables and then double-click the Create table in Design view option. The Design view gives you more control over the structure of the table and the type of information each field will contain. For information on working in the Design view, see pages 418 to 445.

Can Access help me create a table?

✔ You can use the Table Wizard to have Access take you step by step through the process of creating a table. For more information on the Table Wizard, see page 396.

Can I use a table I created in another database?

✔ You can import a table from another database. This saves you from having to create a new table. From the File menu, select Get External Data and then click Import. Click the name of the database that contains the table you want to import and then click the Import button. Click the name of the table you want to import and then click OK.

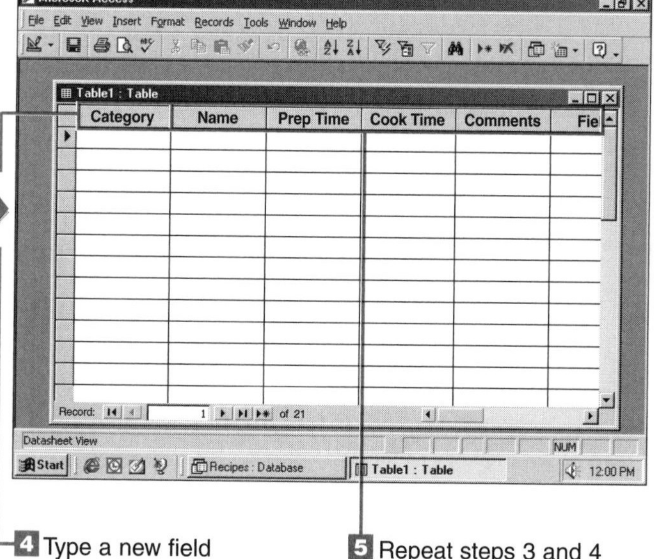

4 Type a new field name and then press the Enter key.

5 Repeat steps 3 and 4 for each field name you want to appear in the table.

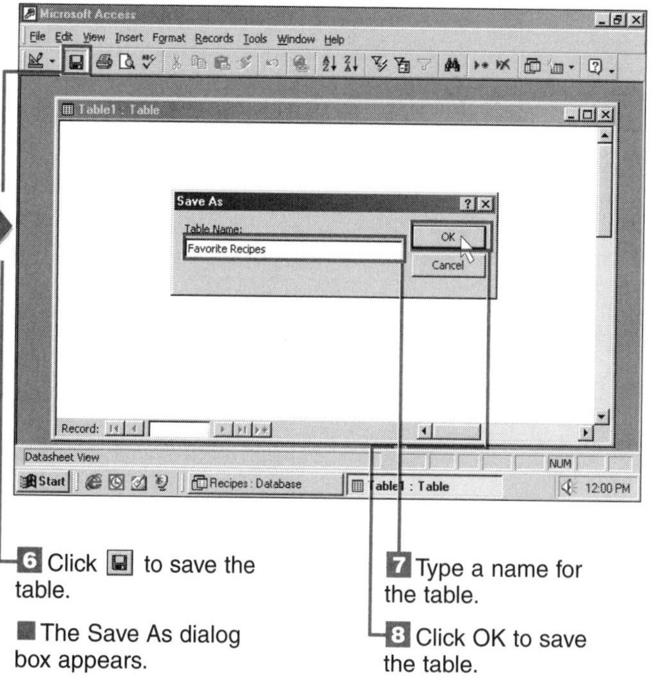

6 Click [save icon] to save the table.

■ The Save As dialog box appears.

7 Type a name for the table.

8 Click OK to save the table.

CONTINUED

CREATE A TABLE IN THE DATASHEET VIEW CONTINUED

You can have Access set a primary key in your table for you. A primary key is one or more fields that uniquely identifies each record in a table, such as an ID number. Each table you create should have a primary key. You can use the primary key to establish relationships between the tables in a database.

The first time you save your table, Access removes the rows and columns that do not contain data. This reduces the clutter in the table and makes it easier to enter your data.

You can enter data into a table in Access as you would enter data into a worksheet in Excel. Access adds a new row to the table each time you enter another record, so you can enter as many records as you need. Access automatically saves each record you enter.

When you finish entering the records for a table, you can close the table. The name of the table appears in the Database window.

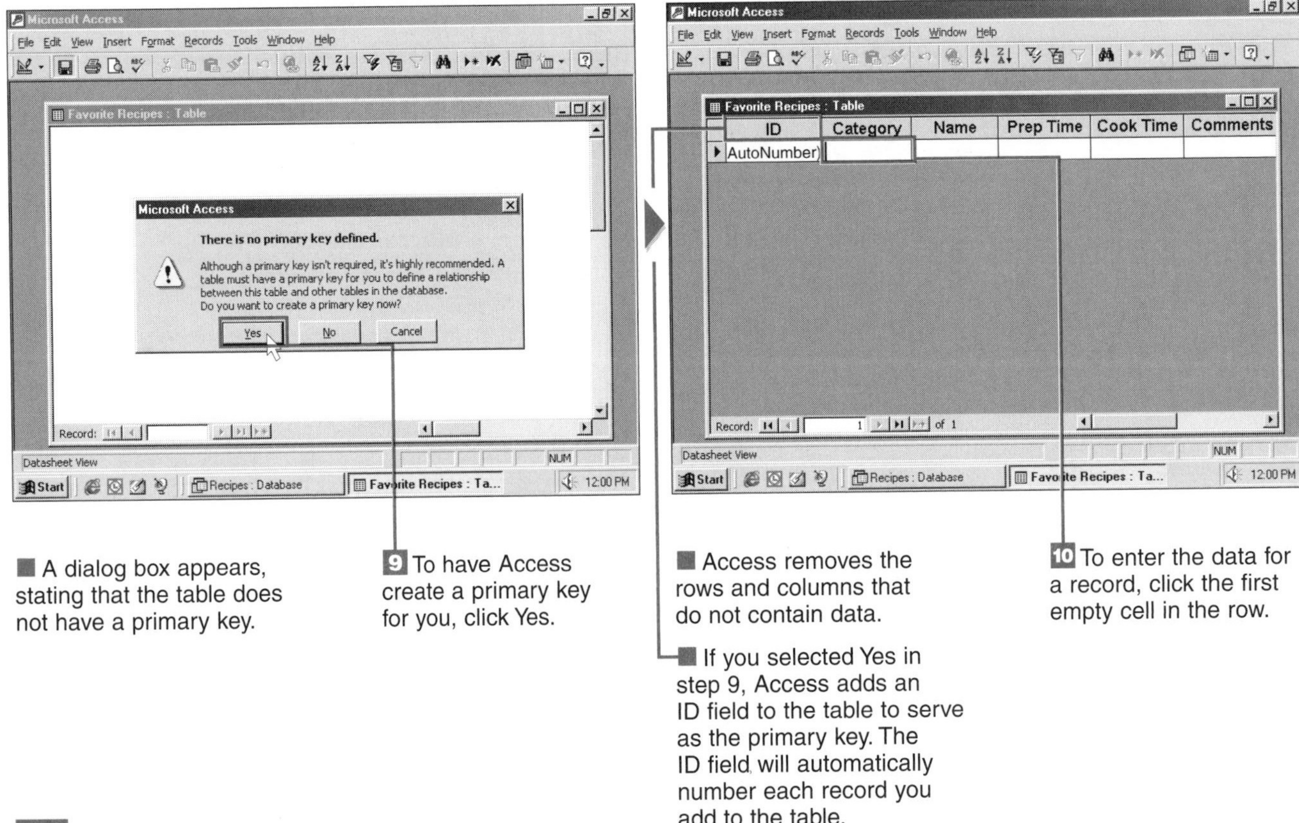

■ A dialog box appears, stating that the table does not have a primary key.

9 To have Access create a primary key for you, click Yes.

■ Access removes the rows and columns that do not contain data.

■ If you selected Yes in step 9, Access adds an ID field to the table to serve as the primary key. The ID field will automatically number each record you add to the table.

10 To enter the data for a record, click the first empty cell in the row.

TIPS

I did not choose to have Access create a primary key for me. Can I set a primary key later?

✔ You can set the primary key at any time. To set the primary key, see page 441.

What are the symbols that appear to the left of a record?

✔ The arrow (▶) indicates the current record. The pencil (✎) indicates the record you are editing. The asterisk (✱) indicates where you can enter data for a new record.

How do I insert a column?

✔ You can insert a column to add a new field to your table. Click the field name for the column you want to appear after the new column. Select the Insert menu and then choose Column.

How do I delete a table?

✔ Before you delete a table, make sure other objects in your database, such as a form or report, do not use the table. In the Database window, click Tables. Click the name of the table you want to delete and then press the Delete key.

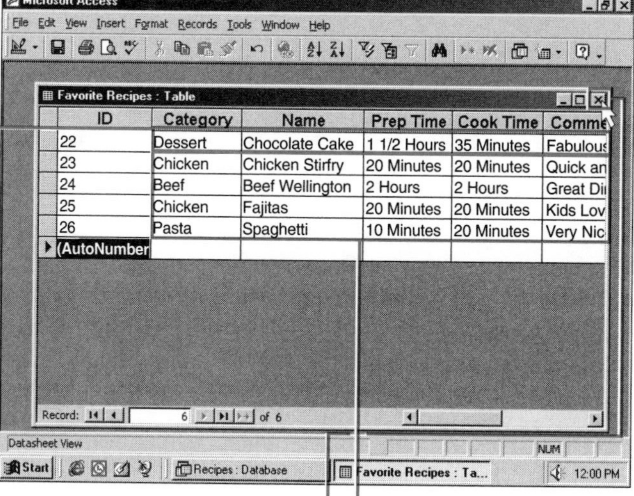

11 Type the data that corresponds to the field and then press the Enter key to move to the next cell. Repeat this step until you finish entering all the data for the record.

12 Repeat steps 10 and 11 for each record. Access automatically saves each record you enter.

13 When you finish entering records, click ☒ to close the table.

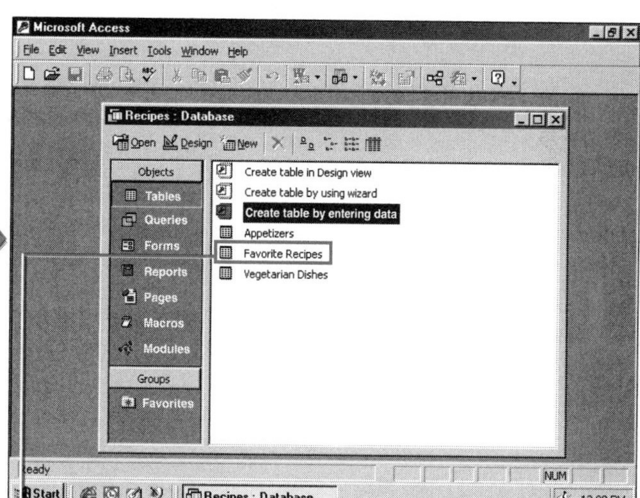

■ The name of the table appears in the Database window.

CREATE A TABLE USING THE WIZARD

The Table Wizard helps you quickly create a table that suits your needs. The wizard asks you a series of questions and then sets up a table based on your answers.

The Table Wizard can help you create a table for business or personal use. The wizard provides sample business tables such as Customers, Products, Orders and Deliveries. For your personal needs, the wizard offers sample tables such as Recipes, Plants, Wine List and Investments. You can select a sample table that is similar to the table you want to create.

The Table Wizard displays the available fields for the sample table you selected. You can include all or only some of the available fields in your table. You should make sure each field you include is directly related to the subject of the table. If you accidentally include a field in your table you do not need, you can remove the field.

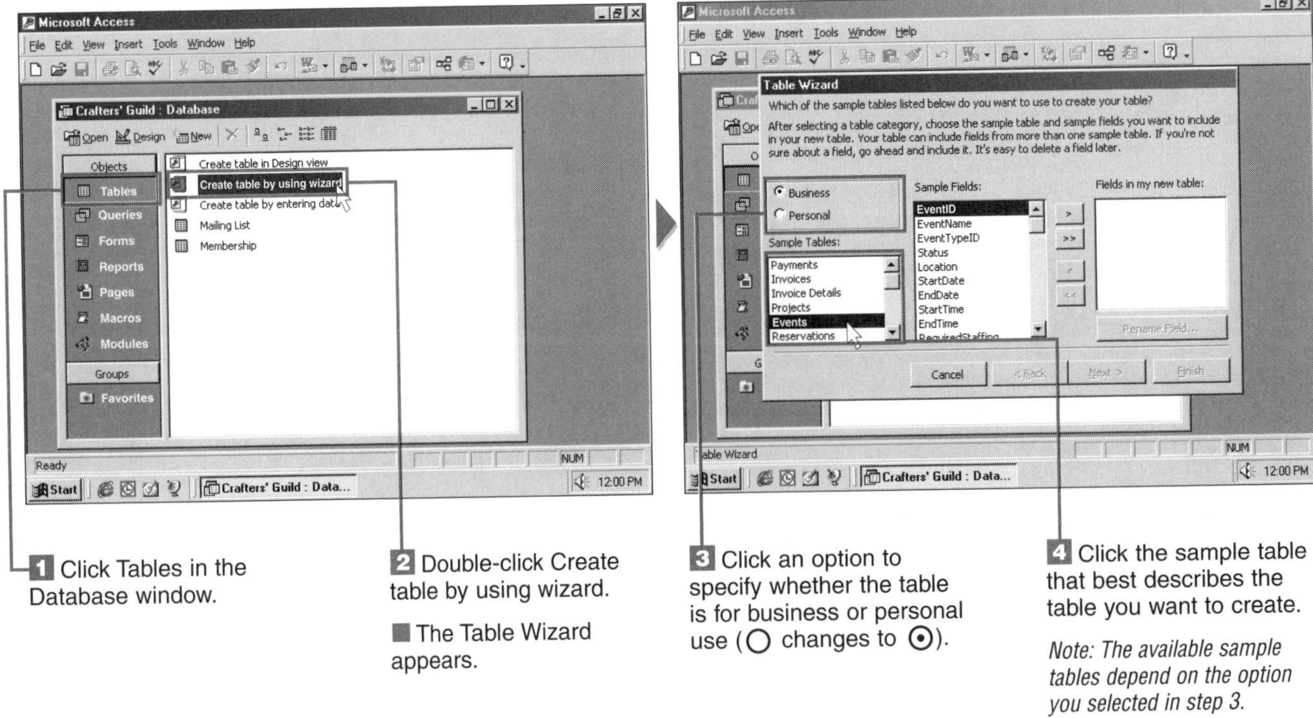

1 Click Tables in the Database window.

2 Double-click Create table by using wizard.

■ The Table Wizard appears.

3 Click an option to specify whether the table is for business or personal use (○ changes to ⊙).

4 Click the sample table that best describes the table you want to create.

Note: The available sample tables depend on the option you selected in step 3.

TIPS

How can I quickly include all the available fields in my table?

✔ In the Table Wizard, click >> to quickly include all the available fields from the sample table in your table.

Can I rename a field in the Table Wizard?

✔ Yes. In the Fields in my new table area, click the field you want to rename and then click the Rename Field button. Type a new name for the field and then click OK.

How can I quickly remove all the fields I included in my table?

✔ In the Table Wizard, click << to quickly remove all the fields you included.

Do I have to complete all the steps in the Table Wizard?

✔ After you select the fields you want to include, you can click the Finish button at any time to create your table based on the information you have provided.

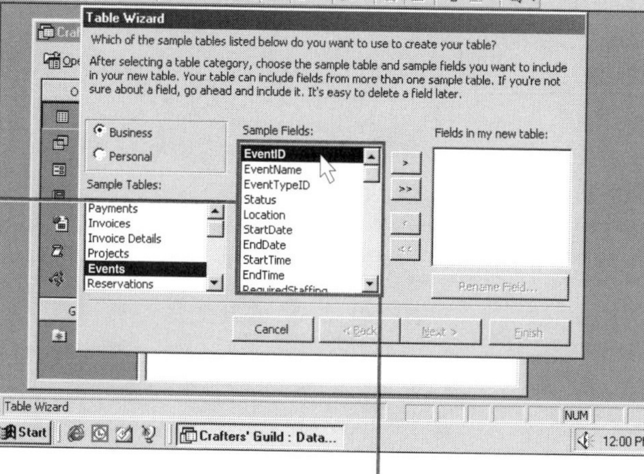

■ This area displays the available fields for the sample table you selected.

5 Double-click each field you want to include in the table.

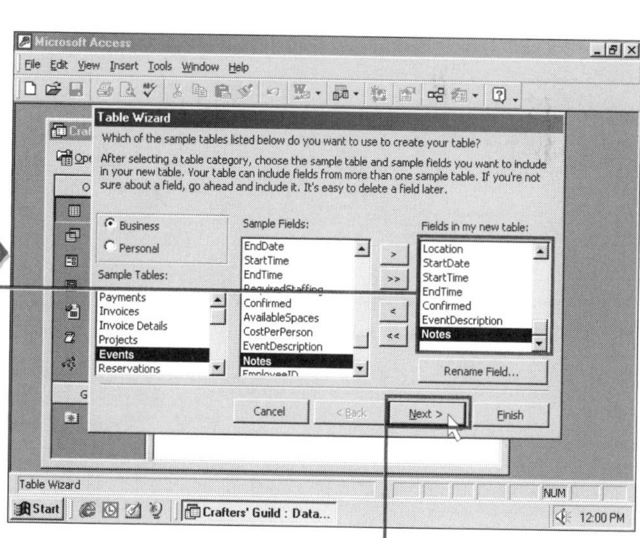

■ Each field you select appears in this area.

6 To remove a field you accidentally included, double-click the field in this area.

7 Click Next to continue.

CONTINUED

CREATE A TABLE USING THE WIZARD

CONTINUED

The Table Wizard asks you to name your table. You can use up to 64 characters to name a table. The name you specify will appear in the Tables area of the Database window.

You can set a primary key for your table. A primary key is a field that uniquely identifies each record in a table. Each table in a database should have a primary key. If you do not know which field to set as the primary key, you should allow the wizard to set the primary key for you. You can later change the primary key the wizard sets. See page 441.

If other tables already exist in the database, the Table Wizard will show you how your new table relates to the other tables.

Access allows you to choose what you want to do when the wizard finishes creating your table. You can modify the table design, start entering data directly into the table or enter data using a form the wizard creates.

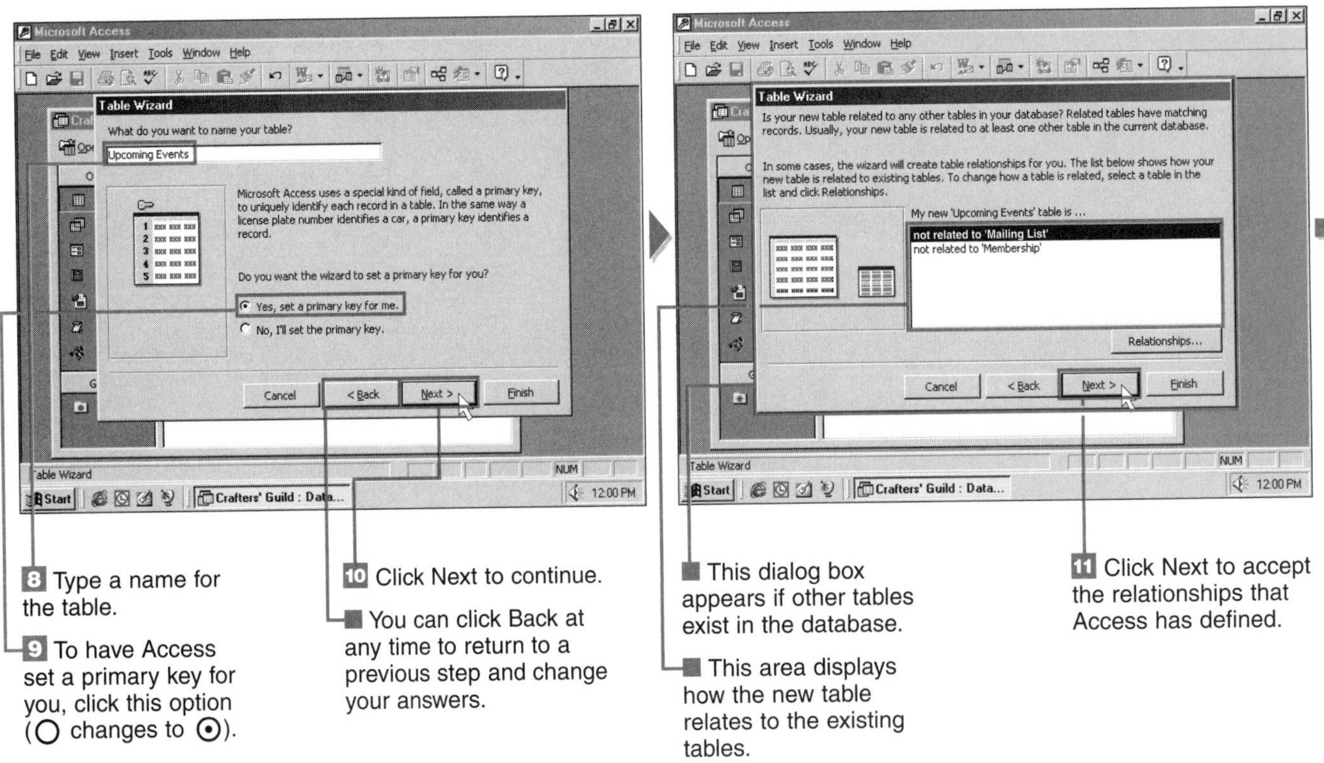

8 Type a name for the table.

9 To have Access set a primary key for you, click this option (○ changes to ⊙).

10 Click Next to continue.

■ You can click Back at any time to return to a previous step and change your answers.

■ This dialog box appears if other tables exist in the database.

■ This area displays how the new table relates to the existing tables.

11 Click Next to accept the relationships that Access has defined.

TIPS

I want to set the primary key. Which field should I use as the primary key?

✔ You should use a field that will hold a unique value for each record. For example, in a table that stores data related to inventory, you could use the Serial Number field as the primary key, since each product has its own unique serial number.

Can I change how my table relates to another table in the database?

✔ Yes. In the Table Wizard, select the table you want to change the relationship for and then click the Relationships button. Select the type of relationship you want to create (○ changes to ⊙). For more information on relationships, see page 442.

How do I delete a table?

✔ Before you delete a table, make sure the table does not contain information you will need in the future and is not used by any other objects in your database, such as a form or report. Click Tables in the Database window, select the table you want to delete and then press the Delete key.

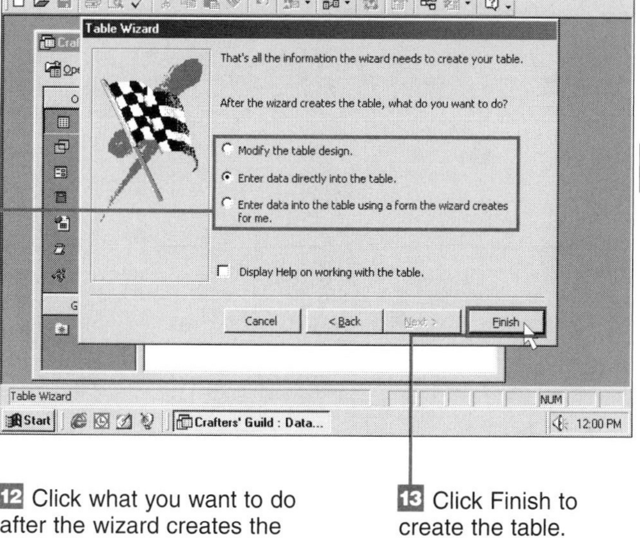

12 Click what you want to do after the wizard creates the table (○ changes to ⊙).

13 Click Finish to create the table.

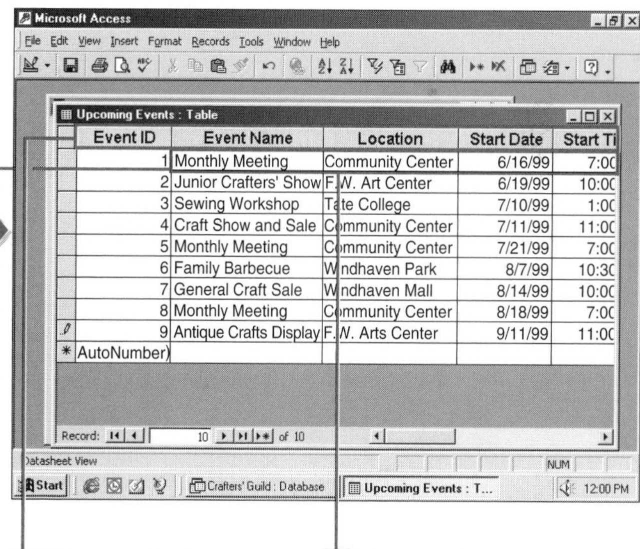

■ This area displays the field names for the table.

14 To add a record, click the first empty cell in a row.

15 Type the data that corresponds to the field and then press the Enter key to move to the next cell. Repeat this step until you finish entering all the data for the record.

16 Repeat steps 14 and 15 for each record.

RENAME A FIELD

You can give a field a different name to more accurately describe the contents of the field. This can help prevent confusion between two similar fields in a table.

If you rename a field that is used in other objects in the database, such as a form or report, Access will automatically change the references in the database to ensure the objects will be able to access the information in the renamed field.

You can use up to 64 characters to name a field. You cannot use the . ! [or] character to name a field.

You should also avoid including spaces when you rename a field if you plan to enter the field name in an expression for a calculation. A field name that contains spaces is more likely to be entered incorrectly than one without spaces. For more information on using expressions in calculations, see page 486.

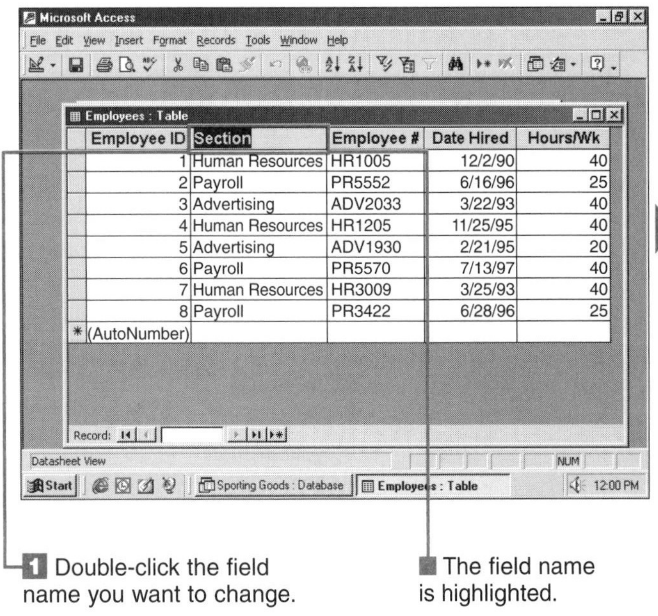

1 Double-click the field name you want to change.

■ The field name is highlighted.

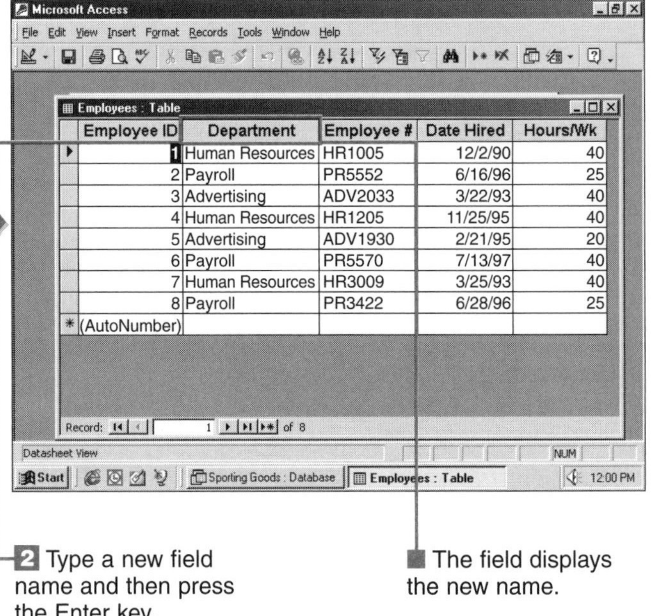

2 Type a new field name and then press the Enter key.

■ The field displays the new name.

REARRANGE FIELDS

You can change the order of fields to better organize the information in your table.

For example, in a table that stores employee names and phone numbers, you may want to move the field containing work phone numbers in front of the field containing home phone numbers.

Rearranging the fields in a table will not affect how the fields are displayed in other objects in the database, such as a form. Rearranging fields in the Datasheet view will also not affect the arrangement of fields in the Design view.

A thick line indicates the new location of the field you are moving. If you move a field to an area of your table that is not displayed on the screen, Access will scroll through the table to show you the new location of the field.

After you change the order of fields in your table, you must save the table to keep the new arrangement of fields.

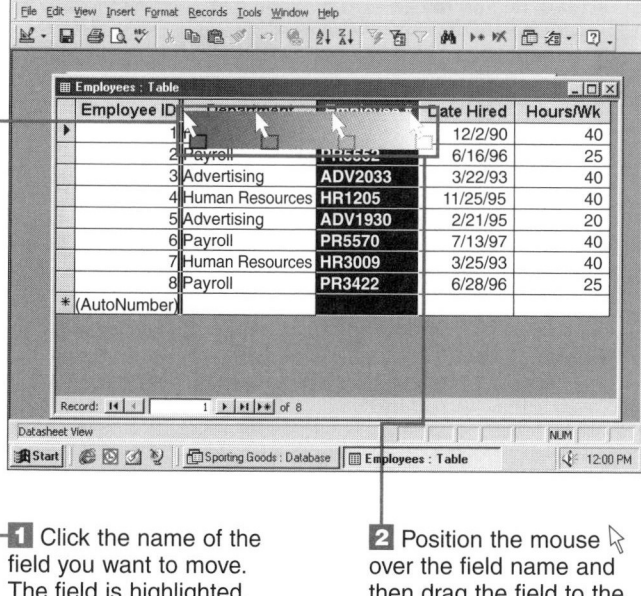

1 Click the name of the field you want to move. The field is highlighted.

2 Position the mouse over the field name and then drag the field to the new location.

Note: A thick line shows where the field will appear.

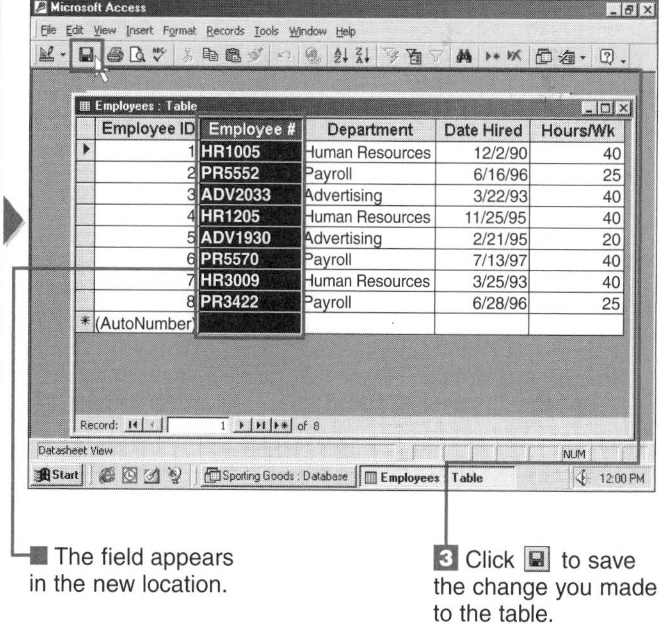

■ The field appears in the new location.

3 Click 💾 to save the change you made to the table.

ADD OR DELETE A FIELD

You can add a field to a table when you want the table to include an additional category of information. For example, you may want to add a field for e-mail addresses to a table that contains client information.

If you no longer need a field, you can delete the field from your table. Deleting a field will permanently delete all the data in the field. Deleting unneeded fields will make your database smaller and may speed up the searches you perform.

Before you delete a field, you should make sure the field is not used in any other objects in the database, such as a form, query or report. If you delete a field used in another object, Access will not be able to find all the data for the object.

When you add or delete a field, Access automatically saves the changes for you.

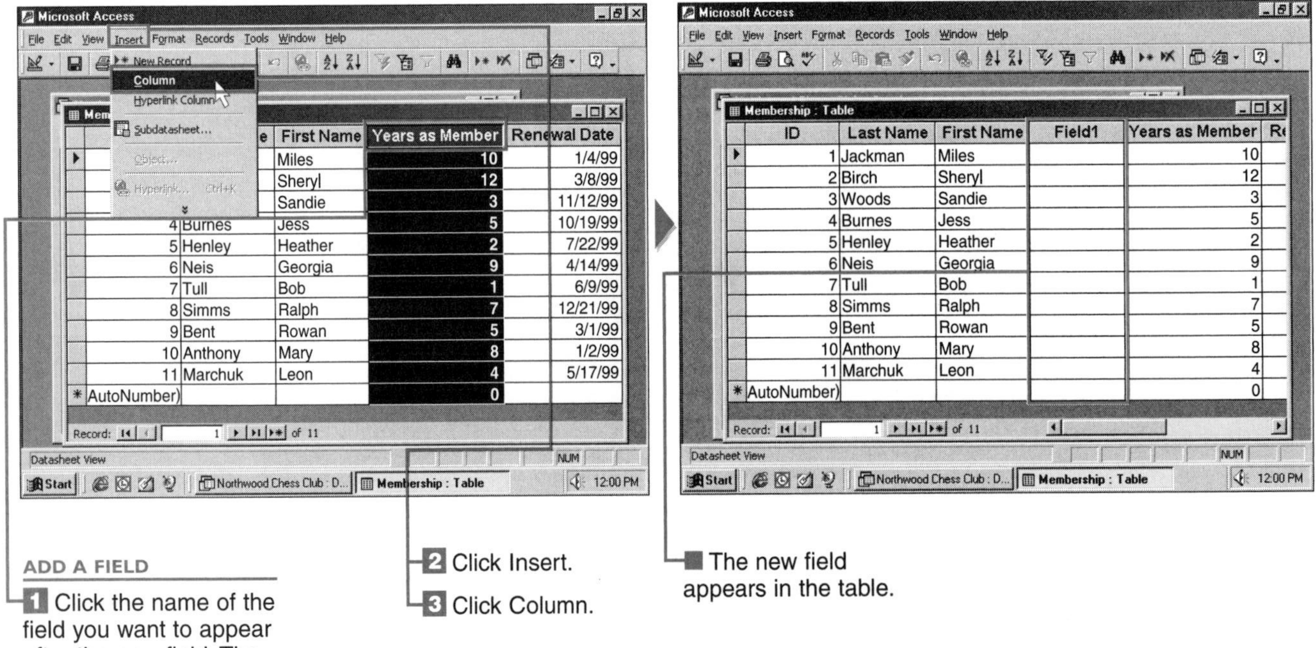

ADD A FIELD

1 Click the name of the field you want to appear after the new field. The field is highlighted.

2 Click Insert.

3 Click Column.

■ The new field appears in the table.

TIPS

How do I change the name of a field I added to my table?

✔ Access automatically assigns a default name to each new field you add to a table. To rename a field, double-click the field name, type a new name and then press the Enter key. For more information on field names, see page 400.

After I delete a field from a table, can I undo the change?

✔ You cannot use the Undo feature to reverse the results of deleting a field. If you regret deleting a field from your table, you must add the field to the table again.

Why won't Access let me delete a field?

✔ Access will not allow you to delete a field that is part of a relationship. A relationship tells Access how to bring together related information from more than one table in a database. You must delete the relationship before you can delete the field. To delete a relationship, see the top of page 469.

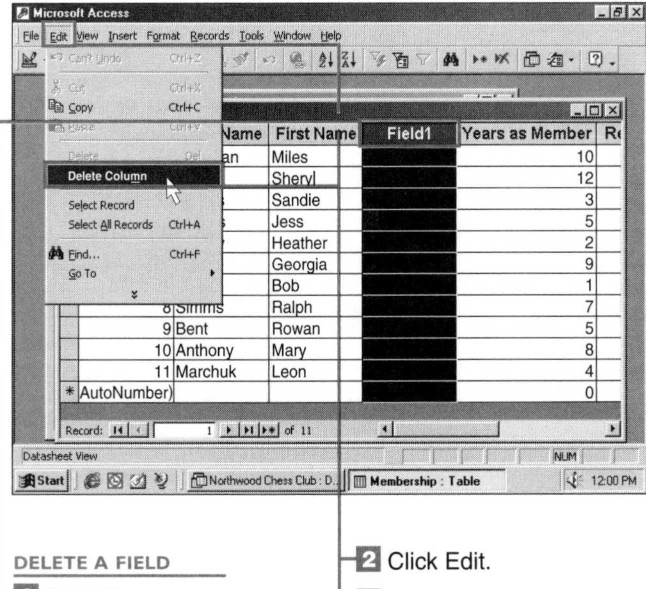

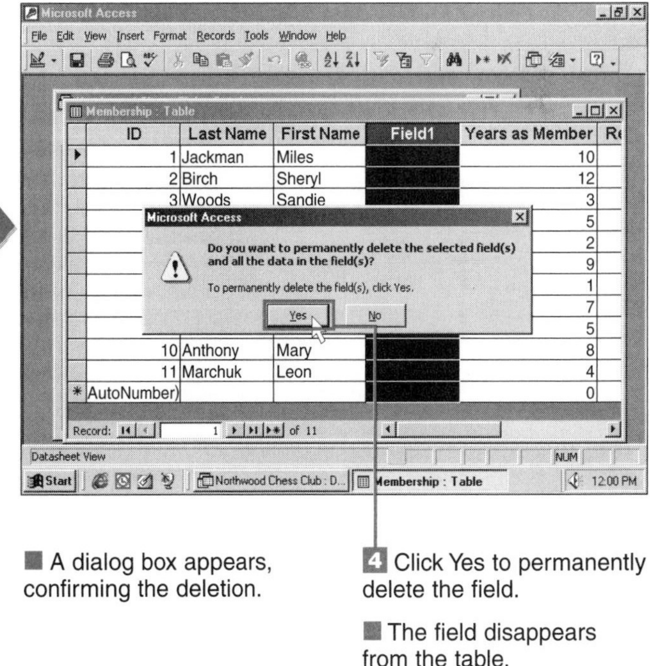

DELETE A FIELD

1 Click the name of the field you want to delete. The field is highlighted.

2 Click Edit.

3 Click Delete Column.

■ A dialog box appears, confirming the deletion.

4 Click Yes to permanently delete the field.

■ The field disappears from the table.

CHANGE COLUMN WIDTH

You can change the width of a column in your table. Increasing the width of a column lets you view data that is too long to display in the column. Reducing the width of a column allows you to display more fields on your screen at once.

You can have Access automatically adjust the width of a column to fit the longest item in the column.

After you change the width of a column, you must save the table to have Access save the new column width.

You can also change the height of rows in your table. Position the mouse over the bottom edge of the gray area to the left of the row you want to change (↖ changes to ‡). You can then drag the row edge to a new location. When you change the height of a row, all the rows in the table automatically change to the new height. You cannot change the height of a single row.

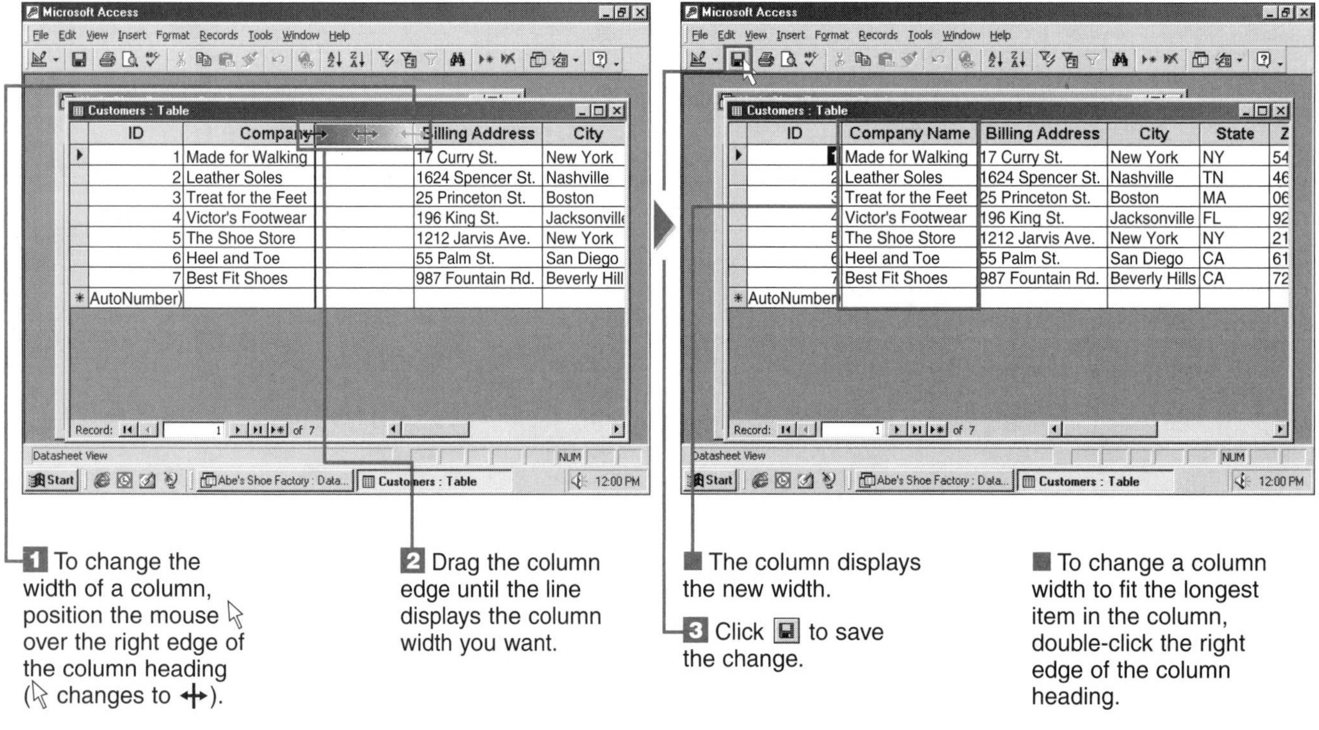

1 To change the width of a column, position the mouse ↖ over the right edge of the column heading (↖ changes to ↔).

2 Drag the column edge until the line displays the column width you want.

■ The column displays the new width.

3 Click 💾 to save the change.

■ To change a column width to fit the longest item in the column, double-click the right edge of the column heading.

OPEN A TABLE

You can open a table and display its contents on your screen. This lets you review and make changes to the table.

You can open a table in the Datasheet or Design view. The Datasheet view displays all the records in a table. You can enter, edit and review records in the Datasheet view.

The Design view displays the structure of a table. You can change settings in the Design view to specify the kind of data you want to enter in each field of a table. For example, you can change settings for a field so you can enter only numbers in the field. For more information on the Design view, see pages 418 to 445.

When you have finished working with a table, you can close the table to remove it from your screen. A dialog box appears if you have not saved changes you made to the layout of the table, such as changing the column width or rearranging fields.

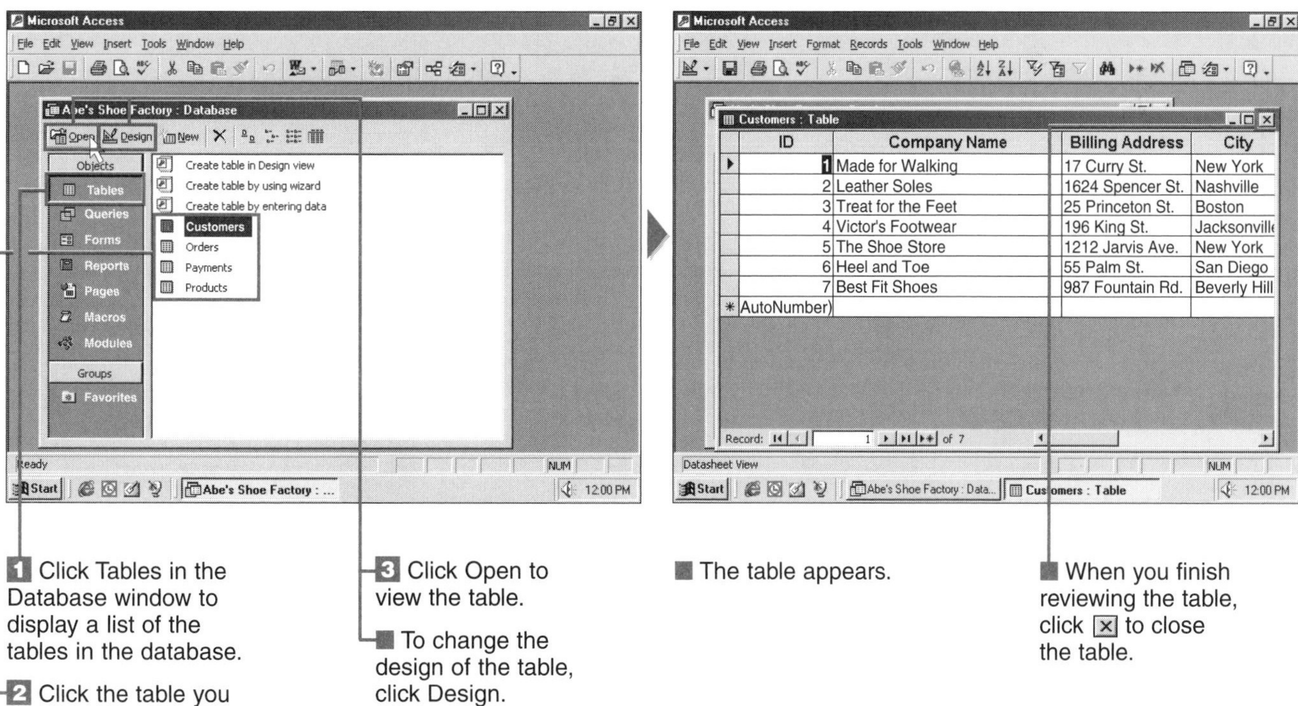

1 Click Tables in the Database window to display a list of the tables in the database.

2 Click the table you want to open.

3 Click Open to view the table.

■ To change the design of the table, click Design.

■ The table appears.

■ When you finish reviewing the table, click ☒ to close the table.

MOVE THROUGH RECORDS

You can easily move through the records in your table when reviewing or editing information.

You can change the location of the insertion point in your table. The insertion point is the flashing line on your screen that indicates where the text you type will appear. The insertion point must be located in the cell you want to edit. Access provides buttons that allow you to instantly move the insertion point to the first, last, previous or next record.

If your table contains a large amount of information, your computer screen may not be able to display all of the fields and records at once. You can use the scroll bars to view the fields and records that are not displayed. You can scroll one field or record at a time. You can also quickly scroll to any field or record in your table. The scroll bars will not appear if all of the fields and records are displayed on your screen.

Scrolling allows you to move to another location in the table but does not move the insertion point.

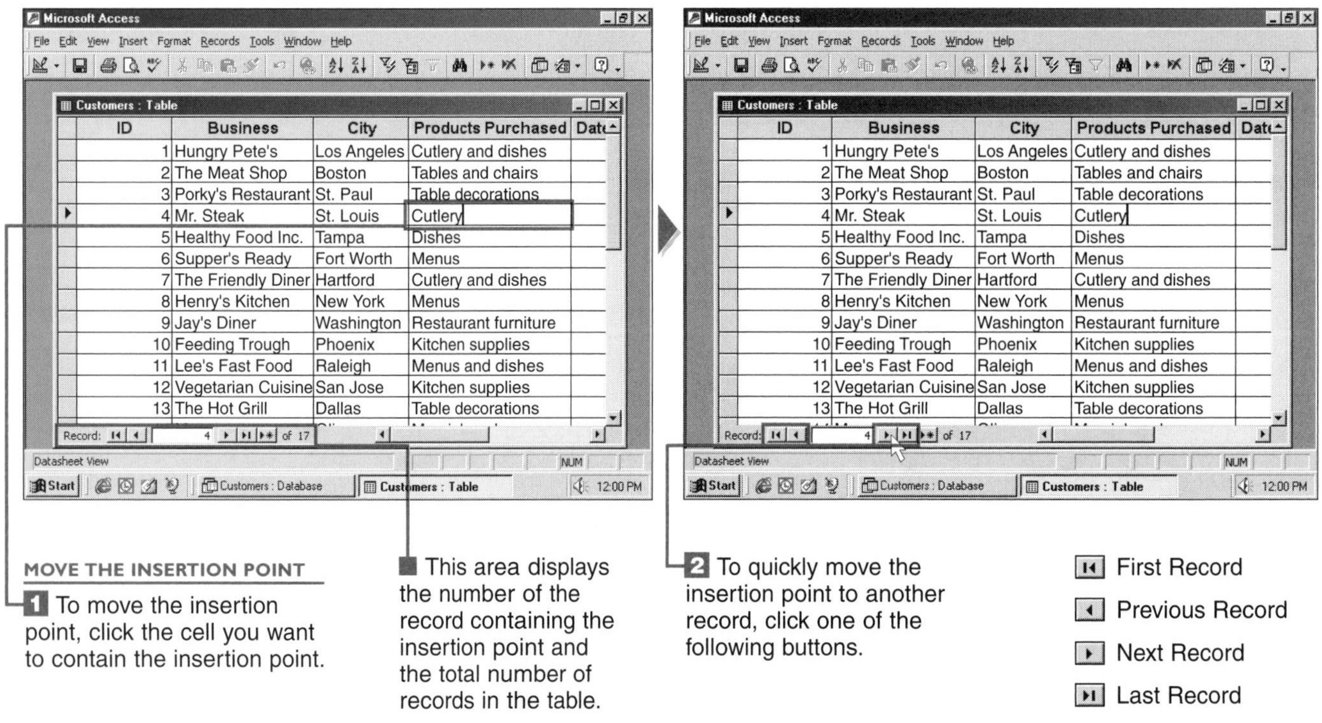

MOVE THE INSERTION POINT

1 To move the insertion point, click the cell you want to contain the insertion point.

■ This area displays the number of the record containing the insertion point and the total number of records in the table.

2 To quickly move the insertion point to another record, click one of the following buttons.

- First Record
- Previous Record
- Next Record
- Last Record

TIPS

How do I use my keyboard to move through fields and records?

✔ Press the Tab key to move to the next field in the current record. Press the ↑ or ↓ key to move up or down one record. Press the Page Up or Page Down key to move up or down one screen of records.

Can I quickly display a specific record?

✔ Yes. This is useful if you know the number of the record you want to display. In the Record area at the bottom of the table, double-click the current number. Type the number of the record you want to display and then press the Enter key.

How can I quickly display a specific field?

✔ You can use the Formatting toolbar to quickly display a specific field. To display the Formatting toolbar, click the View menu, select Toolbars and then select Formatting (Datasheet). In the Go To Field area on the Formatting toolbar, click ▾ and then select the name of the field you want to display.

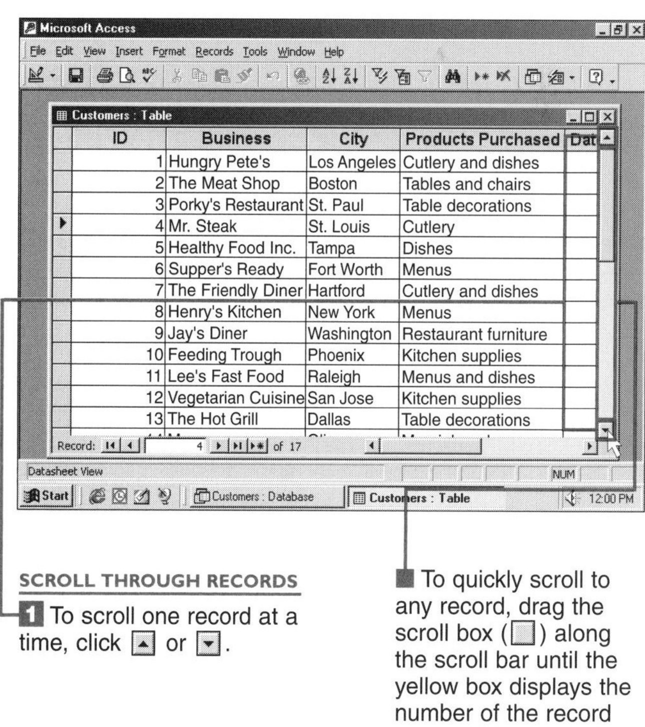

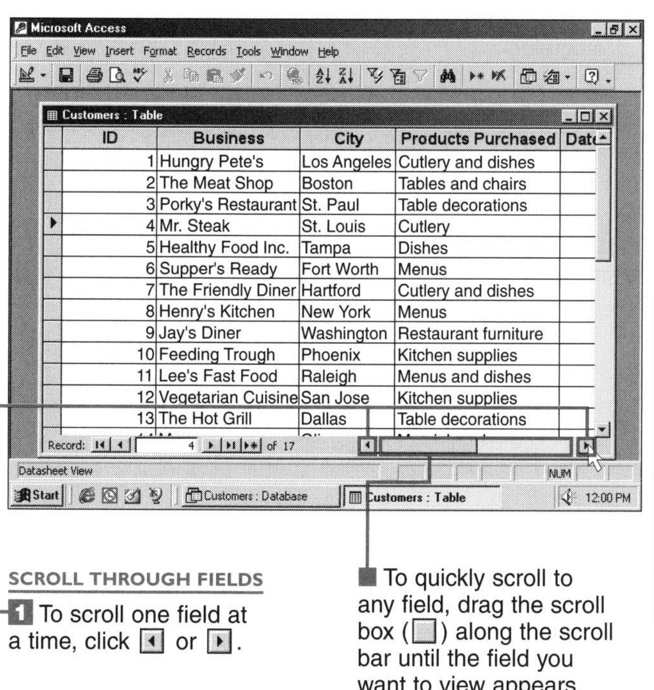

SCROLL THROUGH FIELDS

1 To scroll one field at a time, click ◂ or ▸.

■ To quickly scroll to any field, drag the scroll box (□) along the scroll bar until the field you want to view appears.

SCROLL THROUGH RECORDS

1 To scroll one record at a time, click ▴ or ▾.

■ To quickly scroll to any record, drag the scroll box (□) along the scroll bar until the yellow box displays the number of the record you want to view.

SELECT DATA

Before performing many tasks in a table, you must select the data you want to work with. For example, you must select data you want to move or copy.

Selected data appears highlighted on your screen. This makes data you select stand out from the rest of the data in your table.

You can select the part of the table you want to work with. You can select a field, record, cell or data in a cell. Selecting a field or record is useful when you need to delete a field or record from your table. Selecting one cell or data in a cell is useful when you are editing data in your table.

You can select multiple fields, records or cells to perform the same task on all the fields, records or cells at once. This saves you from having to perform the same task again and again.

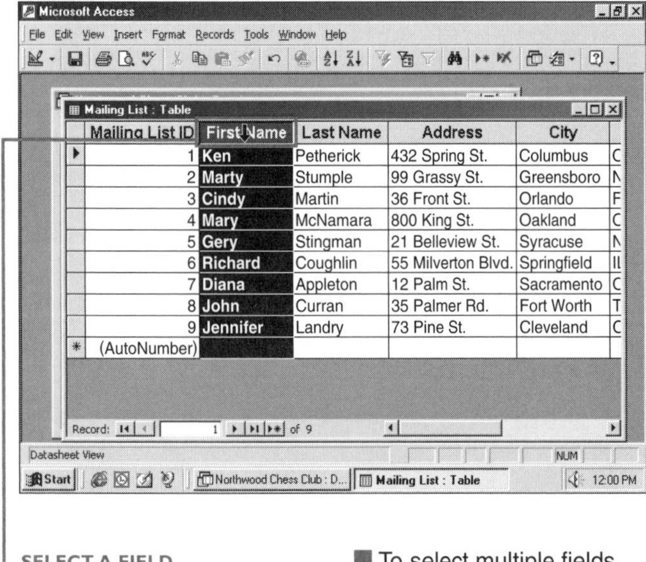

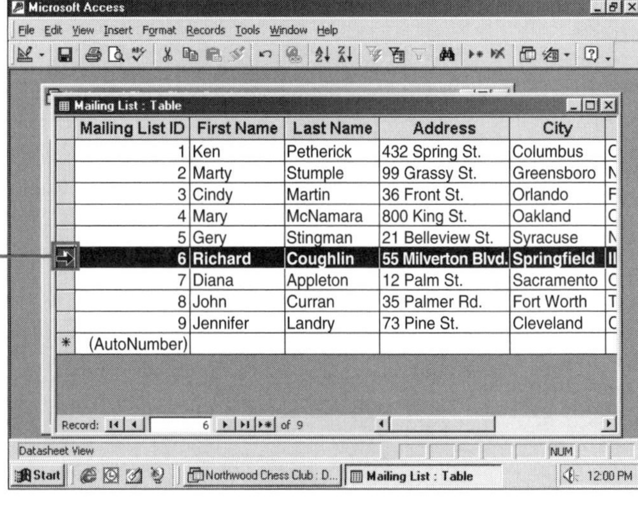

SELECT A FIELD

1 Position the mouse over the name of the field you want to select (changes to ⬇) and then click to select the field.

■ To select multiple fields, position the mouse over the name of the first field (changes to). Then drag the mouse until you highlight all the fields you want to select.

SELECT A RECORD

1 Position the mouse over the area to the left of the record you want to select (changes to ➡) and then click to select the record.

■ To select multiple records, position the mouse over the area to the left of the first record (changes to ➡). Then drag the mouse ➡ until you highlight all the records you want to select.

TIPS

How do I deselect data?

✔ To deselect data, click anywhere in the table.

How do I select all the records in a table?

✔ To select all the records in a table, click the blank area (▢) to the left of the field names. You can also press the Ctrl+A keys to select all the records in a table.

Is there a fast way to select a word in a cell?

✔ To quickly select a word, double-click the word.

How can I quickly select a large group of cells?

✔ To quickly select a large group of cells, click the first cell in the group you want to select and then scroll to the end of the group. Hold down the Shift key as you click the last cell in the group. Access highlights all the cells between the first and last cell you select.

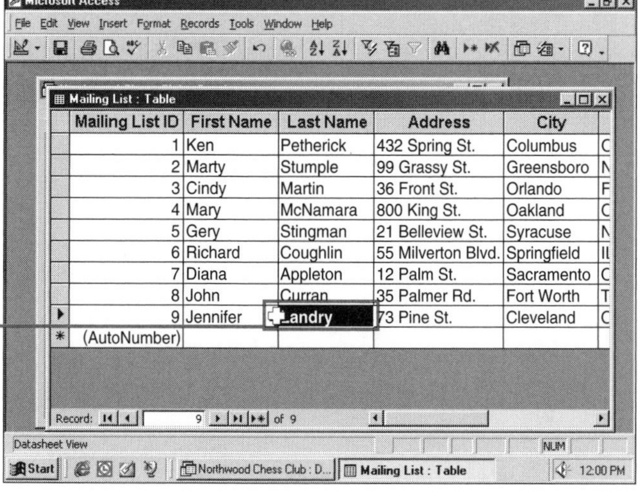

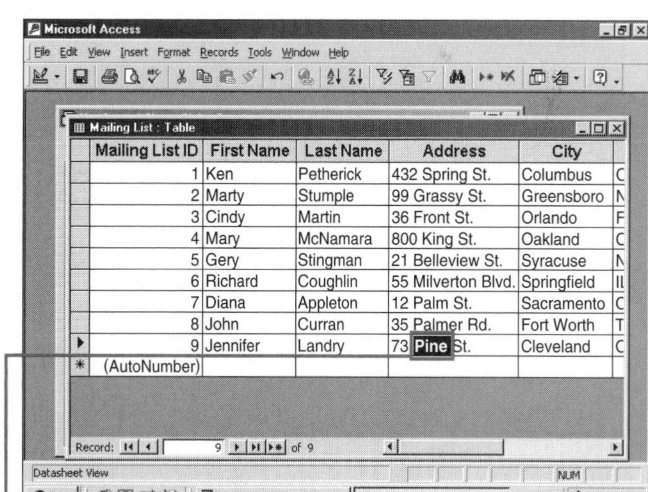

SELECT A CELL

1 Position the mouse I over the left edge of the cell you want to select (I changes to ✚) and then click to select the cell.

■ To select multiple cells, position the mouse I over the left edge of the first cell (I changes to ✚). Then drag the mouse ✚ until you highlight all the cells you want to select.

SELECT DATA IN A CELL

1 Position the mouse I over the data. Then drag the mouse I until you highlight all the data you want to select.

EDIT DATA

After you enter data into your table, you can change the data to correct a mistake or update the data.

The flashing insertion point in a cell indicates where Access will remove or add data. When you remove data using the Backspace key, Access removes the character to the left of the insertion point. When you insert data, Access adds the characters you type at the location of the insertion point.

You can quickly replace all the data in a cell with new data.

As you edit data, Access displays symbols to the left of the records. The arrow (▶) indicates the current record. The pencil (✎) indicates the record you are editing. The asterisk (✱) indicates where you can enter data for a new record.

If you make a mistake while editing data, you can use the Undo feature to immediately undo your most recent change.

You do not have to save the changes you make. When you move from the record you are editing to another record, Access automatically saves your changes.

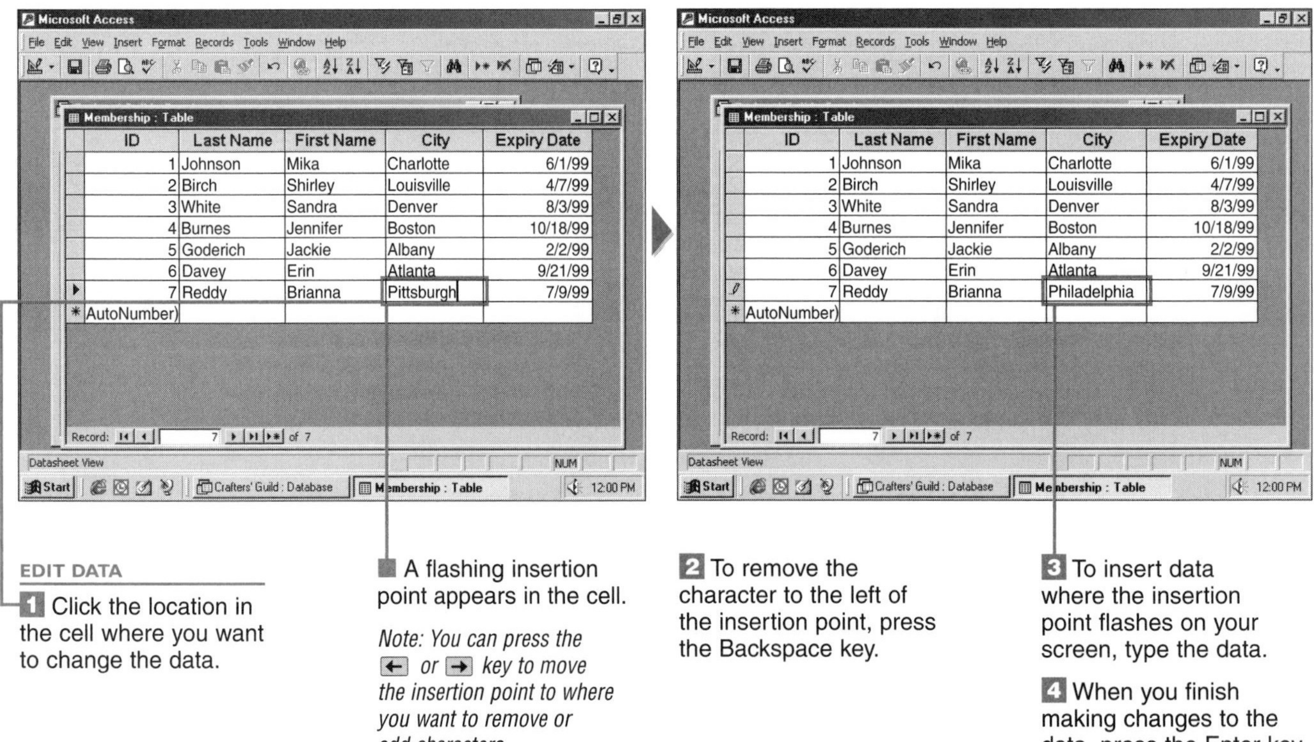

EDIT DATA

1 Click the location in the cell where you want to change the data.

■ A flashing insertion point appears in the cell.

Note: You can press the ← or → key to move the insertion point to where you want to remove or add characters.

2 To remove the character to the left of the insertion point, press the Backspace key.

3 To insert data where the insertion point flashes on your screen, type the data.

4 When you finish making changes to the data, press the Enter key.

TIPS

How can I quickly find data I want to edit?

✔ Click a cell in the field containing the data you want to find. Click the Find button (). Type the data you want to find and then click the Find Next button.

Can I check my table for spelling errors?

✔ You can find and correct all the spelling errors in a table. Click the Spelling button () to start the spell check. To spell check a single field or record, select the field or record before you begin.

Can I copy data in a table?

✔ Yes. Copying data is useful when you want several records in a table to display the same information. After you edit the data in one record, you can copy the data to other records. Select the data you want to copy and then click the Copy button (). Click the location where you want to place the data and then click the Paste button ().

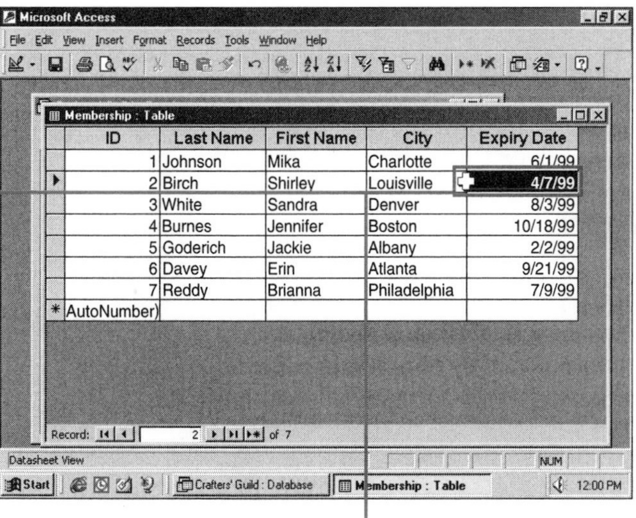

REPLACE ALL DATA IN A CELL

1 Position the mouse I over the left edge of the cell you want to replace with new data (I changes to ✚) and then click to select the cell.

■ The cell is highlighted.

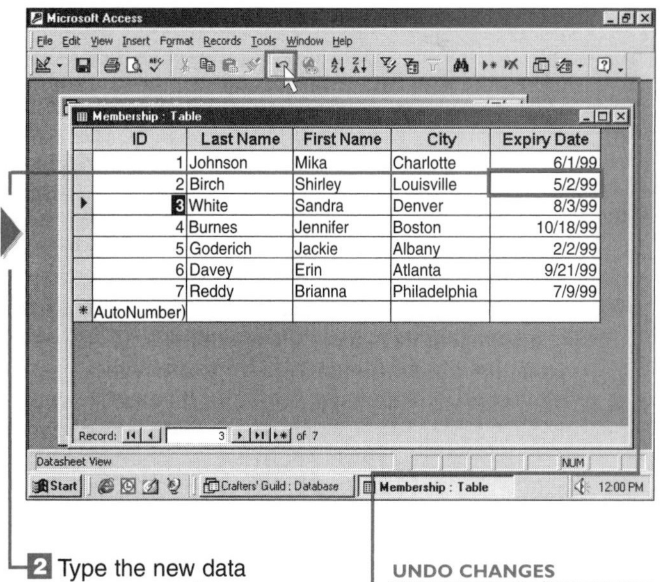

2 Type the new data and then press the Enter key.

UNDO CHANGES

1 Click to undo your most recent change.

ZOOM INTO A CELL

You can zoom into any cell in a table. This can make the contents of the cell easier to review and edit.

Zooming into a cell is useful when the columns in your table are not wide enough to display the entire contents of a cell. For example, a cell may contain a long address or a long description that Access cannot completely display.

When you zoom into a cell, Access displays the contents of the cell in the Zoom dialog box. You can edit the contents of the cell directly in the Zoom dialog box.

If you plan to enter a large amount of data into a cell, you can also zoom into an empty cell. This lets you easily view all the data you are typing into the cell at once.

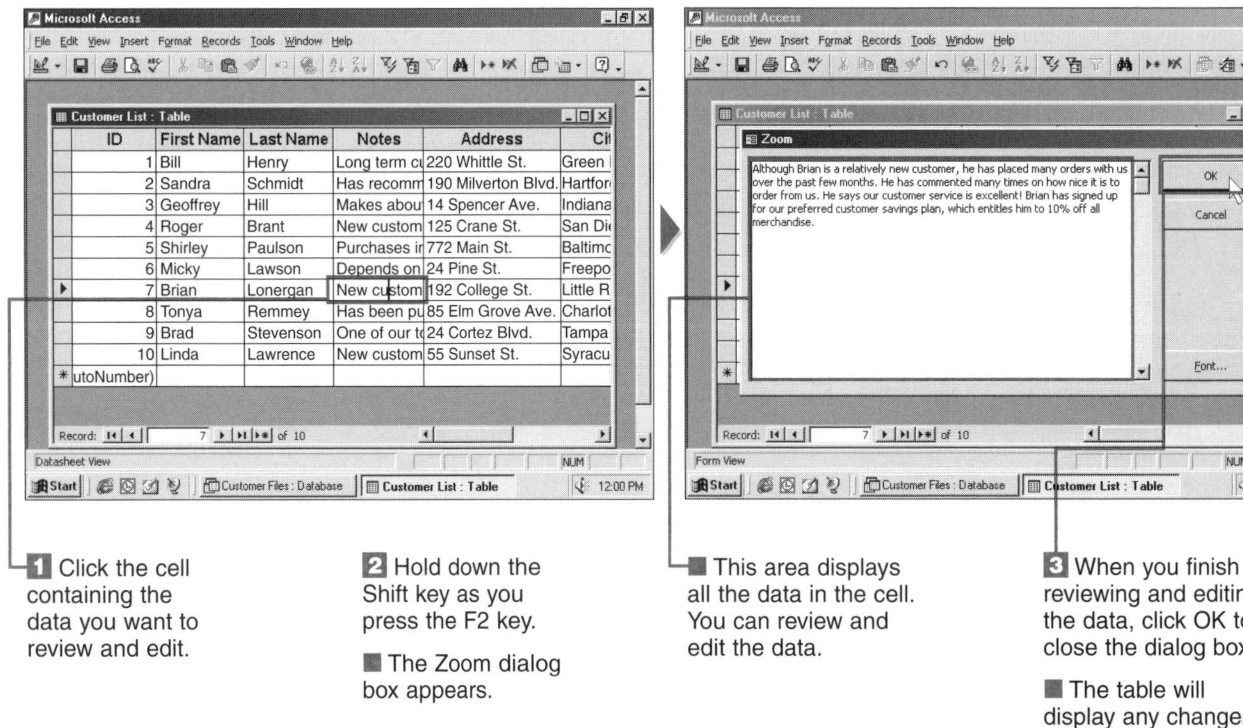

1 Click the cell containing the data you want to review and edit.

2 Hold down the Shift key as you press the F2 key.

■ The Zoom dialog box appears.

■ This area displays all the data in the cell. You can review and edit the data.

3 When you finish reviewing and editing the data, click OK to close the dialog box.

■ The table will display any changes you made to the data.

DISPLAY A SUBDATASHEET

When viewing the records in a table, you can display a subdatasheet to view and edit related data from another table.

Access only displays subdatasheets for tables that have a relationship. If you used the Database Wizard to create your database, the wizard automatically defined relationships between tables for you. For more information on relationships, see page 442.

A plus sign (⊞) appears beside each record that has related data. You can click a plus sign to display the related data in a subdatasheet. For example, a table containing customer information may be related to a table containing product orders. When viewing the customer table, you can click the plus sign beside the record for a customer. A subdatasheet will appear, displaying information about the products the customer has ordered.

When you finish viewing and editing the data in a subdatasheet, you can hide the subdatasheet to remove it from your screen.

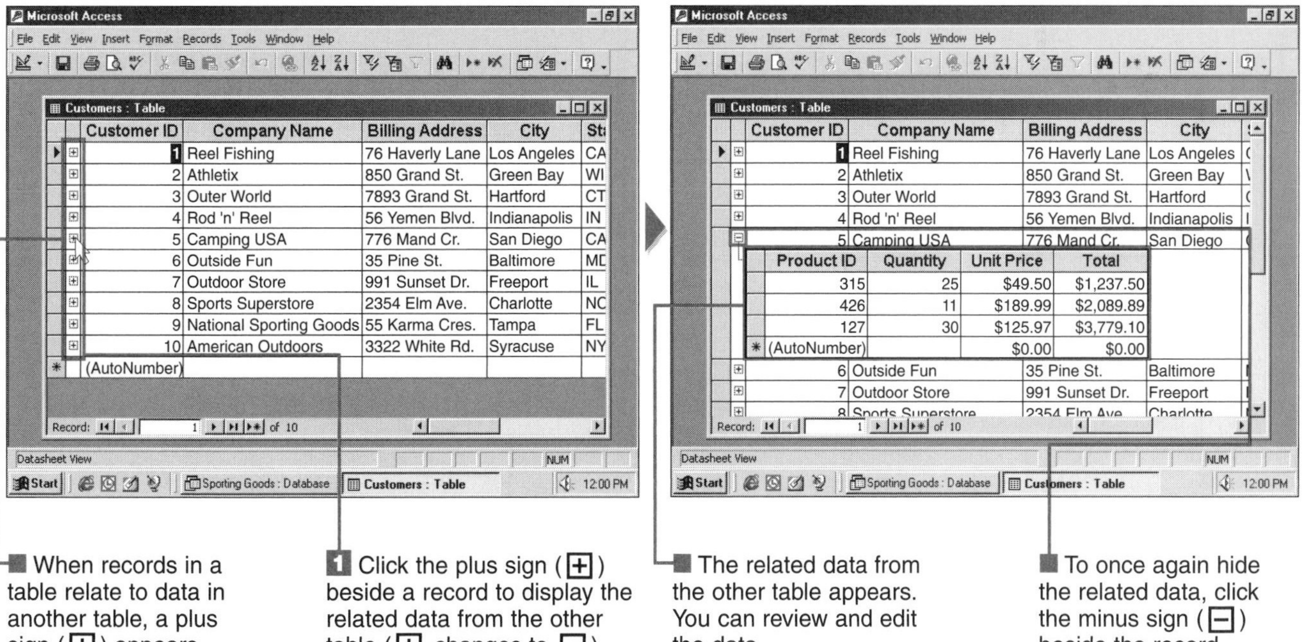

■ When records in a table relate to data in another table, a plus sign (⊞) appears beside each record.

1 Click the plus sign (⊞) beside a record to display the related data from the other table (⊞ changes to ⊟).

■ The related data from the other table appears. You can review and edit the data.

■ To once again hide the related data, click the minus sign (⊟) beside the record.

ADD OR DELETE A RECORD

You can add a new record to insert additional information into your table. Access automatically saves each new record you add to a table.

You can use the blank row at the bottom of a table to add a record. You cannot add a record to the middle of a table. If you want to change the order of the records, you can sort the records at any time. To sort records, see page 466.

If your table has an AutoNumber field, Access will automatically enter a number for each record you add.

You can delete a record to remove information you no longer need. For example, you can delete a record containing a company you no longer deal with from your supplier table.

When you delete a record, you may also want to delete any related records in other tables. For example, if you delete a company from your supplier table, you may also want to delete records containing information about the products the company supplies from your product table.

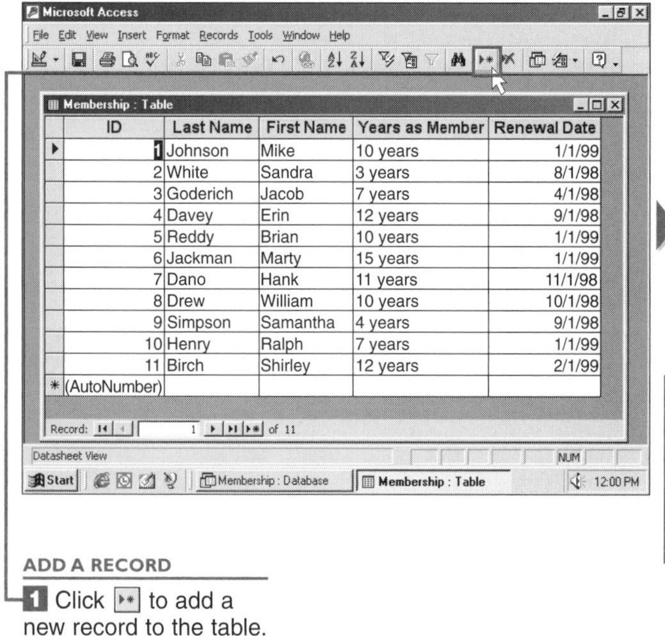

ID	Last Name	First Name	Years as Member	Renewal Date
1	Johnson	Mike	10 years	1/1/99
2	White	Sandra	3 years	8/1/98
3	Goderich	Jacob	7 years	4/1/98
4	Davey	Erin	12 years	9/1/98
5	Reddy	Brian	10 years	1/1/99
6	Jackman	Marty	15 years	1/1/99
7	Dano	Hank	11 years	11/1/98
8	Drew	William	10 years	10/1/98
9	Simpson	Samantha	4 years	9/1/98
10	Henry	Ralph	7 years	1/1/99
11	Birch	Shirley	12 years	2/1/99
(AutoNumber)				

ADD A RECORD

1 Click ▶* to add a new record to the table.

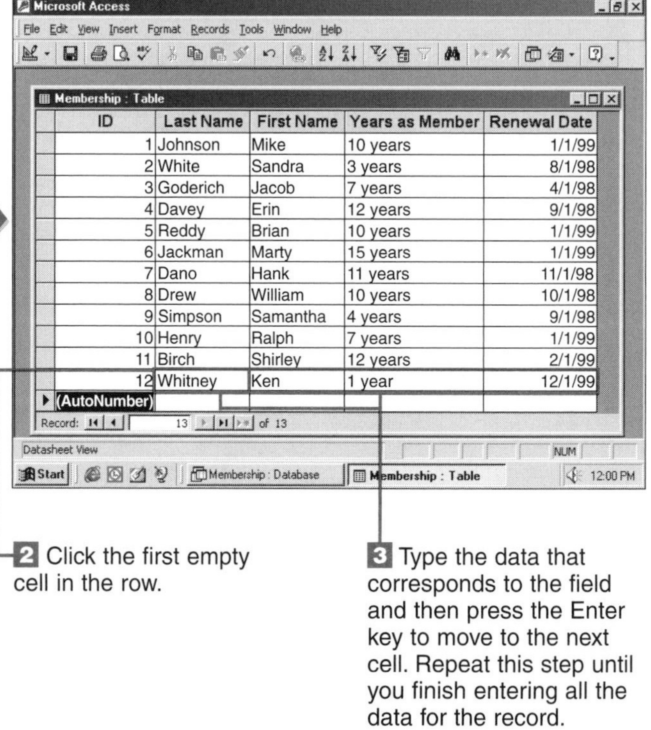

ID	Last Name	First Name	Years as Member	Renewal Date
1	Johnson	Mike	10 years	1/1/99
2	White	Sandra	3 years	8/1/98
3	Goderich	Jacob	7 years	4/1/98
4	Davey	Erin	12 years	9/1/98
5	Reddy	Brian	10 years	1/1/99
6	Jackman	Marty	15 years	1/1/99
7	Dano	Hank	11 years	11/1/98
8	Drew	William	10 years	10/1/98
9	Simpson	Samantha	4 years	9/1/98
10	Henry	Ralph	7 years	1/1/99
11	Birch	Shirley	12 years	2/1/99
12	Whitney	Ken	1 year	12/1/99
(AutoNumber)				

2 Click the first empty cell in the row.

3 Type the data that corresponds to the field and then press the Enter key to move to the next cell. Repeat this step until you finish entering all the data for the record.

TIPS

Is there a faster way to enter data into cells in a new record?

✔ To copy the data from the cell above into the current cell, press the Ctrl+'(Apostrophe) keys. To insert the current date, press the Ctrl+;(Semicolon) keys.

Is there another way to add a record?

✔ You can use a form to add a record to a table. For more information, see page 452.

How do I delete several records at once?

✔ Select the records you want to delete and then perform steps 2 and 3 on this page.

Is there a way to ensure that related data in the database is removed when I delete a record?

✔ You can specify that if you delete a record in one table, related records in another table will also be removed. To do this, you must establish a relationship between the two tables. You must then enforce referential integrity and turn on the Cascade Delete Related Records option. For more information, see page 442.

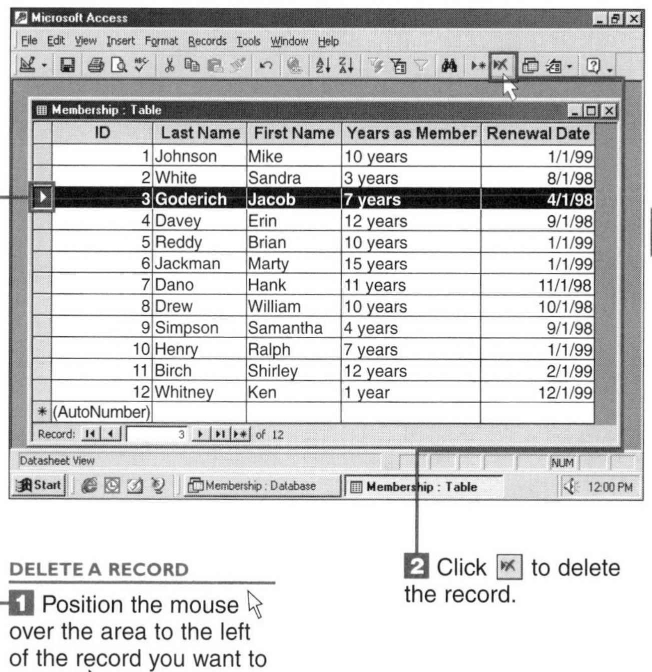

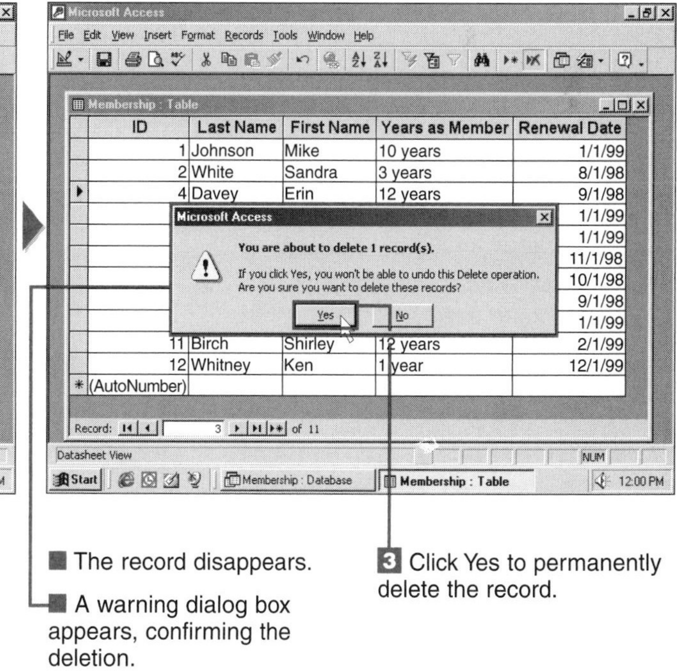

DELETE A RECORD

1 Position the mouse over the area to the left of the record you want to delete (changes to ➡) and then click to select the record.

2 Click ✕ to delete the record.

■ A warning dialog box appears, confirming the deletion.

3 Click Yes to permanently delete the record.

■ The record disappears.

HIDE OR FREEZE A FIELD

You can temporarily hide a field in your table to reduce the amount of data displayed on your screen. This can help you work with specific data and can make your table easier to read.

Hiding a field allows you to review only fields of interest. For example, if you want to browse through the names and telephone numbers of your clients, you can hide fields displaying other information.

When you hide a field, Access does not delete the field. The data in the hidden field remains intact.

You can freeze a field so it will remain on your screen at all times. Freezing a field allows you to keep important data displayed on your screen as you move through a large table. For example, you can freeze a field containing the names of your clients so that the names will remain on your screen while you scroll through the rest of the data for the clients.

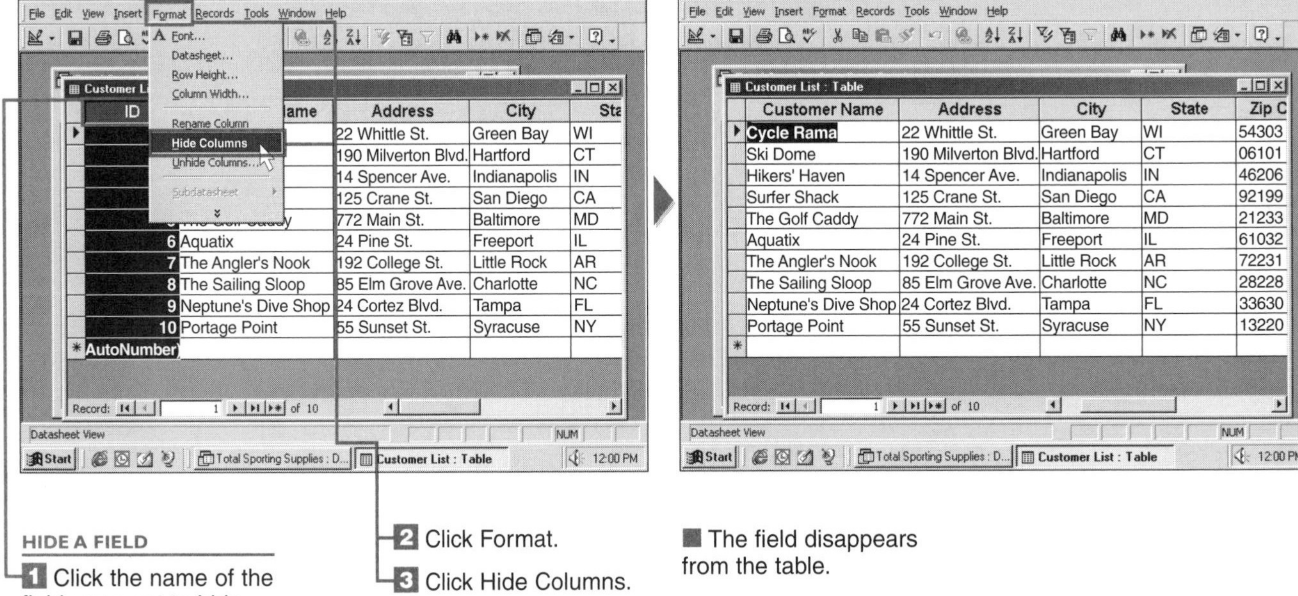

HIDE A FIELD

1 Click the name of the field you want to hide.

2 Click Format.

3 Click Hide Columns.

■ The field disappears from the table.

How do I redisplay a hidden field?

✔ You can redisplay a hidden field to once again view the data in the field. From the Format menu, select Unhide Columns. A dialog box appears, displaying a list of the fields in your table. A check mark beside a field indicates the field is displayed on your screen. Click the box beside the field you want to redisplay (☐ changes to ☑) and then click Close.

How do I unfreeze a field?

✔ You can unfreeze a field at any time. From the Format menu, select Unfreeze All Columns.

Can I hide or freeze more than one field at a time?

✔ Yes. To hide or freeze multiple fields, you must first select the fields you want to hide or freeze. You can then hide or freeze the fields as you would hide or freeze a single field.

FREEZE A FIELD

1 Click the name of the field you want to freeze.

2 Click Format.

3 Click Freeze Columns.

Note: If Freeze Columns does not appear on the menu, position the mouse over the bottom of the menu to display all the menu commands.

4 Click any cell in the table to deselect the field.

■ Access moves the field to the left side of the table. A dark vertical line to the right of the field indicates that the field is frozen.

■ You can use this scroll bar to move through the fields to the right of the dark vertical line.

CHANGE VIEW OF TABLE

There are two ways you can view a table. Each view allows you to perform different tasks.

The Datasheet view displays all the records in a table. You can enter, edit and review records in this view.

The Design view displays the structure of a table. You can change the data type and field property settings in this view. The data type determines the type of information you can enter in a field, such as text, numbers or dates. Specifying a data type helps ensure that you enter the correct information in a field.

The field properties are a set of characteristics that provide additional control over the information you can enter in a field. For example, you can specify the maximum number of characters a field will accept.

Access allows you to quickly switch between the Datasheet and Design views.

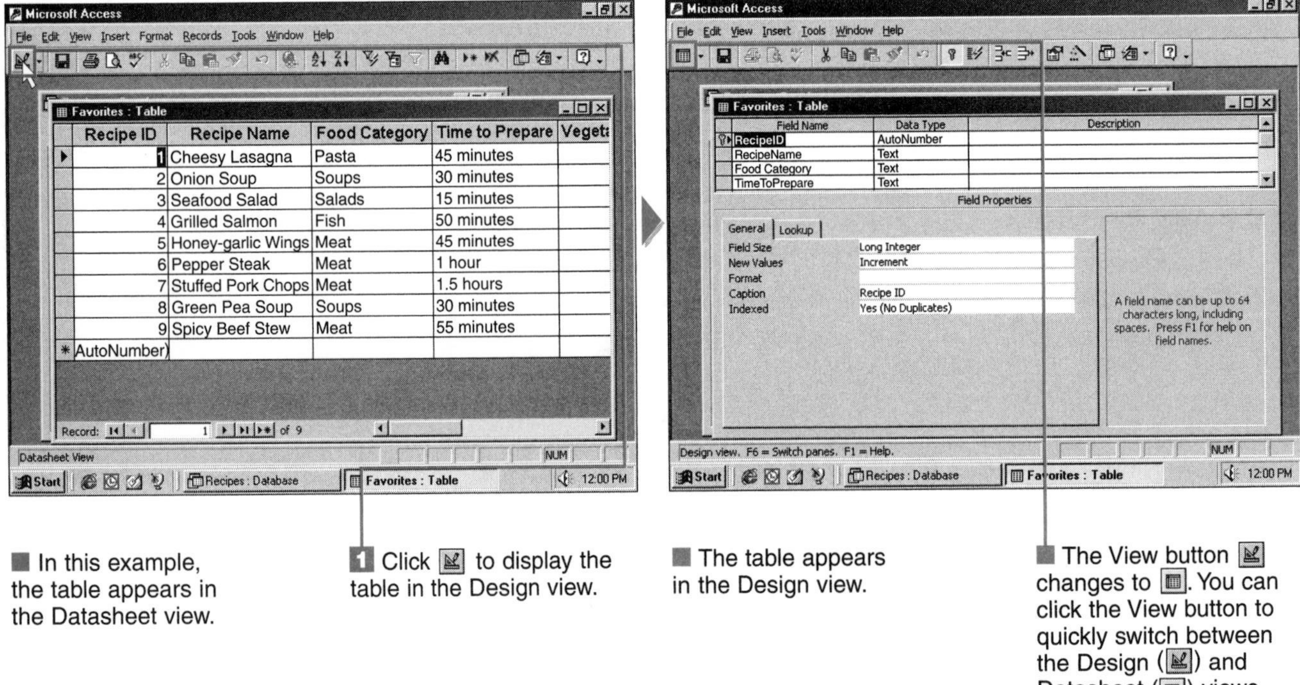

■ In this example, the table appears in the Datasheet view.

1 Click to display the table in the Design view.

■ The table appears in the Design view.

■ The View button changes to . You can click the View button to quickly switch between the Design () and Datasheet () views.

REARRANGE FIELDS

You can rearrange the fields in a table to better organize your information.

When you rearrange fields in the Design view, the fields are also rearranged in the Datasheet view.

Rearranging the fields in your table allows you to place fields in a logical order. For example, in a table that stores client information, you may want to move the field containing first names in front of the field containing last names.

Rearranging fields can also help you work with your table more efficiently. For example, you may want to place fields containing fax numbers and mobile phone numbers beside the field for telephone numbers so you can easily manage the related information.

A thick line indicates where the field you are moving will appear.

Rearranging the fields in a table will not affect how the fields are displayed in other objects based on the table in the database, such as forms.

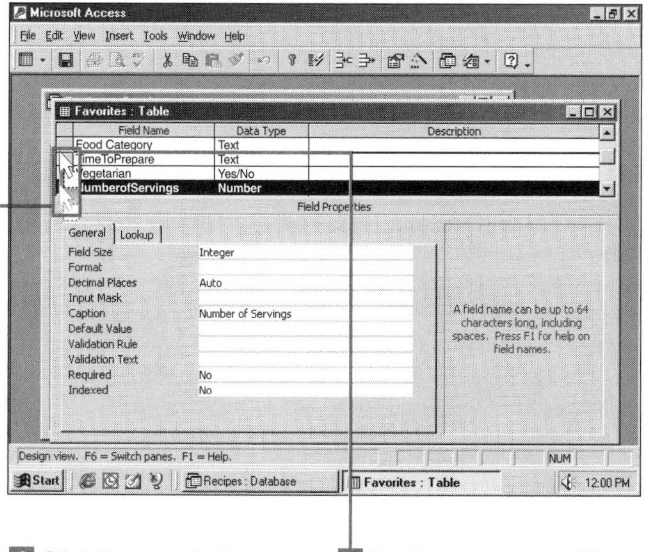

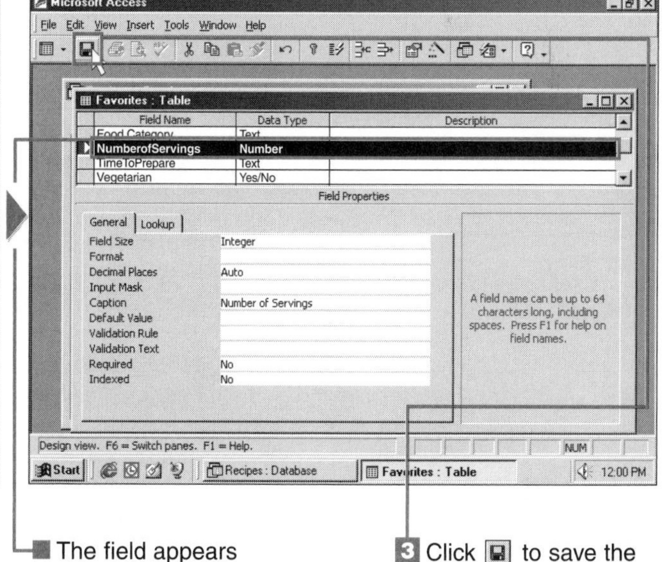

1 Click the area to the left of the field you want to move.

2 Position the mouse I over the area to the left of the field (I changes to ↖) and then drag the field to a new location.

Note: A thick line shows where the field will appear.

■ The field appears in the new location.

3 Click 💾 to save the changes to the table.

ADD A FIELD DESCRIPTION

You can add a description to a field to identify the type of information the field contains. You can use up to 255 characters, including spaces, to describe a field.

Adding a description to a field can help you determine what kind of information you should enter in the field. For example, if a field has an abbreviated field name such as CNum, you can add a description such as "This field contains customer numbers" to help you enter information in the field.

After you add a description to a field, you must save the table to have Access save the description.

When you display your table in the Datasheet view, you can click anywhere in the field to display the description you added. The description will appear on the status bar at the bottom of your screen.

If you use the field in another object in the database, such as a form, the other object will display the description when you are working with the field.

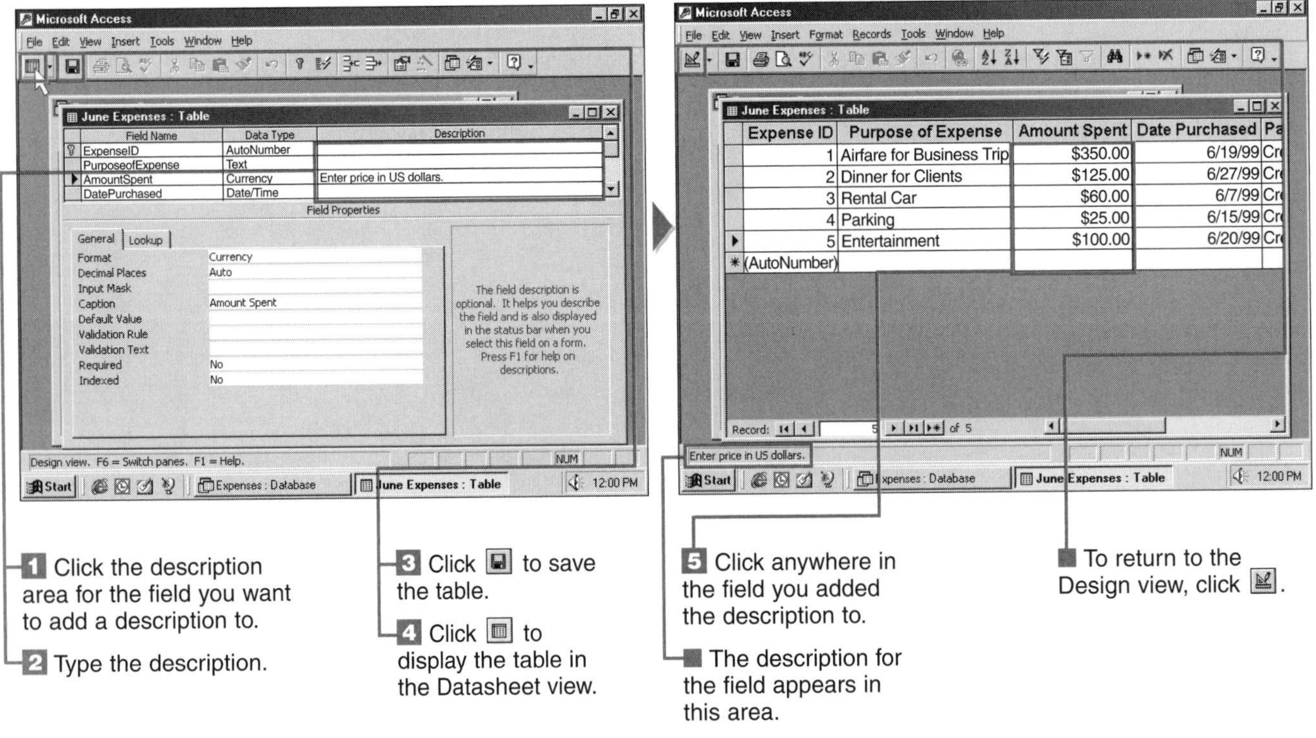

1 Click the description area for the field you want to add a description to.

2 Type the description.

3 Click the save button to save the table.

4 Click the datasheet button to display the table in the Datasheet view.

5 Click anywhere in the field you added the description to.

■ The description for the field appears in this area.

■ To return to the Design view, click the design button.

DISPLAY FIELD PROPERTIES

Each field in a table has properties that you can display. The field properties are a set of characteristics that provide additional control over the kind of information you can enter in a field. For example, the Field Size property tells Access the maximum number of characters a field can contain.

The properties available for a field depend on the type of data the field contains. For example, the Field Size property is available for a field containing text but is not available for a field containing currency. The Decimal Places property is available for a field containing currency but is not available for a field containing text. You can display the available properties for any field in your table.

If you use a field in other objects in the database, such as a form or report, the other objects will also use the properties for the field.

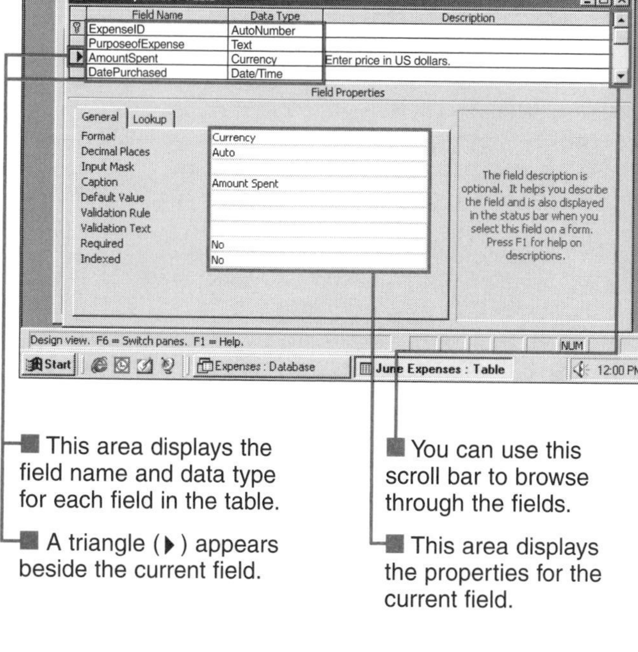

■ This area displays the field name and data type for each field in the table.

■ A triangle (▸) appears beside the current field.

■ You can use this scroll bar to browse through the fields.

■ This area displays the properties for the current field.

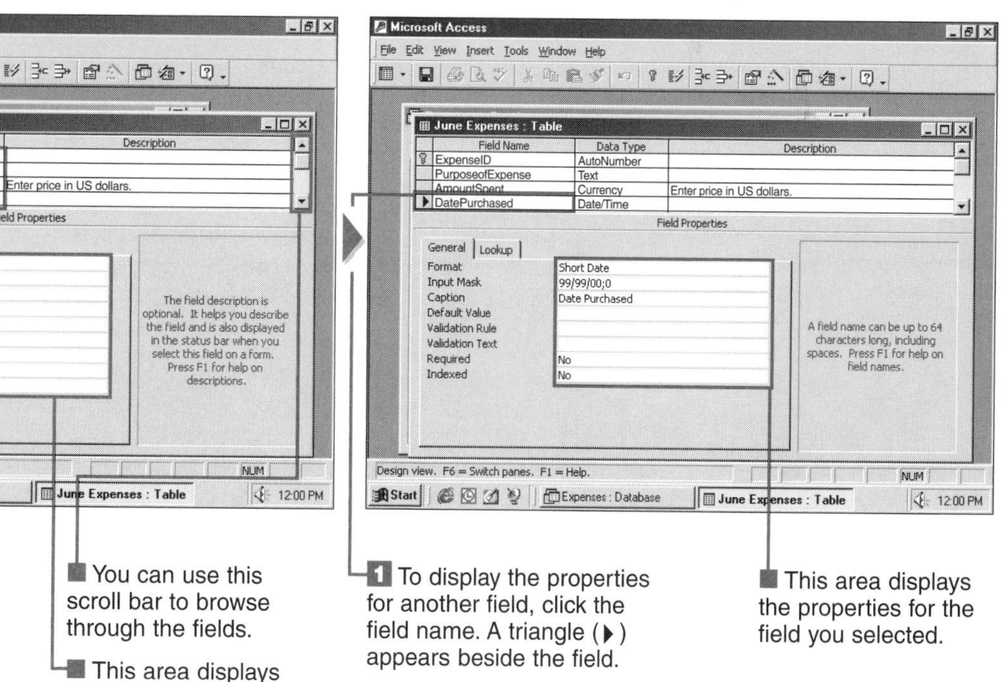

1 To display the properties for another field, click the field name. A triangle (▸) appears beside the field.

■ This area displays the properties for the field you selected.

CHANGE A DATA TYPE

You can change the type of data you can enter in a field.

Before you change the data type for a field, you should consider what type of data you want to be able to enter in the field. Access will not accept entries that do not match the data type you specify. This helps prevent errors when entering data. For example, you cannot enter text in a field with the Number data type.

You should also determine whether you want to be able to perform calculations using the data in the field. For example, Access can calculate numbers in a Number or Currency field but cannot calculate numbers in a Text field.

The ability to sort records is also a consideration. Some data types, such as Memo, Hyperlink and OLE Object, cannot be sorted.

If you change the data type for a field that contains data, Access may delete data in the field. Access will display a warning message before deleting any data.

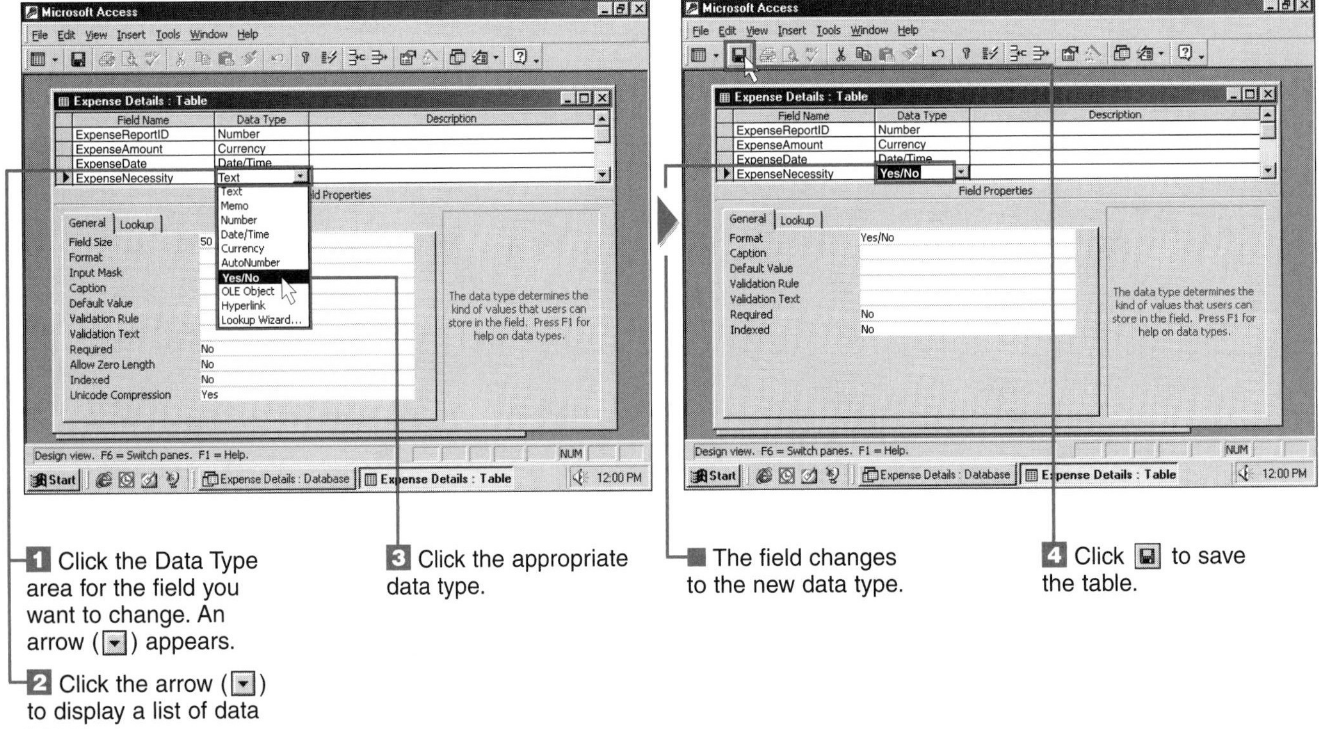

1 Click the Data Type area for the field you want to change. An arrow (▾) appears.

2 Click the arrow (▾) to display a list of data types.

3 Click the appropriate data type.

■ The field changes to the new data type.

4 Click 💾 to save the table.

DATA TYPES

Text

Accepts entries up to 255 characters long that include any combination of text and numbers, such as an address. Make sure you use this data type for numbers you do not want to use in calculations, such as phone numbers or zip codes.

Memo

Accepts entries up to 64,000 characters long that include any combination of text and numbers. The Memo data type is useful for notes, comments or lengthy descriptions.

Number

Accepts only numbers. You can enter numbers you want to be able to use in calculations in a field using the Number data type. By default, this data type does not accept decimal numbers.

Date/Time

Accepts only dates and times.

Currency

Accepts only monetary values. This data type accepts up to 15 numbers to the left of the decimal point and 4 numbers to the right of the decimal point. The Currency data type automatically displays data as currency. For example, if you type 3428, the data will be displayed as $3,428.00.

AutoNumber

Automatically numbers each record for you. The AutoNumber data type automatically assigns a unique number in a sequential or random order to each record in a table.

Yes/No

Accepts only one of two values–Yes/No, True/False or On/Off.

OLE Object

Accepts OLE objects. An OLE object is an item created in another program, such as a document created in Word or a chart created in Excel. OLE objects can also include sounds and pictures.

Hyperlink

Accepts hyperlinks. You can select a hyperlink to jump to another document on an intranet or a Web page on the World Wide Web. You can enter a Web site address, such as www.maran.com, in a field using the Hyperlink data type to be able to quickly access the Web site from the table.

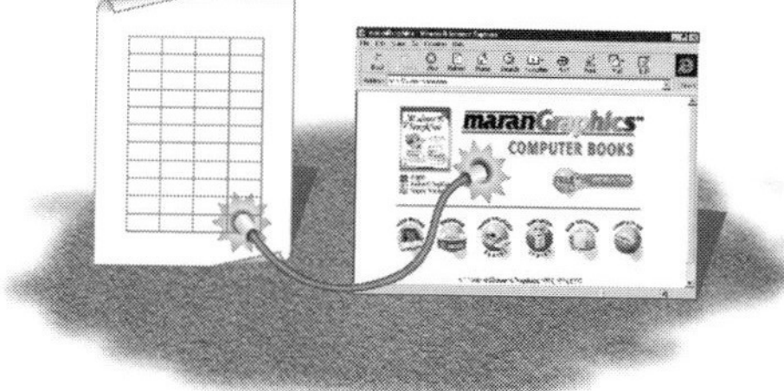

SELECT A FORMAT

You can select a format to customize the way information appears in a field. When you select a format, you only change the way Access displays information on the screen. The values in the field do not change.

You can select a format for Number, Date/Time, Currency, AutoNumber and Yes/No fields.

Access does not provide formats for Text, Memo, OLE Object or Hyperlink fields.

In a Number field, you can choose to display numbers in a format such as 1234.00 or $1,234.00. If you want a number to display decimal places, you may also need to change the field size. For information on changing the field size, see page 426.

In a Date/Time field, you can choose to display a date as Tuesday, July 20, 1999 or 7/20/99. A Yes/No field can display values as True/False, Yes/No or On/Off.

After you select a format, Access will automatically change any data you enter in the field to the new format. For example, if you type 3456, Access will automatically display the data as $3,456.00.

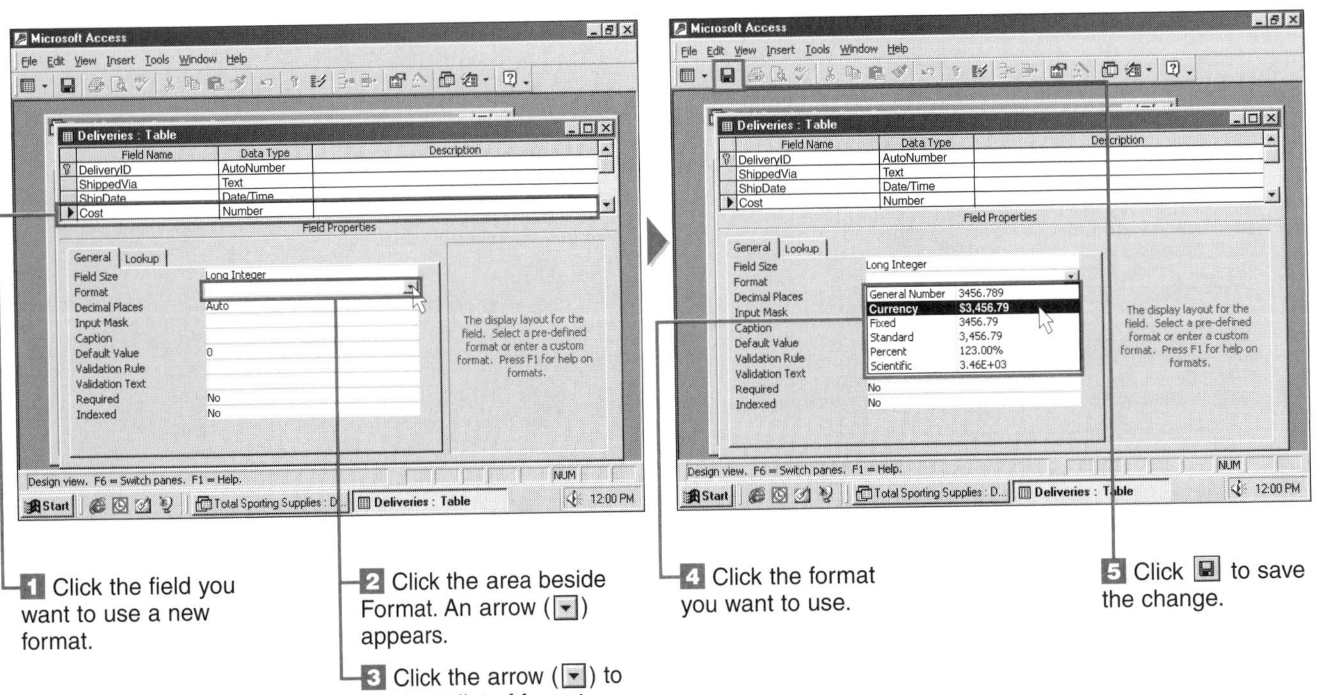

1 Click the field you want to use a new format.

2 Click the area beside Format. An arrow (▾) appears.

3 Click the arrow (▾) to display a list of formats.

4 Click the format you want to use.

5 Click 💾 to save the change.

CHANGE NUMBER OF DECIMAL PLACES

You can specify how many decimal places Access will use to display numbers in a field. Some numbers, such as prices, require only two decimal places. Numbers used in scientific calculations may require more decimal places.

You can choose to display between 0 and 15 decimal places after the decimal point.

Changing the number of decimal places only affects how a number is displayed on the screen, not how a number is stored or used in calculations. For example, if you change the number of decimal places to 1, the number 2.3456 will be displayed as 2.3. However, Access will store and perform calculations using the number 2.3456.

If the Format property of a field is blank or set to General Number, changing the number of decimal places will not affect the field. For information on selecting a format, see page 424.

You may also need to change the field size before the field will display numbers with decimal places. For information on changing the field size, see page 426.

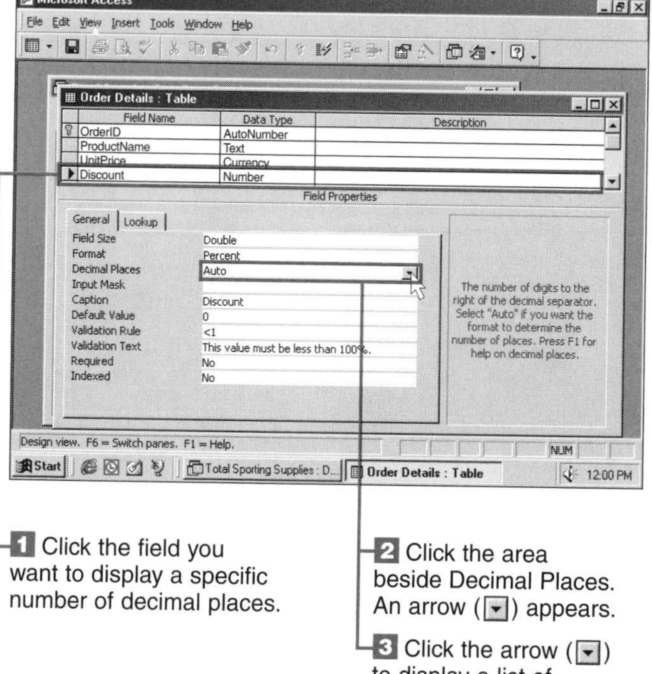

1 Click the field you want to display a specific number of decimal places.

2 Click the area beside Decimal Places. An arrow (▾) appears.

3 Click the arrow (▾) to display a list of decimal place options.

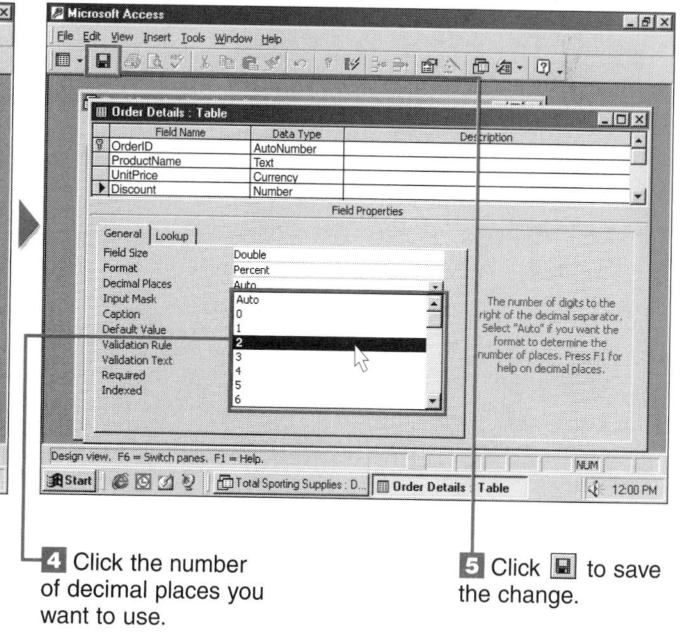

4 Click the number of decimal places you want to use.

5 Click 💾 to save the change.

CHANGE THE FIELD SIZE

You can change the field size of a text or number field to specify the maximum size of data you can enter into the field.

You can change the maximum number of characters that a text field will accept. Access allows you to specify a field size of up to 255 characters.

You can change the size of a number field to specify the size and type of numbers that can be entered into the field. Most field size options allow you to enter whole numbers only. If you want to be able to enter decimal numbers, such as 1.234, you must select the Single or Double field size option.

Access processes smaller field sizes more quickly than larger field sizes. Using smaller field sizes can help speed up tasks such as searching for data in a field.

Using small field sizes can also reduce the amount of space required to store a table on your computer. For example, if a table contains thousands of records, reducing the size of a text field by one or two characters may save a considerable amount of space.

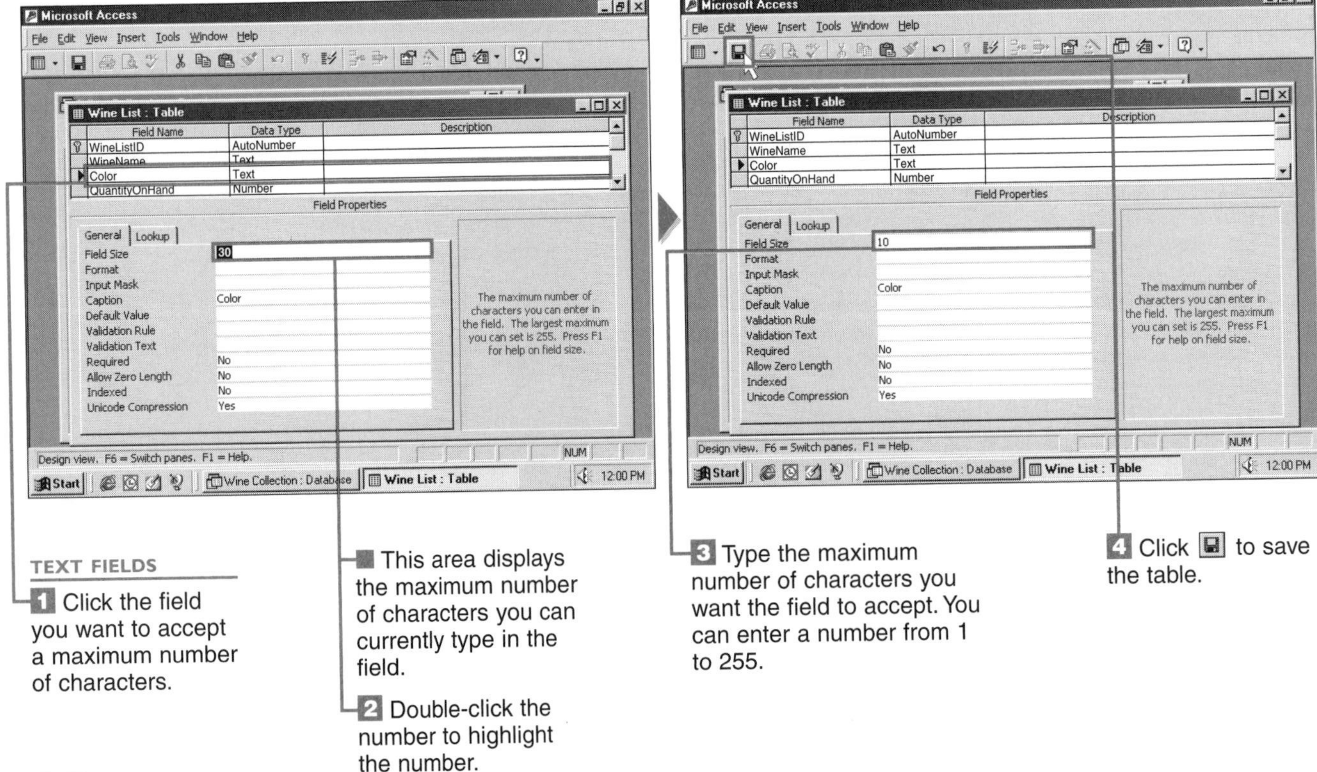

TEXT FIELDS

1 Click the field you want to accept a maximum number of characters.

■ This area displays the maximum number of characters you can currently type in the field.

2 Double-click the number to highlight the number.

3 Type the maximum number of characters you want the field to accept. You can enter a number from 1 to 255.

4 Click 💾 to save the table.

TIPS

What are some commonly used size settings for number fields?

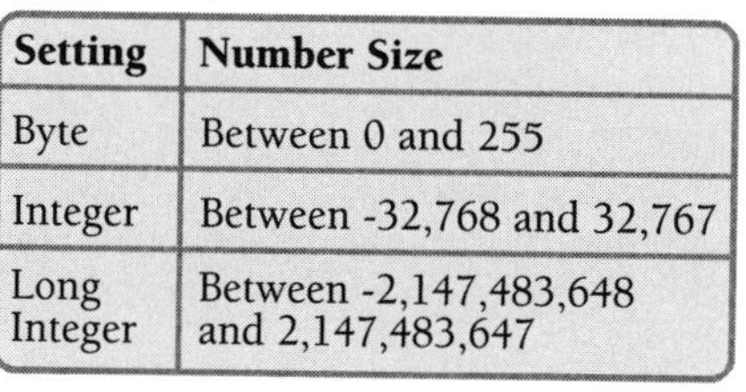

Setting	Number Size
Byte	Between 0 and 255
Integer	Between -32,768 and 32,767
Long Integer	Between -2,147,483,648 and 2,147,483,647

Can I change the size of a field that already contains data?

✔ Yes. If you reduce the size of a text field containing data, Access will shorten any data that is longer than the new field size. If you reduce the size of a number field containing data, Access may change or delete data that is larger than the new field size. Access will display a warning message before changing any data.

Can I change the field size that Access automatically uses for new text or number fields?

✔ Yes. From the Tools menu, select Options and then choose the Tables/Queries tab. To change the size of text fields, double-click the Text area and type the new size. To change the size of number fields, click the Number area and choose a new size setting. Then click OK.

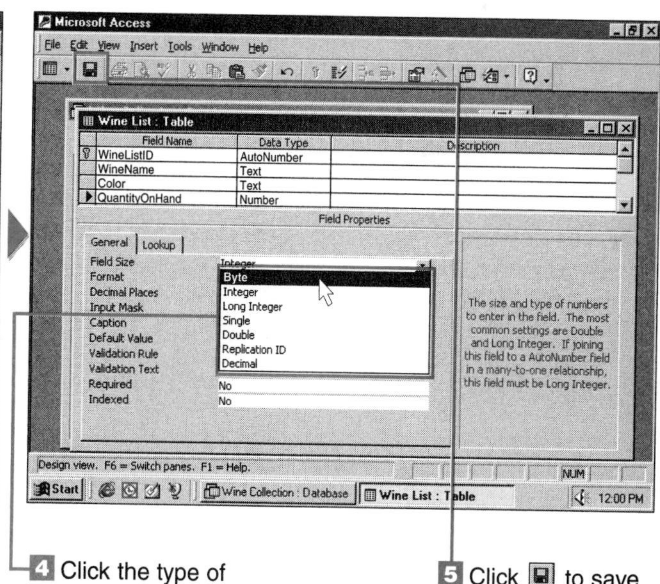

NUMBER FIELDS

1 Click the field you want to accept only a certain type of number.

2 Click the area beside Field Size. An arrow (▼) appears.

3 Click the arrow (▼) to display a list of options.

4 Click the type of number you want the field to accept.

5 Click 💾 to save the table.

ADD A CAPTION

You can create a caption for a field. The caption will appear as the heading for the field instead of the field name.

Adding a caption to a field is useful when you want the heading for a field to be longer and more descriptive than the field name allows. This can help you recognize the field more easily when you are entering or reviewing data in your table. For example, the caption Home Phone Number is much easier to understand than the field name HPhone.

A caption can be up to 2,048 characters in length, including letters, numbers and spaces.

After adding a caption to a field, any forms, reports or queries you create that use the field will display the caption instead of the field name. Any forms or reports you created before adding the caption will continue to display the field name.

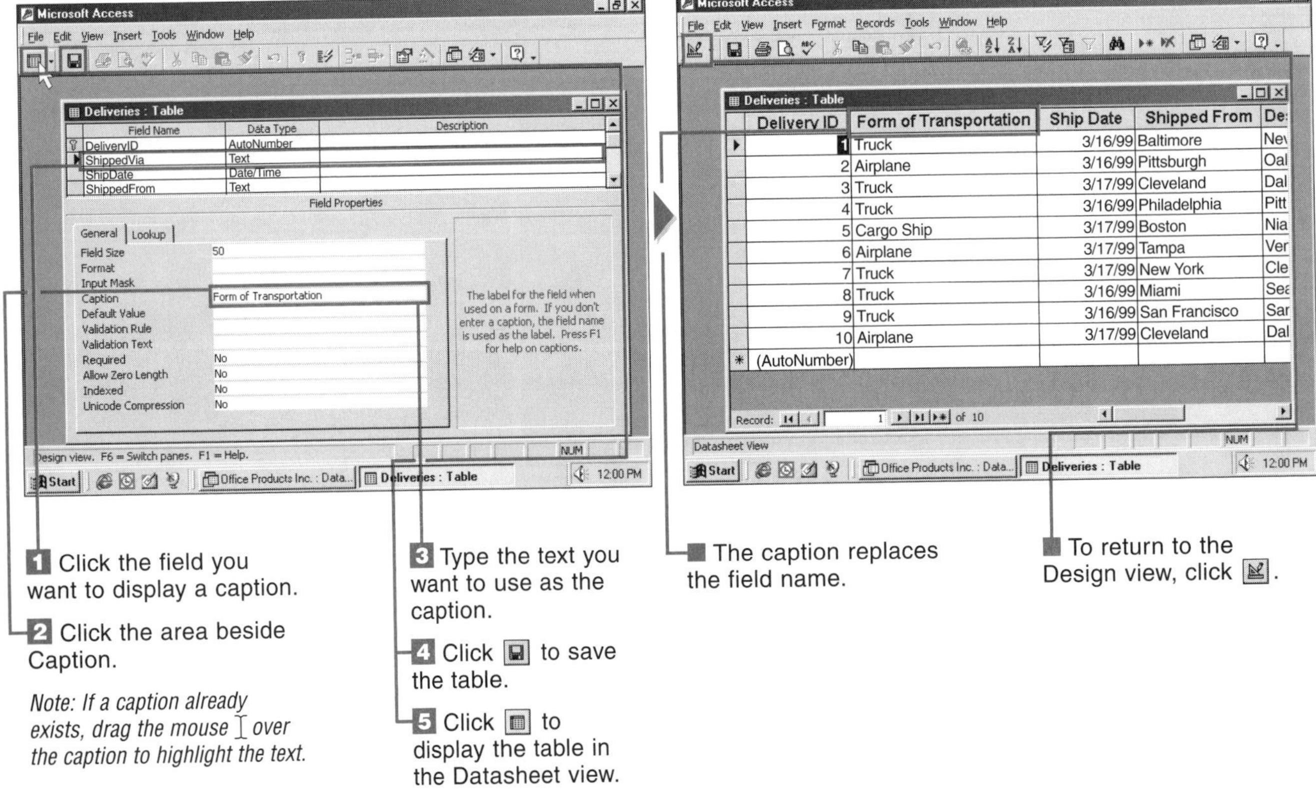

1 Click the field you want to display a caption.

2 Click the area beside Caption.

Note: If a caption already exists, drag the mouse I over the caption to highlight the text.

3 Type the text you want to use as the caption.

4 Click 💾 to save the table.

5 Click ▦ to display the table in the Datasheet view.

■ The caption replaces the field name.

■ To return to the Design view, click ✎.

ADD A DEFAULT VALUE

You can specify a value that you want to appear automatically in a field each time you add a new record. This saves you from having to type the same data over and over again.

For example, a table containing the addresses of your clients may contain a field for the country each client lives in. If the majority of your clients live in the United States, you can set United States as the default value for the field. This can save you a considerable amount of time if the table will contain a large number of records.

You do not have to accept the default value for each new record you add to your table. You can enter another value in the field.

Setting a default value will not affect the existing data in a field. To change existing data to the default value, click a cell containing data you want to change and then press the Ctrl+Alt+Spacebar keys.

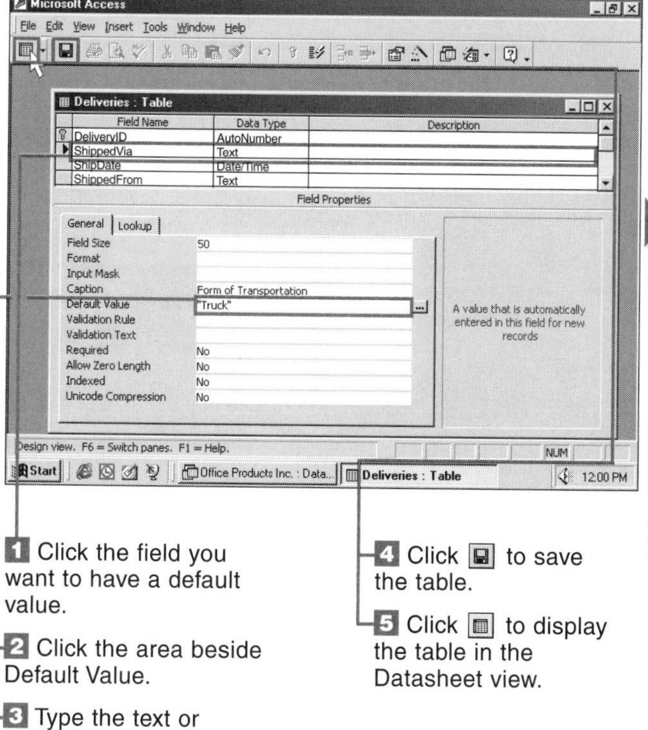

1 Click the field you want to have a default value.

2 Click the area beside Default Value.

3 Type the text or number you want to set as the default value.

4 Click [save icon] to save the table.

5 Click [datasheet icon] to display the table in the Datasheet view.

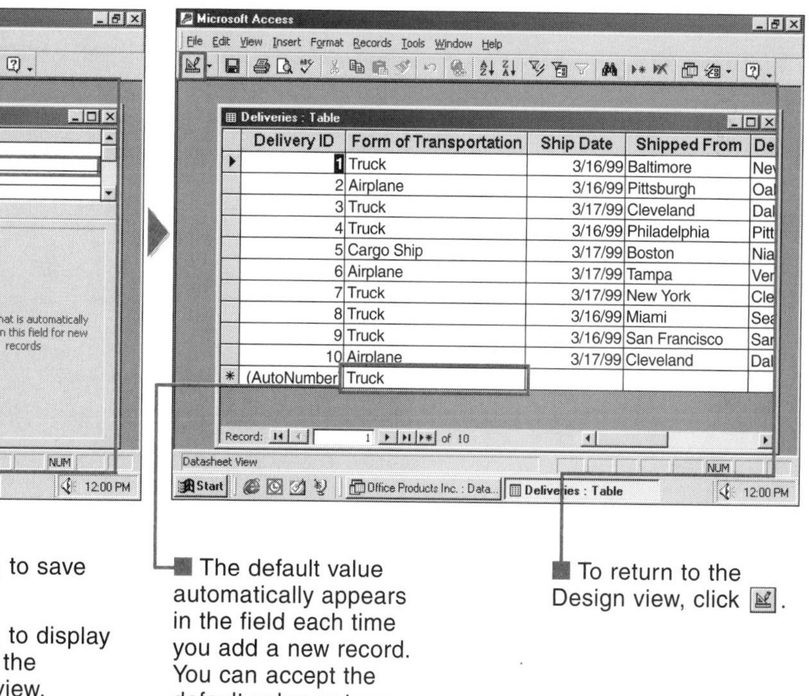

■ The default value automatically appears in the field each time you add a new record. You can accept the default value or type another value.

■ To return to the Design view, click [design view icon].

DATA ENTRY REQUIRED

You can specify that a field must contain data for each record.

Fields that require data prevent you from leaving out important information. For example, in a table that stores invoice information, you can specify that data must be entered in the Invoice Number field.

After you specify that a field must contain data, Access can check to see if the field contains data for all the existing records in the table. When you enter a new record in the table, an error message will appear if you do not enter data in the field.

You can also specify that a field requiring data may accept zero-length strings. A zero-length string indicates that no data exists for the field. For example, if you set the Fax Number field to require data, but one of your clients does not have a fax machine, you will need to enter a zero-length string in the field.

To enter a zero-length string in a cell, type "" in the cell. When you enter a zero-length string, the cell in the table will appear empty.

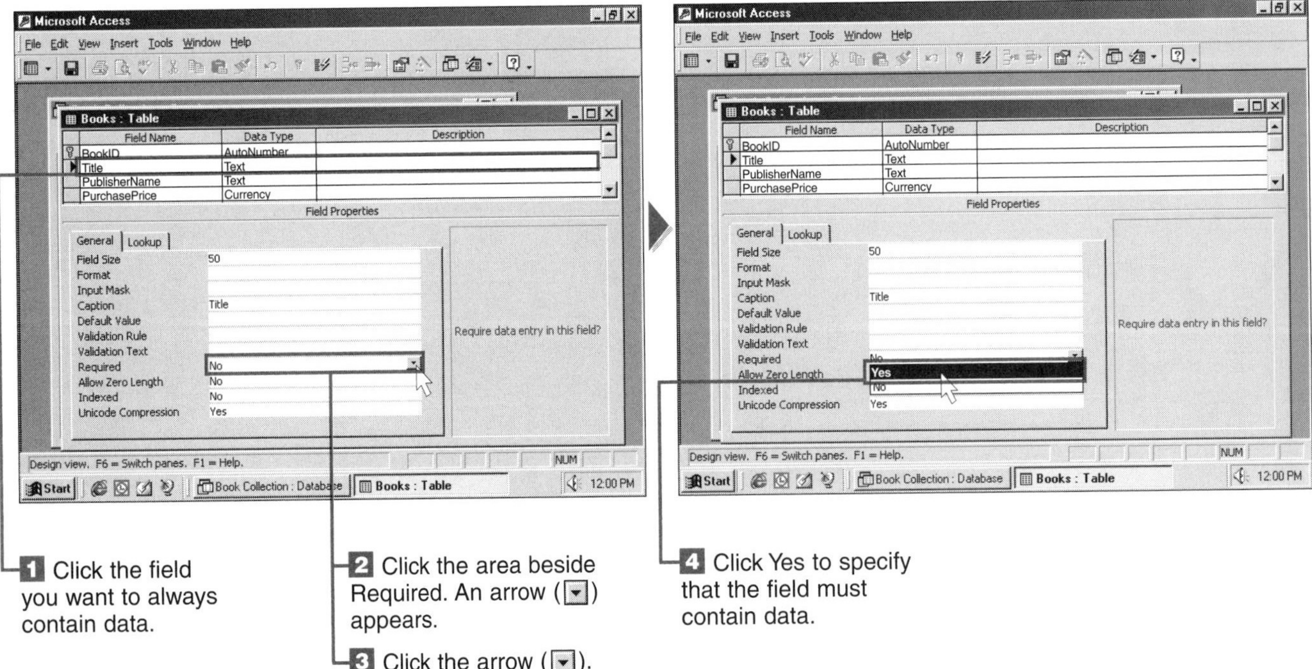

1 Click the field you want to always contain data.

2 Click the area beside Required. An arrow (▼) appears.

3 Click the arrow (▼).

4 Click Yes to specify that the field must contain data.

What is the difference between a null value and a zero-length string?

✔ A null value indicates that you do not know the information for the field. If the field is not set to require data, you can enter a null value by pressing the Enter key. This will leave the cell blank and allow you to move to the next field. A zero-length string indicates that no data exists for the field. If the field is set to require data, you can type "" to enter a zero-length string in the field.

I set a field in my table to require data and accept zero-length strings. Will these properties also be used in my forms?

✔ Properties you specify for a table also apply to forms that use data from the table. You should make sure you set the properties for a table before using the table to create a form.

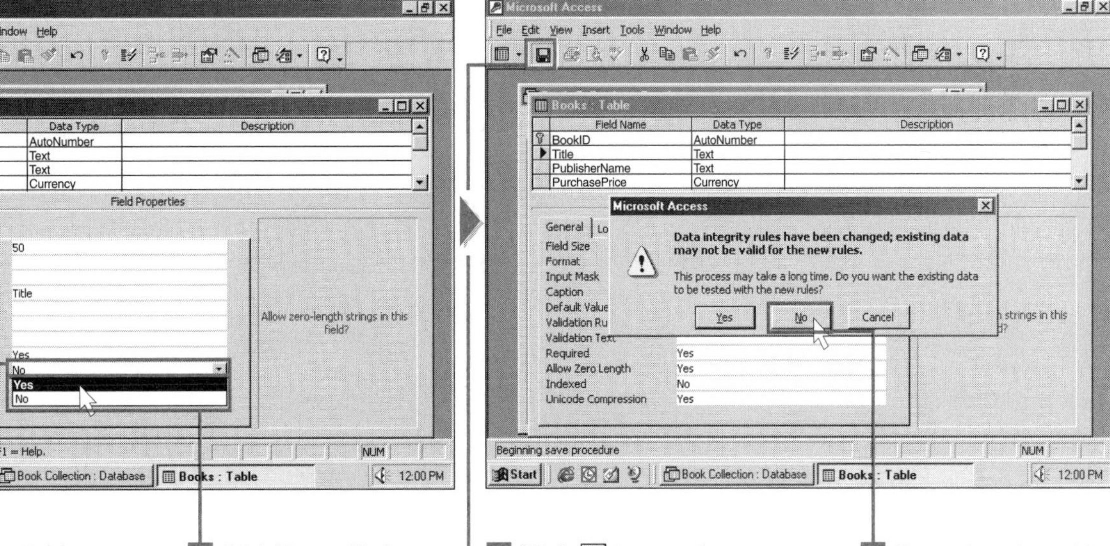

5 To specify if the field can accept a zero-length string, click the area beside Allow Zero Length. An arrow (▾) appears.

6 Click the arrow (▾).

7 Click Yes or No to specify if the field can accept a zero-length string.

8 Click (💾) to save the table.

■ A dialog box appears, asking if you want to check if the field contains data for all existing records.

9 If you do not want to check the field, click No.

Note: If you want to check the field, click Yes.

ADD A VALIDATION RULE

You can add a validation rule to a field to help reduce errors when entering data. A field that uses a validation rule can only accept data that meets certain requirements.

Access automatically sets rules based on the data type of the field. For example, you cannot enter text in a field that has a Number data type. You can use a validation rule to set more specific rules. For example, you can type <50 to specify that numbers entered in the field must be less than 50.

Access will display an error message if the data you enter does not meet the requirements of the field. You can specify the error message you want Access to display. The error message can contain up to 255 characters. If you do not specify an error message, Access will display a standard error message.

When you add a validation rule, you can check to see if the existing data in the field meets the requirements of the new rule. Access notifies you if any existing data violates the new rule.

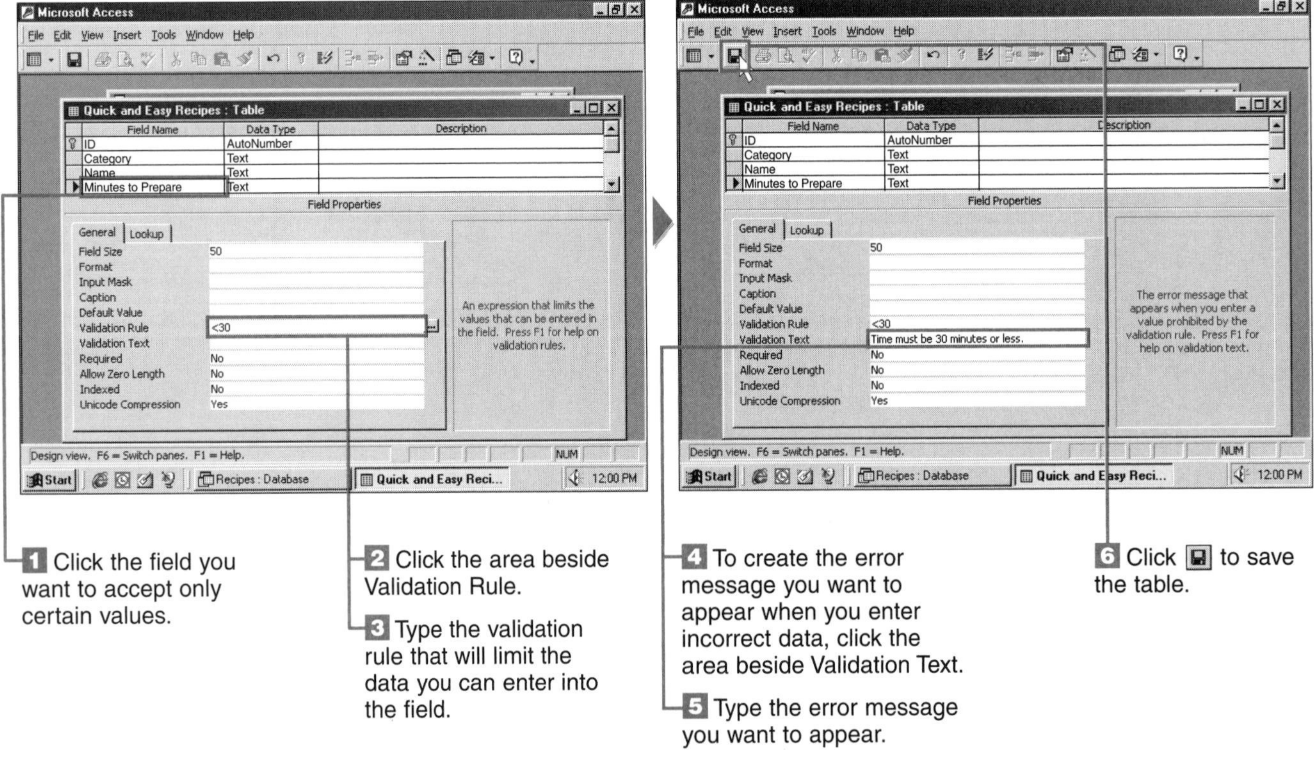

1 Click the field you want to accept only certain values.

2 Click the area beside Validation Rule.

3 Type the validation rule that will limit the data you can enter into the field.

4 To create the error message you want to appear when you enter incorrect data, click the area beside Validation Text.

5 Type the error message you want to appear.

6 Click the Save button to save the table.

TIPS

What types of validation rules can I use?

✔ Examples of validation rules include the following.

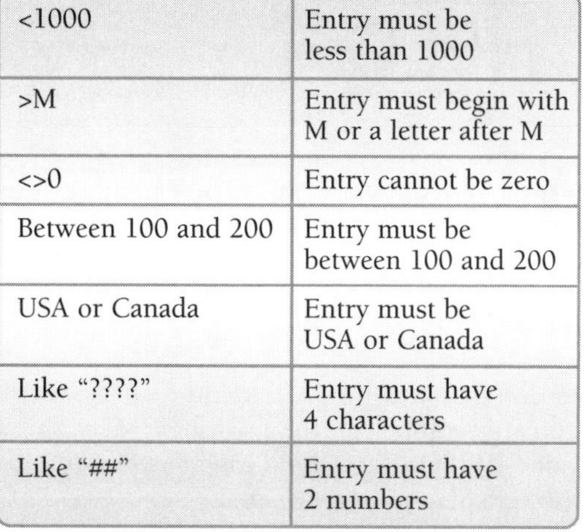

<1000	Entry must be less than 1000
>M	Entry must begin with M or a letter after M
<>0	Entry cannot be zero
Between 100 and 200	Entry must be between 100 and 200
USA or Canada	Entry must be USA or Canada
Like "????"	Entry must have 4 characters
Like "##"	Entry must have 2 numbers

What type of error message should I create?

✔ You should create an error message that explains exactly why the data violates the validation rule. For example, the error message "You must enter a number between 0 and 9", is more informative than the message "Data Rejected".

■ A dialog box appears, asking if you want to check if the existing data meets the new requirements.

7 If you do not want to check the existing data, click No.

Note: If you want to check the existing data, click Yes.

8 Click ▦ to display the table in the Datasheet view.

■ When you enter data that does not meet the requirements of the field, the error message you typed in step 5 will appear.

■ Click OK to close the dialog box and then retype the data.

■ Click ▦ to return to the Design view.

CREATE A YES/NO FIELD

You can create a field that accepts only one of two values, such as Yes or No. Creating a Yes/No field is useful when a field in your table requires a simple answer. For example, a table that stores product information could contain a Yes/No field that indicates whether or not a product has been discontinued.

You can choose one of three available formats for a Yes/No field–Yes/No, True/False or On/Off.

Access offers three ways to display data in a Yes/No field. The Check Box option displays a check box to indicate a value, such as Yes (☑) or No (☐). The Text Box option displays a text value, such as "Yes" or "No". The Combo Box option displays a text value, such as "Yes" or "No", and allows you to select the value you want from a drop-down list.

When you display your table in the Datasheet view, the Yes/No field displays the options you selected.

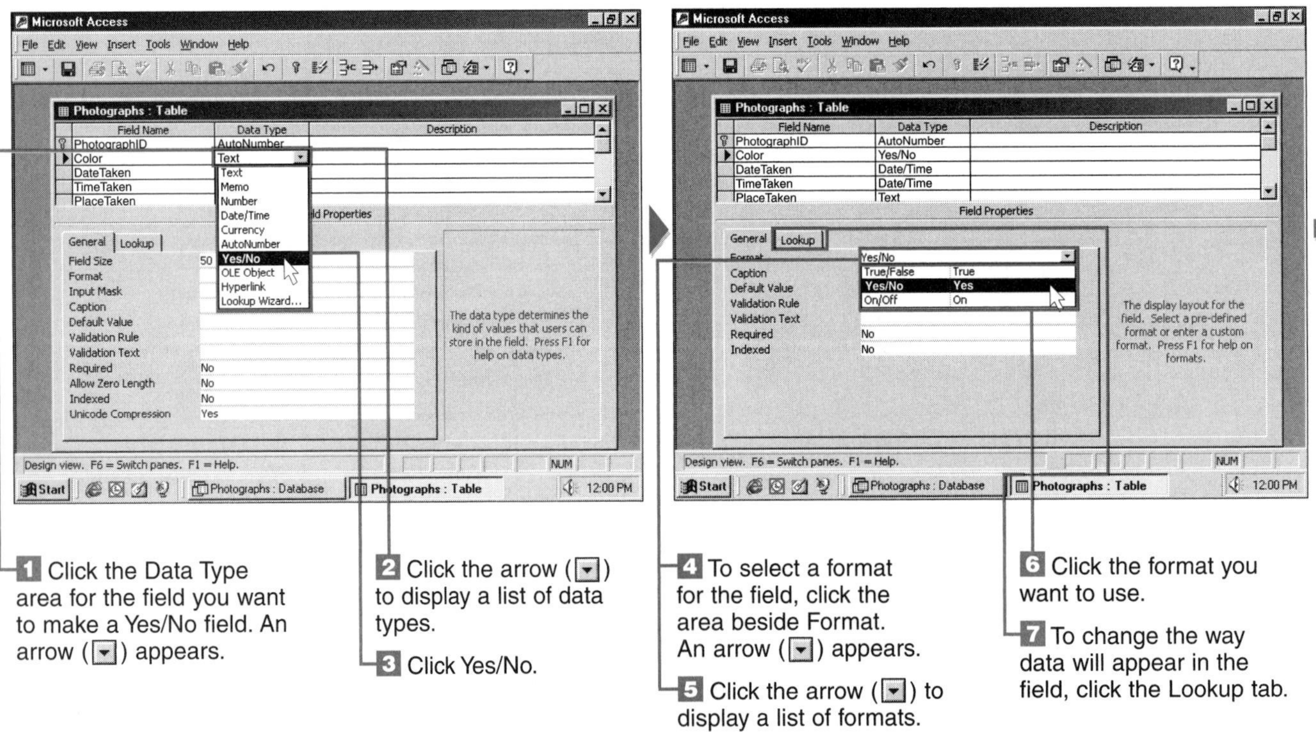

1 Click the Data Type area for the field you want to make a Yes/No field. An arrow (▾) appears.

2 Click the arrow (▾) to display a list of data types.

3 Click Yes/No.

4 To select a format for the field, click the area beside Format. An arrow (▾) appears.

5 Click the arrow (▾) to display a list of formats.

6 Click the format you want to use.

7 To change the way data will appear in the field, click the Lookup tab.

TIPS

When would I use the True/False format?

✔ The True/False format is often used to determine if an action is required. For example, a True/False format could be used to indicate whether or not you should send mailings, such as newsletters, to a client.

How can I speed up the entry of data in a Yes/No field?

✔ By default, Access displays the No value in Yes/No fields. If most of your records require a Yes value, you can change the default value to Yes. For information on setting the default value for a field, see page 429.

In the Datasheet view, why doesn't the Combo Box drop-down list display any values?

✔ You must specify the values you want the drop-down list to display. In the Design view, click the Lookup tab and then click the area beside Row Source Type. Click the arrow (▾) that appears and then select Value List. Click the area beside Row Source and then type the values you want to display in the drop-down list, separated by a semicolon. For example, type **Yes;No**.

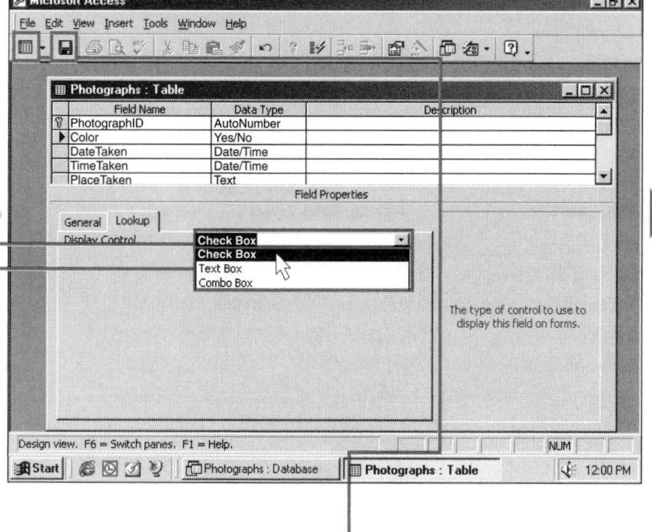

8 Click the area beside Display Control. An arrow (▾) appears.

9 Click the arrow (▾) to display a list of options.

10 Click the display option you want to use.

11 Click 💾 to save the table.

12 Click ▦ to display the table in the Datasheet view.

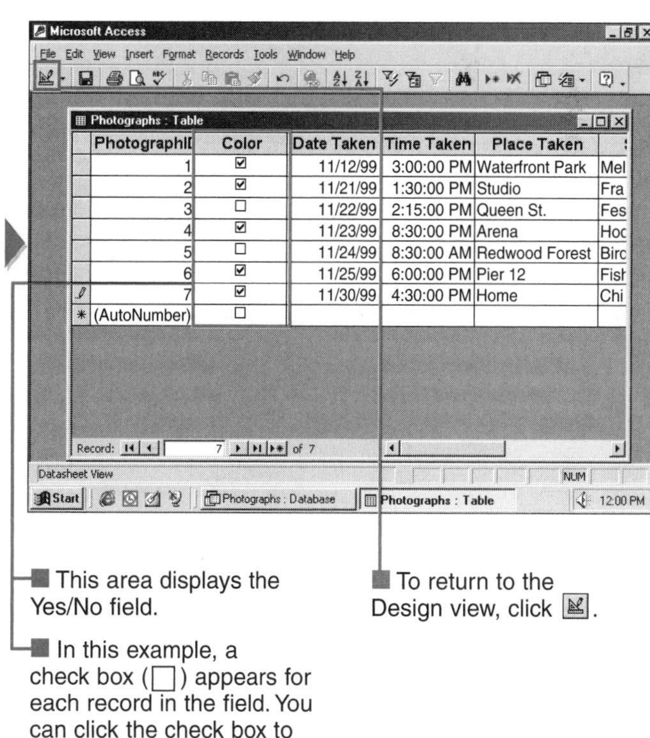

■ This area displays the Yes/No field.

■ In this example, a check box (☐) appears for each record in the field. You can click the check box to indicate Yes (☑) or No (☐).

■ To return to the Design view, click 📐.

CREATE A LOOKUP COLUMN

You can create a list of values, called a lookup column, that you can choose from when entering information in a field. This can save you time since you do not have to type the values for each record.

Creating a lookup column is very useful if you repeatedly enter the same values in a field.

For example, if you always use one of three methods to ship your orders, you can create a lookup column that displays the three shipping methods, such as land, sea and air. In a table that stores the names of your clients, you may want to create a lookup column that displays the Mr., Ms. and Mrs. values.

The Lookup Wizard guides you through the process of creating a lookup column. You can enter the values you want to appear in the lookup column using the Lookup Wizard.

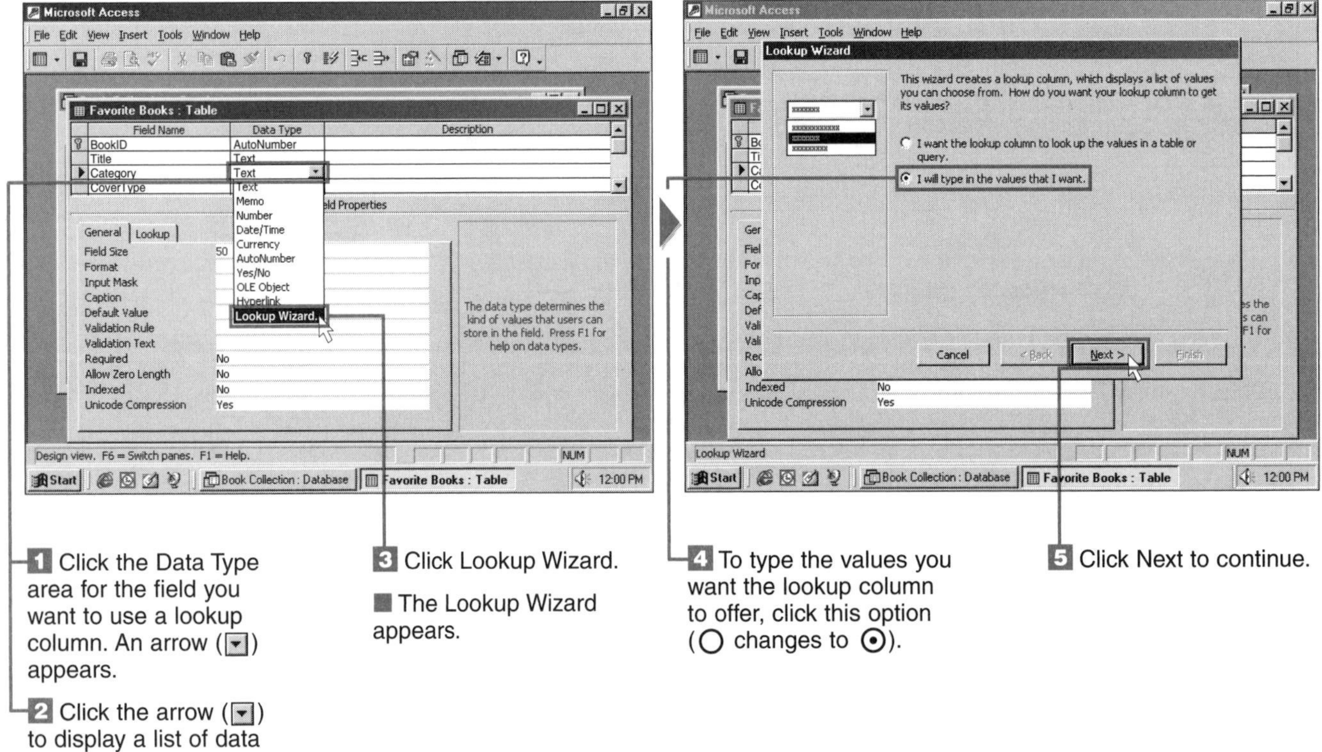

1 Click the Data Type area for the field you want to use a lookup column. An arrow (▼) appears.

2 Click the arrow (▼) to display a list of data types.

3 Click Lookup Wizard.

■ The Lookup Wizard appears.

4 To type the values you want the lookup column to offer, click this option (○ changes to ⊙).

5 Click Next to continue.

TIPS

Can I create a lookup column that contains more than one column?

✔ Yes. For example, the first column could contain shipping methods and the second column could contain costs. Perform steps 1 to 5 below. In the Number of columns area, type the number of columns you want to use. Then enter the values for the columns. The wizard will ask which column contains the values you want to use in the field.

How can I adjust the width of a lookup column?

✔ Perform steps 1 to 8 below. Position the mouse (↖) over the right edge of the column heading (↖ changes to ✛) and then drag the column edge to a new location.

Is there another way to enter values for a lookup column?

✔ You can create a lookup column that uses values from a table or query in your database. In the Lookup Wizard, choose the I want the lookup column to look up the values in a table or query option.

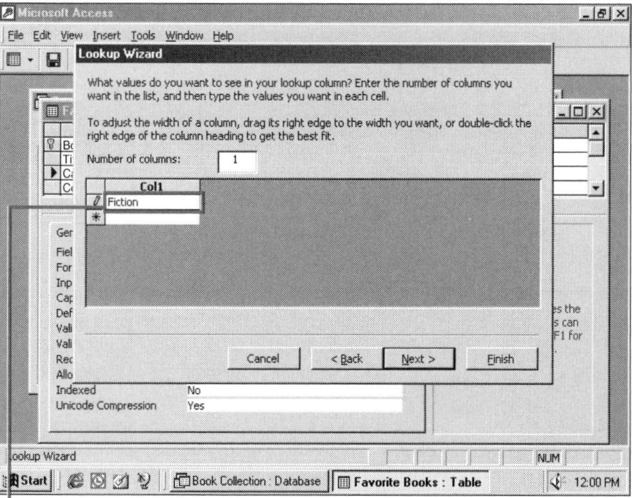

6 Click this area and then type the first value you want to appear in the lookup column.

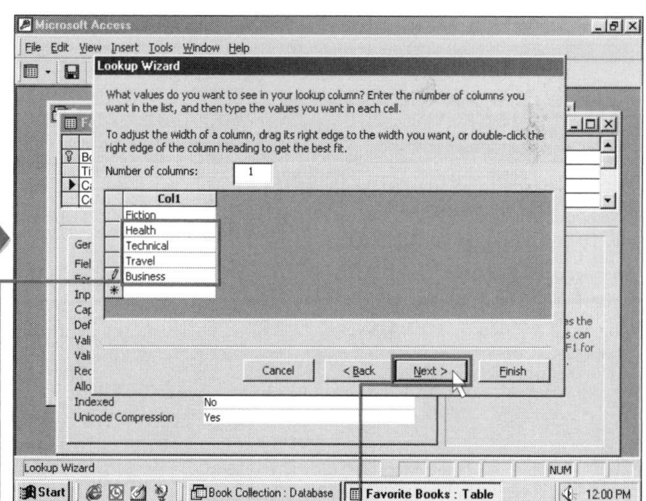

7 To enter the next value, press the Tab key and then type the value.

8 Repeat step 7 for each value you want to appear in the lookup column.

9 Click Next to continue.

CONTINUED

CREATE A LOOKUP COLUMN
CONTINUED

The Lookup Wizard displays the name of the field that will offer the lookup column. If you want the field to display a different field name, you can enter a new name.

After creating a lookup column, you must save the table to have Access save the lookup column.

When your table is displayed in the Datasheet view, users will be able to display the lookup column and select the value they want to enter in the field. Entering information by selecting a value from a lookup column can help prevent errors such as spelling mistakes. Using a lookup column can also ensure that users enter the correct type of information in a field.

If a lookup column does not display the value you want to use, you can type a different value in the field. To hide a lookup column you displayed without selecting a value, you can click outside the lookup column.

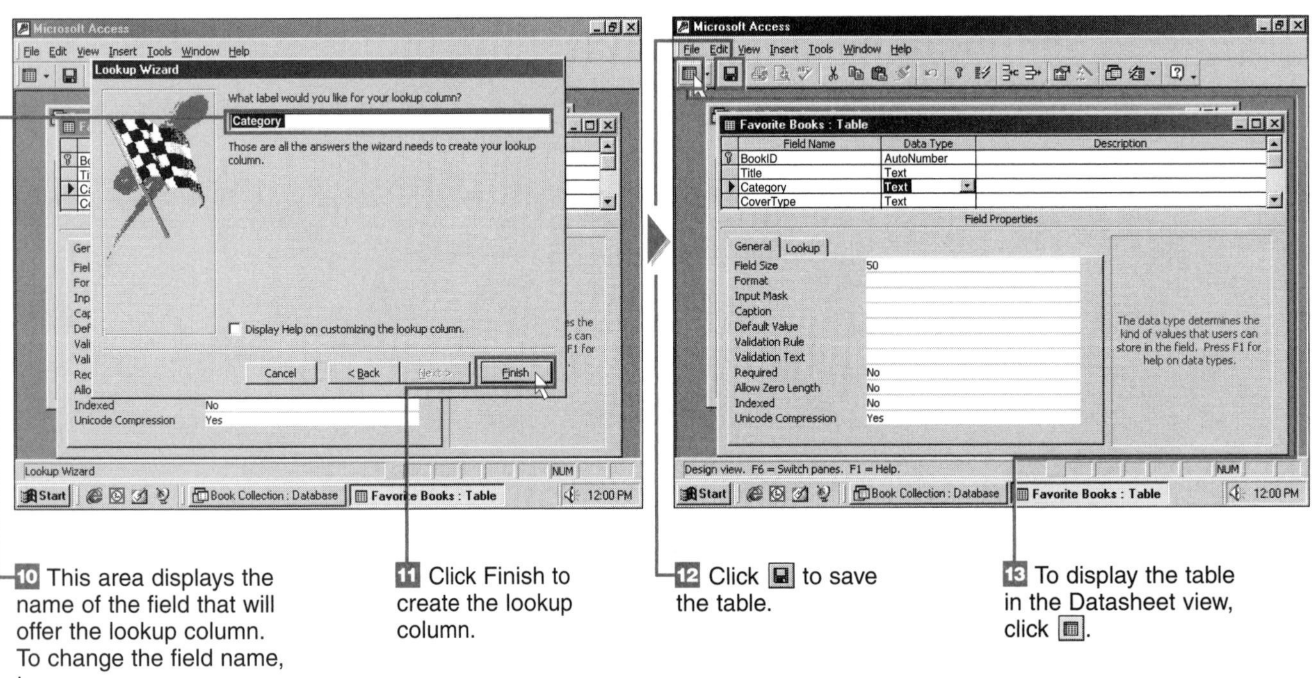

10 This area displays the name of the field that will offer the lookup column. To change the field name, type a new name.

11 Click Finish to create the lookup column.

12 Click 💾 to save the table.

13 To display the table in the Datasheet view, click ▦.

How can I ensure that users will only enter a value from the lookup column?

✔ You can have Access display an error message when a user enters a value that is not displayed in the lookup column. In the Design view, click the field that offers the lookup column, select the Lookup tab and then click the area beside Limit To List. Click the arrow (▼) that appears and then select Yes.

Can I change the values in an existing lookup column?

✔ Yes. In the Design view, click the field that offers the lookup column and then select the Lookup tab. The area beside Row Source displays the values that currently appear in the lookup column. You can delete, edit or add values in this area. You must use a semicolon (;) to separate the values.

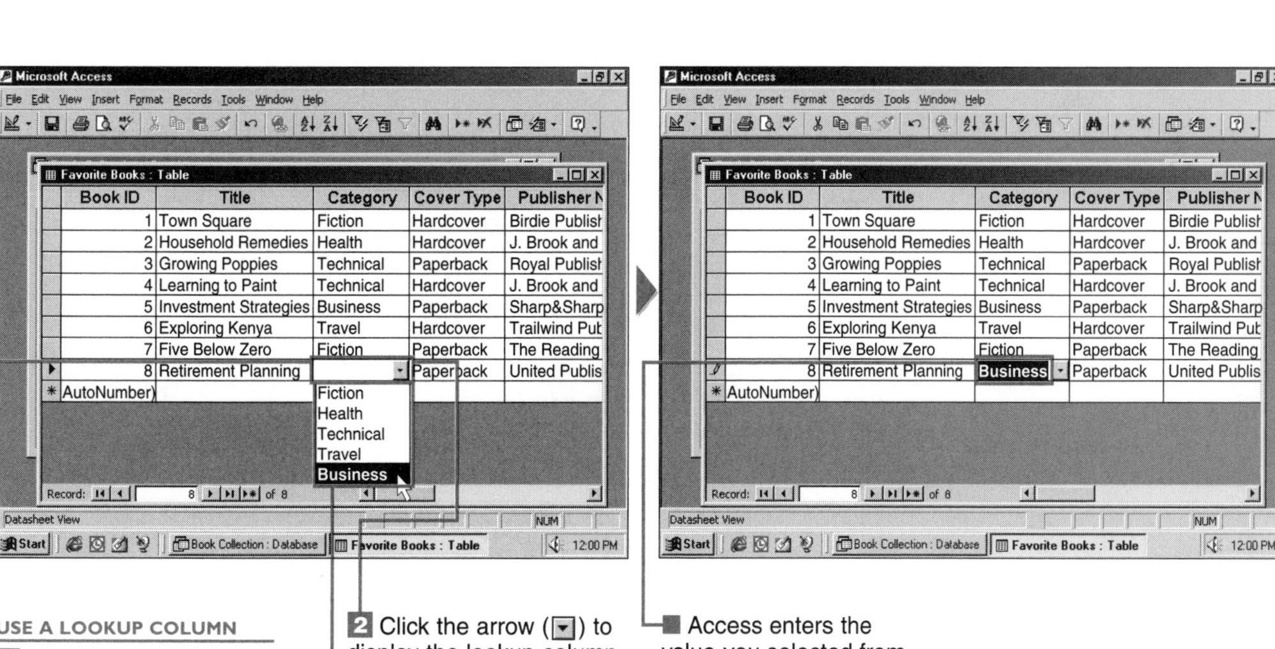

USE A LOOKUP COLUMN

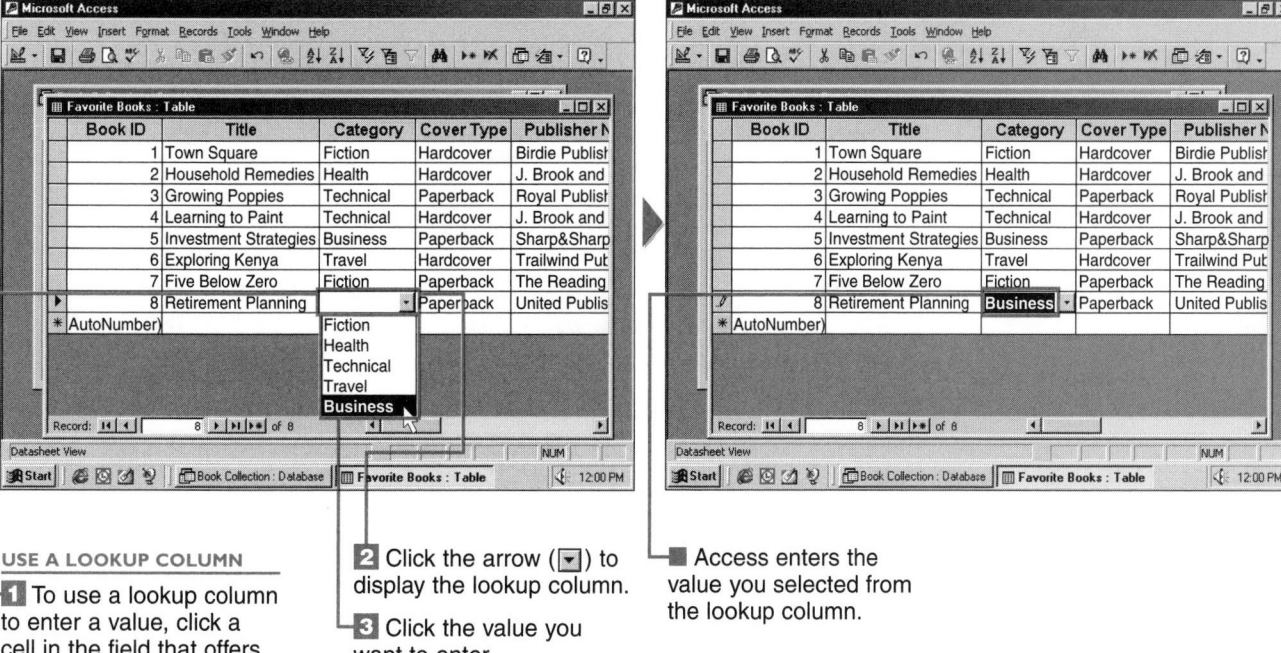

1 To use a lookup column to enter a value, click a cell in the field that offers the lookup column. An arrow (▼) appears.

2 Click the arrow (▼) to display the lookup column.

3 Click the value you want to enter.

■ Access enters the value you selected from the lookup column.

CREATE AN INDEX

You can create an index for a field to speed up searching and sorting information in the field. Access uses the index to find the location of information.

You should index the fields you will frequently search. For example, in a table containing client information, you should index the Last Name field since it is likely you will search for a client using the last name.

You can specify if the field you want to index can contain duplicates. The Yes (Duplicates OK) option allows you to enter the same data in more than one cell in a field. The Yes (No Duplicates) option does not allow you to enter the same data in more than one cell in a field.

The primary key is automatically indexed. The primary key is a field that uniquely identifies each record in a table. The index for the primary key is automatically set to Yes (No Duplicates).

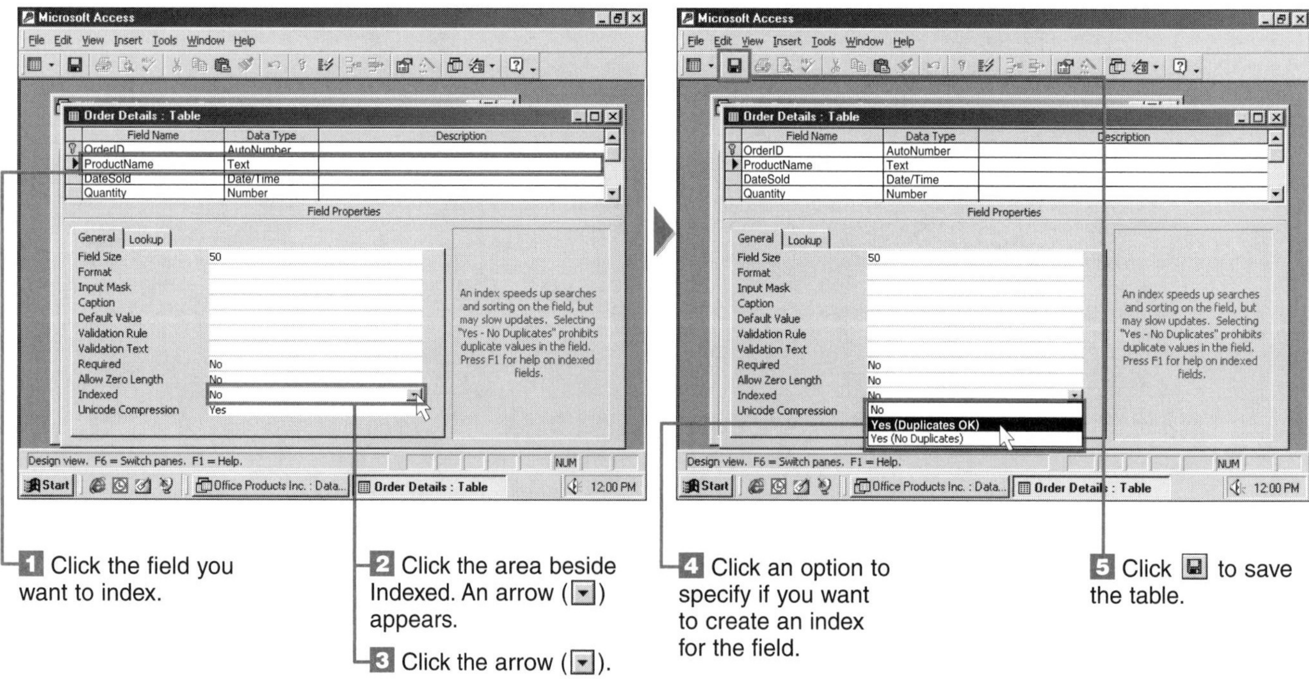

1 Click the field you want to index.

2 Click the area beside Indexed. An arrow (▾) appears.

3 Click the arrow (▾).

4 Click an option to specify if you want to create an index for the field.

5 Click 💾 to save the table.

SET THE PRIMARY KEY

A primary key is one or more fields that uniquely identifies each record in a table. Each table in a database should have a primary key. You should not change the primary key in a table that has a relationship with another table in the database.

There are three types of primary keys you can create–AutoNumber, single-field and multiple-field.

The AutoNumber primary key field automatically assigns a unique number to each record you add. When you create a table, Access can create an AutoNumber primary key field for you.

A single-field primary key is a field that contains a unique value for each record, such as a social security number.

A multiple-field primary key is two or more fields that together make up a unique value for each record.

Access will not allow you to enter the same value in the primary key field more than once. If you create a primary key for a field that already contains data, Access will display a warning message if the field contains duplicate values or an empty cell.

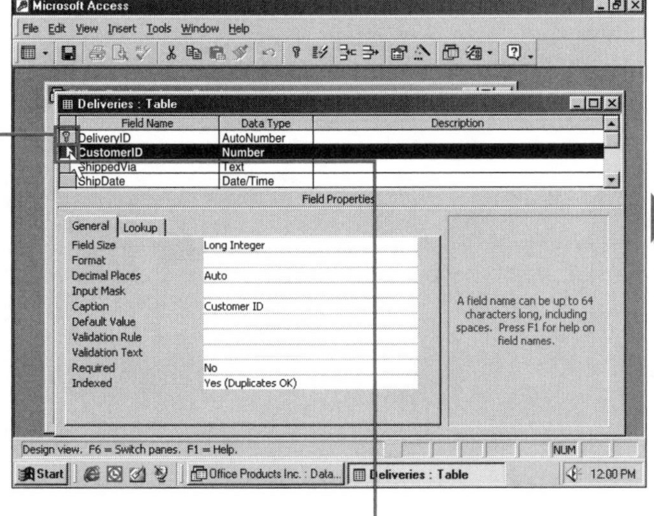

■ The field that is currently set as the primary key displays a key symbol (🔑).

1 To set another field as the primary key, click the area to the left of the field.

Note: To set more than one field as the primary key, hold down the Ctrl key as you click the area to the left of each field.

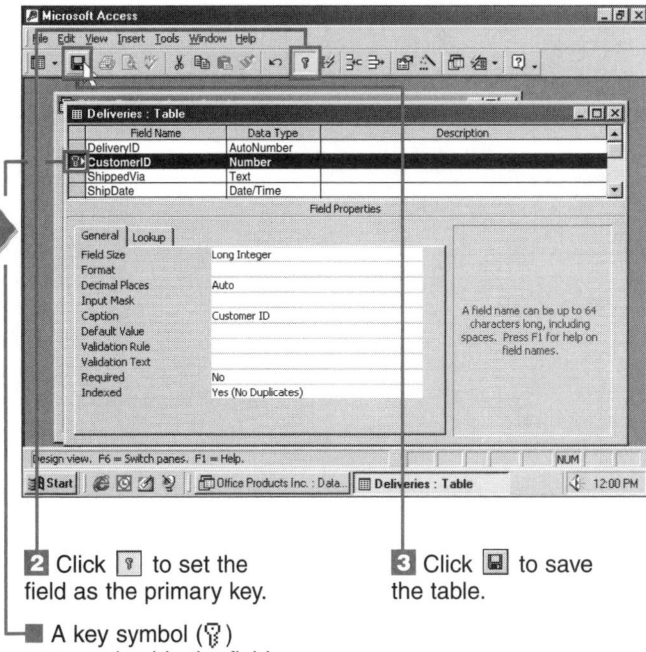

2 Click 🔑 to set the field as the primary key.

■ A key symbol (🔑) appears beside the field.

3 Click 💾 to save the table.

DEFINE RELATIONSHIPS BETWEEN TABLES

You can create relationships between tables to bring together related information. Relationships between tables are essential for creating a form, report or query that uses information from more than one table in a database.

For example, one table in the database could contain the names and addresses of your clients, while the other table could contain the phone numbers of your clients. After you define a relationship between the two tables, you can create a query to have Access display client names, addresses and phone numbers.

The Relationships window shows the relationships that exist between the tables in your database. You can add tables to this window.

You establish a relationship by identifying matching fields in two tables. The fields do not need to have the same name, but they must use the same data type and contain the same kind of information. You will usually relate the primary key in one table to a matching field in the other table. A primary key is a field that uniquely identifies each record in a table.

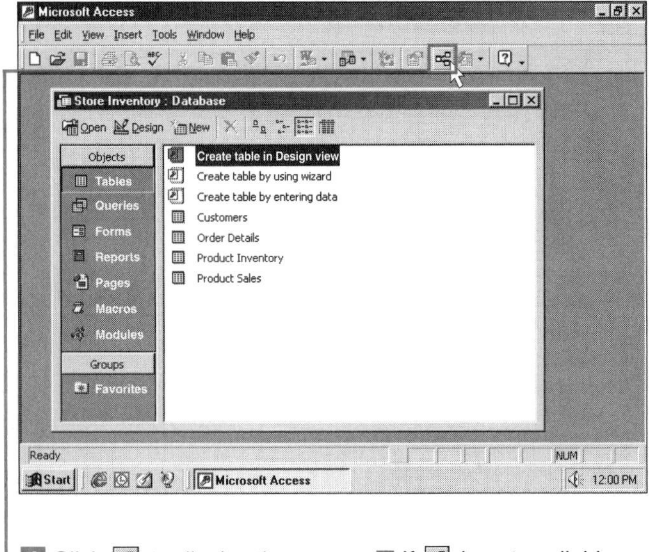

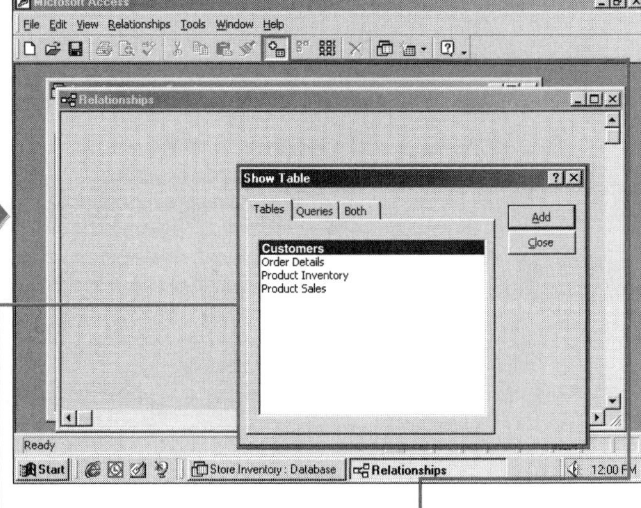

1 Click to display the Relationships window.

■ If is not available, make sure the Database window is open and no other windows are open on the screen.

■ The Relationships window appears. If any relationships exist between the tables in the database, a box for each table appears in the window.

■ The Show Table dialog box may also appear, listing all the tables in the database.

2 If the Show Table dialog box does not appear and you want to add tables to the Relationships window, click to display the dialog box.

TIPS

Why do relationships already exist between tables in my database?

✔ If you used the Database Wizard to create your database, the wizard automatically created relationships between tables for you.

The Relationships window is cluttered. How can I view the relationships for just one table?

✔ Click the Clear Layout button (☒) to remove all the tables from the Relationships window. Click Yes in the dialog box that appears and then perform steps 2 to 4 below to add a table to the Relationships window. Close the Show Table dialog box and then click the Show Direct Relationships button (▦) to view the relationships for the table.

How can I quickly display all the relationships in the database?

✔ To view all the relationships in the database, click the Show All Relationships button (▦).

How do I remove a table from the Relationships window?

✔ Click the box for the table you want to remove and then press the Delete key. This table and any relationships defined for the table are removed from the Relationships window, but not from the database.

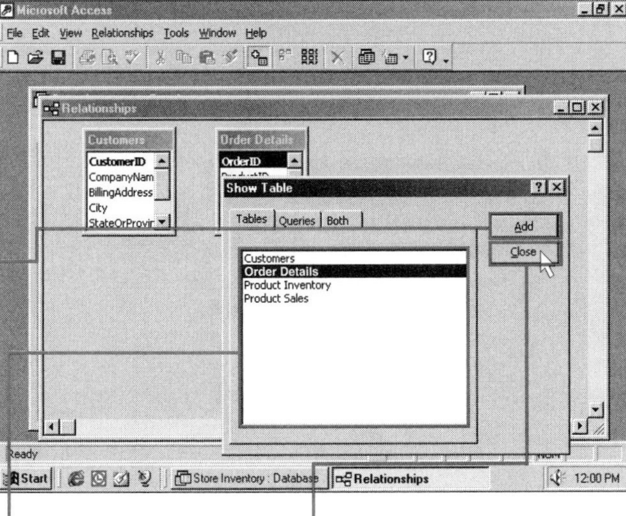

3 Click a table you want to add to the Relationships window.

4 Click Add to add the table to the window.

5 Repeat steps 3 and 4 for each table you want to add.

6 Click Close to remove the dialog box.

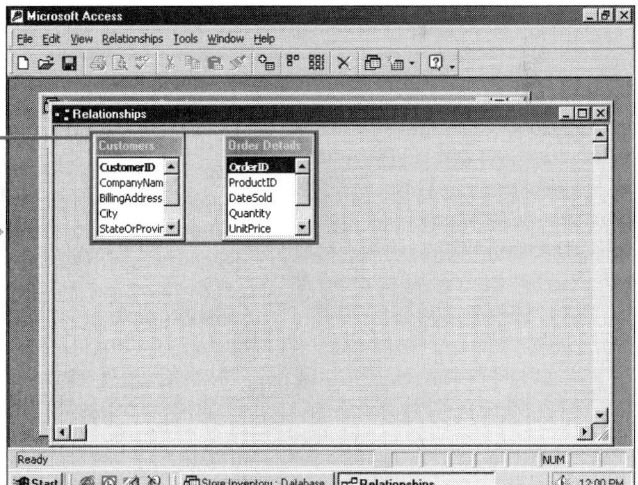

■ The Relationships window displays a box for each table. Each box displays the fields for one table.

■ The primary key in each table appears in **bold**.

CONTINUED

DEFINE RELATIONSHIPS BETWEEN TABLES CONTINUED

The type of relationship Access creates between two tables depends on the fields you use to create the relationship.

If only one field in the relationship is a primary key, Access creates a one-to-many relationship. In this type of relationship, each record in a table relates to one or more records in the other table. For example, if one table stores the names of clients and the other table stores orders, the one-to-many relationship allows each client to have more than one order. This is the most common type of relationship.

If both fields in the relationship are primary keys, Access creates a one-to-one relationship. In this type of relationship, each record in a table relates to just one record in the other table. For example, if one table stores available rental cars and the other table stores the dates the cars are reserved, the one-to-one relationship allows each car to have only one reserve date.

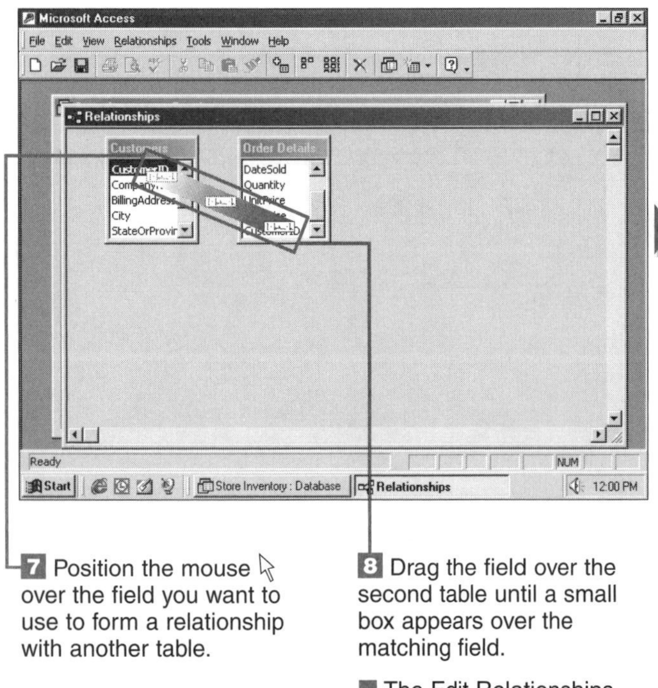

7 Position the mouse over the field you want to use to form a relationship with another table.

8 Drag the field over the second table until a small box appears over the matching field.

■ The Edit Relationships dialog box appears.

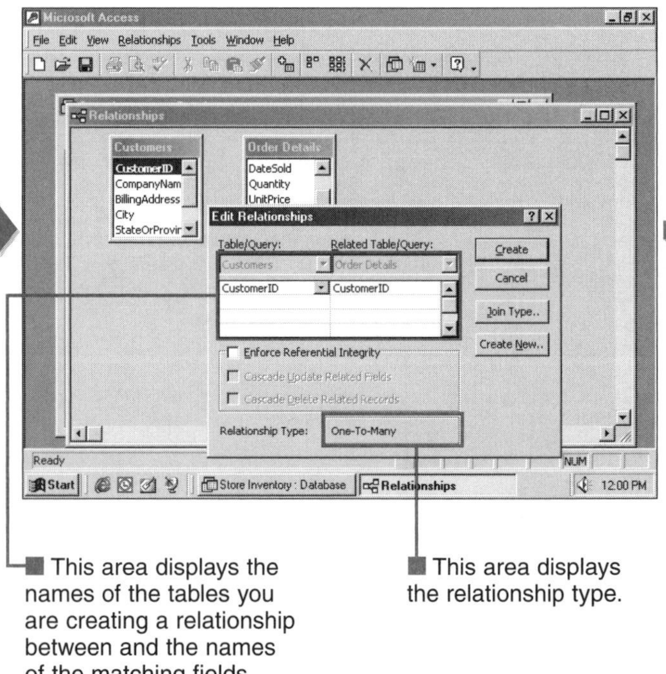

■ This area displays the names of the tables you are creating a relationship between and the names of the matching fields.

■ This area displays the relationship type.

What is referential integrity?

✔ Referential integrity is a set of rules that prevent you from changing or deleting a record if matching records exist in a related table. Access provides two options that let you override the rules of referential integrity but still protect data from accidental changes or deletions. The Cascade Update Related Fields option allows Access to update matching data in all related records when you change the data in the primary key. The Cascade Delete Related Records option allows Access to delete matching records in related tables when you delete a record.

Can I change the referential integrity options later?

✔ Yes. To redisplay the Edit Relationships dialog box so you can change these options, double-click the line representing the relationship you want to change.

How do I delete a relationship?

✔ In the Relationships window, click the line representing the relationship you want to delete and then press the Delete key.

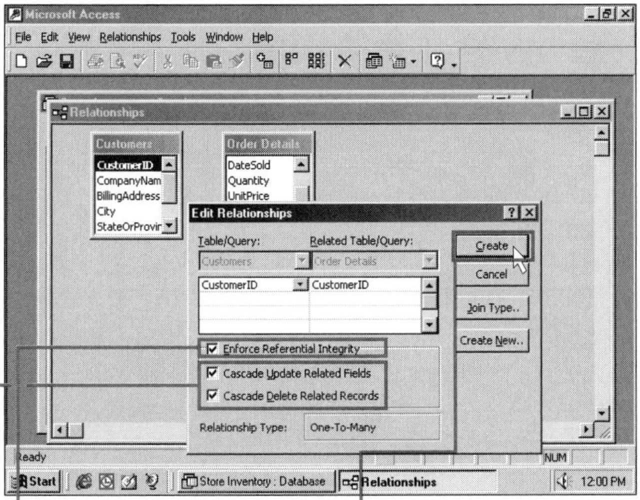

9 To enforce referential integrity between the tables, click this option (☐ changes to ☑).

10 To have Access automatically update related fields or delete related records, click each option you want to use (☐ changes to ☑).

11 Click Create to establish the relationship.

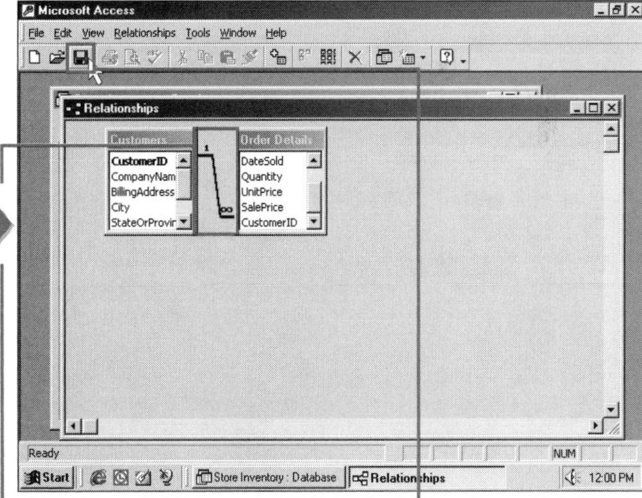

■ A line connects the fields in the two tables to show the relationship.

■ The symbols above the line indicate the type of relationship. In this example, a single record in the Customers table (1) relates to one or more records in the Order Details table (∞).

Note: If you did not perform steps 9 and 10, the symbols above the line do not appear.

12 Click 💾 to save the changes.

CREATE A FORM USING THE FORM WIZARD

The Form Wizard helps you create a form that suits your needs. The wizard asks you a series of questions and then sets up a form based on your answers.

A form presents information from a table in your database in an attractive format. You can use a form to add, edit and delete information in a table. You may find that a form is easier to work with than a table.

The Form Wizard allows you to choose the table containing the fields you want to include in the form. After you choose a table, you can select the fields you want to include. A form can include all or only some of the fields in a table.

If you accidentally select a field you do not want to include in the form, you can easily remove the field from the list of selected fields in the wizard.

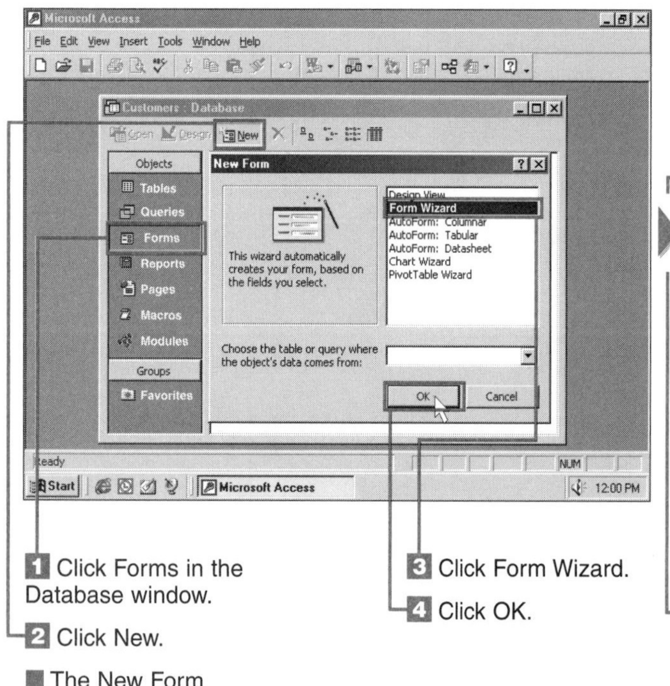

1 Click Forms in the Database window.

2 Click New.

■ The New Form dialog box appears.

3 Click Form Wizard.

4 Click OK.

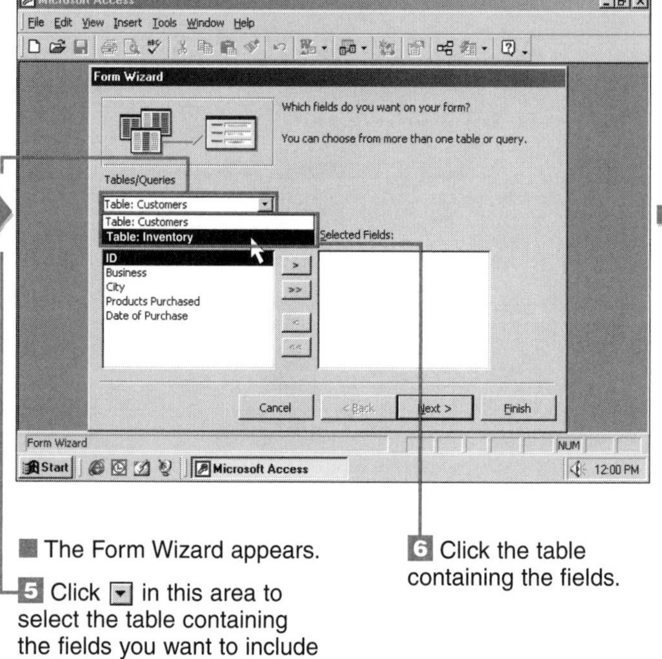

■ The Form Wizard appears.

5 Click ▼ in this area to select the table containing the fields you want to include in the form.

6 Click the table containing the fields.

Can I create a form that uses fields from more than one table?

✔ Yes. Perform steps 1 to 7 below to select the fields you want to include from one table. Then repeat steps 5 to 7 until you have chosen all the tables and selected all the fields you want to include in the form. To use more than one table to create a form, relationships must exist between the tables. For information on defining relationships between tables, see page 442.

In what order will the fields I select appear in the form?

✔ The fields will appear in the form in the order you select them. You can rearrange the fields after you create the form. See page 456.

Is there another way to start the Form Wizard?

✔ Yes. In the Database window, click Forms and then double-click the Create form by using wizard option. This option is not available for some types of databases.

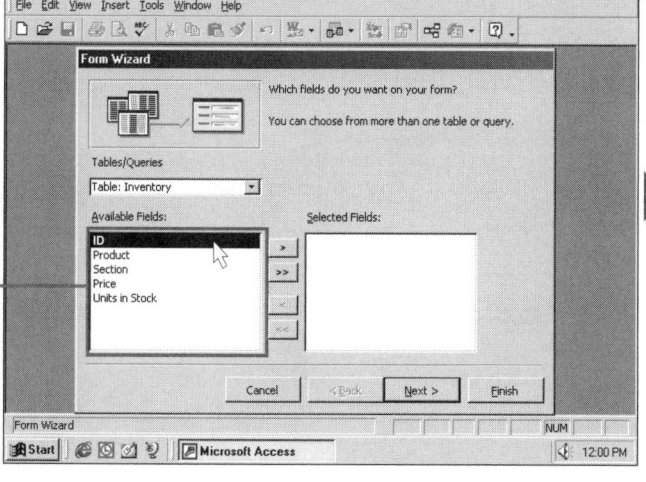

■ This area displays the fields from the table you selected.

7 Double-click each field you want to include in the form.

Note: To add all the fields at once, click >>.

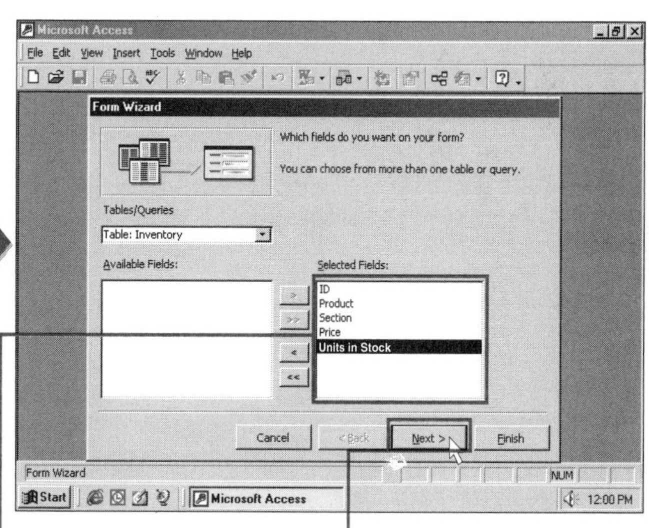

■ Each field you select appears in this area.

8 To remove a field you accidentally selected, double-click the field in this area.

Note: To remove all the fields at once, click <<.

9 Click Next to continue.

CREATE A FORM USING THE FORM WIZARD CONTINUED

When you use the Form Wizard to create a form, you can choose between several layouts for the form. The layout of a form determines the arrangement of information on the form.

The Form Wizard offers four layouts for you to choose from. The Columnar layout displays one record at a time and lines up information in a column. The Tabular layout displays multiple records and presents information in rows and columns. The Datasheet layout displays multiple records and is similar to the Datasheet view for tables. The Justified layout displays one record at a time and aligns information along both the left and right sides of a form.

You can apply a style to the form, such as Blends, International or Stone. Most styles use colors and patterns to enhance the appearance of a form.

You must specify a name for the form. You can use up to 64 characters to name a form. The name you specify will appear at the top of the form and in the Forms area of the Database window.

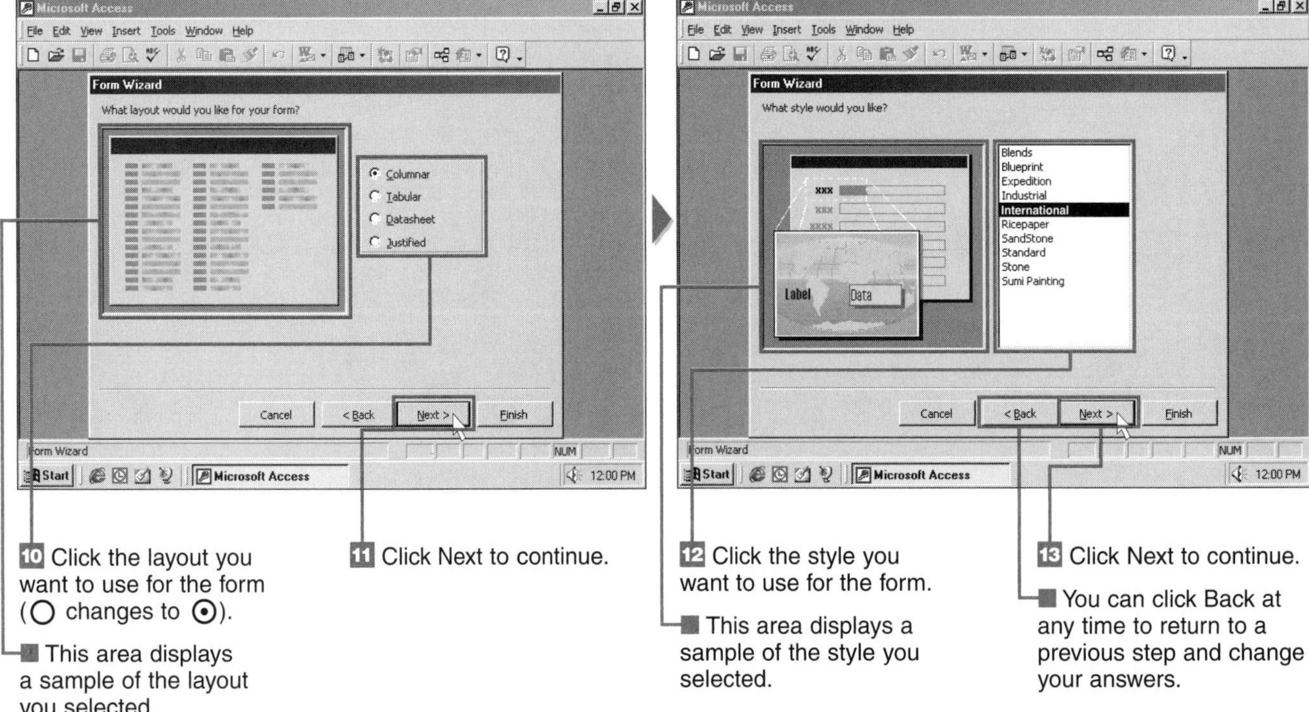

10 Click the layout you want to use for the form (○ changes to ⊙).

■ This area displays a sample of the layout you selected.

11 Click Next to continue.

12 Click the style you want to use for the form.

■ This area displays a sample of the style you selected.

13 Click Next to continue.

■ You can click Back at any time to return to a previous step and change your answers.

TIPS

Can I later change the style of a form?

✔ You can use the AutoFormat feature to later change the style of a form. Display the form you want to change in the Design view and then click the AutoFormat button (). In the AutoFormat dialog box, select the style you want to use and then click OK. For more information on the AutoFormat feature, see page 463.

How do I rename a form I have created?

✔ In the Database window, click Forms and then right-click the form you want to rename. From the menu that appears, select Rename. Type a new name for the form and then press the Enter key.

Is there a faster way to create a form?

✔ You can use an AutoForm to quickly create a form based on one table in your database. In the Database window, select Forms and then click New. Choose the Columnar, Tabular or Datasheet AutoForm style. Click ▾ and then select the table that will supply the information for the form. Then click OK.

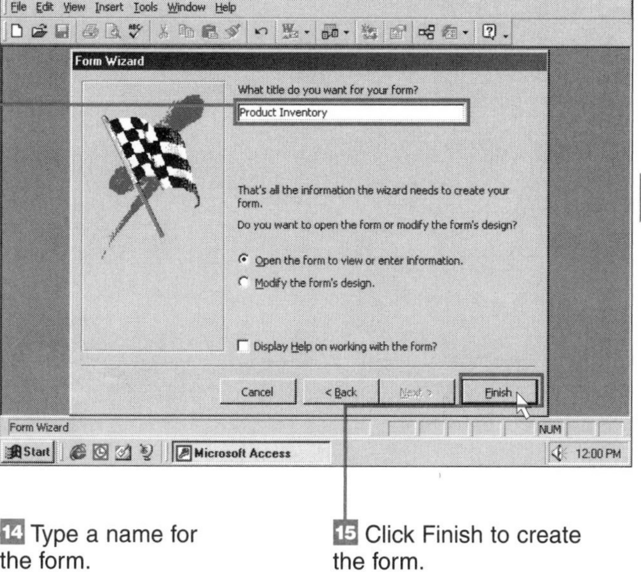

14 Type a name for the form.

15 Click Finish to create the form.

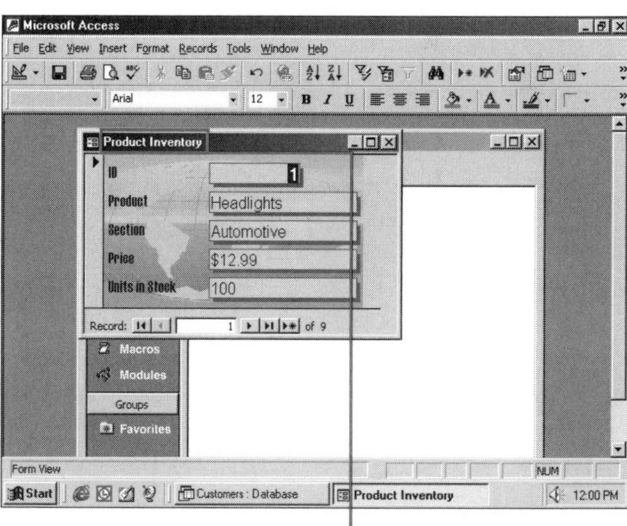

■ The form appears, displaying the field names you selected and the first record.

■ The name of the form appears in this area.

MOVE THROUGH RECORDS

You can easily move through the records in a form to review or edit information. Any changes you make to the information in a form will also appear in the table you used to create the form.

Access displays the number of the current record and the total number of records in the form.

Access also displays buttons you can use to move through the records in the form. You can quickly move to the first, last, previous or next record. If you know the number of the record you want to view, you can quickly move to that record.

You can also use the keyboard to move through records. Use the Page Up or Page Down key to move to the previous or next record. Use the Ctrl+↑ keys or the Ctrl+↓ keys to move to the first or last record.

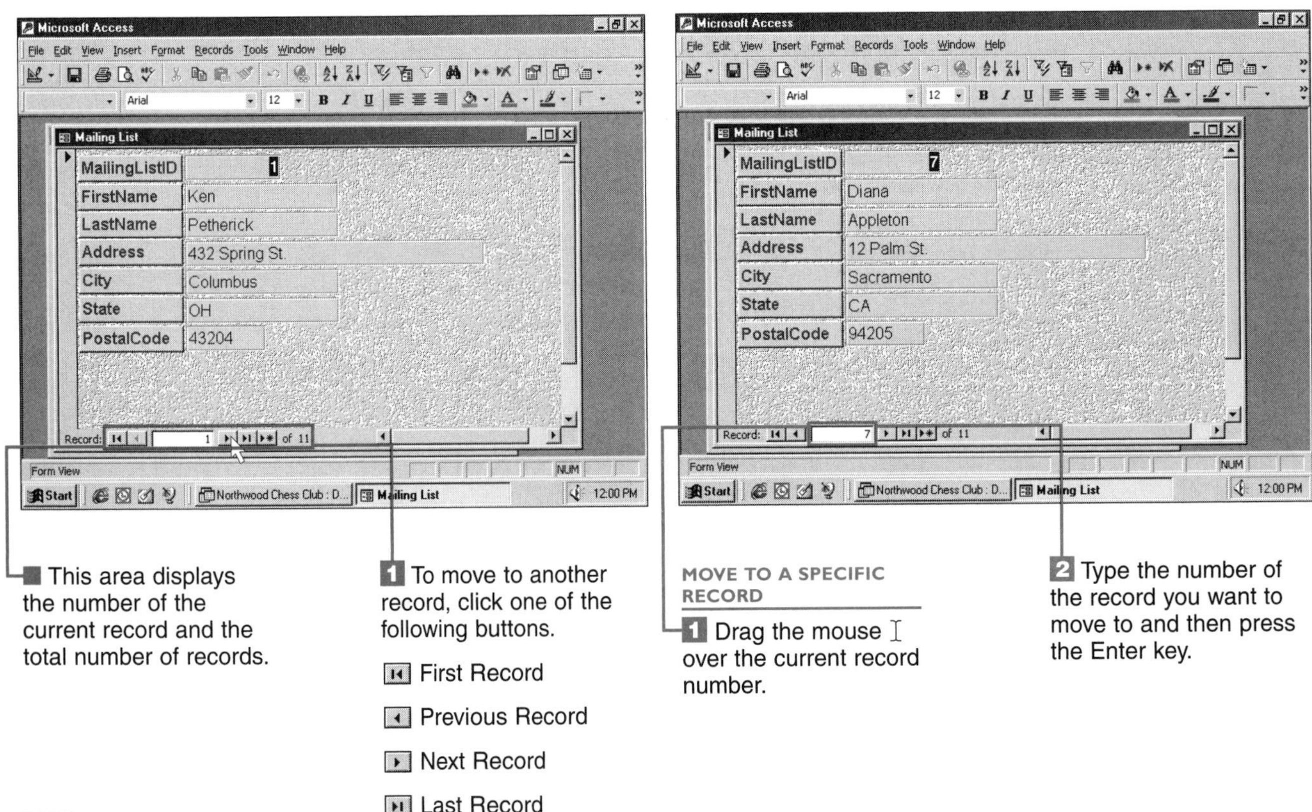

■ This area displays the number of the current record and the total number of records.

1 To move to another record, click one of the following buttons.

- First Record
- Previous Record
- Next Record
- Last Record

MOVE TO A SPECIFIC RECORD

1 Drag the mouse I over the current record number.

2 Type the number of the record you want to move to and then press the Enter key.

EDIT DATA

Access allows you to edit the data in a form. This lets you correct a mistake or update the data in a record.

You can insert new data in a cell. The flashing insertion point in a cell indicates where Access will insert new data. You can also delete data you no longer need from a cell.

You can delete all or part of the data in a cell.

Access remembers the changes you make to a record. If you make a mistake while editing data in a cell, you can use the Undo feature to immediately undo the changes in the current cell. If you move the insertion point to another cell and then select the Undo button (↶), Access will undo all the changes you made to the entire record.

You do not have to save the changes you make. When you move from the record you are editing to another record, Access automatically saves your changes.

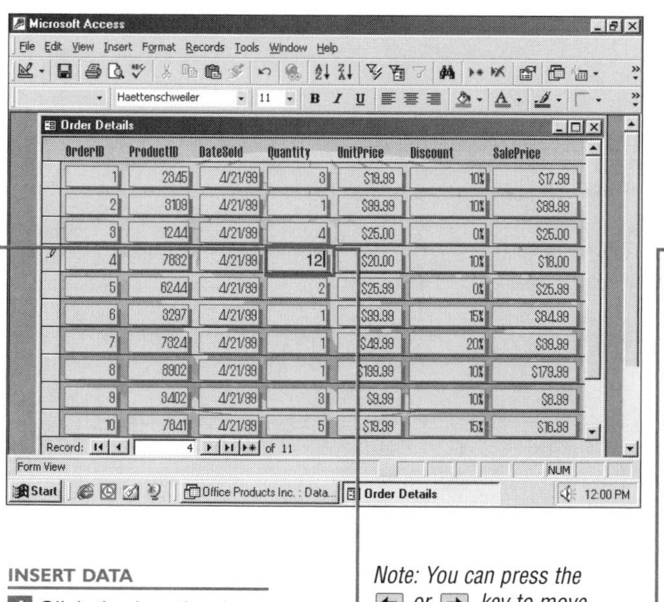

INSERT DATA

1 Click the location in the cell where you want to insert data.

■ A flashing insertion point appears in the cell, indicating where the data you type will appear.

Note: You can press the ← or → key to move the insertion point.

2 Type the data you want to insert.

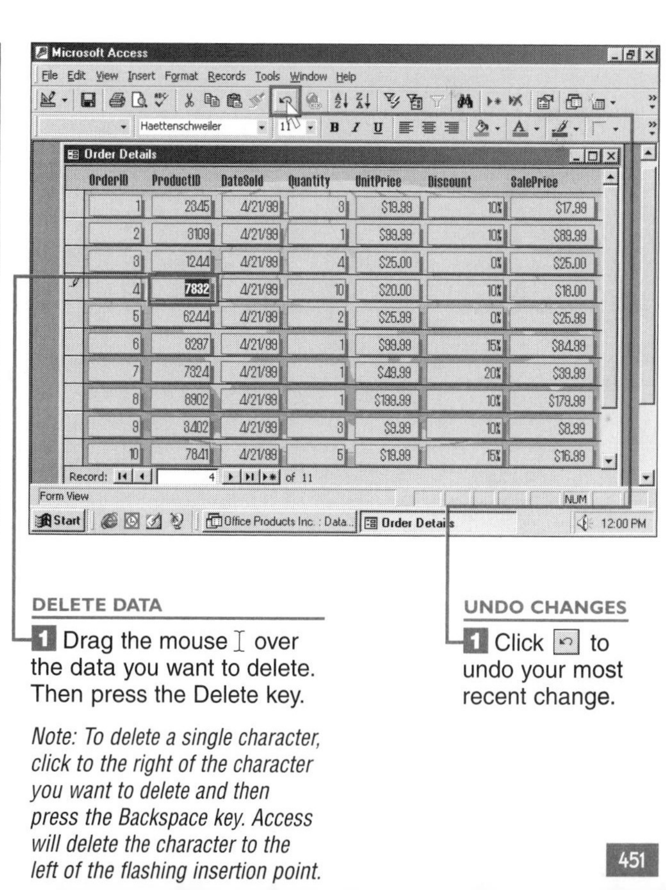

DELETE DATA

1 Drag the mouse I over the data you want to delete. Then press the Delete key.

Note: To delete a single character, click to the right of the character you want to delete and then press the Backspace key. Access will delete the character to the left of the flashing insertion point.

UNDO CHANGES

1 Click ↶ to undo your most recent change.

ADD OR DELETE A RECORD

You can use a form to add a record to the table you used to create the form. For example, you may want to add information about a new client.

Access checks to make sure the data you enter in each field is valid for the specified data type and field properties. If an entry is invalid, Access notifies you before you move to the next field or record. For example, Access will notify you if you try to enter text in a Number field.

You can delete a record to remove information you no longer need. Deleting records saves storage space on your computer and keeps the database from becoming cluttered with unnecessary information.

When you delete a record using a form, you may also want to delete any related data in other tables in the database. For example, if you use a form to delete a company you no longer deal with from your supplier table, you may also want to delete information about the products the company supplies from your product table.

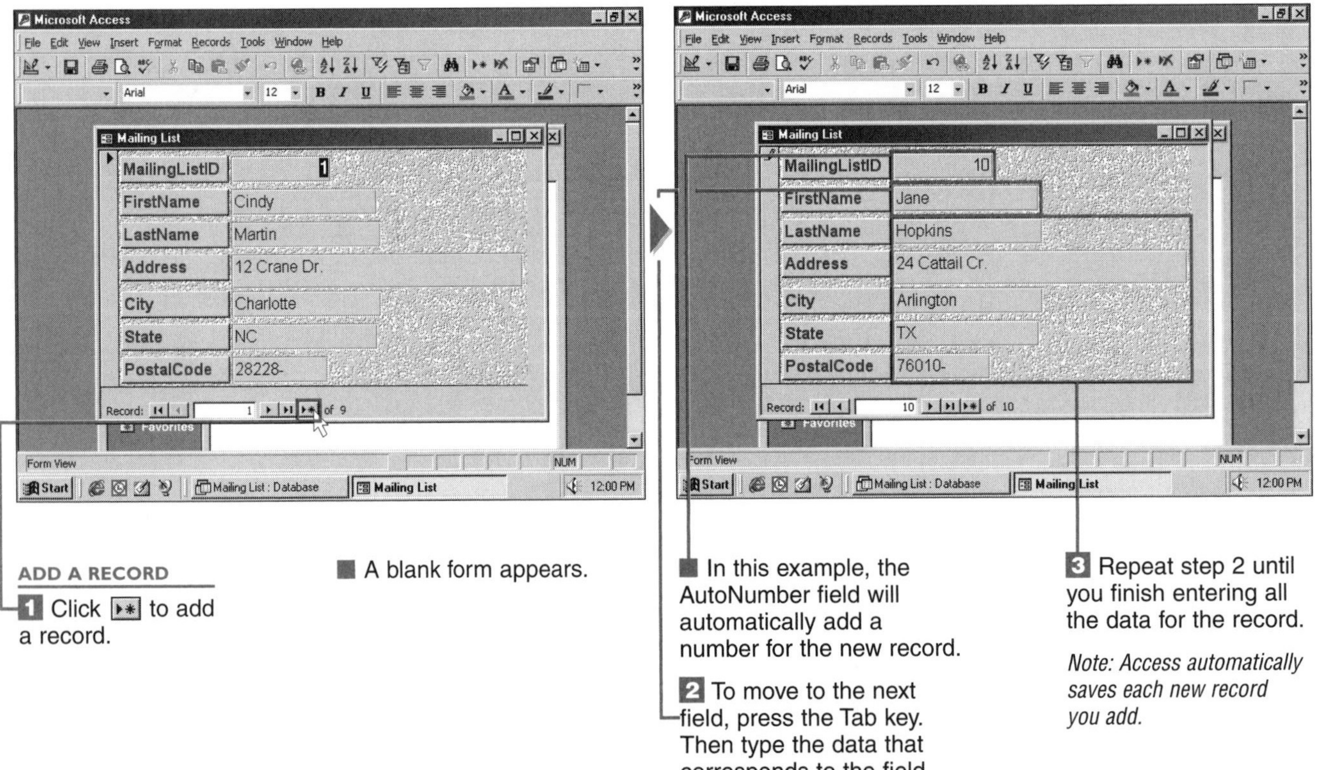

ADD A RECORD

1 Click ▶* to add a record.

■ A blank form appears.

■ In this example, the AutoNumber field will automatically add a number for the new record.

2 To move to the next field, press the Tab key. Then type the data that corresponds to the field.

3 Repeat step 2 until you finish entering all the data for the record.

Note: Access automatically saves each new record you add.

TIPS

How many records can I add to a database?

✔ Since each table can contain up to 1 gigabyte of information, table size does not limit the number of records you can add. The number of records you can add to a database is normally determined by the storage capacity of your computer.

Can I restore a record I accidentally deleted?

✔ When you delete a record from the database, you cannot undo the deletion. If you have a backup copy of the database, you may be able to use the backup to restore a record you deleted.

Is there a way to ensure that related data in the database is removed when I delete a record?

✔ You can specify that if you delete a record from one table, related records from another table will also be removed. To do this, you must establish a relationship between the two tables. You must then enforce referential integrity and turn on the Cascade Delete Related Records option. For more information, see page 442.

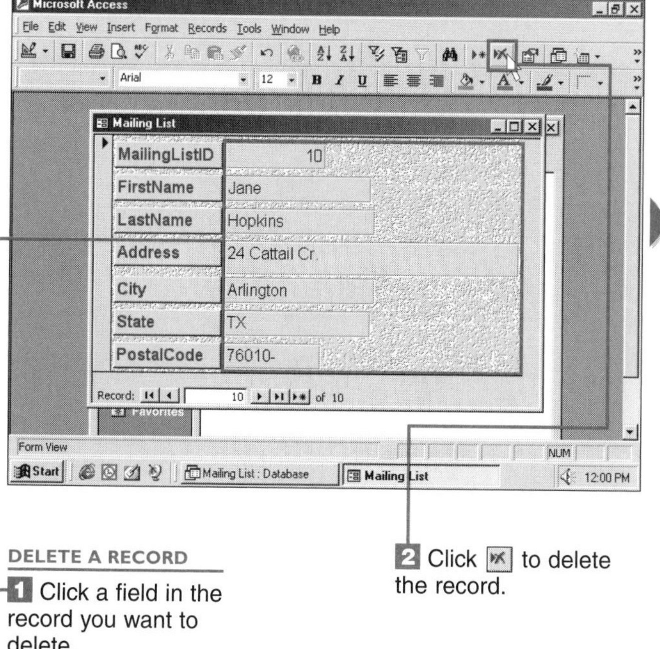

DELETE A RECORD

1 Click a field in the record you want to delete.

2 Click [delete record button] to delete the record.

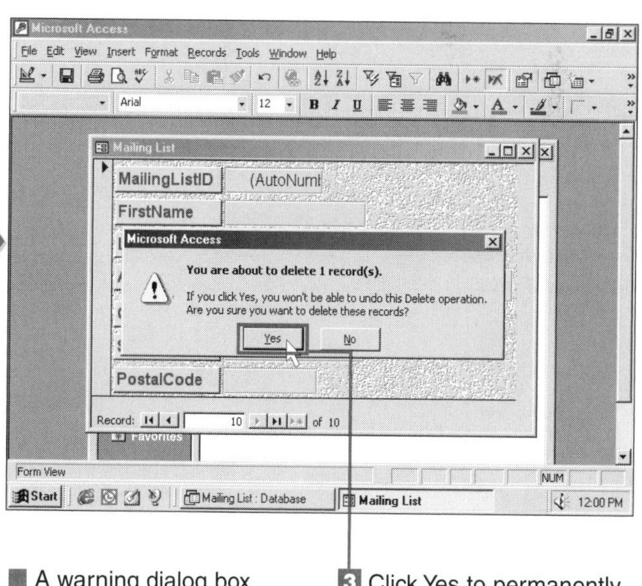

■ A warning dialog box appears, confirming the deletion.

3 Click Yes to permanently delete the record.

■ The record disappears.

OPEN A FORM

You can open a form and display its contents on your screen. This lets you review and make changes to the form.

You can open a form in the Form or Design view. The Form view usually displays one record at a time in an organized and attractive format. This view is useful for entering, editing and reviewing records.

The Design view displays the structure of a form. This view lets you customize the design of a form to make the form easier to use and enhance the appearance of the form.

When you have finished working with a form, you can close the form to remove it from your screen. A dialog box appears if you have not saved changes you made to the design of the form, such as adding a record to the form or moving items on the form.

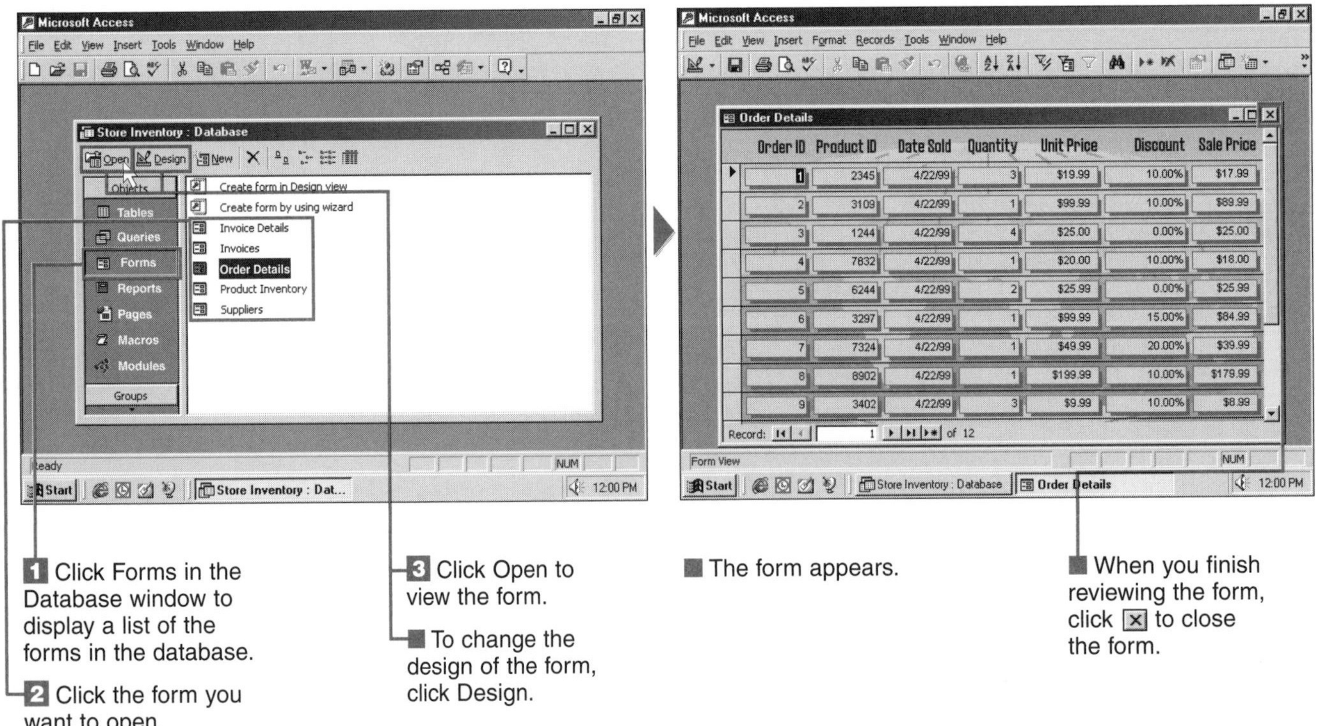

1 Click Forms in the Database window to display a list of the forms in the database.

2 Click the form you want to open.

3 Click Open to view the form.

■ To change the design of the form, click Design.

■ The form appears.

■ When you finish reviewing the form, click ☒ to close the form.

CHANGE VIEW OF FORM

There are three ways you can view a form. Each view allows you to perform different tasks.

The Design view allows you to change the design of a form. You can customize a form in this view to make the form easier to use or to enhance the appearance of the form.

The Form view usually displays one record at a time in an organized and attractive format. The Form view may display all the records at once, depending on the layout you selected when you created the form. This view is often used to enter, edit and review records.

The Datasheet view displays all the records in rows and columns. Each row displays the information for one record. The field names appear directly above the first record. You can enter, edit and review records in this view.

■ In this example, the form appears in the Form view.

1 Click ▾ in this area to display the form in another view.

Note: If the View button is not displayed, click » on the Form View toolbar to display all the buttons.

2 Click the view you want to use.

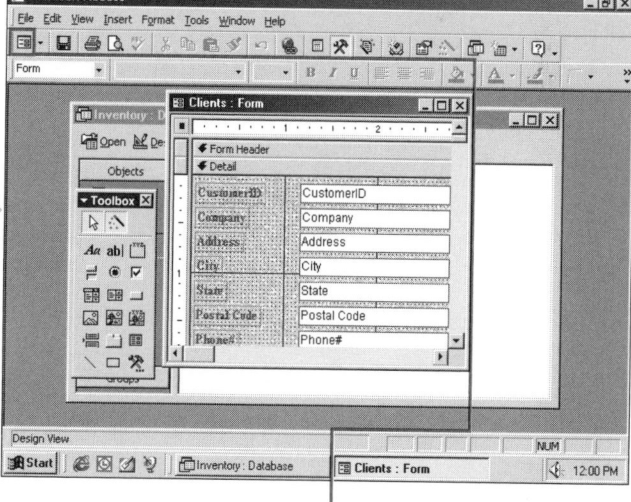

■ The form appears in the view you selected.

■ In this example, the View button changes to the Form View button. You can click the View button to quickly switch between the Design and Form views.

MOVE, RESIZE OR DELETE A CONTROL

You can move, resize or delete a control to enhance the appearance of a form and make the form easier to use. A control is an item on a form, such as a label that displays a field name or a text box that displays data from a field.

You can change the location of a control on a form. You can move a label and its corresponding text box together or individually.

You can change the size of a control. Larger controls allow you to display longer entries. For example, you may want to resize a text box that displays long Web page addresses.

When you move or resize a control, Access automatically aligns the control with the dots on the form. This allows you to neatly arrange controls on the form.

You can delete a control you no longer want to appear on a form. Access allows you to delete just a label or a label and its corresponding text box.

Before you close a form, make sure you save the changes you made to the form.

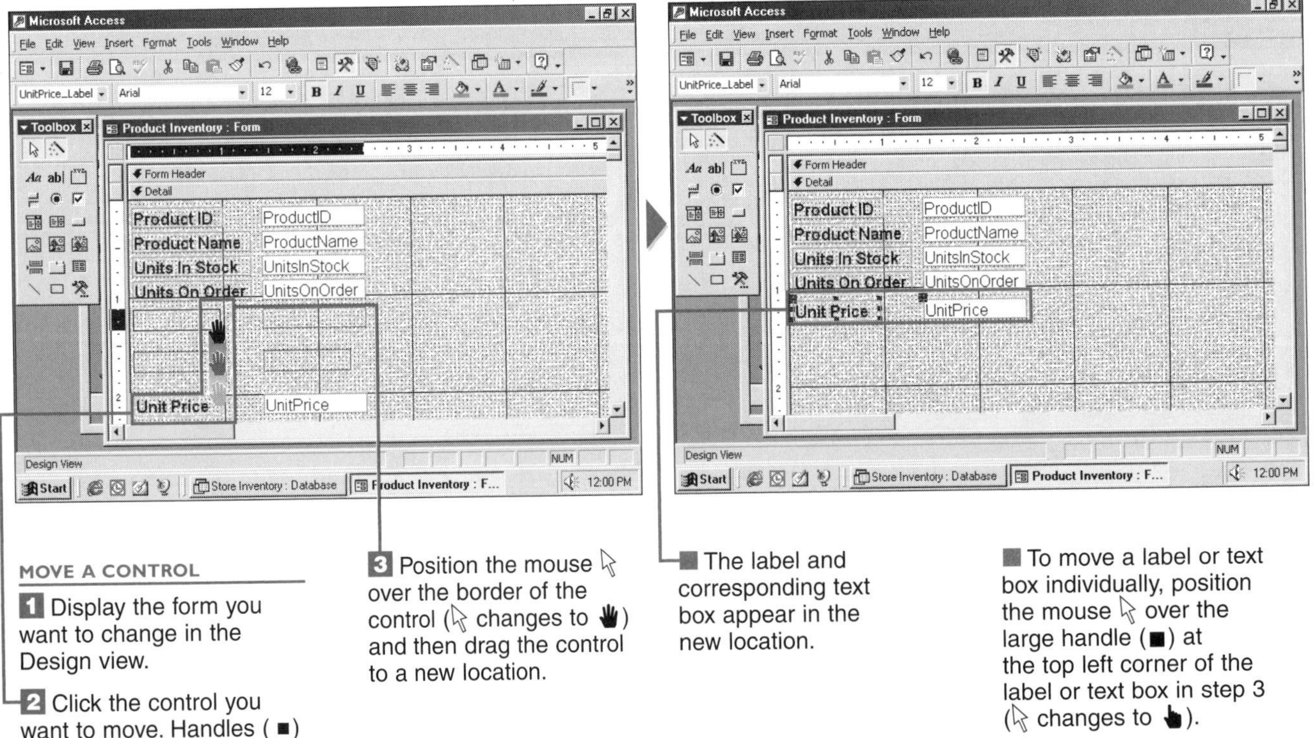

MOVE A CONTROL

1 Display the form you want to change in the Design view.

2 Click the control you want to move. Handles (■) appear around the control.

3 Position the mouse over the border of the control (changes to a hand) and then drag the control to a new location.

■ The label and corresponding text box appear in the new location.

■ To move a label or text box individually, position the mouse over the large handle (■) at the top left corner of the label or text box in step 3 (changes to a pointing hand).

TIPS

How do I move, resize or delete several controls at once?

✔ You must first select the controls you want to move, resize or delete. To select multiple controls, hold down the Shift key as you click each control.

Can I resize an entire form?

✔ Yes. Resizing a form is useful when you want to increase the space available for moving and resizing controls. Position the mouse over an edge of the form (changes to ✛, ‡ or ✥) and then drag the mouse until the form is the size you want.

Can I increase the space between the dots on a form?

✔ Yes. Double-click ☐ or ▣ in the top left corner of the form and then select the Format tab. Scroll through the contents of the tab until you reach the Grid X option. Enter the horizontal dots per inch you want to use. Beside the Grid Y option, enter the vertical dots per inch. You must enter a smaller number to increase the space between the dots.

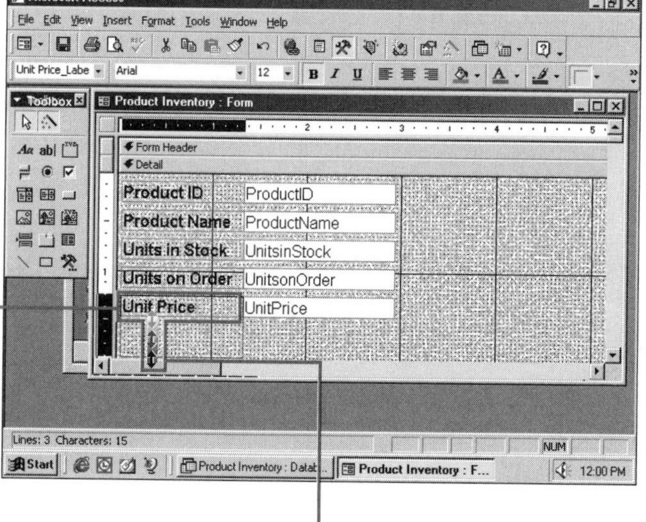

RESIZE A CONTROL

1 Click the control you want to resize. Handles (■) appear around the control.

2 Position the mouse over a handle (changes to ↕, ↔ or ⤡) and then drag the mouse until the control is the size you want.

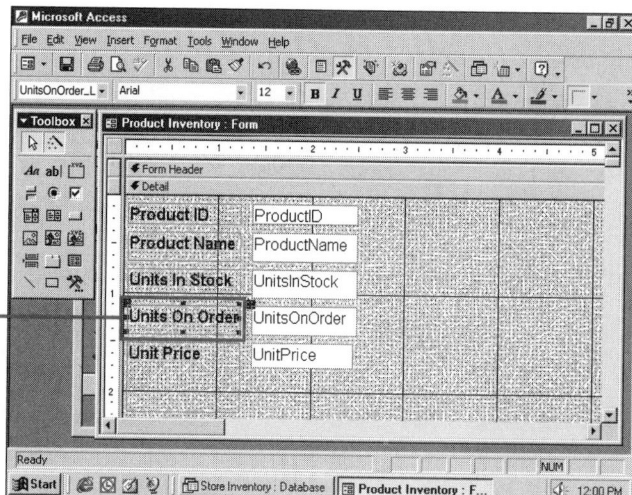

DELETE A CONTROL

1 Click the control you want to delete. Handles (■) appear around the control.

Note: Clicking a label will delete only the label. Clicking a text box will delete the label and the corresponding text box.

2 Press the Delete key.

CHANGE APPEARANCE OF CONTROLS

You can change the font, size, style and alignment of text in a control to customize the appearance of a form. You must display the form in the Design view before you can format the text in a control.

Changing the font can help you enhance the appearance of a form. Access provides a list of fonts for you to choose from.

The fonts appear in the list as they will appear in the control. This lets you preview a font before you select it.

You can increase or decrease the size of text in a control. Access measures the size of text in points. There are 72 points in an inch.

You can use the Bold, Italic and Underline features to change the style of text in a control. This can help you emphasize important information on a form.

Access automatically aligns text to the left and numbers to the right in a control. You can choose to align data to the left, to the right or in the center of a control.

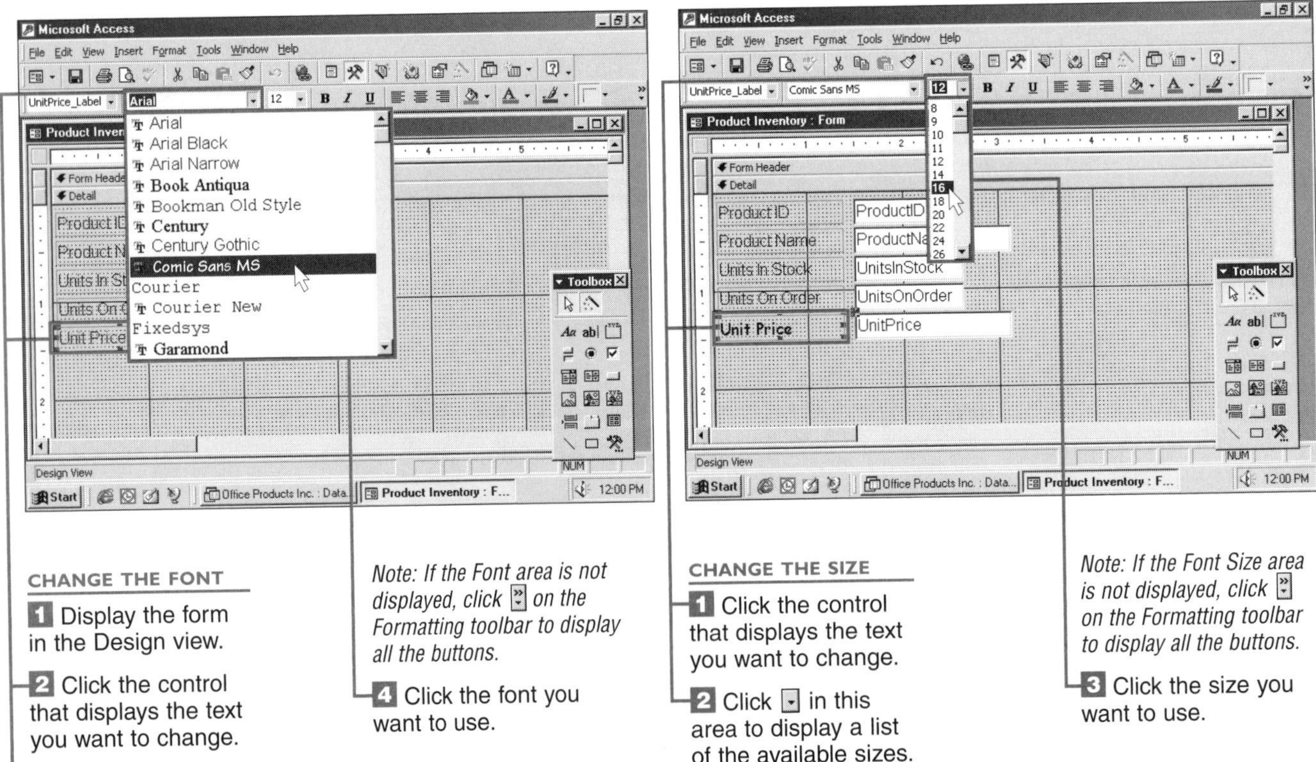

CHANGE THE FONT

1 Display the form in the Design view.

2 Click the control that displays the text you want to change.

3 Click ▾ in this area to display a list of the available fonts.

Note: If the Font area is not displayed, click » on the Formatting toolbar to display all the buttons.

4 Click the font you want to use.

CHANGE THE SIZE

1 Click the control that displays the text you want to change.

2 Click ▾ in this area to display a list of the available sizes.

Note: If the Font Size area is not displayed, click » on the Formatting toolbar to display all the buttons.

3 Click the size you want to use.

TIPS

Why is the text I formatted no longer fully displayed in the control?

✔ If you changed the font or size of the text, the text may be too large to be fully displayed in the control. To display all the text, you can resize the control. Click the control you want to resize. From the Format menu, select Size and then click To Fit.

Can I format several controls at once?

✔ Yes. Select the controls you want to format before you begin. To select multiple controls, hold down the Shift key as you click each control.

Can I copy formatting from one control to another?

✔ You can copy formatting to give the controls on a form a consistent appearance. Click the control that displays the formatting you want to copy and then click the Format Painter button (). Then click the control you want to copy the formatting to.

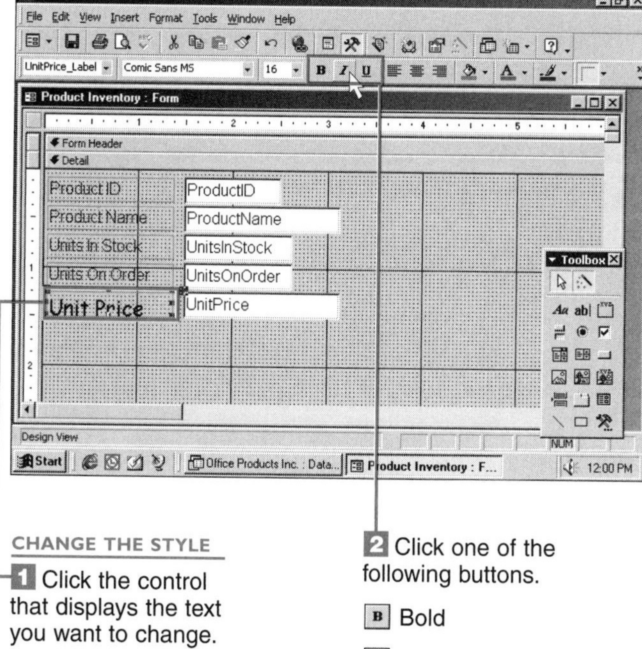

CHANGE THE STYLE

1 Click the control that displays the text you want to change.

2 Click one of the following buttons.

B Bold

I Italic

U Underline

Note: If the button you want is not displayed, click » on the Formatting toolbar to display all the buttons.

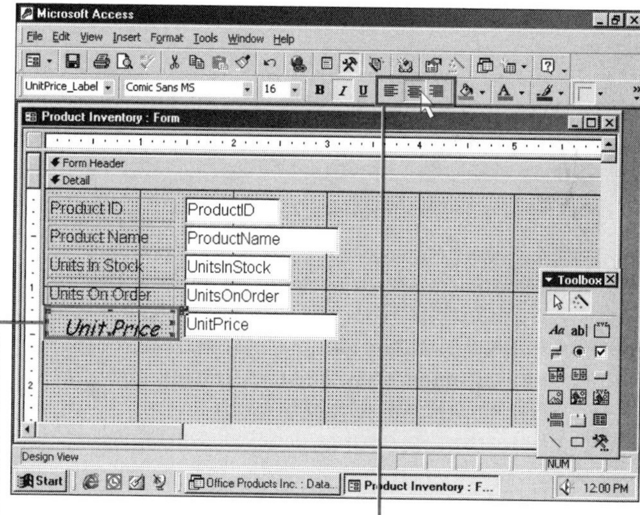

CHANGE ALIGNMENT

1 Click the control that displays the text you want to change.

2 Click one of the following buttons.

Left Align

Center

Right Align

Note: If the button you want is not displayed, click » on the Formatting toolbar to display all the buttons.

CHANGE APPEARANCE OF CONTROLS

You can change the background, text and border colors of a control on a form. You can also change the width of a control's border. Before formatting a control, you must display the form in the Design view.

Changing the background and text colors of a control can help draw attention to important information on a form. Access provides several background and text colors for you to choose from. Make sure you select background and text colors that work well together. For example, red text on a blue background can be difficult to read.

You can change the color and width of a control's border to make the control stand out.

If you are printing a form using a black-and-white printer, any colors you add to the text, background or border of a control will appear as shades of gray.

When you close a form, make sure you save the changes you made to the controls.

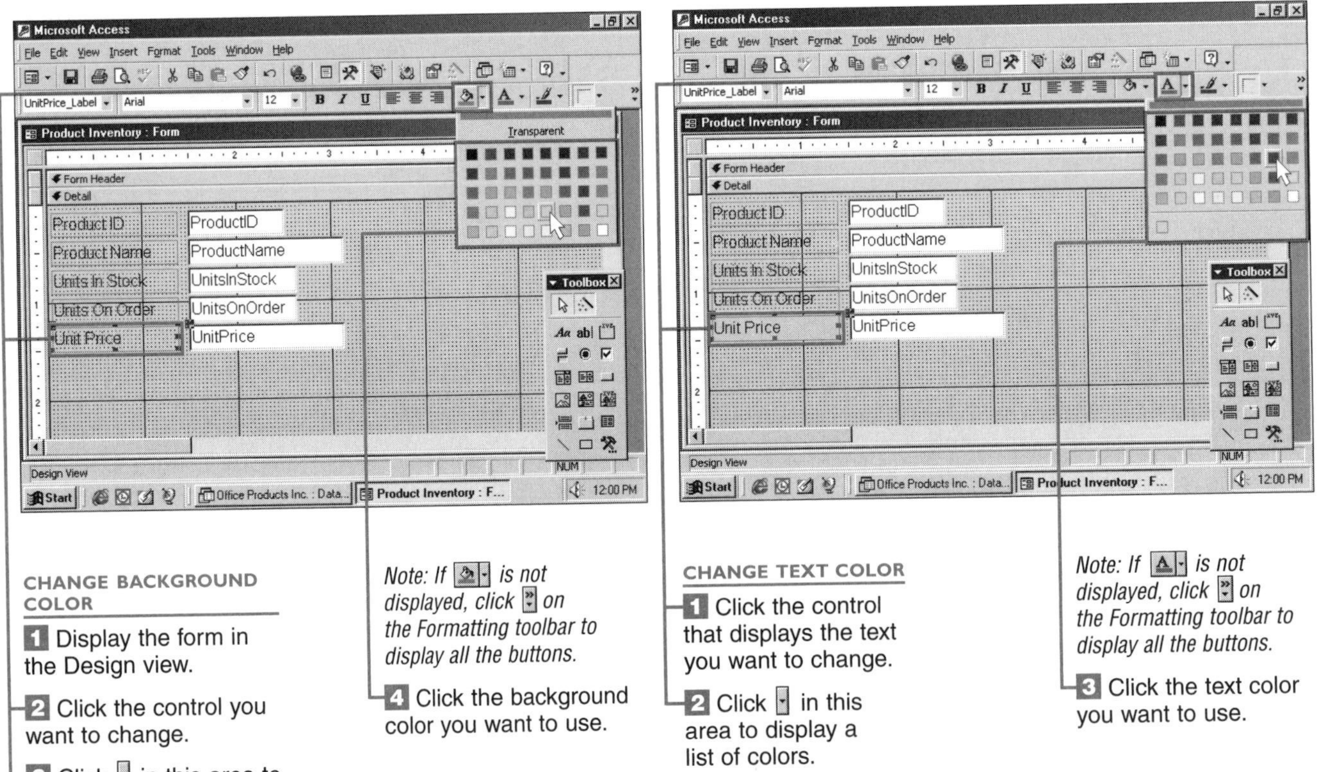

CHANGE BACKGROUND COLOR

1 Display the form in the Design view.

2 Click the control you want to change.

3 Click ▾ in this area to display a list of colors.

Note: If ▾ *is not displayed, click* ▾ *on the Formatting toolbar to display all the buttons.*

4 Click the background color you want to use.

CHANGE TEXT COLOR

1 Click the control that displays the text you want to change.

2 Click ▾ in this area to display a list of colors.

Note: If ▾ *is not displayed, click* ▾ *on the Formatting toolbar to display all the buttons.*

3 Click the text color you want to use.

TIPS

Is there another way to enhance the appearance of a control?

✔ You can make a control appear raised, sunken or shadowed to enhance the appearance of the control. Click the control you want to enhance. Click ▾ beside the Special Effect button (▭▾) on the Formatting toolbar and then click the effect you want to use.

Can I have a list of colors displayed on my screen at all times?

✔ Yes. Display the list of colors you want to appear on your screen at all times. Position the mouse pointer over the bar at the top of the list of colors and then drag the list to a new location on your screen.

How can I quickly change the text color in a control?

✔ The Font/Fore Color button (A) on the Formatting toolbar displays the last text color you selected. To quickly add this color to text in a control, click the control you want to change and then click the Font/Fore Color button (A).

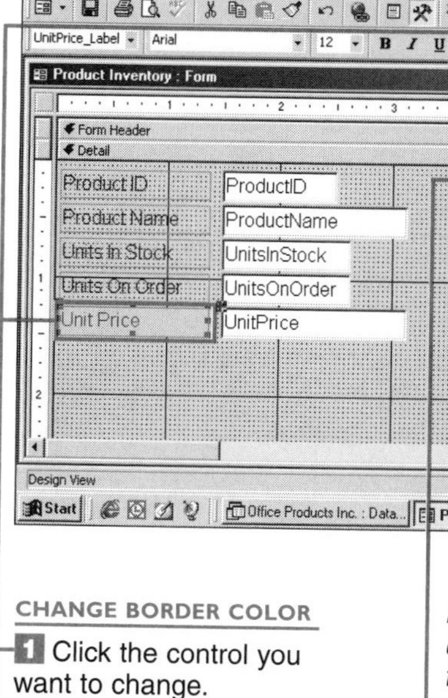

CHANGE BORDER COLOR

1 Click the control you want to change.

2 Click ▾ in this area to display a list of colors.

Note: If ▾ is not displayed, click » on the Formatting toolbar to display all the buttons.

3 Click the border color you want to use.

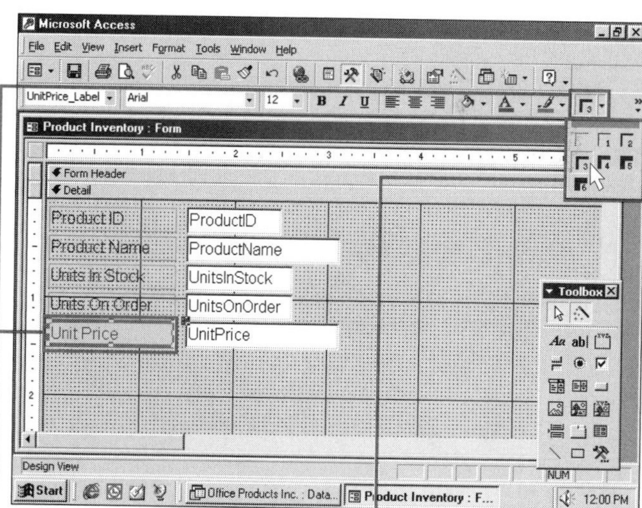

CHANGE BORDER WIDTH

1 Click the control you want to change.

2 Click ▾ in this area to display a list of border widths.

Note: If ▾ is not displayed, click » on the Formatting toolbar to display all the buttons.

3 Click the border width you want to use.

ADD A FIELD

If you left out a field when you created a form, you can add the field later. For example, you may want to add a telephone number field to a form that displays client addresses.

Before you can add a field to a form, you must display the form in the Design view. Access allows you to add a field from the table you used to create the form.

Access uses labels and text boxes to display information on a form. When you add a field, Access adds a label and its corresponding text box for you.

Access automatically uses the correct data type and field properties for a field you add to a form. For example, if you add a field that has the Yes/No data type with the Check Box option, Access adds a check box (☑) to the form instead of a text box.

You may need to resize a form to make room for a field you add. For information on resizing a form, see the top of page 457.

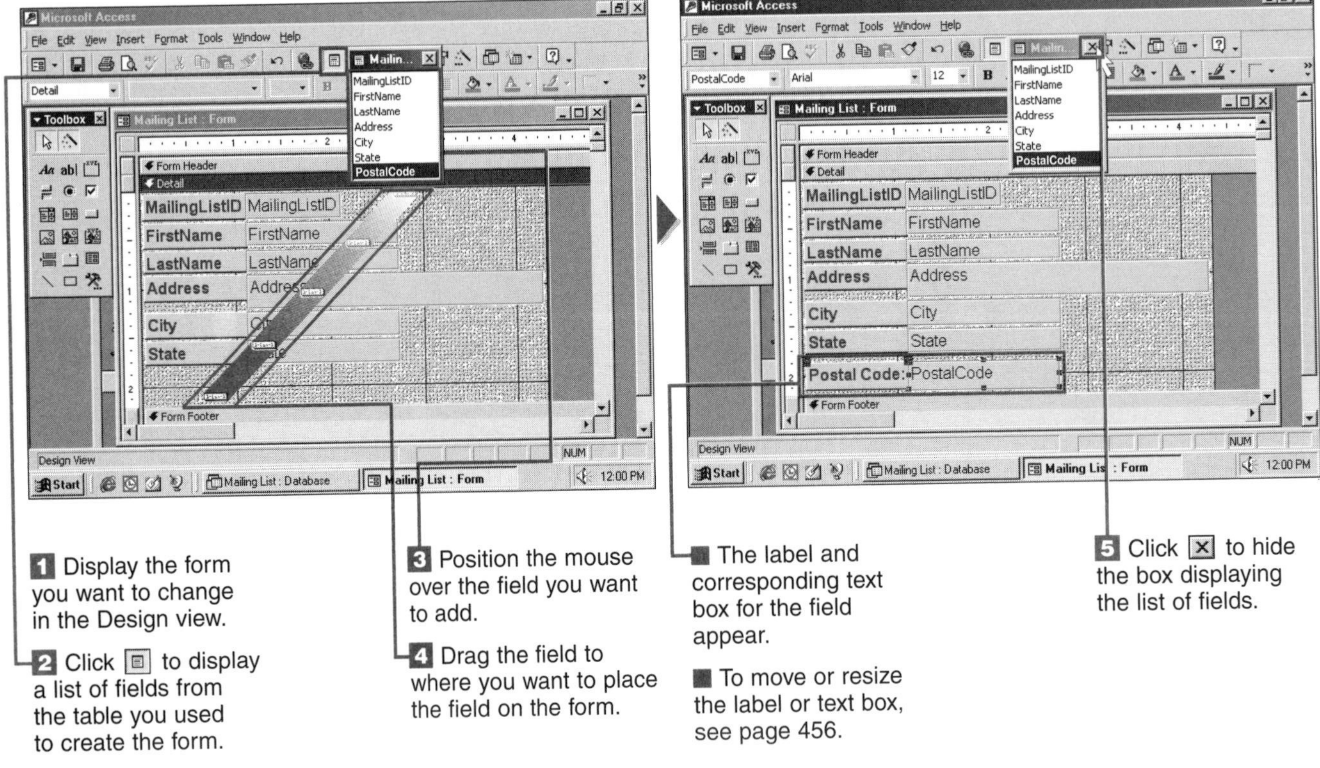

1 Display the form you want to change in the Design view.

2 Click ▤ to display a list of fields from the table you used to create the form.

3 Position the mouse over the field you want to add.

4 Drag the field to where you want to place the field on the form.

■ The label and corresponding text box for the field appear.

■ To move or resize the label or text box, see page 456.

5 Click ☒ to hide the box displaying the list of fields.

SELECT AN AUTOFORMAT

You can select an autoformat to instantly change the overall look of a form. Selecting an autoformat changes the background and text colors of a form.

Before you can select an autoformat, you must display the form in the Design view. You must also select the form to ensure that Access will apply the autoformat you choose to the entire form.

There are several autoformats you can choose from, including Blends, Industrial, International and Stone.

You should use the same autoformat for all the forms in your database. Using one autoformat for all the forms will give the database a more consistent appearance.

Access allows you to preview a sample of the autoformat you select before you apply it to a form. This can help you determine if the autoformat suits your needs.

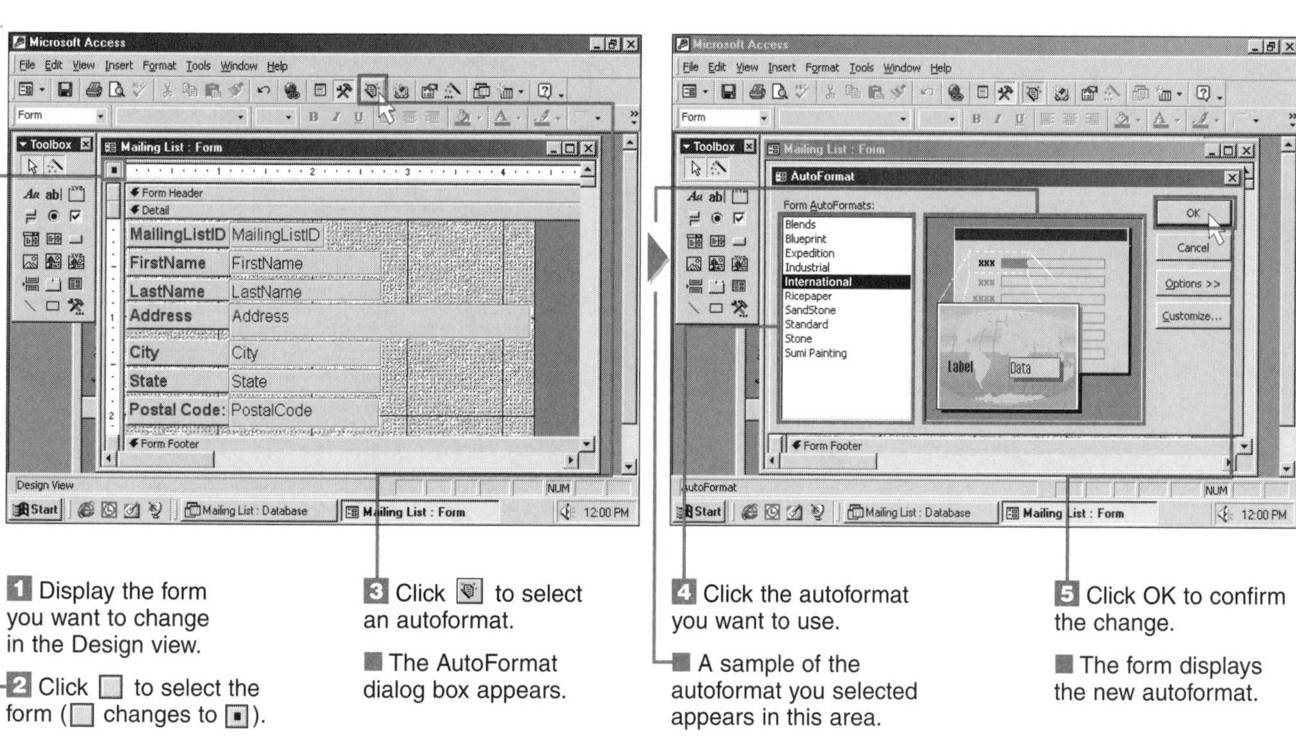

1 Display the form you want to change in the Design view.

2 Click ▢ to select the form (▢ changes to ▣).

3 Click [AutoFormat] to select an autoformat.

■ The AutoFormat dialog box appears.

4 Click the autoformat you want to use.

■ A sample of the autoformat you selected appears in this area.

5 Click OK to confirm the change.

■ The form displays the new autoformat.

FIND DATA

You can search for records that contain specific data. You can search for data in tables, queries and forms.

By default, Access performs a search of the current field. To perform a more advanced search, you can create a query. For more information, see page 472.

You can specify how you want Access to search for data in a field. The Any Part of Field option allows you to find data anywhere in a field. For example, a search for smith finds Smithson and Macsmith. The Whole Field option allows you to find data that is exactly the same as the data you specify. For example, a search for smith finds Smith but not Smithson. You can also choose the Start of Field option to find data only at the beginning of a field. For example, a search for smith finds Smithson but not Macsmith.

After you start the search, Access finds and highlights the first instance of the data. You can continue the search to find the next instance of the data.

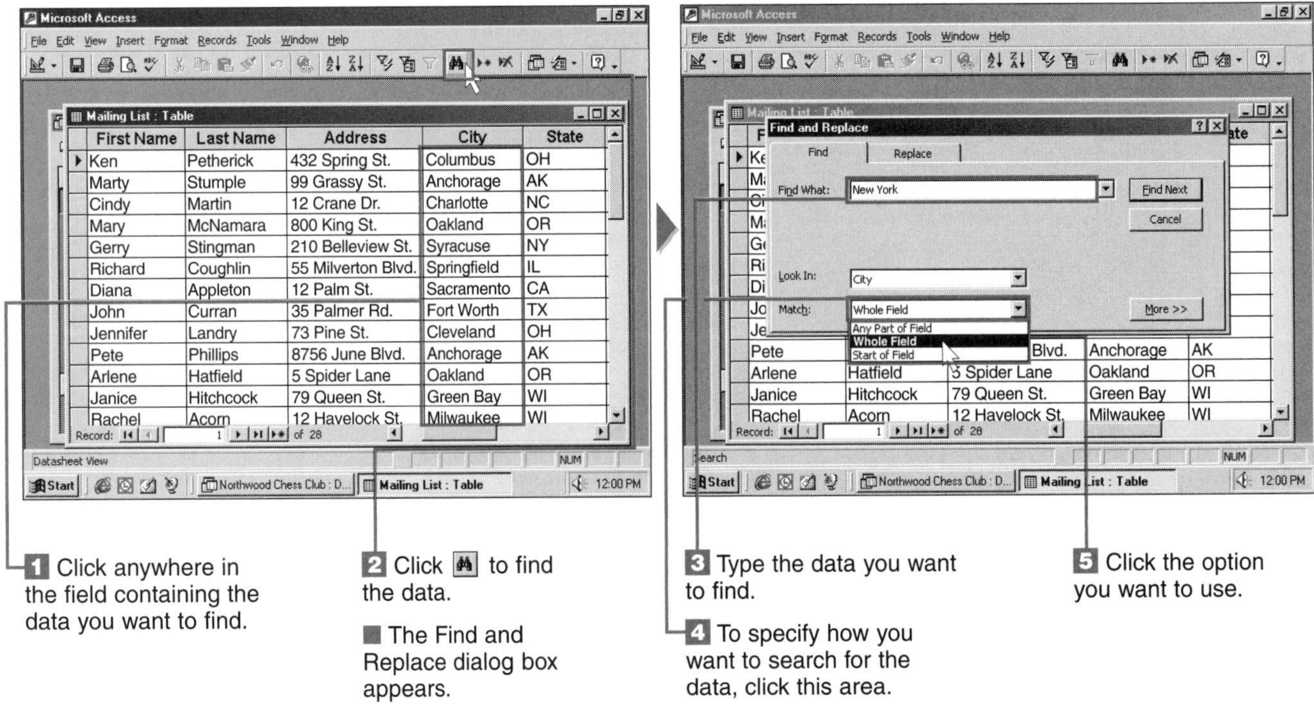

1 Click anywhere in the field containing the data you want to find.

2 Click [binoculars icon] to find the data.

■ The Find and Replace dialog box appears.

3 Type the data you want to find.

4 To specify how you want to search for the data, click this area.

5 Click the option you want to use.

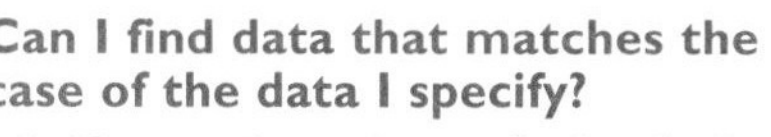

TIPS

Can I find data that matches the case of the data I specify?

✔ You can have Access find only data with exactly matching uppercase and lowercase letters. Click the More button in the Find and Replace dialog box and then select the Match Case option (☐ changes to ☑).

How do I search only part of a field?

✔ Click the More button in the Find and Replace dialog box and then click the Search area. Select Up or Down to search above or below the current record.

How can I have Access replace the data I find with new data?

✔ Perform steps 1 to 3 below and then click the Replace tab. In the Replace With area, type the new data. Click the Find Next button to start the search. To replace the data Access finds with the new data, click the Replace button. To ignore the data and continue with the search, click Find Next.

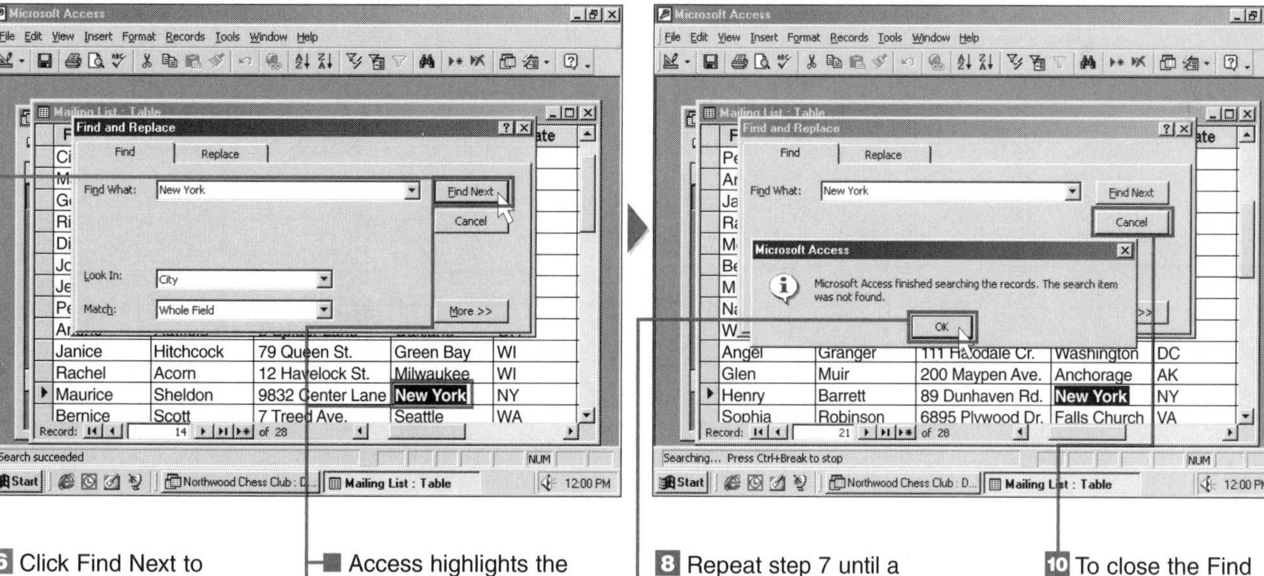

6 Click Find Next to start the search.

■ Access highlights the data in the first matching record it finds.

7 Click Find Next to find the next matching record.

8 Repeat step 7 until a dialog box appears, telling you the search is complete.

9 Click OK to close the dialog box.

10 To close the Find and Replace dialog box, click Cancel.

SORT RECORDS

You can change the order of records in a table, query or form. This can help you find, organize and analyze data.

You can sort by one or more fields. Sorting by more than one field can help you refine the sort. For example, if several of your clients have the same last name, you can sort by the last name field and the first name field. When you sort by multiple fields, you must place the fields side-by-side and in the order you want to perform the sort. Access sorts the records in the far left field first.

You can sort records in ascending or descending order. Sorting in ascending order displays text in alphabetical order from A to Z and displays numbers from smallest to largest. The opposite occurs when you sort text or numbers in descending order.

When you save the table, query or form, Access saves the sort order you specified.

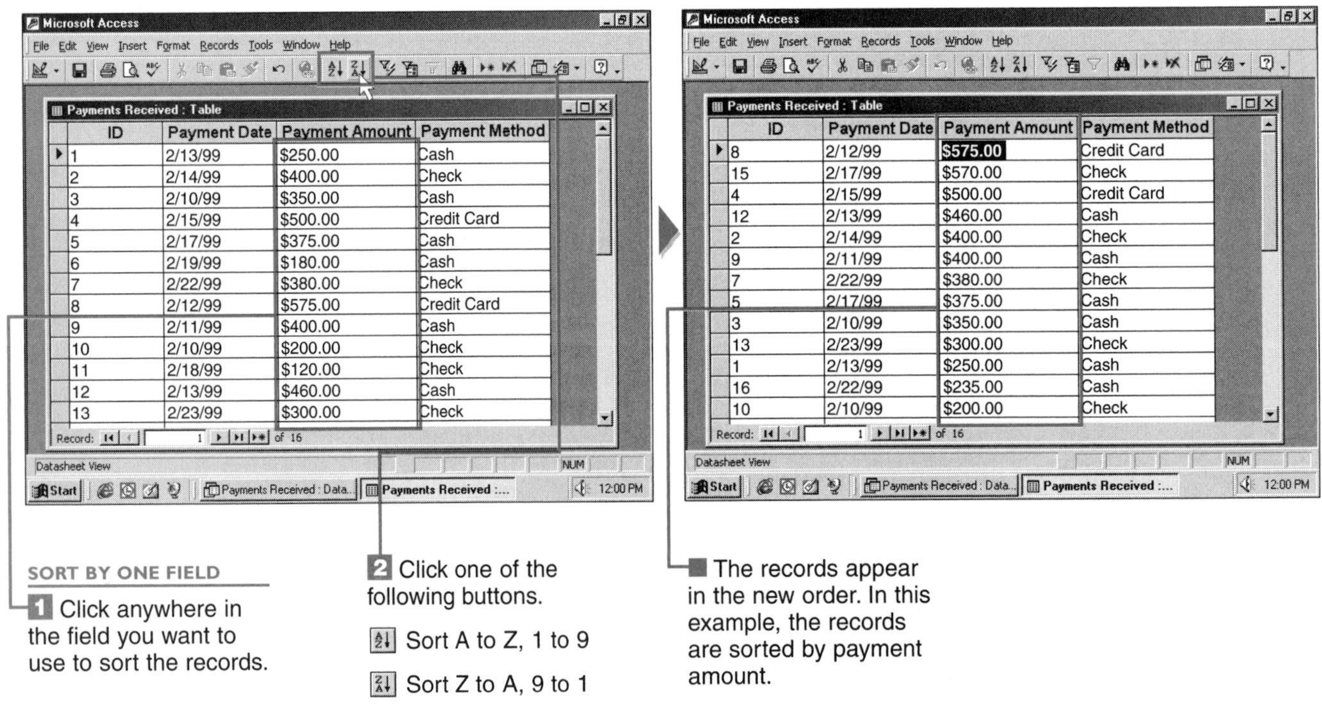

SORT BY ONE FIELD

1 Click anywhere in the field you want to use to sort the records.

2 Click one of the following buttons.

Sort A to Z, 1 to 9

Sort Z to A, 9 to 1

■ The records appear in the new order. In this example, the records are sorted by payment amount.

TIPS

How do I rearrange the fields in a table?

✔ You may need to rearrange the fields when sorting records by two fields. Click the name of the field you want to move. Position the mouse pointer over the field name and then drag the field to a new location. A thick black line shows where the field will appear.

Why are the Sort buttons (A↓Z and Z↓A) unavailable?

✔ The Sort buttons are not available when you select a field that has a Hyperlink, Memo or OLE Object data type. Access will not allow you to sort a field that has one of these data types.

How do I remove a sort from my records?

✔ If you no longer want to display your records in the sort order you specified, you can return your records to the primary key order at any time. From the Records menu, click Remove Filter/Sort.

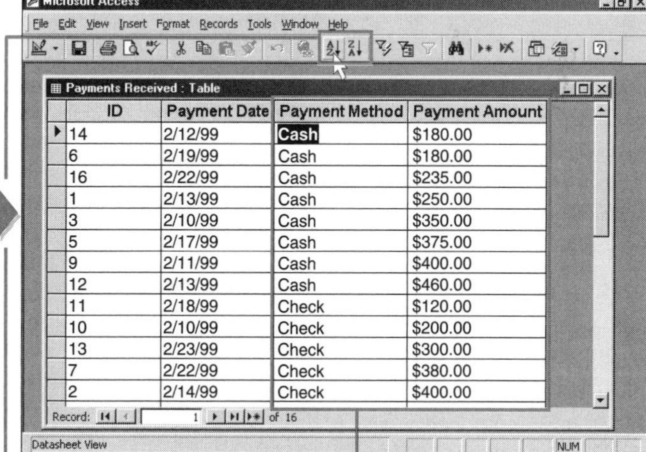

SORT BY TWO FIELDS

1 Place the fields you want to use to sort the records side-by-side and in the order you want to perform the sort.

2 Position the mouse ⬇ over the name of the first field you want to use to sort the records and then drag the mouse ⬇ until you highlight the second field.

3 Click one of the following buttons.

A↓Z Sort A to Z, 1 to 9

Z↓A Sort Z to A, 9 to 1

■ The records appear in the new order. In this example, the records are sorted by payment method. All records with the same payment method are sorted by payment amount.

FILTER DATA

You can filter records in a table, form or query to display only specific records. Filtering data can help you review and analyze information in your database by temporarily hiding information not currently of interest. For example, in a table that stores client addresses, you can filter the data to display only the records for clients who live in California.

When you filter by selection, you select data and have Access display only the records that contain the same data. Filtering by selection is useful when you want to find records containing specific data.

When you filter by input, you enter data or criteria and have Access display only the records containing matching data or data that meets the criteria. Filtering by input is useful when you want to specify exact data or find records containing data within a specific range.

Filtering data does not change how the records are stored in the database.

You can add, delete or edit records when you are viewing filtered records.

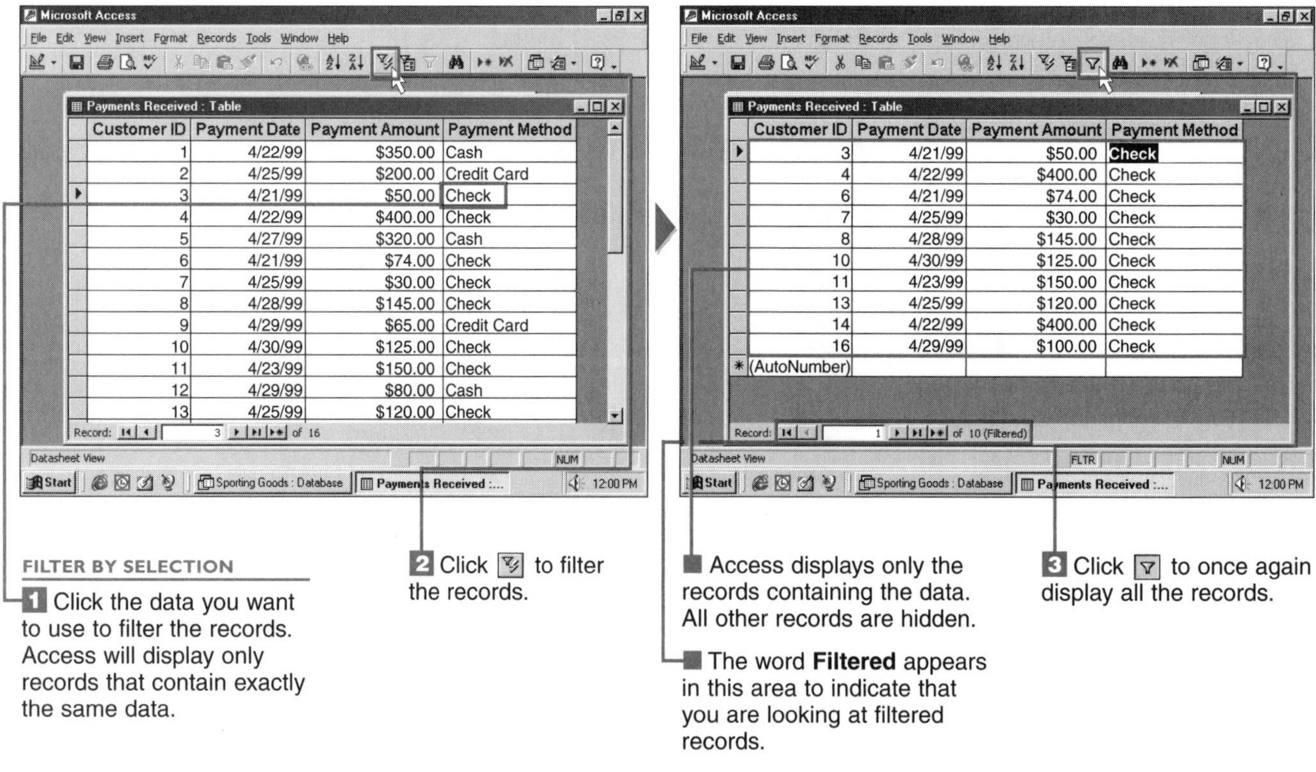

FILTER BY SELECTION

1 Click the data you want to use to filter the records. Access will display only records that contain exactly the same data.

2 Click [icon] to filter the records.

■ Access displays only the records containing the data. All other records are hidden.

■ The word **Filtered** appears in this area to indicate that you are looking at filtered records.

3 Click [icon] to once again display all the records.

TIPS

Is there another way to filter by selection?

✔ Yes. You can select specific characters you want to use to filter the records. For example, select "Smi" in Smith to display records containing data that starts with "Smi", such as Smidley and Smithson. If you do not select the first character, Access will display all the records containing the characters. For example, select "one" in Jones to display records containing Oneida and Stone.

How can I use criteria to filter data?

✔ When filtering by input, you can use criteria to define which records Access displays. For example, type **<1/1/99** to display records containing dates before 1-Jan-99. For examples of criteria, see page 484.

Can I filter records that have already been filtered?

✔ Yes. When Access displays filtered records, you can filter the records again. You can continue to filter records until Access displays the records you want to view.

Can I use a filter to hide records that contain specific data?

✔ Yes. Click the data you do not want to display. From the Records menu, click Filter and then select Filter Excluding Selection.

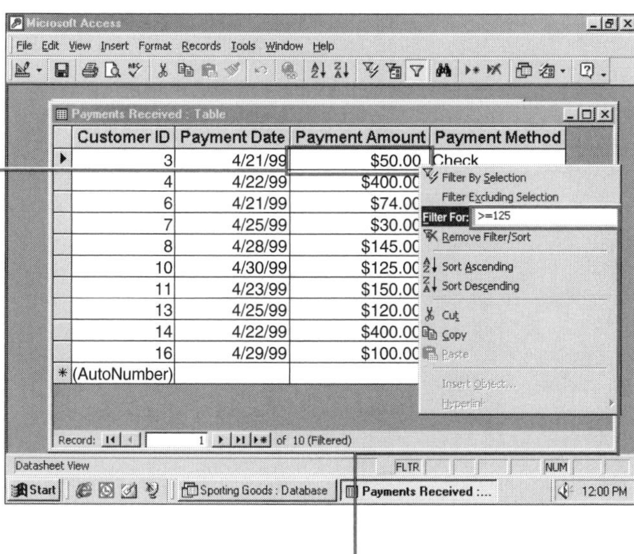

FILTER BY INPUT

1 Right-click the field you want to use to filter the records. A menu appears.

2 Click this area.

3 Type the data or criteria to specify which records you want to find and then press the Enter key.

■ Access displays only the records containing the data. All other records are hidden.

■ The word **Filtered** appears in this area to indicate that you are looking at filtered records.

4 Click ▽ to once again display all the records.

FILTER DATA CONTINUED

You can use the Filter by Form feature to perform powerful searches of a table, form or query in a database. Filtering records allows you to quickly find and display records of interest in a database.

When you filter by form, you can specify the criteria that records must meet to be displayed. For example, you can have Access find clients who made purchases of more than $100.00.

You can specify multiple criteria to filter records. Access will display only records that meet all of the criteria you specify. For example, you can have Access find clients living in California who made purchases of more than $100.00. For examples of criteria you can use, see page 484.

When you save a table, form or query, the last filter you performed is also saved. You can quickly apply the same filter the next time you open the table, form or query.

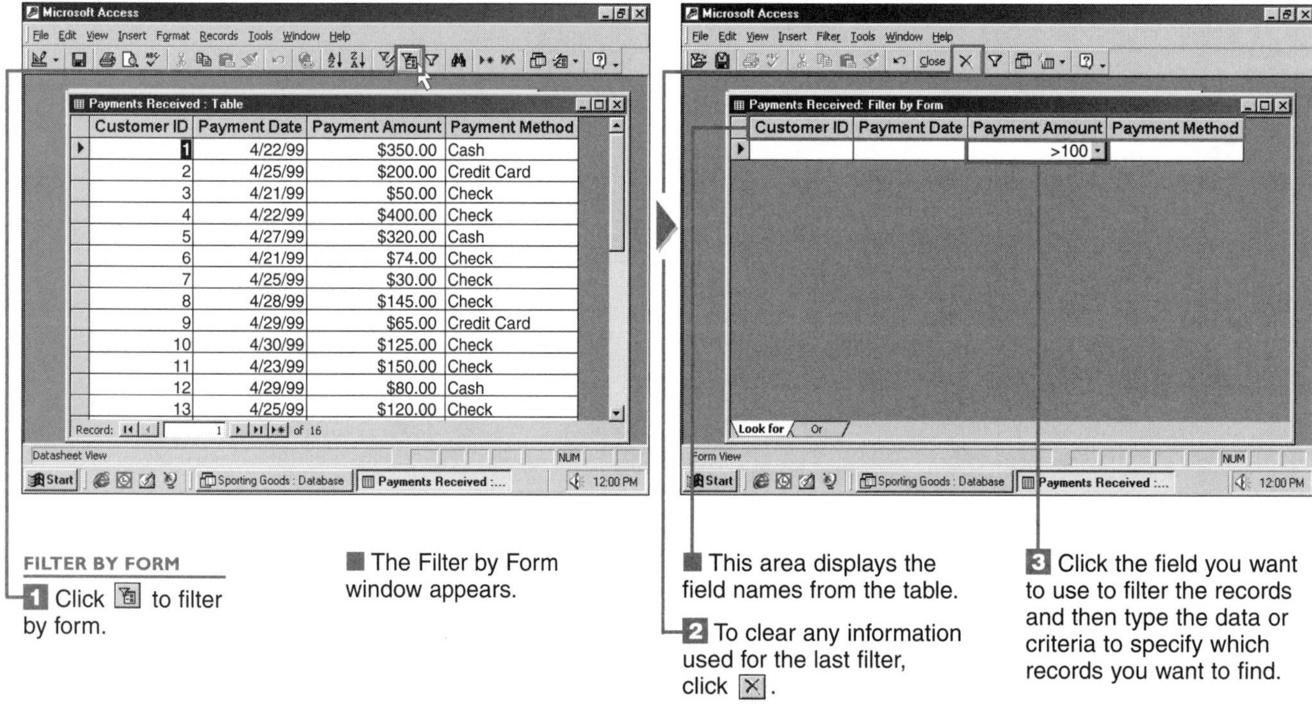

FILTER BY FORM

1 Click the Filter by Form button to filter by form.

■ The Filter by Form window appears.

■ This area displays the field names from the table.

2 To clear any information used for the last filter, click ☒.

3 Click the field you want to use to filter the records and then type the data or criteria to specify which records you want to find.

TIPS

Can I display records that meet one of the criteria I specified?

✔ When you use the steps below to filter by form, Access displays records that meet all of the criteria you specify. You can use the Or tab when filtering by form to display records that meet at least one of the criteria. For example, you can find clients with the first name Bill or William. Perform steps 1 to 3 below to enter the first criteria you want the records to meet. Click the Or tab in the bottom left corner of the Filter by Form window and then enter the second criteria.

How can I quickly enter the data I want to use to filter records?

✔ Click the field you want to use to filter records. To display a list of the values in the field, click the arrow (▾) that appears. Then click the value you want to use to filter the records.

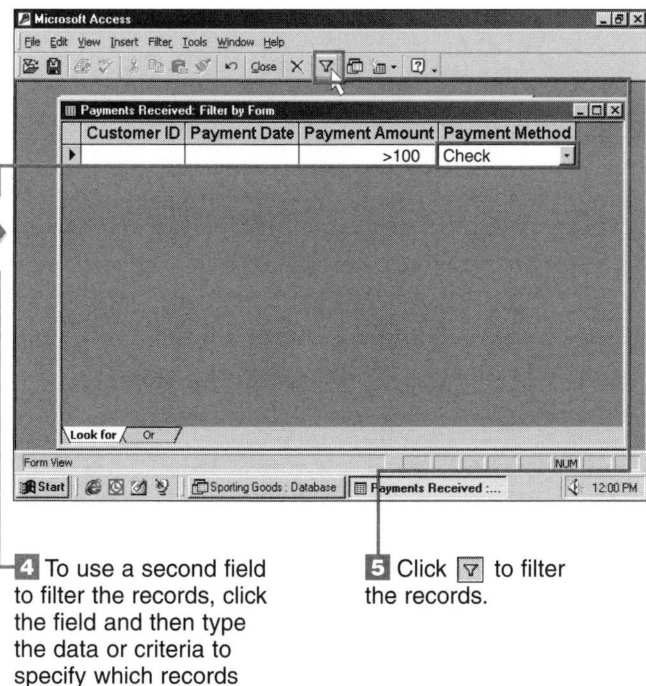

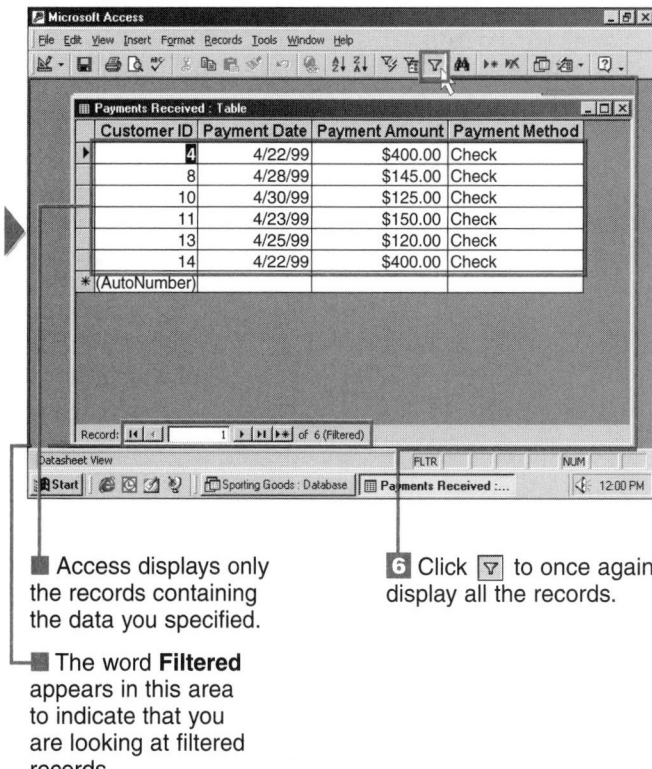

4 To use a second field to filter the records, click the field and then type the data or criteria to specify which records you want to find.

5 Click ▽ to filter the records.

Payments Received : Table

Customer ID	Payment Date	Payment Amount	Payment Method
4	4/22/99	$400.00	Check
8	4/28/99	$145.00	Check
10	4/30/99	$125.00	Check
11	4/23/99	$150.00	Check
13	4/25/99	$120.00	Check
14	4/22/99	$400.00	Check
(AutoNumber)			

Record: 1 of 6 (Filtered)

■ Access displays only the records containing the data you specified.

■ The word **Filtered** appears in this area to indicate that you are looking at filtered records.

6 Click ▽ to once again display all the records.

CREATE A QUERY IN THE DESIGN VIEW

You can create a query to find information of interest in a database. When you create a query, you ask Access to find information that meets certain conditions. The Design view allows you to plan and set up your own query.

A query brings together information from different tables in a database. This makes queries one of the most powerful features of Access. The results of a query are often used to create forms and reports.

You can select each table that contains information you want to use in a query. To perform a query on more than one table, the tables you select should be related. Access displays a line joining the related fields in the tables you select.

The tables you will use in the query appear in the top half of the Select Query window. The bottom half of the window displays a grid, called the design grid, where you can specify the information you want the query to display.

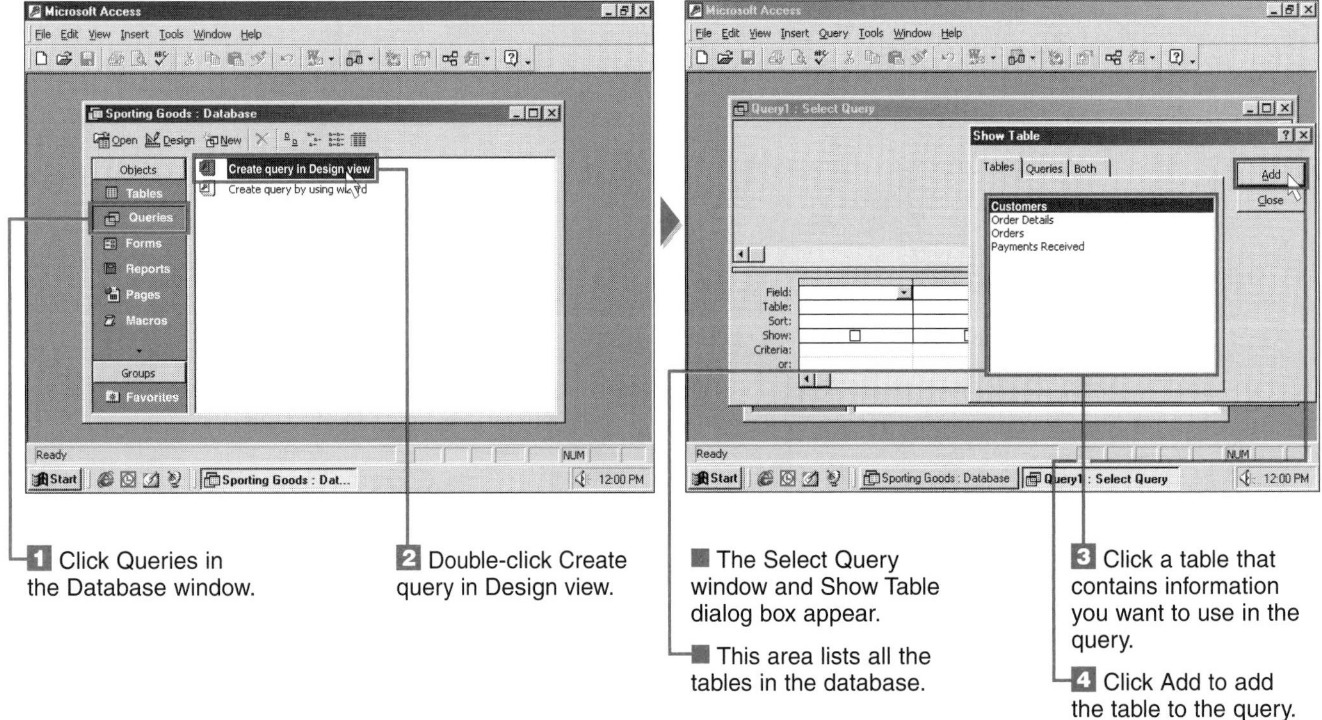

1 Click Queries in the Database window.

2 Double-click Create query in Design view.

■ The Select Query window and Show Table dialog box appear.

■ This area lists all the tables in the database.

3 Click a table that contains information you want to use in the query.

4 Click Add to add the table to the query.

TIPS

How do I add another table to a query?

✔ Click the Show Table button ( ) on the toolbar to redisplay the Show Table dialog box. Double-click the table you want to add to the query and then click the Close button.

How do I remove a table from a query?

✔ In the Select Query window, click the box displaying the fields for the table you want to remove and then press the Delete key. The table is removed from the query but not from the database.

Can I use an existing query to create a new query?

✔ Yes. This is useful if you want to refine an existing query to produce fewer records. In the Show Table dialog box, click the Queries tab and then double-click the name of the query you want to use. Click the Close button and then perform steps 7 to 9 on page 474 to create the new query.

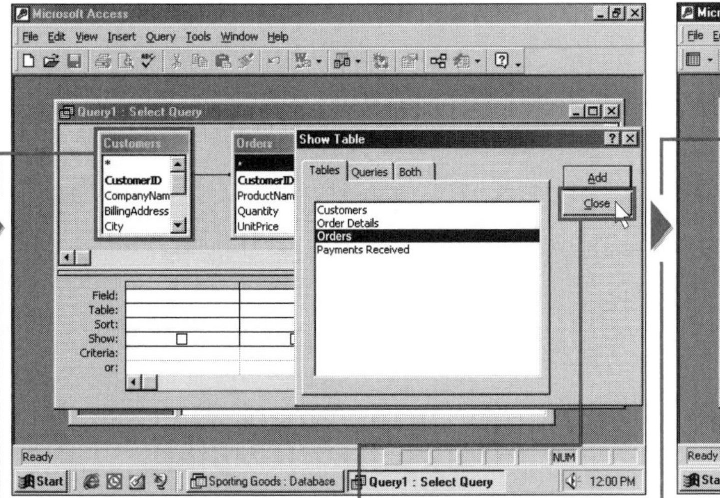

■ A box appears in the Select Query window, displaying the fields for the table you selected.

5 Repeat steps 3 and 4 for each table you want to use in the query.

6 Click Close to hide the Show Table dialog box.

■ Each box in this area displays the fields for one table.

■ If the tables you selected are related, Access displays a line joining the related fields.

CONTINUED

CREATE A QUERY IN THE DESIGN VIEW CONTINUED

You can select the fields you want to include in a query.

After you select the fields you want to include, you can choose to hide a field. Hiding a field is useful when you need to use a field to find information in the database but do not want the field to appear in the results of the query.

When you run a query, Access displays the results of the query in the Datasheet view. If you change the information when the query is displayed in the Datasheet view, the table that supplies the information for the query will also change.

If you want to run a query later, you must save the query. When you save a query, you save only the conditions you specified. You do not save the information gathered by the query. This allows you to view the most current information each time you run the query.

You can give the query a name. Make sure you use a descriptive name that allows you to distinguish the query from the other queries in the database.

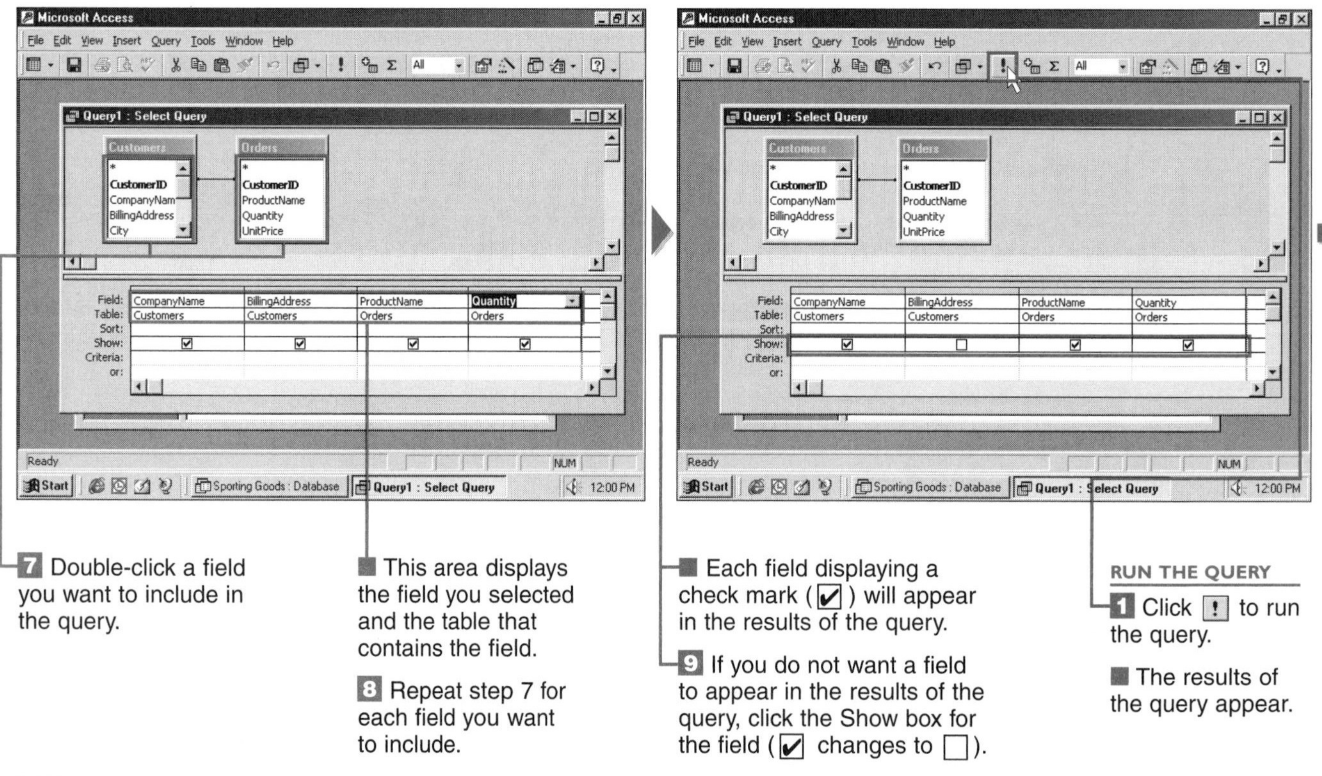

7 Double-click a field you want to include in the query.

■ This area displays the field you selected and the table that contains the field.

8 Repeat step 7 for each field you want to include.

■ Each field displaying a check mark (✔) will appear in the results of the query.

9 If you do not want a field to appear in the results of the query, click the Show box for the field (✔ changes to ☐).

RUN THE QUERY

1 Click ! to run the query.

■ The results of the query appear.

TIPS

How do I quickly include all the fields from a table in a query?

✔ In the Select Query window, double-click the title bar of the box displaying the fields for the table. Position the mouse pointer over the selected fields and then drag the fields to the first empty column in the design grid.

How do I remove a field I included in a query?

✔ Click anywhere in the field. Select the Edit menu and then click Delete Columns.

Can I change the order of fields in a query?

✔ Yes. Rearranging fields in a query will affect the order the fields appear in the results. In the design grid, position the mouse over the top of the field you want to move (changes to ⬇) and click to select the field. Then position the mouse directly above the selected field and drag the field to a new location.

Can I clear a query and start over?

✔ If you make mistakes while selecting fields for a query, you can start over by clearing the design grid. From the Edit menu, click Clear Grid.

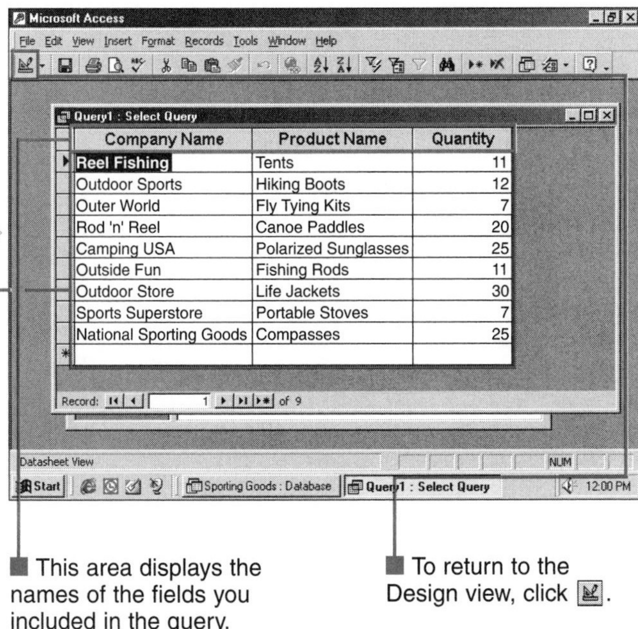

■ This area displays the names of the fields you included in the query.

■ The records that meet the conditions you specified appear in this area.

■ To return to the Design view, click .

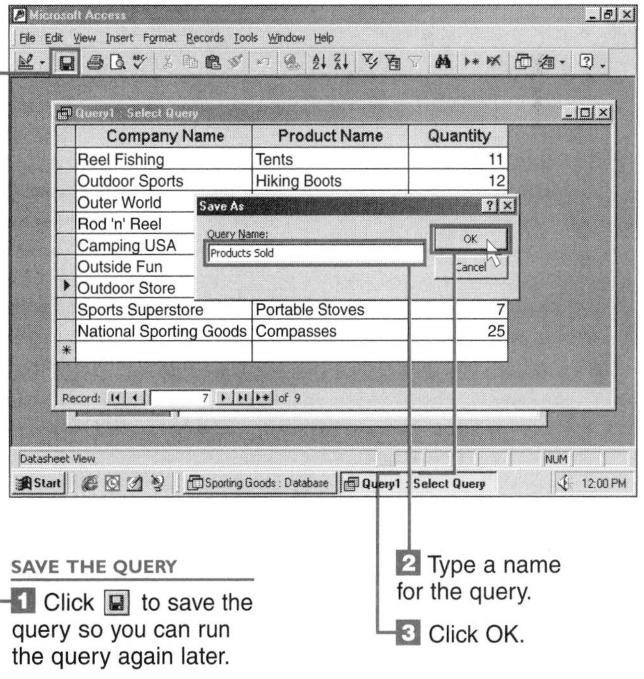

SAVE THE QUERY

1 Click to save the query so you can run the query again later.

■ The Save As dialog box appears.

2 Type a name for the query.

3 Click OK.

CREATE A QUERY USING THE SIMPLE QUERY WIZARD

You can use the Simple Query Wizard to gather information from one or more tables in a database. The wizard asks you a series of questions and then sets up a query based on your answers. The Simple Query Wizard is useful when you want to perform simple calculations in a query, such as finding the sum of values.

The Simple Query Wizard allows you to choose the table containing the fields you want to include in the query. After you choose a table, you can select the fields you want to include. A query can include all or only some of the fields in a table. If you accidentally select a field you do not want to include in the query, you can remove the field from the list of selected fields in the wizard.

You can select fields from multiple tables. If you include fields from more than one table, the tables must be related. For information on relationships between tables, see page 442.

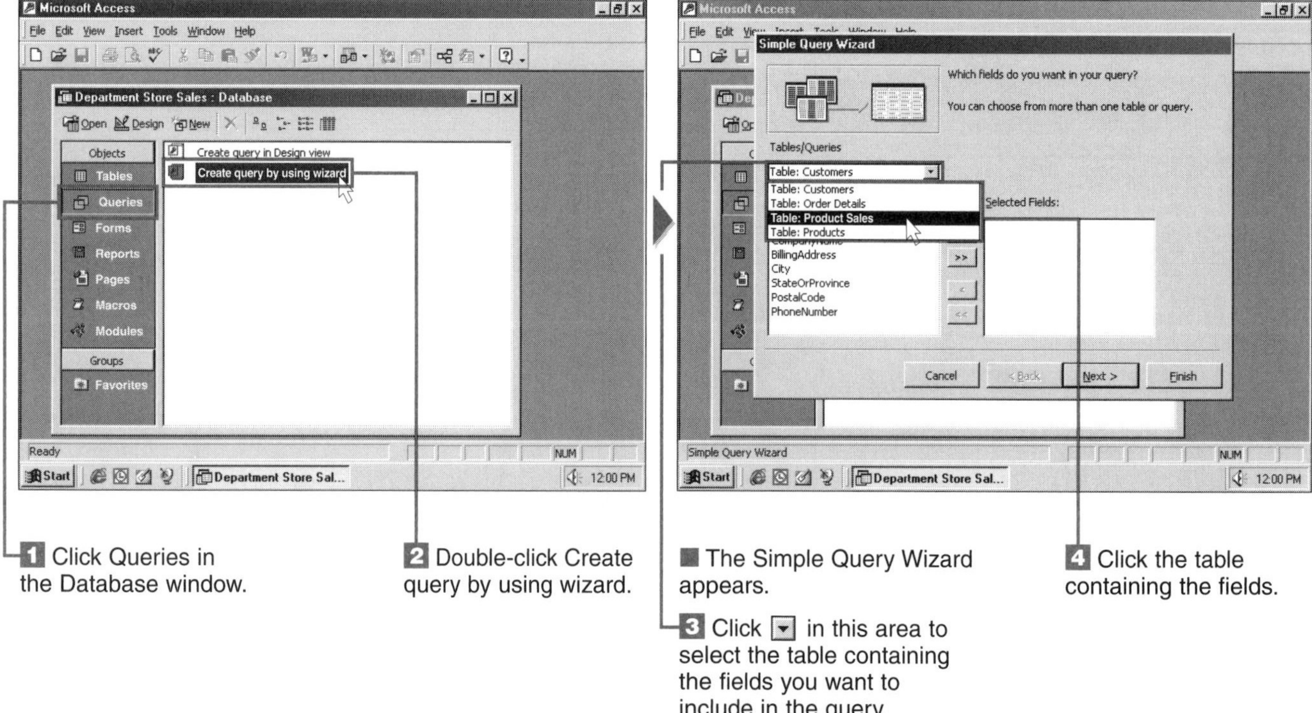

1 Click Queries in the Database window.

2 Double-click Create query by using wizard.

■ The Simple Query Wizard appears.

3 Click ▾ in this area to select the table containing the fields you want to include in the query.

4 Click the table containing the fields.

Are there any other wizards I can use to create a query?

✔ Yes. In the Database window, click Queries and then click the New button. The Crosstab Query Wizard allows you to create a query that groups related information together and displays summarized information. The Find Duplicates Query Wizard allows you to find records that contain the same values to avoid duplication. The Find Unmatched Query Wizard allows you to compare two tables to find records in one table that do not have related records in the other table.

Why should I use a wizard instead of creating my own query?

✔ Using a wizard is a fast way to create a basic query. If you want to plan and set up your own query, you can create a query in the Design view. For more information, see page 472.

■ This area displays the fields from the table you selected.

5 Double-click each field you want to include in the query.

Note: To add all the fields at once, click [>>] .

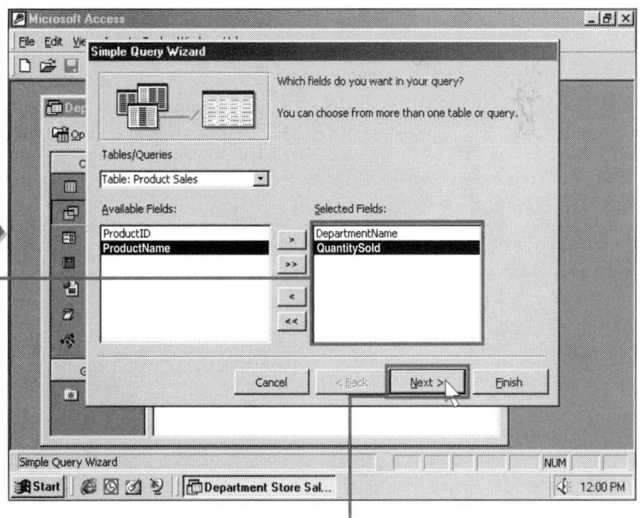

■ Each field you select appears in this area.

■ To remove a field you accidentally selected, double-click the field in this area.

Note: To remove all the fields at once, click [<<].

6 You can add fields from other tables by performing steps 3 to 5 for each table.

7 Click Next to continue.

CONTINUED

CREATE A QUERY USING THE SIMPLE QUERY WIZARD CONTINUED

If the fields you selected for a query contain information that can be calculated, you can choose to display all the records or a summary of the records in the results of the query.

You can calculate values in a query to summarize information. The Sum option adds values. The Avg option calculates the average value. The Min and Max options find the smallest or largest value.

When you calculate values in a query, Access groups related records together. For example, in a query that contains an Employee Name field and a Products Sold field, Access will group together the records for each employee to find the total number of products each employee sold.

You can have Access count the number of records used in each group to perform a calculation. The count appears as a field in the query results.

To finish creating a query, you must name the query. You should choose a descriptive name that will help you recognize the query in the future.

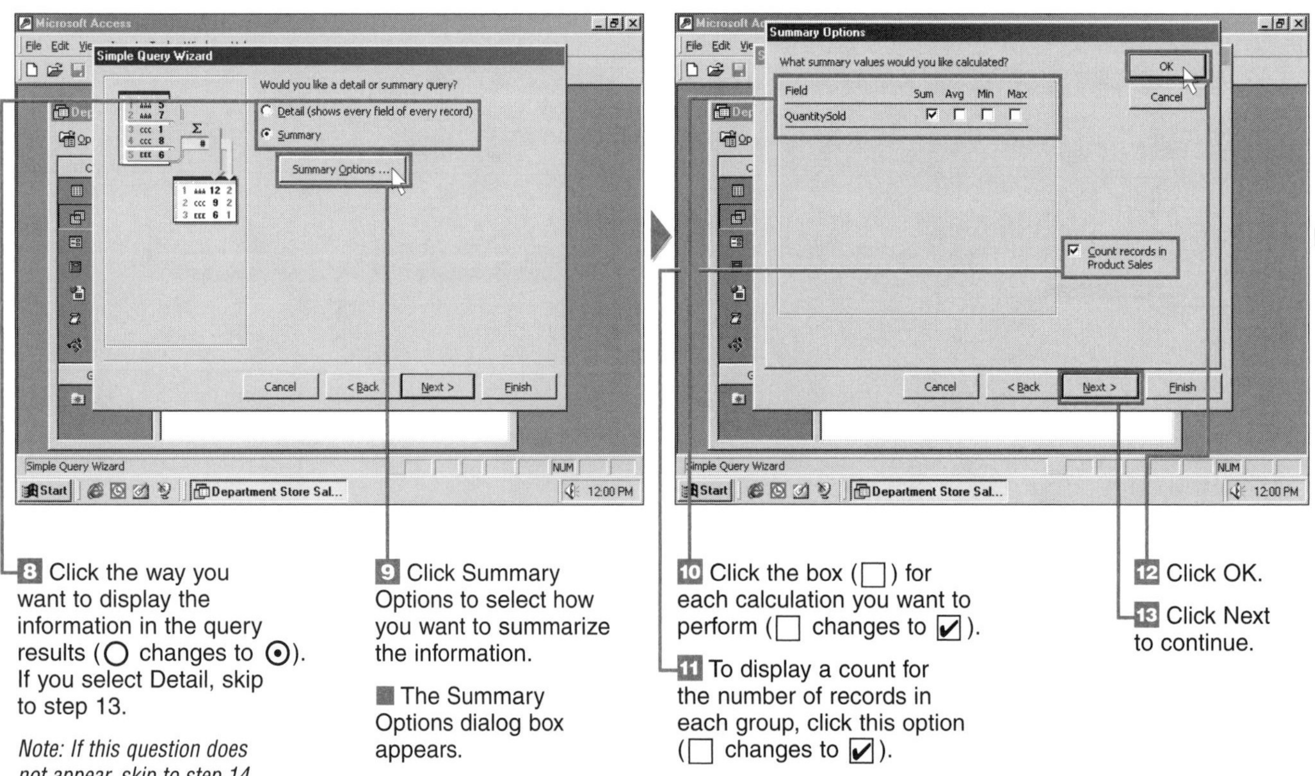

8 Click the way you want to display the information in the query results (○ changes to ⊙). If you select Detail, skip to step 13.

Note: If this question does not appear, skip to step 14.

9 Click Summary Options to select how you want to summarize the information.

■ The Summary Options dialog box appears.

10 Click the box (☐) for each calculation you want to perform (☐ changes to ☑).

11 To display a count for the number of records in each group, click this option (☐ changes to ☑).

12 Click OK.

13 Click Next to continue.

TIPS

Why didn't Access summarize my information properly in the query?

✔ To ensure Access will properly summarize information, you must make sure you only include the fields you need to create the query. Also make sure you select the field you want to group the records by first. Access will group records starting with the first field and then consider the data in each of the following fields.

How can I make changes to a query I created using the Simple Query Wizard?

✔ You can use the Design view to make changes to any query you create. You can sort records, add and remove fields and more. To display the query in the Design view, see page 481.

Why does another dialog box appear, asking me how I would like to group dates in my query?

✔ If one of the fields in your query stores dates, the Simple Query Wizard may ask you how you want to group the dates. You can choose to group the dates in your query by the individual date, day, month, quarter or year.

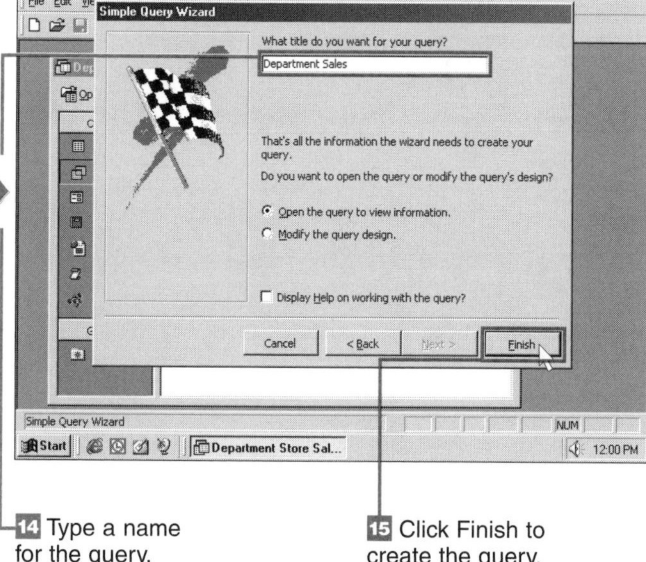

14 Type a name for the query.

15 Click Finish to create the query.

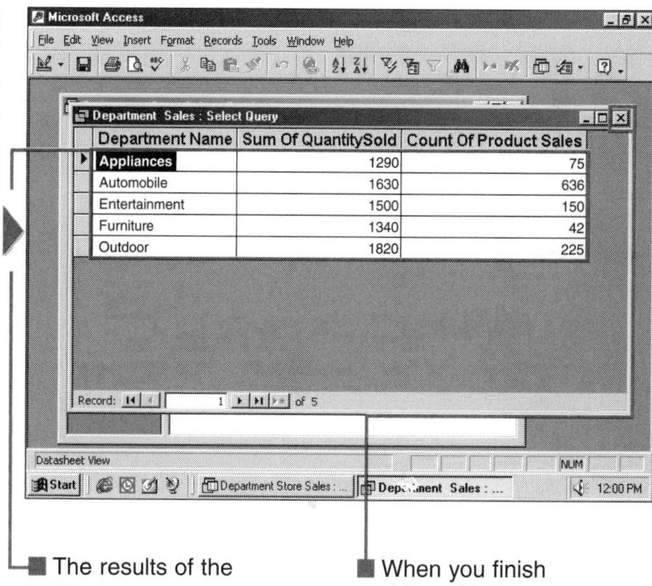

■ The results of the query appear.

■ When you finish working with the query, click ☒ to close the query.

OPEN A QUERY

You can open a query to display the results of the query or change the design of the query. You can open a query in the Datasheet or Design view.

When you open a query in the Datasheet view, Access runs the query and displays the results. This view is similar to the Datasheet view for tables but displays only the information that meets the criteria or conditions of the query.

In the Design view, you can make changes to the structure of a query. You can use this view to tell Access what data you want to find, where to find the data and how you want to display the results.

When you have finished working with a query, you can close the query to remove it from your screen. A dialog box appears if you have not saved changes you made to the query.

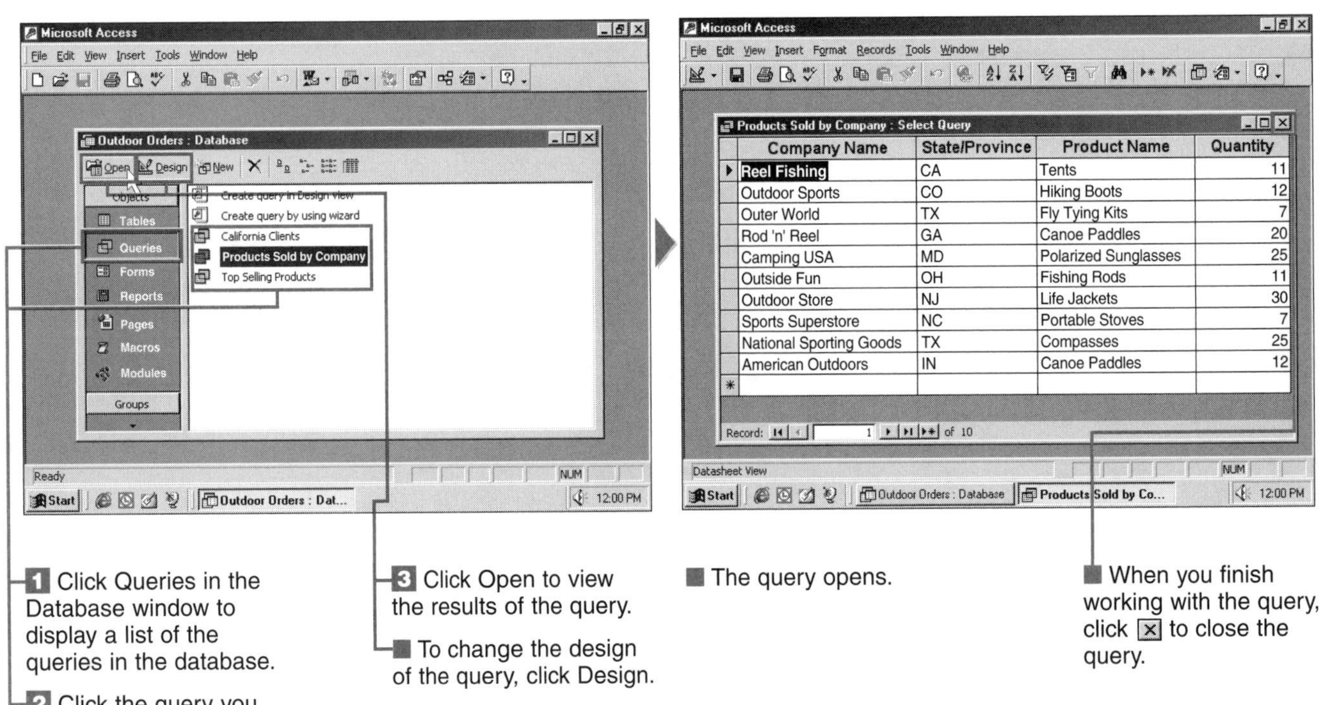

1 Click Queries in the Database window to display a list of the queries in the database.

2 Click the query you want to open.

3 Click Open to view the results of the query.

■ To change the design of the query, click Design.

■ The query opens.

■ When you finish working with the query, click ☒ to close the query.

CHANGE VIEW OF QUERY

There are three ways you can view a query. Each view allows you to perform different tasks.

The Design view allows you to plan your query. You can use this view to tell Access what data you want to find, where Access can find the data and how you want to display the results.

The Datasheet view allows you to review the results of a query. The field names appear across the top of the window. Each row shows the information for a record that meets the criteria or conditions you specified.

The SQL view displays the SQL statement for the current query. Structured Query Language (SQL) is a computer language. When you create a query, Access creates the SQL statement that describes your query. You do not need to use this view to effectively use Access.

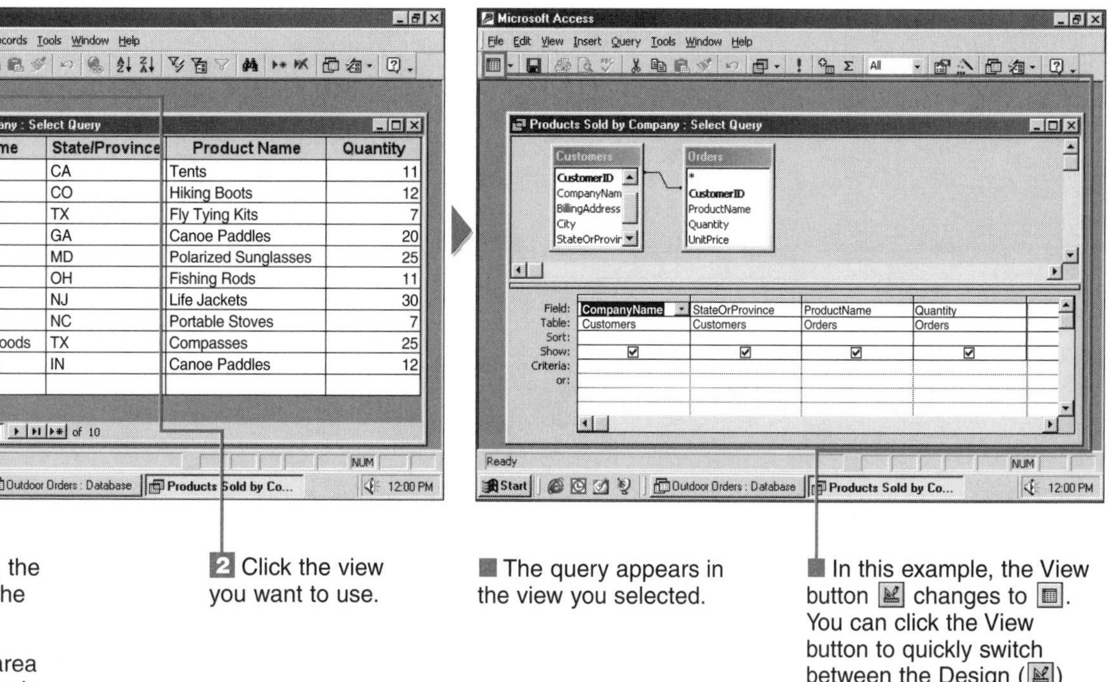

■ In this example, the query appears in the Datasheet view.

1 Click ▾ in this area to display the query in another view.

2 Click the view you want to use.

■ The query appears in the view you selected.

■ In this example, the View button changes to ▦. You can click the View button to quickly switch between the Design and Datasheet (▦) views.

SET CRITERIA

You can use criteria to find specific records in a database. Criteria are conditions that identify which records you want to find. For examples of criteria you can use, see page 484.

To set criteria, you must display the query you want to change in the Design view. You can set criteria for the field you want to use to find specific records. For example, you can set criteria for the State field to find all the clients who live in California.

You can use multiple criteria to find information in the database. Using the "Or" condition allows you to find records that meet at least one of the criteria you specify. For example, you can find clients living in California or Texas.

You can use the "Or" condition with one or more fields.

Using the "And" condition allows you to find records that meet all of the criteria you specify. You can use the "And" condition with one or more fields. For example, you can find clients living in California who bought more than 500 units of a product.

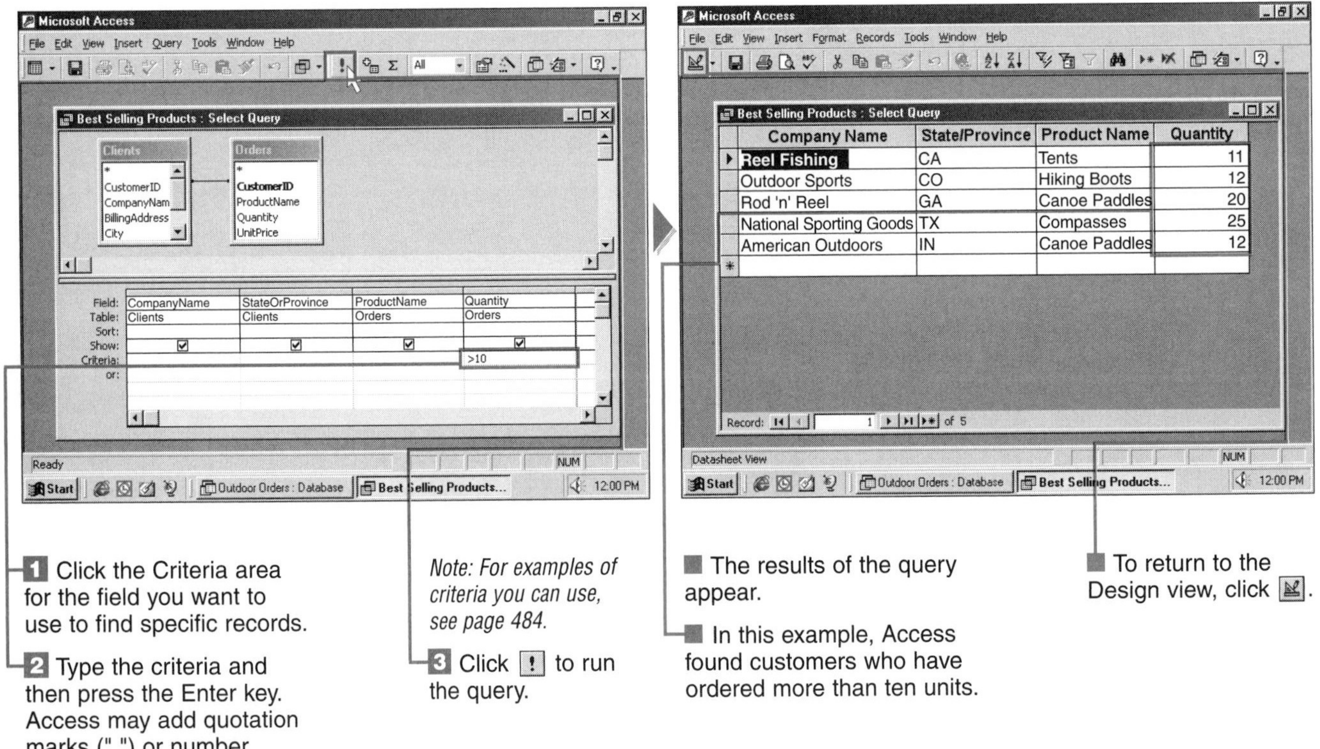

1 Click the Criteria area for the field you want to use to find specific records.

2 Type the criteria and then press the Enter key. Access may add quotation marks (" ") or number signs (#) to the criteria you type.

Note: For examples of criteria you can use, see page 484.

3 Click ! to run the query.

■ The results of the query appear.

■ In this example, Access found customers who have ordered more than ten units.

■ To return to the Design view, click the View button.

TIPS

Can I have Access display only a portion of the records in the results?

✔ When you know there will be many records in the results of a query, you may want to have Access display only the top or bottom values in the results. Click the Sort area for the field you want to show the top or bottom values. Click the arrow (▼) that appears. Select Ascending to display the bottom values or Descending to display the top values. In the Top Values box on the toolbar, click ▼ and then select the values you want to display. You can display the top or bottom 5, 25 or 100 records. You can also display the top or bottom 5 or 25 percent.

How do I use the "And" condition in one field?

✔ In the Criteria area for the field, enter both criteria separated by the word "And". For example, to find records that contain invoice numbers between 100 and 150, type **>100 And <150** in the Criteria area of the Invoice Number field.

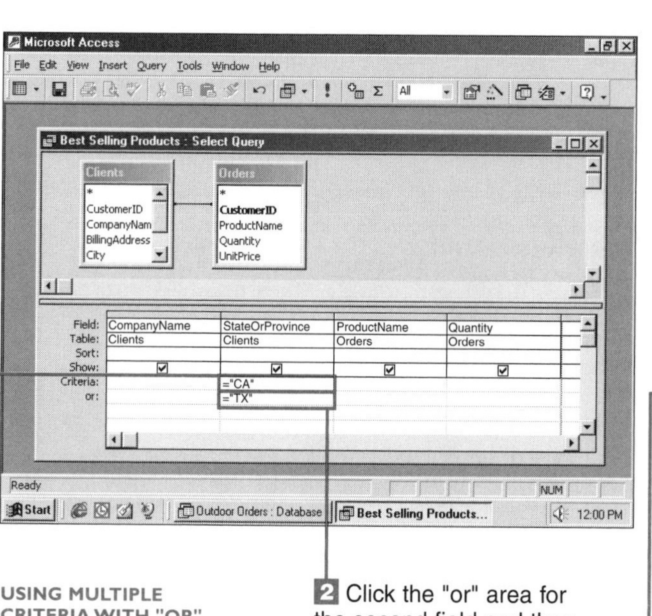

USING MULTIPLE CRITERIA WITH "OR"

1 Enter the criteria for the first field.

2 Click the "or" area for the second field and then type the second criteria.

■ In this example, Access will find customers who live in California or Texas.

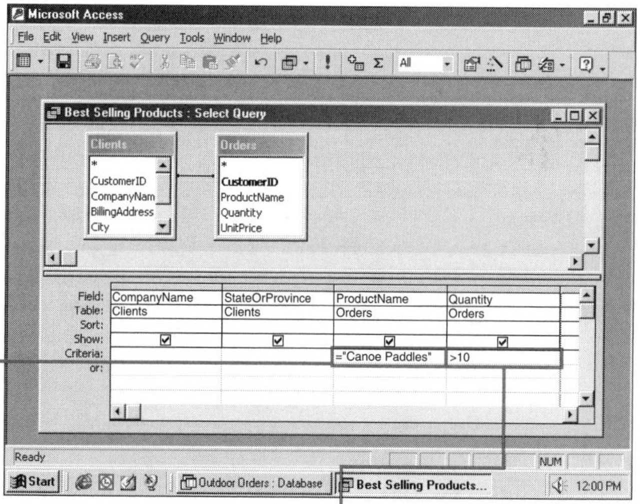

USING MULTIPLE CRITERIA WITH "AND"

1 Enter the criteria for the first field.

2 Click the Criteria area for the second field and then type the second criteria.

■ In this example, Access will find customers who have ordered canoe paddles and purchased more than ten units.

EXAMPLES OF CRITERIA

Exact matches

Criteria	Result
=100	Finds the number 100.
=California	Finds California.
=1/5/99	Finds the date 5-Jan-99.

Less than

Criteria	Result
<100	Finds numbers less than 100.
<N	Finds text starting with the letters A to M.
<1/5/99	Finds dates before 5-Jan-99.

Less than or equal to

Criteria	Result
<=100	Finds numbers less than or equal to 100.
<=N	Finds the letter N and text starting with the letters A to M.
<=1/5/99	Finds dates before and on 5-Jan-99.

Greater than

Criteria	Result
>100	Finds numbers greater than 100.
>N	Finds text starting with the letters N to Z.
>1/5/99	Finds dates after 5-Jan-99.

Greater than or equal to

Criteria	Result
>=100	Finds numbers greater than or equal to 100.
>=N	Finds the letter N and text starting with the letters N to Z.
>=1/5/99	Finds dates on and after 5-Jan-99.

Not equal to

Criteria	Result
<>100	Finds numbers not equal to 100.
<>California	Finds text not equal to California.
<>1/5/99	Finds dates not on 5-Jan-99.

Empty fields

Criteria	Result
Is Null	Finds records that do not contain data in the field.
Is Not Null	Finds records that contain data in the field.

Find list of items

Criteria	Result
In (100,101)	Finds the numbers 100 and 101.
In (California,CA)	Finds California and CA.
In (#1/5/99#,#1/6/99#)	Finds the dates 5-Jan-99 and 6-Jan-99.

Between...And...

Criteria	Result
Between 100 And 200	Finds numbers from 100 to 200.
Between A And D	Finds the letter D and text starting with the letters A to C.
Between 1/5/99 And 1/15/99	Finds dates on and between 5-Jan-99 and 15-Jan-99.

Wildcards

The asterisk (*) wildcard represents one or more characters. The question mark (?) wildcard represents a single character.

Criteria	Result
Like Br*	Finds text starting with **Br**, such as **Br**enda or **Br**own.
Like *ar*	Finds text containing **ar**, such as **Ar**nold or M**ar**c.
Like Wend?	Finds 5 letter words starting with **Wend**, such as **Wend**i or **Wend**y.

SORT THE QUERY RESULTS

You can sort the results of a query to better organize the results. This can help you find information of interest more quickly.

The results of a query can be sorted in ascending or descending order. Sorting in ascending order sorts text in alphabetical order from A to Z and sorts numbers from smallest to largest. When you sort in descending order, the opposite occurs.

You can choose not to sort the results of a query. If you do not sort the results, Access displays the results in the order they are found.

You can sort by one or more fields. When you sort by more than one field, you must place the fields in the order you want to perform the sort. Access sorts the records in the far left field first.

You cannot sort a field that has a Hyperlink, Memo or OLE Object data type.

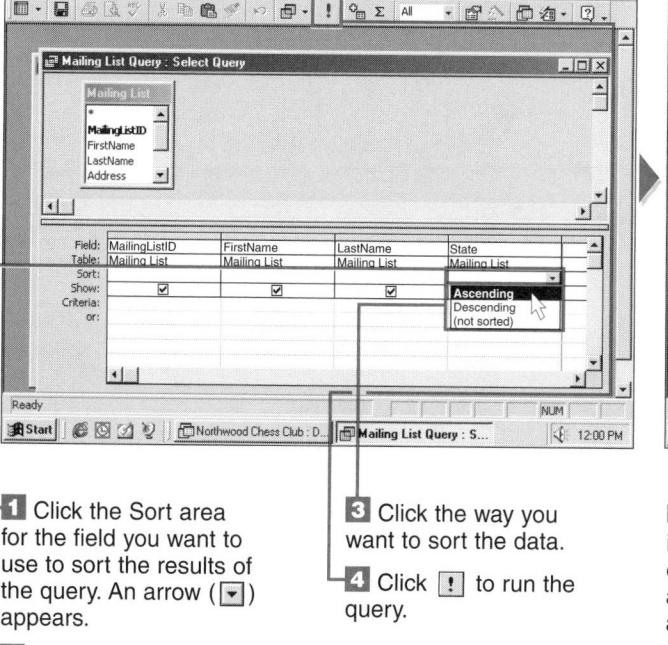

■1 Click the Sort area for the field you want to use to sort the results of the query. An arrow (▼) appears.

■2 Click the arrow (▼).

■3 Click the way you want to sort the data.

■4 Click ! to run the query.

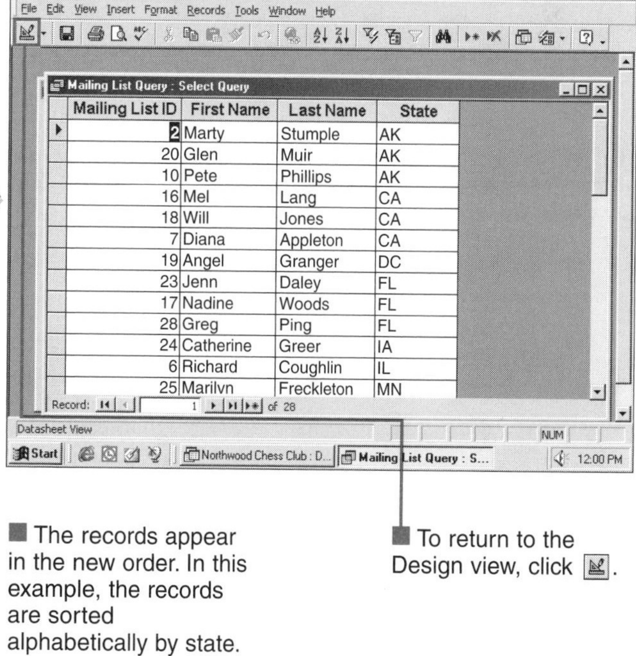

■ The records appear in the new order. In this example, the records are sorted alphabetically by state.

■ To return to the Design view, click .

PERFORM CALCULATIONS

You can perform calculations on records in a database. You can then review and analyze the results.

In a blank field, you can type a name for the field that will display the results of the calculation, followed by an expression. An expression tells Access which items to use in the calculation. An expression also contains operators that tell Access to multiply (*), add (+), subtract (-), divide (/) or raise values to a power (^).

To enter a field name in an expression, type the field name in square brackets. For example, type **[Quantity]*[Cost]** to multiply the Quantity field by the Cost field. Make sure you type the field names exactly.

If the same field name is found in more than one table, type the table name in square brackets followed by a period (.) and the field name in square brackets. For example, type **[Products].[Quantity]** to ensure Access uses the Quantity field in the Products table.

The results of a calculation are not stored in the database. If you run the query again, Access will use the most current data in the database to perform the calculation.

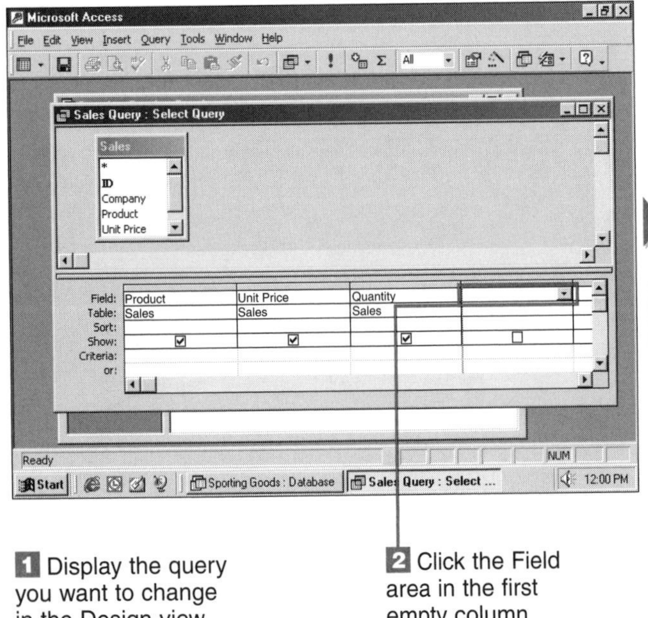

1 Display the query you want to change in the Design view.

2 Click the Field area in the first empty column.

3 Type a name for the field that will display the results of the calculation, followed by a colon (:). Then press the Spacebar to leave a blank space.

TIPS

How can I display an entire expression?

✔ An expression you type may be too long to fit in the Field area. To display the entire expression, click the cell containing the expression and then press the Shift+F2 keys. The Zoom dialog box appears, displaying the entire expression. You can edit an expression in the Zoom dialog box.

Can I change the format of calculated information?

✔ You can change the way calculated information appears in the query results. In the Design view, click anywhere in the calculated field. Click the Properties button (▣) and then select the Format area. Click the arrow (▼) that appears and then select the format you want to use.

What types of expressions can I use?

✔ Here are some examples of expressions you can use.

Inventory Value: [Price]*[Quantity]

Total Price: [Cost]+[Profit]

New Price: [Price]-[Discount]

Item Cost: [Price of Case]/[Items]

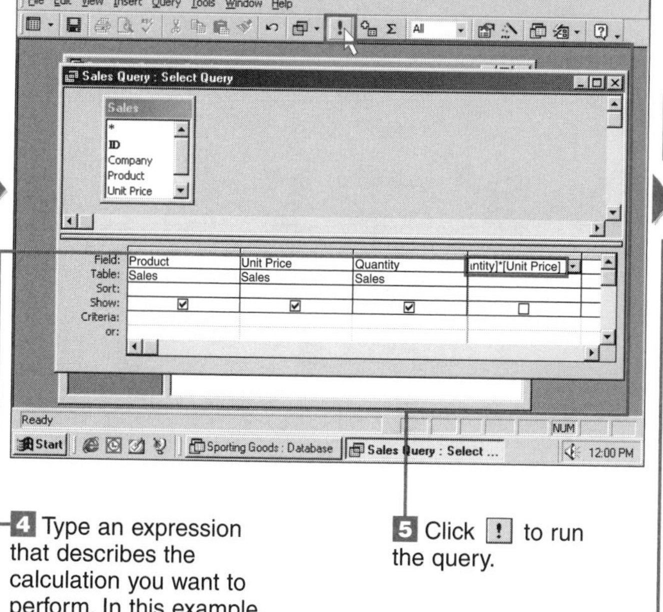

4 Type an expression that describes the calculation you want to perform. In this example, type the expression **[Quantity]*[Unit Price]**.

5 Click ! to run the query.

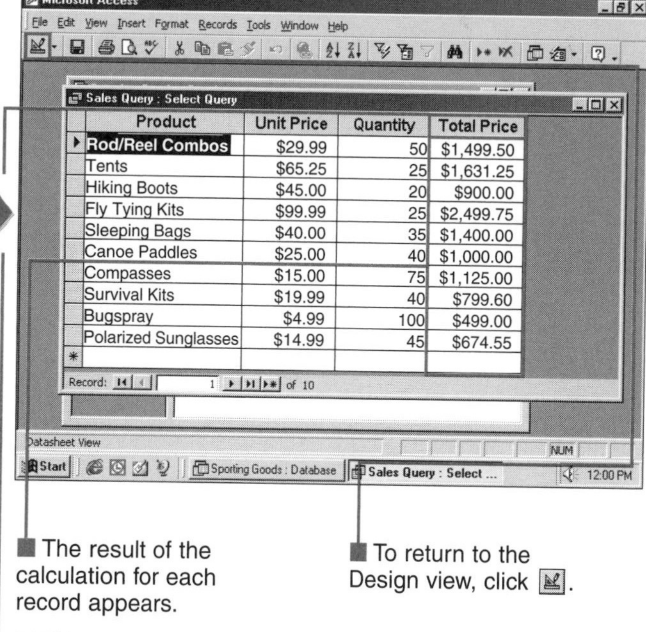

Product	Unit Price	Quantity	Total Price
Rod/Reel Combos	$29.99	50	$1,499.50
Tents	$65.25	25	$1,631.25
Hiking Boots	$45.00	20	$900.00
Fly Tying Kits	$99.99	25	$2,499.75
Sleeping Bags	$40.00	35	$1,400.00
Canoe Paddles	$25.00	40	$1,000.00
Compasses	$15.00	75	$1,125.00
Survival Kits	$19.99	40	$799.60
Bugspray	$4.99	100	$499.00
Polarized Sunglasses	$14.99	45	$674.55

■ The result of the calculation for each record appears.

■ This area displays the field name you typed in step 3.

■ To return to the Design view, click ▣.

SUMMARIZE DATA

You can summarize the information in a database to help you analyze the information.

You can divide records into groups and summarize the information for each group. For example, you can summarize information grouped by date to determine the number of orders for each day.

To group records, you must display the Total row. The words "Group By" automatically appear in each field in the Total row. You can leave the words "Group By" in the field you want Access to use to group the records. In the other field, you can specify the calculation you want to perform on the group to summarize the information.

Access provides several calculations you can perform.

The Sum option adds the values. The Avg option calculates the average value. You can use the Min or Max option to find the smallest or largest value. The Count option calculates the number of values, excluding empty records. You can use the StDev (standard deviation) or Var (variance) option to perform statistical functions. You can use the First or Last option to find the value of the first or last record.

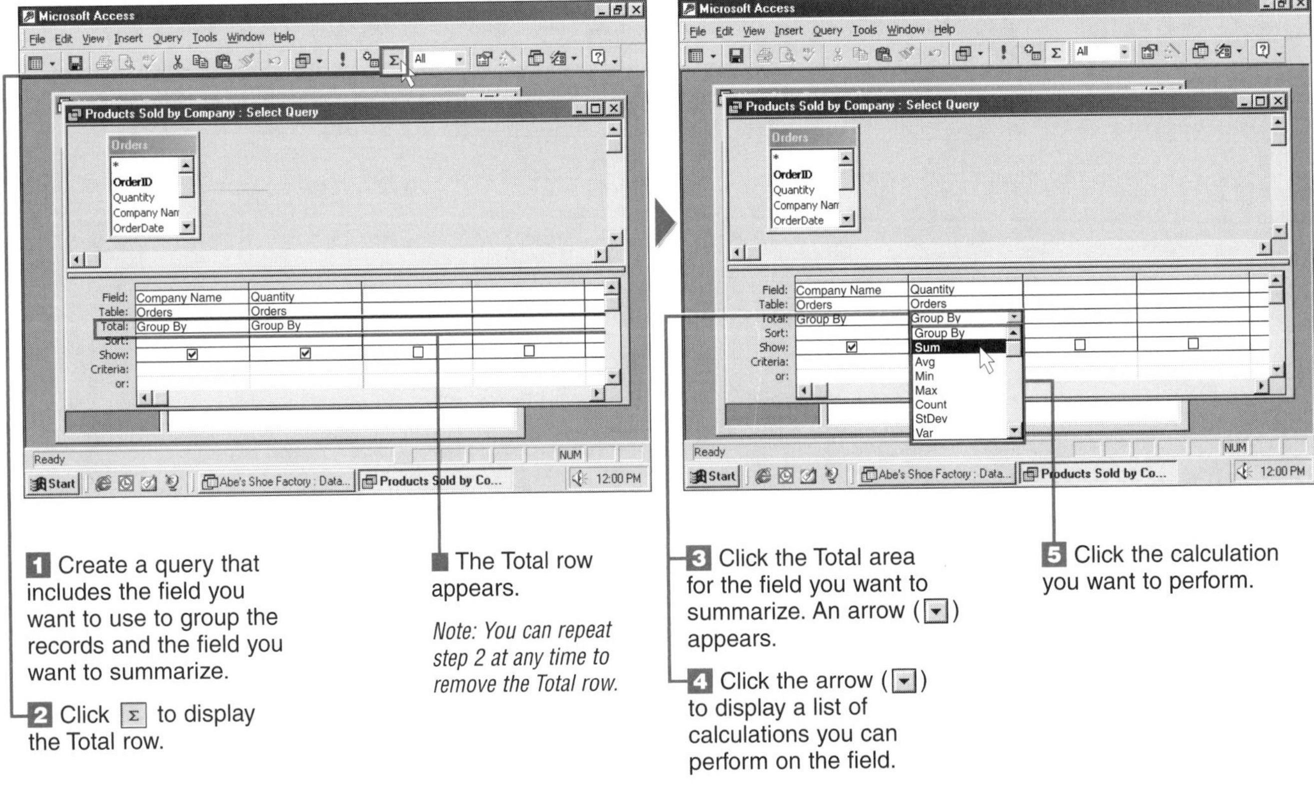

1 Create a query that includes the field you want to use to group the records and the field you want to summarize.

2 Click Σ to display the Total row.

■ The Total row appears.

Note: You can repeat step 2 at any time to remove the Total row.

3 Click the Total area for the field you want to summarize. An arrow (▾) appears.

4 Click the arrow (▾) to display a list of calculations you can perform on the field.

5 Click the calculation you want to perform.

TIPS

Can I use more than one field to group records?

✔ You can group records using more than one field. For example, you can use the Company and Product fields to group the records and the Quantity Ordered field to summarize the data. This lets you display the total amount of each product purchased by each company. Access groups records using fields from left to right. In the Design view, place each field in the order you want to group the records.

Can I limit the records that appear in the results?

✔ You can summarize all the records in a query but show only some of the records in the results. For example, you may want to display only the companies who had orders totaling more than $100.00. In the Criteria area of the field you are summarizing, type the criteria you want to limit the records that will be shown in the results. For examples of criteria, see page 484.

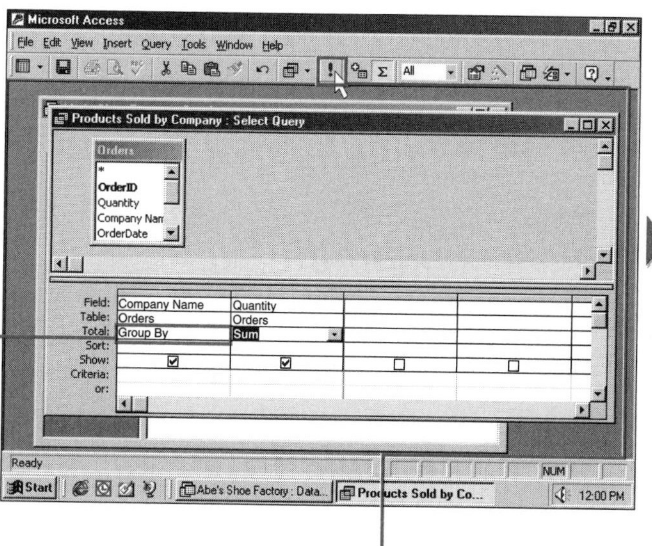

■ Access will use the field that displays "Group By" to group the records.

6 Click [!] to run the query.

Microsoft Access — Products Sold by Company : Select Query

Company Name	SumOfQuantity
Best Fit Shoes	329
Fast Track Footwear	430
Heel and Toe	281
Leather Soles	246
Made for Walking	223
The Shoe Store	327
Treat for the Feet	125
Victor's Footwear	296

Record: 1 of 8

■ The results of the calculations appear. In this example, Access calculates the sum of products purchased by each company.

■ To return to the Design view, click [Design view icon].

CREATE A REPORT USING THE REPORT WIZARD

You can use the Report Wizard to help you create a professionally designed report that summarizes the data from a table. The Report Wizard asks you a series of questions and then creates a report based on your answers.

You can choose the table containing the fields you want to include in the report. After you choose a table, you can select the fields you want to include. For example, in a report that will display monthly sales, you may want to select the Date, Product, Unit Price and Quantity Sold fields. A report can include all or only some of the fields in a table.

The Report Wizard can help you organize the data that will appear in the report by grouping related data together. If you choose to group related data together, Access automatically places the data in the appropriate sections in the report. For example, you can group data by the Date field to have Access place all the sales for the same month together.

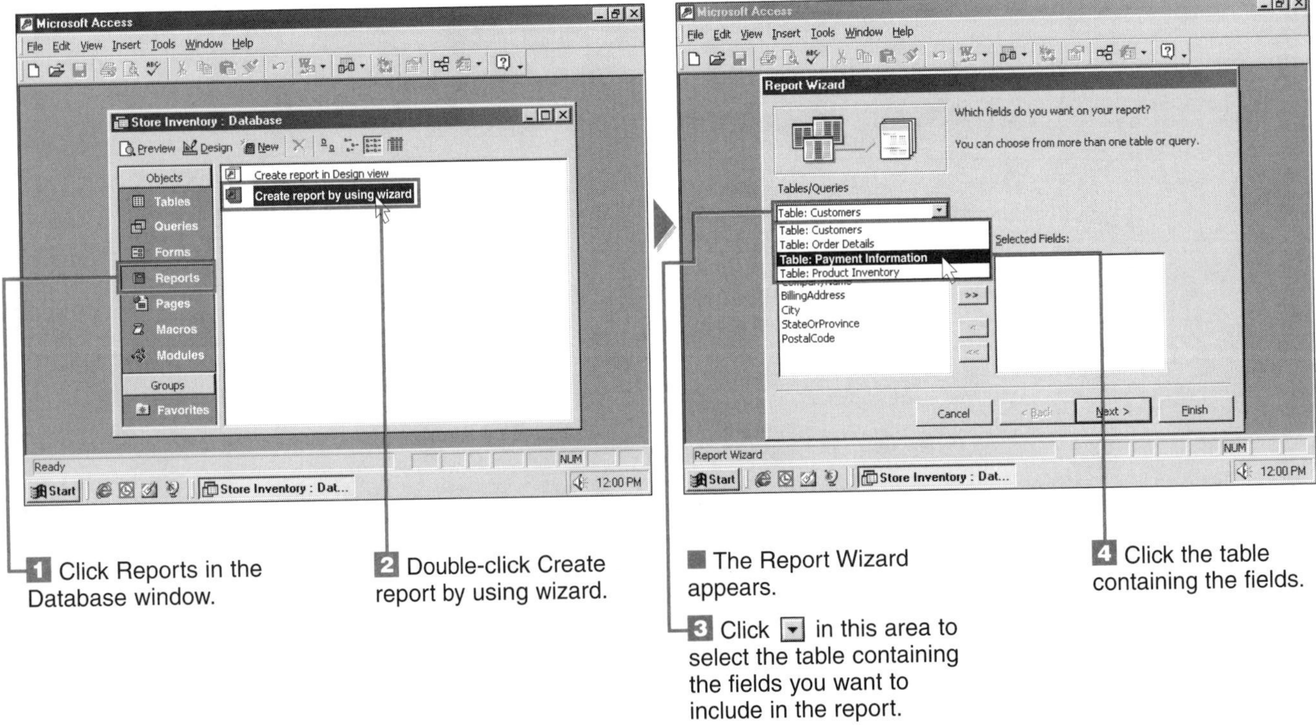

1 Click Reports in the Database window.

2 Double-click Create report by using wizard.

■ The Report Wizard appears.

3 Click ▼ in this area to select the table containing the fields you want to include in the report.

4 Click the table containing the fields.

TIPS

Can I specify how I want Access to group data in my report?

✔ After you select the field you want to use to group related data, you can click the Grouping Options button to specify how you want Access to group the data. In the Grouping intervals area, click ▾ and then select the way you want to group the data. The available options depend on the type of field you selected. For example, you can group data in a Date field by day, month or year.

Can I create a report based on more than one table?

✔ Yes. Relationships must exist between the tables you use. For information on relationships, see page 442. To create the report, perform steps 1 to 5 below and then repeat steps 3 to 5 until you have chosen all the tables and fields you want to include. Then click Next. If the Report Wizard asks how you want to view your data, click the fields in the area below the question until the preview area displays the view you want to use. Then perform steps 6 to 25 to finish creating the report.

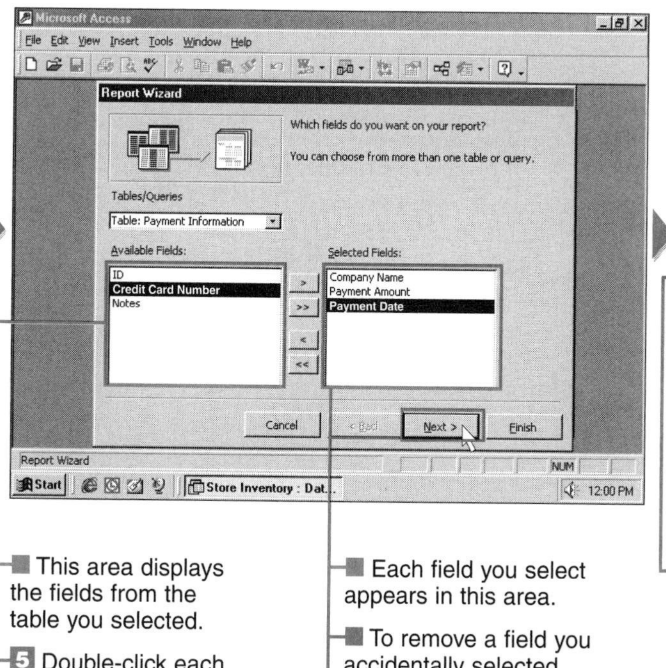

■ This area displays the fields from the table you selected.

5 Double-click each field you want to include in the report.

Note: To add all the fields at once, click ≫.

■ Each field you select appears in this area.

■ To remove a field you accidentally selected, double-click the field in this area.

6 Click Next to continue.

7 To group related data together in the report, double-click the field you want to use to group the data.

■ This area displays how Access will group the data.

8 Click Next to continue.

CONTINUED

CREATE A REPORT USING THE REPORT WIZARD CONTINUED

You can sort the records in a report to better organize the records. The Report Wizard lets you select the fields you want to use to sort the records. For example, you can alphabetically sort records by the Last Name field. If the same data appears more than once in the field, you can sort by a second field, such as First Name.

You can sort records in ascending or descending order. When you sort in ascending order, text is sorted from A to Z and numbers are sorted from 1 to 9. When you sort in descending order, the opposite occurs.

You can perform calculations to summarize the data in a report. When you perform calculations, you can have Access display all the records and the calculated summary for each group of records or just the calculated summaries in the report.

You can also choose to display the percentage of the total that each group represents. For example, in a database that stores sales information, you can calculate the percent of total sales for each region.

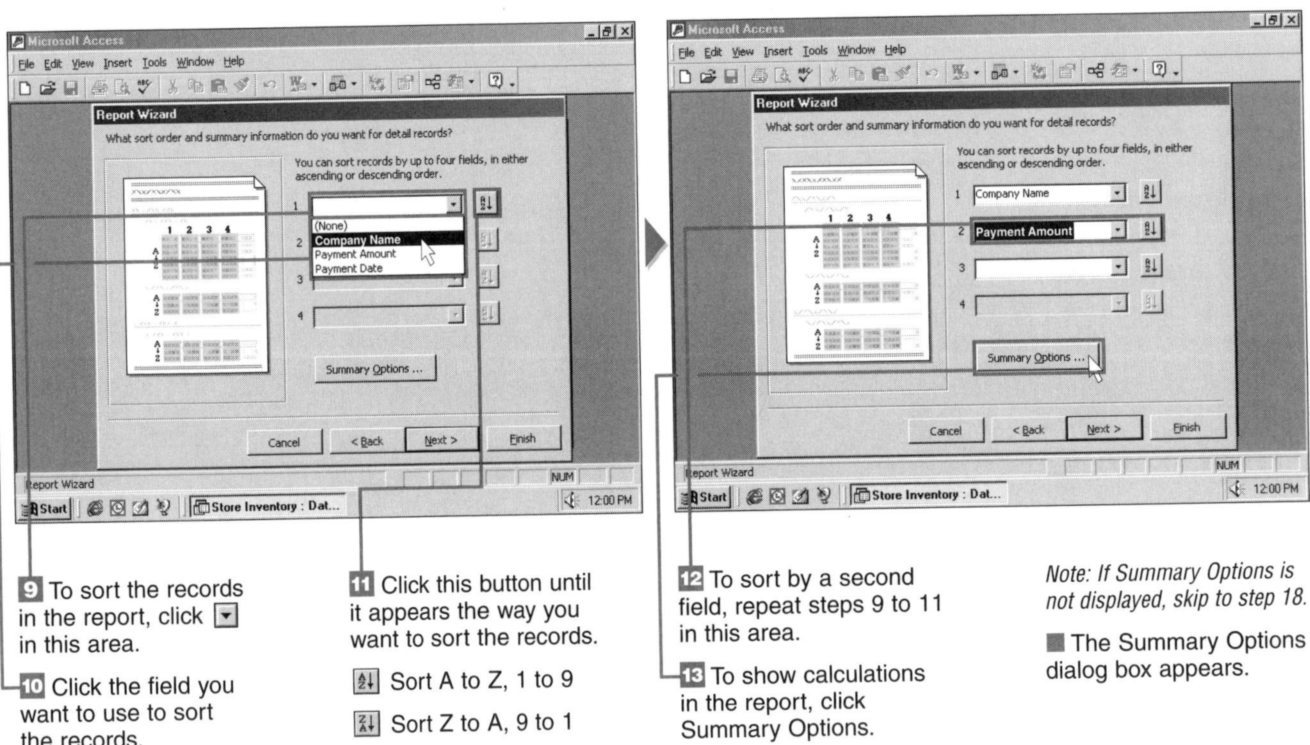

9 To sort the records in the report, click ▾ in this area.

10 Click the field you want to use to sort the records.

11 Click this button until it appears the way you want to sort the records.

- Sort A to Z, 1 to 9
- Sort Z to A, 9 to 1

12 To sort by a second field, repeat steps 9 to 11 in this area.

13 To show calculations in the report, click Summary Options.

Note: If Summary Options is not displayed, skip to step 18.

■ The Summary Options dialog box appears.

TIPS

Why isn't the Summary Options button displayed?

✔ The Summary Options button will not be displayed if you did not include any fields that store numbers in the report. The button will also not be displayed if you did not choose to group related data together in your report. For information on grouping related data, see page 488.

What calculations can I perform on the data in my report?

✔ Access offers several calculations you can perform. The Sum option adds values. The Avg option calculates the average value. The Min and Max options find the smallest or largest value.

Is there a faster way to create a report?

✔ You can use an AutoReport to quickly create a report based on one table in your database. In the Database window, select Reports and then click New. Choose the Columnar or Tabular AutoReport style. Click ▾ and select the table that will supply the information for the report. Then click OK.

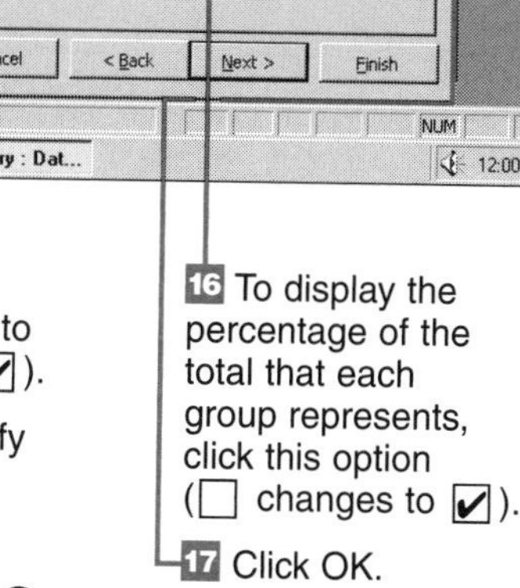

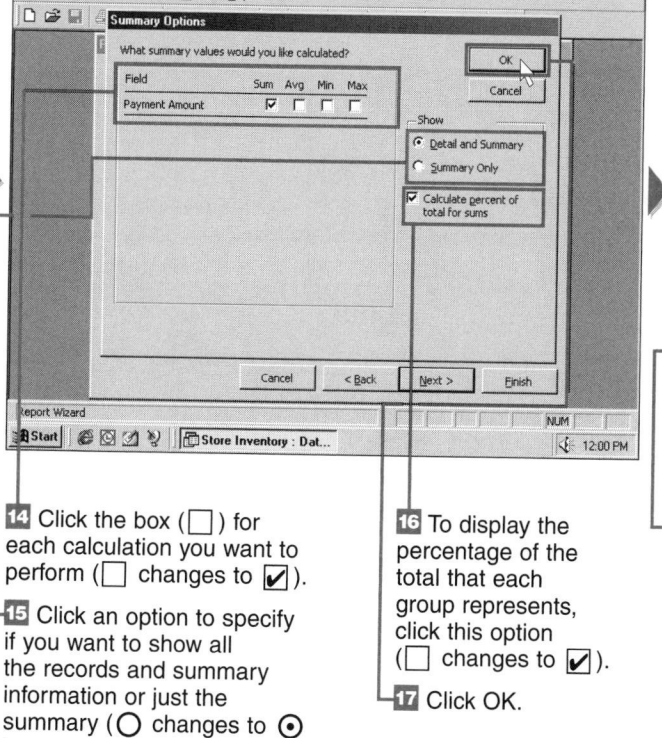

14 Click the box (☐) for each calculation you want to perform (☐ changes to ☑).

15 Click an option to specify if you want to show all the records and summary information or just the summary (○ changes to ⦿).

16 To display the percentage of the total that each group represents, click this option (☐ changes to ☑).

17 Click OK.

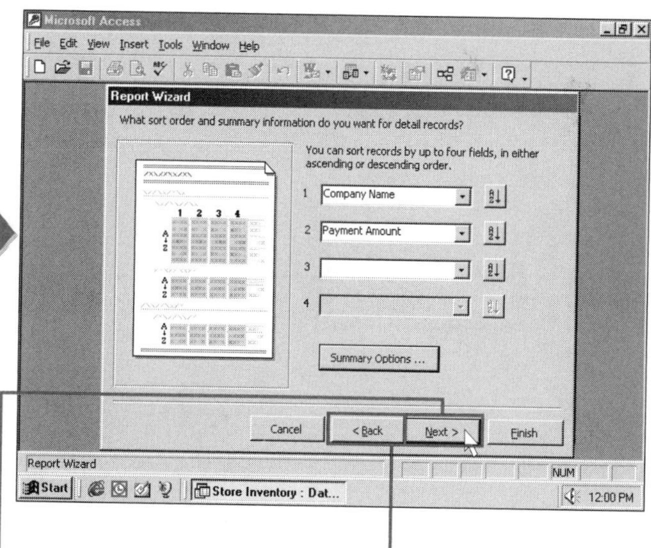

18 Click Next to continue.

■ You can click Back at any time to return to a previous step and change your answers.

CREATE A REPORT USING THE REPORT WIZARD CONTINUED

You can choose between several layouts for a report. The layout you choose determines the arrangement of data in the report.

The available layouts depend on the options you previously selected for the report. If you chose to group related data, the Stepped, Block, Outline and Align Left layouts are available. If you chose not to group related data, the Columnar, Tabular and Justified layouts are available.

You can specify the page orientation of the printed report. The portrait orientation prints data across the short side of a page. The landscape orientation prints data across the long side of a page.

You can choose a style for the report, such as Casual, Corporate or Formal. Most styles use colors and patterns to enhance the appearance of a report.

The Report Wizard asks you to name your report. The name you select will appear in the Reports area of the Database window.

The report appears in a window on your screen. If the report consists of more than one page, you can move through the pages in the report.

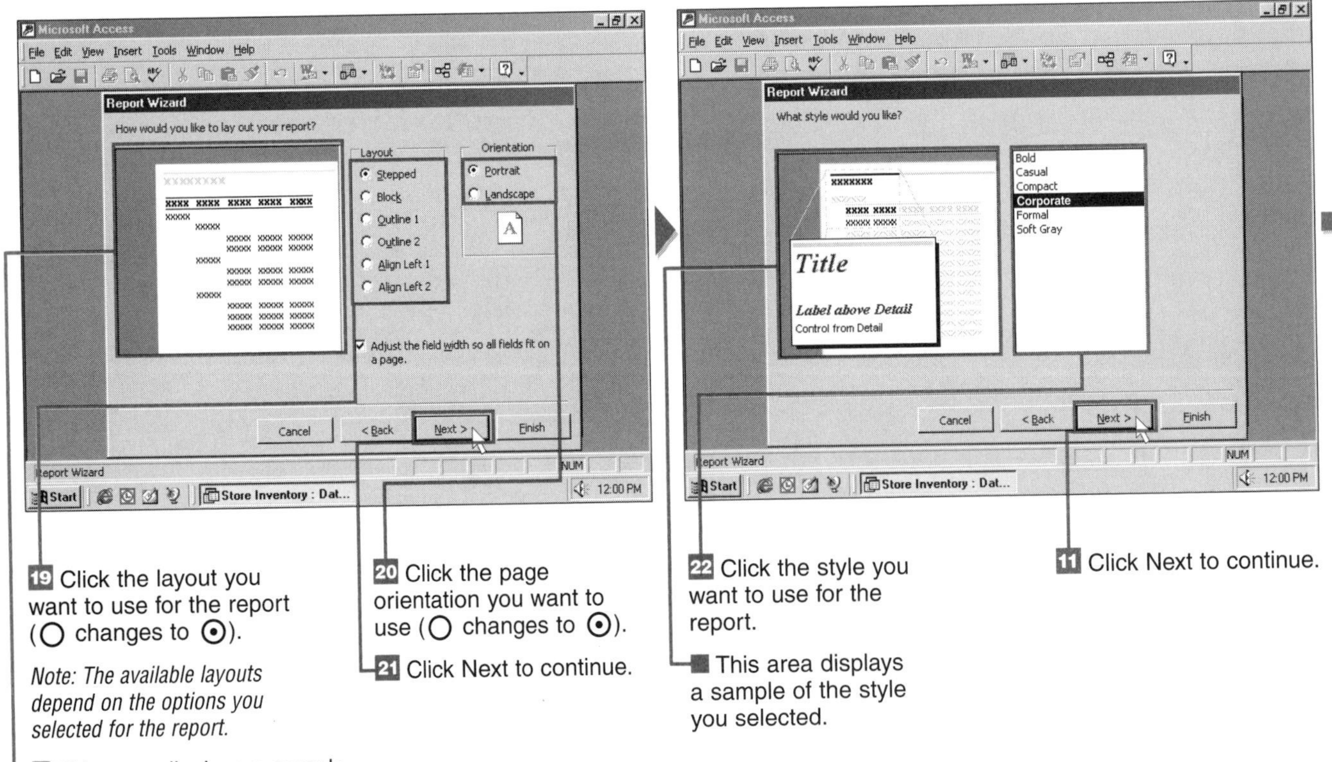

19 Click the layout you want to use for the report (○ changes to ⊙).

Note: The available layouts depend on the options you selected for the report.

■ This area displays a sample of the layout you selected.

20 Click the page orientation you want to use (○ changes to ⊙).

21 Click Next to continue.

22 Click the style you want to use for the report.

■ This area displays a sample of the style you selected.

11 Click Next to continue.

TIPS

Can I later change the style of a report?

✔ Yes. In the Database window, click Reports. Select the name of the report you want to change and then click the Design button. Click the AutoFormat button ( ) and select the style you want to use. Then click OK.

When viewing my report, how can I display an entire page on my screen?

✔ You can click the Zoom button ( ) to display the entire page on your screen. For more information on changing the magnification of a page, see page 498.

How do I print a report?

✔ When the report is displayed on your screen, you can click the Print button ( ) to print the report.

I changed data in a table I used to create a report. How do I update the report?

✔ When you open the report, Access will automatically gather the most current data from the table(s) you used to create the report. Access will also update the date displayed in the report.

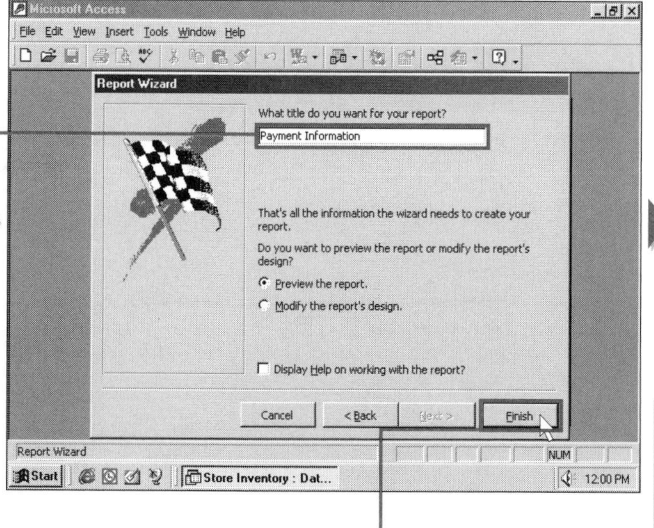

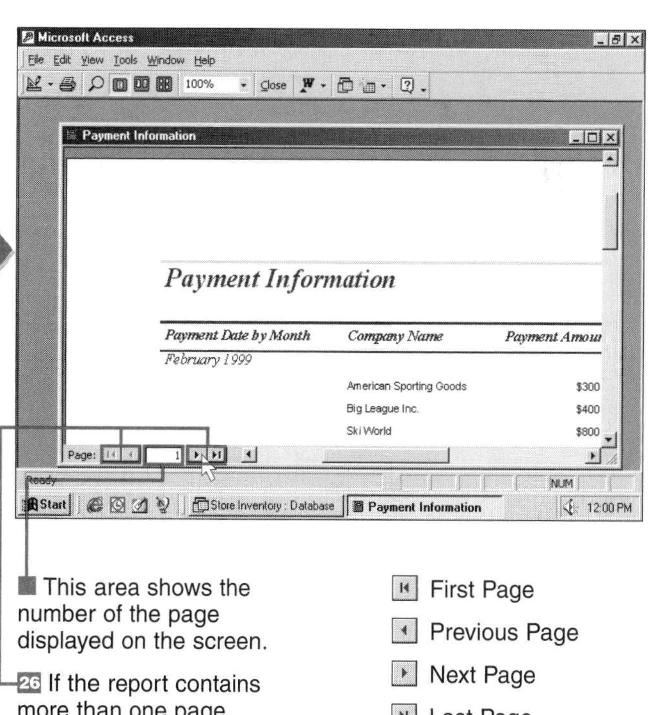

24 Type a name for the report.

25 Click Finish to create the report.

■ A window appears, displaying the report.

■ This area shows the number of the page displayed on the screen.

26 If the report contains more than one page, click one of the following options to display another page.

First Page

Previous Page

Next Page

Last Page

Note: If an option is dimmed, the option is currently not available.

OPEN A REPORT

You can open a report to display the contents of the report on your screen. This allows you to review the information in the report.

You can open a report in the Print Preview or Design view. The Print Preview view allows you to see how a report will look when printed. The Design view allows you to change the design of a report.

When you open a report, Access gathers the most current data from the table or query used to create the report. If the table or query contains a large amount of data, it may take a few moments for the report to appear on your screen.

When you finish working with a report, you can close the report to remove it from your screen. A dialog box appears if you have not saved changes you made to the design of the report, such as changing the font or size of text.

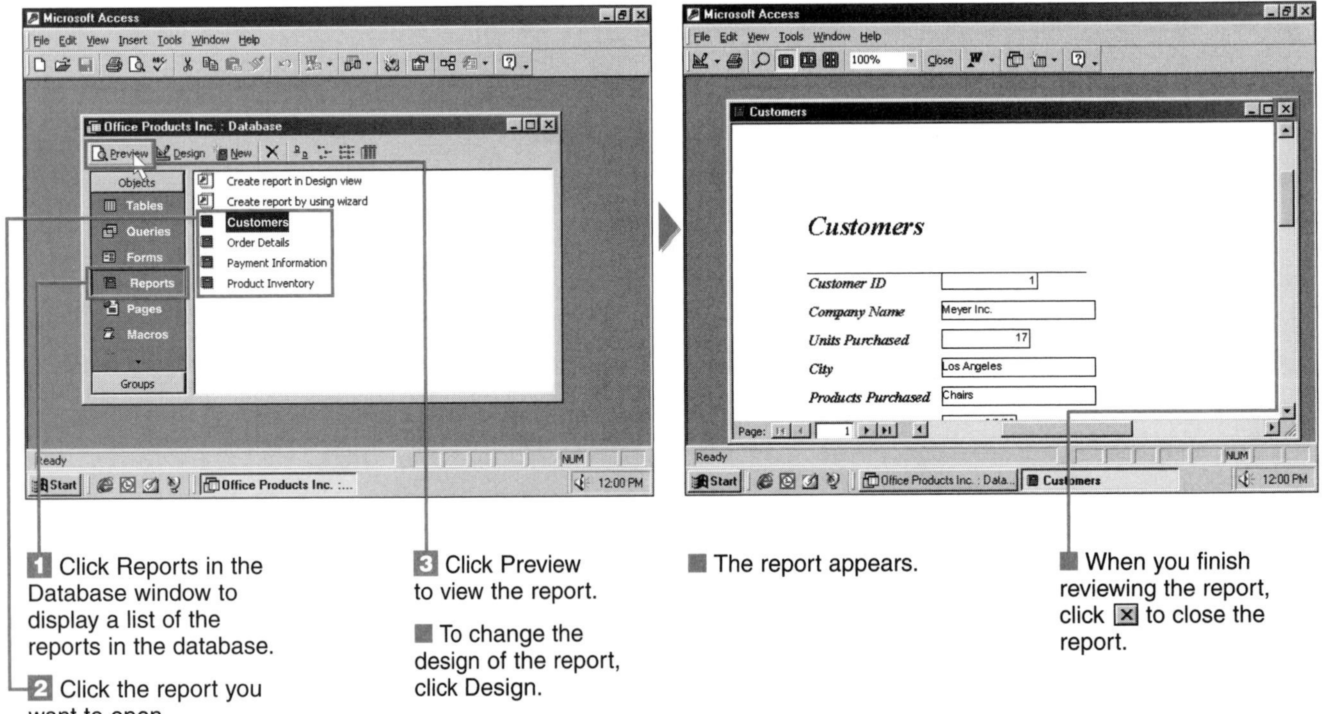

1 Click Reports in the Database window to display a list of the reports in the database.

2 Click the report you want to open.

3 Click Preview to view the report.

■ To change the design of the report, click Design.

■ The report appears.

■ When you finish reviewing the report, click ☒ to close the report.

CHANGE VIEW OF REPORT

There are three ways you can view a report. Each view allows you to perform a different task.

The Design view allows you to change the layout and design of a report. The Design view displays a grid of small, evenly spaced dots to help you line up the items in a report. This view displays information in several sections, such as the report header and page footer sections.

The Print Preview view allows you to see how a report will look when printed. You can use this view to display all the pages in the report and examine how each page will print.

The Layout Preview view allows you to quickly view the layout and style of a report. The Layout Preview view is only available when a report is displayed in the Design view. The Layout Preview view is similar to the Print Preview view, but only allows you to see a few pages of a report. The data from the table or query used to create the report may not update properly in the Layout Preview view.

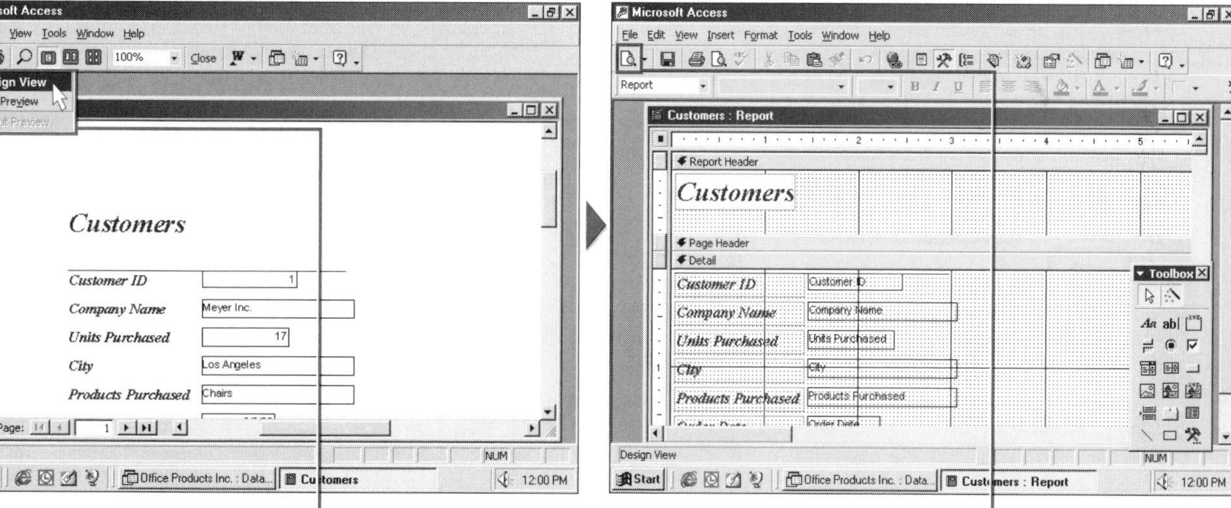

■ In this example, the report appears in the Print Preview view.

1 Click ▾ in this area to display the report in another view.

Note: The available views depend on the view you are currently using.

2 Click the view you want to use.

Note: If the view you want does not appear on the menu, position the mouse over the bottom of the menu to display all the views.

■ The report appears in the view you selected.

■ In this example, the View button changes. You can click the View button to quickly switch between the Design and Print Preview views.

PREVIEW BEFORE PRINTING

You can use the Print Preview feature to see how your tables, queries, forms and reports will look when printed. Using the Print Preview feature can help you confirm that the printed pages will appear the way you want.

The Print Preview window indicates which page you are currently viewing. If an object contains more than one page, you can easily view the other pages.

You can magnify an area of a page. This allows you to view the area in more detail. When you magnify a page, Access displays scroll bars that you can use to move through the information on the page.

You can have Access display several pages in the Print Preview window at once. This gives you an overall view of the pages in an object.

When you have finished using the Print Preview feature, you can close the Print Preview window to return to the Database window.

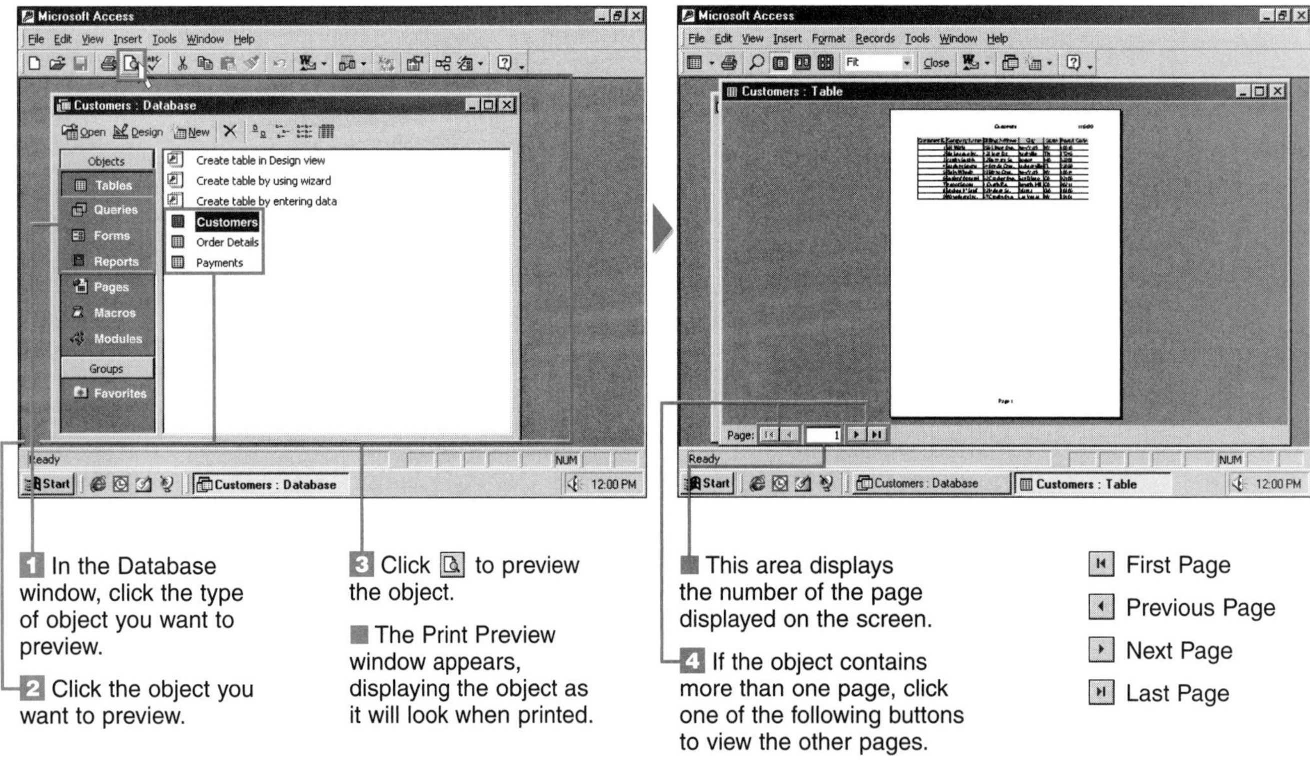

1 In the Database window, click the type of object you want to preview.

2 Click the object you want to preview.

3 Click to preview the object.

■ The Print Preview window appears, displaying the object as it will look when printed.

■ This area displays the number of the page displayed on the screen.

4 If the object contains more than one page, click one of the following buttons to view the other pages.

First Page

Previous Page

Next Page

Last Page

TIPS

Can I preview an object at different magnification levels?

✔ Yes. In the Print Preview window, you can select a new zoom setting to change the level of magnification. Click ▾ in the Zoom area and then select the zoom setting you want to use. By default, Access displays an object in the Fit zoom setting. This zoom setting allows Access to use the magnification level that best fits the currently displayed page(s).

Can I print directly from the Print Preview window?

✔ To print an object directly from the Print Preview window, click the Print button (🖨).

How can I quickly display two pages of an object in the Print Preview window?

✔ To quickly display two pages, click the Two Pages button (▯▯).

How do I preview only one page of an object after displaying multiple pages?

✔ To preview one page of an object, click the One Page button (▯) in the Print Preview window.

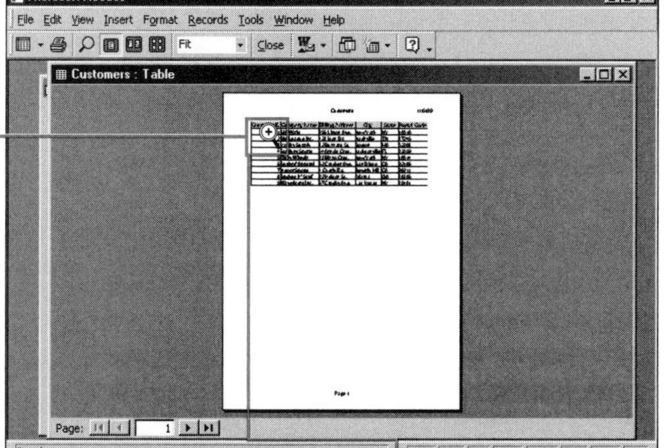

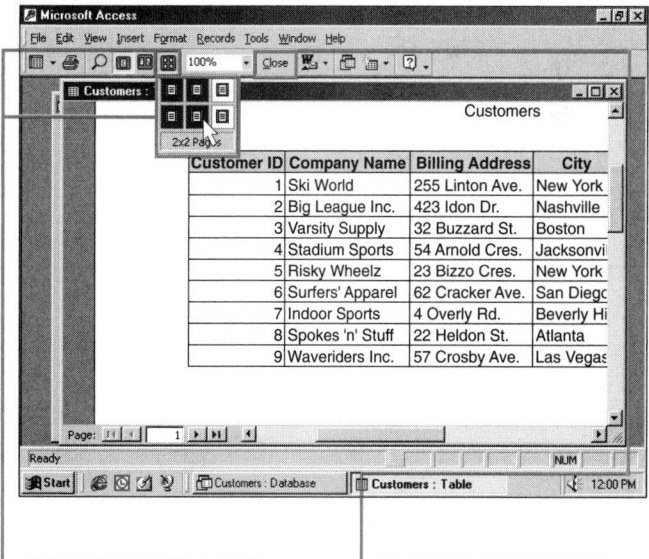

MAGNIFY A PAGE

1 Position the mouse ↖ over the area of the page you want to magnify (↖ changes to 🔍).

2 Click the area to magnify the area.

■ To once again display the entire page, click anywhere on the page.

DISPLAY MULTIPLE PAGES

1 Click ⊞ to display multiple pages.

2 Drag the mouse ↖ down and to the right until you select the number of pages you want to display.

CLOSE PRINT PREVIEW

1 Click Close to close the Print Preview window.

PRINT INFORMATION

You can produce a paper copy of a table, query, form or report. A paper copy is often referred to as a hard copy.

Before printing, make sure your printer is turned on and contains an adequate supply of paper.

You can choose the information you want to print. Access allows you to print all the records, specific pages or specific records. Printing only specific records saves you from printing information you do not want to review. To print only specific records, you must select the records before you begin.

If the current printer settings suit your needs, you can use the Print button ( ) to quickly print all the records without displaying the Print dialog box.

When you print a table or query, Access prints the title, date and page number on each page. This information can help you organize the printed data.

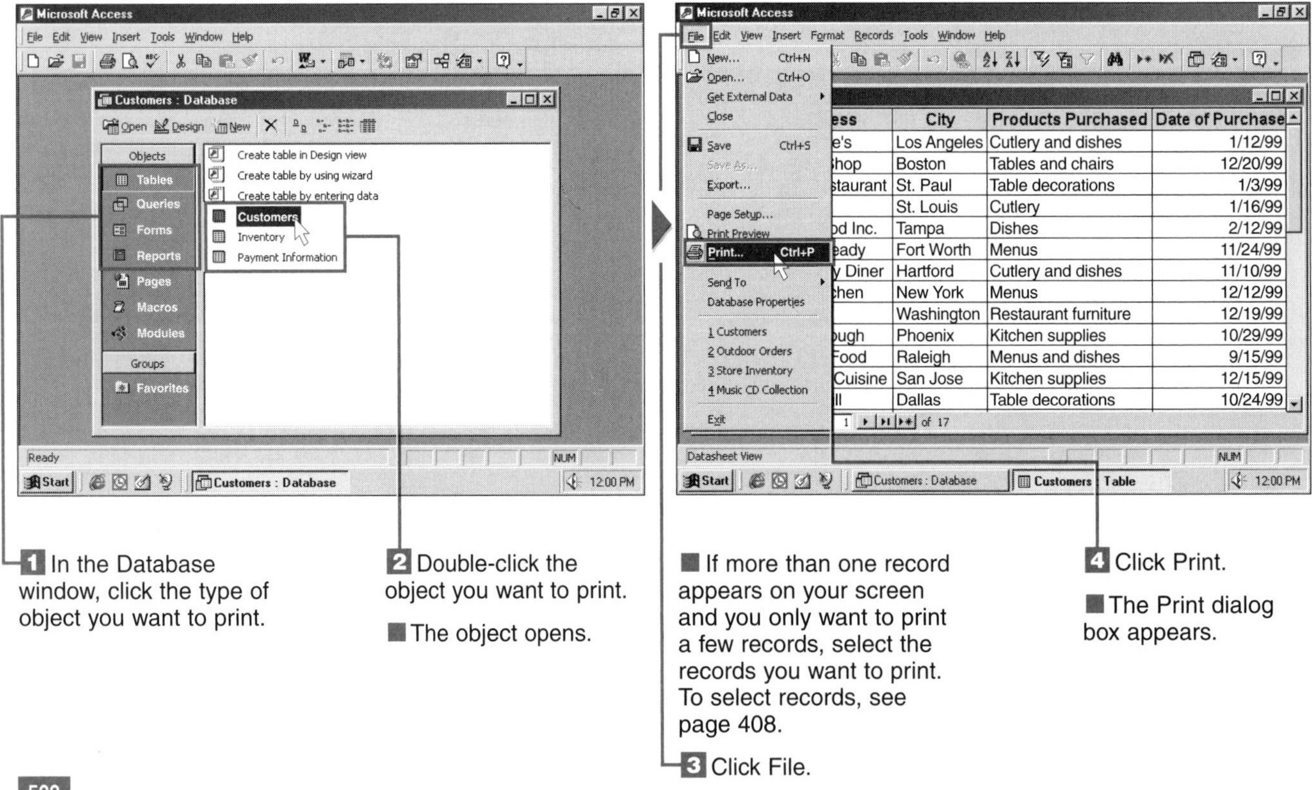

1 In the Database window, click the type of object you want to print.

2 Double-click the object you want to print.

■ The object opens.

■ If more than one record appears on your screen and you only want to print a few records, select the records you want to print. To select records, see page 408.

3 Click File.

4 Click Print.

■ The Print dialog box appears.

TIPS

Can I specify the printer I want to use to print information?

✔ If you have more than one printer installed on your computer, you can select the printer you want to use. This is useful when you use different printers to print different types of information. For example, you may want to use a color printer to print forms and a black-and-white printer to print tables. In the Print dialog box, click the Name area and then select the printer you want to use.

Can I print multiple copies?

✔ Yes. In the Print dialog box, double-click the Number of Copies area and then type the number of copies you want to print.

Can I prevent Access from printing the title, date and page number when I print tables and queries?

✔ Yes. In the Print dialog box, select the Setup button. On the Margins tab, click the Print Headings option (☑ changes to ☐) and then click OK.

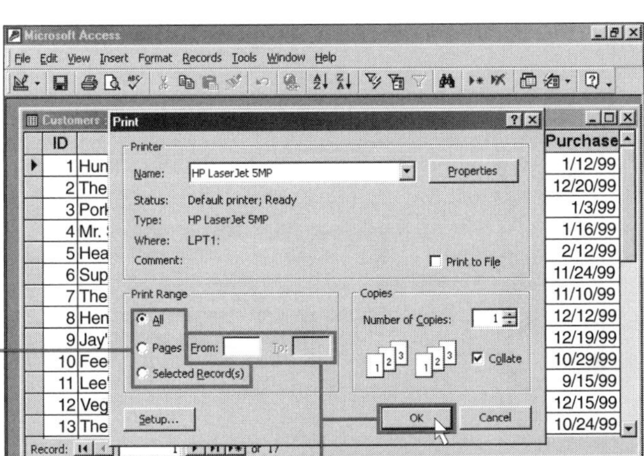

5 Click the print option you want to use (○ changes to ⊙).

■ If you selected Pages in step 5, type the number of the first page you want to print. Press the Tab key and then type the number of the last page you want to print.

6 Click OK.

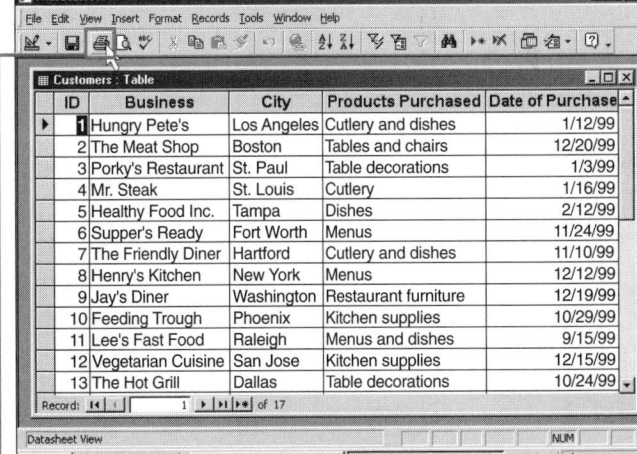

ID	Business	City	Products Purchased	Date of Purchase
1	Hungry Pete's	Los Angeles	Cutlery and dishes	1/12/99
2	The Meat Shop	Boston	Tables and chairs	12/20/99
3	Porky's Restaurant	St. Paul	Table decorations	1/3/99
4	Mr. Steak	St. Louis	Cutlery	1/16/99
5	Healthy Food Inc.	Tampa	Dishes	2/12/99
6	Supper's Ready	Fort Worth	Menus	11/24/99
7	The Friendly Diner	Hartford	Cutlery and dishes	11/10/99
8	Henry's Kitchen	New York	Menus	12/12/99
9	Jay's Diner	Washington	Restaurant furniture	12/19/99
10	Feeding Trough	Phoenix	Kitchen supplies	10/29/99
11	Lee's Fast Food	Raleigh	Menus and dishes	9/15/99
12	Vegetarian Cuisine	San Jose	Kitchen supplies	12/15/99
13	The Hot Grill	Dallas	Table decorations	10/24/99

QUICKLY PRINT ALL RECORDS

1 Click 🖨 to quickly print all the records.

CREATE MAILING LABELS

You can create a mailing label for every person in a table. You can use labels for addressing envelopes and packages, labeling file folders and creating name tags.

The Label Wizard asks you a series of questions and then creates labels based on your answers.

You can choose the table that contains the names and addresses you want to appear on the labels.

There are two types of labels you can use–sheet feed and continuous. Sheet feed labels are individual sheets of labels. Continuous labels are connected sheets of labels, with holes punched along each side. You can consult the manual that came with your printer to determine which type of labels your printer can use.

You can select the label size you want to use. Check your label packaging to determine which label size to select.

The wizard allows you to change the appearance of the text that will appear on the labels. You can choose between various fonts, sizes, weights and colors. The text appearance you choose affects all the text on every label.

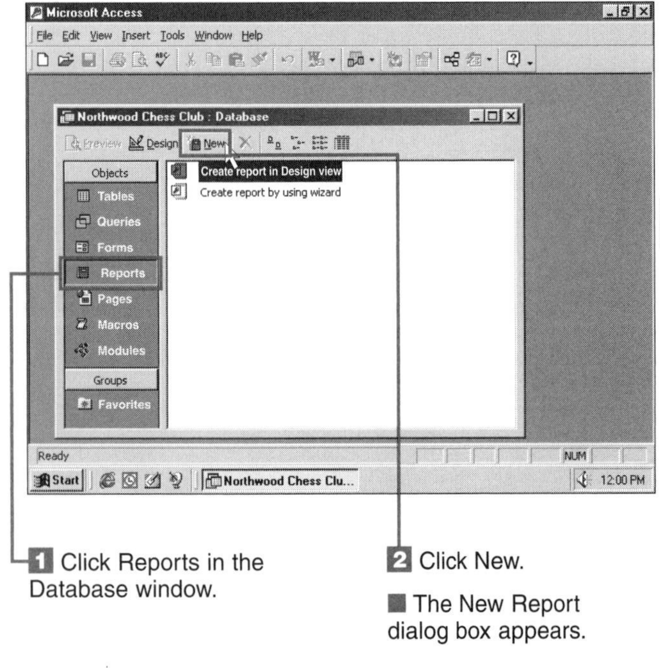

1 Click Reports in the Database window.

2 Click New.

■ The New Report dialog box appears.

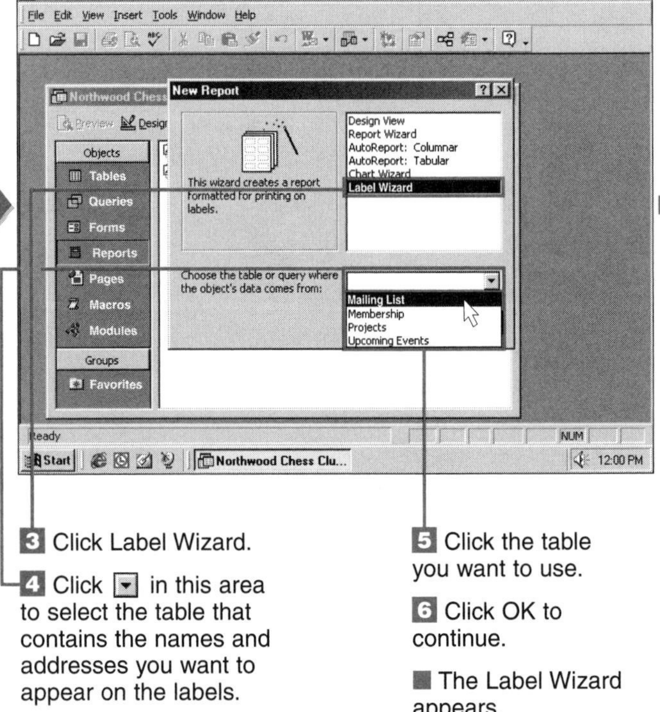

3 Click Label Wizard.

4 Click ▼ in this area to select the table that contains the names and addresses you want to appear on the labels.

5 Click the table you want to use.

6 Click OK to continue.

■ The Label Wizard appears.

TIPS

I cannot find the label size I want in the Label Wizard. What is wrong?

✔ By default, the Label Wizard displays standard Avery labels. You can display a list of label sizes for a different manufacturer. Click ▾ in the Filter by manufacturer area and then select the manufacturer of the labels you are using.

How do I specify a custom label size in the Label Wizard?

✔ Click the Customize button and then click New. A dialog box appears, displaying sample labels and areas where you can enter measurements for your labels. Enter the measurements you want to use and then click OK.

How do I change the Text appearance options in the Label Wizard?

✔ You can click ▾ in the Font name, Font size or Font weight areas to display a list of options. You can then select the option you want to use. Click ... beside the Text color area to display a list of colors and then select the color you want to use. To italicize or underline text, click the appropriate option (☐ changes to ☑).

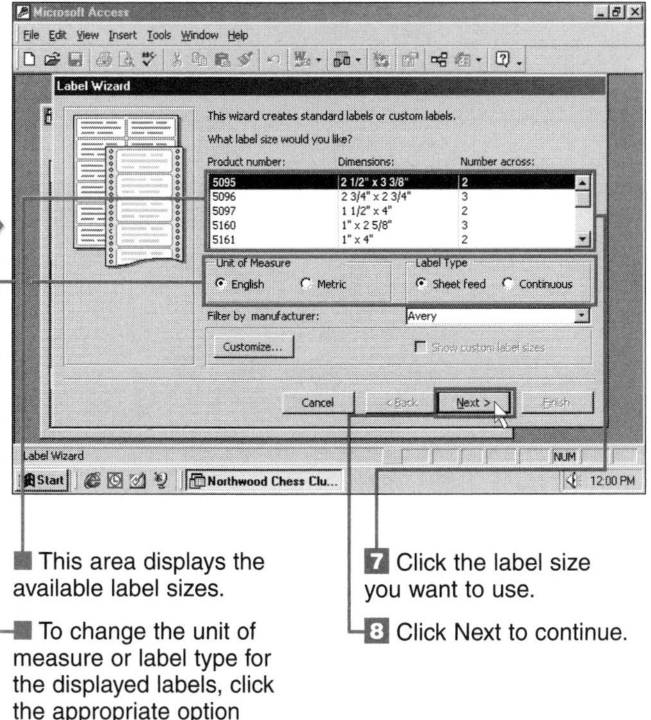

■ This area displays the available label sizes.

■ To change the unit of measure or label type for the displayed labels, click the appropriate option (◯ changes to ⊙).

7 Click the label size you want to use.

8 Click Next to continue.

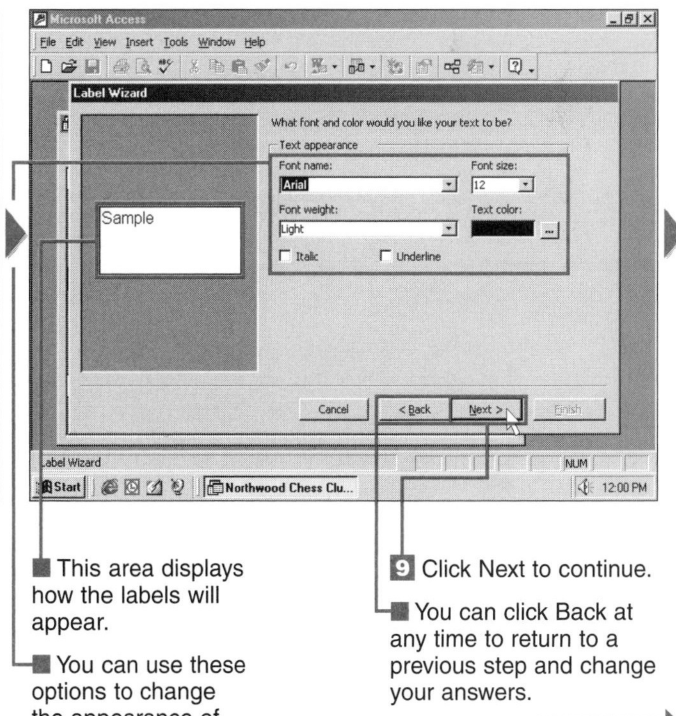

■ This area displays how the labels will appear.

■ You can use these options to change the appearance of the text on the labels.

9 Click Next to continue.

■ You can click Back at any time to return to a previous step and change your answers.

CONTINUED

CREATE MAILING LABELS CONTINUED

The Label Wizard asks you to select the fields you want to appear on the labels. You do not have to select all the fields from the table.

The fields you select should appear in the Label Wizard in the order and location that you want them to print on the labels. Make sure you add spaces or commas where needed, such as a space between the first and last name.

You can specify how you want to sort the labels. Sorting the labels determines the order that Access arranges the labels on a printed sheet. For example, you may want to sort mailing labels by city to place all labels for the same city together.

You can type a name for the labels. Access stores the labels as a report that you can open as you would open any report. To open a report, see page 496.

The labels appear on your screen as they will look when printed. This allows you to preview the labels before you print them.

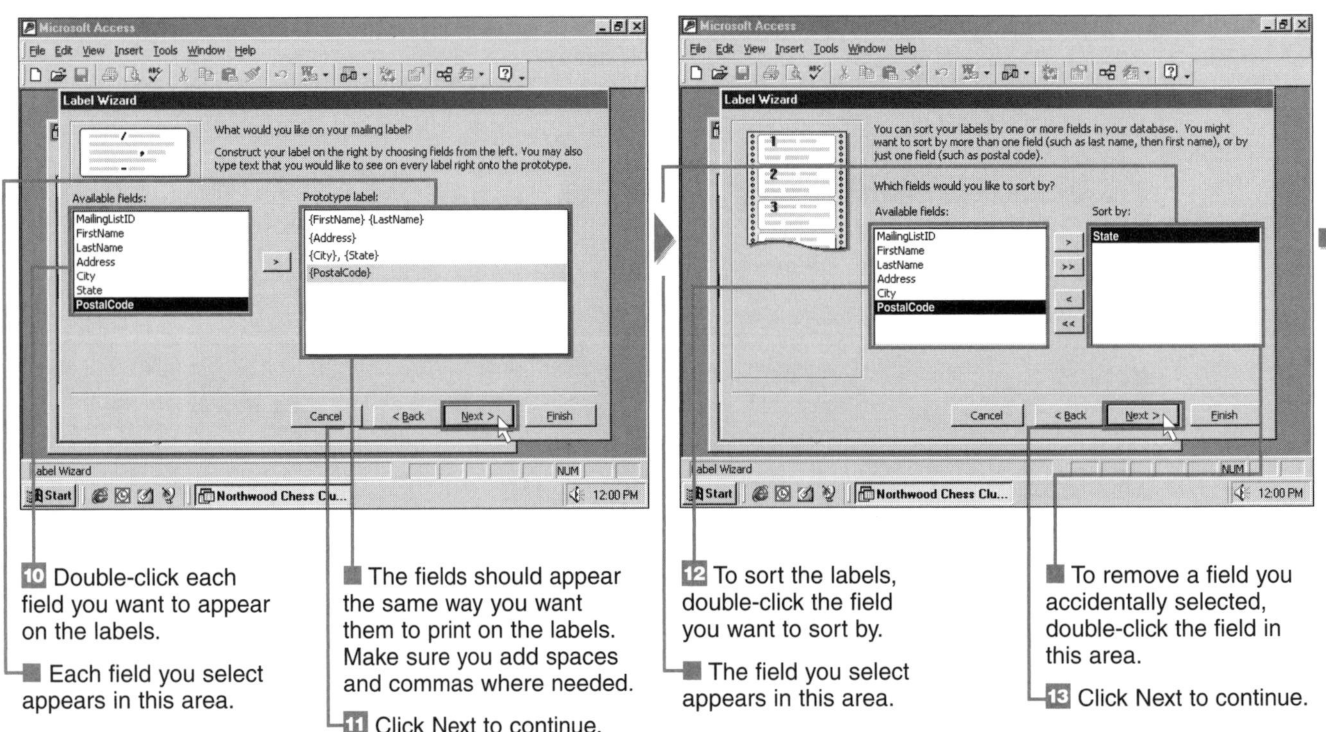

10 Double-click each field you want to appear on the labels.

■ Each field you select appears in this area.

■ The fields should appear the same way you want them to print on the labels. Make sure you add spaces and commas where needed.

11 Click Next to continue.

12 To sort the labels, double-click the field you want to sort by.

■ The field you select appears in this area.

■ To remove a field you accidentally selected, double-click the field in this area.

13 Click Next to continue.

TIPS

Can I sort the labels by more than one field?

✔ Yes. If the first field you are using to sort the labels contains matching data, you can sort by a second field. For example, you may want to sort by state and then by city. In the Label Wizard, double-click the first field you want to sort by and then double-click the second field you want to sort by.

How do I print labels I created?

✔ When viewing the labels, click the Print button (🖨). Before you begin printing, make sure the printer is turned on and the labels are in the printer. For more information on printing, see page 500.

How do I edit labels I created?

✔ To edit labels, you must change the data in the table you used to create the labels. For example, to change the address of a client, you must change the data in the table that stores the client's address. Changes you make to the data in the table will automatically appear in the labels.

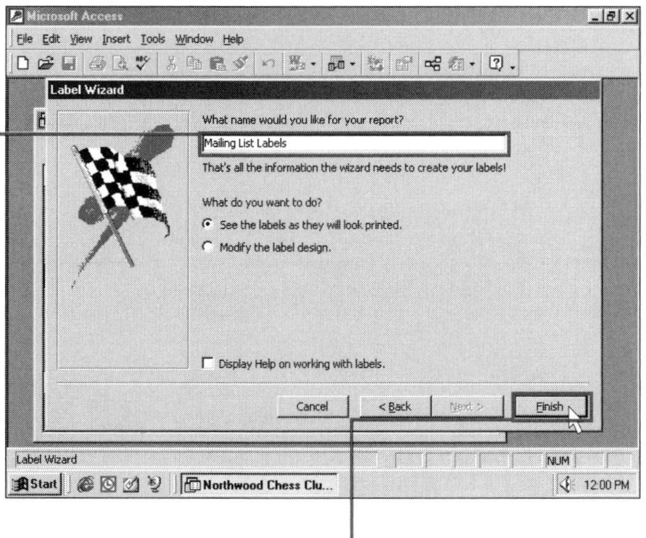

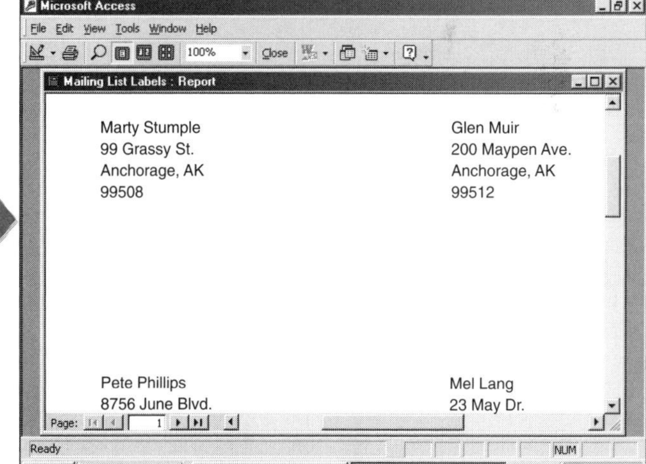

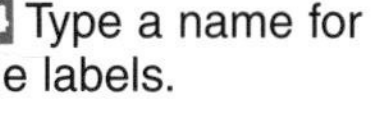

14 Type a name for the labels.

15 Click Finish to create the labels.

■ A new window opens, displaying a personalized label for each person in the table.

SECTION VI

1) EXCHANGE E-MAIL

2) MANAGE INFORMATION

USING OUTLOOK

START OUTLOOK

Outlook can help you manage your messages, appointments, contacts, tasks and notes.

The Microsoft Outlook window is divided into two areas. The area on the left side of the window contains the Outlook Bar. The Outlook Bar displays icons you can select to access the features included with Outlook. The area on the right side of the window displays the current feature.

You can use Outlook's features to manage many different types of information. The Inbox lets you send and receive e-mail messages. The Calendar helps you keep track of your appointments. You can use Contacts to store information about people you correspond with. Tasks allows you to create a list of duties you want to accomplish. Notes lets you create brief reminder notes. Deleted Items stores items you have deleted.

You can use Outlook Today to display a summary of your day. You can see your upcoming appointments, a list of your tasks and a summary of your e-mail messages.

When you start Outlook, the Office Assistant may appear. For more information on the Office Assistant, see page 16.

For more information on Outlook, you can visit the following Web site: www.microsoft.com/outlook

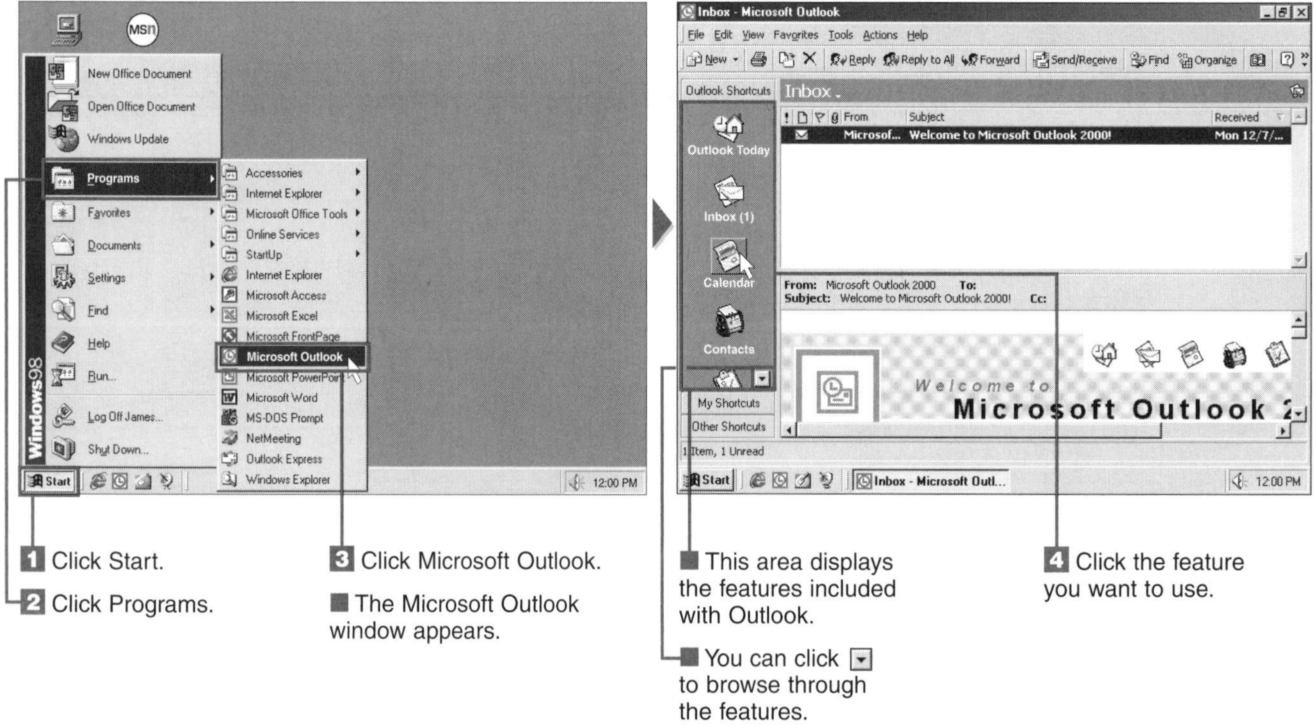

1 Click Start.

2 Click Programs.

3 Click Microsoft Outlook.

■ The Microsoft Outlook window appears.

■ This area displays the features included with Outlook.

■ You can click ▾ to browse through the features.

4 Click the feature you want to use.

TIPS

Why did a dialog box appear when I tried to start Outlook?

✔ The first time you start Outlook, a wizard appears that allows you to set up Outlook on your computer. Follow the instructions on your screen to set up Outlook.

Can I hide the Outlook Bar?

✔ You can hide the Outlook Bar to increase the viewing area of the current feature. From the View menu, select Outlook Bar to remove the check mark (✔). Repeat this procedure to once again view the Outlook Bar.

Can I view all the features in the Outlook Bar at once?

✔ Yes. Outlook automatically displays large icons in the Outlook Bar. To be able to view all the features at once, right-click a blank area in the Outlook Bar and then select Small Icons.

Can I change the way Outlook Today displays information about my day?

✔ Yes. When the Outlook Today feature is displayed, click Customize Outlook Today. Choose the options for the items you want to display differently and then click Save Changes.

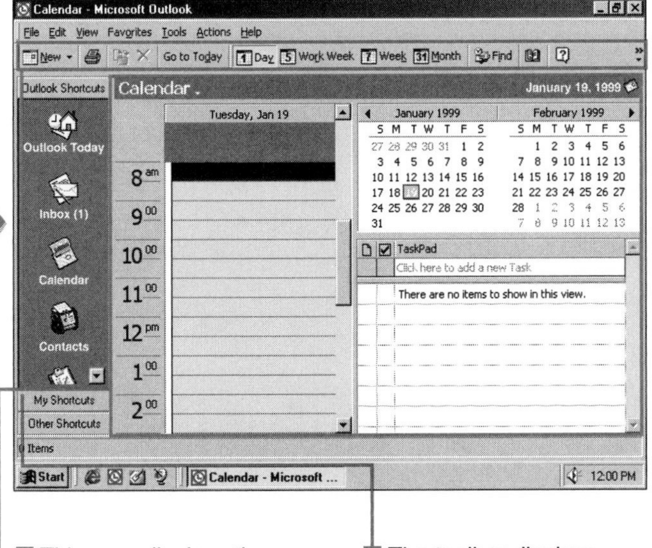

■ This area displays the feature you selected.

■ The toolbar displays the buttons for the feature you selected.

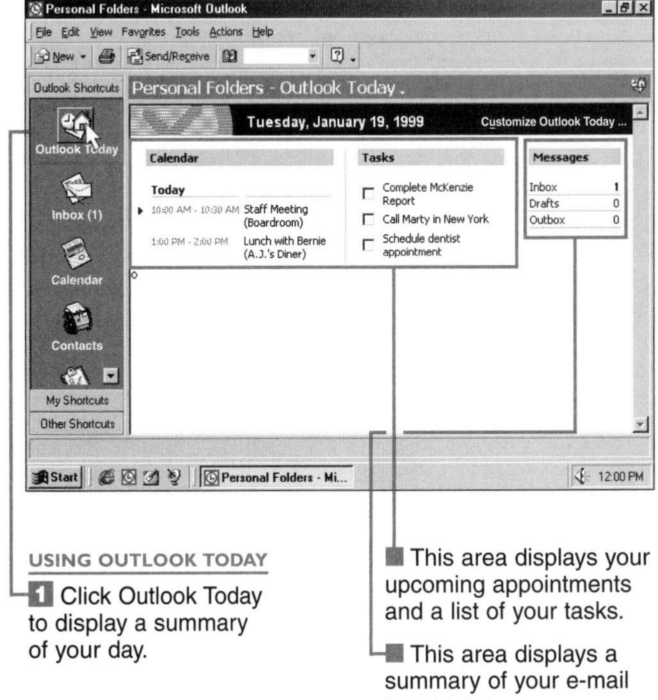

USING OUTLOOK TODAY

1 Click Outlook Today to display a summary of your day.

■ This area displays your upcoming appointments and a list of your tasks.

■ This area displays a summary of your e-mail messages.

READ MESSAGES

Outlook allows you to exchange electronic mail (e-mail) with friends, family members, colleagues and clients.

When you receive new e-mail messages, Outlook displays an envelope icon (✉) in the bottom right corner of your screen.

Outlook stores the messages you receive in the Inbox. You can use the Inbox to open the messages and read their contents. The number in brackets beside the Inbox indicates the number of unread messages the Inbox contains.

Each unread message displays a closed envelope and appears in bold type. After you read a message, it displays an open envelope and appears in regular type. Outlook displays the author, subject and date of each message.

Outlook stores messages you have sent or are planning to send in three mail folders. The Drafts folder stores messages you have not completed. The Outbox folder stores messages that have not yet been sent. The Sent Items folder stores messages you have sent.

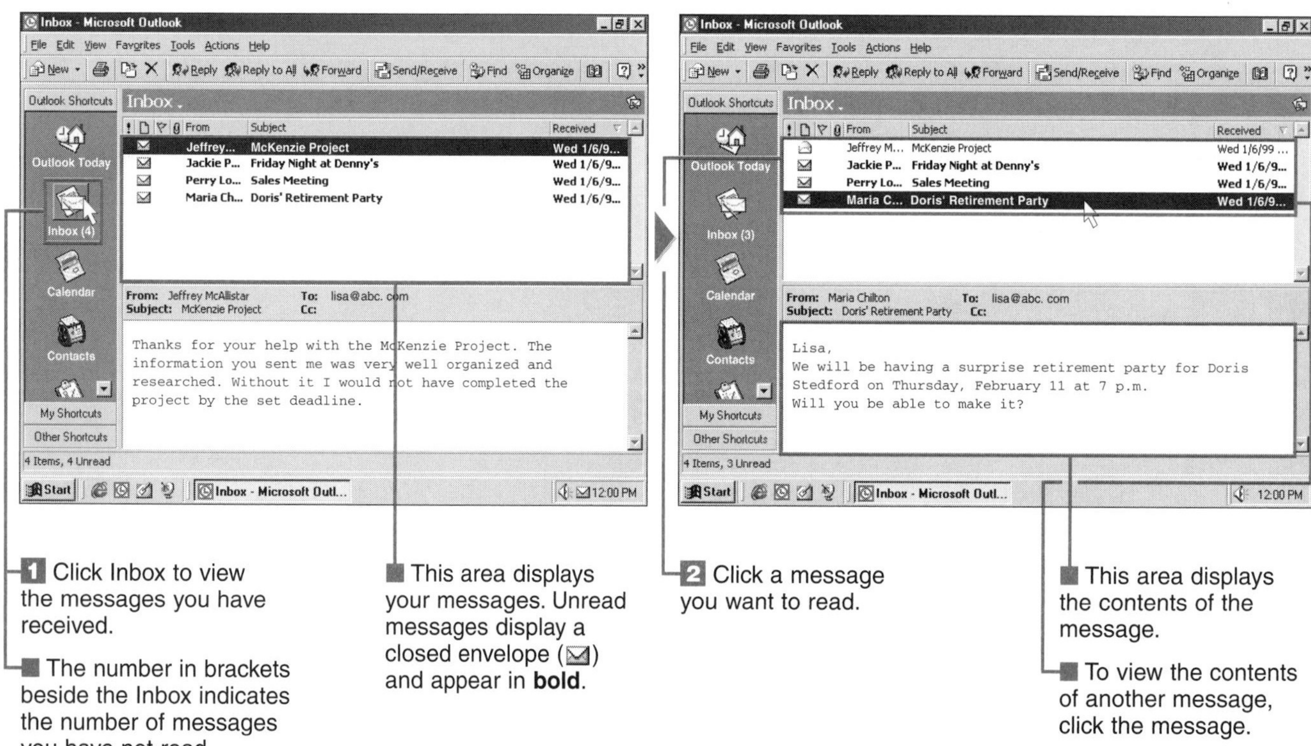

1 Click Inbox to view the messages you have received.

■ The number in brackets beside the Inbox indicates the number of messages you have not read.

■ This area displays your messages. Unread messages display a closed envelope (✉) and appear in **bold**.

2 Click a message you want to read.

■ This area displays the contents of the message.

■ To view the contents of another message, click the message.

TIPS

How do I check for new messages?

- ✔ To check for new messages immediately, click the Send/Receive button. You can also press the F5 key to check for new messages.

What are the Journal and Outlook Update items displayed below the mail folders?

- ✔ The Journal feature helps you keep track of the activities you perform in Office, such as saving a Word document or sending an e-mail message. The Outlook Update feature allows you to automatically connect to the Microsoft Office Update page on the World Wide Web to fix bugs and add new capabilities to Office 2000.

Does Outlook ever automatically check for new messages?

- ✔ If you are connected to your e-mail server through a network, Outlook checks for new messages at regular intervals. To change how often Outlook checks for messages, choose the Tools menu, select Options and then click the Mail Delivery tab. In the minutes area beside the Check for new messages every option, double-click the number and then type the number of minutes you want to use. Then click OK.

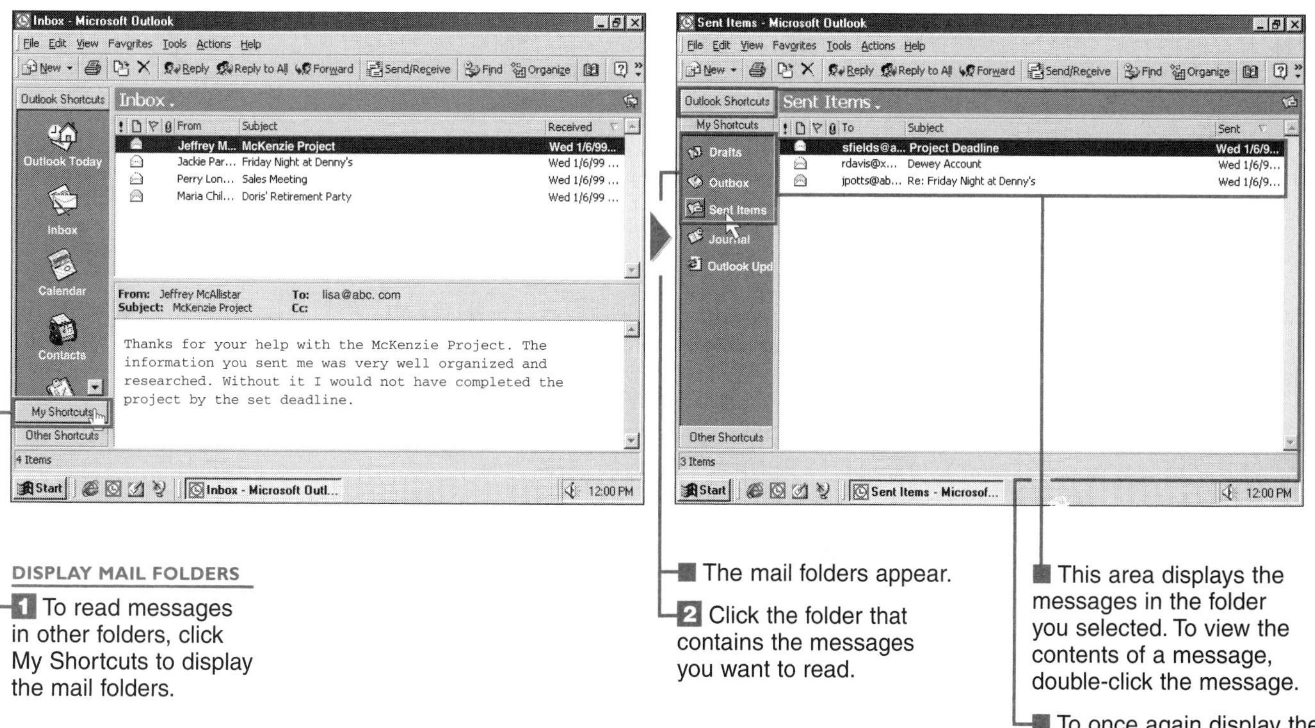

DISPLAY MAIL FOLDERS

1. To read messages in other folders, click My Shortcuts to display the mail folders.

- The mail folders appear.

2. Click the folder that contains the messages you want to read.

- This area displays the messages in the folder you selected. To view the contents of a message, double-click the message.
- To once again display the Outlook features and hide the mail folders, click Outlook Shortcuts.

WORK WITH MESSAGES

You can sort messages in Outlook so they are easier to find. You can sort by the name of the people who sent the messages, the subjects of the messages or the dates the messages were received. Messages can be sorted in ascending or descending order. Messages are usually sorted by the date they were received, in descending order.

You can delete a message you no longer need. Deleting messages prevents your mail folders from becoming cluttered with messages. When you delete a message, Outlook places the deleted message in the Deleted Items folder.

You can produce a paper copy of a message. A printed message is useful when you need a reference copy of the message. Outlook prints information such as the date and time the message was sent on the first page of the message. The page number appears at the bottom of each page of the printed message.

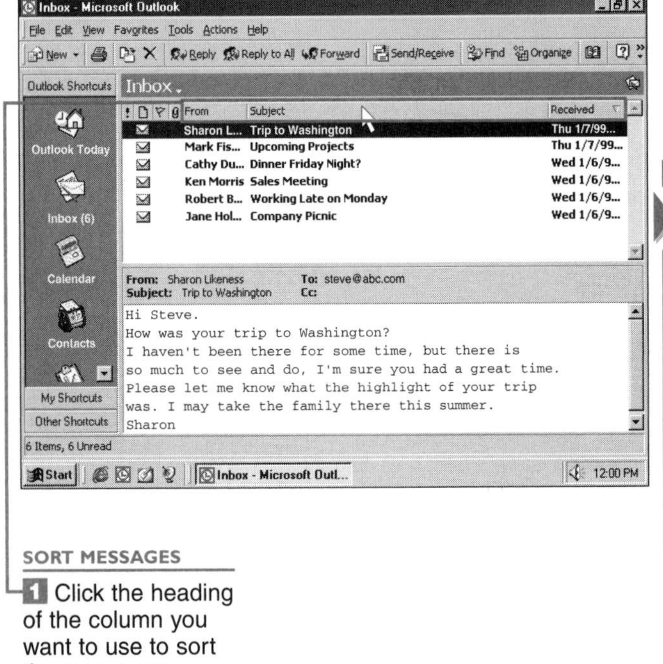

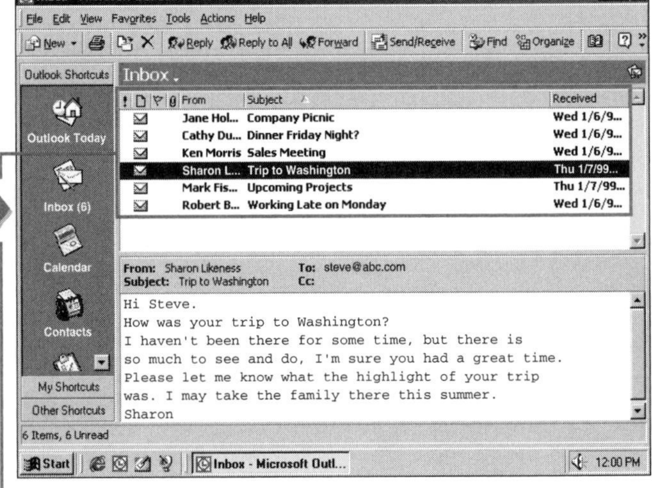

SORT MESSAGES

1 Click the heading of the column you want to use to sort the messages.

■ The messages appear in the new order. A small arrow (▲) appears in the heading of the column you used to sort the messages.

■ You can click the heading again to sort the messages in the opposite order.

TIPS

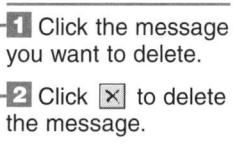

How can I change the width of a column?

✔ Position the mouse (pointer) over the right edge of the column heading you want to change (pointer changes to ✛). Drag the edge of the column until it displays the size you want.

Can I empty the Deleted Items folder?

✔ You can empty the Deleted Items folder to permanently remove deleted messages and all other items you deleted in Outlook from your computer. Click the Tools menu and then select Empty "Deleted Items" Folder.

Can I make a message appear as if I have not read it?

✔ Yes. This is useful if you want to remind yourself to review the message later. Click the message you want to appear as unread. From the Edit menu, select Mark as Unread.

Can I work with a message in another program?

✔ You can save a message as a file so you can work with the message in another program, such as Word. From the File menu, select Save As to save the message as a file. Type a name for the file and then click Save.

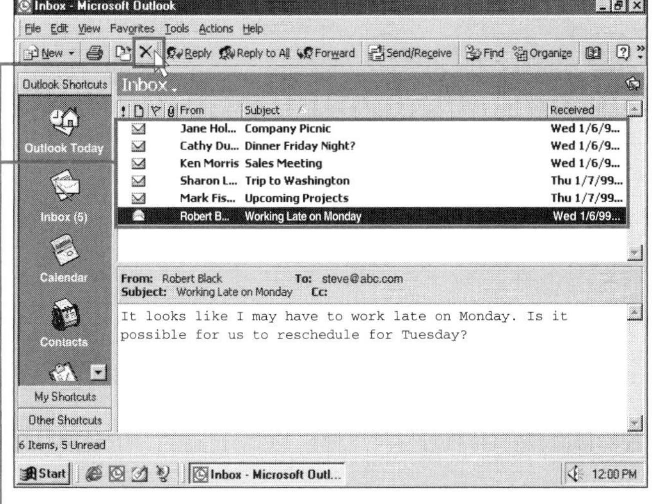

DELETE A MESSAGE

1. Click the message you want to delete.
2. Click ✕ to delete the message.

Note: If ✕ is not displayed, click » on the toolbar to display all the buttons.

■ Outlook places the message in the Deleted Items folder.

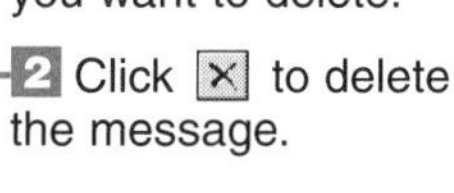

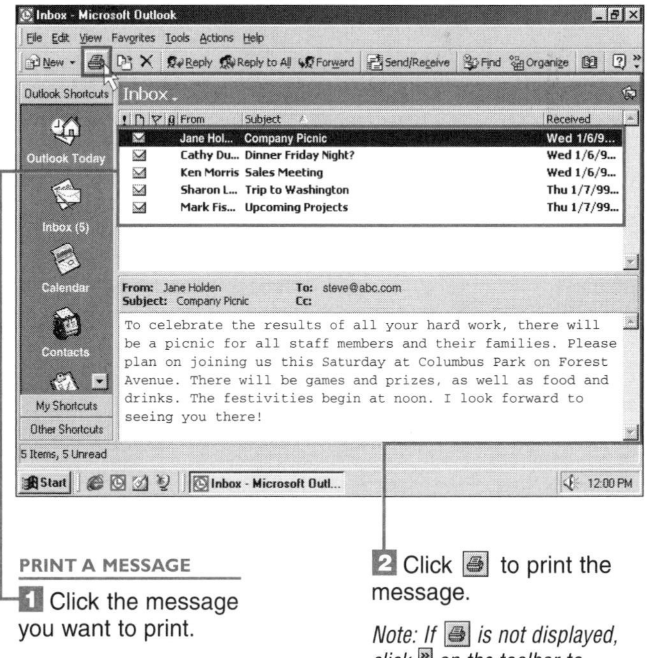

PRINT A MESSAGE

1. Click the message you want to print.
2. Click 🖨 to print the message.

Note: If 🖨 is not displayed, click » on the toolbar to display all the buttons.

CREATE A MESSAGE

You can create and send an e-mail message to exchange ideas or request information. To practice sending a message, you can send a message to yourself.

Outlook allows you to send a message to more than one person. You can enter the address of each person you want to receive the message in the To area. Entering an address in the Cc area allows you to send a copy of the message to a person who is not directly involved but would be interested in the message. Cc stands for carbon copy.

When you create a message, you should enter a subject that will help the reader quickly identify the contents of your message.

You can change the importance of a message to indicate its priority. You can select a low or high importance for the message. Depending on the e-mail program the recipient uses, the reader will see an arrow (↓) for a low importance message and an exclamation mark (!) for a high importance message.

Outlook stores a copy of the messages you send in the Sent Items folder.

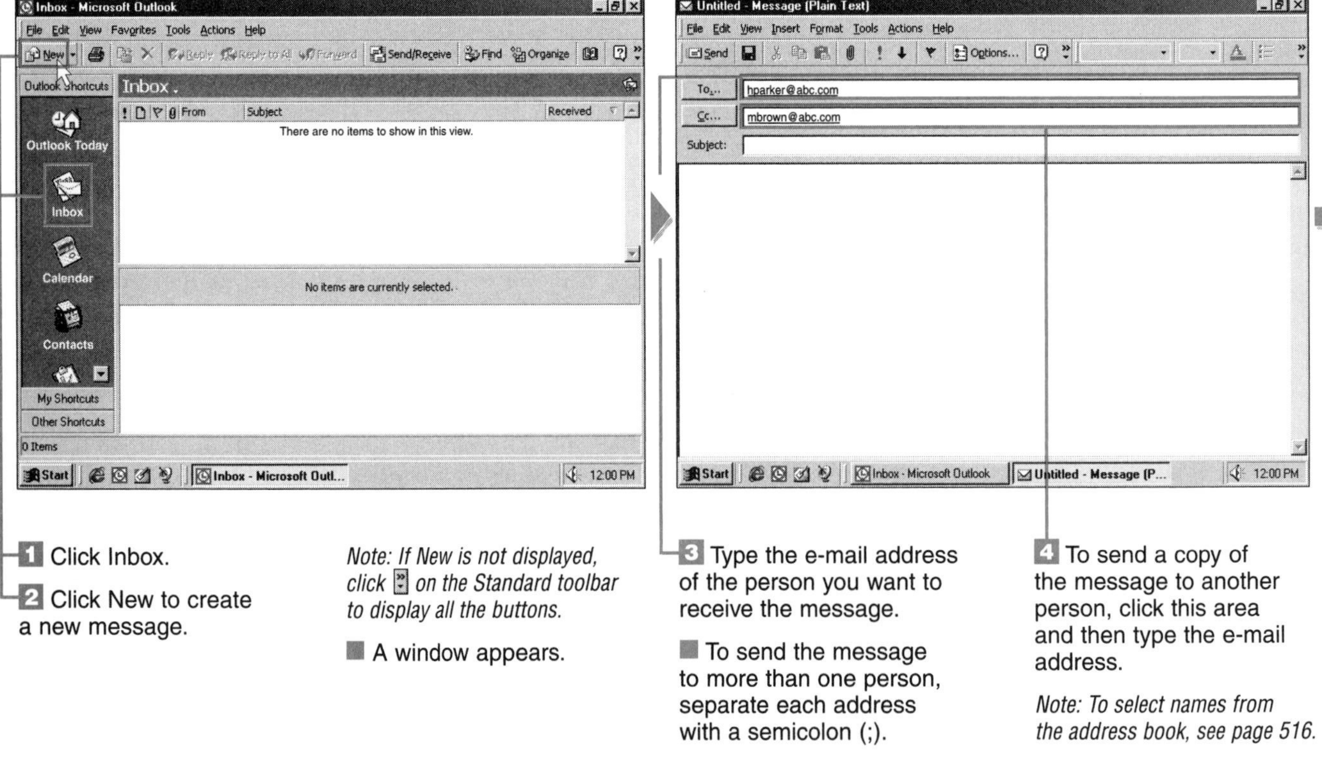

1 Click Inbox.

2 Click New to create a new message.

Note: If New is not displayed, click » on the Standard toolbar to display all the buttons.

■ A window appears.

3 Type the e-mail address of the person you want to receive the message.

■ To send the message to more than one person, separate each address with a semicolon (;).

4 To send a copy of the message to another person, click this area and then type the e-mail address.

Note: To select names from the address book, see page 516.

TIPS

Can I correct spelling errors in my message?

✔ To find and correct spelling errors in a message, select the Tools menu and then click Spelling to start the spell check.

How can I prevent Outlook from saving my messages in the Sent Items folder?

✔ In the Microsoft Outlook window, select the Tools menu, click Options and then choose the Preferences tab. Click the E-mail Options button and click the Save copies of messages in Sent Items folder option (☑ changes to ☐). Then click OK.

Can I use Word to edit my e-mail messages?

✔ Yes. Using Word to edit your e-mail messages lets you use Word's powerful editing features, such as automatic spell checking. In the Microsoft Outlook window, select the Tools menu, click Options and then choose the Mail Format tab. Click the Use Microsoft Word to edit e-mail messages option (☐ changes to ☑) and then click OK.

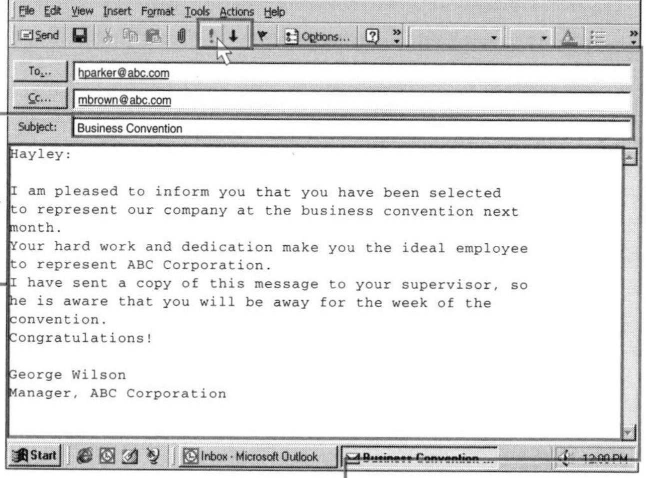

5 Click this area and then type the subject of the message.

6 Click this area and then type the message.

7 To indicate the importance of the message, click one of the following buttons.

! High importance

↓ Low importance

Note: If the button you want is not displayed, click » on the Standard toolbar to display all the buttons.

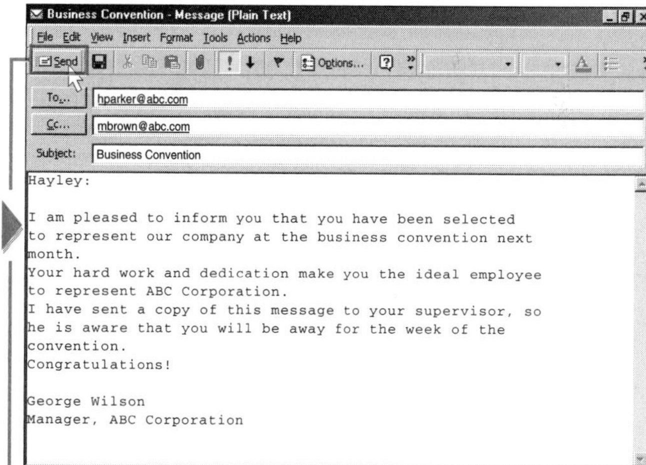

8 Click Send to send the message.

Note: If Send is not displayed, click » on the Standard toolbar to display all the buttons.

■ Outlook stores a copy of the message in the Sent Items folder.

SELECT A NAME FROM THE ADDRESS BOOK

When creating a message, you can select the name of the person you want to receive the message from an address book.

Using an address book makes it easy to send a message when you do not remember the exact spelling of the recipient's address. Using an address book also reduces the possibility that a message will be undeliverable because of a typing mistake in the address.

You can use an address book to send a message to more than one person. You can specify each person you want to receive the original message. You can also send a copy of the message, called a carbon copy (Cc), to another person. This is useful if you want to send a copy of the message to someone who would be interested in the message but is not directly involved. Using an address book also allows you to send a blind carbon copy (Bcc) of the message. A blind carbon copy lets you send a copy of the message to a person without anyone else knowing that the person received the message.

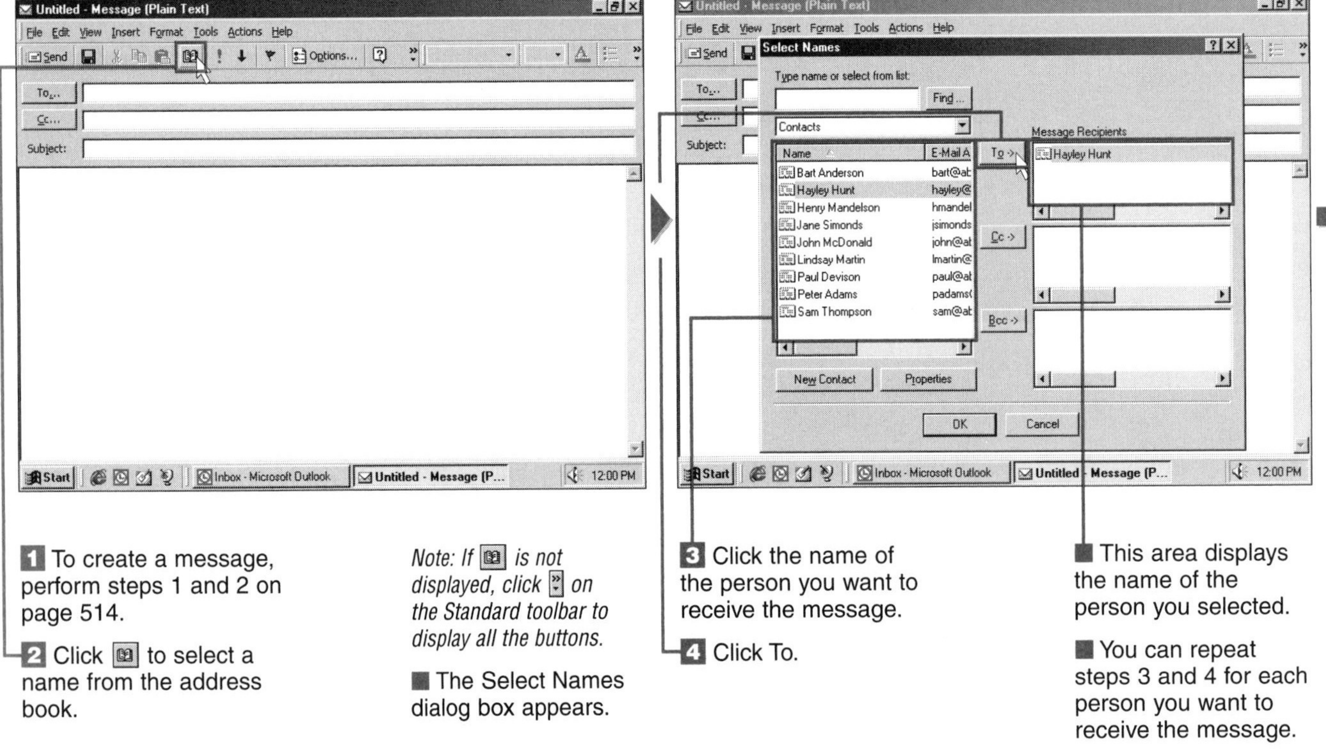

1 To create a message, perform steps 1 and 2 on page 514.

2 Click [address book icon] to select a name from the address book.

Note: If [address book icon] is not displayed, click [»] on the Standard toolbar to display all the buttons.

■ The Select Names dialog box appears.

3 Click the name of the person you want to receive the message.

4 Click To.

■ This area displays the name of the person you selected.

■ You can repeat steps 3 and 4 for each person you want to receive the message.

TIPS

How do I add a name to the address book?

✔ To add a name to the address book, you must add the person to your contact list. To add a person to your contact list, see page 532. To add a person to your contact list while working in the Select Names dialog box, click the New Contact button.

How can I quickly select a group of people from my address book?

✔ If you frequently send messages to the same group of people, you can create a distribution list to store information for all the people in the group. Choose the File menu, select New and then click Distribution List. Type a name for the list and then click the Select Members button. Double-click the name of each person you want to add to the list and then click OK. Click Save and Close to add the list to the address book. In the Select Names dialog box, you can select the name of the distribution list to send the message to the entire group.

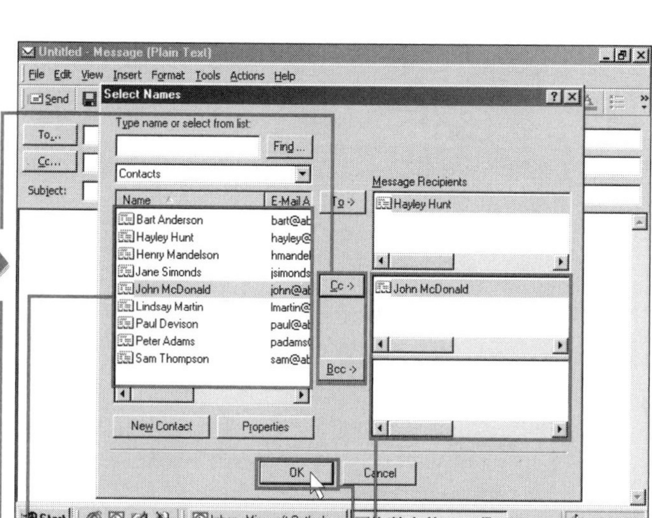

5 To send a copy of the message to another person, click the name of the person.

6 Click the type of copy you want to send.

■ This area displays the name of the person you selected.

■ You can repeat steps 5 and 6 for each person you want to receive a copy of the message.

7 Click OK.

■ This area displays the name of each person you selected from the address book.

■ You can now finish creating the message.

ATTACH A FILE TO A MESSAGE

You can attach a file to a message you are sending. Attaching a file is useful when you want to include additional information with a message.

Outlook allows you to attach many different types of files to a message, including images, documents, videos, sound recordings and program files.

The recipient of your message must have the necessary hardware and software installed on their computer to display or play the file you attach.

When you receive a message with an attached file, you can display or play the file. Messages with an attached file display a paper clip icon (📎). When you select an attached file you want to view, Outlook will ask if you want to open the file or save the file on your computer.

Some files, such as program files, can contain viruses. If you open and run a file that contains a virus, the virus could damage information on your computer. You should only open files sent by people you trust.

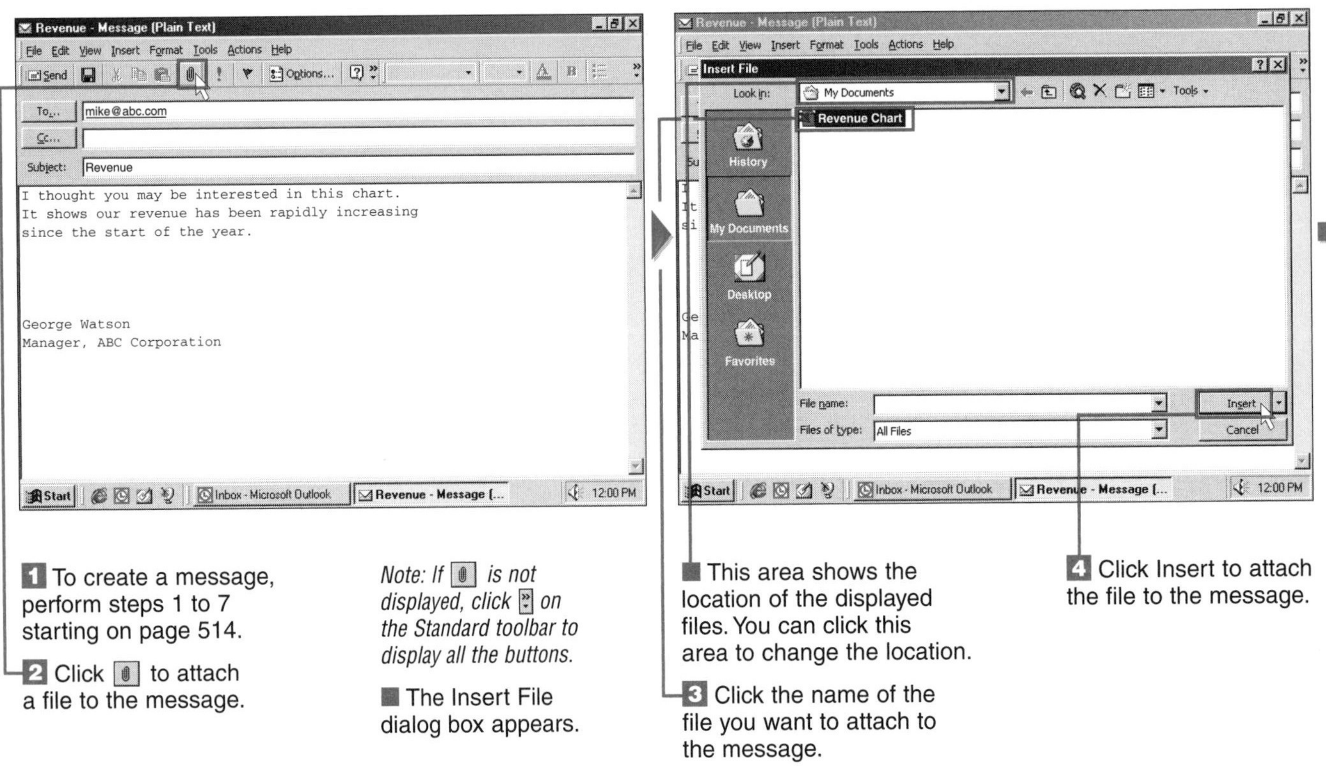

1 To create a message, perform steps 1 to 7 starting on page 514.

2 Click 📎 to attach a file to the message.

Note: If 📎 is not displayed, click » on the Standard toolbar to display all the buttons.

■ The Insert File dialog box appears.

■ This area shows the location of the displayed files. You can click this area to change the location.

3 Click the name of the file you want to attach to the message.

4 Click Insert to attach the file to the message.

TIPS

How do I remove a file I attached to a message?

✔ Click the icon for the file in the message and then press the Delete key.

Can I send a message with many attachments?

✔ While there is no restriction on the number of attachments you can send with a message, you may not be able to send a message that is very large. Many e-mail servers on the Internet will not transfer large messages properly, if at all. When sending e-mail messages over the Internet, you should keep the total size of attachments to less than 150 kilobytes.

How can I check an attached file for viruses before opening the file?

✔ You can use an anti-virus program to check a file for viruses. Anti-virus programs are available in computer stores and on the Internet. When Outlook asks if you want to open or save the attached file, save the file to a folder on your computer. You can then use an anti-virus program to check the file for viruses.

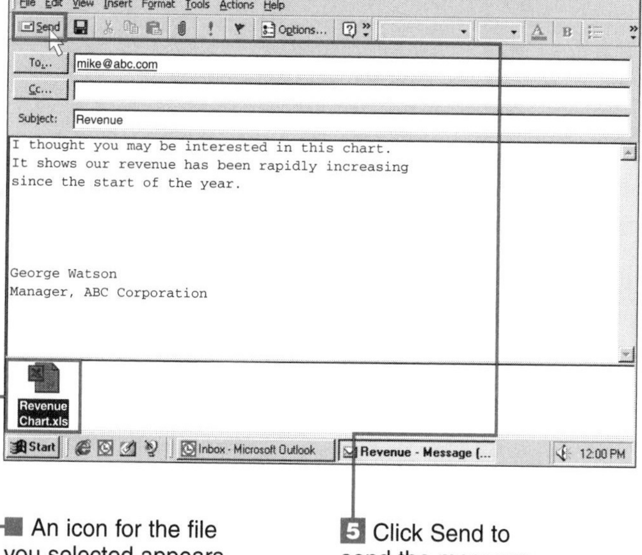

■ An icon for the file you selected appears in the message.

5 Click Send to send the message.

Note: If Send is not displayed, click ⁝ on the Standard toolbar to display all the buttons.

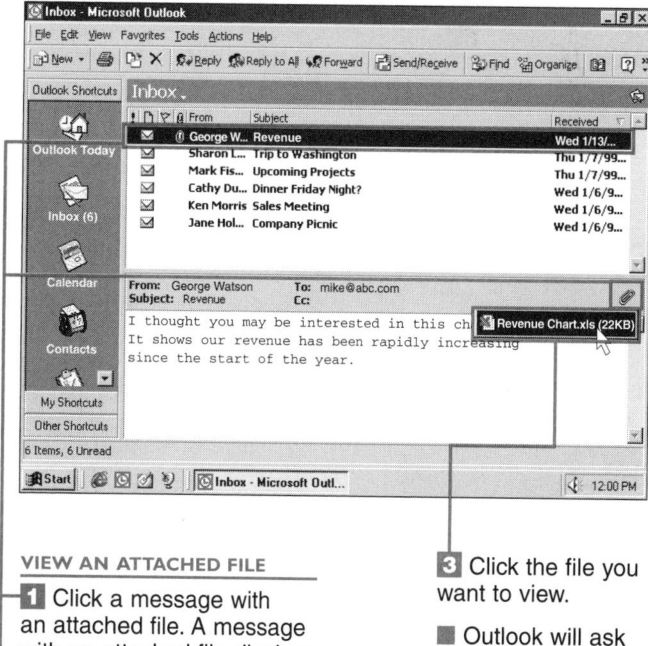

VIEW AN ATTACHED FILE

1 Click a message with an attached file. A message with an attached file displays a paper clip icon (📎).

2 Click this area to display a list of the files attached to the message.

3 Click the file you want to view.

■ Outlook will ask if you want to open or save the file.

REPLY TO OR FORWARD A MESSAGE

You can reply to a message to answer a question, express an opinion or supply additional information.

You can send a reply to just the person who sent the message or to the sender and everyone who received the original message.

When you reply to a message, a new window appears, displaying the name of the recipient(s) and the subject of the message you are replying to. The reply includes a copy of the original message. This is called quoting. Including a copy of the original message helps the reader identify which message you are replying to. To save the reader time, you should delete all parts of the original message that do not directly relate to your reply.

You can also forward a message to another person. When you forward a message, you can add your own comments to the original message. Forwarding a message is useful if you know that another person would be interested in the contents of the message.

Outlook stores a copy of each message you send in the Sent Items folder. For information on the mail folders, see page 511.

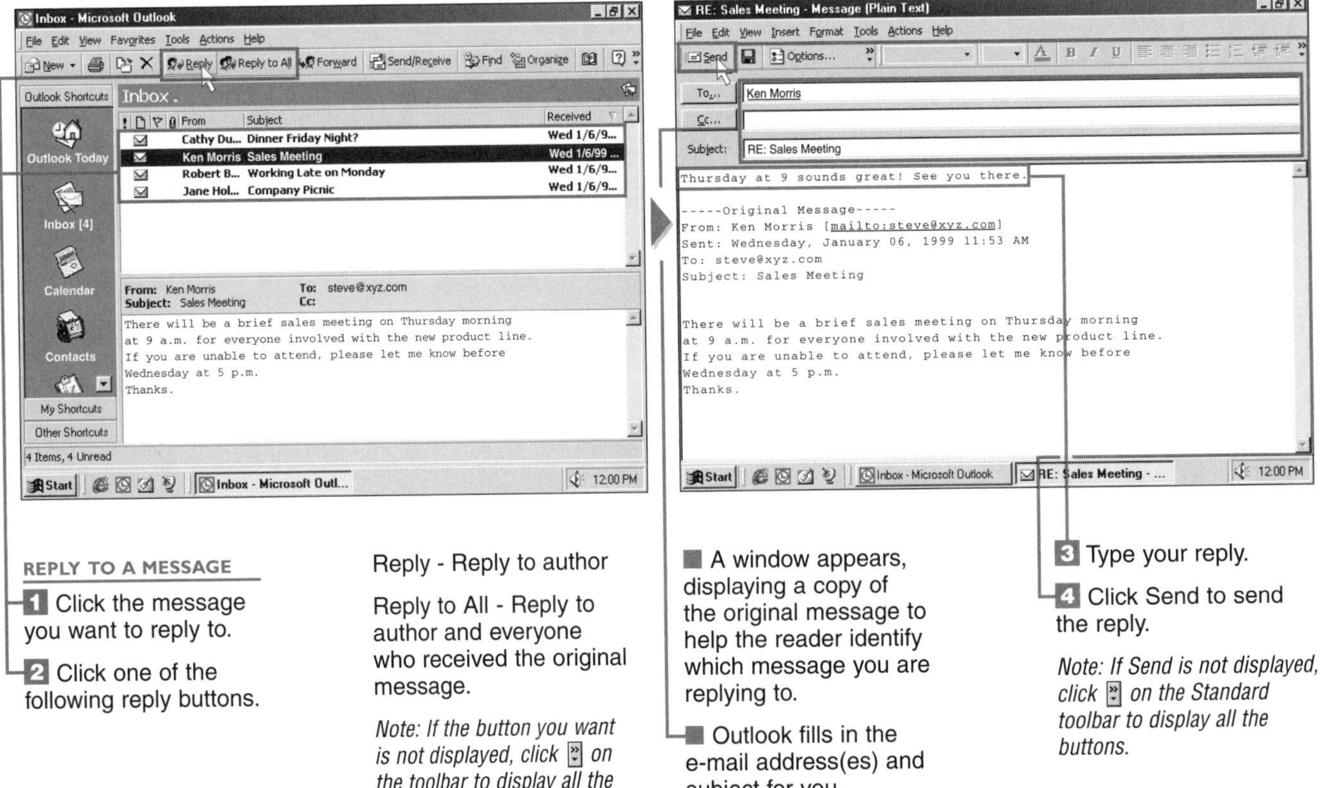

REPLY TO A MESSAGE

1 Click the message you want to reply to.

2 Click one of the following reply buttons.

Reply - Reply to author

Reply to All - Reply to author and everyone who received the original message.

Note: If the button you want is not displayed, click » on the toolbar to display all the buttons.

■ A window appears, displaying a copy of the original message to help the reader identify which message you are replying to.

■ Outlook fills in the e-mail address(es) and subject for you.

3 Type your reply.

4 Click Send to send the reply.

Note: If Send is not displayed, click » on the Standard toolbar to display all the buttons.

TIPS

Can I have Outlook automatically place people I reply to in my Contacts list?

✔ Yes. Choose the Tools menu and then click Options. Select the Preferences tab and then click the E-mail Options button. In the E-mail Options dialog box, select the Automatically put people I reply to in option (☐ changes to ☑). Then click OK.

How do I forward multiple messages?

✔ Hold down the Ctrl key as you click each message you want to forward. Then perform steps 2 to 5 on this page. If you forward more than one message at a time, the messages will be sent as attachments.

Can I prevent Outlook from including a copy of the original message in my replies?

✔ Yes. Choose the Tools menu and then click Options. Select the Preferences tab and then click the E-mail Options button. In the E-mail Options dialog box, click the When replying to a message area and select Do not include original message. Then click OK.

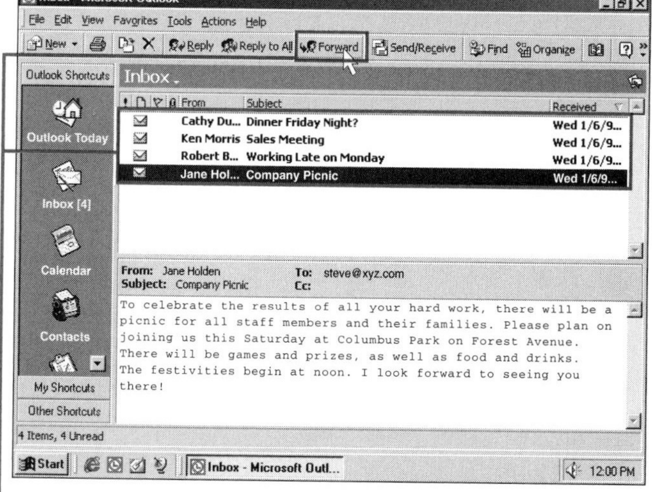

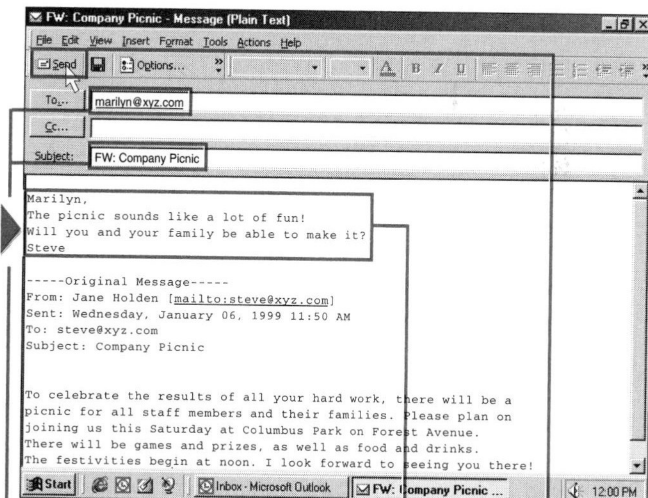

FORWARD A MESSAGE

1 Click the message you want to forward.

2 Click Forward.

Note: If Forward is not displayed, click » on the toolbar to display all the buttons.

■ A window appears, displaying the message you are forwarding.

3 Type the e-mail address of the person you want to receive the message.

Note: To select a name from the address book, see page 516.

■ Outlook fills in the subject for you.

4 Click this area and then type any comments about the message you are forwarding.

5 Click Send to forward the message.

Note: If Send is not displayed, click » on the Standard toolbar to display all the buttons.

NOTES

You can create electronic notes that are similar to the paper sticky notes often used in offices.

Notes are useful for storing small pieces of information such as reminders, questions, ideas and anything else you would record on note paper. Notes are often used to store information on a temporary basis.

When you create a note, Outlook records and saves the current date and time at the bottom of the note. This information helps you keep track of your notes and identify notes that are outdated.

You can open a note to read or edit the contents of the note. When you make changes to the contents of a note, the changes are automatically saved.

You can delete a note you no longer need. Deleting old notes reduces the number of notes on your screen and makes it easier to see new or important notes.

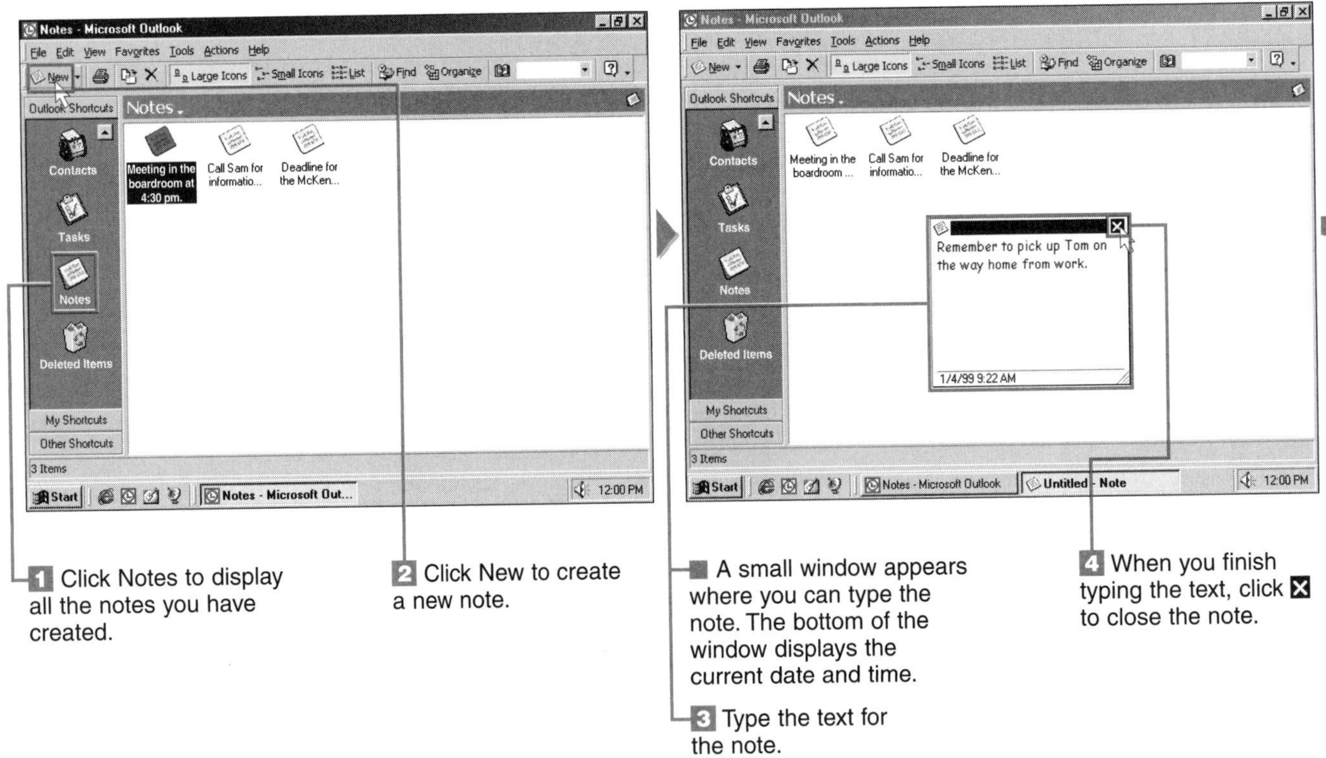

1 Click Notes to display all the notes you have created.

2 Click New to create a new note.

■ A small window appears where you can type the note. The bottom of the window displays the current date and time.

3 Type the text for the note.

4 When you finish typing the text, click ☒ to close the note.

TIPS

How do I change the size of a note?

✔ Display the contents of the note. Position the mouse over the bottom right corner of the note window (changes to ↘) and then drag the corner until the note displays the size you want.

Can I change the color of a note?

✔ By default, Outlook displays notes in yellow. You can change the color of a note to blue, green, pink or white. Display the contents of the note and then click the note icon in the top left corner of the note window. From the menu that appears, click Color and then select the color you want to use.

Can I locate a specific word or phrase in my notes?

✔ Yes. Click the Find button on the toolbar. The Find items in Notes pane appears at the top of the screen. In the Look for area, type the word or phrase you want to locate and then click Find Now. Outlook lists the notes that contain the word or phrase you specified. You can double-click a note to display its contents.

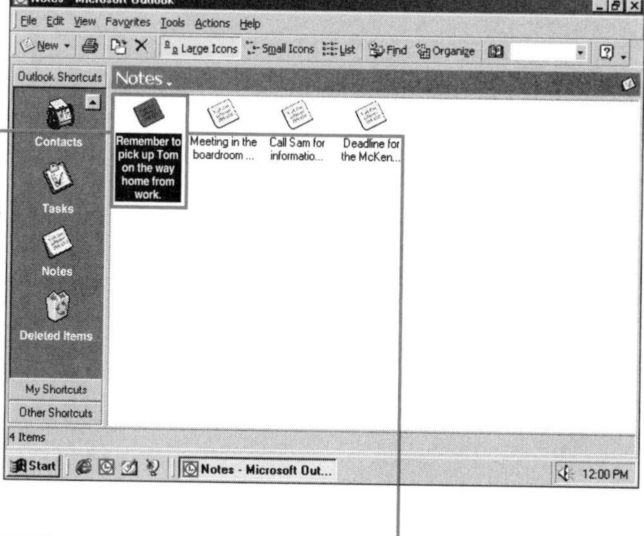

■ The note appears on the screen.

■ To open the note to display its contents, double-click the note.

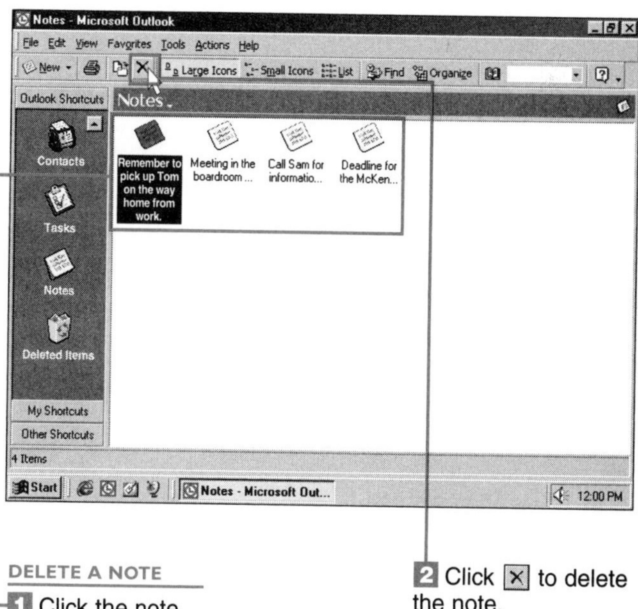

DELETE A NOTE

1 Click the note you want to delete.

2 Click ✕ to delete the note.

TASKS

The Tasks feature allows you to create an electronic to-do list of personal and work-related tasks that you want to accomplish. A task is a duty or errand you want to keep track of until it is complete.

When you create a new task, you should enter a descriptive subject that will help you recognize the task later, such as "submit marketing report" or "book airline reservations". The subject will appear in your task list.

You can specify a due date for a task. The due date will appear in your task list and can help remind you of upcoming deadlines.

Outlook allows you to specify the status and priority of a task. Setting the status of a task can help you monitor your progress. Assigning a priority can help you organize your tasks and budget your time. You can also add comments to a task to record details about the task.

You can change the information for a task at any time.

Outlook also displays your task list in the Calendar. For information on the Calendar, see page 528.

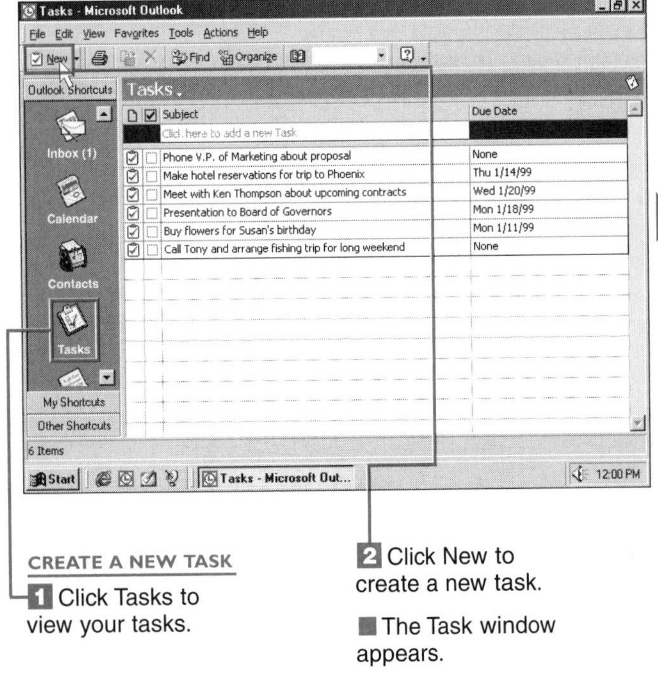

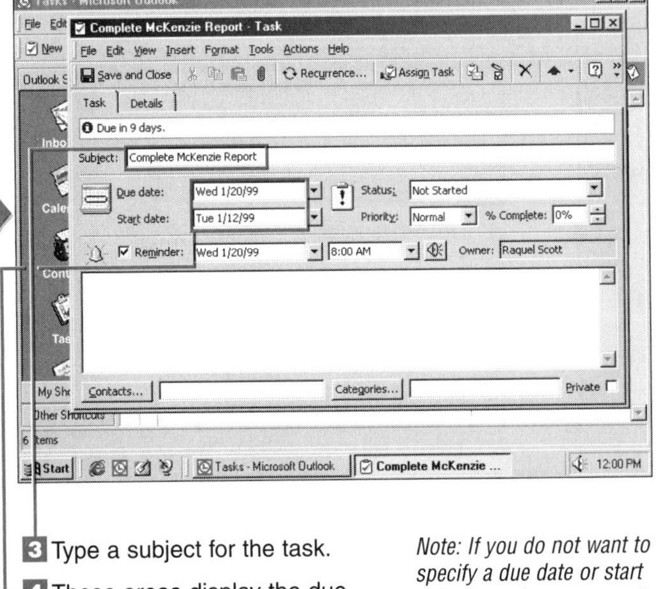

CREATE A NEW TASK

1 Click Tasks to view your tasks.

2 Click New to create a new task.

■ The Task window appears.

3 Type a subject for the task.

4 These areas display the due date and start date for the task. To change the information, drag the mouse I over the existing information and type the dates.

Note: If you do not want to specify a due date or start date, leave these areas set to "None".

Can I create a recurring task?

✔ Yes. Click the Recurrence button in the Task window. In the Task Recurrence dialog box, click the Daily, Weekly, Monthly or Yearly option to specify the frequency of the task (○ changes to ⊙). The available options vary depending on your selection. Select the options you want to use to specify when the task occurs.

Is there another way to create a new task?

✔ In the task list, click the area that says "Click here to add a new Task" and then type a subject for the task. To specify a due date, press the Tab key and then type the due date. Then press the Enter key.

Can I have Outlook remind me of a task?

✔ Yes. In the Task window, click the Reminder option (☐ changes to ☑). Then set the date and time for the reminder in the appropriate areas. Outlook will display a Reminder dialog box on your screen at the time you specify. If you specify a due date or start date after today's date, Outlook automatically turns on the Reminder option.

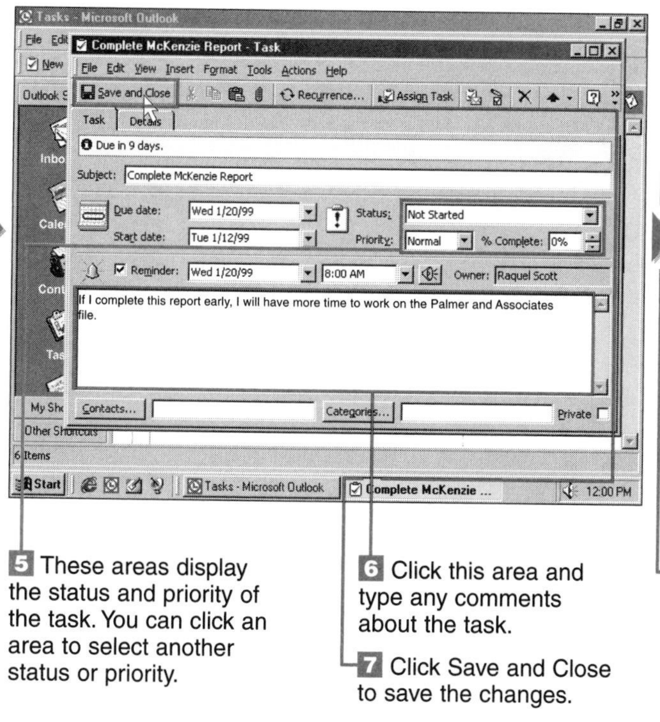

5 These areas display the status and priority of the task. You can click an area to select another status or priority.

6 Click this area and type any comments about the task.

7 Click Save and Close to save the changes.

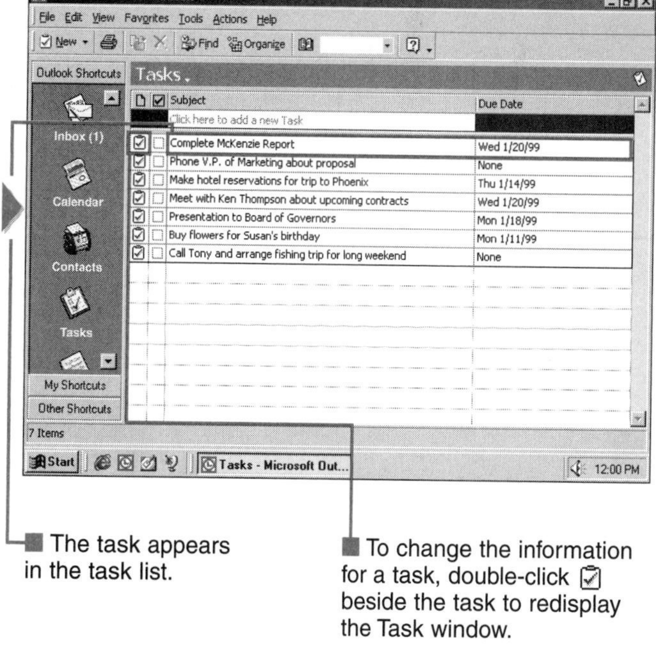

■ The task appears in the task list.

■ To change the information for a task, double-click ☑ beside the task to redisplay the Task window.

TASKS CONTINUED

You can sort the tasks in your task list by subject or due date to help you find tasks of interest. Tasks can be sorted in ascending or descending order.

Once you have accomplished a task, you can mark the task as complete. Outlook draws a line through each completed task. This allows you to see at a glance which tasks are outstanding and which tasks are complete.

You can delete a task you no longer want to display in your task list. Deleting tasks reduces clutter in your task list.

By default, Outlook displays your task list in the Simple List view. You can change the view of your tasks at any time. Outlook offers several views for you to choose from. For example, the Detailed List view displays details about each task, including the priority of the tasks. The Active Tasks view displays only tasks that are incomplete. The Next Seven Days view displays tasks that are due in the next week.

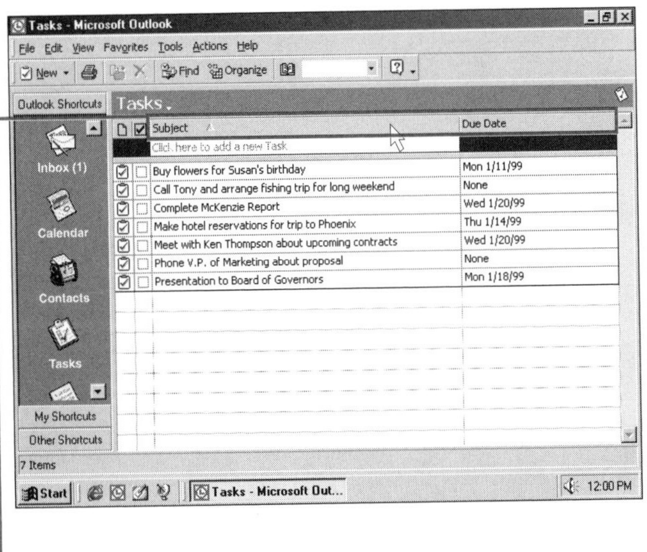

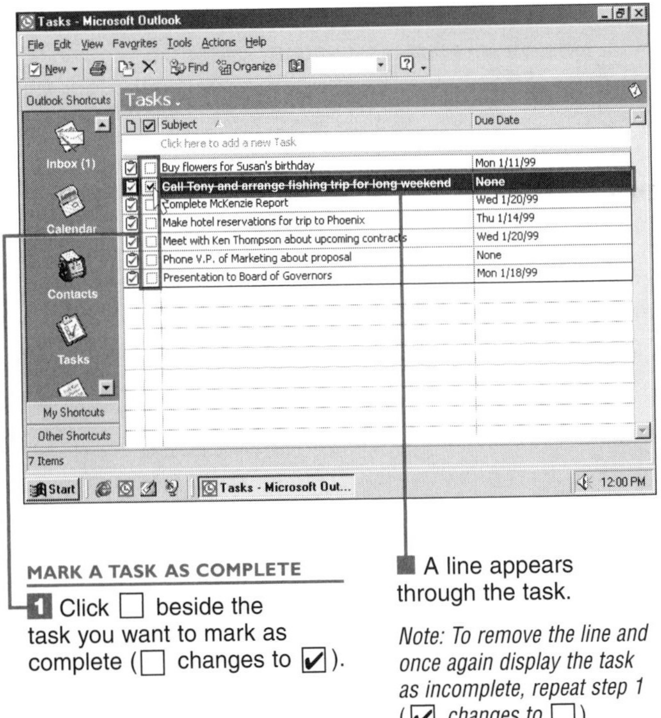

SORT TASKS

1 Click the heading of the column you want to use to sort the tasks. A small arrow (△) appears in the heading of the column.

■ You can click the heading again to sort the tasks in the opposite order.

MARK A TASK AS COMPLETE

1 Click ☐ beside the task you want to mark as complete (☐ changes to ☑).

■ A line appears through the task.

Note: To remove the line and once again display the task as incomplete, repeat step 1 (☑ changes to ☐).

Can I restore a task I have deleted?

✔ When you delete a task, Outlook places the task in the Deleted Items folder. To restore a task, click the Deleted Items icon in the Microsoft Outlook window and then drag the task you want to restore to the Tasks icon.

How do I display comments in my task list?

✔ If you entered comments about a task, you can display the first few lines of the comments in your task list. From the View menu, select AutoPreview. Repeat this procedure to once again hide the comments.

Can I change the color of tasks?

✔ You can change the color of overdue and completed tasks. Select the Tools menu, click Options and then choose the Preferences tab. Click the Task Options button to display the Task Options dialog box. Click the Overdue tasks area to select a new color for overdue tasks. Click the Completed tasks area to select a new color for completed tasks. Then click OK.

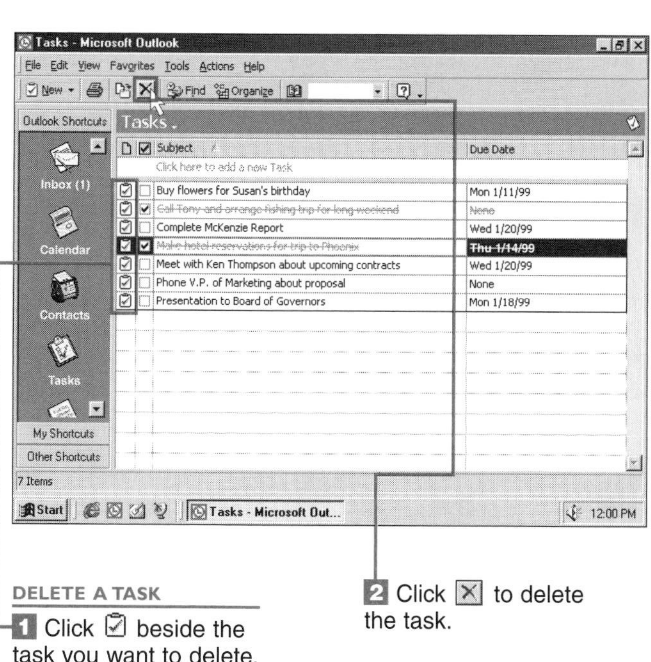

DELETE A TASK

1 Click ☑ beside the task you want to delete.

2 Click ☒ to delete the task.

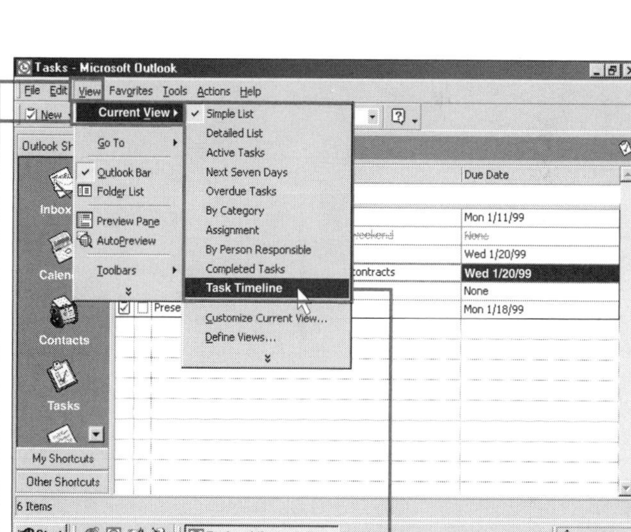

CHANGE VIEW OF TASKS

1 Click View.

2 Click Current View.

3 Click the way you want to view the tasks.

Note: A check mark (✔) appears beside the current view.

CALENDAR

You can use the Calendar to keep track of your appointments. An appointment can be an activity such as going to the dentist, attending a meeting or having lunch with a friend.

The Calendar displays the appointments you have scheduled for today. The Calendar also displays all the days in the current month and the next month. Today's date displays a red outline and days with appointments appear in bold. You can easily display the appointments for another day.

You can flip through all the months in the Calendar to view past or future appointments. Viewing past appointments is useful when you have to report the amount of time you spent working on a particular project.

The Calendar also displays a list of tasks you created using the Tasks feature. A task is a duty or errand you want to accomplish. For information on the Tasks feature, see page 524.

By default, the Calendar displays your appointments in the Day view. You can change the view to display your appointments in the Work Week, Week or Month view.

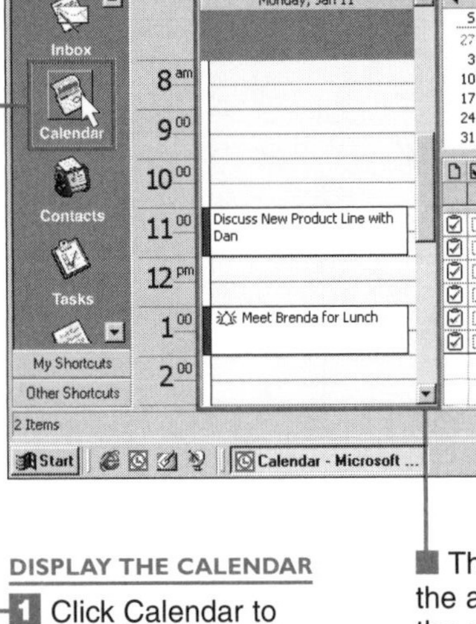

DISPLAY THE CALENDAR

1 Click Calendar to display the Calendar.

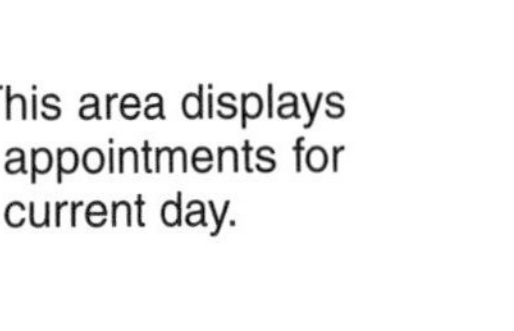

■ This area displays the appointments for the current day.

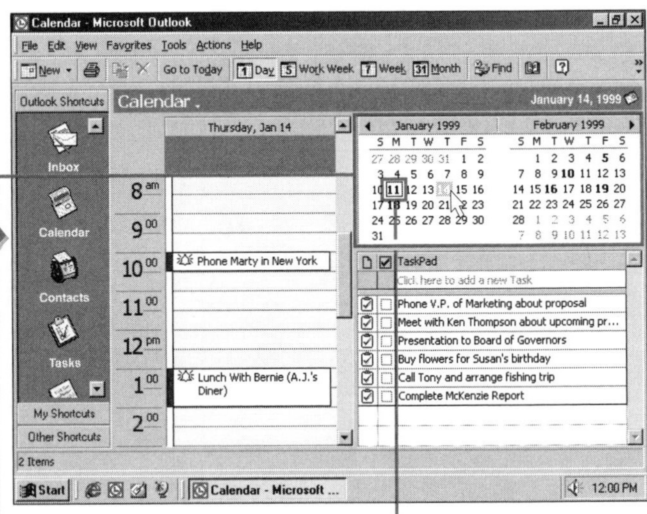

■ This area displays the days in the current month and the next month. Days with appointments are shown in bold.

2 To display the appointments for another day, click the day. The day you select is highlighted.

■ The current day displays a red outline.

Why is the Calendar displaying the wrong date for today?

✔ Outlook uses the date and time set in your computer to determine today's date. Your computer's clock may be set incorrectly. Refer to your Windows documentation to set the correct date and time.

Are there other views available in the Calendar?

✔ The Calendar also offers the Active Appointments, Events, Annual Events, Recurring Appointments and By Category views. To change to one of these views, choose the View menu and select Current View. Then select the view you want to use.

How do I quickly display today's appointments?

✔ You can click the Go to Today button at any time to display today's appointments.

How do I add holidays to the Calendar?

✔ Click the Tools menu and select Options. Choose the Preferences tab and then click the Calendar Options button. Click the Add Holidays button and then select the country for the holidays you want to add (☐ changes to ☑).

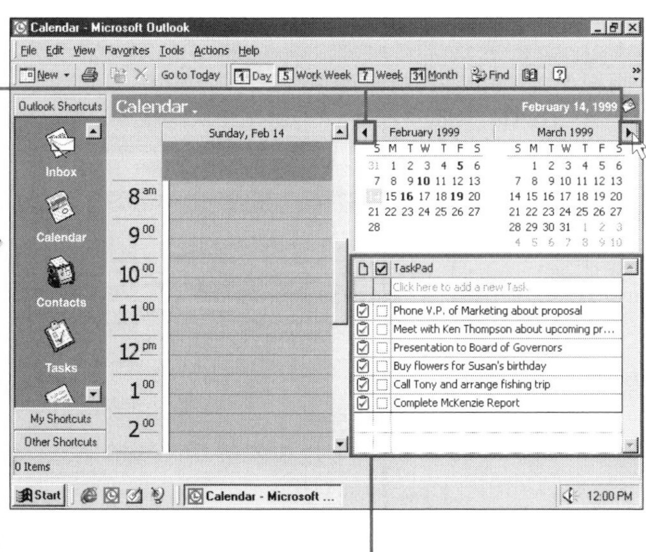

3 To display the days in the previous or next month, click ◄ or ►.

■ This area displays tasks. See page 524 for information on tasks.

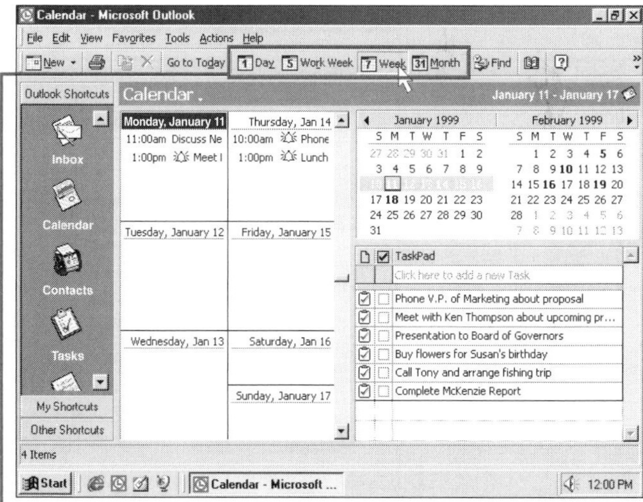

CHANGE VIEW OF CALENDAR

1 Click the way you want to view the Calendar.

1 Day	Day
5 Work Week	Work Week
7 Week	Week
31 Month	Month

Note: If the button you want is not displayed, click » on the toolbar to display all the buttons.

CALENDAR CONTINUED

You can add an appointment to the Calendar to remind you of an activity such as a seminar or doctor's appointment.

The Calendar allows you to enter information about each appointment you want to schedule. You should enter a subject for an appointment. The subject is the description of an appointment that appears in the Calendar. You can also enter the location for an appointment and add comments about the appointment.

When you enter a start date, end date or time for an appointment, you can type text such as "next Tuesday", "tomorrow" or "noon" instead of typing a date or time. Outlook will play a brief sound and display a dialog box 15 minutes before a scheduled appointment.

If an appointment will last an entire day, you can make the appointment an all day event. Outlook displays an all day event just below the date in the Calendar. You can still schedule other appointments after scheduling an all day event.

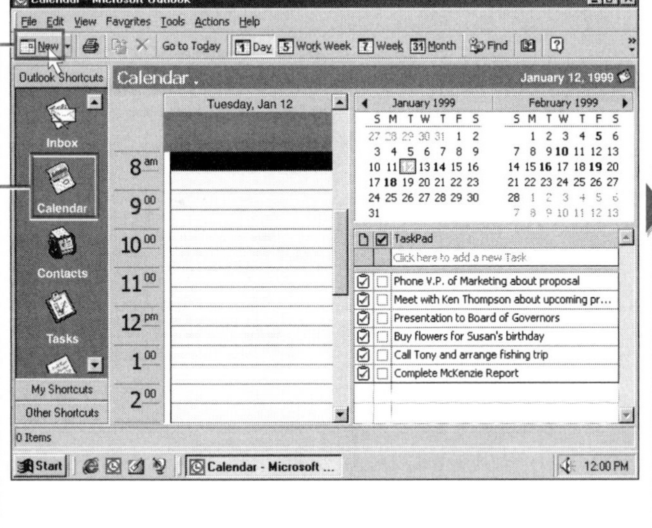

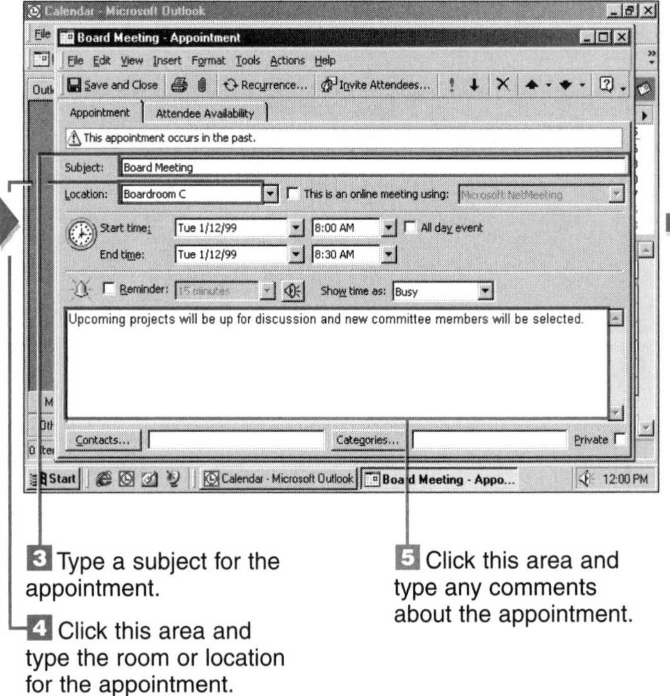

SCHEDULE AN APPOINTMENT

1 Click Calendar to display the Calendar.

2 Click New to schedule an appointment.

Note: If New is not displayed, click » on the toolbar to display all the buttons.

■ The Appointment window appears.

3 Type a subject for the appointment.

4 Click this area and type the room or location for the appointment.

5 Click this area and type any comments about the appointment.

How can I quickly schedule an appointment?

✔ In the Day view, drag the mouse pointer over the yellow area to select the time for the appointment. Type a subject for the appointment and then press the Enter key.

How do I print the information in the Calendar?

✔ Click the Print button (🖨) on the toolbar to display the Print dialog box. In the Print Style area, click the print style you want to use. Click ▾ in the Start area and choose the first date you want to print. Click ▾ in the End area and choose the last date you want to print. Then click OK.

Can I schedule a recurring appointment?

✔ You can schedule a recurring appointment, such as a birthday or weekly meeting. In the Appointment window, click the Recurrence button. In the Appointment Recurrence dialog box, specify the information about the recurring appointment.

How do I delete an appointment?

✔ You can delete an appointment that has been cancelled or that you no longer want to keep. Click the left side of the appointment and then click the Delete button (☒).

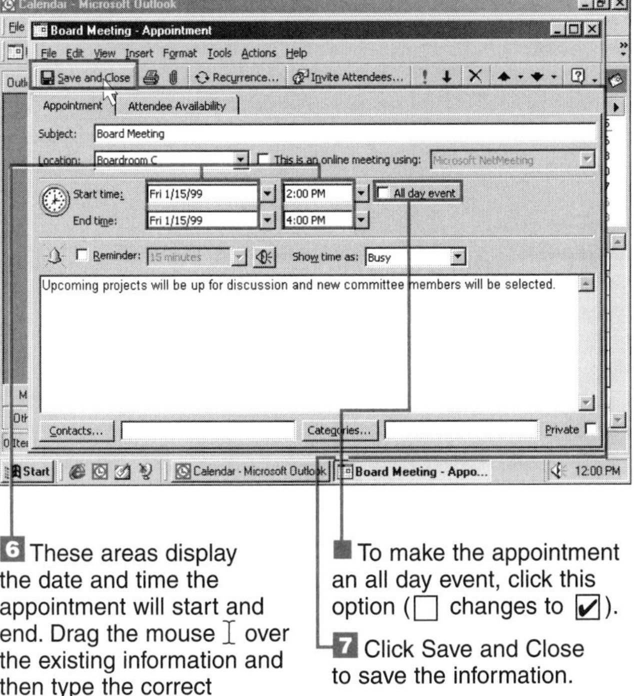

6 These areas display the date and time the appointment will start and end. Drag the mouse I over the existing information and then type the correct information.

■ To make the appointment an all day event, click this option (☐ changes to ☑).

7 Click Save and Close to save the information.

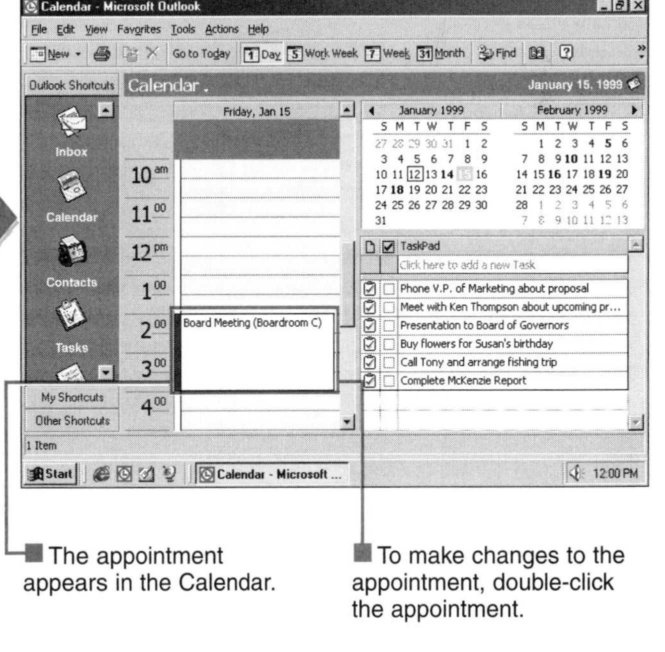

■ The appointment appears in the Calendar.

■ To make changes to the appointment, double-click the appointment.

CONTACTS

Outlook supplies a contacts list where you can keep detailed information about your friends, family members, colleagues and clients.

When you add a contact to the list, Outlook provides spaces for you to enter information about the contact. You can enter the contact's full name, job title, company name and address. You can also enter the contact's business phone, home phone, business fax and mobile phone numbers. The contact's e-mail address, comments about the contact and the contact's Web page address can also be included. You do not need to enter information in all the spaces Outlook provides.

You can update or add additional information to a contact in your list at any time. Over time, friends and colleagues may move and you will need to record their new addresses. Also, as you learn more about your contacts, you can add information such as directions to their house or the names of their children.

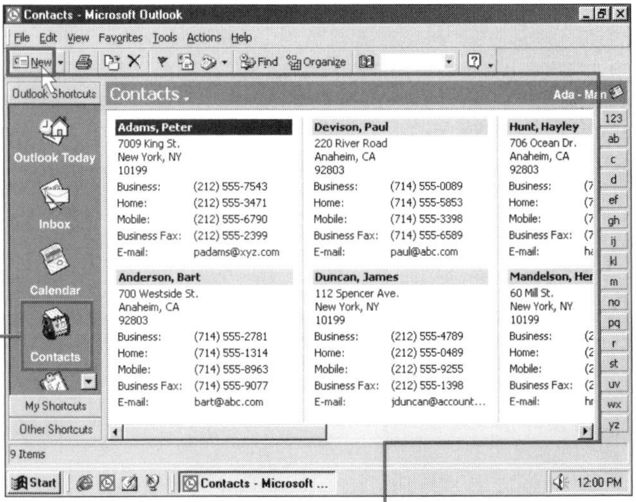

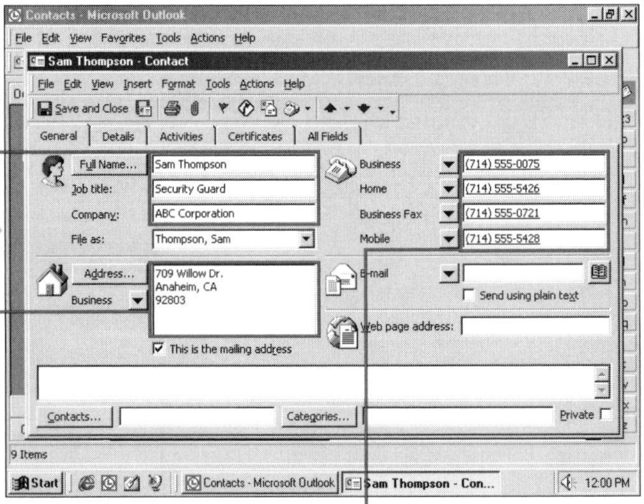

CREATE A NEW CONTACT

1 Click Contacts to display your contacts.

2 Click New to create a new contact.

■ The Contact window appears.

3 Click an area and type the contact's full name, job title and company name.

4 Click this area and type the contact's address.

5 Click an area and type the business, home, business fax and mobile phone numbers.

Why did the Check Address dialog box appear after I entered an address?

✔ If the address you entered is incomplete, the Check Address dialog box appears, to help you complete the address.

Where can I enter more information about a contact?

✔ In the Contact window, click the Details tab. You can enter personal information about the contact, such as the contact's birthday and the name of the contact's spouse.

Can I view a list of e-mail messages I have exchanged with a contact?

✔ Yes. In the Contact window, click the Activities tab. This tab displays a summary of Outlook items, such as e-mail messages and tasks, that relate to the contact.

Can I display a map showing a contact's address?

✔ If a contact's address is in the United States, you can view a map for the address. In the Contact window, click the Display Map of Address button ( ). Your Web browser opens and displays the map.

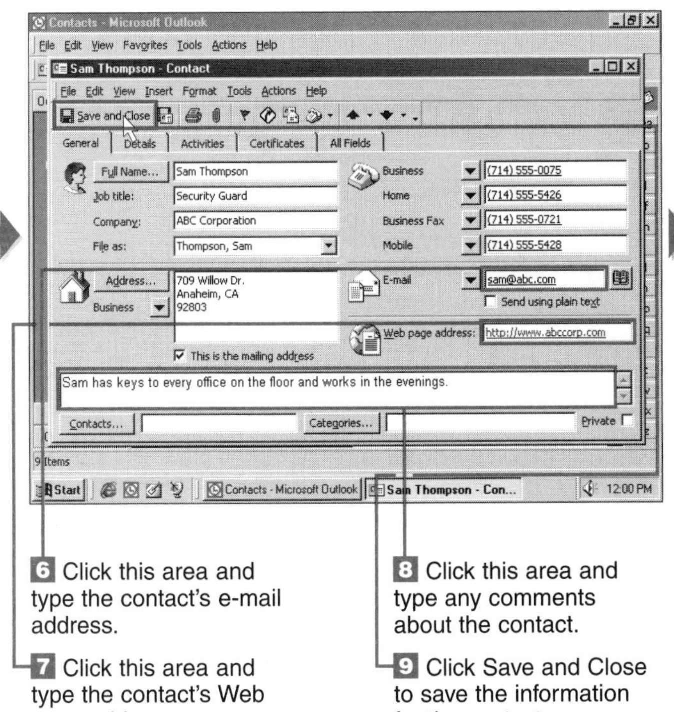

6 Click this area and type the contact's e-mail address.

7 Click this area and type the contact's Web page address.

8 Click this area and type any comments about the contact.

9 Click Save and Close to save the information for the contact.

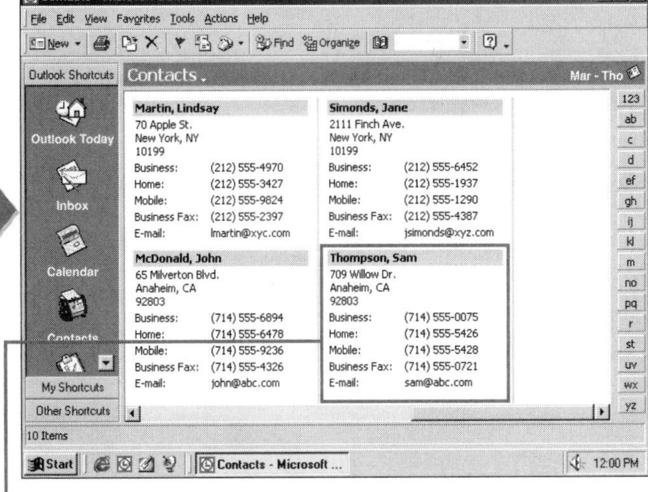

■ The contact appears in the contact list.

■ To change the information for a contact, double-click the contact to redisplay the Contact window.

CONTACTS CONTINUED

Like a paper address book, the contact list displays tabs you can use to browse through your contacts alphabetically. When you select a tab, Outlook displays all the contacts that begin with the letters on the tab.

You can delete a contact you no longer need. This can help make the contact list smaller and easier to manage.

Outlook offers several ways you can display the contact list. You can choose the view that best suits your needs. The Address Cards view displays the mailing address, phone numbers and e-mail address for each contact. The Detailed Address Cards view is useful when you want to display all the information for each contact. The Phone List view lists the business phone, business fax, home phone and mobile phone numbers for each contact. You can also choose a view that groups related contacts together, such as the By Category, By Company or By Location view.

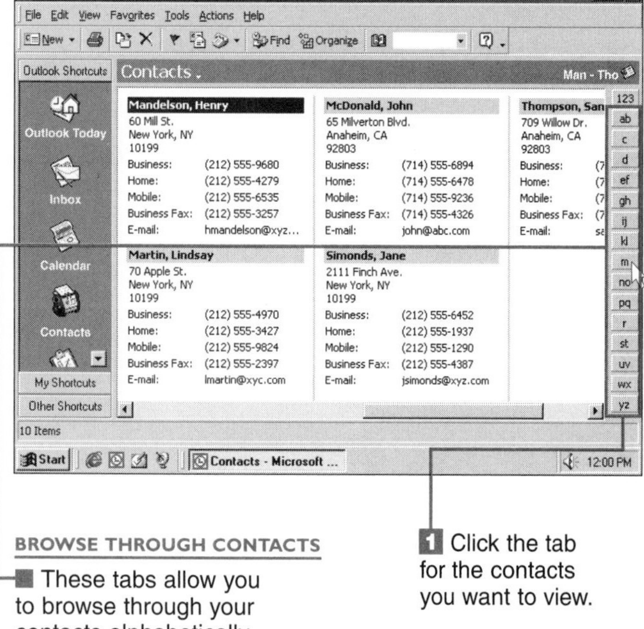

BROWSE THROUGH CONTACTS

■ These tabs allow you to browse through your contacts alphabetically.

1 Click the tab for the contacts you want to view.

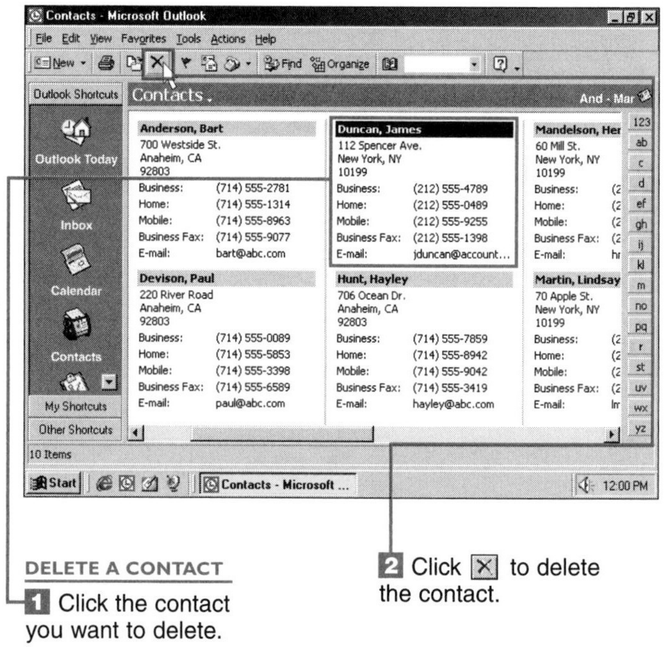

DELETE A CONTACT

1 Click the contact you want to delete.

2 Click ☒ to delete the contact.

Can I restore a contact I have deleted?

✔ When you delete a contact, Outlook places the contact in the Deleted Items folder. To restore a contact, click the Deleted Items icon in the Microsoft Outlook window and then drag the contact you want to restore to the Contacts icon.

How do I print the information for a contact?

✔ In the contact list, click the contact whose information you want to print and then click the Print button (🖨). In the Print range area, click the Only selected items option (○ changes to ⦿) and then click OK.

Can I quickly send an e-mail message to a contact?

✔ You can quickly send an e-mail message to a contact if you entered an e-mail address for the contact. In the contact list, click the contact you want to send a message to and then click the New Message to Contact button (). Outlook automatically displays the contact's e-mail address in the To area of the message.

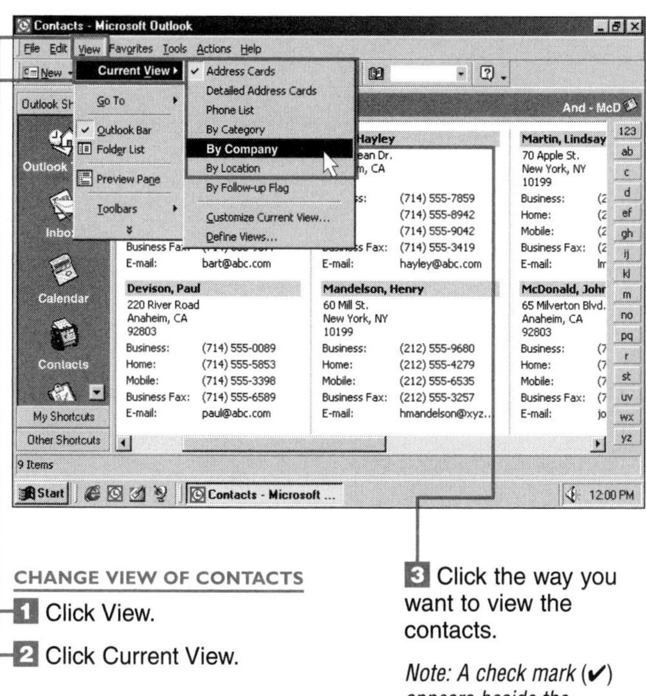

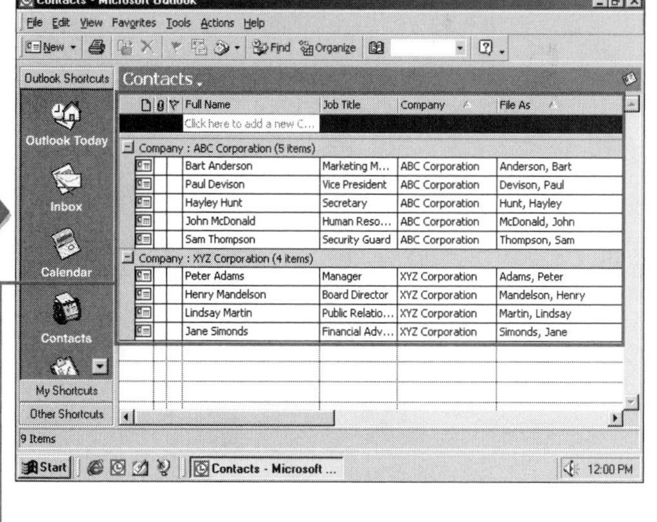

CHANGE VIEW OF CONTACTS

1 Click View.

2 Click Current View.

3 Click the way you want to view the contacts.

Note: A check mark (✔) appears beside the current view.

■ The contacts appear in the new view.

SECTION VII

1) GETTING STARTED

2) ENHANCE A PUBLICATION

USING PUBLISHER

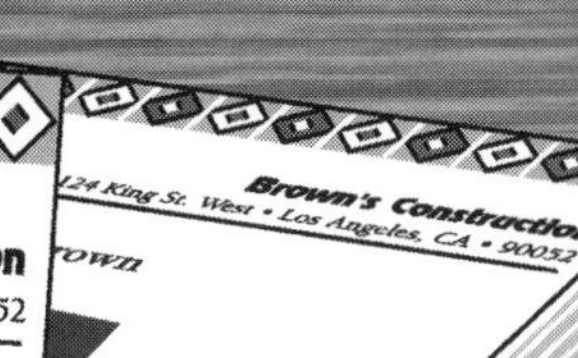

START PUBLISHER

Publisher is a desktop publishing program that helps you design professional publications. You can use Publisher to produce a wide variety of publications, such as newsletters, brochures, catalogs, flyers, invitations and banners.

Each time you start Publisher, the Catalog dialog box appears. This dialog box allows you to create a new publication or open an existing publication.

You can create a new publication using a wizard. The wizard takes you step by step through the process of creating a publication and provides sample text and formatting for the publication.

Using the wizards included with Publisher can help you easily create publications that share a common design and color scheme. This lets you give your organization's publications a consistent and professional appearance.

You can also create a new publication using a blank publication. Using a blank publication lets you create a publication without any sample text or formatting provided by Publisher.

For more information on Publisher, you can visit the following Web site: www.microsoft.com/publisher

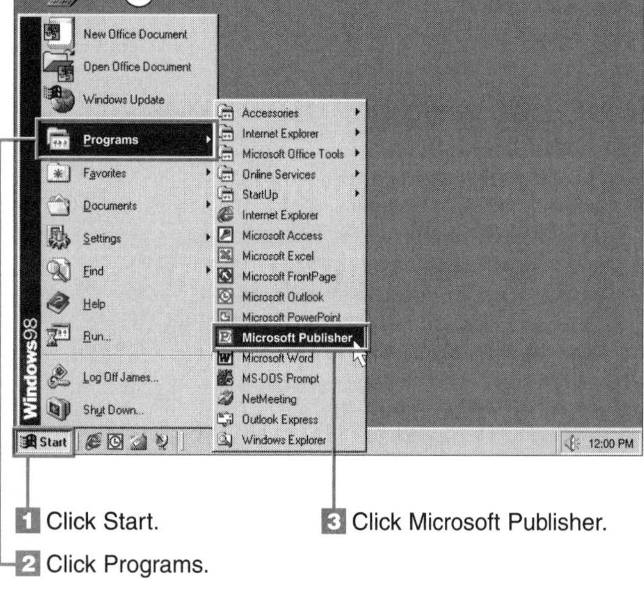

1 Click Start.

2 Click Programs.

3 Click Microsoft Publisher.

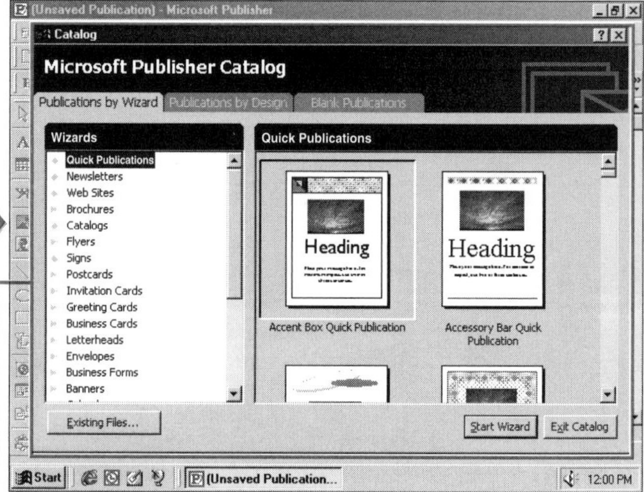

■ The Microsoft Publisher window appears.

■ The Catalog dialog box appears each time you start Publisher, allowing you to create a new publication or open an existing publication.

Note: To create a new publication, see page 540 or 544. To open an existing publication, see page 550.

THE PUBLISHER SCREEN

The Publisher screen displays several items to help you perform tasks efficiently.

Menu Bar

Provides access to lists of commands available in Publisher.

Standard Toolbar

Contains buttons to help you select common commands, such as Save and Print.

Formatting Toolbar

Contains buttons to help you select formatting commands. The available buttons depend on the currently selected object.

Objects Toolbar

Contains buttons to help you add objects, such as text frames, pictures and shapes, to the publication.

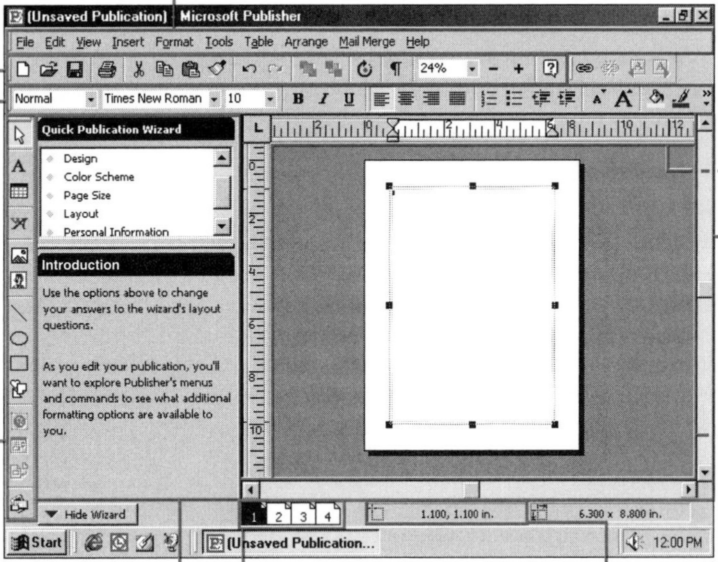

Rulers

Help you align objects in the publication.

Scroll Bars

Allow you to move through the current page in the publication.

Publication Area

Displays the publication you are currently working with.

Wizard

Allows you to change the options for the current publication, such as the design and color scheme.

Page Navigation Control

Allows you to switch between the pages in the publication.

Object Position

Displays the position of the currently selected object or the mouse pointer from the left and top edges of the current page, in inches.

CREATE A PUBLICATION USING A WIZARD

You can use a wizard to save time when creating a publication. A wizard guides you step by step through the process of creating a publication. A wizard also provides the layout and formatting of a publication so you can concentrate on the content.

Publisher provides wizards to help you create many common types of publications, such as newsletters, brochures, business cards and advertisements. Each type of publication offers various designs you can choose from.

Each time you start Publisher, the Catalog dialog box appears, displaying the available wizards. When you select a wizard, you will be asked a series of questions. The wizard uses your answers to create the publication. Publisher displays your publication beside the wizard's questions. As you answer the wizard's questions, the results of your choices immediately appear in the publication. If you do not like the results, you can return to a previous question and change your answers at any time.

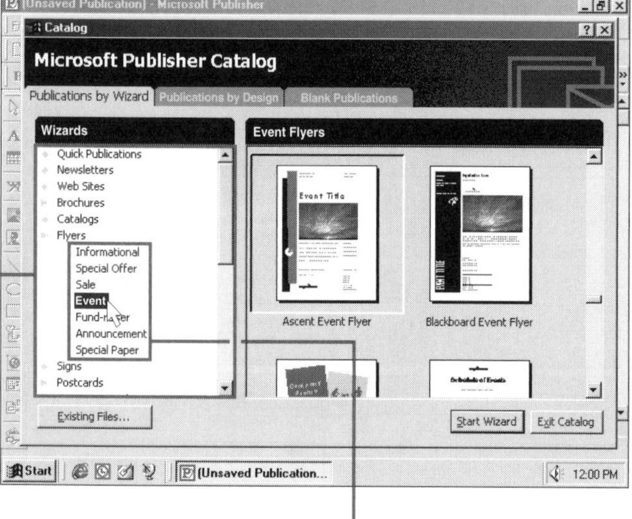

■ The Catalog dialog box appears each time you start Publisher.

1 Click the wizard for the type of publication you want to create.

2 Additional wizards may appear. Click the wizard you want to use.

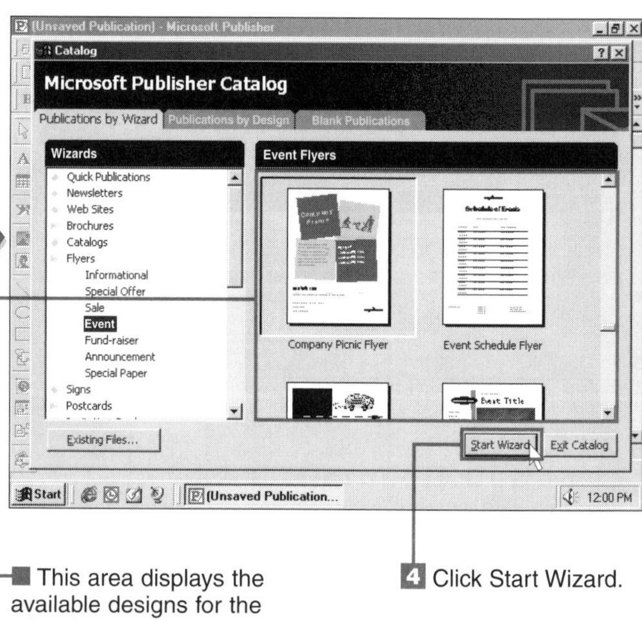

■ This area displays the available designs for the wizard you selected.

3 Click the design you want to use.

4 Click Start Wizard.

Why did a message appear, asking for my personal information?

✔ Publisher asks you for your personal information the first time you use a wizard. Some publications, such as business cards, require personal information. Click OK to display the Personal Information dialog box. Enter your information and then click Update.

Can I use a wizard to create a new publication while working in Publisher?

✔ Yes. From the File menu, select New to display the Catalog dialog box. You can then perform the steps below to create a new publication. Publisher will ask you to save the publication displayed on your screen before creating a new publication.

Can Publisher help me create publications that share a similar design?

✔ Publisher provides design sets that contain a variety of publications with a similar design. For example, the Holiday design set contains invitations, greeting cards and newsletters with a holiday theme. To create a publication from a design set, select the Publication by Design tab in the Catalog dialog box and choose a design set. Select the type of publication you want to create and then click Start Wizard.

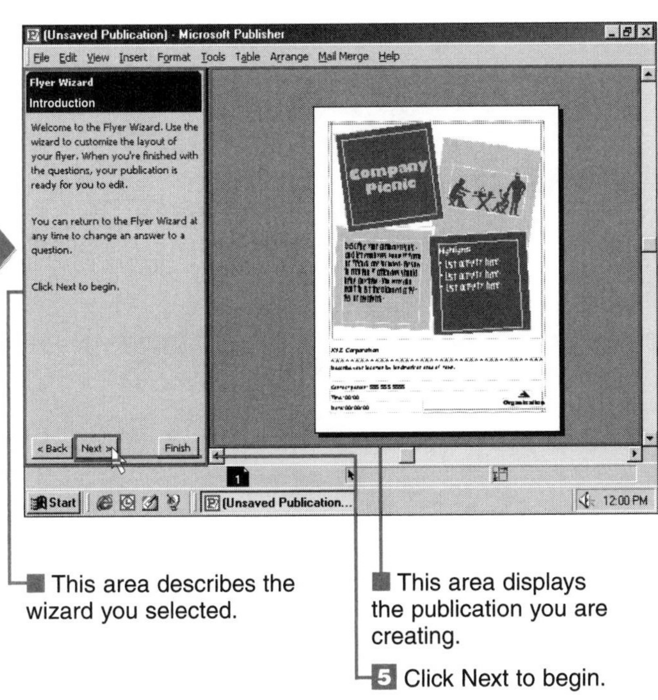

■ This area describes the wizard you selected.

■ This area displays the publication you are creating.

5 Click Next to begin.

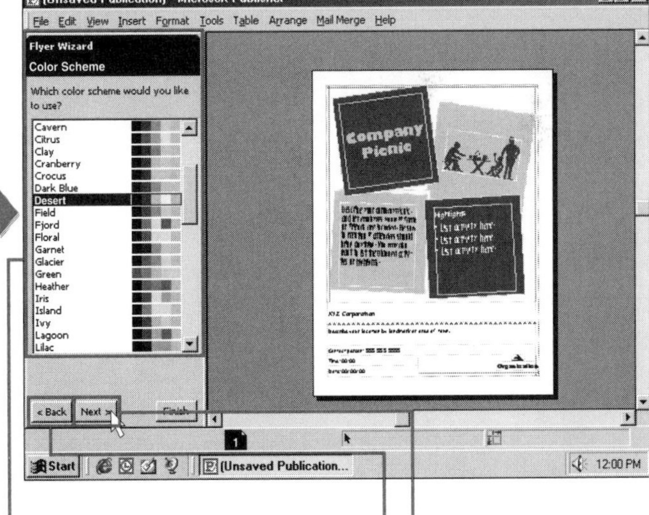

6 Answer each question asked by the wizard. Each wizard will ask you a different set of questions.

■ The results of the choices you make instantly appear in the publication.

7 When you finish answering a question, click Next to continue.

■ You can click Back at any time to return to a previous step and change your answers.

CONTINUED

CREATE A PUBLICATION USING A WIZARD CONTINUED

When you have answered all the wizard's questions, you can finish creating the publication.

Publisher displays the publication on the right side of the window. The layout and formatting of the publication reflect the options you selected in the wizard. Publisher also displays sample text in the publication. You can replace this sample text with your own information.

The left side of the window displays the wizard. You can hide or display the wizard at any time. Hiding the wizard gives you a larger and less cluttered working area. Displaying the wizard lets you quickly make changes to your publication.

The topics you covered when you answered the wizard's questions appear at the top of the wizard. The topics displayed depend on the wizard you used. For example, the Newsletter Wizard includes the Design, Color Scheme, Number of Columns and Personal Information topics. You can redisplay the options for a topic and change your selections at any time. Changes you make in the wizard instantly appear in your publication.

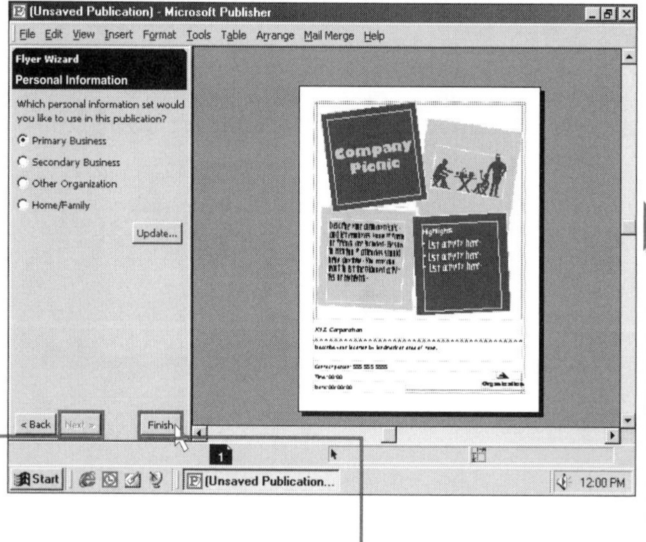

■ When you finish answering all the wizard's questions, the Next button becomes dimmed.

8 Click Finish to create the publication.

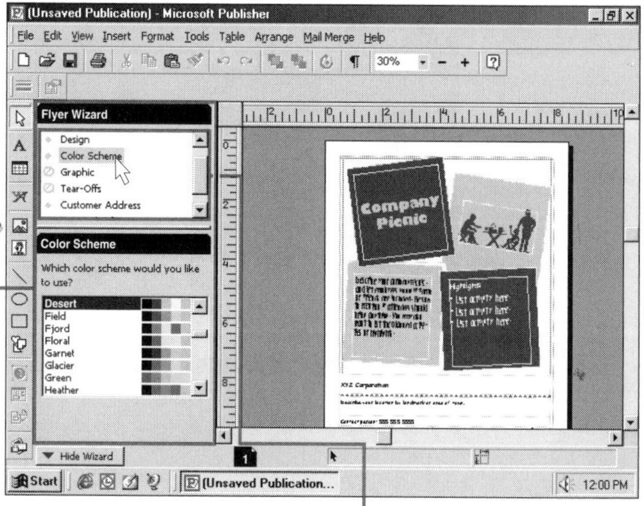

■ Publisher creates the publication.

■ This area displays the wizard. You can use the wizard to make quick changes to the publication.

9 This area displays each topic you covered in the wizard. To once again view the options for a topic, click the topic.

How do I replace the sample text in the publication with my own information?

✔ Click the sample text to highlight the text. Then type your own information. When you begin typing your information, the highlighted text disappears. For information on working with text in a publication, see page 552.

Why did a yellow box appear on my screen when I began typing text in my publication?

✔ As you work with your publication, Publisher may display a yellow box containing a tip to help you work more efficiently. For example, when you enter text using a small font size, Publisher may display a tip telling you how to magnify the page to better view the text.

Can I add text I wrote in another application, such as Word, to my publication?

✔ Yes. Select the text in the other application and click the Copy button (📋). In your publication, click the text frame where you want to enter the text and then click the Paste button (📋).

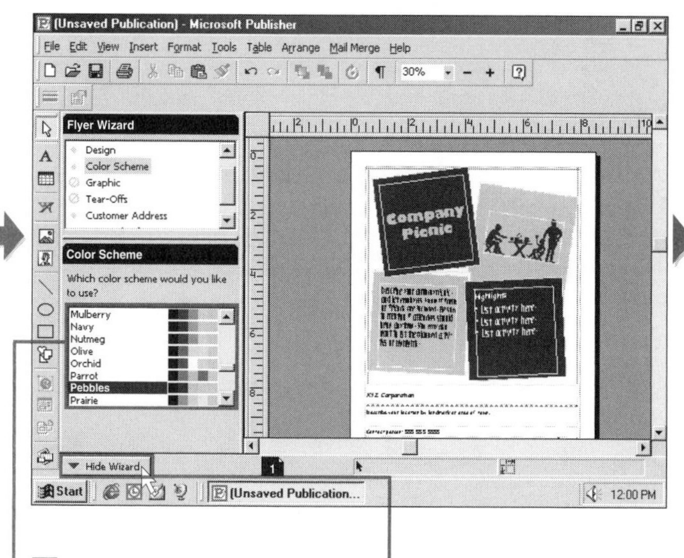

10 This area displays the options for the topic you selected. To select a different option, click the option.

■ The publication displays the change.

HIDE THE WIZARD

1 To hide the wizard to provide a larger area for working with the publication, click Hide Wizard.

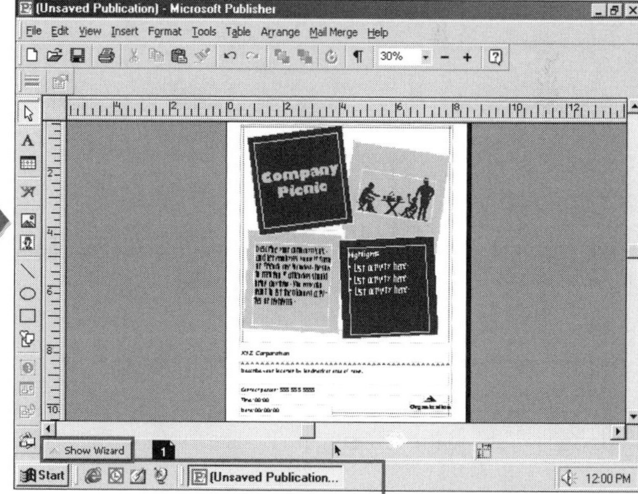

■ The wizard disappears.

■ To once again display the wizard, click Show Wizard.

CREATE A BLANK PUBLICATION

You can use Publisher to create a blank publication. Blank publications are useful when you want Publisher to set up the dimensions for the publication but want to specify the text and design for the publication yourself.

Each time you start Publisher, the Catalog dialog box appears on your screen. This dialog box displays several types of blank publications for you to choose from, including a full page, postcard, business card, poster or banner.

Some types of publications, such as the side-fold card, require folding. These types of publications print multiple pages on one sheet of paper that you can fold into a card or booklet. When you select a folded publication, Publisher indicates how many pages you need to add to the publication and creates the additional blank pages for you.

When you finish creating a blank publication, the Quick Publication Wizard may appear on your screen. You can use this wizard to make changes to your publication, such as selecting a design, color scheme, page size and layout. The options you select will instantly appear in your publication.

■ The Catalog dialog box appears each time you start Publisher.

1 Click the Blank Publications tab.

2 Click the type of publication you want to create.

■ The type of publication you selected is indicated in this area.

3 Click Create to create the publication.

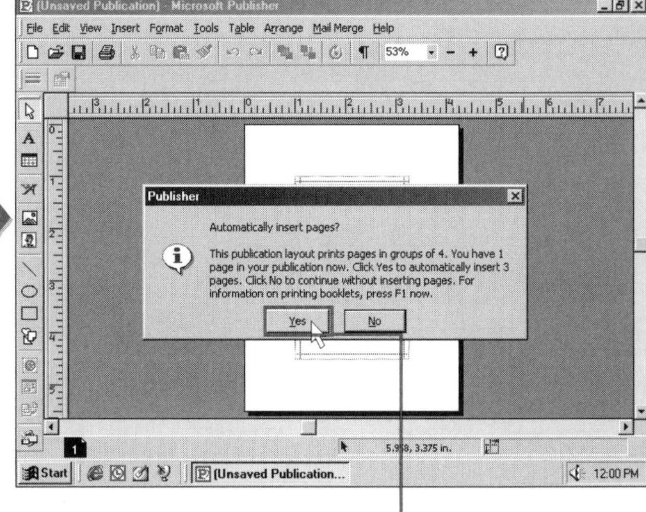

■ A dialog box appears if the type of publication you selected requires more than one page.

4 Click Yes to have Publisher add the necessary pages to the publication.

Note: Click No if you want to create only one page.

Can I display the Catalog dialog box while working in Publisher?

✔ Yes. Click the File menu and then select New. Publisher lets you work with only one publication at a time. Make sure you save the publication displayed on your screen before creating a new publication.

Can I temporarily hide the Quick Publication Wizard?

✔ Yes. Hiding the Quick Publication Wizard provides a larger area for viewing your publication. Click the Hide Wizard button below the wizard. To once again display the wizard, click the Show Wizard button.

Can I create a blank publication that is not available in the Catalog dialog box?

✔ If the Catalog dialog box does not display the type of publication you want to create, you can set up your own blank publication. On the Blank Publications tab, click the Custom Page button. In the Page Setup dialog box, you can specify the dimensions for your new publication. You can also use this dialog box to set up a blank publication for labels or envelopes.

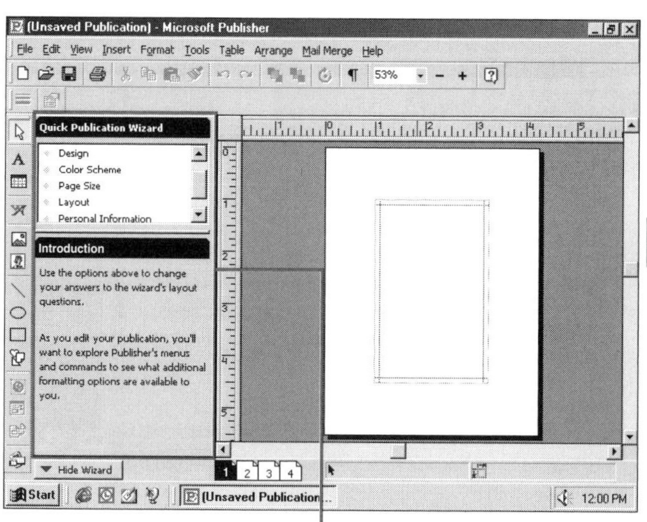

■ Publisher creates the publication.

■ This area may display the Quick Publication Wizard. You can use the wizard to make quick changes to the publication.

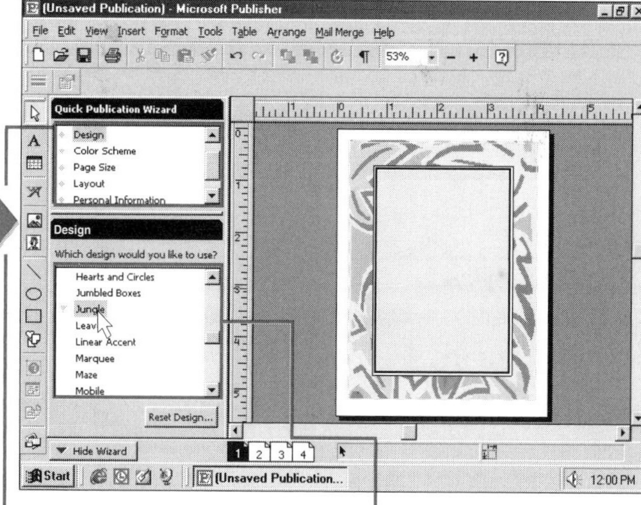

5 To use the wizard to change the publication, click a topic of interest.

6 This area displays the options for the topic you selected. To select an option, click the option.

■ The publication displays the change.

MOVE THROUGH PAGES

Publisher displays an icon for each page in your publication at the bottom of the screen. If your publication contains more than one page, you can use these icons to move through the pages.

When you create a publication using a wizard, the wizard may create multiple pages for you.

You can also add pages to your publication. For information on adding a new page, see page 547.

If your publication contains many pages, Publisher may not be able to display all the page icons on your screen. An arrow (▶) appears if Publisher cannot show all the page icons at once.

TIP

Why did two pages appear when I selected a page icon?

✔ Some publications, such as newsletters and catalogs, have facing pages like those in a book. When you select a page icon, the two facing pages may appear. If you want to view only one page at a time, click the View menu and select Two-Page Spread. Repeat this process to once again view two facing pages.

■ This area displays an icon for each page in the publication. The icon for the current page is highlighted.

■ An arrow (▶) appears if Publisher cannot show all the page icons. You can click the arrow to display the other page icons.

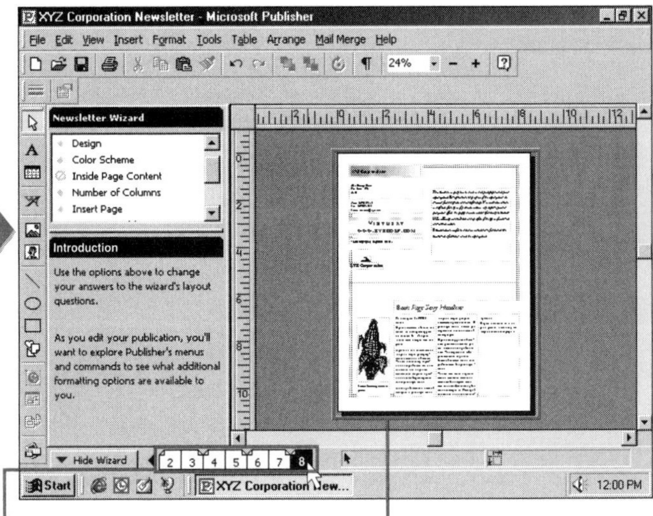

1 Click the icon for the page you want to view.

■ The page you selected appears.

ADD A NEW PAGE

You can add a new page to a publication to include additional information.

Publisher allows you to add a new page before or after the page displayed on your screen. You can add a single page or many pages at once.

Publisher also allows you to specify the way you want to add the new page. If you want to create all the content for the page, you can add a new blank page. If you want to immediately start adding text to the page, you can add a new page containing a text frame that fills the page. If you want to create a new page based on the content and appearance of an existing page, you can add a new page that is a duplicate of the current page.

Some publications, such as newsletters, Web sites and catalogs, may display an Insert Page dialog box that looks and works differently than the method described here.

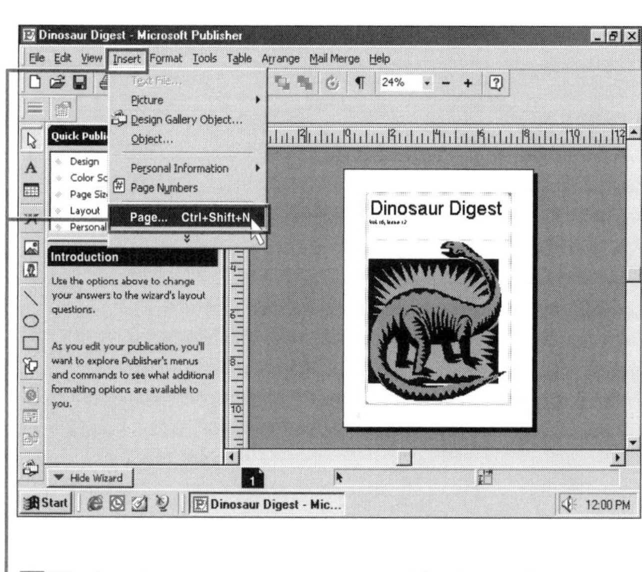

1 Display the page you want to appear before or after a new page.

2 Click Insert.

3 Click Page.

■ The Insert Page dialog box appears.

Note: This dialog box may look different, depending on the type of publication you are working with.

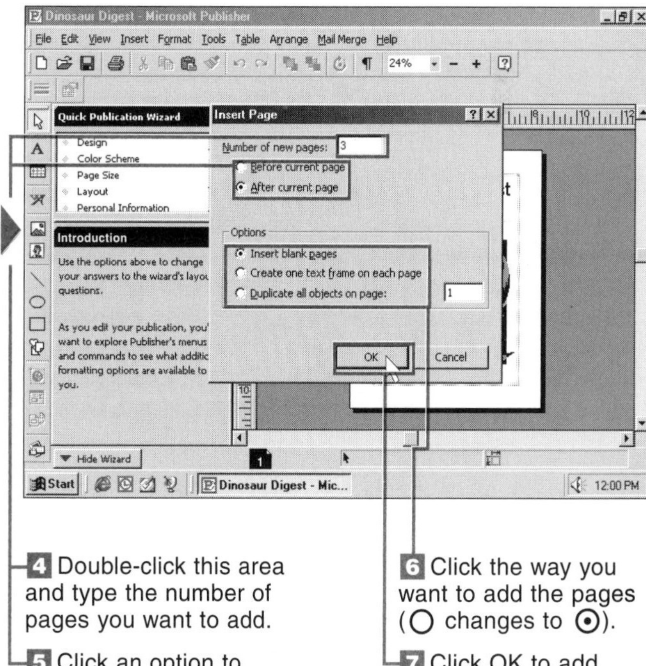

4 Double-click this area and type the number of pages you want to add.

5 Click an option to specify if you want to add the pages before or after the current page (○ changes to ⊙).

6 Click the way you want to add the pages (○ changes to ⊙).

7 Click OK to add the pages.

SAVE A PUBLICATION

You can save your publication to store it for future use. This allows you to later review and make changes to the publication.

You can specify where you want to save your publication. The Places Bar in the Save As dialog box lets you quickly access commonly used folders. The History folder lets you access folders you recently used. The My Documents folder provides a convenient place to save your publication. The Desktop folder lets you quickly save your publication on the Windows desktop. The Favorites folder provides a place to save a publication you will frequently access. You can use Web Folders to save your publication on a computer called a Web server. Once the publication is saved on a Web server, it will be available for other people to view.

To avoid losing your work, you should regularly save changes you make to a publication. If you do not regularly save your changes, Publisher will display a dialog box every 15 minutes to remind you to save your publication.

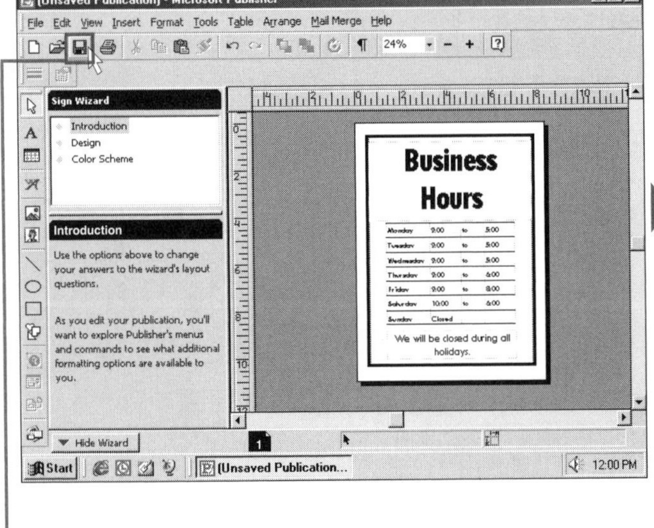

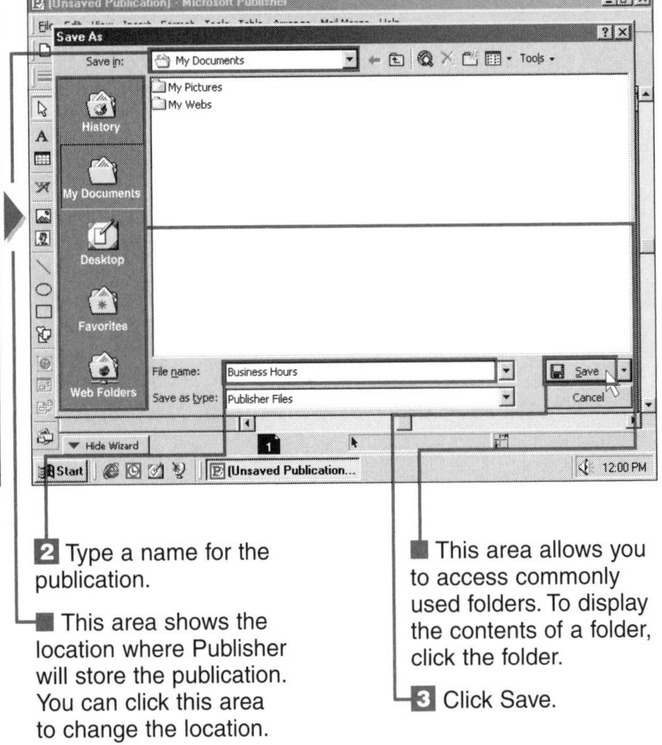

1 Click [save icon] to save the publication.

■ The Save As dialog box appears.

Note: If you previously saved the publication, the Save As dialog box will not appear since you have already named the publication.

2 Type a name for the publication.

■ This area shows the location where Publisher will store the publication. You can click this area to change the location.

■ This area allows you to access commonly used folders. To display the contents of a folder, click the folder.

3 Click Save.

PRINT A PUBLICATION

You can produce a paper copy of the publication displayed on your screen.

Before you print your publication, make sure the printer is turned on and contains an adequate supply of paper. You should also make sure that the printer contains the type and size of paper your publication requires. For example, you may want to use specialty paper to print a postcard. The type and size of paper you can print on depends on your printer. You can consult the manual that came with your printer to determine which types and sizes of paper your printer can use.

Publisher allows you to specify the part of your publication you want to print. You can print all the pages in the publication, a range of pages or only the currently displayed page. Printing a range of pages is useful if you only want to print new pages you added to an existing publication.

You can also click the Print button (🖨) on the Standard toolbar to quickly print your entire publication.

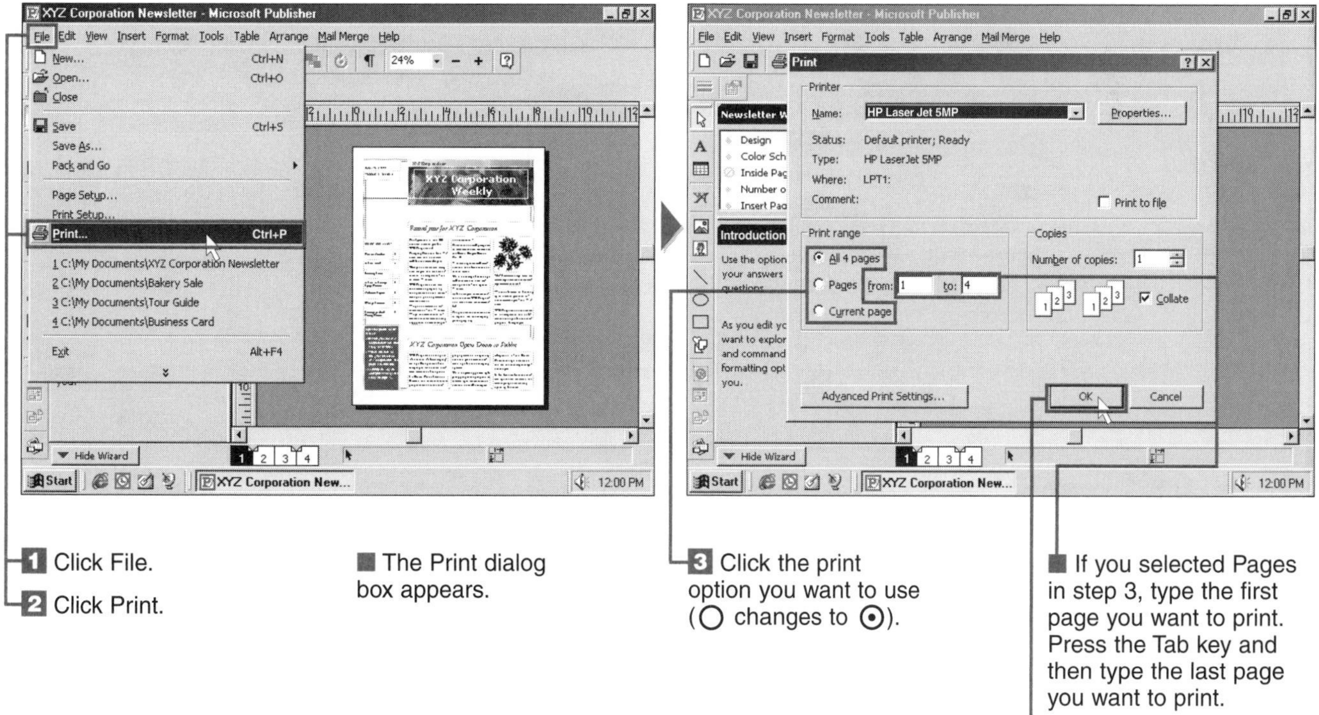

1 Click File.

2 Click Print.

■ The Print dialog box appears.

3 Click the print option you want to use (○ changes to ⊙).

■ If you selected Pages in step 3, type the first page you want to print. Press the Tab key and then type the last page you want to print.

4 Click OK.

OPEN A PUBLICATION

You can open a saved publication and display it on your screen. This lets you review and make changes to the publication.

Each time you start Publisher, the Catalog dialog box appears. You can use the Catalog dialog box to access a list of publications you previously created from the Open Publication dialog box.

The Open Publication dialog box allows you to specify where the publication you want to open is located on your computer. You can use the Places Bar to quickly display the contents of commonly used folders. For information on the Places Bar, see page 548.

After you open a publication, Publisher displays the name of the publication at the top of your screen.

You can have only one publication open at a time. Publisher will close a publication displayed on your screen when you open another publication.

■ The Catalog dialog box appears each time you start Publisher.

1 Click Existing Files to open a publication you previously created.

■ The Open Publication dialog box appears.

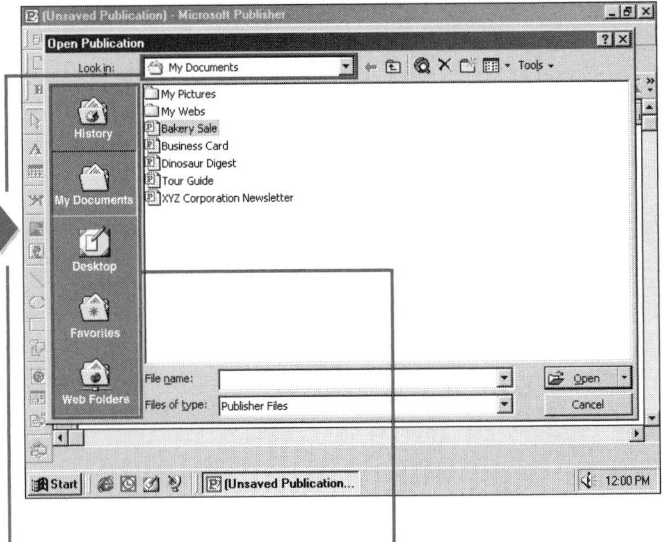

■ This area shows the location of the displayed publications. You can click this area to change the location.

■ This area allows you to access commonly used folders. To display the contents of a folder, click the folder.

How can I open a publication while working in Publisher?

✔ Click the Open button (📂) on the Standard toolbar to display the Open Publication dialog box. Click the name of the publication you want to open and then click Open.

Can I sort the icons in the Open Publication dialog box?

✔ You can sort the icons by name, type, size or date to help you find the publication you want to open. Click ▾ beside the Views button (▦▾) in the Open Publication dialog box and select Arrange Icons. Then click the way you want to sort the icons.

Can I change the way publications are displayed in the Open Publication dialog box?

✔ Yes. Click ▾ beside the Views button (▦▾) in the Open Publication dialog box and then select a new view. The List view displays the names of publications. The Details view displays information about publications, such as size and type. The Properties view displays information about the currently selected publication. The Preview view displays a preview of the currently selected publication.

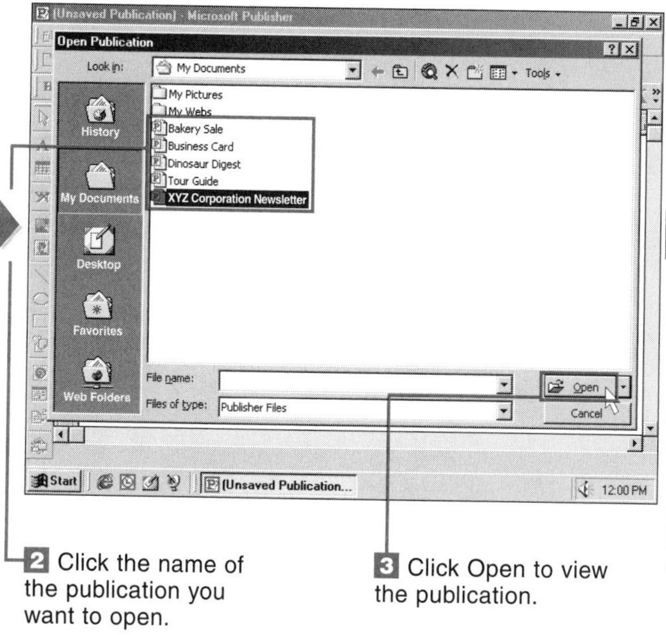

2 Click the name of the publication you want to open.

3 Click Open to view the publication.

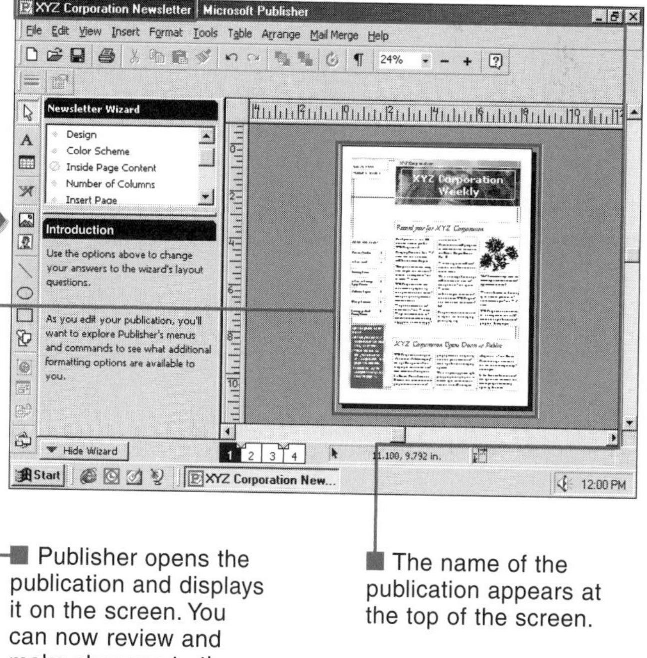

■ Publisher opens the publication and displays it on the screen. You can now review and make changes to the publication.

■ The name of the publication appears at the top of the screen.

ADD A TEXT FRAME

Before you can add text to your publication, you must first add a text frame to hold the text.

You can specify a location and size for a text frame you add to your publication. You can later move and resize the text frame to better suit the publication. You can also delete a text frame you no longer need. For information on moving, resizing or deleting an object, see page 564.

To be able to clearly view the text you type in a text frame, you can magnify the text frame.

As you type text in a text frame, Publisher automatically wraps the text to fit the width of the frame. Publisher also automatically checks the text for spelling errors and underlines any misspelled words in red. For information on correcting spelling errors in your publication, see page 554.

If you used a wizard to create your publication, Publisher may have added sample text frames for you. You can select the text in a text frame and type your own information to replace the text.

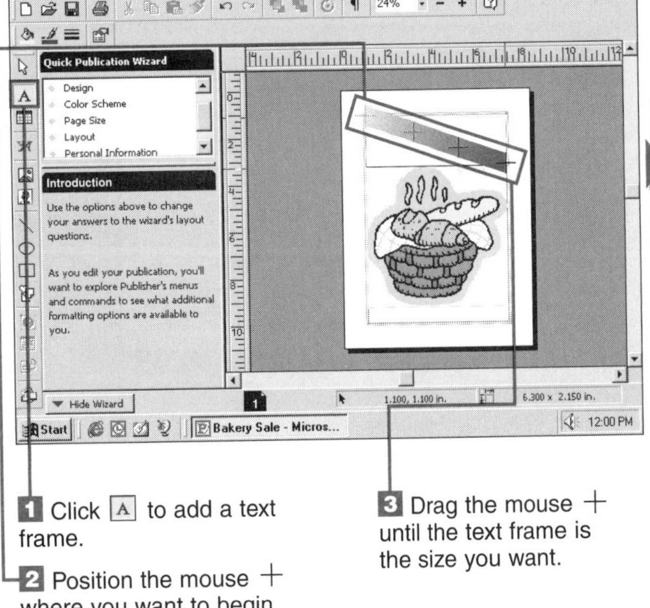

1 Click A to add a text frame.

2 Position the mouse + where you want to begin drawing the text frame.

3 Drag the mouse + until the text frame is the size you want.

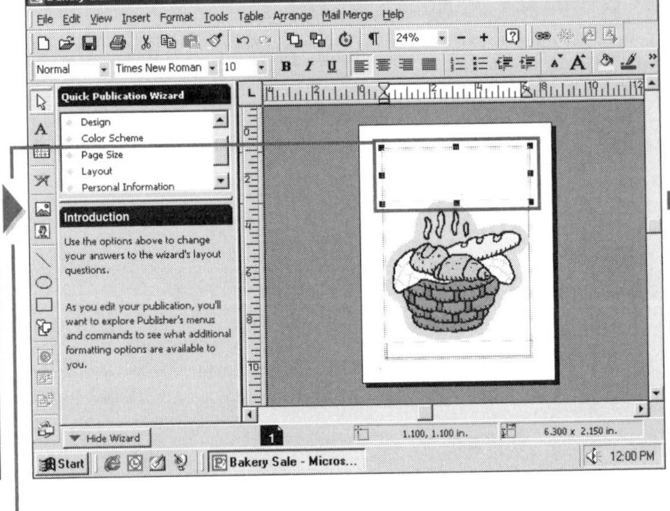

■ The text frame appears in the publication.

4 Press the F9 key to increase the size of the publication so you can clearly view the text you type.

TIPS

Why does the [A···] symbol appear at the bottom of a text frame?

✔ When you type more text than a frame can hold, Publisher displays the overflow indicator ([A···]). You can resize the text frame to display the extra text. To resize an object, see page 564.

Can I change the magnification for my publication?

✔ Yes. You may want to select a higher magnification setting to view a text frame in more detail. Click [▼] in the Zoom box and then click the magnification setting you want to use.

How do I format the text in a text frame?

✔ To select the text you want to format, drag the mouse I over the text. You can then use the buttons on the Formatting toolbar, such as Bold ([B]) or Center ([≡]), to format the text.

How can I add a border to a text frame?

✔ Double-click the border of the text frame to display the Border Style dialog box. Click the BorderArt tab and in the Available Borders area, click the border you want to use. Then click OK.

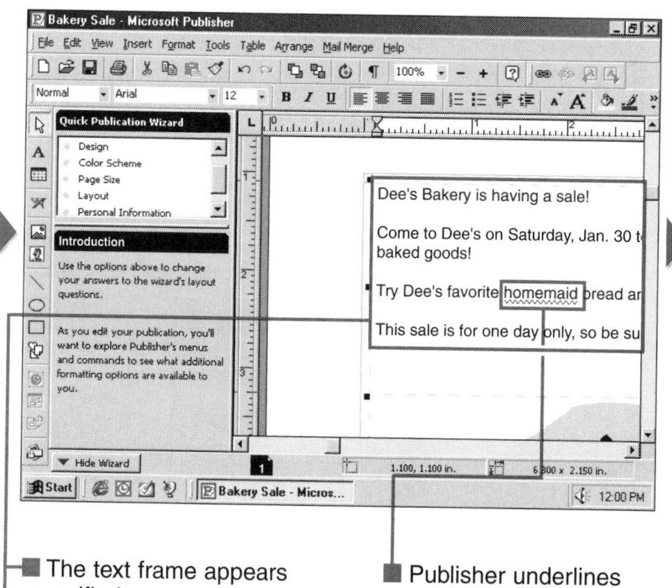

■ The text frame appears magnified.

5 Type the text you want to appear in the text frame. The text you type will appear where the insertion point flashes on the screen.

■ Publisher underlines misspelled words in red. The red underlines will not appear when you print the publication.

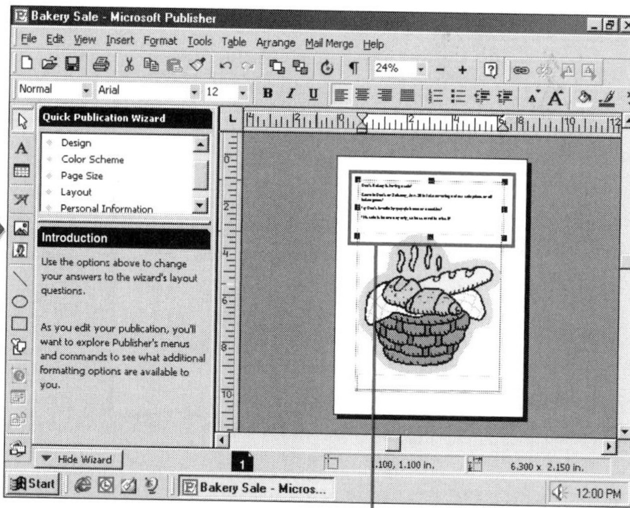

6 When you finish typing the text, press the F9 key to decrease the size of the publication so you can clearly view the publication.

■ The handles (■) around the text frame let you change the size of the frame.

7 To hide the handles, click outside the text frame.

CHECK SPELLING

When you finish entering text in a text frame, you can locate and correct all the spelling errors in the text frame. Correcting spelling errors can help make your publication appear more professional.

When you check the spelling of text in a text frame, Publisher compares every word in the text frame to words in its dictionary to find spelling errors. When Publisher finds a misspelled word, it provides a list of suggestions to correct the word. You can replace the word with a suggestion or ignore the word and continue checking the text frame. If Publisher repeatedly finds a misspelled word you know is correct, such as a name, you can choose to ignore all occurrences of the word in the publication.

Publisher automatically checks your publication for spelling errors as you type and underlines misspelled words in red. The underlines only appear on your screen and will not appear when you print your publication. Publisher also automatically corrects common spelling errors as you type. For example, Publisher automatically replaces "frmo" with "from".

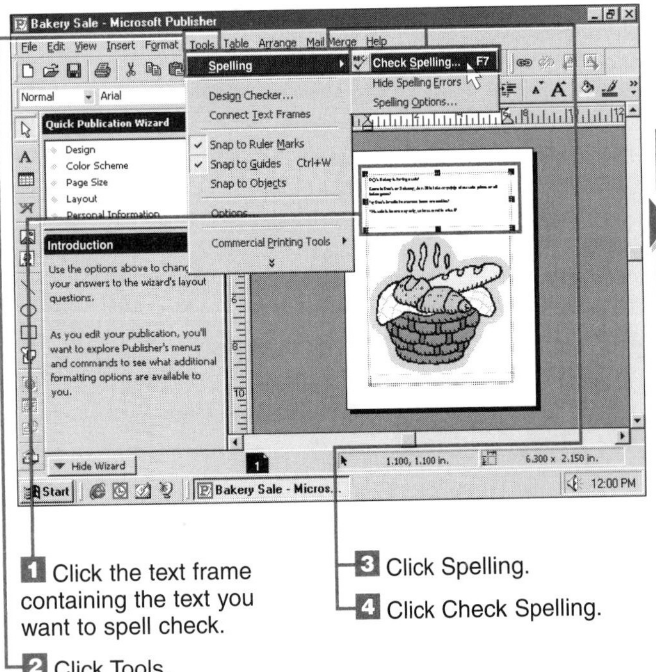

1 Click the text frame containing the text you want to spell check.

2 Click Tools.

3 Click Spelling.

4 Click Check Spelling.

■ The Check Spelling dialog box appears if Publisher finds a misspelled word.

■ This area displays the first misspelled word.

■ This area displays suggestions for correcting the word.

Why does a dialog box appear, asking if I want to check the rest of my publication?

✔ This dialog box appears if you have more than one text frame in your publication. Click Yes to spell check the entire publication. When you click Yes, you also turn on the Check all stories option in the Check Spelling dialog box (☐ changes to ☑). This option will remain on until you exit Publisher.

Can I correct a single error in my publication?

✔ Yes. Right-click a word that displays a red underline. A list of suggestions to correct the error appears. Click the suggestion you want to use.

Why did Publisher underline a correctly spelled word?

✔ Publisher considers any words that do not exist in its dictionary to be misspelled. You can add a word to the dictionary so Publisher will recognize the word during future spell checks. Right-click the word you want to add to the dictionary and then select Add.

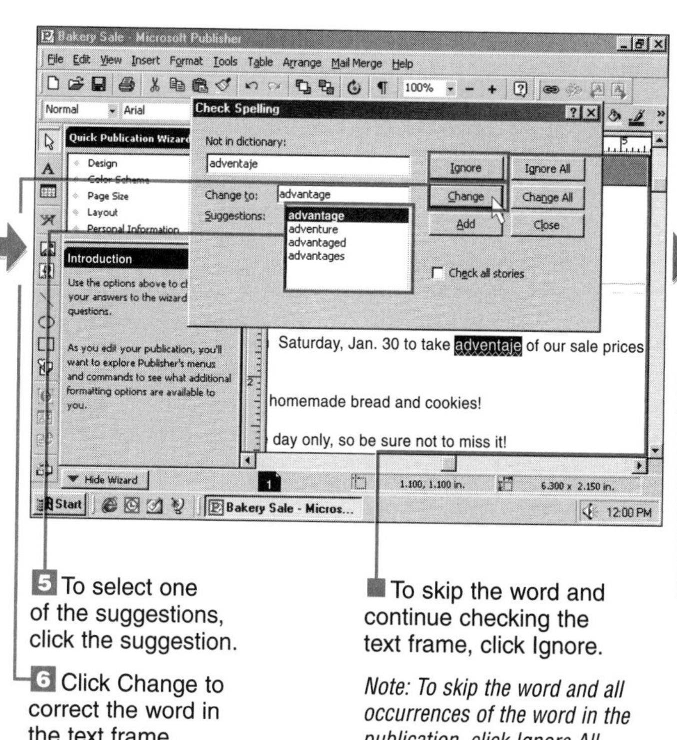

5 To select one of the suggestions, click the suggestion.

6 Click Change to correct the word in the text frame.

■ To skip the word and continue checking the text frame, click Ignore.

Note: To skip the word and all occurrences of the word in the publication, click Ignore All.

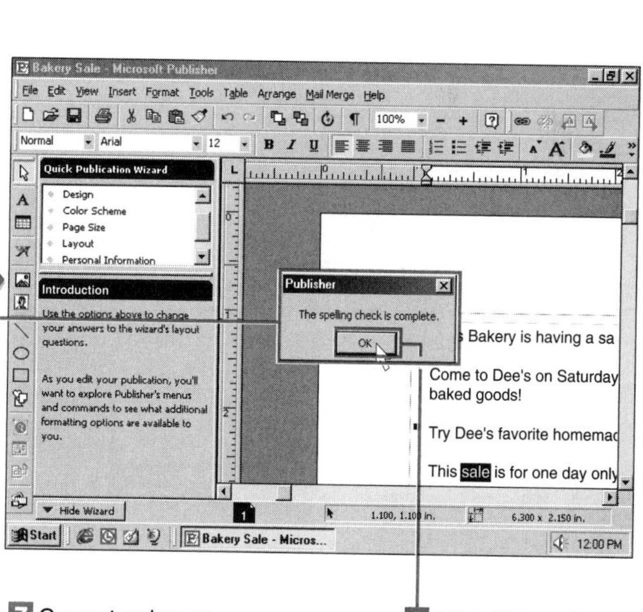

7 Correct or ignore misspelled words until this dialog box appears, telling you the spell check is complete.

8 Click OK to close the dialog box.

ADD A SHAPE

You can add a ready-made shape, called a custom shape, to your publication. Adding a custom shape can enhance the appearance of your publication and draw attention to important information.

Publisher offers several custom shapes you can choose from, including triangles, arrows, stars and banners.

Publisher also allows you to quickly add a line, oval or rectangle to your publication.

When you add a shape to your publication, Publisher lets you specify the location for the shape and the size you want the shape to display. You can later move and resize the shape to better suit your publication. You can also delete a shape you no longer need. For information on moving, resizing or deleting an object, see page 564.

After you create a shape, you can add text to the shape by adding a text frame on top of the shape. This is useful for creating attractive banners in your publication. For information on adding a text frame, see page 552.

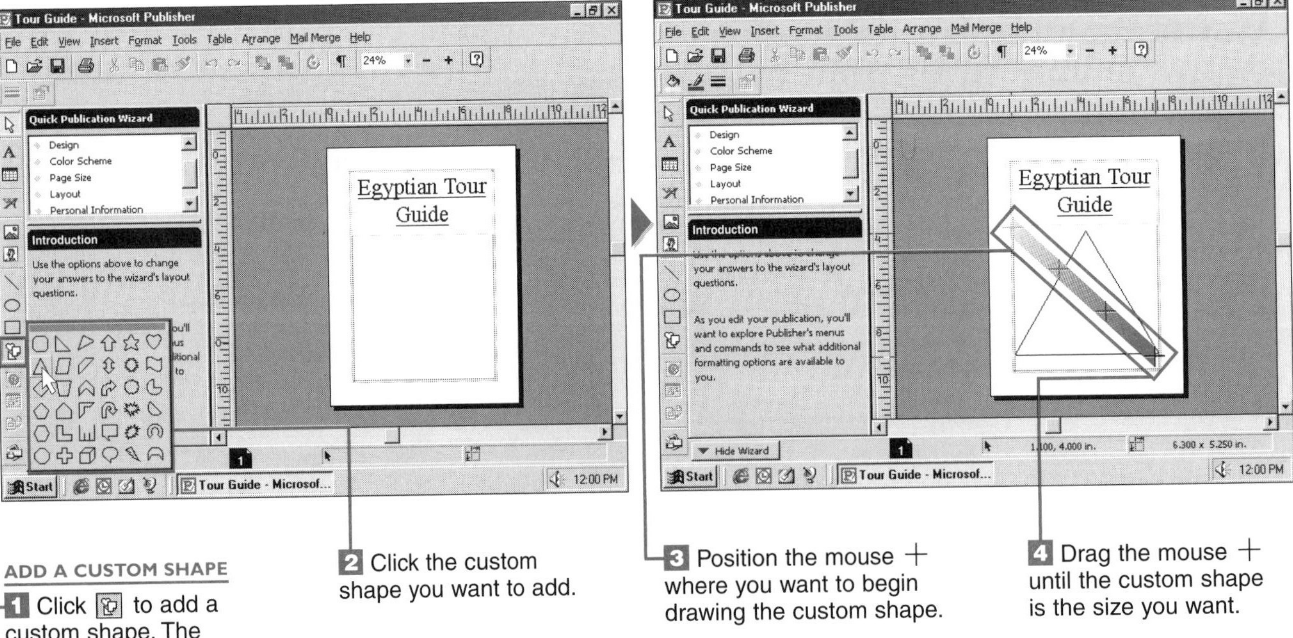

ADD A CUSTOM SHAPE

1 Click to add a custom shape. The available custom shapes appear.

2 Click the custom shape you want to add.

3 Position the mouse + where you want to begin drawing the custom shape.

4 Drag the mouse + until the custom shape is the size you want.

Why does a diamond-shaped handle (◈) appear on a shape I added?

✔ Some custom shapes display diamond-shaped handles (◈) when you click the shape. These handles allow you to adjust the shape of a custom shape. Position the mouse over a diamond-shaped handle (↖ changes to ⇕ or ⇔) and then drag the handle to a new location.

How do I draw a square or circle?

✔ Click the Rectangle Tool button (▢) to draw a square. Click the Oval Tool button (◯) to draw a circle. Then hold down the Shift key as you draw the shape.

Can I add color to a shape?

✔ You can easily fill a shape with color. Click the shape you want to change and then click the Fill Color button (🖌). You can then select a color for the shape.

Can I change the color of the outline around a shape?

✔ Yes. Click the shape you want to change and then click the Line Color button (🖉). You can then select a color for the outline of the shape.

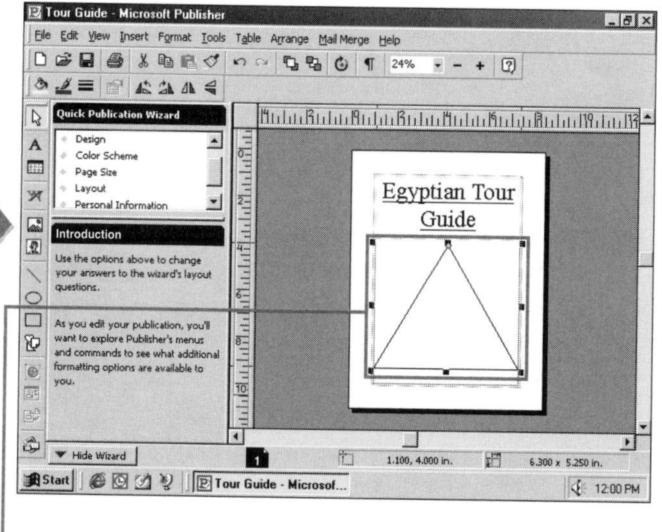

■ The custom shape appears in the publication. The handles (■) around the custom shape let you change the size of the shape.

5 To hide the handles, click outside the custom shape.

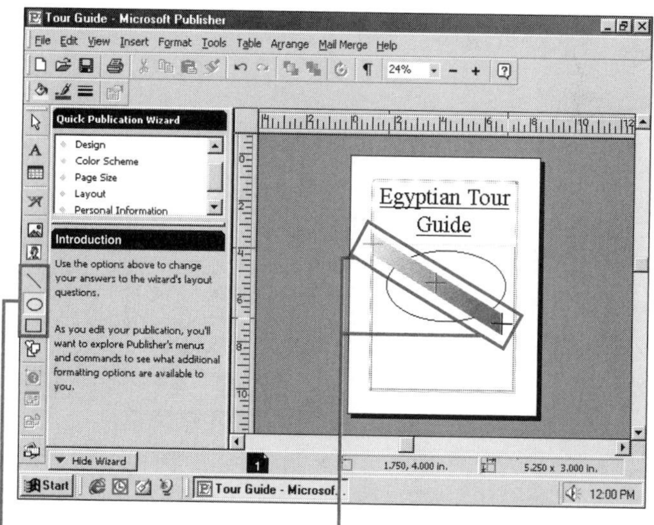

ADD A LINE, OVAL OR RECTANGLE

1 Click one of the following buttons.

- ╲ Line
- ◯ Oval
- ▢ Rectangle

2 Position the mouse + where you want to begin drawing the shape.

3 Drag the mouse + until the shape is the size you want.

ADD CLIP ART

Publisher includes professionally designed clip art images you can add to your publication. You can add clip art images to make your publication more interesting and entertaining. Clip art images can also help convey information. For example, you can add a clip art image of a light bulb to illustrate an idea.

The Microsoft Clip Gallery contains a wide variety of images divided into categories. Some of the categories include Cartoons, Music and Travel. You can select a category to find the clip art image you want to add to your publication.

When adding a clip art image, you can draw a frame for the clip art image in your publication. This lets you specify a location and size for the clip art image. You can later move and resize the clip art image to suit the layout of your publication. You can also delete a clip art image you no longer need. For information on moving, resizing or deleting an object, see page 564.

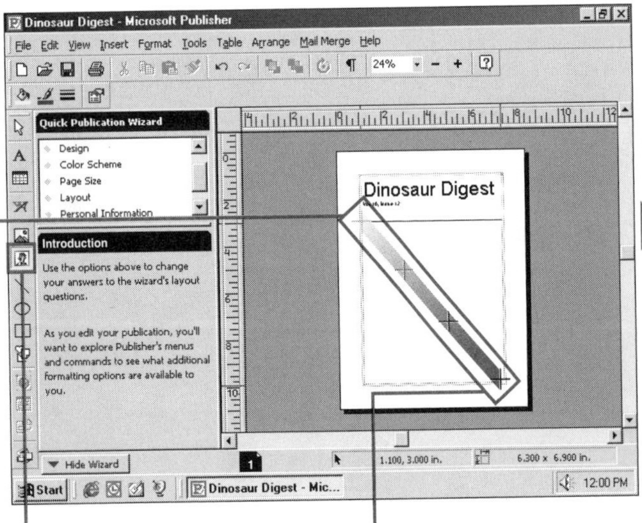

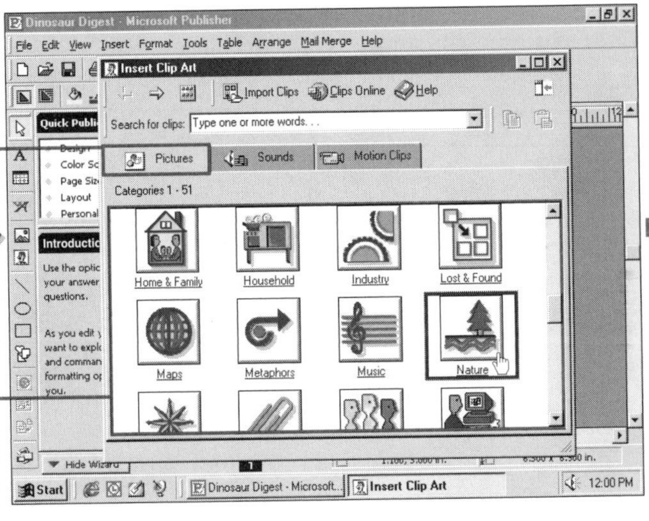

1 Click [icon] to add a clip art image.

2 Position the mouse + where you want to begin drawing the frame for the clip art image.

3 Drag the mouse + until the frame for the clip art image is the size you want.

■ The Insert Clip Art window appears.

4 Click the Pictures tab.

5 Click the category of clip art images you want to display.

■ The clip art images in the category you selected appear.

Can I have the text in my publication wrap tightly around a clip art image?

✔ Yes. When a text frame and a clip art image overlap, the text in the text frame will automatically wrap around the frame for the clip art image. To have the text wrap tightly around the clip art image, click the image and then click the Wrap Text to Picture button (▣).

Is there another way to find clip art images in the Insert Clip Art window?

✔ You can search for clip art images of interest in the Insert Clip Art window. Click the Search for clips area, type a word or phrase describing the clip art image you want to find and then press the Enter key.

Where can I find more clip art images?

✔ If you are connected to the Internet, you can visit Microsoft's Clip Gallery Live Web site to find additional clip art images. In the Insert Clip Art window, click the Clips Online button and then follow the instructions on your screen.

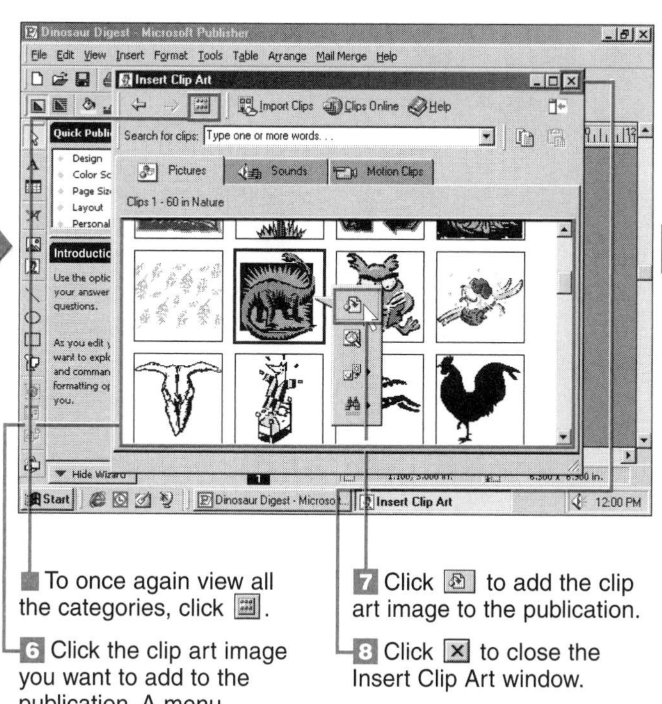

■ To once again view all the categories, click ▦.

6 Click the clip art image you want to add to the publication. A menu appears.

7 Click ▣ to add the clip art image to the publication.

8 Click ☒ to close the Insert Clip Art window.

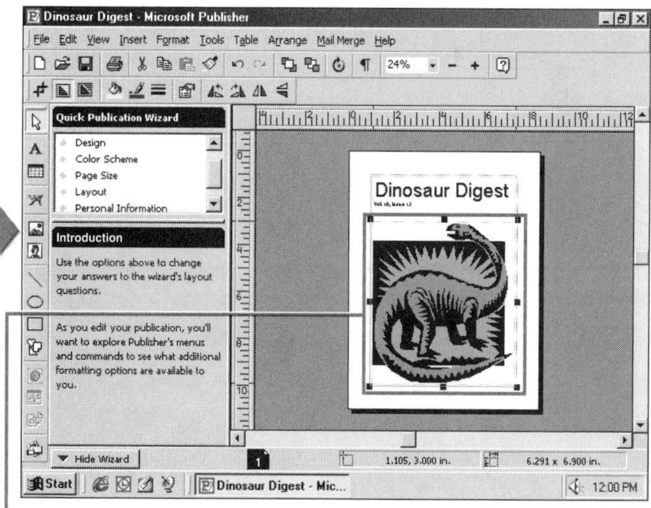

■ The clip art image appears in the publication. The handles (■) around the image let you change the size of the image.

9 To hide the handles, click outside the clip art image.

ADD A PICTURE

You can add a picture stored on your computer to your publication. Adding a picture is useful if you want to display your company logo or a picture of your products in your publication.

Publisher allows you to use many popular graphics file formats, including Enhanced Metafile (.emf), Graphics Interchange Format (.gif), JPEG (.jpg), Windows Bitmap (.bmp) and Windows Metafile (.wmf).

When adding a picture, you can draw a frame for the picture in your publication. This lets you specify the location for the picture and the size you want the picture to display. You can later move and resize the picture to better suit your publication.

You can also delete a picture you no longer need. For information on moving, resizing or deleting an object, see page 564.

You can specify where the picture you want to add is stored on your computer. You can use the Places Bar to quickly locate the picture in a folder you frequently use. For information on the Places Bar, see page 548.

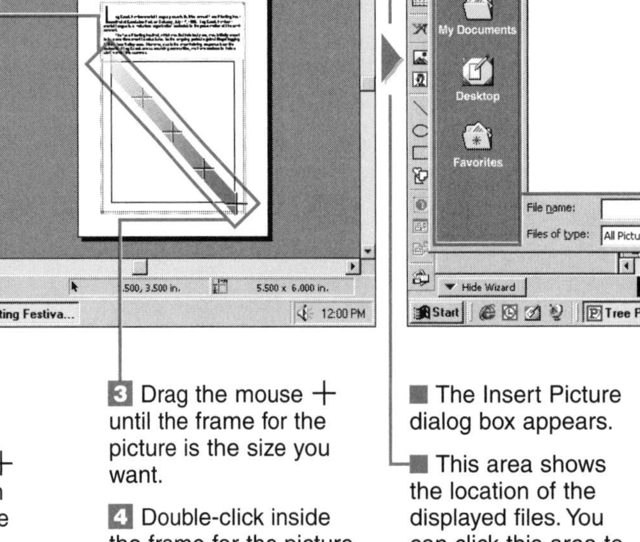

1 Click [icon] to add a picture.

2 Position the mouse + where you want to begin drawing the frame for the picture.

3 Drag the mouse + until the frame for the picture is the size you want.

4 Double-click inside the frame for the picture.

■ The Insert Picture dialog box appears.

■ This area shows the location of the displayed files. You can click this area to change the location.

■ This area allows you to access commonly used folders. To display the contents of a folder, click the folder.

TIPS

Can I trim the edges of a picture?

✔ You can trim the edges of a picture to remove unneeded parts of the picture. Click the picture and then click the Crop Picture button. Position the mouse over one of the handles around the picture (changes to) and then drag the handle to a new location.

How can I rotate a picture?

✔ Click the picture you want to rotate and then click the Rotate Left button or Rotate Right button. You can also flip a picture using the Flip Horizontal button or the Flip Vertical button.

Can I add a border around a picture?

✔ Yes. Adding a border can help make a picture stand out in your publication. Click the picture you want to change and then click the Line/Border Style button. Select a border style from the list or click More Styles to display more borders.

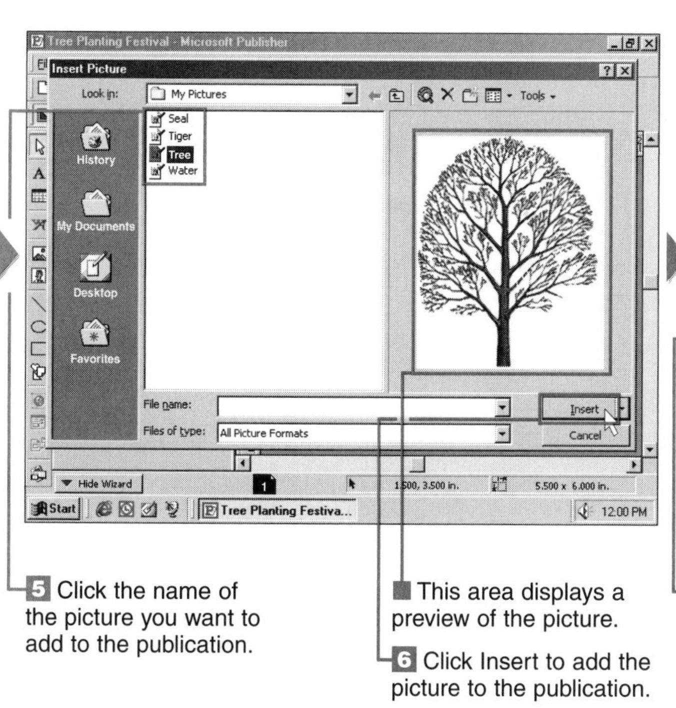

5 Click the name of the picture you want to add to the publication.

■ This area displays a preview of the picture.

6 Click Insert to add the picture to the publication.

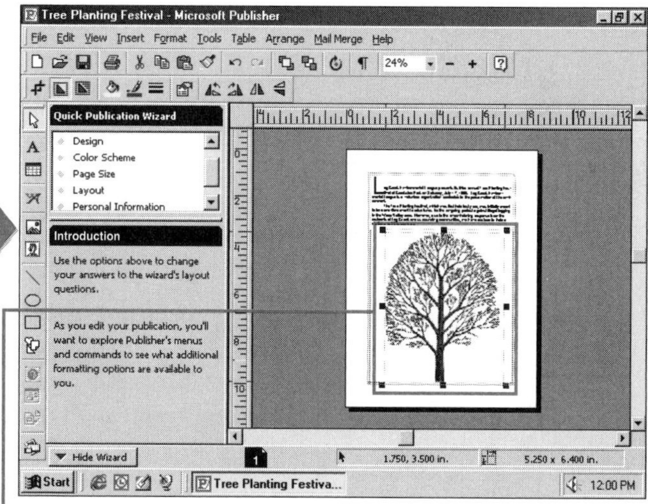

■ The picture appears in the publication. The handles (■) around the picture let you change the size of the picture.

7 To hide the handles, click outside the picture.

ADD A TEXT EFFECT

You can use the WordArt feature to add text effects to your publication. For example, you can add a text effect that slants up, arches down or fades to the right. Text effects are useful for emphasizing headlines or creating banners in a publication.

You can draw a frame for a text effect you add to your publication. This lets you specify the location for the text effect and the size you want the text effect to display.

When typing the text for a text effect, you should be careful not to make any spelling errors. You cannot use Publisher's spell check feature to check the spelling of a text effect.

After you type the text you want the text effect to display, you can select a shape for the text effect. Publisher offers several shapes to choose from, such as Stop Sign, Circle and Triangle. If the shape you select makes the text effect smaller, you may want to stretch the text effect to the edges of the frame.

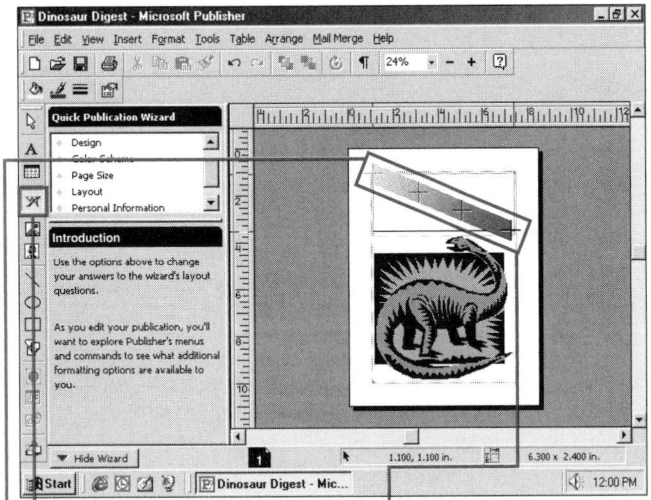

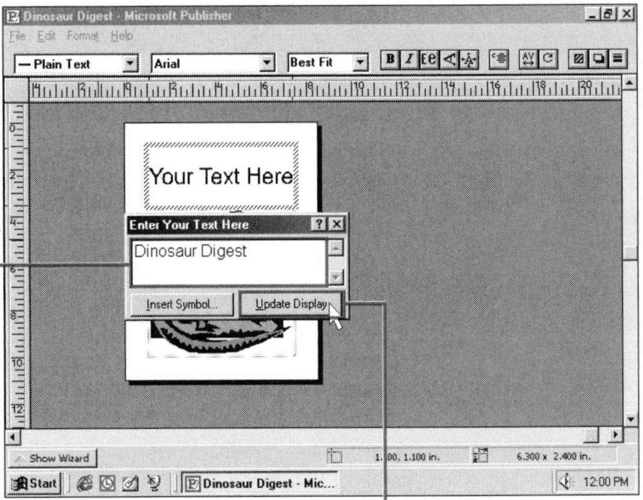

1 Click to add a text effect.

2 Position the mouse where you want to begin drawing the frame for the text effect.

3 Drag the mouse until the frame for the text effect is the size you want.

■ The Enter Your Text Here dialog box appears.

4 Type the text you want the text effect to display.

5 Click Update Display to see the text you typed in the publication.

Can I change the text displayed in the text effect?

✔ Yes. To redisplay the Enter Your Text Here dialog box, double-click the text effect. Type the new text and then click outside the frame.

Can I move a text effect to a new location?

✔ You can easily move or resize a text effect to suit your publication. You can also delete a text effect you no longer need. For information on moving, resizing or deleting an object, see page 564.

How can I change the appearance of my text effect?

✔ Double-click your text effect. The toolbar that appears offers many buttons to help you change the appearance of the text effect. For example, you can bold (B) or italicize (I) text. You can make uppercase and lowercase letters the same height (Ee) or add a shadow (❑) to the text. You can also use the drop-down lists on the toolbar to change the font and size of the text effect. If you increase the size of the text beyond the size of the frame, you can have Publisher resize the frame to fit the text.

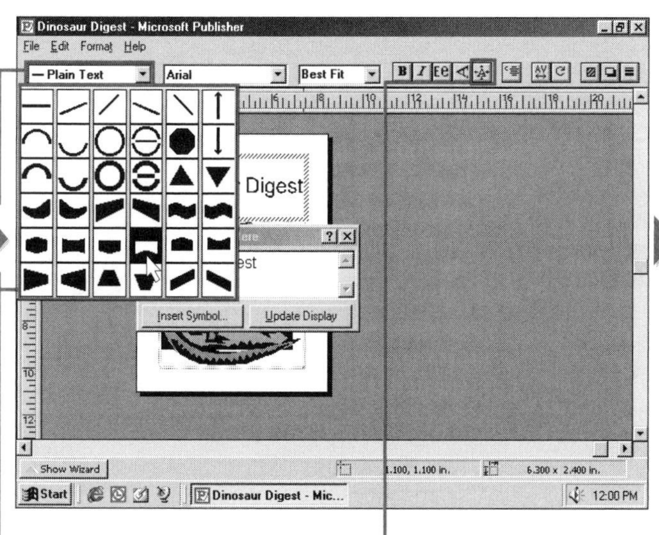

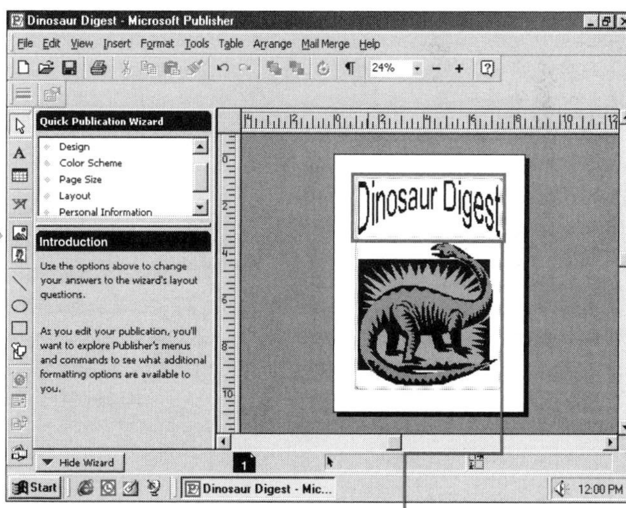

6 Click this area to select a shape for the text effect.

7 Click the shape you want to use.

8 To stretch the text effect to the edges of the frame, click the stretch button.

Note: To undo a stretch, click the stretch button again.

9 When you finish making changes to the text effect, click outside the frame for the text effect.

■ You can now clearly see the text effect in the publication.

MOVE, RESIZE OR DELETE AN OBJECT

You can move or copy an object from one location in your publication to another. When you move an object, the object disappears from its original location in your publication. When you copy an object, the object appears in both the original and new locations.

You can change the size of an object in your publication. For example, you may want to increase the size of a text frame to display more text or reduce the size of a picture to better suit your publication.

When you select an object, handles (■) appear around the object. These handles allow you to resize the object. The handles at the top and bottom of an object allow you to change the height of the object. The handles at the sides of an object allow you to change the width of the object. The handles at the corners of an object allow you to change the height and width of the object at the same time.

You can also delete an object you no longer need from your publication.

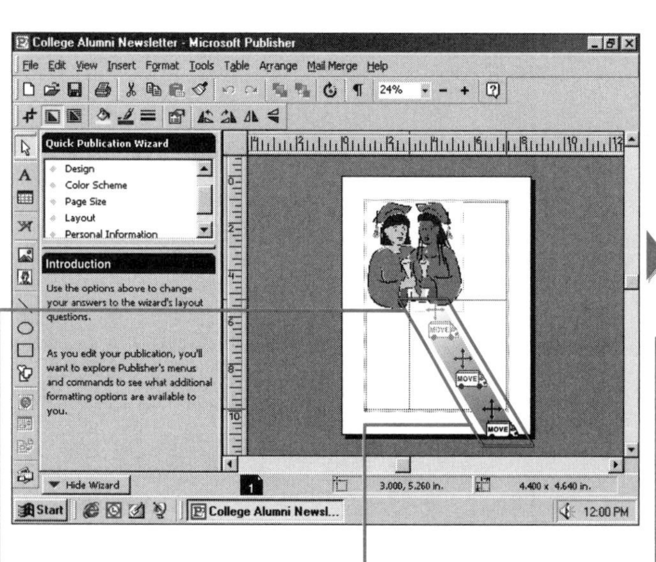

MOVE AN OBJECT

1 Position the mouse ↖ over the border of the object you want to move (↖ changes to ✥MOVE).

2 Drag the object to a new location.

■ The object appears in the new location.

■ To copy an object, hold down the Ctrl key as you perform step 2.

How can I cancel a change I made to an object?

✔ Publisher remembers the last changes you made. You can click the Undo button ( ) to immediately cancel a change you regret.

How can I prevent an object from appearing distorted when I resize it?

✔ Most objects in a publication will maintain their height-to-width ratio if you drag the corner handle when you resize the object. If you want to maintain the height-to-width ratio of a text frame or shape, you must hold down the Shift key as you drag the corner handle.

How can I quickly delete an object?

✔ To quickly delete an object, click the object and then press the Delete key. You cannot use this method to delete a text frame.

Can I move or delete several objects at the same time?

✔ Yes. Click the first object you want to move or delete. Hold down the Shift key as you click the other objects. You can now move or delete all the objects at the same time.

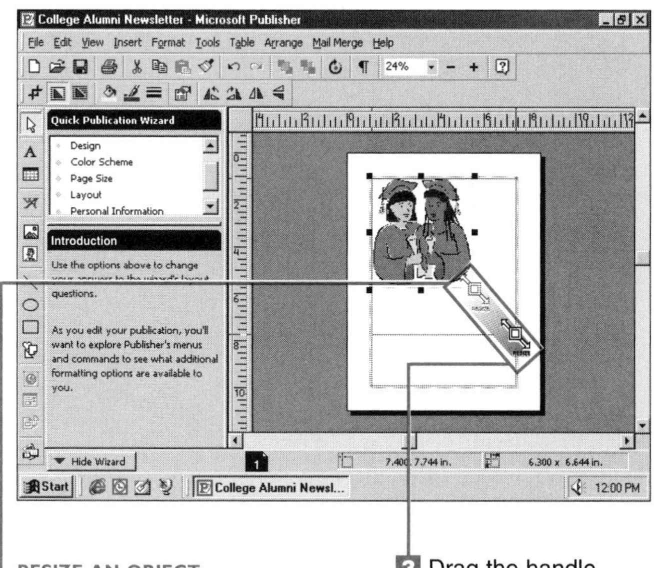

RESIZE AN OBJECT

1 Click the object you want to resize. Handles (■) appear around the object.

2 Position the mouse over one of the handles (changes to , or).

3 Drag the handle until the object is the size you want.

■ The object appears in the new size.

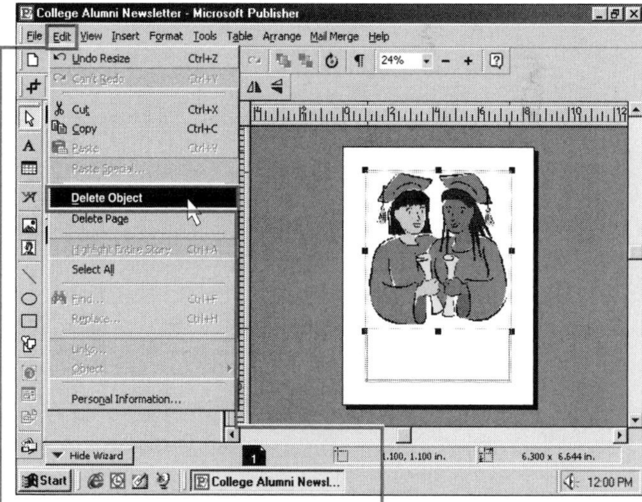

DELETE AN OBJECT

1 Click the object you want to delete. Handles (■) appear around the object.

2 Click Edit.

3 Click Delete Object.

Note: If Delete Object does not appear on the menu, position the mouse over the bottom of the menu to display all the menu commands.

SECTION VIII

1) MANAGE A WEB SITE USING FRONTPAGE

2) ENHANCE A WEB SITE USING FRONTPAGE

CREATE WEB PAGES

3) SAVE OFFICE DOCUMENTS AS WEB PAGES

INTRODUCTION TO FRONTPAGE

FrontPage is a program that you can use to create and edit Web pages. A Web page is a document on the World Wide Web. FrontPage also allows you to create and maintain Web sites. A Web site is a collection of Web pages.

The World Wide Web is part of the Internet and consists of a huge collection of pages stored on hundreds of thousands of computers around the world. A computer that stores Web pages is called a Web server.

For more information on FrontPage, you can visit the following Web site: www.microsoft.com/frontpage

Web Pages

A Web page can contain text, pictures, sound and video. A Web page can also contain highlighted text and images, called hyperlinks, that connect the page to other pages on the Web. When you select a hyperlink, the connected page appears on the screen. Hyperlinks allow you to easily navigate through a vast amount of information by jumping from one Web page to another.

You can find Web pages on every subject imaginable. Each page has a unique address, called a Uniform Resource Locator (URL). You can quickly display any page if you know its URL.

Publish Web Pages

FrontPage lets you publish your pages on the Web so people around the world can view the pages. You can also place pages you create on a corporate intranet. An intranet is a small version of the Internet within a company or organization.

When you finish creating all the pages for your Web site, you can transfer the Web site to a Web server. Once the pages are stored on the server, they will be available to everyone on the Web.

Reasons for Publishing

Publishing pages on the Web allows you to share information with millions of people around the world. Companies often place pages on the Web to keep the public informed about new products, interesting news and job openings within the company. Companies can also allow readers to use their Web pages to place orders for products and services.

Many individuals use the Web to share information about a topic that interests them. For example, you can create pages to discuss a favorite celebrity or hobby, show your favorite pictures, promote a club you belong to or present a resume to potential employers.

START FRONTPAGE

You can use FrontPage to create and maintain Web sites. A Web site is a collection of Web pages.

The FrontPage screen is similar to the screens in other Office programs. This can help you quickly learn to use FrontPage. For example, like the screens in Word and Excel, the FrontPage screen displays toolbars that allow you to quickly select common commands.

The FrontPage screen also contains icons you can use to change the view of a Web site. For more information on the views, see pages 576 to 581.

After you start FrontPage, you can create a Web site using a template or wizard. For information on creating a Web site, see page 570.

Once you have created a Web site, you can work with pages in the Web site. You can edit and format the pages or add items such as pictures and horizontal lines.

After you have created all the pages for your Web site, you can publish the Web site on the World Wide Web.

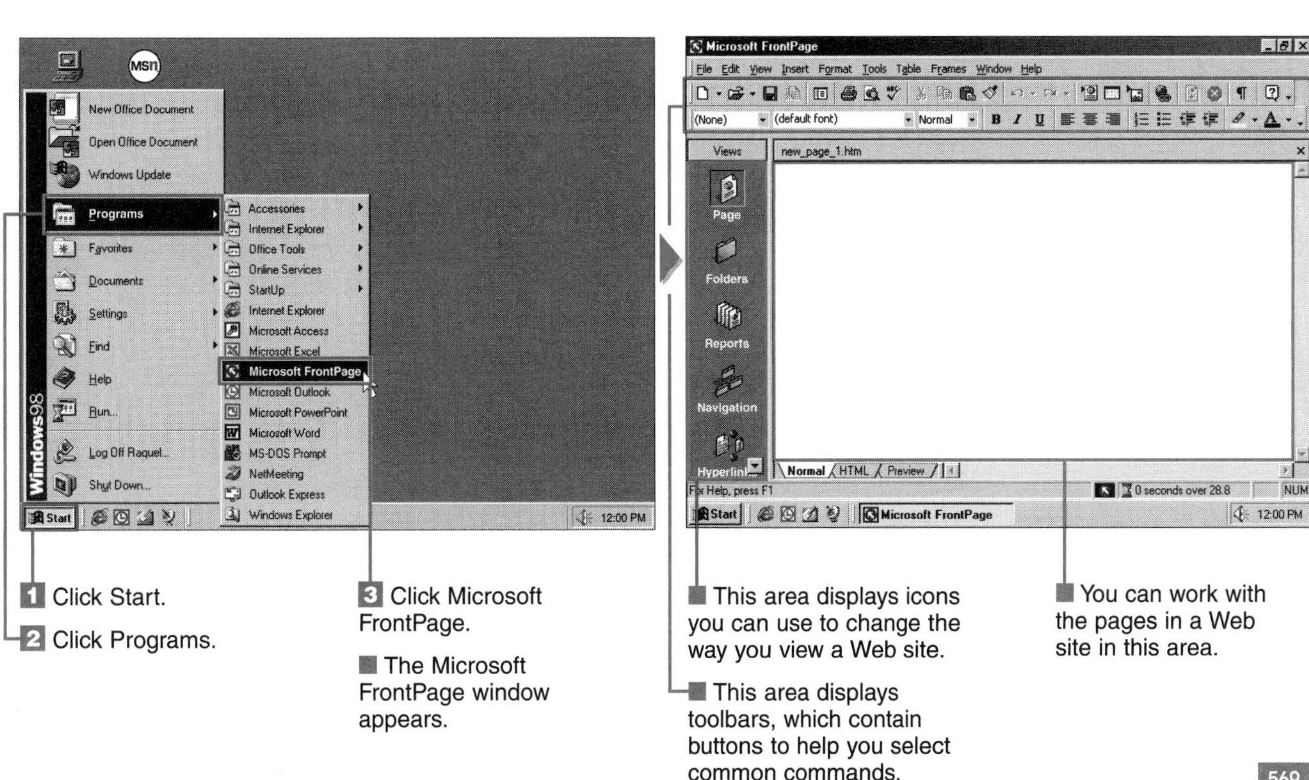

1 Click Start.

2 Click Programs.

3 Click Microsoft FrontPage.

■ The Microsoft FrontPage window appears.

■ This area displays icons you can use to change the way you view a Web site.

■ This area displays toolbars, which contain buttons to help you select common commands.

■ You can work with the pages in a Web site in this area.

CREATE A NEW WEB SITE

FrontPage provides several templates and wizards you can use to create a new Web site.

The One Page Web template creates a Web site containing a single blank page. The Empty Web template creates a Web site with nothing in it. These templates are useful when you want to design your own Web site one page at a time.

The Customer Support Web, Personal Web and Project Web templates create Web sites with multiple pages. These templates provide the layout and formatting for your site so you can concentrate on the content of your pages.

When you use a wizard to create a Web site, the wizard asks you a series of questions and then sets up a Web site based on your answers. FrontPage offers the Corporate Presence Wizard, Discussion Web Wizard and Import Web Wizard.

Some templates and wizards provide sample text for the Web site. You can select the sample text on a page and type your own information to replace the text.

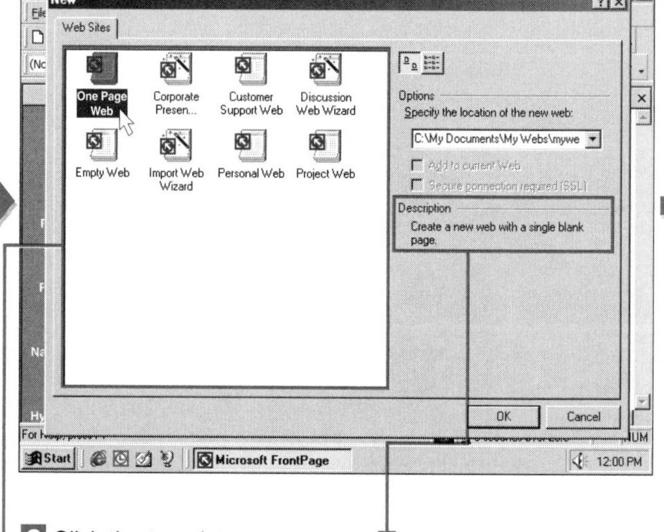

1 Click [icon] in this area to create a new Web site.

2 Click Web.

■ The New dialog box appears.

3 Click the template or wizard you want to use to create the new Web site.

Note: A wizard displays a magic wand ([icon]) and will take you step by step through the process of creating a Web site.

■ This area displays a description of the template or wizard you selected.

Can I use more than one template or wizard to create a Web site?

✔ You can add a new Web site to an existing Web site to combine features from two templates or wizards. For example, you can add a customer support Web site to a corporate presence Web site. Open the Web site you want to add another Web site to. Perform the steps below to create the new Web site, except click the Add to current Web option in step 4 (☐ changes to ☑). If the Web sites contain duplicate features, such as page borders, FrontPage will ask if you want to replace the current feature with the new one.

Can I have my Web site open automatically the next time I start FrontPage?

✔ Yes. From the Tools menu, select Options and then click the Open last Web automatically when FrontPage starts option (☐ changes to ☑). Each time you start FrontPage, the last Web site you worked with will automatically appear on your screen.

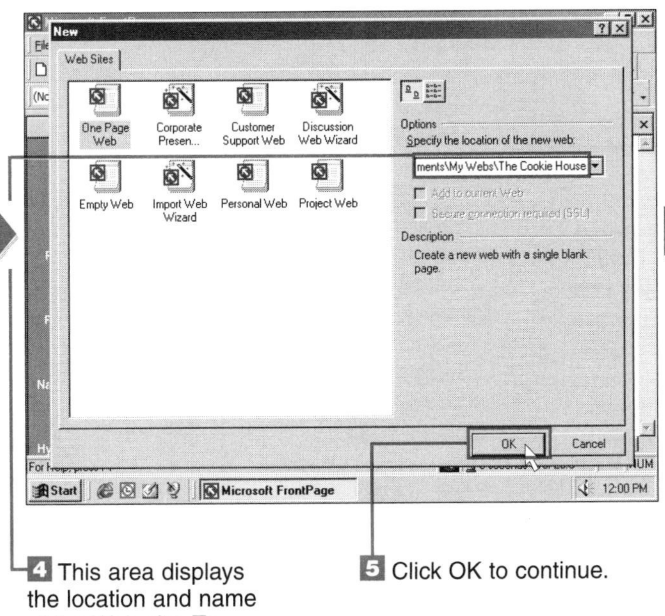

4 This area displays the location and name of the Web site. To change this information, drag the mouse I over the existing text and then type the new information.

5 Click OK to continue.

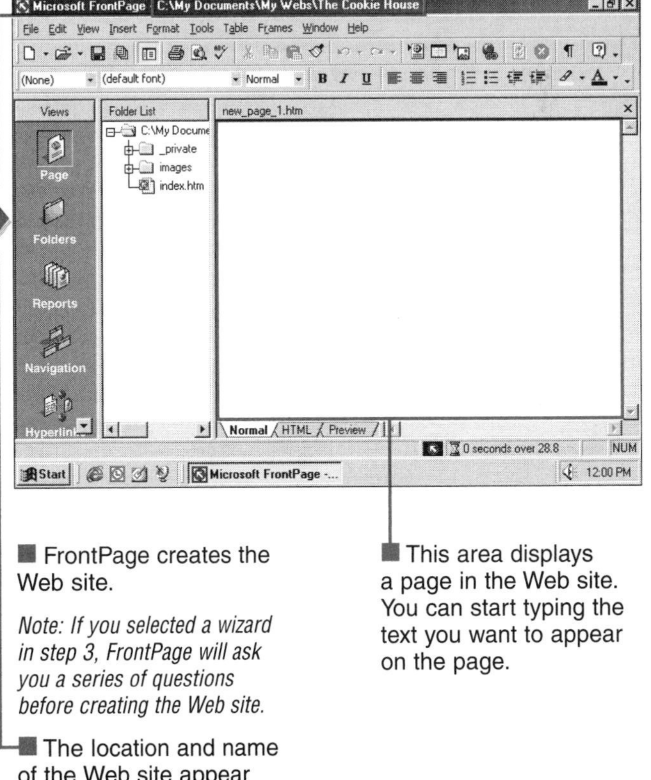

■ FrontPage creates the Web site.

Note: If you selected a wizard in step 3, FrontPage will ask you a series of questions before creating the Web site.

■ The location and name of the Web site appear at the top of the screen.

■ This area displays a page in the Web site. You can start typing the text you want to appear on the page.

SAVE A PAGE

You can save a page to store it for future use. This allows you to later review and make changes to the page.

To avoid losing your work, you should regularly save changes you make to a page.

The first time you save a page, the Save As dialog box appears, allowing you to name the page.

FrontPage may suggest a name for the page based on the first line of text on the page. You can give the page another name. You should choose a descriptive name that will help you identify the page in the future.

By default, FrontPage saves the page in the current Web site in the My Webs folder.

The next time you save the page, the Save As dialog box will not appear since you have already named the page.

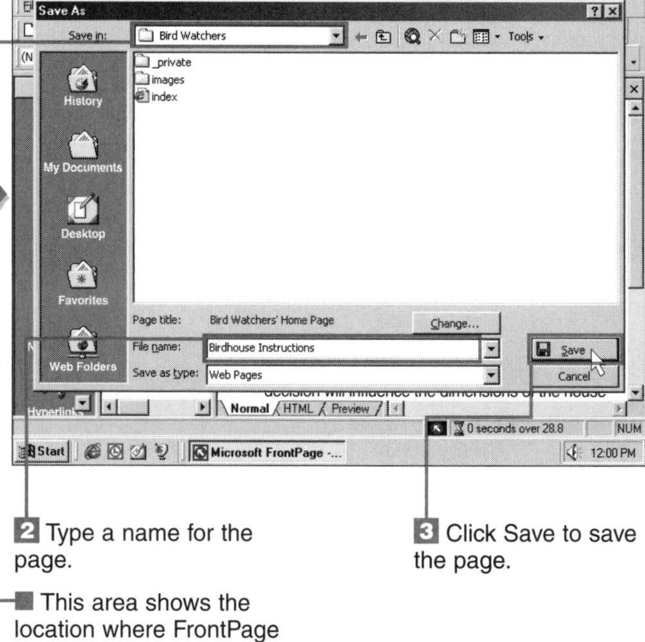

1 Click [save icon] to save the displayed page.

■ The Save As dialog box appears.

Note: If you previously saved the page, the Save As dialog box will not appear since you have already named the page.

2 Type a name for the page.

■ This area shows the location where FrontPage will store the page.

3 Click Save to save the page.

CHANGE THE PAGE TITLE

When you create a page, FrontPage gives the page a temporary title, such as New Page 1. You should change this title to reflect the content of your page.

Do not confuse the page title with the file name. The page title is the text that appears in the title bar at the top of the Web browser window when a reader views your page. The file name is the name you used to store the page as a file on your computer.

When changing the page title, you should use a brief, descriptive title that will interest people in reading your page. For example, the title "Advanced Golf Techniques" is more interesting and informative than "Chapter Two" or "My Home Page".

Using a descriptive page title can also help people find your page on the Web, since many search tools use page titles in their searches.

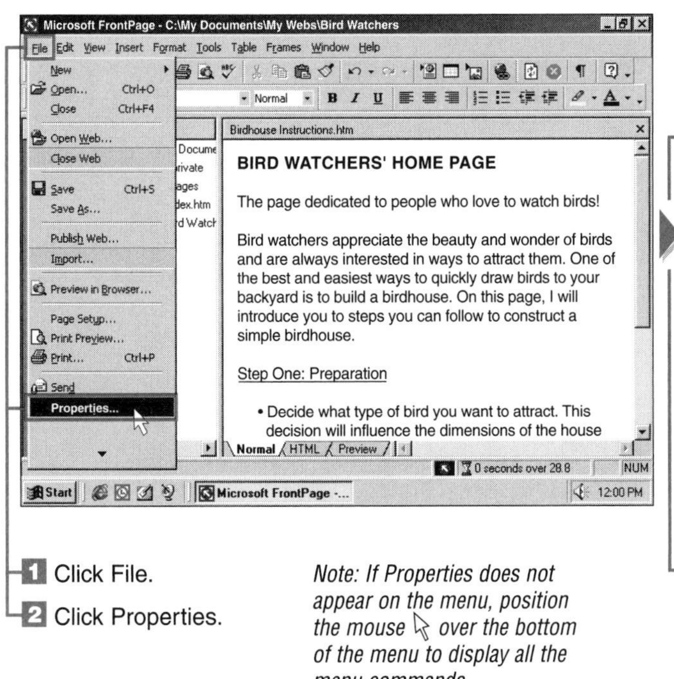

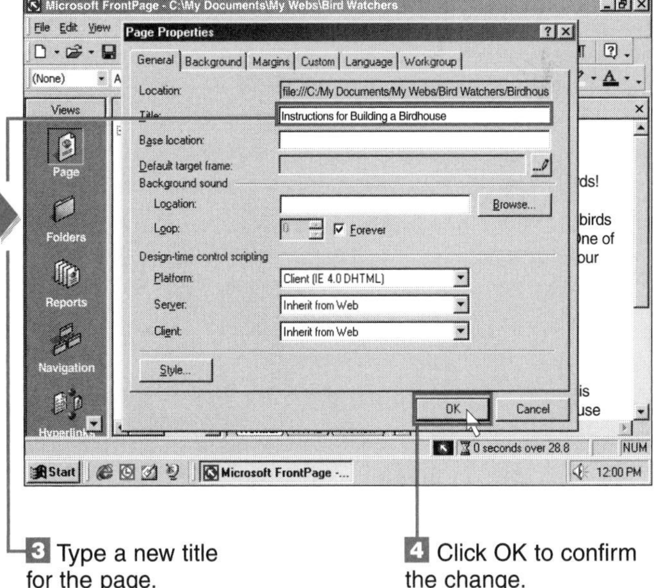

1 Click File.

2 Click Properties.

Note: If Properties does not appear on the menu, position the mouse over the bottom of the menu to display all the menu commands.

■ The Page Properties dialog box appears.

3 Type a new title for the page.

4 Click OK to confirm the change.

CREATE A NEW PAGE

You can create a new page to include information such as product details, company information or a resume.

FrontPage gives each new page a temporary name, such as new_page_2.htm. You can change the temporary name when you save the page. For information on saving a page, see page 572.

When you create a new page, FrontPage displays a blank page on your screen. You can immediately start typing the text you want to appear on the new page.

TIP

Can FrontPage help me create a new page?

✔ FrontPage provides page templates to help you create a new, professional-looking page. Click the File menu, select New and then click Page. Click the General tab and then click the page template you want to use. FrontPage displays a preview of the page template you selected. Click OK to confirm your selection. FrontPage provides a design and sample text for the page. You can replace the sample text with your own information.

1 Click ▾ in this area to create a new page.

2 Click Page.

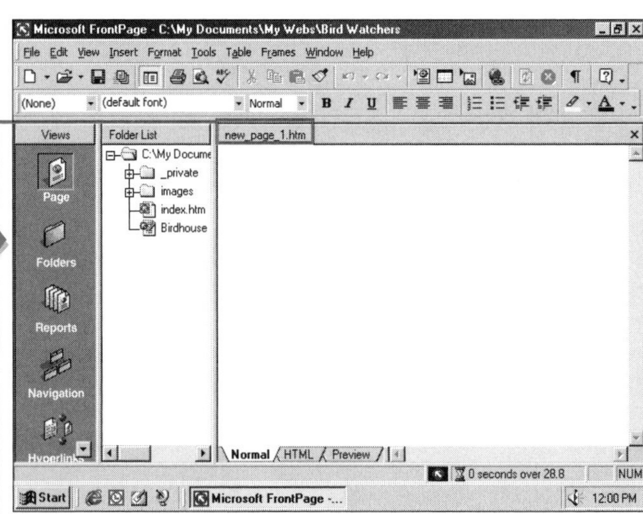

■ A new page appears.

■ This area displays a temporary name for the new page.

■ You can start typing the text you want to appear on the new page.

OPEN A WEB SITE

You can open a saved Web site and display it on your screen.

The Open Web dialog box allows you to specify where the Web site you want to open is located on your computer. By default, FrontPage stores Web sites in the My Webs folder.

FrontPage uses icons to indicate the different items that appear in the Open Web dialog box. Web sites display the icon.

When you open a Web site, FrontPage displays the Web site on your screen. You can then review and make changes to the pages in the Web site. If you make changes to a page, you should save the page. For information on saving a page, see page 572.

You can have more than one Web site open at a time. The name and location of the current Web site appear at the top of the screen. FrontPage displays a button on the taskbar for each open Web site.

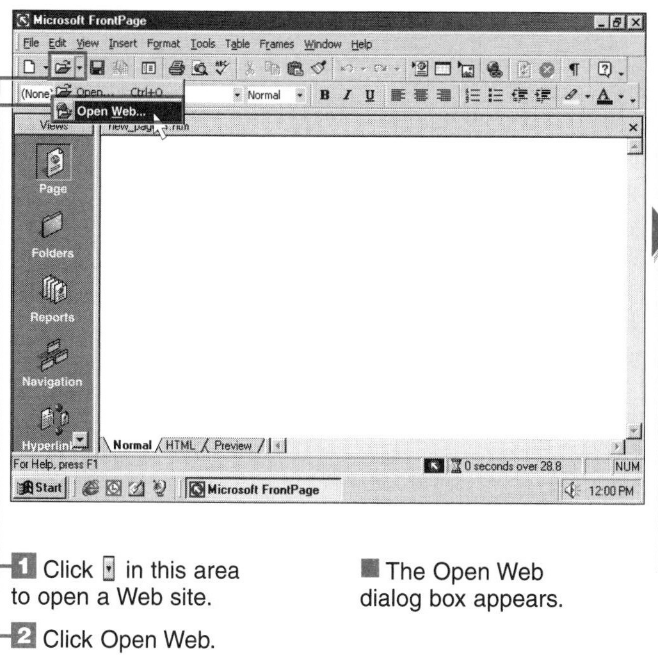

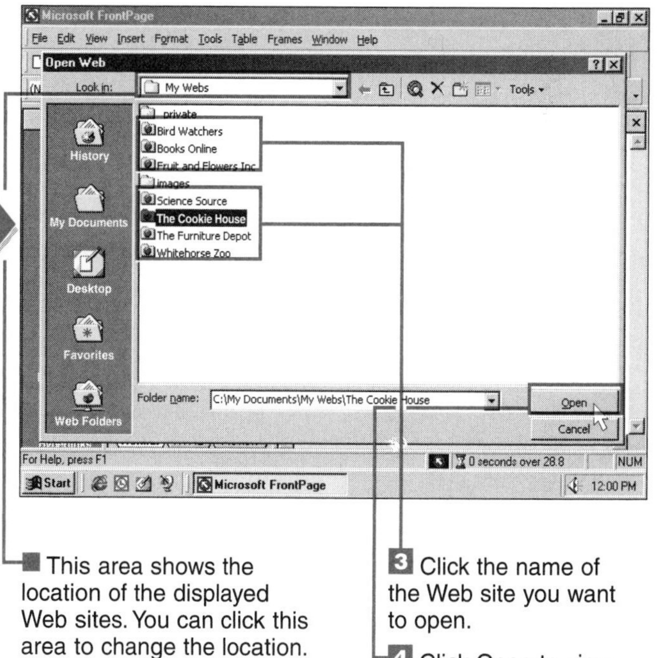

1 Click ▾ in this area to open a Web site.

2 Click Open Web.

■ The Open Web dialog box appears.

■ This area shows the location of the displayed Web sites. You can click this area to change the location.

3 Click the name of the Web site you want to open.

4 Click Open to view the Web site.

USING THE PAGE VIEW

FrontPage offers several ways you can display your Web site. Each view is useful for performing specific tasks. When you want to view and edit the contents of the pages in your Web site, you can display the Web site in the Page view.

The Page view displays a list of the folders and pages in your Web site on the left side of the window and the current page on the right side of the window. In the list of folders and pages, folders display the icon and pages display the icon.

You can hide or display the list of folders and pages at any time. Hiding the list gives you a larger and less cluttered working area.

Displaying the list lets you easily browse through the pages in your Web site.

After you display a page of interest in the Page view, you can edit and format the contents of the page. For example, you can change the font of text and add items such as pictures and horizontal lines.

1 Click Page to display the Web site in the Page view.

■ This area displays the folders and pages in the Web site.

■ If the area displaying the folders and pages does not appear, click to display the area.

Note: You can click again to hide the area.

2 Double-click a page you want to view. Pages display the icon.

■ This area displays the contents of the page you selected.

Note: You can repeat step 2 to view the contents of another page.

USING THE FOLDERS VIEW

When you create a Web site using a template or wizard, FrontPage automatically creates a folder structure for the Web site. You can display your Web site in the Folders view to see the folder structure FrontPage created.

The Folders view displays the folder structure for the Web site on the left side of the window and the contents of the current folder on the right side of the window.

The folder structure includes a main folder for the Web site, a private folder and an images folder. The main folder stores all the folders and pages in your Web site. The private folder stores information you do not want to appear on your pages, such as the results of forms. The images folder stores pictures and other images.

When you display the contents of a folder, you can view information about the contents, such as the name, title and size of each item. You can also sort the contents of a folder to help you find an item of interest.

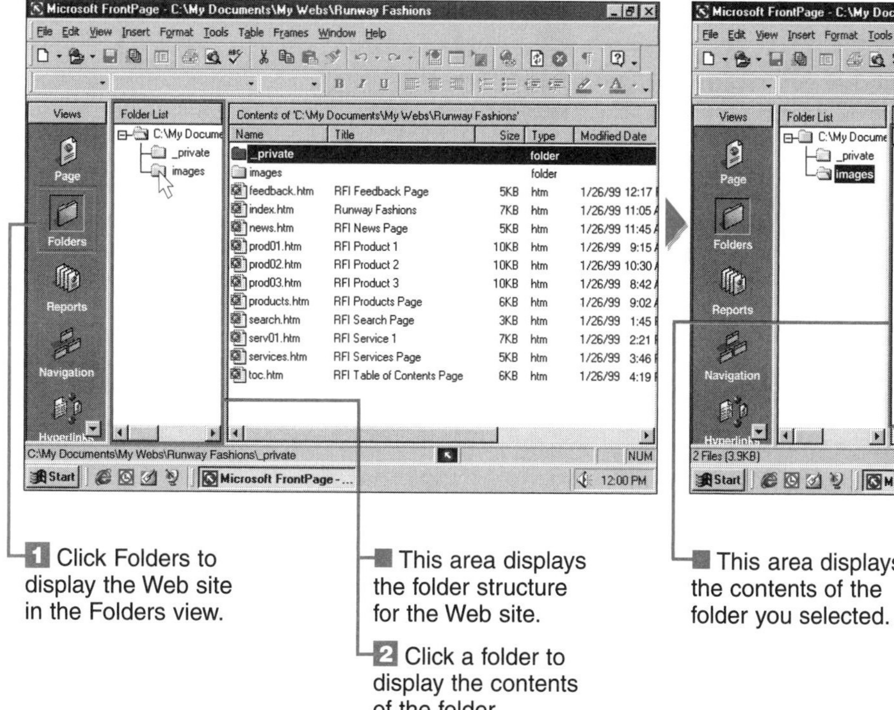

1 Click Folders to display the Web site in the Folders view.

■ This area displays the folder structure for the Web site.

2 Click a folder to display the contents of the folder.

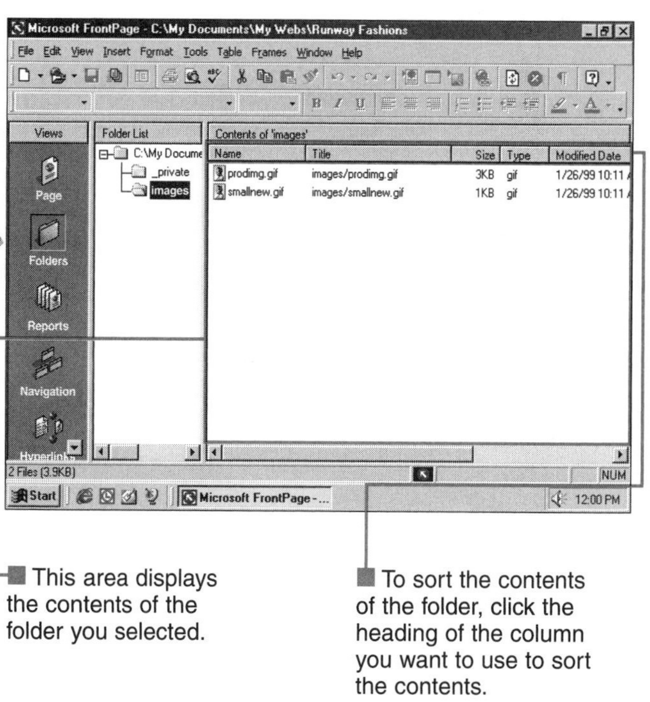

■ This area displays the contents of the folder you selected.

■ To sort the contents of the folder, click the heading of the column you want to use to sort the contents.

USING THE REPORTS VIEW

You can use the Reports view to see information about your Web site. FrontPage offers many reports you can display in the Reports view. Each report displays different information about the Web site.

The Site Summary report displays an overview of your Web site, including information such as the number of pictures and hyperlinks in the Web site.

The All Files, Recently Added Files and Recently Changed Files reports display details about the files in your Web site. For example, you can view the title, size and type of each file.

The Broken Hyperlinks report displays the status of the hyperlinks in your Web site. This lets you quickly determine if your hyperlinks are working.

The Reports view also offers reports that show the publishing status of pages, older files that may need to be updated and pages that will take a long time to display in a Web browser.

You can quickly display the last report you worked with. This is useful if you frequently use the same report.

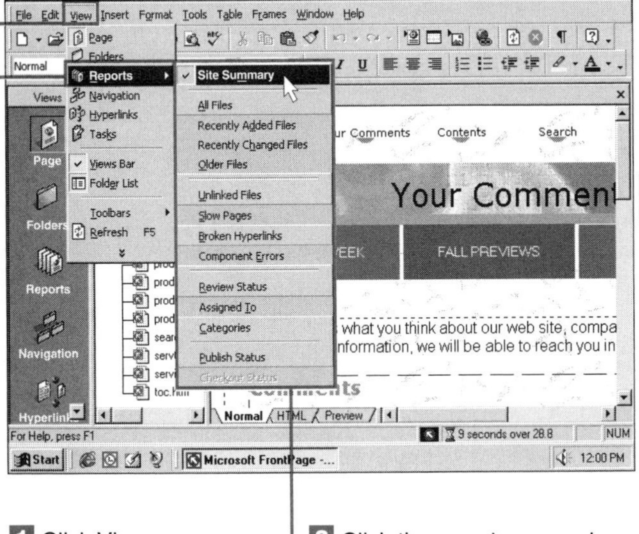

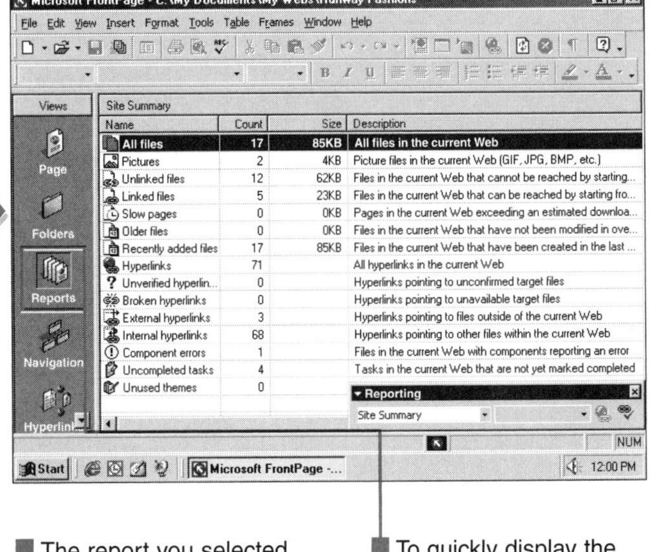

1 Click View.

2 Click Reports.

3 Click the report you want to view.

■ A check mark (✔) appears beside the currently selected report.

Note: If the report you want does not appear on the menu, position the mouse over the bottom of the menu to display all the reports.

■ The report you selected appears.

■ To quickly display the last report you worked with, click Reports.

USING THE HYPERLINKS VIEW

A hyperlink connects information on a page to another page in the Web site or to related information on the Web. When a reader selects a hyperlink in a Web browser, the other page appears on the screen. You can display your Web site in the Hyperlinks view to see the hyperlinks that connect a page to other information.

If you used a template or wizard to create your Web site, FrontPage may have automatically added hyperlinks to the pages for you. You can also add your own hyperlinks to pages. For information on creating a hyperlink, see page 600.

The Hyperlinks view displays a list of the folders and pages in your Web site on the left side of the window and a map of the hyperlinks to and from the current page on the right side of the window. You can hide or display the list of folders and pages. Hiding the list gives you more room to see the hyperlinks for a page. Displaying the list lets you quickly display the hyperlinks for another page.

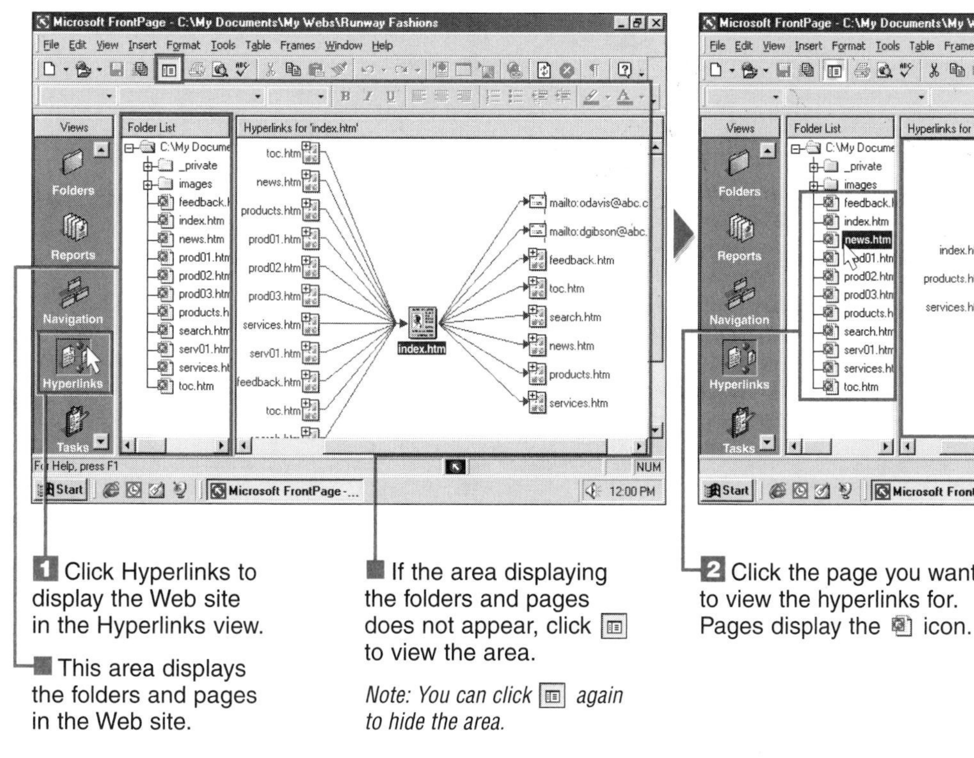

1 Click Hyperlinks to display the Web site in the Hyperlinks view.

■ This area displays the folders and pages in the Web site.

■ If the area displaying the folders and pages does not appear, click ▤ to view the area.

Note: You can click ▤ again to hide the area.

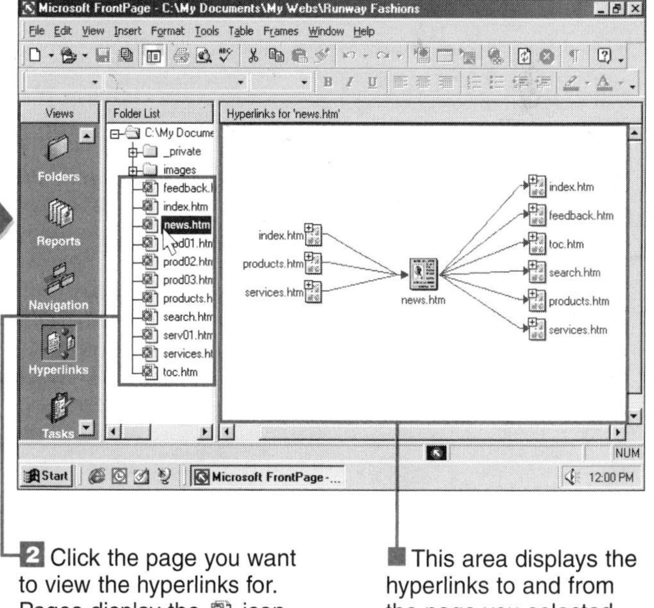

2 Click the page you want to view the hyperlinks for. Pages display the ▣ icon.

■ This area displays the hyperlinks to and from the page you selected.

Note: You can repeat step 2 to view the hyperlinks for another page.

USING THE NAVIGATION VIEW

You can use the Navigation view to work with the navigational structure of your Web site. The navigational structure shows how the pages in your Web site are related. Some templates and wizards automatically set up a navigational structure for you.

The navigational structure of your Web site determines the layout of navigation bars on your pages. A navigation bar is a set of hyperlinks at the top or left edge of each page that readers can use to move through your Web site. When you change the navigational structure of your Web site, FrontPage automatically updates the navigation bars for you.

The Navigation view displays the folders and pages in your Web site on the left side of the window and the navigational structure on the right side of the window. Boxes represent pages in the navigational structure. A line between boxes indicates the pages are related.

While working in the Navigation view, you can add new pages to the navigational structure. You can also move pages to change the way the pages are related.

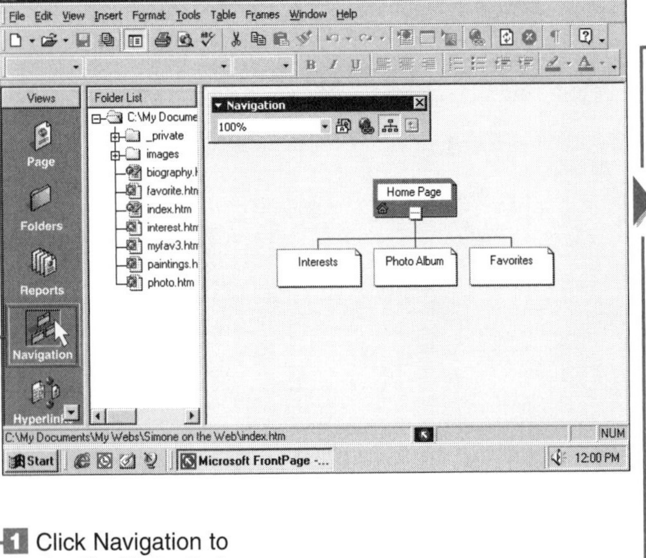

1 Click Navigation to display the Web site in the Navigation view.

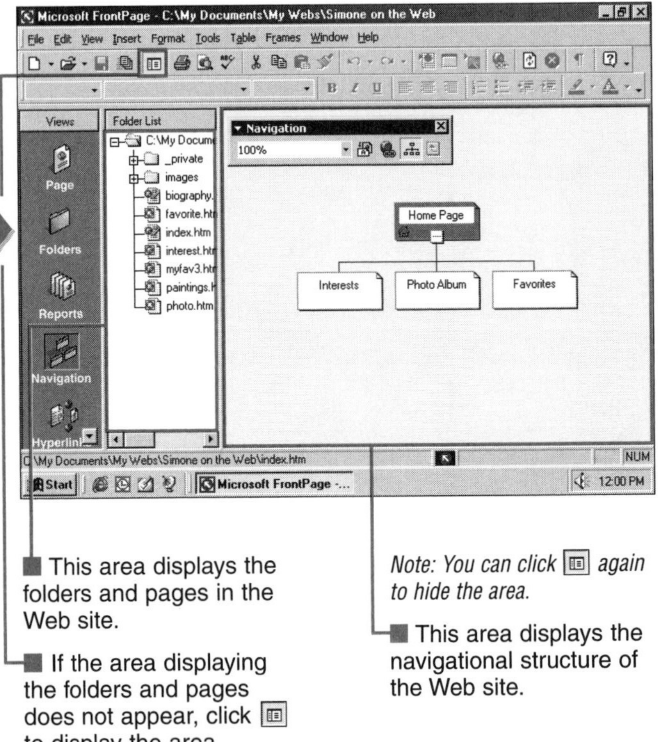

■ This area displays the folders and pages in the Web site.

■ If the area displaying the folders and pages does not appear, click ▤ to display the area.

■ This area displays the navigational structure of the Web site.

Note: You can click ▤ again to hide the area.

How can I add navigation bars to my pages?

✔ If your pages do not display navigation bars, you can have FrontPage automatically add navigation bars to the pages. From the Format menu, select Shared Borders and then choose All Pages (○ changes to ⊙). Click Top or Left to specify where you want the navigation bars to appear (☐ changes to ☑). Then click Include navigation buttons (☐ changes to ☑).

Is there an easier way to work with the navigational structure of a large Web site?

✔ If the navigational structure of your Web site is too large to fit on the screen, you can click the minus sign (⊟) on a page in the structure to hide the pages below the page (⊟ changes to ⊞). To once again display the pages, click the plus sign (⊞).

How do I remove a page from the navigational structure?

✔ Click the page in the navigational structure and then press the Delete key. Click the Remove this page from all navigation bars option (○ changes to ⊙) and then click OK.

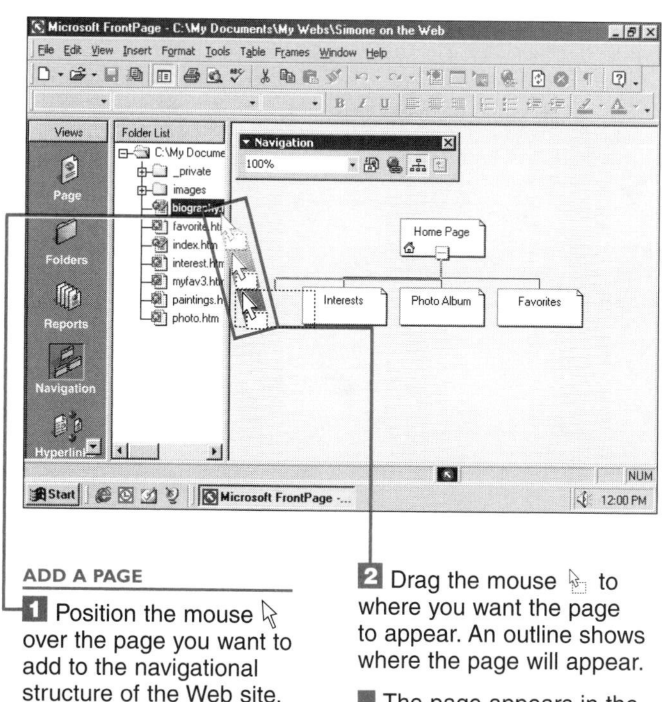

ADD A PAGE

1 Position the mouse over the page you want to add to the navigational structure of the Web site.

2 Drag the mouse to where you want the page to appear. An outline shows where the page will appear.

■ The page appears in the navigational structure.

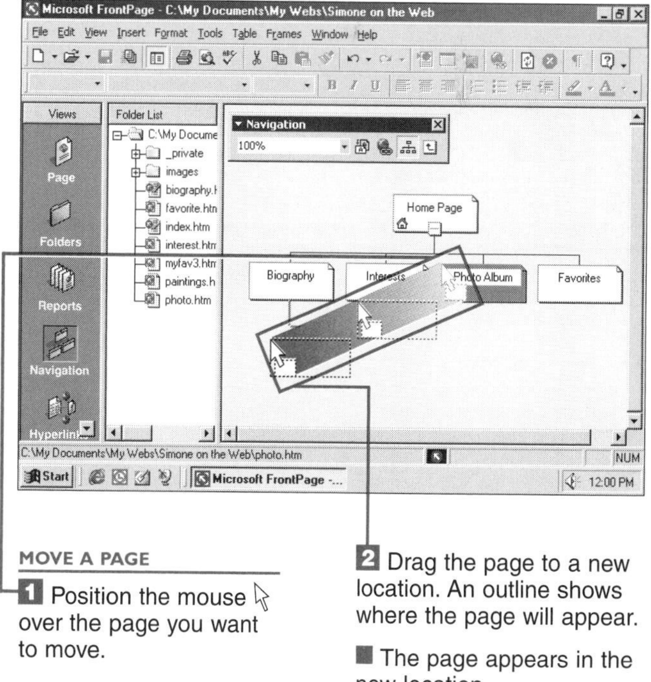

MOVE A PAGE

1 Position the mouse over the page you want to move.

2 Drag the page to a new location. An outline shows where the page will appear.

■ The page appears in the new location.

CHECK SPELLING

You can find and correct spelling errors on your page. Correcting spelling errors will make your page appear more professional.

FrontPage's spell check feature compares every word on your page to words in its dictionary. If a word on your page does not exist in FrontPage's dictionary, FrontPage considers the word misspelled.

FrontPage automatically checks your page for spelling errors as you type and underlines misspelled words in red. The underlines only appear on your screen and will not appear when you view the page in a Web browser or print the page.

When you finish creating your page, you can locate and correct all the spelling errors at once. When FrontPage finds a misspelled word, it provides a list of suggestions to correct the word. You can replace the word with a suggestion or ignore the word and continue checking your page. If FrontPage repeatedly finds a misspelled word you know is correct, such as a name, you can choose to ignore all occurrences of the word on your page.

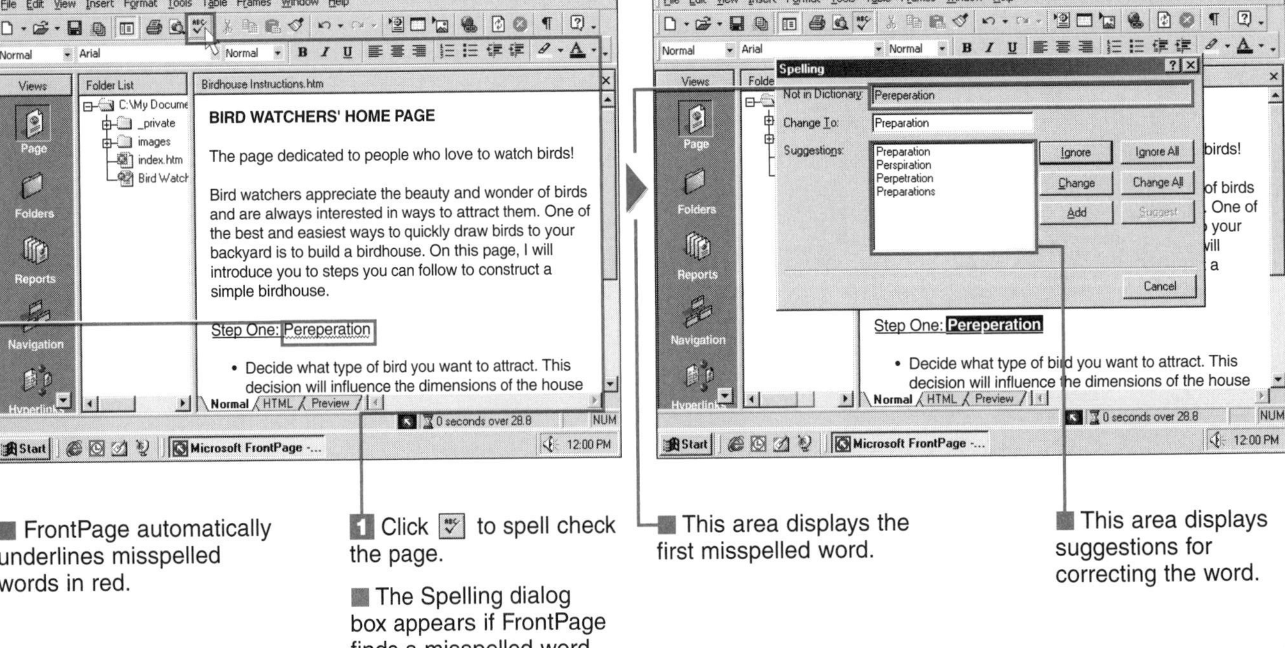

■ FrontPage automatically underlines misspelled words in red.

1 Click [spelling icon] to spell check the page.

■ The Spelling dialog box appears if FrontPage finds a misspelled word.

■ This area displays the first misspelled word.

■ This area displays suggestions for correcting the word.

Why did FrontPage underline a correctly spelled word?

✔ FrontPage considers any word that does not exist in its dictionary to be misspelled. You can add a word to the dictionary so FrontPage will recognize the word during future spell checks. Right-click the word you want to add to the dictionary and then select Add.

Can I correct a single error on my page?

✔ Yes. Right-click a word that displays a red underline. A list of suggestions to correct the error appears. Click the suggestion you want to use.

How can I spell check all the pages in my Web site at once?

✔ From the View menu, select Folders. Click the Spelling button (✓) and select the Entire web option. Then click Start. FrontPage displays a list of pages that contain spelling errors. To correct the errors, double-click the first page in the list. When you have finished correcting the errors on the first page, FrontPage asks if you want to continue with the next page. Click Next Document to continue. When you finish correcting all the pages, click ☒ to close the Spelling dialog box.

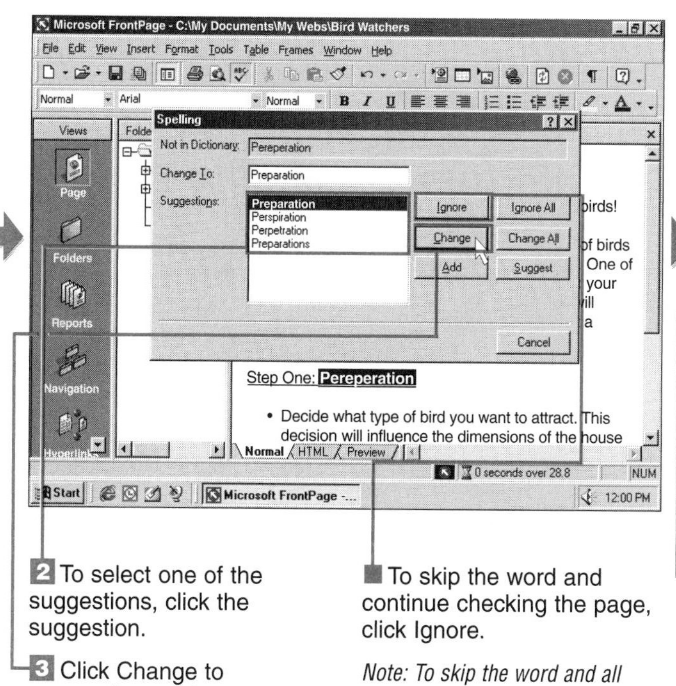

2 To select one of the suggestions, click the suggestion.

3 Click Change to correct the word on the page.

■ To skip the word and continue checking the page, click Ignore.

Note: To skip the word and all occurrences of the word on the page, click Ignore All.

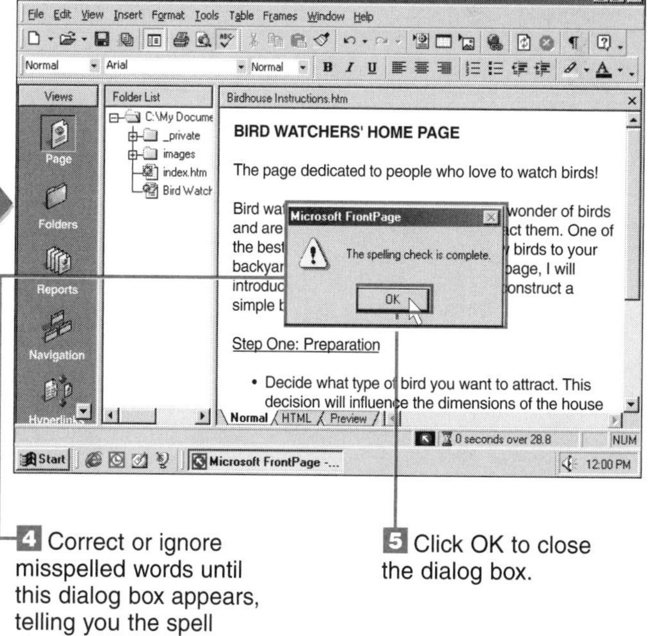

4 Correct or ignore misspelled words until this dialog box appears, telling you the spell check is complete.

5 Click OK to close the dialog box.

PREVIEW A PAGE

You can preview your page to see how the page will appear when readers view the page on the Web. This lets you make sure your page appears the way you want.

You should always save your page before previewing the page.

FrontPage offers two ways you can preview your page–in a Web browser and in FrontPage. When you preview a page in your Web browser, the Web browser opens and displays the page. When you preview a page in FrontPage, FrontPage displays the page on the Preview tab as it will appear on the Web.

FrontPage also lets you view the HTML code used to construct your page. HTML code consists of text and special instructions called tags. As you work with a page, FrontPage automatically enters the HTML code for you and keeps it hidden from view so you can concentrate on the content of your page. If you are familiar with HTML code, you can display and edit the code using the HTML tab.

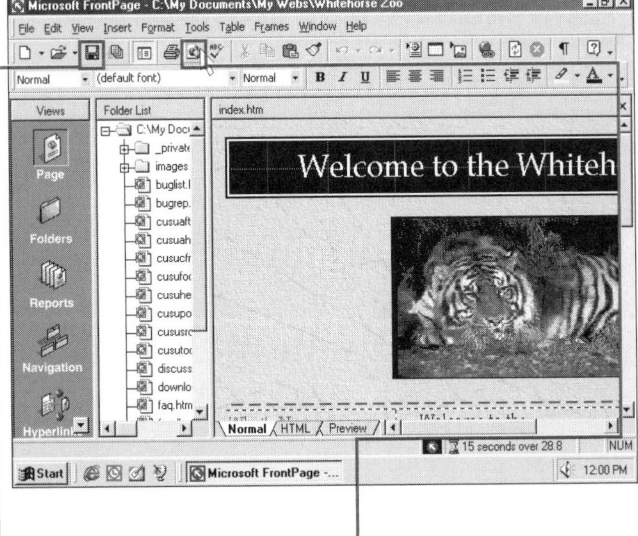

PREVIEW A PAGE IN A WEB BROWSER

1. Click to save any changes you made to the displayed page.

2. Click to preview the page in your Web browser.

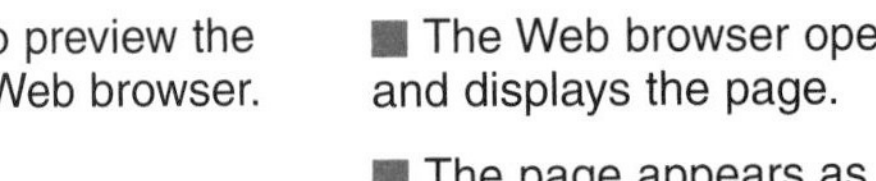

- The Web browser opens and displays the page.
- The page appears as it will look on the Web.

3. When you finish reviewing the page, click to close the Web browser.

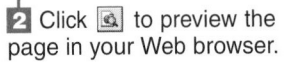

The preview in my Web browser looks different than the preview in FrontPage. What is wrong?

✔ Different Web browsers may display items such as text and tables differently. If your Web browser is different than the Web browser FrontPage uses, the previews may not look the same. You should make sure you are satisfied with the way your page appears in both your Web browser and FrontPage before you publish your Web site.

Can I preview my page in a different Web browser?

✔ If you have more than one Web browser installed on your computer, you can preview your page with a different browser. From the File menu, select Preview in Browser. Choose the browser you want to use and then click Preview.

Can I display the HTML code while I work on my page in the Normal view?

✔ Yes. This can help you understand how FrontPage creates pages using HTML code. From the View menu, select Reveal Tags. You can repeat this process to hide the HTML code.

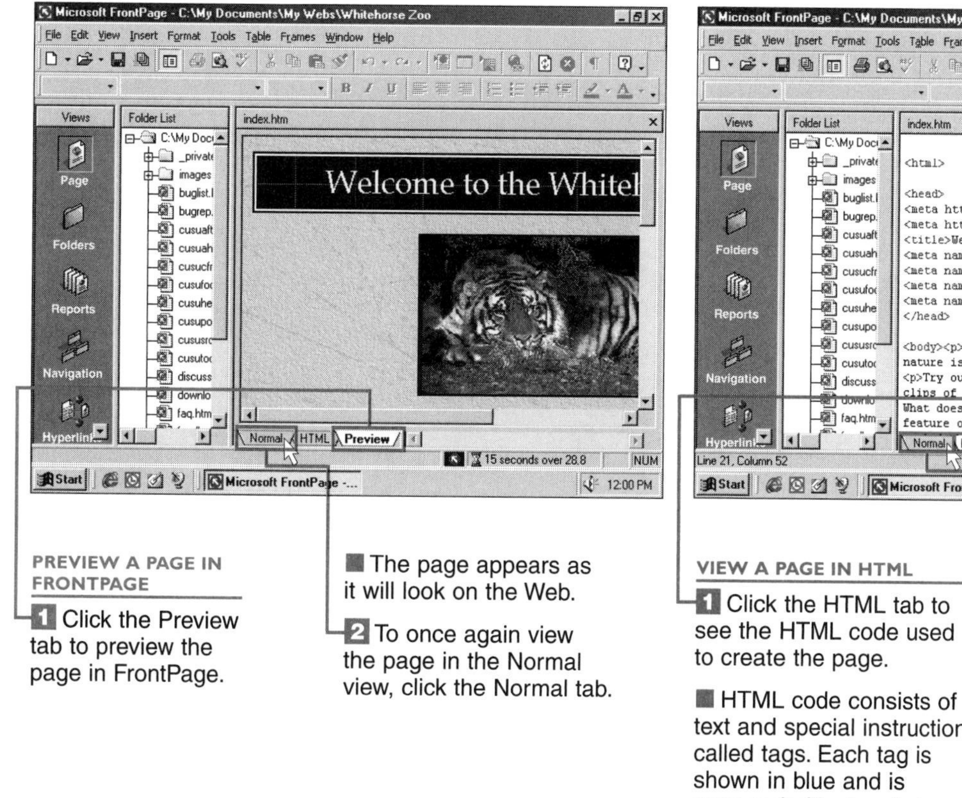

PREVIEW A PAGE IN FRONTPAGE

1 Click the Preview tab to preview the page in FrontPage.

■ The page appears as it will look on the Web.

2 To once again view the page in the Normal view, click the Normal tab.

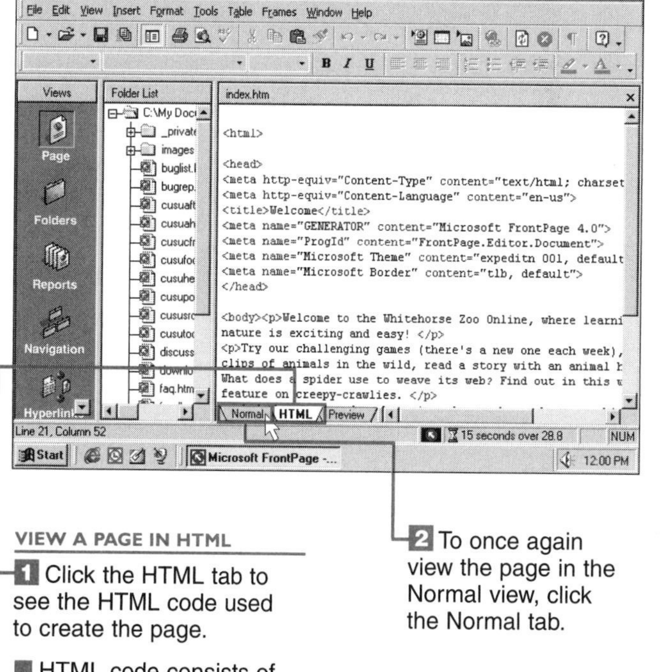

VIEW A PAGE IN HTML

1 Click the HTML tab to see the HTML code used to create the page.

■ HTML code consists of text and special instructions called tags. Each tag is shown in blue and is surrounded by brackets < >.

2 To once again view the page in the Normal view, click the Normal tab.

PUBLISH A WEB SITE

When you finish creating your Web site, you can transfer the pages to a computer called a Web server. Once the pages are stored on the Web server, the pages will be available for other people to view. You can publish your Web site to a Web server on the Internet or on your company's intranet.

The company that gives you access to the Internet usually offers space on its Web server where you can publish your Web site. There are also places on the Internet that will publish your Web site for free, such as GeoCities (www.geocities.com).

Before publishing your Web site, you should preview the pages to ensure they look the way you want. For information on previewing pages, see page 584.

To publish your Web site, you must enter the Internet address of the Web server where you want to publish your Web site. You must also enter your user name and password. If you do not know this information, you can contact your Internet Service Provider (ISP) or system administrator.

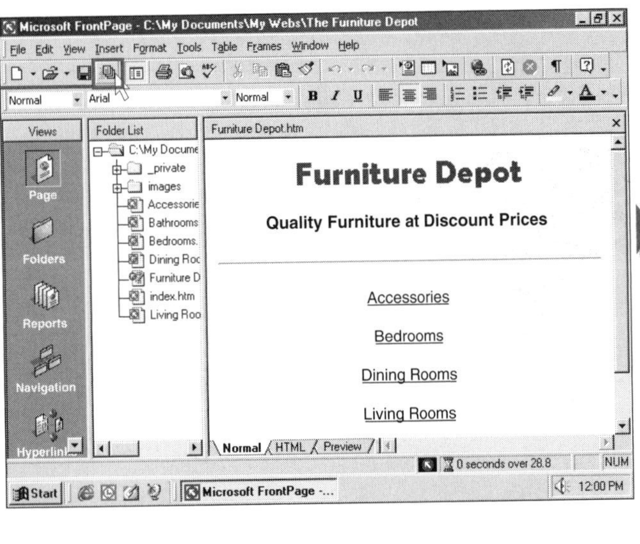

1 Click to publish the current Web site.

■ The Publish Web dialog box appears.

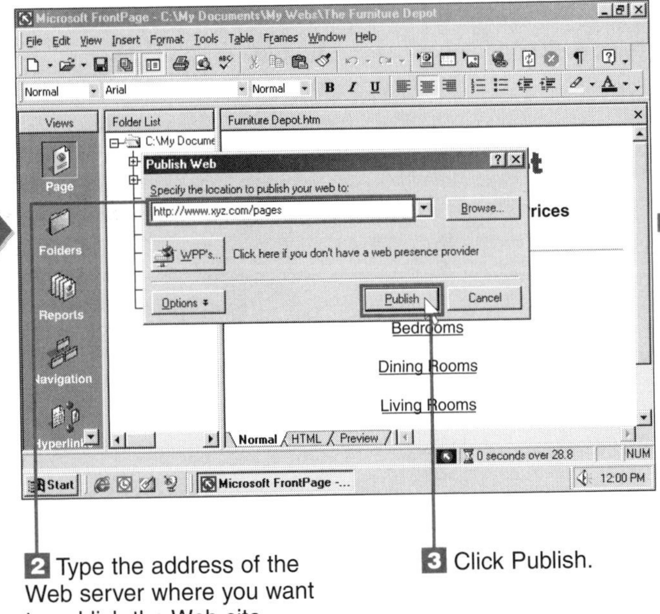

2 Type the address of the Web server where you want to publish the Web site.

3 Click Publish.

TIPS

Do I have to publish all the pages in my Web site?

✔ No. You may not want to publish a page you are still working on. From the View menu, select Reports and then click Publish Status. Right-click the name of the page you do not want to publish and select Properties. Choose the Workgroup tab and click the Exclude this file when publishing the rest of the Web option (☐ changes to ☑). Then click OK.

After publishing my Web site, I updated some of the pages. How do I publish my changes?

✔ You can click the Publish Web button ( ) to publish the changes. FrontPage will not redisplay the Publish Web dialog box. To redisplay the dialog box so you can change your options, select the File menu and then click Publish Web.

How do I determine if my Web server uses FrontPage Server Extensions?

✔ You can contact your Internet service provider or system administrator to find out if your Web server uses FrontPage Server Extensions. If your Web server does not use FrontPage Server Extensions, you may not be able to use some of FrontPage's advanced features. For example, a hit counter you added to a page may not work properly. For information on hit counters, see page 606.

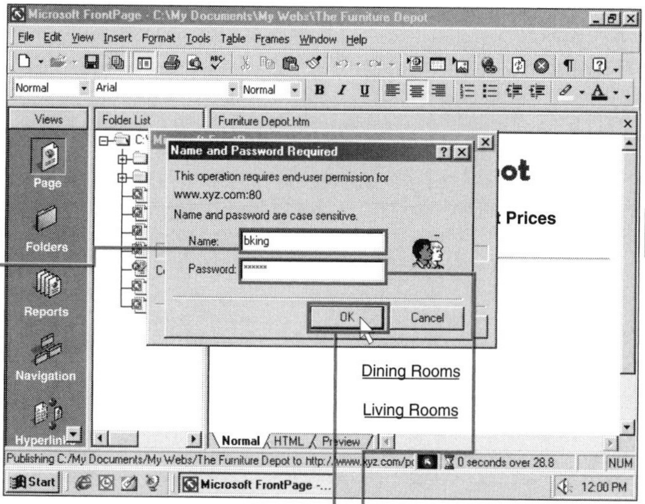

■ A dialog box appears, asking for your name and password.

4 Double-click this area and type your name.

5 Click this area and type your password.
A symbol (*) appears for each character you type to prevent others from seeing your password.

6 Click OK.

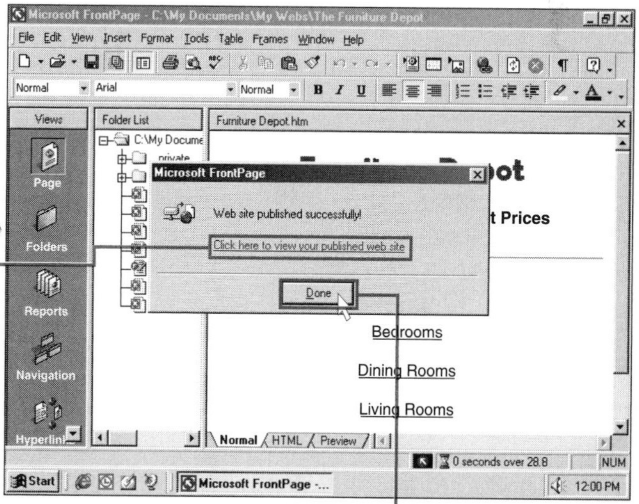

■ A dialog box appears when the Web site has been published successfully.

■ You can click this option to view the published Web site.

7 Click Done to close the dialog box.

SELECT TEXT

Before performing many editing and formatting tasks in FrontPage, you must select the text you want to work with. For example, you must select text you want to change to a different font or size.

Selected text appears highlighted on your screen.

FrontPage highlights selected text in a color that contrasts the background color of your page. This makes the selected text stand out from the rest of the text on the page.

You can select the part of your page you want to work with. You can select a single word or any amount of text on the page.

After you finish working with selected text, you should deselect the text. If you begin typing when text on your screen is selected, FrontPage will delete the selected text and replace it with the text you type.

SELECT A WORD

1 Double-click the word you want to select.

■ To deselect text, click outside the selected area.

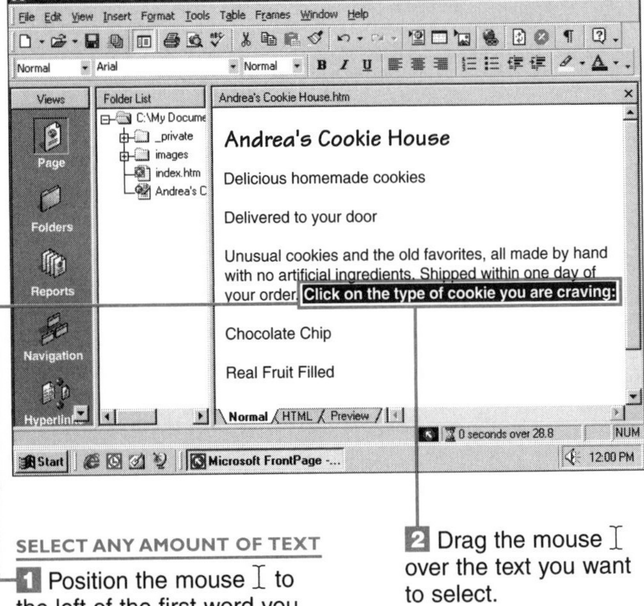

SELECT ANY AMOUNT OF TEXT

1 Position the mouse I to the left of the first word you want to select.

2 Drag the mouse I over the text you want to select.

BOLD, ITALIC OR UNDERLINE

You can use the Bold, Italic and Underline features to change the style of text on your page. These features help you emphasize information and enhance the appearance of the page.

You can use one feature at a time or any combination of the three formatting features to change the style of text.

The Bold feature makes text appear darker and thicker than other text. You can bold headings and titles to make them stand out from the rest of the text on the page.

The Italic feature tilts text to the right. You may want to italicize quotations and definitions on the page.

The Underline feature adds a line underneath text. You should use underlines only when necessary, since people viewing your page may confuse underlined text with hyperlinks.

You should only emphasize important information. If you emphasize too many words and phrases on a page, the important information will not stand out.

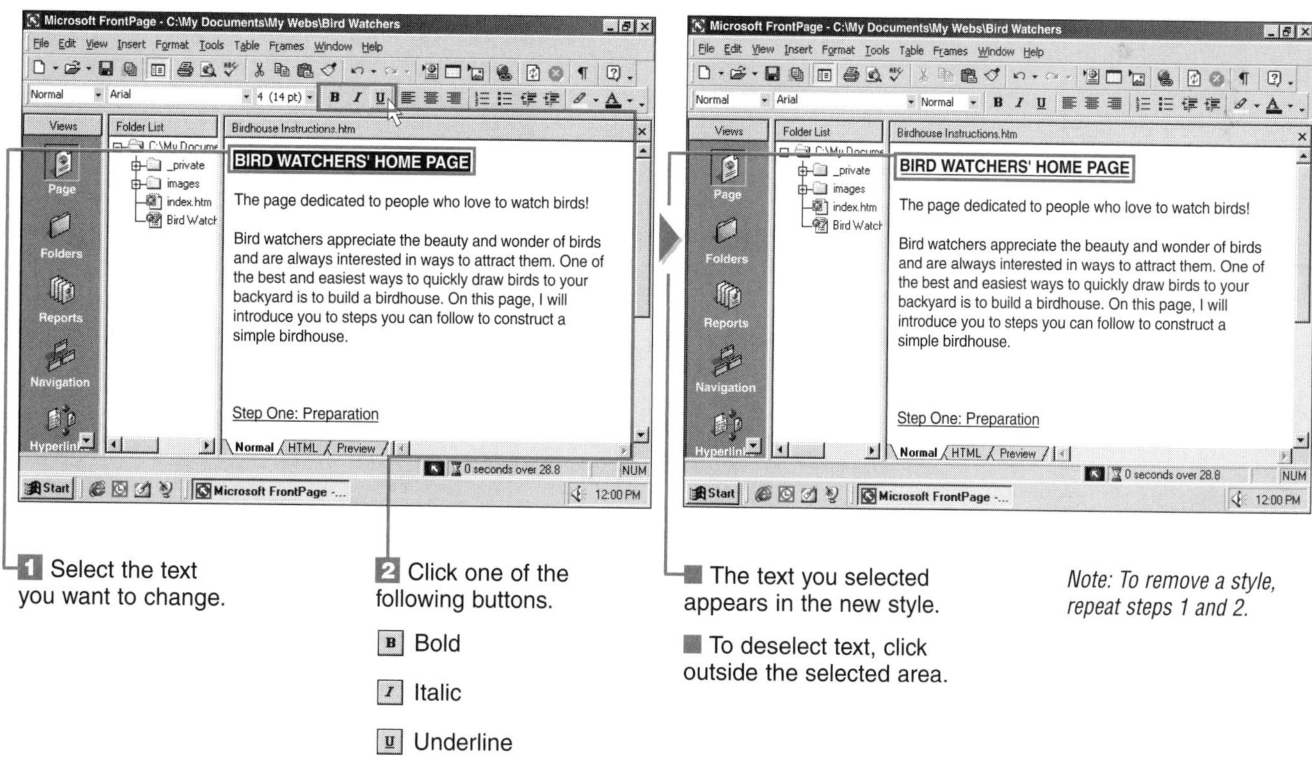

1 Select the text you want to change.

2 Click one of the following buttons.

- B Bold
- I Italic
- U Underline

■ The text you selected appears in the new style.

■ To deselect text, click outside the selected area.

Note: To remove a style, repeat steps 1 and 2.

CHANGE FONT AND SIZE OF TEXT

You can enhance the appearance of your page by changing the font and size of text.

FrontPage automatically uses the (default font) setting and sets the font size to Normal. Using these settings allows a reader's Web browser to determine the font and size of text displayed on a page.

FrontPage provides a list of fonts you can use to give your text a different look. The fonts appear in the list as they will appear on your page. To avoid problems when people view your page, you should use common fonts such as Arial, Times New Roman and Courier.

You can increase or decrease the size of text on your page. Larger text is easier to read, but smaller text allows you to fit more information on a screen.

FrontPage offers seven font sizes. Size 1 is the smallest and size 7 is the largest.

Web browsers can be set to override the formatting you define so readers can display pages with the formatting they prefer. Therefore, the formatting you choose for your page may not appear the way you expect on some computers.

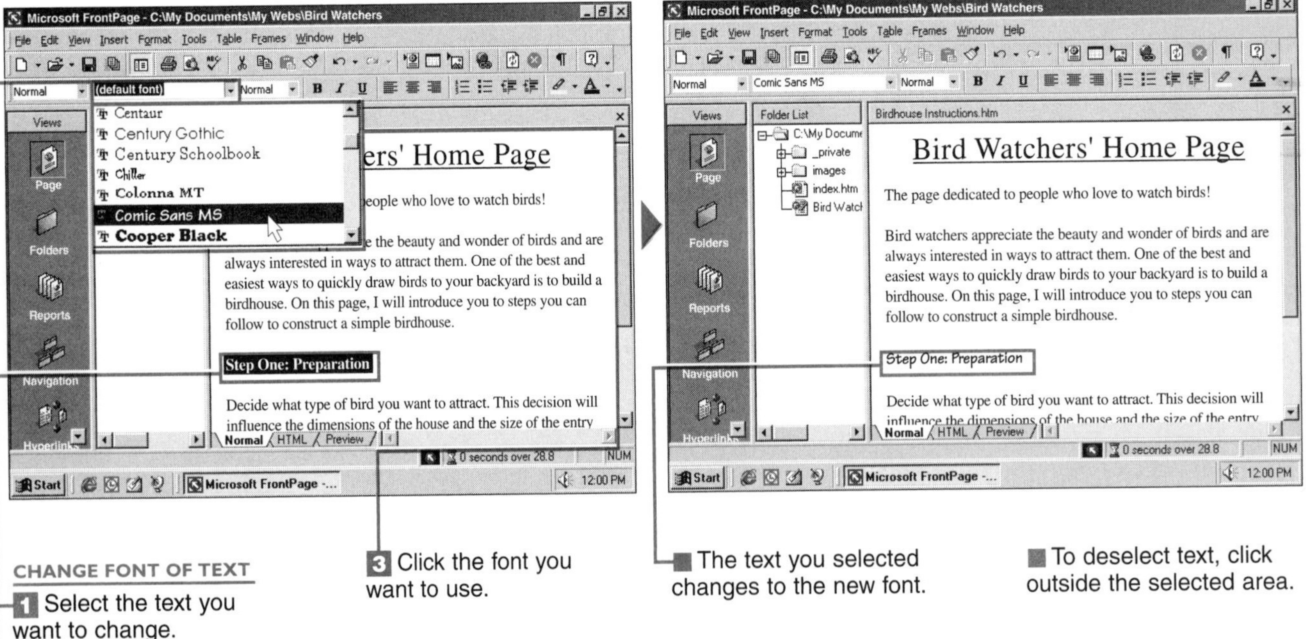

CHANGE FONT OF TEXT

1 Select the text you want to change.

2 Click ▼ in this area to display a list of the available fonts.

3 Click the font you want to use.

■ The text you selected changes to the new font.

■ To deselect text, click outside the selected area.

How can I change the font and size of text while typing?

✔ Before you begin typing the text you want to display a different font and size, select the font and size you want to use. Any text you type after making the changes will display the new font and size.

I changed the font of text, but I do not like the result. Can I cancel the change?

✔ You can immediately click the Undo button (↶) to cancel the last change you made to your page.

Can I quickly remove all the formatting I added to text?

✔ Yes. Select the text you want to remove formatting from. Choose the Format menu and then click Remove Formatting.

Is there another way to change the font and size of text?

✔ Yes. Select the text you want to change. Choose the Format menu and then click Font. The Font dialog box appears, allowing you to select a font and size as well as many other options. FrontPage displays a preview of how the text will look once the formatting is applied.

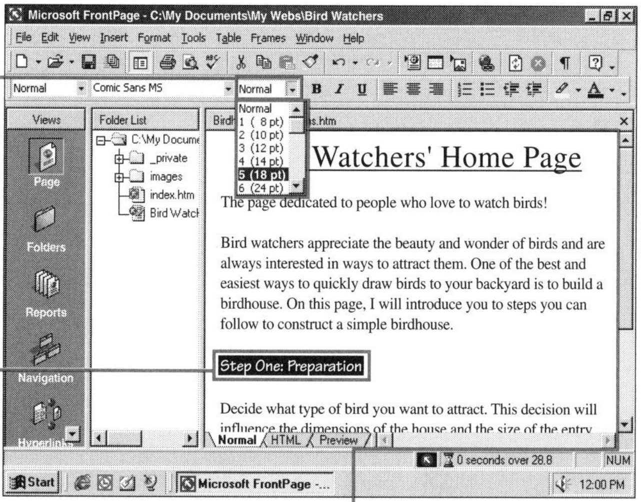

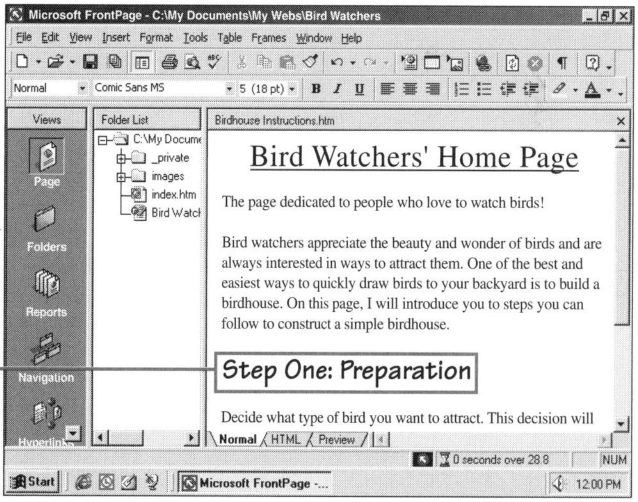

CHANGE SIZE OF TEXT

1 Select the text you want to change.

2 Click ▾ in this area to display a list of the available sizes.

3 Click the size you want to use.

■ The text you selected changes to the new size.

■ To deselect text, click outside the selected area.

CHANGE ALIGNMENT OF TEXT

You can use the alignment buttons on the Formatting toolbar to change the alignment of text on your page. Changing the alignment of text can help organize your page and make the page easier to read.

By default, FrontPage aligns text along the left side of a page.

FrontPage allows you to center text between the left and right sides of your page. This is useful for making headings and titles on your page stand out. You should center only short sections of text, since long paragraphs can be difficult to read when centered.

You can align text along the right side of your page. You may want to right align a column of text, such as a description of a product, to make the text stand out from the rest of the text on your page.

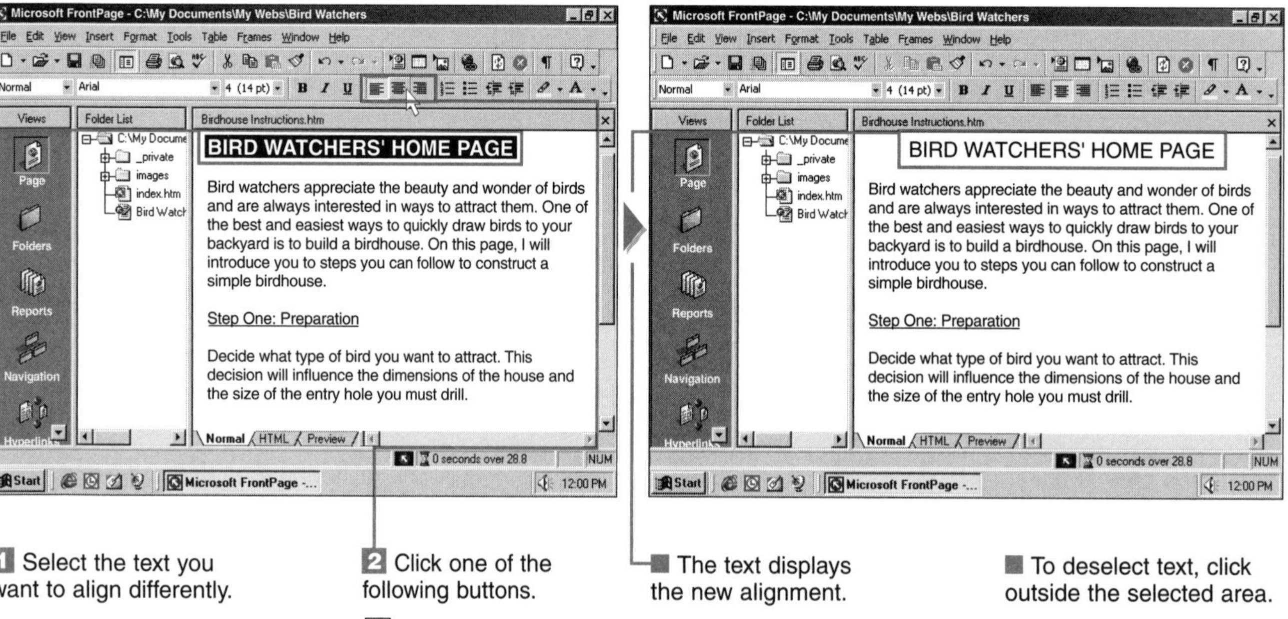

1 Select the text you want to align differently.

2 Click one of the following buttons.

- Left align
- Center
- Right align

■ The text displays the new alignment.

■ To deselect text, click outside the selected area.

INDENT TEXT

You can use the Indent feature to make important text on your page stand out.

FrontPage allows you to quickly move text away from or closer to the left and right edges of your page. This lets you position text where you want it to appear on your page. Increasing the indent moves text away from the edges of your page. Decreasing the indent moves text closer to the edges of your page.

When you indent a paragraph, all the lines of text in the paragraph are indented together.

Indenting text is useful when you want to set quotations or references apart from the rest of the text on your page. Indenting text can also help you emphasize where the content of your page changes. For example, you may want to indent your e-mail address or copyright information to separate it from the rest of the text on your page.

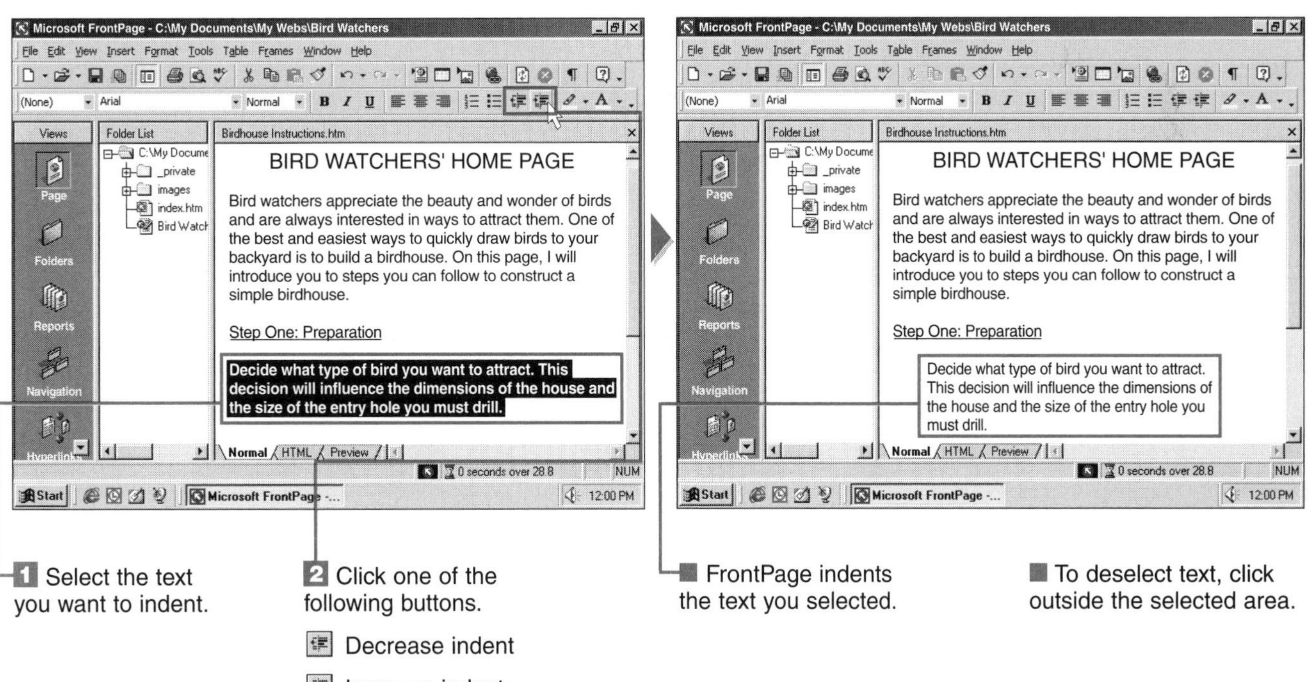

1 Select the text you want to indent.

2 Click one of the following buttons.

- Decrease indent
- Increase indent

■ FrontPage indents the text you selected.

■ To deselect text, click outside the selected area.

CHANGE COLOR OF TEXT

You can change the color of text on a page. FrontPage provides a variety of colors for you to choose from.

You can change the color of text to draw attention to headings or important information on your page. Changing the color of text also allows you to enhance the appearance of your page.

Make sure the text color you choose works well with the background color of the page. For example, red text on a blue background can be difficult to read.

When selecting the text color you want to use, consider that the colors you choose for your page may not appear the way you expect on some computers. Web browsers can be set to override the colors used on a page. This allows people to display your page in the colors they prefer.

If the color you select does not suit your needs, you can return to the default color at any time.

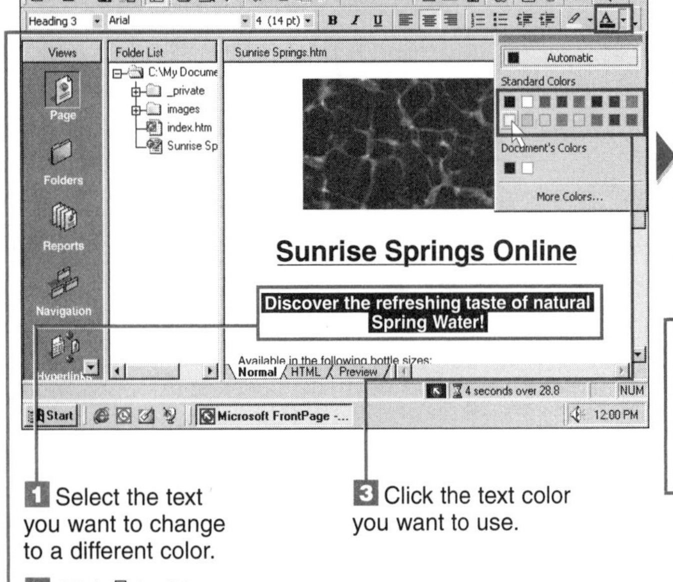

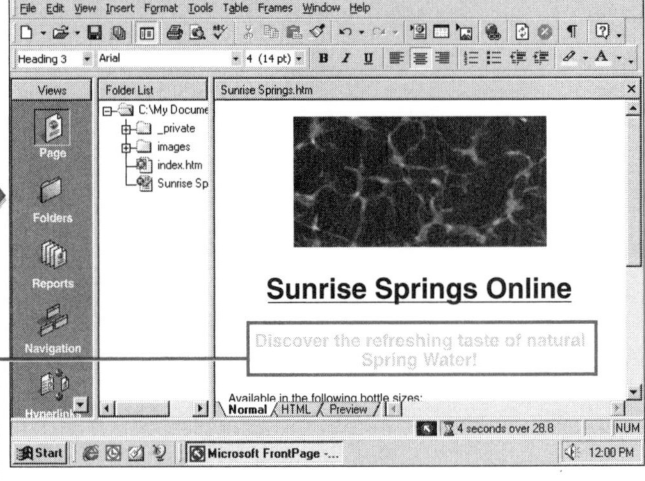

1 Select the text you want to change to a different color.

2 Click ▾ in this area to select a color.

3 Click the text color you want to use.

■ The text appears in the color you selected.

■ To deselect text, click outside the selected area.

Note: To once again display the text in the default color, repeat steps 1 to 3, except select Automatic in step 3.

COPY FORMATTING

You can copy formatting to make one area of text on a page look exactly like another.

You can copy formatting to text on the same page or on a different page. To switch to another page in the Web site, see page 576.

You may want to copy the formatting of text to make all the headings or important words on your page look the same. This will give your page a consistent appearance.

If you copy the formatting of text that contains more than one type of the same formatting, such as multiple fonts, FrontPage will only copy the first type of formatting. For example, if you select a paragraph that contains the Times New Roman font followed by the Arial font, FrontPage will only copy the Times New Roman font.

You can copy formatting to several areas on your page at once. To do so, perform the steps below, except double-click the Format Painter button (✓) in step 2. When you have finished selecting all the text you want to display the formatting, press the Esc key to stop copying the formatting.

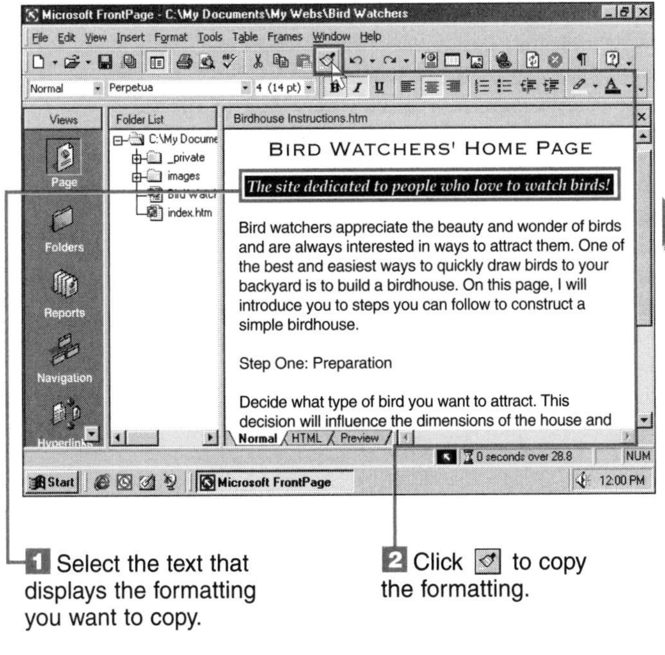

1 Select the text that displays the formatting you want to copy.

2 Click ✓ to copy the formatting.

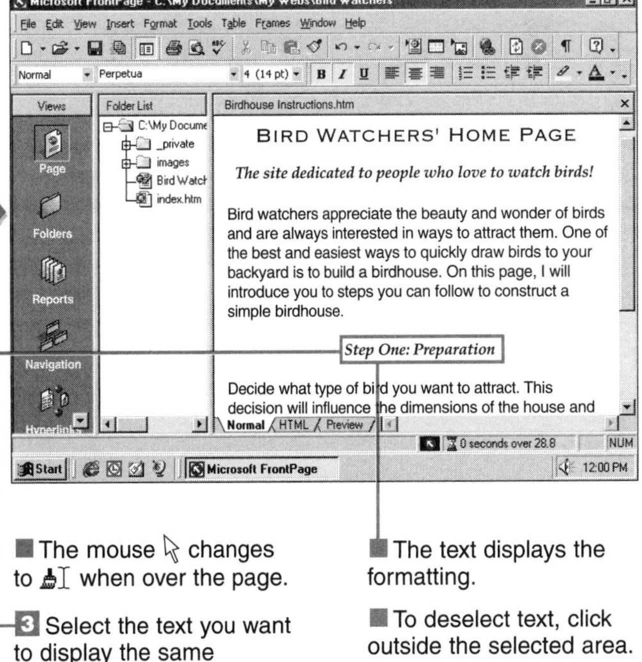

■ The mouse ↖ changes to ♙I when over the page.

3 Select the text you want to display the same formatting.

■ The text displays the formatting.

■ To deselect text, click outside the selected area.

ADD NUMBERS OR BULLETS

You can separate items in a list by beginning each item with a number or a bullet. This can help make the list easier to read.

Numbers are useful for items in a specific order, such as a set of instructions or a table of contents. Bullets are useful for items in no particular order, such as a list of products or a series of hyperlinks. By default, FrontPage displays bullets as dots.

When you add numbers or bullets to a list, FrontPage indents the list slightly. This enhances the appearance of the list and separates the list from the other text on the page.

When you add a new item to a list displaying numbers or bullets, FrontPage automatically adds a number or bullet to the new item. If you add an item within a numbered list, FrontPage automatically renumbers all the items in the list for you.

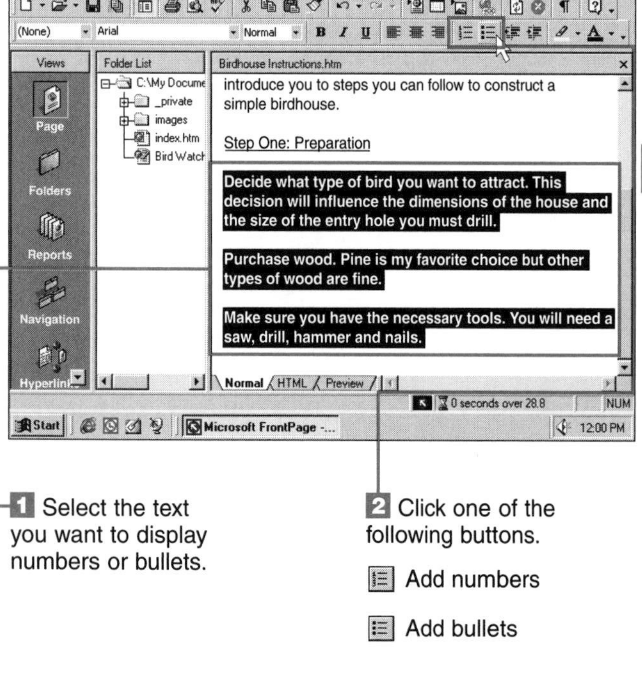

1 Select the text you want to display numbers or bullets.

2 Click one of the following buttons.

Add numbers

Add bullets

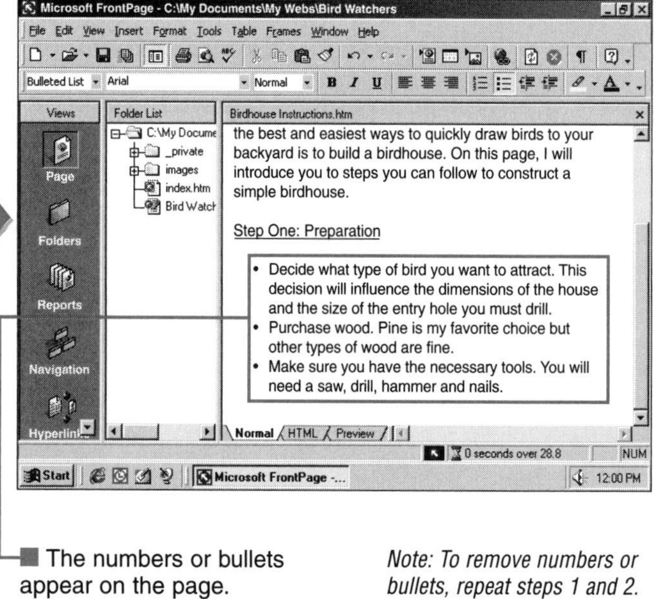

■ The numbers or bullets appear on the page.

■ To deselect text, click outside the selected area.

Note: To remove numbers or bullets, repeat steps 1 and 2.

CREATE A HEADING

You can use headings to indicate the importance of text, such as section titles, on your page.

You can create headings to separate the text on a page into smaller sections. There are six heading levels, ranging in size from very large to very small. Levels 1, 2 and 3 are large and are often used for page and section titles. Level 4 is the same size as the main text on a page. Levels 5 and 6 are smaller and are often used for copyright information. Most pages use a maximum of three heading levels.

Make sure you use the same heading level for all the text of equal importance. This helps your readers determine the importance of the text on the page.

You can also create headings to provide an outline of the page for your readers. By scanning the headings, a reader should get a general overview of the information covered on the page and be able to quickly locate topics of interest.

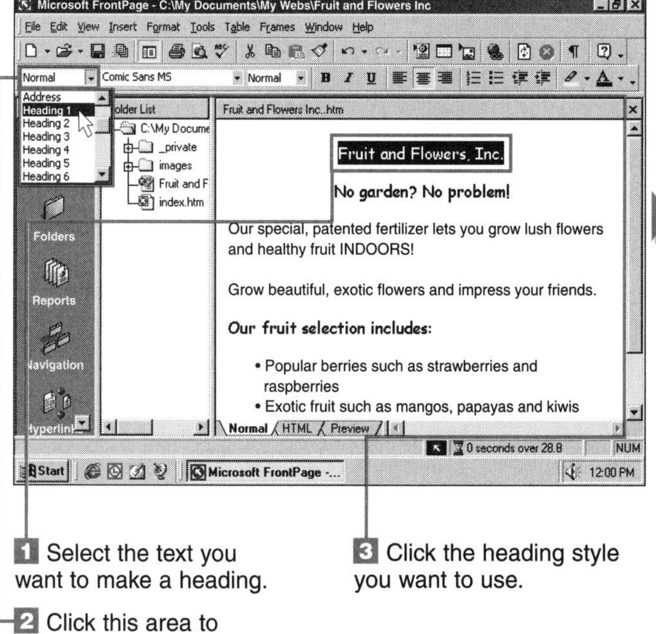

1 Select the text you want to make a heading.

2 Click this area to display a list of the available heading styles.

3 Click the heading style you want to use.

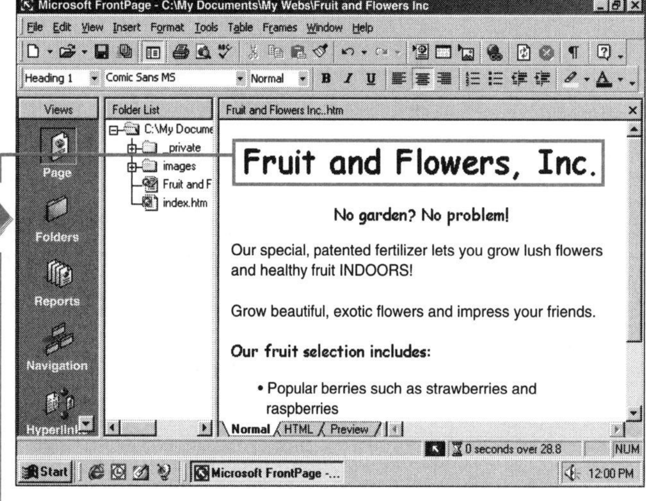

■ The text displays the heading style you selected.

■ To deselect text, click outside the selected area.

Note: To once again display the text in the normal heading style, perform steps 1 to 3, except select Normal in step 3.

ADD A HORIZONTAL LINE

You can place a horizontal line across your page to visually separate sections of the page. Using horizontal lines can help you enhance the appearance of your page or make a long page easier to read.

You can use a horizontal line to separate the main page from a header or footer. A header appears at the top of a page and often includes the title of the page and a table of contents. A footer appears at the bottom of a page and often includes copyright information and the author's name.

You should avoid placing more than one or two horizontal lines on each page. Using too many horizontal lines can make a page difficult to read and annoy your readers.

If you decide that you no longer want to display a horizontal line on your page, you can remove the horizontal line at any time.

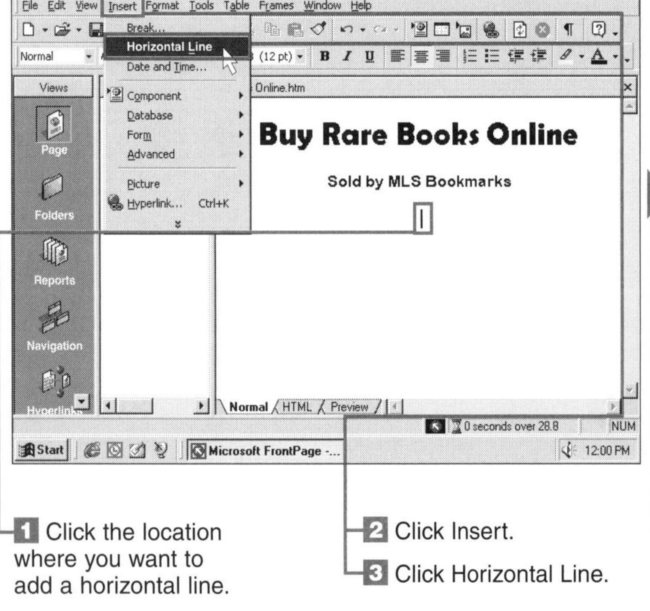

1 Click the location where you want to add a horizontal line.

2 Click Insert.

3 Click Horizontal Line.

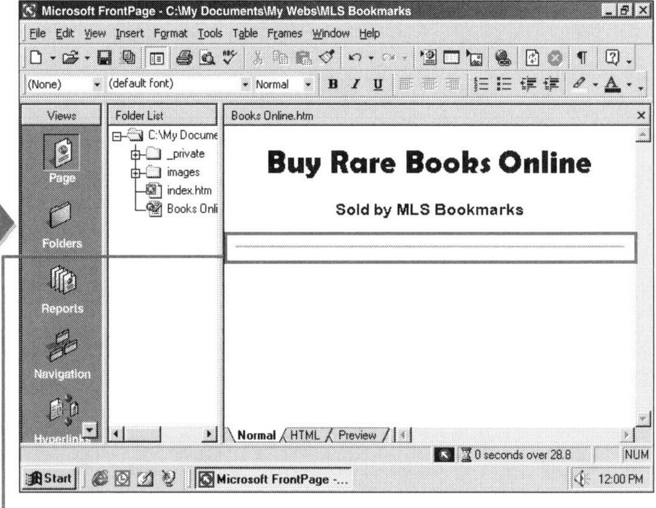

■ A horizontal line appears on the page.

Note: To remove a horizontal line, click the line and then press the Delete key.

PRINT A PAGE

You can produce a paper copy of the page displayed on your screen. A paper copy is often referred to as a hard copy. Producing a hard copy of a page lets you exchange information with people who do not have access to the Web.

Before you print your page, make sure the printer is turned on and contains an adequate supply of paper.

You can print your entire page or only part of the page. If your page is long, it may consist of several printed pages. You can specify the range of printed pages you want to produce. For example, if you want to print information from the beginning of a long page, you may only want to produce the first two printed pages.

Your printed page may look different than the page displayed on your screen. For example, FrontPage may adjust the layout of text and graphics on the printed page due to the size difference between the paper and your computer screen.

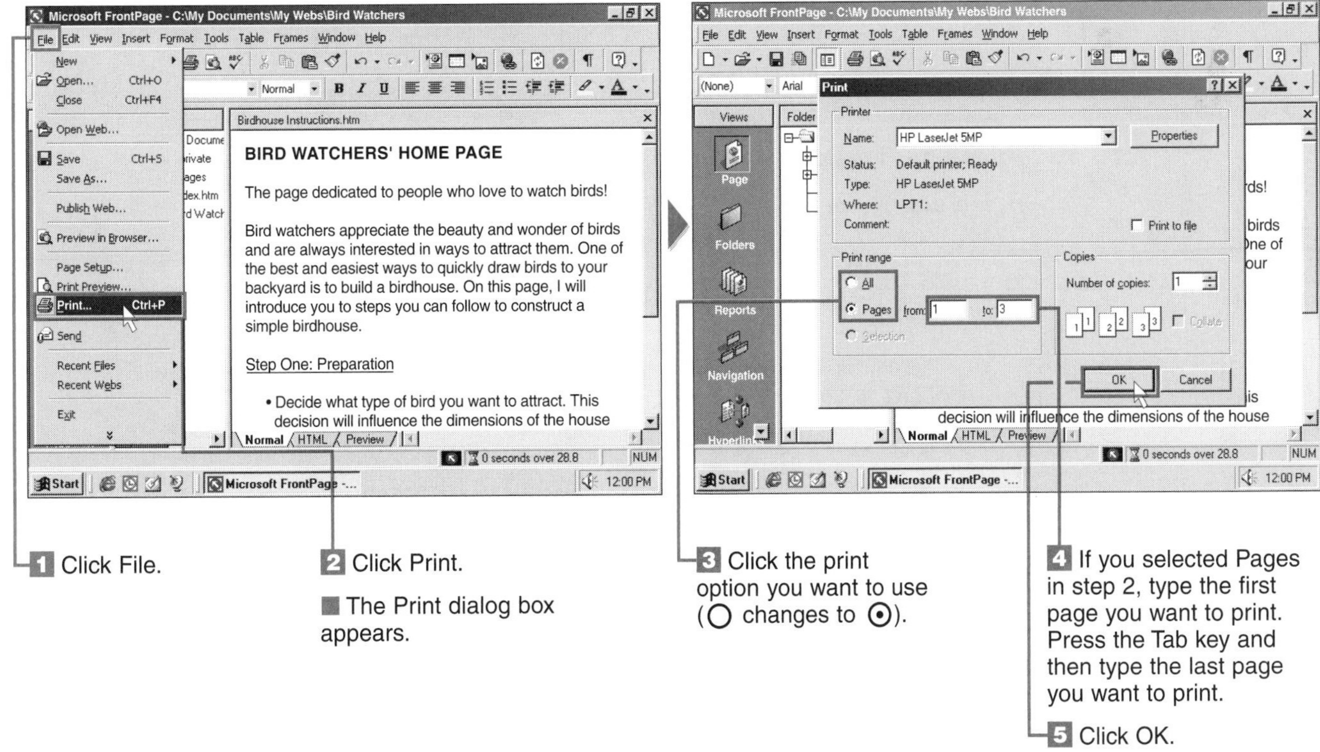

1 Click File.

2 Click Print.

■ The Print dialog box appears.

3 Click the print option you want to use (○ changes to ⦿).

4 If you selected Pages in step 2, type the first page you want to print. Press the Tab key and then type the last page you want to print.

5 Click OK.

CREATE A HYPERLINK

You can create a hyperlink to connect a word, phrase or picture on your page to another page in your Web site or to related information on the Web. When a reader selects the word, phrase or picture in a Web browser, the other page appears on the screen. Adding a hyperlink to your page gives readers quick access to information that relates to the page.

You can use any text or picture on your page as a hyperlink. Make sure the text or picture you choose clearly indicates where the hyperlink will take the reader.

You can also create a hyperlink by typing a Web page address or e-mail address on your page. FrontPage will automatically convert the address to a hyperlink for you.

After creating a hyperlink, you should save your page.

By default, text hyperlinks appear underlined and blue in color. When you position the mouse pointer over a hyperlink in FrontPage, the bottom of your screen displays where the hyperlink will take you.

You can use the Preview tab to test your hyperlinks. This lets you make sure the correct page will appear when you click a hyperlink.

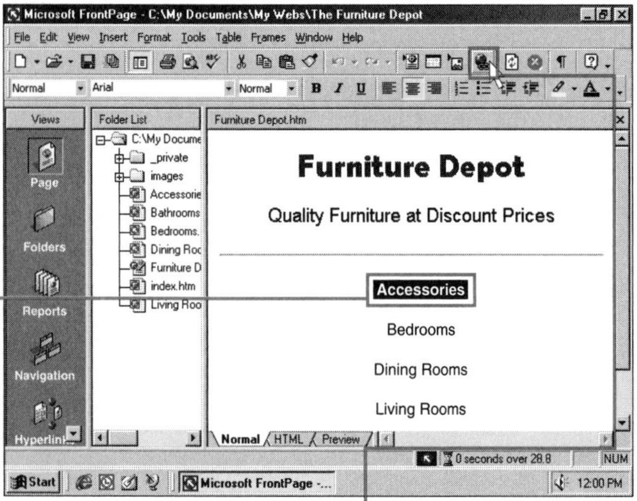

1 Select the text or click the picture you want to make a hyperlink.

2 Click to create a hyperlink.

■ The Create Hyperlink dialog box appears.

3 To link the text or picture to a page in the current Web site, click the page.

■ To link the text or picture to a page on the Web, click this area and then type the address of the page.

4 Click OK to create the hyperlink.

Can I verify all the hyperlinks in my Web site at once?

✔ Yes. From the View menu, click Reports and then choose Broken Hyperlinks. On the Reporting toolbar, click the Verify Hyperlinks button (). Click the Verify all hyperlinks option (○ changes to ⦿) and then click Start. FrontPage displays a list of hyperlinks in your Web site. Hyperlinks with a Broken status must be repaired. Double-click a broken hyperlink in the list. In the Replace hyperlink with area, type the correct address or click Browse to locate the correct file. Then click Replace.

Can I create a hyperlink that sends e-mail?

✔ Yes. Select the text you want to make a hyperlink and then click the Hyperlink button (). In the Create Hyperlink dialog box, click and then type the e-mail address you want to use.

How do I remove a hyperlink without removing the text or picture from my page?

✔ Select the hyperlink on your page and then click the Hyperlink button (). Drag the mouse I over the text in the URL area and then press the Delete key.

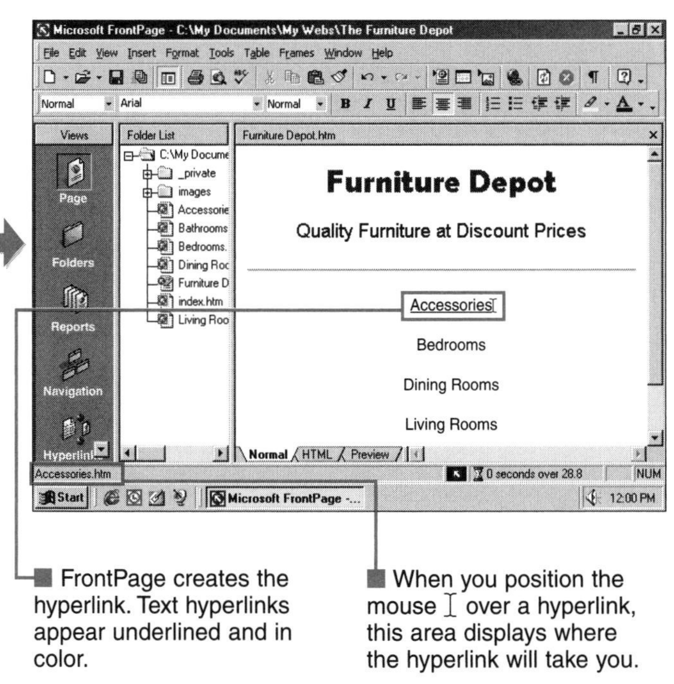

■ FrontPage creates the hyperlink. Text hyperlinks appear underlined and in color.

■ To deselect text, click outside the selected area.

■ When you position the mouse I over a hyperlink, this area displays where the hyperlink will take you.

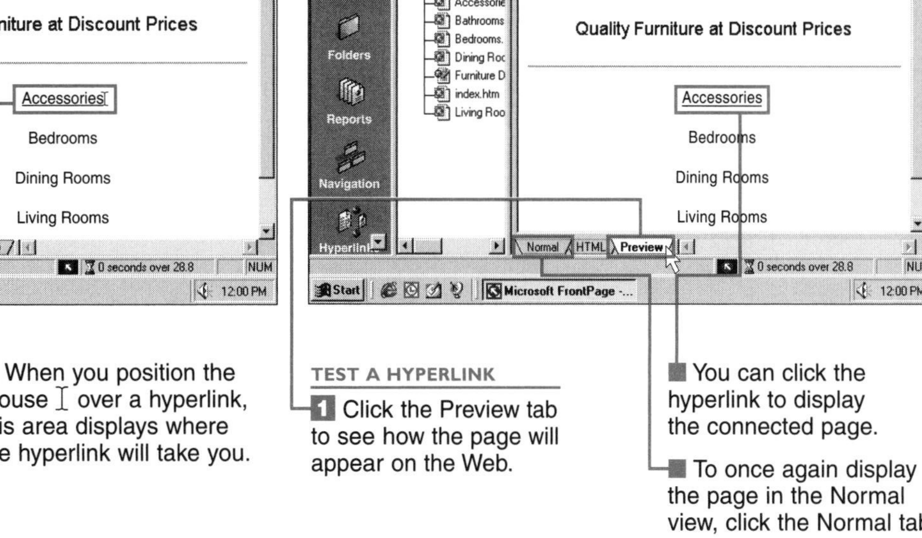

TEST A HYPERLINK

1 Click the Preview tab to see how the page will appear on the Web.

■ You can click the hyperlink to display the connected page.

■ To once again display the page in the Normal view, click the Normal tab.

ADD A PICTURE

You can add a picture to your page to make the page more interesting and attractive. Pictures can also help clarify a concept. For example, you can add a diagram to explain a product.

There are many places you can find pictures to add to your page. Many pages on the Web offer pictures you can use for free. You can also use a scanner to scan pictures into your computer or use a drawing program to create your own pictures. Make sure you have permission to use any pictures you did not create yourself.

Adding pictures increases the time it takes for a page to appear on a screen. The bottom right corner of the Microsoft FrontPage window indicates how long it will take to display your page using a 28.8 Kbps modem. Whenever possible, you should use pictures with a small file size to reduce the time required to display the page.

When adding pictures to your page, you should select pictures in the GIF or JPG format. These picture formats are supported in all Web browsers.

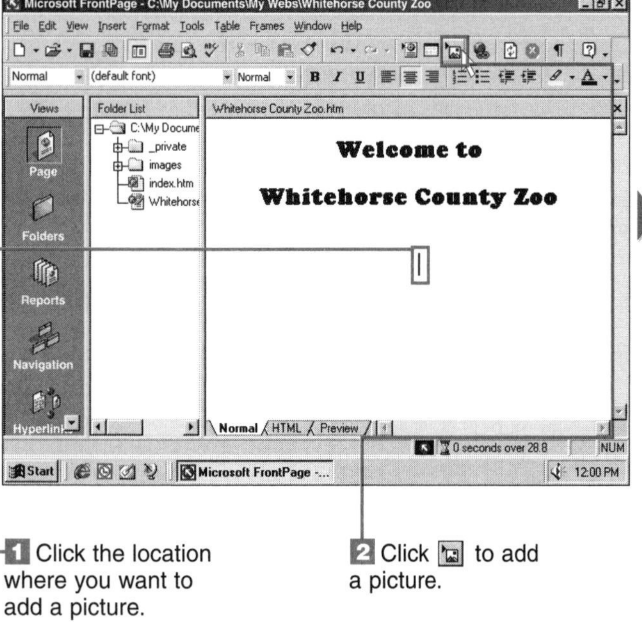

1 Click the location where you want to add a picture.

2 Click [picture icon] to add a picture.

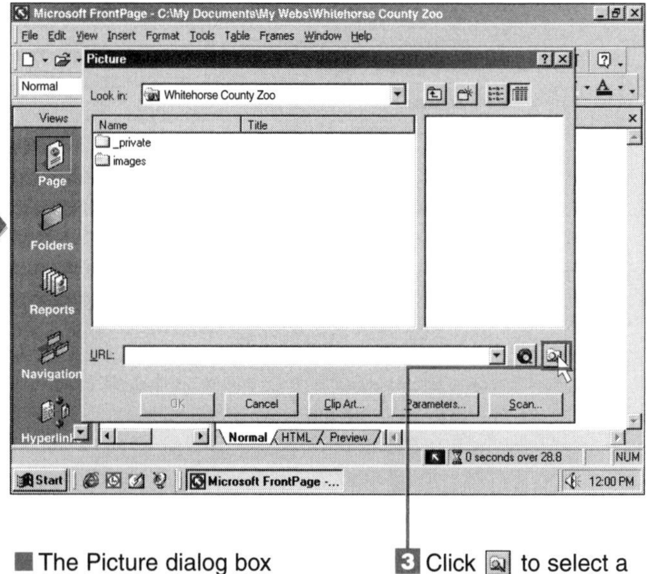

■ The Picture dialog box appears.

Note: If the Select File dialog box also appears, skip to step 4.

3 Click [browse icon] to select a picture stored on your computer.

How do I move a picture on my page?

✔ Position the mouse pointer over the picture and then drag the picture to a new location on your page.

Can I add a clip art image to my page?

✔ Yes. Office includes many ready-made clip art images that you can add. In the Picture dialog box, click the Clip Art button. Select the category of clip art you want to display and then click the clip art image you want to add. From the menu that appears, click [icon] to add the image.

How can I resize a picture?

✔ Click the picture to display handles (■) around the picture. Position the mouse over one of the handles (changes to ↕, ↔ or ↘) and then drag the handle until the picture is the size you want.

Why does the Save Embedded Files dialog box appear when I try to save the page where I added the picture?

✔ You must save pictures and pages as separate files in your Web site. Click OK to save the picture you added.

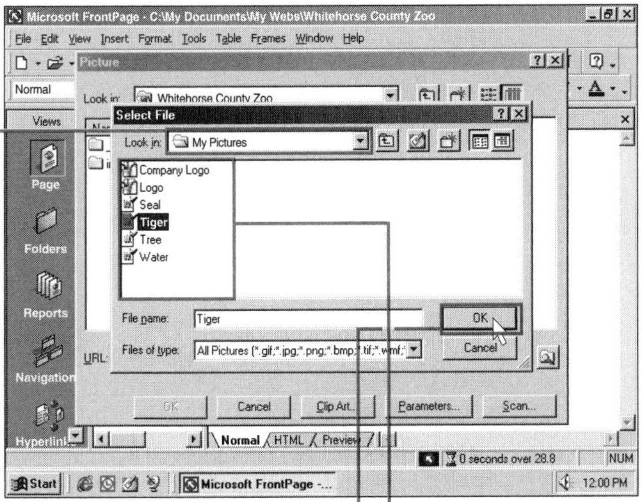

■ The Select File dialog box appears.

■ This area shows the location of the displayed files. You can click this area to change the location.

4 Click the name of the picture you want to add to the page.

5 Click OK to add the picture to the page.

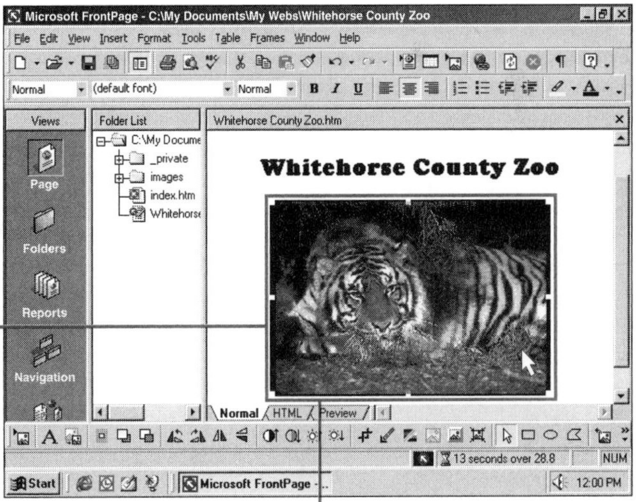

■ The picture appears on the page.

DELETE A PICTURE

1 Click the picture you want to delete. Handles (■) appear around the picture.

2 Press the Delete key.

INSERT A TABLE

You can insert a table to neatly display information on a page. Tables can help you organize lists of information, such as a price list or table of contents. You can also use a table to control the placement of text and pictures on a page.

A table is made up of rows, columns and cells. A row is a horizontal line of cells. A column is a vertical line of cells. A cell is the area where a row and column intersect.

You can enter any amount of text in a cell. When the text you enter reaches the end of a line, FrontPage automatically wraps the text to the next line in the cell and increases the size of the cell to accommodate the text.

FrontPage also increases the width of a column to fit long words in a cell.

You can edit and format text in a table as you would edit and format any text on your page.

If you want to insert additional information into your table, you can insert rows or columns at any time.

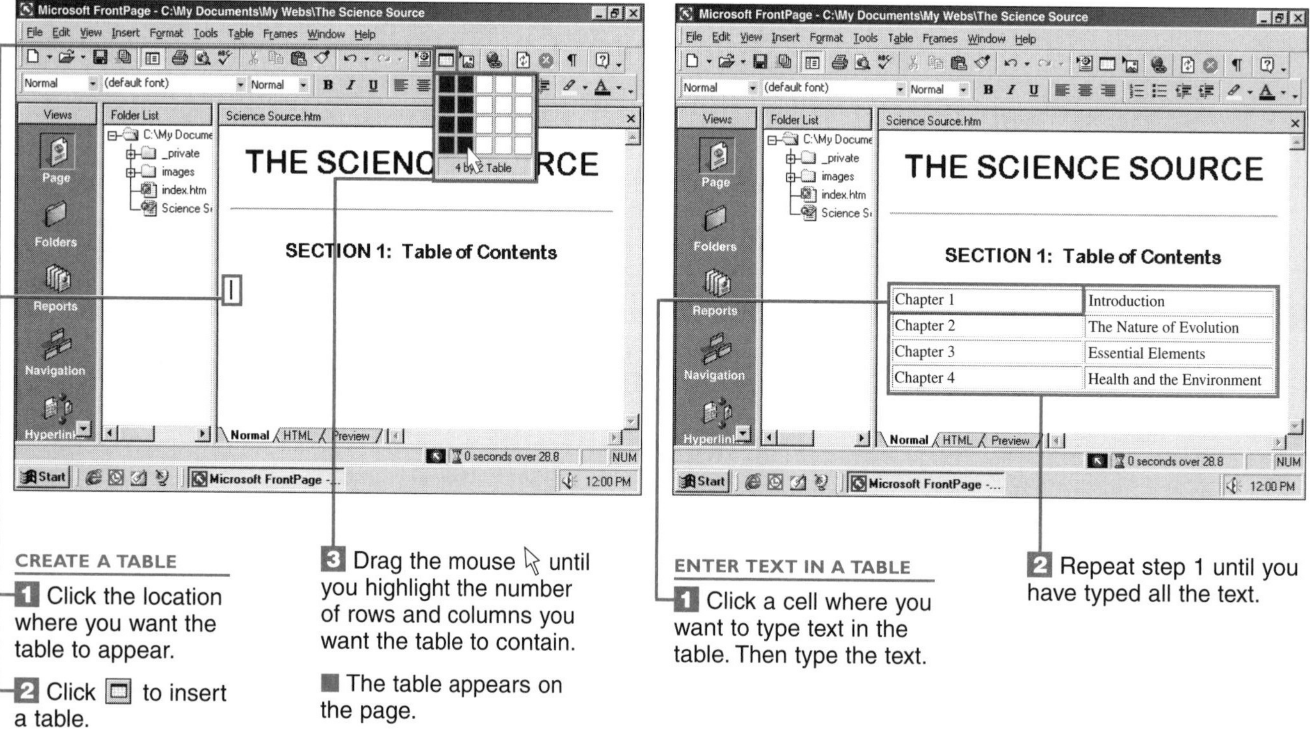

CREATE A TABLE

1 Click the location where you want the table to appear.

2 Click ▭ to insert a table.

3 Drag the mouse ↖ until you highlight the number of rows and columns you want the table to contain.

■ The table appears on the page.

ENTER TEXT IN A TABLE

1 Click a cell where you want to type text in the table. Then type the text.

2 Repeat step 1 until you have typed all the text.

TIPS

Can I change the row height or column width?

✔ Yes. Position the mouse over the bottom edge of the row or the right edge of the column you want to change (changes to ↕, ↔). Then drag the row or column edge to a new position.

How do I delete a row or column?

✔ To select the row or column you no longer need, drag the mouse I over all the cells in the row or column. Then choose the Table menu and select Delete Cells.

Can I change the background color of my table?

✔ Yes. Click anywhere in the table. From the Table menu, select Properties and then click Table. In the Background area, click the area beside Color and select the color you want to use. Then click OK.

Can I change the width of the border around a table?

✔ Yes. Click anywhere in the table. From the Table menu, select Properties and then click Table. Double-click the area beside Size. Type the width you want to use for the border and then click OK.

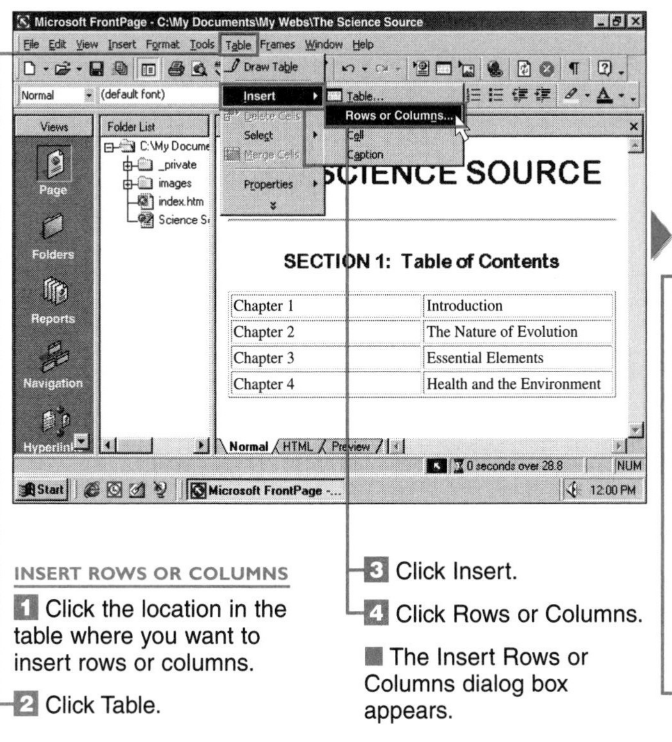

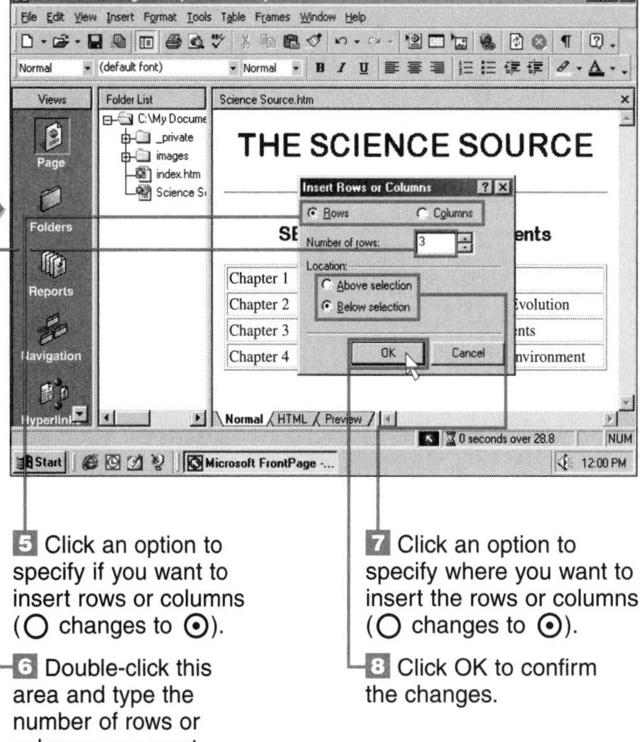

INSERT ROWS OR COLUMNS

1 Click the location in the table where you want to insert rows or columns.

2 Click Table.

3 Click Insert.

4 Click Rows or Columns.

■ The Insert Rows or Columns dialog box appears.

5 Click an option to specify if you want to insert rows or columns (○ changes to ⊙).

6 Double-click this area and type the number of rows or columns you want to insert.

7 Click an option to specify where you want to insert the rows or columns (○ changes to ⊙).

8 Click OK to confirm the changes.

ADD A HIT COUNTER

You can use a hit counter to keep track of the number of people who have visited a page in your Web site. This can help you determine how popular the page is.

FrontPage provides five counter styles you can choose from. You should choose a counter style that works well with the design of your page.

You can start your hit counter at any number. By default, FrontPage starts the hit counter at 0.

You can limit the number of digits your hit counter can display. For example, if you limit the number of digits to five, the hit counter will reset to 00000 after 99999.

You must publish your page before you can view a hit counter you added to the page. For information on publishing Web sites, see page 586.

In order to display a hit counter, your Web server must use FrontPage Server Extensions. You can consult your Web Presence Provider (WPP) to determine if your Web server uses FrontPage Server Extensions.

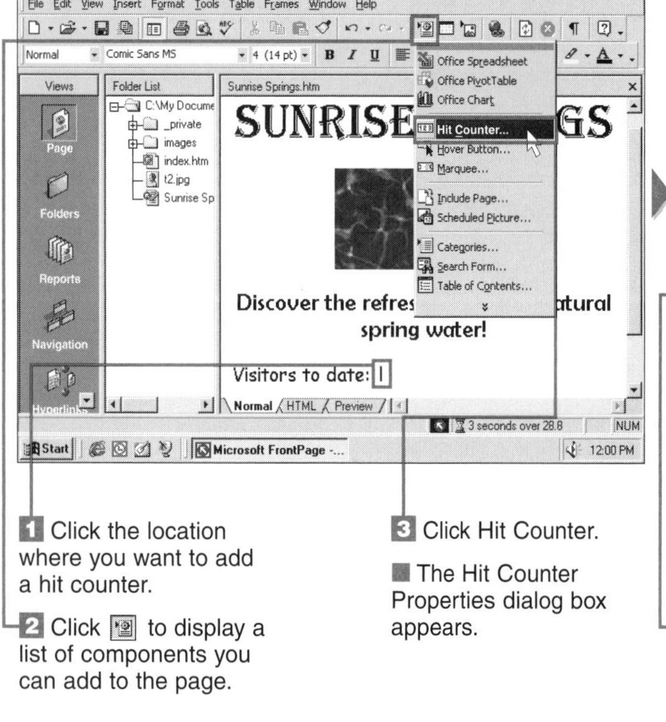

1 Click the location where you want to add a hit counter.

2 Click [icon] to display a list of components you can add to the page.

3 Click Hit Counter.

■ The Hit Counter Properties dialog box appears.

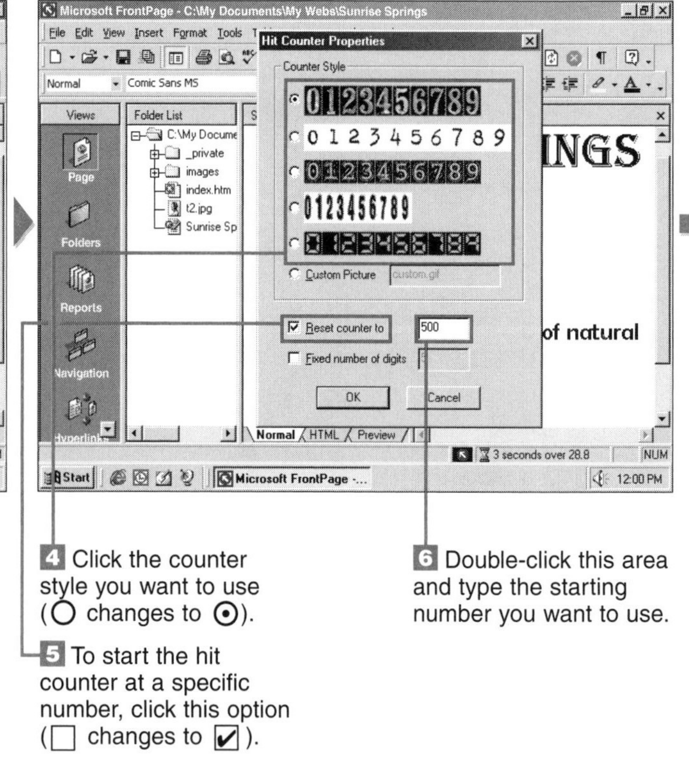

4 Click the counter style you want to use (○ changes to ⊙).

5 To start the hit counter at a specific number, click this option (☐ changes to ☑).

6 Double-click this area and type the starting number you want to use.

What page in my Web site should I add a hit counter to?

✔ A hit counter keeps track of the number of people who visit the page the counter is located on. Your home page is the first page people who visit your site will view, so you should add the hit counter to your home page.

Will adding a hit counter slow the display of my page?

✔ A hit counter is a small program that must run each time your page is displayed in a Web browser. As a result, the page may take slightly longer to be displayed.

Will changing the theme of a page change the appearance of my hit counter?

✔ No. If you change the theme of a page containing a hit counter, you must change the counter style to one that works well with the new theme. Double-click [Hit Counter] on your page to open the Hit Counter Properties dialog box. Choose a new counter style and then click OK.

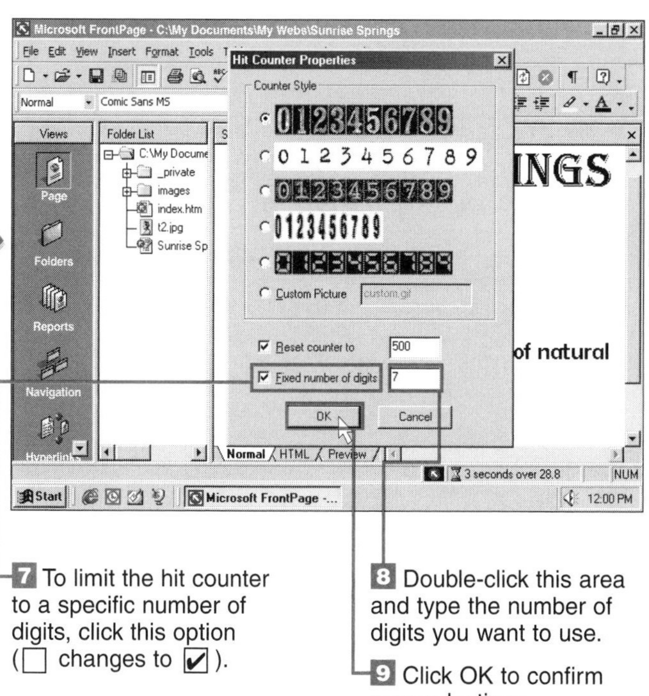

7 To limit the hit counter to a specific number of digits, click this option (☐ changes to ☑).

8 Double-click this area and type the number of digits you want to use.

9 Click OK to confirm your selections.

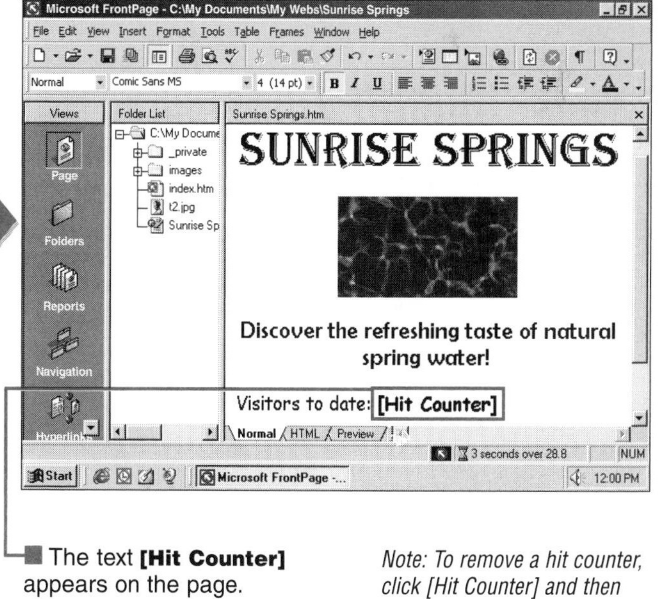

■ The text **[Hit Counter]** appears on the page.

Note: To remove a hit counter, click [Hit Counter] and then press the Delete key.

APPLY A THEME

FrontPage offers many themes that you can choose from to give the pages in your Web site a new appearance. A theme consists of a coordinated set of design elements, including fonts, background images, navigation buttons, bullets, banners and a color scheme.

You can apply a theme to all the pages in your Web site. This is useful when you want to keep the appearance of your Web site consistent. After you apply a theme to the Web site, FrontPage will automatically apply the theme to any new pages you create.

You can also apply a theme to only the current page. This is useful when you want to make an important page stand out from the rest of the pages in your Web site. To apply a theme to only one page, you must first display the page you want to change.

Some of the available themes include Blueprint, Expedition and Romanesque. You can view a sample of a theme to help you choose the theme that best suits the content of your pages and your intended audience.

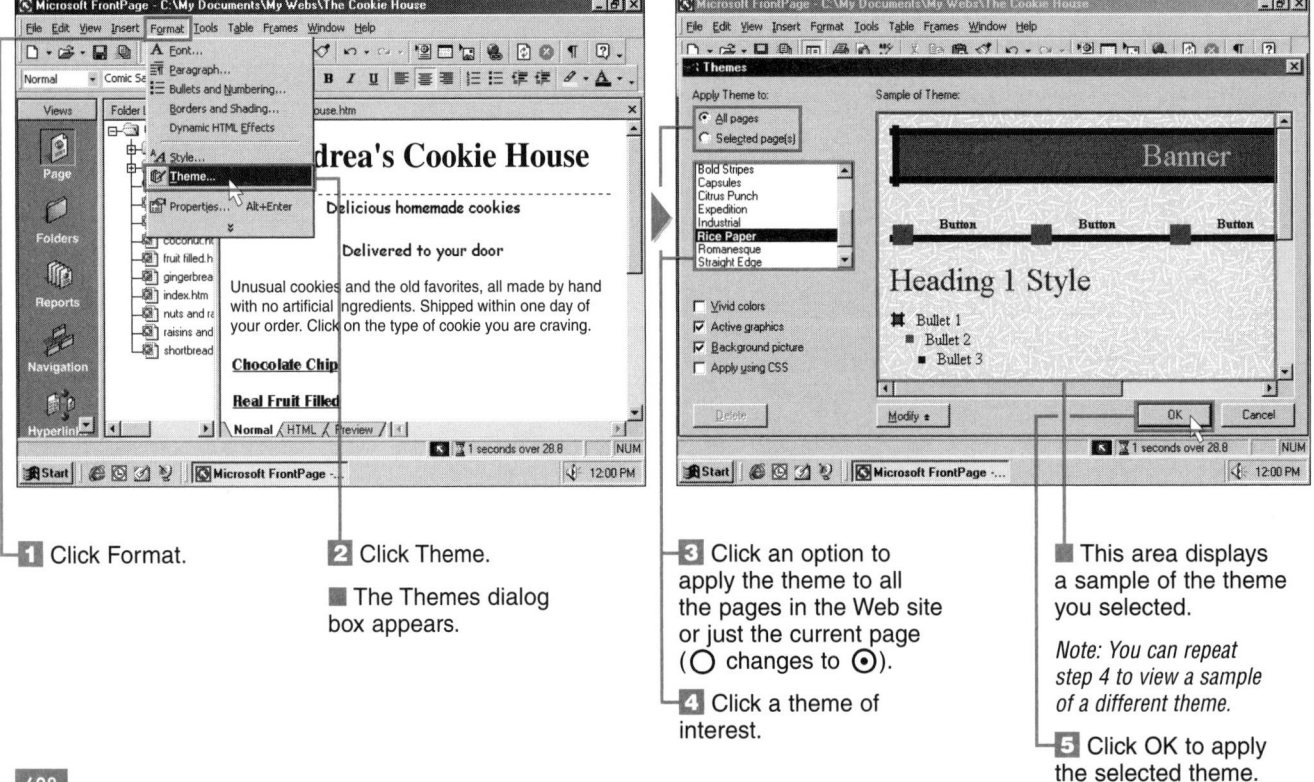

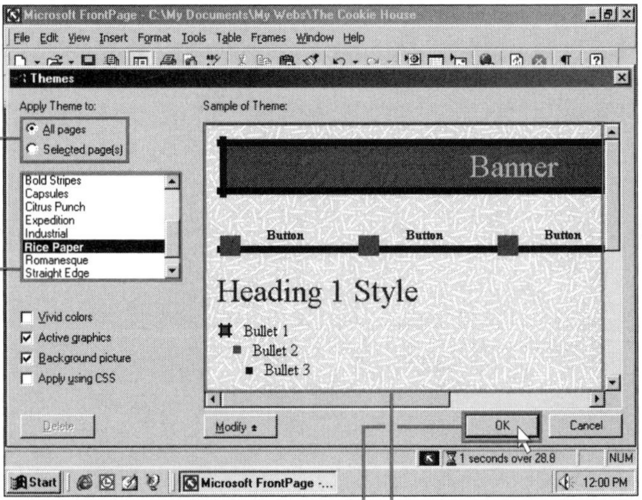

1 Click Format.

2 Click Theme.

■ The Themes dialog box appears.

3 Click an option to apply the theme to all the pages in the Web site or just the current page (○ changes to ⊙).

4 Click a theme of interest.

■ This area displays a sample of the theme you selected.

Note: You can repeat step 4 to view a sample of a different theme.

5 Click OK to apply the selected theme.

Can I personalize a theme to suit my pages?

✔ Yes. FrontPage provides additional options for the themes in the Themes dialog box. The options include Vivid colors, Active graphics, Background picture and Apply using CSS. Each option that displays a check mark (☑) is included in the current theme. You can click an option to add or remove a check mark.

The Apply using CSS option applies the current theme using an external style sheet rather than changing the HTML code for the page(s). Some Web browsers and Web servers cannot properly display pages that use this option.

Does FrontPage offer any other themes?

✔ Yes. When choosing the theme you want to use in the Themes dialog box, you can click Install Additional Themes to have FrontPage display more themes. Click Yes to install the themes. A Microsoft Office 2000 dialog box appears, asking you to insert the CD-ROM disc you used to install Office. Insert the CD-ROM disc and click OK.

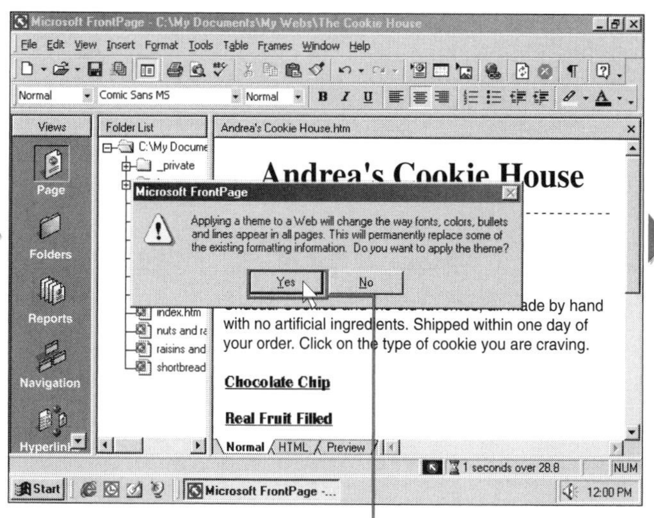

■ A dialog box may appear, indicating that applying the theme will change the way fonts, colors, bullets and lines appear on the page(s) in the Web site.

6 Click Yes to continue.

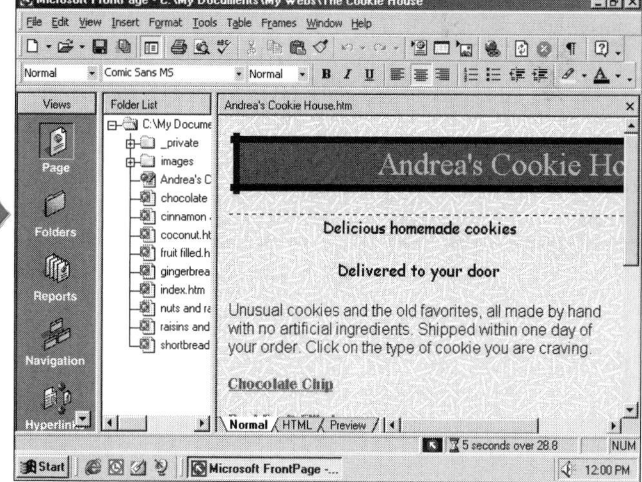

■ The page(s) in the Web site display the theme.

■ To remove a theme from page(s) in the Web site, perform steps 1 to 5, except select [No Theme] in step 4.

CREATE A HYPERLINK

You can create a hyperlink to connect a word, phrase or graphic in your document to another document on your computer, network, corporate intranet or the Internet. An intranet is a small version of the Internet within a company. You can create a hyperlink in Word, Excel, PowerPoint or Access.

You can use any text or graphic in your document as a hyperlink. Make sure the text or graphic you choose clearly indicates where the hyperlink will take you.

You can also create a hyperlink by typing a Web page address or e-mail address in your document. The program will automatically convert the address to a hyperlink for you.

You can easily identify hyperlinks in a document. By default, hyperlinks appear underlined and in color. When you position the mouse pointer over a hyperlink, a yellow box appears, displaying where the hyperlink will take you.

When you select a hyperlink, the connected document appears on your screen. If the hyperlink is connected to a Web page, your Web browser will open and display the page.

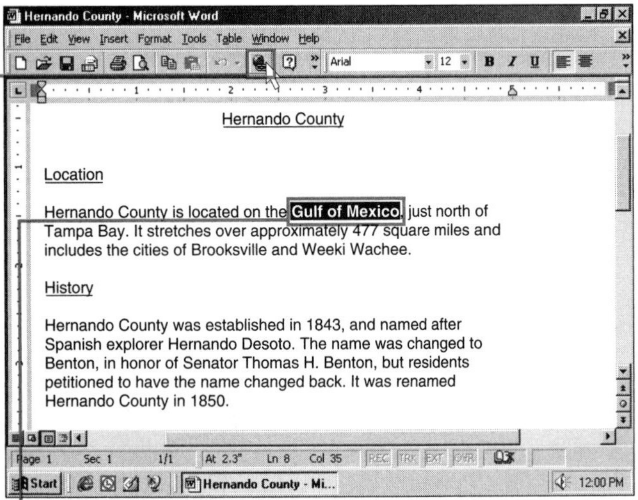

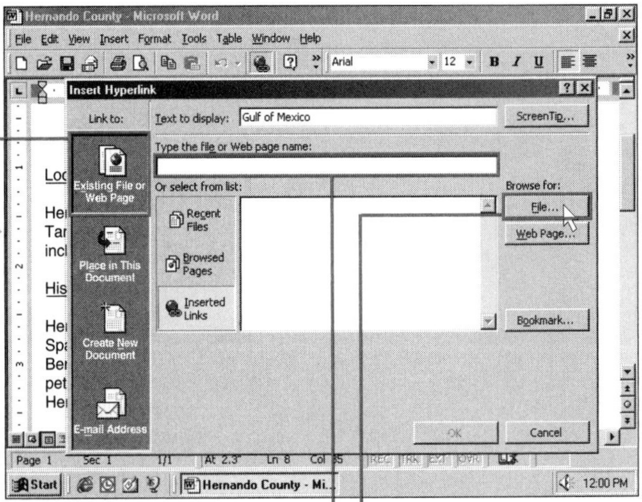

1 Select the text or click the graphic you want to make a hyperlink.

2 Click to create a hyperlink.

Note: If is not displayed, click on the Standard toolbar to display all the buttons.

■ The Insert Hyperlink dialog box appears.

3 Click Existing File or Web Page to link the text or graphic to an existing document.

4 To link the text or graphic to a file on your computer or network, click File.

■ To link the text or graphic to a page on the Web, click this area and type the address of the Web page. Then skip to step 7.

Can I create a hyperlink that allows people to send me e-mail?

✔ Yes. Select the text or graphic you want to make a hyperlink and then click the Insert Hyperlink button (🌐) on the Standard toolbar. Click E-mail Address and type the e-mail address you want to use. Then click OK.

How do I remove a hyperlink?

✔ Right-click the hyperlink in your document. A menu appears. Click Hyperlink and then click Remove Hyperlink.

How can I create a hyperlink in an Access table?

✔ Display the table you want to contain the hyperlink in the Design view. To change the view, see page 418. Change the data type of the appropriate field to Hyperlink. To change the data type, see page 422. Display the table in the Datasheet View and then position the insertion point in the cell containing the text you want to make a hyperlink. Click the Insert Hyperlink button (🌐) and delete any existing text in the Type the file or Web page name area. Then perform steps 4 to 7 below.

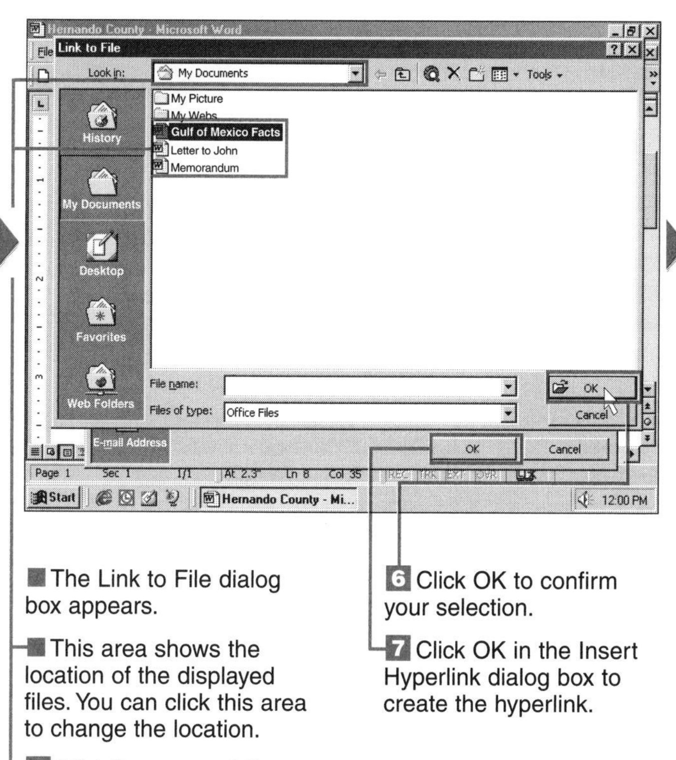

■ The Link to File dialog box appears.

■ This area shows the location of the displayed files. You can click this area to change the location.

5 Click the name of the file you want to link the text or graphic to.

6 Click OK to confirm your selection.

7 Click OK in the Insert Hyperlink dialog box to create the hyperlink.

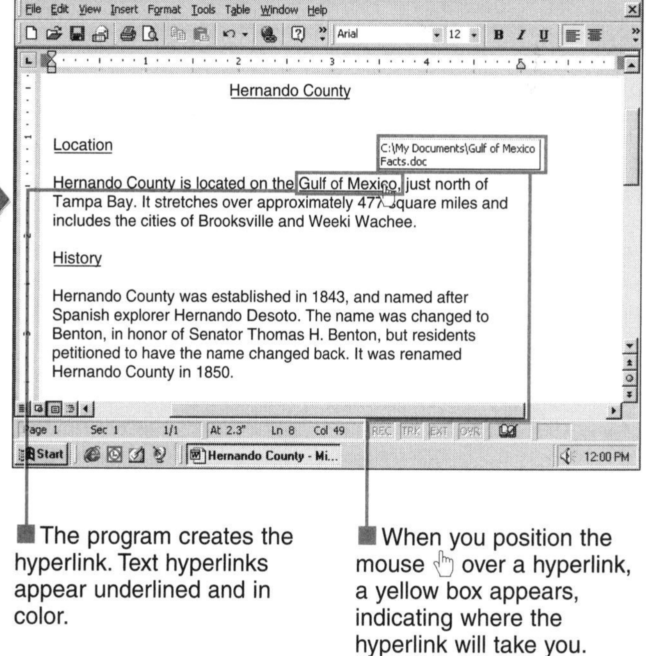

■ The program creates the hyperlink. Text hyperlinks appear underlined and in color.

■ When you position the mouse 👆 over a hyperlink, a yellow box appears, indicating where the hyperlink will take you.

SAVE A DOCUMENT AS A WEB PAGE

You can save a Word document, Excel workbook or PowerPoint presentation as a Web page. This lets you place information on the Internet or on your company's intranet.

When saving information as a Web page, you can specify a file name and title for the page. The file name is the name you use to store the page on your computer.

The title is the text that will appear at the top of the Web browser window when a reader views your page.

You can specify where you want to save the Web page. The Places Bar in the Save As dialog box lets you quickly access commonly used folders, such as My Documents and Favorites.

After you save information as a Web page, you can transfer the page to a computer that stores Web pages, called a Web server. Once the page is published on a Web server, it will be available for other people to view. You may be able to use the Web Folders folder on the Places Bar to save the page directly on a Web server.

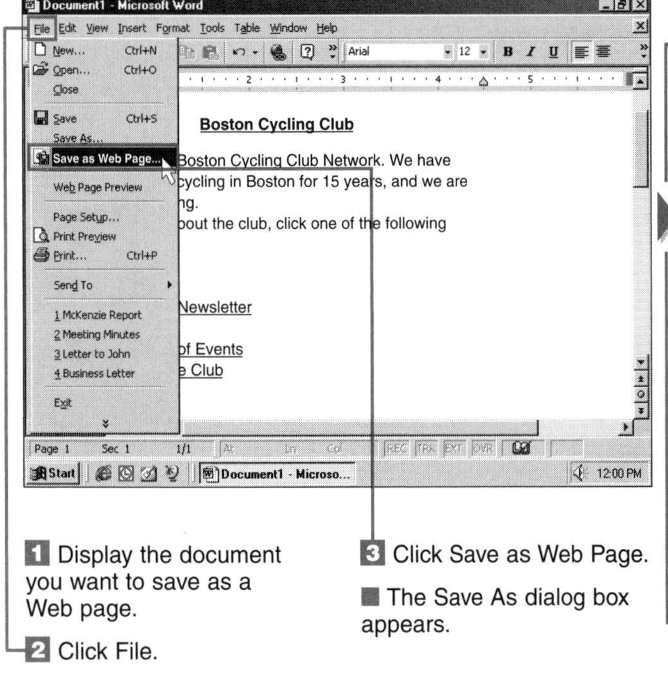

1 Display the document you want to save as a Web page.

2 Click File.

3 Click Save as Web Page.

■ The Save As dialog box appears.

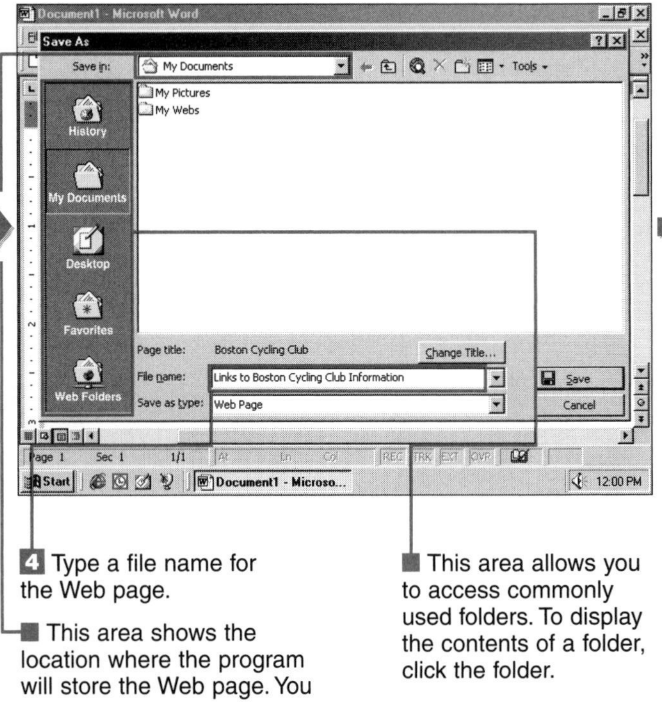

4 Type a file name for the Web page.

■ This area shows the location where the program will store the Web page. You can click this area to change the location.

■ This area allows you to access commonly used folders. To display the contents of a folder, click the folder.

Can I see how a page will look on the Internet?

✔ Before publishing a page, you can preview the page in a Web browser to make sure it will appear the way you want. From the File menu, select Web Page Preview.

Can I save an Access report as a Web page?

✔ Yes. Display the report you want to save as a Web page. From the File menu, select Export. Click the Save as type area, select HTML Documents and click Save. Then click OK in the HTML Output Options dialog box.

Can I save an individual Excel worksheet as a Web page?

✔ When you save an Excel file as a Web page, you can choose whether you want to save the entire workbook or just the current worksheet. To save a worksheet as a Web page, click the Selection: Sheet option in the Save As dialog box (○ changes to ⊙). To save the entire workbook as a Web page, click the Entire Workbook option (○ changes to ⊙).

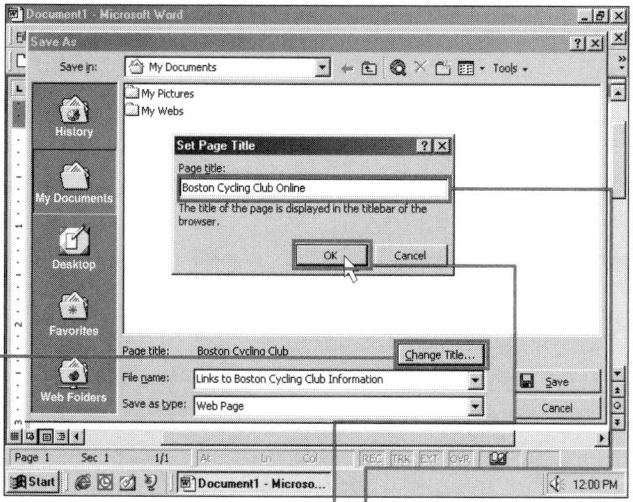

5 Click Change Title to specify a title for the Web page.

■ The Set Page Title dialog box appears.

6 Type a title for the Web page.

7 Click OK to confirm the title.

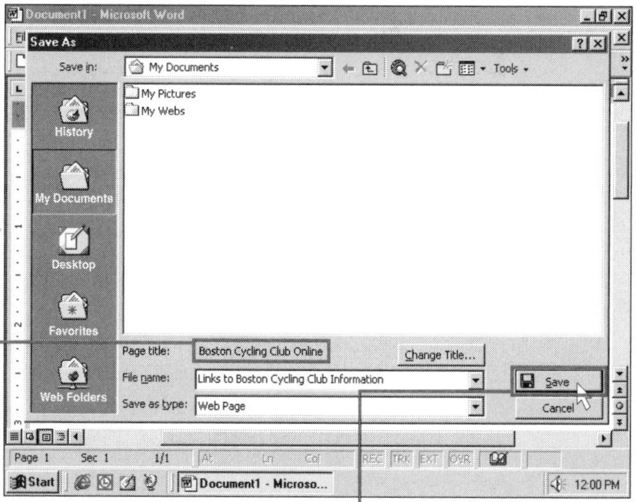

■ This area displays the title for the Web page.

8 Click Save to save the document as a Web page.

SECTION IX

1) EXCHANGE INFORMATION BETWEEN DOCUMENTS

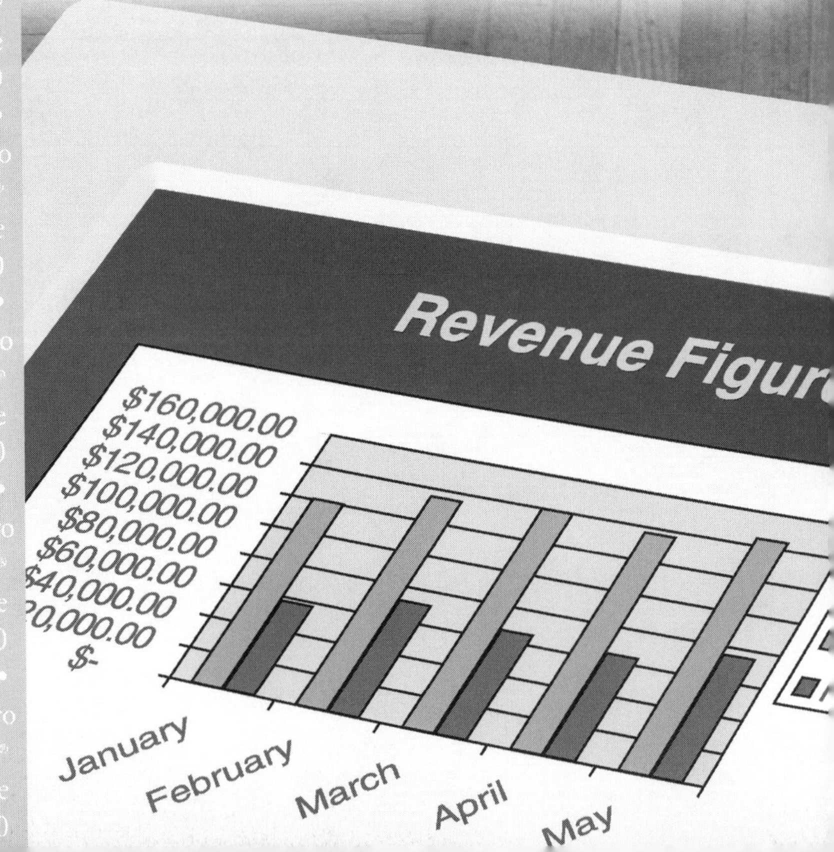

EXCHANGE INFORMATION BETWEEN DOCUMENTS

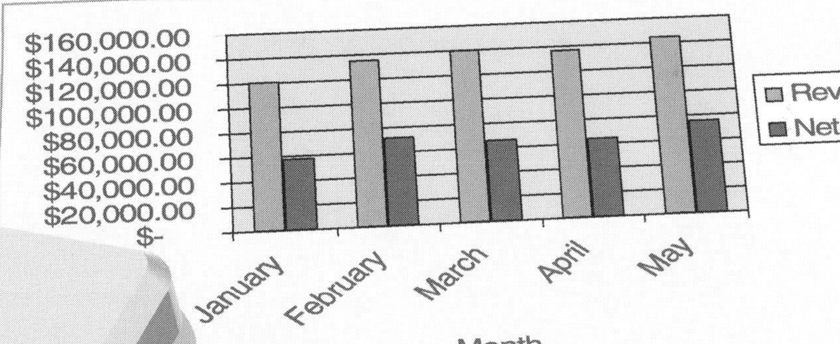
Steve:
Sales have been rising since we began our new marketing plan in January.
Hopefully this trend will continue.
In May, sales exceeded $140,000 for the first time in company history!
It looks like we can expect another incredible year at XYZ Corporation!
Sheila
$160,000.00
$140,000.00
$120,000.00
$100,000.00
$80,000.00
$60,000.00
$40,000.00
$20,000.00
$-
January
February
March
April
May
Month
Revenue
Net

MOVE OR COPY INFORMATION BETWEEN DOCUMENTS

You can move or copy information from one document to another. This saves you time when you want to use the same information in more than one document.

Moving or copying information allows you to use text and objects from one document in another document without having to retype or recreate the information. You can also move or copy information between Office programs, such as Word, Excel, PowerPoint and Access. For example, you can move a chart created in Excel to a Word document.

The information you move or copy is placed in a temporary storage area, called the Office Clipboard. When you move information, the information disappears from the original document and is placed on the Office Clipboard. When you copy information, the information remains in the original document and a copy of the information is placed on the Office Clipboard.

When you paste information into a document, the information from the Office Clipboard appears in the document.

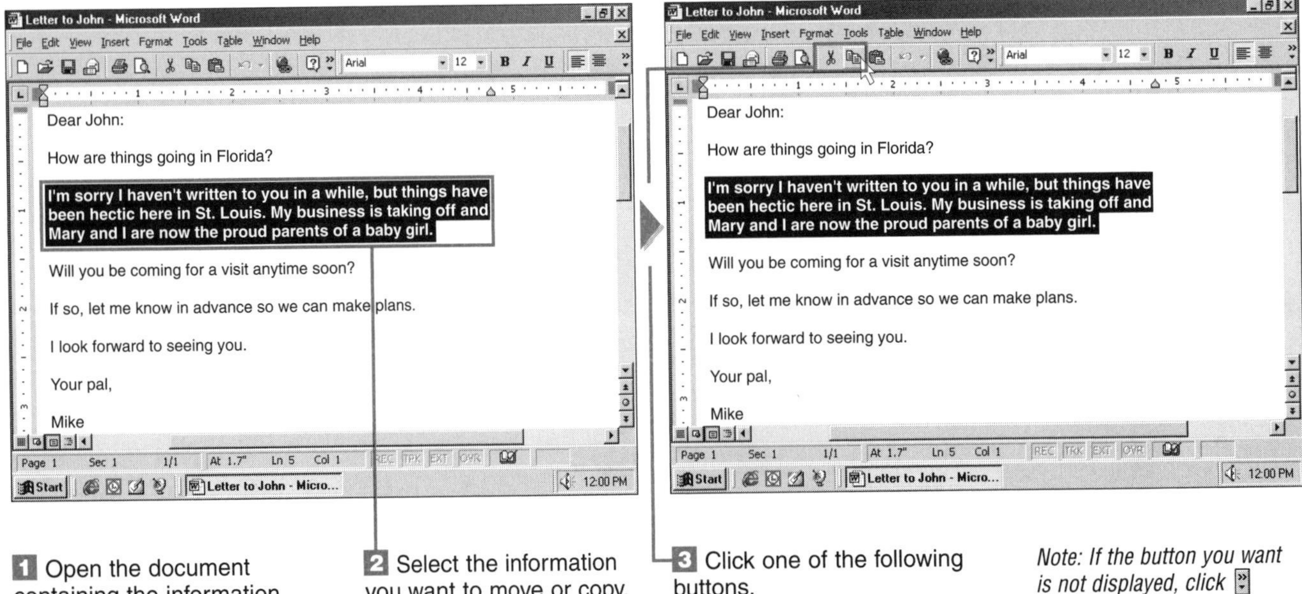

1 Open the document containing the information you want to appear in another document.

2 Select the information you want to move or copy.

3 Click one of the following buttons.

Move information

Copy information

Note: If the button you want is not displayed, click » on the Standard toolbar to display all the buttons.

■ The information is placed on the Office Clipboard.

How do I select the information I want to move or copy?

✔ To select text in most Office programs, drag the mouse I over the text. Selected text appears highlighted on your screen. To select an object in most Office programs, click the object. Handles (□) appear around the selected object.

Is there another way to move or copy information between documents?

✔ Yes. Display both documents side-by-side on your screen. Select the information you want to move or copy. To move the information, drag the information to the other document. To copy the information, hold down the Ctrl key as you drag the information.

Why does the Clipboard toolbar appear when I click the Cut (✂) or Copy (⧉) button?

✔ The Clipboard toolbar may appear when you cut or copy two pieces of information in a row, copy the same information twice or paste copied information and then immediately copy other information. To see the information an icon on the Clipboard toolbar represents, position the mouse pointer over the icon. To place the information in a new location, click the icon.

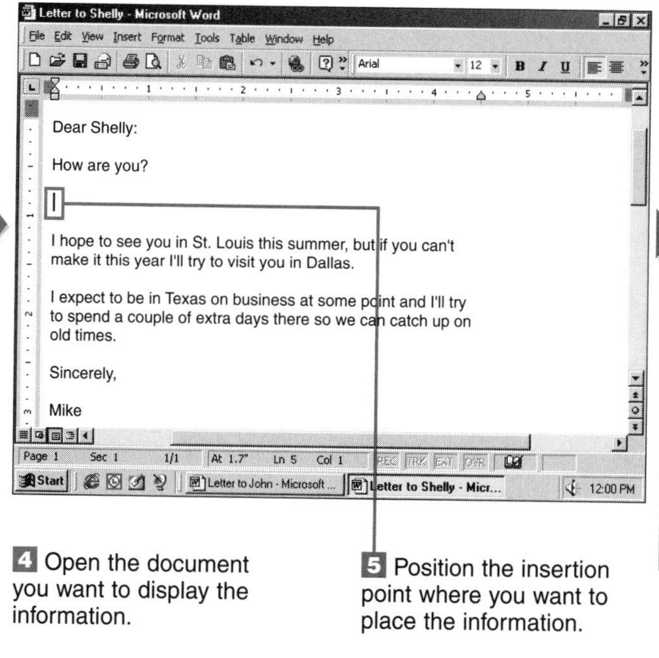

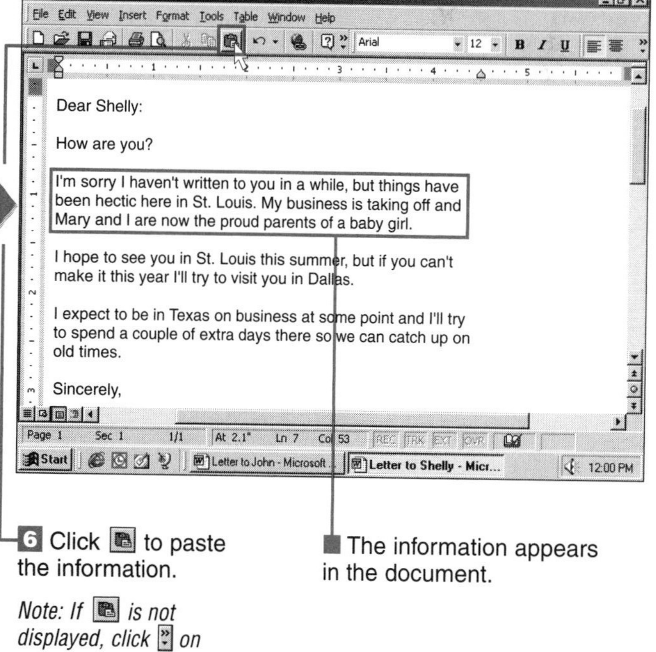

4 Open the document you want to display the information.

5 Position the insertion point where you want to place the information.

6 Click ⧉ to paste the information.

Note: If ⧉ is not displayed, click » on the Standard toolbar to display all the buttons.

■ The information appears in the document.

EMBED INFORMATION

You can use Object Linking and Embedding (OLE) to create a document that contains information from several programs.

Each piece of information you embed in a document is called an object. You can embed objects such as text, charts, images, sounds and video clips in a document.

Each program on your computer is designed to work with a specific type of object. You can use a program on your computer to create an object and then embed the object in another document. For example, you can use Excel to create a chart and then embed the chart in a Word document.

The document you used to create the object is called the source file. The document you embed the object in is called the destination file.

When you embed an object, the object becomes part of the destination file and is no longer connected to the source file.

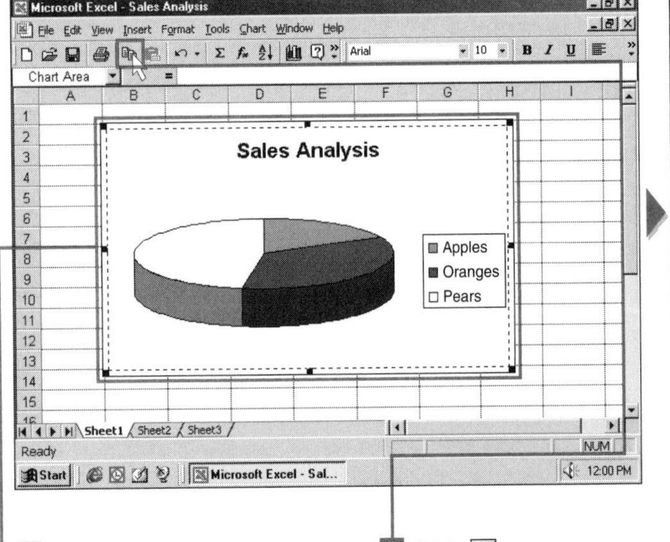

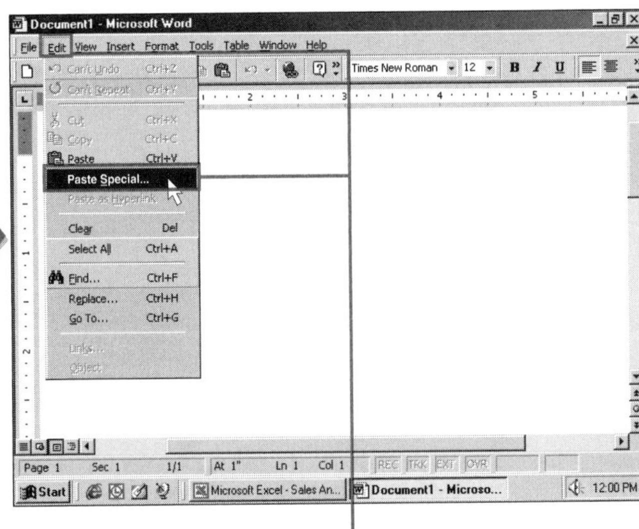

1 Select the information you want to place in another document.

2 Click to copy the information.

Note: If is not displayed, click on the Standard toolbar to display all the buttons.

3 Open the document you want to display the information.

4 Click the location where you want to place the information.

5 Click Edit.

6 Click Paste Special.

Note: If Paste Special does not appear on the menu, position the mouse over the bottom of the menu to display all the menu commands.

How can I tell if a program supports OLE?

✔ Display the Edit menu in the program. If the Paste Special command appears in the menu, the program supports OLE.

Can I use drag and drop to embed objects?

✔ When you move or copy an object by dragging and dropping, the object is embedded in the destination file. Display the source and destination files side-by-side on your screen. Select the object in the source file. To move the object, drag the object to the destination file. To copy the object, hold down the Ctrl key as you drag the object to the destination file.

Can I embed a new object?

✔ Open the document you want to display the new object. From the Insert menu, select Object. Click the Create New tab and then select the type of object you want to create.

Can I embed an entire file in a document?

✔ Yes. From the Insert menu, select Object. Click the Create from File tab and then click Browse to find the file you want to embed.

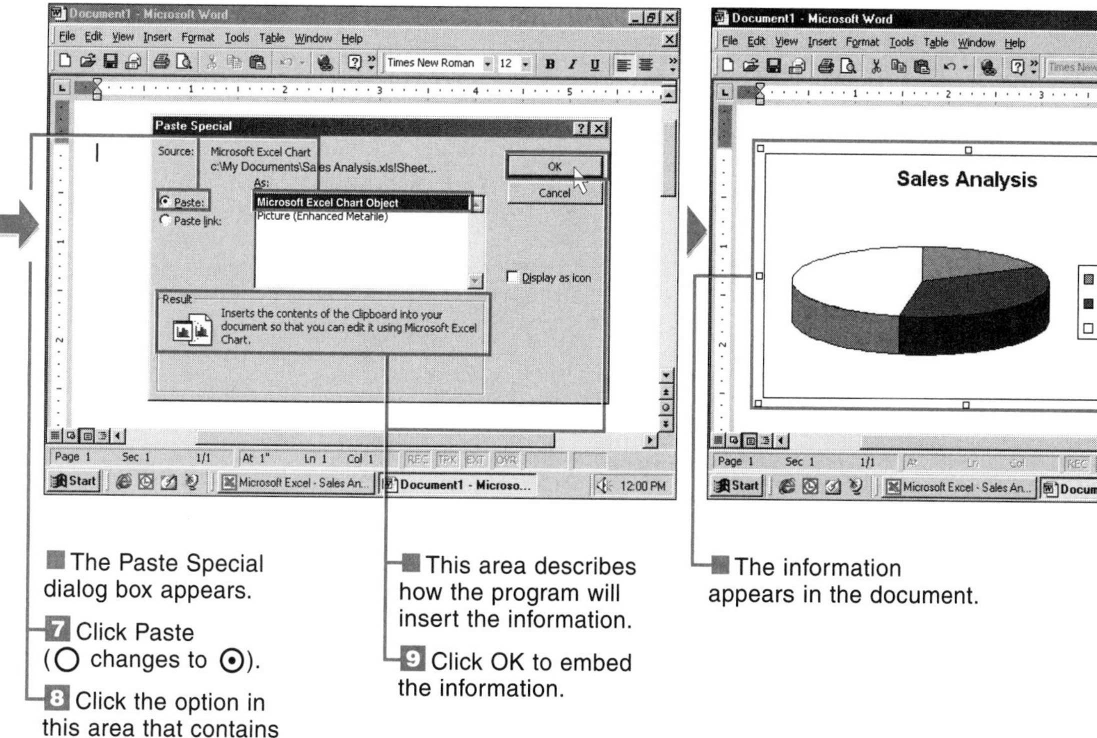

■ The Paste Special dialog box appears.

7 Click Paste (○ changes to ⦿).

8 Click the option in this area that contains the word "Object".

■ This area describes how the program will insert the information.

9 Click OK to embed the information.

■ The information appears in the document.

EDIT EMBEDDED INFORMATION

You can change an object you have embedded in a document. You can edit the object using the same tools you used to create the object.

The file you created an embedded object in is called the source file. The file you embedded the object in is called the destination file. An embedded object is part of the destination file. When you change an embedded object, the object in the source file does not change.

When you double-click an embedded object, the menus and toolbars from the program you used to create the object appear on your screen. You can use these menus and toolbars to edit the embedded object.

When you finish editing the embedded object, the menus and toolbars from the source program are replaced by the menus and toolbars from the destination program.

A document containing an embedded object is often large because it stores information about the object and the program that was used to create the object.

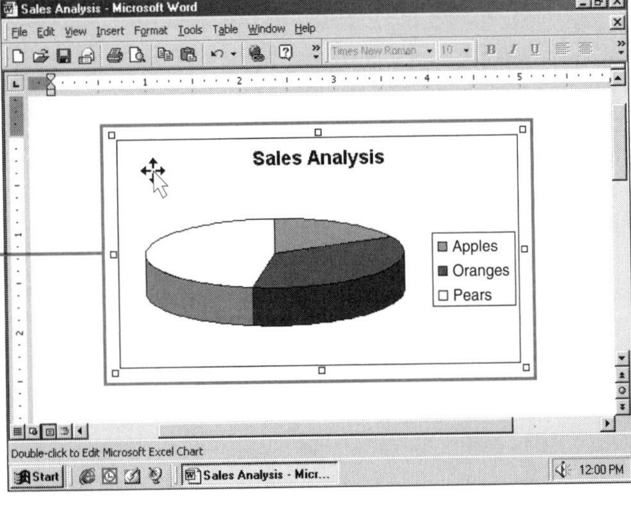

1 Double-click the embedded information you want to change.

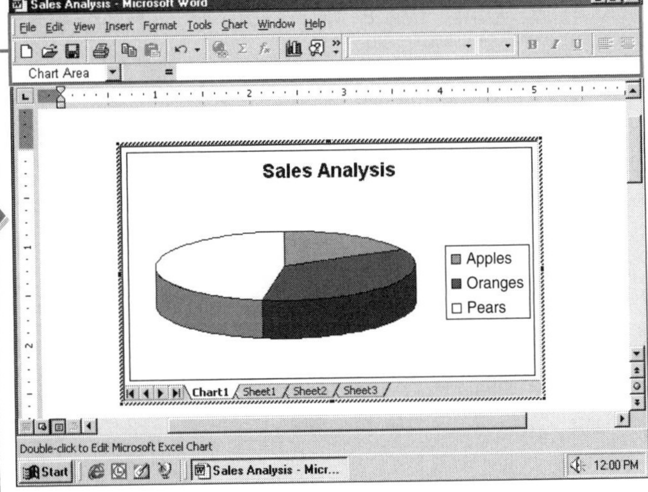

■ The menus and toolbars from the program you used to create the information appear. You can access all the commands you need to make the necessary changes.

When I double-click an embedded object, it appears in a separate window. What should I do?

✔ When you double-click some types of embedded objects, the source program opens and displays the object in a separate window. You can edit the object in the window. When you have finished editing the object, select the File menu and then click Exit to return to the destination file.

Can I change the size of an embedded object?

✔ Yes. Click the object. Handles (□) appear around the object. Position the mouse ↖ over one of the handles (↖ changes to ↕, ↔ or ⤢) and then drag the handle to a new location.

How do I edit an embedded sound or video clip?

✔ Some embedded objects, such as sound and video clips, play automatically when you double-click them. To edit an embedded sound or video clip, right-click the object. Select the object type and then click Edit.

Can I edit an embedded object that someone else created?

✔ You will only be able to edit the object if you have the program that was used to create the object installed on your computer.

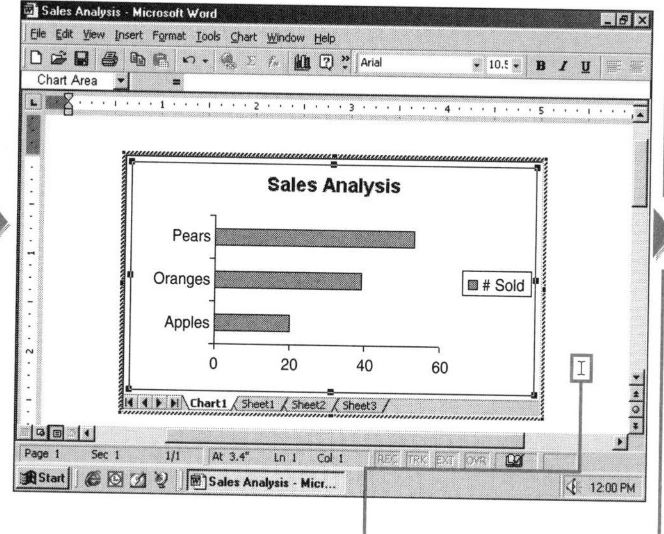

2 Make the necessary changes. In this example, we changed the pie chart to a bar chart.

3 When you finish making the changes, click outside the embedded information.

■ The menus and toolbars from the program containing the embedded information reappear.

LINK INFORMATION

You can use Object Linking and Embedding (OLE) to link the information in one document, called a source file, to another document, called a destination file. A destination file can contain linked information from several source files.

Each piece of information you link between documents is called an object. An object can be an item such as a picture, chart, worksheet or text. You can link an object between documents in the same program or in different programs. For example, you can link a chart in a worksheet to another worksheet in Excel or to a report in Word.

When you link an object, the destination file displays the object but does not contain the object itself. The object remains in the source file. A connection, or link, exists between the source file and the destination file. Since the linked object remains a part of the source file, you should not delete, move or rename the source file.

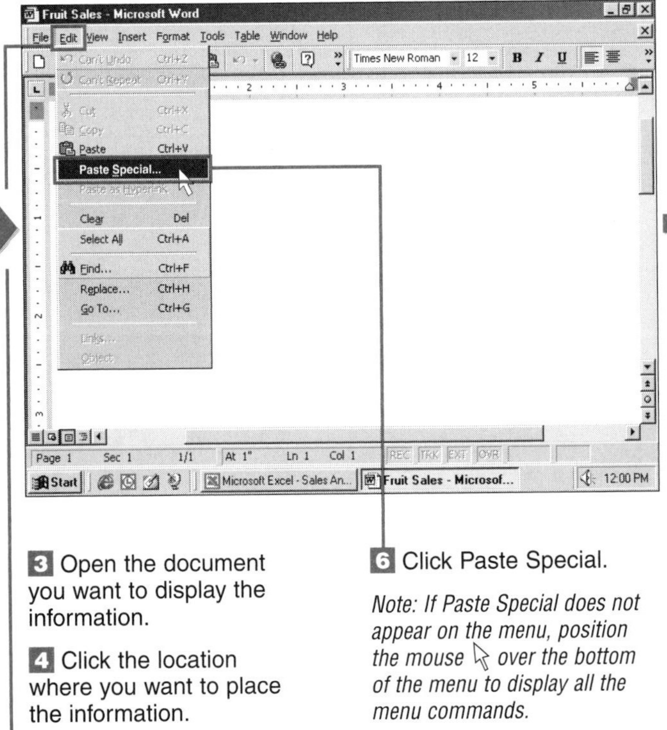

1 Select the information you want to link to another document.

2 Click the Copy button to copy the information.

Note: If the Copy button is not displayed, click the » button on the Standard toolbar to display all the buttons.

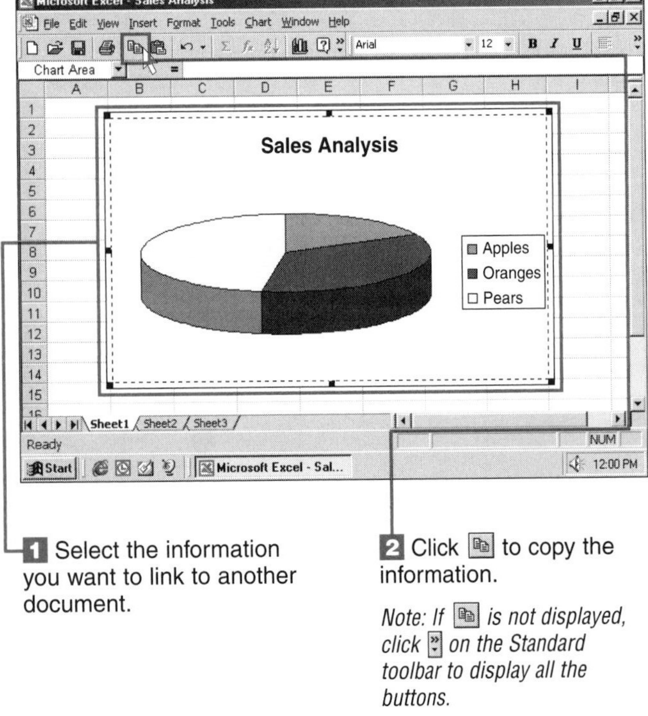

3 Open the document you want to display the information.

4 Click the location where you want to place the information.

5 Click Edit.

6 Click Paste Special.

Note: If Paste Special does not appear on the menu, position the mouse pointer over the bottom of the menu to display all the menu commands.

TIPS

How should I insert information I want to link?

✔ The available options for inserting information depend on the information you select. Inserting information as an object is ideal if you later want to edit the linked information. Some of the other available options include formatted text, unformatted text, picture, bitmap and HTML format.

Can I use drag and drop to link objects?

✔ No. When you drag and drop an object, the object is embedded in the destination file, not linked. For information on embedding an object, see page 618.

What is the difference between linking and embedding?

✔ When you link an object, the object remains a part of the source file. Changes you make to the object in the source file appear in the destination file. When you embed an object, the object becomes part of the destination file and is no longer connected to the source file. Changes you make to the object in the source file do not appear in the destination file.

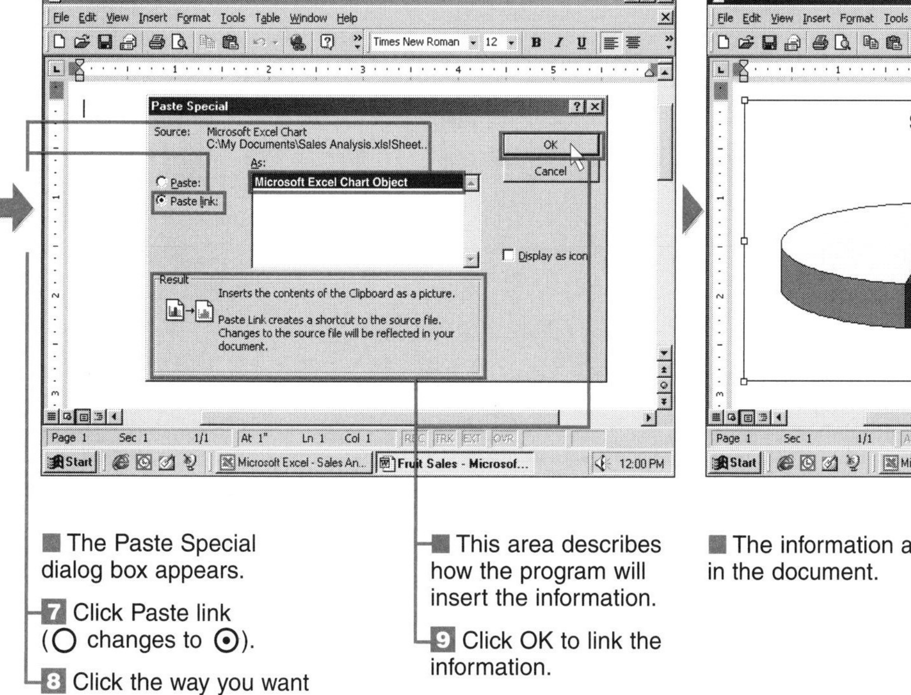

■ The Paste Special dialog box appears.

7 Click Paste link (○ changes to ⊙).

8 Click the way you want to insert the information.

■ This area describes how the program will insert the information.

9 Click OK to link the information.

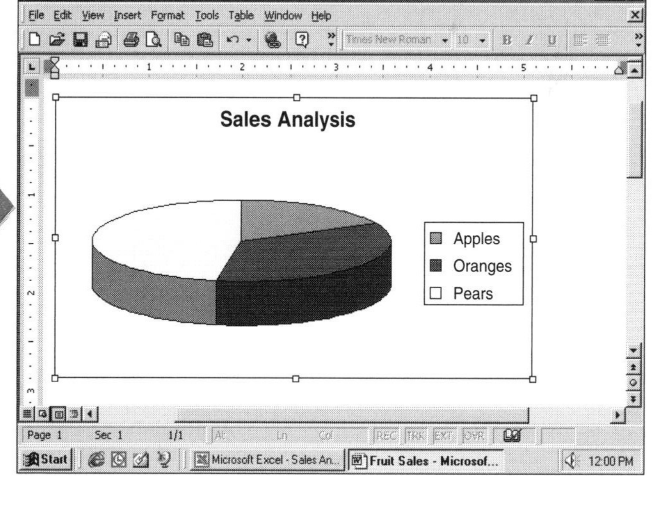

■ The information appears in the document.

EDIT LINKED INFORMATION

You can make changes to a linked object. When you edit a linked object, both the original document and the document you linked the object to display the changes. If you linked the same object to several documents, all the documents will display the changes. This is useful when you want several documents to display the same up-to-date information.

The file you linked the object to is called the destination file. The destination file displays the linked object but does not contain the object itself. The file you created the object in is called the source file. To edit the linked object, the source file must be available on your computer or network and the program used to create the object must be installed on your computer.

To edit a linked object, you can select the linked object in the destination file and then display the object in the source file. You can also go directly to the source program to open the source file and display the object.

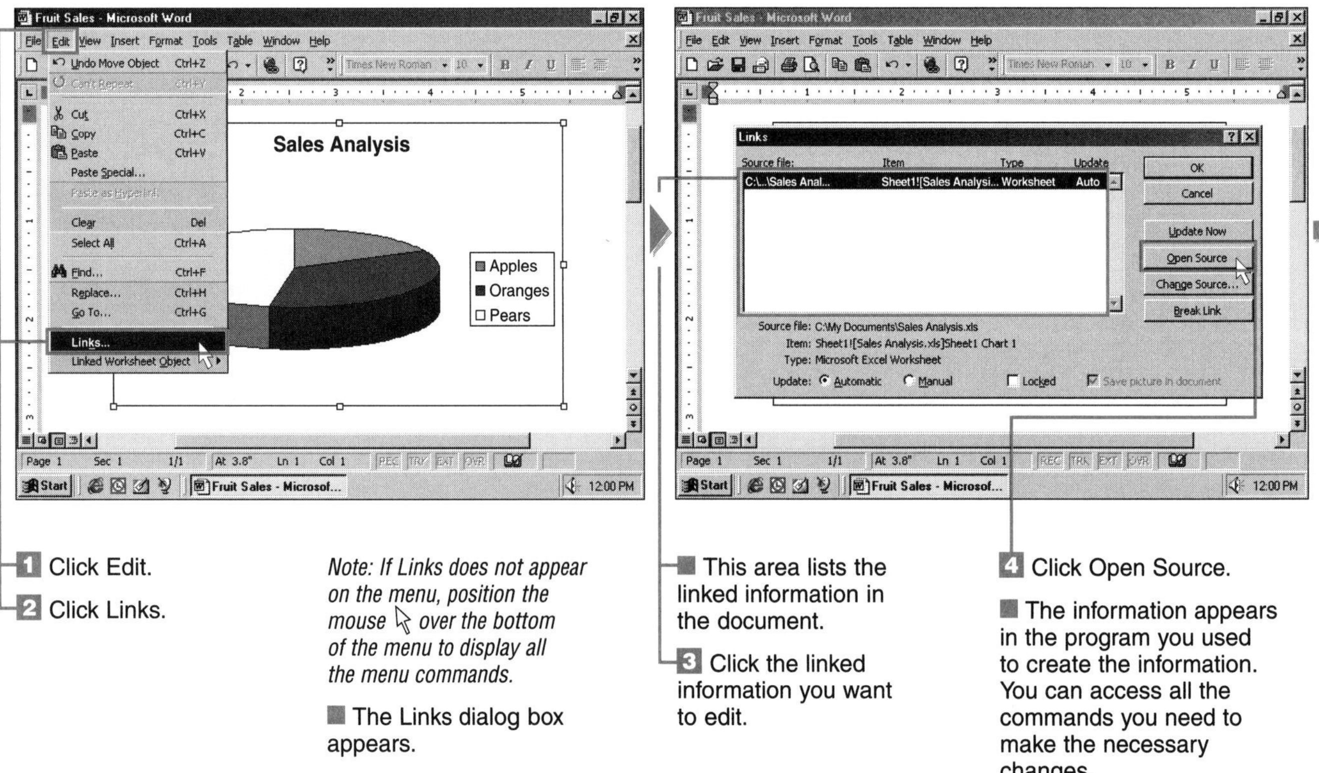

1 Click Edit.

2 Click Links.

Note: If Links does not appear on the menu, position the mouse over the bottom of the menu to display all the menu commands.

■ The Links dialog box appears.

■ This area lists the linked information in the document.

3 Click the linked information you want to edit.

4 Click Open Source.

■ The information appears in the program you used to create the information. You can access all the commands you need to make the necessary changes.

Is there another way to edit linked information in the destination file?

✔ If you inserted the linked information as an object, you can double-click the information to quickly open the source file and edit the information.

Can I break a link?

✔ You can break the connection between linked information and the source file. From the Edit menu, select Links. Click the linked information and then click Break Link. The object becomes part of the destination file and will no longer be updated when you change the object in the source file.

Can I manually update linked information?

✔ By default, when you change linked information in the source file, the information is automatically updated in the destination file. You can have linked information update only when you choose to update the information. From the Edit menu, select Links. Click the linked information you want to update manually and click Manual (○ changes to ⊙). When you want to update the linked information, display the Links dialog box, click the linked information and then click Update Now.

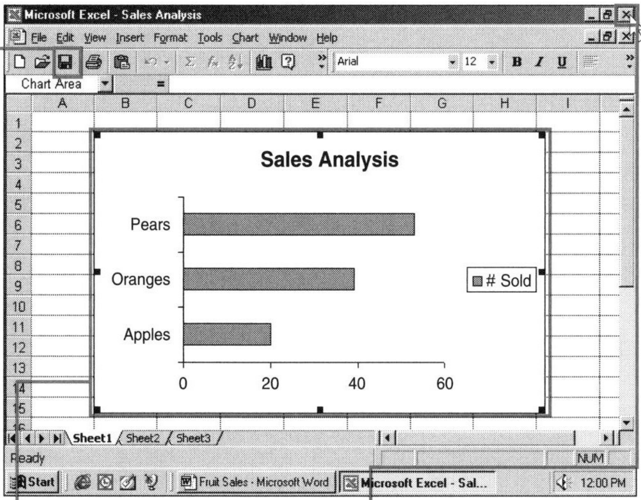

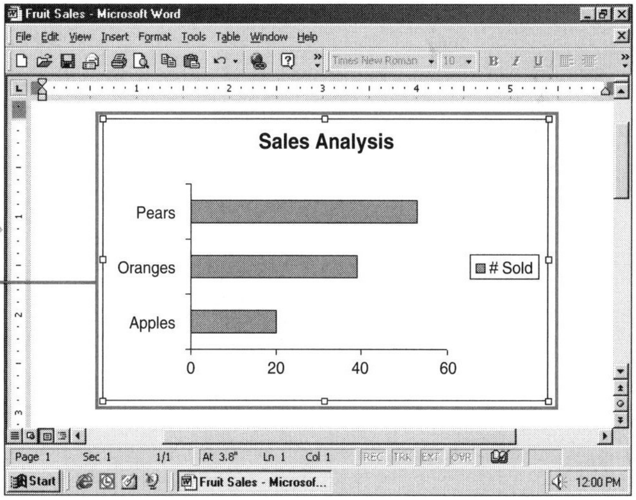

5 Make the necessary changes to the information. In this example, we changed the pie chart to a bar chart.

6 Click 💾 to save the changes.

Note: If 💾 is not displayed, click » on the Standard toolbar to display all the buttons.

7 Click ☒ to exit the program.

■ The document displaying the linked information reappears, showing the changes.

SECTION X

I) CUSTOMIZE OFFICE

CUSTOMIZE OFFICE

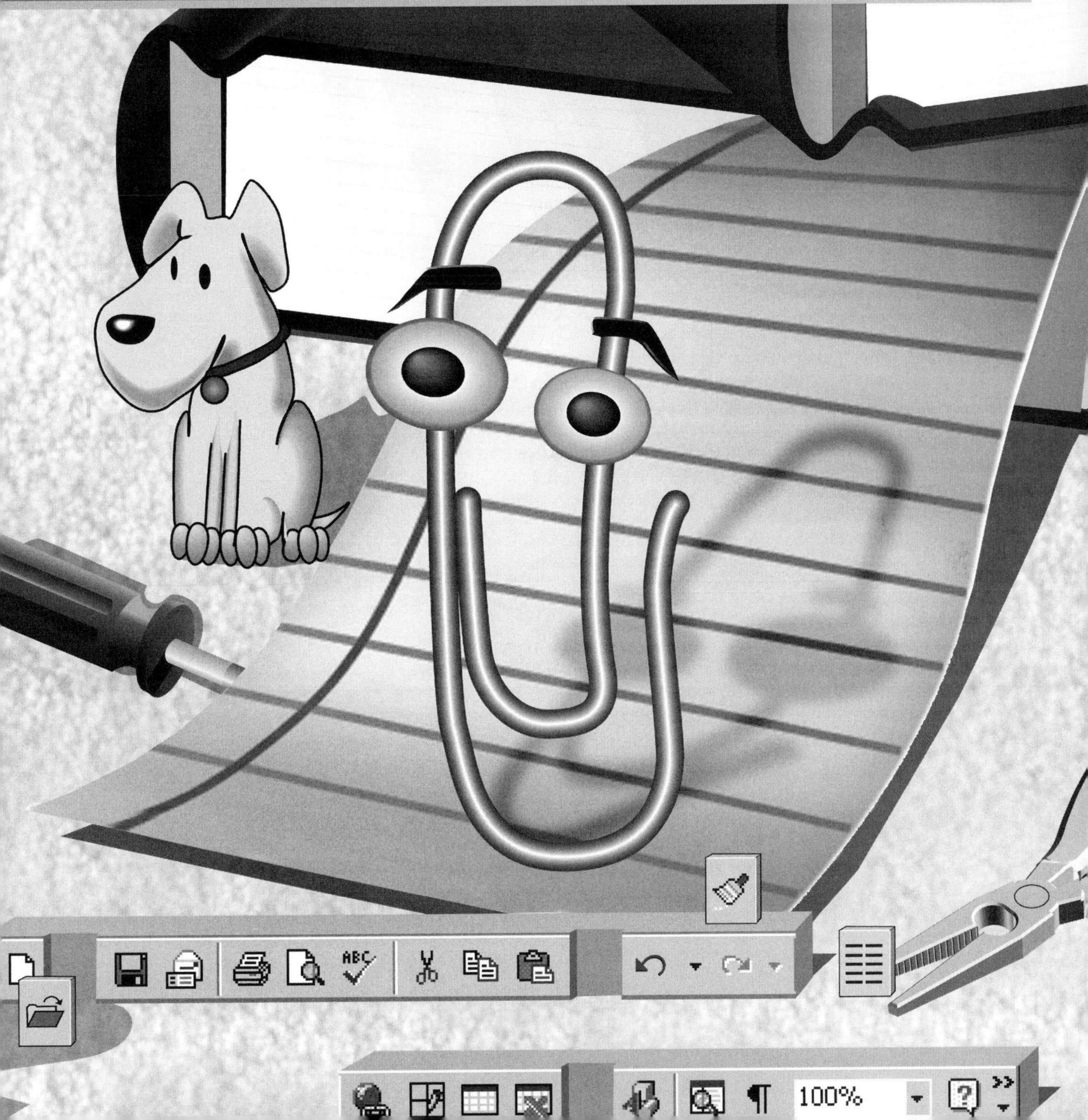

CUSTOMIZE THE OFFICE ASSISTANT

You can customize the Office Assistant to suit your needs.

Changing the capabilities of the Office Assistant allows you to determine how it will act. You can prevent the Office Assistant from displaying messages. If you want to always be able to view the Office Assistant, you can have it automatically move out of the way of other items on your screen, such as dialog boxes. You can also control whether the Office Assistant makes sounds.

You can determine the types of tips the Office Assistant displays. If you primarily use the keyboard, you can tell the Office Assistant not to display tips about using the mouse, but to display tips about keyboard shortcuts. You can also choose to have the Office Assistant display only important tips or display a tip each time you start an Office program.

You can change the animated character that appears as the Office Assistant. You can choose from several different characters, such as Clippit, The Dot, The Genius, Mother Nature or Rocky.

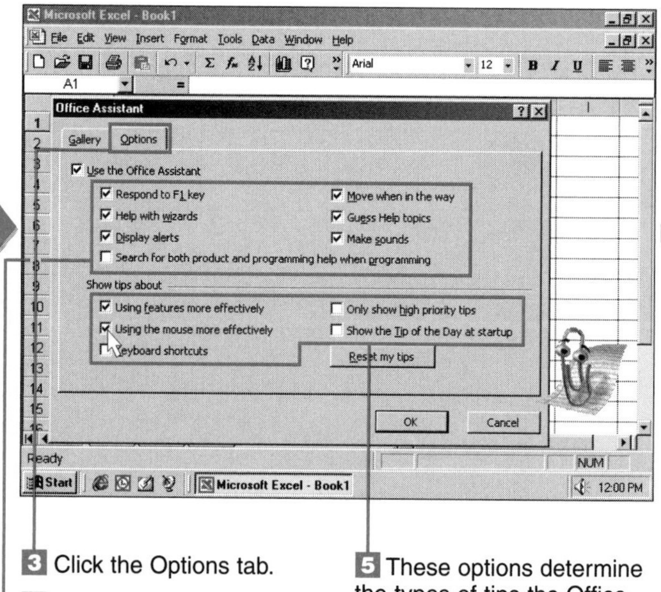

1 Click [?] to display the Office Assistant.

Note: If [?] is not displayed, click [»] on the Standard toolbar to display all the buttons.

2 Click Options.

■ The Office Assistant dialog box appears.

3 Click the Options tab.

4 These options determine the capabilities of the Office Assistant. You can click an option to turn the option on (☑) or off (☐).

5 These options determine the types of tips the Office Assistant offers. You can click an option to turn the option on (☑) or off (☐).

If I make changes to the Office Assistant in one program, are the other Office programs affected by the changes?

✔ The changes you make to the Office Assistant in one program affect most of the other Office programs installed on your computer.

Where can I get more animated characters?

✔ If you have access to the Internet, you can get more animated characters from the Microsoft Office Update Web site. To open your Web browser and display the Web site, click the Help menu and then select Office on the Web.

How can I quickly display the Office Assistant?

✔ You can press the F1 key to quickly display the Office Assistant at any time.

How do I turn off the Office Assistant?

✔ In the Office Assistant dialog box, click the Use the Office Assistant option (☑ changes to ☐). To once again turn on the Office Assistant, click the Help menu and then select Show the Office Assistant.

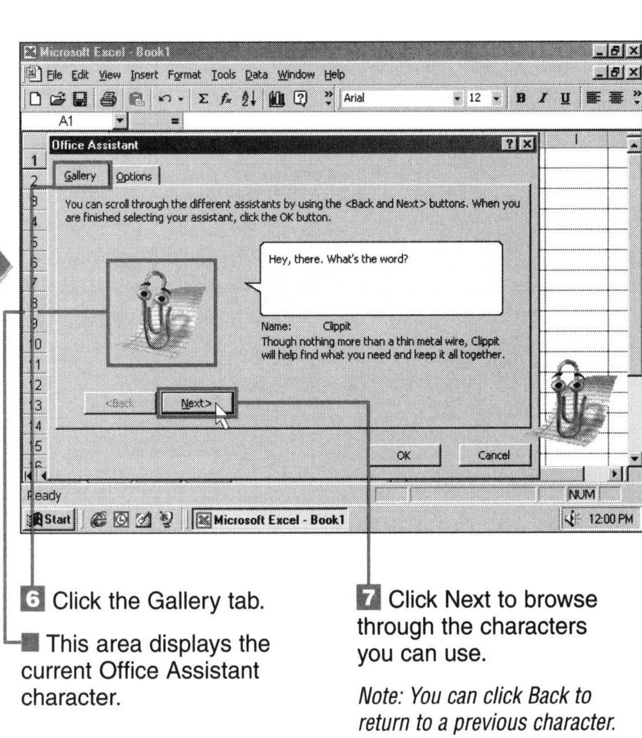

6 Click the Gallery tab.

■ This area displays the current Office Assistant character.

7 Click Next to browse through the characters you can use.

Note: You can click Back to return to a previous character.

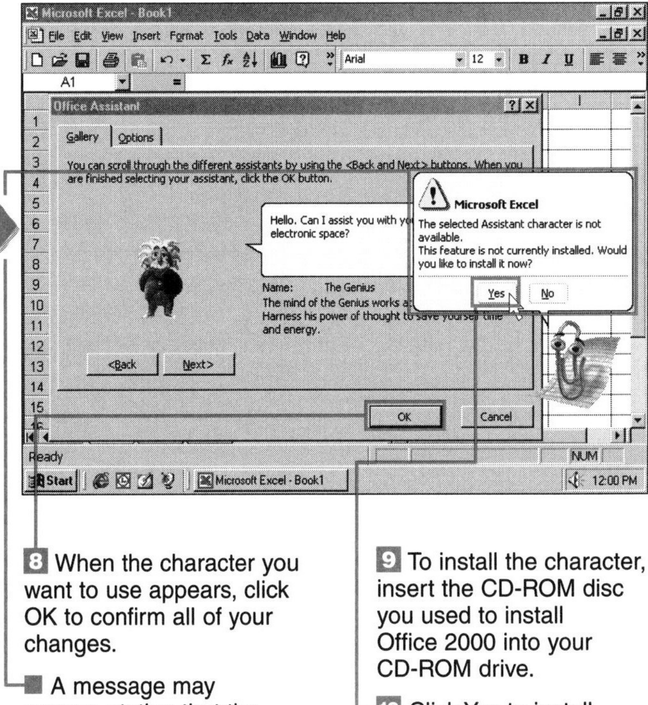

8 When the character you want to use appears, click OK to confirm all of your changes.

■ A message may appear, stating that the character you selected is not installed.

9 To install the character, insert the CD-ROM disc you used to install Office 2000 into your CD-ROM drive.

10 Click Yes to install the character.

CUSTOMIZE A TOOLBAR

You can customize the toolbars in an Office program to help you work more efficiently.

Office provides similar toolbars in each of its programs. Although some toolbar buttons are unique to only one program, there are several buttons that are common to most Office programs, such as the Cut (✂), Copy (📋) and Paste (📋) buttons.

You can remove buttons you do not frequently use from a toolbar. When you remove a button, you do not disable the command associated with the button. For example, if you remove the Spelling and Grammar button (✓) from the Standard toolbar in Word, you can still access the Spelling and Grammar command on the Tools menu.

You can move buttons on a toolbar to place buttons for related tasks together. This can help make it easier to find the commands you need. For example, you can place all the buttons that allow you to access help information together and all the buttons that deal with printing together.

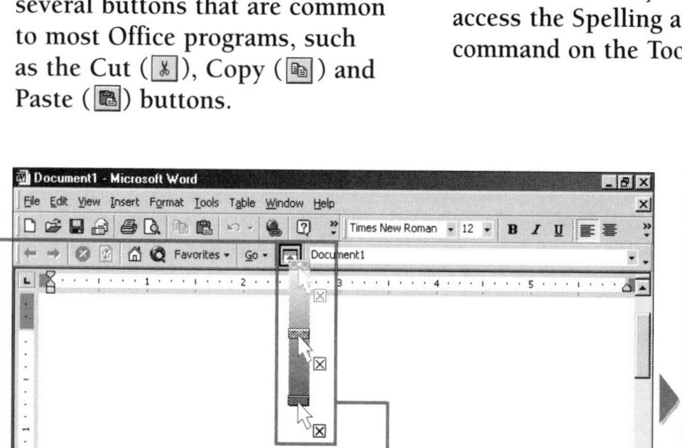

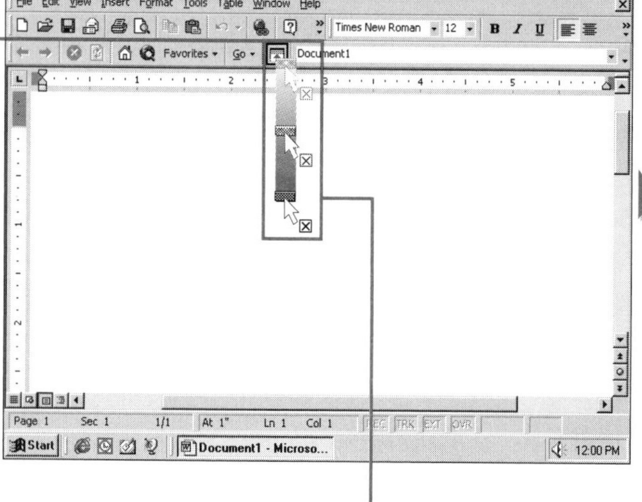

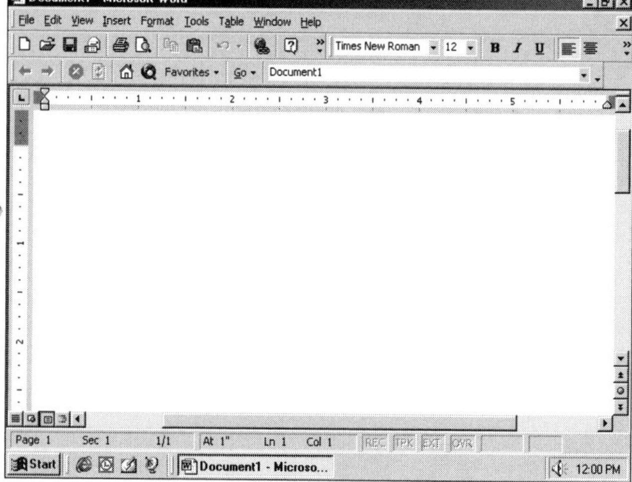

REMOVE A BUTTON

1 Display the toolbar you want to customize.

2 Position the mouse over the button you want to remove from the toolbar.

3 Hold down the Alt key as you drag the button downward off the toolbar.

■ The button disappears from the toolbar.

Can I copy a button from one toolbar to another?

✔ Yes. Display both toolbars on your screen. Position the mouse pointer over the button you want to copy. Hold down the Ctrl+Alt keys as you drag the button to the other toolbar.

Can I move a menu?

✔ Yes. Like moving a toolbar button, moving a menu can help you work more efficiently. Position the mouse pointer over the name of the menu you want to move. Hold down the Alt key as you drag the menu to a new location.

How do I return a toolbar to its original settings?

✔ You can undo all the changes you made to a toolbar. From the Tools menu, select Customize and then choose the Toolbars tab. Select the toolbar you want to return to its original settings and then click Reset. Click OK in the dialog box that appears and then click Close.

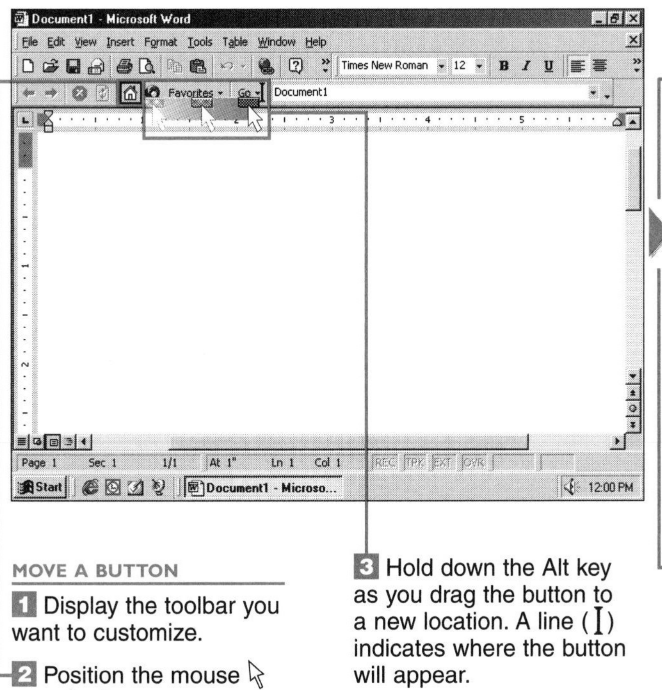

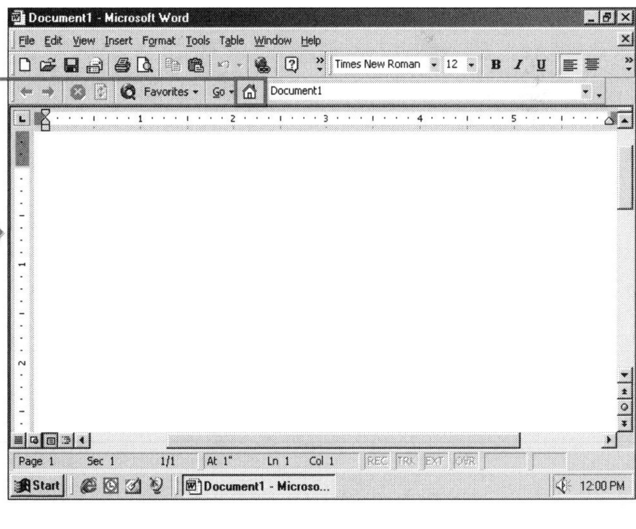

MOVE A BUTTON

1 Display the toolbar you want to customize.

2 Position the mouse over the button you want to move to a new location.

3 Hold down the Alt key as you drag the button to a new location. A line (I) indicates where the button will appear.

■ The button appears in the new location.

CUSTOMIZE A TOOLBAR CONTINUED

You can add buttons to a toolbar to provide quick access to the commands you use most often. You can add buttons to a toolbar you created or to any toolbar included with Office, such as the Formatting toolbar.

Office provides hundreds of commands for you to choose from. The commands are grouped into categories. Each category contains commands to help you perform a specific type of task. For example, the Format category contains commands that will help you format text, including font, underline and alignment commands. If you do not know which category contains the command you want, you can select the All Commands category to see a list of all the commands.

You can add as many buttons to a toolbar as you need. However, if you add too many buttons to a toolbar, the toolbar may become too long to display all the buttons on your screen.

Buttons you add to a toolbar may display images, text or both.

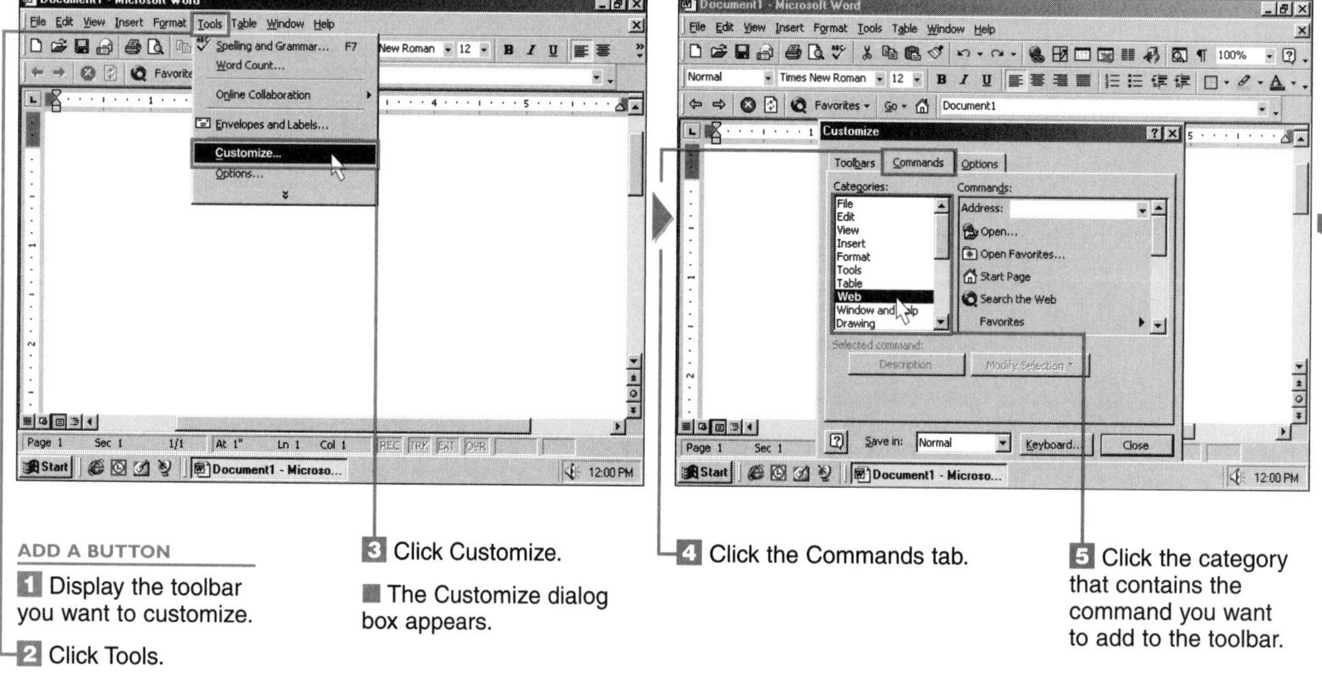

ADD A BUTTON

1 Display the toolbar you want to customize.

2 Click Tools.

3 Click Customize.

■ The Customize dialog box appears.

4 Click the Commands tab.

5 Click the category that contains the command you want to add to the toolbar.

Is there another way to add a button to a toolbar?

✔ Click the More Buttons button (or) on the toolbar you want to customize and then click Add or Remove Buttons. A list of commands for the toolbar appears. A check mark (✔) beside a command indicates a button for the command is currently displayed on the toolbar. Click the command you want to add to the toolbar.

Can I display a description of a command in the Customize dialog box?

✔ Yes. Click the command and then select the Description button.

Can I change the image on a button?

✔ Yes. Changing the image on a button can help draw attention to the button. Office provides several interesting and fun button images. From the Tools menu, select Customize to display the Customize dialog box. On the toolbar, right-click the button you want to change. Select Change Button Image on the menu that appears and then choose the image you want the button to display. To redisplay the original image, right-click the button again and then select Reset Button Image.

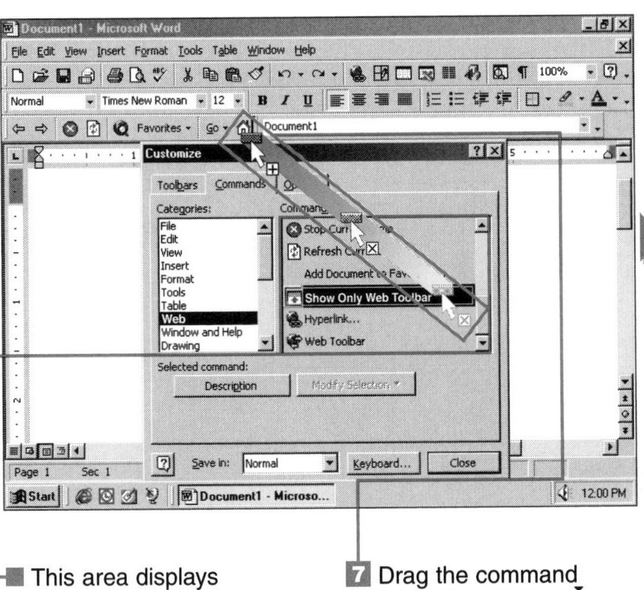

■ This area displays the commands in the category you selected.

6 Position the mouse over the command you want to add to the toolbar.

7 Drag the command to the toolbar. A line (I) indicates where the button for the command will appear.

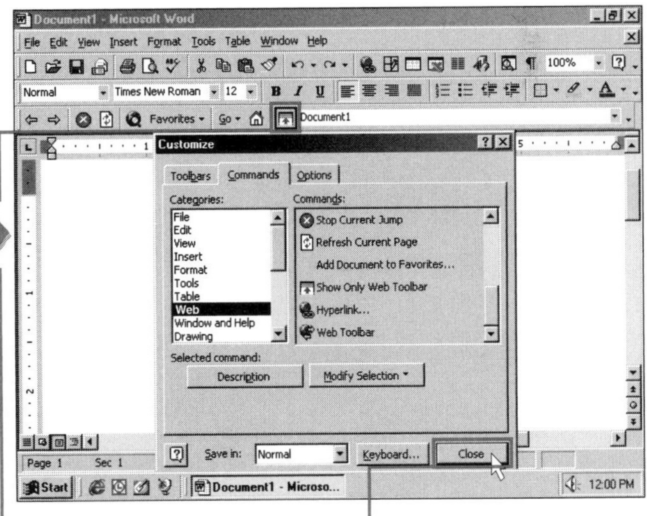

■ The button for the command appears on the toolbar.

8 To add another button to the toolbar, repeat steps 5 to 7.

9 When you finish adding buttons to the toolbar, click Close to close the Customize dialog box.

CREATE A CUSTOM TOOLBAR

You can create a custom toolbar containing buttons you frequently use. This allows you to have a specific toolbar for each type of task you regularly perform, such as printing documents or adding AutoShapes.

A toolbar you create in one Office program will not be available in the other programs. For example, if you create a toolbar containing printing commands in Excel, you will not be able to use the toolbar to print documents in Word. If you want to use the same type of toolbar in Word, you must create a toolbar containing printing commands in Word.

You can name a toolbar you create. A descriptive name will help you identify the toolbar in the future.

A custom toolbar you create does not contain any buttons. You can add, remove or move buttons on a custom toolbar as you would on any toolbar. For more information, see pages 630 to 633.

You can also display or hide a custom toolbar as you would any toolbar. To display or hide a toolbar, see page 13.

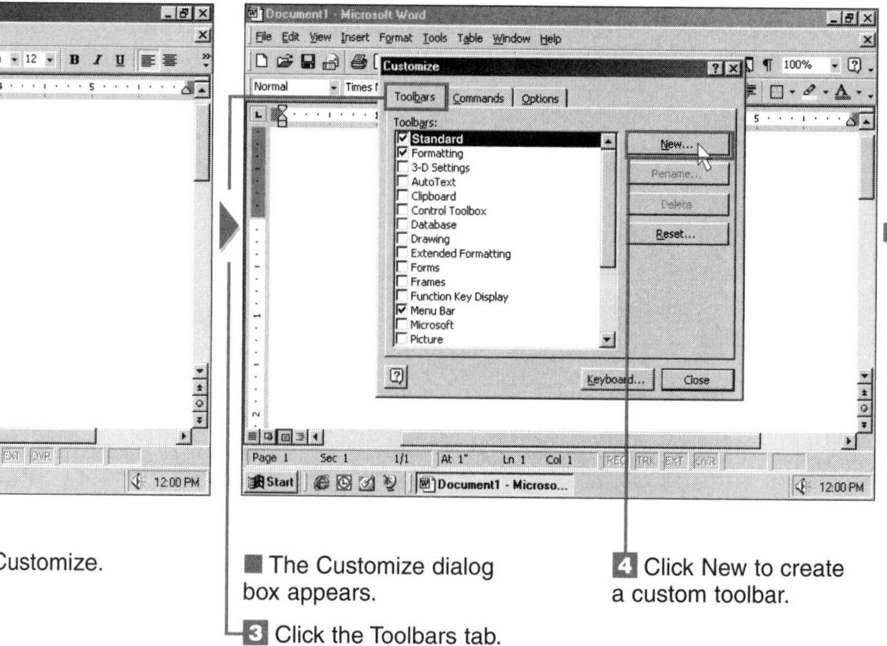

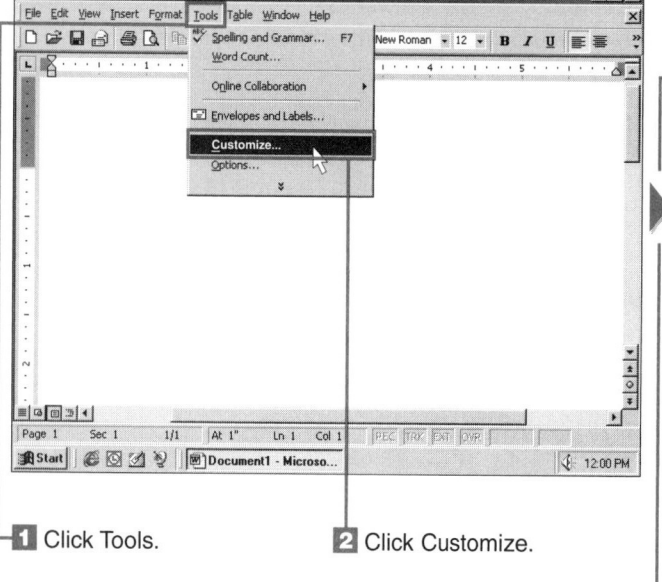

1 Click Tools.

2 Click Customize.

■ The Customize dialog box appears.

3 Click the Toolbars tab.

4 Click New to create a custom toolbar.

Can I place my custom toolbar at the top of the screen with the built-in toolbars?

✔ Yes. Position the mouse pointer over a blank area on the title bar of your toolbar and then drag the toolbar to the top of your screen.

Can I add a built-in menu to my custom toolbar?

✔ Yes. In the Customize dialog box, click the Commands tab. In the Categories area, select Built-in Menus. In the Commands area, position the mouse pointer over the menu you want to add and then drag the menu to your toolbar.

Can I rename a custom toolbar?

✔ Yes. In the Customize dialog box, click the Toolbars tab. Select the name of the custom toolbar you want to rename and then click the Rename button. Type a new name and then click OK. You cannot rename a built-in toolbar.

How do I delete a custom toolbar?

✔ In the Customize dialog box, click the Toolbars tab. Select the name of the custom toolbar you want to delete and then click the Delete button. You cannot delete a built-in toolbar.

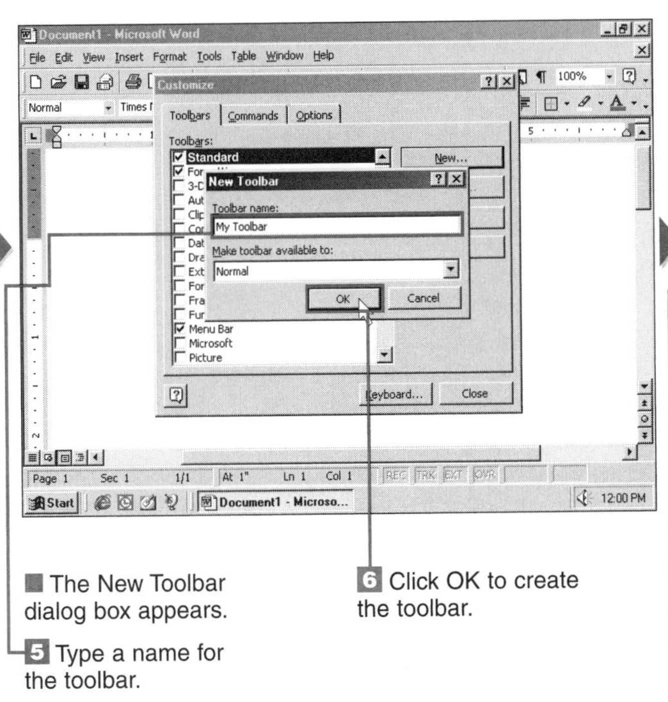

■ The New Toolbar dialog box appears.

5 Type a name for the toolbar.

6 Click OK to create the toolbar.

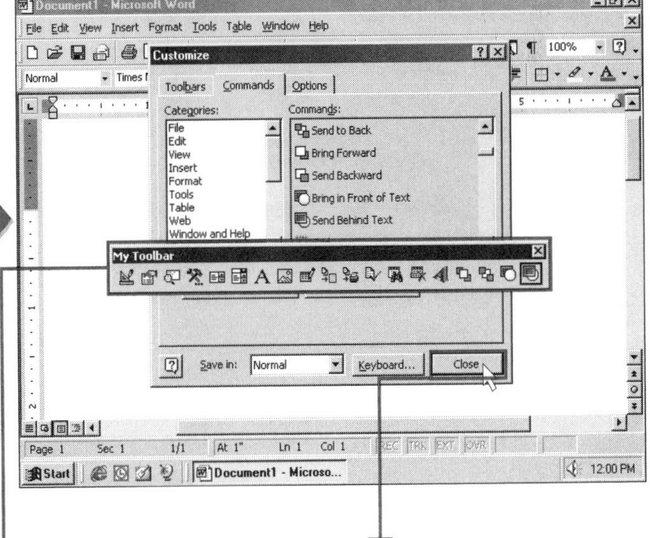

■ The custom toolbar appears on the screen.

■ You can add buttons to the custom toolbar as you would to any toolbar. To add buttons to a toolbar, see page 632.

7 When you finish adding buttons to the toolbar, click Close to close the Customize dialog box.

ADD OR REMOVE OFFICE 2000 FEATURES

You can install Office 2000 features on your computer to add capabilities and enhancements to Office. You can also remove Office 2000 features to free up storage space on your computer.

Office organizes the available features by program. You can display or hide the features for a program. Many features have subfeatures you can add or remove.

Each feature displays an icon that indicates how the feature is currently installed. A feature that displays the icon is installed on your computer. A feature that displays the icon will be installed only when you first use the feature. The ✕ icon indicates a feature is not installed on your computer. A feature that displays the icon is not installed on your computer, but will run using the CD-ROM disc.

You can select a different icon for a feature to change the way the feature is installed. When you select an icon that displays two small squares, such as or , you change the way a feature and all its subfeatures are installed. For example, you can choose the icon to quickly install a feature and all its subfeatures.

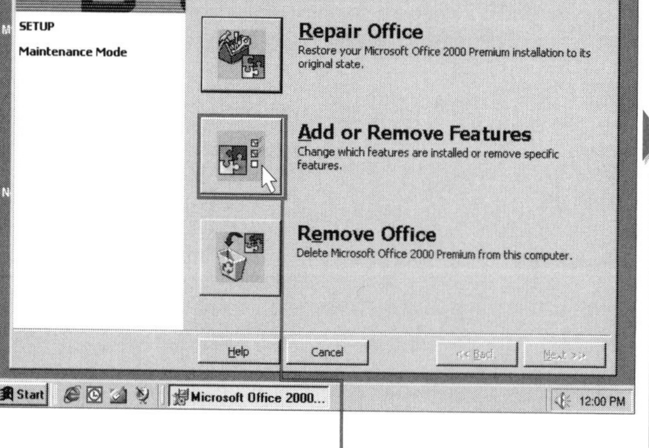

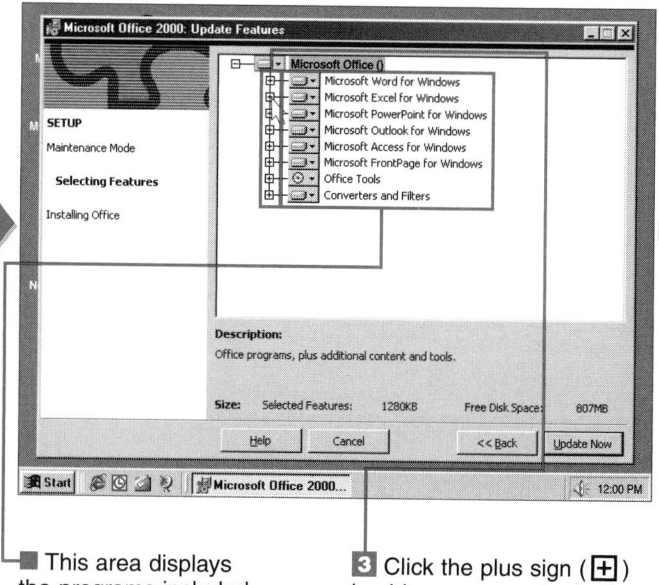

1 Insert the CD-ROM disc you used to install Microsoft Office 2000 into your CD-ROM drive.

■ After a few seconds, the Microsoft Office 2000 Maintenance Mode window appears.

2 Click the button beside Add or Remove Features.

■ This area displays the programs included with Office.

3 Click the plus sign (⊞) beside a program to display the features for the program (⊞ changes to ⊟).

Is there anything I should do before adding or removing Office features?

✔ You should close all open Office programs before adding or removing features.

Why are the icons for some features gray?

✔ When the icon for a feature is gray, the feature has subfeatures that are not all installed the same way. For example, some of the subfeatures may be installed on your computer ( ), while others may only be installed the first time you use the feature ( ). To display the subfeatures for a feature, click the plus sign (⊞) beside the feature.

The Microsoft Office 2000 Maintenance Mode window did not appear. What is wrong?

✔ Your computer may not be set up to automatically run a CD-ROM disc. To display the Microsoft Office 2000 Maintenance Mode window, double-click My Computer on your desktop and then double-click the icon for your CD-ROM drive.

Can I close the window without adding or removing any Office features?

✔ Yes. Click Cancel to exit without making any changes. Then click Yes in the confirmation dialog box that appears.

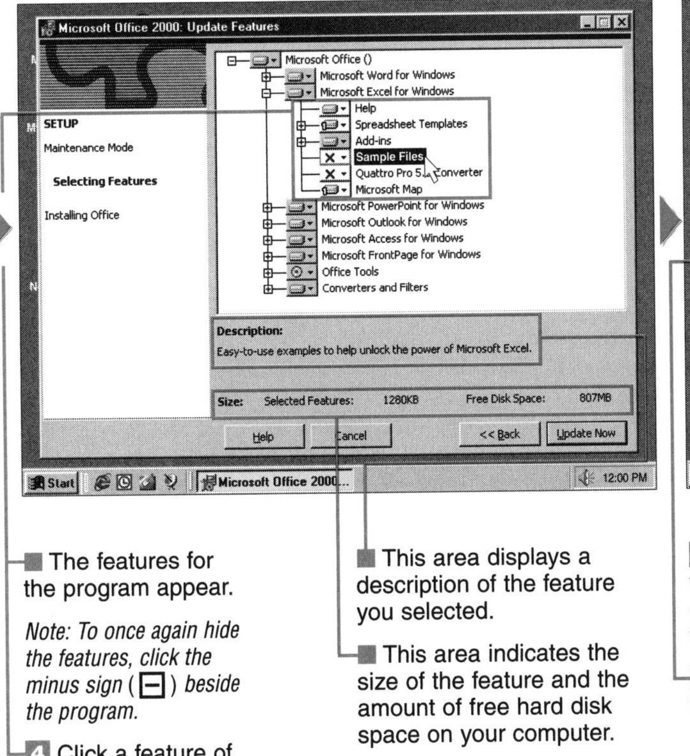

■ The features for the program appear.

Note: To once again hide the features, click the minus sign (⊟) beside the program.

4 Click a feature of interest.

■ This area displays a description of the feature you selected.

■ This area indicates the size of the feature and the amount of free hard disk space on your computer.

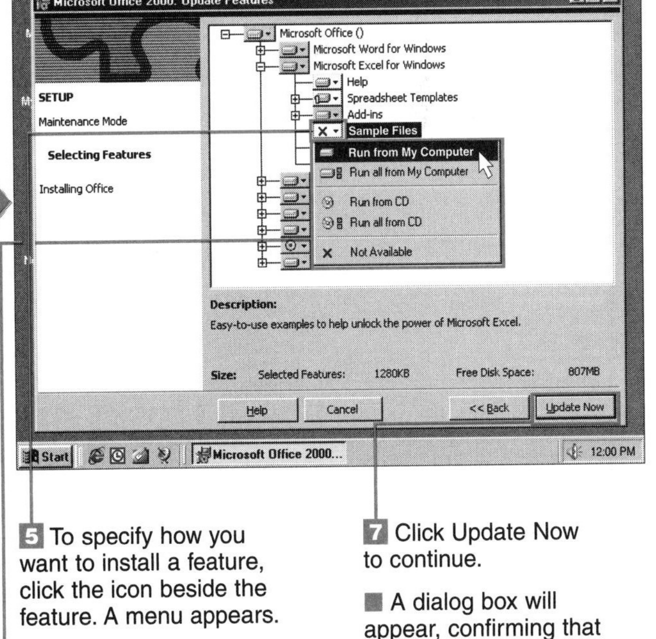

5 To specify how you want to install a feature, click the icon beside the feature. A menu appears.

6 Click the way you want to install the feature.

7 Click Update Now to continue.

■ A dialog box will appear, confirming that the update was completed successfully. Click OK to close the dialog box.

ADDITIONAL OFFICE 2000 PROGRAMS AND FEATURES

Microsoft Internet Explorer 5.0

Microsoft Internet Explorer is a Web browser that allows you to efficiently access information on your computer, your corporate intranet or the Internet. An intranet is a small version of the Internet within a company or organization.

Internet Explorer 5.0 may be installed by default when you install Microsoft Office 2000.

Browsing Features

Internet Explorer includes several features that can help you quickly locate information. You can use the search services on the Internet to locate Web pages of interest. Internet Explorer provides access to popular search services such as Excite, Yahoo! and Lycos.

The Favorites feature allows you to quickly access Web pages and documents you frequently visit. This saves you from having to remember and retype the same addresses over and over.

The History list keeps track of the Web pages and documents you have viewed over the last 20 days so you can quickly return to a page or document.

Communication Features

Internet Explorer includes the Outlook Express e-mail program. Outlook Express allows you to exchange electronic mail with people around the world and read articles in newsgroups.

If your intranet Web server is set up to use Office Server Extensions, you can use Internet Explorer to communicate with other people who are working on the same document stored on the Web server. For more information on Office Server Extensions, see page 639.

Security Features

Internet Explorer offers features that can help make accessing and exchanging information on the Internet more secure. You can assign Web sites to different security zones to restrict the transfer of information to and from the Web sites. For example, you could assign Web sites on your intranet to a zone with a low security level, but assign Web sites on the Internet to a high-security zone. This helps to protect your computer by restricting the transfer of possibly damaging information from the Internet.

The Content Advisor allows you to restrict access to Web sites depending on the content of the site. This is useful if you want to allow children to browse through information on the Internet while restricting their access to offensive material.

Office Server Extensions

Office Server Extensions provide a Web server with additional capabilities designed to help you work more efficiently with your colleagues. A Web server is a computer that stores Web pages and Office documents published on the Internet or a corporate intranet. An intranet is a small version of the Internet within a company or organization.

Office Server Extensions make it easy for you to publish and work with documents directly on a Web server. While you work with a document stored on a Web server, Office Server Extensions allow you to communicate with other people working on the same document. You can have a

discussion with other people in a pane at the bottom of the document or in your Web browser.

You can also have Office notify you by e-mail when a document on the Web server changes.

Office Server Extensions must be installed on the Web Server. You can find the Office Server Extensions on the Microsoft Office 2000 installation CD-ROM disc.

Web Components

Web components allow you to publish interactive Excel worksheets, PivotTables and charts as Web pages on the Internet or a corporate intranet.

With Web components, users can interact with a Web page by making changes to the information on the Web page, such as rearranging data or updating values in a worksheet. Without Web components, people would be able to view your Web page content, but not interact with the content.

Users interact with the Web page content using their Web browser, so they do not need to have Excel installed on their computer. Users who want to interact with your Web page content must use Internet Explorer 4.01 or later and have Web components installed on their computer.

In order for your Web page to be interactive, your Web page must be published on a Web server that has Office Server Extensions installed.

If Web components are not installed on your computer, you can install them from the Microsoft Office 2000 installation CD-ROM disc.

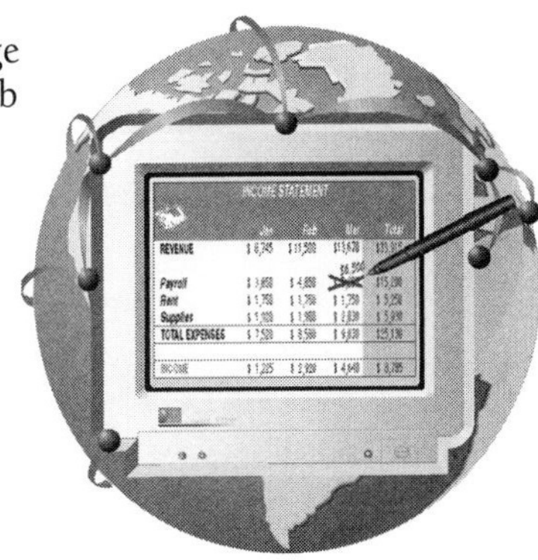

CONTINUED

ADDITIONAL OFFICE 2000 PROGRAMS AND FEATURES CONTINUED

Microsoft PhotoDraw

You can use Microsoft PhotoDraw to create and edit images on your computer. PhotoDraw allows you to work with several different types of images including clip art, photographs, shapes and text.

If PhotoDraw is not installed on your computer, you can install the program from the Microsoft Office 2000 installation CD-ROM disc.

PhotoDraw Features

PhotoDraw offers many features to help you quickly get started. You can use PhotoDraw's tutorial to learn about the PhotoDraw screen, composing images and adding text to images. When you are ready to start creating images, you can use one of PhotoDraw's professionally designed templates to quickly create an image. The templates are divided into categories, including Web Graphics, Business Graphics and Designer Clip Art.

You can save the images you create for use in other programs. PhotoDraw provides a wizard to help you save an image in the correct format for use on the Web, in Office documents, PowerPoint presentations or Publisher publications.

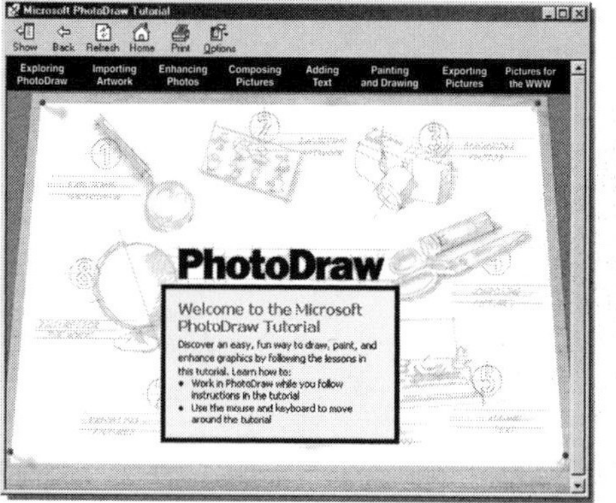

Create Images

PhotoDraw includes the Microsoft Clip Gallery, which offers a wide selection of clip art images for you to choose from. The Microsoft Clip Gallery contains categories of clip art images such as Animals, People at Work and Travel. You can also use clips from PhotoDraw Content, which includes categories such as Academic, Metaphor and Seasons.

You can use PhotoDraw to scan images or work with images captured using a digital camera. PhotoDraw also allows you to paint and draw images. You can paint an image you want to create freehand or draw an image you want to be a precise shape. AutoShapes, including lines, arrows and stars, are also available. You can create a text object to add text to an image.

Edit Images

The type of image you are working with determines how you can edit the image. When working with a photograph, you can crop out unwanted parts, correct red eye problems, sharpen the focus or create a blur effect.

When working with clip art, drawn or painted images and text you can add 3-D or shadow effects. You can also enhance the outline of these images by softening the edges of the image or applying an artistic brush style.

Microsoft Photo Editor

Microsoft Photo Editor is a program that allows you to scan images and then work with the images on your computer.

Photo Editor includes many tools you can use to change the appearance of an image. For example, you can resize or rotate an image. You can also smudge colors in an image, make an area of an image transparent or change the contrast of an image. Photo Editor also includes several special effects you can use. For example, you can emboss an image or apply a watercolor or stained glass effect to an image.

You can save an image as you would any file on your computer. Photo Editor supports many popular image file formats, including Graphics Interchange Format (.gif), JPEG (.jpeg), Tag Image File Format (.tif) and Windows Bitmap (.bmp). You can also print an image or e-mail an image to a colleague.

Photo Editor is available on the Start menu when you select Programs and then Microsoft Office Tools. The first time you start Photo Editor, you may be asked to install the program from the Microsoft Office 2000 installation CD-ROM disc.

Microsoft Binder

Microsoft Binder is a program that enables you to bring together related documents from different Office programs to create a single document, called a binder. For example, a binder could include a Word document that provides background information about your company, an Excel worksheet that displays your company's sales figures and a PowerPoint presentation about your company's objectives.

You can add a copy of an existing document to a binder. You can also add a new, blank document to a binder.

One advantage of using a binder to organize documents is that you can add a header or footer to display the same information, such as page numbers, on each page of every document in the binder. This can help you keep the contents of the printed binder together.

After a binder contains all the documents you want, you can save the binder so you can work with it in the future or print the binder to produce a paper copy.

Binder may not be installed on your computer. You can install Binder from the Microsoft Office 2000 installation CD-ROM disc.

CONTINUED

ADDITIONAL OFFICE 2000 PROGRAMS AND FEATURES CONTINUED

Program Maintenance

Office 2000 programs are self-repairing applications. When you start an Office 2000 program, the program determines whether any essential files are missing and then re-installs the files if necessary. The program may also check your registry files and make any necessary repairs.

You can also use the Detect and Repair feature to find and correct problems with a program's files. This feature is available on the Help menu of most Office programs. Detect and Repair compares the program files on your computer to the files that were installed when you installed Office 2000. The feature then automatically replaces any corrupt or missing files.

When Office is repairing a program, you may be asked to insert the Microsoft Office 2000 installation disc into your CD-ROM drive.

Microsoft Office Shortcut Bar

The Microsoft Office Shortcut Bar allows you to quickly access the Office features and programs you frequently use.

By default, the Office Shortcut Bar displays the Office toolbar. The Office toolbar allows you to perform tasks such as creating a new document, using an Outlook feature or starting FrontPage. You can have the Office Shortcut Bar display a different toolbar, such as a toolbar containing buttons for the items found in your Favorites folder or on your desktop.

The Microsoft Office Shortcut Bar is available on the Start menu when you select Programs and then Microsoft Office Tools. The first time you display the Office Shortcut Bar, you may be asked to install the feature from the Microsoft Office 2000 installation CD-ROM disc. You can set up the Office Shortcut Bar to start automatically every time you start Windows.

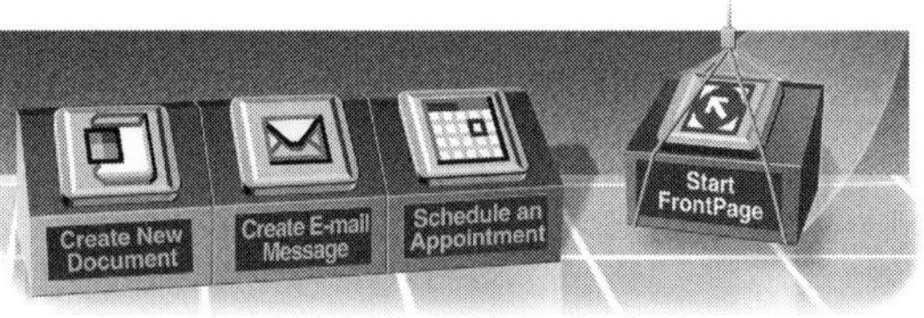

Scanner and Camera Add-In

The Scanner and Camera Add-In allows you to scan an image or download an image from a digital camera while working in an Office program and then insert the image directly into the current document. This saves you from having to leave the Office program to scan or download an image.

In an Office program, you can access the From Scanner or Camera option by selecting the Insert menu and then Picture. The first time you use the From Scanner or Camera option, you may be asked to install the feature from the Microsoft Office 2000 installation CD-ROM disc.

Text Converters

Text converters allow Office programs to work with a wide variety of file formats. For example, you can create a document in Word and then save the document in a format that can be used by another program, such as WordPerfect or an earlier version of Word. Text converters make it easy to exchange data with friends and colleagues who do not use Office 2000.

The first time you use a text converter, you may be asked to install the text converter from the Microsoft Office 2000 installation CD-ROM disc. Some text converters are automatically installed when you install Office 2000.

Microsoft Office Language Settings

Microsoft Office Language Settings allow you to change the language displayed in Office programs.

You can select the language you want to display in the menus, dialog boxes and Help feature of a program. The program will also use the dictionary for the new language so you can use features such as the spell checker.

The Microsoft Office Language Settings feature is available on the Start menu when you select Programs and then Microsoft Office Tools. The first time you start Microsoft Office Language Settings, you may be asked to install the feature from the Microsoft Office 2000 installation CD-ROM disc. You may also need to install the MultiLanguage Pack, which is found on the Microsoft Office 2000 installation CD-ROM disc.

Small Business Tools

Small Business Tools is a collection of programs and utilities designed for the small business user. The Small Business Financial Manager is a popular feature included in Small Business Tools.

The Small Business Financial Manager works with Excel to help you review, manipulate and analyze your organization's financial information. For example, you can convert data from other accounting programs into data that you can use with Excel. You can also create detailed reports so you can view your financial data more easily. This feature also allows you to create scenarios to see how changes in your financial data, such as increased profits or hiring a new employee, can affect your business.

If Small Business Tools is not installed on your computer, you can install it from the Microsoft Office 2000 installation CD-ROM disc.

APPENDIX

WHAT'S ON THE CD-ROM DISC

The CD-ROM disc included in this book contains many useful files and programs. You will find a Web page providing one-click access to all the Internet links mentioned in the book. This disc also includes Internet sign up offers, a version of the book that you can view using Adobe Acrobat Reader and trial versions of popular programs. Before installing any of the programs on the disc, make sure a newer version of the program is not already installed on your computer. For information on installing different versions of the same program, contact the program's manufacturer.

System Requirements

You can use this disc on any computer running Windows that has a CD-ROM drive. To get the most out of the items on the disc, you should have a 486 or Pentium computer with at least 32 MB of RAM. You should have at least 200 MB of free hard disk space and your system should be able to display at least 256 colors.

Use the My Computer or Windows Explorer window to display the contents of the CD.

Note: If you have trouble viewing the directory structure of the CD, or if the directory names are truncated (example: \directo~), your CD-ROM drive is currently using 16-bit drivers instead of the necessary 32-bit drivers. Please contact your CD-ROM drive vendor for information on upgrading the CD-ROM drivers.

Web Links

This CD contains a Web page that provides one-click access to all the Web pages and Internet references in the book. To use these links, you must have an Internet connection and a Web browser, such as Internet Explorer, installed.

To display the Web links page, open the Web Links folder on the CD and then double-click Web Links.html. Your Web browser opens and displays the page.

Master Office 2000 Visually–Acrobat Version

The CD-ROM disc contains a version of this book that you can view and search using Adobe Acrobat Reader. You cannot print the pages or copy text from the Acrobat files. A full and free version of Adobe Acrobat Reader 3.01 is also included on the disc. For information about how to install Acrobat Reader and view the book on the CD-ROM disc, see page 646.

Internet Explorer 5

This disc contains a full version of Internet Explorer 5. Internet Explorer 5 is Microsoft's latest Web browser. It offers new and improved features that make browsing the Web faster and easier.

To install Internet Explorer 5, open the IE5 folder. Double-click IE.exe and then follow the instructions on your screen.

EarthLink Network® Internet Sign Up Offer

If you are not yet connected to the Internet, you can use the CD to set up an account and start using the *EarthLink Network*® Internet service. You can set up your account to use Internet Explorer 4.0 or Netscape 4.5 as your Web browser.

Open the EarthLink folder on the CD. To install Microsoft Internet Explorer 4.0 and set up an Internet account, open the EarthLink MSIE4 folder. Double-click Setup.exe and then follow the instructions on your screen.

To install Netscape 4.5 and set up an Internet account, open the EarthLink Netscape folder. Double-click Setup.exe and then follow the instructions on your screen.

Programs

The Programs folder on the CD-ROM disc contains seven useful programs.

Before installing a program from this CD, you should exit all other programs. In order to use most of the programs, you must accept the license agreement provided with the program. Make sure you read any Readme files provided with each program.

Acrobat Reader

This disc contains a full version of Acrobat Reader 3.01. For more information about using Acrobat Reader, see page 646.

In the Programs folder, open the Acrobat Reader with Search folder. To install the program, double-click rs32e301.exe and then follow the instructions on your screen.

Paint Shop Pro

Paint Shop Pro is a graphics program you can use to edit and create pictures. This disc contains version 5.01 of Paint Shop Pro. You may use the program for free for 30 days. If you wish to continue using the program, you must then purchase the licensed version.

In the Programs folder, open the Paint Shop Pro folder. To install the program, double-click Psp501ev.exe and then follow the instructions on your screen.

WinZip

WinZip compresses files to make it easier and faster to transfer information from one computer to another. This disc contains version 7.0 of WinZip. You may use the program for free for 21 days. If you wish to continue using the program, you must pay a registration fee.

In the Programs folder, open the WinZip folder. To install the program, double-click winzip70.exe and then follow the instructions on your screen.

WinFax PRO

WinFax PRO uses advanced technology to send and receive faxes using your computer's fax modem. This disc contains version 9.0 of WinFax PRO. You may use the program for free for 30 days. If you wish to continue using the program, you must then purchase the licensed version.

In the Programs folder, open the WinFax Pro folder. To install the program, double-click setup.exe and then follow the instructions on your screen.

Norton Utilities

Norton Utilities includes several components to help you with computer maintenance tasks. This disc contains a trial version of Norton Utilities. If you wish to continue using the program, you must then purchase the licensed version.

In the Programs folder, open the Norton Utilities folder. To install the program, double-click nu3_trybuy.exe and then follow the instructions on your screen.

TalkWorks Pro

You can use TalkWorks Pro to bring professional voice and fax messaging to your home or office. This disc contains a trial version of TalkWorks Pro. If you wish to continue using the program, you must then purchase the licensed version.

In the Programs folder, open the TalkWorks Pro folder. To install the program, double-click Twtrybuy.exe and then follow the instructions on your screen.

RealPlayer

RealPlayer speeds up the delivery of audio and video files from the Internet. This disc contains a full version of RealPlayer 5.0.

In the Programs folder, open the RealPlayer folder. To install the program, double-click rp32_50.exe and then follow the instructions on your screen.

MASTER OFFICE 2000 VISUALLY ON CD

You can view Master Office 2000 VISUALLY on your screen using the CD included at the back of this book. The CD allows you to search the contents of the book for a specific word or phrase. The CD also provides a convenient way of keeping the book handy while traveling.

You must install Acrobat Reader on your computer before you can view the information on the CD. This program is also provided on the CD. Acrobat Reader allows you to view Portable Document Format (.pdf) files. These files can display books and magazines on your screen exactly as they appear in printed form.

To install Acrobat Reader, open the Programs folder on the CD and then open the Acrobat Reader with Search folder. Double-click the rs32e301.exe file and then follow the instructions on your screen.

After Acrobat Reader is installed, you can view the contents of the book, found on the CD in the folder named Acrobat Version of Book. The contents are divided into ten sections that correspond to the sections of this book. To view the contents of a section, double-click the section.

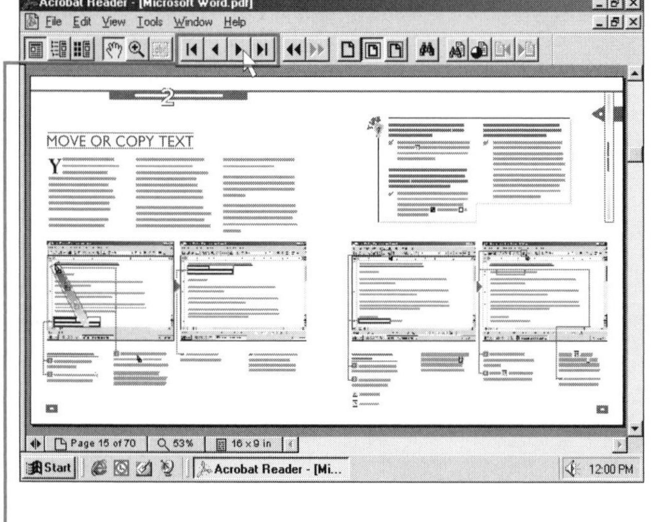

FLIP THROUGH PAGES

1 Click one of the following options to flip through the pages of a section.

- First Page
- Previous Page
- Next Page
- Last Page

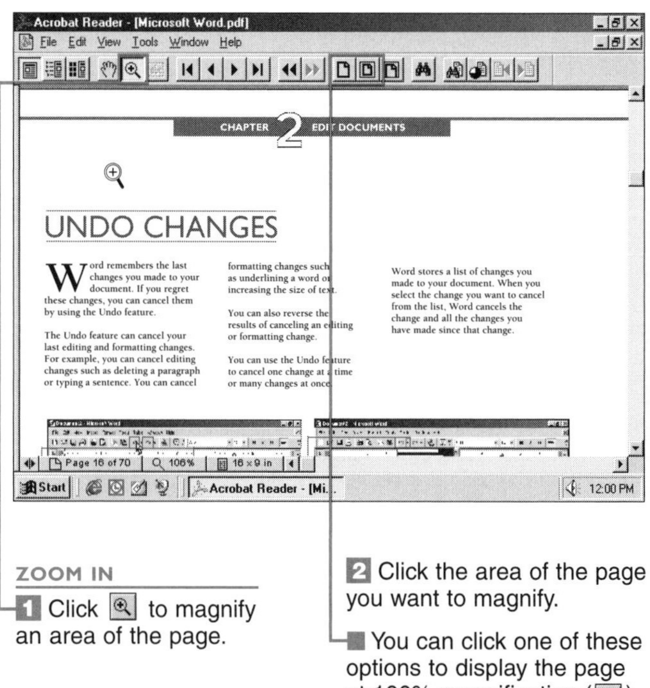

ZOOM IN

1 Click (zoom tool) to magnify an area of the page.

2 Click the area of the page you want to magnify.

■ You can click one of these options to display the page at 100% magnification (actual size button) or to fit the entire page inside the window (fit page button).

Can I use an older version of Acrobat Reader to view the information on the CD?

✔ Yes, but the latest version of Acrobat Reader offers more features, such as the ability to search all the sections at once.

How do I search all the sections on the CD at once?

✔ You must first locate the index. While viewing the contents of the book, click [search icon] in the Acrobat Reader window. Click Indexes and then click Add. Click index.pdx, click Open and then click OK. You need to locate the index only once. After locating the index, you can click [search icon] to search all the sections.

How can I make searching the CD more convenient?

✔ Copy the Acrobat Version of Book folder from the CD to your hard drive. This allows you to easily access the contents of the book at any time.

Can I use Acrobat Reader for anything else?

✔ Acrobat Reader is a popular and useful program. There are many files available on the Web that are designed to be viewed using Acrobat Reader. Look for files with the .pdf extension.

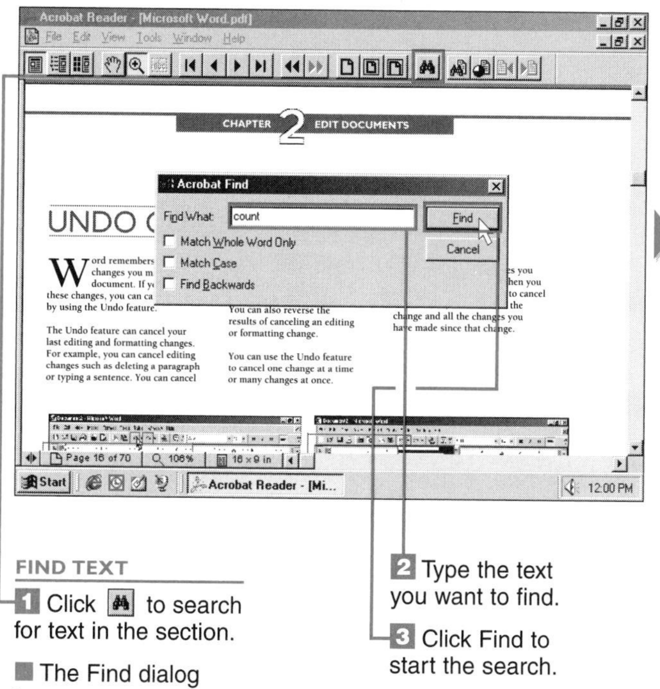

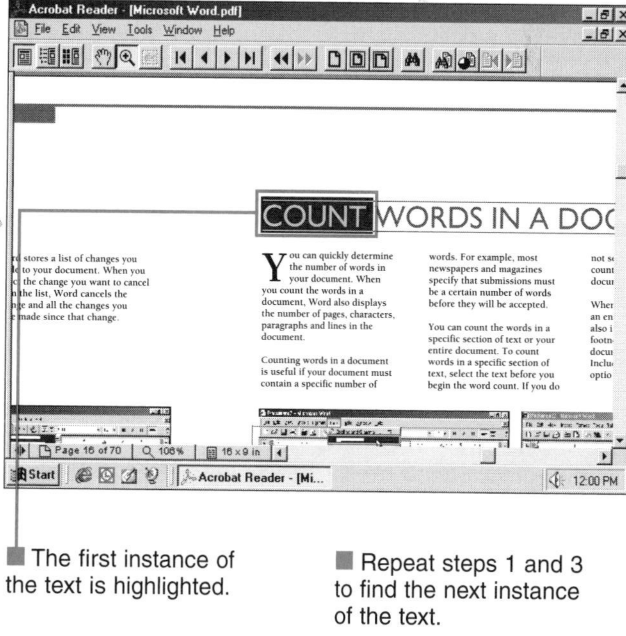

FIND TEXT

1 Click [search icon] to search for text in the section.

■ The Find dialog box appears.

2 Type the text you want to find.

3 Click Find to start the search.

■ The first instance of the text is highlighted.

■ Repeat steps 1 and 3 to find the next instance of the text.

APPENDIX

IDG BOOKS WORLDWIDE, INC. END-USER LICENSE AGREEMENT

Read This. You should carefully read these terms and conditions before opening the software packet(s) included with this book ("Book"). This is a license agreement ("Agreement") between you and IDG Books Worldwide, Inc. ("IDGB"). By opening the accompanying software packet(s), you acknowledge that you have read and accept the following terms and conditions. If you do not agree and do not want to be bound by such terms and conditions, promptly return the Book and the unopened software packet(s) to the place you obtained them for a full refund.

1. License Grant. IDGB grants to you (either an individual or entity) a nonexclusive license to use one copy of the enclosed software program(s) (collectively, the "Software") solely for your own personal or business purposes on a single computer (whether a standard computer or a workstation component of a multi-user network). The Software is in use on a computer when it is loaded into temporary memory (i.e., RAM) or installed into permanent memory (e.g., hard disk, CD-ROM or other storage device). IDGB reserves all rights not expressly granted herein.

2. Ownership. IDGB is the owner of all right, title and interest, including copyright, in and to the compilation of the Software recorded on the CD-ROM. Copyright to the individual programs on the CD-ROM is owned by the author or other authorized copyright owner of each program. Ownership of the Software and all proprietary rights relating thereto remain with IDGB and its licensors.

3. Restrictions On Use and Transfer.

(a) You may only (i) make one copy of the Software for backup or archival purposes, or (ii) transfer the Software to a single hard disk, provided that you keep the original for backup or archival purposes. You may not (i) rent or lease the Software, (ii) copy or reproduce the Software through a LAN or other network system or through any computer subscriber system or bulletin-board system, or (iii) modify, adapt or create derivative works based on the Software.

(b) You may not reverse engineer, decompile, or disassemble the Software. You may transfer the Software and user documentation on a permanent basis, provided that the transferee agrees to accept the terms and conditions of this Agreement and you retain no copies. If the Software is an update or has been updated, any transfer must include the most recent update and all prior versions.

4. Restrictions on Use of Individual Programs. You must follow the individual requirements and restrictions detailed for each individual program. These limitations are contained in the individual license agreements recorded on the CD-ROM. These restrictions include a requirement that after using the program for the period of time specified in its text, the user must pay a registration fee or discontinue use. By opening the Software packet(s), you will be agreeing to abide by the licenses and restrictions for these individual programs. None of the material on this disk(s) or listed in this Book may ever be distributed, in original or modified form, for commercial purposes.

5. Limited Warranty.

(a) IDGB warrants that the Software and CD-ROM are free from defects in materials and workmanship under normal use for a period of sixty (60) days from the date of purchase of this Book. If IDGB receives notification within the warranty period of defects in materials or workmanship, IDGB will replace the defective CD-ROM.

(b) IDGB AND THE AUTHOR OF THE BOOK DISCLAIM ALL OTHER WARRANTIES, EXPRESS OR IMPLIED, INCLUDING WITHOUT LIMITATION IMPLIED WARRANTIES OF MERCHANTABILITY AND FITNESS FOR A PARTICULAR PURPOSE, WITH RESPECT TO THE SOFTWARE, THE PROGRAMS, THE SOURCE CODE CONTAINED THEREIN, AND/OR THE TECHNIQUES DESCRIBED IN THIS BOOK. IDGB DOES NOT WARRANT THAT THE FUNCTIONS CONTAINED IN THE SOFTWARE WILL MEET YOUR

REQUIREMENTS OR THAT THE OPERATION OF THE SOFTWARE WILL BE ERROR FREE.

(c) This limited warranty gives you specific legal rights, and you may have other rights which vary from jurisdiction to jurisdiction.

6. Special note about the WinFax Pro trialware on the CD: This program was reproduced by IDG Books Worldwide, Inc. under a special arrangement with Symantec Corporation. If your diskette is defective, please return it to IDG Books Worldwide Inc., which will arrange for its replacement. PLEASE DO NOT RETURN IT TO Symantec CORPORATION. PLEASE DO NOT CONTACT Symantec CORPORATION FOR PRODUCT SUPPORT. End users of this Symantec program shall not be considered "registered owners" of a Symantec product and therefore shall not be eligible for upgrades, promotions or other benefits available to "registered owners" of Symantec products.

7. Remedies.

(a) IDGB's entire liability and your exclusive remedy for defects in materials and workmanship shall be limited to replacement of the Software. This Limited Warranty is void if failure of the Software has resulted from accident, abuse, or misapplication. Any replacement Software will be warranted for the remainder of the original warranty period or thirty (30) days, whichever is longer. If you experience problems with the Software, contact IDG Technical Support at 1-800-762-2974.

(b) In no event shall IDGB or the author be liable for any damages whatsoever (including without limitation damages for loss of business profits, business interruption, loss of business information, or any other pecuniary loss) arising out of the use of or inability to use the Book or the Software, even if IDGB has been advised of the possibility of such damages.

(c) Because some jurisdictions do not allow the exclusion or limitation of liability for consequential or incidental damages, the above limitation or exclusion may not apply to you.

8. U.S. Government Restricted Rights. Use, duplication, or disclosure of the Software by the U.S. Government is subject to restrictions stated in paragraph (c) (1) (ii) of the Rights in Technical Data and Computer Software clause of DFARS 252.227-7013, and in subparagraphs (a) through (d) of the Commercial Computer—Restricted Rights clause at FAR 52.227-19, and in similar clauses in the NASA FAR supplement, when applicable.

9. General. This Agreement constitutes the entire understanding of the parties, and revokes and supersedes all prior agreements, oral or written, between them and may not be modified or amended except in a writing signed by both parties hereto which specifically refers to this Agreement. This Agreement shall take precedence over any other documents that may be in conflict herewith. If any one or more provisions contained in this Agreement are held by any court or tribunal to be invalid, illegal or otherwise unenforceable, each and every other provision shall remain in full force and effect.

INDEX

Numbers & Symbols

A

B

C

INDEX

INDEX

D

INDEX

INDEX

E

F

G

H

M

INDEX

N

O

P

INDEX

Q

R

S

INDEX

U

V

W

Y

Z

Visual

Read Less-Learn More
ASP.NET
HTML
JavaScript
Your visual blueprint for creating Web applications on the .NET framework
Your visual blueprint for designing effective Web pages
Your visual blueprint for building dynamic Web pages